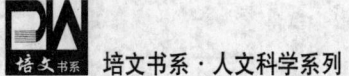
培文书系·人文科学系列

MEN'S LIVES
男性的世界

第六版

[美]迈克尔·基梅尔　迈克尔·梅斯纳　著
MICHAEL S. KIMMEL　MICHAEL A. MESSNER

北京大学出版社
PEKING UNIVERSITY PRESS

北京市版权局著作权合同登记图字：01-2004-6695 号

图书在版编目(CIP)数据

男性的世界(第 6 版)/(美)迈克尔·基梅尔(Michael S. Kimmel)等著. —影印本.
—北京：北京大学出版社，2005.1
(培文书系·人文科学系列)

ISBN 7-301-08218-5

I. 男… II. 迈… III. 男性-生活-研究-英文 IV. C913

中国版本图书馆 CIP 数据核字(2004)第 115096 号

English reprint edition copyright © 2004 by PEARSON EDUCATION ASIA LIMITED and PEKING UNIVERSITY PRESS.
Original English language title from Proprietor's edition of the Work.

Original English language title: Men's Lives, Michael S. Kimmel, Michael A. Messner
Copyright © 2004

ISBN: 0-205-37902-8
All Rights Reserved.

Published by arrangement with the original publisher, Pearson Education, Inc., publishing as Allyn And Bacon Inc.

This edition is authorized for sale and distribution only in the People's Republic of China exclusively (except Hong Kong SAR, Macao SAR and Taiwan).
仅限于中华人民共和国境内(不包括中国香港、澳门特别行政区和中国台湾地区)销售发行。

书　　　名：	男性的世界(第 6 版)
著作责任者：	[美] Michael S. Kimmel, Michael A. Messner　著
责 任 编 辑：	曹媛媛
标 准 书 号：	ISBN 7-301-08218-5/G·1321
出　版　者：	北京大学出版社
地　　　址：	北京市海淀区中关村北京大学校内　100871
网　　　址：	http://cbs.pku.edu.cn　电子信箱：pw@pup.pku.edu.cn
电　　　话：	邮购部 62752015　发行部 62750672　编辑部 58874097 58874098
印　刷　者：	山东新华印刷厂临沂厂
发　行　者：	北京大学出版社
经　销　者：	新华书店
	850毫米×1168 毫米　16 开　38.625 印张　550 千字
	2005 年 1 月第 1 版　2006 年 1 月第 2 次印刷
定　　价：	55.00 元

版权所有，翻印必究
本书封面贴有 Pearson Education(培生教育出版集团)激光防伪标签，无标签者不得销售。

出 版 说 明

　　培文书系人文科学系列旨在面向国内人文领域的师生和广大人文爱好者,推介国外经典的和新近的英文原版和中文翻译版优秀著作和教材,使我国读者得以从中了解、学习和借鉴国外先进研究成果。

　　需要重申的是,作者本人的有些观点和结论尚需商榷,有些甚至是不可取的,为此我们对个别段落或语句有所删节,同时也提请读者加以甄别。书中的观点均不代表出版社观点。

北京大学出版社
2005 年 1 月

CONTENTS

Preface **vii**

Introduction **ix**

PART ONE   Perspectives on Masculinity   1

ARTICLE 1   Varieties of "Real Men"   **James Messerschmidt**   3

ARTICLE 2   The Black Male: Searching Beyond Stereotypes   **Manning Marable**   21

ARTICLE 3   "Macho": Contemporary Conceptions   **Alfredo Mirandé**   28

ARTICLE 4   All Men Are *Not* Created Equal: Asian Men in U.S. History   **Yen Le Espiritu**   39

ARTICLE 5   Lives at the Center of the Periphery, Lives at the Periphery of the Center: Chinese American Masculinities and Bargaining with Hegemony   **Anthony S. Chen**   48

ARTICLE 6   (In) Secure Times: Constructing White Working-Class Masculinities in the Late 20th Century   **Michelle Fine, Lois Weis, Judi Addelston, and Julia Marusza Hall**   66

ARTICLE 7   Gender, Class, and Terrorism   **Michael S. Kimmel**   79

PART TWO   Boyhood   85

ARTICLE 8   Barbie Girls versus Sea Monsters: Children Constructing Gender   **Michael A. Messner**   87

ARTICLE 9   Warrior Narratives in the Kindergarten Classroom: Renegotiating the Social Contract?   **Ellen Jordan and Angela Cowan**   103

ARTICLE 10   Memories of Same-Sex Attractions   **Ritch C. Savin-Williams**   116

ARTICLE 11   The Puerto Rican Dummy and the Merciful Son   **Martín Espada**   133

ARTICLE 12   Girls Will Be Girls and Boys Will Be First   **Pat Mahony**   140

ARTICLE 13   Making a Name for Yourself: Transgressive Acts and Gender Performance   **Ann Ferguson**   154

PART THREE Collegiate Masculinities: Privilege and Peril 167

ARTICLE 14 The Fraternal Bond as a Joking Relationship: A Case Study of the Role of Sexist Jokes in Male Group Bonding **Peter Lyman** 169

ARTICLE 15 Fraternities and Collegiate Rape Culture: Why Are Some Fraternities More Dangerous Places for Women? **A. Ayres Boswell and Joan Z. Spade** 179

ARTICLE 16 Why College Men Drink: Alcohol, Adventure, and the Paradox of Masculinity **Rocco L. Capraro** 190

ARTICLE 17 Fraternal Bonding in the Locker Room: A Profeminist Analysis of Talk About Competition and Women **Timothy Jon Curry** 204

ARTICLE 18 The Antirape Rules **Jason Schultz** 218

PART FOUR Men and Work 225

ARTICLE 19 The Glass Escalator: Hidden Advantages for Men in the "Female" Professions **Christine L. Williams** 227

ARTICLE 20 Rambo Litigators: Emotional Labor in a Male-Dominated Occupation **Jennifer Pierce** 241

ARTICLE 21 Hitting Bottom: Homelessness, Poverty, and Masculinity **Timothy Nonn** 258

ARTICLE 22 Being the "Go-To Guy": Fatherhood, Masculinity, and the Organization of Work in Silicon Valley **Marianne Cooper** 268

ARTICLE 23 "Why Marcia You've Changed!" Male Clerical Temporary Workers Doing Masculinity in a Feminized Occupation **Kevin D. Henson and Jackie Krasas Rogers** 289

ARTICLE 24 Sexual Harassment and Masculinity: The Power and Meaning of "Girl Watching" **Beth A. Quinn** 305

PART FIVE Men and Health: Body and Mind 319

ARTICLE 25 Masculinities and Men's Health: Moving Toward Post-Superman Era Prevention **Don Sabo** 321

ARTICLE 26 Confessions of a Nice Negro, or Why I Shaved My Head **Robin D. G. Kelley** 335

CONTENTS v

ARTICLE 27 How to Build a Man **Anne Fausto-Sterling** 342

ARTICLE 28 If Men Could Menstruate **Gloria Steinem** 347

ARTICLE 29 Coming to Terms: Masculinity and Physical Disability
Thomas J. Gerschick and Adam Stephen Miller 349

ARTICLE 30 Trips to Fantasy Island: Contexts of Risky Sex for San Francisco Gay Men **Rafael M. Diaz** 363

PART SIX   Men in Relationships   381

ARTICLE 31 The Approach–Avoidance Dance: Men, Women, and Intimacy
Lillian B. Rubin 383

ARTICLE 32 "I'm Not Friends the Way She's Friends": Ideological and Behavioral Constructions of Masculinity in Men's Friendships
Karen Walker 389

ARTICLE 33 The Politics of Gay Men's Friendships **Peter M. Nardi** 402

ARTICLE 34 Men on Rape **Tim Beneke** 406

ARTICLE 35 Rape and the Prison Code **Terry A. Kupers** 412

PART SEVEN   Male Sexualities   419

ARTICLE 36 Becoming 100 Percent Straight **Michael A. Messner** 421

ARTICLE 37 The Heterosexual Questionnaire **M. Rochlin** 427

ARTICLE 38 Stereotypes of Black Male Sexuality: The Facts Behind the Myths
Robert Staples 428

ARTICLE 39 Chicano Men: A Cartography of Homosexual Identity and Behavior
Tomás Almaguer 433

ARTICLE 40 Sociocultural Facets of the Black Gay Male Experience
Susan D. Cochran and Vickie M. Mays 447

ARTICLE 41 Fantasy Islands: Exploring the Demand for Sex Tourism **Julia O'Connell Davidson and Jacqueline Sanchez Taylor** 454

PART EIGHT   Men in Families   467

ARTICLE 42 Strategies Men Use to Resist **Francine M. Deutsch** 469

ARTICLE 43 Life-Styles of Gay Husbands and Fathers **Brian Miller** 476

| ARTICLE 44 | A Place Called Home: A Queer Political Economy: Mexican Immigrant Men's Family Experiences **Lionel Cantú** 484 |
| ARTICLE 45 | On "Good" Black Fathers **Michael C. Hanchard** 497 |

PART NINE Masculinities in the Media 505

ARTICLE 46	The Morality/Manhood Paradox: Masculinity, Sport, and the Media **Shari Lee Dworkin and Faye Linda Wachs** 507
ARTICLE 47	In an Imperfect World, Men with Small Penises Are Unforgiven **Peter Lehman** 522
ARTICLE 48	Beer Commercials: A Manual on Masculinity **Lance Strate** 533
ARTICLE 49	Looking for My Penis: The Eroticized Asian in Gay Video Porn **Richard Fung** 543

PART TEN Men, Movements, and the Future 553

ARTICLE 50	Men: Comrades in Struggle **bell hooks** 555
ARTICLE 51	Statement of Principles **The National Organization for Men Against Sexism** 564
ARTICLE 52	Clarence, William, Iron Mike, Tailhook, Senator Packwood, Spur Posse, Magic . . . and Us **Michael S. Kimmel** 565
ARTICLE 53	It's Raining Men? **Robert Reid-Pharr** 580

Contributors 587

PREFACE

Over the past twenty years, we have been teaching courses on the male experience, or "men's lives." Our courses have reflected both our own education and recent research by feminist scholars and profeminist men in U.S. society. (By profeminist men, we mean active supporters of women's efforts against male violence and claims for equal opportunity, political participation, sexual autonomy, family reform, and equal education.) Gender, scholars have demonstrated, is a central feature of social life—one of the chief organizing principles around which our lives revolve. Gender shapes our identities and the institutions in which we find ourselves. In the university, women's studies programs and courses about women in traditional disciplines have explored the meaning of gender in women's lives. But what does it mean to be a man in contemporary U.S. society?

This anthology is organized around specific themes that define masculinity and the issues men confront over the course of their lives. In addition, a social-constructionist perspective has been included that examines how men actively construct masculinity within a social and historical context. Related to this construction and integrated in our examination are the variations that exist among men in relation to class, race, and sexuality.

We begin Part One with issues and questions that unravel the "masculine mystique" and reveal various dimensions of men's position in society and their relationships with women and with other men. Parts Two through Nine examine the different issues that emerge for men at different times of their lives and the ways in which their lives change over time. We touch on central moments related to boyhood, adolescence, sports, occupations, marriage, and fatherhood, and explore men's emotional and sexual relationships with women and with other men. The final part, "Men, Movements, and the Future," explores some of the ways in which men are changing and some possible directions by which they might continue to change.

Although a major component of the traditional, normative definition of masculinity is independence, we are pleased to acknowledge those colleagues and friends whose criticism and support have been a constant help throughout our work on this project. Karen Hanson and Jeff Lasser, our editors at Allyn and Bacon, inherited this project and have embraced it as their own, facilitating our work at every turn. Chris Cardone and Bruce Nichols, our original editors, were supportive from the start and helped get the project going. Many other scholars who work on issues of masculinity, such as Bob Blauner, Robert Brannon, Harry Brod, Rocco Capraro, Bob Connell, James Harrison, Jeff Hearn, Joe Pleck, Tony Rotundo, Don Sabo, and Peter Stein, have contributed to a supportive intellectual community in which to work.

We also thank the following reviewers for their helpful comments and suggestions: Parvin Abyanch, California State University, Pomona; Alice Abelkemp, University of New Orleans; Eric Anderson, University of California, Irvine; Ron Matson, Wichita State University; Gul Ozyegin, College of William and Mary; Jessica Maguire, Ohio State University; Mindy Stombler, Texas Technical University; and Regina E. Werum, Emory University. Colleagues at the State University of New York at Stony Brook and the University of Southern California have also been supportive of this project. We are especially grateful to Diane Barthel, Ruth Schwartz Cowan, John Gagnon, Barry Glassner, Norman Goodman, Nilufer Isvan, Carol Jacklin, and Barrie Thorne. A fellowship from the Lilly Foundation supported Kimmel's work on pedagogical issues of teaching about men and masculinity.

This book is the product of the profeminist men's movement as well—a loose network of men who support a feminist critique of traditional masculinity and women's struggles to enlarge the scope of their personal autonomy and public power. These men are engaged in a variety of efforts to transform masculinity in ways that allow men to live fuller, richer, and healthier lives. The editors of *Changing Men* (with whom we worked as Book Review Editor and Sports Editor), the late Mike Biernbaum and Rick Cote, labored for more than a decade to provide a forum for antisexist men. We acknowledge their efforts with gratitude and respect.

Our families, friends, and colleagues have provided a rare atmosphere that combines intellectual challenge and emotional support. We are grateful to Martin Duberman, "Eli Zal," Pam Hatchfield, Sandi Kimmel, Mary Morris and Larry O'Connor, Lillian and Hank Rubin, and Mitchell Tunick. We want especially to acknowledge our fathers and mothers for providing such important models—not of being women or men, but of being adults capable of career competence, emotional warmth, and nurturance (these are not masculine or feminine traits).

Finally, we thank Amy Aronson and Pierette Hondagneu-Sotelo, who have chosen to share our lives, and our sons, who didn't have much of a choice about it. Together they fill our lives with so much joy.

M.S.K.
M.A.M.

INTRODUCTION

This is a book about men. But, unlike other books about men, which line countless library shelves, this is a book about men *as men*. It is a book in which men's experiences are not taken for granted as we explore the "real" and significant accomplishments of men, but a book in which those experiences are treated as significant and important in themselves.

Men as "Gendered Beings"

But what does it mean to examine men "as men"? Most courses in a college curriculum are about men, aren't they? But these courses routinely deal with men only in their public roles, so we come to know and understand men as scientists, politicians, military figures, writers, and philosophers. Rarely, if ever, are men understood through the prism of gender.

But listen to some male voices from some of these "ungendered" courses. Take, for example, composer Charles Ives, debunking "sissy" types of music; he said he used traditional tough guy themes and concerns in his drive to build new sounds and structures out of the popular musical idiom (cf. Wilkinson 1986: 103). Or architect Louis Sullivan, describing his ambition to create "masculine forms": strong, solid, commanding respect. Or novelist Ernest Hemingway, retaliating against literary enemies by portraying them as impotent or homosexual.

Consider also political figures, such as Cardinal Richelieu, the seventeenth-century French First Minister to Louis XIII, who insisted that it was "necessary to have masculine virtue and do everything by reason" (cited in Elliott 1984: 20). Closer to home, recall President Lyndon Baines Johnson's dismissal of a political adversary: "Oh him. He has to squat to piss!" Or his boast that during the Tet offensive in the Vietnam War, he "didn't just screw Ho Chi Minh. I cut his pecker off!"

Democrats have no monopoly on unexamined gender coloring their political rhetoric. Indeed, recent political campaigns have revolved, in part, around gender issues, as each candidate attempted to demonstrate that he was not a "wimp" but was a "real man." (Of course, the few successful female politicians face the double task of convincing the electorate that they are not the "weak-willed wimps" that their gender implies in the public mind while at the same time demonstrating that they are "real women.")

These are just a few examples of what we might call gendered speech, language that uses gender terms to make its case. And these are just a few of the thousands of examples one could find in every academic discipline of how men's lives are organized around gender issues and how gender remains one of the organizing principles of social life. We come to know ourselves and our world through the prism of gender. Only we act as if we didn't know it.

Fortunately, in recent years, the pioneering work of feminist scholars, both in traditional disciplines and in women's studies, and of feminist women in the political arena has made us aware of the centrality of gender in our lives. In the social sciences, gender has now taken its place alongside class and race as one of the three central mechanisms by which power and resources are distributed in our society and the three central themes out of which we fashion the meanings of our lives.

We certainly understand how this works for women. Through women's studies courses and also in courses about women in traditional disciplines, students have explored the complexity of women's lives, the hidden history of exemplary women, and the daily experiences of women in the routines of their lives. For women, we know how gender works as one of the formative elements out of which social life is organized.

The Invisibility of Gender: A Sociological Explanation

Too often, though, we treat men as if they had no gender, as if only their public personae were of interest to us as students and scholars, as if their interior experience of gender was of no significance. This became evident when one of us was in a graduate seminar on feminist theory several years ago. A discussion between a white woman and a black woman revolved around the question of whether their similarities as women were greater than their racial differences as black and white. The white woman asserted that the fact that they were both women bonded them, in spite of their racial differences. The black woman disagreed.

"When you wake up in the morning and look in the mirror, what do you see?" she asked.

"I see a woman," replied the white woman.

"That's precisely the issue," replied the black woman. "I see a black woman. For me, race is visible every day, because it is how I am not privileged in this culture. Race is invisible to you, which is why our alliance will always seem somewhat false to me."

Witnessing this exchange, Michael Kimmel was startled. When he looked in the mirror in the morning, he saw, as he put it, "a human being: universally generalizable. The generic person." What had been concealed—that he possessed both race and gender—had become strikingly visible. As a white man, he was able not to think about the ways in which gender and race had affected his experiences.

There is a sociological explanation for this blind spot in our thinking: the mechanisms that afford us privilege are very often invisible to us. What makes us marginal (unempowered, oppressed) are the mechanisms that we understand, because those are the ones that are most painful in daily life. Thus, white people rarely think of themselves as "raced" people, and rarely think of race as a central element in their experience. But people of color are marginalized by race, and so the centrality of race both is painfully obvious and needs study urgently. Similarly, middle-class people do not acknowledge the importance of social class as an organizing principle of social life, largely because for them class is an invisible force that makes everyone look pretty much the same. Working-class people, on the other hand, are often painfully aware of the centrality of class in their lives. (Interestingly, upper-class people are often more aware of class dynamics than are middle-class people. In part, this may be the result of the emphasis on status within the upper class, as lineage, breeding, and family honor take center stage. In part, it may also be the result of a peculiar marginalization of the upper class in our society, as in the overwhelming number of television shows and movies that are ostensibly about just plain [i.e., middle-class] folks.)

In this same way, men often think of themselves as genderless, as if gender did not matter in the daily experiences of our lives. Certainly, we can see the biological sex of individuals, but we rarely understand the ways in which *gender*—that complex of social meanings that is attached to biological sex—is enacted in our daily lives. For example, we treat male scientists as if their being men had nothing to do with the organization of their experiments, the logic of scientific inquiry, or the questions posed by science itself. We treat male political figures as if masculinity were not even remotely in their consciousness as they do battle in the political arena.

This book takes a position directly opposed to such genderlessness for men. We believe that men are also "gendered," and that this gendering process, the transformation of biological males into socially interacting men, is a central experience for men. That we are unaware of it only helps to perpetuate the inequalities based on gender in our society.

In this book, we will examine the various ways in which men are gendered. We have gathered together some of the most interesting, engaging, and convincing materials from the past decade that have been written about men. We believe that *Men's Lives* will allow readers to explore the meanings of masculinity in contemporary U.S. culture in a new way.

Earlier Efforts to Study Men

Certainly, researchers have been examining masculinity for a long time. Historically, there have been three general models that have governed social scientific research on men and masculinity. *Biological models* have focused on the ways in which innate biological differences between males and females program different social behaviors. *Anthropological models* have examined masculinity cross-culturally, stressing the variations in the behaviors and attributes associated with being a man. And, until recently, *sociological models* have stressed how socialization of boys and girls includes accommodation to a "sex role" specific to one's biological sex. Although each of these perspectives helps us to understand the meaning of masculinity and femininity, each is also limited in its ability to explain fully how gender operates in any culture.

Relying on differences in reproductive biology, some scholars have argued that the physiological organization of males and females makes inevitable the differences we observe in psychological temperament and social behaviors. One perspective holds that differences in endocrine functioning are the cause of gender difference, that testosterone predisposes males toward aggression, competition, and violence, whereas estrogen predisposes females toward passivity, tenderness, and exaggerated emotionality. Others insist that these observed behavioral differences derive from the differences between the size or number of sperm and eggs. Since a male can produce 100 million sperm with each ejaculation, whereas a female can produce fewer than 20 eggs capable of producing healthy offspring over the course of her life, these authors suggest that men's "investment" in their offspring is significantly less than women's investment. Other authors arrive at the same conclusion by suggesting that the different size of egg and sperm, and the fact that the egg is the source of the food supply, impels temperamental differences. Reproductive "success" to males means the insemination of as many females as possible; to females, reproductive success means carefully choosing one male to mate with and insisting that he remain present to care for and support their offspring. Still other authors argue that male and female behavior is governed by different halves of the brain; males are ruled by the left hemisphere, which controls rationality and abstract thought, whereas females are governed by the right hemisphere, which controls emotional affect and creativity. (For examples of these works, see Trivers 1972; Goldberg 1975; Wilson 1976; and Goldberg, 1986.)

Observed normative temperamental differences between women and men that are assumed to be of biological origin are easily translated into political prescriptions. In this ideological sleight of hand, what is *normative* (i.e., what is prescribed) is translated into what is *normal*, and the mechanisms of this transformation are the assumed biological imperative. George Gilder, for example, assembles the putative biological differences between women and men into a call for a return to traditional gender roles. Gilder believes that male sexuality is, by nature, wild and lusty, "insistent" and "incessant," careening out of control and threatening anarchic disorder, unless it can be controlled and constrained. This is the task of women. When women refuse to apply the brakes to male sexuality—by asserting their own or by choosing to pursue a life outside the domestic sphere—they abandon their "natural" function for illusory social gains. Sex education, abortion, and birth control are all condemned as facilitating women's escape from biological necessity. Similarly, he argues against women's employment, since the "unemployed man can contribute little to the community and will often disrupt it, but the woman may even do more good without a job than with one" (Gilder 1986: 86).

The biological argument has been challenged by many scholars on several grounds. The implied causation between two observed sets of differences (biological differences and different behaviors) is misleading, since there is no logical reason to assume that one caused the other, or that the line of causation moves only from the biological to the social. The selection of biological evidence is partial, and generalizations from "lower" animal species to human beings are always suspect. One sociologist asks, if these differences are "natural," why must their enforcement be coercive, and why must males and females be forced to assume the rules that they are naturally supposed to play (see Epstein 1986:8)? And one primatologist argues that the evidence adduced to support the current status quo might also lead to precisely the opposite conclusions, that biological differences would impel female promiscuity and male fragility (see Hardy 1981). Biological differences between males and females would appear to set some parameters for differences in social behavior, but would not dictate the temperaments of men and women in any one culture. These psychological and social differences would appear to be the result far more of the ways in which cultures interpret, shape, and modify these biological inheritances. We may be born males or females, but we become men and women in a cultural context.

Anthropologists have entered the debate at this point, but with different positions. For example, some anthropologists have suggested that the universality of gender differences comes from specific cultural adaptations to the environment, whereas others describe the cultural variations of gender roles, seeking to demonstrate the fluidity of gender and the primacy of cultural organization. Lionel Tiger and Robin Fox argue that the sexual division of labor is universal because of the different nature of bonding for males and females. "Nature," they argue, "intended mother and child to be together" because she is the source of emotional security and food; thus, cultures have prescribed various behaviors for women that emphasize nurturance and emotional connection (Tiger and Fox 1984: 304). The bond between men is forged through the necessity of "competitive cooperation" in hunting; men must cooperate with members of their own tribe in the hunt and yet compete for scarce resources with men in other tribes. Such bonds predispose men toward the organization of the modern corporation or governmental bureaucracy.

Such anthropological arguments omit as much as they include, and many scholars have pointed out problems with the model. Why didn't intelligence become sex linked, as this model (and the biological model) would imply? Such positions also reveal a marked conservatism: the differences between women and men are the differences that nature or cultural evolution intended, and are therefore not to be tampered with.

Perhaps the best known challenge to this anthropological argument is the work of Margaret Mead. Mead insisted that the variations among cultures in their prescriptions of gender roles required the conclusion that culture was the more decisive cause of these differences. In her classic study, *Sex and Temperament in Three Primitive Societies* (1935), Mead observed such wide variability among gender role prescriptions—and such marked differences from our own—that any universality implied by biological or anthropological models had to be rejected. And although the empirical accuracy of Mead's work has been challenged in its specific arguments, the general theoretical arguments remain convincing.

Psychological theories have also contributed to the discussion of gender roles, as psychologists have specified the developmental sequences for both males and females. Earlier theorists observed psychological distancing from the mother as the precondition for independence and autonomy, or suggested a sequence that placed the capacity for abstract reason as the developmental stage beyond relational reasoning. Since it is normative for males to exhibit independence and the capacity for abstract reason, it was argued that males are more successful at negotiating these psychological passages, and implied that women somehow lagged behind men on the ladder of developmental success. (Such arguments may be found in Freud, Erikson, and Kohlberg.)

But these models, too, have been challenged, most recently by sociologist Nancy Chodorow, who argued that women's ability to connect contains a more fundamentally human trait than the male's need to distance, and by psychologist

Carol Gilligan, who claimed that women's predisposition toward relational reasoning may contain a more humane strategy of thought than recourse to abstract principles. Regardless of our assessment of these arguments, Chodorow and Gilligan rightly point out that the highly ideological assumptions that make masculinity the normative standard against which the psychological development of *both* males and females was measured would inevitably make femininity problematic and less fully developed. Moreover, Chodorow explicitly insists that these "essential" differences between women and men are socially constructed and thus subject to change.

Finally, sociologists have attempted to synthesize these three perspectives into a systematic explanation of "sex roles." These are the collection of attitudes, attributes, and behaviors that is seen as appropriate for males and appropriate for females. Thus, masculinity is associated with technical mastery, aggression, competitiveness, and cognitive abstraction, whereas femininity is associated with emotional nurturance, connectedness, and passivity. Sex role theory informed a wide variety of prescriptive literature (self-help books) that instructed parents on what to do if they wanted their child to grow up as a healthy boy or girl.

The strongest challenge to all these perspectives, as we have seen, came from feminist scholars, who have specified the ways in which the assumptions about maturity, development, and health all made masculinity the norm against which both genders were measured. In all the social sciences, these feminist scholars have stripped these early studies of their academic facades to reveal the unexamined ideological assumptions contained within them. By the early 1970s, women's studies programs began to articulate a new paradigm for the study of gender, one that assumed nothing about men or women beforehand, and that made no assumptions about which gender was more highly developed. And by the mid-1970s, the first group of texts about men appeared that had been inspired by these pioneering efforts by feminist scholars.

Thinking About Men: The First Generation

In the mid-1970s, the first group of works on men and masculinity appeared that was directly influenced by these feminist critiques of the traditional explanations for gender differences. Some books underscored the costs to men of traditional gender role prescriptions, exploring how some aspects of men's lives and experiences are constrained and underdeveloped by the relentless pressure to exhibit other behaviors associated with masculinity. Books such as Marc Feigen-Fasteau's *The Male Machine* (1974) and Warren Farrell's *The Liberated Man* (1975) discussed the costs to men's health—both physical and psychological—and to the quality of relationships with women, other men, and their children of the traditional male sex role.

Several anthologies explored the meanings of masculinity in the United States by adopting a feminist-inspired prism through which to view men and masculinity. For example, Deborah David and Robert Brannon's *The Forty-Nine Percent Majority* (1976) and Joseph Pleck and Jack Sawyer's *Men and Masculinity* (1974) presented panoramic views of men's lives, from within a framework that accepted the feminist critique of traditional gender arrangements. Elizabeth Pleck and Joseph Pleck's *The American Man* (1980) suggested a historical evolution of contemporary themes. These works explored both the "costs" and the privileges of being a man in modern U.S. society.

Perhaps the single most important book to criticize the normative organization of the male sex role was Joseph Pleck's *The Myth of Masculinity* (1981). Pleck carefully deconstructed the constituent elements of the male sex role and reviewed the empirical literature for each component part. After demonstrating that the empirical literature did not support these normative features,

Pleck argued that the male sex role model was incapable of describing men's experiences. In its place, he posited a male "sex role strain" model that specified the contemporary sex role as problematic, historically specific, and also an unattainable ideal.

Building on Pleck's work, a critique of the sex role model began to emerge. Sex roles had been cast as the static containers of behaviors and attitudes, and biological males and females were required to fit themselves into these containers, regardless of how ill-fitting these clusters of behaviors and attitudes felt. Such a model was ahistorical and suggested a false cultural universalism, and was therefore ill equipped to help us understand the ways in which sex roles change, and the ways in which individuals modify those roles through the enactments of gender expectations. Most telling, however, was the way in which the sex role model ignored the ways in which definitions of masculinity and femininity were based on, and reproduced, relationships of power. Not only do men as a group exert power over women as a group, but the definitions of masculinity and femininity reproduce those power relations. Power dynamics are an essential element in both the definition and the enactments of gender.

This first generation of research on masculinity was extremely valuable, particularly since it challenged the unexamined ideology that made masculinity the gender norm against which both men and women were measured. The old models of sex roles had reproduced the domination of men over women by insisting on the dominance of masculine traits over feminine traits. These new studies argued against both the definitions of either sex and the social institutions in which those differences were embedded. Shapers of the new model looked at "gender relations" and understood how the definition of either masculinity or femininity was relational, that is, how the definition of one gender depended, in part, on the understanding of the definition of the other.

In the early 1980s, the research on women again surged ahead of the research on men and masculinity. This time, however, the focus was not on the ways in which sex roles reproduce the power relations in society, but rather on the ways in which femininity is experienced differently by women in various social groups. Gradually, the notion of a single femininity—which was based on the white middle-class Victorian notion of female passivity, langorous beauty, and emotional responsiveness—was replaced by an examination of the ways in which women differ in their gender role expectations by race, class, age, sexual orientation, ethnicity, region, and nationality.

The research on men and masculinity is now entering a new stage, in which the variations among men are seen as central to the understanding of men's lives. The unexamined assumption in earlier studies had been that one version of masculinity—white, middle-aged, middle-class, heterosexual—was the sex role into which all men were struggling to fit in our society. Thus, working-class men, men of color, gay men, and younger and older men were all observed as departing in significant ways from the traditional definitions of masculinity. Therefore, it was easy to see these men as enacting "problematic" or "deviant" versions of masculinity. Such theoretical assertions, however, reproduce precisely the power relationships that keep these men in subordinate positions in our society. Not only does middle-class, middle-aged, heterosexual white masculinity become the standard against which all men are measured, but this definition, itself, is used against those who do not fit as a way to keep them down. The normative definition of masculinity is not the "right" one, but it is the one that is dominant.

The challenge to the hegemonic definition of masculinity came from men whose masculinity was cast as deviant: men of color, gay men, and ethnic men. We understand now that we cannot speak of "masculinity" as a singular term, but must examine *masculinities*: the ways in which different men construct different versions of masculinity. Such a perspective can be seen in several recent works, such as Harry Brod's *The Making of Masculinities* (1987), Michael Kimmel's *Changing Men: New Directions in Research on Men and Masculinity* (1987), and Tim Carrigan, Bob Connell, and John Lee's "Toward a New Sociology of Masculinity" (1985). Bob Connell's *Gender and Power* (1987) and Jeff Hearn's *The Gender of Oppression* (1987) represent the most sophisticated theoretical statements of this perspective. Connell argues that the oppression of women is a chief mechanism that links the various masculinities, and that the marginalization of certain masculinities is an important component of the reproduction of male power over women. This critique of the hegemonic definition of masculinity as a perspective on men's lives is one of the organizing principles of our book, which is the first college-level text in this second generation of work on men and masculinities.

Now that we have reviewed some of the traditional explanations for gender relations and have situated this book within the research on gender in general, and men in particular, let us briefly outline exactly the theoretical perspective we have employed in the book.

The Social Construction of Masculinities

Men are not born, growing from infants through boyhood to manhood, to follow a predetermined biological imperative encoded in their physical organization. To be a man is to participate in social life as a man, as a gendered being. Men are not born; they are made. And men make themselves, actively constructing their masculinities within a social and historical context.

This book is about how men are made and how men make themselves in contemporary U.S. society. It is about what masculinity means, about how masculinity is organized, and about the social institutions that sustain and elaborate it. It is a book in which we will trace what it means to be a man over the course of men's lives.

Men's Lives revolves around three important themes that are part of a social scientific perspective. First, we have adopted a *social constructionist* perspective. By this we mean that the important fact of men's lives is not that they are biological males, but that they become men. Our sex may be male, but our identity as men is developed through a complex process of interaction with the culture in which we both learn the gender scripts appropriate to our culture and attempt to modify those scripts to make them more palatable. The second axis around which the book is organized follows from our social constructionist perspective. As we have argued, the experience of masculinity is not uniform and universally generalizable to all men in our society. Masculinity differs dramatically in our society, and we have organized the book to illustrate the *variations* among men in the construction of masculinity. Third, we have adopted a *life course* perspective, to chart the construction of these various masculinities in men's lives and to examine pivotal developmental moments or institutional locations during a man's life in which the meanings of masculinity are articulated. Social constructionism, variations among men, and the life course perspective define the organization of this book and the criteria we have used to select the articles included.

The Social Constructionist Model

The social constructionist perspective argues that the meaning of masculinity is neither transhistorical nor culturally universal, but rather varies from culture to culture and within any one culture over time. Thus, males become men in the United States in the early twenty-first century in a way that is very different from men in Southeast Asia, or Kenya, or Sri Lanka.

Men's lives also vary within any one culture over time. The experience of masculinity in the contemporary United States is very different from that experience 150 years ago. Who would argue that what it meant to be a "real man" in seventeenth-century France (at least among the upper classes)—high-heeled patent leather shoes, red velvet jackets covering frilly white lace shirts, lots of rouge and white powder makeup, and a taste for the elegant refinement of ornate furniture—bears much resemblance to the meaning of masculinity among a similar class of French men today?

A perspective that emphasizes the social construction of gender is, therefore, both *historical* and *comparative*. It allows us to explore the ways in which the meanings of gender vary from culture to culture, and how they change within any one culture over historical time.

Variations Among Men

Masculinity also varies *within* any one society according to the various types of cultural groups that compose it. Subcultures are organized around other poles, which are the primary way in which people organize themselves and by which resources are distributed. And men's experiences differ from one another according to what social scientists have identified as the chief structural mechanisms along which power and resources are distributed. We cannot speak of masculinity in the United States as if it were a single, easily identifiable commodity. To do so is to risk positing one version of masculinity as normative and making all other masculinities problematic.

In the contemporary United States, masculinity is constructed differently by class culture, by race and ethnicity, and by age. And each of these axes of masculinity modifies the others. Black masculinity differs from white masculinity, yet each of them is also further modified by class and age. A 30-year-old middle-class black man will have some things in common with a 30-year-old middle-class white man that he might not share with a 60-year-old working-class black man, although he will share with him elements of masculinity that are different from those of the white man of his class and age. The resulting matrix of *masculinities* is complicated by cross-cutting elements; without understanding this, we risk collapsing all masculinities into one hegemonic version.

The challenge to a singular definition of masculinity as the normative definition is the second axis around which the readings in this book revolve.

The Life Course Perspective

The meaning of masculinity is not constant over the course of any man's life, but will change as he grows and matures. The issues confronting a man about proving himself and feeling successful and the social institutions in which he will attempt to enact his definitions of masculinity will change throughout his life. Thus, we have adopted a *life course perspective* to discuss the ways in which different issues will emerge for men at different times of their lives, and the ways in which men's lives, themselves, change over time. The life course perspective we have employed will examine men's lives at various pivotal moments in their development from young boys to adults. Like a slide show, these points will freeze the action for a short while, to afford us the opportunity to examine in more detail the ways in which different men in our culture experience masculinity at any one time.

The book's organization reflects these three concerns. Part One sets the context through which we shall examine men's lives. Parts Two through Nine follow those lives through their full course, examining central moments experienced by men in the United States today. Specifically, Parts Two and Three touch on boyhood and adolescence, discussing some of the institutions organized to embody and reproduce masculinities in the United States, such as fraternities, the Boy Scouts, and sports groups. Part Four, "Men and Work," explores the ways in which masculinities are constructed in relation to men's occupations. Part Five, "Men and Health: Body and Mind," deals with heart attacks, stress, AIDS, and other health problems among men. Part Six, "Men in Relationships," describes men's emotional and sexual relationships. We deal with heterosexuality and homosexuality, mindful of the ways in which variations are based on specific lines (class, race, ethnicity). Part Seven, "Male Sexualities," studies the normative elements of heterosexuality and probes the controversial political implications of pornography as a source of both straight and gay men's sexual information. Part Eight, "Men in Families," concentrates on masculinities within the family and the role of men as husbands, fathers, and senior citizens. Part Nine, "Masculinities in the Media," explores the different ways the media presents modes of masculinity. Part Ten, "Men, Movements, and the Future," examines some of the ways in which men are changing and points to some directions in which men might continue to change.

Our perspective, stressing the social construction of masculinities over the life course, will, we believe, allow a more comprehensive understanding of men's lives in the United States today.

References

Brod, Harry, ed. *The Making of Masculinities.* Boston: Unwin, Hyman, 1987.

Carrigan, Tim, Bob Connell, and John Lee. "Toward a New Sociology of Masculinity" in *Theory and Society,* 1985, 5(14).

Chodorow, Nancy. *The Reproduction of Mothering.* Berkeley: University of California Press, 1978.

Connell, R. W. *Gender and Power.* Stanford, CA: Stanford University Press, 1987.

David, Deborah, and Robert Brannon, eds. *The Forty-Nine Percent Majority.* Reading, MA: Addison-Wesley, 1976.

Elliott, J. H. *Richelieu and Olivares.* New York: Cambridge University Press, 1984.

Epstein, Cynthia Fuchs. "Inevitability of Prejudice" in *Society,* Sept./Oct., 1986.

Farrell, Warren. *The Liberated Man.* New York: Random House, 1975.

Feigen-Fasteau, Marc. *The Male Machine.* New York: McGraw-Hill, 1974.

Gilligan, Carol. *In a Different Voice.* Cambridge, MA: Harvard University Press, 1982.

Gilder, George. *Men and Marriage.* Gretna, LA: Pelican Publishers, 1986.

Goldberg, Steven. *The Inevitability of Patriarchy.* New York: William Morrow & Co., 1975.

——— "Reaffirming the Obvious" in *Society,* Sept./Oct., 1986.

Hearn, Jeff. *The Gender of Oppression.* New York: St. Martin's Press, 1987.

Hrdy, Sandra Blaffer. *The Woman That Never Evolved.* Cambridge, MA: Harvard University Press, 1981.

Kimmel, Michael S., ed. *Changing Men: New Directions in Research on Men and Masculinity.* Newbury Park, CA: Sage Publications, 1987.

Mead, Margaret. *Sex and Temperament in Three Primitive Societies.* New York: McGraw-Hill, 1935.

Pleck, Elizabeth, and Joseph Pleck, eds. *The American Man.* Englewood Cliffs, NJ: Prentice-Hall, 1980.

Pleck, Joseph. *The Myth of Masculinity.* Cambridge, MA: M.I.T. Press, 1981.

——— and Jack Sawyer, eds. *Men and Masculinity.* Englewood Cliffs, NJ: Prentice-Hall, 1974.

Tiger, Lionel, and Robin Fox. *The Imperial Animal.* New York: Holt, Rinehart & Winston, 1984.

Trivers, Robert. "Parental Investment and Sexual Selection" in *Sexual Selection and the Descent of Man* (B. Campbell, ed.). Chicago: Aldine Publishers, 1972.

Wilkinson, Rupert. *American Tough: The Tough Guy Tradition and American Character.* New York: Harper & Row, 1986.

Wilson, E. O. *Sociobiology: The New Synthesis.* Cambridge, MA: Harvard University Press, 1976.

Part One

Perspectives on Masculinities

A quick glance at any magazine rack or television talk-show is enough to make you aware that these days, men are confused. What does it mean to be a "real man"? How are men supposed to behave? What are men supposed to feel? How are men to express their feelings? Who are we supposed to be like: Eminem or Boys II Men? Jimmy Kimmel or "Will"? Derek Jeter or John Rocker? Rhett Butler or Ashley Wilkes?

We are daily bombarded with images and handy rules to help us negotiate our way through a world in which all the rules seem to have suddenly vanished or changed. Some tell us to reassert traditional masculinity against all contemporary challenges. But a strength built only on the weakness of others hardly feels like strength at all. Others tell us that men are in power, the oppressor. But if men are in power as a group, why do individual men often feel so powerless? Can men change?

These questions will return throughout this book. These articles in Part One begin to unravel the "masculine mystique" and suggest various dimensions of men's position in society, their power, their powerlessness, and their confusion.

But we cannot speak of "masculinity" as some universal category that is experienced in the same ways by each man. "All men are alike," runs a popular wisdom. But are they really? Are gay men's experiences with work, relationships, love, and politics similar to those of heterosexual men? Do black and Chicano men face the same problems and conflicts in their daily lives that white men face? Do middle-class men have the same political interests as blue-collar men? The answers to these questions, as the articles in this part suggest, are not simple.

Although earlier studies of men and masculinity focused on the apparently universal norms of masculinity, recent work has attempted to demonstrate how different the worlds of various men are. Men are divided along the same lines that divide any other group: race, class, sexual orientation, ethnicity, age, and geographic region. Men's lives vary in crucial ways, and understanding these variations will take us a long way toward understanding men's experiences.

Earlier studies that suggested a single universal norm of masculinity reproduced some of the problems they were trying to solve. To be sure, *all* benefit from the inequality between women and men; for example, think of how rape jokes or male-exclusive sports culture provide contexts for the bonding of men across class, race, and ethnic lines while denying full participation to women. But the single, seemingly universal masculinity obscured ways in which some men hold and maintain power over other men in our society, hiding the fact that

all men do not share equally in the fruits of gender inequality.

Here is how sociologist Erving Goffman put it in his important book *Stigma* (New York: Doubleday, 1963, p. 128):

> In an important sense there is only one complete unblushing male in America: a young, married, white, urban, northern, heterosexual Protestant father of college education, fully employed, of good complexion, weight, and height, and a recent record in sports. Every American male tends to look out upon the world from this perspective, this constituting one sense in which one can speak of a common value system in America. Any male who fails to qualify in any one of these ways is likely to view himself—during moments at least—as unworthy, incomplete, and inferior.

As Goffman suggests, middle-class, white, heterosexual masculinity is used as the marker against which other masculinities are measured, and by which standard they may be found wanting. What is *normative* (prescribed) becomes translated into what is *normal*. In this way, heterosexual men maintain their status by the oppression of gay men; middle-aged men can maintain their dominance over older and younger men; upper-class men can exploit working-class men; and white men can enjoy privileges at the expense of men of color.

The articles in this section explore the variety of masculinities. James Messerschmidt discusses what sorts of experiences, behaviors, and traits are associated with being "real men" for a number of different men. Manning Marable, Alfredo Mirande, Yen Le Espiritu, and Anthony Chen focus on the different ways in which different groups of men (African American, Latino, and Asian American) experience masculinities. Michelle Fine and her colleagues examine the same questions for white working-class men in a world that seems to be passing them by. Taken together, they suggest that an understanding of class, ethnic, and racial minorities requires and understanding of how political, social, and economic factors shape and constrain the possibilities and personal lifestyle choices for different groups of men. Calls for "changing masculinities," these articles suggest, must involve an emphasis on *institutional* transformation, to which Marable's arguments give a special political urgency.

Michael Kimmel's article explores the gendered dimensions to terrorism, particularly examining the similarities between the perpetrators of America's two most horrific acts of terrorism: the bombing of the Murrah Federal Building in Oklahoma City in 1995 and the attack on the World Trade Center and the Pentagon on September 11, 2001.

ARTICLE 1

James Messerschmidt

Varieties of "Real Men"

It was a theoretical breakthrough in social theory when the family came to be recognized generally as both gendered and political. Feminist work has now begun to reveal theoretically what we have known for some time in practice—that other social milieux, such as the street and workplace, are not only political but also gendered (Cockburn 1983; Connell 1987; Acker 1990). I extend this theoretical insight through an analysis of how the social structures of labor, power, and sexuality constrain and enable social action within three specific social settings: the street, the workplace, and the family. I focus on how some men, within particular social situations, can make use of certain crimes to construct various public and private adult masculinities.

Research reveals that men construct masculinities in accord with their position in social structures and, therefore, their access to power and resources. Because men situationally accomplish masculinity in response to their socially structured circumstances, various forms of crime can serve as suitable resources for doing masculinity within the specific social contexts of the street, the workplace, and the family. Consequently, I emphasize the significant differences among men and how men utilize different types of crimes to situationally construct distinct forms of masculinities. We begin with the street and an examination of pimping.

From *Masculinities and Crime: Critique and Reconceptualization of Theory*, pp. 119–153. Rowman and Littlefield Publishers, 1993. Reprinted by permission.

The Street

Middle-class, working-class, and lower-working-class young men exhibit unique types of public masculinities that are situationally accomplished by drawing on different forms of youth crime. Moreover, class and race structure the age-specific form of resources employed to construct the cultural ideals of hegemonic masculinity. Such public arenas as the school and street are lush with gendered meanings and signals that evoke various styles of masculinity and femininity. Another type of public masculinity found in the social setting of the street is that of the adult pimp. This particularized form of masculinity is examined here within the context of "deviant street networks."

The Pimp and His Network

Eleanor Miller's (1986, 35–43) respected work *Street Women* reports that in Milwaukee, Wisconsin, African American men in their mid to late twenties and early thirties dominate what she calls "deviant street networks." Deviant street networks are groups of men and women assembled to conduct such illegal profit-making ventures as prostitution, check and credit-card fraud, drug trafficking, burglary, and robbery. Although both men and women engage in various aspects of these "hustling activities," gender relations are unequal, reflecting the social structures of labor, power, and normative heterosexuality. Miller (p. 37) found that a major source of continuous income in these networks "derives from the hustling activity of women who turn their earnings over to the men in exchange for affection, an allowance, the status of their company, and some measure of protection." Commonly referred to as "pimps," the men act as agents and/or companions of these women, substantially profiting from their labor. Miller found that to work as street hustlers, it is essential that women have a "male" sponsor and protector. However, this "essential" has not always existed in the history of prostitution.

Throughout the 1800s, U.S. prostitution was condemned but not classified as a criminal offense, and was conducted primarily under the direction of a "madam" in brothels located in specific red-light districts (Rosen 1982, 27–30). In an attempt to halt prostitution, state legislatures enacted laws in the early 1900s in order to close down these red-light districts and, contemporaneously, women-controlled brothels. Predictably, rather than halting prostitution, new forms of prostitution emerged from this attempt at legislating morality. As Rosen (p. 32) shows in *The Lost Sisterhood,* the closing of the brothels simply increased streetwalking for women; because prostitutes could no longer receive "johns" "in the semiprotected environment of the brothel or district, . . . they had to search for business in public places—hotels, restaurants, cabarets, or on the street." This search for customers in public places exposed prostitutes to violent clients and police harassment. Consequently, these women turned to men for help in warding off dangers, providing legal assistance, and offering some emotional support. Eventually, the overall prostitution business came to be dominated by individual pimp entrepreneurs or masculine-dominated syndicated crime.

In today's deviant street network, the pimp usually controls two to three women (labeled "wives-in-law") on the street (Miller 1986, 37–38). The women turn over their earnings to the pimp and he decides how it will be spent. The disciplinarian of the network, the pimp also "decides upon and metes out the punishment" (Romenesko and Miller 1989, 120). Indeed, as Romenesko and Miller (p. 117) show in their interviews with street hustlers, the pimp demands unquestioned respect:

Showing respect for "men" means total obedience and complete dedication to them. Mary reports that in the company of "men" she had to "talk mainly to the women—try not to look at the men if possible at all—try not to have conversations with them." Rita, when asked about the rules of the street, said, "Just basic, obey. Do what he wants to do. Don't disrespect him. . . . I could not disrespect him in any verbal or physical way. I never attempted to hit him back. Never." And, in the same vein, Tina said that when her "man" had others over to socialize, the women of the family were relegated to the role of servant. "We couldn't speak to them when we wasn't spoken to, and we could not foul up on orders. And you cannot disrespect them."

This authority and control exercised by pimps over women is also clearly exemplified in biographies of pimp life (Malcolm X, 1965; Slim, 1967). Christina Milner and Richard Milner (1972, 52–53) reported a similar form of gendered power in their study of African American pimps in San Francisco:

First and foremost, the pimp must be in complete control of his women; this control is made conspicuous to others by a series of little rituals which express symbolically his woman's attitude. When in the company of others she must take special pains to treat him with absolute deference and respect. She must light his cigarettes, respond to his every whim immediately, and never, never, contradict him. In fact, a ho [prostitute] is strictly not supposed to speak in the company of pimps unless spoken to.

Gender is a situated accomplishment in which we produce forms of behavior seen by others in the same immediate situation as masculine or feminine. Within the confines and social setting of the street, economically marginal men and women create street networks for economic survival, yet simultaneously "do gender" in the process of surviving. In this manner, deviant street networks become the condition that produces material survival as well as the social setting that reaffirms one's gender. The result is a gendered, deviant street network in which men and women do masculinity and femininity, albeit in a distinct manner.

In short, the division of street network labor is concerned both with rationally assigning specific tasks to network members and with the symbolic affirmation and assertion of specific forms of masculinity and femininity (discussed further below). Consequently, pimps simultaneously do pimping and masculinity. As marginalized men, street pimps choose pimping in preference to unemployment and routine labor for "the man." Lacking other avenues and opportunities for accomplishing gender, the pimp lifestyle is a survival strategy that is exciting and rewarding for them as men. The deviant street network provides the context within which to construct one's "essential nature" as a man and to survive as a human being.

The Cool Pose of the Badass

African American street pimps engage in specific practices (constrained by class and race) intended to construct a specific "cool pose" as an important aspect of their specific type of masculinity (Majors 1986; Majors and Billson 1992). In the absence of resources that signify other types of masculinity, sex category is held more accountable and physical presence, personal style, and expressiveness take on an increased importance (Messner 1989, 82). Consequently, as Richard Majors (1986, 5) argues, many "black males have learned to make great use of 'poses' and 'postures' that connote control, toughness and detachment," adopting a specific carriage that exemplifies an expressive and distinct assertion of masculinity.

The often flamboyant, loud, and ostentatious style of African American pimps signifies aspects of this cool pose. The exaggerated display of luxury (for example, in the form of flashy clothing) is also a specific aspect of the cool pose distinctively associated with African American pimps. Majors and Billson (1992, 81–84) argue that the "sharp" and "clean" look of pimps is intended to upstage other men in the highly competitive arena of the street where they earn street applause for their style, providing an "antidote to invisibility." Pimps literally prance above their immediate position in the class and race divisions of labor and power, thereby constructing a specific masculine street upper-crust demeanor.

Notwithstanding, this cool presence complements an intermittent and brutal comportment to construct masculinity and, in the process, show that the pimp means business. In other words, the African American pimp must always be prepared to employ violence both for utilitarian reasons and for constructing and maintaining a formidable, portentious profile (Katz 1988, 97). The following account by Milner and Milner (1972, 232) illustrates this unpredictable use of violence:

> One ho known as Birthday Cake said she worked for a pimp for four years, gave him a new Cadillac every year, and one night came home from work with her money "funny" and got the beating of her life. She walked in and handed over the money; he counted it and said, "That's all right, honey," drew her a bath, laid her down afterwards on the bed, went to the closet and got a tire iron and beat her senseless with it. She showed us the long scars which required hundreds of stitches and demonstrated her permanent slight limp.

This "badass" form of masculinity (Katz 1988, 80–113) is also publicly displayed for, and supported by, other pimps. Milner and Milner (1972, 56) discuss how a pimp took one of "his" prostitutes (who was also a dancer) into the dancer's dressing room and "began to shout at her and slap her around" loud enough for everyone in the bar to hear. "The six pimps sitting at the back of the bar near the dressing room began to clap and whistle loudly," seemingly for the current dancer, "but in reality to cover the noise of the beating from the ears of the straight customers" (p. 56). Emerging from the dressing room and joining the others, the pimp exclaimed, "Well, I took care of that bitch." Then they all began to "joke around." In contrast, when the prostitute emerged, not "one of them (pimps) felt it proper to comfort her in any way" (p. 56). Such violence, neither out-of-control nor ungovernable, is situationally determined and regulated. Thus, pimp violence becomes a means of disciplining the prostitute and of constructing a badass public masculinity.

The combined cool pose and badass identity of African American pimps clearly represent a specialized means with which to transcend class and race domination. Yet, it also demonstrates the socially constrained nature of social action, and how African American pimps rework the ideals of hegemonic masculinity as a vehicle for achieving that transcendence. Pimping, then, is a resource for surmounting oppressive class and race conditions and for reasserting the social dominance of men. Moreover, like other men, pimps associate masculinity with work, with authority and control, and with explicit heterosexuality.

Within deviant street networks, the prostitute/pimp relationship represents a reworking of these hegemonic masculine ideals under specifically structured social possibilities/constraints. Through their authority and control within deviant street networks, pimps create a class- and race-specific type of masculine meaning and configuration, resulting in a remodeling of heterosexual monogamy in which the pimp provides love, money, and an accompanying sense of security for his "wives-in-law" (Romenesko and Miller 1989, 123).

Normative heterosexuality is the major focus of activities: wives-in-law are expected to be sexually seductive to men, receptive to the sexual "drives" and special "needs" of men (including the pimp), and to work for men who "protect" them and negotiate the "rough spots."[1] Pimping, as a resource for demonstrating that one is a "real man," distinguishes pimps from prostitutes in a specific way. Within the social context of the deviant street network, this pimp type of masculinity is sustained by means of collective and gendered practices that subordinate women, manage the expression of violence against women, and exploit women's labor and sexuality. Indeed, the individual style of the pimp is somewhat meaningless outside the group (Connell 1991, 157); it is the deviant street network that provides meaning and currency for this type of masculinity.[2] Pimping, in short, is a practice that facilitates a particular gender strategy.

In spite of the above, in attempting to transcend oppressive social structures, African American pimps ultimately reproduce them. Their masculine style is at once repugnant to "conventionality"—their source of wealth anathema to traditional morality (Katz 1988, 97)—yet simultaneously reactionary and reproductive of the gendered social order. In other words, African American pimps respond in a gender-specific manner to race and class oppression, which in turn locks them into the very structured constraints they attempt to overcome. Thus, pimping becomes a form of social action that ultimately results in the reproduction of the gender divisions of labor and power as well as normative heterosexuality.

The following section examines two distinct types of masculinity constructed in the workplace.

The Workplace

The gender divisions of labor and power and normative heterosexuality structure gender relations in the workplace. The workplace not only produces goods and provides services but is the site of gendered control and authority. Because women historically have been excluded from paid work or segregated within it, today the gender division in the workplace is both horizontally and vertically segregated (Game and Pringle 1984; Walby 1986; Reskin and Roos 1987).[3] The result is that women are concentrated overwhelmingly at the lower levels of the occupational hierarchy in terms of wages and salary, status, and authority. Indeed, a recent study of nearly four hundred firms revealed that the vast majority of women were either completely or nearly completely segregated by gender (Bielby and Baron 1986). Consequently, gender relations throughout much of the paid-labor market—like gender relations in schools, youth groups, and deviant street networks—embody relations of power: the domination of men and the subordination of women. Moreover, the creation of "male" and "female" jobs helps to maintain and reproduce this power relationship. Accordingly, gender differences are maintained through gender segregation, and occupational segregation is born of practices ultimately based on conceptions of what constitutes the "essential" natures of men and women.

In addition, the concepts "worker" and "a job" are themselves gendered. As Joan Acker (1990) recently demonstrated, these concepts embody the gender divisions of labor and power. Historically, the idea of a job and who works it has assumed a specific gendered organization or public and private life: a man's life centers on full-time work at a job outside the household; a woman's life focuses on taking care of all his other needs. Consequently, as the abstract worker is masculinized (p. 152):

> it is the man's body, his sexuality, minimal responsibility in procreation, and conventional control of emotions that pervades work and organizational processes. Women's bodies—female sexuality, their ability to procreate and their pregnancy, breast feeding, childcare, menstruation, and mythic "emotionality"—are suspect, stigmatized, and used as grounds for control and exclusion.

Because organization and sexuality occur simultaneously, the workplace is sexualized and normative heterosexuality actually conditions work activities (Hearn and Parkin 1987). As Rosemary Pringle (1989, 162) recently reported, heterosexuality in the workplace is actively perpetuated in a range of practices and interactions exemplified in "dress and self-presentation, in jokes and gossip, looks and flirtations, secret affairs and dalliances, in fantasy and in the range of coercive behaviors that we now call sexual harassment."

Within the social situation of gendered segregation, power, and normative heterosexuality, men and women in the paid-labor market actively construct specific types of masculinity and femininity, depending upon their position in the workplace. In other words, social action is patterned in the workplace in terms of a distinction between masculine and feminine. Regarding men specifically, a power hierarchy exists in the workplace among men and, not surprisingly, different forms of masculinity correspond to particular positions in this hierarchy.

Let us now look at two differing forms of masculinity in the workplace: (1) workers and their relation to a specific type of sexual harassment and (2) corporate executives and their involvement in a variant form of sexual harassment. In each case, I demonstrate how specific crimes are a resource for constructing particularized representations of private masculinity—those that are occluded from the vision, company, or intervention of outsiders.

Workers and Sexual Harassment

Studies highlight the persistence and dominance of normative heterosexuality on the shop floor—such practices as exhibiting men's sexuality as biologically driven and perpetually incontinent, whereas women are the objects of a sexuality that precipitates men's "natural urges" (Willis 1979; Cockburn 1983; Hearn 1985; Gray 1987). This macho sexual prowess, mediated through bravado and sexist joking, is constructed and encouraged on the shop floor (Collinson and Collinson 1989, 95–98). Moreover, failure to participate in this specific interaction raises serious questions about one's masculinity. In this way, situationally specific notions of heterosexuality are reproduced through the construction of shop-floor masculinity and center on men's insistence on exercising power over women.

Under such conditions, when women enter the shop floor as coworkers, a threatening situation (for the men, that is) results. In this situation, some shop-floor men are likely to engage in forms of interaction quite different from their interaction with women outside the workplace. Not surprising, sexual harassment is more prevalent in this type of social setting. For example, one study of a manufacturing firm (in which the vast majority of manual laborers were men) found (DiTomaso 1989, 81):

> the men in the plant acted differently than they would if they interacted with these women in any other context. Their behavior, in other words, was very much related to the work context itself. It appeared to provide a license for offensive behavior and an occasion for attempting to take advantage of many of the women in the plant.

In DiTomaso's study, the younger women on the shop floor were perceived by the men as the most threatening because they were competing directly for the same kinds of jobs as were the men. Consequently, these women were more likely than other women to be subjected to demeaning forms of social interaction: the men's behavior was more likely to exceed simple flirtation and to involve specific forms of sexual harassment. The following are comments from several women in the plant (pp. 80–81):

> "The men are different here than on the street. It's like they have been locked up for years."

> "It's like a field day."

> "A majority of the men here go out of their way to make you feel uneasy about being inside the plant and being a female; nice guys are a minority."

Research reveals that sexual harassment occurs at all levels in the workplace—from shop floor to management. However, sexual harassment by men on the shop floor generally is twice as serious and persistent, and is different from sexual harassment by managers (Hearn 1985, 121). In the shop-floor setting (where men are the majority), sexual harassment is "a powerful form of economic protection and exclusion from men's territory. Women workers are perceived as a threat to solidarity between men" (pp. 121–122). Studies of shop-floor sexual harassment suggest that 36 to 53 percent of women workers report some type of sexual harassment (Gruber and Bjorn 1982); furthermore, a recent study of workplace sexual assault suggests that manual workers (as opposed to other men in the firm) committed the overwhelming majority of both attempted and completed assaults within the entire firm (Schneider 1991, 539).

Notwithstanding, the most common types of sexual harassment on the shop floor involve such demeaning acts as sexual slurs, pinches or grabs, and public displays of derogatory images of women (Carothers and Crull 1984, 222; Schneider 1991, 539). Perceptively, women shop-floor coworkers are more likely than women coworkers in other occupational settings to describe this sexual harassment as designed to label them as "outsiders." The "invasion" of women on the shop floor poses a threat to men's monopoly over these jobs, and one way to discourage women from attempting to compete in this domain is to remind them, through remarks and behavior, of their "female fragility" (Carothers and Crull 1984, 224). In this way, then, shop-floor men attempt to secure the "maleness" of the job by emphasizing the "femaleness" of women coworkers (DiTomaso 1989, 88).

Although most shop-floor workers clearly do not engage in sexual harassment, the unique social setting of the shop floor increases the likelihood that this particular type of sexual harassment will occur. Indeed, this specific shop-floor sexual harassment must be seen as a practice communicating anger against women for invading a "male" bastion and for threatening the economic and social status of men (Carothers and Crull 1984, 224). In addition, however, the shop floor is an ideal arena for differentiating between masculinity and femininity—performing manual labor demonstrates to others that such workers are "real men." The presence of women on the shop floor dilutes this gender distinction: if women can do what "real men" do, the value of the practice for accomplishing masculinity is effectively challenged. Because "doing gender" means creating differences between men and women, by maintaining and emphasizing the "femaleness" of women coworkers, shop-floor men are attempting to distinguish clearly between women and men manual laborers, thus preserving the peculiar masculinity of the shop floor. This type of sexual harassment serves as an effective (albeit primitive) resource for solidifying, strengthening, and validating a specific type of heterosexual shop-floor masculinity, while simultaneously excluding, disparaging, and ridiculing women (Segal 1990, 211).[4]

Moving from shop floor to boardroom, we will next consider how a different type of sexual harassment provides certain white corporate executives with resources for constructing a specific form of private masculinity.

White Corporate Executives and Sexual Harassment

Sexual harassment is a resource available to corporate executives for constructing a specific type of masculinity. Because of their subordinate position in the corporation, women "are vulnerable to the whim and fancy of male employers or organizational superiors, who are in a position to reward or punish their female subordinate economically" (Box 1983, 152). In other words, corporate-executive men are in a unique position to sexually exploit, if they desire, women subordinates. Executive exploitation of sexuality is often a means of reinforcing men's power at the same time as making profits. For example, secretaries frequently are treated as conspicuous "possessions"; therefore, by hiring the "best looking" instead of the most competent secretary, managers exploit secretarial sexuality to "excite the envy of colleagues, disarm the opposition and obtain favors from other departments" (Hearn 1985, 118). Thus, as Jeff Hearn (p. 118) points out, exploitation of secretarial sexuality is not only a matter of directly objectifying women but also of using their sexuality for the eyes of other men. Economic and gender relations are produced simultaneously through the same ongoing sexual practices.

In addition to this direct exploitation of secretarial sexuality, corporate executives sometimes engage in specific types of sexual harassment. While shop-floor men who engage in sexual harassment are more likely to undertake practices that create a sexually demeaning work environment characterized by slurs, pictures, pinches, and grabs, white corporate-executive men are more likely to threaten women workers and lower-level managers who refuse to comply with demands for sexual favors with the loss of their jobs (Carothers and Crull 1984, 222). One secretary described this type of sexual harassment from a corporate executive as follows (cited in Carothers and Crull 1984, 222):

> He always complimented me on what I wore. I thought he was just being nice. It got to the place that every time he buzzed for me to come into his office for dictation, my stomach turned. He had a way of looking at me as if he were undressing me. This time as his eyes searched up and down my body and landed on my breast, he said. "Why should your boyfriend have all the fun. You could have fun with me *and* it could pay off for you. *Good* jobs are really scarce these days."

The harassment of women in subordinate positions by an executive man more likely involves hints and requests for dates or sexual favors, which, when rejected, are likely followed by work retaliation (p. 224). Essentially, this particular type of sexual harassment involves economic threats by white, corporate-executive men such that if a woman employee or would-be employee refuses to submit, she will, on the one hand, not be hired, retained, or promoted or, on the other hand, will be fired, demoted, or transferred to a less-pleasant work assignment. Assuming that the woman employee or potential employee does not desire a sexual relationship with the executive, such threats are extremely coercive. Given the economic position of many of these women, termination, demotion, or not being hired is economically devastating. When women depend on men for their economic well-being, some men take advantage of their economic vulnerability and engage in this particular practice of sexual harassment.

Although the imbalance of corporate gender power can be exercised coercively, sexual harassment is by no means automatic. Women often enter into genuine and humane relationships with men in the workplace, notwithstanding the fact that these men may be in supervisory positions vis-à-vis the women.[5] Nevertheless, the general power imbalance within the corporation often creates conditions such that men in supervisory positions may exercise economic coercion to gain sexual access without genuine overt consent. Indeed, the corporate structural position of white executive men ensures that such exploitation will more likely be manipulative than violent.

One recent study of workplace assaults found that shop-floor workers utilized physical force more often than other forms of coercion because they lack the institutionalized economic means with which to force compliance. Corporate executives are much more likely to use economic coercion than physical force as a means with which to obtain sexual access to women subordinates (Schneider 1991). Two women who experienced this type of sexual assault stated in part (cited in MacKinnon 1979, 32):

> "If I wasn't going to sleep with him, I wasn't going to get my promotion."

> "I was fired because I refused to give at the office."

When women refuse to "give at the office," some corporate executives retaliate by exercising their power over women's careers. In one case, an executive, "following rejection of his elaborate sexual advances, barraged the woman with unwarranted reprimands about her job performance, refused routine supervision or task direction, which made it impossible for her to do her job, and then fired her for poor work performance" (MacKinnon 1979, 35).

The social construction of masculinity/femininity in the executive/secretary relationship shows clearly how this specific type of sexual harassment comes about. A secretary is often expected to nurture the executive by stroking his ego, making his coffee, cleaning the office, and ensuring he is presentable (Sokoloff 1980, 220). Secretaries are often symbolically hired as "office wives." In one case, an executive had his secretary do all his grocery shopping and even go to his home and take his washing off the line! (Pringle 1989, 169–170)

Rosabeth Moss Kanter (1977, 88) noted some time ago that a "tone of emotional intensity" pervades the relationship between secretary and executive. The secretary comes to "feel for" the executive, "to care deeply about what happens to him and to do his feeling for him." In fact, according to Kanter (p. 88), secretaries are rewarded for their willingness "to take care of bosses' personal needs." In other words, women subordinates construct a specific type of femininity by performing an extensive nurturing service for the executive.[6] Women do in the workplace what they traditionally have done in the home. It should come as no surprise that some executives come to expect such nurturance from women subordinates, just as they do from their wives, and that some take this nurturance further to include sexual nurturing. The result is that some women are coerced to exchange sexual services for material survival. As Carothers and Crull (1984, 223) observe in their important study of sexual harassment:

> The male boss can use his power over women within the organizational structure to impose sexual attentions on a woman, just as he can coerce her into getting his coffee. They both know that if she does not go along, she is the one who will lose in terms of job benefits.

Corporate-executive harassment and sexual coercion are practices that simultaneously construct a specific form of masculinity. This type of sexual harassment arrogantly celebrates hegemonic masculinity, its presumed heterosexual urgency, and the "normality of pursuing women aggressively. In an attempt to "score" with "his" secretary, the corporate-executive sexual harasser strengthens gender hierarchy, thereby "affirming in men a shared sense of themselves as the dominant, assertive and active sex" (Segal 1990, 244). The corporate executive enjoys an immediate sensation of power derived from this practice, power that strengthens his masculine self-esteem.

In this way, in addition to normative heterosexuality, white, corporate-executive sexual harassers attempt to reproduce their gender power.

Through the practice of corporate sexual harassment, executives exhibit, as MacKinnon (1979, 162) argues, "that they can go this far any time they wish and get away with it." White, corporate-executive sexual harassment, constructed differently than by shop-floor men, provides a resource for constructing this specific type of heterosexual masculinity that centers on the "driven" nature of "male" sexuality and "male" power.

Although clearly most corporate executives do not engage in sexual harassment, the social setting of the executive/secretary relationship increases the probability that this specific form of sexual harassment will occur. Corporate executives engage in sexual harassment to reinforce their power by sexualizing women subordinates, creating "essential" differences between women and men by constructing this particular type of masculinity.

The Family

In addition to the street and the workplace, the divisions of labor and power frame social interactions and practices in the contemporary nuclear family where, for example, women remain responsible primarily for unpaid housework and child care while men remain responsible primarily for paid labor. Indeed, the gender division of household labor defines not only who does most of the unpaid household labor but also the kind of household labor assigned to men and women. Moreover, the sociological evidence indicates clearly that in Western industrialized societies gender asymmetry in the performance of household labor continues to exist (Hartmann 1981; Berk 1985; Messerschmidt 1986, 74; Andersen 1988, 141–145; Hochschild 1989, 1992) and women share less in the consumption of household goods (from food to leisure time) than do men (Walby 1989, 221).

It is true that barely 10 percent of all U.S. heterosexual households consist of a husband and wife with two children living at home, where the husband is the sole breadwinner (Messerschmidt 1986, 74). Further, as fertility is delayed or declines, and with more and more women working during pregnancy and child-rearing years, active motherhood is shrinking as a component of most women's lives (Petchesky 1984, 246). Nevertheless, evidence indicates that women continue to perform most of the household labor, even as these demographic changes occur and women's participation in the paid-labor market increases dramatically. Indeed, Arlie Hochschild (1992, 512) concluded in her study of fifty-two heterosexual couples over an eight-year period that just as "there is a wage gap between men and women in the work place, there is a 'leisure gap' between them in the home. Most women work one shift at the office or factory and a 'second shift' at home."

This gender division of labor embodies the husband's power to define the household setting in his terms. While conscious efforts are being made in many households to dismantle familial power relations (Connell 1987, 124), especially in the middle class (Ehrenreich 1983), for most couples the capacity of each spouse to determine the course of their shared life is unequal: men alone make the "very important" decisions in the household; women alone make few "important" decisions (Komter 1989). In many dual-career families, men's power is deemed authentic and an acceptable part of social relations. This legitimized power in the family provides men with considerably greater authority (Bernard 1982; Komter 1989; Pahl 1992). Concomitantly, the marital sexual relationship, as with other aspects of marriage, likely embodies power, unless consciously dismantled, and "in most cases it is the husband who holds the initiative in defining sexual practice" (Connell 1987, 123).

The concept of patriarchy has lost its strength and usefulness as a theoretical starting point for comprehending gender inequality in Western industrialized societies. Nevertheless, the concept is helpful to describe a certain type of masculinity that persists today: some men are simply *patriarchs* in the traditional sense. Patriarchs fashion configurations of behavior and pursue a gender strategy within the family setting that control women's labor and/or sexuality. Moreover, these men will most likely use violence against women in the family. In the final section of this chapter, the discussion focuses on two forms of violence against women in the family—wife beating and wife rape—and analyzes how these crimes serve as a resource for the construction of specific types of patriarchal masculinities.

Wife Beating and Battering Rape

Victimization surveys indicate that in the home, wives are assaulted much more often by their husbands than husbands are by their wives (less than 5 percent of domestic violence involves attacks on husbands by their wives) and women are much more likely than men to suffer injury from these assaults (Dobash, Dobash, Wilson, and Daly 1992).[7] Wife beating also develops within a setting of prolonged and persistent intimidation, domination, and control over women (Dobash and Dobash 1984; Pagelow 1984; Dobash et al. 1992). Accordingly, wife beating is the "chronic battering of a person of inferior power who for that reason cannot effectively resist" (Gordon 1988, 251).

Violence by men in the household derives from the domestic authority of men and is intimately linked to the traditional patriarchal expectation (1) that men are the credible figures within monogamous relationships and (2) that men possess the inherent right to control those relationships. As Susan Schechter (1982, 222) argues, "a man beats to remind a woman that the relationship will proceed in the way he wants or that ultimately he holds the power."

Katz's (1988, 18–31) discussion of "righteous slaughter"—killing among family members, friends, and acquaintances—by men aids in understanding how this focus on household authority and control results in wife beating as a resource for masculine construction. Katz argues that for the typical killer, murder achieves *Good* by obliterating *Bad*. Moreover, the killer has no capacity to "ignore a fundamental challenge" to his self-worth and identity. From the killer's perspective, the victim teases, dares, defies, or pursues the killer. Accordingly, the killer sees himself as simply "defending his rights." In other words, the killer's identity and self-worth have been taken away—by an insult, losing an argument, an act of infidelity—and such events attack an "eternal human value" that calls for a "last stand in defense of his basic worth." The "eternally humiliating situation" is transformed into a blinding rage and the compulsion to wipe away the stigmatizing stain through the act of murder. And the rage is not random and chaotic but, rather, "coherent, disciplined action, cunning in its moral structure" (p. 30). The killer "does not kill until and unless he can fashion violence to convey the situational meaning of defending his rights" (p. 31).

Investigations of wife beating indicate further the application of the notion "defending his rights." Violence is regarded by the husband as achieving *Good* by pulverizing *Bad;* such men engage in a coherent and disciplined rage to defend what they consider to be their rights. According to interviews with wife beaters, their wife is perceived as not "performing well," not accomplishing what her "essential nature" enjoins and stipulates. Women are beaten for not cooking "up to standards," for not being obeisant and deferential, and for not completing or performing housework sufficiently—for not being a "good wife" (Ptacek 1988, 147). According to the offender, the "privileges of male entitlement have been unjustly denied" because the wife is not submissive and, therefore, not conforming to his standards of "essential femininity" (p. 148). Irene Frieze's (1983, 553) interviews with wife beaters found that they believe "it is their right as men to batter wives who disobey them."

Dobash and Dobash (1984, 274) similarly found that most wife beating is precipitated by verbal confrontations centering on possessiveness and jealousy on the part of the husband and a husband's demand concerning domestic labor and services. During an argument over such issues, "the men were most likely to become physically violent at the point when the woman could be perceived to be questioning his authority or challenging the legitimacy of his behavior or at points when she asserted herself in some way" (p. 274).

In other words, wife beating arises not solely from gendered subordination but also from women actively contesting that subordination (Gordon 1988, 286). In such situations, the wife beater is punishing "his wife" for her failure to fulfill adequately her "essential" obligations in the gender division of labor and power and for her challenge to his dominance. The wife beater perceives that he has an inherent patriarchal right to punish "his woman" for her alleged wrongdoing.

Wife beaters are piously sure of their righteousness, and thus fashion their violence to communicate the situational meaning of defending their patriarchal rights. Indeed, the more traditional the gender division of labor (regardless of class and race position) the greater the likelihood of wife beating (Edleson, Eisikovits, and Guttman, 1986; Messerschmidt 1986; Smith 1990a). In such traditional patriarchal households, both husband and wife tend to perceive the lopsided gender division of labor and power as "fair" (Berk 1985). Linda Gordon's (1988, 260–261) historical study of family violence found that in households where wife beating is prevalent:

> Women as well as men professed allegiance to male-supremacist understandings of what relations between the sexes should be like. These shared assumptions, however, by no means prevented conflict. Women's assumptions of male dominance did not mean that they quit trying to improve their situations.

The wife beater attempts to resolve in *his* way what he regards as a conflict over this "fair" arrangement, even when the wife is not actively or consciously contesting that "fair" household organization.[8] Accordingly, as West and Zimmerman (1987, 144) argue, "It is not simply that household labor is designated as 'women's work,' but that a woman to engage in it and a man not to engage in it is to draw on and exhibit the 'essential nature' of each." By engaging in practices that maintain gender divisions of labor and power, husbands and wives do not simply produce household goods and services, but also produce gender. Indeed, husbands and wives develop gendered rationalizations and justifications for this asymmetrical household labor. What follows are selected but representative examples (Komter 1989, 209):

> *By wives:*
> "He has no feeling for it."
> "He is not born to it."
> "It does not fit his character."
>
> *By husbands:*
> "She has more talent for it."
> "It is a woman's natural duty."

When this asymmetry is questioned (whether consciously or not), the wife beater assumes that his "essential rights" are being denied—an injustice has occurred, a violation of the "natural" order of things. The "essential nature" of wife beaters is that they control familial decision making and thus dominate the family division of labor and power. When wives "question" this decision making, through words or actions, they threaten their husband's control of the gender division of labor and power. In other words, the husband interprets such behavior as a threat to his "essential nature"—control and domination of the household. Because spousal domestic labor is a symbolic affirmation of a patriarch's masculinity and his wife's femininity, such men are extremely vulnerable to disappointment when that labor is not performed as they expect (Gordon 1988, 268).

According to the wife beater, it is his duty to determine, for example, what constitutes a satisfactory meal, how children are cared for, when and how often sexual relations occur, and the nature of leisure activities (Ferraro 1988, 134). Women are beaten for some of the most insignificant conduct imaginable: for example, preparing a casserole instead of a meat dish for dinner, wearing their hair in a ponytail, or remarking that they do not like the pattern on the wallpaper. Kathleen Ferraro (p. 135) discusses a case in which even the issue of wearing a particular piece of clothing was perceived by the husband as a threat to his control:

> On her birthday, she received a blouse from her mother that she put on to wear to a meeting she

was attending without Steven. He told her she could not wear the blouse, and after insisting that she would, Steven beat her. It was not only her insistence on wearing the blouse that evening that triggered Steven's abuse. It was the history of his symbolic control, through determining her appearance that was questioned by wearing the new blouse.

Wife beaters (regardless of class and race position) presume they have the patriarchal right—because it is part of their "essential nature"—to dominate and control their wives, and wife beating serves both to ensure continued compliance with their commands and as a resource for constructing a "damaged" patriarchal masculinity. Thus, wife beating increases (or is intended to do so) their control over women and, therefore, over housework, child care, and sexual activity.

Yet wife beating is related not only to the husband's control over familial decision making, but also develops from another form of control, possessiveness. For some wife beaters, spousal demonstration of loyalty is a focal concern and is closely monitored. For instance, time spent with friends may be interpreted by a wife beater simply as disloyalty. Indeed, sexual jealousy of friends is a common theme in the literature on wife beating (Dobash and Dobash 1979, 1984; Frieze 1983; Ferraro 1988), and indicates the importance of the social structure of normative heterosexuality to understanding wife beating. The wife's uncommitted wrong is the potential to be unfaithful, which to her husband is not only a serious challenge to his patriarchal ideology, but his very real fear that his wife will choose another man and, thereby, judge him less "manly" than his "competitor." Thus, because time spent with friends endangers his ongoing interest in heterosexual performance, wife beating reassures him that his wife is his to possess sexually.

Moreover, not only potential sexual competitors can threaten a patriarchal husband, but relatives may also pose threats to a wife's loyalty. Pregnancy, for example, is closely associated with wife beating, and reflects the husband's resentment of the fetal intruder (Ferraro 1988). Walker (1979, 83–84) offers an example of a husband and wife who planned to spend the day together, but the wife broke off the plans, choosing instead to baby-sit her three-year-old granddaughter. Her husband (Ed) seems to have interpreted this choice as disloyal behavior and a challenge to his ultimate control.

> Ed became enraged. He began to scream and yell that I didn't love him, that I only loved my children and grandchildren. I protested and said, "Maybe you would like to come with me," thinking that if he came, he might feel more a part of the family. He just became further enraged. I couldn't understand it.... He began to scream and yell and pound me with his fists. He threw me against the wall and shouted that he would never let me leave, that I had to stay with him and could not go. I became hysterical and told him that I would do as I saw fit.... Ed then became even further enraged and began beating me even harder.

Thus, under conditions where labor services are "lacking" and possessiveness is "challenged," a wife beater's masculinity is threatened. In such a scenario, predictably, the wife beater attempts to reestablish control by reconstructing his patriarchal masculinity through the practice of wife beating.

Approximately 30 to 40 percent of battered women are also victims of wife rape (Walker 1979; Russell 1982b; Frieze 1983). These "battering rapes," as Finkelhor and Yllö (1985) describe them, do not result from marital conflicts over sex; rather, the rape is an extension of other violence perpetrated on the victim. The wife beating/rape represents punishment and degradation for challenging his authority and, thus, the traditional division of labor and power. In fact, although wife beating and battering rapes extend across all classes and races (for the reasons discussed above), they occur most frequently in working-class and lower-working-class households wherein the traditional patriarchal gender division of labor and power—husband decision maker and wife caretaker—is strongest (Walker 1977–1978; Straus, Gelles, and Steinmetz 1980; Finkelhor and Yllö

1985; Messerschmidt 1986, 144; Smith 1990b). Research consistently shows that class conditions are associated with wife beating: for example, low-income (Straus et al. 1980; DeKeseredy and Hinch 1991) and working-class wives are approximately twice as likely as middle-class wives to experience wife beating (Stets and Straus 1989; Smith 1990a). Moreover, among couples in which the husband is unemployed or employed part-time, the level of husband-to-wife violence is three times as high as the level among couples in which the husband is fully employed (Straus et al. 1980; DeKeseredy and Hinch 1991).

Finally, Michael Smith's (1990b, 49) study of risk factors in wife beating found that "the lower the income, the higher the probability of abuse." This same study went on to report that the chances of a low-income woman being severely battered during marriage exceed those of a middle-class woman by a factor of ten. Smith's (1990b, 267) data reveals that "men with relatively low incomes, less educated men, and men in low-status jobs were significantly more likely than their more privileged counterparts to subscribe to an ideology of familial patriarchy. These men were also more likely to have beaten their wives."

Although at work he is individually powerless, at home the working-class battering rapist is a patriarch endowed with individual authority. His ability to earn money (if available) "authorizes" his patriarchal power as husband/father. But his masculine identity depends on the demarcation of public and private responsibility; consequently, any challenge to the status quo in the home is taken personally as a confrontation (Tolson 1977, 70). In seeking to sustain this specific type of patriarchal masculinity, working-class men develop an intense emotional dependency on the family/household (Donaldson 1987), demanding nurturance, services, and comfort on their terms when at home. As Lynne Segal (1990, 28) points out, "the sole site of authority" for such men is in the home. And when their power and authority are threatened or perceived to be threatened at home, working-class men are more likely than other men to employ battering rapes to accomplish gender and reestablish their control. As Harris and Bologh (1985, 246) point out in their examination of "blue collar battering," "If he can establish an aura of aggression and violence, then he may be able to pass as a 'real man,' for surely it is admirable to use violence in the service of one's honor."

Battering in this sense is a resource for affirming "maleness." Because of their structural position in the class division of labor, working-class men—in particular, lower-working-class men—lack traditional resources for constructing their masculinity and, as a result, are more likely than are middle-class men to forge a particular type of masculinity that centers on ultimate control of the domestic setting through the use of violence. Moreover, unemployment and low occupational status undermine the patriarchal breadwinner/good provider masculinity: he cannot provide for his wife and children. Such men are more likely than are economically advantaged husbands to engage in wife beating and battering rapes to reestablish their masculinity. As Kathleen Ferraro (1988, 127) puts it, "for men who lack any control in the civil realm, dominance within the private realm of the home becomes their sole avenue for establishing a sense of self in control of others."[9]

In sum, most working- and lower-working-class husbands do not abuse their wives, nor is this particular type of abuse limited to this class of men. Nevertheless, the peculiar social conditions prevalent in working- and lower-working-class families increase the incidence of this type of abuse. For these men, power is exercised in the home in ways that hegemonic masculinity approves: men are allowed to be aggressive and sexual. Lacking dominance over others at work or the ability to act out a breadwinner (or even economic contributor) masculinity, sex category is particularly important, and working- and lower-working-class men are more likely to express their masculinity as patriarchs, attempting to control the labor and sexuality of "their women." Consequently, when patriarchal relations are "challenged," their taken-for-granted "essential nature" is undermined and, accordingly, doing masculinity requires extra effort. Wife beating/rape is a specific practice designed with an eye to one's accountability as a "real man" and, therefore, serves as a suitable resource for simultaneously accomplishing gender and affirming patriarchal masculinity.

Force-only Rape

However, wife rape is not limited to the victims of wife beating. Indeed, in Finkelhor and Yllö's (1985) study, 40 percent of their sample were "force-only rapes"—situations in which husbands use only the force necessary to coerce their wives into submission. The perpetrators and victims of force-only rapes were significantly more educated than those of battering rapes, more often middle-class, and almost half held business- or professional-level jobs.[10] Moreover, the perpetrators and victims of force-only rapes were much less likely to have been in a relationship based on the traditional gender divisions of labor and power. Sex was usually the issue in force-only rapes, and the offenders were "acting on some specifically sexual complaint," such as how often to have sex or what were acceptable sexual activities (p. 46).

In some sectors of the "progressive" middle class, there have been serious attempts to become truly equal marriage partners, where the wife has a career and where the husband participates equally in child care and housework. However, the greater the income differential between husbands and wives, the less involved some husbands are in parenting and housework, and there exists greater equality in dual-career families than in dual-income families (Segal 1990, 38). Consequently, as Barbara Ehrenreich (1989, 218–220; see also 1983, 1984) argues, a new heterosexual masculinity on the part of certain progressive, middle-class men has emerged, consisting of choosing a mate who can "pull her own weight" economically and who is truly committed to sharing household labor equally.

Notwithstanding, this progressive "dual-career" relationship is not supplemented, in many cases, by a progressive sexual relationship. As Andrew Tolson (1977, 121) argued as early as 1977, for many progressive, middle-class men, sexual passion is "still acted out in familial terms of masculine 'conquest'—to which women could only 'respond.'" Although many progressive, middle-class men seriously seek "free women" who live for themselves and their careers (Ehrenreich 1984), in bed they continue to demand submission and the affirmation of masculinity through heterosexual performance (Tolson 1977, 121). That is, many progressive, middle-class men continue to adhere t the hegemonic masculine ideology that "entitles" them to sex with their wives whenever they want it. For example, Finkelhor and Yllö (1985, 62–70) discuss the case of Ross, a middle-class businessman who somewhat represents this progressive middle class, yet who frequently raped his wife. Ross describes below how one such rape occurred during an argument over sex that his wife was winning (p. 66):

> She was standing there in her nightie. The whole thing got me somewhat sexually stimulated, and I guess subconsciously I felt she was getting the better of me. It dawned on me to just throw her down and have at her . . . which I did. I must have reached out and grabbed at her breast. She slapped my hand away. So I said, "Lay down. You're going to get it." She replied, "Oh, no, you don't," so I grabbed her by the arms and she put up resistance for literally fifteen seconds and then just resigned herself to it. There were no blows or anything like that. It was weird. I felt very animalistic, and I felt very powerful. I had the best erection I'd had in years. It was very stimulating. . . . I walked around with a smile on my face for three days.

Ross believed his wife not only controlled the sexuality in their lives, but that she had "completely and totally emasculated" him (p. 68). The rape was both a way to overcome that loss of power in his life and a means to construct a specific type of patriarchal masculinity centering on heterosexual performance and the domination and control of women's sexuality.

Another businessman, Jack, stated to Finkelhor and Yllö (p. 72), "When she would not give it freely, I would take it." He felt that his wife did not have the right to deny sex, he had the right to sex when he pleased, and it was her duty to satisfy his sexual needs. Similarly, in Irene Frieze's (1983, 544, 553) study of wife rape, the vast majority of wife rapists engaged in this form of violence in order to prove their "manhood," believing "that their wives were obligated to service them sexually in whatever ways they desired."

Thus, in force-only rapes, the assaults are practices of masculine control based on expectations that sex is a right. Both battering and force-only rapists consciously choose such violent action to facilitate a patriarchal gender strategy and to protect what they view as their "essential" privileges. The resulting masculine construction is not only an exhibition of their "essential nature," but also illustrates the seductive quality of violence for displaying that "essential nature." For these men, masculine authority is quite simply expressed through the violent control of women.

Nevertheless, such personal choices become enigmatic when detached from social structures. In battering rapes, because the traditional division of labor and power is prevalent and the struggle is over authority and control of that division, these men construct a patriarchal form of masculinity that punishes and degrades the wife for deviating from her "essential" duties. In force-only rapes, however, the gender division of labor is not the issue: this is the classic, middle-class, dual-career family in which both partners participate in decision making and household tasks, and in which the husband accepts, in a general way, his wife's autonomous right to develop her own interests. However, the force-only rapist feels specifically wronged, cheated, and deprived in the sexual realm. Some progressive, middle-class men simply adhere to the hegemonic masculine ideology that entitles them to sex whenever they want it. Sex is considered a marriage right by which gender is accomplished through effective performance in the sexual realm. Like sexual harassment, a similar type of crime, wife rape can be a resource for accomplishing masculinity differently. And as the social setting within the nuclear family changes, so does the conceptualization of what is normative masculine behavior. Different social settings generate different masculinities, even when the particular resource (crime) is similar.

In sum, the structure of the gender division of labor and power and normative heterosexuality impinges on the construction of masculinity. These structural features both preclude and permit certain forms of crime as resources that men may use to pursue a gender strategy and construct their masculinity. Although both battering and force-only rapists try to control their wives, they do so in qualitatively different ways. The social relations extant within their respective gender divisions of labor and power are different, and different options exist for maintaining their control. The choices made by each type of rapist, and the resources available to carry out those choices, develop in response to the specific social circumstances in which they live. For these reasons, then, these men employ different forms of violence to construct different types of private masculinities.

This chapter has attempted to demonstrate that men produce specific configurations of behavior that can be seen by others within the same immediate social setting as "essentially male." These different masculinities emerge from practices that utilize different resources, and class and race relations structure the resources available to construct specific masculinities. Pimps, workers, executives, and patriarchs generate situationally accomplished, unique masculinities by drawing on different types of crime indigenous to their distinct positions within the structural divisions of labor and power. Because men experience their everyday world from a uniquely individualistic position in society, they construct the cultural ideals of hegemonic masculinity in different ways.

Social structures are framed through social action and, in turn, provide resources for constructing masculinity. As one such resource, specific types of crime ultimately are based on these social structures. Thus, social structures both enable and constrain social action and, therefore, masculinities and crime.

Notes

1. Prostitutes, or "wives-in-law," are constructing a femininity that both confirms and violates stereotypical "female" behavior. In addition to the conventional aspects of femininity just mentioned, prostitute femininity also ridicules conventional morality by advocating sex outside marriage, sex for pleasure, anonymous sex, and sex that is not limited to reproduction and the domesticated couple. This construction of a specific type of femininity clearly challenges, in certain respects, stereotypical femininity. Nevertheless, the vast majority of prostitutes do not consider themselves feminists: they know very little about the feminist movement, do not share its assumptions, and believe men and women are "naturally" suited for different types of work (Miller 1986, 160).

2. The masculinity constructed by African American pimps is fittingly comparable to the masculinity associated with men (usually from working-class backgrounds) who are members of white motorcycle gangs. The men in such groups act extremely racist and similarly exploit the sexuality and labor of "biker women." However, biker men do not display a "cool pose" with an accompanying show of luxury in the form of flashy clothing and exotic hairstyles. On the contrary, a biker usually has long unkempt hair, a "rough" beard, and his "colors" consist of black motorcycle boots, soiled jeans, and a simple sleeveless denim jacket with attached insignia (see Willis 1978; Hopper and Moore 1990).

3. Horizontal segregation allocates men and women to different types of jobs; vertical segregation concentrates men and women in different occupations at different steps in an occupational hierarchy.

4. Nevertheless, it should be pointed out that increasing numbers of men are attempting to counter sexism on the shop floor and, therefore, reconstruct shop-floor masculinity. For an excellent example, see Gray 1987.

5. Indeed, office romances seem to be flourishing because women more routinely work beside men in professional and occupational jobs (Ehrenreich 1989, 219).

6. This particular form of femininity has been explored by Pringle (1988).

7. Despite devastating criticisms of the Conflict Tactics Scale as a methodological tool (Dobash, Dobash, Wilson, and Daly 1992), some researchers (remarkably) continue to use it to guide their work, concluding that women are about as violent as men in the home (Straus and Gelles 1990) or even, in some cases, that more men are victimized in the home than are women (McNeely and Mann 1990).

8. Unfortunately, there is scant research on wife beating in racial-minority households. Nevertheless, what evidence there is on African American households suggests that when violence does occur, both husband and wife are likely to accept the traditional patriarchal division of labor and power as natural and that complete responsibility for the battering, when questioned, "lies with white society" (Richie 1985, 42; see also Asbury 1987). Consequently, I am forced to concentrate solely on class and wife beating.

9. This is not to deny that many middle-class men engage in wife beating for the reasons discussed earlier in this section. What I suggest, following Segal (1990, 255) and others, is that it is clearly less common in middle-class households because such men have access to other resources, possibly more effective resources, through which they exert control over women without employing violence.

10. Because Finkelhor and Yllö (1985, 9) found no significantly higher rate of marital rape among African Americans than among whites, I do not distinguish by race.

References

Andersen, Margaret. (1988). *Thinking About Women*. New York: Macmillan.

Berk, Sarah Fenstermaker. (1985). *The Gender Factory: The Apportionment of Work in American Households*. New York: Plenum Press.

Bernard, Jessie. (1992). "The Good-Provider Role: Its Rise and Fall." In *Men's Lives,* ed. Michael S. Kimmel and Michael A. Messner, 203–21. New York: Macmillan.

Bielby, William, and James N. Baron. (1986). "A Woman's Place Is with Other Women: Sex Segregation within Organizations." In *Sex Segregation in the Workplace: Trends, Explanations, Remedies,* ed. Barbara Reskin, 27–55. Washington, DC: National Academy Press.

Box, Steven. (1983). *Power, Crime and Mystification.* New York: Tavistock.

Carothers, Suzanne C., and Peggy Crull. (1984). "Contrasting Sexual Harassment in Female- and Male-Dominated Occupations." In *My Troubles Are Going to Have Trouble with Me,* ed. Karen Brodkin Sacks and Dorothy Remy, 219–28. New Brunswick, NJ: Rutgers University Press.

Cockburn, Cynthia. (1983). *Brothers: Male Dominance and Technological Change.* London: Pluto Press.

Collinson, David L., and Margaret Collinson. (1989). "Sexuality in the Workplace: The Domination of Men's Sexuality." In *The Sexuality of Organization,* ed. Jeff Hearn, Deborah L. Sheppard, Peta Tancred-Sheriff, and Gibson Burrell, 91–109. Newbury Park, CA: Sage.

Connell, R. W. (1991). "Live Fast and Die Young: The Construction of Masculinity among Young Working-Class Men on the Margin of the Labour Market." *Australian and New Zealand Journal of Sociology* 27 (2): 141–71.

Connell, R. W. (1987). *Gender and Power.* Stanford, CA: Stanford University Press.

DeKeseredy, Walter, and Ronald Hinch. (1991). *Woman Abuse: Sociological Perspectives.* Lewiston, NY: Thompson Educational Pub., Inc.

D'Emilio, John, and Estelle B. Freedman. (1988). *Intimate Matters: A History of Sexuality in America.* New York: Harper and Row.

DiTomaso, Nancy. (1989). "Sexuality in the Workplace: Discrimination and Harassment." In *The Sexuality of Organization,* eds. Jeff Hearn, Deborah L. Sheppard, Peta Tancred-Sheriff, and Gibson Burrell, 71–90. Newbury Park, CA: Sage.

Dobash, R. Emerson, and Russell P. Dobash. (1984). "The Nature and Antecedents of Violent Events." *British Journal of Criminology* 24 (3): 269–88.

Dobash, R. Emerson, and Russell P. Dobash. (1979). *Violence Against Wives.* New York: Free Press.

Dobash, Russell P., R. Emerson Dobash, Margo Wilson, and Martin Daly. (1992). "The Myth of Sexual Symmetry in Marital Violence." *Social Problems* 39 (1): 71–91.

Donaldson, Mike. (1987). "Labouring Men: Love, Sex and Strife." *Australian and New Zealand Journal of Sociology* 23 (2): 165–84.

Edleson, Jeffrey L., Zvi Eisikovits, and Edna Guttman. (1986). "Men Who Batter Women: A Critical Review of the Evidence." *Journal of Family Issues* 6 (2): 229–47.

Ehrenreich, Barbara. (1983). *The Hearts of Men.* New York: Doubleday.

Ferraro, Kathleen J. (1988). "An Existential Approach to Battering." In *Family Abuse and its Consequences,* ed. Gerald T. Hotaling, David Finkelhor, John T. Kirkpatrick, and Murray Straus, 126–38. Newbury Park, CA: Sage.

Finkelhor, David, and Kristi Yllö. (1985). *License to Rape: Sexual Abuse of Wives.* New York: Holt, Rinehart and Winston.

Frieze, Irene H. (1983). "Investigating the Causes and Consequences of Marital Rape." *Signs* 8 (3): 532–53.

Game, Ann, and Rosemary Pringle. (1984). *Gender at Work.* Boston: Allen and Unwin.

Gordon, Linda. (1988). *Heroes of Their Own Lives.* New York: Viking.

Gray, Stan. (1987). "Sharing the Shop Floor." In *Beyond Patriarchy,* ed. Michael Kaufman, 216–34. New York: Oxford University Press.

Gruber, James, and Lars Bjorn. (1982). "Blue Collar Blues: The Sexual Harassment of Women Autoworkers." *Work and Occupations* 9 (3): 271–98.

Harris, Richard N., and Roslyn Wallach Bologh. (1985). "The Dark Side of Love: Blue and White Collar Wife Abuse." *Victimology* 10 (1–4): 242–52.

Hartmann, Heidi. (1981). "The Unhappy Marriage of Marxism and Feminism: Towards a More Progressive Union." In *Women and Revolution,* ed. Lydia Sargent, 1–41. Boston: South End Press.

Hearn, Jeff. (1985). "Men's Sexuality at Work." In *The Sexuality of Men,* ed. Andy Metcalf and Martin Humphries, 110–28. London: Pluto Press.

Hochschild, Arlie. (1992). "The Second Shift: Employed Women Are Putting in Another Day of Work at Home." In *Men's Lives,* ed. Michael S. Kimmel and Michael A. Messner, 511–15. New York: Macmillan.

Hochschild, Arlie. (1989). *The Second Shift.* New York: Viking.

Kanter, Rosabeth Moss. (1977). *Men and Women of the Corporation.* New York: Basic Books.

Katz, Jack. (1988). *Seductions of Crime: Moral and Sensual Attractions in Doing Evil.* New York: Basic Books.

Komter, Aafke. (1989). "Hidden Power in Marriage." *Gender and Society* 3 (2): 187–216.

MacKinnon, Catherine A. (1979). *Sexual Harassment of Working Women.* New Haven, CT: Yale University Press.

Majors, Richard. (1986). "Cool Pose: The Proud Signature of Black Survival." *Changing Men* 17: 5–6.

Majors, Richard, and Janet Mancini Billson. (1992). *Cool Pose: The Dilemma's of Black Manhood in America.* New York: Macmillan.

Messerschmidt, James W. (1986). *Capitalism, Patriarchy and Crime: Toward a Socialist Feminist Criminology.* Totowa, NJ: Rowman and Littlefield.

Miller, Eleanor. (1986). *Street Woman.* Philadelphia: Temple University Press.

Milner, Christina, and Richard Milner. (1972). *Black Players: The Secret World of Black Pimps.* Boston: Little, Brown.

Pagelow, Mildred D. (1984). *Family Violence.* New York: Praeger.

Pahl, Jan. (1992). "Money and Power in Marriage." In *Gender, Power and Sexuality,* ed. Pamela Abbott and Claire Wallace, 41–57. London: Macmillan.

Petchesky, Rosalind. (1984). *Abortion and Woman's Choice.* New York: Longman.

Pringle, Rosemary. (1989). "Bureaucracy, Rationality and Sexuality: The Case of Secretaries." In *The Sexuality of Organization,* ed. Jeff Hearn, Deborah L. Sheppard, Peta Tancred-Sheriff, and Gibson Burell, 158–77. Newbury Park, CA: Sage.

Ptacek, James. (1988). "Why Do Men Batter Their Wives?" In *Feminist Perspectives on Wife Abuse,* ed. Kersti Yllö and Michele Bogard, 133–57. Newbury Park, CA: Sage.

Reskin, Barbara, and Patricia Roos. (1987). "Status Hierarchies and Sex Segregation." In *Ingredients for Women's Employment Policy,* ed. Christine Bose and Glenna Spitze, 3–21. Albany: State University of New York Press.

Romenesko, Kim, and Eleanor M. Miller. (1989). "The Second Step in Double Jeopardy: Appropriating the Labor of Female Street Hustlers." *Crime and Delinquency* 35 (1): 109–35.

Rosen, Ruth. (1982). *The Lost Sisterhood: Prostitution in America: 1900–1918.* Baltimore: Johns Hopkins University Press.

Russell, Diana E. H. (1982). *Rape in Marriage.* New York: Macmillan.

Schechter, Susan. (1982). *Women and Male Violence.* Boston: South End Press.

Schneider, Beth E. (1991). "Put up and Shut Up: Workplace Sexual Assaults." *Gender and Society* 5 (4): 533–48.

Segal, Lynne. (1990). *Slow Motion: Changing Masculinities, Changing Men.* New Brunswick, NJ: Rutgers University Press.

Smith, Michael D. (1990). "Patriarchal Ideology and Wife Beating: A Test of a Feminist Hypothesis." *Violence and Victims* 5 (4): 257–73.

Smith, Michael D. (1990a). "Sociodemographic Risk Factors in Wife Abuse: Results from a Survey of Toronto Women." *Canadian Journal of Sociology* 15 (1): 39–58.

Sokoloff, Natalie J. (1980). *Between Money and Love.* New York: Praeger.

Stets, Jan E., and Murray A. Straus. (1989). "The Marriage License as a Hitting License: A Comparison of Assaults in Dating, Cohabitating and Married Couples." In *Violence in Dating Relationships,* ed. Maureen A. Pirog-Good and Jan E. Stets, 38–52. New York: Praeger.

Straus, Murray A., and Richard J. Gelles. (1990). "How Violent Are American Families? Estimates from the National Family Violence Survey and Other Studies." In *Physical Violence in American Families,* ed. Murray A. Straus and Richard J. Gelles, 95–112. New Brunswick, NJ: Transaction.

Straus, Murray A., Richard J. Gelles, and Susan Steinmetz. (1980). *Behind Closed Doors.* New York: Doubleday.

Tolson, Andrew. (1977). *The Limits of Masculinity.* New York: Harper and Row.

Walby, Sylvia. (1986). *Patriarchy at Work: Patriarchal and Capitalist Relations in Employment.* Minneapolis: University of Minnesota Press.

Walker, Lenore E. (1979). *The Battered Woman.* New York: Harper and Row.

Walker, Lenore E. (1977–78). "Battered Women and Learned Helplessness." *Victimology* 2 (4): 525–34.

West, Candace, and Don H. Zimmerman. (1987). "Doing Gender." *Gender and Society* 1 (2): 125–51.

Willis, Paul E. (1979). "Shop Floor Culture, Masculinity and the Wage Form." In *Working Class Culture,* ed. John Clarke, Chas Critcher, and Richard Johnson, 185–98. London: Hutchinson.

ARTICLE 2

Manning Marable

The Black Male: Searching Beyond Stereotypes

What is a Black man? Husband and father. Son and brother. Lover and boyfriend. Uncle and grandfather. Construction worker and sharecropper. Minister and ghetto hustler. Doctor and mine-worker. Auto mechanic and presidential candidate.

What is a Black man in an institutionally racist society, in the social system of modern capitalist America? The essential tragedy of being Black and male is our inability, as men and as people of African descent, to define ourselves without the stereotypes the larger society imposes upon us, and through various institutional means perpetuates and permeates within our entire culture. Our relations with our sisters, our parents and children, and indeed across the entire spectrum of human relations are imprisoned by images of the past, false distortions that seldom if ever capture the essence of our being. We cannot come to terms with Black women until we understand the half-hidden stereotypes that have crippled our development and social consciousness. We cannot challenge racial and sexual inequality, both within the Black community and across the larger American society, unless we comprehend the critical difference between the myths about ourselves and the harsh reality of being Black men.

From *The American Black Male*, R. Majors and J. Gordon, eds., pp. 69–78. Chicago: Nelson-Hall, 1993.

Confrontation with White History

The conflicts between Black and white men in contemporary American culture can be traced directly through history to the earliest days of chattel slavery. White males entering the New World were ill adapted to make the difficult transition from Europe to the American frontier. As recent historical research indicates, the development of what was to become the United States was accomplished largely, if not primarily, by African slaves, men and women alike. Africans were the first to cultivate wheat on the continent; they showed their illiterate masters how to grow indigo, rice, and cotton; their extensive knowledge of herbs and roots provided colonists with medicines and preservatives for food supplies. It was the Black man, wielding his sturdy axe, who cut down most of the virgin forest across the southern colonies. And in times of war, the white man reluctantly looked to his Black slave to protect him and his property. As early as 1715, during the Yemassee Indian war, Black troops led British regulars in a campaign to exterminate Indian tribes. After another such campaign in 1747, the all-white South Carolina legislature issued a public vote of gratitude to Black men, who "in times of war, behaved themselves with great faithfulness and courage, in repelling the attacks of his Majesty's enemies." During the American Revolution, over two thousand Black men volunteered to join the beleaguered Continental Army of George Washington, a slaveholder. A generation later, two thousand Blacks from New York joined the state militia's segregated units during the War of 1812, and Blacks fought bravely under Andrew Jackson at the Battle of New Orleans. From Crispus Attucks to the 180,000 Blacks who fought in the Union Army during the Civil War, Black men gave their lives to preserve the liberties of their white male masters.

The response of white men to the many sacrifices of their sable counterparts was, in a word, contemptuous. Their point of view of Black males was conditioned by three basic beliefs. Black men were only a step above the animals—possessing awesome physical power but lacking in intellectual ability. As such, their proper role in white society was as laborers, not as the managers of labor. Second, the Black male represented a potential political threat to the entire system of slavery. And third, but by no means last, the Black male symbolized a lusty sexual potency that threatened white women. This uneven mixture of political fears and sexual anxieties was reinforced by the white males' crimes committed against Black women, the routine rape and sexual abuse that all slave societies permit between the oppressed and the oppressor. Another dilemma, seldom discussed publicly, was the historical fact that some white women of social classes were not reluctant to request the sexual favors of their male slaves. These inherent tensions produced a racial model of conduct and social context that survived the colonial period and continued into the twentieth century. The white male–dominated system dictated that the only acceptable social behavior of any Black male was that of subservience—the loyal slave, the proverbial Uncle Tom, the ever-cheerful and infantile Sambo. It was not enough that Black men must cringe before their white masters; they must express open devotion to the system of slavery itself. Politically, the Black male was unfit to play even a minor role in the development of democracy. Supreme Court Chief Justice Roger B. Tawney spoke for his entire class in 1857: "Negroes [are] beings of an inferior order, and altogether unfit to associate with the white race, either by social or political relations; and so far inferior that they have no rights which the white man was bound to respect." Finally, Black males disciplined for various crimes against white supremacy—such as escaping from the plantation, or murdering their masters—were often punished in a sexual manner. On this point, the historical record is clear. In the colonial era, castration of Black males was required by the legislatures of North and South Carolina, Virginia, Pennsylvania, and New Jersey. Black men were castrated simply for striking a white man or for attempting to learn to read and write. In the late nineteenth century, hundreds of Black male victims of lynching were first sexually mutilated before being executed. The impulse to castrate Black males was popularized in white literature and folklore, and even today, instances of such crimes are not entirely unknown in the rural South.

The relations between Black males and white women were infinitely more complex. Generally, the vast majority of white females viewed Black men through the eyes of their fathers and husbands. The Black man was simply a beast of burden, a worker who gave his life to create a more comfortable environment for her and her children. And yet, in truth, he was still a man. Instances of interracial marriage were few, and were prohibited by law even as late as the 1960s. But the fear of sexual union did not prohibit many white females, particularly indentured servants and working-class women, from soliciting favors from Black men. In the 1840s, however, a small group of white middle-class women became actively involved in the campaign to abolish slavery. The founders of modern American feminism—Susan B. Anthony, Elizabeth Cady Stanton, and Lucretia Mott—championed the cause of emancipation and defended Blacks' civil rights. In gratitude for their devotion to Black freedom, the leading Black abolitionist of the period, Frederick Douglass, actively promoted the rights of white women against the white male power structure. In 1848, at the Seneca Falls, New York, women's rights convention, Douglass was the only man, Black or white, to support the extension of voting rights to all women. White women looked to Douglass for leadership in the battle against sexual and racial discrimination. Yet curiously, they were frequently hostile to the continued contributions of Black women to the cause of freedom. When the brilliant orator Sojourner Truth, second only to Douglass as a leading figure in the abolitionist movement, rose to lecture before an 1851 women's convention in Akron, Ohio, white women cried out, "Don't let her speak!" For these white liberals, the destruction of slavery was simply a means to expand democratic rights to white women: the goal was defined in racist terms. Black men like Douglass were useful allies only so far as they promoted white middle-class women's political interests.

The moment of truth came immediately following the Civil War, when Congress passed the Fifteenth Amendment, which gave Black males the right to vote. For Douglass and most Black leaders, both men and women, suffrage was absolutely essential to preserve their new freedoms. While the Fifteenth Amendment excluded females from the electoral franchise, it nevertheless represented a great democratic victory for all oppressed groups.

For most white suffragists, however, it symbolized the political advancement of the Black male over white middle-class women. Quickly their liberal rhetoric gave way to racist diatribes. "So long as the Negro was lowest in the scale of being, we were willing to press his claims," wrote Elizabeth Cady Stanton in 1865. "But now, as the celestial gate to civil rights is slowly moving on its hinges, it becomes a serious question whether we had better stand aside and see 'Sambo' walk into the kingdom first." Most white women reformists concluded that "it is better to be the slave of an educated white man than of a degraded, ignorant black one." They warned whites that giving the vote to the Black male would lead to widespread rape and sexual assaults against white women of the upper classes. Susan B. Anthony vowed, "I will cut off this right arm of mine before I will ever work for or demand the ballot for the Negro and not the [white] woman." In contrast, Black women leaders like Sojourner Truth and Frances E. Watkins Harper understood that the enfranchisement of Black men was an essential step for the democratic rights of all people.

The division between white middle-class feminists and the civil rights movement of Blacks, beginning over a century ago, has continued today in debates over affirmative action and job quotas. White liberal feminists frequently use the rhetoric of racial equality but often find it difficult to support public policies that will advance Black males over their own social group. Even in the 1970s, such liberal women writers as Susan Brownmiller continued to resurrect the myth of the "Black male-as-rapist" and sought to define white women in crudely racist terms. The weight of white history, from white women and men alike, has been an endless series of stereotypes used to frustrate the Black man's images of himself and to blunt his constant quest for freedom.

Confronting the Black Woman

Images of our suffering—as slaves, sharecroppers, industrial workers, and standing in unemployment lines—have been intermingled in our relationship with the Black woman. We have seen her straining under the hot southern sun, chopping cotton row upon row, and nursing our children on the side. We have witnessed her come home, tired and weary after working as a nurse, cook, or maid in white men's houses. We have seen her love of her children, her commitment to the church, her beauty and dignity in the face of political and economic exploitation. And yet, so much is left unsaid. All too often the Black male, in his own silent suffering, fails to communicate his love and deep respect for the mother, sister, grandmother, and wife who gave him the courage and commitment to strive for freedom. The veils of oppression, and the illusions of racial stereotypes, limit our ability to speak the inner truths about ourselves and our relationships to Black women.

The Black man's image of the past is, in most respects, a distortion of social reality. All of us can feel the anguish of our great-grandfathers as they witnessed their wives and daughters being raped by their white masters, or as they wept when their families were sold apart. But do we feel the double bondage of the Black woman, trying desperately to keep her family together and yet at times distrusted by her own Black man? Less than a generation ago, most Black male social scientists argued that the Black family was effectively destroyed by slavery; that the Black man was much less than a husband or father; and that the result was a "Black matriarchy" that crippled the economic, social, and political development of the Black community. Back in 1965, Black scholar C. Eric Lincoln declared that the slavery experience had "stripped the Negro male of his masculinity" and "condemned him to a eunuch-like existence in a culture that venerates masculine primacy." The rigid rules of Jim Crow applied more to Black men than to their women, according to Lincoln: "Because she was frequently the white man's mistress, the Negro woman occasionally flaunted the rules of segregation. . . . The Negro [male] did not earn rewards for being manly, courageous, or assertive, but for being accommodating—for fulfilling the stereotype of what he has been forced to be." The social by-product of Black demasculinization, concluded Lincoln, was the rise of Black matriarchs, who psychologically castrated their husbands and sons. "The Negro female has had the responsibility of the Negro family for so many generations that she accepts it, or assumes it, as second nature. Many older women have forgotten why the responsibility developed upon the Negro woman in the first place, or why it later became institutionalized," Lincoln argues. "And young Negro women do not think it absurd to reduce the relationship to a matter of money, since many of them probably grew up in families where the only income was earned by the mothers: the fathers may not have been in evidence at all." Other Black sociologists perpetuated these stereotypes, which only served to turn Black women and men against each other instead of focusing their energies and talents in the struggle for freedom.

Today's social science research on Black female–male relations tells us what our common sense should have indicated long ago—that the essence of Black family and community life has been a positive, constructive, and even heroic experience. Andrew Billingsley's *Black Families in White America* illustrates that the Black "extended family" is part of our African heritage that was never eradicated by slavery or segregation. The Black tradition of racial cooperation, the collectivist rather than individualistic ethos, is an outgrowth of the unique African heritage that we still maintain. It is clear that the Black woman was the primary transmitter and repositor of the cultural heritage of our people and played a central role in the socialization and guidance of Black male and female children. But this fact does not in any way justify the myth of a "Black matriarchy." Black women suffered from the economic exploitation and racism Black males experienced—but they also were trapped by institutional sexism and all of the various means of violence that have been used to oppress all women, such as rape, "wife beating," and sterilization. The majority of the Black poor throughout history have been overwhelmingly female; the lowest paid major group within the labor force in America is Black women, not men.

In politics, the sense of the Black man's relations with Black women are again distorted by stereotypes. Most of us can cite the achievement of the great Black men who contributed to the freedom of our people: Frederick Douglass, W. E. B. Du Bois, Marcus Garvey, Martin Luther King, Jr., Malcolm X, Paul Robeson, Medgar Evers, A. Philip Randolph. Why then are we often forgetful of Harriet Tubman, the fearless conductor on the Underground Railroad, who spirited over 350 slaves into the North? What of Ida B. Wells, newspaper editor and antilynching activist; Mary Church Terrell, educator, member of the Washington, D.C., Board of Education from 1895 to 1906, and civil rights leader; Mary McLeod Bethune, college president and director of the Division of Negro Affairs for the National Youth Administration; and Fannie Lou Hamer, courageous desegregation leader in the South during the 1960s? In simple truth, the cause of Black freedom has been pursued by Black women and men equally. In Black literature, the eloquent appeals to racial equality penned by Richard Wright, James Baldwin, and Du Bois are paralleled in the works of Zora Neale Hurston, Alice Walker, and Toni Morrison. Martin Luther King, Jr., may have expressed for all of us our collective vision of equality in his "I Have a Dream" speech at the 1963 March on Washington—but it was the solitary act of defiance by the Black woman, Rosa Parks, that initiated the great Montgomery bus boycott in 1955 and gave birth to the modern civil rights movement. The struggle of our foremothers and forefathers transcends the barrier of gender, as Black women have tried to tell their men for generations. Beyond the stereotypes, we find a common heritage of suffering, and a common will to be free.

The Black Man Confronts Himself

The search for reality begins and ends with an assessment of the actual socioeconomic condition of Black males within the general context of the larger society. Beginning in the economic sphere, one finds that the illusion of Black male achievement in the marketplace is undermined by statistical evidence. Of the thousands of small businesses initiated by Black entrepreneurs each year, over 90 percent go bankrupt within thirty-six months. The Black businessman suffers from redlining policies of banks, which keep capital outside his hands. Only one out of two hundred Black businessmen have more than twenty paid employees, and over 80 percent of all Black men who start their own firms must hold a second job, working sixteen hours and more each day to provide greater opportunities for their families and communities. In terms of actual income, the gap between the Black man and the white man has increased in the past decade. According to the Bureau of Labor Statistics, in 1979 only forty-six thousand Black men earned salaries between $35,000 and $50,000 annually. Fourteen thousand Black men (and only two thousand Black women) earned $50,000 to $75,000 that year. And in the highest income level, $75,000 and above, there were four thousand Black males compared to five hundred and forty-eight thousand white males. This racial stratification is even sharper at the lower end of the income scale. Using 1978 poverty statistics, only 11.3 percent of all white males under fourteen years old live in poverty, while the figure for young Black males is 42 percent. Between the ages of fourteen and seventeen, 9.6 percent of white males and 38.6 percent of Black males are poor. In the age group eighteen to twenty-one years, 7.5 percent of white males and 26.1 percent of all Black males are poor. In virtually every occupational category, Black men with identical or superior qualifications earn less than their white male counterparts. Black male furniture workers, for example, earn only 69 percent of white males' average wages; in printing and publishing, 68 percent; in all nonunion jobs, 62 percent.

Advances in high-technology leave Black males particularly vulnerable to even higher unemployment rates over the next decades. Millions of Black men are located either in the "old line" industries such as steel, automobiles, rubber, and textiles, or in the public sector—both of which have experienced severe job contractions. In agriculture, to cite one typical instance, the disappearance of Black male workers is striking. As late as forty years ago, two out of every five Black men were either farmers or farm workers. In 1960, roughly 5 percent of all Black men were still employed in agriculture, and another 3 percent owned their own farms. By 1983, however, less than 130,000 Black men worked in agriculture. From 1959 to 1974, the number of Black-operated cotton farms in the South dropped from 87,074 to 1,569. Black tobacco farmers declined in number from 40,670 to barely 7,000 during the same period. About three out of four black men involved in farming today are not self-employed.

From both rural and urban environments, the numbers of jobless Black adult males have soared since the late 1960s. In 1969, for example, only 2.5 percent of all Black married males with families were unemployed. This percentage increased to about 10 percent in the mid-1970s, and with the recession of 1982–1984 exceeded 15 percent. The total percentage of all Black families without a single income earner jumped from 10 percent in 1968 to 18.5 percent in 1977—and continued to climb into the 1990s.

These statistics fail to convey the human dimensions of the economic chaos of Black male joblessness. Thousands of jobless men are driven into petty crime annually, just to feed their families; others find temporary solace in drugs or alcohol. The collapse of thousands of Black households and the steady proliferation of female-headed, single-parent households is a social consequence of the systematic economic injustice inflicted upon Black males.

Racism also underscores the plight of Black males within the criminal justice system. Every year in this country there are over 2 million arrests of Black males. About three hundred thousand Black men are currently incarcerated in federal and state prisons or other penal institutions. At least half of the Black prisoners are less than thirty years of age, and over one thousand are not even old enough to vote. Most Black male prisoners were unemployed at the time of their arrests; the others averaged less than $8,000 annual incomes during the year before they were jailed. And about 45 percent of the thirteen hundred men currently awaiting capital punishment on death row are Afro-Americans. As Lennox S. Hinds, former National Director of the National Conference of Black Lawyers has stated, "Someone black and poor tried for stealing a few hundred dollars has a 90 percent likelihood of being convicted of robbery with a sentence averaging between 94 to 138 months. A white business executive who embezzled hundreds of thousands of dollars has only a 20 percent likelihood of conviction with a sentence averaging about 20 to 48 months." Justice is not "color blind" when Black males are the accused.

What does the economic and social destruction of Black males mean for the Black community as a whole? Dr. Robert Staples, associate professor of sociology at the University of California–San Francisco, cites some devastating statistics of the current plight of younger Black males:

> Less than twenty percent of all Black college graduates in the early 1980s are males. The vast majority of young Black men who enter college drop out within two years.
>
> At least one-fourth of all Black male teenagers never complete high school.
>
> Since 1960, Black males between the ages of 15 to 20 have committed suicide at rates higher than that of the general white population. Suicide is currently the third leading cause of death, after homicides and accidents, for Black males aged 15 to 24.
>
> About half of all Black men over age 18 have never been married [or are] separated, divorced, or widowed.
>
> Despite the fact that several million Black male youths identify a career in professional athletics as a desirable career, the statistical probability of any Black man making it to the pros exceeds 20,000 to one.
>
> One half of all homicides in America today are committed by Black men—whose victims are other Black men.
>
> The typical Black adult male dies almost three years before he can even begin to collect Social Security.

Fred Clark, a staff psychologist for the California Youth Authority, states that the social devastation of an entire generation of Black males has made it extremely difficult for eligible Black women to locate partners. "In Washington, D.C., it is estimated that there is a one to twelve ratio of Black [single] males to eligible females," Clark observes. "Some research indicates that the female is better suited for surviving alone than the male. There are more widowed and single Black females than males. Males die earlier and more quickly than females when single. Single Black welfare mothers seem to live longer than single unemployed Black males."

Every socioeconomic and political indicator illustrates that the Black male in America is facing an unprecedented crisis. Despite singular examples of successful males in electoral politics, business, labor unions, and the professions, the overwhelming majority of Black men find it difficult to acquire self-confidence and self-esteem within the chaos of modern economic and social life. The stereotypes imposed by white history and by the lack of knowledge of our own past often convince many younger Black males that their struggle is too overwhelming. Black women have a responsibility to comprehend the forces that destroy the lives of thousands of their brothers, sons, and husbands. But Black men must understand that they, too, must overcome their own inherent and deeply ingrained sexism, recognizing that Black women must be equal partners in the battle to uproot injustice at every level of the society. The strongest ally Black men have in their battle to achieve Black freedom is the Black woman. Together, without illusions and false accusations, without racist and sexist stereotypes, they can achieve far more than they can ever accomplish alone.

References

Billingsley, A. 1968. *Black Families in White America*. Englewood Cliffs, NJ: Prentice-Hall.

Clark, K. 1965. *Dark Ghetto*. New York: Harper and Row.

Davis, A. Y. 1981. *Women, Race and Class*. New York: Random House.

Lincoln, C. E. 1965. "The Absent Father Haunts the Negro Family." *New York Times Magazine*, Nov. 28.

Marable, M. 1983. *How Capitalism Underdeveloped Black America*. Boston: South End Press.

ARTICLE 3

Alfredo Mirandé

"Macho": Contemporary Conceptions

Mi Noche Triste

My own *noche triste* occurred when my father returned from location on the film *Capitán de Castilla* (Captain from Castille). I remember that he had been gone for a long time, that he came back from Morelia with a lot of presents, and that at first, I was very happy to see him. Then there was a big fight; my parents argued all night, and they separated shortly thereafter. One night when my mother was very sad and depressed, she went to *el árbol de la noche triste*. As she cried by the tree she thought about how she and Hernán Cortés both had been in the same situation: depressed, weeping, and alone.

After my parents separated, my brothers and I went with my father and moved to Tacubaya to live with his mother, Anita, and her mother (my great-grandmother), Carmela (Mamá Mela). Grandmother Anita, or *Abillá*, as we called her, was a petite, energetic little woman, but Mamá Mela was tall, dark, and stately. In Tacubaya we were also surrounded by family, but now it was my father's family, Mirandé-Salazar. His family was smaller because he was an only child and because his father's two siblings, Concha (Consuelo) and Lupe (Guadalupe), never married or had children. My grandfather, Alfredo, died when I was about two years old, but I remember him.

In Tacubaya we first lived in a big, long house with a large green entrance, *El Nueve* (nine), on a street called Vicente Eguía, before moving to an apartment house, *El Trece* (thirteen), down the street. At *El Trece* we lived in the first apartment, and my great-aunts, Concha and Lupe, lived in *El Seis* (six). Concha had been an elementary school teacher and Lupe was an artist. They were retired but very active; both did a lot of embroidering and Lupe was always painting. I was very fond of *las tías*. To me *las tías* always seemed old and very religious, but I was very close to my aunts and loved them deeply. They wore black shawls and went to church early each morning. When I wasn't playing in the courtyard, I was often visiting with my aunts. They taught me catechism, and Tía Lupe was my *madrina*, or godmother, for my first communion.

I would spend hours with *las tías,* fascinated by their conversation. It seemed that every minute was filled with stories about the Mexican Revolution and about my grandfather, Alfredo. I especially liked it when they spoke about him, as I had been named Alfredo and identified with him. They said he was a great man and that they would be very proud and happy if I grew up to be like him someday. No, it was actually that I had no choice—I was destined to be like him. Because I had the good fortune of being named after Alfredo, I had to carry on his name, and, like him, I too would be a great man someday. I should add that my aunts stressed *man* when they talked about him. In other words, I had a distinct impression that my grandfather and I were linked not only because we were both named Mirandé and Alfredo, but also because we were both men. I did not realize it at the time, but my teachers (who were mostly women)—*las tías,* my *Abillá,* Mamá Mela, and my mother—were socializing me into my "sex role." But I don't remember anyone describing Grandfather Alfredo as "macho." Per-

From *Hombres y Machos: Masculinity and Latino Culture* by Alfredo Mirandé. Copyright © 1997. Reprinted by permission of Westview Press, a member of Perseus Books, L.L.C.

haps my *tías* took his being "macho" for granted, since he was obviously male.

I do not know very much about Alfredo's family, except that his father, Juan, or *Jean*, came to Mexico from France and married a *mexicana*, María. I also learned from my mother that Alfredo was of humble origins and was, in a very real sense, a self-made man who studied and pursued a career as a civil engineer. He was committed to bringing about social justice and distributing the land held by the *hacendados* (landowners) among the Mexican *peones*. As a civilian he served under Emiliano Zapata, making cannons and munitions. According to historian John Womack . . . , Alfredo Mirandé was one of Zapata's key assistants and worked as a spy in Puebla for some time under the code name "Delta." While he was in hiding, my *Abillá* would take in other people's clothes to mend and to launder to earn money so that the family could survive. My grandfather grew to be disillusioned, however, as the Revolution did not fulfill its promise of bringing about necessary economic and social reforms.

My *tías* had a photograph of Alfredo standing proudly in front of a new, experimental cannon that he had built. They related that a foolish and headstrong general, anxious to try out the new cannon, pressured Alfredo to fire it before it was ready. My grandfather reluctantly complied and received severe burns all over his body, almost dying as a result of the explosion. It took him months to recover from the accident.

As I think back, most of the stories they told me had a moral and were designed, indirectly at least, to impart certain values. What I learned from my *tías* and, indirectly, from my grandfather was that although one should stand up for principles, one should attempt to avoid war and personal conflicts, if at all possible. One should also strive to be on a higher moral plane than one's adversaries. Alfredo was intelligent, strong, and principled. But what impressed me most is that he was said to be incredibly just and judicious. Everyone who knew him said he treated people of varying educational and economic levels fairly, equally, and with dignity and respect.

I realize that Alfredo lived in a society and a historical period in which women were relegated to an inferior status. Yet I also know that he and my grandmother shared a special intimacy and mutual respect such as I have never personally encountered. By all accounts they loved and respected each other and shared an incredible life together. I have read letters that my grandfather wrote to my grandmother when they were apart, and they indicate that he held her in very high regard and treated her as an equal partner.

"Macho": An Overview

Mexican folklorist Vicente T. Mendoza suggested that the word "macho" was not widely used in Mexican songs, *corridos* (folk ballads), or popular culture until the 1940s. . . . Use of the word was said to have gained in popularity after Avila Camacho became president. The word lent itself to use in *corridos* because "macho" rhymed with "Camacho."

While "macho" has traditionally been associated with Mexican or Latino culture, the word has recently been incorporated into American popular culture, so much so that it is now widely used to describe everything from rock stars and male sex symbols in television and film to burritos. When applied to entertainers, athletes, or other "superstars," the implied meaning is clearly a positive one that connotes strength, virility, masculinity, and sex appeal. But when applied to Mexicans or Latinos, "macho" remains imbued with such negative attributes as male dominance, patriarchy, authoritarianism, and spousal abuse. Although both meanings connote strength and power, the Anglo macho is clearly a much more positive and appealing symbol of manhood and masculinity. In short, under current usage the Mexican macho oppresses and coerces women, whereas his Anglo counterpart appears to attract and seduce them.

This [reading] focuses on variations in perceptions and conceptions of the word "macho" held by Mexican and Latino men. Despite all that has been written and said about the cult of masculinity and the fact that male dominance has been assumed to be a key feature of Mexican and Latino culture, very little research exists to support this assumption. Until recently such generalizations were based on stereotypes, impressionistic evidence, or the observations of ethnographers such as Oscar Lewis . . . , Arthur Rubel . . . , and William Madsen. . . . These Anglo ethnographers were criticized by noted Chicano folklorist Américo Paredes . . . for the persistent ignorance and insensitivity to Chicano language and culture that is reflected in their work. Paredes contended, for example, that although most anthropologists present themselves as politically liberal and fluent in Spanish, many are only minimally fluent and fail to grasp the nuance and complexity of Chicano language. There is, it seems, good reason to be leery of their findings and generalizations regarding not only gender roles but also all aspects of the Mexican/Latino experience.

Utilizing data obtained through qualitative open-ended questions, I look in this chapter at how Latino men themselves perceive the word "macho" and how they describe men who are considered "*muy machos.*" Although all of the respondents were living in the United States at the time of the interviews, many were foreign-born and retained close ties with Mexican/Latino culture. Since they had been subjected to both Latino and American influences, I wondered whether they would continue to adhere to traditional Mexican definitions of "macho" or whether they had been influenced by contemporary American conceptions of the word.

Specifically, an attempt was made in the interviews to examine two polar views. The prevailing view in the social science literature of the Mexican macho is a negative one. This view holds that the origins of the excessive masculine displays and the cult of masculinity in México and other Latino countries can be traced to the Spanish Conquest, as the powerless colonized man attempted to compensate for deep-seated feelings of inadequacy and inferiority by assuming a hypermasculine, aggressive, and domineering stance. There is a second and lesser-known view that is found in Mexican popular culture, particularly in film and music, one that reflects a more positive, perhaps idyllic, conception of Mexican culture and national character. Rather than focusing on violence and male dominance, this second view associates macho qualities with the evolution of a distinct code of ethics.

Un hombre que es macho is not hypermasculine or aggressive, and he does not disrespect or denigrate women. Machos, according to the positive view, adhere to a code of ethics that stresses humility, honor, respect of oneself and others, and courage. What may be most significant in this second view is that being "macho" is not manifested by such outward qualities as physical strength and virility but by such inner qualities as personal integrity, commitment, loyalty, and, most importantly, strength of character. Stated simply, a man who acted like my Tío Roberto would be macho in the first sense of the word but certainly not in the second. It is not clear how this code of ethics developed, but it may be linked to nationalist sentiments and Mexican resistance to colonization and foreign invasion. Historical figures such as Cuauhtémoc, *El Pipíla, Los Niños Héroes,* Villa, and Zapata would be macho according to this view. In music and film positive macho figures such as Pedro Infante, Jorge Negrete, and even Cantinflas are patriots, but mostly they are *muy hombres,* men who stand up against class and racial oppression and the exploitation of the poor by the rich.

Despite the apparent differences between the two views, both see the macho cult as integral to Mexican and Latino cultures. Although I did not formulate explicit hypotheses, I entered the field expecting that respondents would generally identify with the word "macho" and define it as a positive trait or quality in themselves and other persons. An additional informal hypothesis proposed was that men who had greater ties to Latino culture and the Spanish language would be more likely to identify and to have positive associations with the word. I expected, in other words, that respondents would be more likely to adhere to the positive view of macho.

Findings: Conceptions of Macho

Respondents were first asked the following question: "What does the word 'macho' mean to you?" The interviewers were instructed to ask this and all other questions in a neutral tone, as we wanted the respondents to feel that we really were interested in what they thought. We stressed in the interviews that there were no "right" or "wrong" answers to any of the questions. This first question was then followed by a series of follow-up questions that included: "Can you give me an example (or examples) of someone you think is really macho?"; "What kinds of things do people who are really macho do?"; and "Can a woman be macha?"

Each person was assigned an identification number, and the responses to the above questions were typed on a large index card. Three bilingual judges, two men and one woman, were asked to look at the answers on the cards and to classify each respondent according to whether they believed the respondent was generally "positive," "negative," or "neutral" toward the word "macho." Those respondents classified as "positive" saw the term as a desirable cultural or personal trait or value, identified with it, and believed that it is generally good to be, or at least to aspire to be, macho. But those respondents classified as "negative" by the judges saw it as an undesirable or devalued cultural or personal trait, did not identify with being macho, and believed that it is generally bad or undesirable to be macho. In the third category, respondents were classified as "neutral" if they were deemed to be indifferent or ambivalent or to recognize both positive and negative components of the word "macho." For these respondents, macho was "just a word," or it denoted a particular male feature without imputing anything positive or negative about the feature itself.

Overall there was substantial agreement among the judges. In 86 percent of 105 cases the judges were in complete agreement in their classifications, and in another 12 percent two out of three agreed. In other words, in only two instances was there complete disagreement among the judges in which one judge ranked the respondents positive, another negative, and still another neutral.

One of the most striking findings is the extent to which the respondents were polarized in their views of macho. Most had very strong feelings; very few were neutral or indifferent toward the word. In fact, only 11 percent of the 105 respondents were classified as neutral by our judges. No less surprising is the fact that, contrary to my expectations, very few respondents viewed the word in a positive light. Only 31 percent of the men were positive in their views of macho, compared to 57 percent who were classified as negative. This means, in effect, that more than two-thirds of the respondents believed that the word "macho" had either negative or neutral connotations.

My expectation that those individuals with greater ties to Latino culture would be more likely to identify and to have positive associations with "macho" was also not supported by the data. Of the thirty-nine respondents who opted to be interviewed in Spanish, only 15 percent were seen as having a positive association with macho, whereas 74 percent were negative and 10 percent were neutral toward the term. In contrast, of the sixty-six interviewed in English, 41 percent were classified as positive, 47 percent as negative, and 12 percent as neutral toward the term.

Although negative views of the word "macho" were more prevalent than I had expected, the responses closely parallel the polar views of the word "macho" discussed earlier. Responses classified as "negative" by our judges are consistent with the "compensatory" or "deficit" model, which sees the emphasis on excessive masculinity among Mexicans and Latinos as an attempt to conceal pervasive feelings of inferiority among native men that resulted from the Conquest and the ensuing cultural, moral, and spiritual rape of the indigenous population. Those classified as "positive," similarly, are roughly consistent with an "ethical" model, which sees macho behavior as a positive, nationalist response to colonization, foreign intervention, and class exploitation.

Negative Conceptions of "Macho"

A number of consistent themes are found among the men who were classified as viewing the word "macho" in a negative light. Though I divide them into separate themes to facilitate the presentation of the findings, there is obviously considerable overlap between them.

Negative Theme 1: Synthetic/Exaggerated Masculinity

A theme that was very prevalent in the responses is that machos are men who are insecure in themselves and need to prove their manhood. It was termed a "synthetic self-image," "exaggerated masculinity," "one who acts tough and is insecure in himself," and an "exaggerated form of manliness or super manliness." One respondent described a macho as

> one who acts "bad." One who acts tough and who is insecure of himself. I would say *batos* [dudes] who come out of the *pinta* [prison] seem to have a tendency to be insecure with themselves, and tend to put up a front. [They] talk loud, intimidate others, and disrespect the meaning of a man.

Another person described it as

> being a synthetic self-image that's devoid of content.... It's a sort of facade that people use to hide the lack of strong, positive personality traits. To me, it often implies a negative set of behaviors.... I have a number of cousins who fit that. I have an uncle who fits it. He refuses to have himself fixed even though he was constantly producing children out of wedlock.

Negative Theme 2: Male Dominance Authoritarianism

A second, related theme is that of male dominance, chauvinism, and the double standard for men and women. Within the family, the macho figure is viewed as authoritarian, especially relative to the wife. According to one respondent, "They insist on being the dominant one in the household. What they say is the rule. They treat women as inferior. They have a dual set of rules for women and men." Another respondent added:

> It's someone that completely dominates. There are no two ways about it; it's either his way or no way. My dad used to be a macho. He used to come into the house drunk, getting my mother out of bed, making her make food, making her cry.

A Spanish-speaker characterized the macho as follows:

> *Una persona negativa completamente. Es una persona que es irresponsable en una palabra. Que anda en las cantinas. Es no es hombre. Si, conozco muchos de mi tierra; una docena. Toman, pelean. Llegan a la case gritando y golpeando a la señora, gritando, cantando. Eso lo vi yo cuando era chavalillo y se me grabó. Yo nunca vi a mi papá que golpeara a mi mamá* (A completely negative person. In a word, it's a person who is irresponsible. Who is out in the taverns. That's not a man. Yes, I know many from my homeland; a dozen. They drink, fight. They come home yelling and hitting the wife, yelling, singing. I saw this as a child and it made a lasting impression on me. I never saw my father hit my mother).

Negative Theme 3: Violence/Aggressiveness

A third, related theme is macho behavior manifested in expressions of violence, aggressiveness, and irresponsibility, both inside and outside the family. It is "someone that does not back down, especially if they fear they would lose face over the most trivial matters." Another person saw macho as the exaggeration of perceived masculine traits and gave the example of a fictional figure like Rambo and a real figure like former president Ronald Reagan. This person added that it was "anyone who has ever been in a war," and "it's usually associated with dogmatism, with violence, with not showing feelings." A Spanish-speaking man summarized it succinctly as "*el hombre que sale de su trabajo los vierns, va a la cantina, gasta el cheque, y llega a su casa gritando, pegándole a su esposa diciendo que él es el macho*" (the man who gets out of work on Friday, goes to a bar, spends his check, and comes home yelling and hitting his wife and telling her that he is the macho [i.e., man]). Still another felt that men who were macho did such things as "drinking to excess," and that associated with the word "macho" was "the notion of physical prowess or intimidation of others. A willingness to put themselves and others at risk, particularly physically. For those that are married, the notion of having women on the side."

One of our Spanish-speaking respondents mentioned an acquaintance who lost his family because he would not stop drinking. "*Él decía, 'La mujer se hizo para andar en la casa y yo pa' andar en las cantinas'*" (He used to say, "Woman was made to stay at home and I was made to stay in taverns"). This respondent also noted that men who are real machos tend not to support their families or tend to beat them, to get "dandied up," and to go out drinking. Another said that they "drink tequila" and "have women on their side kissing them."

Negative Theme 4: Self-Centeredness/*Egoísmo*

Closely related is the final theme, which views someone who is macho as being self-centered, selfish, and stubborn, a theme that is especially prevalent among respondents with close ties to México. Several men saw machismo as *un tipo de egoísmo* (a type of selfishness) and felt that it referred to a person who always wanted things done his way—*a la mía*. It is someone who wants to impose his will on others or wants to be right, whether he is right or not. It is viewed, for example, as

> *un tipo de egoísmo que nomás "lo mío" es bueno y nomás mis ideas son buenas. Como se dice, "Nomás mis chicharrones truenan."... Se apegan a lo que ellos creen. Todo lo que ellos dicen está correcto. Tratan que toda la gente entre a su manera de pensar y actuar, incluyendo hijos y familia* (A type of selfishness where only "mine" is good and only my ideas are worthwhile. As the saying goes, "Whatever I say goes."... They cling to their own beliefs. Everything they say is right. They try to get everyone, including children and family, to think and act the way they do).

Some respondents who elaborated on the "self-centeredness" or *egoísta* theme noted that some men will hit their wives "just to prove that they are machos," while others try to show that they "wear the pants" by not letting their wives go out. One person noted that some men believe that wives and daughters should not be permitted to cut their hair because long hair is considered "a sign of femininity," and another made reference to a young man who actually cut off a finger in order to prove his love to his sweetheart.

Because the word "macho" literally means a "he-mule" or a "he-goat," respondents often likened macho men to a dumb animal such as a mule, goat, or bull: "Somebody who's like a bull, or bullish"; "The man who is strong as though he were an animal"; "It's an ignorant person, like an animal, a donkey or mule"; and "It's a word that is outside of that which is human." One person described a macho as

> the husband of the mule that pulls the plow. A macho is a person who is dumb and uneducated. *Hay tienes a* [There you have] Macho Camacho [the boxer]. He's a wealthy man, but that doesn't make a smart man. I think he's dumb!... They're aggressive, and they're harmful, and insensitive.

Another respondent said, "Ignorant, is what it means to me, a fool. They're fools, man. They act bully type." Another similarity linked it to being "ignorant, dumb, stupid," noting that they "try to take advantage of their physical superiority over women and try to use that as a way of showing that they are right."

Given that these respondents viewed "macho" in a negative light, it is not surprising to find that most did not consider themselves macho. Only eight of the sixty men in this category reluctantly acknowledged that they were "somewhat" macho. One said, "Yes, sometimes when I drink, I get loud and stupid," and another, "Yes, to an extent because I have to be headstrong, and bullish as a teacher."

Positive Conceptions of Macho: Courage, Honor, and Integrity

As previously noted, only about 30 percent of the respondents were classified as seeing macho as a desirable cultural or personal trait or value, and those who did so were much more apt to conduct the interview in English. Some 82 percent of the men who had positive conceptions were interviewed in English.

As was true of men who were classified as negative toward the word "macho," several themes were discernible among those classified as positive. And as with the negative themes, they are separate but overlapping. A few respondents indicated that it meant "masculine" or "manly" (*varonil*), a type of masculinity (*una forma de masculinidad*), or male. The overriding theme, however, linked machismo to internal qualities like courage, valor, honor, sincerity, respect, pride, humility, and responsibility. Some went so far as to identify a distinct code of ethics or a set of principles that they saw as being characteristic of machismo.

Positive Theme 1: Assertiveness/Standing Up for Rights A more specific subtheme is the association of machismo with being assertive, courageous, standing up for one's rights, or going "against the grain" relative to other persons. The following response is representative of this view:

> To me it means someone that's assertive, someone who stands up for his or her rights when challenged. . . . Ted Kennedy because of all the hell he's had to go through. I think I like [Senator] Feinstein. She takes the issues by the horns. . . . They paved their own destiny. They protect themselves and those that are close to them and attempt to control their environment versus the contrast.

It is interesting to note that this view of being macho can be androgynous. Several respondents mentioned women who exemplified "macho qualities" or indicated that these qualities may be found among either gender. Another man gave John Kennedy and Eleanor Roosevelt as examples and noted that people who are macho

> know how to make decisions because they are confident of themselves. They know their place in the world. They accept themselves for what they are and they are confident in that. They don't worry about what others think. . . . They know what to do, the things that are essential to them and others around them.

A Spanish-speaking respondent added:

> *En respecto a nuestra cultra es un hombre que defiende sus valores, en total lo físico, lo emocional, lo psicológico. En cada mexicano hay cierto punto de macho. No es arrogante, no es egoísta excepto cuando tiene que defender sus valores. No es presumido* (Relative to our culture, it's a man that stands up for what he believes, physically, emotionally, and psychologically. Within every Mexican there is a certain sense of being macho. He is not arrogant, not egotistic, except when he has to defend his values. He is not conceited).

Positive Theme 2: Responsibility/Selflessness
A second positive macho theme is responsibility, selflessness, and meeting obligations. In direct opposition to the negative macho who is irresponsible and selfish, the positive macho is seen as having a strong sense of responsibility and as being very concerned with the welfare and well-being of other persons. This second positive macho theme was described in a number of ways: "to meet your obligations"; "someone who shoulders responsibility"; "being responsible for your family"; "a person who fulfills the responsibility of his role . . . irrespective of the consequences"; "they make firm decisions . . . that take into consideration the well-being of others." According to one respondent:

> A macho personality for me would be a person that is understanding, that is caring, that is trustworthy. He is all of those things and practices them as well as teaches them, not only with family but overall. It encompasses his whole life.

> It would be a leader with compassion. The image we have of Pancho Villa. For the Americans it would be someone like Kennedy, as a strong person, but not because he was a womanizer.

Positive Theme 3: General Code of Ethics The third theme we identified embodies many of the same traits mentioned in the first and second themes, but it differs in that respondents appear to link machismo not just to such individual qualities as selflessness but to a general code of ethics or a set of principles. One respondent who was married to an Israeli woman offered a former defense minister of Israel as exemplifying macho qualities. He noted that

> It's a man responsible for actions, a man of his word.... I think a macho does not have to be a statesman, just a man that's known to stand by his friends and follow through. A man of action relative to goals that benefit others, not himself.

Another said that it means living up to one's principles to the point of almost being willing to die for them. One of the most extensive explications of this code of ethics was offered by the following respondent:

> To me it really refers to a code of ethics that I use to relate values in my life and to evaluate myself in terms of my family, my job, my community. My belief is that if I live up to my code of ethics, I will gain respect from my family, my job, and my community. Macho has nothing to do with how much salsa you can eat, how much beer you can drink, or how many women you fuck!
>
> They have self-pride, they hold themselves as meaningful people. You can be macho as a farmworker or judge. It's a real mixture of pride and humility. Individualism is a part of it—self-awareness, self-consciousness, responsibility.

Positive Theme 4: Sincerity/Respect The final positive theme overlaps somewhat with the others and is often subsumed under the code of ethics or principles. A number of respondents associated the word "macho" with such qualities as respect for oneself and others, acting with sincerity and respect, and being a man of your word. One of our interviewees said,

> *Macho significa una persona que cumple con su palabra y que es un hombre total.... Actúan con sinceridad y con respeto* (Macho means a person who backs up what he says and who is a complete man.... They act with sincerity and respect).

Another mentioned self-control and having a sense of oneself and the situation.

> Usually they are reserved. They have kind of an inner confidence, kind of like you know you're the fastest gun in town so you don't have to prove yourself. There's nothing to prove. A sense of self.

Still another emphasized that physical prowess by itself would not be sufficient to identify one as macho. Instead, "It would be activities that meet the challenge, require honor, and meet obligations." Finally, a respondent observed:

> Macho to me means that you understand your place in the world. That's not to say that you are the "he-man" as the popular conception says. It means you have respect for yourself, that you respect others.

Not surprisingly, all of the respondents who viewed machismo in a positive light either already considered themselves to have macho qualities or saw it as an ideal they hoped to attain.

Neutral Conceptions of Macho

Twelve respondents could not be clearly classified as positive or negative in their views of "macho." This so-called neutral category is somewhat of a residual one, however, because it includes not only men who were, in fact, neutral but also those who gave mixed signals and about whom the judges could not agree. One said that "macho" was just a word that didn't mean anything; another said that it applied to someone strong like a boxer or a wrestler, but he did not know anyone who was macho, and it was not clear whether he considered it to be a positive or negative trait. Others were either ambivalent or pointed to both positive and negative components of being macho. A street-wise young man in his mid-twenties, for example, indicated that

> The word macho to me means someone who won't take nothing from no one. Respects others, and expects a lot of respect from others.

The person is willing to take any risk. . . . They always think they can do anything and everything. They don't take no shit from no one. They have a one-track mind. Never want to accept the fact that women can perform as well as men.

Significantly, the judges were divided in classifying this respondent; one classified him as negative, another as positive, and the third as neutral. The fact is that rather than being neutral, this young man identifies both positive ("respects others and self") and negative ("never want to accept the fact that women can perform as well as men") qualities with being macho.

Another person observed that there were at least two meanings of the word—one, a brave person who is willing to defend his ideals and himself, and the other, a man who exaggerates his masculinity—but noted that "macho" was not a term that he used. Another respondent provided a complex answer that distinguished the denotative (i.e., macho) and connotative (i.e., machismo) meanings of the term. He used the word in both ways, differentiating between being macho or male, which is denotative, and machismo, which connotes male chauvinism. He considered himself to be macho but certainly not *machista*.

> *Ser macho es ser valiente o no tener miedo. La connotación que tiene mal sentido es poner los intereses del hombre adelante de los de la mujer o del resto de la familia. Representa egoísmo. . . . Macho significa varón, hombre, pero el machismo es una manera de pensar, y es negativo* (To be macho is to be brave or to not be afraid. The connotation that is negative is to put the interests of the man ahead of those of the woman or the rest of the family. It represents selfishness. . . . Macho means male, man, but machismo is a way of thinking, and it is negative).

Another person similarly distinguished between being macho and being *machista*.

> *Pues, en el sentido personal, significa el sexo masculino y lo difiere del sexo femenino. La palabra machismo existe solamente de bajo nivel cultural y significa un hombre valiente, borracho y pendenciero* (Well, in a personal sense, it means the masculine gender and it distinguishes it from the feminine. The word machismo exists only at a low cultural level and it means a brave man, a drunkard, and a hell-raiser).

Six of the twelve respondents who were classified as neutral considered themselves to be at least somewhat macho.

Regional and Socioeconomic Differences in Conceptions of Macho

Conceptions of the word "macho" do not vary significantly by region, but there are significant differences according to socioeconomic status. Men with more education, with a higher income, and in professional occupations were more likely to have a positive conception of the word. This is not to suggest that they are necessarily more *machista,* or chauvinistic, but that they simply see the word in a more positive light. Almost half (42 percent) of the respondents who were professionals associated the word "macho" with being principled or standing up for one's rights, whereas only 23 percent of nonprofessionals had a positive conception of the word.

Place of birth and language were also significantly associated with attitudes toward machismo, but, ironically, those respondents who were born in the United States and those who were interviewed in English were generally more positive toward the word "macho." Forty-two percent of those born in the United States have positive responses, compared with only 10 percent of those who were foreign-born.

An English-speaking respondent said that "macho equals to me chivalry associated with the Knights of the Round Table, where a man gives his word, defends his beliefs, etc." Another noted that machos were people who "stand up for what they believe, try things other people are afraid to do, and defend the rights of others." But one Mexican man saw it as the opposite—"*Mexicanos que aceptan que la mujer 'lleve los pantalones,' irresponsables, les dan mas atención a sus aspectos sociales que a sus responsabilidades*" (Mexicans who accept that the women "wear the pants," they are irresponsible, these men pay more attention to their social lives than to their responsibilities).

Regional and Socioeconomic Differences in "How Machos Act"

After defining the word "macho," respondents were asked to give an example of how people who are macho act or behave. The answers ranged from drinking to excess, acting "bad" or "tough," being insecure in themselves, to having a "synthetic self-image," a code of ethics, and being sincere and responsible. Because responses typically were either negative or positive rather than neutral or indifferent, they were grouped into two broad categories.

Regional differences were not statistically significant, although southern Californians were more likely than Texans or northern Californians to see macho behavior as aggressive or negative and to associate it with acting tough, drinking, or being selfish.

The general pattern that was observed with regard to occupation, education, and income was that professionals, those with more education, and those with higher incomes were less likely to associate the word "macho" with negative behaviors such as drinking and trying to prove one's masculinity.

Place of birth and the language in which the interview was conducted were also related to the type of behavior that was associated with the word "macho." Men born in the United States and those who opted to conduct the interview in English were significantly more likely to associate such positive behaviors as being responsible, honorable, or respectful of others with people they considered to be macho.

Conclusion

These data provide empirical support for two very different and conflicting models of masculinity. The compensatory model sees the cult of virility and the Mexican male's obsession with power and domination as futile attempts to mask feelings of inferiority, powerlessness, and failure, whereas the second perspective associates being macho with a code of ethics that organizes and gives meaning to behavior. The first model stresses external attributes such as strength, sexual prowess, and power; the second stresses internal qualities like honor, responsibility, respect, and courage.

Although the findings are not conclusive, they have important implications. First, and most importantly, the so-called Mexican/Latino masculine cult appears to be a more complex and diverse phenomenon than is commonly assumed. But the assumption that being macho is an important Mexican cultural value is seriously called into question by the findings. Most respondents did not define macho as a positive cultural or personal trait or see themselves as being macho. Only about one-third of the men in the sample viewed the word "macho" positively. If there is a cultural value placed on being macho, one would expect that those respondents with closer ties to Latino culture and the Spanish language would be more apt to identify and to have positive associations with macho, but the opposite tendency was found to be true. Respondents who preferred to be interviewed in English were much more likely to see macho positively and to identify with it, whereas the vast majority of those who elected to be interviewed in Spanish viewed it negatively.

A major flaw of previous conceptualizations has been their tendency to treat machismo as a unitary phenomenon. The findings presented here suggest that although Latino men tend to hold polar conceptions of macho, these conceptions may not be unrelated. In describing the term, one respondent observed that there was almost a continuum between a person who is responsible and one who is chauvinistic. If one looks more closely at the two models, moreover, it is clear that virtually every trait associated with a negative macho trait has its counterpart in a positive one. Some of the principal characteristics of the negative macho and the positive counterparts are highlighted in Table 3.1.

TABLE 3.1
Negative and Positive Macho Traits

Negative	Positive
Bravado	Brave
Cowardly	Courageous
Violent	Self-defensive
Irresponsible	Responsible
Disrespectful	Respectful
Selfish	Altruistic
Pretentious	Humble
Loud	Soft-spoken
Boastful	Self-effacing
Abusive	Protective
Headstrong/bullish	Intransigent
Conformist	Individualistic
Chauvinistic	Androgynous
Dishonorable	Honorable
External qualities	Internal qualities

The close parallel between negative and positive macho traits is reminiscent of Vicente T. Mendoza's distinction between genuine and false macho. According to Mendoza, the behavior of a genuine machismo is characterized by true bravery or valor, courage, generosity, stoicism, heroism, and ferocity; the negative macho simply uses the appearance of semblance of these traits to mask cowardliness and fear....

From this perspective much of what social scientists have termed "macho" behavior is not macho at all, but its antithesis. Rather than attempting to isolate a modal Mexican personality type of determining whether macho is a positive or a negative cultural trait, social scientists would be well served to see Mexican and Latino culture as revolving around certain focal concerns or key issues such as honor, pride, dignity, courage, responsibility, integrity, and strength of character. Individuals, in turn, are evaluated positively or negatively according to how well they are perceived to respond to these focal concerns. But because being macho is ultimately an internal quality, those who seek to demonstrate outwardly that they are macho are caught in a double bind. A person who goes around holding his genitals, boasting about his manliness, or trying to prove how macho he is would not be considered macho by this definition. In the final analysis it is up to others to determine the extent to which a person lives up to these expectations and ideals.

It is also important to note that to a great extent, the positive internal qualities associated with the positive macho are not the exclusive domain of men but extend to either gender. One can use the same criteria in evaluating the behavior of women and employ parallel terminology such as *la hembra* (the female) and *hembrismo* (femaleness). *Una mujer que es una hembra* (a woman who is a real "female") is neither passive and submissive nor physically strong and assertive, for these are external qualities. Rather, *una hembra* is a person of strong character who has principles and is willing to defend them in the face of adversity. Thus, whereas the popular conception of the word "macho" refers to external male characteristics such as exaggerated masculinity or the cult of virility, the positive conception isolated here sees being macho as an internal, androgynous quality.

ARTICLE 4

Yen Le Espiritu

All Men Are *Not* Created Equal: Asian Men in U.S. History

Today, virtually every major metropolitan market across the United States has at least one Asian American female newscaster. In contrast, there is a nearly total absence of Asian American men in anchor positions (Hamamoto, 1994, p. 245; Fong-Torres, 1995). This gender imbalance in television news broadcasting exemplifies the racialization of Asian American manhood: Historically, they have been depicted as either asexual or hypersexual; today, they are constructed to be less successful, assimilated, attractive, and desirable than their female counterparts (Espiritu, 1996, pp. 95–98). The exclusion of Asian men from Eurocentric notions of the masculine reminds us that not all men benefit—or benefit equally—from a patriarchal system designed to maintain the unequal relationship that exists between men and women. The feminist mandate for gender solidarity tends to ignore power differentials among men, among women, and between white women and men of color. This exclusive focus on gender bars traditional feminists from recognizing the oppression of men of color: the fact that there are men, and not only women, who have been "feminized" and the fact that some white middle-class women hold cultural power and class power over certain men of color (Cheung, 1990, pp. 245–246; Wiegman, 1991, p. 311). Presenting race and gender as relationally constructed, King-Kok Cheung (1990) exhorted white scholars to acknowledge that, like female voices, "the voices of many men of color have been historically silenced or dismissed" (p. 246). Along the same line, black feminists have referred to "racial patriarchy"—a concept that calls attention to the white/patriarch master in U.S. history and his dominance over the black male as well as the black female (Gaines, 1990, p. 202).

Throughout their history in the United States, Asian American men, as immigrants and citizens of color, have faced a variety of economic, political, and ideological racism that have assaulted their manhood. During the pre–World War II period, racialized and gendered immigration policies and labor conditions emasculated Asian men, forcing them into womanless communities and into "feminized" jobs that had gone unfilled due to the absence of women. During World War II, the internment of Japanese Americans stripped *Issei* (first generation) men of their role as the family breadwinner, transferred some of their power and status to the U.S.-born children, and decreased male dominance over women. In the contemporary period, the patriarchal authority of Asian immigrant men, particularly those of the working class, has also been challenged due to the social and economic losses that they suffered in their transition to life in the United States. As detailed below, these three historically specific cases establish that the material existences of Asian American men have historically contradicted the Eurocentric, middle-class constructions of manhood.

Asian Men in Domestic Service

Feminist scholars have argued accurately that domestic service involves a three-way relationship between privileged white men, privileged white women, and poor women of color (Romero,

Reprinted by permission of the author.

1992). But women have not been the only domestic workers. During the pre–World War II period, racialized and gendered immigration policies and labor conditions forced Asian men into "feminized" jobs such as domestic service, laundry work, and food preparation.[1] Due to their noncitizen status, the closed labor market, and the shortage of women, Asian immigrant men, first Chinese and later Japanese, substituted to some extent for female labor in the American West. David Katzman (1978) noted the peculiarities of the domestic labor situation in the West in this period: "In 1880, California and Washington were the only states in which a majority of domestic servants were men" (p. 55).

At the turn of the twentieth century, lacking other job alternatives, many Chinese men entered into domestic service in private homes, hotels, and rooming houses (Daniels, 1988, p. 74). Whites rarely objected to Chinese in domestic service. In fact, through the 1900s, the Chinese houseboy was the symbol of upper-class status in San Francisco (Glenn, 1986, p. 106). As late as 1920, close to 50 percent of the Chinese in the United States were still occupied as domestic servants (Light, 1972, p. 7). Large numbers of Chinese also became laundrymen, not because laundering was a traditional male occupation in China, but because there were very few women of any ethnic origin—and thus few washerwomen—in gold-rush California (Chan, 1991, pp. 33–34). Chinese laundrymen thus provided commercial services that replaced women's unpaid labor in the home. White consumers were prepared to patronize a Chinese laundryman because as such he "occupied a status which was in accordance with the social definition of the place in the economic hierarchy suitable for a member of an 'inferior race'" (cited in Siu, 1987, p. 21). In her autobiographical fiction *China Men*, Maxine Hong Kingston presents her father and his partners as engaged in their laundry business for long periods each day—a business considered so low and debased that, in their songs, they associate it with the washing of menstrual blood (Goellnicht, 1992, p. 198). The existence of the Chinese houseboy and launderer—and their forced "bachelor" status—further bolstered the stereotype of the feminized and asexual or homosexual Asian man. Their feminization, in turn, confirmed their assignment to the state's labor force which performed "women's work."

Japanese men followed Chinese men into domestic service. By the end of the first decade of the twentieth century, the U.S. Immigration Commission estimated that 12,000 to 15,000 Japanese in the western United States earned a living in domestic service (Chan, 1991, pp. 39–40). Many Japanese men considered housework beneath them because in Japan only lower-class women worked as domestic servants (Ichioka, 1988, p. 24). Studies of Issei occupational histories indicate that a domestic job was the first occupation for many of the new arrivals; but unlike Chinese domestic workers, most Issei eventually moved on to agricultural or city trades (Glenn, 1986, p. 108). Filipino and Korean boys and men likewise relied on domestic service for their livelihood (Chan, 1991, p. 40). In his autobiography *East Goes West*, Korean immigrant writer Younghill Kang (1937) related that he worked as a domestic servant for a white family who treated him "like a cat or a dog" (p. 66).

Filipinos, as stewards in the U.S. Navy, also performed domestic duties for white U.S. naval officers. During the ninety-four years of U.S. military presence in the Philippines, U.S. bases served as recruiting stations for the U.S. armed forces, particularly the navy. Soon after the United States acquired the Philippines from Spain in 1898, its navy began actively recruiting Filipinos—but only as stewards and mess attendants. Barred from admissions to other ratings, Filipino enlistees performed the work of domestics, preparing and serving the officers' meals, and caring for the officers' galley, wardroom, and living spaces. Ashore, their duties ranged from ordinary housework to food services at the U.S. Naval Academy hall. Unofficially, Filipino stewards also have been ordered to perform menial chores such as walking the officers' dogs and acting as personal servants for the officers' wives (Espiritu, 1995, p. 16).

As domestic servants, Asian men became subordinates of not only privileged white men but also privileged white women. The following testimony from a Japanese house servant captures this unequal relationship:

> Immediately the ma'am demanded me to scrub the floor. I took one hour to finish. Then I had to wash windows. That was very difficult job for me. Three windows for another hour! . . . The ma'am taught me how to cook. . . . I was sitting on the kitchen chair and thinking what a change of life it was. The ma'am came into the kitchen and was so furious! It was such a hard work for me to wash up all dishes, pans, glasses, etc., after dinner. When I went into the dining room to put all silvers on sideboard, I saw the reflection of myself on the looking glass. In a white coat and apron! I could not control my feelings. The tears so freely flowed out from my eyes, and I buried my face with my both arms (quoted in Ichioka, 1988, pp. 25–26).

The experiences of Asian male domestic service workers demonstrate that not all men benefit equally from patriarchy. Depending on their race and class, men experience gender differently. While male domination of women may tie all men together, men share unequally in the fruits of this domination. For Asian American male domestic workers, economic and social discriminations locked them into an unequal relationship with not only privileged white men but also privileged white women (Kim, 1990, p. 74).

The racist and classist devaluation of Asian men had gender implications. The available evidence indicates that immigrant men reasserted their lost patriarchal power in racist America by denigrating a weaker group: Asian women. In *China Men*, Kingston's immigrant father, having been forced into "feminine" subject positions, lapses into silence, breaking the silence only to utter curses against women (Goellnicht, 1992, pp. 200–201). Kingston (1980) traces her father's abuse of Chinese women back to his feeling of emasculation in America: "We knew that it was to feed us you had to endure demons and physical labor" (p. 13). On the other hand, some men brought home the domestic skills they learned on the jobs. Anamaria Labao Cabato relates that her Filipino-born father, who spent twenty-eight years in the navy as a steward, is "one of the best cooks around" (Espiritu, 1995, p. 143). Leo Sicat, a retired U.S. Navy man, similarly reports that "we learned how to cook in the Navy, and we brought it home. The Filipino women are very fortunate because the husband does the cooking. In our household, I do the cooking, and my wife does the washing" (Espiritu, 1995, p. 108). Along the same line, in some instances, the domestic skills which men were forced to learn in their wives' absence were put to use when husbands and wives reunited in the United States. The history of Asian male domestic workers suggests that the denigration of women is only one response to the stripping of male privilege. The other is to institute a revised domestic division of labor and gender relations in the families.

Changing Gender Relations: The Wartime Internment of Japanese Americans

Immediately after the bombing of Pearl Harbor, the incarceration of Japanese Americans began. On the night of 7 December 1941, working on the principle of guilt by association, the Federal Bureau of Investigation (FBI) began taking into custody persons of Japanese ancestry who had connections to the Japanese government. On 19 February 1942, President Franklin Delano Roosevelt signed Executive Order 9066, arbitrarily suspending civil rights of U.S. citizens by authorizing the "evacuation" of 120,000 persons of Japanese ancestry into concentration camps, of whom approximately 50 percent were women and 60 percent were U.S.-born citizens (Matsumoto, 1989, p. 116).

The camp environment—with its lack of privacy, regimented routines, and new power hierarchy—inflicted serious and lasting wounds on Japanese American family life. In the crammed twenty-by-twenty-five-foot "apartment" units, tensions were high as men, women, and children struggled to recreate family life under very trying conditions. The internment also transformed the balance of power in families: husbands lost some of their power over wives, as did parents over children. Until the internment, the Issei man had been the undisputed authority over his wife and children: he was both the breadwinner and the decision maker for the entire family. Now "he had no rights, no home, no control over his own life" (Houston and Houston, 1973, p. 62). Most important, the internment reverted the economic roles—and thus the status and authority—of family members. With their means of livelihood cut off indefinitely, Issei men lost their role as breadwinners. Despondent over the loss of almost everything they had worked so hard to acquire, many Issei men felt useless and frustrated, particularly as their wives and children became less dependent on them. Daisuke Kitagawa (1967) reports that in the Tule Lake relocation center, "the [Issei] men looked as if they had suddenly aged ten years. They lost the capacity to plan for their own futures, let alone those of their sons and daughters" (p. 91).

Issei men responded to this emasculation in various ways. By the end of three years' internment, formerly enterprising, energetic Issei men had become immobilized with feelings of despair, hopelessness, and insecurity. Charles Kikuchi remembers his father—who "used to be a perfect terror and dictator"—spending all day lying on his cot: "He probably realizes that he no longer controls the family group and rarely exerts himself so that there is little family conflict as far as he is concerned" (Modell, 1973, p. 62). But others, like Jeanne Wakatsuki Houston's father, reasserted their patriarchal power by abusing their wives and children. Stripped of his roles as the protector and provider for his family, Houston's father "kept pursuing oblivion through drink, he kept abusing Mama, and there seemed to be no way out of it for anyone. You couldn't even run" (Houston and Houston, 1973, p. 61). The experiences of the Issei men underscore the intersections of racism and sexism—the fact that men of color live in a society that creates sex-based norms and expectations (i.e., man as breadwinner) which racism operates simultaneously to deny (Crenshaw, 1989, p. 155).

Camp life also widened the distance and deepened the conflict between the Issei and their U.S.-born children. At the root of these tensions were growing cultural rifts between the generations as well as a decline in the power and authority of the Issei fathers. The cultural rifts reflected not only a general process of acculturation, but were accelerated by the degradation of everything Japanese and the simultaneous promotion of Americanization in the camps (Chan, 1991, p. 128; see also Okihiro, 1991, pp. 229–232). The younger *Nisei* also spent much more time away from their parents' supervision. As a consequence, Issei parents gradually lost their ability to discipline their children, whom they seldom saw during the day. Much to the chagrin of the conservative parents, young men and women began to spend more time with each other unchaperoned—at the sports events, the dances, and other school functions. Freed from some of the parental constraints, the Nisei women socialized more with their peers and also expected to choose their own husbands and to marry for "love"—a departure from the old customs of arranged marriage (Matsumoto, 1989, p. 117). Once this occurred, the prominent role that the father plays in marriage arrangements—and by extension in their children's lives—declined (Okihiro, 1991, p. 231).

Privileging U.S. citizenship and U.S. education, War Relocation Authority (WRA) policies regarding camp life further reverted the power hierarchy between the Japan-born Issei and their U.S.-born children. In the camps, only Nisei were eligible to vote and to hold office in the Community Council; Issei were excluded because of their alien status. Daisuke Kitagawa (1967) records the impact of this policy on parental authority: "In the eyes of young children, their parents were definitely inferior to their grown-up brothers and sisters, who as U.S. citizens could elect and be elected members of the Community

Council. For all these reasons many youngsters lost confidence in, and respect for, their parents" (p. 88). Similarly, the WRA salary scales were based on English-speaking ability and on citizenship status. As a result, the Nisei youths and young adults could earn relatively higher wages than their fathers. This shift in earning abilities eroded the economic basis for parental authority (Matsumoto, 1989, p. 116).

At war's end in August 1945, Japanese Americans had lost much of the economic ground that they had gained in more than a generation. The majority of Issei women and men no longer had their farms, businesses, and financial savings; those who still owned property found their homes dilapidated and vandalized and their personal belongings stolen or destroyed (Broom and Riemer, 1949). The internment also ended Japanese American concentration in agriculture and small businesses. In their absence, other groups had taken over these ethnic niches. This loss further eroded the economic basis of parental authority since Issei men no longer had businesses to hand down to their Nisei sons (Broom and Riemer, 1949, p. 31). Historian Roger Daniels (1988) declared that by the end of World War II, "the generational struggle was over: the day of the Issei had passed" (286). Issei men, now in their sixties, no longer had the vigor to start over from scratch. Forced to find employment quickly after the war, many Issei couples who had owned small businesses before the war returned to the forms of manual labor in which they began a generation ago. Most men found work as janitors, gardeners, kitchen helpers, and handymen; their wives toiled as domestic servants, garment workers, and cannery workers (Yanagisako, 1987, p. 92).

Contemporary Asian America: The Disadvantaged

Relative to earlier historical periods, the economic pattern of contemporary Asian America is considerably more varied, a result of both the postwar restructured economy and the 1965 Immigration Act.[2] The dual goals of the 1965 Immigration Act—to facilitate family reunification and to admit educated workers needed by the U.S. economy—have produced two distinct chains of emigration from Asia: one comprising the relatives of working-class Asians who had immigrated to the United States prior to 1965; the other of highly trained immigrants who entered during the late 1960s and early 1970s (Liu, Ong, and Rosenstein, 1991). Given their dissimilar backgrounds, Asian Americans "can be found throughout the income spectrum of this nation" (Ong, 1994, p. 4). In other words, today's Asian American men both join whites in the well-paid, educated, white collar sector of the workforce *and* join Latino immigrants in lower-paying secondary sector jobs (Ong and Hee, 1994). This economic diversity contradicts the model minority stereotype—the common belief that most Asian American men are college educated and in high-paying professional or technical jobs.

The contemporary Asian American community includes a sizable population with limited education, skills, and English-speaking ability. In 1990, 18 percent of Asian men and 26 percent of Asian women in the United States, age 25 and over, had less than a high school degree. Also, of the 4.1 million Asians 5 years and over, 56 percent did not speak English "very well" and 35 percent were linguistically isolated (U.S. Bureau of the Census, 1993, Table 2). The median income for those with limited English was $20,000 for males and $15,600 for females; for those with less than a high school degree, the figures were $18,000 and $15,000, respectively. Asian American men and women with both limited English-speaking ability and low levels of education fared the worst. For a large portion of this disadvantaged population, even working full-time, full-year brought in less than $10,000 in earnings (Ong and Hee, 1994, p. 45).

The disadvantaged population is largely a product of immigration: Nine tenths are immigrants (Ong and Hee, 1994). The majority enter as relatives of the pre-1956 working-class Asian immigrants. Because immigrants tend to have socioeconomic backgrounds similar to those of their sponsors, most family reunification immigrants represent a continuation of the unskilled and semiskilled Asian labor that emigrated before 1956 (Liu, Ong, and Rosenstein, 1991). Southeast Asian refugees, particularly the second-wave refugees who arrived after 1978, represent another largely disadvantaged group. This is partly so because refugees are less likely to have acquired readily transferable skills and are more likely to have made investments (in training and education) specific to the country of origin (Chiswick, 1979; Montero, 1980). For example, there are significant numbers of Southeast Asian military men with skills for which there is no longer a market in the United States. In 1990, the overall economic status of the Southeast Asian population was characterized by unstable, minimum-wage employment, welfare dependency, and participation in the informal economy (Gold and Kibria, 1993). These economic facts underscore the danger of lumping all Asian Americans together because many Asian men do not share in the relatively favorable socioeconomic outcomes attributed to the "average" Asian American.

Lacking the skills and education to catapult them into the primary sector of the economy, disadvantaged Asian American men and women work in the secondary labor market—the labor-intensive, low-capital service, and small manufacturing sectors. In this labor market, disadvantaged men generally have fewer employment options than women. This is due in part to the decline of male-occupied manufacturing jobs and the concurrent growth of female-intensive industries in the United States, particularly in service, microelectronics, and apparel manufacturing. The garment industry, microelectronics, and canning industries are top employers of immigrant women (Takaki, 1989, p. 427; Mazumdar, 1989, p. 19; Villones, 1989, p. 176; Hossfeld, 1994, pp. 71–72). In a study of Silicon Valley (California's famed high-tech industrial region), Karen Hossfeld (1994) reported that the employers interviewed preferred to hire immigrant women over immigrant men for entry-level, operative jobs (p. 74). The employers' "gender logic" was informed by the patriarchal and racist beliefs that women can afford to work for less, do not mind dead-end jobs, and are more suited physiologically to certain kinds of detailed and routine work. As Linda Lim (1983) observes, it is the "*comparative disadvantage* of women in the wage-labor market that gives them a comparative advantage vis-à-vis men in the occupations and industries where they are concentrated—so-called female ghettoes of employment" (p. 78). A white male production manager and hiring supervisor in a California Silicon Valley assembly shop discusses his formula for hiring:

> Just three things I look for in hiring [entry-level, high-tech manufacturing operatives]: small, foreign, and female. You find those three things and you're pretty much automatically guaranteed the right kind of work force. These little foreign gals are grateful to be hired—very, very grateful—no matter what (Hossfeld, 1994, p. 65).

Refugee women have also been found to be more in demand than men in secretarial, clerical, and interpreter jobs in social service work. In a study of Cambodian refugees in Stockton, California, Shiori Ui (1991) found that social service agency executives preferred to hire Cambodian women over men when both had the same qualifications. One executive explained his preference, "It seems that some ethnic populations relate better to women than men. . . . Another thing is that the pay is so bad" (cited in Ui, 1991, p. 169). As a result, in the Cambodian communities in Stockton, it is often women—and not men—who have greater economic opportunities and who are the primary breadwinners in their families (Ui, 1991, p. 171).

Due to the significant decline in the economic contributions of Asian immigrant men, women's earnings comprise an equal or greater share of the family income. Because the wage each earns is low, only by pooling incomes can a husband and wife earn enough to support a family (Glenn, 1983, p. 42). These shifts in resources have challenged the patriarchal authority of Asian men. Men's loss of status and power—not only in the public but also in the domestic arena—places severe pressure on their sense of well-being. Responding to this pressure, some men accepted the new division of labor in the family (Ui, 1991, pp. 170–173); but many others resorted to spousal abuse and divorce (Luu, 1989, p. 68). A Korean immigrant man describes his frustrations over changing gender roles and expectations:

> In Korea [my wife] used to have breakfast ready for me.... She didn't do it any more because she said she was too busy getting ready to go to work. If I complained she talked back at me, telling me to fix my own breakfast.... I was very frustrated about her, started fighting and hit her (Yim, 1978, quoted in Mazumdar, 1989, p. 18).

Loss of status and power has similarly led to depression and anxieties in Hmong males. In particular, the women's ability—and the men's inability—to earn money for households "has undermined severely male omnipotence" (Irby and Pon, 1988, p. 112). Male unhappiness and helplessness can be detected in the following joke told at a family picnic, "When we get on the plane to go back to Laos, the first thing we will do is beat up the women!" The joke—which generated laughter by both men and women—drew upon a combination of "the men's unemployability, the sudden economic value placed on women's work, and men's fear of losing power in their families" (Donnelly, 1994, pp. 74–75). As such, it highlights the interconnections of race, class, and gender—the fact that in a racist and classist society, working-class men of color have limited access to economic opportunities and thus limited claim to patriarchal authority.

Conclusion

A central task in feminist scholarship is to expose and dismantle the stereotypes that traditionally have provided ideological justifications for women's subordination. But to conceptualize oppression only in terms of male dominance and female subordination is to obscure the centrality of classism, racism, and other forms of inequality in U.S. society (Stacey and Thorne, 1985, p. 311). The multiplicities of Asian men's lives indicate that ideologies of manhood and womanhood have as much to do with class and race as they have to do with sex. The intersections of race, gender, and class mean that there are also hierarchies among women and among men and that some women hold power over certain groups of men. The task for feminist scholars, then, is to develop paradigms that articulate the complicity among these categories of oppression, that strengthen the alliance between gender and ethnic studies, and that reach out not only to women, but also to men, of color.

Notes

1. One of the most noticeable characteristics of pre–World War II Asian America was a pronounced shortage of women. During this period, U.S. immigration policies barred the entry of most Asian women. America's capitalist economy also wanted Asian male workers but not their families. In most instances, families were seen as a threat to the efficiency and exploitability of the workforce and were actively prohibited.

2. The 1965 Immigration Act ended Asian exclusion and equalized immigration rights for all nationalities. No longer constrained by exclusion laws, Asian immigrants began arriving in much larger numbers than ever before. In the 1980s, Asia was the largest source of U.S. legal immigrants, accounting for 40 percent to 47 percent of the total influx (Min, 1995, p. 12).

References

Broom, Leonard and Ruth Riemer. 1949. *Removal and Return: The Socio-Economic Effects of the War on Japanese Americans*. Berkeley: University of California Press.

Chan, Sucheng. 1991. *Asian Americans: An Interpretive History*. Boston: Twayne.

Cheung, King-Kok. 1990. "The Woman Warrior Versus the Chinaman Pacific: Must a Chinese American Critic Choose Between Feminism and Heroism?" In *Conflicts in Feminism*, edited by

Marianne Hirsch and Evelyn Fox Keller (pp. 234–251). New York and London: Routledge.

Chiswick, Barry. 1979. "The Economic Progress of Immigrants: Some Apparently Universal Patterns." In W. Fellner (Ed.), *Contemporary Economic Problems* (pp. 357–399). Washington, DC: American Enterprise Institute.

Crenshaw, Kimberlee. 1989. "Demarginalizing the Intersection of Race and Sex: A Black Feminist Critique of Antidiscrimination Doctrine, Feminist Theory and Antiracist Politics." In *University of Chicago Legal Forum: Feminism in the Law: Theory, Practice, and Criticism* (pp. 139–167). Chicago: University of Chicago Press.

Daniels, Roger. 1988. *Asian America: Chinese and Japanese in the United States Since 1850*. Seattle: University of Washington Press.

Donnelly, Nancy D. 1994. *Changing Lives of Refugee Hmong Women*. Seattle: University of Washington Press.

Espiritu, Yen Le. 1995. *Filipino American Lives*. Philadelphia: Temple University Press.

Espiritu, Yen Le. 1996. *Asian American Women and Men: Labor, Laws, and Love*. Thousand Oaks, CA: Sage.

Fong-Torres, Ben. 1995. "Why Are There No Male Asian Anchor*men* on TV?" In *Men's Lives*, 3rd ed., edited by Michael S. Kimmel and Michael A. Messner (pp. 208–211). Boston: Allyn and Bacon.

Gaines, Jane. 1990. "White Privilege and Looking Relations: Race and Gender in Feminist Film Theory." In *Issues in Feminist Film Criticism*, edited by Patricia Erens (pp. 197–214). Bloomington: Indiana University Press.

Glenn, Evelyn Nakano. 1983. "Split Household, Small Producer and Dual Wage Earner: An Analysis of Chinese-American Family Strategies." *Journal of Marriage and the Family*, February: 35–46.

Glenn, Evelyn Nakano. 1986. *Issei, Nisei, War Bride: Three Generations of Japanese American Women at Domestic Service*. Philadelphia: Temple University Press.

Goellnicht, Donald C. 1992. "Tang Ao in America: Male Subject Positions in *China Men*." In *Reading the Literatures of Asian America*, edited by Shirley Geok-lin-Lim and Amy Ling (pp. 191–212). Philadelphia: Temple University Press.

Gold, Steve and Nazli Kibria. 1993. "Vietnamese Refugees and Blocked Mobility." *Asian and Pacific Migration Review* 2:27–56.

Hamamoto, Darrell. 1994. *Monitored Peril: Asian Americans and the Politics of Representation*. Minneapolis: University of Minnesota Press.

Hossfeld, Karen J. 1994. "Hiring Immigrant Women: Silicon Valley's 'Simple Formula.' " In *Women of Color in U.S. Society*, edited by Maxine Baca Zinn and Bonnie Thornton Dill (pp. 65–93). Philadelphia: Temple University Press.

Houston, Jeanne Wakatsuki and James D. Houston. 1973. *Farewell to Manzanar*. San Francisco: Houghton Mifflin.

Ichioka, Yuji. 1988. *The Issei: The World of the First Generation Japanese Immigrants, 1885–1924*. New York: The Free Press.

Irby, Charles and Ernest M. Pon. 1988. "Confronting New Mountains: Mental Health Problems Among Male Hmong and Mien Refugees. *Amerasia Journal* 14: 109–118.

Kang, Younghill. 1937. *East Goes West*. New York: C. Scribner's Sons.

Katzman, David. 1978. "Domestic Service: Women's Work." In *Women Working: Theories and Facts in Perspective*, edited by Ann Stromberg and Shirley Harkess (pp. 377–391). Palo Alto: Mayfield.

Kim, Elaine. 1990. " 'Such Opposite Creatures': Men and Women in Asian American Literature." *Michigan Quarterly Review*, 68–93.

Kingston, Maxine Hong. 1980. *China Men*. New York: Knopf.

Kitagawa, Daisuke. 1967. *Issei and Nisei: The Internment Years*. New York: Seabury Press.

Kitano, Harry H. L. 1991. "The Effects of the Evacuation on the Japanese Americans." In *Japanese Americans: From Relocation to Redress*, edited by Roger Daniels, Sandra C. Taylor, and Harry Kitano (pp. 151–162). Seattle: University of Washington Press.

Light, Ivan. 1972. *Ethnic Enterprise in America: Business and Welfare Among Chinese, Japanese, and Blacks*. Berkeley and Los Angeles: University of California Press.

Lim, Linda Y. C. 1983. "Capitalism, Imperialism, and Patriarchy: The Dilemma of Third-World Women Workers in Multinational Factories." In *Women, Men, and the International Division of Labor*, edited by June Nash and Maria Patricia Fernandez-Kelly (pp. 70–91). Albany: State University of New York.

Liu, John, Paul Ong, and Carolyn Rosenstein. 1991. "Dual Chain Migration: Post-1965 Filipino Immigration to the United States." *International Migration Review* 25 (3): 487–513.

Luu, Van. 1989. "The Hardships of Escape for Vietnamese Women." In *Making Waves: An Anthology of Writings by and about Asian American Women*, edited by Asian Women United of California (pp. 60–72). Boston: Beacon Press.

Matsumoto, Valerie. 1989. "Nisei Women and Resettlement During World War II." In *Making Waves: An Anthology of Writings by and about Asian American Women*, edited by Asian Women United of California (pp. 115–126). Boston: Beacon Press.

Mazumdar, Sucheta. 1989. "General Introduction: A Woman-Centered Perspective on Asian American History." In *Making Waves: An Anthology by and about Asian American Women*, edited by Asian Women United of California (pp. 1–22). Boston: Beacon Press.

Min, Pyong Gap. 1995. "Korean Americans." In *Asian Americans: Contemporary Trends and Issues*, edited by Pyong Gap Min (pp. 199–231). Thousand Oaks, CA: Sage.

Modell, John, ed. 1973. *The Kikuchi Diary: Chronicle from an American Concentration Camp*. Urbana: University of Illinois Press.

Montero, Darrell. 1980. *Vietnamese Americans: Patterns of Settlement and Socioeconomic Adaptation in the United States*. Boulder, CO: Westview.

Okihiro, Gary Y. 1991. *Cane Fires: The Anti-Japanese Movement in Hawaii, 1865–1945*. Philadelphia: Temple University Press.

Ong, Paul. 1994. "Asian Pacific Americans and Public Policy." In *The State of Asian Pacific America: Economic Diversity, Issues, & Policies*, edited by Paul Ong (pp. 1–9). Los Angeles: LEAP Asian Pacific American Public Policy Institute and UCLA Asian American Studies Center.

Ong, Paul and Suzanne Hee. 1994. "Economic Diversity." In *The State of Asian Pacific America: Economic Diversity, Issues, & Policies*, edited by Paul Ong (pp. 31–56). Los Angeles: LEAP Asian Pacific American Public Policy Institute and UCLA Asian American Studies Center.

Romero, Mary. 1992. *Maid in the U.S.A.* New York: Routledge.

Siu, Paul. 1987. *The Chinese Laundryman: A Study in Social Isolation*. New York: New York University Press.

Stacey, Judith and Barrie Thorne. 1985. "The Missing Feminist Revolution in Sociology." *Social Problems* 32: 301–316.

Takaki, Ronald. 1989. *Strangers from a Different Shore: A History of Asian Americans*. Boston: Little, Brown.

Ui, Shiori. 1991. " 'Unlikely Heroes': The Evolution of Female Leadership in a Cambodian Ethnic Enclave." In *Ethnography Unbound: Power and Resistance in the Modern Metropolis*, edited by Michael Burawoy et al. (pp. 161–177). Berkeley: University of California Press.

U.S. Bureau of the Census. 1993. *We the American Asians*. Washington, DC: U.S. Government Printing Office.

Villones, Rebecca. 1989. "Women in the Silicon Valley." In *Making Waves: An Anthology of Writings by and about Asian American Women*, edited by Asian Women United of California (pp. 172–176). Boston: Beacon Press.

Wiegman, Robyn. 1991. "Black Bodies/American Commodities: Gender, Race, and the Bourgeois Ideal in Contemporary Film." In *Unspeakable Images: Ethnicity and the American Cinema*, edited by Lester Friedman (pp. 308–328). Urbana and Chicago: University of Illinois Press.

Yanagisako, Sylvia Junko. 1987. "Mixed Metaphors: Native and Anthropological Models of Gender and Kinship Domains." In *Gender and Kinship: Essays Toward a Unified Analysis*, edited by Jane Fishburne Collier and Sylvia Junko Yanagisako (pp. 86–118). Palo Alto, CA: Stanford University Press.

ARTICLE 5

Anthony S. Chen

Lives at the Center of the Periphery, Lives at the Periphery of the Center: Chinese American Masculinities and Bargaining with Hegemony

More than a decade has passed since the "new sociology of masculinity" (NSM) was proposed as a paradigmatic alternative to sex role therapy. It has since come to serve as a tremendously productive analytical and theoretical foundation for much recent scholarship. But even as empirical work on masculinities has advanced apace, the animating theoretical concern of the NSM—understanding the hegemonic power relations among men and between men and women—has been left behind. One key consequence has been an uneven and incomplete view of subaltern masculinities. This article tries to address the lacunae by linking the original theoretical impetus of the NSM with an empirical focus on subaltern masculinities. In particular, it presents a theoretically informed analysis of life history interviews with Chinese American men.

This article begins with the argument that there is still a need for additional theoretically engaged work on subaltern masculinities, particularly if our concern is to fully interrogate the conceptual implications of deploying hegemony in the study of gender. Since they are forged at both the center and periphery of vast systems of power, Chinese American masculinities make a fitting object of inquiry. I explore the construction of Chinese American masculinities through an examination of life history interviews conducted with Chinese American men who live in large cities on the northeastern seaboard. The interviews are analyzed using Hochschild's (1989) concept of "gender strategy," which describes the way that men and women solve problems in their everyday lives using culturally constructed notions of gender. Specifically, I adopt her concept to ask how Chinese American men "solve" the problem of "achieving" masculinity when faced with an abundance of negative stereotypes of them as men. Four primary gender strategies are evident: compensation, deflection, denial, and repudiation. Each one is presented through a focused life history narrative of one respondent.

I then proceed to analyze and theorize these empirical findings with an eye toward understanding how hegemony unfolds and works in the lives of Chinese American men. Here I introduce

Author's Note: This work was supported in part by the Graduate Division, University of California, Berkeley, and The Paul and Daisy Soros Fellowships for New Americans. I am enormously grateful to Arlie Hochschild and Barrie Thorne for their discerning supervision of the research. For feedback and encouragement, special thanks go to Robert Blauner, Michael Burawoy, Jachinson Chan, Nancy Chodorow, Robert Connell, Troy Duster, Jerome Karabel, Michael Kimmel, Elizabeth Long, Michael Messner, Michael Omi, Lisa Stulberg, Sau-Ling Wong, and Mayling Nu. Many thanks to Beth Schneider, Jane Ward, and the anonymous reviewers for their editorial guidance. My deepest appreciation goes to the men who so generously permitted me, a total stranger, to interview them about such deeply personal matters.

From *Gender & Society*, 13(2): 584–607. Copyright © 1999. Copyright © Anthony S. Chen. Reprinted by permission of Sage Publications, Inc.

the concept of the "hegemonic bargain" as the specific mechanism by which hegemony can be understood to operate in the social order. A hegemonic bargain occurs when a Chinese American man's gender strategy involves "achieving manhood" by consciously trading on, or unconsciously benefiting from, the privileges afforded by his race, gender, class, generation, and/or sexuality. Three observed gender strategies—compensation, deflection, and denial—participate in a hegemonic bargain; a fourth, repudiation, does not. The article concludes with a discussion of the empirical, analytical, and theoretical contributions of the research to the new sociology of masculinity as well as the sociological study of gender.

Bringing Hegemony Back In

For more than a decade, the "new sociology of masculinity" (Carrigan, Connell, and Lee 1985) has been the reigning framework for feminist-inspired research on men and masculinities. Its influence has been impressive. Nearly all recent work invokes the plural term *masculinities* to signify a paradigmatic break with sex role theory (Parsons and Bales 1955), the functionalist orthodoxy that had dominated research on gender until it was largely discredited by feminist criticism in the late 1960s and early 1970s (e.g., Lopata and Thorne 1978).[1]

Since the mid-1980s, the NSM has largely supplanted sex role theory in the study of masculinities. This is partly because it affords scholars analytical flexibility. Rather than viewing gender in terms of a preordained script with participants acting out their apposite sex role, it focuses on the system of "hegemonic power relations" (Carrigan, Connell, and Lee 1985) among different men (e.g., of different classes) and between men and women. This approach implies the need to treat masculinity as heterogeneous rather than monolithic—hence the use of the plural "masculinities" over the singular "masculine sex role." The NSM also gives scholars important theoretical leverage by stressing the historical relations of hegemonic power in which men and women, individually and collectively, are bound up. Gender is made in a "historical situation, a set of circumstances in which power is won and held" (Carrigan, Connell, and Lee 1985, 94). Masculinity is therefore not a homogeneous, static object divested of struggle; rather, it must be seen as a multifaceted, dynamic process suffused with power relations (Carrigan, Connell, and Lee 1985, 181). This process is said to be hegemonic because it involves not only pure coercion but also struggle over prevailing conceptions of the world—for example, definitions of what is masculine and what is feminine—to which the oppressor and oppressed consent.

Despite being regularly cited as a source of inspiration, however, the NSM has yielded little empirical research that properly applies the framework or enhances our grasp of it. Several problems are currently evident in the NSM. Most generally, it is not clear how the concept of hegemony is being used to explain the nature and type of domination at work in gender relations. The term is now so loosely bandied about that it has merely become a convenient way of designating a generic relationship of domination and subordination. Yet hegemony is anything but generic, referring as it does to a distinctive kind of domination. Broadly speaking, the term describes the historical process of establishing a commonsense *Weltanschauung* (worldview) that functions to secure the consent of the oppressed in their own oppression (Gramsci 1971, 12, 326).[2] Domination is achieved not solely through "the violence of the ruling class or the coercive power of the state, as it had been in the past, but through the acceptance by the ruled of a 'conception of the world' which belongs to the ruler" (Fiori [1970] 1990, 238). Hegemony thus refers to an advanced mode of domination in late capitalist societies that "is characterised by [a] combination of force and consent" that is used to promulgate a view of the world to which the oppressed and the oppressor both submit (Gramsci 1971, 80). The "mechanisms of control for securing this consent," Perry Anderson (1976, 79–80) has written, "[lie] in a ramified network of cultural institutions—schools, churches, newspapers, parties, associations." In discussions of gender, hegemony is associated with the taken-for-granted conceptions about the "nature" of men and women, of masculinity and femininity.

Presently, the NSM cleaves to such a framework mainly in theory and rarely in practice; empirical research on masculinities frequently fails to seriously engage the theoretical impetus behind the NSM. One common result is that scholars have implicitly conflated the study of hegemonic power relations with the study of hegemonic masculinities, that is, implicitly confusing an analysis of hegemony with an analysis of the masculinities of men who occupy elite or ruling-class positions in society (e.g., Donaldson 1993; Kilduff and Mehra 1996). The distinction is not irrelevant. The category "hegemonic masculinities" is a Weberian ideal type that designates the set of masculinities that are dominant in a given society. It refers to masculinities that are chiefly, though not exclusively, associated with men located in the uppermost reaches of a society's ascriptive hierarchies. Erving Goffman offers a vivid definition:

> In an important sense there is only one unblushing male in America: a young, married, white, urban, northern, heterosexual, Protestant father of college education, fully employed, of good complexion, weight, and height, and a recent record in sports. Every American male tends to look out upon the world from this perspective. . . . Any male who fails to qualify in any one of these ways is likely to view himself—during moments at least—as unworthy, incomplete, and inferior. (1963, 128)

The foregoing qualities are characteristic of hegemonic masculinity in America after World War II, even though not all of the qualities must necessarily be present for a given masculinity to achieve hegemonic status. In fact, it is more precise to think of hegemonic masculinities as a position in the social order—one that is seen as worthy, complete, and superior—rather than a fixed set of essential characteristics. The content of hegemonic masculinity varies extensively across time and place, which is a vital source of its strength.[3]

But hegemonic masculinities are not analytically identical to hegemonic power relations. Grasping the latter means more than simply studying the former; it surely means far more than studying "unblushing" American men. At the very least, it must imply addressing a set of complex, interrelated questions. How is hegemony achieved? How is it structured? By what mechanisms? At the individual level? At the societal level? How are notions of superiority and inferiority defined and given content? What makes some masculinities hegemonic and some men the beneficiaries of hegemony? How do dominant men contribute to their dominance? What marginalizes or subordinates some men, and how do they participate in their own oppression? In what ways do hegemonic masculinities depend on other masculinities and vice versa? How do men contribute to the oppression of women?

A closely related problem, also stemming from want of sustained engagement between theoretical and empirical work, is the incomplete view of subaltern men in the NSM. This is not to say that scholarship on subaltern men is utterly lacking. To be sure, our understanding of subaltern men has sharpened considerably because of recent work in the area. Two themes in particular have received substantial attention: how subaltern men are exploited and how subaltern men resist their exploitation. But comparatively less is known about how subaltern men, particularly men of color, can contribute to their own oppression and the oppression of women. The subaltern has been understood as a victim and a resistor, but how fully has he been understood as an accomplice or even a perpetrator? Some authors have touched on the question, and others have recently made signal contributions on which I draw heavily (Peña 1991; Hondagneu-Sotelo and Messner 1994; Kleinberg [1980] 1995; Fine et al. 1997). A balance sheet of the field as a whole, however, would show that attention to the question of complicity has been less concentrated and sustained than attention to other aspects of subaltern masculinities. This unevenness can be partly attributed to a failure to reckon with the full theoretical implications of hegemony. Since hegemony is now simply trafficked as a generic synonym for domination, the prevailing emphasis in scholarship has been on understanding the side of coercion (how conceptions of masculinity are imposed from without or, alternatively, how such conceptions from without are triumphantly resisted) and not consent (how those same conceptions are actively taken up from within).

Of course, some scholarship does show subaltern men as active agents in the construction of their masculinity. But on the whole it has not fully explored the ways in which subaltern men, some more than others, seek to construct their own masculinity in the image of hegemonic masculinity. This is part and parcel of a theme in the NSM—that subaltern men not only resist but also abet their own oppression and the oppression of women—that remains decidedly underdeveloped. I propose that it is vital to renew concern for the theme. If it has been convincingly demonstrated that the dominant culture sets "white, middle-class, early middle-aged, heterosexual" as the "standards for other men, against which other men are measured and, more often than not, found wanting" (Kimmel 1994, 124; cited in Cheng 1996, 180), then it is also necessary to show how such standards are also used by subaltern men to measure themselves—and to find themselves wanting.

This article, it is hoped, will help to raise afresh questions about hegemony in the empirical study of masculinity. For if the concept is to be meaningful, it is essential to examine the tangled and complex interplay of different masculinities as well as their collaboration or collusion in the oppression of women and each other. It is crucial to parse out the key sociological ligatures that bind together differently constituted masculinities, through a delicate balance of coercion and consent, in a common project of domination. In short, it is necessary to explore and extend the original insights of the NSM articulated more than a decade ago.

Research Design and Methodology

Choosing the Object of Inquiry: Why Study Chinese American Men and Masculinities?

I take up the challenge of interrogating the dynamics of hegemony in gender relations by following a line of scholarship in the NSM that focuses on men whose lives have come under tremendous pressure and exhibit the "crisis tendencies" of the modern gender order with the greatest clarity (Connell 1992, 1995). It is where and when "things fall apart" that we can see how—and under what sociological conditions and contingencies—they came to be made and put together (Kandiyoti 1988, 286; Messner 1993). This article rests on the premise that the lives of Chinese American men are apt material for studying masculinity. Chinese American men live at the intersection and interstices of vast systems of power: patriarchy, racism, colonialism, and capitalism, to adduce a few. They live at the center and periphery of these (sometimes) countervailing systems, at precisely the paradoxical locations where the social order is likely to experience "crisis tendencies" most intensely. This is one reason why I have chosen to focus on them. The other reason is that studying Chinese American men permits us to explore hegemony relationally. As the findings below will attest, Chinese American men experience a "moment of engagement" (Connell 1995, 145) with hegemonic masculinity—usually in deciding how to deal with negative stereotypes of them as men, which are themselves founded against images of hegemonic masculinity. This moment of engagement leaves traces in one's life history that are useful for studying how hegemony enters into social relations among men and between men and women.

Determining the Unit of Analysis: Gender Strategies

My analytical approach in examining the lives of Chinese American men is to focus on their gender strategies, which constitutes the unit of analysis for this research. The concept of "gender strategies" comes from Hochschild (1989), whose study *The*

Second Shift traces how husbands and wives negotiate and rationalize the apportionment of domestic labor. Hochschild defines a gender strategy as "a plan of action through which a person tries to solve problems at hand, given the cultural notions of gender at play" (p. 15). "To pursue a gender strategy," Hochschild tells us:

> a man draws on beliefs about manhood and womanhood, beliefs that are forced in early childhood and thus anchored to deep emotions. He makes a connection between how he thinks about his manhood, what he feels about it, and what he does. (p. 15)

Thus, a man might adopt a gender strategy of cooperation in regards to the second shift, sharing the load at home with his wife. Alternatively, a man might resist his wife's calls for sharing and adopt a range of different gender strategies: disaffiliating himself from mundane household tasks or decreasing his needs.

My use of the term, however, differs slightly from Hochschild's. I adapt it to look at how Chinese American men, given their cultural beliefs about gender, adopt a "plan of action" to solve the problem of dealing with negative stereotypes of them as men. To be sure, the stereotypes are astonishingly heterogeneous and malleable. One need only consider images of the shrieking martial arts expert, Armani-clad drug dealer, bumbling computer nerd, or the stony-faced patriarch to touch on a diverse few. The content of stereotypes about Chinese American men—much as the content of hegemonic masculinity itself—varies fluidly across time and place. Stereotypes themselves often belie far more complicated social realities (Chow 1994). But it is also essential to note that nearly all of the stereotypes are founded against images of hegemonic masculinity and portray Chinese American men by turns as "unworthy, incomplete, or inferior" (Goffman, 1963, 128). Schematically speaking, they are seen as socially unskilled, grossly unathletic, and sexually unattractive when younger but publicly inhibited and privately despotic when older. Clearly, while the content of stereotypes may change—across the individual life course as well as the history of whole societies—their negative valorization does not. My empirical question thus remains, "How do Chinese American men 'achieve' masculinity in the face of negative stereotypes of them as men?" Put differently, "What gender strategies do Chinese American men adopt to 'achieve' masculinity?"

Collecting the Data

To explore the gender strategies of Chinese American men, I conducted life history interviews in the spring of 1995 with men living in the northeastern United States. A nonrandom snowball sample was generated using a local organizational directory of Asian/Pacific organizations. This yielded a sample of nine men, all of whom identified themselves as Chinese or Chinese American. Eight of the men were heterosexual, and one was gay. Three men were married, and two of the married men had children. Ages ranged from the mid-20s to mid-40s. All of the men were salaried professionals—engineers, lawyers, executives, accountants, government officials—at the beginning or midpoint of their careers. Gay, young, and lower-class men were underrepresented in the sample. The limited nature of the sample, particularly its size and lack of representativeness, does not permit strong, definitive claims. Accordingly, the analysis in the following pages, however suggestive, is to be treated as exploratory.

Each interview lasted from one to three hours; the interviews were held in the respondent's workplace, when possible. Before the actual interview, a basic questionnaire was administered to obtain relevant biographical information. The interview was then given using an open-ended interview schedule and followed a basic chronological pattern, beginning with a man's boyhood and concluding with his current situation. Importantly, during the interview, I tried not to mention the subject of negative stereotypes to each respondent, waiting instead for him to address it on his own. In the event that a respondent failed to raise the subject himself, I would then raise it. I used a tape recorder during the interviews and later transcribed them.

Constructing the Typology and Presenting the Data

Examining the interview data revealed four analytically distinct gender strategies. But a few remarks are necessary here to clarify the analysis. Some interviews revealed only one gender strategy, while other interviews contained evidence of multiple gender strategies. Complicating matters further, the gender strategies of some men clearly changed over time. That said, a clear pattern of gender strategies did nonetheless emerge within and across interviews; they should be regarded as Weberian ideal types.

In presenting the gender strategies, I have proceeded by depicting each strategy as it emerges in the life history of a single respondent, not by weaving together material from several different respondents, which is the conventional technique.[4] This was done for several reasons. First, it is compelling to provide a contextual, diachronic view of each gender strategy as it flows from the now converging, now diverging forces of biography and history. Second, concentrating on a smaller set of life histories yields greater analytical clarity than traditional techniques; such clarity is essential to theoretically informed empirical research. Lastly, each of the four life histories exemplifies a particular gender strategy with especial lucidity.

Clearly, I am neither concerned with comprehensively mapping out the universe of gender strategies nor with predicting the gender strategies that men will adopt given their social backgrounds. But such a decision has drawbacks. It diminishes generalizability, although such a claim is inappropriate to such a small sample ($N = 9$). What is also sacrificed is an appreciation of how a given gender strategy might look and feel in the lives of different men. Finally, the decision to present each strategy through a single life history runs the risk of implying that each man's life can be fully comprehended in terms of the gender strategy that he is made to represent. It is therefore necessary to stress that I have deliberately created a one-dimensional portrait of my respondents only for the purposes of analytical and theoretical precision. Their actual lives are terrifically complicated, ceaselessly changing, and replete with myriad stories: joy and sadness, pleasure and pain, triumph and failure, exploitation and liberation. I have chosen not to tell some stories. My respondents have chosen not to tell me certain others. Still other stories may have been long forgotten. Only the surface of things has been broached.

Nevertheless, the original purpose of the research project, motivated by larger theoretical concerns, is to shift our angle of vision to bring into fuller view what had formerly remained out of sight. Now it is true that the object of study is always in motion, "freezing" only at the moment of analysis. Perhaps, too, the new view may conceal as much as it reveals. It certainly may be said to be as "biased" as the view from which the project started. But at least the selective shift in perception does help to cast differently what had once been an old and familiar scene.

Engendering and Race-ing Chinese American Men

Four main gender strategies were evident in the interviews: compensation, which is meant to undermine negative stereotypes by meeting the ideals of hegemonic masculinity; deflection, which tries to divert attention away from self-perceived stereotypical behavior; denial, which rejects the existence of stereotypes or their applicability to the actor himself; and repudiation, which disavows the cultural assumptions about masculinity that make such stereotypes possible. I present each in turn.

Compensation: "I Was Nondenominational. You Had to Be Good-Looking and a Lot of Fun!"

A Chinese American man may follow a strategy of compensation when he is aware of the negative stereotypes about himself and consciously tries to undermine them by conforming par excellence to the hegemonic ideal.[5] Gary Chu was born in the early 1950s and grew up in a northeastern metropolis. His father was a hard-working contractor; his mother stayed at home to raise him. Now a prominent trial attorney, he speaks with great self-assurance throughout the interview.

Gary attended Catholic school as a boy. Like other Chinese kids in the 1950s, he faced "a definite problem" at school with name-calling. "Chink" and "slanty-eyes" were some favorite epithets. That would seem to have boded ill for his social life. But he quickly points out to me that he was never ostracized from his peers as an "outsider," partly because he was a "jockish type." Gary was athletic and got along with everyone, which made things easier for him. In college, he was elected president of the student association. Handsome and personable, he dated a "fair amount"—even had a few steady girlfriends. "You had to be good-looking and a lot of fun!" he says of his romantic interests. "It was a great time." He went to law school after college, and soon thereafter he married a "very accomplished" Chinese American businesswoman named Jennifer. Gary still gets along with everyone, and he now works at a well-regarded, modestly sized law firm of which he is a founding partner. The position permits him the luxury of juggling his schedule to spend time with his young children.

Negative stereotypes of Chinese American men have decisively influenced Gary's life. A desire to "cut against" these stereotypes drove him not simply to participate in sports but to excel at them as a proclamation that he could be as good as white men. "Although I like[d] to play sports," he says, "I made a point of excelling at it. And in American society, the kind of stereotype of Asians being smart, being academic, very intellectual, it was probably working. Having done athletics and saw that I was good at it, it drove me to kind of excel at it."

The decision to develop his athleticism—in response to images of the Asian academic overachiever—has paid enormous dividends for his career, and he knows it. Gary still stays in touch with his former teammates, and most of them still "network together, send business to each other." Deciding to cut against stereotypes has also structured his career in other ways. Aside from helping him cultivate a wide circle of friends and associates, it has helped him to decide what kind of lawyer to become. Here, too, Gary expresses a desire to cut against the stereotype:

> Well, I think the stereotype is that Asian men are docile, that they are retiring, that they are doctors and engineers, that if they go into law, they'll be corporate types, do deals, do transactional work. And I can tell you that that is the reason I decided to go into litigation. That is the reason I decided to be a trial attorney—to cut against that. I was going to go out and eventually start to develop my own clients: have some visibility, have some independence, and to be a litigator.

But his decision is not cost-free. Going against the grain is no longer a matter of youthful rebellion; it is now a matter of professional survival. Now that he is a bona fide litigator, Gary must confront the stereotypes endlessly, with each new client and colleague:

> Early on, when I first got to be a prosecutor, I was a unique commodity, so they thought they could walk all over me because "He's Asian." Here's the stereotype: "The guy's soft, not aggressive." Or, "Never heard of a Chinese lawyer, let alone someone who has trial experience as a litigator." So that was something I had to overcome. Do I have to overcome it every day? Yes, I do. With clients, all the time. With new clients. Has it shaped sociologically the way I practice? Absolutely it does. Because I have a reputation as being very, very aggressive, and very no-nonsense. Won't be personally abusive to another lawyer, but I only go in one direction: I only go forward, for good or for bad.

For Gary, the decision to become a highly visible, highly aggressive litigator who had some degree of personal freedom in his own law practice was directly "shaped" by his strategy of compensation.

So, too, it seems, was his whole professional persona.

Starting his own law firm has had benefits other than financial independence. One benefit is more free time to spend with his children. Gary's own father was "very driven by work" and "wasn't around all that much." That strained their relationship. For his own part, Gary has tried to become intimately involved in raising his own children, becoming "very, very close" to his son. This makes Gary a perfect embodiment of the "New Man of the 90s"—strong but sensitive, equally engaged in breadwinning and child rearing. Appropriately, he expresses aversion to the notion of leaving domestic chores to his wife as "women's work" and tries "to be as equal as I can be." So he cooks, does housework, rears the children. But this happens mainly on the weekends. During the weekdays, an Asian nanny takes care of the kids; she also cooks. Every now and then, a cleaning woman comes in to straighten up and clean the bathrooms. This frees up time so that Gary can visit with his children.

His love for them is impossible to deny. Throughout the interview, his face radiates at the mere mention of his children. He speaks effusively of his five-year-old son, who is "a clone of me." Gary says that his son "dresses like I do," has the "same mannerisms," and even has the "same walk." Above all, he "has the same kind of athletic ability as me." Like his father, his son has taken to tennis "like a duck to water," showing every sign of the family athleticism. "Even at an early age," Gary avers, "some of the local pros in the area have begun to take a look at him."

Deflection: "The Person to Make 'the Big Money'"

A man engages in a strategy of deflection when he tries to divert attention from personal shortcomings associated with negative stereotypes of Chinese American men. In the mid-1970s, Ming-Yao Wang emigrated from his native Asian island to pursue a better education in the United States, which he did with astonishing success. Spending a number of years at several prestigious East Coast universities, Wang collected several postbaccalaureate degrees. "I was a professional student," he jokes about his protracted sortie in higher education. His slender frame quivers as he laughs. Ming-Yao now works for a large engineering firm.

Our conversation revolves largely around financial matters. Ming-Yao makes a good living. This is fortunate since he and his wife Shiu live in a large home in a nice neighborhood with extremely well-to-do neighbors. "Our home is very expensive," he says frankly. But he admits that he would not have been able to afford to live in the neighborhood were it not for a generous inheritance that helped out with the down payment. "Actually my position [did] not fit that neighborhood," he concedes. "My neighbors are rich people. I am not."

Consequently, his wife works also: "In order to live in that neighborhood, my wife, she has to work, too, to pay the mortgage." His salary as an engineer is not enough by itself to support their lifestyle. By contrast, other husbands in the neighborhood are "vice presidents." "Their wives just stay at home," he says of them. "Only [the] husbands work. [This] may be the typical American family." The trend, of course, is precisely the opposite. Two-income families in the United States are becoming increasingly dominant. But the 1950s image of the family, celebrating the complementary roles of a male breadwinner and female homemaker, still has an iron grip on his memory, as it does for many Americans. Nevertheless, Ming-Yao badly wants to live the image:

> My thinking is that—this is the traditional Chinese thinking—the husband usually work outside the house, the wife should be working inside the house. So wife should be a housewife. Based upon that kind of concept, I usually work very hard.

There is a close correspondence here between his perceived American and Chinese familial ideals. Ming-Yao sees a patriarchal family structure as a cornerstone of both American and Chinese culture.

But there is another reason that he wants his wife to be responsible for the second shift, and he is perfectly honest about it: "That is boring work!" Ming-Yao hastily qualifies himself. He is not backwards, and he says that he would be perfectly fine doing household chores if Shiu were prepared to be the primary breadwinner. "If you want to be the person to makes the major money for the house," he says. "[and] by major money I mean 'big money' for this house, then I follow you." But for now, neither partner makes enough. Even though he earns more than his wife, she must also work to support the house. This presents a problem for Ming-Yao because it means Shiu can negotiate with him about the second shift. It gives her leverage, and he cannot legitimately insist that she do all the work. So he must help her with the cooking and cleaning.

Meanwhile, he tries to "study very hard" to improve his chances at getting a raise or promotion. A significant reason why Ming-Yao must work so hard is racial discrimination. Even though he does not believe that he will ever openly witness discrimination, he suspects that it manifests itself privately: "I think that in public of course nobody dare treat me differently, but in private it should have some kind of difference here." This prejudice—and he suggests that it is not entirely unjustified on the part of Americans—has two main sources: first, it is due to the fact that "Orientals" have an "English problem"; second, it happens because "Chinese people are not aggressive enough." He quips self-deprecatingly, "I got that two problems."

To cope with racial prejudice at work, Ming-Yao deflects his own self-perceived deficiencies by doing other things that make him vital to the success and well-being of the company:

> My way to solve that problem, I study very hard, always update myself. Because my knowledge is updated, always in front, those people have to treat me well, they have to respect me.

Ultimately, when he gets the promotion and begins to earn the "big money," he will be able to "let his wife stay at home." He explains this to me earnestly, leaving little doubt about his resolve and willpower. But the weight of staying "updated" at work does take a toll on him. "It's not that easy," he said, to "concentrate" and "spend all of my efforts" on trying to "get a promotion" and "get a big salary." This is even harder because he feels that he needs to do more than his white peers to achieve the same visibility. Circumventing racism at work is taxing and it drains him. Keeping "updated" and staying "in front" leaves Ming-Yao spent: "Because I spend too much time and effort on work in the office, I don't have energy to work at home."

Denial: "I'm a White Boy!"

A Chinese American man may exercise a strategy of denial when he rejects the existence of negative stereotypes about Chinese American men or claims a kind of racial and gender exceptionalism about them, maintaining that the stereotypes do not apply to him.[6] Mark Wong, a 40-year-old technical specialist for a large telecommunications firm, says that he felt that the company had not given him a "fair shake" the last time promotions to higher management were decided. Instead, he was passed up. But he is quick to point out that "it's not just being Asian that's doing it. Technical people don't move up as quickly as salespeople." "I'm sure that [being Asian American] is a part of it," he assures me, "but it is really the corporate structure." Our interview takes place in a war room on his floor in the office building. Mark is a gregarious, ruddy-faced man, with a shock of black hair that he halfway subdues with gel. Like Gary, he speaks with great confidence and self-possession.

What is most remarkable about the entire interview is Mark's repeated admission that he always "felt" more white than Chinese. Growing up, he "felt more white [than Chinese] because I had all white friends." He tells me that he had lived for years as a boy without "knowing what being Chinese was." Even today, when he serves as the primary coordinator for a large Asian American cultural organization, he would probably surprise most of his Asian American colleagues by identifying as white: "If you were to ask the same crowd that I hang around with [now], they might think I consider myself Chinese, but I think I'm really white. My values, the way I think, are mostly white."

That feeling of being white seems to come from badly wanting to be white, a sentiment that reaches back to his youth. Mark grew up in a strict, working-class Chinese household. His father owned a hand laundry, and his mother was a seamstress. They both worked long hours. Like Gary, he thought his parents were too "controlling." "It was always very cold," he says, "very business-at-hand. Very regimented." There were no signs of emotional support to be found: "You always felt that there wasn't any love in the family; you never heard them say to you, 'I love you.'" In lieu of such support was the weighty expectation that Mark would excel in school. Yet, no matter how hard he tried or how well he did, he could never "get the love" that he wanted. "I was always striving to get to some place you could never get to," he said. "Like you would try and get the best grades you could in school—and even if you got that hundred, [you would still get asked,] 'Well wasn't there an extra credit question you could have answered?'"

But Mark wanted more than just praise for work well done in school. He wanted everything else too—the beatific pageant of American life presented in glossy monthly magazines and weekly television sitcoms:

> I don't remember things like going to parades with my folks. I don't remember doing a lot of those things that kids do with their parents. I can count how many times we went out as a family on one hand.

When he has his own kids one day, Mark wants "to make things a lot different. I grew up in front of *Ozzie and Harriet, Leave It to Beaver.* I want what I see there." What he did not get as a son he wants to give as a father.

Perhaps as a result of his strict upbringing at home, Mark cut up a bit when he went outside. One set of close friends was a group of rowdy and carefree local boys:

> They were all pretty wild. They were all white. A lot of them were musicians. I was almost a musician. We did a lot of crazy things, like beer blasts and what not. Mooning people from the cars. So it was pretty crazy. Yeah, we mooned folks, went to beer parties. I guess an occasional smoking a doobie in the back of the field, you know. A lot of practical jokes.

Smiling a little, he speaks more fondly of these friends than his parents. It seems that in their youthful carousing, they provided him with something important that he had not found at home.

And yet despite his nearly all-white affiliations in high school, Mark was somehow—and for some reason—elected president of the "Asian Club." At the time, he was uncertain why he started socializing with them. "In a way, I was like them," he says,

> but in other ways, I wasn't like them. I knew some of their problems. I heard some of the problems they had in their families: not being close, everybody's always working, everybody's always trying to top everybody else with grades. But what I didn't see in them that I knew that I had was . . . I was very white. And a lot of them were very Chinese, were not American born, were born on the other side. So I saw a big difference there. So in a way, I fit in, and in a way, I really didn't fit in.

Now, however, he claims to know himself better. As an adult, he likes to make friends with Chinese people because "I really seek out my own kind of people."

But he is still careful to disclaim any apparent racial motivation here: "I don't want to make it sound like it's very racial or anything." Instead, something else drives his associations with Chinese Americans. It is mainly because they are the kind of people "who would understand the kind of problems I have. Like relative problems. Like Chinese problems in general." I ask for an example of a Chinese problem. "I'm not sure that I can pin one down right now," he laughs, and then offers an ill-considered one instead: "Does this sauce go with this food?" Pausing for a moment and pursing his lips in dissatisfaction, he returns to his earlier, vaguer formulation: "It's having people around you who have had similar life experiences." This seems a fine line to walk, attributing his desire to hang out with his "own kind" to common "life experiences" but not willing to posit racial identity as a source of solidarity. But it is not a fine line for Mark. "I'm a white boy!" he bursts out in a lighter moment at the end of the interview.

Repudiation: "Proud of Being Asian"

A Chinese American man may engage in a strategy of repudiation by rejecting the symbolic or material premises of hegemonic masculinity. Nigel Chan, now a successful media executive in a large city on the East Coast, once wanted to be white. This is partly because he had grown up "English educated." Raised in a former British colony in Asia, Nigel went to Catholic schools and "learned English in a proper English way." That gave him access to the whole Anglophone world of television, children's novels, and magazines, all of which greatly influenced him. In fact, he says that the country was "indiscriminately" flooded with Western culture. When I ask for an example of a childhood favorite, he smiles distantly and mentions Enid Blyton.

Nigel speaks in staccato bursts, with a distinguished Chinese-British accent. His coarse hair is cropped fairly short, and he is dressed in a fashionable turquoise sport coat. He speaks to me with great aplomb, as though he is making a business presentation; it seems that he has told his story several times before.

"For a very long time," he says, "I would only date white guys because to me the concept of beauty was purely white." As a kid, he was often teased good-naturedly by his brother, who would wryly observe that Nigel preferred "English men." It was only after Nigel had spent some time in America that he realized—much to his naive dismay—that white men did not prefer him. He had trouble getting dates. Curious, he asked his friends why. Many of them replied, "It's not you, honey, it's your race." Asian men were simply seen as unattractive. "Well, you're good-looking for an Asian guy," he heard once. Another time someone told him, "You'd make a great boyfriend, but I've always wanted a blonde." Still another said to him, "I never thought of Asians as being sexual or sexy or interesting." These blunt rejections precipitated a kind of self-loathing that he had never felt before. Nigel desired white men while growing up, but he never considered the possibility that he would be regarded by them as an inadequate or undesirable partner—perhaps because he identified with them so completely.

According to Nigel, his erstwhile feelings are not uncommon: "An entire [younger] generation of Asian American gay men think they should have a white boyfriend." The attempt to obtain one is a widespread pursuit. He says, "I would say that 90 percent of all the gay Asian men I know in the United States are chasing after white boyfriends." Nigel once did so himself. For his first 10 years here, he spent most of his time "trying to be white, trying to fit in, trying to find a white boyfriend." During his "hazy days of self-loathing," as he calls them, he strove frantically to meet the masculine ideal. The key to dating success was "to be big," which is to say, having "a young white man's body." And so Nigel and his friends worked out constantly, even though "Asians have smaller bones and don't put on muscles in the same way."

But musculature alone would not have been sufficient: Everything about their (racialized) appearance mattered, from dress to hygiene and grooming. "We all bought *GQ* magazine, we certainly followed all the beauty rules," he says. "We all had our hair cut the same way, but of course those haircuts would never work on Asian hair." Many of his friends had perms "to get out hair to be like that." Nigel tried so hard he eventually succeeded in getting accepted. "My last year there," he says, "I started working out at the gym—you know, part of my ongoing effort to get a white boyfriend, and for the first time I was really accepted in a very superficial way. I was accepted into this clique of what they called the Yummy Boys. The A-list."

The success was short-lived. Nigel soon started to question his own desire to be desired by white men. Initially provoked by the constant rejection he faced, the questioning only grew stronger as a result of business trips he began taking to Asia. On one trip he discovered that his "race" meant almost nothing to prospective romantic partners. "When I go back [to Asia]," he says, "the reaction I get there is so different than what I have from men in America—even in, say, in places like New York or Los Angeles." In Asia, he saw gay Asian couples dating each other unself-consciously and without self-hate.

This was a startling contrast to what he had expected to find, which was based on his memories of growing up inundated by Western culture and values. One possible reason for the dramatic change was a shift in government policy, which has begun to actively promote Asian self-pride since he left: "The government [there] . . . felt that there were too many white role models . . . so they instituted a lot of programs there to develop Asian talent in culture." One major development involved television programming. Companies there began to produce "homegrown TV programs featuring sexy Asian men and beautiful Asian women in a way that you'd never see in the United States."

Visiting his former home in Asia helped him to sense some of the racial prejudices built into his previously commonsensical notion of beauty. As a consequence, his former adulation of whiteness has subsided. He says to me, "There is something about American gay culture, and this transcends racial lines, that is incredibly superficial and very, very mired in an obsession with youth and beauty." This realization of the hegemonic ideal has enabled him to establish highly meaningful relationships with Asian men and has made him more comfortable with his racial identity. "I have come to a point right now in my life," he says, "where I basically date Asians and am proud of being Asian."

But his new feelings of self-pride extend to more than simply the question of whom he chooses to date. It also means adopting a broadly "Asian American" identity that for him is based less on the inherent cultural affinities than on a shared experience of being an American of Asian descent. It means seeking out and appreciating others similarly identified. What brings them together is a sense of their difference from the "larger white society." "Many Asians I know hang out with white people [and are] completely . . . completely . . . acculturated," he says, "[but] a realization [eventually] comes about that they will never be white and that there is a kind of discrimination and prejudice . . . that will continue to exist." The realization also consists of the sense that "there is greater political power when you band together with other Asian groups." This mutual recognition, based as it is on a shared experience of discrimination and political awareness, forms the basis of a "pan-Asian" identity to which Nigel feels increasingly attached. The best word to describe it, he says, is not English but Italian: *simpatico*.

Toward a New(er) Sociology of Masculinity: Bargaining with Hegemony

After closely considering the stories of Gary, Ming-Yao, Mark, and Nigel, one begins to sense, perhaps only fleetingly, that there is something hegemonic at work. Goffman's (1963) image of the blushing man is instructive here. Gary avoids having to blush, Ming-Yao blushes but then tries to make up for it, Mark denies that he has to blush, and Nigel repudiates the notion of blushing itself. But what precisely is hegemonic in their gender strategies? What are the specific mechanisms by which hegemony is effectuated?

I would like to suggest one possible mechanism by introducing the concept of the hegemonic bargain, which builds on Kandiyoti's (1988) notion of the patriarchal bargain.[7] Let me develop the former by relating it to the latter. In a comparative analysis of how women adapt to the structures of a patriarchal society. Kandiyoti defines a patriarchal bargain as the "concrete set of constraints" in a given society that shape "women's gendered subjectivity and determine the nature of gender ideology" (p. 275). The term designates the "set of rules and scripts regulating gender relations, to which both genders accommodate and acquiesce," and it also names the array of rewards and privileges conferred to women (and men too) as an incentive for them to accept the social order (Kandiyoti 1988, 286). A society's patriarchal bargain therefore establishes the terms for "women's active or passive resistance in the face of their oppression" (Kandiyoti 1988, 275).

Slightly modifying her concept, I argue that a Chinese American man enters into a hegemonic bargain when his gender strategy involves trading on (or benefiting from) the advantages conferred by his race, gender, sexuality, class, accent, and/or generational status to achieve "unblushing" manhood. This bargain is possible because Chinese American men occupy a variety of positions in the social order, enabling them to deploy their given social advantages, whatever they may be, for the purposes of bolstering their masculinity. When a Chinese American man is located at the dominant end of at least one social hierarchy—whether it be race, class, sexuality, or generational status—he is in a position to strike a hegemonic bargain.

Notwithstanding obvious semantic similarities, the hegemonic and patriarchal bargains are not identical. The term *hegemonic bargain* is fairly narrow in scope, referring to Chinese American men's exchange of social advantage for the elevation of their manhood. On the other hand, the term *patriarchal bargain* is relatively broad, designating as it does the conditions under which women strategically cope with and adapt to patriarchal oppression. A hegemonic bargain more or less conforms to the conventional definition of a bargain, that is, an exchange between two relatively equal parties. But a patriarchal bargain does not since "women as a rule bargain from a weaker position" (Kandiyoti 1988, 286). The term therefore obscures the "asymmetrical exchange" in women's negotiation with and accommodation to the patriarchal bargain in their given society.

But what precisely makes a hegemonic bargain hegemonic? It is hegemonic because it involves a kind of domination that crucially depends on historically emergent, commonsensical conceptions of gender to which the dominant and dominated both accede. These conceptions of gender represent a powerful force of consent that is but one side of a two-sided hegemonic process. The other side of that hegemonic process, coercion, articulates with consent to strengthen "the general direction imposed on social life" (Gramsci 1971, 12) and thereby gives the system of domination a hegemonic quality. Importantly, hegemonic domination does not involve gender alone but also involves other aspects of difference—race, class, sexuality—that together constitute the social order.

And what makes it a bargain? It is a bargain because a Chinese American man exchanges or trades in the advantages conferred to him by his position in the social order for "real," "unblushing" manhood. This is the general, abstract model of a hegemonic bargain, but it does take more specific forms, depending on exactly what a Chinese American man uses as his strategy to "achieve" manhood. For instance, a Chinese American man striking a hegemonic bargain might think, "Real men are rich and successful. Even though I am a Chinese American man, and Chinese American men are seen as inadequate or incomplete men, I am rich. Therefore, I am a real man." Here, his class privilege (e.g., a large bank account, an expensive car, the accouterments of worldly success) is exchanged for "true" manhood.

Given this understanding of the concept, how might we reinterpret the gender strategies contained in the life histories of these four Chinese Americans? As someone who compensates, Gary Chu challenges negative stereotypes of Chinese American men by rising to meet the ideals of hegemonic masculinity. From his days in grade school to his career as a respected attorney, he has made it a point to cut against images of the "typical" Chinese guy: unathletic and sexually unappealing when younger, publicly reserved and privately domineering when older. It is in compensating that Gary has struck a hegemonic bargain. As a young man, he traded on his athleticism and good looks to escape the fate of "typical" Chinese American men. Gary achieved manhood by holding his own against, if not altogether besting, white men at their own game: He played sports, participated in student government, and dated frequently.

A similar strategy holds true for him now. As a married middle-aged man, he spends time constantly with his children and tries to help around the house with the cooking, thereby distinguishing himself from his father and other "typical" Chinese fathers and husbands. Unlike them, he seems modern and enlightened. Domestic chores must not be "women's work," he says. But in a sense, what he means is that these activities are not his woman's work. They are other women's work. It may be true that he is a bona fide "New Man," but this is true in large measure because he has the economic capacity to purchase women's labor.[8] This irony involves a hegemonic bargain on at least two levels. First and perhaps most clearly, Gary has taken advantage of one form of his class privilege, a high level of income, to hire domestic help. But in doing so, he is also clearly benefiting from a gendered division of (international) labor in which women, primarily from the developing world, constitute the major source of cheap labor from which domestic workers are drawn. Were it not for these women, the price of enlightenment might be even higher. The hegemonic bargain he has struck thus contains a class and gender dimension, if not also one rooted in the inequality between poor and rich countries.

For Gary, the cost of compensating is minimal, the benefit maximal. But for other Chinese American men—those who are not gifted with quick reflexes or who are less well-to-do—achieving manhood is not so easy. Not everyone can follow suit. And so Gary does appear to be exceptional for a Chinese American man. This result simply reinscribes the very set of perceptions that he originally wanted to cut against: that a man is rightly measured by his athleticism, his sexual conquests, his pocketbook, and his social enlightenment; that in these respects, Chinese American men do not measure up; and that their failure to do so is typical.

Ming-Yao Wang has made a hegemonic bargain, too, though of a different sort. Unlike Gary Chu, he simply cannot meet the hegemonic ideal. He consequently deflects attention away from his deficiencies as a man by making himself indispensable to the office.

The logic of hegemony is worth following closely here. Enraptured by the mythical image of the American Dream, Ming-Yao pursues it with steady resolve. He wants a capacious house in the suburbs, surrounded by secure sidewalks, verdant parks, and genteel neighbors. He wants Shiu to care for him and their home. Since he has a greater earning potential than his wife, he accepts the responsibility of bringing home the kind of "big money" that will allow them to realize his dream. But racial (and gender) prejudice exists at work. There is prejudice against people who speak with an accent or who seem too passive. This makes things challenging for him. But rather than seeing the workplace as discriminatory, however, he sees himself as the source of the problem. He does not have a decent command of English. He is not aggressive enough. To surmount the problem, Ming-Yao accepts the inferiority of Chinese American men—that is, his own inferiority—and deflects attention away from it by making himself indispensable to the company in other ways. He learns everything he can about computers and publishes papers. He keeps "updated." With his work ethic, a promotion might still be in the offing. Maybe he could even become vice president, like his wealthy neighbor, and his wife could stay home. Then they could easily afford the house—maybe even hire someone to take care of the chores. Then Ming-Yao could be more like Gary.

But unlike Gary, Ming-Yao has neither the sinewy good looks nor the easygoing manner to convert into hegemonic masculinity, although he does have a high-powered education. And so he is forced into a different bargain. In exchange for accepting the inferiority of Chinese men, Ming-Yao is given a shot at attaining the dream of American manhood (a home in the suburbs, a wife in the home) by keeping himself "updated" and his knowledge "upfront." Rather than cutting against the grain of stereotype as Gary does, Ming-Yao accepts his deficiencies as inevitable and immutable. Conceding that he cannot beat Americans at their own game—a concession rejected by Gary—Ming-Yao instead uses his willpower and smarts to find other ways to achieve his objectives. An intellect honed by years of education, which constitutes a kind of class privilege, is what he trades in for a chance at achieving masculinity.

Mark strikes a hegemonic bargain through his gender strategy of denial. This may not appear to be the case at first, for he seems genuinely ambivalent about his racial(ized) identity. On one hand, he claims repeatedly that he is white. And yet he confesses in guarded moments that he seeks out his "own kind of people." This state of existential dualism seems an inescapable predicament, something on the order of the "double consciousness" of which W. E. B. DuBois (1989, 5) wrote so poignantly. Nonetheless, a hegemonic bargain arises here as well. Mark is undeniably Chinese American, the kind of well-assimilated, middle-class Chinese American that is dispersed throughout suburbs and cities all around the United States. But in his own view, he is definitely not that kind of Chinese American—the kind that speaks with an accent, the kind whose parents cannot relate to their kids, the kind that do not know how to relax and kick back or how to "moon people" or light up a "doobie" out back. Mark will consent to lead these Chinese Americans. But he is not, emphatically not, one of them himself. That is what he means when he says that he is white—but not Chinese. There is no small irony here: The reason he has not been given a "fair shake" at work is probably the same reason thousands of other Asian American "technical specialists" have not been promoted to higher management either.[9] Institutional racism likely holds them back as much as it holds him back. But to recognize their shared fate would be tantamount to announcing that he is not a "white boy." And so he insists that he was "passed over" because of the "corporate structure."

It is in denying his racial(ized) identity that Mark has struck a hegemonic bargain. What he exchanges to achieve masculinity are the social and cultural experiences of his formative years, during which he assimilated into a peer group of mostly white friends. To distinguish himself from those who come from the "other side," Mark draws on his associations with and knowledge of "white" society. What once enabled him to be a cool (read: white) boy and what will make him a caring (read: white) father is his conviction that in most matters of social and cultural life, he simply knows better than the "average" Chinese American guy. That confidence in knowing better, partly resulting from being a second-generation Chinese American, sustains his strategy of denial. Like Gary, Mark becomes more of a man by being less "Chinese," and similarly his gender strategy may have the effect of reinforcing the stereotype of the "typical Chinese guy" from which he is trying to escape.

Not all of the gender strategies evident in the life histories necessarily lead to a hegemonic bargain; some illustrate the potential to refuse it. Nigel once chose to compensate. Pining constantly after white men, he did everything in his power to make himself more attractive to them. After 10 years of trying to assimilate, he finally found limited acceptance in the white gay community. But the acceptance felt empty and hollow. This became even clearer to him after his trips to Southeast Asia, where he was no longer judged by the same aesthetic yardstick. In Asia, he was treated as an equal to his peers, as a whole human being. The experience was powerful enough that Nigel adopted a different gender strategy, repudiation, which consisted of rejecting some of the basic assumptions or premises that underlie hegemonic masculinity: that white men are superior to Chinese American men, that Chinese American men have an inherent reason to be embarrassed and to feel inadequate. This shift extended beyond his romantic life, however. It was related to his broader embrace of a wider pan-Asian identity, an Asian American identity that was rooted in a common experience of anti-Asian discrimination and recognition of shared political interests.

Conclusion

This article has been at once empirical, analytical, and theoretical. Its empirical contribution can be found in the life history interviews of Chinese American men, who, along with Asian American men more broadly, have been understudied in the NSM. The life histories of Gary, Ming-Yao, Mark, and Nigel are therefore instructive for their own sake. Its analytical contribution can be found in the use of Hochschild's (1989) concept of "gender strategies" to guide the conduct of the interviews and to facilitate their subsequent examination. Using the concept not only helped to focus the interviews but also provided a suitable unit of analysis for framing and exploring the chief empirical and theoretical questions.

The article's theoretical contribution is threefold. First, by revisiting the writings of Gramsci (1971), it has developed a general conceptual model of hegemony as a two-sided process involving the ever-shifting balance of coercion and consent. This dualistic conceptualization of hegemony has opened up a space for exploring how subaltern men, particularly men of color, can be understood as contributing to their own oppression and the oppression of women. Second, this article has demonstrated the theoretical value of treating hegemony not simply as a function of class relations but as the convergence of race, gender, class, sexual, and (post)colonial relations—in their ideological and material manifestations.

Third, and perhaps most concretely, this article has not simply ended with the now-commonplace call for understanding how race, class, and gender intersect, but it has gone on to outline a specific mechanism by which their intersection takes on a hegemonic effect, that is, through the hegemonic bargain. A Chinese American man enters into a hegemonic bargain when he trades on or unconsciously benefits from the "privileges" of race, gender, class, generation, and/or sexuality for the purpose of "achieving" his masculinity. The mechanism is a bargain because it involves trading advantages conferred by one part of the social order for the advantages of another. The mechanism is hegemonic because it draws on and reinforces a worldview that regards Chinese American men as inadequate and incomplete. Most important, it is hegemonic because it reinforces a worldview by which many Chinese American men regard themselves as inadequate and incomplete. Such a finding reminds us of the power exerted by hegemonic masculinity in the lives of men subordinate to it, and it suggests one of the ways in which the oppressed—by turns wittingly and unwittingly—come to be agents in their own oppression.

Still, many more questions have been raised here than answered. Some pertain directly to the object of our analysis. What encourages the adoption of a given gender strategy and not others? Why and how do gender strategies change? Why and how do some men come to repudiate the lure of hegemonic masculinity? Are compensation, deflection, and denial necessarily linked to a hegemonic bargain? How would the present analysis change (or remain the same) if the experiences of lower-class, gay, or younger Chinese American men were included? How comprehensive is the foregoing typology?

Broader theoretical questions about hegemony also remain. How do coercion and consent work together? Against one another? Following the work of Pyke (1996), how do microlevel social relations reflect but also reconstitute those at the macrolevel? In what further ways do race, class, gender, and sexuality articulate to reinforce the hegemonic social order? In what ways do such forces run at cross-purposes? That is, are there contradictions in the articulation of race, class, gender, and sexuality? If so, what are the origins of such contradictions? What is their potential as sites for reconfiguring social relations?

While many more questions remain to be answered, all of them share an important emphasis on exploring a central paradox of hegemony: how a world inhabited by so many decent-minded people can nonetheless be riven with so much injustice and suffering. This article shares the same concern. All of the men I interviewed were honest and well intentioned. All of them struggled valiantly against racial prejudice. But in their own personal struggles against racism, in their struggles to fight off negative stereotypes about Asian American men, some of them may have inadvertently reproduced those stereotypes and given succor to certain views on masculinity that made those racial stereotypes possible. This is no reason to abandon a modest faith in the possibility of changing men.[10] That is because in coming to an understanding of the intricate and complicated ways that we have made and continue to make our own oppression—whether consciously or unconsciously—we empower ourselves in no small measure to unmake it.

Notes

1. For a recent discussion of sex role theory and its influence on the study of masculinity, see Messner (1997, 275–260).

2. As Anderson (1976) notes, Antonio Gramsci did not invent the term *hegemony* himself but rather borrowed it, with important modifications, from Plekhanov and Axelrod. Gramsci (1971) used the term to describe the system of capitalist domination at work in the industrialized societies of the West. An analysis of hegemony was to serve as the foundation for a "Revolution against *Capital*," that is, an effort to undermine the fatalistic notion (in certain readings of Marx) that a revolution in the West would be an inevitable consequence of anonymous, transcendent economic processes. In Gramsci's view, a protracted and complicated "war of position" against the "earthenworks" of civil society in Western nation-states would be necessary to undo hegemony there. A massive seizure of state power (a "war of movement"), as in Russia, would simply not succeed by itself in the West. For an evocative application of Gramsci to the study of race and ethnicity, see Hall (1986).

3. Thanks to Teresa Gowan and Georg Tillner for reminding me of this important point.

4. The names of the respondents, along with telltale biographical details, have been altered to preserve their privacy.

5. The term *compensatory* has been used in connection with subaltern masculinities before. Most prominently, Pyke (1996) examines the social foundations of compensatory, lower-class masculinities.

6. Thanks to Cynthia Liu for suggesting that I use the term *exceptionalism* here.

7. Lisa Stulberg recommended the Kandiyoti (1988) article to me and challenged me to think through the concept of the "patriarchal bargain." For examples of how it has been put to work previously, see the excellent articles by Hondagneu-Sotelo (1992) and Kibria (1990). Thanks also to an anonymous reviewer for the references.

8. For a sharp analysis of the emergence of the "New Man," see Messner (1993, 733), who argues that changes in men's behavior may simply represent "a shift in style—and not the social position of power—of hegemonic masculinity."

9. For a report on racial discrimination of the kind likely encountered by Mark, see *Good for Business: A Fact-Finding Report of the Federal Glass Ceiling Commission* (Federal Glass Ceiling Commission [FGCC] 1995). As the report plainly notes, "97 percent of all senior managers in *Fortune* 1000 industrial and service companies are white; 95 to 97 percent are male. In *Fortune* 2000 industrial and service companies, 5 percent of senior managers are women—and of that 5 percent, virtually all are white" (pp. iii–iv). Like other people of color, Asian Americans tend to be severely underrepresented in the managerial ranks: a survey of *Fortune* 1000 industrial and *Fortune* 500 service companies showed that 0.3 percent of senior-level managers were Asian American (FGCC 1995, 9). Of that minuscule percentage, most were doubtless men. In sum, "today's American labor force is still gender and race segregated—white men fill most top management positions in corporations" (FGCC 1995, 12).

10. The wonderfully evocative phrase, "changing men," comes from the titles of books by Kimmel (1987) and Segal (1990).

References

Anderson, P. 1976. *Considerations on Western Marxism*. London: Verso.

Carrigan, T., R. W. Connell, and J. Lee. 1985. Toward a new sociology of masculinity. *Theory and Society* 14:551–604.

Cheng, Cliff. 1996. "We choose not to compete": The "merit" discourse in the selection process, and Asian and Asian American men and their masculinity. In *Masculinities in organizations*, edited by C. Cheng. Thousand Oaks, CA: Sage.

Chow, E. Ngan-ling. 1994. Asian American women at work. In *Women of color in U.S. society*, edited by M. Baca Zinn and B. Thornton Dill. Philadelphia: Temple University Press.

Connell, R. W. 1992. A very straight gay: Masculinity, homosexual experience, and the dynamics of gender. *American Sociological Review* 57:735–751.

———. 1995. *Masculinities*. University of California Press.

Donaldson, M. 1993. What is hegemonic masculinity? *Theory and Society* 22:643–657.

DuBois, W. E. B. 1989. *The souls of black folk*. New York: Penguin.

Federal Glass Ceiling Commission (FGCC). 1995. *Good for business: A fact-finding report of the federal glass-ceiling commission*. Washington, DC: Department of Labor, Government Printing Office.

Fine, M., L. Weis, J. Addelston, and J. Marusza. 1997. (In) Secure times: Constructing white working-class masculinities in the late-20th century. *Gender & Society* 11:52–68.

Fiori, G. [1970] 1990. *Antonio Gramsci: Life of a revolutionary*. Reprint, New York: Verso.

Goffman, E. 1963. *Stigma*. Englewood Cliffs, NJ: Prentice Hall.

Gramsci, A. 1971. *Selections from prison notebooks*. New York: International.

Hall, S. 1986. Gramsci's relevance for the study of race and ethnicity. *Journal of Communication Inquiry* 10:5–27.

Hochschild, A. 1989. *The second shift*. New York: Viking.

Hondagneu-Sotelo, P. 1992. Overcoming patriarchal constraints: The reconstruction of gender relations among Mexican immigrant women and men. *Gender & Society* 6:393–415.

Hondagneu-Sotelo, P., and M. Messner. 1994. Gender displays and men's power: The "new man" and the Mexican immigrant man. In *Theorizing masculinities*, edited by H. Brod and M. Kaufman. Thousand Oaks, CA: Sage.

Kandiyoti, D. 1988. Bargaining with patriarchy. *Gender & Society* 2:274–290.

Kibria, N. 1990. Power, patriarchy, and gender conflict in the Vietnamese immigrant community. *Gender & Society* 4:9–24.

Kilduff, M., and A. Mehra. 1996. Hegemonic masculinity among the elite. In *Masculinities in organizations*, edited by C. Cheng. Thousand Oaks, CA: Sage.

Kimmel, M. 1987. *Changing men*. Newbury Park, CA: Sage.

———. 1994. Masculinities as homophobia: Fear, shame, and silence in the construction of gender identity. In *Theorizing masculinities*, edited by H. Brod and M. Kaufman. Thousand Oaks, CA: Sage.

Kleinberg, S. [1980] 1995. The new masculinity of gay men and beyond. In *Men's lives*, edited by M. Kimmel and M. Messner. Reprint, Boston: Allyn and Bacon.

Lopata, H. Z., and B. Thorne. 1978. On the term sex rules. *Signs: Journal of Women in Culture and Society* 3:718–721.

Messner, M. 1993. "Changing men" and feminist politics in the United States. *Theory and Society* 22:723–737.

———. 1997. The limits of "the male sex role": An analysis of the men's liberation and men's rights movements' discourse. *Gender & Society* 12:255–276.

Parsons, T., and R. F. Bales. 1955. *Family, socialization and interaction process*. London: Routledge & Kegan Paul.

Peña, M. 1991. Class, gender, and machismo: The "treacherous-woman" folklore of Mexican male workers. *Gender & Society* 5:30–46.

Pyke, Karen. 1996. Class-based masculinities: The interdependence of gender, class, and interpersonal power. *Gender & Society* 10:527–549.

Segal, L. 1990. *Slow motion: Changing masculinities, changing men*. London: Virago.

ARTICLE 6

Michelle Fine
Lois Weis
Judi Addelston
Julia Marusza Hall

(In) Secure Times:
Constructing White Working-Class Masculinities in the Late 20th Century

In the late 1980s and early 1990s, the poor and working-class white boys and men whom we interviewed have narrated "personal identities" as if they were wholly independent of corroding economic and social relations. Drenched in a kind of postindustrial, late twentieth-century individualism, the discourse of "identity work" appears to be draped in Teflon. The more profoundly that economic and social conditions invade their personal well-being, the more the damage and disruption is denied. Hegemony works in funny ways, especially for white working-class men who wish to think they have a continued edge on "Others"—people of color and white women.

Amid the pain and anger evident in the United States in the 1990s, we hear a desperate desire to target, to pin the tail of blame on these "Others" who have presumably taken away economic and social guarantees once secure in a nostalgic yesteryear. Our work in this article follows this pain and anger, as it is narrated by two groups of poor and working-class white boys in the Northeast, in high school and at their public sector jobs. Through pooled analyses of two independent qualitative studies, we look at the interiors and fragilities of white working-class male culture, focusing on the ways in which both whiteness and maleness are constructed through the setting up of "Others." Specifically, the two populations in this study include white working-class boys in high school and poor and working-class white men in their communities and workplaces—including a group of firefighters—between the ages of 24 and 35. These two groups were purposefully selected to demonstrate how white working-class men construct identities at different stages of adulthood. Although some of the men in this study are poor, the analytic focus remains on the identity formation of white working-class men, as the poor men come from working-class backgrounds and, as their articulations indicate, they routinely fluctuate between poor and working-class status.

Through these narratives we cut three analytic slices, trying to hear how personal and collective identities are formed today by poor and working-class white men. The first slice alerts us to their wholesale *refusal to see themselves inside history*, drowning in economic and social relations, corroding the ever-fragile "privilege" of white working-class men. The second slice takes us to the *search for scapegoats* and the ways in which these men scour their "local worlds" for those who have robbed them of their presumed privilege—finding answers in historically likely suspects,

From *Gender & Society* 11(1) © 1998 by Michelle Fine et al. pp. 52–68. Reprinted by permission of Sage Publications, Inc.

Blacks and white women. The third slice, taken up in the conclusion, distressingly reveals the erosion of union culture in the lives of these boys and men and the *refusal to organize along lines of class or economic location,* with women and men across racial/ethnic groups, in a powerful voice of protest or resistance. These themes document the power of prevailing ideologies of individualism and meritocracy—as narrated by men who have, indeed, lost their edge but refuse to look up and fetishistically only look "down" to discover who stole their edge. These are men who belong to a tradition of men who think they "did it right," worked hard and deserve a wife, a house, a union job, a safe community, and public schools. These are men who confront the troubled pastiche of the 1990s, their "unsettled times," and lash out at pathetically available "Others." By so doing, they aspire toward the beliefs, policies, and practices of a white elite for whom their troubles are as trivial as those of people of color. Yet, these boys and men hold on, desperate and vigilant, to identities of white race and male gender as though these could gain them credit in increasingly class-segregated worlds.

The poor and working-class white boys and men in this [study] belong to a continuum of white working-class men who, up until recently in U.S. history, have been relatively privileged. These men, however, do not articulate a sense of themselves inside that history. In current economic and social relations that felt sense of privilege is tenuous at best. Since the 1970s, the U.S. steel industry has been in rapid decline as have other areas of manufacturing and production, followed by the downward spiral of businesses that sprang up and around larger industry (Bluestone and Harrison 1982). In the span of a few decades, foreign investment, corporate flight, downsizing, and automation have suddenly left members of the working class without a steady family wage, which, compounded with the dissipation of labor unions, has left many white working-class men feeling emasculated and angry (Weis 1990; Weis, Proweller, and Centrie 1996). It seems that overnight, the ability to work hard and provide disappeared. White working-class men, of course, are not more racist or sexist than middle-class and upper-class white men. In this analysis, however, we offer data that demonstrate how white working-class male anger takes on virulent forms as it is displaced in a climate of reaction against global economic change.

As they search for someone who has stolen their presumed privilege, we begin to understand ways in which white poor and working-class men in the 1980s and 1990s manage to maintain a sense of self in the midst of rising feminism, affirmative action, and gay/lesbian rights. We are given further insight into ways in which they sustain a belief in a system that has, at least for working- and middle-class white men, begun to crumble, "e-racing" their once relatively secure advantage over white women and women and men of color (Newman 1993). As scholars of the dominant culture begin to recognize that "white is a color" (Roman 1993; Wong 1994), our work makes visible the borders, strategies, and fragilities of white working-class male culture, in insecure times, at a moment in history when many feel that this identity is under siege.

Many, of course, have theorized broadly about the production of white working-class masculinity. Willis (1977), for example, focuses on how white working-class "lads" in the industrial English Midlands reject school and script their futures on the same shopfloor on which their fathers and older brothers labor. Because of the often tense and contradictory power dynamics inherent in any single cultural context, Connell (1995) draws attention to the multiplicity of masculinities among men. In the absence of concrete labor jobs in which poor and working-class white men partially construct a sense of manhood, Connell also explores how the realm of compulsory heterosexuality becomes a formidable context for the production of white working-class male subjectivities. Various strands within the literature on masculine identity formation consider the construction of the "Other." For instance, researchers who explore all-male spaces in schools for white working-class and middle-class boys indicate that they often become potent breeding grounds for negative attitudes toward white women and gay men, whether in college fraternities (Sanday 1990), high school and college sports teams (Messner and Sabo 1994), or on an all-male college campus (Addelston and Stirratt, forthcoming). The look at the formation of white working-class masculinity in this study draws on this significant literature, while bringing to the forefront of analysis the current effects that the deindustrializing economy has on the meaning-making processes among poor and working-class white boys and men, particularly as it translates to the construction of a racial "Other."

On Whiteness

In the United States, the hierarchies of race, gender, and class are embodied in the contemporary "struggle" of working-class white men. As their stories reveal, these boys and men are trying to sustain a *place* within this hierarchy and secure the very *hierarchies* that assure their place. Among the varied demographic categories that spill out of this race/gender hierarchy, white men are the only ones who have a vested interest in maintaining both their position and their hierarchy—even, ironically, working-class boys and men who enjoy little of the privilege accrued to their gender/race status.

Scholars of colonial thought have highlighted the ways in which notions about non-Western "Others" are produced simultaneously with the production of discourse about the Western white "self," and these works become relevant to our analyses of race/gender domination. Analysts of West European expansion document the cultural disruptions that took place alongside economic appropriation, as well as the importance of the production of knowledge about groups of people that rendered colonization successful. As Frankenberg states,

> The notion of "epistemic violence" captures the idea that associated with West European colonial expansion is the production of modes of knowing that enabled and rationalized colonial domination from the standpoint of the West, and produced ways of conceiving other societies and cultures whose legacies endure into the present (1993, 16).

Central, then, to the colonial discourse is the idea of the colonized "Other" being wholly and hierarchically different from the "white self." In inventing discursively the colonial "Other," whites were parasitically producing an apparently stable Western white self out of a previously nonexistent self. Thus the Western (white) self and the colonial "Other" both were products of discursive construction. The work of Chakravorty Spivak (1985), which explores how Europe positioned itself as sovereign in defining racial "Others" for the purposes of administration and expanding markets, is useful on this point.

One continuing effect of colonial discourse is the production of an unnamed, unmarked white/Western self against which all others can be named and judged. It is the unmarked self that must be deconstructed, named, and marked (Frankenberg 1993). This article takes up this challenge. As we will argue here, white working-class male identity is parasitically coproduced as these men name and mark others, largely African Americans and white women. Their identity would not exist in its present form (and perhaps not at all) if these simultaneous productions were not taking place. At a moment of economic crisis in which white working-class men are being squeezed, the disparaging constructions of others proliferate.

Racism and the Construction of the "Other"

The first study we focus on involves an ethnographic investigation conducted by Lois Weis in the mid-1980s. This is an exploration of white working-class high school students in a deindustrializing urban area called "Freeway." Data were collected in the classrooms, study halls, during extracurricular activities, and through in-depth interviews with over 60 juniors, most of their teachers, the vice-principal, social workers, guidance counselors, and others over the course of an academic year. Data collection centered on the junior class since this is the year when some students begin to plan for further schooling, and in the state where Freeway is located, college entrance exams are administered.

While there are several facets to the production of the boys' identity, we focus on the ways in which young white boys coproduce African American male identities and their own identities. For the most part, these young white boys narrate a sense of self grounded in the sphere of sexuality, in which they script themselves as the protectors of white women whom they feel are in danger of what they regard as a deviant African American male sexuality. Not only are these young working-class boys unable to see themselves as belonging to a tradition of privilege in their being white and male, their felt loss of that historic status in a restructuring economy leaves them searching in their school, their neighborhood, and surrounding communities for those responsible. Perhaps due, in part, to student peer culture contextualized within the lived culture of the school in which these interviews took place, this examination of white male working-class youths of high school age reveals meaning-making processes that are strikingly uniform, at least in relation to the construction of a racial "Other."

Freeway is a divided city and a small number of Arabs and Hispanics live among African Americans largely on one side of the "tracks," and whites on the other, although there are whites living in one section of Freeway just adjacent to the steel mill, which is in the area populated by people of color. Virtually no people of color live in the white area, unlike many large cities in the United States, where there are pockets of considerable mix. Most African Americans came up from the South during and after World War II, drawn by the lure of jobs in the steel industry. Having been relegated to the dirtiest and lowest paid jobs, most are now living in large public housing projects, never having been able to amass the necessary capital to live elsewhere. Although we have no evidence to this effect, we also assume that even had they been able to accumulate capital, mortgages would have been turned down if African Americans had wished to move into the white area. Also, there are no doubt informal agreements among those who rent, not to rent to African Americans in the white areas, further contributing to the segregated nature of the town. Today, most of project residents receive welfare and have done so for a number of years.

Among these white adolescent men, people of color are used consistently as a foil against which acceptable moral, and particularly sexual, standards are established. The goodness of white is always contrasted with the badness of Black—Blacks are involved with drugs, Blacks are unacceptable sexually, Black men attempt to "invade" white sexual space by talking with white women, Black women are simply filthy. The binary translates in ways that complement white boys. As described by Jim, there is a virtual denial of anything at all good being identified with Blackness and of anything bad identified with whiteness:[1]

The minorities are really bad into drugs. You're talking everything. Anything you want, you get from them. A prime example, the _____ ward of Freeway; about 20 years ago, the _____ ward was predominately white, my grandfather used to live there. Then Italians, Polish, the Irish people, everything was fine. The houses were maintained; there was a good standard of living. . . . The Blacks brought drugs. I'm not saying white people didn't have drugs; they had drugs, but to a certain extent. But drugs were like a social thing. But now you go down to the _____ ward; it's amazing; it's a ghetto. Some of the houses are okay. They try to keep them up. Most of the homes are really, really terrible. They throw garbage on the front lawn; it's sickening. You talk to people from [surrounding suburbs]. Anywhere you talk to people, they tend to think the majority of our school is Black. They think you hang with Black people, listen to Black music. . . . A few of them [Black] are starting to go into the _____ ward now [the white side], so they're moving around. My parents will be around there when that happens, but I'd like to be out of there.

Much expressed racism centers on white men's entitled access to white women, thus serving the dual purpose of fixing Blacks and white women on a ladder of social relations. Clint expresses these sentiments as he relays that the fighting between Blacks and white in the community is a result of white men protecting white women:

> [The Blacks] live on the other side of town. . . . A lot of it [fights] starts with Blacks messing with white girls. That's how a lot of them start. Even if they [white guys] don't know the white girl, they don't like to see [it] . . . I don't like it. If I catch them [Blacks] near my sister, they'll get it. I don't like to see it like that. Most of them [my friends] see it that way [the same way he does] . . . I don't know many white kids that date Black girls.

This felt need to protect white girls also translates as a code of behavior for white male students inside school. Within school walls, white working-class male anger toward African American men is magnified. As Bill bitterly accounts, white male students are not seen as doing the right thing:

> Like my brother, he's in ninth grade. He's in trouble all the time. Last year he got jumped in school . . . about his girlfriend. He don't like Blacks. They come up to her and go, "Nice ass," and all that shit. My brother don't like that when they call her "nice ass" and stuff like that. He got suspended for saying "fucking nigger"; but it's all right for a Black guy to go up to whites and say stuff like that ["nice ass"]. . . . Sometimes the principals aren't doing their job. Like when my brother told [the assistant principal] that something is going to happen, Mr. _____ just said, "Leave it alone, just turn your head." . . . Like they [administrators] don't know when fights start in this school. Like there's this one guy's kid sister, a nigger [correction]—a Black guy—grabbed her ass. He hit him a couple of times. Did the principal know about it? No!

These young white men construct white women as if they were in need of their protection. The young men fight for these young women. Their complaints are communicated through a language of property rights. Black boys intruding onto *white property*. It is the fact that *Black* men are invading *white* women, the property of *white* men, that is at issue here. The discursive construction of Black men as oversexualized enables white men to elaborate their own "appropriate" heterosexuality. At a time of heightened concern with homosexuality, by virtue of their age, the collective nature of their lives, the fear of being labeled homosexual, and the violence that often accompanies such labeling in high school, these boys assert virulently and publicly their concern with Black men, while expressing their own heterosexuality and their ability to "take care of their women."

There is a grotesqueness about this particular set of interactions, a grotesqueness that enables white men to write themselves as pure, straight, and superior, while authoring Black men as dirty, oversexualized, and almost animal-like. The white female can be put on a pedestal, in need of protection. The Black female disparaged; the Black male avenged. The elevation of white womenhood, in fact, has been irreducibly linked to the debasement of both Black women and men (Davis 1990). By this Davis asserts that in the historic positioning of Black females as unfeminine and Black males as predators, the notion of what is feminine has become an idealized version of white womanhood. It is most interesting that not one white female in this study ever discussed young Black men as a "problem." This is not to say that white women were not racist, but this discursive rendering of Black men was quite noticeably the terrain of white men.

The word *nigger* flows freely from the lips of white men and they treat Black women far worse than they say Black men treat white women. During a conversation at the lunch table, for example, Mike says that Yolanda [a Black female] should go to "Niggeria" [Nigeria]. In another conversation about Martin Luther King Day, Dave says, "I have a wet dream—about little white boys and little Black girls." On another occasion, when two African American women walk into the cafeteria, Pete comments that "Black people . . . they're yecch. They smell funny and they [got] hair under their arms." The white boys at this table follow up their sentiment by making noises to denote disgust.

Young white men spend a great deal of time expressing and exhibiting disgust for people of color. This is done at the same time they elaborate an uninvited protectionist stance toward white women. If white women are seen as the property of white men, it is all the more acceptable for them to say and do anything they like. This set of discursive renditions legitimates their own "cultural wanderings" since they are, without question, "on the top." For the moment, this symbolic dominance substitutes for the real material dominance won during the days of heavy industry. Most important, for present purposes, is the coproduction of the "white self," white women, and the African American male "Other."

Young Adults: White Poor and Working-Class Men in an Economic Stranglehold

The second set of narratives stems from an ongoing study of poor and working-class young adults who grew up in the Reagan–Bush years, conducted by Michelle Fine, Lois Weis, and a group of graduate students, including Judi Addelston. In broad strokes we are investigating constructions of gender, race, ethnic, and class identities; participation in social and community-based movements for change; participation in self-help groups; participation in religious institutions; experiences within and outside the family; and experiences within and outside the new economy. We have adopted a quasi-life history approach in which a series of in-depth interviews are conducted with young people—poor and working-class—of varying racial backgrounds. Data were gathered in Buffalo, New York, and Jersey City, New Jersey. Seventy-five to 80 adults were interviewed in each city. While the larger aspects of the project are as stated above, in this [study] we focus on the bordered constructions of whiteness as articulated by young white men—a combined sample of poor and working-class men, some of whom are firefighters.[2]

As with the Freeway boys, we hear from these somewhat older men a set of identities that are carved explicitly out of territory bordered by African Americans and white women. Similar to the Freeway study, these groups are targeted by young white adult men as they search their communities, work sites, and even the local social service office for those who are responsible for stealing their presumed privilege. While most of these men narrate hostile comparisons with "Others," some offer sympathetic, but still bordered, views. Like cartographers working with different tools on the same geopolitical space, all these men—from western New York and northern New Jersey—sculpt their identities as if they were discernibly framed by, and contrasted through, race, gender, and sexuality.

As with the teens, the critique by young adult white men declares the boundaries of acceptable behavior at themselves. The white male critique is, by and large, a critique of the actions/behaviors taken by African Americans, particularly men. This circles around three interrelated points: "not working," welfare abuse or "cheats," and affirmative action.

Because many, if not most, of the white men interviewed have themselves been out of work and/or received welfare benefits and food stamps, their critique serves to denigrate African Americans. It also draws the limits of what constitutes "deserving" circumstances for not working, receiving welfare, and relying on government-sponsored programs at themselves.

By young adulthood, the target site for this white male critique shifts from sexuality to work but remains grounded *against* men of color. When asked about the tensions in their neighborhood, Larry observes,

> Probably not so much [tension] between them [Blacks and Hispanics]. But like for us. I mean, it gets me angry sometimes. I don't say I'm better than anybody else. But I work for the things that I have, and they [Blacks and Hispanics]

figure just because you're ahead, or you know more and you do more, [that it's] because you're white. And that's not really it. We're all equal, and I feel that what I've done, I've worked for myself to get to where I'm at. If they would just really try instead of just kind of hanging out on the street corners. That's something that really aggravates me, to see while I'm rushing to get to work, and everybody is just kind of milling around doing nothing.

In Larry's view, he is a hardworking man, trying to live honestly, while African Americans and Hispanics do nothing all day long. Larry talks about the anger he feels for those who are Black and Hispanic and in so doing sets up a binary opposition between whites and "Others," with whites as morally superior. From this flows an overt racial critique of affirmative action programs, as well as a more racially coded critique of welfare abusers and cheats.

We take up the issue of affirmative action first. Many of these white men focus on what they consider to be unfair hiring practices, which they see as favoring people of color and white women. Pete, for example, has a great deal to say about his experience at work and the Civil Rights movement more generally, and then how such movements have hurt him as a white man:

> For the most part, it hasn't been bad. It's just that right now with these minority quotas, I think more or less, the white male has become the new minority. And that's not to point a finger at the Blacks, Hispanics, or the women. It's just that with all these quotas, instead of hiring the best for the job, you have to hire according to your quota system, which is still wrong . . . Civil rights, as far as I'm concerned, is being way out of proportion . . . granted, um, the Afro-Americans were slaves over 200 years ago. They were given their freedom. We as a country, I guess you could say, has tried to, well, I can't say all of us, but most of us, have tried to, like, make things a little more equal. Try to smooth over some of the rough spots. You have some of these militants who are now claiming that after all these years, we still owe them. I think the owing time is over for everybody. Because if we go into that, then the Poles are still owed [he is Polish]. The Germans are still owed. Jesus, the Jews are definitely still owed. I mean, you're, you're getting cremated, everybody wants to owe somebody. I think it's time to wipe the slate clean . . . it's all that, um, you have to hire a quota of minorities. And they don't take the best qualified, they take the quota number first . . . . So that kind of puts you behind the eight ball before you even start. . . . Well, I'm a minority according to some people now, because they consider the white male now a minority.

Larry focuses on what he interprets as a negative effect of the Civil Rights movement—government-sponsored civil service tests. For Larry, these exams favor white women and "minorities" and exclude qualified white men from employment:

> I mean, in theory, a whole lot of it [Civil Rights movement] is good. I feel that is worthwhile, and there has to be some, not some, there has to be equality between people. And just because of . . . I feel that the federal government sometimes makes these laws or thinks that there's laws that are bad, but they themselves break them. I mean, I look at it as where—this is something that has always irked me—taking civil service exams. I feel that, I mean, I should be given a job based on my abilities and my knowledge, my background, my schooling, everything as a whole, rather than sometimes a Black man has to have a job just because he's Black. And really you're saying, you're not basing it on being Black or whether you're a male or female, but that's exactly what they're doing . . . I really, I completely disagree with quotas. I don't feel it's, they're fair. I mean, me as a white male, I'm really being pushed, turned into a minority. I mean, it doesn't matter. We have to have so many Blacks working in the police department or in the fire department, or women. And even though, well, say, I'm not just saying this because I'm a white male, but white males, you know, will be pushed, you know, pushed away from the jobs or not given

the jobs even though they might qualify more so for them, and have more of the capabilities to do the job. And they just won't get it because they're white males.

According to Tom, "color" is not an issue—there are lazy people all over and he even has friends who are Black. Tom, however, accuses African Americans and white women of unfairly playing up minority status to get jobs. From politicians to other lazy minorities, in Tom's view, Blacks in particular have a lock hold on all the good jobs:

> I have nothing against Blacks. Whether you're Black, white, you know, yellow, whatever color, whatever race. But I don't like the Black movement where, I have Black friends. I talk to them and they agree. You know, they consider themselves, you know. There's white trash and there's white, and there's Black trash, and there's Blacks. And the same in any, you know, any race. But as soon as they don't get a job, they right away call, you know, they yell discrimination. That's where I think some of our, you know, politicians come in too. You have your [council members in Buffalo], and I think they do that. But I think maybe if you went out there, and educated yourself. And you know, there's a lot of educated Blacks, and you don't hear them yelling discrimination because they've got good jobs. Because they got the know-how behind them. But the ones that are really lazy, don't want it, they, they start yelling discrimination so they can just get the job and they're not even qualified for it. And then they might take it away from, whether it's a, you know, a woman or a guy.

The white male critique off affirmative action is that it is not "fair." It privileges Blacks, Hispanics, and at times white women, above white men. According to these men, white men are today being set up as the "new minority," which contradicts their notions of equal opportunity. Nowhere in these narratives is there any recognition that white men as a group have historically been privileged, irrespective of individual merit. These assertions about affirmative action offer white men a way of "Othering" African Americans, in particular. This theme is further elaborated in discussions of welfare abusers and cheats. Like talk of sexuality among the younger men, as exemplified by Pete, the primary function of discussions about welfare abusers is to draw the boundaries of acceptable welfare at their own feet:

> [The Welfare system] is a joke. . . . They treat you like absolute garbage. They ask you everything except your sexual preference to be quite honest with you. They ask how many people are in the house. What time do you do this? What time do you do that? Where do you live? Do you pay your gas? Do you pay your electric? Um, how come you couldn't move into a cheaper apartment? Regardless of how much you're paying to begin with. If you ask them for a menial item, I mean . . . like your stove and refrigerator. They give me a real hard time. . . . There's definitely some people who abuse the system, I can see that. But then there are people who, when you need it, you know, it's like they have something to fall on to. And they're [the case workers] basically shoving everybody into one category. They're all users. But these [case workers] are the same people that if the country closes them off, they won't have a job and they're going to be there next too.

Ron, a white working-class man who has been in and out of instances of stable employment, makes observations on welfare and social services that are based on his own varied experiences. Ron says that he has never applied for welfare and takes pride in this fact, and he compares himself with those who abuse the system—who he believes are mostly Black. Later, Ron reveals that he has used social services:

> You know, we [spouse] look at welfare as being something, um, less than admirable . . . I think for the most part, I think most people get out of life what they put into it. You know, because some people have more obstacles than others, there's no doubt about it. But I think a lot of people just expect things to come to them, and when it doesn't, you know, they've got the gov-

ernment to fall back on.... You know I think it [falling back on the government] is more common for Black people. I mean social services, in general, I think, is certainly necessary, and Kelly and I have taken advantage of them. We've got food stamps several times. Um, one of the things about the home improvement [business he was in], when I first got into that, before I really developed my skills better and, and the first company, like I said, when they were doing some change over. And, just before they left [the city], we were at a point where business was starting to slack off and um, especially in the winter time. So, a lot of times in the winter when my income was quite low, we'd go on food stamps, and I think, I think that's the way it should be used. I mean, it's help there for people. But, you know, as soon as I was able to get off it, I did. And not for any noble reasons, but just, you know, I think I'd rather be able to support myself than have things handed to me.

Since most of the case workers are white, Ron is aligning himself with the hardworking white people who have just fallen on hard times, unlike the abusers, largely Black, who exploit the system. Along these same lines, Pete's criticism of the case workers is that they treat *all* welfare recipients as cheats. Many of the white men who have been out of work, or are now in a precarious economic state, speak with a strong disdain for African American men and, if less so, for white women as well. Others, however, narrate positions relative to white women and people of color within a discourse of concern and connection. This more liberal discourse is typically spoken by working-class men who occupy positions of relative economic security. But even here the borders of their identity nevertheless fall along the same fault lines of race and gender (Roediger 1994).

The white working-class firefighters interviewed in our study narrate somewhat similar views. Joe, for instance, works in a fire department in Jersey City. He, like so many of our informants, insists that he is "not a racist," but he vehemently feels that "Civil Rights has [sic] gone far enough."

As we discovered, the fire and police departments in Jersey City have historically garnered a disproportionate share of the city's public sector investment and growth over the last decade, and they employ a disproportionate share of white men. We began to hear these departments as the last public sector spaces in which white working-class men could at once exercise identities as white, working, and men. Joe offers these words to describe his raced and gendered identity:

> No, I'm not racist. I'm not prejudiced. There are definitely lowlifes in this community where we live in. If you see somebody do something stupid, you call them stupid. You don't call them a stupid Black person because there's no need for those extra words. Just stupid. That's how I feel, I look at things. I'm not racist at all. If there is such a thing, racist towards a person. That's how I see it.

Although Joe makes the disclaimer that he is not racist, ironically, he specifically marks the Black person "who does something stupid." Later, in his interview, we hear greater clarity. Joe is tired of hearing about race and has come to some frightening conclusions about how such issues should be put to rest:

> Civil rights, I think they're going overboard with it. Everything is a race issue now. Everything you see on TV, all of the talk shows. You have these Black Muslims talking, preaching hate against whites, the whites should be dead. And then you got these Nazi fanatics who say Blacks and Jews should be dead. That's fine, let them [Blacks and Jews] go in their own corner of the world.

In characterizing African Americans as "lowlifes" and "stupid," Joe ostensibly creates a subclass used to buttress what he sees as the higher moral character of whites. Sick of the race "issue," Joe also critiques gains won during progressive movements for social change. On the streets of his community and on television, Joe maintains that he is bombarded with examples of irresponsible African Americans and others whom he feels are taking over and, therefore, should be pushed back into "their own corner of the world." Interestingly, Joe revised his otherwise critical look at affirmative action because it *positively* affected him:

> I would say, what you call affirmative action, I would say that helped me to get this job. Because if it wasn't for minorities pressing the issue two or three years ago about the test being wrong, I would have scored a 368 on the test [and would have failed].

Joe passed the exam only after it had been modified to be more equitable. For Joe, public sector commitments to equity, including affirmative action and welfare, could be helpful if they help whites. But they are racist if they don't. In talking about his sister, Joe points out how she is being discriminated against because she is white. In Joe's logic, because so many Blacks and Asians are using and abusing the system, whites, unfairly, are the ones who are being cheated. Again, Joe places his sister in a position of superiority in relation to people of color. While his sister is a hard worker, "Others," who do not really need the assistance, are simply bilking the system:

> She just had a baby. She works as a waitress. Not too much cash in there because they cut her hours, and she's getting welfare and from what I understand from her, there are people, Black or Asian people, that aren't having as much problems as she is. It seems that the system is trying to deter her from using it. The impression she gets is you're white, you can get a job. If it's true, and I think that's definitely not right. You could be Black, white, gold, or brown, if you need it, you should have it.

Mark is another white firefighter. Echoing much of what Joe has said, Mark portrays the firehouse as a relatively protected and defended space for whiteness. By extension, the firehouse represents the civic goodness of [white] public institutions. In both Joe's and Mark's interviews, there is a self-consciousness about "not sounding racist," yet both consistently link any mention of people of color and the mention of social problems—be it child neglect, violence, or vandalism. Whiteness preserves the collective good, whereas people of color periodically threaten the collective good:

> I wouldn't say there is tension in the fire department but people are prejudiced. I guess I am to a certain degree. I don't think I'm that bad. I think there's good Blacks and bad Blacks, there's good whites and bad whites. I don't know what the percentage of minorities are, but Jersey City is linked with other cities and they have to have a certain percentage of minorities. Where I live right now, it's not too bad. I don't really hang out. . . . I have no problems with anybody. Just the vandalism. You just got to watch for that.

Mark doesn't describe how he got to be a firefighter, and he also does not know how Joe successfully landed the job. Although he is secure in his vocation, Joe is somehow certain that "minorities" have gained access unfairly. When asked what he might like to see changed about the job, Mark responds,

> Have probably testing be more well-rounded. More straightforward and fair. It seems to be a court fight every time to take a test. Everybody takes the same test. I just don't understand why it's so difficult. I understand you have to have certain minorities in the job and that's only fair, but sometimes I think that's not fair. It's not the fire department, it's the people that fight it . . . I think everybody should take the same test and that's it. The way you score is the way you score.

Frank, on the other hand, embodies the white working-class "success" story. He has completed college and graduate school and speaks from an even greater distance about his community's sentiments about race, safety and crime. Frank complicates talk of race/ethnicity by introducing social class as the social border that cannot easily be crossed. His narrative of growing up unravels as follows:

Well, because, you know, we were white, and these other places were, were much less white, and I think there was kind of that white fear of, minorities, um, particularly Blacks and Hispanics. And you know, I'm not proud of that, but I mean, that's just, that's part of the history of it. But it was also perceiving that things were changing, very radically, very dramatically. And what's happened over the years is that a lot of people who lived there for generations have moved away. But, you know, it was, I think, they just, a fear of, of the changes going on in the 60s and 70s, and seeing, you know, crime increase. . . . And wanting to keep, you know, this neighborhood as intact as possible. . . . I sense that there's a lot of apprehension [among whites]. You know, I think . . . I mean, a lot of it comes out of people talking about, um, their fear, you know, um, getting mugged, or getting their, you know their car stolen.

Seemingly embarrassed by racialized biases embedded in the community in which he was raised, Frank nevertheless shifts responsibly off of whites and onto "minorities" when he discusses solutions to racial problems:

Indian women have these . . . marks on their foreheads. And um, you know, they're apparently, just racists (referring to white youths who beat on these women). . . . You know, ignorant. Yeah, they're, they're young white, ignorant people who go around beating up Indians, in particular because the Indians tend to be passive. Um, it's something they need to learn to do, which is to be more assertive, I think and to be, um, you know, to stand up for their, their basic human rights.

We hear, from these young white males, a set of identities carved inside, and against, demographic and political territories. The borders of gender, race/ethnicity, and, for Frank, class, mark the borders of self, as well as "Other." While all of our interviewees are fluent in these comparisons, those who sit at the collapsing "bottom" of the economy or in sites of fragile employment rehearse identities splintered with despair, verbal violence, and hostile comparisons of self and "Other." Those more economically secure also speak through these traditional contours of identity but insist that they have detached from the moorings of hostile attitudes and oppositional identities. Even this last group, however, has little social experience from which to invent novel constructions of self, as white, working-class, male, and positively engaged with others.

From men like Frank we hear the most stretch, the greatest desire to connect across borders. But even these men feel the pull of tradition, community, historic, and contemporary fears. They are simply one job away from the narrations of their more desperate and hostile or perhaps more honest white brothers. With few noticing that the economy has produced perverse relations of scarcity, along lines of race, class, and gender, these white men are the mouths that uphold, as if truth, the rhetoric of the ruling class. Elite white men have exploited these men's fears and provided them with the language of hate and the ideology of the "Other." To this end, many of the working-class men in this sample believe that there are still good jobs available for those who work hard, only "minorities" are blocking any chance for access to such employment. Refusing analyses of collapsing urban economies and related race relations, these young adult white men hold Black and Latino men accountable for their white misery and disappointments.

Conclusion

The U.S. economy is rapidly changing, moving from an industrial to a postindustrial society. Jobs that once served to secure the lives and identities of many working-class people are swiftly becoming a thing of the past. The corrosion of white working-class male felt privilege—as experienced by the boys and men in this analysis—has also been paralleled by the dissipation of labor unions, which are being washed away as quickly as industry. Even though capital has traditionally used fundamental cleavages such as racism and sexism as tools to fracture a working-class consciousness from forming, labor unions have typically played a strong role in U.S. history in creating a space for some workers to organize against capital for change (Roediger 1994). Historical ties to white working-class union activity are fading fast, particularly among young white working-class men, whose fathers, uncles, and older brothers no longer have a union tradition to pass on to the next generation. With the erosion of union culture and no formal space left to develop and refine meaningful critique, some white working-class men, instead, scramble to reassert their assumed place of privilege on a race-gender hierarchy in an economy that has ironically devalued all workers. Unorganized and angry, our data indicate that white working-class boys and men consistently displace their rage toward historically and locally available groups.

We have offered two scenes in which white men in various stages of adulthood, poor and working-class, are constructing identities on the backs of people of color and white women. Clearly this is not only the case for white working-class men, nor is it generalizable to *all* white working-class men, but these men are among the best narrators of virulent oppositional hostility. It is important that the boys and young adult men in both studies in different geographic locations exhibit similar sentiments. These white men are a race/class/gender group that has been dramatically squeezed relative to their prior positions. Meanwhile, the fantasies and stereotypes of "Others" continue to be promoted, and these delicate, oppositional identities constantly require "steroids" of denigration to be maintained. As the Freeway data suggest, white working-class men also virulently construct notions of identity around another historically available "Other"—gays. Many studies, such as that by Messner and Sabo (1994), evidence how homophobia is used as a profound foil around which to forge aggressive forms of heterosexuality. Heteromasculinity, for the working class in the United States, may indeed be endangered.

As these white boys and men comment on their sense of mistreatment, we reflect, ironically, on their stone-faced fragility. The 1980s and 1990s have marked a time when the women they associate with got independent, their jobs got scarce, their unions got weak, and their privileged access to public institutions was compromised by the success of equal rights and affirmative action. Traditional bases of white male material power—head of the family, productive worker, and exclusive access to "good" public sector and/or unionized jobs—eroded rapidly. Sold out by elites, they are in panic and despair. Their reassertions of status reveal a profound fragility masked by the protection of "their women," their fight for "fairness" in the workplace, and their demand for "diversity" among (but not within) educational institutions. As they narrate a precarious white heteromasculinity, perhaps they speak for a narrow slice of men sitting at the white working-class nexus. More likely, they speak for a gendered and raced group whose privilege has been rattled and whose wrath is boiling over. Their focus, almost fetishistically, is on themselves as victims and "Others" as perpetrators. Research conducted by Janoff-Bulman (1979) documents that an exclusive focus on individual "perpetrators" of injustice [real or imagined] is the *least* likely strategy for transforming inequitable social conditions and the *most* likely strategy for creating poor mental health outcomes. Comforted by Howard Stern and Rush Limbaugh, these men are on a treacherous course for self, "Others," and the possibilities for broad-based social change.

The responsibility of educators, researchers, and citizens committed to democratic practice is not simply to watch passively or interrupt responsively when these boys/men get "out of hand." We must embark on serious social change efforts aimed at both understanding and transforming what we uncover here. Spaces must be located in which men/boys are working together to affirm white masculinity that does not rest on the construction of the viral "Other." Such spaces must be imagined and uncovered, given the attention that they deserve. Schools, churches, and work sites all offer enormous potential for such transformative cultural activity. We need to make it our task to locate spaces in which white men and boys are reimagining what it means to be white and male in the 1990s. Activists and researchers can profitably work with such groups to chronicle new images of white masculinity that are not based on the aggressive "Othering" that we find to be so prevalent.

Notes

1. We must point out that although we focus on only the white boys' construction of Blacks, we do not mean to imply that they authored the race script in its entirety nor that they wrote the meaning of Black for the African American students. We are, for present purposes, simply focusing on the ways in which young white men discursively construct the "Other."

2. We include men of different ages and statuses to represent an array of voices that are white, male, and working-class.

References

Addelston, J., and M. Stirratt. Forthcoming. The last bastion of masculinity: Gender politics and the construction of hegemonic masculinity at the Citadel. In *Masculinities and organizations,* edited by C. Change. Thousand Oaks, CA: Sage.

Bluestone, B., and B. Harrison. 1982. *The deindustrialization of America.* New York: Basic Books.

Connell, R. 1995. *Masculinities.* Berkeley: University of California Press.

Davis, A. 1990. *Women, culture, and politics.* New York: Vintage.

Frankenberg, R. 1993. *The social construction of whiteness: White women, race matters.* Minneapolis: University of Minnesota Press.

Janoff-Bulman, R. 1979. Characterological versus behavioral self-blame: Inquiries into depression and rape. *Journal of Social Psychology* 37:1798–1809.

Messner, M., and D. Sabo. 1994. *Sex, violence, and power in sports: Rethinking masculinity.* Freedom, CA: Crossing.

Newman, K. 1993. *Declining fortunes: The withering of the American dream.* New York: Basic Books.

Roediger, D. 1994. *The wages of whiteness: Race and the making of the American working class.* New York: Verso.

Roman, L. 1993. White is a color!: White defensiveness, postmodernism, and anti-racist pedagogy. In *Race, identity and representation in education.* New York: Routledge.

Sanday, P. R. 1990. *Fraternity gang rape: Sex, brotherhood, and privilege on campus.* New York: New York University Press.

Spivak, C. 1985. The Rani of Sirmur. In *Europe and its others,* edited by F. Barker. Colchester, UK: University of Essex Press.

Weis, L. 1990. *Working class without work: High school students in a de-industrializing economy.* New York: Routledge.

Weis, L., A. Proweller, and C. Centrie. 1996. Re-examining a moment in history: Loss of privilege inside white, working class masculinity in the 1990s. In *Off white,* edited by M. Fine, L. Powell, L. Weis, and M. Wong. New York: Routledge.

Willis, Paul. 1977. *Learning to labor: How working-class kids get working-class jobs.* New York: Columbia University Press.

Wong, L. M. 1994. Di(s)-secting and di(s)-closing whiteness. Two tales from psychology. *Feminism and Psychology* 4:133–153.

ARTICLE 7

Michael S. Kimmel

Gender, Class, and Terrorism

The events of September 11 [2001] have sent scholars and pundits alike scrambling to make sense of those seemingly senseless acts. While most analyses have focused on the political economy of globalization or the perversion of Islamic teachings by Al Qaeda, several commentators have raised gender issues.

Some have reminded us that in our haste to lionize the heroes of the World Trade Center collapse, we ignored the many women firefighters, police officers, and rescue workers who also risked their lives. We've been asked to remember the Taliban's vicious policies toward women; indeed, even Laura Bush seems to be championing women's emancipation.

A few have asked us to consider the other side of the gender coin: men. Some have rehearsed the rather tired old formulae about masculine bloodlust or the drive for domination and conquest, with no reference to the magnificent humanity displayed by so many on September 11. In an article in *Slate*, the Rutgers anthropologist Lionel Tiger trotted out his old male-bonding thesis but offered no understanding of why Al Qaeda might appeal to some men and not others. Only the journalist Barbara Ehrenreich suggests that there may be a link between the misogyny of the Taliban and the masculinity of the terrorists.

As for myself, I've been thinking lately about a letter to the editor of a small, upstate–New York newspaper, written in 1992 by an American GI after his return from service in the Gulf War. He complained that the legacy of the American middle class had been stolen by an indifferent government. The American dream, he wrote, has all but disappeared; instead, most people are struggling just to buy next week's groceries.

That letter writer was Timothy McVeigh from Lockport, N.Y. Two years later, he blew up the Murrah federal building in Oklahoma City in what is now the second-worst act of terrorism ever committed on American soil.

What's startling to me are the ways that McVeigh's complaints were echoed in some of the fragmentary evidence that we have seen about the terrorists of September 11, and especially in the portrait of Mohammed Atta, the suspected mastermind of the operation and the pilot of the first plane to hit the World Trade Center.

Looking at these two men through the lens of gender may shed some light on both the method and the madness of the tragedies they wrought.

McVeigh was representative of the small legion of white supremacists—from older organizations like the John Birch Society, the Ku Klux Klan, and the American Nazi Party, to newer neo-Nazi, racist-skinhead, white-power groups like Posse Comitatus and the White Aryan Resistance, to radical militias.

These white supremacists are mostly younger (in their early 20s), lower-middle-class men, educated at least through high school and often beyond. They are the sons of skilled workers in industries like textiles and tobacco, the sons of the owners of small farms, shops, and grocery stores. Buffeted by global political and economic forces, the sons have inherited little of their fathers' legacies. The family farms have been lost to foreclosure, the small shops squeezed out by

From *The Chronicle of Higher Education* (Feb. 8, 2002): B11–B12. Copyright © Michael Kimmel. Reprinted by permission of Chronicle of Higher Education and the author.

Wal-Marts and malls. These young men face a spiral of downward mobility and economic uncertainty. They complain that they are squeezed between the omnivorous jaws of global capital concentration and a federal bureaucracy that is at best indifferent to their plight and at worst complicit in their demise.

As one issue of *The Truth at Last,* a white-supremacist magazine, put it:

> Immigrants are flooding into our nation willing to work for the minimum wage (or less). Super-rich corporate executives are flying all over the world in search of cheaper and cheaper labor so that they can lay off their American employees. . . . Many young White families have no future! They are not going to receive any appreciable wage increases due to job competition from immigrants.

What they want, says one member, is to "take back what is rightfully ours."

Their anger often fixes on "others"—women, members of minority groups, immigrants, gay men, and lesbians—in part because those are the people with whom they compete for entry-level, minimum-wage jobs. Above them all, enjoying the view, hovers the international Jewish conspiracy.

What holds together these "paranoid politics"—antigovernment, anti-global capital but pro-small capitalist, racist, sexist, anti-Semitic, homophobic—is a rhetoric of masculinity. These men feel emasculated by big money and big government—they call the government "the Nanny State"—and they claim that "others" have been handed the birthright of native-born white men.

In the eyes of such downwardly mobile white men, most white American males collude in their own emasculation. They've grown soft, feminized, weak. White supremacists' Web sites abound with complaints about the "whimpering collapse of the blond male"; the "legions of sissies and weaklings, of flabby, limp-wristed, non-aggressive, non-physical, indecisive, slack-jawed, fearful males who, while still heterosexual in theory and practice, have not even a vestige of the old macho spirit."

American white supremacists thus offer American men the restoration of their masculinity—a manhood in which individual white men control the fruits of their own labor and are not subject to emasculation by Jewish-owned finance capital or a black- and feminist-controlled welfare state. Theirs is the militarized manhood of the heroic John Rambo, a manhood that celebrates their God-sanctioned right to band together in armed militias if anyone, or any government agency, tries to take it away from them. If the state and the economy emasculate them, and if the masculinity of the "others" is problematic, then only "real" white men can rescue America from a feminized, multicultural, androgynous melting pot.

Sound familiar? For the most part, the terrorists of September 11 come from the same class, and recite the same complaints, as American white supremacists.

Virtually all were under 25, educated, lower middle class or middle class, downwardly mobile. The journalist Nasra Hassan interviewed families of Middle Eastern suicide bombers (as well as some failed bombers themselves) and found that none of them had the standard motivations ascribed to people who commit suicide, such as depression.

Although several of the leaders of Al Qaeda are wealthy—Osama bin Laden is a multimillionaire, and Ayman al-Zawahiri, the 50-year-old doctor thought to be bin Laden's closest adviser, is from a fashionable suburb of Cairo—many of the hijackers were engineering students for whom job opportunities had been dwindling dramatically. (Judging from the minimal information I have found, about one-fourth of the hijackers had studied engineering.) Zacarias Moussaoui, who did not hijack one of the planes but is the first man to be formally charged in the United States for crimes related to September 11, earned a degree at London's South Bank University. Marwan al-Shehhi, the chubby, bespectacled 23-year-old from the United Arab Emirates who flew the second plane into the World Trade Center, was an engineering student, while Ziad Jarrah, the 26-year-old Lebanese who flew the plane that crashed in Pennsylvania, had studied aircraft design.

Politically, these terrorists opposed globalization and the spread of Western values; they opposed what they perceived as corrupt regimes in several Arab states (notably Saudi Arabia and Egypt), which they claimed were merely puppets of American domination. "The resulting anger is naturally directed first against their rulers," writes the historian Bernard Lewis, "and then against those whom they see as keeping those rulers in power for selfish reasons."

Central to their political ideology is the recovery of manhood from the emasculating politics of globalization. The Taliban saw the Soviet invasion and westernization of Afghanistan as humiliations. Bin Laden's October 7 videotape describes the "humiliation and disgrace" that Islam has suffered "for more than 80 years." And over and over, Nasra Hassan writes, she heard the refrain: "The Israelis humiliate us. They occupy our land, and deny our history."

Terrorism is fueled by a fatal brew of antiglobalization politics, convoluted Islamic theology, and virulent misogyny. According to Ehrenreich, while these formerly employed or self-employed males "have lost their traditional status as farmers and breadwinners, women have been entering the market economy and gaining the marginal independence conferred by even a paltry wage." As a result, "the man who can no longer make a living, who has to depend on his wife's earnings, can watch Hollywood sexpots on pirated videos and begin to think the world has been turned upside down."

The Taliban's policies thus had two purposes: to remasculinize men and to refeminize women. Another journalist, Peter Marsden, has observed that those policies "could be seen as a desperate attempt to keep out that other world, and to protect Afghan women from influences that could weaken the society from within." The Taliban prohibited women from appearing in public unescorted by men, from revealing any part of their body, and from going to school or holding a job. Men were required to grow their beards, in accordance with religious images of Muhammad, yes; but also, perhaps, because wearing beards has always been associated with men's response to women's increased equality in the public sphere, since beards symbolically reaffirm biological differences between men and women, while gender equality tends to blur those differences.

The Taliban's policies removed women as competitors and also shored up masculinity, since they enabled men to triumph over the humiliations of globalization and their own savage, predatory, and violently sexual urges that might be unleashed in the presence of uncovered women.

All of these issues converged in the life of Mohammed Atta, the terrorist about whom the most has been written and conjectured. Currently, for example, there is much speculation about Atta's sexuality. Was he gay? Was he a repressed homosexual, too ashamed of his sexuality to come out? Such innuendoes are based on no more than a few circumstantial tidbits about his life. He was slim, sweet-faced, neat, meticulous, a snazzy dresser. The youngest child of an ambitious lawyer father and a pampering mother, Atta grew up shy and polite, a mama's boy. "He was so gentle," his father said. "I used to tell him, 'Toughen up, boy!'"

When such revelations are offered, storytellers seem to expect a reaction like "Aha! So that explains it!" (Indeed, in a new biography of Adolf Hitler, *The Hidden Hitler,* Lothar Machtan offers exactly that sort of explanation. He argues that many of Hitler's policies—such as the killing of longtime colleague and avowed homosexual Ernst Rohm, or even the systematic persecution and execution of gay men in concentration camps—were, in fact, prompted by a desire to conceal his own homosexuality.)

But what do such accusations actually explain? Do revelations about Hitler's or Atta's possible gay propensities raise troubling connections between homosexuality and mass murder? If so, then one would also have to conclude that the discovery of Shakespeare's "gay" sonnet explains the Bard's genius at explicating Hamlet's existential anguish, or that Michelangelo's sexuality is the decisive factor in his painting of God's touch in the Sistine Chapel.

Such revelations tell us little about the Holocaust or September 11. They do, however, address the consequences of homophobia—both official and informal—on young men who are exploring their sexual identities. What's relevant is not the possible fact of Hitler's or Atta's gayness, but the shame and fear that surround homosexuality in societies that refuse to acknowledge sexual diversity.

Even more troubling is what such speculation leaves out. What unites Atta, McVeigh, and Hitler is not their repressed sexual orientation but gender—their masculinity, their sense of masculine entitlement, and their thwarted ambitions. They accepted cultural definitions of masculinity, and needed someone to blame when they felt that they failed to measure up. (After all, being called a mama's boy, a sissy, and told to toughen up are demands for gender conformity, not matters of sexual desire.) Gender is the issue, not sexuality.

All three failed at their chosen professions. Hitler was a failed artist—indeed, he failed at just about every job he ever tried except dictator. McVeigh, a business-college dropout, found his calling in the military during the Gulf War, where his exemplary service earned him commendations; but he washed out of Green Beret training—his dream job—after only two days. And Atta was the odd man out in his family. His two sisters both became doctors—one a physician and one a university professor. His father constantly reminded him that he wanted "to hear the word 'doctor' in front of his name. We told him, your sisters are doctors and their husbands are doctors and you are the man of the family."

Atta decided to become an engineer, but his degree meant little in a country where thousands of college graduates were unable to find good jobs. After he failed to find employment in Egypt, he went to Hamburg, Germany, to study architecture. He was "meticulous, disciplined, and highly intelligent, an ordinary student, a quiet, friendly guy who was totally focused on his studies," according to another student in Hamburg.

But his ambitions were constantly undone. His only hope for a good job in Egypt was to be hired by an international firm. He applied and was continually rejected. He found work as a draftsman—highly humiliating for someone with engineering and architectural credentials and an imperious and demanding father—for a German firm involved with razing low-income Cairo neighborhoods to provide more scenic vistas for luxury tourist hotels.

Defeated, humiliated, emasculated, a disappointment to his father and a failed rival to his sisters, Atta retreated into increasingly militant Islamic theology. By the time he assumed the controls of American Airlines Flight 11, he evinced a hysteria about women. In the message he left in his abandoned rental car, he made clear what mattered to him in the end. "I don't want pregnant women or a person who is not clean to come and say good-bye to me," he wrote. "I don't want women to go to my funeral or later to my grave." Of course, Atta's body was instantly incinerated, and no burial would be likely.

The terrors of emasculation experienced by lower-middle-class men all over the world will no doubt continue, as they struggle to make a place for themselves in shrinking economies and inevitably shifting cultures. They may continue to feel a seething resentment against women, whom they perceive as stealing their rightful place at the head of the table, and against the governments that displace them. Globalization feels to them like a game of musical chairs, in which, when the music stops, all the seats are handed to others by nursemaid governments.

The events of September 11, as well as of April 19, 1995 (the Oklahoma City bombing), resulted from an increasingly common combination of factors—the massive male displacement that accompanies globalization, the spread of American consumerism, and the perceived corruption of local political elites—fused with a masculine sense of entitlement. Someone else—some "other"—had to be held responsible for the terrorists' downward mobility and failures, and the failure of their fathers to deliver their promised inheritance. The terrorists didn't just get mad. They got even.

Such themes were not lost on the disparate bands of young, white supremacists. American Aryans admired the terrorists' courage and chastised their own compatriots. "It's a disgrace that in a population of at least 150 million White/Aryan Americans, we provide so few that are willing to do the same [as the terrorists]," bemoaned Rocky Suhayda, the chairman of the American Nazi Party. "A bunch of towel head/sand niggers put our great White Movement to shame."

It is from such gendered shame that mass murderers are made.

PART TWO

Boyhood

"One is not born, but rather becomes, a woman," wrote the French feminist thinker Simone de Beauvoir in her ground-breaking book *The Second Sex* (New York: Vintage, 1958). The same is true for men. And the social processes by which boys become men are complex and important. How does early childhood socialization differ for boys and girls? What specific traits are emphasized for boys that mark their socialization as different? What types of institutional arrangements reinforce those traits? How do the various institutions in which boys find themselves—school, family, and circles of friends—influence their development? What of the special institutions that promote "boy's life" or an adolescent male subculture?

During childhood and adolescence, masculinity becomes a central theme in a boy's life. *New York Times* editor A. M. Rosenthal put the dilemma this way: "So there I was, 13 years old, the smallest boy in my freshman class at DeWitt Clinton High School, smoking a White Owl cigar. I was not only little, but I did not have longies—long trousers—and was still in knickerbockers. Obviously, I had to do something to project my fierce sense of manhood" (*New York Times*, 26 April 1987). That the assertion of manhood is part of a boy's natural development is suggested by Roger Brown, in his textbook *Social Psychology* (New York: Free Press, 1965, p. 161):

> In the United States, a *real* boy climbs trees, disdains girls, dirties his knees, plays with soldiers, and takes blue for his favorite color. When they go to school, real boys prefer manual training, gym, and arithmetic. In college the boys smoke pipes, drink beer, and major in engineering or physics. The real boy matures into a "man's man" who plays poker, goes hunting, drinks brandy, and dies in the war.

The articles in this section address the question of how boys develop, focusing on the institutions that shape boys' lives. Mike Messner observes the opening ceremony of a local American Youth Soccer League season and analyzes a moment of gender construction among four- and five-year-old girls and boys. Ellen Jordan and Angela Cowan describe the gender socialization of schooling, both inside and outside the classroom. Ritch Savin-Williams, Martin Espada, Pat Mahoney, and Ann Ferguson examine issues of boys' development from the perspectives of different groups of boys—those who feel different and those who are made to feel different.

Photo by Mike Messner.

ARTICLE 8

Michael A. Messner

Barbie Girls versus Sea Monsters: Children Constructing Gender

In the past decade, studies of children and gender have moved toward greater levels of depth and sophistication (e.g., Thorne 1993; Jordan and Cowan 1995; McGuffy and Rich 1999). In her groundbreaking work on children and gender, Thorne (1993) argued that previous theoretical frameworks, although helpful, were limited: The top-down (adult-to-child) approach of socialization theories tended to ignore the extent to which children are active agents in the creation of their worlds—often in direct or partial opposition to values or "roles" to which adult teachers or parents are attempting to socialize them. Developmental theories also had their limits due to their tendency to ignore group and contextual factors while overemphasizing "the constitution and unfolding of *individuals* as boys or girls" (Thorne 1993, 4). In her study of grade school children, Thorne demonstrated a dynamic approach that examined the ways in which children actively construct gender in specific social contexts of the classroom and the playground. Working from emergent theories of performativity, Thorne developed the concept of "gender play" to analyze the social processes through which children construct gender. Her level of analysis was not the individual but "*group life*—with social relations, the organization and meanings of social situations, the collective practices through which children and adults create and recreate gender in their daily interactions" (Thorne 1993, 4).

A key insight from Thorne's research is the extent to which gender varies in salience from situation to situation. Sometimes, children engage in "relaxed, cross sex play"; other times—for instance, on the playground during boys' ritual invasions of girls' spaces and games—gender boundaries between boys and girls are activated in ways that variously threaten or (more often) reinforce and clarify these boundaries. However, these varying moments of gender salience are not free-floating; they occur in social contexts such as schools and in which gender is formally and informally built into the division of labor, power structure, rules, and values (Connell 1987).

The purpose of this article is to use an observation of a highly salient gendered moment of group life among four- and five-year-old children as a point of departure for exploring the conditions under which gender boundaries become activated and enforced. I was privy to this moment as I observed my five-year-old son's first season (including weekly games and practices) in organized soccer. Unlike the long-term, systematic ethnographic studies of children conducted by Thorne (1993) or Adler and Adler (1998), this article takes one moment as its point of departure.

Author's Note: Appreciative thanks to Pierrette Hondagneu-Sotelo, Lynn Spigel, Leslie Cole, Barrie Thorne, and the students in my sociology-of-sex-and-gender seminar for helpful comments on the first draft of this article. Christine Bose and the three anonymous reviewers at *Gender & Society* added additional suggestions that sharpened the article considerably. Special thanks to Sasha Hondagneu-Messner and Miles Hondagneu-Messner for making it possible for me to witness events like the one analyzed in this article.

From *Gender & Society* 14(6): 765–784. Copyright © 2000 Sociologists for Women in Society. Reprinted by permission of Sage Publications, Inc.

I do not present this moment as somehow "representative" of what happened throughout the season; instead, I examine this as an example of what Hochschild (1994, 4) calls "magnified moments," which are "episodes of heightened importance, either epiphanies, moments of intense glee or unusual insight, or moments in which things go intensely but meaningfully wrong. In either case, the moment stands out; it is metaphorically rich, unusually elaborate and often echoes [later]." A magnified moment in daily life offers a window into the social construction of reality. It presents researchers with an opportunity to excavate gendered meanings and processes through an analysis of institutional and cultural contexts. The single empirical observation that serves as the point of departure for this article was made during a morning. Immediately after the event, I recorded my observations with detailed notes. I later slightly revised the notes after developing the photographs that I took at the event.

I will first describe the observation—an incident that occurred as a boys' soccer team of four- and five-year-olds waited next to a girls' team of four- and five-year-olds for the beginning of the community's American Youth Soccer League (AYSO) season's opening ceremony. I will then examine this moment using three levels of analysis.

1. *The interactional level:* How do children "do gender," and what are the contributions and limits of theories of performativity in understanding these interactions?
2. *The level of structural context:* How does the gender regime, particularly the larger organizational level of formal sex segregation of AYSO, and the concrete, momentary situation of the opening ceremony provide a context that variously constrains and enables the children's interactions?
3. *The level of cultural symbol:* How does the children's shared immersion in popular culture (and their differently gendered locations in this immersion) provide symbolic resources for the creation, in this situation, of apparently categorical differences between the boys and the girls?

Although I will discuss these three levels of analysis separately, I hope to demonstrate that interaction, structural context, and culture are simultaneous and mutually intertwined processes, none of which supersedes the others.

Barbie Girls versus Sea Monsters

It is a warm, sunny Saturday morning. Summer is coming to a close, and schools will soon reopen. As in many communities, this time of year in this small, middle- and professional-class suburb of Los Angeles is marked by the beginning of another soccer season. This morning, 156 teams, with approximately 1,850 players ranging from 4 to 17 years old, along with another 2,000 to 3,000 parents, siblings, friends, and community dignitaries have gathered at the local high school football and track facility for the annual AYSO opening ceremonies. Parents and children wander around the perimeter of the track to find the assigned station for their respective teams. The coaches muster their teams and chat with parents. Eventually, each team will march around the track, behind their new team banner, as they are announced over the loudspeaker system and are applauded by the crowd. For now though, and for the next 45 minutes to an hour, the kids, coaches, and parents must stand, mill around, talk, and kill time as they await the beginning of the ceremony.

The Sea Monsters is a team of four- and five-year-old boys. Later this day, they will play their first-ever soccer game. A few of the boys already know each other from preschool, but most are still getting acquainted. They are wearing their new uniforms for the first time. Like other teams, they were assigned team colors—in this case, green and blue—and asked to choose their team name at their first team meeting, which occurred a week ago. Although they preferred "Blue

Sharks," they found that the name was already taken by another team and settled on "Sea Monsters." A grandmother of one of the boys created the spiffy team banner, which was awarded a prize this morning. As they wait for the ceremony to begin, the boys inspect and then proudly pose for pictures in front of their new award-winning team banner. The parents stand a few feet away—some taking pictures, some just watching. The parents are also getting to know each other, and the common currency of topics is just how darned cute our kids look, and will they start these ceremonies soon before another boy has to be escorted to the bathroom?

Queued up one group away from the Sea Monsters is a team of four- and five-year-old girls in green and white uniforms. They too will play their first game later today, but for now, they are awaiting the beginning of the opening ceremony. They have chosen the name "Barbie Girls," and they also have a spiffy new team banner. But the girls are pretty much ignoring their banner, for they have created another, more powerful symbol around which to rally. In fact, they are the only team among the 156 marching today with a team float—a red Radio Flyer wagon base, on which sits a Sony boom box playing music, and a 3-foot-plus-tall Barbie doll on a rotating pedestal. Barbie is dressed in the team colors—indeed, she sports a custom-made green-and-white cheerleader-style outfit, with the Barbie Girls' names written on the skirt. Her normally all-blonde hair has been streaked with Barbie Girl green and features a green bow, with white polka dots. Several of the girls on the team also have supplemented their uniforms with green bows in their hair.

The volume on the boom box nudges up and four or five girls begin to sing a Barbie song. Barbie is now slowly rotating on her pedestal, and as the girls sing more gleefully and more loudly, some of them begin to hold hands and walk around the float, in sync with Barbie's rotation. Other same-aged girls from other teams are drawn to the celebration and, eventually, perhaps a dozen girls are singing the Barbie song. The girls are intensely focused on Barbie, on the music, and on their mutual pleasure.

As the Sea Monsters mill around their banner, some of them begin to notice, and then begin to watch and listen as the Barbie Girls rally around their float. At first, the boys are watching as individuals, seemingly unaware of each other's shared interest. Some of them stand with arms at their sides, slack-jawed, as though passively watching a television show. I notice slight smiles on a couple of their faces, as though they are drawn to the Barbie Girls' celebratory fun. Then, with sideglances, some of the boys begin to notice each others' attention on the Barbie Girls. Their faces begin to show signs of distaste. One of them yells out, "NO BARBIE!" Suddenly, they all begin to move—jumping up and down, nudging and bumping one other—and join into a group chant: "NO BARBIE! NO BARBIE! NO BARBIE!" They now appear to be every bit as gleeful as the girls, as they laugh, yell, and chant against the Barbie Girls.

The parents watch the whole scene with rapt attention. Smiles light up the faces of the adults, as our glances sweep back and forth, from the sweetly celebrating Barbie Girls to the aggressively protesting Sea Monsters. "They are SO different!" exclaims one smiling mother approvingly. A male coach offers a more in-depth analysis: "When I was in college," he says, "I took these classes from professors who showed us research that showed that boys and girls are the same. I believed it, until I had my own kids and saw how different they are." "Yeah," another dad responds, "Just look at them! They are so different!"

The girls, meanwhile, show no evidence that they hear, see, or are even aware of the presence of the boys who are now so loudly proclaiming their opposition to the Barbie Girls' songs and totem. They continue to sing, dance, laugh, and rally around the Barbie for a few more minutes, before they are called to reassemble in their groups for the beginning of the parade.

After the parade, the teams reassemble on the infield of the track but now in a less organized manner. The Sea Monsters once again find themselves in the general vicinity of the Barbie Girls and take up the "NO BARBIE!" chant again. Perhaps put out by the lack of response to their chant, they begin to dash, in twos and threes, invading the girls' space, and yelling menacingly. With this, the Barbie Girls have little choice but to recognize the presence of the boys—some look puzzled and shrink back, some engage the boys and chase them off. The chasing seems only to incite more excitement among the boys. Finally, parents intervene and defuse the situation, leading their children off to their cars, homes, and eventually to their soccer games.

The Performance of Gender

In the past decade, especially since the publication of Judith Butler's highly influential *Gender Trouble* (1990), it has become increasingly fashionable among academic feminists to think of gender not as some "thing" that one "has" (or not) but rather as situationally constructed through the performances of active agents. The idea of gender as performance analytically foregrounds the agency of individuals in the construction of gender, thus highlighting the situational fluidity of gender: here, conservative and reproductive, there, transgressive and disruptive. Surely, the Barbie Girls versus Sea Monsters scene described above can be fruitfully analyzed as a moment of crosscutting and mutually constitutive gender performances: The girls—at least at first glance—appear to be performing (for each other?) a conventional four- to five-year-old version of emphasized femininity. At least on the surface, there appears to be nothing terribly transgressive here. They are just "being girls," together. The boys initially are unwittingly constituted as an audience for the girls' performance but quickly begin to perform (for each other?—for the girls, too?) a masculinity that constructs itself in opposition to Barbie, and to the girls, as not feminine. They aggressively confront—first through loud verbal chanting, eventually through bodily invasions—the girls' ritual space of emphasized femininity, apparently with the intention of disrupting its upsetting influence. The adults are simultaneously constituted as an adoring audience for their children's performances and as parents who perform for each other by sharing and mutually affirming their experience-based narratives concerning the natural differences between boys and girls.

In this scene, we see children performing gender in ways that constitute themselves as two separate, opposed groups (boys vs. girls) and parents performing gender in ways that give the stamp of adult approval to the children's performances of difference, while constructing their own ideological narrative that naturalizes this categorical difference. In other words, the parents do not seem to read the children's performances of gender as social constructions of gender. Instead, they interpret them as the inevitable unfolding of natural, internal differences between the sexes. That this moment occurred when it did and where it did is explicable, but not entirely with a theory of performativity. As Walters (1999, 250) argues:

> The performance of gender is never a simple voluntary act.... Theories of gender as play and performance need to be intimately and systematically connected with the power of gender (really, the power of male power) to constrain, control, violate, and configure. Too often, mere lip service is given to the specific historical, social, and political configurations that make certain conditions possible and others constrained.

Indeed, feminist sociologists operating from the traditions of symbolic interactionism and/or Goffmanian dramaturgical analysis have anticipated the recent interest in looking at gender as a dynamic performance. As early as 1978, Kessler and McKenna developed a sophisticated analysis of gender as an everyday, practical accomplishment of people's interactions. Nearly a decade later, West and Zimmerman (1987) argued that in people's everyday interactions, they were "doing gender" and, in so doing, they were constructing masculine dominance and feminine deference. As these ideas have been taken up in sociology, their tendencies toward a celebration of the "freedom" of agents to transgress and reshape the fluid boundaries of gender have been put into play with theories of social structure (e.g., Lorber 1994; Risman 1998). In these accounts, gender is viewed as enacted or created through everyday interactions, but crucially, as Walters suggested above, within "specific historical, social, and political configurations" that constrain or enable certain interactions.

The parents' response to the Barbie Girls versus Sea Monsters performance suggests one of the main limits and dangers of theories of performativity. Lacking an analysis of structural and cultural context, performances of gender can all too easily be interpreted as free agents' acting out the inevitable surface manifestations of a natural inner essence of sex difference. An examination of structural and cultural context, though, reveals that there was nothing inevitable about the girls' choice of Barbie as their totem, nor in the boys' response to it.

The Structure of Gender

In the entire subsequent season of weekly games and practices, I never once saw adults point to a moment in which boy and girl soccer players were doing the *same* thing and exclaim to each other, "Look at them! They are *so similar*!" The actual similarity of the boys and the girls, evidenced by nearly all of the kids' routine actions throughout a soccer season—playing the game, crying over a skinned knee, scrambling enthusiastically for their snacks after the games, spacing out on a bird or a flower instead of listening to the coach at practice—is a key to understanding the salience of the Barbie Girls versus Sea Monsters moment for gender relations. In the face of a multitude of moments that speak to similarity, it was this anomalous Barbie Girls versus Sea Monsters moment—where the boundaries of gender were so clearly enacted—that the adults seized to affirm their commitment to difference. It is the kind of moment—to use Lorber's (1994, 37) phrase—where "believing is seeing," where we selectively "see" aspects of social reality that tell us a truth that we prefer to believe, such as the belief in categorical sex difference. No matter that our eyes do not see evidence of this truth most of the rest of the time.

In fact, it was not so easy for adults to actually "see" the empirical reality of sex similarity in everyday observations of soccer throughout the season. That is due to one overdetermining factor: an institutional context that is characterized by informally structured sex segregation among the parent coaches and team managers, and by formally structured sex segregation among the children. The structural analysis developed here is indebted to Acker's (1990) observation that organizations, even while appearing "gender neutral," tend to reflect, recreate, and naturalize a hierarchical ordering of gender. Following Connell's (1987, 98–99) method of structural analysis, I will examine the "gender regime"—that is, the current "state of play of sexual politics"—within the local AYSO organization by conducting a "structural inventory" of the formal and informal sexual divisions of labor and power.[1]

Adult Divisions of Labor and Power

There was a clear—although not absolute—sexual division of labor and power among the adult volunteers in the AYSO organization. The board of directors consisted of 21 men and 9 women, with the top two positions—commissioner and assistant commissioner—held by men. Among the league's head coaches, 133 were men and 23 women. The division among the league's assistant coaches was similarly skewed. Each team also had a team manager who was responsible for organizing snacks, making reminder calls about games and practices, organizing team parties and the end-of-the-year present for the coach. The vast majority of team managers were women. A common slippage in the language of coaches and parents revealed the ideological assumptions underlying this position: I often noticed people describe a team manager as the "team mom." In short, as Table 8.1 shows, the vast majority of the time, the formal authority of the head coach and assistant coach was in the hands of a man, while the

TABLE 8.1
Adult Volunteers as Coaches and Team Managers, by Gender (in percentages) ($N = 156$ teams)

	Head Coaches	Assistant Coaches	Team Managers
Women	15	21	86
Men	85	79	14

backup, support role of team manager was in the hands of a woman.

These data illustrate Connell's (1987, 97) assertion that sexual divisions of labor are interwoven with, and mutually supportive of, divisions of power and authority among women and men. They also suggest how people's choices to volunteer for certain positions are shaped and constrained by previous institutional practices. There is no formal AYSO rule that men must be the leaders, women the supportive followers. And there are, after all, *some* women coaches and *some* men team managers.[2] So, it may appear that the division of labor among adult volunteers simply manifests an accumulation of individual choices and preferences. When analyzed structurally, though, individual men's apparently free choices to volunteer disproportionately for coaching jobs, alongside individual women's apparently free choices to volunteer disproportionately for team manager jobs, can be seen as a logical collective result of the ways that the institutional structure of sport has differentially constrained and enabled women's and men's previous options and experiences (Messner 1992). Since boys and men have had far more opportunities to play organized sports and thus to gain skills and knowledge, it subsequently appears rational for adult men to serve in positions of knowledgeable authority, with women serving in a support capacity (Boyle and McKay 1995). Structure—in this case, the historically constituted division of labor and power in sport—constrains current practice. In turn, structure becomes an object of practice, as the choices and actions of today's parents recreate divisions of labor and power similar to those that they experienced in their youth.

The Children: Formal Sex Segregation

As adult authority patterns are informally structured along gendered lines, the children's leagues are formally segregated by AYSO along lines of age and sex. In each age group, there are separate boys' and girls' leagues. The AYSO in this community included 87 boys' teams and 69 girls' teams. Although the four- to five-year-old boys often played their games on a field that was contiguous with games being played by four- to five-year-old girls, there was never a formal opportunity for cross-sex play. Thus, both the girls' and the boys' teams could conceivably proceed through an entire season of games and practices in entirely homosocial contexts.[3] In the all-male contexts that I observed throughout the season, gender never appeared to be overtly salient among the children, coaches, or parents. It is against this backdrop that I might suggest a working hypothesis about structure and the variable salience of gender: The formal sex segregation of children does not, in and of itself, make gender overtly salient. In fact, when children are absolutely segregated, with no opportunity for cross-sex interactions, gender may appear to disappear as an overtly salient organizing principle. However, when formally sex-segregated children are placed into immediately contiguous locations, such as during the opening ceremony, highly charged gendered interactions between the groups (including invasions and other kinds of border work) become more possible.

Although it might appear to some that formal sex segregation in children's sports is a natural fact, it has not always been so for the youngest age-groups in AYSO. As recently as 1995, when my older son signed up to play as a five-year-old,

I had been told that he would play in a coed league. But when he arrived to his first practice and I saw that he was on an all-boys team, I was told by the coach that AYSO had decided this year to begin sex segregating all age-groups, because "during half-times and practices, the boys and girls tend to separate into separate groups. So the league thought it would be better for team unity if we split the boys and girls into separate leagues." I suggested to some coaches that a similar dynamic among racial ethnic groups (say, Latino kids and white kids clustering as separate groups during halftimes) would not similarly result in a decision to create racially segregated leagues. That this comment appeared to fall on deaf ears illustrates the extent to which many adults' belief in the need for sex segregation—at least in the context of sport—is grounded in a mutually agreed-upon notion of boys' and girls' "separate worlds," perhaps based in ideologies of natural sex difference.

The gender regime of AYSO, then, is structured by formal and informal sexual divisions of labor and power. This social structure sets ranges, limits, and possibilities for the children's and parents' interactions and performances of gender, but it does not determine them. Put another way, the formal and informal gender regime of AYSO made the Barbie Girls versus Sea Monsters moment possible, but it did not make it inevitable. It was the agency of the children and the parents within that structure that made the moment happen. But why did this moment take on the symbolic forms that it did? How and why do the girls, boys, and parents construct and derive meanings from this moment, and how can we interpret these meanings? These questions are best grappled with in the realm of cultural analysis.

The Culture of Gender

The difference between what is "structural" and what is "cultural" is not clear-cut. For instance, the AYSO assignment of team colors and choice of team names (cultural symbols) seem to follow logically from, and in turn reinforce, the sex segregation of the leagues (social structure). These cultural symbols such as team colors, uniforms, songs, team names, and banners often carried encoded gendered meanings that were then available to be taken up by the children in ways that constructed (or potentially contested) gender divisions and boundaries.

Team Names

Each team was issued two team colors. It is notable that across the various age groups, several girls' teams were issued pink uniforms—a color commonly recognized as encoding feminine meanings—while no boys' teams were issued pink uniforms. Children, in consultation with their coaches, were asked to choose their own team names and were encouraged to use their assigned team colors as cues to theme of the team name (e.g., among the boys, the "Red Flashes," the "Green Pythons," and the blue-and-green "Sea Monsters"). When I analyzed the team names of the 156 teams by age group and by sex, three categories emerged:

1. *Sweet names:* These are cutesy team names that communicate small stature, cuteness, and/or vulnerability. These kinds of names would most likely be widely read as encoded with feminine meanings (e.g., "Blue Butterflies," "Beanie Babes," "Sunflowers," "Pink Flamingos," and "Barbie Girls").
2. *Neutral or paradoxical names:* Neutral names are team names that carry no obvious gendered meaning (e.g., "Blue and Green Lizards," "Team Flubber," "Galaxy," "Blue Ice"). Paradoxical names are girls' team names that carry mixed (simultaneously vulnerable *and* powerful) messages (e.g., "Pink Panthers," "Flower Power," "Little Tigers").
3. *Power names:* These are team names that invoke images of unambiguous strength, aggression, and raw power (e.g., "Shooting Stars," "Killer Whales," "Shark Attack," "Raptor Attack," and "Sea Monsters")

As Table 8.2 illustrates, across all age-groups of boys, there was only one team name coded as

TABLE 8.2
Team Names, by Age-Groups and Gender

	4–5		6–7		8–13		14–17		Total	
	n	%	n	%	n	%	n	%	n	%
Girls										
Sweet names	5	42	3	17	2	7	0	0	10	15
Neutral/paradoxical	5	42	6	33	7	25	5	45	23	32
Power names	2	17	9	50	19	68	6	55	36	52
Boys										
Sweet names	0	0	0	0	1	4	0	0	1	1
Neutral/paradoxical	1	7	4	15	4	12	4	31	13	15
Power names	13	93	22	85	29	85	9	69	73	82

a sweet name—"The Smurfs," in the 10- to 11-year-old league. Across all age categories, the boys were far more likely to choose a power name than anything else, and this was nowhere more true than in the youngest age groups, where 35 of 40 (87 percent) of boys' teams in the four-to-five and six-to-seven age groups took on power names. A different pattern appears in the girls' team name choices, especially among the youngest girls. Only 2 of the 12 four- to five-year-old girls' teams chose power names, while 5 chose sweet names and 5 chose neutral/paradoxical names. At age six to seven, the numbers begin to tip toward the boys' numbers but still remain different, with half of the girls' teams now choosing power names. In the middle and older girls' groups, the sweet names all but disappear, with power names dominating, but still a higher proportion of neutral/paradoxical names than among boys in those age groups.

Barbie Narrative versus Warrior Narrative

How do we make sense of the obviously powerful spark that Barbie provided in the opening ceremony scene described above? Barbie is likely one of the most immediately identifiable symbols of femininity in the world. More conservatively oriented parents tend to happily buy Barbie dolls for their daughters, while perhaps deflecting their sons' interest in Barbie toward more sex-appropriate "action toys." Feminist parents, on the other hand, have often expressed open contempt—or at least uncomfortable ambivalence—toward Barbie. This is because both conservative and feminist parents see dominant cultural meanings of emphasized femininity as condensed in Barbie and assume that these meanings will be imitated by their daughters. Recent developments in cultural studies, though, should warn us against simplistic readings of Barbie as simply conveying hegemonic messages about gender to unwitting children (Seiter 1995; Attfield 1996). In addition to critically analyzing the cultural values (or "preferred meanings") that may be encoded in Barbie or other children's toys, feminist scholars of cultural studies point to the necessity of examining "reception, pleasure, and agency," and especially "the fullness of reception contexts" (Walters 1999, 246). The Barbie Girls versus Sea Monsters moment can be analyzed as a "reception context," in which differently situated boys, girls, and parents variously used Barbie to construct pleasurable intergroup bonds, as well as boundaries between groups.

Barbie is plastic both in form and in terms of cultural meanings children and adults create around her (Rogers 1999). It is not that there are not hegemonic meanings encoded in Barbie: Since its introduction in 1959, Mattel has been successful in selling millions[4] of this doll that "was recognized as a model of ideal teenhood" (Rand 1998, 383) and "an icon—perhaps *the* icon—of true white womanhood and femininity" (DuCille 1994, 50). However, Rand (1998) argues that "we condescend to children when we analyze Barbie's content and then presume that it passes untransformed into their minds, where, dwelling beneath the control of consciousness or counterargument, it generates self-image, feelings, and other ideological constructs." In fact, people who are situated differently (by age, gender, sexual orientation, social class, race/ethnicity, and national origin) tend to consume and construct meanings around Barbie variously. For instance, some adult women (including many feminists) tell retrospective stories of having rejected (or even mutilated) their Barbies in favor of boys' toys, and some adult lesbians tell stories of transforming Barbie "into an object of dyke desire" (Rand 1998, 386).

Mattel, in fact, clearly strategizes its marketing of Barbie not around the imposition of a singular notion of what a girl or woman should be but around "hegemonic discourse strategies" that attempt to incorporate consumers' range of possible interpretations and criticisms of the limits of Barbie. For instance, the recent marketing of "multicultural Barbie" features dolls with different skin colors and culturally coded wardrobes (DuCille 1994). This strategy broadens the Barbie market, deflects potential criticism of racism, but still "does not boot blond, white Barbie from center stage" (Rand 1998, 391). Similarly, Mattel's marketing of Barbie (since the 1970s) as a career woman raises issues concerning the feminist critique of Barbie's supposedly negative effect on girls. When the AAUW recently criticized Barbie, adult collectors defended Barbie, asserting that "Barbie, in fact, is a wonderful role model for women. She has been a veterinarian, an astronaut, and a soldier—and even before real women had a chance to enter such occupations" (Spigel forthcoming). And when the magazine *Barbie Bazaar* ran a cover photo of its new "Gulf War Barbie," it served "as a reminder of Mattel's marketing slogan: 'We Girls Can Do Anything'" (Spigel forthcoming). The following year, Mattel unveiled its "Presidential Candidate Barbie" with the statement "It is time for a woman president, and Barbie had the credentials for the job." Spigel observes that these liberal feminist messages of empowerment for girls run—apparently unambiguously—alongside a continued unspoken understanding that Barbie must be beautiful, with an ultraskinny waist and long, thin legs that taper to feet that appear deformed so that they may fit (only?) into high heels.[5] "Mattel does not mind equating beauty with intellect. In fact, so long as the 11½ inch Barbie body remains intact, Mattel is willing to accessorize her with a number of fashionable perspectives—including feminism itself" (Spigel forthcoming).

It is this apparently paradoxical encoding of the all-too-familiar oppressive bodily requirements of feminine beauty alongside the career woman role modeling and empowering message that "we girls can do anything" that may inform how and why the Barbie Girls appropriated Barbie as their team symbol. Emphasized femininity—Connell's (1987) term for the current form of femininity that articulates with hegemonic masculinity—as many Second Wave feminists have experienced and criticized it, has been characterized by girls' and women's embodiments of oppressive conceptions of feminine beauty that symbolize and reify a thoroughly disempowered stance vis-à-vis men. To many Second Wave feminists, Barbie seemed to symbolize all that was oppressive about his femininity—the bodily self-surveillance, accompanying eating disorders, slavery to the dictates of the fashion industry, and compulsory heterosexuality. But Rogers (1999, 14) suggests that rather than representing an unambiguous image of emphasized femininity, perhaps Barbie represents a more paradoxical image of "emphatic femininity" that:

> takes feminine appearances and demeanor to unsustainable extremes. Nothing about Barbie ever looks masculine, even when she is on the police force.... Consistently, Barbie manages impressions so as to come across as a proper

feminine creature even when she crosses boundaries usually dividing women from men. Barbie the firefighter is in no danger, then, of being seen as "one of the boys." Kids know that; parents and teachers know that; Mattel designers know that too.

Recent Third Wave feminist theory sheds light on the different sensibilities of younger generations of girls and women concerning their willingness to display and play with this apparently paradoxical relationship between bodily experience (including "feminine" displays) and public empowerment. In Third Wave feminist texts, displays of feminine physical attractiveness and empowerment are not viewed as mutually exclusive or necessarily opposed realities, but as lived (if often paradoxical) aspects of the same reality (Heywood and Drake 1997). This embracing of the paradoxes of post–Second Wave femininity is manifested in many punk, or Riot Grrrl, subcultures (Klein 1997) and in popular culture in the resounding late 1990s' success of the Spice Girls' mantra of "Girl Power." This generational expression of "girl power" may today be part of "the pleasures of girl culture that Barbie stands for" (Spigel forthcoming). Indeed, as the Barbie Girls rallied around Barbie, their obvious pleasure did not appear to be based on a celebration of quiet passivity (as feminist parents might fear). Rather, it was a statement that they—the Barbie Girls—were here in this public space. They were not silenced by the boys' oppositional chanting. To the contrary, they ignored the boys, who seemed irrelevant to their celebration. And, when the boys later physically invaded their space, some of the girls responded by chasing the boys off. In short, when I pay attention to what the girls *did* (rather than imposing on the situation what I *think* Barbie "should" mean to the girls), I see a public moment of celebratory "girl power."

And this may give us better basis from which to analyze the boys' oppositional response. First, the boys may have been responding to the threat of displacement they may have felt while viewing the girls' moment of celebratory girl power. Second, the boys may simultaneously have been responding to the fears of feminine pollution that Barbie had come to symbolize to them. But why might Barbie symbolize feminine pollution to little boys? A brief example from my older son is instructive. When he was about three, following a fun day of play with the five-year-old girl next door, he enthusiastically asked me to buy him a Barbie like hers. He was gleeful when I took him to the store and bought him one. When we arrived home, his feet had barely hit the pavement getting out of the car before an eight-year-old neighbor boy laughed at and ridiculed him: "A *Barbie*? Don't you know that Barbie is a *girl's toy*?" No amount of parental intervention could counter this devastating peer-induced injunction against boys' playing with Barbie. My son's pleasurable desire for Barbie appeared almost overnight to transform itself into shame and rejection. The doll ended up at the bottom of a heap of toys in the closet, and my son soon became infatuated, along with other boys in his preschool, with Ninja Turtles and Power Rangers.

Research indicates that there is widespread agreement as to which toys are appropriate for one sex and polluting, dangerous, or inappropriate for the other sex. When Campenni (1999) asked adults to rate the gender appropriateness of children's toys, the toys considered most appropriate to girls were those pertaining to domestic tasks, beauty enhancement, or child rearing. Of the 206 toys rated, Barbie was rated second only to Makeup Kit as a female-only toy. Toys considered most appropriate to boys were those pertaining to sports gear (football gear was the most masculine-rated toy, while boxing gloves were third), vehicles, action figures (G. I. Joe was rated second only to football gear), and other war-related toys. This research on parents' gender stereotyping of toys reflects similar findings in research on children's toy preferences (Bradbard 1985; Robinson and Morris 1986). Children tend to avoid cross-sex toys, with boys' avoidance of feminine-coded toys appearing to be stronger than girls' avoidance of masculine-coded toys (Etaugh and Liss 1992). Moreover, preschool-age boys who perceive their fathers to be opposed to cross-gender-typed play are more likely than girls or other boys to think that it is "bad" for boys to play with toys that are labeled as "for girls" (Raag and Rackliff 1998).

By kindergarten, most boys appear to have learned—either through experiences similar to my son's, where other male persons police the boundaries of gender-appropriate play and fantasy and/or by watching the clearly gendered messages of television advertising—that Barbie dolls are not appropriate toys for boys (Rogers 1999, 30). To avoid ridicule, they learn to hide their desire for Barbie, either through denial and oppositional/pollution discourse and/or through sublimation of their desire for Barbie into play with male-appropriate "action figures" (Pope et al. 1999). In their study of a kindergarten classroom, Jordan and Cowan (1995, 728) identified "warrior narratives . . . that assume that violence is legitimate and justified when it occurs within a struggle between good and evil" to be the most commonly agreed-upon currency for boys' fantasy play. They observe that the boys seem commonly to adapt story lines that they have seen on television. Popular culture—film, video, computer games, television, and comic books—provides boys with a seemingly endless stream of Good Guys versus Bad Guys characters and stories—from cowboy movies, Superman and Spiderman to Ninja Turtles, Star Wars, and Pokémon—that are available for the boys to appropriate as the raw materials for the construction of their own warrior play.

In the kindergarten that Jordan and Cowan studied, the boys initially attempted to import their warrior narratives into the domestic setting of the "Doll Corner." Teachers eventually drove the boys' warrior play outdoors, while the Doll Corner was used by the girls for the "appropriate" domestic play for which it was originally intended. Jordan and Cowan argue that kindergarten teachers' outlawing of boys' warrior narratives inside the classroom contributed to boys' defining schools as a feminine environment, to which they responded with a resistant, underground continuation of masculine warrior play. Eventually though, boys who acquiesce and successfully sublimate warrior play into fantasy or sport are more successful in constructing what Connell (1989, 291) calls "a masculinity organized around themes of rationality and responsibility [that is] closely connected with the 'certification' function of the upper levels of the education system and to a key form of masculinity among professionals."

In contrast to the "rational/professional" masculinity constructed in schools, the institution of sport historically constructs hegemonic masculinity as *bodily superiority* over femininity and nonathletic masculinities (Messner 1992). Here, warrior narratives are allowed to publicly thrive—indeed, are openly celebrated (witness, for instance, the commentary of a televised NFL [National Football League] football game or especially the spectacle of televised professional wrestling). Preschool boys and kindergartners seem already to know this, easily adopting aggressively competitive team names and an us-versus-them attitude. By contrast, many of the youngest girls appear to take two or three years in organized soccer before they adopt, or partially accommodate themselves to, aggressively competitive discourse, indicated by the 10-year-old girls' shifting away from the use of sweet names toward more power names. In short, where the gender regime of preschool and grade school may be experienced as an environment in which mostly women leaders enforce rules that are hostile to masculine fantasy play and physicality, the gender regime of sport is experienced as a place where masculine styles and values of physicality, aggression, and competition are enforced and celebrated by mostly male coaches.

A cultural analysis suggests that the boys' and the girls' previous immersion in differently gendered cultural experiences shaped the likelihood that they would derive and construct different meanings from Barbie—the girls through pleasurable and symbolically empowering identification with "girl power" narratives; the boys through oppositional fears of feminine pollution (and fears of displacement by girl power?) and with aggressively verbal, and eventually physical, invasions of the girls' ritual space. The boys' collective response thus constituted them differently, *as boys*, in opposition to the girls' constitution of themselves *as girls*. An individual girl or boy, in this moment, who may have felt an inclination to dissent from the dominant feelings of the group (say, the Latina Barbie Girl who, her mother later told me, did not want the group to be identified with Barbie, or a boy whose immediate inner response to the Barbie Girls' joyful celebration might be to join in) is most likely silenced into complicity in this powerful moment of border work.

What meanings did this highly gendered moment carry for the boys' and girls' teams in the ensuing soccer season? Although I did not observe the Barbie Girls after the opening ceremony, I did continue to observe the Sea Monsters' weekly practices and games. During the boys' ensuing season, gender never reached this "magnified" level of salience again—indeed, gender was rarely raised verbally or performed overtly by the boys. On two occasions, though, I observed the coach jokingly chiding the boys during practice that "if you don't watch out, I'm going to get the Barbie Girls here to play against you!" This warning was followed by gleeful screams of agony and fear, and nervous hopping around and hugging by some of the boys. Normally, though, in this sex-segregated, all-male context, if boundaries were invoked, they were not boundaries between boys and girls but boundaries between the Sea Monsters and other boys' teams, or sometimes age boundaries between the Sea Monsters and a small group of dads and older brothers who would engage them in a mock scrimmage during practice. But it was also evident that when the coach was having trouble getting the boys to act together, as a group, his strategic and humorous invocation of the dreaded Barbie Girls once again served symbolically to affirm their group status. They were a team. They were the boys.

Conclusion

The overarching goal of this article has been to take one empirical observation from everyday life and demonstrate how a multilevel (interactionist, structural, cultural) analysis might reveal various layers of meaning that give insight into the everyday social construction of gender. This article builds on observations made by Thorne (1993) concerning ways to approach sociological analyses of children's worlds. The most fruitful approach is not to ask why boys and girls are so different but rather to ask how and under what conditions boys and girls constitute themselves as separate, oppositional groups. Sociologists need not debate whether gender is "there"—clearly, gender is always already there, built as it is into the structures, situations, culture, and consciousness of children and adults. The key issue is under what conditions gender is activated as a salient organizing principle in social life and under what conditions it may be less salient. These are important questions, especially since the social organization of categorical gender difference has always been so clearly tied to gender hierarchy (Acker 1990; Lorber 1994). In the Barbie Girls versus Sea Monsters moment, the performance of gendered boundaries and the construction of boys' and girls' groups as categorically different occurred in the context of a situation systematically structured by sex segregation, sparked by the imposing presence of a shared cultural symbol that is saturated with gendered meanings, and actively supported and applauded by adults who basked in the pleasure of difference, reaffirmed.[6]

I have suggested that a useful approach to the study of such "how" and "under what conditions" questions is to employ multiple levels of analysis. At the most general level, this project supports the following working propositions.

Interactionist theoretical frameworks that emphasize the ways that social agents "perform" or "do" gender are most useful in describing how groups of people actively create (or at times disrupt) the boundaries that delineate seemingly categorical differences between male persons and female persons. In this case, we saw how the children and the parents interactively performed gender in a way that constructed an apparently natural boundary between the two separate worlds of the girls and the boys.

Structural theoretical frameworks that emphasize the ways that gender is built into institutions through hierarchical sexual divisions of labor are most useful in explaining under what conditions social agents mobilize variously to disrupt or to affirm gender differences and inequalities. In this case, we saw how the sexual division of labor among parent volunteers (grounded in their own histories in the gender regime of sport), the formal sex segregation of the children's leagues, and the structured context of the opening ceremony created conditions for possible interactions between girls' teams and boys' teams.

Cultural theoretical perspectives that examine how popular symbols that are injected into circulation by the culture industry are variously taken up by differently situated people are most useful in analyzing how the meanings of cultural symbols, in a given institutional context, might trigger or be taken up by social agents and used as resources to reproduce, disrupt, or contest binary conceptions of sex difference and gendered relations of power. In this case, we saw how a girls' team appropriated a large Barbie around which to construct a pleasurable and empowering sense of group identity and how the boys' team responded with aggressive denunciations of Barbie and invasions.

Utilizing any one of the above theoretical perspectives by itself will lead to a limited, even distorted, analysis of the social construction of gender. Together, they can illuminate the complex, multileveled architecture of the social construction of gender in everyday life. For heuristic reasons, I have falsely separated structure, interaction, and culture. In fact, we need to explore their constant interrelationships, continuities, and contradictions. For instance, we cannot understand the boys' aggressive denunciations and invasions of the girls' space and the eventual clarification of categorical boundaries between the girls and the boys without first understanding how these boys and girls have already internalized four or five years of "gendering" experiences that have shaped their interactional tendencies and how they are already immersed in a culture of gendered symbols, including Barbie and sports media imagery. Although "only" preschoolers, they are already skilled in collectively taking up symbols from popular culture as resources to be used in their own group dynamics—building individual and group identities, sharing the pleasures of play, clarifying boundaries between in-group and out-group members, and constructing hierarchies in their worlds.

Furthermore, we cannot understand the reason that the girls first chose "Barbie Girls" as their team name without first understanding the fact that a particular institutional structure of AYSO soccer preexisted the girls' entrée into the league. The informal sexual division of labor among adults, and the formal sex segregation of children's teams, is a preexisting gender regime that constrains and enables the ways that the children enact gender relations and construct identities. One concrete manifestation of this constraining nature of sex segregated teams is the choice of team names. It is reasonable to speculate that if the four- and five-year-old children were still sex integrated, as in the pre-1995 era, no team would have chosen "Barbie Girls" as its team name, with Barbie as its symbol. In other words, the formal sex segregation created the conditions under which the girls were enabled—perhaps encouraged—to choose a "sweet" team name that is widely read as encoding feminine meanings. The eventual interactions between the boys and the girls were made possible—although by no means fully determined—by the structure of the gender regime and by the cultural resources that the children variously drew on.

On the other hand, the gendered division of labor in youth soccer is not seamless, static, or immune to resistance. One of the few woman head coaches, a very active athlete in her own right, told me that she is "challenging the sexism" in AYSO by becoming the head of her son's league. As post–Title IX women increasingly become mothers and as media images of competent, heroic female athletes become more a part of the cultural landscape for children, the gender regimes of children's sports may be increasingly challenged (Dworkin and Messner 1999). Put another way, the dramatically shifting opportunity structure and cultural imagery of post–Title IX sports have created opportunities for new kinds of interactions, which will inevitably challenge and further shift institutional structures. Social structures simultaneously constrain and enable, while agency is simultaneously reproductive and resistant.

Notes

1. Most of the structural inventory presented here is from a content analysis of the 1998–1999 regional American Youth Soccer League (AYSO) yearbook, which features photos and names of all of the teams, coaches, and managers. I counted the number of adult men and women occupying various positions. In the three cases where the sex category of a name was not immediately obvious (e.g., Rene or Terry), or in the five cases where simply a last name was listed, I did not count it. I also used the AYSO yearbook for my analysis of the children's team names. To check for reliability, another sociologist independently read and coded the list of team names. There was disagreement on how to categorize only 2 of the 156 team names.

2. The existence of some women coaches and some men team managers in this AYSO organization manifests a less extreme sexual division of labor than that of the same community's Little League baseball organization, in which there are proportionally far fewer women coaches. Similarly, Saltzman Chafetz and Kotarba's (1999, 52) study of parental labor in support of Little League baseball in a middle-class Houston community revealed an apparently absolute sexual division of labor, where nearly all of the supportive "activities off the field were conducted by the women in the total absence of men, while activities on the field were conducted by men and boys in the absence of women." Perhaps youth soccer, because of its more recent (mostly post–Title IX) history in the United States, is a more contested gender regime than the more patriarchally entrenched youth sports like Little League baseball or youth football.

3. The four- and five-year-old kids' games and practices were absolutely homosocial in terms of the kids, due to the formal structural sex segregation. However, 8 of the 12 girls' teams at this age level had male coaches, and 2 of the 14 boys' teams had female coaches.

4. By 1994, more than 800 million Barbies had been sold worldwide. More than $1 billion was spent on Barbies and accessories in 1992 alone. Two Barbie dolls were purchased every second in 1994, half of which were sold in the United States (DuCille 1994, 49).

5. Rogers (1999, 23) notes that if one extrapolates Barbie's bodily proportions to "real woman ones," she would be "33-18-31.5 and stand five feet nine inches tall, with fully half of her height accounted for by her 'shapely legs.'"

6. My trilevel analysis of structure, interaction, and culture may not be fully adequate to plumb the emotional depths of the magnified Barbie Girls versus Sea Monsters moment. Although it is beyond the purview of this article, an adequate rendering of the depths of pleasure and revulsion, attachment and separation, and commitment to ideologies of categorical sex difference may involve the integration of a fourth level of analysis: gender at the level of personality (Chodorow 1999). Object relations theory has fallen out of vogue in feminist sociology in recent years, but as Williams (1993) has argued, it might be most useful in revealing the mostly hidden social power of gender to shape people's unconscious predispositions to various structural contexts, cultural symbols, and interactional moments.

References

Acker, Joan. 1990. Hierarchies, jobs, bodies: A theory of gendered organizations. *Gender & Society* 4:139–158.

Adler, Patricia A., and Peter Adler. 1998. *Peer power: Preadolescent culture and identity.* New Brunswick, NJ: Rutgers University Press.

Attfield, Judy. 1996. Barbie and Action Man: Adult toys for girls and boys, 1959–93. In *The gendered object,* edited by Pat Kirkham, 80–89. Manchester, UK, and New York: Manchester University Press.

Boyle, Maree, and Jim McKay. 1995. "You leave your troubles at the gate": A case study of the exploitation of older women's labor and "leisure" in sport. *Gender & Society* 9:556–576.

Bradbard, M. 1985. Sex differences in adults' gifts and children's toy requests. *Journal of Genetic Psychology* 145:283–284.

Butler, Judith. 1990. *Gender trouble: Feminism and the subversion of identity.* New York and London: Routledge.

Campenni, C. Estelle. 1999. Gender stereotyping of children's toys: A comparison of parents and nonparents. *Sex Roles* 40:121–138.

Chodorow, Nancy J. 1999. *The power of feelings: Personal meanings in psychoanalysis, gender, and culture.* New Haven and London: Yale University Press.

Connell, R. W. 1987. *Gender and power.* Palo Alto, CA: Stanford University Press.

———. 1989. Cool guys, swots and wimps: The interplay of masculinity and education. *Oxford Review of Education* 15:291–303.

DuCille, Anne. 1994. Dyes and dolls: Multicultural Barbie and the merchandising of difference. *Differences: A Journal of Cultural Studies* 6:46–68.

Dworkin, Shari L., and Michael A. Messner. 1999. Just do . . . what?: Sport, bodies, gender. In *Revisioning gender,* edited by Myra Marx Ferree, Judith Lorber, and Beth B. Hess, 341–361. Thousand Oaks, CA: Sage.

Etaugh, C., and M. B. Liss. 1992. Home, school, and playroom: Training grounds for adult gender roles. *Sex Roles* 26:129–147.

Heywood, Leslie, and Jennifer Drake, Eds. 1997. *Third wave agenda: Being feminist, doing feminism.* Minneapolis: University of Minnesota Press.

Hochschild, Arlie Russell. 1994. The commercial spirit of intimate life and the abduction of feminism: Signs from women's advice books. *Theory, Culture & Society* 11:1–24.

Jordan, Ellen, and Angela Cowan. 1995. Warrior narratives in the kindergarten classroom: Renegotiating the social contract? *Gender & Society* 9:727–743.

Kessler, Suzanne J., and Wendy McKenna. 1978. *Gender: An ethnomethodological approach.* New York: John Wiley.

Klein, Melissa. 1997. Duality and redefinition: Young feminism and the alternative music community. In *Third wave agenda: Being feminist, doing feminism,* edited by Leslie Heywood and Jennifer Drake, 207–225. Minneapolis: University of Minnesota Press.

Lorber, Judith. 1994. *Paradoxes of gender.* New Haven and London: Yale University Press.

McGuffy, C. Shawn, and B. Lindsay Rich. 1999. Playing in the gender transgression zone: Race, class, and hegemonic masculinity in middle childhood. *Gender & Society* 13:608–627.

Messner, Michael A. 1992. *Power at play: Sports and the problem of masculinity.* Boston: Beacon.

Pope, Harrison G., Jr., Roberto Olivarda, Amanda Gruber, and John Borowiecki. 1999. Evolving ideals of male body image as seen through action toys. *International Journal of Eating Disorders* 26:65–72.

Raag, Tarja, and Christine L. Rackliff. 1998. Preschoolers' awareness of social expectations of gender: Relationships to toy choices. *Sex Roles* 38:685–700.

Rand, Erica. 1998. Older heads on younger bodies. In *The children's culture reader,* edited by Henry Jenkins, 382–393. New York: New York University Press.

Risman, Barbara. 1998. *Gender vertigo: American families in transition.* New Haven and London: Yale University Press.

Robinson, C. C., and J. T. Morris. 1986. The gender-stereotyped nature of Christmas toys received by 36-, 48-, and 60-month-old children: A comparison between nonrequested vs. requested toys. *Sex Roles* 15:21–32.

Rogers, Mary F. 1999. *Barbie culture.* Thousand Oaks, CA: Sage.

Saltzman Chafetz, Janet, and Joseph A. Kotarba. 1999. Little League mothers and the reproduction of gender. In *Inside sports,* edited by Jay Coakley and Peter Donnelly, 46–54. London and New York: Routledge.

Seiter, Ellen. 1995. *Sold separately: Parents and children in consumer culture.* New Brunswick, NJ: Rutgers University Press.

Spigel, Lynn. Forthcoming. Barbies without Ken: Femininity, feminism, and the art-culture system. In *Sitting room only: Television, consumer culture and the suburban home,* edited by Lynn Spigel. Durham, NC: Duke University Press.

Thorne, Barrie. 1993. *Gender play: Girls and boys in school.* New Brunswick, NJ: Rutgers University Press.

Walters, Suzanna Danuta. 1999. Sex, text, and context: (In) between feminism and cultural studies.

In *Revisioning gender,* edited by Myra Marx Ferree, Judith Lorber, and Beth B. Hess, 222–257. Thousand Oaks, CA: Sage.

West, Candace, and Don Zimmerman. 1987. Doing gender. *Gender & Society* 1:125–151.

Williams, Christine. 1993. Psychoanalytic theory and the sociology of gender. In *Theory on gender, gender on theory,* edited by Paula England, 131–149. New York: Aldine.

ARTICLE 9

Ellen Jordan
Angela Cowan

Warrior Narratives in the Kindergarten Classroom: Renegotiating the Social Contract?

The "social contract" becomes part of the lived experience of little boys when they discover that the school forbids the warrior narratives through which they initially define masculinity and imposes a different, public sphere: masculinity of rationality and responsibility. They learn that these narratives are not to be lived but only experienced symbolically through fantasy and sport in the private sphere of desire. Little girls, whose gender-defining fantasies are not repressed by the school, have less lived awareness of the social contract.

Since the beginning of second wave feminism, the separation between the public (masculine) world of politics and the economy and the private (feminine) world of the family and personal life has been seen as highly significant in establishing gender difference and inequality (Eisenstein 1984). Twenty years of feminist research and speculation have refined our understanding of this divide and how it has been developed and reproduced. One particularly striking and influential account is that given by Carole Pateman in her book *The Sexual Contract* (1988).

Pateman's broad argument is that in the modern world, the world since the Enlightenment, a "civil society" has been established. In this civil society, patriarchy has been replaced by a fratriarchy, which is equally male and oppressive of women. Men now rule not as fathers but as brothers, able to compete with one another, but presenting a united front against those outside the group. It is the brothers who control the public world of the state, politics, and the economy. Women have been given token access to this world because the discourses of liberty and universalism made this difficult to refuse, but to take part they must conform to the rules established to suit the brothers.

This public world in which the brothers operate together is conceptualized as separate from the personal and emotional. One is a realm where there is little physicality—everything is done rationally, bureaucratically, according to contracts that the brothers accept as legitimate. Violence in this realm is severely controlled by agents of the state, except that the brothers are sometimes called upon for the supreme sacrifice of dying to preserve freedom. The social contract redefines the brawling and feuding long seen as essential characteristics of masculinity as deviant, even

Author's Note: The research on which this article is based was funded by the Research Management Committee of the University of Newcastle. The observation was conducted at East Maitland Public School and the authors would like to thank the principal, teachers, and children involved for making our observer so welcome.

From *Gender & Society* 9(6): 727–743. Copyright © 1995 by Sage Publications. Reprinted by permission of Sage Publications, Inc.

criminal, while the rest of physicality—sexuality, reproduction of the body, daily and intergenerationally—is left in the private sphere. Pateman quotes Robert Unger, "The dichotomy of the public and private life is still another corollary of the separation of understanding and desire.... When reasoning, [men] belong to a public world.... When desiring, however, men are private beings" (Pateman 1989, 48).

This is now widely accepted as the way men understand and experience their world. On the other hand, almost no attempt has been made to look at how it is that they take these views on board, or why the public/private divide is so much more deeply entrenched in their lived experience than in women's. This article looks at one strand in the complex web of experiences through which this is achieved. A major site where this occurs is the school, one of the institutions particularly characteristic of the civil society that emerged with the Enlightenment (Foucault 1980, 55–57). The school does not deliberately condition boys and not girls into this dichotomy, but it is, we believe, a site where what Giddens (1984, 10–13) has called a cycle of practice introduces little boys to the public/private division.

The article is based on weekly observations in a kindergarten classroom. We examine what happens in the early days of school when the children encounter the expectations of the school with their already established conceptions of gender. The early months of school are a period when a great deal of negotiating between the children's personal agendas and the teacher's expectations has to take place, where a great deal of what Genovese (1972) has described as accommodation and resistance must be involved.

In this article, we focus on a particular contest, which, although never specifically stated, is central to the children's accommodation to school: little boys' determination to explore certain narratives of masculinity with which they are already familiar—guns, fighting, fast cars—and the teacher's attempts to outlaw their importation into the classroom setting. We argue that what occurs is a contest between two definitions of masculinity: what we have chosen to call "warrior narratives" and the discourses of civil society—rationality, responsibility, and decorum—that are the basis of school discipline.

By "warrior narratives," we mean narratives that assume that violence is legitimate and justified when it occurs within a struggle between good and evil. There is a tradition of such narratives, stretching from Hercules and Beowulf to Superman and Dirty Harry, where the male is depicted as the warrior, the knight-errant, the superhero, the good guy (usually called a "goody" by Australian children), often supported by brothers in arms, and always opposed to some evil figure, such as a monster, a giant, a villain, a criminal, or, very simply, in Australian parlance, a "baddy." There is also a connection, it is now often suggested, between these narratives and the activity that has come to epitomize the physical expression of masculinity in the modern era: sport (Duthie 1980, 91–94; Crosset 1990; Messner 1992, 15). It is as sport that the physicality and desire usually lived out in the private sphere are permitted a ritualized public presence. Even though the violence once characteristic of the warrior has, in civil society and as part of the social contract, become the prerogative of the state, it can still be re-enacted symbolically in countless sporting encounters. The mantle of the warrior is inherited by the sportsman.

The school discipline that seeks to outlaw these narratives is, we would suggest, very much a product of modernity. Bowles and Gintis have argued that "the structure of social relations in education not only inures the student to the discipline of the work place, but develops the types of personal demeanor, modes of self-presentation, self-image, and social-class identifications which are the crucial ingredients of job adequacy" (1976, 131). The school is seeking to introduce the children to the behavior appropriate to the civil society of the modern world.

An accommodation does eventually take place, this article argues, through a recognition of the split between the public and the private. Most boys learn to accept that the way to power and respectability is through acceptance of the conventions of civil society. They also learn that warrior narratives are not a part of this world; they can only be experienced symbolically as fantasy or sport. The outcome, we will suggest, is that little boys learn that these narratives must be left behind in the private world of desire when they participate in the public world of reason.

The Study

The school where this study was conducted serves an old-established suburb in a country town in New South Wales, Australia. The children are predominantly Australian born and English speaking, but come from socioeconomic backgrounds ranging from professional to welfare recipient. We carried out this research in a classroom run by a teacher who is widely acknowledged as one of the finest and most successful kindergarten teachers in our region. She is an admired practitioner of free play, process writing, and creativity. There was no gender definition of games in her classroom. Groups composed of both girls and boys had turns at playing in the Doll Corner, in the Construction Area, and on the Car Mat.

The research method used was nonparticipant observation, the classic mode for the sociological study of children in schools (Burgess 1984; Thorne 1986; Goodenough 1987). The group of children described came to school for the first time in February 1993. The observation sessions began within a fortnight of the children entering school and were conducted during "free activity" time, a period lasting for about an hour. At first we observed twice a week, but then settled to a weekly visit, although there were some weeks when it was inconvenient for the teacher to accommodate an observer.

The observation was noninteractive. The observer stationed herself as unobtrusively as possible, usually seated on a kindergarten-sized chair, near one of the play stations. She made pencil notes of events, with particular attention to accurately recording the words spoken by the children, and wrote up detailed narratives from the notes, supplemented by memory, on reaching home. She discouraged attention from the children by rising and leaving the area if she was drawn by them into any interaction.

This project thus employed a methodology that was ethnographic and open-ended. It was nevertheless guided by certain theories, drawn from the work on gender of Jean Anyon, Barrie Thorne, and R. W. Connell, of the nature of social interaction and its part in creating personal identity and in reproducing the structures of a society.

Anyon has adapted the conceptions of accommodation and resistance developed by Genovese (1972) to understanding how women live with gender. Genovese argued that slaves in the American South accommodated to their contradictory situation by using certain of its aspects, for example, exposure to the Christian religion, to validate a sense of self-worth and dignity. Christian beliefs then allowed them to take a critical view of slavery, which in turn legitimated certain forms of resistance (Anyon 1983, 21). Anyon lists a variety of ways in which women accommodate to and resist prescriptions of appropriate feminine behavior, arguing for a significant level of choice and agency (Anyon 1983, 23–26).

Thorne argues that the processes of social life, the form and nature of the interactions, as well as the choices of the actors, should be the object of analysis. She writes, "In this book I begin not with individuals, although they certainly appear in the account, but with *group life*—with social relations, the organization and meanings of social situations, the collective practices through which children and adults create and recreate gender in their daily interactions" (1993, 4).

These daily interactions, Connell (1987, 139–141) has suggested, mesh to form what Giddens (1984, 10–13) has called "cyclical practices." Daily interactions are neither random nor specific to particular locations. They are repeated and recreated in similar settings throughout a society. Similar needs recur, similar discourses are available, and so similar solutions to problems are adopted; thus, actions performed and discourses adopted to achieve particular ends in particular situations have the unintended consequence of producing uniformities of gendered behavior in individuals.

In looking at the patterns of accommodation and resistance that emerge when the warrior narratives that little boys have adapted from television encounter the discipline of the classroom, we believe we have uncovered one of the cyclical practices of modernity that reveal the social contract to these boys.

Warrior Narratives in the Doll Corner

In the first weeks of the children's school experience, the Doll Corner was the area where the most elaborate acting out of warrior narratives was observed. The Doll Corner in this classroom was a small room with a door with a glass panel opening off the main area. Its furnishings—stove, sink, dolls' cots, and so on—were an attempt at a literal re-creation of a domestic setting, revealing the school's definition of children's play as a preparation for adult life. It was an area where the acting out of "pretend" games was acceptable.

Much of the boys' play in the area was domestic:

> Jimmy and Tyler were jointly ironing a tablecloth. "Look at the sheet is burnt, I've burnt it," declared Tyler, waving the toy iron above his head. "I'm telling Mrs. Sandison," said Jimmy worriedly. "No, I tricked you. It's not really burnt. See," explained Tyler, showing Jimmy the black pattern on the cloth. (February 23, 1993)

> "Where is the baby, the baby boy?" Justin asked, as he helped Harvey and Malcolm settle some restless teddy babies. "Give them some potion." Justin pretended to force feed a teddy, asking "Do you want to drink this potion?" (March 4, 1993)

On the other hand, there were attempts from the beginning by some of the boys and one of the girls to use this area for nondomestic games and, in the case of the boys, for games based on warrior narratives, involving fighting, destruction, goodies, and baddies.

> The play started off quietly, Winston cuddled a teddy bear, then settled it in a bed. Just as Winston tucked in his bear, Mac snatched the teddy out of bed and swung it around his head in circles. "Don't hurt him, give him back," pleaded Winston, trying vainly to retrieve the teddy. The two boys were circling the small table in the center of the room. As he ran, Mac started to karate chop the teddy on the arm, and then threw it on the floor and jumped on it. He then snatched up a plastic knife, "This is a sword. Ted is dead. They all are." He sliced the knife across the teddy's tummy, repeating the action on the bodies of two stuffed dogs. Winston grabbed the two dogs, and with a dog in each hand, staged a dog fight. "They are alive again." (February 10, 1993)

> Three boys were busily stuffing teddies into the cupboard through the sink opening. "They're in jail. They can't escape," said Malcolm. "Let's pour water over them." "Don't do that. It'll hurt them," shouted Winston, rushing into the Doll Corner. "Go away, Winston. You're not in our group," said Malcolm. (February 12, 1993)

The boys even imported goodies and baddies into a classic ghost scenario initiated by one of the girls:

> "I'm the father," Tyler declared. "I'm the mother," said Alanna. "Let's pretend it's a stormy night and I'm afraid. Let's pretend a ghost has come to steal the dog." Tyler nodded and placed the sheet over his head. Tyler moaned, "ooooOOOOOOOAHHHH!!!" and moved his outstretched arms toward Alanna. Jamie joined the game and grabbed a sheet from the doll's cradle, "I'm the goody ghost." "So am I," said Tyler. They giggled and wrestled each other to the floor. "No! you're the baddy ghost," said Jamie. Meanwhile, Alanna was making ghostly noises and moving around the boys. "Did you like the game? Let's play it again," she suggested. (February 23, 1993)

In the first two incidents, there was some conflict between the narratives being invoked by Winston and those used by the other boys. For

Winston, the stuffed toys were the weak whom he must protect knight-errant style. For the other boys, they could be set up as the baddies whom it was legitimate for the hero to attack. Both were versions of a warrior narrative.

The gender difference in the use of these narratives has been noted by a number of observers (Paley 1984; Clark 1989, 250–252; Thorne 1993, 98–99). Whereas even the most timid, least physically aggressive boys—Winston in this study is typical—are drawn to identifying with the heroes of these narratives, girls show almost no interest in them at this early age. The strong-willed and assertive girls in our study, as in others (Clark 1990, 83–84; Walkerdine 1990, 10–12), sought power by commandeering the role of mother, teacher, or shopkeeper, while even the highly imaginative Alanna, although she enlivened the more mundane fantasies of the other children with ghosts, old widow women, and magical mirrors, seems not to have been attracted by warrior heroes.[1]

Warrior narratives, it would seem, have a powerful attraction for little boys, which they lack for little girls. Why and how this occurs remains unexplored in early childhood research, perhaps because data for such an explanation are not available to those doing research in institutional settings. Those undertaking ethnographic research in preschools find the warrior narratives already in possession in these sites (Paley 1984, 70–73, 116; Davies 1989, 91–92). In this research, gender difference in the appeal of warrior narratives has to be taken as a given—the data gathered are not suitable for constructing theories of origins; thus, the task of determining an explanation would seem to lie within the province of those investigating and theorizing gender differentiation during infancy, and perhaps, specifically, of those working in the tradition of feminist psychoanalysis pioneered by Dinnerstein (1977) and Chodorow (1978). Nevertheless, even though the cause may remain obscure, there can be little argument that in the English-speaking world for at least the last hundred years—think of Tom Sawyer playing Robin Hood and the pirates and Indians in J. M. Barrie's *Peter Pan*—boys have built these narratives into their conceptions of the masculine.

Accommodation Through *Bricolage*

The school classroom, even one as committed to freedom and self-actualization as this, makes little provision for the enactment of these narratives. The classroom equipment invites children to play house, farm, and shop, to construct cities and roads, and to journey through them with toy cars, but there is no overt invitation to explore warrior narratives.

In the first few weeks of school, the little boys un-self-consciously set about redressing this omission. The method they used was what is known as *bricolage*—the transformation of objects from one use to another for symbolic purposes (Hebdige 1979, 103). The first site was the Doll Corner. Our records for the early weeks contain a number of examples of boys rejecting the usages ascribed to the various Doll Corner objects by the teacher and by the makers of equipment and assigning a different meaning to them. This became evident very early with their use of the toy baby carriages (called "prams" in Australia). For the girls, the baby carriages were just that, but for many of the boys they very quickly became surrogate cars:

> Mac threw a doll into the largest pram in the Doll Corner. He walked the pram out past a group of his friends who were playing "crashes" on the Car Mat. Three of the five boys turned and watched him wheeling the pram toward the classroom door. Mac performed a sharp three-point turn; raced his pram past the Car Mat group, striking one boy on the head with the pram wheel. (February 10, 1993)

> "Brrrrmmmmmm, brrrrrmmmmm," Tyler's revving engine noises grew louder as he rocked the pram back and forth with sharp jerking movements. The engine noise grew quieter as he left the Doll Corner and wheeled the pram around the classroom. He started to run with the pram when the teacher could not observe him. (March 23, 1993)

The boys transformed other objects into masculine appurtenances: knives and tongs became weapons, the dolls' beds became boats, and so on.

Mac tried to engage Winston in a sword fight using Doll Corner plastic knives. Winston backed away, but Mac persisted. Winston took a knife but continued to back away from Mac. He then put down the knife, and ran away half-screaming (semi-seriously, unsure of the situation) for his teacher. (February 10, 1993)

In the literature on youth subcultures, bricolage is seen as a characteristic of modes of resistance. Hebdige writes:

> It is through the distinctive rituals of consumption, through style, that the subculture at once reveals its "secret" identity and communicates its forbidden meanings. It is predominantly the way commodities are *used* in subculture which mark the subculture off from more orthodox cultural formations. . . . The concept of *bricolage* can be used to explain how subcultural styles are constructed. (1979, 103)

In these early weeks, however, the boys did not appear to be aware that they were doing anything more than establishing an accommodation between their needs and the classroom environment.

This mode of accommodation was rejected by the teacher, however, who practiced a gentle, but steady, discouragement of such bricolage. Even though the objects in this space are not really irons, beds, and cooking pots, she made strong efforts to assert their cultural meaning, instructing the children in the "proper" use of the equipment and attempting to control their behavior by questions like "Would you do that with a tea towel in your house?" "Cats never climb up on the benches in *my* house." It was thus impressed upon the children that warrior narratives were inappropriate in this space.

The children, our observations suggest, accepted her guidance, and we found no importation of warrior narratives into the Doll Corner after the first few weeks. There were a number of elaborate and exciting narratives devised, but they were all to some degree related to the domestic environment. For example, on April 20, Justin and Nigel used one of the baby carriages as a four-wheel drive, packed it with equipment and went off for a camping trip, setting out a picnic with Doll Corner tablecloths, knives, forks, and plates when they arrived. On May 18, Matthew, Malcolm, Nigel, and Jonathan were dogs being fed in the Doll Corner. They then complained of the flies, and Jonathan picked up the toy telephone and said, "Flycatcher! Flycatcher! Come and catch some flies. They are everywhere." On June 1, the following was recorded:

> "We don't want our nappies [diapers] changed," Aaron informed Celia, the mum in the game. "I'm poohing all over your clothes mum," Mac declared, as he grunted and positioned himself over the dress-up box. Celia cast a despairing glance in Mac's direction, and went on dressing a doll. "I am too; poohing all over your clothes mum," said Aaron. "Now mum will have to clean it all up and change my nappy," he informed Mac, giggling. He turned to the dad [Nigel], and said in a baby voice, "Goo-goo; give him [Mac] the feather duster." "No! give him the feather duster; he did the longest one all over the clothes," Mac said to Nigel. (June 1, 1993)

Although exciting and imaginative games continued, the bricolage virtually disappeared from the Doll Corner. The intention of the designer of the Doll Corner equipment was increasingly respected. Food for the camping trip was bought from the shop the teacher had set up and consumed using the Doll Corner equipment. The space invaded by flies was a domestic space, and appropriate means, calling in expert help by telephone, were used to deal with the problem. Chairs and tables were chairs and tables, clothes were clothes and could be fouled by appropriate inhabitants of a domestic space, babies. Only the baby carriages continued to have an ambiguous status, to maintain the ability to be transformed into vehicles of other kinds.

The warrior narratives—sword play, baddies in jail, pirates, and so on—did not vanish from the boys' imaginative world, but, as the later observations show, the site gradually moved from the Doll Corner to the Construction Area and the Car Mat. By the third week in March (that is, after about six weeks at school), the observer noticed the boys consistently using the construction toys to develop these narratives. The bricolage was now restricted to the more amorphously defined construction materials.

> Tyler was busy constructing an object out of five pieces of plastic straw (clever sticks). "This is a water pistol. Everyone's gonna get wet," he cried as he moved into the Doll Corner pretending to wet people. The game shifted to guns and bullets between Tyler and two other boys. "I've got a bigger gun," Roger said, showing off his square block object. "Mine's more longer. Ehehehehehehehe, got you," Winston yelled to Roger, brandishing a plastic straw gun. "I'll kill your gun," Mac said, pushing Winston's gun away. "No Mac. You broke it. No," cried Winston. (March 23, 1993)

> Two of the boys picked up swords made out of blue- and red-colored plastic squares they had displayed on the cupboard. "This is my sword," Jamie explained to Tyler. "My jumper [sweater] holds it in. Whichever color is at the bottom, well that's the color it shoots out. Whoever is bad, we shoot with power out of it." "Come on Tyler," he went on. "Get your sword. Let's go get some baddies." (March 30, 1993)

The toy cars on the Car Mat were also pressed into the service of warrior narratives:

> Justin, Brendan, and Jonathan were busy on the Car Mat. The game involved police cars that were chasing baddies who had drunk "too much beers." Justin explained to Jonathan why his car had the word "DOG" written on the front. "These are different police cars, for catching robbers taking money." (March 4, 1993)

> Three boys, Harvey, Maurice, and Marshall, were on the Car Mat. "Here comes the baddies," Harvey shouted, spinning a toy car around the mat. "Crasssshhhhh everywhere." He crashed his car into the other boys' cars and they responded with laughter. "I killed a baddie everyone," said Maurice, crashing his cars into another group of cars. (May 24, 1993)

A new accommodation was being proposed by the boys, a new adaptation of classroom materials to the needs of their warrior narratives.

Classroom Rules and Resistance

Once again the teacher would not accept the accommodation proposed. Warrior narratives provoked what she considered inappropriate public behavior in the miniature civil society of her classroom. Her aim was to create a "free" environment where children could work independently, learn at their own pace, and explore their own interests, but creating such an environment involved its own form of social contract, its own version of the state's appropriation of violence. From the very first day, she began to establish a series of classroom rules that imposed constraints on violent or disruptive activity.

The belief underlying her practice was that firmly established classroom rules make genuine free play possible, rather than restricting the range of play opportunities. Her emphasis on "proper" use of equipment was intended to stop it being damaged and consequently withdrawn from use. She had rules of "no running" and "no shouting" that allowed children to work and play safely on the floor of the classroom, even though other children were using equipment or toys that demanded movement, and ensured that the noise level was low enough for children to talk at length to one another as part of their games.

One of the outcomes of these rules was the virtual outlawing of a whole series of games that groups of children usually want to initiate when they are playing together, games of speed and body contact, of gross motor self-expression and skill. This prohibition affected both girls and boys and was justified by setting up a version of public and private spaces: The classroom was not the proper place for such activities, they "belong" in the playground.[2] The combined experience of many teachers has shown that it is almost impossible for children to play games involving car crashes and guns without violating these rules; therefore, in this classroom, as in many others (Paley 1984, 71, 116), these games were in effect banned.

These rules were then policed by the children themselves, as the following interchange shows:

> "Eeeeeeheeeeeeheeeeh!" Tyler leapt about the room. A couple of girls were saying, "Stop it Tyler" but he persisted. Jane warned, "You're not allowed to have guns." Tyler responded saying, "It's not a gun. It's a water pistol, and that's not a gun." "Not allowed to have water pistol guns," Tony reiterated to Tyler. "Yes, it's a water pistol," shouted Tyler. Jane informed the teacher, who responded stating, "NO GUNS, even if they are water pistols." Tyler made a spear out of Clever Sticks, straight after the banning of gun play. (March 23, 1993)

The boys, however, were not prepared to abandon their warrior narratives. Unlike gross motor activities such as wrestling and football, they were not prepared to see them relegated to the playground, but the limitations on their expression and the teacher disapproval they evoked led the boys to explore them surreptitiously; they found ways of introducing them that did not violate rules about running and shouting.

As time passed, the games became less visible. The warrior narratives were not so much acted out as talked through, using the toy cars and the construction materials as a prompt and a basis:

> Tyler was showing his plastic straw construction to Luke. "This is a Samurai Man and this is his hat. A Samurai Man fights in Japan and they fight with the Ninja. The bad guys who use cannons and guns. My Samurai is captain of the Samurai and he is going to kill the sergeant of the bad guys. He is going to sneak up on him with a knife and kill him." (June 1, 1993)

> Malcolm and Aaron had built boats with Lego blocks and were explaining the various components to Roger. "This ship can go faster," Malcolm explained. "He [a plastic man] is the boss of the ship. Mine is a goody boat. They are not baddies." "Mine's a steam shovel boat. It has wheels," said Aaron. "There it goes in the river and it has to go to a big shed where all the steam shovels are stopping." (June 11, 1993)

It also became apparent that there was something covert about this play. The cars were crashed quietly. The guns were being transformed into water pistols. Swords were concealed under jumpers and only used when the teacher's back was turned. When the constructed objects were displayed to the class, their potential as players in a fighting game was concealed under a more mundane description. For example:

> Prior to the free play, the children were taking turns to explain the Clever Stick and Lego Block constructions they had made the previous afternoon. I listened to Tyler describe his Lego robot to the class: "This is a transformer robot. It can do things and turn into everything." During free play, Tyler played with the same robot explaining its capacities to Winston: "This is a terminator ship. It can kill. It can turn into a robot and the top pops off." (March 23, 1993)

Children even protested to one another that they were not making weapons, "This isn't a gun, it's a lookout." "This isn't a place for bullets, it's for petrol."

The warrior narratives, it would seem, went underground and became part of a "deviant" masculine subculture with the characteristic "secret" identity and hidden meanings (Hebdige 1979, 103). The boys were no longer seeking accommodation but practicing hidden resistance. The classroom, they were learning, was not a place where it was acceptable to explore their gender identity through fantasy.

This, however, was a message that only the boys were receiving. The girls' gender-specific fantasies (Paley 1984, 106–108; Davies 1989, 118–122) of nurturing and self-display—mothers, nurses, brides, princesses—were accommodated easily within the classroom. They could be played out without contravening the rules of the miniature civil society. Although certain delightful activities—eating, running, hugging, and kissing (Best 1983, 110)—might be excluded from this public sphere, they were not ones by means of which their femininity, and thus their subjectivity, their conception of the self, was defined.

Masculinity, the School Regime, and the Social Contract

We suggest that this conflict between warrior narratives and school rules is likely to form part of the experience of most boys growing up in the industrialized world. The commitment to such narratives was not only nearly 100 percent among the boys we observed, but similar commitment is, as was argued above, common in other sites. On the other hand, the pressure to preserve a decorous classroom is strong in all teachers (with the possible exception of those teaching in "alternative" schools) and has been since the beginnings of compulsory education. Indeed, it is only in classrooms where there is the balance of freedom and constraint we observed that such narratives are likely to surface at all. In more formal situations, they would be defined as deviant and forced underground from the boys' first entry into school.

If this is a widely recurring pattern, the question then arises: Is it of little significance or is it what Giddens (1984, 10–3) would call one of the "cyclical practices" that reproduce the structures of our society? The answer really depends on how little boys "read" the outlawing of their warrior narratives. If they see it as simply one of the broad constraints of school against which they are continually negotiating, then perhaps it has no significance. If, on the other hand, it has in their minds a crucial connection to the definition of gender, to the creation of their own masculine identity, to where they position particular sites and practices on a masculine to feminine continuum, then the ostracism of warrior narratives may mean that they define the school environment as feminine.

There is considerable evidence that some primary school children do in fact make this categorization (Best 1983, 14–15; Brophy 1985, 118; Clark 1990, 36), and we suggest here that the outlawry of the masculine narrative contributes to this. Research by Willis (1977) and Walker (1988) in high schools has revealed a culture of resistance based on definitions of masculinity as *antagonistic* to the demands of the school, which are construed as feminine by the resisters. It might therefore seem plausible to see the underground perpetuation of the warrior narrative as an early expression of this resistance and one that gives some legitimacy to the resisters' claims that the school is feminine.

Is the school regime that outlaws the warrior narratives really feminine? We would argue, rather, that the regime being imposed is based on a male ideal, an outcome of the Enlightenment and compulsory schooling. Michel Foucault has pointed out that the development of this particular regime in schools coincided with the emergence of the prison, the hospital, the army barracks, and the factory (Foucault 1980, 55–57). Although teachers in the first years of school are predominantly female, the regime they impose is perpetuated by male teachers (Brophy 1985, 121), and this preference is endorsed by powerful and influential males in the society at large. The kind of demeanor and self-management that teachers are trying to inculcate in the early school years is the behavior expected in male-dominated public arenas like boardrooms, courtrooms, and union mass meetings.[3]

Connell (1989, 291) and Willis (1977, 76, 84) provide evidence that by adolescence, boys from all classes, particularly if they are ambitious, come to regard acquiescence in the school's demands as compatible with constructing a masculine identity. Connell writes:

> Some working class boys embrace a project of mobility in which they construct a masculinity organized around themes of rationality and responsibility. This is closely connected with the "certification" function of the upper levels of the education system and to a key

form of masculinity among professionals. (1989, 291)

Rationality and responsibility are, as Weber argued long ago, the primary characteristics of the modern society theorized by the Enlightenment thinkers as based on a social contract. This prized rationality has been converted in practice into a bureaucratized legal system where "responsible" acceptance by the population of the rules of civil society obviates the need for individuals to use physical violence in gaining their ends or protecting their rights, and where, if such violence is necessary, it is exercised by the state (Weber 1978, 341–354). In civil society, the warrior is obsolete, his activities redefined bureaucratically and performed by the police and the military.

The teacher in whose classroom our observation was conducted demonstrated a strong commitment to rationality and responsibility. For example, she devoted a great deal of time to showing that there was a cause and effect link between the behavior forbidden by her classroom rules and classroom accidents. Each time an accident occurred, she asked the children to determine the cause of the accident, its result, and how it could have been prevented. The implication throughout was that children must take responsibility for the outcomes of their actions.

Mac accidentally struck a boy, who was lying on the floor, in the head with a pram wheel. He was screaming around with a pram, the victim was playing on the Car Mat and lying down to obtain a bird's eye view of a car crash. Mac rushed past the group and struck Justin on the side of the head. Tears and confusion ensued. The teacher's reaction was to see to Justin, then stop all play and gain children's attention, speaking first to Mac and Justin plus Justin's group:

T. How did Justin get hurt?
M. [No answer]
T. Mac, what happened?
M. I was wheeling the pram and Justin was in the way.
T. Were you running?
M. I was wheeling the pram.

The teacher now addresses the whole class:
T. Stop working everyone, eyes to me and listen. Someone has just been hurt because someone didn't remember the classroom rules. What are they Harvey?
(Harvey was listening intently and she wanted someone who could answer the question at this point).
H. No running in the classroom.
T. Why?
Other children offer an answer.
Chn. Because someone will get hurt.
T. Yes, and that is what happened. Mac was going too quickly with the pram and Justin was injured. Now how can we stop this happening next time?
Chn. No running in the classroom, only walk. (February 10, 1993)

Malcolm, walking, bumped Winston on the head with a construction toy. The teacher intervened:
T. [To Malcolm and Winston] What happened?
W. Malcolm hit me on the head.
M. But it was an accident. I didn't mean it. I didn't really hurt him.
T. How did it happen?
M. It was an accident.
W. He [Malcolm] hit me.
T. Malcolm, I know you didn't mean to hurt Winston, so how did it happen?
M. I didn't mean it.
T. I know you didn't mean it, Malcolm, but why did Winston get hurt?
Chn. Malcolm was running.
M. No I wasn't.
T. See where everyone was sitting? There is hardly enough room for children to walk. Children working on the floor must remember to leave a walking path so that other children can move safely around the room. Otherwise someone will be hurt, and that's what has happened today. (February 23, 1993)

This public-sphere masculinity of rationality and responsibility, of civil society, of the social contract is not the masculinity that the boys are bringing into the classroom through their warrior narratives. They are using a different, much older version—not the male as responsible citizen, the producer and consumer who keeps the capitalist system going, the breadwinner, and caring father of a family. Their earliest vision of masculinity is the male as warrior, the bonded male who goes out with his mates and meets the dangers of the world, the male who attacks and defeats other males characterized as baddies, the male who turns the natural products of the earth into weapons to carry out these purposes.

We would argue, nevertheless, that those boys who aspire to become one of the brothers who wield power in the public world of civil society ultimately realize that conformity to rationality and responsibility, to the demands of the school, is the price they must pay. They realize that although the girls can expect one day to become the brides and mothers of their pretend games, the boys will never, except perhaps in time of war, be allowed to act out the part of warrior hero in reality.

On the other hand, the school softens the transition for them by endorsing and encouraging the classic modern transformation and domestication of the warrior narrative, sport (Connell 1987, 177; Messner 1992, 10–12). In the school where this observation was conducted, large playground areas are set aside for lunchtime cricket, soccer, and basketball; by the age of seven, most boys are joining in these games. The message is conveyed to them that if they behave like citizens in the classroom, they can become warriors on the sports oval.

Gradually, we would suggest, little boys get the message that resistance is not the only way to live out warrior masculinity. If they accept a public/private division of life, it can be accommodated within the private sphere; thus, it becomes possible for those boys who aspire to respectability, figuring in civil society as one of the brothers, to accept that the school regime and its expectations are masculine and to reject the attempts of the "resisters" to define it (and them) as feminine. They adopt the masculinity of rationality and responsibility as that appropriate to the public sphere, while the earlier, deeply appealing masculinity of the warrior narratives can still be experienced through symbolic reenactment on the sports field.

Conclusion

We are not, of course, suggesting that this is the only way in which the public/private division becomes part of the lived awareness of little boys. We do, however, believe that we have teased out one strand of the manner in which they encounter it. We have suggested that the classroom is a major site where little boys are introduced to the masculinity of rationality and responsibility characteristic of the brothers in civil society; we have been looking at a "cycle of practice" where, in classroom after classroom, generation after generation, the mode of masculinity typified in the warrior narratives is first driven underground and then transferred to the sports field. We are, we would suggest, seeing renegotiated for each generation and in each boy's own life the conception of the "social contract" that is characteristic of the era of modernity, of the Enlightenment, of democracy, and of capitalism. We are watching reenacted the transformation of violence and power as exercised by body over body, to control through surveillance and rules (Foucault 1977, 9; 1984, 66–67), the move from domination by individual superiors to acquiescence in a public sphere of decorum and rationality (Pateman 1988).

Yet, this is a social *contract*, and there is another side to the bargain. Although they learn that they must give up their warrior narratives of masculinity in the public sphere, where rationality and responsibility hold sway, they also learn that in return they may preserve them in the private realm of desire as fantasy, as bricolage, as a symbolic survival that is appropriate to the spaces of leisure and self-indulgence, the playground, the backyard, the television set, the sports field. Although this is too large an issue to be explored in detail here, there may even be a reenactment in the school setting of what Pateman (1988, 99–115) has defined as the sexual contract, the male right to dominate women in return for accepting the constraints of civil society. Is this, perhaps, established for both boys and girls by means of the endemic misogyny—invasion of girls' space (Thorne 1986, 172; 1993, 63–88), overt expressions of aversion and disgust (Goodenough 1987, 422; D'Arcy 1990, 81), disparaging sexual innuendo (Best 1983, 129; Goodenough 1987, 433; Clark 1990, 38–46)—noted by so many observers in the classrooms and playgrounds of modernity? Are girls being contained by the boys' actions within a more restricted, ultimately a private, sphere because, in the boys' eyes, they have not earned access to the public sphere by sharing their ordeal of repression, resistance, and ultimate symbolic accommodation of their gender-defining fantasies?

Notes

1. Some ethnographic studies describe a "tomboy" who wants to join in the boys' games (Best 1983, 95–97; Davies 1989, 93, 123; Thorne 1993, 127–129), although in our experience, such girls are rare, rarer even than the boys who play by choice with girls. The girls' rejection of the warrior narratives does not appear to be simply the result of the fact that the characters are usually men. Bronwyn Davies, when she read the role-reversal story *Rita the Rescuer* to preschoolers, found that many boys identified strongly with Rita ("they flex their muscles to show how strong they are and fall to wrestling each other on the floor to display their strength"), whereas for most girls, Rita remained "other" (Davies 1989, 57–58).

2. This would seem to reverse the usual parallel of outdoor/indoor with public/private. This further suggests that the everyday equation of "public" with "visible" may not be appropriate for the specialized use of the term in sociological discussions of the public/private division. Behavior in the street may be more visible than what goes on in a courtroom, but it is nevertheless acceptable for the street behavior to be, to a greater degree, personal, private, and driven by "desire."

3. There are some groups of men who continue to reject these modes of modernity throughout their lives. Andrew Metcalfe, in his study of an Australian mining community, has identified two broad categories of miner, the "respectable," and the "larrikin" (an Australian slang expression carrying implications of nonconformism, irreverence, and impudence). The first are committed to the procedural decorums of union meetings, sporting and hobby clubs, welfare groups, and so on; the others relate more strongly to the less disciplined masculinity of the pub, the brawl, and the racetrack (Metcalfe 1988, 73–125). This distinction is very similar to that noted by Paul Willis in England between the "ear'oles" and the "lads" in a working-class secondary school (Willis 1977). It needs to be noted that this is not a *class* difference and that demographically the groups are identical. What distinguishes them is, as Metcalfe points out, their relative commitment to the respectable modes of accommodation and resistance characteristic of civil society of larrikin modes with a much longer history, perhaps even their acceptance or rejection of the social contract.

References

Anyon, Jean. 1983. Intersections of gender and class: Accommodation and resistance by working-class and affluent females to contradictory sex-role ideologies. In *Gender, class and education*, edited by Stephen Walker and Len Barton. Barcombe, Sussex: Falmer.

Best, Raphaela. 1983. *We've all got scars: What girls and boys learn in elementary school*. Bloomington: Indiana University Press.

Bowles, Samuel, and Herbert Gintis. 1976. *Schooling in capitalist America: Educational reform and the contradictions of economic life*. London: Routledge and Kegan Paul.

Brophy, Jere E. 1985. Interactions of male and female students with male and female teachers. In *Gender influences in classroom interaction*, edited by L. C. Wilkinson and C. B. Marrett. New York: Academic Press.

Burgess, R. G., ed. 1984. *The research process in educational settings: Ten case studies*. Lewes: Falmer.

Chodorow, Nancy. 1978. *The reproduction of mothering: Psychoanalysis and the sociology of gender*. Berkeley: University of California Press.

Clark, Margaret. 1989. Anastasia is a normal developer because she is unique. *Oxford Review of Education* 15:243–255.

———. 1990. *The great divide: Gender in the primary school*. Melbourne: Curriculum Corporation.

Connell, R. W. 1987. *Gender and power: Society, the person and sexual politics*. Sydney: Allen and Unwin.
———. 1989. Cool guys, swots and wimps: The interplay of masculinity and education. *Oxford Review of Education* 15:291–303.
Crosset, Todd. 1990. Masculinity, sexuality, and the development of early modern sport. In *Sport, men and the gender order*, edited by Michael E. Messner and Donald F. Sabo. Champaign, IL: Human Kinetics Books.
D'Arcy, Sue. 1990. Towards a non-sexist primary classroom. In *Dolls and dungarees: Gender issues in the primary school curriculum*, edited by Eva Tutchell. Milton Keynes: Open University Press.
Davies, Bronwyn. 1989. *Frogs and snails and feminist tales: Preschool children and gender*. Sydney: Allen and Unwin.
Dinnerstein, Myra. 1977. *The mermaid and the minotaur: Sexual arrangements and human malaise*. New York: Harper and Row.
Duthie, J. H. 1980. Athletics: The ritual of a technological society? In *Play and culture*, edited by Helen B. Schwartzman. West Point, NY: Leisure.
Eisenstein, Hester. 1984. *Contemporary feminist thought*. London: Unwin Paperbacks.
Foucault, Michel. 1977. *Discipline and punish: The birth of the prison*. Translated by Alan Sheridan. New York: Pantheon.
———. 1980. Body/power. In *power/knowledge: Selected interviews and other writings 1972–1977*, edited by Colin Gordon. Brighton: Harvester
———. 1984. Truth and power. In *The Foucault reader*, edited by P. Rabinow. New York: Pantheon.
Genovese, Eugene E. 1972. *Roll, Jordan, roll: The world the slaves made*. New York: Pantheon.
Giddens, Anthony. 1984. *The constitution of society: Outline of the theory of structuration*. Berkeley: University of California Press.

Goodenough, Ruth Gallagher. 1987. Small group culture and the emergence of sexist behaviour: A comparative study of four children's groups. In *Interpretive ethnography of education*, edited by G. Spindler and L. Spindler. Hillsdale, NJ: Lawrence Erlbaum.
Hebdige, Dick. 1979. *Subculture: The meaning of style*. London: Methuen.
Messner, Michael E. 1992. *Power at play: Sports and the problem of masculinity*. Boston: Beacon.
Metcalfe, Andrew. 1988. *For freedom and dignity: Historical agency and class structure in the coalfields of NSW*. Sydney: Allen and Unwin.
Paley, Vivian Gussin. 1984. *Boys and girls: Superheroes in the doll corner*. Chicago: University of Chicago Press.
Pateman, Carole. 1988. *The sexual contract*. Oxford: Polity.
———. 1989. The fraternal social contract. In *The disorder of women*. Cambridge: Polity.
Thorne, Barrie. 1986. Girls and boys together . . . but mostly apart: Gender arrangements in elementary schools. In *Relationships and development*, edited by W. W. Hartup and Z. Rubin. Hillsdale, NJ: Lawrence Erlbaum.
———. 1993. *Gender play: Girls and boys in school*. New Brunswick, NJ: Rutgers University Press.
Walker, J. C. 1988. *Louts and legends: Male youth culture in an inner-city school*. Sydney: Allen and Unwin.
Walkerdine, Valerie. 1990. *Schoolgirl fictions*. London: Verso.
Weber, Max. 1978. *Selections in translation*. Edited by W. G. Runciman and translated by Eric Matthews. Cambridge: Cambridge University Press.
Willis, Paul. 1977. *Learning to labour: How working class kids get working class jobs*. Farnborough: Saxon House.

ARTICLE 10

Ritch C. Savin-Williams

Memories of Same-Sex Attractions

Recalling their childhood, gay/bisexual youths often report the pervasiveness of distinct, early memories of same-sex attractions. They remember particular feelings or incidents from as young as four or five years of age that, in retrospect, reflect the first manifestations of sexual orientation. These memories often comprise some of the youths' earliest recollections of their lives, present in some rudimentary form for many years before the ability to label sexual feelings and attractions emerges, usually after pubertal onset.[1]

Indeed, over 80 percent of the interviewed youths reported same-sex attractions prior to the physical manifestations of puberty. By the completion of puberty, all youths recalled attractions that they later labeled as "homosexual." Nearly half noted that their feelings for other males were some of their very first memories, present prior to beginning elementary school. Revelation for one youth came through his kindergarten naps: "Dreams of naked men and curious about them. Really wanting to look at them." Another youth was acting on his sexually charged feelings at age four: "I particularly remember an incident with a cousin in the bathroom and we both having hard-ons and feeling a tingling sensation when we rubbed against each other. I wanted to repeat it, and did!"

The origins of these feelings and their meanings are difficult to discern because prepubertal children are seldom asked if they have sexual attractions for other boys or girls. Thus, clinicians, educators, researchers, and other interested professionals must rely on retrospective data from adolescents and young adults. Although these later recollections may be distorted by an awareness of current sexual identity, they provide an invaluable source of information.

Gay/bisexual youths often recall a vague but distinct sense of *being different* from other boys. Indeed, characterizing most developmental models of sexual identity is an introductory stage in which an individual has an unequivocal cognitive and/or emotional realization that he or she is "different" from others. An individual may feel alienated from others with very little awareness that homosexuality is the relevant issue.[2] For example, sociologist and sex educator Richard Troiden proposes a coming-out model that begins with an initial sense that one is marginalized in conjunction with perceptions of being different from peers.[3] This undeniable feeling may be the first internal, emotional revelation of sexual orientation, although it is not likely to be perceived initially as sexual but rather as a strongly experienced sense of not fitting in or of not having the same interests as other boys/girls.

The existence of these early feelings implies that youths have both an awareness of a normative standard of how boys are supposed to act, feel, and behave and a belief that they violate this ideal. Troiden describes this conflation of feeling different and gender inappropriate:

> It is not surprising that "prehomosexuals" used gender metaphors, rather than sexual metaphors, to interpret and explain childhood feelings of difference. . . . Children do not appear to define their sexual experimentation in heterosexual or homosexual terms. The socially created categories of homosexual, heterosexual,

From *And Then I Became Gay* by Ritch Savin-Williams. Copyright © 1997. Reproduced by permission of Taylor & Francis/Routledge, Inc.

and bisexual hold little or no significance for them. (p. 52)

Retrospectively, the gay/bisexual youths interviewed for this book reported three somewhat overlapping sources as a basis for their initial awareness of differentness:

- a pervasive and emotional captivation with other boys that felt passionate, exotic, consuming, and mysterious;
- a strongly felt desire to engage in play activities and to possess traits usually characteristic of girls;
- disinterest or, in more extreme cases, a revulsion in typical boys' activities, especially team sports and rough-and-tumble physical play.[4]

These three sources are not mutually exclusive—many youths recalled instances of all three during their childhood. For example, one youth who felt apart and isolated during his childhood was obsessed with wanting to be around adult men, frequently developed crushes on male teachers, and spent considerable time with neighborhood girls, particularly enjoying their games of hopscotch and jump rope. He was called "sissy" and "girly" by other boys, and he detested team sports and all things athletic, especially locker rooms.

The prevalence of these three is difficult to determine because few researchers have systematically asked boys the relevant questions that probe these issues. It also bears noting that not all gay or bisexual individuals recall this sense of being different during childhood and adolescence and that these feelings and attractions are not solely the domain of sexual-minority youths. Heterosexual boys may also feel different, have same-sex attractions or desires, enjoy feminine activities, and avoid aggressive pursuits.

Youths interviewed for this book easily and at times graphically remembered these same-sex attractions that emanated from their earliest childhood memories. Despite the dramatic significance that these early homoerotic attractions would have, at the time they felt natural, omnipresent. Many recalled these attractions to other males by identifying concrete, distinct memories prior to first grade. Without great fanfare, with no clashing of cymbals, and with no abiding shock, later homoerotic attractions were felt to be contiguous with these early feelings.

Captivation with Masculinity

Of the three sources for feeling different, the vast majority of the gay/bisexual youths interviewed for this book attributed to themselves an early sense that in some fundamental way they differed from other boys. This difference was an obsession of always wanting to be near other males. Most boys did not at the time believe that these attractions were sexually motivated; they were just overwhelmed with an all-consuming desire to be with other males. Some became flushed or excited when they made contact, especially physical, with other boys or men; some arranged their lives so as to increase time spent with males, while others avoided males because they were frightened by the male aura. Above all else, their obsession with males was mysterious and pervasive. It was also present from an early age, from first memories.

One youth's childhood was one massive memory of men. He decided that the death of his father ten years earlier was the reason that he would always need guys in his life.

> I can remember wanting the men who visited us to hug me when I was real little, maybe three or four. I've always wanted to touch and be touched by guys, and I was a lot. Guys loved to manhandle me. They would throw me up in the air and I'd touch the ceiling and I'd scream and would love it and would do anything to make it happen more and more. It never was enough and I'd tire them out or I'd go to someone else who would toss me. Sometimes I would be teased for the "little points" [erections] in my pants, but no one, including myself, made much of it.
>
> I think I spent my childhood fantasizing about men, not sexually of course, but just being close to them and having them hold me or hug me. I'd feel safe and warm. My dad gave me this

and my older brother Mitchell gave me this but all of this was never enough. With the other men I'd feel flushed, almost hot. Maybe those were hot flashes like what women get! Those were good days.

Although he may have been an extreme case, other youths also recalled distinct attractions to men that a decade or more later were still vivid, emotional, and construed as significant. This obsession with males remained at the time nameless for the following three youths:

> I was seven at the time and Will, who was working for us doing yard work, was twenty-one and a college student/athlete. One night when my parents went to a hotel for their anniversary dinner and whatever, they asked Will to stay the night to watch over me. He was in a sleeping bag on the floor and I knew he was nude and he was next to my bed and I kept wondering what was in the sleeping bag. I just knew that I wanted to get in with him but I didn't know why or that I could because I didn't want to bother him. I didn't sleep the whole night.

> Maybe it was third grade and there was an ad in the paper about an all-male cast for a movie. This confused me but fascinated—intrigued—me so I asked the librarian and she looked all flustered, even mortified, and mumbled that I ought to ask my parents.

> It was very clear to me around six years of age. There was a TV beer commercial which featured several soccer players without shirts on. I mentioned to my brother how much I liked this TV show because the guys didn't have shirts on. I remember this but I'm sure I had thoughts before this.

Those who monopolized their attention were occasionally same-age boys, but were more often older teenagers and adults—male teachers, coaches, cousins, or friends of the family. Public male figures were also sources of fantasies—Superman, Scott Baio, Duran Duran, John Ritter, Bobby Ewing, and Hulk Hogan. Others turned pages in magazines and catalogs to find male models in various stages of undress; especially popular were underwear advertisements. The captivation with men had a familiar tone—a drive for male contact or the male image from an early age with little understanding of what it meant—and a common emotional quality—excitement, euphoria, mystery.

These same-sex attractions were not limited to gay boys. Bisexual youths recalled similar early homoerotic captivation with men.

> Technically it could be either male or female, no matter. I just was into naked bodies. I had access and took, without him knowing it, dad's *Penthouse* magazines. Such a big fuss, but actually in them and whatever else I could find, turned on by both the girls and the men. The men I recall most vividly. It was the hairless, feminine guys with big penises and made-up faces. I loved make-up on my guys, the eyelashes and the eyes, blue shadow, but mostly it was the look. Tight jeans, lean bodies.

Homoerotic desires were often interpreted as natural and hence characteristic of all boys. Many youths articulated that their desire for the "male touch" was deeply embodied in their natural self. By this they implied that their attractions to boys were not a matter of choice or free will but were of early and perhaps, they speculated, genetic origins. For example, one youth never felt that he had a choice regarding his intense attractions to adult males:

> My infatuation with my day camp counselor I didn't choose. Why him and not his girlfriend? I never chose my love objects but I was always attracted to guys. In all of my early dreams and fantasies I always centered on guys whether they were sexual or not. What I wanted to do was to get close to them and I knew that innately, perhaps even by the age of six or seven. I felt it was okay because God said it was okay.

Similarly, many other youths noted that their homoerotic desires were never a matter of choice but "just were." Most believed that they were gay or bisexual in large part because of genetic factors or the "way the cards were dealt—luck of the draw, like something in the neuro-structure or hormonal."

I'd dream of my uncle and wake up all euphoric and sweaty and eroticized. Another dream that I had at six was of my [boy] classmates playing around in their underwear with these big cocks sticking out. It just happened. How could I choose these things to dream about, to check out the cocks in my mom's *Playgirl*, and to cut out pictures of guys from movie magazines? I was very intrigued by all of this and knew somehow it related to me.

Maybe my child sex play taught me how to be gay but then maybe it only reinforced what already was. I know that I've been gay for a long time, probably I was born with it. I assumed when I was young that all people had a pee pee. It doesn't have to be genetic but then it could happen during the first year of life. I think I was born being gay, leaning toward homosexuality, and development just sort of pushed it further.

My brother is gay, my uncle is gay, my father acts like he is gay sometimes, and my mother is hanging out with feminist support groups and really butch-looking women. Did I really have a choice?!

I can't stand the smell of women. Who really cares? I could have gone straight but it would have been torture. I am what I am, from birth.

Some youths simply assumed, based on the egocentric principle that their thoughts and feelings were shared by others, that all boys must feel as they do but were simply not talking about their desires. With age, however, they came to realize that perhaps they were more "into it."

I guess I was pretty touchable—and I still am based on what guys I know or am with tell me. I didn't understand why because I thought all kids liked it. Others have told me that they liked it too but somehow I think I liked it more. I craved and adored it and my day would not be a good one unless I had this contact. Only later did I find out why I liked being touched by guys.

Another youth decided that he would simply "outgrow" his obsession with males. He was not, however, going to let this future keep him from enjoying this wonderful pleasure at the moment.

As a child I knew I was attracted to males. I was caught by my mother looking at nude photographs of men in her magazines and I heard my father say to her that, "He'll grow out of it," and so I thought and hoped I would. But until then I just settled back and enjoyed my keen curiosity to see male bodies.

You see, it did not feel threatening because (a) it felt great, and (b) father said I would grow out of it, and he was always right. So why not enjoy it until it went away?

Other youths, however, recognized that these undeniably homoerotic attractions were not typical of other boys. They knew they were extreme cases but they "could not help it."

Even at eight I could tell that my interest in guys was way beyond normal. Like this time that we were out with my friend Chad's big brother catching fireflies and he took off his shirt and I forgot about the fireflies and just stared at his chest. Chad got really irritated and called out, "Hey homo give me the jar!" I'm sure I blushed.

When we played truth-or-dare I always wanted to be dared to kiss one of the guys. No one ever dared me to do that, probably because they knew that I'd like it. And I would have! I knew it was strange of me and that they didn't want to kiss boys. They all knew that too but I really didn't care.

Eventually, most youths understood that these undeniable attractions were the wrong ones to have. Despite the belief that they had no choice in matters of their attractions, most inevitably came to appreciate that they should hide their attractions. Snide remarks made by peers, prohibitions taught by parents, and the silence imposed by religion and by teachers all contributed to this realization. Thus, although early obsessions with males were experienced as instinctive, most of the gay/bisexual youths acknowledged from an early age that their impulses were somehow "wrong" but not necessarily "bad."

Despite the presence of an older gay brother, one youth was vulnerable to society's negative messages about homosexuality. His concern centered on being "strike two" for his mother.

Well, I knew enough to hide Sean's *Jock* after I looked at it. It was not guilt—it was too much fun!—but fear that I felt. I was afraid if mother found out that she would feel bad that she had two failures and that Sean would kill me for getting into his stockpile.

Very few youths made the connection during their childhood that these attractions that felt so natural and significant placed them in the stigmatized category of "homosexual." Although most had a passing acquaintance with the concept and had seen "homosexuals" displayed in the media, relatively few would have situated themselves in this category at this point in their lives. One youth believed that "it" was something to be outgrown: "I thought maybe that it was just a stage that I was going through. But if it wasn't a stage then it was probably no problem for me to worry about now." Other youths, however, were worried.

> Something was different about me. I knew that. I was afraid of what it meant, and I prayed to God that whatever it was that He would take it away. It was a burden but I liked it, and so I felt guilty about liking it.

It was not until many years later, with the onset of sexual maturations that these attractions would be fully linked with sexuality and perhaps a sexual identity. Homosensuality for these youths was not foreign but natural, a lifelong intrigue with men's bodies. However, as the societal wrongness of their intuitive obsession with masculinity became increasingly apparent, many youths hoped that their attractions were a phase to be outgrown or that their feelings would make sense in some distant future.

The feared repercussions from family members and peers if they were known to have gay traits served as a powerful reason for the boys to feel that their same-sex desires and acts were improper and should not be shared with others. Acting on them was thought to be wrong because if caught, punishment would likely ensue. Balancing desire and fear became a significant dilemma. Eventually, many of the youths recognized that others rarely shared or understood their same-sex desires. This pact of secrecy with themselves was a major theme for many of the youths. It did not, however, always inhibit their sexual behavior; a significant number of the boys acted on their sexual desires during childhood. . . .

Acting Like a Girl

A second source of feeling different, not explicitly linked with same-sex attractions, involved cultural definitions of gender—how a boy should *not* act, think, and feel. Characteristics deemed not appropriate for boys included observable behaviors such as play with girl-typed toys, especially dolls; involvement in female activities and games; cross-dressing; sex-role motor behavior including limp wrists, high-pitched voices, and dramatic gestures; and stated interests such as wishing to be a girl, imagining self as dancer or model, and preferring female friends and being around older women. These boys did not wonder, "Why am I gay?" but "Why do I act like a girl?"[5] For example, one youth recalled his childhood in the following way:

> I knew that a boy wasn't supposed to kiss other boys, although I did. I knew it was wrong, so this must be some indication that I knew. I also knew that I wasn't supposed to cross my legs at the knees, but I wouldn't like quickly uncross my legs whenever that was the case. So this is certainly at a young age that I noticed this. I think I knew that it was sort of a female thing, sort of an odd thing, and I knew that boys weren't supposed to do that.

Many boys who fit the category of gender bending were at once erotically drawn to boys and men (the first source) but were repelled by their behavior, their standard of dress and cleanliness, and their barbarian nature. They felt ambivalent regarding their attractions to males; intrigued by male bodies and the masculinity mystique, these youths saw men as enigmatic and unapproachable.

Psychotherapist Richard Isay characterizes this sense of gender atypicality in some pregay boys: "They saw themselves as more sensitive than other boys; they cried more easily, had their feelings more readily hurt, had more aesthetic interests, enjoyed nature, art, and music, and were drawn to other 'sensitive' boys, girls, and adults" (p. 23).[6] Indeed, research amply demonstrates that gender nonconformity is one of the best childhood predictors of adult homosexuality in men.[7] Findings from prospective studies are fairly straightforward: The proportion of *extremely* feminine boys who eventually profess a same-sex sexual orientation approaches 100 percent. However, the fraction of these gender-nonconforming boys in the total population remains considerably below that of gay men. Thus, while the vast majority of extremely feminine boys eventually adopt a gay or bisexual identity in adulthood, so do an unknown number of boys who are not particularly feminine.

Feeling more similar to girls than to boys, one youth described his experience "as if I was from a different planet than other boys." He was not alone; a substantial proportion of the gay/bisexual youths recalled that this "girl-like syndrome" was the basis of how they differed from their male peers. Of all boys interviewed, over one-third described their self-image as being more similar to that of girls than boys, and nearly all of these boys reported that this sense of themselves permeated areas of their lives.

One consequence of having more culturally defined feminine than masculine interests was that many boys with gender-atypical characteristics felt most comfortable in the company of girls and women or preferred spending time alone. Two youths described their gender nonconformity during their childhood years.

I had mostly friends who were girls and I can remember playing jump rope, dolls, and hopscotch with them, and I can remember being very interested in hairstyling and practicing on dolls. I got into sewing and knitting. I played make-believe, read spy and adventure stories, house with my sisters. I had a purse and dolls that they gave me. We did everything together. I was never close with my brother and we never did anything together. I was always accepted by girls and few other boys were.

Thinking back I did play with girls in the neighborhood a lot. I loved actually to kiss girls and I was always wanting to kiss girls and I thought this might be a little strange or weird because I liked girls so much at such a young age. I just felt very comfortable with them. I felt more self-conscious around boys because I always wondered what they were thinking about.

The extent to which such behavior could produce a gender-bender who is accepted by girls as one of them is illustrated by a third youth:

I was even invited to slumber parties and I always went. They were so much fun! Just the five of us in our gowns, with lace and bows that my mom had made for my sister and I "borrowed," laughing, sneaking cigarettes, and gossiping about other girls.

Thus, almost without exception boys who displayed early gender-atypical behavior strongly preferred hanging out with girls rather than with boys. Girls were far less likely to reject the "feminine" boys, a reaction that has been confirmed by research studies.[8] If such youths had male friends it was usually one best friend, perhaps a neighbor who also disliked masculine activities.

I have always been gay although I did not know what that meant at the time. But I knew that I always felt queer, out of place in my hometown.... Mostly I spent my time alone in the house or with girls at school. We ate lunch together and talked in between classes. I always felt that girls received the short end of the stick. I really did not have many friends because I lived in a rural area. I felt rejected and I feared being rejected.

I have usually had one best male friend, who might change every other year or so but who always was like me in hating sports. Like Tim who was one of my best friends because he lived across the street and was handy, someone so I would not be alone. We spent time together but I am not sure what else we ever did. Otherwise I hung with girls.

Not uncommonly, boys who displayed interest in gender-atypical pursuits fervently expressed strong preferences for solo activities such as reading and make-believe games, or for artistic endeavors.

But my major activity during childhood was drawing and I was sort of known as "The Artist," even as early as third and fourth grades. Today I can see some very gay themes in my drawings! Whenever anyone in the class wanted anything drawn then they asked me. No matter how much they had ridiculed me I agreed to do it.

A second youth made up plays for the neighborhood, role-played TV characters, and cartooned.

I took part in dance, ballet, singing, and had good manners. I liked Broadway musicals, Barbra, Bette, Joan, Liz, Judy, and Greta . . . I did drama, lots and lots of drama! Anything pretend. I did lots of skits for the Mickey Mouse Club, play writing, and office decorating.

Unclear from these accounts is whether the decision to spend time alone was one freely chosen by the gay/bisexual youths or was a consequence of exclusion dictated by others. That is, were they loners by choice or by circumstance? Although most evidence supports the banishment hypothesis, time alone may have been desired and pursued for creative reasons; time alone may have enhanced their creative efforts. One youth found that he spent a lot of time "doing nothing, just being alone, playing the violin, planting flowers, and arranging flowers." Another youth loved "building and creating things like castles and bridges and rivers in the backyard. Maybe it was because I was an only child but I was into any kind of art and I also composed on the piano." When asked about his childhood activities, a third youth was merely succinct: "Shopped. Homework. Masturbated. Read."

Most difficult for many gender-atypical gay/bisexual boys was the almost universal harassment they received from their peers. As a consequence of associating with girls and not boys, spending considerable time alone, and appreciating female activities, they faced almost daily harassment from peers, usually boys but sometimes girls, teachers, parents, and siblings. Perhaps most insufferable to their male peers was the gay/bisexual boys' feminine gross and fine motor behavior. Their hand gestures, standing and sitting posture, leg and hip movement, voice pitch and cadence, and head tilt conveyed to others that these boys were girllike and hence weak and deplorable. The reactions they received from peers went beyond mere teasing, which most youths receive during childhood and adolescence as a mechanism for social bonding, to outright verbal abuse that was harassing and sometimes extremely destructive to a sense of self. The abuse was occasionally physically expressed and always had emotional and self-image consequences.

Below is a list of names that boys with gender-atypical characteristics reported that they were called by age mates. Not all youths recalled or wanted to remember the exact names.

- sissy
- queer
- gayson
- fruitcake
- schoolboy
- fairy
- girly
- wimp
- Tinkerbell

- clumsy
- little girl
- faggot
- wimpy
- pansy
- softy
- homo
- gay guy
- flamer

- bitchy
- cry baby
- super fem
- fruit
- gaylord
- girl
- cocksucker
- Avon Lady
- mommy's boy

- fag
- fem
- queer bait
- gay
- Janus
- fag boy
- lisp
- Safety Girl

One youth reported that in grammar school he was voted "The Person Most Likely to Own a Gay Bar."

The specific provocation that elicited these names during school, on the bus, and in the neighborhood varied, but several patterns are discernible. The abuse usually occurred because a boy was perceived as a misfit, as acting too much "like a girl." Three youths provided testimonies from their lives:

Because I was somewhat effeminate in my behavior and because I wore "girly" shoes. Some said that I was a little girl because I couldn't play baseball. I played the clarinet in school and this was defined as a female instrument so I got some teasing for that. I thought I could control my behavior but it got so bad that my family decided to pull me out of the public school to go to a private Catholic school where the teasing receded.

Because I was weak and a cry baby. I was not in the "in" crowd. Also because of the way I dressed and that I got good grades. I was very thin and got every disease that came around. I had all sorts of allergies and was always using all sorts of drugs. I was told I looked like a girl. I played with Barbies and taught her how to sit up and later how to fly. I just wasn't masculine enough I guess.

People thought that perhaps I might be gay because they thought I was just way too nice and also because I was flamboyant. They really didn't think I was like homosexually gay. It was just a term they used for me because it seemed to fit my personality. People said I'm gay because of my mannerisms, also because I slur my s's and I'm so flamboyant. I think it's the way that I walked, the way I talked, the way I carried myself. I had a soft voice. Lots of boys blew me kisses. My voice is just not masculine. Also I tended to be very giggly and flighty and flaky and silly at times.

One youth believed that "most kids were just looking for a laugh" and that he was the easiest target, because of his femininity, they could find. He was their "amusement for the day."

In no story were girls the only ones who verbally abused a youth for being gender nonconforming. On many occasions, however, boys acted alone. Perhaps the most usual pattern was for boys, or a subset of boys, to be the persistent ridiculers with a few girls chiming in when present.

Some of the jocks really bothered me but mostly it was these three guys every day making my life miserable. Always done by males who really had this pecking order. Real bullies!

This was mostly males—this one guy seemed to have it out for me. But some of the girls who hung out with him also did it. The girls thought I was bitchy and called me "fag" and "homo."

Although reactions to being victimized by peer ridicule were diverse, the most common responses, illustrated by three youths, were to ignore, withdraw, or cry.

I took it without saying anything back. I'd pretend that I didn't hear them or hide my feelings. I hated it but didn't say anything back. Guess I was benign to it. Just sat there and took it. I did that for protection. I was so much of a misfit that bullies did it to me. I offended them in some way. Just a horrible, wrenching experience.

I became more withdrawn and thus more of an outcast. I'd cower and keep my distance, keeping it inside myself. I did nothing or remained silent or said "leave me alone." Once I fought back and lost, which made me withdraw even more.

I was very, very sensitive and would cry very easily. I had very little emotional control at the time. Cry, yell at them, cry some more. I would tell my mother and cry and she'd try to comfort me or she'd just dismiss it all. I would tell the guys that I had told my mother and they would make more fun of me.

Not all boys reacted so passively to the verbal assault. Several developed innovative, self-enhancing ways to cope with peer harassment. For example, one youth noted an unusual situation:

All my boyfriends, the jock types, always protected me and punished those who teased me. I would just turn away as if I never gave notice because I knew that I would be protected by all the guys, the jocks, that I was having sex with. I never did try to get back at them [the harassers]. Once they realized this then they kept quiet.

Another used his intelligence and experience as strategies for coping with peer harassment.

I think it was because I was so flamboyant and I was not so sports-oriented. If they said it to my face then I would say "get out of my face!" Or I would point out their stupidity. I considered them to be rather stupid, so immature. I'd been around the world and I knew I could say things that would damage them because I was smarter than them and because I had so many female friends. I tried to ignore it because I knew that I was better than them. I sort of got respect for not fighting back or sometimes I would say, "I like girls! What's *your* problem?"

It is difficult to ascertain the true impact on a youth of this constant bombardment of negative peer review. Few of the boys thought it was anything but negative. Most felt that the most significant effect of the verbal harassment was what it did to their personality: They became increasingly withdrawn from social interactions, despondent, and self-absorbed. The aftermath for the four youths below was a decrease in their self-image and self-worth.

> I felt very conscious about my voice and somewhat shameful that I wasn't masculine enough. I actually just sort of retreated more and became more introverted. I felt rejected and it hurt my self-esteem. I took the ridicule to heart and I blamed myself.
>
> Because I knew that indeed I had the attractions to guys I knew that they were right and that I was a disgusting human being. I just spent a lot more time alone to avoid the pain. I just sort of blocked it all internally because it hurt so much. I just sort of erased all my memories of my childhood so I can't give you much detail.
>
> A real nightmare! I really felt like I had no friends. It really did lower my self-esteem and it made me focus on sort of my outer appearance and ignore the inner. It devastated me because I felt everything they said was true. I was quiet and kept it inside.
>
> Heightened my sense of being different. Caused me to withdraw and not feel good about myself. Cut off from people and became shy. Became introverted, guilty. I hated that time. Childhood was supposed to be happy times but it was not. Later, I dropped out of school, thought about suicide, and ran away from home.

Although none of the boys felt that the labeling made him gay, many believed that the name-calling contributed to their negative image of homosexuality. Hence, the ridicule became a central factor in who they are. The abuse also kept them in the closet for a considerably longer period of time. These effects are apparent in the two narratives below:

> It just sort of reinforced that men are scum. I viewed being a fag as so negative that it hurt my self-image for them to call me that. I didn't like myself, so being gay is bad and what they're saying I knew it to be true because I am bad and being gay is bad and I'm gay. It's made me think of males only as sex objects because I wanted to be hated by men because I didn't like myself. I started back in elementary school to believe it was true.
>
> I had such a hostile view towards homosexuality, so it was hard to come out as a result of this stigma because I had really low self-esteem. It affected me by not having a positive attitude about homosexuality in general. I needed at least a positive or even neutral point of view and that would have made my gay life so much easier. I continue to suppress things.

It was the rare youth for whom anything positive emerged from the verbal ridicule. One youth noted that "teasing sort of helped me to deal with my gay identity at a very early age because everyone was calling my attention to it." He was proud to be effeminate; he reported that the teasing made him stronger and was thus beneficial.

> I wore stylish clothes and was my own individual self. My teachers appreciated this but not the slobs. Because of this a lot of them said that I was gay and so I thought I must be, although I did not know what this meant except that it meant I would not be shoveling cow shit!

Unfortunately, few youths could recall such positive aspects to their gender atypicality. More often, the consequences of being true to their nature were that other boys viewed them as undesirable playmates and as "weird." Labeled sissy or effeminate, they were rejected by boys, and, equally important, they had little desire to fraternize with their male peers. Because other boys did not constitute an enjoyable or safe context for play or socializing, the youths often turned to girls for activities and consolation. They preferred to dance rather than shovel shit, to sing rather than yell "hike," and to draw rather than bash heads. Thus, childhood was usually experienced as a traumatizing time by youths who did not conform to cultural sex roles. The fortunate ones sought and found girls for solace and support. Girls became their saviors, offering sources of emotional sustenance as the male world of childhood became increasingly distasteful. It was to these girls that many gay/bisexual males subsequently disclosed their sexual affiliations during middle or late adolescence. . . .

Not Acting Like a Boy

A third source of feeling different among the interviewed youths originated from a disinterest or abhorrence of typical masculine activities, which may or may not have occurred in the presence of a captivation with masculinity (first source) or of high levels of femininity (second source). Thus, a lack of masculinity did not necessarily imply that such youths were fond of female activities or were drawn to or hung out with girls. Many reported never playing house, dressing up as a girl, or having a passing acquaintance with Barbie. In the absence of typical expressions of femininity, boys without masculine interests were usually loners or spent time with one or several best male friends.

Compared with what is known about gender-atypical boys, considerably less is known concerning those who during childhood do not fit cultural images of how a boy should act, think, and feel. Characteristics labeled as unmasculine or as failure to conform to gender expectations include observable behaviors such as avoidance of rough-and-tumble play, typical boys' games, and athletic activities; no imagining of oneself as a sports figure; and no desire to grow up to be like one's father. These boys did not wonder, "Why am I gay?" but "Why don't I act like a boy?"[9]

Childhood activities that constitute "unmasculine" all share the characteristic of being gender neutral by North American standards, suitable for both boys and girls. Within this gender non-partisanship, active and passive patterns were evident in the interviews. Some boys were as active as masculine-inclined peers but in nonmasculine, nonathletic—at least in a team sports sense—activities.

> My friend and me made roads and gardens. I liked to sort of build cities and bridges outside and in the garden. Played in the woods, hiked in the woods, camped out, and hide and seek. Ted and I were almost inseparable for a couple of years. I also biked, swam a lot, jumped on the trampoline. Biking was my way of dealing with stress. I was into matchbox cars.

> I enjoyed playing office, playing grow-up, walking around the city basically looking at other people. Mind games and chess with my brothers. Creative imaginative play. Discovering and enjoying spending a lot of time on bike trips, going to new places. Getting out of the house and being outside, just wandering off by myself.

More common were boys who spent considerable time alone pursuing passive activities. This passivity should not be equated, however, with having a bad time or having a bad childhood. Many recalled an enjoyable if unconventional life during childhood.

> At school I hung out with myself but on weekends it was primarily guys in the neighborhood and we would like watch TV and videos. They were like my best friends and we were not really into moving sports. We were more into passive activities like music and cards. I've always been in the band. Hanging out at the mall. A couple of us guys would do this.

> Very quiet pursuits, stamps, cooking, which my mother liked. Guess I played verbal games, board games with the family, Risk and Candyland, and crossword puzzles. Did a lot with my family, like family vacations, visiting historical things. I read, played with Lincoln Logs, fantasizing, spending time by myself, drawing, and swinging. I loved the freedom of the swing and I'd do it for hours. Oh yes, I loved croquet!

> I read a lot—like the encyclopedia, the phone book, science fiction, science, mystery, and

gothic novels. I had a comic book collection and Star Wars cards. I spent most of my other time drawing maps. I was really into getting any information anywhere I could, even from the atlas or an almanac. I can remember actually setting out to read the dictionary, although I don't think I got very far. Almost every book in the public library later on.

Most explicitly, unmasculine youths felt particularly ill at ease with archetypal male sports, especially loathing team sports such as baseball, basketball, and football. If they became involved in competitive, aggressive sports it was in response to family or peer pressure. Perhaps forced by a father or coach to participate in sports as a right fielder, a defensive back, or a bench warmer, they deeply resented such coercion and their inevitable failure. Severely repulsed by many typical masculine pursuits, this source of trauma was to be avoided at all costs, even at the price of disappointing parents. Unmasculine youths often shared with the following very gender-atypical youth his rejection of masculine activities and hence of masculinity.

> I did not play basketball or wrestle and I was not a farmer nor a slob nor did I shovel cow shit like my classmates. Girl, they would come in smelling like they looked and you can be sure it was not a number Chanel ever heard of! There was no way that I was going to let this be a part of what I wanted for my life.

> Well they [parents] wanted me to try at least one sport but I was always sort of the last chosen. I knew I was effeminate and clumsy and my father ridiculed me for it. So I avoided sports and I did this by going home for lunch and visiting my female friends rather than playing sports with the other guys during recess.

For one youth, the appeal or even logic of sports baffled and befuddled him.

> I really did not care about most sports and I still do not. I liked more intellectual than physical things. I enjoyed more talking philosophy, writing poetry, and drawing than spending time throwing stupid balls away, then running after the stupid balls, trying to find the stupid balls, and then throwing the stupid balls back to the same person so that he could throw it away again and have somebody run after it, find it, and throw it back to him again. Sounds real intelligent does it not?! Doing these stupid ball tricks made Bill [twin brother] real popular and me really unpopular. Where is the fairness in that?

> I only played sports during recess when I had to. I hated little boy games such as basketball, kickball, football, baseball, or anything that had a ball or a peck order. It was very aggressive and used all of the wrong parts of my anatomy and my personality.

The most aversive aspect of sports was its aggressive, dominant, physical nature. One youth remarked that in sports someone always has to lose—"and it was usually me!" This reflected not only his own personal experience of losing but also an antipathy to his life philosophy of peace, harmony, cooperation. Another youth astutely recognized another reason not to become involved in sports—his true nature might emerge and become figuratively and physically visible.

> I was not on any team sport because I was so self-conscious about being around other males. I was afraid of how I might be looked upon by them and what I might do or say or look at if I was around them a lot. What would I do in the locker room? What would happen to "George," who has a mind of his own? Maybe my feelings might come out and then where would I be?

Other youths reported that they wanted to participate in sports but could not because of physical problems. One noted, "I could never much be a sports person because I had a coordination problem because of my vision that caused me to be physically awkward." Another compensated by reading about sports: "Well, I read the sports pages and sports books! I hated gym because I was overweight. I could not do sports because I felt so evil watching men strip naked in the locker room and I couldn't take it." A third youth was on the swim team before getting pneumonia, forcing him to quit. His restitution was to remain active: "I hung out at the beach (yes, looking at the guys!), played Atari, skateboarded, and played Pogo."

Those who became involved in sports almost preferred individual to team sports. These "jocks" included the two youths below.

> Some track, cross-country, swimming. I never liked the team sports. I had to do soccer in fourth grade because my best friends were into it but I disliked it immensely. Guess I was mid-level in ability and lower than that in interest but it gave me something to do and kept me around guys. I lived in a very sex-segregated rural area. I gave all of these up in junior high, except swimming in the Scout pool.
>
> I was really into sports. Let's see. Gymnastics in fourth to sixth grades; bowling in third; darts in third; ping pong whenever; dodge the ball in second to fourth; volleyball in sixth.

Perhaps because of their paltry athleticism and low levels of masculine interests, these boys were not immune to peer ridicule and teasing. They were not, however, ridiculed nearly to the degree that gender-noncomforming boys were. They were often teased for non-gender-related characteristics or for individualized perceived deficits in physical features ("fatty"), in normative masculine behavior ("wimp"), or in desirable kinds of intelligence ("nerd"). Some were also called names more typical of effeminate youths ("fag") without, they almost universally acknowledged, the connotation of sexuality. One youth defended himself by asserting, "Being called a fag really was not a sexual thing. It was more that it reflected on my low self-esteem and that I was so wimpy."

The most common name callers were same-age, same-sex peers, although occasionally girls also participated. One youth had an unusual experience. Called "nerd" by three girls who were making his life miserable, "several boys seemed to go out of their way to protect me and shield me from this kind of teasing. Of course I was giving them answers on their exams!" Otherwise he simply withdrew. Because ridicule was seemingly random and seldom daily, it was sometimes difficult for unmasculine youths to understand what provoked the name calling.

One youth reported that he enjoyed his life as a loner and that others seemed more upset than he was that he was spending so much time alone. With his involvement in computers, the complaints lessened, perhaps, he guessed, because others envied his knowledge and saw it as a means to earn a good living. He was subject, however, to the taunts of male peers. Occasionally he was ridiculed by several boys on the school bus and during recess for reasons that were beyond his control.

> At first I didn't understand why they were on my case, but since I didn't fit in in a lot of ways, they had their way. It was just the usual thing. Probably because I wasn't good at sports but I can't remember what I was called. In gym classes primarily by macho males. Nothing I didn't want to remember. I really can't remember too much of it or certainly not the names. It just seemed like I was teased about as much as anyone else was. Not every day, maybe once a month, and I just sort of reacted passively. Never really a major thing or very threatening, just sort of stupid kids' stuff. Just sort of let it go away.
>
> I didn't fit in because I was against the intellectualism of the smart kids and I wasn't a jock. Hence I was not respected. I have no real memories of the exact names but I think they weren't happy ones because I was thin and, oh yes, my ears stuck out so I was called "monkey face."

The name-calling message might be that the boy was too feminine or not masculine enough, but more commonly it was because he was simply different or had undesirable characteristics. Very few felt that being gay was a cause of the verbal abuse. The following youths recounted the reasons they believed they suffered at the hands of their peers.

> I was awkward and wore glasses. I had a speech impediment and a birthmark. I was ostracized, sort of left out because I wasn't conforming and I was very shy. I was sort of known as an only

child and thus a spoiled brat with very little social skills. I was never teased about being gay.

For being fat and overweight. Maybe I was teased more than average. It did hurt. I reacted by just crying because I really couldn't ignore it. It was a weight issue and not a sexual identity issue.

Because I was quiet, shy, and geekish. For being physically awkward, being different, bookish. As a kid I was teased for having cow eyes because my eyes were large. For not going to church. Very low-class assholes, mostly males. Then I went to a school for gifted children and it stopped.

I was ridiculed about being a softy and brain box because I was so intellectual or consumed in the books. They said I got good grades because I was kissing teachers' asses. I think I was just different from all of them and the teachers liked me because I liked learning. Perhaps it happened because I went to an all-male Catholic school.

I was shy and I got called Spock a lot because of my eyes which were real dark. They thought I was wearing eye shadow.

The most common response of the youths was to remain silent. One youth felt scared and frightened but "later it just got to be an annoyance. My response was to remain rather stoic." Another hated gym because he was not "graceful" and because of a particular nemesis.

A classic case of one guy on my case which I usually ignored. But one day he threw me to the gym floor but a guy came to my rescue. He was bigger than me so my reaction was basically to brave it, to try to show that it did not affect me by just walking away. I would usually not talk back and I would not cry.

A second common response was to simply avoid situations where one might be ridiculed. This was not always an easy task.

Being not good at sports, I tried to avoid all sporting situations if at all possible. I just felt like I was left out of everything. I sort of internalized it but I can't really remember how I reacted. I dreaded going to the gym. I was afraid and felt that I was bullied. I was not verbally equipped to deal with this kind of teasing. I really didn't fight back until high school.

A third response, somewhat less prevalent, was to feel extremely hurt and cry, either publicly or in private. One youth grew to hate and fear school. "It was very painful and I was upset by it and I cried. In fact, so much so I didn't want to go to school." Another cried in private.

I was teased for being very heavy and for being slow. I reacted by being very hurt; I couldn't accept it. I cried a lot, not in front of them but in the bathroom or my room. My out was always, "Well, I'm smart."

Finally, several youths reported that they surprised their tormentors by behaving in a very masculine way, fighting back against the name-calling.

I rode the bus. I felt singled out and ridiculed. Initially what I did was simply relax and ignore it but then at one point I actually fought back, physically and verbally attacking sort of the main person who was ridiculing me the most. If I did fight back, which was the case occasionally, I would usually win. Because it was a small school, the word got out and after that I had no problems. I gained in popularity and the teasing tapered off to almost nothing.

There were rumors about me being gay. I got teasing when my friend told others that we had slept together. I confronted these people but it didn't help. I ended up going back at others or attacking them. I confronted them, "Why are you so interested in my sexuality?" After awhile they left me alone. I denied being gay but I knew I was. I wasn't ashamed but I wanted the ridiculing to stop. I was very wicked to others.

The immediate effects of the ridicule are difficult to determine. However, based on their reports, consequences appear far less severe than they were for youths who enacted femininity, perhaps because the ridicule was not as frequent and did not focus on a central aspect of their sexuality. For example, one youth noted that the name-calling had no repercussion on his sexuality because he did not interpret the ridicule as emanating from his unconventional sexuality. He did not feel that the abuse made him gay or caused him to delay self-identifying as gay. He felt, however, that the ridicule contributed to this tendency to withdraw from social settings, causing him to be more introverted and self-effacing.

> It had no real implications for my sexual identification. Everybody in my school was teased; everyone was called faggot, so I really didn't feel like I was singled out. But it made me trust people less. Hurt my self-esteem. I still need to be liked by others and if not, it upsets me. Maybe why I spent so much time alone. People hurt you. On the good side, I developed good sarcastic skills and a dry wit.

Including those who had many feminine characteristics during childhood, as many as three-quarters of the gay/bisexual youths interviewed had few interests or characteristics usually attributed to men in North American culture. Being *neither* particularly masculine *nor* feminine resulted in youths occupying the middle rung of the peer-group status hierarchy. When not alone, they were usually with a best buddy or a small group of male friends with whom they spend considerable time. Although they were seldom as frequently ridiculed by peers as were youths who were gender atypical in their lifestyle, such youths still faced verbal abuse, usually from same-age boys. The personal characteristics that became targets of abuse were notably analogous to those that heterosexual boys also receive teasing about if they are "unconventional": physical features, personality characteristics, and intelligence. Similar to other gay/bisexual youths, however, most recalled early, intense, natural attractions to other boys and men.

Acting Like a Boy

Not all of the gay/bisexual boys felt different from peers, acted in gender-atypical ways, expressed effeminate gestures and postures, or disliked team sports during their childhood. One in ten was masculine in appearance, behavior, and interests—nearly indistinguishable from their childhood masculine heterosexual peers. Although these relatively rare boys recalled, in retrospect, that they might have had "nonsexual" attractions to males during early childhood, they had few memories of *sexual* attractions to girls, boys, or anything else. Now, however, they believe that their same-sex attractions have always been a natural part of who they are.

Many of these youths reminisced that as children they chased girls, but this was more of a game that they joined with other boys than a statement about their sexuality or their true sexual interests. As adolescents they were simply disinterested in sexual relations with girls, in being emotionally intimate with girls, or in developing romantic relationships with girls. Most never fantasized about girls. The gay youths with masculine characteristics often had difficulty articulating precisely what it was about sexuality that excited them. Many failed to recall any prepubertal sexual or erotic attractions; thus, in some respects, they appeared to be asexual, especially during the years preceding adolescence. One youth reported "a vague sense that although I did not desire intimate relations with girls, I was not sure what I wanted." Unsure of how they "became gay," the youths characterized their life before puberty as "sexless" and as deeply invested in masculine activities, especially sports.

One youth, who would later run track and play high-school baseball and football, remembered his childhood as his "glory years." Girls were not an integral part of his life.

> As a child I used to run a lot, just everywhere I could, and play tag, swimming, kickball, and softball. Loved making forts. Building blocks, Legos, war games. Just like my best buddy, which changed from time to time, well at least every year I would develop a best buddy, and it was always the best looking guy in my class who was my best friend—always an athlete. I hung around totally guys.

> Maybe I just did not have time but I was not into sex. I would have to say that I was sexless because I cannot remember any sexual thoughts. I

was not interested in girls even though I had several girlfriends. In general I felt left out of what my teammates said they were going through.

When asked during the interview to elaborate *any* aspect of his childhood sexuality, he drew a blank. He had many stories of athletic exploits but no sexual ones. Years after pubertal onset he discovered his sexuality and expressed wonderment regarding the location of his sexual desires during childhood.

Similar to this youth, others appeared in most respects to be the traditional, heterosexual boy next door. This was especially evident in their play activities and partners. They enjoyed their popularity with other boys, and they often developed a best friendship with another boy, usually a teammate on a sports team. One swimmer noted that the time he spent "with Jared and the other guys on the swim team was the happiest time of my life."

The sports acumen of these youths was equal or superior to many of their heterosexual peers. However, a distinct bias existed in terms of liking and participating in individual rather than team sports. While many played competitive team sports, their participation appeared more obligatory as an important aspect of male culture than a real choice. Their true love was more apparent in individual sports, especially swimming, track, tennis, and wrestling. Similar to other gay/bisexual youths, many disliked the aggressive, competitive nature of team sports.

> For Dad I did baseball—and it wasn't that I was bad, because I made the team and started—but I just couldn't get into it. Like I refused to slide because I was afraid I'd hurt the other guy, and I was just not going to go crashing into fences to catch a ball! I didn't like being challenged at sports because I was afraid I wasn't good enough so I went into individual sports like tennis, track, and swimming. Dad and I reached a compromise with my track, especially when I won the state 1000M.

> As a child I really liked horseplay, tag, and wrestling. I have to admit that I hated the Little League but as a kid I played Little League for five years, usually at second base. Later tennis, two years of which were on varsity and I lettered. Also track and lifted weights. I was accepted by everyone, but the baseball guys who were so cutthroat; every game was the end of the universe for them!

As a result of their peer status, few of these boys were teased by others. When they were, it was usually within the context of normative male bonding—teasing in good humor. Although relatively few heard references to being gay, they nonetheless dreaded such accusations. One youth feared that his friends would notice his head turning when a good-looking guy passed by.

In contrast to the gay/bisexual youths previously discussed, masculine youths by disposition looked and acted like other boys their age, participated in typical masculine pursuits, and "fooled" peers into believing that they were heterosexual. They claimed no memories of homoerotic or even sexual attractions during childhood, perhaps, one might speculate, because the realization that the true objects of their sexual desires were boys would have caused them considerable grief and confusion. They were often perceived to be social butterflies and they actively engaged in male–male competitive sports, although their preference was individual sports. Their male friendships were critical to maintain; they wanted and needed to be members of the "male crowd." From all appearances they succeeded in creating a facade of heterosexuality, in being accepted as "one of the guys."

Reflections on the Childhood of Gay/Bisexual Youths

From an early age, the vast majority of the gay/bisexual youths believed that they were different from other boys their age and that regardless of the source of this feeling, it was a natural, instinctual, and omnipresent aspect of themselves. The pattern that most characterized the youths' awareness, interpretation, and affective responses to childhood attractions consisted of an overwhelming desire to be in the company of men. They wanted to touch, smell, see, and hear masculinity. This awareness originated from earliest childhood memories; in this sense, they "always felt gay."

Most ultimately recognized, however, that these feelings were not typical of other boys and that it would be wrong or unwise to express them because of family and peer prohibitions. Others simply assumed that all boys felt as they did and could not understand why their friends were not as preoccupied as they were with homoerotic desires. Although these attractions may have felt natural, the youths were told by parents, friends, religious leaders, teachers, and dogma that such desires were evil and sinful. Many knew that their homosensuality was ill-advised, but they did not thus conclude that it made them sick or immoral.

Beyond this common pattern, two other sources of "feeling different" characterized the vast majority of the gay/bisexual youths. Many were dominated by an overwhelming sense that their difference was attributed to their feminine appearance, behavior, and interests. In many respects these characteristics typify the stereotype that many, gay and nongay alike, have of gay males. Youths so feminized felt natural and true to self, despite the fact that their gender noncomformity was frequently and severely punished with ostracism. Most of these youths detested cultural definitions of masculinity and felt at odds with other boys because they did not share their peers' interest in team sports, competition, and aggressive pursuits. Being an outcast in the world of male peers was usually felt to be unfair and unnecessary, but also inevitable. To avoid becoming expatriated, these boys developed friendships with girls, perhaps because of common interests such as attractions to boys and appreciation of the arts, creativity, clothing, and manners. They felt more comfortable and had greater comradery with girls than with boys. Few wanted to change either their genitalia or their behavior; they did not view themselves as women in disguise—they were simply repulsed by the "grossness" of masculinity and attracted to the sensitivities of femininity.

Other youths failed to duplicate standard masculine characteristics without necessarily assuming feminine traits. In this they may well have resembled heterosexual peers who were also neither particularly masculine nor feminine in behavior. They differed, however, in the direction of their sexual attractions. Being disinterested in team sports and other typical aggressive and competitive pursuits caused them to feel unmasculine, but they did not thus necessarily construe themselves as feminine. Relatively few spent time with girls or participated in girl games. Rather, their activities can be characterized as "appropriate" for either girls or boys.

Many of these youths felt that they simply faded into the background when with peers. Most were loners for a considerable period during their childhood; when they socialized with peers they were usually with one or two male friends. Although they were spared the vicious, pervasive verbal abuse that their effeminate counterparts received during childhood, they were not immune from harassment. Boys still ridiculed them for their physical features, lack of ability in athletic pursuits, and unconventional behavior or intelligence.

In contrast to these gay/bisexual youths was a much smaller group of youths who were nearly indistinguishable from masculine heterosexual boys their age. Constituting at least one of every ten youths interviewed, their participation in typical masculine pursuits, especially individual and team sports, blended them into the fabric of male culture. Many were socially active and one might speculate that their male friendships were an enjoyable sublimation of homoerotic attractions that they only later, often during adolescence or young childhood, recognized. Their failure to recognize any sexual feelings during childhood could be attributed to the direction their sexual attractions might take if they were allowed into consciousness. In this respect, their psychic investment was to conceal this secret from themselves and others.

Unknown is the etiology of these patterns and their long-term effects on other aspects of development, including participation in sexual activities, self-recognition of a sexual identity, disclosure of that identity to others, romantic relationships with other males, and developing a positive sense of self.

Although several of the interviewed youths experienced same-sex attractions as arising abruptly and unexpectedly, for the vast majority these feelings emerged as gradual, inevitable, and not particularly surprising. In this sense, these findings are at odds with the theme of this book—diversity in developmental patterns. Few if any youths believed that they could control the direction of their sexual feelings and no youth believed that he ultimately chose his sexual orientation or sexual attractions. The incorporation of the various masculine and feminine behavioral patterns was felt by youths to be less a matter of choice than an experienced naturalness that was derived from their biological heritage and, less commonly, from early socialization processes beyond their control. On his emerging sexuality, one youth reflected, "It was like being visited by an old friend." This awareness may have emerged early or late, surfaced gradually or arrived instantaneously, felt normal or wrong, motivated sexual activity or abstinence—but it was one aspect of the self that was present without invitation. Future development [. . .] was simply an unfolding of that which was already present, with puberty playing a crucial turning point for many youths in clarifying for them that their homosensuality had a sexual component. From this awareness often loomed first sexual encounters, which occurred during the earliest years of childhood or waited until young adulthood. They too were interpreted by the youths in diverse ways, thus having a differential impact on the eventual incorporation of a gay or bisexual identity.

Notes

1. See early account in A. P. Bell, M. S. Weinberg, and S. K. Hammersmith (1981), *Sexual Preference: Its Development in Men and Women* (Bloomington, IN: Indiana University Press). For data on gay youths see G. Herdt and A. Boxer (1993), *Children of Horizons: How Gay and Lesbian Teens Are Leading a New Way Out of the Closet* (Boston: Beacon) and R. C. Savin-Williams (1990), *Gay and Lesbian Youth: Expressions of Identity* (New York: Hemisphere).

2. J. Sophie presents a synthesis of coming-out models in her 1985–1986 article, "A Critical Examination of Stage Theories of Lesbian Identity Development," *Journal of Homosexuality, 12,* 39–51.

3. Revised in his 1989 article, R. R. Troiden, "The Formation of Homosexual Identities," *Journal of Homosexuality, 17,* 43–73. Additional empirical evidence is available in references in note 1 and B. S. Newman and P. G. Muzzonigro (1993), "The Effects of Traditional Family Values on the Coming Out Process of Gay Male Adolescents," *Adolescence, 28,* 213–226, and S. K. Tellijohann and J. P. Price (1993), "A Qualitative Examination of Adolescent Homosexuals' Life Experiences: Ramifications for Secondary School Personnel," *Journal of Homosexuality, 26,* 41–56.

4. For a comprehensive review of this literature see J. M. Bailey and K. J. Zucker (1995), "Childhood Sex-Typed Behavior and Sexual Orientation: A Conceptual Analysis and Quantitative Review," *Developmental Psychology, 31,* 43–55.

5. For a review of studies using these measures, see note 4 and J. M. Bailey (1996), "Gender Identity," in R. C. Savin-Williams and K. M. Cohen (Eds.), *The Lives of Lesbians, Gays, and Bisexuals: Children to Adults,* pp. 71–93 (Fort Worth, TX: Harcourt Brace); R. Green (1987), *The "Sissy Boy Syndrome" and the Development of Homosexuality* (New Haven: Yale University Press); G. Phillips and R. Over (1992), "Adult Sexual Orientation in Relation to Memories of Childhood Gender Conforming and Gender Nonconforming Behaviors," *Archives of Sexual Behavior, 21,* 543–558; and B. Zuger (1984), "Early Effeminate Behavior in Boys: Outcome and Significance for Homosexuality," *Journal of Nervous and Mental Disease, 172,* 90–97.

6. From R. A. Isay (1989), *Being Homosexual: Gay Men and Their Development* (New York: Farrar Straus Grove).

7. See sources in notes 1 and 4.

8. Experimental evidence is supplied in K. J. Zucker, D. N. Wilson-Smith, J. A. Kurita, and A. Stern (1995), "Children's Appraisals for Sex-Typed Behavior in their Peers," *Sex Roles, 33,* 703–725.

9. See references in notes 4 and 5.

The Puerto Rican Dummy and the Merciful Son

Martín Espada

I have a four-year-old son named Clemente. He is not named for Roberto Clemente, the baseball player, as many people are quick to guess, but rather for a Puerto Rican poet. His name, in translation, means "merciful." Like the cheetah, he can reach speeds of up to 60 miles an hour. He is also, demographically speaking, a Latino male, a "macho" for the twenty-first century.

Two years ago, we were watching television together when a ventriloquist appeared with his dummy. The ventriloquist was Anglo; the dummy was a Latino male, Puerto Rican, in fact, like me, like my son. Complete with pencil mustache, greased hair, and jawbreaking Spanish accent, the dummy acted out an Anglo fantasy for an Anglo crowd that roared its approval. My son was transfixed; he did not recognize the character onscreen because he knows no one who fits that description, but he sensed my discomfort. Too late, I changed the channel. The next morning, my son watched Luis and María on *Sesame Street*, but this was inadequate compensation. *Sesame Street* is the only barrio on television, the only neighborhood on television where Latino families live and work, but the comedians are everywhere, with that frat-boy sneer, and so are the crowds.

However, I cannot simply switch off the comedians, or explain them (how do you explain to a preschooler that a crowd of strangers is angrily laughing at the idea of *him*?). We live in western Massachusetts, not far from Springfield and Holyoke, hardscrabble small cities that, in the last generation, have witnessed a huge influx of Puerto Ricans, now constituting some of the poorest Puerto Rican communities in the country. The evening news from Springfield features what I call "the Puerto Rican minute." This is the one minute of the newscast where we see the faces of Puerto Rican men, the mug shot or the arraignment in court or witnesses pointing to the bloodstained sidewalk, while the newscaster solemnly intones the mantra of gangs, drugs, jail. The notion of spending the Puerto Rican minute on a teacher or a health care worker or an artist in the community never occurs to the television journalists who produce this programming.

The Latino male is the bogeyman of the Pioneer Valley, which includes the area where we live. Recently, there was a rumor circulating in the atmosphere that Latino gangs would be prowling the streets on Halloween, shooting anyone in costume. My wife, Katherine, reports that one Anglo gentlemen at the local swimming pool took responsibility for warning everyone, a veritable Paul Revere in swim trunks wailing that "The Latinos are going to kill kids on Halloween!" Note how 1) Latino gangs became "Latinos" and 2) Latinos and "kids" became mutually exclusive categories. My wife wondered if this warning contemplated the Latino males in her life, if this racially paranoid imagination included visions of her professor husband and his toddling offspring as gunslingers in full macho swagger, hunting for "gringos" in Halloween costumes. The rumor, needless to say, was unfounded.

Copyright © 1998 by Martín Espada. Reprinted by permission of the author.

From *Muy Macho: Latino Men Confront Their Manhood* Ray Gonzalez, ed. New York: Anchor Books, 1996, pp. 75–90.

Then there is the national political climate. In 1995, we saw the spectacle of a politician, California Governor Pete Wilson, being seriously considered for the presidency on the strength of his support for Proposition 187, the most blatantly anti-Latino initiative in recent memory. There is no guarantee, as my son grows older, that this political pendulum will swing back to the left; if anything, the pendulum may well swing farther to the right. That means more fear and fury and bitter laughter.

Into this world enters Clemente, which raises certain questions: How do I think of my son as a Latino male? How do I teach him to disappoint and disorient the bigots everywhere around him, all of whom have bought tickets to see the macho pantomime? At the same time, how do I teach him to inoculate himself against the very real diseases of violence and sexism and homophobia infecting our community? How do I teach Clemente to be Clemente?

My son's identity as a Puerto Rican male has already been reinforced by a number of experiences I did not have at so early an age. At age four, he has already spent time in Puerto Rico, whereas I did not visit the island until I was ten years old. From the time he was a few months old, he has witnessed his Puerto Rican father engaged in the decidedly nonstereotypical business of giving poetry readings. We savor new Spanish words together the same way we devour mangos together, knowing the same tartness and succulence.

And yet, that same identity will be shaped by negative as well as positive experiences. The ventriloquist and his Puerto Rican dummy offered Clemente a glimpse of his inevitable future: Not only bigotry, but his growing awareness of that bigotry, his realization that some people have contempt for him because he is Puerto Rican. Here his sense of maleness will come into play, because he must learn to deal with his own rage, his inability to extinguish the source of his torment.

My father has good reason for rage. A brown-skinned man, he learned rage when he was arrested in Biloxi, Mississippi, in 1950, and spent a week in jail for refusing to go to the back of the bus. He learned rage when he was denied a college education and instead struggled for years working for an electrical contractor, hating his work and yearning for so much more. He learned rage as the political triumphs of the 1960s he helped to achieve were attacked from without and betrayed from within. My father externalized his rage. He raged at his enemies and he raged at us. A tremendous ethical and cultural influence for us nonetheless, he must have considered himself a failure by the male career-obsessed standards of the decade into which I was born: the 1950s.

By adolescence, I had learned to internalize my rage. I learned to do this, not so much in response to my father, but more in response to my own growing awareness of bigotry. Having left my Brooklyn birthplace for the town of Valley Stream, Long Island, I was dubbed a spic in an endless torrent of taunting, bullying, and brawling. To defend myself against a few people would have been feasible; to defend myself against dozens and dozens of people deeply in love with their own racism was a practical impossibility. So I told no one, no parent or counselor or teacher or friend, about the constant racial hostility. Instead, I punched a lamp, not once but twice, and watched the blood ooze between my knuckles as if somehow I could leech the poison from my body. My evolving manhood was defined by how well I could take punishment, and paradoxically I punished myself for not being man enough to end my own humiliation. Later in life, I would emulate my father and rage openly. Rarely, however, was the real enemy within earshot, or even visible.

Someday, my son will be called a spic for the first time; this is as much a part of the Puerto Rican experience as the music he gleefully dances to. I hope he will tell me. I hope that I can help him handle the glowing toxic waste of his rage. I hope that I can explain clearly why there are those waiting for him to explode, to confirm their stereotypes of the hot-blooded, bad-tempered Latino male who has, without provocation, injured the Anglo innocents. His anger—and that anger must come—has to be controlled, directed, creatively channeled, articulated—but not all-consuming, neither destructive nor self-destructive. I keep it between the covers of the book I write.

The anger will continue to manifest itself as he matures and discovers the utter resourcefulness of bigotry, the ability of racism to change shape and survive all attempts to snuff it out. "Spic" is a crude expression of certain sentiments that become subtle and sophisticated and insidious at other levels. Speaking of crudity, I am reminded of a group organized by white ethnics in New York during the 1960s under the acronym of SPONGE: The Society for the Prevention of the Niggers Getting Everything. When affirmative action is criticized today by Anglo politicians and pundits with exquisite diction and erudite vocabulary, that is still SPONGE. When and if my son is admitted to school or obtains a job by way of affirmative action, and is resented for it by his colleagues, that will be SPONGE, too.

Violence is the first cousin to rage. If learning to confront rage is an important element of developing Latino manhood, then the question of violence must be addressed with equal urgency. Violence is terribly seductive; all of us, especially males, are trained to gaze upon violence until it becomes beautiful. Beautiful violence is not only the way to victory for armies and football teams; this becomes the solution to everyday problems as well. For many characters on the movie or television screen, problems are solved by *shooting* them. This is certainly the most emphatic way to win an argument.

Katherine and I try to minimize the seductiveness of violence for Clemente. No guns, no soldiers, and so on. But his dinosaurs still eat each other with great relish. His trains still crash, to their delight. He is experimenting with power and control, with action and reaction, which brings him to an imitation of violence. Needless to say, there is a vast difference between stegosaurus and Desert Storm.

Again, all I can do is call upon my own experience as an example. I not only found violence seductive; at some point, I found myself enjoying it. I remember one brawl in Valley Stream when I snatched a chain away from an assailant, knocked him down, and needlessly lashed the chain across his knees as he lay sobbing in the street. That I was now the assailant with the chain did not occur to me.

I also remember the day I stopped enjoying the act of fistfighting. I was working as a bouncer in a bar, and found myself struggling with a man who was so drunk that he appeared numb to the blows bouncing off his cranium. Suddenly, I heard my first echo: *thok*. I was sickened by the sound. Later, I learned that I had broken my right ring finger with that punch, but all I could recall was the headache I must have caused him. I never had a fistfight again. Parenthetically, that job ended another romance: the one with alcohol. Too much of my job consisted of ministering to people who had passed out at the bar, finding their hats and coats, calling a cab, dragging them in their stupor down the stairs. Years later, I channeled those instincts cultivated as a bouncer into my work as a legal services lawyer, representing Latino tenants, finding landlords who forgot to heat buildings in winter or exterminate rats to be more deserving targets of my wrath. Eventually, I even left the law.

Will I urge my son to be a pacifist, thereby gutting one of the foundations of traditional manhood, the pleasure taken in violence and the power derived from it? That is an ideal state. I hope that he lives a life that permits him pacifism. I hope that the world around him evolves in such a way that pacifism is a viable choice. Still, I would not deny him the option of physical self-defense. I would not deny him, on philosophical grounds, the right to resistance in any form that resistance must take to be effective. Nor would I have him deny the right to others, with the luxury of distance. Too many people in this world still need a revolution.

When he is old enough, Clemente and I will talk about matters of justification, which must be carefully and narrowly defined. He must understand that abstractions like "respect" and "honor" are not reasons to fight in the street, and abstractions like "patriotism" and "country" are not reasons to fight on the battlefield. He must understand that violence against women is not acceptable, a message which will have to be somehow repeated every time another movie trailer blazes the art of misogyny across his subconscious mind. Rather than sloganizing, however, the best way I can communicate that message is by the way I treat his mother. How else will he know that jealousy is not love, that a lover is not property?

Knowing Katherine introduced me to a new awareness of many things: compassion and intimacy, domestic violence and recovery. Her history of savage physical abuse as a child—in a Connecticut farming community—compelled me to consider what it means to heal another human being, or to help that human being heal herself. What small gestures begin to restore humanity?

When the Leather Is a Whip

At night,
with my wife
sitting on the bed,
I turn from her
to unbuckle
my belt
so she won't see
her father
unbuckling
his belt

Clemente was born on December 28, 1991. This was a difficult birth. Katherine's coccyx, or tailbone, broken in childhood, would break again during delivery. Yet only with the birth could we move from gesture to fulfillment, from generous moments to real giving. The extraordinary healing that took place was not only physical but emotional and spiritual as well. After years of constant pain, her coccyx bone set properly, as if a living metaphor for the new opportunity represented by the birth of this child.

White Birch

Two decades ago rye whiskey
scalded your father's throat,
stinking from the mouth
as he stamped his shoe
in the groove between your hips,
dizzy flailing cartwheel down the stairs.

The tail of your spine split,
became a scraping hook.
For twenty years a fire raced
across the boughs of your bones,
his drunken mouth a movie
flashing with every stabbed gesture.

Now the white room of birth is throbbing:
the numbers of palpitating red on the
    screen of machinery
tentacled to your arm; the oxygen mask
    wedged
in a wheeze on your face; the numbing
    medication
injected through the spine.
The boy was snagged on that spiraling bone.

Medical fingers prodded your raw pink
    center
while you stared at a horizon of water
no one else could see, creatures leaping
    silver
with tails that slashed the air
like your agonized tongue.

You were born in the river valley,
hard green checkerboard of farms,
a town of white birches
and a churchyard from the workhorse time,
weathered headstones naming women
drained of blood with infants coiled inside
the caging hips, hymns swaying
as if lanterns over the mounded earth.

Then the white birch of your bones,
resilient and yielding, yielded again,
root snapped as the boy spilled out of you
into hands burst open by beckoning
and voices pouring praise like water,
two beings tangled in exhaustion,
blood-painted, but full of breath.
After a generation of burning
the hook unfurled in your body,
the crack in the bone dissolved:
One day you stood, expected again

the branch of nerves
fanning across your back to flame,
and felt only the grace of birches.

Obviously, my wife and son had changed me, had even changed my poetry. This might be the first Puerto Rican poem swaying with white birch trees instead of coconut palms. On the other hand, Katherine and I immediately set about making this a Puerto Rican baby. I danced him to sleep with blaring salsa. Katherine painted *coquís*—tiny Puerto Rican frogs—on his pajamas. We spoon-fed him rice and beans. He met his great-grandmother in Puerto Rico.

The behavior we collectively refer to as "macho" has deep historical roots, but the trigger is often a profound insecurity, a sense of being threatened. Clemente will be as secure as possible, and that security will stem in large part from self-knowledge. He will know the meaning of his name.

Clemente Soto Vélez was a great Puerto Rican poet, a fighter for the independence of Puerto Rico who spent years in prison as a result. He was also our good friend. The two Clementes met once, when the elder Clemente was eighty-seven years old and the younger Clemente was nine months. Fittingly, it was Columbus Day, 1992, the five-hundredth anniversary of the conquest. We passed the day with a man who devoted his life and his art to battling the very colonialism personified by Columbus. The two Clementes traced the topography of one another's faces. Even from his sickbed, the elder Clemente was gentle and generous. We took photographs, signed books. Clemente Soto Vélez died the following spring, and eventually my family and I visited the grave in the mountains of Puerto Rico. We found the grave unmarked but for a stick with number and letter, so we bought a gravestone and gave the poet his name back. My son still asks to see the framed photograph of the two Clementes, still asks about the man with the long white hair who gave him *his* name. This will be family legend, family ritual, the origins of the name explained in greater and greater detail as the years pass, a source of knowledge and power as meaningful as the Book of Genesis.

Thankfully, Clemente also has a literal meaning: "merciful." Every time my son asks about his name, an opportunity presents itself to teach the power of mercy, the power of compassion. When Clemente, in later years, consciously acts out these qualities, he does so knowing that he is doing what his very name expects of him. His name gives him the beginnings of a moral code, a goal to which he can aspire. "Merciful": Not the first word scrawled on the mental blackboard next to the phrase "Puerto Rican male." Yet how appropriate, given that, for Katherine and me, the act of mercy has become an expression of gratitude for Clemente's existence.

Because Clemente Means Merciful

—*for Clemente Gilbert-Espada
February 1992*

At three AM, we watched
the emergency room doctor
press a thumb against your cheekbone
to bleach your eye with light.
The spinal fluid was clear, drained
from the hole in your back,
but the X ray film
grew a stain on the lung,
explained the seizing cough,
the wailing heat of fever:
pneumonia at the age
of six weeks, a bedside vigil.
Your mother slept beside you,
the stitches of birth still burning.
When I asked, "Will he be OK?"
no one would answer: "Yes."
I closed my eyes and dreamed
my father dead, naked on a steel table
as I turned away. In the dream,
when I looked again,
my father had become my son.

So the hospital kept us: the oxygen mask,
a frayed wire taped to your toe
for reading the blood,
the medication forgotten from shift to shift,

a doctor bickering with radiology over the
    film,
the bald girl with a cancerous rib removed,
the pediatrician who never called, the
    yawning intern,
the hospital roommate's father
from Guatemala, ignored by the doctors
as if he had picked their morning coffee,
the checkmarks and initials of five AM,
the pages of forms flipping like a deck of
    cards,
recordkeeping for the records office,
the lawyers and the morgue.

One day, while the laundry
in the basement hissed white sheets,
and sheets of paper documented dwindling
    breath,
you spat mucus, gulped air, and lived.
We listened to the bassoon of your lungs,
the cadenza of the next century, resonate.
The Guatemalan father
did not need a stethoscope to hear
the breathing, and he grinned.
I grinned too, and because Clemente
means merciful, stood beside the
    Guatemalteco,
repeating in Spanish everything
that was not said to him.

I know someday you'll stand beside
the Guatemalan fathers,
speak in the tongue
of all the shunned faces,
breathe in a music
we have never heard, and live
by the meaning of your name.

Inevitably, we try to envision the next century. Will there be a men's movement in twenty years, when my son is an adult? Will it someday alienate and exclude Clemente, the way it has alienated and excluded me? The counterculture can be as exclusive and elitist as the mainstream; to be kept out of both is a supreme frustration. I sincerely do not expect the men's movement to address its own racism. The self-congratulatory tone of that movement drowns out any significant self-criticism. I only wish that the men's movement wouldn't be so *proud* of its own ignorance. The blatant expropriation of Native American symbols and rituals by certain factions of the movement leaves me with a twitch in my face. What should Puerto Rican men do in response to this colonizing definition of maleness, particularly considering the presence of our indigenous Taíno blood?

I remember watching one such men's movement ritual, on public television, I believe, and becoming infuriated because the drummer couldn't keep a beat. I imagined myself cloistered in a tent with some Anglo accountant from the suburbs of New Jersey, stripped to the waist and whacking a drum with no regard for rhythm, the difference being that I could hear Mongo Santamaría in my head, and he couldn't. I am torn between hoping that the men's movement reforms itself by the time my son reaches adulthood, or that it disappears altogether, its language going the way of Esperanto.

Another habit of language that I hope is extinct by the time Clemente reaches adulthood is the Anglo use of the term "macho." Before this term came into use to define sexism and violence, no particular ethnic or racial group was implicated by language itself. "Macho," as employed by Anglos, is a Spanish word that particularly seems to identify Latino male behavior as the very standard of sexism and violence. This connection, made by Anglos both intuitively and explicitly, then justifies a host of repressive measures against Latino males, as our presence on the honor roll of many a jail and prison will attest. In nearby Holyoke, police officers routinely round up Puerto Rican men drinking beer on the stoop, ostensibly for violating that city's "open container" ordinance, but also as a means of controlling the perceived threat of macho volatility on the street. Sometimes, of course, that perception turns deadly. I remember at age fifteen, hearing about a friend of my father's, Martín "Tito" Pérez, who was "suicided" in a New York City jail cell. A grand jury determined that it is possible for a man to hang himself with his hands cuffed behind him.

While Latino male behavior is, indeed, all too often sexist and violent, Latino males in this country are in fact no worse in that regard than their Anglo counterparts. Arguably, European and European-American males have set the world standard for violence in the twentieth century, from the Holocaust to Hiroshima to Vietnam.

Yet, any assertiveness on the part of Latino males, especially any form of resistance to Anglo authority, is labeled macho and instantly discredited. I can recall one occasion, working for an "alternative" radio station in Wisconsin, when I became involved in a protest over the station's refusal to air a Spanish-language program for the local Chicano community. When a meeting was held to debate the issue, the protesters, myself included, became frustrated and staged a walkout. The meeting went on without us, and we later learned that we were *defended*, ironically enough, by someone who saw us as acting macho. "It's their culture," this person explained apologetically to the gathered liberal intelligentsia. We got the program on the air.

I return, ultimately, to that ventriloquist and his Puerto Rican dummy, and I return, too, to the simple fact that my example as a father will have much to do with whether Clemente frustrates the worshippers of stereotype. To begin with, my very *presence*—as an attentive father and husband—contradicts the stereotype. However, too many times in my life, I have been that Puerto Rican dummy, with someone else's voice coming out of my mouth, someone else's hand in my back making me flail my arms. I have read aloud a script of cruelty or rage, and swung wildly at imagined or distant enemies. I have satisfied audiences who expected the macho brute, who were thrilled when my shouting verified all their anthropological theories about my species. I served the purposes of those who would see the Puerto Rican species self-destruct, become as rare as the parrots of our own rain forest.

But, in recent years, I have betrayed my puppeteers and disappointed the crowd. When my new sister-in-law met me, she pouted that I did not look Puerto Rican. I was not as "scary" as she expected me to be; I did not roar and flail. When a teacher at a suburban school invited me to read there, and openly expressed the usual unspoken expectations, the following incident occurred, proving that sometimes a belly laugh is infinitely more revolutionary than the howl of outrage that would have left me pegged, yet again, as a snarling, stubborn macho.

My Native Costume

When you come to visit,
said a teacher
from the suburban school,

don't forget to wear
your native costume.

But I'm a lawyer,
I said.
My native costume
is a pinstriped suit.

You know, the teacher said,
a Puerto Rican costume.

Like a guayabera?
The shirt? I said.
But it's February.

The children want to see
a native costume,
the teacher said.

So I went
to the suburban school,
embroidered guayabera
short sleeved shirt
over a turtleneck,
and said, Look kids,
cultural adaptation.

The Puerto Rican dummy brought his own poems to read today. *Claro que sí*. His son is always watching.

ARTICLE 12

Pat Mahony

Girls Will Be Girls and Boys Will Be First

In this chapter I explore some of the underlying themes and negative consequences of the ways that the "underachievement of boys" are currently being expressed. My argument is not that the education of boys is unimportant but that the assumptions and purposes underpinning the current obsession with their academic performance are misconceived. As a consequence, key questions concerning the role of schools in the social construction of masculinities are omitted; the practices and consequences of different masculinities in relation to women become invisible; and the effects on different groups of boys of the internal orderings of masculinities are obscured. In relation to the last and sensitized by recent work on women and social class (Mahony and Zmroczek 1997), there is, for example, a great deal of work to be done in identifying how boys from working-class backgrounds are subordinated by the practices, values, and conceits of white, middle-class modes of masculinity. This chapter is critical of the way that the debates about boys are currently being expressed while welcoming the fact that after generations of breaking their bodies by providing fodder for coal mines, factories, and battlefields, serious questions are being forced on us about the education of working-class boys.

At the present time, a number of interdependent issues and themes tumble over each other, coalesce around and find expression in current concerns about boys. The "problem" emerges differently in different countries depending on how issues inherent in the restructurings of patriarchal capitalism are being perceived, experienced, and responded to. In order to trace such themes, I look first at the different and sometimes contradictory claims made in relation to the "evidence" on the underachievement of boys. Next, I place the concern with academic achievement within the wider context of the changing global economy which is framing the education and social policies of national governments. In this I consider the effects of the restructuring of capitalism and some patriarchal investments in and anxieties about these. I move on to explore some of the negative consequences of the English response to these wider changes before moving on to draw out some of the dilemmas involved both in current policy and in proposals for change.

Noisy Data

First, it is important to note that Michèle Cohen's work (1996: 8–9) demonstrates that the preoccupation with masculinity is not new:

> The question then, is not why there was an anxiety about masculinity at a specific time, say the eighteenth century, but how the anxiety about masculinity is articulated at any particular historical moment—or geographical space.

Second, it is interesting to note that the current preoccupation with the "what about the boys?" debate is not confined to the United Kingdom. Heard from an international perspective, there is a din of anxiety but with enough variations on a theme to alert us to the possibility that a number of concerns are gathering round this one issue. Only in some countries is the examination performance of boys being played in a major key and even here, there are conflicting claims about which

Reprinted from *Failing Boys?*, D. Epstein, J. Elwood, V. Hey, & J. Maw (eds.), pp. 37–55, Open University Press 1998. Copyright © Pat Mahony. Reprinted by permission.

groups of boys are underachieving, in which curriculum areas, at which level of qualification, according to which definitions of underachievement, and according to what evidence.

In Australia, Martin Mills and Bob Lingard (1997: 278) describe the debate as developing in response to the claim that girls were outperforming boys in the public exam held at the end of secondary schooling. They suggest that closer analysis of the data revealed that:

> a small group of mainly middle class girls are now performing as well as, and thus challenging, the dominance of middle class boys in the high status, "masculinist" subjects such as Maths, Chemistry and to a lesser extent Physics.

In another article they alert us to the existence of "a particular version of masculinity politics" which is "a recuperative, reactionary politics which seeks to reassert male dominance and traditional sex roles and in some manifestations is explicitly anti-feminist, even misogynist" (Lingard and Mills 1997: 4).

In England, the problem has been defined by the Chief Inspector of Schools as "the failure of boys and in particular white working class boys" (Pyke 1996: 2). In this case the evidence does not support the claim that boys *per se* are underachieving once we move beyond the public examinations at 16 plus. In relation to A level, for example, Patricia Murphy and Jannette Elwood (1998: 19) point out that, "whilst males continue to outperform females in mathematics, males now outperfom females in English." In fact, as Arnot, David, and Weiner (1996) demonstrate, male students continue to achieve higher performances in relation to their entry than female students in nearly all subjects.

Odette Parry's discussion of Caribbean examination results adds a further dimension to the debate. She cites evidence from the World Bank claiming that "females do better than males at both primary and secondary levels of schooling" (Parry 1996: 2–3). She goes on to note that "subject choices follow the traditional pattern with girls highly visible in arts and boys in science."

When she compares English grade results with physics we find that "81.4% of the grade one (English) results were taken by females and 60.7% of the grade one physics went to males." These figures bear a striking resemblance to patterns of gender-segregated achievement identified in the United Kingdom in the 1980s (Mahony 1985). However, at the time, such data was taken as signifying the "underachievement of girls." Seen in its historical context, similar evidence is being used across time and place to signify opposite conclusions. This raises a separate but related issue.

When the focus was on the alleged underachievement of girls, it took a good deal of persuasion by (mainly) feminists before policy makers would look beyond the innate capacities of girls themselves for explanations of "failure" in maths and science. Such responses have not figured highly in relation to the "underachievement of boys" though, inflamed by racist accounts of intelligence, they may lurk behind some teachers' explanations of the achievement gap "between the Black and white boys in this school" (MA student's statement in class). By and large what was once evidence of the problem *of* girls has now become, not even the problem *of* boys but the problem *for* boys. The first casualty is that many of the gains made for girls, such as sensitivity to the messages contained in course materials, are increasingly being eroded as the belief takes hold that "girls have had it too good for too long" (Barber 1994: 2). Some educationists argued in the 1980s that these messages matter, not because of any causal relationship between girls' achievement and images in textbooks (if this had been the case girls would never have succeeded in anything), but because the images were degrading and distorting in portraying boys as adventurous and active while girls dripped around waiting for the first opportunity to serve them (Moys 1980). I will return to this point later but for the moment we need only to note that "achievement" and "underachievement" like other relational concepts, drifts into finer and finer specificity the more data becomes available. We could commit the rest of our lives in trying to find out which boys are underachieving, in relation to whom, in what areas, when, in which countries and why. Or we could ask another question. Why is there such a concern, even an obsession with academic achievement in the first place? I shall now go on to locate this obsession within the rise of the "competition state." This in turn has generated a whole variety of education policy reforms within which the "underachievement of boys" can be partly (but not entirely) understood.

Education and the Global Community

The "underachievement of boys" has to be seen in part within a broader context of change.

> As the world is characterised by increasing interpenetration and the crystallisation of transnational markets and structures, the state itself is having to act more and more like a market player, that shapes its policies to promote, control, and maximise returns from market forces in an international setting. (Cerny 1990: 230)

In the United Kingdom (as elsewhere) the preoccupation with increasing the competitiveness of the nation state plc in the global economy is pervasive and although the precise contribution of schooling to such competitiveness is controversial, the belief that national prosperity depends on high levels of knowledge and skill (one of the principles of microeconomic reform) is clearly presumed in the major educational policy documents of governments as far apart as Australia or New Zealand and the United Kingdom (Grace 1991; Knight et al. 1994).

In England it is a belief which is evident in the education policies of the Labour government (albeit set alongside a new concern with inequality):

> The Government's policy decisions, and the framework within which the DfEE [Department for Education and Employment] operates, will be shaped by powerful economic, social and technological forces. We believe the most important are:
>
> - globalisation—new opportunities and risks in an increasingly global economy where goods, services, capital and information are highly mobile and success depends more and more on the skills of the workforce. (DfEE 1997a)

Within this and in the words of David Blunkett, the Secretary of State for Education:

> We are talking about investing in human capital in the age of knowledge. To compete in the global economy, to live in a civilised society and to develop the talents of each and every one of us, we will have to unlock the potential of every young person. (DfEE 1997b: 3)

In this respect there has been little change in government policy from the former Conservative government in which competition in the global economy clearly underpinned the school effectiveness movement and defined the priorities of schooling. As the Chief Executive of the Teacher Training Agency (the body responsible for teacher training in England) put it:

> everyone is now agreed that the top priority in education is the need to raise pupils' standards of learning. . . . And there is a widespread awareness that, in a competitive world, constant progress is necessary just to maintain parity with other nations. (Millett 1996)

Finally, as has been argued elsewhere (Hextall and Mahony 1998), it has provided a dominant theme within the Teacher Training Agency's (TTA) reconstruction of what it means to teach and of what constitutes career progression in teaching.[1]

At the time of writing, it is too early to identify the continuities and discontinuities in the recently elected Labour government's policies but the former Conservative government's strategy for levering up standards of achievement in school is well known. In pursuit of global competitiveness, the drive to school effectiveness was directly tied to the National Curriculum and judged in accordance with criteria derived from it, mediated through performance indicators of published league tables of examination results and inspection reports. In a context of competition between schools for students, academic achievement becomes highly visible and even heightened through such mechanisms as parental choice and "measures" of individual teacher effectivity while explanations of, and solutions to, underachievement proliferate. Individual students or groups of students (such as boys) thus become crucial in determining the overall academic performance of schools, geared to the demands of the competition state. Since the demands of the global economy have become one of the major new plausibilities in Britain, it is worth noting (Mahony and Moos 1997: 12) that the Danish Minister for Education, Ole Vig Jensen has been very direct in rejecting a model of education based on the economic rationalism underpinning so much of recent education policy in the United Kingdom: "Our educational system shall not be a product of a global educational race without thinking of the goals and ideals we want in Denmark." But the "global race" is not the end of the story.

Lean, Mean, and Flexible

If one driving force in policy reform has been the need to increase "effectiveness" then the other two of the "virtuous three Es of economy, efficiency, and effectiveness" (Pollitt 1993: 59) have involved the need to reduce public expenditure. To this end new public management (NPM) or New Managerialism has been introduced across all parts of the UK public sector, in most OECD countries (Shand 1996) and may even be having an impact further afield in countries such as Pakistan and Kenya (Davies 1994). There is increasing evidence that different countries and sectors have introduced NPM in different ways according to their diverse historical and cultural traditions (Ferlie et al. 1996). For example, changes in the United Kingdom have been marked in particular ways by the influence of the New Right and their nostalgia for a fictitious age when "traditional values" were beyond question and by a particularly hard version of market liberalism. Broadly conceived, NPM in the United Kingdom is viewed as a way of dispersing the management, reporting and accounting approaches of the public sector and modeling them by different degrees along the lines of "best," i.e. "efficient," commercial practice.

The imperative to reduce public expenditure marks a change of view in which public spending, for example, on unemployment benefit, is no longer seen as an entitlement of citizens or as a social investment but as an unproductive cost. Such expenditure becomes identified as a drain on the public purse along with those who "consume" it. Here the call for a highly skilled labour force connects with the demonization of the "work shy" in the need for an increased inculcation of the work ethic. The slide from "unemployment" to an assumption of "unemployability" easily passes unnoticed giving rise to the assumption that the conditions creating both are the same. Today's underachieving boy stands at the brink of tomorrow's unemployed youth in the form of public burden number one. I shall return later to say more about the labour market, but for the moment I want to pick up another strand of the argument.

Me Tarzan, You Jane

One of the issues in the movement towards various forms of NPM is how the values and motivations of particular powerful groups of white, male elites (Hutton 1995) have connected with the "efficiency fetish" (Lingard 1995). Such men are powerful within the transnational organizations such as the World Bank as well as influencing policy in or behind national governments and their departments.

Within a restructuring of capitalism the patriarchal cage seems to have been rattled by a belief that men are losing economic ground to women. There is indeed an issue emerging in some areas of the labour market which, as I shall suggest later, forms a significant element in the concerns about "underachieving" boys. But for white male elites the "natural order" is not about to be overturned and any panic in that direction is unfortunately unwarranted with women constituting fewer than 5 percent of senior management in the United Kingdom and United States (2 percent in Australia), 5 percent of UK Institute of Directors and less than 1 percent of chief executives (Collinson and Hearn 1996).

Weiner et al. (1997: 13) note that when it was newly formed in 1995, appointments to the Department for Education and Employment were "overwhelmingly male at all senior levels despite the fact that the Secretary of State was a woman." In an age of the calculative frameworks of managerialism, it would be pertinent to know whether these DfEE officials mirror the new generation of economics graduates described in Pusey's study of government restructuring in Canberra (1991), for as Prue Hyman (1994: 33–4) argues:

> free rider behaviour (selfish unwillingness to pay for public goods) was more prevalent in economics graduates . . . selfish behaviour in an experimental game was more common both among economics majors than others and among men than women.

It would also be interesting to know how far they reject offensive modes of management-speak "full of lurid gender terminology: thrusting entrepreneurs, opening up virgin territory, aggressive lending, etc." (Connell 1993: 614) and how far the sexualized discourse of management has connected for male managers in education with the "pre-pubescent boy's fantasy of being 'big,' one's potency being judged according to the size of one's budget" (Hoggett 1996: 15).

Collinson and Hearn (1996: 3–4) suggest that the 1990s has brought an increased evaluation of managers and their performance, one criterion being "the masculinist concern with personal power and the ability to control others and self." They too argue that conventional managerial discourse has become redolent with highly (hetero) sexualized talk of "penetrating markets" and "getting into bed with suppliers/customers/competitors."

Given the restructuring of the public sector in line with "best commercial practice," it is not surprising to find similar versions of masculinism in evidence. According to Clarke and Newman (1997: 70):

many public sector organisations have taken on images of competitive behaviour as requiring hard, macho or "cowboy" styles of working. It is as if the unlocking of the shackles of bureaucratic constraints has at last allowed public sector managers to become "real men," released from the second-class status of public functionaries by their exposure to the "real world" of the market place.

There are other indications that while capitalism has fiddled, patriarchy has burned, even without the help of the efficiency fetish or its first cousin, the achievement fetish. This provides further evidence that the economic argument is not the only or indeed a sufficient explanatory framework for understanding the current concern about boys. In Denmark anxieties have been expressed about the demise of the "Real Man":

> The newest tendencies in Denmark support the statement that: "Real men are a scarce commodity," and that boys ought to be allowed to be more "macho" . . . Projects aimed at and for boys are being initiated in kindergartens at a rate unheard of up to now, because the predominantly women staff have been exposed to a good deal of male criticism. This criticism has made the women preschool teachers battle with their own insecurity and many of them now allow "boys' anxiety-based aggression" to run free by buying weapons and war toys and encouraging boys to let loose their wild ideas. Furthermore there is a call for more men teachers. In Viborg the head of a preschool teachers training college in the media has advertised not only for men or for qualified men, but for "Real Men" . . . (Kruse 1996: 438–9)

Kruse goes on to decide the arguments of a number of prominent men among whom is former teacher and author Bertill Nordahl:

> school is a terrible place for boys. In school they are trapped by "The Matriarchy" and are dominated by women who cannot accept boys as they are. The women teachers mainly wish to control and to suppress boys. According to him, men teachers are not a lot better off, over-run as

they are by women and female values, which undermine their masculinity and self-esteem. In order to survive in the workplace dominated by women, they submit themselves to female values—thereby becoming *vatpikke* (cotton wool pricks). (Kruse 1996: 439)

As I have suggested, what is interesting about this version of the "what about the boys?" movement is its independence from any statistics on achievement.

I now move on to discuss some of the negative effects of NPM on schools. I have written elsewhere about the negative effects of NPM on feminist work in teacher education (Mahony 1997) so I shall limit my comments to the school context.

The Problem with Basics

The blinkered preoccupation with achievement, defined narrowly as subject knowledge, literacy, and numeracy has been the subject of some criticism both within the United Kingdom and elsewhere. Commenting on issues which arose from a school effectiveness research project McGraw et al. (1992: 174) concluded that:

> School effectiveness is about a great deal more than maximizing academic achievement. Learning and the love of learning; personal development and self-esteem; life skills, problem solving and learning how to learn; the development of independent thinkers and well rounded confident individuals; all rank as highly or more highly as the outcomes of effective schooling as success in a narrow range of academic disciplines.

Even within the school effectiveness "movement," a major figure in the United Kingdom has argued that:

> In Britain and internationally, there is a sense in which the entire enterprise of school effectiveness appears in a "time warp." The studies that have been conducted are all aging rapidly and are of less and less use in the educational world of the 1990's. This world has new needs at the level of pupil outcomes from schools—the skills to access information and to work collaboratively in groups, and the social outcomes of being able to cope in a highly complex world are just three new educational goals which are never used as outcomes in the school effectiveness literature. (Reynolds 1994: 23)

The effects of current UK plc definitions of what it means to "become educated" are highlighted when one works with teachers in other countries, many of whom cite UK research and development from the 1980s (derided by our own Government) as inspiring their current initiatives. Much of that work was undertaken by classroom teachers, yet such is the degree of centralization of educational policy in this country that teachers' voices have increasingly been removed from policy-making circles, their professionalism undermined and their creativity stifled (Mahony and Hextall 1997a).

In addition, teacher "efficiency" is in the process of being reconstructed through a revised appraisal system, performance-related pay, inspection reports on individual teachers, development of teaching standards, and the restructuring of the profession into four stages.

None of this is likely to foster a climate in which teachers will find it easy to be creative about developing different ways of working with different groups of young people. Nor will they be thoroughly prepared or motivated to engage in the kind of progressive work which I suggest later is necessary if we are seriously asking "What about the boys?" Such work which may well "rock the boat" will require a fresh look at gender relations in a context where over the last few years, we have witnessed a full frontal *attack* on such work in schools. Many new teachers in the United Kingdom have never known a time when the purposes of schooling went beyond the pursuit of higher academic standards. They do not remember that in the run-up to the 1987 general election "equal opportunities" were derided as the invention of the "loony Left" and our alleged intention to deprive children of a good education.

They probably do not remember that one book in one teachers' centre in one London borough, which told the story of a girl visiting her father and his male lover, became a *cause célèbre*; that lies abounded in the tabloid press which told of gay sex being taught to 5-year-olds and of traditional children's stories being rewritten by teachers obsessed with sex equality (Cooper 1989). They may believe along with a first-year undergraduate student teacher that "being OK about gays in school is against the law" or that "teachers in the old days" (defined as the 1980s!) "were too political." Thus when John Major (Chitty and Simon 1993) dismissed the politics of "gender, race and class" as diverting schools from their "true purposes," his words probably fell on uncritical ears. It will take time and considerable political will to put issues of social justice back on the agenda for schools and there is no guarantee that our first-year student will ever come to understand the following quotation as located precisely within the politics of gender (and class).

> In 1995 the proportion of men receiving 1st class honours degrees in History at Cambridge was three times that of women . . . men fare better because they adopt a punchy, aggressive and adversarial approach in their essays. (Targett 1996: 3)

There are further problems with our obsession with narrow definitions of academic achievement. It leads to a "sex war" mentality in which our ever increasing preoccupation with who is doing better than whom leads each year to a media panic expressed in such headlines in the *Times Educational Supplement* as "Male brain rattled by curriculum oestrogen" (15 March 1996), "Perils of ignoring our lost boys" (28 June 1996) and in the *Guardian* "Girls on top of the learning curve" (19 October 1996). It is a short step from this kind of headline to the conclusion expressed by our Chief Inspector for Schools in *The Times* and repeated in the *Times Educational Supplement* that "the failure of boys and in particular white working class boys is one of the most disturbing problems we face within the whole education system."

It fuels the claim made the year before that "girls have had their way for long enough, now it's time for the boys" and the call for "reverse discrimination" (Smith 1995). And it heightens the pressure to pour resources into researching the causes of the "underachievement of boys," and to change classroom practice in ways which benefit boys (Klein 1995).

Furthermore, it is not clear where the contexts exist in which different value positions about the purposes of schooling or the different needs of young people, positioned differently by class, "race," gender, sexuality or ability, could even be debated.

We have seen so far that the concern about boys fits into a wider set of issues about the relationship of the nation state to the global economy and into a range of anxieties concerned with reasserting patriarchal dominance. Having outlined some of the negative responses in the United Kingdom, I now move on to a consideration of the terrain between schools and the global economy constituted by the world of paid work. This forms the immediate context into which young people move and to which the achievement effort is partly directed. Here again we see an interweaving of the issues I have raised so far as we reflect on what it means to be prepared for, and positioned within, a changing labour market.

The World of McWork

> A quiet revolution is going on which is transforming the lives of millions of workers in Britain. The world of full-time pensionable employment is retreating before their eyes; and in its stead is emerging an insecure world of contract work, part-time jobs and casualised labour. (Hutton 1995: 20)

This "quiet revolution" has had dramatic effects on economic inequality in the United Kingdom. Lean and Ball (1996: 1) note that according to the Human Development Report published by the UN Development Programme:

> Britain is now the most unequal country in the Western world . . . The report shows that the

poorest 40 per cent of Britons share a lower proportion of the national wealth—14.6 per cent—than any other Western country. The richest fifth of Britons enjoy on average, incomes 10 times as high as the poorest fifth.

The gendered effects of poverty within these statistics are not mentioned nor, conversely, have the effects on children's educational potential featured highly within the school-effectiveness movement. The displacement of the "masculine" manufacturing base by the "feminine" service sector has meant that an increasing proportion of casualized work is being carried out by white and black working class women (EOC 1997). It would seem that since 1977 when Paul Willis wrote *Learning to Labour: How Working Class Kids Get Working Class Jobs*, it is the world which has changed, not the boys and there is no longer a fit between large areas of it and many of the boys. This raises the spectre of the "traditional" heterosexual nuclear family being made unstable by the "underachievement of boys."

If such employment as is available for groups for young working-class people exists largely in the service industries, then it has to be recognized that these require high levels of expertise in the expressive aspects of customer service. Qualities such as "warmth, empathy, sensitivity to unspoken needs and high levels of interpersonal skills to build an effective relationship with customers" (Devereux 1996: 13) would seem to be at odds with masculinities encouraged in, and adopted by, some adolescent boys. The latter poses a really difficult challenge for the demands of the labour market, the problem for some boys seems to be that they are not more like girls. It would follow that some masculinities need to change. On the other hand any attempt to critique or transform such masculinities strikes at the heart of the gender regime from which men earn the "patriarchal dividend" (Connell 1995: 41). How far there really is a need for everyone to achieve high levels of academic knowledge in order to ensure UK plc's competitiveness in the global economy and how far the real problem lies in the threat to the "natural order" of the working class male breadwinner would be a question worthy of further pursuit.

Evidence from one region in the south-east of England indicates that the reconstruction of masculinities will be hard to achieve. In a project undertaken with 130 14-years-olds, about their attitudes to school subjects and their ambitions for the future (Mahony and Frith 1995), it emerged that for many boys, biological accounts of gender were alive and kicking. Being good at (or bad at) different subjects was a matter beyond their control—"It's in yer brain" as one boy said and there was nothing to be done for some boys from whom it was not "in yer brain" but to "f— about." Girls on the other hand tended to think that if "you work harder maybe you get to like it and get better at it."

Students of both sexes thought that some subjects were easier for girls or boys though their reasons differed; boys again tended to blame the gendered nature of "natural ability" whereas girls cited "what you're used to since you were little."

Whether the boys really did believe in "nature" rather than "nurture" is a moot point. In one report: "Staff felt that boys appeared more concerned with preserving an image of reluctant involvement or disengagement; for many boys, it is not acceptable for them to be seen to be interested or stimulated by academic work" (Hofkins 1995: 5). Two points need to be interjected here about the ways in which biological determinism rolls on and off the explanatory stage. First, biological determinism is not the quaint prerogative of 14-year-old boys in south-east England but pervasive across other sites. One recent example occurred during my recent period of jury service on a case involving violent assault, when a barrister said, "You may think there is a little too much testosterone in this case, but unfortunately that is natural." It remains unclear what would have been the point of punishing the accused, if found guilty, but then perhaps it is a mistake to seek logical argument in the legitimating discourses of male violence.

In an opposite tendency, anecdotal evidence from teachers suggests that girls are increasingly acting in ways conventionally associated with particular forms of masculinity (for example, in their increased tendency to resort to physical violence). Here, femininities and masculinities are not regarded as biologically fixed but as fluid and (in the case of the girls) as both amenable to, and in need of, reconstruction. That such a strategy (to eliminate masculinist behaviour) should not have occurred to our money conscious policy makers as a way of cutting the cost of policing, prosecuting and imprisoning men (and a few women) is perhaps no surprise. It would after all undercut one of the major props in the maintenance of patriarchal power.

To return to the study, it was predominantly the male students who wanted to get a job at 16 rather than continuing into further education and mostly the boys who were unclear about the future. They also tended to be less informed than the girls about relevant pathways to different occupations, despite the fact that all the students had spent a considerable amount of time studying "careers." For example, one student who wanted to be a PE teacher said he would either go to college to study English, media, and art or get a job.

Where they had them, the ambitions of the white working-class boys clustered simultaneously round two poles of the male labour market. On the one hand they aspired to enter the middle-class professions even though 40 percent of them could not accurately spell their chosen "career." Given what is known about the widening social class divisions in access to higher education and the social class backgrounds and exclusionary networking practices of members of the legal and medical professions, it is highly unlikely that the opportunity will really exist for these boys to become a "barraster," "solister," "docter," or "arcatec." Perhaps knowing this, they nearly always proposed alternatives to their preferred futures such as "getting a practical job," "a physical job," "a job using my body," "being a courier," or "driving a big lorry." Not one of them wanted to work in the service industries, a common aspiration for the girls and none predicted that he would find employment there. This raises a further set of complexities. Does the future lie in the reskilling (and "feminization"?) of working-class boys so that they can displace working-class women at the edge of the labour market or does it reside in encouraging them into modes of perceived middle-class masculinity so that they can enter the more stable ranks of the managerial classes? These dilemmas are further cross-cut by the recognition that masculinities are neither fixed nor framed solely by social class but by sexuality, region, age, ability, and by ethnicity as well as by the availability and nature of work, being shaped in part by economic policies geared to the needs of multinational companies, operating across national borders. In any event, there are real problems in the 1990s around the claim that some masculinities need to be reconstructed. Let us briefly explore these.

From Pen to Practice

First, a perspective favouring the reconstruction of particular masculinities will not be easy to introduce, even if the grounds on which it is advanced were reframed in terms of the employability of boys. The attack on the equity work of the 1980s at least in the United Kingdom has probably left too much detritus in the popular imagination for the arguments to be taken seriously and the anti-feminist backlash inherent in some forms of masculinity politics seems set to exploit this (Connell 1997). Second, though recent literature has stressed the transformational potential of "variety, difference and plurality, both between men and men and within individual boys and men" (Jackson and Salisbury 1996: 109) and though these particular authors make a rare and much welcome foray into suggesting practical strategies for working with boys (Salisbury and Jackson 1996), it is not clear how the cracks and fissures in the constructions of masculinities could be systematically exploited in school to produce new gender regimes. How would this much needed work stand alongside the competition to achieve higher academic results, defined within "Blairjorism" as the true purposes of schooling?

How could the attempt to soften the hard competitive edges of some forms of masculinity sit comfortably within a context where *increased* competitiveness (in the global economy) has all but become the national anthem for the millennium? Within the increasingly managerialist restructuring of schools (Mahony and Hextall 1997b), it may even be that masculinist values are on the increase:

> Organisations clearly reproduce themselves. People in power (who are mostly men) mentor, encourage, and advance people who are most like themselves . . . a number of studies have shown that as women move up the organizational hierarchy, their identification with the masculine model of managerial success becomes so important that they end up rejecting even the few valued feminine managerial traits they may have endorsed. (Kanter 1993: 72)

The second problem in the United Kingdom is that few are now qualified to do such work. Nor is it clear how teachers could become qualified in the current climate. The priorities for continuing professional development for teachers are being centrally defined around the need to increase teachers' subject knowledge and their "leadership" skills and the spaces for thinking about the wider purposes of schooling are not evident within the framework of national standards for teaching currently being developed by the TTA.

The increasing gap between research and practice in the education of teachers does not help matters. As teachers work longer and harder to ensure that theirs is an "effective school" so, in parallel, researchers are striving to meet the demands of the academy for the publication of yet more academically orientated texts. Theory and practice become progressively estranged, to the detriment of both.

Within the academy there is a further problem. Just as it is easy for researchers to get lost in the detailed data on underachievement, so the temptation is to be drawn into the increasingly detailed exploration of masculinities, femininities, ethnicities, sexualities, or class identities. This is an attractive option, to be sure, easier than trying to change the world and allowing a sensitive subject to be avoided. This is that masculinities, for all their variety and internal jockeying, coalesce around a main axis of power relations with women. This awareness and its implications for action are low on both the research and practice agenda, not helped in either case by the way that the "underachievement of boys" debate has been framed. Responsibility for this cannot be laid at the door of the pressing demands of the global economy. Other countries inhabit the same globe without feeling the need to deny that expressions of male power in the form of sexual violence are issues which have to be dealt with in school.

The European Dimension

A European workshop on in-school "prevention" of sexual violence against girls and boys was recently held in Germany. The workshop grew out of the joint local government/European Union financed PETZE project, set up in Schleswig Holstein to develop a teachers' INSET programme on sexual violence against girls and boys (Schmidt and Peter 1996). Sixty men and women (of whom I was one) from thirteen countries participated in the workshop including doctors, government officials, academics, and youth workers. In preparation, a survey was conducted on the activities of the fifteen member states in relation to "prevention work" in school, how questions of sexual violence were discussed and how teachers were supported in this work. The questionnaire from the United Kingdom was not filled in though a note was attached explaining that it was "impossible to fill it in because such work is the responsibility of the LEAs [local education authorities]" (Kavemann 1996). The Leeds Inter-Agency School Project (1996: 1), however, suggests that "LMS has made it difficult to promote and resource such work across the LEA." Delegates from various countries reported that "we are very worried that we will go the same way as the English—obsessed with exams" and the question "How have you in your country let this happen?" was one I could not answer, even in my own language.

Astounding was the similarity of the evidence of sexual violence quoted from many of the countries. As definitions of sexual violence vary and research methods change, so the findings of prevalence studies vary. However, bearing this difficulty in mind, much of the evidence presented at the workshop confirmed the findings of Kelly et al. (1991) that if unwanted sexual events or interactions are included then one in two women and one in four men will have experienced at least one event before the age of 18. If "abuse attempts successfully resisted" and "less serious" forms of abuse are excluded then one in five women and one in fourteen men experienced at least one event before the age of 18.

The outcome of the workshop was that agreement on a five-page resolution was reached and sent off "to Europe." Read out of the context in which it was produced and from a perspective which theorizes the continuum of sexual violence as functioning to maintain patriarchal domination, the first paragraph of the resolution is less than perfect:

> The most far-reaching aim of prevention is to change social structures of power and violence between the sexes and the generations which produce sexual abuse of children, particularly of girls, to abolish the myths around sexual violence and the denial of its devastating consequences. (European Workshop 1996: 81)

On the other hand, as the culmination of the participants' work over three days, in which the predominant theme had been men's sexual violence and its functioning in the social control of women, it provided evidence that perhaps we need to look outside England for examples of broader and more equitable views of the "true purposes of schooling" and of what it means to take a wider view of gender relations. Masculinities form only part of this wider perspective and the "underachievement of boys" an even smaller part.

Conclusion

I have argued that the "underachievement of boys" debate is part of a much bigger bundle of anxieties around "What about the boys?" and that these cannot be understood outside various forms of patriarchal capitalist restructurings occurring within different sites. There is an untidy heap of issues around what it means to engage with the problem which range from the diversionary through to the radical. Even from a radical perspective which explores the potential for transforming masculinities, the danger is that the wider spectrum of gender relations and the positionings of women within it, will be overlooked. In particular, sexual violence, its devastating effects on individuals and its functioning in the social control of women are not high on the agenda in some of the theorizing around masculinities, and the difficulties of educating women and men teachers to undertake transformational work in this country should not be underestimated within the purposes of schooling as defined by Blairjorism.

As a way forward we might explore the potential for exploiting at a national level the contradictions between education policy in the United Kingdom and what is currently being recommended as best practice by transnational organizations such as the OECD (Townshend 1996). We might also consider the possibilities afforded by forging alliances with other groups expressing dissatisfaction with current definitions of the purposes of schooling (Gardiner 1997). Finally, we need to question whether there are spaces in which it might be possible to overcome some of the difficulties I have highlighted in order to engage in radical work at the level of the "local." Some of the work currently being conducted under the banner of "underachieving boys" would be an obvious starting point notwithstanding the fact that teachers willing and able to do it will need time, acknowledgement, and support.

Evidence which gives cause for optimism at the level of the local suggests that parents' views of the purposes of schooling are rather wider than those pursued over recent years (Mahony and Moos 1997). There are also practical examples where such views are being accessed and developed to legitimate a broader view of the purposes of the individual school (MacBeath et al. 1996).

Even though these local spaces may provide opportunities for radical work, such possibilities mark the beginning, not the end of current debates. They raise but do not resolve wide-ranging concerns evident throughout the whole area of public-sector reorganization over patterns of centralization/decentralization and questions of accountability and representation (Mahony and Hextall 1997a). We are led ultimately to questions about forms of social participation and control, the nature of society itself in the late 1990s and the representation of different voices and value positions within it. As is often the case, issues of gender lead ultimately to questions concerned with what kind of society we want, who the "we" is who wants it and the nature of our powers to achieve it.

Note

1. The data on the Teacher Training Agency was gathered during an ESRC funded project "The Policy Context and Impact of the Teacher Training Agency" undertaken with Ian Hextall from September 1995 to November 1996.

References

Arnot, M., David, M. and Weiner, G. (1996) *Educational Reforms and Gender Equality in Schools*. Manchester: Equal Opportunities Commission.

Barber, M. (1994) Report into school students' attitudes, *Guardian*, 23 August.

Cerny, P. (1990) *The Changing Architecture of Politics: Structure, Agency and the Future of the State*. London: Sage Publications.

Chitty, C. and Simon, B. (eds) (1993) Extract from John Major's speech to the 1992 Conservative Party conference, in *Education Answers Back: Critical Responses to Government Policy*. London: Wishart.

Clarke, J. and Newman, J. (1997) *The Managerial State*. London: Sage Publications.

Cohen, M. (1996) *Fashioning Masculinity: National Identity and Language in the Eighteenth Century*. London: Routledge.

Collinson, D. and Hearn J. (eds) (1996) *Men as Managers, Managers as Men*. London: Sage Publications.

Connell, R. W. (1993) The big picture: masculinities in recent world history. *Theory and Society*, 22: 597–624.

Connell, R. W. (1995) *Masculinities*. Sydney: Allen and Unwin.

Connell, R. W. (1997) Men, masculinities and feminism. *Social Alternatives*, 16: 7–10.

Cooper, D. (1989) Positive images in Haringey: a struggle for identity, in C. Jones and P. Mahony (eds) *Learning our Lines: Sexuality and Social Control in Education*. London: The Women's Press.

Davies, L. (1994) *Beyond Authoritarian School Management: The Challenge of Transparency*. Derbyshire: Education Now Publishing Co-operative.

Department for Education and Employment (DfEE) (1997a) *Learning and Working Together for the Future*. London: HMSO.

Department for Education and Employment (DfEE) (1997b) *Excellence in Schools*. London: HMSO.

Devereux, C. (1996) *Cross Cultural Standards of Competence in Customer Service*. Cheam: W. A. Consultants.

Equal Opportunities Commission [EOC] (1997) 'Briefings on Women and Men in Britain: The Labour Market', Manchester: Equal Opportunities Commission.

European Workshop (1996) Prevention of sexual violence against girls and boys in school. Documentation. Ministry of Education, Science, Research and Cultural Affairs of the Land of Schlewig-Holstein, Germany.

Ferlie, E., Pettigrew, A., Ashburner, L. and Fitgerald, L. (1996) *The New Public Management in Action*. Oxford: Oxford University Press.

Gardiner, J. (1997) Editors back new progressivism, *Times Educational Supplement*, 24 January.

Grace, G. (1991) Welfare Labourism versus the New Right: the struggle in New Zealand's educational policy. *International Studies in the Sociology of Education*, 1: 25–41.

Hextall, I. and Mahony, P. (1998) Effective teachers for effective schools, in R. Slee, S. Tomlinson and G. Weiner (eds) *Effective for Whom?* London: Falmer Press.

Hofkins, D. (1995) Why teenage boys think success is sad, *Times Educational Supplement*, 18 August.

Hoggett, P. (1996) New modes of control in the public service. *Public Administration*, 74: 9–31.

Hutton, W. (1995) *The State We're In*. London: Jonathan Cape.

Hyman, P. (1994) *Women and Economics: A New Zealand Feminist Perspective*. Wellington, New Zealand: Bridget Williams Book Ltd.

Jackson, D. and Salisbury J. (1996) Why should secondary schools take working with boys seriously? *Gender and Education*, 8: 103–15.

Kanter, R. M. (1993) *Men and Women of the Corporation*, 2nd ed. New York: Basic Books.

Kavemann, B. (1996) Verbal comment made during presentation of *Evaluation of a Survey of the European Union Member States Concerning Prevention of Sexual Violence against Girls and Boys*. Schleswig-Holstein: Ministry of Education, Science, Research and Culture.

Kelly, L., Regan, L. and Burton, S. (1991) *An Exploratory Study of the Prevalence of Sexual Abuse in a Sample of 16–21 Year Olds*. London: Child Abuse Studies Unit, University of North London.

Klein, R. (1995) Tails of snips and snails, *Times Educational Supplement*, 9 June.

Knight, J., Lingard, B. and Barlett, L. (1994) Reforming teacher education policy under Labor Governments in Australia 1983–93. *British Journal of Sociology of Education*, 15: 451–66.

Kruse, A.-M. (1996) Approaches to teaching girls and boys: current debates, practices and perspectives in Denmark, in P. Mahony (ed.) *Changing Schools: Some International Feminist Perspectives on Working with Girls and Boys*. Special Issue, *Women's Studies International Forum*, 19: 429–45.

Lean, G. and Ball, G. (1996) UK most unequal Country in the West, *Independent on Sunday*, 21 July.

Leeds Inter-Agency School Project (1996) *Summary, Key Issues and Recommendations*. Leeds: Leeds City Council.

Lingard, B. (1995) Re-articulating relevant voices in reconstructing teacher education. The Annual Harry Penny Lecture, University of South Australia.

Lingard, B. and Mills, M. (1997) Masculinity politics: an introduction. *Social Alternatives*, 16: 4–6.

MacBeath, J., Boyd, J., Rand, B. and Bell, S. (1996) *Schools Speak for Themselves: Towards a Framework for Self-Evaluation*. Strathclyde Quality in Education Centre, University of Strathclyde.

McGraw, B., Piper, K., Banks, D. and Evans, B. (1992) *Making Schools More Effective*. Victoria: Australian Council for Educational Research (ACER).

Mahony, P. (1985) *Schools for the Boys?* London: Hutchinson.

Mahony, P. (1997) Talking heads: feminist perspectives on public sector reform in teacher education. *Discourse*, 18: 87–102.

Mahony, P. and Frith, R. (1995) *Factors Influencing Girls' and Boys' Option Choices in Year 9*. Report to Essex Careers and Business Partnership. London: Roehampton Institute.

Mahony, P. and Hextall, I. (1997a) Problems of accountability in reinvented government: a case study of the Teacher Training Agency. *Journal of Education Policy*, 12: 267–78.

Mahony, P. and Hextall, I. (1997b) Sounds of silence: the social justice agency of the Teacher Training Agency. *International Studies in Sociology of Education*, 7: 137–56.

Mahony, P. and Moos, L. (1997) Facts and fictions of school leadership. Paper presented at European Conference on Educational Research, Frankfurt, Germany, 24–26 September.

Mahony, P. and Zmroczek, C. (1997) *Class Matters: "Working Class" Women's Perspectives on Social Class*. London: Taylor and Francis.

Millett, A. (1996) *Chief Executive's Annual Lecture*. London: Teacher Training Agency.

Mills, M. and Lingard, B. (1997) Masculinity politics, myths and boys' schooling. *British Journal of Educational Studies*, 45: 276–92.

Moys, A. (1980) *Modern Languages Examinations at 16+*. London: Centre for Information on Language Teaching Research.

Murphy, P. and Elwood, J. (1998) Gendered experiences, choices and achievement: exploring the links, in D. Epstein, J. Maw, J. Elwood and V. Hey (eds) *International Journal of Inclusive Education: Special Issue on Boys' "Underachievement,"* 2(2): 95–118.

Parry, O. (1996) Cultural contexts and school failure: underachievement of Caribbean males in Jamaica, Barbados and St. Vincent and the Grenadines. Paper presented to ESRC seminar series "Gender and Schooling: Are Boys Now Underachieving?," University of London Institute of Education.

Pollitt, C. (1993) *Managerialism and the Public Services*, 2nd ed. Oxford: Blackwell Publishers.

Pusey, M. (1991) *Economic Rationalism in Canberra: A Nation-Building State Changes its Mind*. New York: Cambridge University Press.

Pyke, N. (1996) Boys "read less than girls," *Times Educational Supplement*, 15 March.

Reynolds, D. (1994) School effectiveness and quality in education, in P. Ribnew and E. Burridge (eds) *Improving Education: Promoting Quality in Schools*. London: Cassell.

Salisbury, J. and Jackson, D. (1996) *Challenging Macho Values: Practical Ways of Working with Adolescent Boys*. London: Falmer Press.

Schmidt, B. and Peter, A. (1996) The Petze Project: working with teachers on the prevention of sexual violence against girls and boys in Germany, in P. Mahony (ed.) *Changing Schools: Some International Feminist Perspectives on Working with Girls and Boys*. Special issue *Women's Studies International Forum*, 19: 395–407.

Shand, D. (1996) The new public management: an international perspective. Paper presented to Public Services Management 2000 Conference, University of Glamorgan, 11 October.

Smith, M. J. (1995) Silence of the lads, *Times Educational Supplement*, 24 March.

Targett, S. (1996) Women told to take risks to get a first, *Times Higher Educational Supplement*, 1 November.

Townshend, J. (1996) An overview of OECD work on teachers, their pay and conditions, teaching quality and the continuing professional development of teachers. Paper presented at UNESCO International Conference on Education, Geneva, October.

Weiner, G., Arnot, M. and David, M. (1997) Is the future female? Female success, male disadvantage and changing gender patterns in education, in A. H. Halsey, P. Brown, H. Lauder and A. Stuart-Wells (eds) *Education: Culture, Economy and Society*. Oxford: Oxford University Press.

Willis, P. (1977) *Learning to Labour: How Working Class Kids Get Working Class Jobs*. Aldershot: Saxon House.

ARTICLE 13

Ann Ferguson

Making a Name for Yourself: Transgressive Acts and Gender Performance

Though girls as well as boys infringe the rules, the overwhelming majority of violations in every single category, from misbehavior to obscenity, are by males. In a disturbing tautology, transgressive behavior is that which constitutes masculinity. Consequently, African American males in the very act of identification, of signifying masculinity, are likely to be breaking rules.

I use the concept of sex/gender not to denote the existence of a stable, unitary category that reflects the presence of fundamental, natural biological difference, but as a socially constructed category whose form and meaning [vary] culturally and historically. We come to know ourselves and to recognize others as of a different sex through an overdetermined complex process inherent in every sphere of social life at the ideological and discursive level, through social structures and institutional arrangements, as well as through the micropolitics of social interactions.[1] We take sex difference for granted, as a natural form of difference as we look for it, recognize it, celebrate it; this very repetition of the "fact" of difference produces and confirms its existence. Indeed, assuming sex/gender difference and identifying as one or the other gender is a precursor of being culturally recognizable as "human."

While all these modes of constituting gender as difference were palpable in the kids' world, in the following analysis of sex/gender as a heightened and highly charged resource for self-fashioning and making a name for oneself, the phenomenological approach developed by ethnomethodologists and by poststructuralist feminist Judith Butler is the most productive one to build on. Here gender is conceptualized as something we do in a performance that is both individually and socially meaningful. We signal our gender identification through an ongoing performance of normative acts that are ritually specific, drawing on well-worked-over, sociohistorical scripts and easily recognizable scenarios.[2]

Butler's emphasis on the coerced and coercive nature of these performances is especially useful. Her work points out that the enactment of sex difference is neither voluntary nor arbitrary in form but is a compulsory requirement of social life. Gender acts follow sociohistorical scripts that are policed through the exercise of repression and taboo. The consequences of an inadequate or bad performance are significant, ranging from ostracism and stigmatization to imprisonment and death. What I want to emphasize in the discussion that follows are the rewards that attach to this playing out of roles; for males, the enactment of masculinity is also a thoroughly embodied display of physical and social power.

Identification as masculine through gender acts, within this framework, is not simply a matter of imitation or modeling, but is better understood as a highly strategic attachment to a social category that has political effects. This attachment involves narratives of the self and of Other, constructed within and through fantasy and imagination, as well as through repetitious, referential acts.

From *Bad Boys: Public Schools in the Making of Black Masculinity,* by Ann Ferguson. Ann Arbor: University of Michigan Press, 2000. © University of Michigan. Reprinted with permission.

The performance signals the individual as socially connected, embedded in a collective membership that always references relations of power.

African American boys at Rosa Parks School use three key constitutive strategies of masculinity in the embrace of the masculine "we" as a mode of self-expression. These strategies speak to and about power. The first is that of heterosexual power, always marked as male. Alain's graffiti become the centerpiece of this discussion. The second involves classroom performances that engage and disrupt the normal direction of the flow of power. The third strategy involves practices of "fighting." All three invoke a "process of iterability, a regularized and constrained repetition of norms," in doing gender, constitute masculinity as a natural, essential, corporeal style; and involve imaginary, fantasmatic identifications.[3]

These three strategies often lead to trouble, but by engaging them a boy can also make a name for himself as a real boy, the Good Bad Boy of a national fantasy. All three illustrate and underline the way that normative male practices take on a different, more sinister inflection when carried out by African American boys. Race makes a significant difference both in the form of the performance as well as its meaning for the audience of adult authority figures and children for whom it is played.

Heterosexual Power: Alain's Graffiti

One group of transgressions specifically involves behavior that expresses sexual curiosity and attraction. These offenses are designated as "personal violations" and given more serious punishment. Inscribed in these interactions are social meanings about relations of power between the sexes as well as assumptions about male and female difference at the level of the physical and biological as well as the representational. It is assumed that females are sexually passive, unlikely to be initiators of sexual passes, while males are naturally active sexual actors with strong sexual drives. Another assumption is that the feminine is a contaminated, stigmatizing category in the sex/gender hierarchy.

Typically, personal violations involved physical touching of a heterosexual nature where males were the "perpetrators" and females the "victims." A few examples from the school files remind us of some of the "normal" displays of sexual interest at this age.

- Boy was cited with "chasing a girl down the hall" [punishment: two days in the Jailhouse].
- Boy pulled a female classmate's pants down during recess [punishment: one and a half days in the Jailhouse].
- Boy got in trouble for, "touching girl on private parts. She did not like" [punishment: a day in the Jailhouse].
- Boy was cited for "forcing girl's hand between his legs" [punishment: two and a half days in the Jailhouse].

In one highly revealing case, a male was cast as the "victim" when he was verbally assaulted by another boy who called him a girl. The teacher described the "insult" and her response to it on the referral form in these words:

During the lesson, Jonas called Ahmed a girl and said he wasn't staying after school for detention because "S" [another boy] had done the same thing. Since that didn't make it ok for anyone to speak this way I am requesting an hour of detention for Jonas. I have no knowledge of "S" saying so in my presence.

This form of insult is not unusual. When boys want to show supreme contempt for another boy they call him a girl or liken his behavior to female behavior. What is more troubling is that adults capitulate in this stigmatization. The female teacher takes for granted that a comment in which a boy is called a girl is a symbolic attack, sufficiently derogatory to merit punishment. All the participants in the classroom exchange witness the uncritical acknowledgment of adult authority to a gender order of female debasement.

Of course, this is not news to them. Boys and girls understand the meaning of being male and being female in the field of power; the binary opposition of male/female is always one that expresses a norm, maleness, and its constitutive outside, femaleness. In a conversation with a group of boys, one of them asserted and then was supported by others that "a boy can be a girl, but a girl can never be a boy." Boys can be teased, controlled, punished by being accused of being "a girl." A boy faces the degradation of "being sissified," being unmanned, transferred to the degraded category of female. Girls can be teased about being a tomboy. But this is not the same. To take on qualities of being male is the access to and performance of power. So females must now fashion themselves in terms of male qualities to partake of that power. Enactments of masculinity signal value, superiority, power.

Let us return to Alain, the 11-year-old boy who while cooling off and writing lines as a punishment in the antechamber of the Punishing Room, writes on the table in front of him: "Write 20 times. I will stop fucking 10 cent teachers and this five cent class. Fuck you. Ho! Ho! Yes Baby." Alain's message can be read in a number of ways. The most obvious way is the one of the school. A child has broken several rules in one fell swoop and must be punished: he has written on school property (punishable); he has used an obscenity (punishable); he has committed an especially defiant and disrespectful act because he is already in the Punishing Room and therefore knows his message is likely to be read (punishable). Alain is sent home both as a signal to him and to the other witnesses as well as to the students and adults who will hear it through the school grapevine that he cannot get away with such flagrant misbehavior.

An alternative reading looks at the content of the message itself and the form that Alain's anger takes at being sent to the Punishing Room. Alain's anger is being vented against his teacher and the school itself, expressing his rejection, his disidentification with school that he devalues as monetarily virtually worthless. His message expresses his anger through an assertion of sexual power—to fuck or not to fuck—one sure way that a male can conjure up the fantasmatic as well as the physical specter of domination over a female of any age. His assertion of this power mocks the authority of the teacher to give him orders to write lines. His use of "baby" reverses the relations of power, teacher to pupil, adult to child; Alain allies himself through and with power as the school/teacher becomes "female," positioned as a sex object, as powerless, passive, infantilized. He positions himself as powerful through identification with and as the embodiment of male power as he disidentifies with school. At this moment, Alain is not just a child, a young boy, but taking the position of "male" as a strategic resource for enacting power, for being powerful. At the same time, this positioning draws the admiring, titillated attention of his peers.

These moments of sex trouble exemplify some of the aspects of the performance of sex/gender difference that is naturalized through what is deemed punishable as well as punishment practices. Judging from the discipline records, girls do not commit sexual violations. It is as if by their very nature they are incapable. To be female is to be powerless, victimizable, chased down the hallway, an object to be acted upon with force, whose hand can be seized and placed between male legs. To be female is also to be sexually passive, coy, the "chaste" rather than the chaser, in relation to male sexual aggressiveness. In reality, I observed girls who chased boys and who interacted with them physically. Girls, in fact, did "pants" boys, but these acts went unreported by the boys. For them to report and therefore risk appearing to be victimized by a girl publicly would be a humiliating outcome that would only undermine their masculinity. In the production of natural difference, boys' performances work as they confirm that they are active pursuers, highly sexualized actors who must be punished to learn to keep their burgeoning sexuality under control. There is a reward for the behavior even if it may be punished as a violation. In the case of African American boys, sex trouble is treated as egregious conduct.

African American males have historically been constructed as hypersexualized within the national imagination. Compounding this is the process of the adultification of their behavior. Intimations of sexuality on their part, especially when directed toward girls who are bused in—white girls from middle-class families—are dealt with as grave transgressions with serious consequences.

Power Reversals: Class Acts

Performance is a routine part of classroom work. Students are called upon to perform in classes by teachers to show off their prowess or demonstrate their ineptitude or lack of preparation. They are required to read passage aloud, for example, before a highly critical audience of their peers. This display is teacher initiated and reflects the official curricula; they are command performances with well-scripted roles, predictable in the outcome of who has and gets respect, who is in control, who succeeds, who fails.

Another kind of performance is the spontaneous outbreaks initiated by the pupils generally defined under the category of "disruption" by the school. These encompass a variety of actions that punctuate and disrupt the order of the day. During the school year about two-thirds of these violations were initiated by boys and a third by girls. Here are some examples from the discipline files of girls being "disruptive":

- Disruptive in class—laughing, provoking others to join her. Purposely writing wrong answers, being very sassy, demanding everyone's attention.
- Constantly talking; interrupting; crumpling paper after paper; loud.

Some examples of boys' disruption:

- Constant noise, indian whoops, face hiccups, rapping.
- Chanting during quiet time—didn't clean up during art [punishment: detention].
- Joking, shouting out, uncooperative, disruptive during lesson.

From the perspective of kids, what the school characterizes as "disruption" on the referral slips is often a form of performance of the self: comedy, drama, melodrama become moments for self-expression and display. Disruption adds some lively spice to the school day; it injects laughter, drama, excitement, a delicious unpredictability to the classroom routine through spontaneous, improvisational outbursts that add flavor to the bland events.

In spite of its improvisational appearance, most performance is highly ritualized with its own script, timing, and roles. Teachers as well as students engage in the ritual and play their parts. Some kids are regular star performers. Other kids are audience. However, when a substitute is in charge of the class and the risk of being marked as a troublemaker is minimal, even the most timid kids "act up." These rituals circulate important extracurricular knowledge about relations of power.

These dramatic moments are sites for the presentation of a potent masculine presence in the classroom. The Good Bad Boy of our expectations engages power, takes risks, makes the class laugh, and the teacher smile. Performances mark boundaries of "essential difference"—risk taking, brinkmanship. The open and public defiance of the teacher in order to get a laugh, make things happen, take center stage, be admired, is a resource for doing masculinity.

These acts are especially meaningful for those children who have already been marginalized as outside of the community of "good," hard-working students. For the boys already labeled as troublemakers, taking control of the spotlight and turning it on oneself so that one can shine, highlights, for a change, one's strengths and talents. Already caught in the limelight, these kids put on a stirring performance.

Reggie, one of the Troublemakers, prides himself on being witty and sharp, a talented performer. He aspires to two careers: one is becoming a Supreme Court justice, the other an actor. He had recently played the role of Caliban in the school production of *The Tempest* that he described excitedly to me:

> I always try to get the main characters in the story 'cause I might turn out to be an actor because I'm really good at acting and I've already

did some acting. Shakespeare! See I got a good part. I was Caliban. I had to wear the black suit. Black pants and top. Caliban was a beast! In the little picture that we saw, he looks like the ... the ... [searching for image] the beast of Notre Dame. The one that rings the bells like *fing! fing! fing!*

Here is one official school activity where Reggie gets to show off something that he is "good at." He is also proud to point out that this is not just a role in any play, but one in a play by Shakespeare. Here his own reward, which is not just doing something that he is good at, but doing it publicly so that he can receive the attention and respect of adults and peers, coincides with the school's educational agenda of creating an interest in Shakespeare among children.

Reggie also plays for an audience in the classroom, where he gets in trouble for disruption. He describes one of the moments for me embellished with a comic imitation of the teacher's female voice and his own swaggering demeanor as he tells the story:

The teacher says [he mimics a high-pitched fussy voice], "You not the teacher of this class." And then I say [adopts a sprightly cheeky tone], "Oh, yes I am." Then she say, "No, you're not, and if you got a problem, you can just leave." I say, "Okay" and leave.

This performance, like others I witnessed, are strategies for positioning oneself in the center of the room in a face-off with the teacher, the most powerful person up to that moment. Fundamental to the performance is engagement with power; authority is teased, challenged, even occasionally toppled from its secure heights for brief moments. Children-generated theatrics allow the teasing challenge of adult power that can expose its chinks and weaknesses. The staged moments heighten tension, test limits, vent emotions, perform acts of courage. For Reggie to have capitulated to the teacher's ultimatum would have been to lose what he perceives as the edge in the struggle. In addition, he has won his escape from the classroom.

Horace describes his challenge to the teacher's authority in a summer school math class:

Just before the end of the period he wrote some of our names on the board and said, "Whoever taught these students when they were young must have been dumb." So I said, "Oh, I didn't remember that was you teaching me in the first grade." Everyone in the room cracked up. I was laughing so hard, I was on the floor. He sent me to the office.

Horace is engaging the teacher in a verbal exchange with a comeback to an insult rather than just passively taking it. In this riposte, Horace not only makes his peers laugh at the teacher, but he also defuses the insult through a quick reversal. The audience in the room, raised on TV sitcom repartee and canned laughter, is hard to impress, so the wisecrack, the rejoinder, must be swift and sharp. Not everyone can get a laugh at the teachers' expense, and to be topped by the teacher would be humiliating, success brings acknowledgment, confirmation, applause from one's peers. For Horace, this is a success story, a moment of gratification in a day that brings few his way.

The tone of the engagement with power and the identity of the actor is highly consequential in terms of whether a performance is overlooked by the teacher or becomes the object of punishment. In a study of a Texas high school, Foley documents similar speech performances.[4] He describes how both teacher and students collaborate to devise classroom rituals and "games" to help pass the time given the context of routinized, alienating classroom work. He observes that upper-middle-class male Anglo students derail boring lessons by manipulating teachers through subtle "making out" games without getting in trouble. In contrast, low-income male Hispanic students, who were more likely to challenge teachers openly in these games, were punished. Foley concluded that one of the important lessons learned by all participants in these ritual games was that the subtle manipulation of authority was a much more effective way of getting your way than openly confronting power.

Style becomes a decisive factor in who gets in trouble. I am reminded of comments made by one of the student specialists at Rosa Parks who explained the high rate of black kids getting in trouble by remarking on their different style of rule breaking: "The white kids are sneaky, black kids are more open."

So why are the black kids "more open" in their confrontations with power? Why not be really "smart" and adopt a style of masculinity that allows them to engage in these rituals that spice the school day and help pass time, but carry less risk of trouble because it is within certain mutually understood limits?

These rituals are not merely a way to pass time, but are also a site for constituting a gendered racial subjectivity. For African American boys, the performance of masculinity invokes cultural conventions of speech performance that draw on a black repertoire. Verbal performance is an important medium for black males to establish a reputation, make a name for yourself, and achieve status.[5] Smitherman points out that black talk in general is

> a functional dynamic that is simultaneously a mechanism for learning about life and the world and a vehicle for achieving group recognition. Even in what appears to be only casual conversation, whoever speaks is highly conscious of the fact that his personality is on exhibit and his status at stake.[6]

Oral performance has a special significance in black culture for the expression of masculinity. Harper points out that verbal performance functions as an identifying marker for masculinity only when it is delivered in the vernacular and that "a too-evident facility in white idiom can quickly identify one as a white-identified uncle Tom who must also be therefore weak, effeminate, and probably a fag."[7] Though the speech performances that I witnessed were not always delivered in the strict vernacular, the nonverbal, bodily component accompanying it was always delivered in a manner that was the flashy, boldly flamboyant popular style essential to a good performance. The body language and spoken idiom openly engage power in a provocative competitive way. To be indirect, "sly," would not be performing masculinity.

This nonstandard mode of self-representation epitomizes the very form the school seeks to exclude and eradicate. It is a masculine enactment of defiance played in a black key that is bound for punishment. Moreover, the process of adultification translates the encounter from a simple verbal clash with an impertinent child into one interpreted as an intimidating threat.

Though few white girls in the school were referred to the office for disruptive behavior, a significant number of African American girls staged performances, talked back to teachers, challenged authority, and were punished. But there was a difference with the cultural framing of their enactments and those of the boys. The bottom line of Horace's story was that "everyone in the room cracked up." He engaged authority through a self-produced public spectacle with an eye for an audience that is at home with the cultural icon of the Good Bad Boy as well as the "real black man." Boys expect to get attention. Girls vie for attention too, but it is perceived as illegitimate behavior. As the teacher described it in the referral form, the girl is "demanding attention." The prevailing cultural framework denies her the rights for dramatic public display.

Male and female classroom performance is different in another respect. Girls are not rewarded with the same kind of applause or recognition by peers or by teachers. Their performance is sidelined; it is not given center stage. Teachers are more likely to "turn a blind eye" to such a display rather than call attention to it, for girls are seen as individuals who operate in cliques at most and are unlikely to foment insurrection in the room. Neither the moral nor the pragmatic principle prods teachers to take action. The behavior is not taken seriously; it is rated as "sassy" rather than symptomatic of a more dangerous disorder. In some classrooms, in fact, risk taking and "feistiness" on the part of girls is subtly encouraged given the prevailing belief that what they need is to become more visible, more assertive in the classroom. The notion is that signs of self-assertion on their part should be encouraged rather than squelched.

Disruptive acts have a complex, multifaceted set of meanings for the male Troublemakers themselves. Performance as an expression of black masculinity is a production of a powerful subjectivity to be reckoned with, to be applauded; respect and ovation are in a context where none is forthcoming. The boys' anger and frustration as well as fear motivate the challenge to authority. Troublemakers act and speak out as stigmatized outsiders.

Ritual Performances of Masculinity: Fighting

Each year a substantial number of kids at Rosa Parks get into trouble for fighting. It is the most frequent offense for which they are referred to the Punishing Room. Significantly, the vast majority of the offenders are African American males.[8]

The school has an official position on fighting; it is the wrong way to handle any situation, at any time, no matter what. Schools have good reasons for banning fights: kids can get hurt and when fights happen they sully the atmosphere of order, making the school seem like a place of danger, of violence.

The prescribed routine for schoolchildren to handle situations that might turn into a fight is to tell an adult who is then supposed to take care of the problem. This routine ignores the unofficial masculine code that if someone hits you, you should solve the problem yourself rather than showing weakness and calling an adult to intervene. However, it is expected that girls with a problem will seek out an adult for assistance. Girls are assumed to be physically weaker, less aggressive, more vulnerable, more needy of self-protection; they must attach themselves to adult (or male) power to survive. This normative gender distinction, in how to handle both problems of a sexual nature and physical aggression, operates as a "proof" of a physical and dispositional gender nature rather than behavior produced through discourses and practices that constitute sex difference.

Referrals of males to the Punishing Room, therefore, are cases where the unofficial masculine code for problem resolution has prevailed. Telling an adult is anathema to these youth. According to their own codes, the act of "telling" is dangerous for a number of reasons. The most practical of these sets it as a statement to the "whole world" that you are unable to deal with a situation on your own—to take care of yourself—an admission that can have disastrous ramifications when adult authority is absent. This is evident from the stance of a Troublemaker who questions the practical application of the official code by invoking knowledge of the proper male response when one is "attacked" that is shared with the male student specialist charged with enforcing the regulation: "I said, 'Mr. B, if somebody came up and hit you, what would you do?' 'Well,' he says, 'We're not talking about me right now, see.' That's the kind of attitude they have. It's all like on you."

Another reason mentioned by boys for not relying on a teacher to take care of a fight situation is that adults are not seen as having any real power to effectively change the relations among kids:

> If someone keep messing with you, like if someone just keep on and you tell them to leave you alone, then you tell the teacher. The teacher can't do anything about it because, see, she can't hit you or nothing. Only thing she can do is tell them to stop. But then he keep on doing it. You have no choice but to hit 'em. You already told him once to stop.

This belief extends to a distrust of authority figures by these young offenders. The assumption that all the children see authority figures such as teachers, police, and psychologists as acting on their behalf and trust they will act fairly may be true of middle- and upper-class children brought up to expect protection from authority figures in society. This is not the case with many of the children at the school. Their mistrust of authority is rooted in the historical and locally grounded knowledge of power relations that come from living in a largely black and impoverished neighborhood.

Fighting becomes, therefore, a powerful spectacle through which to explore trouble as a site for the construction of manhood. The practice takes place along a continuum that ranges from play—spontaneous outbreaks of pummeling and wrestling in fun, ritualistic play that shows off "cool" moves seen on video games, on TV, or in movies—to serious, angry socking, punching, fistfighting. A description of some of these activities and an analysis of what they mean provides the opportunity for us to delve under the surface of the ritualized, discrete acts that make up a socially recognizable fight even into the psychic, emotional, sensuous aspects of gender performativity. The circular, interactive flow between fantasmatic images, internal psychological processes, and physical acts suggest the dynamics of attachment of masculine identification.

Fighting is one of the social practices that add tension, drama, and spice to the routine of the school day. Pushing, grabbing, shoving, kicking, karate chopping, wrestling, fistfighting engage the body and the mind. Fighting is about play and games, about anger, and pain, about hurt feelings, about "messing around." To the spectator, a fight can look like serious combat, yet when the combatants are separated by an adult, they claim, "We were only playing." In fact, a single fight event can move along the continuum from play to serious blows in a matter of seconds. As one of the boys explained, "You get hurt and you lose your temper."

Fighting is typically treated as synonymous with "aggression" or "violence," terms that already encode the moral, definitional frame that obscures the contradictory ways that the practice, in all its manifestations, is used in our society. We, as good citizens, can distance ourselves from aggressive and violent behavior. "Violence" as discourse constructs "fighting" as pathological, symptomatic of asocial, dangerous tendencies, even though the practice of "fighting" and the discourses that constitute this practice as "normal," are in fact taken for granted as ritualized resources for "doing" masculinity in the contemporary United States.

The word *fighting* encompasses the "normal" as well as the pathological. It allows the range of meanings that the children, specifically the boys whom I interviewed and observed, as well as some of the girls, bring to the practice. One experience that it is open to is the sensuous, highly charged embodied experience before, during, and after fighting; the elating experience of "losing oneself" that I heard described in fight stories.

War Stories

I began thinking about fights soon after I started interviews with the Troublemakers and heard "fight stories." Unlike the impoverished and reluctantly told accounts of the school day, these stories were vivid, elaborate descriptions of bodies, mental states, and turbulent emotional feelings. They were stirring, memorable moments in the tedious school routine.

Horace described a fight with an older boy who had kept picking on him. He told me about the incident as he was explaining how he had broken a finger one day when we were trading "broken bones" stories.

> When I broke this finger right here it really hurted. I hit somebody in the face. It was Charles. I hit him in the face. You know the cafeteria and how you walk down to go to the cafeteria. Right there. That's where it happened. Charles picked me up and put me on the wall, slapped me on the wall, and dropped me. It hurt. It hurt bad. I got mad because he used to be messing with me for a long time so I just swung as hard as I could, closed my eyes, and just *pow*, hit him in the face. But I did like a roundhouse swing instead of doing it straight and it got the index finger of my right hand. So it was right there, started right here, and all around this part [he is showing me the back of

his hand] it hurt. It was swollen. Oooh! It was like this! But Charles, he got hurt too. The next day I came to school I had a cast on my finger and he had a bandage on his ear. It was kinda funny, we just looked at each other and smiled.

The thing that most surprised and intrigued me about Horace's story was that he specifically recalled seeing Charles the next day and that they had looked at each other and smiled. Was this a glance of recognition, of humor, of recollection of something pleasing, of all those things? The memory of the exchanged smile derailed my initial assumption that fighting was purely instrumental. This original formulation said that boys fight because they have to fight in order to protect themselves from getting beaten up on the playground. Fighting from this instrumental perspective is a purely survival practice. Boys do fight to stave off the need to fight in the future, to stop the harassment from other boys on the playground and in the streets. However, this explains only a small group of boys who live in certain environments; it relegates fighting to the realm of the poor, the deviant, the delinquent, the pathological. This position fails to address these physical clashes as the central normative practice in the preparation of bodies, of mental stances, of self-reference for manhood and as the most effective form of conflict resolution in the realm of popular culture and international relations.

I listened closely to the stories to try to make sense of behavior that was so outside of my own experience, yet so familiar a part of the landscape of physical fear and vulnerability that I as a female walked around with every day. I asked school adults about their own memories of school and fighting. I was not surprised to find that few women seemed to recall physical fights at school, though they had many stories of boys who teased them or girlfriends whom they were always "fighting" with. This resonated with my own experience. I was struck, however, by the fact that all of the men whom I talked to had had to position themselves in some way with regard to fighting. I was also struck that several of these men framed the memory of fighting in their past as a significant learning experience.

Male adults in school recall fighting themselves, but in the context both of school rules and of hindsight argue that they now know better. One of the student specialists admitted that he used to fight a lot. I found it significant that he saw "fighting" as the way he "learned":

> I used to fight a lot. [Pause.] I used to fight a lot and I used to be real stubborn and silent. I wouldn't say anything to anybody. It would cause me a lot of problems, but that's just the way I learned.

The after-school martial arts instructor also admitted to fighting a lot when he was younger:

> There were so many that I had as a kid that it's hard to remember all of them and how they worked out. But yes, I did have a lot of arguments and fights. A lot of times I would lose my temper, which is what kids normally do, they lose their temper, and before they have a chance to work things out they begin punching and kicking each other. Right? Well I did a lot of those things so I know from experience those are not the best thing to do.

As I explored the meaning of fighting I began to wonder how I, as female, had come to be shaped so fighting was not a part of my own corporeal or mental repertoire. A conversation with my brother reminded me of a long forgotten self that could fight, physically, ruthlessly, inflict hurt, cause tears. "We were always fighting," he recalled. "You used to beat me up." Memories of these encounters came back. I am standing with a tuft of my brother's hair in my hand, furious tears in my eyes. Full of hate for him. Kicking, scratching, socking, feeling no pain. Where had this physical power gone? I became "ladylike," repressing my anger, limiting my physical contact to shows of affection, fearful. I wondered about the meaning of being female in a society in which to be female is to be always conscious of men's physical power and to consciously chart one's everyday routines to avoid becoming a victim of this power, but to never learn the bodily and mental pleasure of fighting back.

Bodily Preparations: Pain and Pleasure

Fighting is first and foremost a bodily practice. I think about fighting and physical closeness as I stand observing the playground at recess noticing a group of three boys, bodies entangled, arms and legs flailing. In another area, two boys are standing locked closely in a wrestling embrace. Children seem to gravitate toward physical contact with each other. For boys, a close, enraptured body contact is only legitimate when they are positioned as in a fight. It is shocking that this bodily closeness between boys would be frowned on, discouraged if it were read as affection. Even boys who never get in trouble for "fighting" can be seen engaging each other through the posturing and miming, the grappling of playfight encounters.

This play can lead to "real" fights. The thin line between play and anger is crossed as bodies become vulnerable, hurt, and tempers are lost. One of the white boys in the school who was in trouble for fighting describes the progression this way:

> Well we were messing with each other and when it went too far, he started hitting me and then I hit him back and then it just got into a fight. It was sorta like a game between me, him and Thomas. How I would get on Thomas's back an—he's a big guy—and Stephen would try to hit me and I would wanta hit him back. So when Thomas left it sorta continued and I forgot which one of us wanted to stop—but one of us wanted to stop and the other one wouldn't.

Fighting is about testing and proving your bodily power over another person, both to yourself and to others through the ability to "hurt" someone as well as to experience "hurt."

> HORACE: You know Claude. He's a bad boy in the school. When I was in the fifth grade, he was in the fifth grade. I intercepted his pass and he threw the ball at my head and then I said, "You're mad," and I twisted the ball on the floor. I said, "Watch this," and y'know spiraled it on the floor, and he kicked it and it hit my leg, and I said, "Claude, if you hit me one more time with the ball or anything I'm going to hurt you." He said. "What if you do?" I said, "Okay, you expect me not to do anything, right?" He said, "Nope." Then I just *pow, pow, pow,* and I got him on the floor and then I got him on his back. I wanted to hurt him badly but I couldn't.
>
> ANN: Why couldn't you?
>
> HORACE: I didn't want to get in trouble. And if I did really hurt him it wouldn't prove anything anyway. But it did. It proved that I could hurt him and he didn't mess with me anymore.

Pain is an integral part of fighting. Sometimes it is the reason for lashing out in anger. This description by Wendell also captures the loss of self-control experienced at the moment of the fight:

> Sometimes it starts by capping or by somebody slams you down or somebody throws a bullet at you. You know what a bullet is, don't you? [He chuckles delightedly because I think of a bullet from a gun.] The bullet I am talking about is a football! You throw it with all your might and it hits somebody. It just very fast and they call it bullets. You off-guard and they throw it at your head, and bullets they throw with all their might so it hurts. Then that sorta gets you all pissed off. Then what happens is, you kinda like, "Why you threw it?" " 'Cause I wanted to. Like, so?" "So you not going to do that to me." Then: "So you going to do something about it?" Real smart. "Yeah!" And then you tap the person on the shoulder and your mind goes black and then *shweeeee* [a noise and hand signal that demonstrates the evaporation of thought] you go at it. And you don't stop until the teacher comes and stops it.

Fighting is a mechanism for preparing masculinized bodies through the playful exercise of bodily moves and postures and the routinized rehearsal of sequences and chains of stances of readiness, attack, and defense. Here it is crucial to emphasize that while many boys in the school never ever engage in an actual physical fight with another boy or girl during school hours, the majority engage in some form of body enactments of fantasized "fight" scenarios. They have observed boys and men on TV, in the movies, in video games, on the street, in the playground adopting these stances.

These drills simultaneously prepare and cultivate the mental states in which corporeal styles are grounded. So for instance, boys are initiated into the protocol of enduring physical pain and mental anguish—"like a man"—through early and small infusions of the toxic substance itself in play fights. The practice of fighting is the site for a hot-wiring together of physical pain and pleasure, as components of masculinity as play and bodily hurt inevitably coincide.

Consequently, it also engages powerful emotions. Lindsey described the feelings he experienced prior to getting into a fight:

> Sometimes it's play. And sometimes it's real. But that's only sometimes, because they can just suddenly make you angry and then, it's like they take control of your mind. Like they manipulate your mind if you angry. Little by little you just lose it and you get in a temper.

One of the white boys in the school who had gotten in trouble for fighting described his thoughts and feelings preceding a fight and the moment of "just going black" in a loss of self:

> My mind would probably be going through how I would do this. If I would stop it now or if I would follow through with it. But once the fight actually happens I sort of go black and just fight 'em.

Fighting is a practice, like sports, that is so symbolically "masculine" that expressions of emotion or behavior that might call one's manhood into question are allowed without danger of jeopardizing one's manliness. Even crying is a permissible expression of "masculinity" under these circumstances. One of the boys who told me he never cried, corrected himself:

> But if I be mad, I cry. Like if I get into a fight or something like that, I cry because I lose my temper and get so mad. But sometimes, I play football and if I cry that mean I'm ready to tumble—throw the ball to me because I'm going.

Fighting in school is a space in which boys can feel free to do emotional work.[9] In a social practice that is so incontrovertibly coded as masculine, behaviors marked as feminine, such as crying, can be called upon as powerful wellsprings for action.

One of the questions that I asked all the boys about fighting came out of my own ignorance. My query was posed in terms of identity work around the winning and losing of fights. Did you ever win a fight? Did you ever lose a fight? How did you feel when you lost? How did you feel when you won? I found the answers slippery, unexpected, contradictory. I had anticipated that winning would be described in proud and boastful ways, as success stories. But there seemed to be a surprising reluctance to embellish victory. I learned that I was missing the point by posing the question the way I had in terms of winning and losing. Trey enlightened me when he explained that what was at stake was not winning or losing per se but in learning about the self:

> I won a lot of fights. You know you won when they start crying and stuff or when they stop and leave. I lost fights. Then you feel a little okay. At least you lost. I mean like you ain't goin' win every fight. At least you fought back instead of just standing there and letting them hit you.

Another boy expressed the function that fighting played in establishing yourself as being a particular kind of respectable person:

> It's probably like dumb, but if somebody wants to fight me, I mean, I don't care even if I know I can't beat 'em. I won't stop if they don't stop. I mean I'm not scared to fight anybody. I'm not a coward. I don't let anybody punk me around. If you let people punk you around, other peoples want to punk you around.

Proving yourself to others is like a game, a kind of competition:

> Me and Leslie used to fight because we used to be the biggest boys, but now we don't care anymore. We used to get friends and try and fight each other. I fought him at Baldwin school all the time. We stopped about the fifth grade [the previous year]. Just got tired, I guess.

Standing and proving yourself today can be insurance against future harassment in the yard as you make a name for yourself through readiness to fight: "Like if somebody put their hands on you, then you have to, you have to hit them back. Because otherwise you going be beat up on for the rest of your life."

Eddie, who has avoided fights because he does not want to get in trouble, is now seen as a target for anyone to beat up, according to one of his friends, who characterized Eddie's predicament this way: "He can't fight. *He can't fight.* Every girl, every boy in the whole school fixing to beat him up. Badly. They could beat him up badly."

Eddie explains his own perspective on how he has come to actually lose a reputation.

> Yeah, I won a fight in preschool. Like somebody this tall [his gesture indicates a very tall someone] I had to go like this [reaches up to demonstrate] so I could hit him. He was older than me. He was the preschool bully. Till I mess him up.

But Eddie's parents came down hard on him for getting in trouble for fighting in elementary school:

> Yeah, I lost fights. See when I got to Rosa Parks my parents told me not to fight unless I had to—so I lost my face. 'Cause I was so used to telling them to stop, don't fight, don't fight.

In constructing the self through fight stories, it is not admirable to represent oneself as the aggressor or initiator in a fight. All the boys whom I talked to about fighting presented themselves as responding to a physical attack that had to be answered in a decisive way. No one presented himself as a "bully," though I knew that Horace had that reputation. Yet he told me that "only fights I been in is if they hit me first."

There are, however, times when it is legitimate to be the initiator. When verbal provocation is sufficient. This is when "family" has been insulted. Talking about "your momma" is tantamount to throwing down the gauntlet:

> Mostly I get in fights if somebody talk about my grandfather because he's dead. And I loved my grandfather more than I love anybody and then he died. [Tears are in Jabari's eyes as we talk.] That's why I try to tell people before they get ready to say anything, I'm like, "Don't say anything about my grandfather, 'cause if you say something about him, I'm goin' hit you."

The boys talked about how they learned to fight. How one learns to fight and what one learns about the meaning of fighting—why fight, to fight or not to fight—involved both racial identity and class positioning. Ricky and Duane, two of the Schoolboys, have been enrolled by their parents in martial arts classes. Fighting remains a necessary accoutrement of masculinity that is "schooled," not a "natural" acquisition of doing. As such, it becomes a marker of higher class position. Fighting takes place in an institutionalized arena rather than spontaneously in just any setting. The mind seems to control the body here, rather than vice versa.

Horace, on the other hand, like the majority of boys with whom I talked, explained that he had learned to fight through observation and practice:

> I watched people. Like when I was younger, like I used to look up to people. I still do. I look up to people and they knew how to fight so I just watched them. I just like saw people fight on TV, you know. Boxing and stuff.

Another boy told me that he thought kids learned to fight "probably from theirselves. Like their mom probably say, if somebody hit you, hit them back." This advice about proper behavior is grounded in the socialization practices that are brought into school as ways of responding to confrontations.

Gender Practice and Identification

Fighting acts reproduce notions of essentially different gendered natures and the forms in which this "difference" is grounded. Though class makes some difference in when, how, and under what conditions it takes place, fighting is the hegemonic representation of masculinity. Inscribed in the male body—whether individual males fight or not, abjure fighting or not—is the potential for this unleashing of physical power. By the same token, fighting for girls is considered an aberration, something to be explained.

Girls do get in fights at school. Boys asserted that girls can fight, even that "sometimes they get in fights easier. Because they got more attitude." Indeed, girls do make a name for themselves this way. One of the girls at Rosa Parks was in trouble several times during the school year for fighting. Most of her scrapes were with the boys who liked to tease her because she was very tall for her age. This, however, was not assumed to be reflective of her "femaleness" but of her individuality. Mr. Sobers, for example, when I asked him about her, made a point of this singularity rather than explaining her in terms of race, class, or gender: "Oh, Stephanie is just Stephanie."

Notes

1. Here are a very few examples of the enormous body of work concerned with the production of gender differences in the last two decades. At the ideological and discursive level see Mullings, "Images, Ideology"; Teresa de Lauretis, *Technologies of Gender: Essays on Theory, Film, and Fiction* (Bloomington: Indiana University Press, 1987); and Michele Barrett, *Women's Oppression Today: Problems in Marxist Feminist Analysis* (London: New Left Books, 1980). For processes of social structure and institutional arrangements see R. W. Connell et al., *Making the Difference: Schools, Families, and Social Division* (London: George Allen and Unwin, 1982); Mariarosa Dalla Costa, "Women and the Subversion of the Community," in *The Power of Women and the Subversion of Community*, ed. Mariarosa Dalla Costa and Selma James (Bristol, England: Falling Wall Press, 1973); Catharine A. MacKinnon, *Feminism Unmodified: Discourses on Life and Law* (Cambridge: Harvard University Press, 1987). For micropolitics see Arlie Russell Hochschild, *The Second Shift: Working Parents and the Revolution at Home* (New York: Viking, 1989); Donna Eder, Catherine Colleen Evans, and Stephen Parker, *School Talk: Gender and Adolescent Culture* (New Brunswick, N.J.: Rutgers University Press, 1995); and Candace West and Don H. Zimmerman, "Doing Gender," *Gender & Society* 1, no. 2 (1987).

2. Judith Butler, "Performative Acts and Gender Constitution: An Essay in Phenomenology and Feminist Theory," *Theatre Journal* 40, no. 4 (1988).

3. Judith Butler, *Bodies That Matter: On the Discursive Limits of "Sex"* (New York: Routledge, 1993), 95.

4. Douglas E. Foley, *Learning Capitalist Culture: Deep in the Heart of Tejas* (Philadelphia: University of Pennsylvania, 1990).

5. Geneva Smitherman, *Talkin and Testifyin: Language of Black America* (Detroit: Wayne State University Press, 1977); Lawrence Levine, *Black Culture and Black Consciousness: Afro-American Folk Thought from Slavery to Freedom* (New York: Oxford University Press, 1977); Philip Brian Harper, *Are We Not Men? Masculine Anxiety and the Problem of African-American Identity* (New York: Oxford University Press, 1996); Keith Gilyard, *Voices of the Self: A Study of Language Competence* (Detroit: Wayne State University Press, 1991).

6. Smitherman, *Talkin and Testifyin*, 80.

7. Harper, *Are We Not Men?* 11.

8. One-quarter of the 1,252 referrals to the Punishing Room were for fighting; four-fifths of the incidents involved boys, nine out of ten of whom were African Americans. All except three of the girls who were in fights were black.

9. Arlie Russell Hochschild, *The Managed Heart: Commercialization of Human Feeling* (Berkeley and Los Angeles: University of California Press, 1983). Hochschild explores the feeling rules that guide and govern our own emotional displays as well as how we interpret the emotional expression of others.

PART THREE

Collegiate Masculinities: Privilege and Peril

The old social science orthodoxy about sex role socialization, from the 1950s until today, held that three institutions—family, church, and school—formed the primary sites of socialization, and the impact of education, family values, and religious training was decisive in shaping people's lives. This view tended to emphasize the centrality of adults in boys' lives. Because adults themselves were constructing the models of socialization, this conclusion seems understandable. But as social scientists began to ask boys and girls about the forces that influenced them, they heard about the increasing importance of peer groups and the media—two arenas where adults had far less reach. In recent years, researchers have begun to explore how homosocial peer groups affect men's lives.

The articles in Part Three focus on masculinities in college, a place where the all-male peer group is especially salient. How does collegiate life organize and reproduce the definitions of masculinity that we learn as young boys? How do specific all-male subcultures develop within these institutions, and what roles do they play? Part Three explores male bonding within collegiate organizations, such as fraternities and athletic teams, and within the traditions of an all-male military institution. In recent years these institutions have been increasingly scrutinized and criticized, and some group members have felt besieged and unfairly picked on. Who's right?

Two of the articles in this section focus specifically on fraternities and the role of fraternity culture in campus life. The articles by Peter Lyman and by A. Ayres Boswell and Joan Spade ask: How is hegemonic masculinity reproduced in fraternity life? Why are fraternity men more likely to be accused of sexual assault? Rocco Capraro provides a fascinating gender analysis of male drinking culture in college, and Timothy Curry describes the ways in which collegiate athletics, both varsity and intramural, create and sustain certain versions of masculinity. Finally, Jason Schultz proposes some new rules of dating etiquette for college men.

167

Photo courtesy of Barbara Kruger.

168

ARTICLE 14

Peter Lyman

The Fraternal Bond as a Joking Relationship: A Case Study of the Role of Sexist Jokes in Male Group Bonding

One evening during dinner, 45 fraternity men suddenly broke into the dining room of a nearby campus sorority, surrounded the 30 women residents, and forced them to watch while one pledge gave a speech on Freud's theory of penis envy as another demonstrated various techniques of masturbation with a rubber penis. The women sat silently, staring downward at their plates, and listened for about 10 minutes, until a woman law student who was the graduate resident in charge of the house walked in, surveyed the scene and demanded, "Please leave immediately!" As she later described that moment, "There was a mocking roar from the men, 'It's tradition.' I said, 'That's no reason to do something like this, please leave!' And they left. I was surprised. Then the women in the house started to get angry. And the guy who made the penis-envy speech came back and said to us, 'That was funny to me. If that's not funny to you I don't know what kind of sense of humor you have, but I'm sorry.'"

That night the women sat around the stairwell of their house discussing the event, some angry and others simply wanting to forget the whole thing. They finally decided to ask the university to require that the men return to discuss the event. When university officials threatened to take action, the men agreed to the meeting. I had served as a faculty resident in student housing for two years and had given several talks in the dorm

From *Changing Men*, Michael Kimmel (ed.). Newbury Park, CA: Sage Publications, 1987. Reprinted by permission.

about humor and gender, and was asked by both the men and the women involved to attend the discussion as a facilitator, and was given permission to take notes and interview the participants later, provided I concealed their identities.

The penis-envy ritual had been considered a successful joke in previous years by both "the guys and the girls," but this year it failed, causing great tension between two groups that historically had enjoyed a friendly joking relationship. In the women's view, the joke had not failed because of its subject; they considered sexual jokes to be a normal part of the erotic joking relationship between men and women. They thought it had failed because of its emotional structure, the mixture of sexuality with aggression and the atmosphere of physical intimidation in the room that signified that the women were the object of a joking relationship between the men. A few women argued that the failed joke exposed the latent domination in men's relation to women, but this view was labeled "feminist" because it endangered the possibility of reconstituting the erotic joking relationship with the men. Although many of the men individually regretted the damage to their relationship with women friends in the group, they argued that the special male bond created by sexist humor is a unique form of intimacy that justified the inconvenience caused the women. In reinterpreting these stories as social constructions of gender, I will focus upon the way the joke form and joking relationships reveal the emotional currents underlying gender in this situation.

The Sociology of Jokes

Although we conventionally think of jokes as a meaningless part of the dramaturgy of everyday life, this convention is part of the way that the social function of jokes is concealed and is necessary if jokes are to "work." It is when jokes fail that the social conflicts that the joke was to reconstruct or "negotiate" are uncovered, and the tensions and emotions that underlie the conventional order of everyday social relations are revealed.

Joking is a special kind of social relationship that suspends the rules of everyday life in order to preserve them. Jokes indirectly express the emotions and tensions that may disrupt everyday life by "negotiating" them (Emerson 1969, 1970), reconstituting group solidarity by shared aggression and cathartic laughter. The ordinary consequences of forbidden words are suspended by meta-linguistic gestures (tones of voice, facial expressions, catch phrases) that send the message "this is a joke," and emotions that would ordinarily endanger a social relationship can be spoken safely within the micro-world created by the "the joke form" (Bateson 1972).

Yet jokes are not just stories, they are a theater of domination in everyday life, and the success or failure of a joke marks the boundary within which power and aggression may be used in a relationship. Nearly all jokes have an aggressive content, indeed shared aggression toward an outsider is one of the primary ways by which a group may overcome internal tension and assert its solidarity (Freud 1960, p. 102). Jokes both require and renew social bonds; thus Radcliffe-Brown pointed out that "joking relationships" between mothers-in-law and their sons-in-law provide a release for tension for people structurally bound to each other but at the same time feeling structural conflict with each other (Radcliffe-Brown 1959). Joking relationships in medicine, for example, are a medium for the indirect expression of latent emotions or taboo topics that if directly expressed would challenge the physician's authority or disrupt the need to treat life and death situations as ordinary work (see Coser 1959; Emerson 1969, 1970).

In each of the studies cited above, the primary focus of the analysis was upon the social function of the joke, not gender, yet in each case the joke either functioned through a joking relationship between men and women, such as in Freud's or Radcliffe-Brown's analysis of mother-in-law jokes, or through the joking relationship between men and women. For example, Coser describes the role of nurses as a safe target of jokes: as a surrogate for the male doctor in patient jokes challenging medical authority; or as a surrogate for the patient in the jokes with which doctors expressed anxiety. Sexist jokes, therefore, should be analyzed not only in general terms of the function of jokes as a means of defending social order, but in specific terms as the mechanism by which the order of gender domination is sustained in everyday life. From this perspective, jokes reveal the way social organizations are gendered, namely, built around the emotional rules of male bonding. In this case study, gender is not only the primary content of men's jokes, but the emotional structures of the male bond is built upon a joking relationship that "negotiates" the tension men feel about their relationship with each other, and with women.

Male bonding in everyday life frequently takes the form of a group joking relationship by which men create a serial kind of intimacy to "negotiate" the latent tension and aggression they feel toward each other. The humor of male bonding relationships generally is sexual and aggressive, and frequently consists of sexist or racist jokes. As Freud (1960, p. 99) observed, the jokes that individual men direct toward women are generally erotic, tend to clever forms (like the double entendre), and have a seductive purpose. The jokes that men tell about women in the presence of other men are sexual and aggressive rather than erotic and use hostile rather than clever verbal forms; and, this paper will argue, have the creation of male group bonding as their purpose. While Freud analyzed jokes in order to reveal the unconscious, in this article, relationships will be analyzed to uncover the emotional dynamics of male friendships.

The failed penis-envy joke reveals two kinds of joking relationships between college men and women. First, the attempted joke was part of an ongoing joking relationship between "the guys and the girls," as they called each other. The guys used the joking relationship to negotiate the tension they felt between sexual interest in the girls and fear of commitment to them. The guys contrasted their sense of independence and play in male friendships to the sense of dependence they felt in their relationships with women, and used hostile joking to negotiate their fear of the "loss of control" implied by intimacy. Second, the failure of the joke uncovered the use of sexist jokes in creating bonds between men; through their own joking relationships (which they called friendship), the guys negotiated the tension between their need for intimacy with other men and their fear of losing their autonomy as men to the authority of the work world.

The Girls' Story

The women frequently had been the target of fraternity initiation rites in the past, and generally enjoyed this joking relationship with the men, if with a certain ambivalence. "There was a naked Christmas Carol event, they were singing 'We wish you a Merry Christmas,' and 'Bring on the hasty pudding' was the big line they liked to yell out. And we had five or six pledges who had to strip in front of the house and do naked jumping jacks on the lawn, after all the women in the house were lined up on the steps to watch." The women did not think these events were hostile because they had been invited to watch, and the men stood with them watching, suggesting that the pledges, not the women, were the targets of the joke. This made the joke sexual, not sexist, and part of the normal erotic joking relationship between the guys and girls. Still, these jokes were ritual events, not real social relationships; one woman said, "We were just supposed to watch, and the guys were watching us watch. The men set up the stage and the women are brought along to observe. They were the controlling force, then they jump into the car and take off."

At the meeting with the men, two of the women spoke for the group while 11 others sat silently in the center, surrounded by about 30 men. Each tried to explain to the men why the joke had not been funny. The first began, "I'm a feminist, but I'm not going to blame anyone for anything. I just want to talk about my feelings." When she said, "these guys pile in, I mean these huge guys," the men exploded in loud cathartic laughter, and the women joined in, releasing some of the tension of the meeting. She continued, "Your humor was pretty funny as long as it was sexual, but when it went beyond sexual to sexist, then it became painful. You were saying 'I'm better than you.' When you started using sex as a way of proving your superiority it hurt me and made me angry."

The second woman speaker criticized the imposition of the joke form itself, saying that the men's raid had the tone of a symbolic rape. "I admit we knew you were coming over, and we were whispering about it. But it went too far, and I felt afraid to say anything. Why do men always think about women in terms of violating them, in sexual imagery? You have to understand that the combination of a sexual topic with the physical threat of all of you standing around terrified me. I couldn't move. You have to realize that when men combine sexuality and force it's terrifying to women." This woman alluded to having been sexually assaulted in the past, but spoke in a nonthreatening tone that made the men listen silently.

The women spoke about feeling angry about the invasion of their space, about the coercion of being forced to listen to the speeches, and about being used as the object of a joke. But they reported their anger as a psychological fact, a statement about a past feeling, not an accusation. Many began by saying, "I'm not a feminist, but . . . ," to reassure the men that although they felt angry, they were not challenging traditional gender relations. The women were caught in a double-bind; if they spoke angrily to the men they would violate the taboo against the expression of anger by women (Miller 1976, p. 102). If they said nothing, they would internalize their anger, and traditional feminine culture would encourage them to feel guilty about feeling angry at all (Bernardez 1978; Lerner 1980). In part they resolved the issue by accepting the men's construction of the event as a joke, although a failed joke; accepting the joke form absolved the men of responsibility, and transformed a debate about gender into a debate about good and bad jokes.

To be accepted as a joke, a cue must be sent to establish a "frame" [for] the latent hostility of the joke content in a safe context; the men sent such a cue when they stood next to the women during the naked jumping jacks. If the cue "this is a joke" is ambiguous, or is not accepted, the aggressive content of the joke is revealed and generally is responded to with anger or aggression, endangering the relationship. In part the women were pointing out to the men that the cue "this is a joke" had not been given in this case, and the aggressive content of the joke hurt them. If the cue is given properly and accepted, the everyday rules of social order are suspended and the rule "this is fun" is imposed on the expression of hostility.

Verbal aggression mediated by the joke form generally will be [accepted] without later consequences in the everyday world, and will be judged in terms of the formal intention of jokes, shared play marked by laughter in the interest of social order. By complaining to the university, the women had suspended the rules of joke culture, and attempted to renegotiate them by bringing in an observer; even this turned out to be too aggressive, and the women retreated to traditional gender relationships. The men had formally accepted this shift of rules in order to avoid punishment from the university, however their defense of the joke form was tacitly a defense of traditional gender rules that would define male sexist jokes toward women as erotic, not hostile.

In accepting the construction of the event as "just a joke" the women absolved the men of responsibility for their actions by calling them "little boys." One woman said, "It's not wrong, they're just boys playing a prank. They're little boys, they don't know what they're doing. It was unpleasant, but we shouldn't make a big deal out of it." In appealing to the rules of the joke form the men were willing to sacrifice their relationship to the women to protect the rules. In calling the men "little boys" the women were bending the rules trying to preserve the relationship through a patient nurturing role (see Gilligan 1982, p. 44).

In calling the guys "little boys," the girls had also created a kind of linguistic symmetry between "the boys and the girls." With the exception of the law student, who called the girls "women," the students called the men "guys" and the women "girls." Earlier in the year the law student had started a discussion about this naming practice. The term "women" had sexual connotations that made "the girls" feel vulnerable, and "gals," the parallel to "guys," connoted "older women" to them. While the term "girls" refers to children, it was adopted because it avoided sexual connotations. Thus the women had no term like "the guys," which is a bonding term that refers to a group of friends as equals; the women often used the term "the guys" to refer to themselves in a group. As the men's speeches were to make clear, the term "guys" refers to a bond that is exclusively male, which is founded upon the emotional structure of the joke form, and which justifies it.

The Guys' Story

Aside from the roar of laughter when a woman referred to their intimidating size, the men interrupted the women only once. When a woman began to say that the men obviously intended to intimidate them, the men loudly protested that the women couldn't possibly judge their intentions, that they intended the whole event only as a joke, and the intention of a joke is, by definition, just fun.

At this point the two black men in the fraternity intervened to explain the rules of male joke culture to the women. The black men said that in a sense they understood what the women meant, it is painful being the object of aggressive jokes. In fact, they said, the collective talk of the fraternity at meals and group events was made up of nothing but jokes, including many racist jokes. One said, "I know what you mean. I've had to listen to things in the house that I'd have hit someone for saying if I'd heard them outside." There was again cathartic laughter among the guys, for the male group bond consisted almost entirely of aggressive words that were barely contained by the responsibility absolving rule of the joke form. A woman responded, "Maybe people should be hit for saying those things, maybe that's the right thing to do." But the black speaker was trying to explain the rules of male joke culture to the women, "if you'd just ignored us, it wouldn't have been any fun." To ignore a joke, even though it makes you feel hurt or angry, is to show strength or coolness, the two primary masculine ideals of the group.

Another man tried to explain the failure of the joke in terms of the difference between the degree of "crudeness" appropriate among the guys and between "guys and girls." He said, "As I was listening at the edge of the room, near the door, and when I looked at the guys I was laughing but when I looked at the girls I was embarrassed. I could see both sides at the same time. It was too crude for your sense of propriety. We have a sense of crudeness you don't have. That's a cultural aspect of the difference between girls and guys."

The other men laughed as he mentioned "how crude we are at the house," and one of the black men added, "you wouldn't believe how crude it gets." Many of the men said privately that while they individually found the jokes about women vulgar, the jokes were justified because they were necessary for the formation of the fraternal bond. These men thought the mistake had been to reveal their crudeness to the women, this was "in bad taste."

In its content, the fraternal bond was almost entirely a joking relationship. In part, the joking was a kind of "signifying" or "dozens," a ritual exchange of insults that functioned to create group solidarity. "If there's one theme that goes on, it's the emphasis on being able to take a lot of ridicule, of shit, and not getting upset about it. Most of the interaction we have is verbally abusing each other, making disgusting references to your mother's sexuality, or the women you were seen with, or your sex organ, the size of your sex organ. And you aren't cool unless you can take it without trying to get back." Being cool is an important male value in other settings as well, such as sports or work; the joke form is a kind of male pedagogy in that, in one guy's words, it teaches "how to keep in control of your emotions."

But the guys themselves would not have described their group as a joking relationship or even as a male bond; they called it friendship. One man said he had found perhaps a dozen guys in the house who were special friends, "guys I could cry in front of." Yet in interviews, no one could recall any of the guys actually crying in front of each other. One said, "I think the guys are very close, they would do nearly anything for each other, drive each other places, give each other money. I think when they have problems about school, their car, or something like that, they can talk to each other. I'm not sure they can talk to each other about problems with women though." The image of crying in front of the other guys was a moving symbol of intimacy to the guys, but in fact crying would be an admission of vulnerability, which would violate the ideals of "strength" and "being cool."

Although the fraternal bond was idealized as a unique kind of intimacy upon which genuine friendship was built, the content of the joking relationship was focused upon women, including much "signifying" talk about mothers. The women interpreted the sexist jokes as a sign of vulnerability. "The thing that struck me the most about our meeting together," one said, "was when the men said they were afraid of trusting women, afraid of being seen as jerks." According to her, this had been the women's main reaction to the meeting by the other women, "How do you tell men that they don't have to be afraid, and what do you do with women who abuse that kind of trust?" One of the men on the boundary of the group remarked that the most hostile misogynist jokes came from the men with the fewest intimate relationships with women. "I think down deep all these guys would love to have satisfying relationships with women. I think they're scared of failing, of having to break away from the group they've become comfortable with. I think being in a fraternity, having close friendships with men is a replacement for having close relationships with women. It'd be painful for them because they'd probably fail."

Joking mobilized the commitment of the men to the group by policing the individual men's commitments to women and minimized the possibility of dyadic withdrawal from the group (see Slater 1963). "One of the guys just acquired a girlfriend a few weeks ago. He's someone I don't think has had a woman to be friends with, maybe ever, at least in a long time. Everybody has been ribbing him intensely the last few weeks. It's good natured in tone. Sitting at dinner they've invented a little song they sing to him. People yell questions about his girlfriend, the size of her vagina, does she have big breasts."

Since both the jokes and the descriptions of the parties have strong homoerotic overtones, including the exchange of women as sexual partners, jokes were also targeted at homosexuality, to draw an emotional line between the homosocial male bond and homosexual relationships. Being called "queer," however, did not require a sexual relationship with another man, but only visible signs of vulnerability or nurturing behavior.

Male Bonding as a Joking Relationship

Fraternal bonding is an intimate kind of male group friendship that suspends the ordinary rules and responsibilities of everyday life through joking relationships. To the guys, dyadic friendship with a woman implied "loss of control," namely, responsibility for work and family. In dealing with women, the group separated intimacy from sex, defining the male bond as intimate but not sexual (homosocial), and relationships with women as sexual but not intimate (heterosexual). The intimacy of group friendship was built upon shared spontaneous action, "having fun," rather than the self-disclosure that marks women's friendships (see Rubin 1983, p. 13). One of the men had been inexpressive as he listened to the discussion, but spoke about fun in a voice filled with emotion, "The penis-envy speech was a hilarious idea, great college fun. That's what I joined the fraternity for, a good time. College is a stage in my life to do crazy and humorous things. In 10 years when I'm in the business world I won't be able to carry on like this [again cathartic laughter from the men]. The initiation was intended to be humorous. We didn't think through how sensitive you women were going to be."

This speech gives the fraternal bond a specific place in the life cycle. The joking relationship is a ritual bond that creates a male group bond in the transition between boyhood and manhood, after the separation from the family, where the authority of mothers limits fun, but before becoming subject to the authority of work. One man later commented on the transitional nature of the male bond, "I think a lot of us are really scared of losing total control over our own lives. Having to sacrifice our individuality. I think we're scared of work in the same way we're scared of women." In this sense individuality is associated with what the guys called "strength," both the emotional strength suggested by being cool, and the physical strength suggested by facing the risks of sports and the paramilitary games they liked to play.

The emotional structure of the joking relationship is built upon the guys' latent anger about the discipline that middle-class male roles imposed upon them, both marriage rules and work rules. The general relationship between organization of men's work and men's domination of women was noted by Max Weber (1958, pp.

345–346), who described "the vocational specialist" as a man mastered by the rules of organization that create an impersonal kind of dependence, and who therefore seeks to create a feeling of independence through the sexual conquest of women. In each of the epochs of Western history, Weber argues, the subordination of men at work has given rise to a male concept of freedom based upon the violation of women. Although Weber tied dependence upon rules to men's need for sexual conquest through seduction, this may also be a clue to the meaning of sexist jokes and joking relationships among men at work. Sexist jokes may not be simply a matter of recreation or a means of negotiating role stress, they may be a reflection of the emotional foundations of organizational life for men. In everyday work life, sexist jokes may function as a ritual suspension of the rules of responsibility for men, a withdrawal into a microworld in which their anger about dependence upon work and women may be safely expressed.

In analyzing the contradictions and vulnerabilities the guys felt about relationships with women and the responsibilities of work, I will focus upon three dimensions of the joking relationship: (1) the emotional content of the jokes; (2) the erotics of rule breaking created by the rules of the joke form; and (3) the image of strength and "being cool" they pitted against the dependence represented by both women and work.

The Emotional Dynamic of Sexist Jokes

When confronted by the women, the men defended the joke by asserting the formal rule that the purpose of jokes is play, then by justifying the jokes as necessary in order to create a special male bond. The defense that jokes are play defines aggressive behavior as play. This defense was far more persuasive to the men than to the women, since many forms of male bonding play are rule-governed aggression, as in sports and games. The second defense, asserting the relation between sexist jokes and male bonds, points out the social function of sexist jokes among the guys, to control the threat that individual men might form intimate emotional bonds with women and withdraw from the group. Each defense poses a puzzle about the emotional dynamics of male group friendship, for in each case male group friendship seems more like a defense against vulnerability than a positive ideal.

In each defense, intimacy is split from sexuality in order to eroticize the male bond, thereby creating an instrumental sexuality directed at women. The separation of intimacy from sexuality transforms women into "sexual objects," which both justifies aggression at women by suspending their relationships to the men and devalues sexuality itself, creating a disgust at women as the sexual "object" unworthy of intimate attention. What is the origin of this conjunction between the devaluation of sexuality and the appropriation of intimacy for the male bond?

Chodorow (1978, p. 182) argues that the sense of masculine identity is constructed by an early repression of the son's erotic bond with his mother; with this repression the son's capacity for intimacy and commitment is devalued as feminine behavior. Henceforth men feel ambivalent about intimate relationships with women, seeking to replicate the fusion of intimacy and sexuality that they had experienced in their primal relationships to their mothers, but at the same time fearing engulfment by women in heterosexual relationships, like the engulfment of their infant selves by their mothers (Chodorow 1976). Certainly the content of the group's joke suggests this repression of the attachment to the mother, as well as hostility to her authority in the family. One man reported, "There're an awful lot of jokes about people's mothers. If any topic of conversation dominates the conversation it's 'heard your mother was with Ray [one of the guys] last night.' The guys will say incredibly vulgar things about their mothers, or they'll talk about the anatomy of a guy's girlfriends, or women they'd like to sleep with." While the guys' signifying mother jokes suggest the repression Chodorow describes, the men realized that their view of women made it unlikely that marriage would be a positive experience. One said, "I think a lot of us expect to marry someone pretty enough that other men will think we got a good catch, someone who is at least marginally interesting to chat with, but not someone we'd view as a friend. But at the same time, a woman who will make sufficient demands that we won't be able to have any friends. So we'll be stuck for the rest of our lives without friends."

While the emotional dynamic of men's "heterosexual knots" may well begin in this primordial separation of infant sons from mothers, its structure is replicated in the guys' ambivalence about their fathers, and their anger about the dependence upon rules in the work world. Yet the guys themselves described the fraternal bond as a way of creating "strength" and overcoming dependence, which suggests a positive ideal of male identity. In order to explore the guys' sense of the value of the male bond, their conception of strength and its consequences for the way they related to each other and to women has to be taken seriously.

Strength

Ultimately the guys justified the penis-envy joke because it created a special kind of male intimacy, but while the male group is able to appropriate its members' needs for intimacy and commitment, it is not clear that it is able to satisfy those needs, because strength has been defined as the opposite of intimacy. "Strength" is a value that represents solidarity rather than intimacy, the solidarity of a shared risk in rule-governed aggressive competition; its value is suggested by the cathartic laughter when the first woman speaker said, "These guys poured in, these huge guys."

The eros detached from sexuality is attached to rules, not to male friends; the male bond consists of an erotic toward rules, and yet the penis-envy joke expresses most of all the guys' ambivalence about rules. Like "the lads," the male gangs who roam the English countryside, "getting in trouble" by enforcing social mores in unsocial ways (Peters 1972), "the guys" break the rules in rule-governed ways. The joke form itself suggests this ambivalence about rules and acts as a kind of pedagogy about the relationship between rules and aggression in male work culture. The joke form expresses emotions and tensions that might endanger the order of the organization, but that must be spoken lest they damage social order. Jokes can create group solidarity only if they allow dangerous things to be said; allow a physical catharsis of tension through laughter; or create the solidarity of an "in group" through shared aggression against an "out group." In each case there is an erotic in joke forms: an erotic of shared aggression, of shared sexual feeling, or an erotic of rule breaking itself.

It has been suggested that male groups experience a high level of excitement and sexual arousal in public acts of rule breaking (Thorne & Luria 1986). The penis-envy speech is precisely such an act, a breaking of conventional moral rules in the interest of group arousal. In each of the versions of the joking relationship in this group there is such an erotic quality: in the sexual content of the jokes, in the need for women to witness dirty talk or naked pledges, in the eros of aggression of the raid and jokes themselves. The penis-envy speech, a required event for all members of the group, is such a collective violation of the rules, and so is the content of their talk, a collective dirty talking that violates moral rules. The cathartic laughter that greeted the words, "You wouldn't believe what we say at the house," testifies to the emotional charge invested in dirty talk.

Because the intimacy of the guys' bond is built around an erotic of rule breaking, it has the serial structure of shared risk rather than the social structure of shared intimacy. In writing about the shared experience of suffering and danger of men at war, J. Glenn Gray (1959, pp. 89–90) distinguishes two kinds of male bonding, comradeship and friendship. Comradeship is based upon an erotic of shared danger, but is based upon the loss of an individual sense of self to a group identity, while friendship is based upon an individual's intellectual and emotional affinity to another individual. In the eros of friendship one's sense of self is heightened; in the eros of comradeship a sense of self is replaced by a sense of group membership. In this sense the guys were seeking comradeship, not friendship, hence the group constructed its bond through an erotic of shared activities with an element of risk, shared danger, or rule breaking: in sports, in paramilitary games, in wild parties, in joking relations. The guys called the performance of these activities "strength," being willing to take risks as a group and remaining cool.

Thus the behavior that the women defined as aggressive was seen by the men as a contest of strength governed by the rules of the joke form, to which the proper response would have been to remain "cool." To the guys, the masculine virtue of "strength" has a positive side, to discover oneself and to discover a sense of the other person through a contest of strength that is governed by rules. To the guys, "strength" is not the same as power or aggression because it is governed by rules, not anger; it is anger that is "uncool."

"Being Cool"

It is striking that the breaking of rules was not spontaneous, but controlled by the rules of the joke form: that aggressive talk replaces action; that talk is framed by a social form that requires the consent of others; that talk should not be taken seriously. This was the lesson that the black men tried to teach the women in the group session: In the male world, aggression is not defined as violent if it is rule governed rather than anger governed. The fraternal bond was built upon this emotional structure, for the life of the group centered upon the mobilization of aggressive energies in rule-governed activities (in sports, games, jokes, parties). In each arena aggression was highly valued (strength) only when it was rule governed (cool). Getting angry was called "losing control" and the guys thought they were most likely to lose control when they experienced themselves as personally dependent, as in relationships with women and at work.

Rule-governed aggression is a conduct that is very useful to organizations, in that it mobilizes aggressive energies but binds them to order by rules (see Benjamin 1980, p. 154). The male sense of order is procedural rather than substantive because the male bond is formal (rule governed), rather than personal (based upon intimacy and commitment). Male groups in this sense are shame cultures, not guilt cultures, because the male bond is a group identity that subordinates the individual to the rules, and because social control is imposed through collective judgments about self-control, such as "strength" and "cool." The sense of order within such male groups is based upon the belief that all members are equally dependent upon the rules and that no personal dependence is created within the group. This is not true of the family or of relations with women, both of which are intimate, and, from the guys' point of view, are "out of control" because they are governed by emotion.

The guys face contradictory demands from work culture about the use of aggressive behavior. Aggressive conduct is highly valued in a competitive society when it serves the interests of the organization, but men also face a strong taboo against the expression of anger at work when it is not rule governed. "Competition" imposes certain rules upon aggressive group processes: Aggression must be calculated, not angry; it must be consistent with the power hierarchy of the organization, serving authority and not challenging it; if expressed, it must be indirect, as in jokes; it must serve the needs of group solidarity, not of individual autonomy. Masculine culture separates anger from aggression when it combines the value "strength" with the value "being cool." While masculine cultures often define the expression of anger as "violent" or "loss of control," anger, properly defined, is speech, not action; angry speech is the way we can defend our sense of integrity and assert our sense of justice. Thus it is anger that challenges the authority of the rules, not aggressive behavior in itself, because anger defends the self, not the organization.

The guys' joking relationship taught them a pedagogy for the controlled use of aggression in the work world, to be able to compete aggressively without feeling angry. The guys recognized the relationship between their male bond and the work world by claiming that "high officials of the university know about the way we act and they understand what we are doing." While this might be taken as evidence that the guys were internalizing their fathers' norms and thus inheriting the mantle of patriarchy, the guys described their fathers as slaves to work and women, not as patriarchs. The guys also asserted themselves against the authority of their fathers by acting out against the authority of rules in the performance of "strength."

The guys clearly benefited from the male authority that gave them the power to impose the penis-envy joke upon the women with essentially no consequences. Men are allowed to direct anger and aggression toward women because social norms governing the expression of anger or humor generally replicate the power order of the group. It is striking, however, that the guys would not accept the notion that men have more power than women do; to them it is not men who rule, but rules that govern men. These men had so internalized the governing of male emotions by rules that their anger itself could emerge only indirectly through rule-governed forms, such as jokes and joking relationships. In these forms their anger could serve only order, not their sense of self or justice.

References

Bateson, G. (1972). A theory of play and fantasy. In *Steps toward an ecology of mind* (pp. 177–193). New York: Ballantine.

Benjamin, J. (1978). Authority and the family revisited, or, A world without fathers. *New German Critique, 4*(3), 13, 35–57.

Benjamin, J. (1980). The bonds of love: Rational violence and erotic domination. *Feminist Studies, 6*(1), 144–174.

Berndardez, T. (1978). Women and anger. *Journal of the American Medical Women's Association, 33*(5), 215–219.

Bly, R. (1982). What men really want: An interview with Keith Thompson. *New Age*, pp. 30–37, 50–51.

Chodorow, N. (1976). Oedipal asymmetries, heterosexual knots. *Social Problems, 23*, 454–468.

Chodorow, N. (1978). *The reproduction of mothering*. Berkeley: University of California Press.

Coser, R. (1959). Some social functions of laughter: A study of humor in a hospital setting. *Human Relations, 12*, 171–182.

Emerson, J. (1969). Negotiating the serious import of humor. *Sociometry, 32*, 169–181.

Emerson, J. (1970). Behavior in private places. In H. P. Dreitzel (Ed.), *Recent sociology: Vol. 2. Patterns in communicative behavior*. New York: Macmillan.

Freud, S. (1960). *Jokes and their relation to the unconscious*. New York: Norton.

Gilligan, C. (1982). *In a different voice*. Cambridge, MA: Harvard University Press.

Gray, G. J. (1959). *The warriors: Reflections on men in battle*. New York: Harper & Row.

Lerner, H. E. (1980). Internal prohibitions against female anger. *American Journal of Psychoanalysis, 40*, 137–148.

Miller, J. B. (1976). *Toward a new psychology of women*. Boston: Beacon.

Peters, E. L. (1972). Aspects of the control of moral ambiguities. In M. Gluckman (Ed.), *The allocation of responsibility* (pp. 109–162). Manchester: Manchester University Press.

Radcliffe-Brown, A. (1959). *Structure and function in primitive society*. Glencoe, IL: Free Press.

Rubin, L. (1983). *Intimate strangers*. New York: Harper & Row.

Slater, P. (1963). On social regression. *American Sociological Review, 28*, 339–364.

Thorne, B., & Luria, Z. (1986). Sexuality and gender in children's daily worlds. *Social Problems*.

Weber, M. (1958). Religions of the world and their directions. In H. Gerth & C. W. Mills (Eds.), *From Max Weber*. New York: Oxford University Press.

ARTICLE 15

A. Ayres Boswell
Joan Z. Spade

Fraternities and Collegiate Rape Culture: Why Are Some Fraternities More Dangerous Places for Women?

Date rape and acquaintance rape on college campuses are topics of concern to both researchers and college administrators. Some estimate that 60 to 80 percent of rapes are date or acquaintance rape (Koss, Dinero, Seibel, and Cox 1988). Further, 1 out of 4 college women say they were raped or experienced an attempted rape, and 1 out of 12 college men say they forced a woman to have sexual intercourse against her will (Koss, Gidycz, and Wisniewski 1985).

Although considerable attention focuses on the incidence of rape, we know relatively little about the context or the *rape culture* surrounding date and acquaintance rape. Rape culture is a set of values and beliefs that provides an environment conducive to rape (Herman 1984; Buchwald, Fletcher, & Roth 1993). The term applies to a generic culture surrounding and promoting rape, not the specific settings in which rape is likely to occur. We believe that the specific settings also are important in defining relationships between men and women.

Some have argued that fraternities are places where rape is likely to occur on college campuses (Martin and Hummer 1989; Sanday 1990; O'Sullivan 1993) and that the students most likely to accept rape myths and be more sexually aggressive are more likely to live in fraternities and sororities, consume higher doses of alcohol and drugs, and place a higher value on social life at college (Gwartney-Gibbs and Stockard 1989; Kalof and Cargill 1991). Others suggest that sexual aggression is learned in settings such as fraternities and is not part of predispositions or preexisting attitudes (Boeringer, Shehan, and Akers 1991). To prevent further incidences of rape on college campuses, we need to understand what it is about fraternities in particular and college life in general that may contribute to the maintenance of a rape culture on college campuses.

Our approach is to identify the social contexts that link fraternities to campus rape and promote a rape culture. Instead of assuming that all fraternities provide an environment conducive to rape, we compare the interactions of men and women at fraternities identified on campus as being especially *dangerous* places for women, where the likelihood of rape is high, to those seen as *safer* places, where the perceived probability of rape occurring is lower. Prior to collecting data for our study, we found that most women students identified some fraternities as having more sexually aggressive

Author's Note: An earlier version of this article was presented at the annual meeting of the American Sociological Association, August 1993. Special thanks go to Barbara Frankel, Karen Hicks, and Jennifer Vochko for their input into the process and final version and to Judith Gerson, Sue Curry Jansen, Judith Lasker, Patricia Yancey Martin, and Ronnie Steinberg for their careful readings of the draft of this article and for many helpful comments.

From *Gender & Society* 10(2): 133–147. Copyright © 1996 A. Ayres Boswell and Joan Z. Spade. Reprinted by permission of Sage Publications, Inc.

members and a higher probability of rape. These women also considered other fraternities as relatively safe houses, where a women could go and get drunk if she wanted to and feel secure that the fraternity men would not take advantage of her. We compared parties at houses identified as high-risk and low-risk houses as well as at two local bars frequented by college students. Our analysis provides an opportunity to examine situations and contexts that hinder or facilitate positive social relations between undergraduate men and women.

The abusive attitudes toward women that some fraternities perpetuate exist within a general culture where rape is intertwined in traditional gender scripts. Men are viewed as initiators of sex and women as either passive partners or active resisters, preventing men from touching their bodies (LaPlante, McCormick, and Brannigan 1980). Rape culture is based on the assumptions that men are aggressive and dominant whereas women are passive and acquiescent (Herman 1984; Buchwald, Fletcher, & Roth 1993). What occurs on college campuses is an extension of the portrayal of domination and aggression of men over women that exemplifies the double standard of sexual behavior in U.S. society (Barthel 1988; Kimmel 1993).

Sexually active men are positively reinforced by being referred to as "studs," whereas women who are sexually active or report enjoying sex are derogatorily labeled as "sluts" (Herman 1984; O'Sullivan 1993). These gender scripts are embodied in rape myths and stereotypes such as "She really wanted it; she just said no because she didn't want me to think she was a bad girl" (Malamuth 1986; Jenkins and Dambrot 1987; Muehlenhard and Linton 1987; Peterson and Franzese 1987; Lisak and Roth 1988; Burke, Stets, and Pirog-Good 1989). Because men's sexuality is seen as more natural, acceptable, and uncontrollable than women's sexuality, many men and women excuse acquaintance rape by affirming that men cannot control their natural urges (Miller and Marshall 1987).

Whereas some researchers explain these attitudes toward sexuality and rape using an individual or a psychological interpretation, we argue that rape has a social basis, one in which both men and women create and recreate masculine and feminine identities and relations. Based on the assumption that rape is part of the social construction of gender, we examine how men and women "do gender" on a college campus (West and Zimmerman 1987). We focus on fraternities because they have been identified as settings that encourage rape (Sanday 1990). By comparing fraternities that are viewed by women as places where there is a high risk of rape to those where women believe there is a low risk of rape as well as two local commercial bars, we seek to identify characteristics that make some social settings more likely places for the occurrence of rape.

Method

We observed social interactions between men and women at a private coeducational school in which a high percentage (49.4 percent) of students affiliate with Greek organizations. The university has an undergraduate population of approximately 4,500 students, just more than one third of whom are women; the students are primarily from upper-middle-class families. The school, which admitted only men until 1971, is highly competitive academically.

We used a variety of data collection approaches: observations of interactions between men and women at fraternity parties and bars, formal interviews, and informal conversations. The first author, a former undergraduate at this school and a graduate student at the time of the study, collected the data. She knew about the social life at the school and had established rapport and trust between herself and undergraduate students as a teaching assistant in a human sexuality course.

The process of identifying high- and low-risk fraternity houses followed Hunter's (1953) reputational approach. In our study, 40 women students identified fraternities that they considered to be high risk, or to have more sexually aggressive members and higher incidence of rape, as well as fraternities that they considered to be safe houses. The women represented all four years of undergraduate college and different living groups (sororities, residence halls, and off-campus housing). Observations focused on the four fraternities named most often by these women as high-risk houses and the four identified as low-risk houses.

Throughout the spring semester, the first author observed at two fraternity parties each weekend at two different houses (fraternities could have parties only on weekends at this campus). She also observed students' interactions in two popular university bars on weeknights to provide a comparison of students' behavior in non-Greek settings. The first local bar at which she observed was popular with seniors and older students; the second bar was popular with first-, second-, and third-year undergraduates because the management did not strictly enforce drinking age laws in this bar.

The observer focused on the social context as well as interaction among participants at each setting. In terms of social context, she observed the following: ratio of men to women, physical setting such as the party decor and theme, use and control of alcohol and level of intoxication, and explicit and implicit norms. She noted interactions between men and women (i.e., physical contact, conversational style, use of jokes) and the relations among men (i.e., their treatment of pledges and other men at fraternity parties). Other than the observer, no one knew the identity of the high- or low-risk fraternities. Although this may have introduced bias into the data collection, students on this campus who read this article before it was submitted for publication commented on how accurately the social scene is described.

In addition, 50 individuals were interviewed including men from the selected fraternities, women who attended those parties, men not affiliated with fraternities, and self-identified rape victims known to the first author. The first author approached men and women by telephone or on campus and asked them to participate in interviews. The interviews included open-ended questions about gender relations on campus, attitudes about date rape, and their own experiences on campus.

To assess whether self-selection was a factor in determining the classification of the fraternity, we compared high-risk houses to low-risk houses on several characteristics. In terms of status on campus, the high- and low-risk houses we studied attracted about the same number of pledges; however, many of the high-risk houses had more members. There was no difference in grade point averages for the two types of houses. In fact, the highest and lowest grade point averages were found in the high-risk category. Although both high- and low-risk fraternities participated in sports, brothers in the low-risk houses tended to play intramural sports whereas brothers in the high-risk houses were more likely to be varsity athletes. The high-risk houses may be more aggressive, as they had a slightly larger number of disciplinary incidents and their reports were more severe, often with physical harm to others and damage to property. Further, in year-end reports, there was more property damage in the high-risk houses. Last, more of the low-risk houses participated in a campus rape-prevention program. In summary, both high- and low-risk fraternities seem to be equally attractive to freshmen men on this campus, and differences between the eight fraternities we studied were not great; however, the high-risk houses had a slightly larger number of reports of aggression and physical destruction in the houses and the low-risk houses were more likely to participate in a rape prevention program.

Results
The Settings
Fraternity Parties We observed several differences in the quality of the interaction of men and women at parties at high-risk fraternities compared to those at low-risk houses. A typical party at a low-risk house included an equal number of women and men. The social atmosphere was friendly, with considerable interaction between women and men. Men and women danced in groups and in couples, with many of the couples

kissing and displaying affection toward each other. Brothers explained that, because many of the men in these houses had girlfriends, it was normal to see couples kissing on the dance floor. Coed groups engaged in conversations at many of these houses, with women and men engaging in friendly exchanges, giving the impression that they knew each other well. Almost no cursing and yelling was observed at parties in low-risk houses; when pushing occurred, the participants apologized. Respect for women extended to the women's bathrooms, which were clean and well supplied.

At high-risk houses, parties typically had skewed gender ratios, sometimes involving more men and other times involving more women. Gender segregation also was evident at these parties, with the men on one side of a room or in the bar drinking while women gathered in another area. Men treated women differently in the high-risk houses. The women's bathrooms in the high-risk houses were filthy, including clogged toilets and vomit in the sinks. When a brother was told of the mess in the bathroom at a high-risk house, he replied, "Good, maybe some of these beer wenches will leave so there will be more beer for us."

Men attending parties at high-risk houses treated women less respectfully, engaging in jokes, conversations, and behaviors that degraded women. Men made a display of assessing women's bodies and rated them with thumbs up or thumbs down for the other men in the sight of the women. One man attending a party at a high-risk fraternity said to another, "Did you know that this week is Women's Awareness Week? I guess that means we get to abuse them more this week." Men behaved more crudely at parties at high-risk houses. At one party, a brother dropped his pants, including his underwear, while dancing in front of several women. Another brother slid across the dance floor completely naked.

The atmosphere at parties in high-risk fraternities was less friendly overall. With the exception of greetings, men and women rarely smiled or laughed and spoke to each other less often than was the case at parties in low-risk houses. The few one-on-one conversations between women and men appeared to be strictly flirtatious (lots of eye contact, touching, and very close talking). It was rare to see a group of men and women together talking. Men were openly hostile, which made the high-risk parties seem almost threatening at times. For example, there was a lot of touching, pushing, profanity, and name calling, some done by women.

Students at parties at the high-risk houses seemed self-conscious and aware of the presence of members of the opposite sex, an awareness that was sexually charged. Dancing early in the evening was usually between women. Close to midnight, the sex ratio began to balance out with the arrival of more men or more women. Couples began to dance together but in a sexual way (close dancing with lots of pelvic thrusts). Men tried to pick up women using lines such as "Want to see my fish tank?" and "Let's go upstairs so that we can talk; I can't hear what you're saying in here."

Although many of the same people who attended high-risk parties also attended low-risk parties, their behavior changed as they moved from setting to setting. Group norms differed across contexts as well. At a party that was held jointly at a low-risk house with a high-risk fraternity, the ambience was that of a party at a high-risk fraternity with heavier drinking, less dancing, and fewer conversations between women and men. The men from both high- and low-risk fraternities were very aggressive; a fight broke out, and there was pushing and shoving on the dance floor and in general.

As others have found, fraternity brothers at high-risk houses on this campus told about routinely discussing their sexual exploits at breakfast the morning after parties and sometimes at house meetings (cf. Martin and Hummer 1989; Sanday 1990; O'Sullivan 1993). During these sessions, the brothers we interviewed said that men bragged about what they did the night before with stories of sexual conquests often told by the same men, usually sophomores. The women involved in these exploits were women they did not know or knew but did not respect, or *faceless victims*. Men usually treated girlfriends with respect and did not talk about them in these storytelling sessions. Men from low-risk houses, however, did not describe similar sessions in their houses.

The Bar Scene The bar atmosphere and social context differed from those of fraternity parties. The music was not as loud, and both bars had places to sit and have conversations. At all fraternity parties, it was difficult to maintain conversations with loud music playing and no place to sit. The volume of music at parties at high-risk fraternities was even louder than it was at low-risk houses, making it virtually impossible to have conversations. In general, students in the local bars behaved in the same way that students did at parties in low-risk houses with conversations typical, most occurring between men and women.

The first bar, frequented by older students, had live entertainment every night of the week. Some nights were more crowded than others, and the atmosphere was friendly, relaxed, and conducive to conversation. People laughed and smiled and behaved politely toward each other. The ratio of men to women was fairly equal, with students congregating in mostly coed groups. Conversation flowed freely and people listened to each other.

Although the women and men at the first bar also were at parties at low- and high-risk fraternities, their behavior at the bar included none of the blatant sexual or intoxicated behaviors observed at some of these parties. As the evenings wore on, the number of one-on-one conversations between men and women increased and conversations shifted from small talk to topics such as war and AIDS. Conversations did not revolve around picking up another person, and most people left the bar with same-sex friends or in coed groups.

The second bar was less popular with older students. Younger students, often under the legal drinking age, went there to drink, sometimes after leaving campus parties. This bar was much smaller and usually not as crowded as the first bar. The atmosphere was more mellow and relaxed than it was at the fraternity parties. People went there to hang out and talk to each other.

On a couple of occasions, however, the atmosphere at the second bar became similar to that of a party at a high-risk fraternity. As the number of people in the bar increased, they removed chairs and tables, leaving no place to sit and talk. The music also was turned up louder, drowning out conversation. With no place to dance or sit, most people stood around but could not maintain conversations because of the noise and crowds. Interactions between women and men consisted mostly of flirting. Alcohol consumption also was greater than it was on the less crowded nights, and the number of visibly drunk people increased. The more people drank, the more conversation and socializing broke down. The only differences between this setting and that of a party at a high-risk house were that brothers no longer controlled the territory and bedrooms were not available upstairs.

Gender Relations

Relations between women and men are shaped by the contexts in which they meet and interact. As is the case on other college campuses, *hooking up* has replaced dating on this campus, and fraternities are places where many students hook up. Hooking up is a loosely applied term on college campuses that had different meanings for men and women on this campus.

Most men defined hooking up similarly. One man said it was something that happens

> when you are really drunk and meet up with a woman you sort of know, or possibly don't know at all and don't care about. You go home with her with the intention of getting as much sexual, physical pleasure as she'll give you, which can range anywhere from kissing to intercourse, without any strings attached.

The exception to this rule is when men hook up with women they admire. Men said they are less likely to press for sexual activity with someone they know and like because they want the relationship to continue and be based on respect.

Women's version of hooking up differed. Women said they hook up only with men they cared about and described hooking up as kissing and petting but not sexual intercourse. Many women said that hooking up was disappointing because they wanted longer-term relationships. First-year women students realized quickly that hook-ups were usually one-night stands with no strings attached, but many continued to hook up because they had few opportunities to develop relationships with men on campus. One first-year woman said that "70 percent of hook-ups never talk again and try to avoid one another; 26 percent may actually hear from them or talk to them again, and 4 percent may actually go on a date, which can lead to a relationship." Another first-year woman said, "It was fun in the beginning. You get a lot of attention and kiss a lot of boys and think this is what college is about, but it gets tiresome fast."

Whereas first-year women get tired of the hook-up scene early on, many men do not become bored with it until their junior or senior year. As one upperclassman said, "The whole game of hooking up became really meaningless and tiresome for me during my second semester of my sophomore year, but most of my friends didn't get bored with it until the following year."

In contrast to hooking up, students also described monogamous relationships with steady partners. Some type of commitment was expected, but most people did not anticipate marriage. The term *seeing each other* was applied when people were sexually involved but free to date other people. This type of relationship involved less commitment than did one of boyfriend/girlfriend but was not considered to be a hook-up.

The general consensus of women and men interviewed on this campus was that the Greek system, called "the hill," set the scene for gender relations. The predominance of Greek membership and subsequent living arrangements segregated men and women. During the week, little interaction occurred between women and men after their first year in college because students in fraternities or sororities live and dine in separate quarters. In addition, many non-Greek upper-class students move off campus into apartments. Therefore, students see each other in classes or in the library, but there is no place where students can just hang out together.

Both men and women said that fraternities dominate campus social life, a situation that everyone felt limited opportunities for meaningful interactions. One senior Greek man said:

> This environment is horrible and so unhealthy for good male and female relationships and interactions to occur. It is so segregated and male dominated.... It is our party, with our rules and our beer. We are allowing these women and other men to come to our party. Men can feel superior in their domain.

Comments from a senior woman reinforced his views: "Men are dominant; they are the kings of the campus. It is their environment that they allow us to enter; therefore, we have to abide by their rules." A junior women described fraternity parties as:

> good for meeting acquaintances but almost impossible to really get to know anyone. The environment is so superficial, probably because there are so many social cliques due to the Greek system. Also, the music is too loud and the people are too drunk to attempt to have a real conversation, anyway.

Some students claim that fraternities even control the dating relationships of their members. One senior woman said, "Guys dictate how dating occurs on this campus, whether it's cool, who it's with, how much time can be spent with the girlfriend and with the brothers." Couples either left campus for an evening or hung out separately with their own same-gender friends at fraternity parties, finally getting together with each other at about 2 A.M. Couples rarely went together to fraternity parties. Some men felt that a girlfriend was just a replacement for a hook-up. According to one junior man, "Basically a girlfriend is someone you go to at 2 A.M. after you've hung out with the guys. She is the sexual outlet that the guys can't provide you with."

Some fraternity brothers pressure each other to limit their time with and commitment to their girlfriends. One senior man said, "The hill [fraternities] and girlfriends don't mix." A brother described a constant battle between girlfriends and brothers over who the guy is going out with for the night, with the brothers usually winning. Brothers teased men with girlfriends with remarks such as "whipped" or "where's the ball and chain?" A brother from a high-risk house said that few brothers at his house had girlfriends; some did, but it was uncommon. One man said that from the minute he was a pledge he knew he would probably never have a girlfriend on this campus because "it was just not the norm in my house. No one has girlfriends; the guys have too much fun with [each other]."

The pressure on men to limit their commitment to girlfriends, however, was not true of all fraternities or of all men on campus. Couples attended low-risk fraternity parties together, and men in the low-risk houses went out on dates more often. A man in one low-risk house said that about 70 percent of the members of his house were involved in relationships with women, including the pledges (who were sophomores).

Treatment of Women

Not all men held negative attitudes toward women that are typical of a rape culture, and not all social contexts promoted the negative treatment of women. When men were asked whether they treated the women on campus with respect, the most common response was "On an individual basis, yes, but when you have a group of men together, no." Men said that, when together in groups with other men, they sensed a pressure to be disrespectful toward women. A first-year man's perception of the treatment of women was that "they are treated with more respect to their faces, but behind closed doors, with a group of men present, respect for women is not an issue." One senior man stated, "In general, college-aged men don't treat women their age with respect because 90 percent of them think of women as merely a means to sex." Women reinforced this perception.

A first-year women stated, "Men here are more interested in hooking up and drinking beer than they are in getting to know women as real people." Another woman said, "Men here use and abuse women."

Characteristic of rape culture, a double standard of sexual behavior for men versus women was prevalent on this campus. As one Greek senior man stated, "Women who sleep around are sluts and get bad reputations; men who do are champions and get a pat on the back from their brothers." Women also supported a double standard for sexual behavior by criticizing sexually active women. A first-year woman spoke out against women who are sexually active: "I think some girls here make it difficult for the men to respect women as a whole."

One concrete example of demeaning sexually active women on this campus is the "walk of shame." Fraternity brothers come out on the porches of their houses the night after parties and heckle women walking by. It is assumed that these women spent the night at fraternity houses and that the men they were with did not care enough about them to drive them home. Although sororities now reside in former fraternity houses, this practice continues and sometimes the victims of hecklings are sorority women on their way to study in the library.

A junior man in a high-risk fraternity described another ritual of disrespect toward women called "chatter." When an unknown woman sleeps over at the house, the brothers yell degrading remarks out the window at her as she leaves the next morning such as "Fuck that bitch" and "Who is that slut?" He said that sometimes brothers harass the brothers whose girlfriends stay over instead of heckling those women.

Fraternity men most often mistreated women they did not know personally. Men and women alike reported incidents in which brothers observed other brothers having sex with unknown women or women they knew only casually. A sophomore woman's experience exemplifies this anonymous state: "I don't mind if 10 guys were watching or it was videotaped. That's expected on this campus. It's the fact that he didn't apologize or even offer to drive me home that really upset me." Descriptions of sexual encounters involved the satisfaction of men by nameless women. A brother in a high-risk fraternity described a similar occurrence:

> A brother of mine was hooking up upstairs with an unattractive woman who had been pursuing him all night. He told some brothers to go outside the window and watch. Well, one thing led to another and they were almost completely naked when the woman noticed the brothers outside. She was then unwilling to go any further, so the brother went outside and yelled at the other brothers and then closed the shades. I don't know if he scored or not, because the woman was pretty upset. But he did win the award for hooking up with the ugliest chick that weekend.

Attitudes Toward Rape

The sexually charged environment of college campuses raises many questions about cultures that facilitate the rape of women. How women and men define their sexual behavior is important legally as well as interpersonally. We asked students how they defined rape and had them compare it to the following legal definition: the perpetration of an act of sexual intercourse with a female against her will and consent, whether her will is overcome by force or fear resulting from the threat of force, or by drugs or intoxicants; or when, because of mental deficiency, she is incapable of exercising rational judgment. (Brownmiller 1975, 368)

When presented with this legal definition, most women interviewed recognized it as well as the complexities involved in applying it. A first-year woman said, "If a girl is drunk and the guy knows it and the girl says, 'Yes, I want to have sex,' and they do, that is still rape because the girl can't make a conscious, rational decision under the influence of alcohol." Some women disagreed. Another first-year woman stated, "I don't think it is fair that the guy gets blamed when both people involved are drunk."

The typical definition men gave for rape was "when a guy jumps out of the bushes and forces himself sexually onto a girl." When asked what date rape was, the most common answer was "when one person has sex with another person who did not consent." Many men said, however, that "date rape is when a woman wakes up the next morning and regrets having sex." Some men said that date rape was too gray an area to define. "Consent is a fine line," said a Greek senior man student. For the most part, the men we spoke with argued that rape did not occur on this campus. One Greek sophomore man said, "I think it is ridiculous that someone here would rape someone." A first-year man stated, "I have a problem with the word rape. It sounds so criminal, and we are not criminals; we are sane people."

Whether aware of the legal definitions of rape, most men resisted the idea that a woman who is intoxicated is unable to consent to sex. A Greek junior man said, "Men should not be responsible for women's drunkenness." One first-year man said, "If that is the legal definition of rape, then it happens all the time on this campus." A senior man said, "I don't care whether alcohol is involved or not; that is not rape. Rapists are people that have something seriously wrong with them." A first-year man even claimed that when women get drunk, they invite sex. He said, "Girls get so drunk here and then come to us. What are we supposed to do? We are only human."

Discussion and Conclusion

These findings describe the physical and normative aspects of one college campus as they relate to attitudes about and relations between men and women. Our findings suggest that an explanation emphasizing rape culture also must focus on those characteristics of the social setting that play a role in defining heterosexual relationships on college campuses (Kalof and Cargill 1991). The degradation of women as portrayed in rape culture was not found in all fraternities on this campus. Both group norms and individual behavior changed as students went from one place to another. Although individual men are the ones who rape, we found that some settings are more likely places for rape than are others. Our findings suggest that rape cannot be seen only as an isolated act and blamed on individual behavior and proclivities, whether it be alcohol consumption or attitudes. We also must consider characteristics of the settings that promote the behaviors that reinforce a rape culture.

Relations between women and men at parties in low-risk fraternities varied considerably from those in high-risk houses. Peer pressure and situational norms influenced women as well as men. Although many men in high- and low-risk houses shared similar views and attitudes about the Greek system, women on this campus, and date rape, their behaviors at fraternity parties were quite different.

Women who are at highest risk of rape are women whom fraternity brothers did not know. These women are faceless victims, nameless acquaintances—not friends. Men said their responsibility to such persons and the level of guilt they feel later if the hook-ups end in sexual intercourse are much lower if they hook up with women they do not know. In high-risk houses, brothers treated women as subordinates and kept them at a distance. Men in high-risk houses actively discouraged ongoing heterosexual relationships, routinely degraded women, and participated more fully in the hook-up scene; thus, the probability that women would become faceless victims was higher in these houses. The flirtatious nature of the parties indicated that women go to these parties looking for available men, but finding boyfriends or relationships was difficult at parties in high-risk houses. However, in the low-risk houses, where more men had long-term relationships, the women were not strangers and were less likely to become faceless victims.

The social scene on this campus, and on most others, offers women and men few other options to socialize. Although there may be no such thing as a completely safe fraternity party for women, parties at low-risk houses and commercial bars encouraged men and women to get to know each other better and decreased the probability that women would become faceless victims. Although both men and women found the social scene on this campus demeaning, neither demanded different settings for socializing, and attendance at fraternity parties is a common form of entertainment.

These findings suggest that a more conducive environment for conversation can promote more positive interactions between men and women. Simple changes would provide the opportunity for men and women to interact in meaningful ways such as adding places to sit and lowering the volume of music at fraternity parties or having parties in neutral locations, where men are not in control. The typical party room in fraternity houses includes a place to dance but not to sit and talk. The music often is loud, making it difficult, if not impossible, to carry on conversations; however, there were more conversations at the low-risk parties, where there also was more respect shown toward women. Although the number of brothers who had steady girlfriends in the low-risk houses as compared to those in the high-risk houses may explain the differences, we found that commercial bars also provided a context for interaction between men and women. At the bars, students sat and talked and conversations between men and women flowed freely, resulting in deep discussions and fewer hook-ups.

Alcohol consumption was a major focus of social events here and intensified attitudes and orientations of a rape culture. Although pressure to drink was evident at all fraternity parties and at both bars, drinking dominated high-risk fraternity parties, at which nonalcoholic beverages usually were not available and people chugged beers and became visibly drunk. A rape culture is strengthened by rules that permit alcohol only at fraternity parties. Under this system, men control the parties and dominate the men as well as the women who attend. As college administrators crack down on fraternities and alcohol on campus, however, the same behaviors and norms may transfer to other places such as parties in apartments or private homes where administrators have much less control. At commercial bars, interaction and socialization with others were as important as drinking, with the exception of the nights when the bar frequented by under-class students became crowded. Although one solution is to offer nonalcoholic social activities, such events receive little support on this campus. Either these alternative events lacked the prestige of the fraternity parties or the alcohol was seen as necessary to unwind, or both.

In many ways, the fraternities on this campus determined the settings in which men and women interacted. As others before us have found, pressures for conformity to the norms and values exist at both high-risk and low-risk houses (Martin and Hummer 1989; Sanday 1990; Kalof and Cargill 1991). The desire to be accepted is not unique to this campus or the Greek system (Horowitz 1988; Moffat 1989; Holland and Eisenhart 1990). The degree of conformity required by Greeks may be greater than that required in most social groups, with considerable pressure to adopt and maintain the image of their houses. The fraternity system intensifies the "groupthink syndrome" (Janis 1972) by solidifying the identity of the in-group and creating an us/them atmosphere. Within the fraternity culture, brothers are highly regarded and women are viewed as outsiders. For men in high-risk fraternities, women threatened their brotherhood; therefore, brothers discouraged relationships and harassed those who treated women as equals or with respect. The pressure to be one of the guys and hang out with the guys strengthens a rape culture on college campus by demeaning women and encouraging the segregation of men and women.

Students on this campus were aware of the contexts in which they operated and the choices available to them. They recognized that, in their interactions, they created differences between men and women that are not natural, essential, or biological (West and Zimmerman 1987). Not all men and women accepted the demeaning treatment of women, but they continued to participate in behaviors that supported aspects of a rape culture. Many women participated in the hook-up scene even after they had been humiliated and hurt because they had few other means of initiating contact with men on campus. Men and women alike played out this scene, recognizing its injustices in many cases but being unable to change the course of their behaviors.

Although this research provides some clues to gender relations on college campuses, it raises many questions. Why do men and women participate in activities that support a rape culture when they see its injustices? What would happen if alcohol were not controlled by groups of men who admit that they disrespect women when they get together? What can be done to give men and women on college campuses more opportunities to interact responsibly and get to know each other better? These questions should be studied on other campuses with a focus on the social settings in which the incidence of rape and the attitudes that support a rape culture exist. Fraternities are social contexts that may or may not foster a rape culture.

Our findings indicate that a rape culture exists in some fraternities, especially those we identified as high-risk houses. College administrators are responding to this situation by providing counseling and educational programs that increase awareness of date rape including campaigns such as "No means no." These strategies are important in changing attitudes, values, and behaviors; however, changing individuals is not enough. The structure of campus life and the impact of that structure on gender relations on campus are highly determinative. To eliminate campus rape culture, student leaders and administrators must examine the situations in which women and men meet and restructure these settings to provide opportunities for respectful interaction. Change may not require abolishing fraternities; rather, it may require promoting settings that facilitate positive gender relations.

References

Barthel, D. 1988. *Putting on appearances: Gender and advertising*. Philadelphia: Temple University Press.
Boeringer, S. B., C. L. Shehan, and R. L. Akers, 1991. Social contexts and social learning in sexual co-

ercion and aggression: Assessing the contribution of fraternity membership. *Family Relations* 40:58–64.

Brownmiller, S. 1975. *Against our will: Men, women and rape.* New York: Simon & Schuster.

Buchwald, E., P. R. Fletcher, and M. Roth, eds. 1993. *Transforming a rape culture.* Minneapolis, MN: Milkweed Editions.

Burke, P., J. E. Stets, and M. A. Pirog-Good. 1989. Gender identity, self-esteem, physical abuse and sexual abuse in dating relationships. In *Violence in dating relationships: Emerging social issues*, edited by M. A. Pirog-Good and J. E. Stets. New York: Praeger.

Gwartney-Gibbs, P., and J. Stockard. 1989. Courtship aggression and mixed-sex peer groups. In *Violence in dating relationships: Emerging social issues*, edited by M. A. Pirog-Good and J. E. Stets. New York: Praeger.

Herman, D. 1984. The rape culture. In *Women: A feminist perspective*, edited by J. Freeman. Mountain View, CA: Mayfield.

Holland, D. C., and M. A. Eisenhart. 1990. *Educated in romance: Women, achievement, and college culture.* Chicago: University of Chicago Press.

Horowitz, H. L. 1988. *Campus life: Undergraduate cultures from the end of the 18th century to the present.* Chicago: University of Chicago Press.

Hunter, F. 1953. *Community power structure.* Chapel Hill: University of North Carolina Press.

Jenkins, M. J., and F. H. Dambrot. 1987. The attribution of date rape: Observer's attitudes and sexual experiences and the dating situation. *Journal of Applied Social Psychology* 17:875–895.

Janis, I. L. 1972. *Victims of groupthink.* Boston: Houghton Mifflin.

Kalof, L., and T. Cargill. 1991. Fraternity and sorority membership and gender dominance attitudes. *Sex Roles* 25:417–423.

Kimmel, M. S. 1993. Clarence, William, Iron Mike, Tailhook, Senator Packwood, Spur Posse, Magic . . . and us. In *Transforming a rape culture*, edited by E. Buchwald, P. R. Fletcher, and M. Roth. Minneapolis, MN: Milkweed Editions.

Koss, M. P., T. E. Dinero, C. A. Seibel, and S. L. Cox. 1988. Stranger and acquaintance rape: Are there differences in the victim's experience? *Psychology of Women Quarterly* 12:1–24.

Koss, M. P., C. A. Gidycz, and N. Wisniewski. 1985. The scope of rape: Incidence and prevalence of sexual aggression and victimization in a national sample of higher education students. *Journal of Consulting and Clinical Psychology* 55:162–170.

LaPlante, M. N., N. McCormick, and G. G. Brannigan. 1980. Living the sexual script: College students' views of influence in sexual encounters. *Journal of Sex Research* 16:338–355.

Lisak, D., and S. Roth. 1988. Motivational factors in nonincarcerated sexually aggressive men. *Journal of Personality and Social Psychology* 55:795–802.

Malamuth, N. 1986. Predictors of naturalistic sexual aggression. *Journal of Personality and Social Psychology* 50:953–962.

Martin, P. Y., and R. Hummer. 1989. Fraternities and rape on campus. *Gender & Society* 3:457–473.

Miller, B., and J. C. Marshall. 1987. Coercive sex on the university campus. *Journal of College Student Personnel* 28:38–47.

Moffat, M. 1989. *Coming of age in New Jersey: College life in American culture.* New Brunswick, NJ: Rutgers University Press.

Muehlenhard, C. L., and M. A. Linton. 1987. Date rape and sexual aggression in dating situations: Incidence and risk factors. *Journal of Counseling Psychology* 34:186–196.

O'Sullivan, C. 1993. Fraternities and the rape culture. In *Transforming a rape culture*, edited by E. Buchwald, P. R. Fletcher, and M. Roth. Minneapolis, MN: Milkweed Editions.

Peterson, S. A., and B. Franzese. 1987. Correlates of college men's sexual abuse of women. *Journal of College Student Personnel* 28:223–228.

Sanday, P. R. 1990. *Fraternity gang rape: Sex, brotherhood, and privilege on campus.* New York: New York University Press.

West, C., and D. Zimmerman. 1987. Doing gender. *Gender & Society* 1:125–151.

ARTICLE 16

Rocco L. Capraro

Why College Men Drink: Alcohol, Adventure, and the Paradox of Masculinity

*And you drink this burning liquor like your life
Your life which you drink like an eau-de-vie.*
    Apollinaire[1]

Though terror speaks to life and death and distress makes of the world a vale of tears, yet shame strikes deepest into the heart of man.
    Tomkins[2]

Given the magnitude of the negative consequences of some college men's drinking—for themselves and for those around them—on campuses across the nation,[3] college health professionals and alcohol prevention educators might well wonder: "Why *do* college men drink?" Because most college men drink in unproblematic ways and only to be sociable,[4] those men who drink in a way that is likely to be harmful to themselves or others are actually the central focus of this article—that is, those men "for whom drinking has become a central activity in their way of life."[5(p100)]

Writing from a men's health studies perspective, I articulate what is necessarily only a tentative answers to the question of men's problem drinking by offering a model for conceptualizing the complex connections between college men and alcohol. Men's health studies, a subfield of men's studies, describes and analyzes men's experience of health, injury, morbidity, and mortality in the context of masculinity.[6,7] I also suggest an answer to the companion question that immediately presents itself to us: "What can we do about it?"

Part one of this article discusses the connections between alcohol, men, and masculinity generally; part two, the cultural and developmental aspects of men in a college setting; and part three, conceptual and programmatic responses to the men's problem drinking.

In general, I conclude that when college men drink, they are simply *being* men in college: that is the best context for understanding why they drink. I further conclude, in what is perhaps my central insight in this article, that college men's drinking appears to be profoundly paradoxical in a way that seems to replicate a larger paradox of masculinity itself: that men's alcohol use is related to both men's power and men's powerlessness. Stated most succinctly, my interpretation of a variety of evidence suggests that many college men may be drinking not only to enact male privilege but also to help them negotiate the emotional hazards of being a man in the contemporary American college.

From *Journal of American College Health* 48: 307–315. Copyright © 2000. Reprinted with permission of the Helen Dwight Reid Foundation. Published by Heldref Publication, Washington, DC.

Alcohol and Masculinity

Drinking as a Male Domain

If we want to understand why college men drink, then we might embed drinking and college in masculinity and ask in what ways each might be seen as a specific male experience.[6] When we look for connections between drinking, men, and masculinity, we observe that the most prominent feature on the social landscape of drinking is that drinking is a "male domain."[3(p6)] By *male domain*, I suggest that drinking is male dominated, male identified, and male centered.[8]

Men outnumber women in virtually every category of drinking behavior u ed in research for comparison—prevalence, consumption, frequency of drinking and intoxication, incidence of heavy and problem drinking, alcohol abuse and dependence, and alcoholism.[4,9–12] Although most college men and women say they drink to be sociable, men are more likely than women to say they drink for escapism or to get drunk.[4(p125)]

These findings hold true for the categories of age, ethnicity, geographic region, religion, education, income, and marital status.[9] Although there has been some speculation that changing gender roles may be narrowing the gap between women and men vis-á-vis alcohol, discussed by scholars as the *convergence hypothesis*, research tends to reject that proposition.[3]

In a classic and often-cited article, Lemle and Miskind[9] asked, "Why should it be that males drink and abuse alcohol in such magnitude and in such marked contrast to females?" Citing empirical research that placed men mostly in the company of other men in the life course of their drinking, they suggested that drinking was a symbol of masculinity and speculated that men may drink to be manly.[9(p215)] They found little or no empirical evidence to support many of the theoretical possibilities they discussed, particularly for any theories concerned with men's abusive drinking, yet they remained intrigued with the idea that men were affirming their manliness by drinking.

More recently, McCreary et al.[10] ask what *specific* aspects of the male gender role correlate with alcohol involvement. In addition to the personality traits of instrumentality and expressiveness, they explore the traits of traditional male-role attitudes and masculine gender-role stress. For their research, traditional male-role attitudes represent a "series of beliefs and assumptions that men should be in high-status positions in society, act in physically and emotionally toughened ways, and avoid anything stereotypically feminine." *Masculine gender-role stress* is a term used to "describe the stress resulting from a man's belief that he is unable to meet society's demands of what is expected from men or the male role or from having to respond to a situation in a feminine-typed manner."[10(pp111–112)]

McCreary et al.[10] identify traditional male-role attitudes as the *one* aspect of the male gender role they studied that predicts alcohol *use* among men. Alcohol use itself correlates with alcohol problems. However, masculine gender-role stress, while statistically unrelated to alcohol *use,* does predict alcohol *problems* for men. (p. 121) In short, this study suggests that, from the point of view of masculinity or culture of manhood as a factor among many others, men *qua* men might arrive at alcohol problems by two routes: one route starts at traditional male-role attitudes, passes through alcohol use, and ends in alcohol problems; another route starts at masculine gender-role stress and ends directly in alcohol problems.

Variations on a Theme: Conflict and Strain, Shame and Fear, Depression, and the Paradox of Masculinity

The Paradox of Masculinity Traditional male-role attitudes and masculine gender-role stress are actually not very far apart; in some aspects, they are correlated.[10,13] Their correlation reveals the contradictory nature of masculinity.[14] Reflecting upon the contradictory nature of the male role, researchers in the field of men's studies have articulated the paradox of masculinity, or the paradox of men's power, as follows: *men are powerful and powerless.*[15-18]

What is the resolution of the apparent contradiction that constitutes the paradox? How can men be both powerful and powerless? Men's studies observe two aspects of men's lives. First, in objective social analysis, *men as a group have power over women as a group:* but, in their subjective experience of the world, *men as individuals do not feel powerful.* In fact, they feel powerless. As at first articulated, and then later resolved by men's studies, the concept of a paradox of men's power offers an important insight into men's lives, one that seems to capture and to explain many of the contradictory claims made by and about men.

Ironically, it is men themselves who make the "rules of manhood" by which men as individuals are "disempowered."[17(p138)] Kaufman[16] aptly concludes that men's power is actually the cause of men's pain: "men's social power is the source of individual power and privilege . . . it is also the source of the individual experience of pain and alienation."[16(pp142-143)]

The paradoxical nature of masculinity is further illuminated in other men's studies research on at least three critical psychosocial aspects of masculinity: gender-role conflict and strain, shame and fear, and depression. Interestingly, those same aspects of masculinity are themselves important possible connections between men and alcohol. Consequently, the concept of the paradox of men's power draws us to an important conceptual understanding of some men's connections to alcohol.

Conflict and Strain O'Neil[19] provides a useful series of interlocking definitions that locate gender-role conflict and strain in relation to the gender role itself. Gender roles are "behaviors, expectations, and values defined by society as masculine or feminine," or "as appropriate behavior for men and women." Gender-role conflict is "a psychological state in which gender roles have negative consequences on the individual or others" through the restriction, devaluation, or violation of oneself or others. Gender-role strain is "physical or psychological tension experienced as an outcome of gender-role conflict." At the bottom of gender-role strain is a "discrepancy between the real self and the gender role." (pp. 24, 25) Strain can follow from both conformity and nonconformity to the male role.

In his writings on strain, Pleck[14,20] provides additional insight into the relation between the masculine gender role and conflict or strain. Pleck maintains that the masculine gender role itself is "dysfunctional,"[14(p147)] fraught with contradictions and negative consequences. Even when men live up to the role, they suffer well-documented adverse consequences. But, very often, men do not live up to the role. In fact, conflict and strain are inherent in the role, and they are actually the best rubrics under which to understand most men's identity and experience.

In Pleck's[14] role-strain paradigm, social approval and situational adaptation replace innate psychological need as the social and psychological mechanisms by which men achieve manhood. Violating gender roles (norms and stereotypes) results in social condemnation, a negative consequence experienced as sex-role strain and anxiety, a negative psychological consequence. (pp. 145, 146) At least one study has connected role conflict and alcohol use. Blazina and Watkins[21] found that masculine gender-role conflict, in particular the factor cluster of "success, power, and competition," were significantly related to college men's reported use of alcohol.

Shame and Fear Krugman,[22] reflecting on Pleck's foundational work on gender-role strain, characterizes male-role strain, with its grounding in feelings of inadequacy and inferiority, as a shame-based experience. "Role strain generates shame affect as males fail to live up to the cultural and peer group standards they have internalized."[22(p95)] The essence of shame for Krugman is "painful self-awareness" or "a judgment against the self." (p. 99) He advises that shame is active in both male gender-role strain and normal male socialization.

Recent research suggests that normative male socialization employs shame to shape boys' and men's behaviors and attitudes.[22,23] In common and nonpathological forms, shame becomes integrated into the self and transformed into a cue that tells us when to modify our behaviors and feelings in response to shame's messages about their appropriateness. But although shame may be the powerful leverage to enforce boys' and men's conformity to the male role, men are less likely than women to transform shame because they find shame to be *repugnant* to their masculinity. Consequently, for Krugman,[22] boys and men internalize male gender roles to avoid shame; but they also learn that dependency needs, for example, are shameful, especially under the gaze of their peer group.

Shame is related to fear.[2] Shame can magnify fear by linking similar episodes of fear into what Tomkins refers to as a family of episodes, creating a behavioral template in which fear can be anticipated and become more pervasive. In adversarial cultures, and I would include our own society generally in that category, fear and shame are conjoined, resulting in the mutually reinforcing "fear of shame" and "shame of fear."[2(p538)]

Kimmel[17] places fear and shame at the very center of the social construction of men's identity. For him, men "fear that other men will unmask us, emasculate us, reveal to us and the world that we do not measure up, that we are not real men. Fear makes us ashamed." (p. 131) To avoid shame, Kimmel writes, men distance themselves from the feminine and all associations with it, including mothers, the world of feelings, nurturing, intimacy, and vulnerability.

Without the transformation of shame, men learn to manage shame in other ways. Alcohol is one of the significant ways men manage shame: drinking is a "maladaptive male solution to the pressure of undischarged shame."[22(p120)] Speaking metaphorically, Krugman observes that alcohol "dissolves acute shame" (p. 94). Referring to Lansky's study of shame in families, Krugman reports that alcohol, as a disinhibitor, is used by some men "to handle vulnerable and exposed states that generate shameful feelings." Krugman, citing M. Horowitz, advises that alcohol "softens ego criticism" and "facilitates interpersonal connections and self-disclosures." (p. 120) Drinking may also reduce fear.[2] It seems to me that shame may also be the mechanism that leads men directly to alcohol, which is used to instill conformity to the dictates of traditional masculinity that encourage men to drink.

Depression In addition to anxiety and shame, male gender-role strain and conflict make themselves known in the lives of men in depression. Depression is significantly related to all four aspects of gender-role conflict: (a) success, power, and competition; (b) restrictive emotionality; (c) restrictive affectionate behavior between men; and (d) conflicts between work and family relations.[13,24] Traditional masculinity insidiously puts men at risk for depression and also masks the depression, should it actually develop.[25,26]

Whereas Kaufman[16] uses a discourse of power to explain men's unacknowledged emotions, Lynch and Kilmartin[25] offer an alternative approach to the pitfalls of masculinity drawn from the point of view of social relations. Men's socialization encourages them to disconnect, or dissociate, from their feelings. An emotionally restrictive masculinity permits men to show their feelings only "in disguised form," and so they become "mostly unrecognized, unexpressed, and misunderstood by self and others." (p. 45) Men, instead, express their feelings in indirect ways, often through behavior that is destructive to themselves or others. Dissociation from feelings and destructive behavior are the two major characteristics of what Lynch and Kilmartin refer to as "masculine depression."[25(pp9,10)]

Heavy drinking, or binge drinking, is one of the ways some depressed men may act out, or manifest, their depression.[4] Lynch and Kilmartin[25] cite research indicating that depression is a strong risk factor for substance abuse problems. Krugman[22] notes a study showing strong correlations between alcohol abuse and major depression, especially among men. Although they do not cite empirical evidence for it, Blazina and Watkins[21] speculate that traditional men may "self-medicate their pain and depression with alcohol." (p. 461) Although research findings suggest only a possible correlation between alcohol use or abuse and depression, perhaps alcohol use or abuse may actually precede depression. Alcohol and depression are certainly connected in the lives of some men.

Alcohol and the Paradox of Men's Power

Men in our society are supposed to be powerful.[27] According to the empirical findings of McClelland et al.,[28] when men are not powerful, they may often compensate for their lack of power or seek an "alternative to obtaining social power" with alcohol. Stated most dramatically by McClelland, drinking is "part of a cluster of actions which is a principal manifestation of the need for power." (p. 119) For this research, feeling powerful means "feeling that one is vigorous and can [have] an impact on others." (p. 84) But men's power motivation can be personalized (i.e., for "the greater glory or influence of the individual") or socialized for "the good of others." (p. 137)

According to McClelland,[28] a few drinks will stimulate socialized power thoughts for most men, and that is one of the reasons they like to drink. Higher levels of drinking tend to decrease inhibitions and stimulate personalized power thoughts. Heavy drinking in men is uniquely associated with personalized power, McClelland says. Heavy drinking makes men feel strong and assertive and, I would argue, the way they are supposed to feel.

Drinking may be related to men's power in a more profound and paradoxical way. In the aggregate, the connection between some men and heavy or problem drinking appears to be of two sorts: (a) that which follows from simple, apparently uncomplicated, conformity to traditional masculinity—drinking simply because men are supposed to drink; and (b) that which is informed by complex, perceived inadequacy as men, either from men's own point of view, or from that of society. If they do not feel inadequate, then at least they experience a kind of doubt, or a sense of falling short of the cultural ideal of manhood—drinking because of gender-role conflicts.

This distinction may be, after all, only a conceptual, or theoretical, distinction; in practice, the two sorts of connection co-occur. I wonder if traditional masculinity does not contain within it, socially constructed over time in the course of men's history, the use of alcohol to accommodate gender-role conflict. Given the way traditional masculinity has been constructed, is not gender-role conflict of the sort described by Pleck[14] and O'Neil[19] and documented in the lives of the men studied by Tomkins,[2] Krugman,[21] Lynch and Kilmartin,[25] Real,[26] and Kimmel[17] inherent in most men's lives? Have not men as historical agents, therefore, made provision for taking care of their own? If so, traditional masculine drinking would encompass conflicted drinking; certainly, in the culture of manhood, it does.

If heavy and problem drinking is associated with conformity, overconformity, or conflicted or strained resistance to the imperatives of traditional masculinity, why should this be the case? It would appear that drinking is a kind of fatally flawed defense mechanism, or compensatory behavior. It protects men's objective power as a group, even as it reveals men's subjective powerlessness as individuals and results in a diminution of men's power, particularly through the loss of control of emotions, health, and a variety of other negative consequences.

If this is the case, then drinking would have much in common with other documented psychological defense mechanisms that correlate with male gender-role conflict. And gender-role conflict, following from either conformity or nonconformity, might itself be seen as a defense mechanism that "protects a man's sense of well-being."[29(p253)] Like men's silence,[30] men's drinking turns out to be in the interest of men's power, even as it disempowers individual men. And alcohol, in my view, is the paradoxical drug that is a part of the larger whole, a trope, of a paradoxical masculinity.

As I ponder this material, then, it seems to me that a significant part of men's drinking, like male gender-role stress and strain, men's shame, and masculine depression themselves, is a reflection of both men's power and men's powerlessness about men's privilege and men's pain. Heavy and problem drinking join other aspects of masculinity as they, too, come to be seen as manifestations of the paradox of masculinity. Drinking thus falls into a line of masculine icons, including body building, sexual assault, and pornography, that reveal the paradoxical nature of masculinity itself.[31-34] As I review those icons, it strikes me that at those times men *appear* most powerful socially, they *feel* most powerless personally.

College and Masculinity

College Drinking

What happens when we look at *college* men? College students, mostly men, are among the heavy drinkers in Rorabaugh's[35] history of drinking in early American society. Contemporary college men drink more than they did in high school and more heavily than their noncollege counterparts, and the gap is widening.[3,36-38] Men have been the primary public purveyors of alcohol to the college campus. All of the differences in drinking behavior for men and women generally hold true for college men and women.[3,4]

Given today's college students' preference for alcohol, one could not really imagine most colleges void of alcohol.[39] However, given the great variety of colleges and universities, the diversity of today's student populations, and the sweeping nature of the concerns I express in this article, most of what follows must necessarily speak primarily to an ideal type, represented for me by the relatively small, residential liberal arts college, occupied by a mostly traditionally aged student population.[40] In the following pages, I shall discuss critical aspects of college that seem to define college men's experience and help explain much of the presence of alcohol on college campuses: adventure, adult development, and permissiveness.

College as Adventure

Green[41] conceptualizes adventure as a domain of transgression. For Green, adventure takes shape around the themes of "eros" and "potestas"—love and power. Following Bataille, Green asks us to think about civil society "as based on the purposes and values of work, which means the denial of all activities hostile to work, such as both the ecstasies of eroticism and those of violence." Adventure lies in the conceptual space where heroes, "men acting with power," break free of ordinary restraints and "sample the repressed pleasures of sex and violence."[42(p17)]

Although Green[41] makes no reference to drinking in his essays on adventure, we can easily recognize that the terrain of adventure is the same terrain as that of alcohol: "a boy's first drink, first prolonged drinking experience, and first intoxication tend to occur with other boys away from home."[9(p214)] Sports and the military are contexts for both adventure and drinking. Drinking games "are an important factor in the socialization of new students into heavy use," particularly for men.[42(p105)] Drinking, in general, can be an adventure, insofar as it takes men through a "breach" of the social contract and into the realms of violence, sex, and other adventure motifs.

In what way might college be conceptualized as an adventure? College is not literally, or predominantly, a scene or eros and potestas. It is, however, a time and place of an imaginative assertion of manhood outside of civil society, away from home and family, where a kind of heroism is possible. By analogy, we can observe that student life in 19th-century American colleges developed outside of the civil society represented by the faculty and administration in what I would regard as the realm of adventure. Horowitz[43] argues that what we think of as student life was actually "born in revolt" (p. 23) against the faculty and administration. It is a "world made by the undergraduates," she says. (p. 3)

Levine and Cureton[39] find that colleges today are occupied by a transitional generation that reflects the changing demographics of contemporary American society. Horowitz's history, however, employs a simple tripartite typology of college students that is still largely applicable as a model for understanding students on many campuses in more recent times. That typology deeply resonates with my own many years of experience in student affairs: (a) college men—affluent men in revolt against the faculty and administration who created campus life as "the culture of the college man" (p. 32); (b) outsiders—hardworking men who identify with the faculty (p. 14); and (c) rebels—creative, modernist, and expressive men who conform neither to campus life nor to the faculty (p. 15). Horowitz[43] observes that these three student types were distinctly *male* when they first made their appearance, but their female counterparts eventually found their place alongside the men.

Nuwer[44] argues that there are historical links between traditional male undergraduate life and danger, a key adventure motif. Social interactions initiating students into various campus communities have continuously subjected college men to high risk. Acceptance by their peers is granted in exchange for successfully undertaking the risk involved. A variety of college rituals and traditions often mix danger and alcohol.[44] Alcohol, itself, is associated with risk in men's lives.[9] Seen this way, college and campus life become an adventurescape, where young men (college men) imagine their manhood in a developmental moment that is socially dominated by alcohol.

Green[41] identifies a number of arenas or institutions of adventure: manhood before marriage, hunting, battle, travel, sports, and politics, to name a few. Although there may be feminine variants, Green links adventure to masculinity because society gives men the freedom to "apply forces to the world to assert power and identity." Adventure is an act of assertion by which men "imagine themselves" in "a breach of the social contract." (p. 19)

College as a Male Developmental Moment

Beyond seeing the sociology of college and student life organized as adventure, we must also consider the role of individual developmental psychology in the college environment. Paradoxically, just at the moment the great adventure begins, college men feel the most vulnerable. Rotundo[45] observes that in the 19th century, "male youth culture" made its appearance in men's development as the vehicle for the transition from boyhood to manhood. Boys' principal developmental task was disengagement from home, which created conflict between the imperatives of wordly ambition young men's psychological needs for attachment. Young men of Rotundo's period gathered in business districts and colleges. Wherever they gathered, a "special culture" developed to support them in a time of need. (pp. 56–62)

Lyman[46] carries us forward from Rotundo's[45] historical analysis to the present. In his essay on male bonding in fraternities, he locates college as a developmental time and place between the authority of home and family (in the high school years), and that of work and family (after graduation). He identifies college men's anger, their "latent anger about the discipline that middle-class male roles impose upon them, both marriage rules and work rules." (p. 157) Their great fear is loss of control and powerlessness. Lyman concludes that joking relationships (banter, sexual humor, etc.) among men allow a needed connection without being self-disclosive or emotionally intimate, that is, with little vulnerability. Recent research on first-year college men has characterized their transition to college as often involving separation anxiety and loss, followed by grieving. Among the significant responses that may manifest some college men's grief, we find self-destructive behaviors, including alcohol use.[47]

Shame theory advises that to avoid shame, boys need to distance themselves from their mothers because of the "considerable discomfort with dependency needs at the level of the peer group."[22(p107)] College men in groups, such as Lyman's fraternity men, perceive homosexuality and intimate emotional relationships with women to be a threat to their homosocial world. Thus, men are encouraged to treat women as sexual objects, which confirms their heterosexuality, but prevents true intimacy with women.

Alcohol plays a role in men's emotional management under these conditions. Drinking remains a "socially acceptable way for men to satisfy their dependency needs while they maintain a social image of independence,"[48(p187)] even as it masks those needs. For example, recent research on drinking games suggests they are actually an environmental context for drinking where a variety of students' social and psychological needs come into play.[49] When men (and women) give reasons for playing drinking games, they are likely to be "tapping into more general motives for drinking" (p. 286). Alcohol may be an effective way to cope in the short term, but it is ultimately "self-destructive."[48(p191)]

For Nuwer,[44] as was true for Horowitz,[43] fraternities are the quintessential emblems of traditional college life. They provide a "feeling of belonging" for students who "crave relationships and acceptance" in their college years (p. 38). They are also the riskiest environments for heavy and problem drinking.[4] Nationally, just over 80 percent of fraternity residents binge drink, whereas just over 40 percent of all college students binge.[50] Drinking in fraternities is perhaps best understood as an extreme on a continuum of college men's drinking, dramatizing what may be going on to a lesser extent in traditional student life among a range of men. From the point of view of men's needs assessments, we have much to learn from the psychology of brotherhood.

Permissiveness—Real and Imagined

Alcohol is "one of the oldest traditions in the American college," and alcohol-related problems have also been a benchmark of campus life. Until very recently, though, college administrations have been permissive about alcohol, voicing "official condemnation tempered by tacit toleration."[51(pp81–83)] Myers[52] provides a model for "institutional (organizational) denial" of the presence (or extent) of alcohol abuse that could easily apply to college campuses nationally. (p. 43) In 1995, Wechsler[11] was explicit about the widespread denial about alcohol on college campuses.

With the increase in the drinking age from 18 to 21 years and increased awareness of the dangers of alcohol abuse, colleges now "typically have policies which promote responsible drinking" and attempt the "management of student drinking and its consequences."[51(pp84–88)] My own informal observations are that liability case law, awareness of the negative impact of alcohol on the achievement of educational mission, and enrollment management concerns for retention have also encouraged colleges to be more vigilant about the role of alcohol in campus cultures.

But among students, permissiveness persists, both in drinking behavior and in attitudes toward drinking. Permissiveness itself is, in part, the result of students' own misperceptions of campus norms for alcohol behavior and attitudes.[53,54] With reference to the consumption of alcohol and the acceptability of intoxication, students generally perceive themselves to be in a permissive environment. In reality, the environment is not as permissive as they think. Misperceiving the norm leads students who are inclined to drink to consume more alcohol than they otherwise would drink were they to perceive the norm correctly.[55] This social norms research indicates that correcting the misperception through public information campaigns can reduce both problem drinking and binge drinking on college campuses.[56,57]

How well do social norms approaches work with college men who are heavy drinkers? How are masculinity, permissive attitudes about drinking, and misperceptions of the norm related? How accurately do college men perceive their campus norms? For social norms theory and research, the heaviest drinking results from the interaction of the most permissive personal attitudes toward alcohol and the greatest misperception of the norm as more permissive than it actually is. Men as a group are the heaviest drinkers on campus. We might conclude that the heaviest drinking men have the most permissive attitudes about drinking and that they misperceive the norm at the greatest rates. But, theoretically, they should also be most susceptible to the benefits of social norms approaches.

However, in one study, the heaviest drinking college men proved to be the least susceptible to social norms interventions. From 1995 to 1998 Western Washington University implemented a campus-wide social norms approach. Although most students on the campus changed their patterns of drinking in positive ways, the "students reporting they had seven or more drinks on peak occasions [the most consumed at one time in the past month] remained virtually unchanged [at about 35 percent]." The most recalcitrant students at Western Washington were underage men: "nearly two thirds of the underage men still reported having seven or more drinks on a peak occasion. Only one third of the underage women reporting the same"[56(p3)] level of consumption.

In view of the significance of personal attitudes toward alcohol,[55] permissive personal attitudes about alcohol in the group of recalcitrant underage men might have been so robust that they simply overwhelmed any other perceptions of the environment. Prentice and Miller[58] found that men and women in their study did respond differently to corrections of misperceptions. Perhaps, in the case of at least some college men, personal attitudes about drinking and misperception of the campus norm are so inextricably linked that research and prevention work that addresses the one (personal attitudes) must necessarily be done in conjunction with the same kind of work on the other (misperception of the norm).

Perkins once characterized "the perceived male stereotype of heavy use as a misperception to which males do not need to conform."[3(p6)] Some college men's misperceptions of their campus alcohol norms may be "contained" in their personal attitudes about drinking. Baer found that differences in the perception of campus drinking norms among students in different housing situations on one campus "*already existed prior to college enrollment*"[42(p98)] [emphasis mine]. Certainly, if "the impact of public behavior and conversation" on campus can generate misperceptions of the norm,[54(p17)] a lifetime of powerful messages about the connection between alcohol and manhood would produce great distortions of its own.

Social norms theory, research, and strategies would be enhanced by a closer look at gender in the creation of drinking attitudes and behaviors, in possible differences in the misperception of norms, and in the social mechanisms that lie behind the actual norms. Social norms research surveys should include measures of traditional masculine role strain and should look for correlations between attitudes and perceptions of the norm and actual drinking behavior.

In addition, surveys should replace the generic "college student" with "male student" or "female student" when asking college students about how much students are drinking and asking about their attitudes toward drinking. So, for example, we should ask, "How many drinks does a *male* [or *female*] student typically have at a party on this campus?" instead of "do *students* typically have" or "Is it acceptable for men [or women] to drink with occasional intoxication as long as it does not interfere with other responsibilities?"[54(p15)]

The results would have implications for norms-based prevention programs. It would make sense if, in fact, masculinity were found to predispose men to misperceive the norm because assumptions and attitudes about drinking and how drinking relates to manhood are built into masculinity. It would also make sense that the actual and perceived social norms be gender specific.

What Is to Be Done?
Concrete Responses

Men, alcohol, and college are connected by the paradoxical nature of men's power. What can we do about college men's frequent, heavy, and problem drinking? Following from the model that has been developed in this essay, nothing short of radical reconstruction of masculinity and a reimagining of the college experience are likely to bring about significant change in college men's drinking. The same paradox that characterizes college men's drinking also provides a pedagogy for change. This is because, while the paradox acknowledges men's pain and powerlessness, it also discourages men from seeing themselves simply as victims, and it insists that men take responsibility for their actions.

Colleges, in collaboration with high schools and community agencies, should integrate gender awareness into alcohol education, prevention, and risk-reduction programs. For men, I recommend a comprehensive educational program that addresses four central themes in men's lives: friendship, health, life/work/family, and sexual ethics (see also, Good and Mintz[24(p20)]).

As in the case of effective rape prevention education workshops for men, the pedagogy should be workshops that are all male, small group, interactive, and peer facilitated. Such programs have been shown to change some men's attitudes and values that are associated with the perpetration of rape.[59] It may be that the rape prevention workshops are changing attitudes because they correct men's misperceived norm of other men's attitudes about women, or vice versa.[60]

Attitudes and values associated with problem drinking could be similarly changed. Developing what Lynch and Kilmartin[25] refer to as "healthy masculinity" that connects men in healthy relationships with other men, family, and intimate partners would be a succinct statement of the goal of such programming. (pp. 46, 47)

The transition to college is a critical juncture in the consumption of alcohol.[4] Programming should therefore begin early in the first year and continue well beyond orientation week. Broad-based, fully integrated, social norms educational programs, interventions, and public information initiatives should be implemented.[55] I would add that such programs should be gender-informed along the lines I have suggested in this article. College men should understand how the paradoxical masculinity I have discussed may orient them to alcohol use and abuse.

College students should be strongly encouraged to get involved in clubs and organizations on campus, to run for office, and to be involved in sports as ways of meeting power orientation needs in socially responsible ways.[23] Those activities themselves must have alcohol education components; otherwise, involvement could have the ironic consequence of promoting heavier drinking.[3] Associations between men and beer in campus media should be discouraged.[61,62] Given their powerful influence over men's drinking in the first year,[43] the hazards of drinking games should be especially discussed in educational programming.

In general, college as adventure is a theme that should be discouraged. A "boys will be boys" permissiveness should be rejected. Recognizing and affirming that alcohol does harm, colleges must assert themselves as "moral communities" and move from permissive to restrictive stances on alcohol by first articulating what the harm is, then establishing policies to prevent college community members from harming themselves or others.[51(pp135,150–159)] Wechsler and associates[63] recommend a comprehensive approach to alcohol use on college campuses, including scrutiny of alcohol marketing, more alcohol-free events and activities, and more restrictive policies that control the flow of alcohol on campus. Their recommendation would benefit from more deeply gendered approaches to the problem because the problem, itself, is deeply gendered.

In addition to promoting social norms approaches, preventive education, and risk-reduction education, college administrators should require that frequent violators of alcohol policy seek treatment or seek their education elsewhere. Although critics of treatment may say it addresses the symptoms and not the real problem, which is the campus culture itself, colleges must offer treatment as part of a comprehensive program for renewed campus life. Treatment should seamlessly integrate men's health studies approaches.[66,67] Unfortunately, some college men will be untouched and untouchable by education or treatment, and they must lose the privilege of attending their chosen college and be asked to leave.

Conceptual Responses

Speaking most globally about solving the problem of college men's drinking and solving the problem of the connections between alcohol and masculinity, I would paraphrase what I have previously written about the problem of rape: Our understanding of the specific act of drinking should be embedded in our understanding of masculinity. Drinking is not an isolated behavior; it is a behavior linked to larger systems of attitudes, values, and modalities of conduct in men's lives that constitute masculinity and men's social position relative to women. In this model, alcohol prevention work with men begins with them *as* men, and with men's questioning of prevailing assumptions about masculinity and what it means to be a man. I am extremely skeptical of any alcohol prevention work that proposes solutions to the problem of drinking that leave masculinity, as we know it, largely intact.[68(p22)]

The educational challenge, which is really the psychological and political resistance to this solution, lies in the fact that alcohol benefits men as a group, even as it injures men as individuals. Men are likely to resist this global approach because we fear losing the benefits of masculinity conferred upon the group. The path to a reconstructed masculinity or alternatives to the dominant masculinity that includes more variety of men's identities and experiences may look something like Helms's[69] stage-development model for a positive racial-cultural identity for minority groups. It will not be easy getting there.

In the meantime, in our work with college men who drink, we must look to the bottom of their glasses and find the *men* inside. For when college men drink, they are simply being men at college, or what they perceive men at college to be. By this I mean that the most useful way to interpret their behavior is not so much in its *content,* but in its *context*—first, the imperatives of manhood, then the psychosocial particulars of college life, both of which put men at risk for drinking. Basically, at the bottom of heavy and problematic drinking among college men are the paradoxical nature of masculinity and the corresponding paradoxical nature of alcohol in men's lives. Once we know college men *as* men, we will know more about why they drink and what we can do about it.

Acknowledgment

This article is dedicated to Alan D. Berkowitz, longtime friend and colleague. I would also like to thank others for their extremely helpful and supportive readings of its various drafts: John Lynch, H. Wesley Perkins, Jan E. Regan, David A. Diana, and David DeVries.

References

1. Apollinaire G. Zone. In: *Selected Writings of Guillaume Apollinaire* (trans. Roger Shattuck). New York: New Directions, 1971.
2. Tomkins S. *Affect, Imagery, Consciousness.* Vol 3, 1962–1992. New York: Springer, 1991.
3. Perkins H. W. Gender patterns in consequences of collegiate alcohol abuse: A 10-year study of trends in an undergraduate population. *J Stud Alcohol.* 1992, September: 458–462.
4. Berkowitz A. D., Perkins H. W. Recent research on gender differences in collegiate alcohol use. *J Am Coll Health.* 1987, 36:123–129.
5. Fingarette H. *Heavy Drinking: The Myth of Alcoholism as a Disease.* Berkeley, CA: University of California Press, 1989.
6. Brod H. The case for men's studies. In: Brod H., ed. *The Making of Masculinities: The New Men's Studies.* Boston: Allen Unwin, 1987.
7. Sabo D., Gordon D. F. Rethinking men's health and illness. In: Sabo D., Gordon D. F. eds. *Men's Health and Illness: Gender, Power, and the Body.* Thousand Oaks, CA: Sage, 1995.
8. Johnson A. G. *The Gender Knot: Unraveling Our Patriarchal Legacy.* Philadelphia: Temple University Press, 1997.
9. Lemle R., Mishkind M. E. Alcohol and masculinity. *Journal of Substance Abuse Treatment.* 1989, 6:213–222.

10. McCreary D. R., Newcomb M. D., Sadave S. The male role, alcohol use, and alcohol problems. *Journal of Counseling Psychology.* 1999, 46(1): 109–124.
11. Wechsler H., Deutsch C., Dowdell G. Too many colleges are still in denial about alcohol abuse. (1995) http://www.hsph.harvard.edu/cas/test/articles/chronicle2.shtm/.
12. Courtenay W. H. Behavioral factors associated with disease, injury, and death among men: Evidence and implications for prevention. *The Journal of Men's Studies.* In press.
13. Sharpe M. J. Heppner P. P. Gender role, gender-role conflict, and psychological well-being in men. *Journal of Counseling Psychology.* 1991, 39(3):323–330.
14. Pleck J. H. *The Myth of Masculinity.* Cambridge, MA: The MIT Press, 1981.
15. Pleck J. Men's power with women, other men, and society: A men's movement analysis. In: Kimmel M. S., Messner M. A. eds. *Men's Lives.* New York: Macmillan, 1989.
16. Kaufman M. Men, feminism, and men's contradictory experiences of power. In: Brod H., Kaufman M., eds. *Theorizing Masculinities.* Newbury Park, CA: Sage, 1994.
17. Kimmel M. S. Masculinity as homophobia: Fear, shame, and silence in the construction of gender identity. In: Brod H., Kaufman M., eds. *Theorizing Masculinities.* Newbury Park, CA: Sage, 1994.
18. Capraro R. L. Review of *Theorizing Masculinities.* Brod H., Kaufman M., eds. Sage; 1994. *Journal of Men's Studies.* 1995, 4(2):169–172.
19. O'Neil J. Assessing men's gender role conflict. In: Moore D., Leafgren F., eds. *Problem Solving Strategies and Interventions for Men in Conflict.* Alexandria, VA: American Association for Counseling and Development, 1990.
20. Pleck J. The gender role strain paradigm: An update. In: Levant R. L., Pollack W. S., eds. *A New Psychology of Men.* New York: Basic, 1995.
21. Blazina C., Watkins C. E. Masculine gender role conflict: Effects on college men's psychological well-being, chemical substance usage, and attitudes toward help-seeking. *Journal of Counseling Psychology.* 1995, 43(4):461–465.
22. Krugman S. Male development and the transformation of shame. In: Levant R. F., Pollack W. S., eds. *A New Psychology of Men.* New York: Basic, 1995.
23. Pollack W. *Real Boys.* New York: Henry Holt, 1999.
24. Good G. E., Mintz L. Gender role conflict and depression in college men: Evidence for compounded risk. *Journal of Counseling and Development.* 1990, 69 (September/October):17–21.
25. Lynch J., Kilmartin C. *The Pain Behind the Mask: Overcoming Masculine Depression.* New York: Haworth, 1999.
26. Real T. *I Don't Want to Talk About It.* New York: Simon & Schuster, 1997.
27. David D. S., Brannon R., eds. *The Forty-Nine Percent Majority: The Male Sex Role.* New York: Random House, 1976.
28. McClelland D. C., David W. N., Kalin R., Wanner E. *The Drinking Man.* New York: The Free Press, 1972.
29. Mahalik J. R., Cournoyer R. J., DeFran W., Cherry M., Napolitano J. M. Men's gender role conflict in relation to their use of psychological defenses. *Journal of Counseling Psychology.* 1998, 45(3):247–255.
30. Sattel J. W. Men, inexpressiveness, and power. In: Thorne K. H. *Language, Gender and Society.* Newbury House, 1983.
31. Fussell W. S. *Muscle: Confessions of an Unlikely Body-builder.* New York: Avon Books, 1991.
32. Berkowitz A. D., Burkhart B. R., Bourg S. E. *Research on College Research and Prevention Education in Higher Education.* San Francisco: Jossey-Bass, 1994.
33. Brod H. Pornography and the alienation of male sexuality. In: Hearn J., Morgan D., eds. *Men, Masculinities and Social Theory.* London: Unwin Hyman, 1990.
34. Kimmel M. S. *Men Confront Pornography.* New York: Crown, 1990.
35. Rorabaugh W. J. *The Alcoholic Republic: An American Tradition.* New York: Oxford University Press, 1981.
36. Maddox G. L., ed. *The Domesticated Drug: Drinking Among Collegians.* New Haven: College and University Press, 1970.
37. Bacon S. D., Strauss R. *Drinking in College.* New Haven: Yale University Press, 1953.
38. Johnston L., Bachman J. G., O'Malley P. M. *Monitoring the Future.* Health and Human Services Dept., US Public Health Service, National Institutes of Health, National Institute of Drug Abuse, 1996.

39. Levine A., Cureton J. S. *When Hope and Fear Collide: A Portrait of Today's College Student.* San Francisco: Jossey-Bass, 1998.

40. *Daedalus.* Distinctively American: The residential liberal arts colleges. Winter 1999.

41. Green M. *The Adventurous Male: Chapters in the History of the White Male Mind.* University Park, PA: The Pennsylvania State University Press, 1993.

42. Adams C. E., Nagoshi C. T. Changes over one semester in drinking game playing and alcohol use and problems in a college sample. *Subst Abuse.* 1999, 20(2):97–106.

43. Horowitz H. L. *Campus Life: Undergraduate Cultures from the End of the Eighteenth Century to the Present.* Chicago: University of Chicago Press, 1987.

44. Nuwer H. *Wrongs of Passage: Fraternities, Sororities, Hazing, and Binge Drinking.* Bloomington, IN: Indiana University Press, 1999.

45. Rotundo E. A. *American Manhood: Transformations in Masculinity from the Revolution to the Modern Era.* New York: HarperCollins, 1993.

46. Lyman P. The fraternal bond as a joking relationship. In: Kimmel M. S., ed. *Changing Men: New Directions in Research on Men and Masculinity.* Newbury Park, CA: Sage, 1987.

47. Gold J., Neururer J., Miller M. Disenfranchised grief among first-semester male university students: Implications for systemic and individual interventions. *Journal of the First Year Experience.* 2000, 12(1):7–27.

48. Burda P. C., Tushup R. J., Hackman P. S. Masculinity and social support in alcoholic men. *Journal of Men's Studies.* 1992, 1(2):187–193.

49. Johnson T. J., Hamilton S., Sheets V. L. College students' self-reported reasons for playing drinking games. *Addict Behav.* 1999, 24(2):279–286.

50. Wechsler H., Dowdall G. W., Maener G., Gledhill-Hoyt J., Lee H. Changes in binge drinking and related problems among American college students between 1993 and 1997. *J Am Coll Health.* 1998, 47:57–68.

51. Hoekema D. A. *Campus Rules and Moral Community: In Place of In Loco Parentis.* Lanham, MD: Rowman & Littlefield, 1994.

52. Myers P. L. Sources and configurations of institutional denial. *Employee Assistance Quarterly.* 1990, 5(3):43–53.

53. Berkowitz, A. D. From reactive to proactive prevention: Promoting an ecology of health on campus. In: Rivers P. C., Shore E. R., eds. *Substance Abuse on Campus: A Handbook for College and University Personnel.* Westport, CT: Greenwood Press, 1997.

54. Perkins H. W. Confronting misperceptions of peer drug use norms among college students: An alternative approach for alcohol and other drug education programs. In: *The Higher Education Leaders/Peer Network Peer Prevention Resource Manual.* US Dept. of Education, FIPSE Drug Prevention Program, 1991.

55. Perkins H. W., Wechsler H. Variation in perceived college drinking norms and its impact on alcohol abuse: A nationwide study. *Journal of Drug Issues.* 1996, 26(4):961–974.

56. Fabiano P. M., McKinney G. R., Hyun Y.-R., Mertz H. K., Rhoads K. Lifestyles, 1998: Patterns of alcohol and drug consumption and consequences among Western Washington University students—An extended executive study. *Focus: A Research Summary.* 1999, 4(3):1–8.

57. Haines M. *A Social Norms Approach to Preventing Binge Drinking at Colleges and Universities.* Newton, MA: The Higher Education Center for Alcohol and Other Drug Prevention, 1998.

58. Prentice D. A., Miller D. T. Pluralistic ignorance and alcohol use on campus: Some consequences of misperceiving the social norms. *J Pers Soc Psychol.* 1993, 65:243–256.

59. Berkowitz A. D. A model acquaintance rape prevention program for men. In: Berkowitz A. D., ed. *Men and Rape: Theory, Research, and Prevention Education in Higher Education.* San Francisco: Jossey-Bass, 1994.

60. Berkowitz A. D. Applications of social norms theory to other health and social justice issues. Paper presented at: Annual Social Norms Conference. July 28–30, 1999, Big Sky, Mont.

61. Postman N., Nystrom C., Strate L., Weingartner C. *Myths, Men, and Beer: An Analysis of Beer Commercials on Broadcast Television, 1987.* Washington, DC: AAA Foundation for Traffic Safety, undated.

62. Courtenay W. H. Engendering health: A social constructionist examination of men's health beliefs and behaviors. *Psychology of Men and Masculinity.* In press.

63. Wechsler H., Kelley K., Weitzman E. R., San Giovanni J. P., Seebring M. What colleges are doing about student binge drinking: A survey of college administrators. (March 2000)

http://www.hsph.Harvard.edu/cas/test/alcohol/surveyrpt.shtm/.
64. Scher M., Steven M., Good G., Eichenfield G. A. *Handbook of Counseling and Psychotherapy with Men.* Newbury Park, CA: Sage, 1987.
65. Moore D., Leafgren F., eds. *Problem Solving Strategies and Intervention for Men in Conflict.* Alexandria, VA: American Association for Counseling and Development, 1990.
66. Levant R. F., Pollack, W. S., eds. *A New Psychology of Men.* New York: Basic, 1995.
67. Mahalik M. R. Incorporating a gender role strain perspective in assessing and treating men's cognitive distortions. *Professional Psychology: Research and Practice.* 1999, 30(4):333–340.
68. Capraro R. L. Disconnected lives: Men, masculinity, and rape prevention. In: Berkowitz A. D., ed. *Men and Rape: Theory, Research, and Prevention Programs in Higher Education.* San Francisco: Jossey-Bass, 1994.
69. Helms J. An Update of Helms' *White and People of Color Racial Identity Models.* In: Ponterretto J., et al., eds. *Handbook of Multicultural Counseling.* Newbury Park, CA: Sage, 1995.

ARTICLE 17

Timothy Jon Curry

Fraternal Bonding in the Locker Room: A Profeminist Analysis of Talk About Competition and Women

The men's locker room is enshrined in sports mythology as a bastion of privilege and a center of fraternal bonding. The stereotyped view of the locker room is that it is a retreat from the outside world where athletes quietly prepare themselves for competition, noisily celebrate an important victory, or silently suffer a defeat. Given the symbolic importance of this sports shrine, it is surprising that there have been so few actual studies of the dynamics of male bonding in locker rooms. The purpose of this study was to explore a new approach to this aspect of fraternal bonding, by collecting locker room talk fragments and interpreting them from a profeminist perspective. Profeminism in this context meant adapting a feminist perspective to men's experience in sport, giving special attention to sexist and homophobic remarks that reveal important assumptions about masculinity, male dominance, and fraternal bonding.

Although seldom defined explicitly, the fraternal bond is usually considered to be a force, link, or affectionate tie that unites men. It is characterized in the literature by low levels of disclosure and intimacy. Sherrod (1987), for example, suggests that men associate different meanings with friendships than women do, and that men tend to derive friendships from doing things together while women are able to maintain friendships through disclosures. This view implies that men need a reason to become close to one another and are uncomfortable about sharing their feelings.

Some of the activities around which men bond are negative toward women and others who are perceived as outsiders to the fraternal group. For example, Lyman (1987) describes how members of a fraternity bond through sexist joking relationships, and Fine (1987) notes the development of sexist, racist, and homophobic attitudes and jokes even among preadolescent Little Leaguers. Sanday (1990) examines gang rape as a by-product of male bonding in fraternities, and she argues that the homophobic and homosocial environments of such all-male groups make for a conducive environment for aggression toward women.

Sport is an arena well suited for the enactment and perpetuation of the male bond (Messner 1987). It affords separation and identity building as individual athletes seek status through making the team and winning games (Dunning 1986), and it also provides group activity essential for male bonding (Sherrod 1987) while not requiring much in the way of intimate disclosures (Sabo & Panepinto 1990). Feminist scholars have pointed out that the status enhancement available to men through sports is not as available to women, and thus sport serves to legitimate men's domination of women and their control of public life (Bryson 1987; Farr 1988). In addition, since most sports are rule bound either by tradition or by explicit

Reprinted by permission from T. J. Curry, 1991, "Fraternal Bonding in the Locker Room: A Profeminist Analysis of Talk about Competition and Women," *Sociology of Sport Journal* 8(2): 119–135.

formal codes, involvement in sports is part of the typical rights-and-rules orientation of boys' socialization in the United States (Gilligan 1982).

For young men, sport is also an ideal place to "do gender"—display masculinity in a socially approved fashion (West & Zimmerman 1987). In fact the male bond is apparently strengthened by an effective display of traditional masculinity and threatened by what is not considered part of standard hegemonic masculinity. For example, as Messner (1989, p. 192) relates, a gay football player who was aggressive and hostile on the field felt "compelled to go along with a lot of locker room garbage because I wanted that image [of attachment to more traditional male traits]—and I know a lot of others who did too . . . I know a lot of football players who very quietly and secretly like to paint, or play piano. And they do it quietly, because this to them is threatening if it's known by others." Since men's bonding is based on shared activity rather than on self-disclosures (Sherrod 1987), it is unlikely that teammates will probe deeply beneath these surface presentations.

Deconstructing such performances, however, is one way of understanding "the interactional scaffolding of social structure and the social control process that sustains it" in displays of masculinity central to fraternal bonding (West & Zimmerman 1987, p. 147). Pronger (1990, pp. 192–213) has provided one such deconstruction of doing gender in the locker room from the perspective of a homosexual. He notes the irony involved in maintaining the public façade of heterosexuality while privately experiencing a different reality.

Two other studies of locker rooms emphasized the cohesive side of male bonding through sports, but neither of these studies was concerned specifically with gender displays or with what male athletes say about women (Snyder 1972; Zurcher 1982). The uproar over the sexual harassment of a woman reporter in the locker room of the NFL's New England Patriots, described by Heymann (1990), suggests that this work is a timely and important undertaking.

Procedures

This study of locker room talk follows Snyder (1972), who collected samples of written messages and slogans affixed to locker room walls. However, since the messages gathered by Snyder were originally selected by coaches and were meant to serve as normative prescriptions that would contribute to winning games, they mostly revealed an idealistic, public side of locker room culture. From reading these slogans one would get the impression that men's sports teams are characterized by harmony, consensus, and "esoteric in-group traditions" (Snyder 1972, p. 99).

The approach taken here focuses on the spoken aspects of locker room culture—the jokes and put-downs typically involved in fraternal bonding (Fine 1987; Lyman 1987). Although this side of locker room culture is ephemeral, situational, and generally not meant for display outside of the all-male peer groups, it is important in understanding how sport contributes to male bonding, status attainment, and hegemonic displays of masculinity.

The Talk Fragments

The talk fragments were gathered in locker rooms from athletes on two teams participating in contact sports at a large midwestern university with a "big time" sports program. The first team was approached at the beginning of its season for permission to do a field study. Permission was granted and assurances were made that anonymity would be maintained for athletes and coaches. I observed the team as a nonparticipant sport sociologist, both at practices and during competition, for well over a month before the first talk fragments were collected. The talk fragments were gathered over a two-month period and the locker room was visited frequently to gather field notes. Note gathering in the locker room was terminated upon saturation; however, the team's progress was followed and field observations continued until the end of the season.

Intensive interviews were conducted with some of the athletes and coaches during all nine months of the research. These interviews concerned not only locker room interaction but also the sport background and life histories of the respondents. Additionally, after the talk fragments were gathered, five of the athletes enrolled in my class on sport sociology and wrote term papers on their experiences in sport. These written documents, along with the interviews and observations made outside the locker room, provided a rich variety of materials for the contextual analysis and interpretation of the conversations held inside the locker room. They also lent insight into how the athletes themselves defined locker room talk.

The talk fragments were collected in plain view of the athletes, who had become accustomed to the presence of a researcher taking notes. Fragments of talk were written down as they occurred and were reconstructed later. Such obvious note taking may have influenced what was said, or more likely what was not said. To minimize the obtrusiveness of the research, eye contact was avoided while taking notes. A comparison between the types of conversations that occurred during note taking versus when note taking was not done yielded few differences. Even so, more talk fragments were gathered from a second locker room as a way of both increasing the validity of the study and protecting the anonymity of the athletes and coaches from the first locker room.

The Second Locker Room

Field notes concerning talk from a second locker room were gathered by a senior who had enjoyed a successful career as a letterman. His presence in the locker room as a participant observer was not obtrusive, and the other student-athletes reacted to him as a peer. He gathered talk fragments over a three-month period while his team was undergoing conditioning and selection procedures similar in intensity to that of the original team. He met with me every week and described his perceptions of interaction in the locker room. His collection of talk fragments was included as part of a written autobiographical account of his experience in sport while at college. These research procedures were modeled after Zurcher's (1983) study of hashers in a sorority house and Shaw's (1972) autobiographical account of his experience in sport.

One additional point needs to be stressed here: Unlike anecdotal accounts of locker room behavior or studies based on the recollections of former athletes, these conversations were systematically gathered live and in context over a relatively brief period of time. Consequently the stories and jokes may not be as extreme as those remembered by athletes who reflect upon their entire career in sport (e.g., Messner 1987; Pronger 1990), or as dramatic as the episode of sexual harassment that took place in the locker room of the New England Patriots (Heymann 1990).

The strength of this study lies in situating the conversations within the context of the competitive environment of elite collegiate sport rather than capturing the drama of a single moment or the recollections of particularly memorable occasions. In other words, no one study, including this one, can hope to cover the entire gambit of locker room culture and various distinctive idiocultures of different teams (Fine 1987). A variety of studies that use different methods and incorporate different perspectives are needed for that endeavor.

Profeminist Perspective

Messner (1990) has recently argued that a profeminist perspective is needed to overcome male bias in research in the sociology of sport. For decades, Messner claims, male researchers have been prone to writing about sport from a masculine standpoint and have neglected gender issues. He further states that since men have exclusive access to much of the social world of sport, they also have the primary responsibility of providing a more balanced interpretation of that world by paying special attention to gender oppression. He maintains that such balance is best achieved at this point by adopting a value-centered feminist perspective rather than a supposedly value-free but androcentric perspective.

Adopting a feminist standpoint requires assuming that "feminist visions of an egalitarian society are desirable" (Messner 1990, p. 149). Ultimately, research guided by such an assumption will contribute to a deeper understanding of the costs and the privileges of masculinity and may help build a more just and egalitarian world. Messner does not offer explicit guidelines as to how an androcentric researcher might begin to undertake such a shift in perspectives, however, although he does refer to a number of exemplary studies.

As a method of consciously adopting a profeminist perspective in this research, a review of feminist literature on sports and socialization was undertaken, feminist colleagues were consulted on early drafts of the manuscript, and a research assistant trained in feminist theory was employed to help with the interpretation of talk fragments. She shared her ideas and observations regarding the talk fragments, written documents, and field notes with me and suggested some additional references and sources that proved useful.

The talk fragments were selected and arranged to provide a sense of the different themes, ideas, and attitudes encountered. In focusing on the talk fragments themselves, two categories emerged (through a grounded theory approach) as especially important for situating and interpreting locker room behavior from a profeminist perspective: (a) the dynamics of competition, status attainment, and bonding among male athletes, and (b) the dynamics of defending one's masculinity through homophobic talk and talk about women as objects. A numbering system for each talk fragment (Athlete 1, 2, Sam, etc.) is used below to keep track of the different speakers. Names have been changed and the numbering system starts over for each talk fragment.

Competition, Status Attainment, and Bonding

Locker room talk is mostly about the common interests that derive from the shared identities of male student-athlete. Underlying these interactions is an ever present sense of competition, both for status and position on the team itself and between the team and its opponents. While sport provides an activity to bond around, one's position on the team is never totally secure. An injury or poor performance may raise doubts about one's ability and lead to one's replacement. Such basic insecurities do not promote positive social relationships in the locker room, and they help explain some of the harshness of the talk that the athletes directed toward each other and toward women.

For example, competition can have a subtle influence on the relationships athletes have with others on the team and cause them to be quite tentative, as illustrated by the following statements obtained from two interviews:

> One of the smaller guys on the team was my best friend . . . maybe I just like having a little power over [him] . . . It doesn't matter if the guy is your best friend, you've got to beat him, or else you are sitting there watching. Nobody wants to watch.

> That's one of my favorite things about the sport, I enjoy the camaraderie. [Who are your friends?] Usually it's just the starters . . . you unite behind each other a lot. The other guys don't share the competition with you like the starters do.

The competition can extend beyond sport itself into other domains. It is not unusual for athletes to have as their closest friends men who are not on the team, which helps them maintain some defensive ego boundaries between themselves and the team. It also provides a relief from the constant competition, as one athlete indicates:

> [My] better friends aren't on the team. Probably because we are not always competing. With my [athlete] friends, we are always competing . . . like who gets the best girls, who gets the best grades . . . Seems like [we] are competitive about everything, and it's nice to have some friends that don't care . . . you can just relax.

Competition, Emotional Control, and Bonding

A variety of studies have indicated that male athletes are likely to incorporate competitive motivation as part of their sport identity (e.g., Curry & Weiss 1989). As competition and status attainment become important for the male athlete in establishing his identity, noninstrumental emotion becomes less useful, perhaps even harmful to his presentation of a conventionally gendered self (Sherrod 1987). In addition, by defining themselves in terms of what is not feminine, men may come to view emotional displays with disdain or even fear (Herek 1987). However, control over emotions in sport is made difficult by the passions created by an intense desire to win. One athlete described his feelings of being consumed by competition while in high school and his need to control the emotions:

> My junior year, I had become so obsessed with winning the district... I was so overcome that I lost control a week before the tournament. I was kicking and screaming and crying on the sofa... since then I have never been the same. True, now I work harder than that year but now when I start to get consumed [with something] I get fearful and reevaluate its importance.

As part of learning to control emotions, the athletes have learned to avoid public expressions of emotional caring or concern for one another even as they bond, because such remarks are defined as weak or feminine. For example, the remarks of the following athlete illustrate how this type of socialization can occur through sport. This athlete's father was very determined that his son would do well in sports, so much so that he forced the boy to practice daily and became very angry with the boy's mistakes. To understand his father's behavior, the boy went to his mother:

> I would come up from the cellar and be upset with myself, and I would talk to my mother and say, "Why does he yell so much?" and she would say, "He only does it because he loves you."

While the father emphasized adherence to rules and discipline, the boy had to depend on his mother to connect him to his father's love. Distancing from each other emotionally is of course dysfunctional for the relationships among male athletes and leads to an impoverishment of relationships (Messner 1987).

Maintaining a "safe" distance from one another also influences what is said and what is not said in front of others about topics of mutual concern, such as grades and women. Failure to address such common problems openly means that they must be dealt with indirectly or by denial. For example, the deriding of academic work by male athletes has been noted by other investigators (Adler & Adler 1991) and is not typical of female athletes (Meyer 1990). The reason may be that when athletes make comments that might be construed as asking for help or encouragement, their behavior is considered nonmasculine. They are thus subject to ridicule, as illustrated in the following two talk fragments:

> *Fragment 1*
> *Athlete 1:* [Spoken to the athlete who has a locker near him, but loud enough to be heard by others] What did you get on your test?
> *Athlete 2:* 13 [pause], that's two D+'s this week. That's a student-athlete for you. [sighs, then laughs quietly]
> *Athlete 1:* That's nothing to laugh about.
> *Athlete 2:* [contritely] I mean an athlete-student, but things are looking up for me. I'm going to do better this week. How did you do on that test?
> *Athlete 1:* Got a 92.
> *Athlete 3:* Yeah, who did you cheat off of? [group laughter]
>
> *Fragment 2*
> *Athlete 1:* [To coach, shouted across room] I'm doing real bad in class.
> *Coach:* Congratulations!
> *Athlete 1:* [serious tone, but joking] Will you call the professor up and tell him to give me an A?
> *Coach:* [Obviously sarcastically] Sure thing, would tonight at nine be all right?

Competition and a Sense of Self

Considering the time-consuming nature of big-time college sports, it is not surprising that they become the central focus of athletes' lives. Approximately 30 hours a week were spent in practice, and often the athletes were too tired after a hard practice to do much else than sleep.

Fragment 3
Athlete 1: [collapses on bench] Shit, I'm going to bed right now, and maybe I'll make my nine o'clock class tomorrow.
Athlete 2: 40 minutes straight! I thought he'd never stop the drills.
Athlete 1: Left you gasping for air at the end, didn't it?
Athlete 2: You mean gasping for energy.

Sports and competition become the greater part of the athlete's world. Through his strivings to excel, to be a part of the team and yet stand out on his own, he develops a conception of who he is. Thus the athlete's sense of self can be seen as being grounded in competition, with few alternative sources of self-gratification (Adler & Adler 1991). The rewards for such diligence are a heightened sense of self-esteem. When one athlete was asked what he would miss most if he were to leave sports, he declared, "the competition . . . the attitude I feel about being [on the team]. It makes me feel special. You're doing something that a lot of people can't do, and wish they could do." In other words, his knowledge of his "self" includes status-enhancing presumptions about character building through sport.

This attitude is not atypical. For example, another man claimed, "I can always tell a [refers to athletes in same sport he plays]. They give off cues—good attitude, they are sure of themselves, bold, not insecure." This sense of specialness and status presumption cements the male bond and may temporarily cut across social class and racial differences. Later in life the experiences and good memories associated with fellowship obtained through sport may further sociability and dominance bonding (Farr 1988). For the elite college athlete, however, this heightened self-esteem is obtained at some costs to other activities. Often academic studies and social or romantic involvements get defined as peripheral to the self and are referred to with contempt in the locker room, as illustrated in the next fragment:

Most everyone has vacated the locker room for the showers. Sam and a few of his friends are left behind. Sam is red shirting (saving a year's eligibility by not participating on the team except for practices) and will not be traveling with the team. What he is going to do instead is the subject of several jokes once all the coaches have left the locker room:

Fragment 4
Athlete 1: What are you going to do, Sam, go to the game?
Sam: I can't, I sold my ticket. [laughs] I'm going to the library so I can study. [cynically] Maybe I'll take my radio so I can listen to the game. [pause] I hate my classes.
Athlete 1: Oh, come on, that's not the right attitude.
Sam: And I hope to get laid a few times too.
Athlete 1: Hey come on, that's not a nice way to talk.
Sam: How else are you supposed to talk in a locker room?

Sam's comment also leads us directly to the question of peer group influence on presentation of a gendered self. A general rule of male peer groups is that you can say and do some things with your peers that would be inappropriate almost anywhere else. For male athletes this rule translates into an injunction to be insulting and antisocial on occasion (Fine 1987; Lyman 1987). You are almost expected to speak sarcastically and offensively in the locker room, as Sam indicates above. Thus, hostile talk about women is blended with jokes and put-downs about classes and each other. In short, while sport leads to self-enhancement, the peer culture of male athletes also fosters antisocial talk, much of which is directed toward the athletes themselves.

Rigidities of the Bond

Competition in sports, then, links men together in a status-enhancing activity in which aggression is valued (Dunning 1986). The bond between male athletes is usually felt to be a strong one, yet it is set aside rather easily. The reason for this is that the bond is rigid, with sharply defined boundaries. For example, when speaking about what it is that bonds athletes to their sport and other athletes, a coach remarks,

> They know they are staying in shape, they are part of something. Some of them stay with it because they don't want to be known as quitters. There's no in-between. You're a [team member or not a team member]. The worst guy on the team is still well thought of if he's out there every day going through it. There's no sympathy in that room. No sympathy if you quit. You might die but you're not going to quit.

This rigid definition of who is or is not a team member reflects Gilligan's (1982) concept of a rights/rules moral system for males, which emphasizes individuality, instrumental relations, achievement, and control. In short the male athlete is either on the team or not. There is no grey area: It is clearly a black or white situation. If one follows the "rules," then he has the "right" to participate in bonding. If one does not follow the rules (i.e., quits), he ceases to exist in a bonding capacity. However, as Coakley (1990) has observed, following the rules to their extremes can lead to "positive" deviance, including a refusal to quit in spite of injury. Athlete 1 below endured a number of small and severe injuries, but throughout his ordeal refused to consider leaving the team.

Fragment 5
Athlete 1: My shin still hurts, can't get it to stop.
Athlete 2: Well, that's it then—time to quit.
Athlete 1: Not me, I'm not a quitter.
Athlete 2: Oh, come on, I can see through that. You'll quit if you have to.
Athlete 1: No way.

Even though injured, an athlete is still a member of the team if he attends practice, even if only to watch the others work out. However, his bond with the others suffers if he cannot participate fully in the sport. Sympathy is felt for such athletes, in that their fate is recognized and understood. As one athlete empathized during an interview, "I feel for the guys who are hurt who are usually starters . . . [They] feel lonely about it, feel like they want to be back out there, feel like they want to prove something."

Perhaps what these athletes need to prove is that they are still a part of the activity around which the bonds are centered. As Sherrod (1987) suggests, the meanings associated with friendship for men are grounded in activities, giving them a reason to bond. Past success or status as a team member is not enough to fully sustain the bond; bonding requires constant maintenance. With boundaries so rigid, the athletes must constantly establish and reestablish their status as members involved in the bond by the only way they know how: through competition.

Rigid definitions of performance requirements in sport combine to form an either/or situation for the athlete and his ability to bond with teammates. If he stays within these boundaries, he is accepted and the bond remains intact. If he fails, he is rejected and the bond is severed. One athlete sums up this position with the following comments: "You lose a lot of respect for guys like that. Seems like anybody who's quit, they just get pushed aside. Like [name deleted], when he used to be [on the team] he hung around with us, and now that he's not, he ain't around anymore." Thus an athlete may find his relations severed with someone he has known for half his life, through participation in sport in junior high and high school, simply because the other person has left the team.

Talk About Women

Competitive pressures and insecurities surrounding the male bond influence talk about women. As discussed above, competition provides an activity bond to other men that is rewarding, even though the atmosphere of competition surrounding big-time sports generates anxiety and other strong emotions that the athletes seek to control or channel. Competition for positions or status on the team also curtails or conditions friendships, and peer group culture is compatible with antisocial talk and behavior, some of which is directed at the athletes themselves.

The fraternal bond is threatened by inadequate role performance, quitting the team, or not living up to the demands of masculinity. Consequently, fear of weakening the fraternal bond greatly affects how athletes "do gender" in the locker room and influences the comments they make about women. In this regard, locker room talk may again be characterized both by what is said and what is not said. Conversations that affirm a traditional masculine identity dominate, and these include talk about women as objects, homophobic talk and talk that is very aggressive and hostile toward women—essentially talk that promotes rape culture.

Woman as Person, Woman as Object

Two additional distinctions now need to be made in categorizing locker room talk about women. One category concerns women as real people, persons with whom the athletes have ongoing social relationships. This category of locker room talk is seldom about sexual acquisition; most often it is about personal concerns athletes might wish to share with their best friend on the team. Because the athletes do not want their comments to be overheard by others who might react with ridicule, this type of talk usually occurs in hushed tones, as described in the following fragment. Talk about women as objects, on the other hand, often refers to sexual conquests. This type of talk is not hushed. Its purpose seems mainly to enhance the athletes' image of themselves to others as practicing heterosexuals.

Fragment 6
Athlete 1 to 2: I've got to talk to you about [whispers name]. They go over to an empty corner of the locker room and whisper. They continue to whisper until the coaches arrive. The athletes at the other end of the locker room make comments:
Athlete 3: Yeah, tell us what she's got.
Athlete 4: Boy, you're in trouble now.

Assistant coach: You'll have to leave our part of the room. This is where the real men are.

The peer culture of the locker room generally does not support much talk about women as persons. Norms of masculinity discourage talking seriously about social relations, so these types of conversations are infrequent (Fine 1987; Sabo & Panepinto 1990). Inevitably, personal revelations will quickly be followed by male athletic posturing, jokes, and put-downs, as in the talk fragment above. While the jokes may be amusing, they do little to enhance personal growth and instead make a real sharing of intimacies quite difficult. The ridicule that follows these interactions also serves to establish the boundaries of gender appropriate behavior. This ridicule tells the athlete that he is getting too close to femaleness, because he is taking relatedness seriously. "Real men" do not do that. Perhaps just taking the view of women as persons is enough to evoke suspicion in the locker room.

To avoid this suspicion, the athlete may choose to present his attitude toward women in a different way, one that enhances his identity as a "real man." The resulting women-as-objects stories are told with braggadocio or in a teasing manner; they are stage performances usually requiring an audience of more than one, and may be told to no one in particular:

Fragment 7
I was taking a shower with my girlfriend when her parents came home. I never got dressed so fast in my life.

These types of stories elicit knowing smiles or guffaws from the audience, and it is difficult to tell whether or not they are true. In any event the actual truth of such a story is probably less important than the function it serves in buttressing the athlete's claim as a practicing heterosexual.

Fragment 8
Athlete 1: How was your Thanksgiving?
Athlete 2: Fine, went home.

Athlete 1: I bet you spent the time hitting high schools!

Athlete 2: Naw, only had to go back to [one place] to find out who was available.

Women's identities as people are of no consequence in these displays. The fact that women are viewed as objects is also evident in the tendency of men to dissect woman's bodies into parts, which are then discussed separately from the whole person. Athlete 1 in Fragment 9 below is describing a part of a woman's body as if it existed separately from the woman, as if it was in the training room and the woman was not:

Fragment 9

Athlete 1: I just saw the biggest set of Ta-Tas in the training room!

Athlete 2: How big were they?

Athlete 1: Bigger than my mouth.

This perspective toward women highlights the fact that the use of women's bodies is more important than knowing them as people. Perhaps this attitude is also based in the athlete's focus on maintaining control, whether physically through athletic performance or mentally through strict adherence to rules and discipline. Since the male athlete's ideas about control center around physical strength and mental discipline, they stand in sharp contrast to ideas about females, who are generally thought of as physically weak and emotional. Following the implications of these ideas a bit further, women as persons are emotional and cannot be easily controlled; women as objects, however, have no volition and can be more easily controlled.

Doing Gender through Homophobic Talk

From Herek's (1987) notion that through socialization boys learn to be masculine by avoiding that which is feminine or homosexual, it follows that in the locker room an athlete may be singled out if his demeanor is identified as unmasculine in any way. The reasoning may be seen as follows: (a) "real men" are defined by what they are *not* (women and homosexuals); (b) it is useful to maintain a separation from femaleness or gayness so as not to be identified as such; (c) expression of dislike for femaleness or homosexuality demonstrates to oneself and others that one is separate from it and therefore must be masculine. For example, when an athlete's purple designer underwear is discovered, a teammate asks, "and did you get earrings for Christmas?" When he protests, this reply, directed to all of the athletes in the room is offered: "Guess I hit a . . . nerve. I won't begin on the footsies today, maybe tomorrow."

This example illustrates that every aspect of the athlete's appearance runs the risk of gender assessment. That which is under suspicion of being at odds with traditional definitions of masculinity threatens the bond and will be questioned. Connell (1990, pp. 88–89) provides further graphic example of gender assessment among athletes. He describes the life of a determinedly heterosexual Australian Iron-Man competitor, whose first coital experience at 17 was both arranged and witnessed by his surf-club friends, and who felt he had to "put on a good show for the boys." Presumably, his performance allowed him and his friends to reaffirm to themselves and others that their sexual preferences remained within the boundaries of the bond.

Not only is being homosexual forbidden, but tolerance of homosexuality is theoretically off limits as well. The sanctions associated with this type of boundary maintenance manifest themselves in jokes and story telling about homosexuals.

Fragment 10

Athlete 1: When I was at [high school] we all lined up to watch the other guys come in. Fred pretended to be interested in one of them and said, "I like that one" [he gestures with a limp wrist] . . . . We were all so fucking embarrassed, nobody would give him a ride home. It was the funniest thing!

Athlete 2: Yeah, once we all stopped in at [a local bar] and Tom got up to dance with one of the fags, actually took his hand and started to dance! Boy was the fag surprised. [group laughter]

Making fun of homosexuals by mimicking stereotyped gay gender displays brings laughter in the locker room partly because it helps distance the athletes from being categorized as gay themselves. Such hegemonic gender displays also take more aggressive forms. Perhaps male athletes are especially defensive because of the physical closeness and nudity in the locker room and the contact between males in sport itself. This latter idea is evident in the following remarks of a coach:

> We do so much touching that some people think we're queer. In 37 years I've never for sure met a queer [athlete]. At [a certain college] we had a [teammate] that some of the fellows thought was queer. I said "pound on him, beat on him, see what happens." He quit after three days. He never approached anyone anyway.

Locker Room Talk Promotes Rape Culture

Maintaining the appearance of a conventional heterosexual male identity then, is of the utmost importance to the athlete who wants to remain bonded to his teammates. Also, as discussed previously, the perception of women as objects instead of persons encourages expressions of disdain or even hatred toward them on the part of the male athletes. Thus, the striving to do gender appropriately within the constraints of the fraternal bond involves talk that manages to put down women while also ridiculing or teasing each other, as the following fragments indicate:

> *Fragment 11*
> *Assistant Coach 1:* [announcement] Shame to miss the big [football] game, but you have to travel this week to keep you out of trouble. Keep you from getting laid too many times this weekend. Here are the itineraries for the trip. They include a picture of Frank's girlfriend. [Picture is of an obese woman surrounded by children. Frank is one of the best athletes on the team.]
> *Assistant Coach 2:* Yeah, when she sits around the house, she really sits around the house.
> *Assistant Coach 3:* She's so ugly that her mother took her everywhere so she wouldn't have to kiss her good-bye. [group laughter]

Jibes and put-downs about one's girlfriend or lack of sexual success are typified by this exchange. Part of the idealized heterosexual male identity consists of "success" with women, and to challenge that success by poking fun at the athlete's girlfriend is an obvious way to insult him. These jibes were directed at one of the best athletes on the team whose girlfriend was not in town. It is important to note that these insults were delivered by the assistant coaches, who are making use of their masculine identity as a common bond they share with the student-athletes. By ridiculing one of the better athletes, they are not threatening any of the more vulnerable team members and at the same time they are removing some of the social distance between themselves and the students. After receiving such an insult, the athlete has to think of a comeback to top it or lose this round of insulting. Fine (1987) also noted such escalation of insults in his study of the Little League. This attitude is recognized and understood by other athletes:

> *Fragment 12*
> You guys harass around here real good. If you knew my mother's name, you would bring her into it too.

Thus a negative view of women prevails in the locker room and serves to facilitate the bond between athletes and their coaches. At times the competition involved with these exchanges does not involve insults directed at one another. The athletes compete instead to see who can express the most negative attitudes toward women, as illustrated by the final comments from a discussion of different types of women:

> *Fragment 13*
> Let me tell you about those [names an ethnic minority] women. They look good until they are 20, then they start pushing out the pups. By the time they're 40, they weigh 400 pounds.

This negative orientation is fed by other related attitudes about women, such as those that concern women's sports, as indicated by the following remarks made by a coach: "[Our sport] has been taking a beating in lots of colleges. It's because of the emphasis on women's sports. Too bad, because [our sport] is cheaper. Could make money . . ." (he continues with comments about women's sports not paying their way).

At their extreme, these attitudes promote aggression toward women and create an environment supportive for rape culture (Beneke 1982; Sanday 1990). A fairly mild form of this aggression is suggested in the following talk fragment, in which two athletes are talking about Jerry, an athlete who is a frequent butt of their jokes. Jerry has just left the locker room and this conversation occurs when he is out of hearing distance:

Fragment 14
Athlete 1: Hey Pete, did you know Jerry is a sexual dynamo?
Pete: Why do you say that?
Athlete 1: He said he was with two different girls in the same day and both girls were begging, and I emphasize begging, for him to stop. He said he banged each of them so hard that they begged for him to stop.
Pete: I think he's becoming retarded.
Athlete 1: Do you believe he said this to me?
Pete: Well, what did you do?
Athlete 1: I laughed in his face.
Pete: What did he do?
Athlete 1: Nothing, he just kept telling me about this; it was hilarious.

The preceding fragment can be seen as describing rape in that the women involved with the athlete "begged for him to stop," and in this case the athletes choose to use the story to put down Jerry and thus negate his claim to sexual dynamism. The rape reference is more obvious in the following fragment. To set the scene, the team was visited by high school athletes and their parents; the athletes were being recruited by the coaches. The mother of one recruit drew attention from a group of athletes because she was extremely attractive. This conversation occurs in the locker room after she left with her son:

Fragment 15
Athlete 1: She's too young to be his mother!
Athlete 2: Man, I'd hurt her if I got ahold of her.
Athlete 3: I'd tear her up.
Athlete 4: I'd break her hips. [all laugh]
Athlete 3: Yeah, she was hot!

Thus locker room talk about women, though serving a function for the bonding of men, also promotes harmful attitudes and creates an environment supportive of sexual assault and rape. Competition among teammates, the emphasis upon women as objects, sexual conquest as enviable achievement, peer group encouragement of antisocial comments and behavior, and anxiety about proving one's heterosexuality—all of these ideas are combined in the preceding fragment to promote a selfish, hostile, and aggressive approach to sexual encounters with women.

Conclusions

Sex and aggression are familiar themes in men's talk, and it is no surprise to find them of paramount importance in the locker room. Fine's (1987) work with preadolescent Little League baseball players indicated that the conversations of 9- to 12-year-old boys reflected similar concerns. What comes through less clearly in the conversations is the fulfillment that men find in such talk. It is an affirmation of one's masculine identity to be able to hold one's own in conversations about women, to top someone else's joke, or to share a story that one's peers find interesting. In this way the athlete's identity as a man worthy of bonding with is maintained.

College athletes often speak of the rewards of team membership as being an important reason for participating in a sport, and one of the rewards is the give and take of the peer culture in the locker room. The combination of revelation and braggadocio requires a shifting interpretation between fantasy and reality, and the ready willingness to insult means that a false interpretation may subject one to ridicule.

There are no definitive studies that document the effects of participating in locker room culture. On the one hand, behavior in locker rooms is both ephemeral and situational and probably does not reflect the actual values of all the participants. From this perspective, the locker room is just a place to change clothing and to shower, and one should not make too much of what goes on there. In discussing locker room interaction with some of the athletes involved, I found that most distanced themselves from it and denied its importance to them, particularly with respect to devaluing academic work. In some cases locker room talk even served as a negative reference for athletes, who quietly went about their business and avoided involvement. However, it is important to note that no one ever publicly challenged the dominant sexism and homophobia of the locker room. Whatever oppositional thoughts there may have been were muttered quietly or remained private.

On the other hand, there is evidence that years of participating in such a culture desensitizes athletes to women's and gay rights and supports male supremacy rather than egalitarian relationships with women. For instance, Connell's (1990) life history of an Iron-Man indicated that this incredibly fit young man was unable to tolerate a "girl" who stood up for her own interests, and so had a series of girlfriends who were compliant with his needs and schedule. Moreover, Connell observes that this attitude is typical among the other male supremacists who constitute the Australian surfing subculture.

Another illustration is provided by the harassment of Lisa Olson in the locker room of the New England Patriots. This episode also supports the idea that locker room talk promotes aggressive antifemale behavior. The details of this case involved grown men parading nude around the seated reporter as she was conducting an interview. Some of the men "modeled themselves" before her, and one "adjusted" his genitals and shook his hips in an exaggerated fashion, and one naked player stood arm's length from her and said "Here's what you want. Do you want to take a bite out of this?"—all to the accompaniment of bantering and derisive laughter (Heymann 1990, p. 9A). No one tried to stop the humiliating activity, nor did management intervene or sincerely apologize until forced to by the NFL Commissioner. In fact, the initial reaction of the team's owner was to support the players. The owner, Victor ("I liked it so much, I bought the company"—Remington) Kiam, was heard to say, "What a classic bitch. No wonder none of the players like her." However, his concern for the sales of his women's shaving products resulted in the following damage control campaign:

> He took out full-page ads in three major U.S. newspapers to protest his innocence, offered testimonials from three people who denied he said anything derogatory about Olson, and blamed the Patriots front office personnel for not telling him of the Olson locker room incident sooner. (Norris 1991, p. 23)

Finally, Sanday (1990, p. 193) concludes her study of gang rape by fraternity members by indicating that "Sexism is an unavoidable by-product of a cultural fascination with the virile, sexually powerful hero who dominates everyone, male and female alike." If this is true, then sexism in locker rooms is best understood as part of a larger cultural pattern that supports male supremacy.

It is my view that sexist locker room talk is likely to have a cumulative negative effect on young men because it reinforces the notions of masculine privilege and hegemony, making that world view seem normal and typical. Moreover, it does so in a particularly pernicious fashion. By linking ideas about masculinity with negative attitudes toward women, locker room culture creates a no-win situation for the athlete who wishes to be masculine and who wants to have successful, loving, nurturing relationships with women: "real men" are not nurturant. Similarly, locker room talk provides no encouragement for the "real man" who seeks egalitarian relationships.

As Pronger (1990) notes, the myth of masculinity prevalent in the locker room cannot be maintained in the face of equitable relations between men and women or in the acceptance of homosexuality.

Finally, by linking ideas about status attainment with male bonding and masculinity, locker room culture makes it more difficult for young men to realize that women also desire success and status attainment through hard work and self-discipline. In other words, through participating in sport young men are taught that discipline and effort are needed for success and that one's acceptance depends on successful performance. But since these lessons are usually learned in all-male groups, they do not generalize easily to women and may create barriers to men's acceptance of women in the workplace.

References

Adler, P. A., & Adler, P. (1991). *Backboards & blackboards: College athletes and role engulfment.* New York: Columbia University Press.

Beneke, T. (1982). *Men on rape.* New York: St. Martin's Press.

Bryson, L. (1987). Sport and the maintenance of masculine hegemony. *Women's Studies International Forum,* 10, 349–360.

Coakley, J. J. (1990). *Sport in society: Issues and controversies.* St. Louis: Mosby.

Connell, R. W. (1990). An Iron Man: The body and some contradictions of hegemonic masculinity. In M. A. Messner & D. F. Sabo (Eds.), *Sport, men, and the gender order* (pp. 83–95). Champaign, IL: Human Kinetics.

Curry, T. J., & Weiss, O. (1989). Sport identity and motivation for sport participation: A comparison between American college athletes and Austrian student sport club members. *Sociology of Sport Journal,* 6, 257–268.

Dunning, E. (1986). Social bonding and violence in sport. In N. Elias & E. Dunning (Eds.), *Quest for excitement: Sport and leisure in the civilizing process* (pp. 224–244). Oxford: Basil Blackwell.

Farr, K. A. (1988). Dominance bonding through the good old boys sociability group. *Sex Roles,* 18, 259–277.

Fine, G. A. (1987). *With the boys: Little League baseball and preadolescent culture.* Chicago: University of Chicago Press.

Gilligan, C. (1982). *In a different voice: Psychological theory and woman's development.* Cambridge, MA: Harvard University Press.

Herek, G. M. (1987). On heterosexual masculinity: Some physical consequences of the social construction of gender and sexuality. In M. S. Kimmel (Ed.), *Changing men: New directions in research on men and masculinity* (pp. 68–82). Beverly Hills: Sage.

Heymann, P. B. (1990, Nov. 28). Report describes what happened in locker room. *USA Today,* pp. 9A, 7C.

Lyman, P. (1987). The fraternal bond as a joking relationship: A case study of the role of sexist jokes in male group bonding. In M. S. Kimmel (Ed.), *Changing men: New directions in research on men and masculinity* (pp. 148–163). Beverly Hills: Sage.

Messner, M. A. (1987). The meaning of success: The athletic experience and the development of male identity. In H. Brod (Ed.), *The making of masculinities: The new men's studies* (pp. 193–209). Boston: Allen and Unwin.

Messner, M. A. (1989). Gay athletes and the gay games: An interview with Tom Waddell. In M. S. Kimmel and M. A. Messner (Eds.), *Men's lives* (pp. 190–193). New York: Macmillian.

Messner, M. A. (1990). Men studying masculinity: Some epistemological issues in sport sociology. *Sociology of Sport Journal,* 7, 136–153.

Meyer, B. B. (1990). From idealism to actualization: The academic performance of female college athletes. *Sociology of Sport Journal,* 7, 44–57.

Norris, M. (1991, Feb. 2). Mr. nice guy. *T.V. Guide,* pp. 22–29.

Pronger, B. (1990). *The arena of masculinity: Sport, homosexuality, and the meaning of sex.* New York: St. Martin's Press.

Sabo, D. F., & Panepinto, J. (1990). Football ritual and the social reproduction of masculinity. In M. A. Messner & D. F. Sabo (Eds.), *Sport, men, and the gender order* (pp. 115–126). Champaign, IL: Human Kinetics.

Sanday, P. R. (1990). *Fraternity gang rapes: Sex, brotherhood, and privilege on campus.* New York: New York University Press.

Shaw, G. (1972). *Meat on the hoof.* New York: St. Martin's Press.

Sherrod, D. (1987). The bonds of men: Problems and possibilities in close male relationships. In H. Brod (Ed.), *The making of masculinities: The new men's studies* (pp. 213–239). Boston: Allen and Unwin.

Snyder, E. E. (1972). Athletic dressing room slogans as folklore: A means of socialization. *International Review of Sport Sociology, 7,* 89–100.

West, C., & Zimmerman, D. H. (1987). Doing gender. *Gender & Society, 1,* 125–149.

Zurcher, L. A. (1983). Dealing with an unacceptable role: Hashers in a sorority house. In L. A. Zurcher (Ed.), *Social roles: Conformity, conflict, and creativity* (pp. 77–89). Beverly Hills: Sage.

Zurcher, L. A. (1982). The staging of emotion: A dramaturgical analysis. *Symbolic Interaction, 5,* 1–19.

ARTICLE 18

Jason Schultz

The Antirape Rules

"This will probably offend you," she said, looking down for a moment, "but I need to ask you something." She clenched her hands together in a small ball as she leaned back against the headboard of my bed and took a deep breath. "I need to know why it doesn't bother you." Her eyes reopened and looked to me for answers. My lips pursed and separated.

I thought back to other conversations I'd had like this one. Six years back. You'd think that after half a decade of educating, counseling, and supporting survivors that you've heard everything—every story, every question, every nightmare. But this was a new one. "Well," I said, "it doesn't bother me because I didn't do it. And because letting it bother me would make us both victims of his attack. It doesn't mean I don't hate him. It means I know the difference between hating him and hating you because of what he did to you."

She stared back at me. "You probably don't believe that," I continued. "But it's the truth and it's the same answer I'm going to give you every time you ask. It may not help you feel any better, and that's fine because I'm not saying it to make you feel better. You're going to have to figure out how to believe me. It's my job to understand how you feel and yours to believe that I care."

Ever since I became a rape educator in 1990, I've been acutely aware of the impact of violence against women in my life. On an external level, I now worry much more about my female friends and family. I always try to offer them a ride or walk home. I always wait for them to get inside safely before driving away. I give way to women on the street at night. I make sure other men know I'm watching when they make their moves.

On a more personal level, I've felt the pain of being mistrusted for no good reason, the frustration when past hurts affect present attempts at intimacy, the disbelief when cycles of violence repeat themselves. I've felt the emotional impact of rape in my relationships, my friendships, even my family.

The Cascade Effect

The first time is always the worst. That cold, hard realization of the effect of rape. The first woman ever to tell me she was raped was a good friend of mine in college. We were both in our first semester at Duke University, giddy with excitement over the future and full of arrogance about our newfound college independence. "No more curfews!" we would shout, fantasizing about all the rules we would break and trouble we would cause.

Eight weeks into the semester, there was a knock at my door. I opened it and in she collapsed, sobbing. She crawled over to my futon and curled up in a shell. "What's wrong?" I asked. "He raped me tonight" was all she could murmur.

In the following months I learned what rape does to friendship. The anger, the sadness, the hurt—it all came flooding out. I tried every method of support I could think of—the strong shoulder to cry on, the overprotective brother, the

From *Just Sex*, Jodi Gold and Susan Villarti (eds.), pp. 135–142, Lanham, MD: Rowman & Littlefield, 2000. Copyright © 2000 by Rowman & Littlefield. Used with permission.

vindictive vigilante. Nothing changed how she felt. "How can I trust you?" she would blurt out in private. "You could be just like him."

"You could be just like him." Those words echo in my ears every time I talk to men about rape and every time I hear them talk about it. "But I'm not a rapist!" they'll say—all the words that I once said myself. They're right, of course. They're always right. But that's the horror of rape. It doesn't change anything. It doesn't make a difference to a survivor that you're not a rapist. They simply don't care.

I joined the Duke Acquaintance Rape Education Program. I felt stronger, more in control. I learned what caused rape: patriarchy, socialization, cycles of violence. I also felt in control of my own emotions. I knew that when survivors talked to me that it wasn't my fault—I hadn't caused their pain. I was helping them. I was part of the solution, not part of the problem.

But they just kept on coming. A friend . . . a classmate . . . a fellow editor at the student newspaper. Someone I met at a party. Someone I hooked up with after a basketball game. My senior-year girlfriend. Her roommate. The numbers started to build and so did the horrors. Child sexual abuse, STDs, gang rape. I started to keep count. The Number kept growing. All the time I kept thinking and saying to myself, "It's okay. You're helping them. You're making a difference."

And I was. I received countless thank-yous from people I helped and from others as well—faculty in the women's studies department, campus administrators who had their hands tied by the legal department. But no matter how hard I tried to help, no matter how much I listened, The Number kept growing. Sisters, old friends from high school, the cab driver on my way home for Thanksgiving. How? I would wonder. How can we live in a world where every woman I meet has been tortured in this way?

In some ways it was a perverse high. I was the savior. I was the good guy. I heard their stories and believed them. If only more men could be like me, I would think to myself, there wouldn't be all this hurt and madness.

December of my senior year, I lost it. I called up a close friend of mine—someone with whom I had shared much of my adolescent and adult life, someone with whom I could break the rules. "I need to ask you a question," I prefaced. "It's going to sound weird and might possibly embarrass you, but I need to know if you've ever been raped." I went on for a minute explaining what was happening to me, how all the violence in the lives of the people around me was overwhelming my sense of hope.

"Jason," she interrupted. "I have *never* been raped. By anyone. Anytime in my life." My stomach relaxed and the air slowly left my chest in relief. "Thank you," I said. "Thank you so much."

I have no idea how one learns to live with being raped. I can't even imagine what it means to carry that around with you. But I know what it means to live with and care for people who have been raped. I know the frantic phone calls, the frustration of starting over, the joy of witnessing recovery. I know that it's hard to be a man and care for women who've been raped. I know how not to blame myself and not to blame them.

As part of the national antirape movement, I've spent the last eight years talking about sexual violence, mostly on college campuses and mostly to men. Looking back on that now, I realize that we don't need to simply educate men on how not to rape. The reality is that most of us don't rape women. But we do need to educate all men on how to live with, love, care for, and communicate with survivors. We need to share the rules we've learned.

The Antirape Rules

When I first heard of *The Rules*, I laughed. *The Rules: Time-Tested Secrets for Capturing the Heart of Mr. Right* was a surprising best-seller self-help book that gave women traditional and prefeminist guidelines for snagging men. Encouraging mind games, *The Rules* include such tidbits as "Let him take the lead," and "Don't call him." What a ridiculous idea, I thought. How could anyone imagine finding the key to a successful relationship in this semblance of pop-cult grocery-store-line pocket trash? I figured the hype about the book was simply the logical outcome of media conspiracy, lack of education, and yet another market built on women's insecurities. Yet as many of us do, I forced myself to read *The Rules,* just to be sure.

I pretty much found what I suspected. Manipulative psychobabble and social conditioning. There were, of course, a few feminist intonations about the "modern girl" and the need to be independent in one's life. But these were couched in the frantic language of the man-crazy woman and the "horror" of being unmarried.

So why was this book selling? I wandered about, asking various female friends. They gave me three reasons: (1) Despite all our good wishes about bicycles and fish, many women *are* frustrated with their attempts to find the right guy; (2) despite the stereotypes, every woman I talked to knew at least one man whom they thought would respond to *The Rules;* and (3) even if you completely disagree with *The Rules,* you still want to read it as a gut check—just to make sure you're still not doing anything wrong.

So while the content of *The Rules* disturbed me, the brilliance of the approach to writing it intrigued me. Then it clicked. Rules . . . that's what men need—not on how to find the right woman (well, maybe, but that's more like a book instead of an essay), but for handling the issue of rape—a topic that makes men about as neurotic as women are made about marriage.

Where to Start

That being said, starting to learn about rape is almost always weird for men. There are so many subtle moments and brief insights that we all need to learn. But every journey starts with a single step, or four in this case. Below are several experiences and "rules" that have helped me support survivors of sexual assault in my own life. I offer them up in the hope that we all will start to think about what "rules" truly help us care for, and about, each other.

Rule #1: Believe the Hype

As much of a cliché as it sounds, you probably know someone who has been raped. They may have told you by now or not, but sooner or later they will. When they do, they will most likely disclose information to you in doses. Maybe just the fact that it happened. Maybe the story leading up to it. They may even disguise it as bad sex or a drunken blur. Whatever they do when they tell you, there's one rule to follow: Don't reject them.

Rape centers on control. After someone is assaulted, it often takes great effort to regain control of her or his life. One of the quickest ways to do this is to control who knows about the rape and what they know about it. That is why it is often difficult to get survivors to talk to the police or a doctor or even answer their phone. There are many other reasons why survivors don't tell anyone, such as fear of retaliation, desire to put it behind them and move on, and so on. But the need to control who knows about the rape is often a primary concern. (Hence the need for rape crisis centers to maintain confidentiality.)

When a survivor tells you about her rape, she is beginning to trust again. She is reaching out to you with one of the few parts of her life that she does feel control over. When she does this, she generally wants two things: (1) to have you believe her, and (2) to have you accept her. Often a survivor's worst fear is that telling someone about the rape will trigger another attack or betrayal, this time a verbal or emotional one.

Marilyn Van Derbur Atler, an incest survivor and former Miss America, once talked at Duke about disclosing her survivor status on an airplane. She was sitting next to a businessman, reading a magazine, when he struck up a conversation with her. At one point in the conversation, he mentioned his occupation. He then proceeded to ask her what she did. "I talk about how I survived child sexual abuse," she replied. As you can imagine, the man was struck silent by her comment.

After taking a moment to compose himself, though, he asked a question I suspect most men think about when a survivor discloses to them: "How should one respond to that?" he asked her.

Ms. Van Derbur Atler calmly looked back at him and said, "You say 'I'm very sorry that happened to you.' And you mean it."

Rule #2: Don't Expect Her to Change, or Try to Change Her

The knock on the door had to be Catherine. I opened it and it was. "Surprise!" she yelled, and marched into the room with not one man in tow, but two—one on each arm. "This is Kevin; and this is Dave! Aren't they cute?" she breathed into my face, fresh and full of keg beer. My heart sank.

"Yeah, I suppose they are. Don't you think you're . . . um . . . a little out of it to be hooking up with two guys?" I asked, regretting each word as I spoke.

"Fuck you," she retorted. "I'm a big girl. I'm in control. I'll do whatever I want." She turned around, pushed the two men out the door, and slammed it behind her.

The next afternoon she came to apologize. We both knew she was having a tough time dating again after the rape, especially on campus. She admitted that last night she had been scared of being alone with her dates and said that she came by my room with the hope that I would intervene. I told her that I can't intervene—that part of being supportive is following her lead and letting her run her own life again, not simply transferring control to me.

I asked her why she chose Kevin and Dave. "They don't particularly seem your type," I said, still trying to tread cautiously. Catherine had always gone for more introverted guys as long as I had known her. She started to list a number of excuses: She was turning over a new leaf. They liked her, so why not? She didn't care who she hooked up with anymore.

Finally, she told the truth. "I knew what they wanted," she said. "I knew they wanted sex, so I knew there wouldn't be any surprises. No rape. No force. No betrayal. I knew that if I took the initiative with them that I would be in control and never out of it. I wouldn't have to be afraid that it would happen again." She leaned against the wall, picking off pieces of paint with her fingernails. "I just can't take that risk anymore."

I sat at my desk. I had no idea what to say. "You'll figure it out," I responded.

Watching survivors make dumb decisions and take horrible risks is probably the most frustrating part of being there for them. When Catherine left with the two men, it took every ounce of self-control not to run after her and make sure she wasn't going to be attacked again. But the number-one rule with survivors is to let them forge their own recovery. Catherine also later admitted that she had been testing me in some ways by bringing the men home—to see if I would trust her. I've learned time and time again to be honest with survivors about how I feel—to express disappointment, concern, anger, fear—but ultimately to leave the decisions up to them. Right or wrong, they will need you as a friend the next day more than a savior the night before.

Rule #3: Ask for It

"I've been thinking about kissing you all night," I said.

"Really?" she asked whimsically, testing the waters a bit more.

"And then touching you. All over."

The wind whistled past our ears as we headed back to the hotel. A sudden silence arose between us. "I hope that's okay," I added.

"Sure," she said. "I just . . . well—no one's ever said that to me so far in advance before." She blushed a little. "Usually we're already drunk and naked and at least somewhere near the bed."

I laughed. "Well, I figured it'd be better to make my intentions clear before we got in the elevator. That way you could decide what floor to get off on . . . so to speak." We laughed again, and I felt the tension ease a bit. I opened the outside door for her and we scurried into the lobby.

"So it's really my choice?"

"Yeah," I replied.

She reached out with one hand for the elevator button, then reached with the other for my arm. She smiled as we waited for the doors to open.

Much has been said about supposed politically correct sex: that asking for consent is unsexy, that talking ruins the mood. And for the most part, I agree—if that's all you do. In the midst of confronting violence, it's easy to forget about the fact that being sexy is important to both men and women, to survivors and nonsurvivors alike. Being too clinical, too cautious, or even too earnest often clashes with our fantasies about what turns us on. And no matter how many rape awareness workshops we attend or late-night dorm conversations we have, antiseptic sexual conversations will rarely hit the right spot.

Being sexy means knowing what you really want. If you truly know what you want with the other person, you'll know how to tell them you want it. And you'll also know when they want it too. Spend some time thinking about it. Fantasize about what you think will make you both happy, then take a deep breath and tell her. Style, nuance, attitude, and mystery are all still important elements of seduction. Don't lose them. Just use them in the way they were meant to be used: to elicit true desire and temptation.

Rule #4: Sometimes the Tough Thing Is the Right Thing

I stayed up very late last night, trying to clean the kitchen. It's something I do when I'm nervous—cleaning. It had been a pretty rough day, with the trip to the hospital and all. I wondered what Laura was doing right now. I thought about the hug she had given me right before they took her to her room. "Don't disappear on me," she said, as if I were the one leaving the rest of the world behind. "Remember, I know where you live," she added as the duty nurse searched her suitcase. I nodded, turned, and walked down the hallway, hands in my pockets, eyes on the red carpet beneath my feet.

The counter was a mess. I emptied the wine bottle from the night before and dumped the ashtray. We'd decided that they probably wouldn't allow her to drink or smoke once she was inside, so we took advantage of her last night to binge a little. At one point I caught her staring at me from her seat near the windowsill, bright blue eyes flickering as she exhaled away form my face. "It really means a lot to me," she said softly, turning back toward the light. "I really don't know who else I can trust."

That was exactly twenty-four hours ago. Now she was tucked away inside the psych ward on the other side of town and I was home, loading dishes into the dishwasher. I felt a tremendous sense of relief, mixed with sadness from the separation. I thought about calling the hallway phone number she had left me. I let the thought pass. I took her last cigarette from off the counter and grabbed a match.

Helping survivors recover can hurt. Many of the men I've talked to over the years have told me about "secondary syndrome"—a condition whereby people who are close to a victim of violence begin to experience similar symptoms of post-traumatic stress disorder—almost like emotional osmosis. Lack of sleep, difficulty concentrating, and depression are a few of the common experiences.

But beyond secondary syndrome is an even greater issue for men who support survivors—our own general health and happiness. No matter how giving you are, no matter how gentle you want to be, there are limits to what any one person can offer to another. Anger, depression, and burnout can creep up on us, and before we know it, we're of little use to them or to ourselves.

The bottom line is always to know your limits and make sure you have support for yourself. Find friends to talk to about the situation. Call a help line whenever you feel like it. Take time away from the crisis. Checking Laura into the psychiatric hospital was a difficult decision for both her and me, but we agreed that she needed more help than I could ever give her. Recognizing that limit not only saved her life, but saved our friendship as well. In the end, we realized we wanted both to survive.

PART FOUR

Men and Work

In what ways is work tied to male identity? Do men gain a sense of fulfillment from their work, or do they view it as necessary drudgery? How might the organization of workplaces play on, reinforce, or sometimes threaten the types of masculinity that males have already learned as youngsters? How does the experience of work (or of not having work) differ for men of different social classes, ethnicities, and sexual preference groups? And how do recent structural changes in society impact upon the masculinity–work relationship? The articles in this section address these issues and more.

The rise of urban industrial capitalism saw the creation of separate "public" and "domestic" spheres of social life. As women were increasingly relegated to working in the home, men were increasingly absent from the home, and the male "breadwinner role" was born. The sexual division of labor, this gendered split between home and workplace, has led to a variety of problems and conflicts for women and for men. Women's continued movement into the paid labor force, higher levels of unemployment, and the rise of a more service-oriented economy have led to dramatic shifts in the quality and the quantity of men's experiences in their work.

Articles by Jennifer Pierce and Marianne Cooper explore how men "do" gender in the workplace; those by Christine Williams, Kevin Henson, and Jackie Krasas Rogers explore how men who do women's work also "do" gender by ensuring that their masculinity is validated. Timothy Nonn explores the gendered meanings of work at the other side of the economic pyramid, among the homeless.

The work world has also become an arena of the battle between the sexes, as the continuing debates over sexual harassment make clear. The article by Beth Quinn examines sexual harassment in that most commonplace behavior—girl watching.

Music, 1985, oil on canvas, 70 × 60. Copyright © 1985 by Greg Drasler.

ARTICLE 19

Christine L. Williams

The Glass Escalator: Hidden Advantages for Men in the "Female" Professions

The sex segregation of the U.S. labor force is one of the most perplexing and tenacious problems in our society. Even though the proportion of men and women in the labor force is approaching parity (particularly for younger cohorts of workers) (U.S. Department of Labor 1991:18), men and women are still generally confined to predominantly single-sex occupations. Forty percent of men or women would have to change major occupational categories to achieve equal representation of men and women in all jobs (Reskin and Roos 1990:6), but even this figure underestimates the true degree of sex segregation. It is extremely rare to find specific jobs where equal numbers of men and women are engaged in the same activities in the same industries (Bielby and Baron 1984).

Most studies of sex segregation in the work force have focused on women's experiences in male-dominated occupations. Both researchers and advocates for social change have focused on the barriers faced by women who try to integrate predominantly male fields. Few have looked at the "flip-side" of occupational sex segregation: the exclusion of men from predominantly female occupations (exceptions include Schreiber 1979;

Author's Note: This research was funded in part by a faculty grant from the University of Texas at Austin. I also acknowledge the support of the sociology departments of the University of California, Berkeley; Harvard University; and Arizona State University. I would like to thank Judy Auerbach, Martin Button, Robert Nye, Teresa Sullivan, Debra Umberson, Mary Waters, and the reviewers at *Social Problems* for their comments on earlier versions of this paper.

From *Social Problems* 39(3): 253–267. Copyright © 1992 by the Society for the Study of Social Problems. Reprinted by permission.

Zimmer 1988; Williams 1989). But the fact is that men are less likely to enter female sex-typed occupations than women are to enter male-dominated jobs (Jacobs 1989). Reskin and Roos, for example, were able to identify 33 occupations in which female representation increased by more than nine percentage points between 1970 and 1980, but only three occupations in which the proportion of men increased as radically (1990:20–21).

In this paper, I examine men's under-representation in four predominantly female occupations—nursing, librarianship, elementary school teaching, and social work. Throughout the twentieth century, these occupations have been identified with "women's work"—even though prior to the Civil War, men were more likely to be employed in these areas. These four occupations, often called the female "semi-professions" (Hodson and Sullivan 1990), today range from 5.5 percent male (in nursing) to 32 percent male (in social work). (See Table 19.1.) These percentages have not changed substantially in decades. In fact, as Table 19.1 indicates, two of these professions—librarianship and social work—have experienced declines in the proportions of men since 1975. Nursing is the only one of the four experiencing noticeable changes in sex composition, with the proportion of men increasing 80 percent between 1975 and 1990. Even so, men continue to be a tiny minority of all nurses.

Although there are many possible reasons for the continuing preponderance of women in these fields, the focus of this paper is discrimination. Researchers examining the integration of women into "male fields" have identified discrimination as a major barrier to women (Reskin and

TABLE 19.1
Percent Male in Selected Occupations, Selected Years

Profession	1990	1980	1975
Nurses	5.5	3.5	3.0
Elementary teachers	14.8	16.3	14.6
Librarians	16.7	14.8	18.9
Social workers	31.8	35.0	39.2

Source: U.S. Department of Labor. Bureau of Labor Statistics. *Employment and Earnings* 38:1 (January 1991), Table 22 (Employed civilians by detailed occupation), 185; 28:1 (January 1981), Table 23 (Employed persons by detailed occupation), 180; 22:7 (January 1976), Table 2 (Employed persons by detailed occupation), 11.

Hartmann 1986; Reskin 1988; Jacobs 1989). This discrimination has taken the form of laws or institutionalized rules prohibiting the hiring or promotion of women into certain job specialties. Discrimination can also be "informal," as when women encounter sexual harassment, sabotage, or other forms of hostility from their male co-workers resulting in a poisoned work environment (Reskin and Hartmann 1986). Women in nontraditional occupations also report feeling stigmatized by clients when their work puts them in contact with the public. In particular, women in engineering and blue-collar occupations encounter gender-based stereotypes about their competence which undermine their work performance (Martin 1980; Epstein 1988). Each of these forms of discrimination—legal, informal, and cultural—contributes to women's underrepresentation in predominantly male occupations.

The assumption in much of this literature is that any member of a token group in a work setting will probably experience similar discriminatory treatment. Kanter (1977), who is best known for articulating this perspective in her theory of tokenism, argues that when any group represents less than 15 percent of an organization, its members will be subject to predictable forms of discrimination. Likewise, Jacobs argues that "in some ways, men in female-dominated occupations experience the same difficulties that women in male-dominated occupations face" (1989:167), and Reskin contends that any dominant group in an occupation will use their power to maintain a privileged position (1988:62).

However, the few studies that have considered men's experience in gender-atypical occupations suggest that men may not face discrimination or prejudice when they integrate predominantly female occupations. Zimmer (1988) and Martin (1988) both contend that the effects of sexism can outweigh the effects of tokenism when men enter nontraditional occupations. This study is the first to systematically explore this question using data from four occupations. I examine the barriers to men's entry into these professions; the support men receive from their supervisors, colleagues, and clients; and the reactions they encounter from the public (those outside their professions).

Methods

I conducted in-depth interviews with 76 men and 23 women in four occupations from 1985–1991. Interviews were conducted in four metropolitan areas: San Francisco/Oakland, California; Austin, Texas; Boston, Massachusetts; and Phoenix, Arizona. These four areas were selected because they show considerable variation in the proportions of men in the four professions. For example, Austin has one of the highest percentages of men in nursing (7.7 percent), whereas Phoenix's percentage is one of the lowest (2.7 percent) (U.S. Bureau of the Census 1980). The sample was generated using "snowballing" techniques. Women were included in the sample to gauge their feelings and responses to men who enter "their" professions.

Like the people employed in these professions generally, those in my sample were predominantly white (90 percent).[1] Their ages ranged from 20 to 66 and the average age was 38. The interview questionnaire consisted of several open-ended questions on four broad topics: motivation to enter the profession; experiences in training;

career progression; and general views about men's status and prospects within these occupations. I conducted all the interviews, which generally lasted between one and two hours. Interviews took place in restaurants, my home or office, or the respondent's home or office. Interviews were tape-recorded and transcribed for the analysis.

Data analysis followed the coding techniques described by Strauss (1987). Each transcript was read several times and analyzed into emergent conceptual categories. Likewise, Strauss's principle of theoretical sampling was used. Individual respondents were purposively selected to capture the array of men's experiences in these occupations. Thus, I interviewed practitioners in every specialty, oversampling those employed in the *most* gender atypical areas (e.g., male kindergarten teachers). I also selected respondents from throughout their occupational hierarchies—from students to administrators to retirees. Although the data do not permit within-group comparisons, I am reasonably certain that the sample does capture a wide range of experiences common to men in these female-dominated professions. However, like all findings based on qualitative data, it is uncertain whether the findings generalize to the larger population of men in nontraditional occupations.

In this paper, I review individuals' responses to questions about discrimination in hiring practices, on-the-job rapport with supervisors and coworkers, and prejudice from clients and others outside their profession.

Discrimination in Hiring

Contrary to the experience of many women in the male-dominated professions, many of the men and women I spoke to indicated that there is a *preference* for hiring men in these four occupations. A Texas librarian at a junior high school said that his school district "would hire a male over a female."

I: Why do you think that is?

R: Because there are so few, and the . . . ones that they do have, the library directors seem to really . . . think they're doing great jobs. I don't know, maybe they just feel they're being progressive or something, [but] I have had a real sense that they really appreciate having a male, particularly at the junior high. . . . As I said, when seven of us lost our jobs from the high schools and were redistributed, there were only four positions at the junior high, and I got one of them. Three of the librarians, some who had been here longer than I had with the school district, were put down in elementary school as librarians. And I definitely think that being male made a difference in my being moved to the junior high rather than an elementary school.

Many of the men perceived their token status as males in predominantly female occupations as an *advantage* in hiring and promotions. I asked an Arizona teacher whether his specialty (elementary special education) was an unusual area for men compared to other areas within education. He said,

> Much more so. I am extremely marketable in special education. That's not why I got into the field. But I am extremely marketable because I am a man.

In several cases, the more female-dominated the specialty, the greater the apparent preference for men. For example, when asked if he encountered any problem getting a job in pediatrics, a Massachusetts nurse said,

> No, no, none. . . . I've heard this from managers and supervisory-type people with men in pediatrics: "It's nice to have a man because it's such a female-dominated profession."

However, there were some exceptions to this preference for men in the most female-dominated specialties. In some cases, formal policies actually barred men from certain jobs. This was the case in some rural Texas school districts, which refused to hire men in the youngest grades (K–3). Some nurses also reported being excluded from positions in obstetrics and gynecology wards, a policy encountered more frequently in private Catholic hospitals.

But often the pressures keeping men out of certain specialties were more subtle than this. Some men described being "tracked" into practice areas within their professions which were considered more legitimate for men. For example, one Texas man described how he was pushed into administration and planning in social work, even though "I'm not interested in writing policy; I'm much more interested in research and clinical stuff." A nurse who is interested in pursuing graduate study in family and child health in Boston said he was dissuaded from entering the program specialty in favor of a concentration in "adult nursing." A kindergarten teacher described the difficulty of finding a job in his specialty after graduation: "I was recruited immediately to start getting into a track to become an administrator. And it was men who recruited me. It was men that ran the system at that time, especially in Los Angeles."

This tracking may bar men from the most female-identified specialties within these professions. But men are effectively being "kicked upstairs" in the process. Those specialties considered more legitimate practice areas for men also tend to be the most prestigious, better paying ones. A distinguished kindergarten teacher, who had been voted city-wide "Teacher of the Year," told me that even though people were pleased to see him in the classroom, "there's been some encouragement to think about administration, and there's been some encouragement to think about teaching at the university level or something like that, or supervisory-type position." That is, despite his aptitude and interest in staying in the classroom, he felt pushed in the direction of administration.

The effect of this "tracking" is the opposite of that experienced by women in male-dominated occupations. Researchers have reported that many women encounter a "glass ceiling" in their efforts to scale organizational and professional hierarchies. That is, they are constrained by invisible barriers to promotion in their careers, caused mainly by sexist attitudes of men in the highest positions (Freeman 1990).[2] In contrast to the "glass ceiling," many of the men I interviewed seem to encounter a "glass escalator." Often, despite their intentions, they face invisible pressures to move up in their professions. As if on a moving escalator, they must work to stay in place.

A public librarian specializing in children's collections (a heavily female-dominated concentration) described an encounter with this "escalator" in his very first job out of library school. In his first six-months' evaluation, his supervisors commended him for his good work in storytelling and related activities, but they criticized him for "not shooting high enough."

Seriously. That's literally what they were telling me. They assumed that because I was a male—and they told me this—and that I was being hired right out of graduate school, that somehow I wasn't doing the kind of management-oriented work that they thought I should be doing. And as a result, really they had a lot of bad marks, as it were, against me on my evaluation. And I said I couldn't believe this!

Throughout his ten-year career, he has had to struggle to remain in children's collections.

The glass escalator does not operate at all levels. In particular, men in academia reported some gender-based discrimination in the highest positions due to their universities' commitment to affirmative action. Two nursing professors reported that they felt their own chances of promotion to deanships were nil because their universities viewed the position of nursing dean as a guaranteed female appointment in an otherwise heavily male-dominated administration. One California social work professor reported his university canceled its search for a dean because no minority male or female candidates had been placed on their short list. It was rumored that other schools on campus were permitted to go forward with their searches—even though they also failed to put forward names of minority candidates—because the higher administration perceived it to be "easier" to fulfill affirmative action goals in the social work school. The interviews provide greater evidence of the "glass escalator" at work in the lower levels of these professions.

Of course, men's motivations also play a role in their advancement to higher professional positions. I do not mean to suggest that the men I talked to all resented the informal tracking they experienced. For many men, leaving the most female-identified areas of their professions helped them resolve internal conflicts involving their masculinity. One man left his job as a school social worker to work in a methadone drug treatment program not because he was encouraged to leave by his colleagues, but because "I think there was some macho shit there, to tell you the truth, because I remember feeling a little uncomfortable there . . . ; it didn't feel right to me." Another social worker, employed in the mental health services department of a large urban area in California, reflected on his move into administration:

> The more I think about it, through our discussion, I'm sure that's a large part of why I wound up in administration. It's okay for a man to do the administration. In fact, I don't know if I fully answered a question that you asked a little while ago about how did being male contribute to my advancing in the field. I was saying it wasn't because I got any special favoritism as a man, but . . . I think . . . because I'm a man, I felt a need to get into this kind of position. I may have worked harder toward it, may have competed harder for it, than most women would do, even women who think about doing administrative work.

Elsewhere I have speculated on the origins of men's tendency to define masculinity through single-sex work environments (Williams 1989). Clearly, personal ambition does play a role in accounting for men's movement into more "male-defined" arenas within these professions. But these occupations also structure opportunities for males independent of their individual desires or motives.

The interviews suggest that men's underrepresentation in these professions cannot be attributed to discrimination in hiring or promotions. Many of the men indicated that they received preferential treatment because they were men. Although men mentioned gender discrimination in the hiring process, for the most part they were channelled into the more "masculine" specialties within these professions, which ironically meant being "tracked" into better paying and more prestigious specialties.

Supervisors and Colleagues: The Working Environment

Researchers claim that subtle forms of workplace discrimination push women out of male-dominated occupations (Reskin and Hartmann 1986; Jacobs 1989). In particular, women report feeling excluded from informal leadership and decision-making networks, and they sense hostility from their male co-workers, which makes them feel uncomfortable and unwanted (Carothers and Crull 1984). Respondents in this study were asked about their relationships with supervisors and female colleagues to ascertain whether men also experienced "poisoned" work environments when entering gender atypical occupations.

A major difference in the experience of men and women in nontraditional occupations is that men in these situations are far more likely to be supervised by a member of their own sex. In each of the four professions I studied, men are overrepresented in administrative and managerial capacities, or, as in the case of nursing, their positions in the organizational hierarchy are governed by men (Grimm and Sterm 1974; Phenix 1987; Schmuck 1987; York, Henley, and Gamble 1987; Williams 1989). Thus, unlike women who enter "male fields," the men in these professions often work under the direct supervision of other men.

Many of the men interviewed reported that they had good rapport with their male supervisors. Even in professional school, some men reported extremely close relationships with their male professors. For example, a Texas librarian described an unusually intimate association with two male professors in graduate school:

I can remember a lot of times in the classroom there would be discussions about a particular topic or issue, and the conversation would spill over into their office hours, after the class was over. And even though there were . . . a couple of the other women that had been in on the discussion, they weren't there. And I don't know if that was preferential or not . . . it certainly carried over into personal life as well. Not just at the school and that sort of thing. I mean, we would get together for dinner . . .

These professors explicitly encouraged him because he was male:

I: Did they ever offer you explicit words of encouragement about being in the profession by virtue of the fact that you were male? . . .

R: Definitely. On several occasions. Yeah. Both of these guys, for sure, including the Dean who was male also. And it's an interesting point that you bring up because it was, oftentimes, kind of in a sign, you know. It wasn't in the classroom, and it wasn't in front of the group, or if we were in the student lounge or something like that. It was . . . if it was just myself or maybe another one of the guys, you know, and just talking in the office. It's like . . . you know, kind of an opening-up and saying, "You know, you are really lucky that you're in the profession because you'll really go to the top real quick, and you'll be able to make real definite improvements and changes. And you'll have a real influence," and all this sort of thing. I mean, really, I can remember several times.

Other men reported similar closeness with their professors. A Texas psychotherapist recalled his relationships with his male professors in social work school:

I made it a point to make a golfing buddy with one of the guys that was in administration. He and I played golf a lot. He was the guy who kind of ran the research training, the research part of the master's program. Then there was a sociologist who ran the other part of the research program. He and I developed a good friendship.

This close mentoring by male professors contrasts with the reported experience of women in nontraditional occupations. Others have noted a lack of solidarity among women in nontraditional occupations. Writing about military academies, for example, Yoder describes the failure of token women to mentor succeeding generations of female cadets. She argues that women attempt to play down their gender difference from men because it is the source of scorn and derision.

Because women felt unaccepted by their male colleagues, one of the last things they wanted to do was to emphasize their gender. Some women thought that, if they kept company with other women, this would highlight their gender and would further isolate them from male cadets. These women desperately wanted to be accepted as cadets, not as *women* cadets. Therefore, they did everything from not wearing skirts as an option with their uniforms to avoiding being a part of a group of women. (Yoder 1989:532)

Men in nontraditional occupations face a different scenario—their gender is construed as a *positive* difference. Therefore, they have an incentive to bond together and emphasize their distinctiveness from the female majority.

Close, personal ties with male supervisors were also described by men once they were established in their professional careers. It was not uncommon in education, for example, for the male principal to informally socialize with the male staff, as a Texas special education teacher describes:

Occasionally I've had a principal who would regard me as "the other man on the campus" and "it's us against them," you know? I mean, nothing really that extreme, except that some male principals feel like there's nobody there to talk to except the other man. So I've been in that position.

These personal ties can have important consequences for men's careers. For example, one California nurse, whose performance was judged marginal by his nursing supervisors, was transferred to the emergency room staff (a prestigious promotion) due to his personal friendship with the physician in charge. A Massachusetts teacher acknowledged that his principal's personal interest in him landed him his current job.

> I: You had mentioned that your principal had sort of spotted you at your previous job and had wanted to bring you here [to this school]. Do you think that has anything to do with the fact that you're a man, aside from your skills as a teacher?
>
> R: Yes, I would say in that particular case, that was part of it. . . . We have certain things in common, certain interests that really lined up.
>
> I: Vis-à-vis teaching?
>
> R: Well, more extraneous things—running specifically, and music. And we just seemed to get along real well right off the bat. It is just kind of a guy thing; we just liked each other . . .

Interviewees did not report many instances of male supervisors discriminating against them, or refusing to accept them because they were male. Indeed, these men were much more likely to report that their male bosses discriminated against the *females* in their professions. When asked if he thought physicians treated male and female nurses differently, a Texas nurse said:

> I think yeah, some of them do. I think the women seem like they have a lot more trouble with the physicians treating them in a derogatory manner. Or, if not derogatory, then in a very paternalistic way than the men [are treated]. Usually if a physician is mad at a male nurse, he just kind of yells at him. Kind of like an employee. And if they're mad at a female nurse, rather than treat them on an equal basis, in terms of just letting their anger out at them as an employee, they're more paternalistic or there's some sexual harassment component to it.

A Texas teacher perceived a similar situation where he worked:

> I've never felt unjustly treated by a principal because I'm a male. The principals that I've seen that I felt are doing things that are kind of arbitrary or not well thought out are doing it to everybody. In fact, they're probably doing it to the females worse than they are to me.

Openly gay men may encounter less favorable treatment at the hands of their supervisors. For example, a nurse in Texas stated that one of the physicians he worked with preferred to staff the operating room with male nurses exclusively—as long as they weren't gay. Stigma associated with homosexuality leads some men to enhance, or even exaggerate their "masculine" qualities, and may be another factor pushing men into more "acceptable" specialties for men.

Not all men who work in these occupations are supervised by men. Many of the men interviewed who had female bosses also reported high levels of acceptance—although levels of intimacy with women seemed lower than with other men. In some cases, however, men reported feeling shut-out from decision making when the higher administration was constituted entirely by women. I asked an Arizona librarian whether men in the library profession were discriminated against in hiring because of their sex:

> Professionally speaking, people go to considerable lengths to keep that kind of thing out of their [hiring] deliberations. Personally, is another matter. It's pretty common around here to talk about the "old girl network." This is one of the few libraries that I've had any intimate knowledge of which is actually controlled by women. . . . Most of the department heads and upper level administrators are women. And there's an "old girl network" that works just like the "old boy network," except that the important conferences take place in the women's room rather than on the golf course. But the political mechanism is the same, the exclusion of the other sex from decision making is the same. The reasons are the same. It's somewhat discouraging . . .

Although I did not interview many supervisors, I did include 23 women in my sample to ascertain their perspectives about the presence of men in their professions. All of the women I interviewed claimed to be supportive of their male colleagues, but some conveyed ambivalence. For example, a social work professor said she would like to see more men enter the social work profession, particularly in the clinical specialty (where they are underrepresented). Indeed, she favored affirmative action hiring guidelines for men in the profession. Yet, she resented the fact that her department hired "another white male" during a recent search. I questioned her about this ambivalence:

I: I find it very interesting that, on the one hand, you sort of perceive this preference and perhaps even sexism with regard to how men are evaluated and how they achieve higher positions within the profession, yet, on the other hand, you would be encouraging of more men to enter the field. Is that contradictory to you, or . . . ?

R: Yeah, it's contradictory.

It appears that women are generally eager to see men enter "their" occupations. Indeed, several men noted that their female colleagues had facilitated their careers in various ways (including mentorship in college). However, at the same time, women often resent the apparent ease with which men advance within these professions, sensing that men at the higher levels receive preferential treatment which closes off advancement opportunities for women.

But this ambivalence does not seem to translate into the "poisoned" work environment described by many women who work in male-dominated occupations. Among the male interviewees, there were no accounts of sexual harassment. However, women do treat their male colleagues differently on occasion. It is not uncommon in nursing, for example, for men to be called upon to help catheterize male patients, or to lift especially heavy patients. Some librarians also said that women asked them to lift and move heavy boxes of books because they were men. Teachers sometimes confront differential treatment as well, as described by this Texas teacher:

As a man, you're teaching with all women, and that can be hard sometimes. Just because of the stereotypes, you know. I'm real into computers . . . and all the time people are calling me to fix their computer. Or if somebody gets a flat tire, they come and get me. I mean, there are just a lot of stereotypes. Not that I mind doing any of those things, but it's . . . you know, it just kind of bugs me that it is a stereotype, "A man should do that." Or if their kids have a lot of discipline problems, that kiddo's in your room. Or if there are kids that don't have a father in their home, that kid's in your room. Hell, nowadays that'd be half the school in my room (laughs). But you know, all the time I hear from the principal or from other teachers, "Well, this child really needs a man . . . a male role model" (laughs). So there are a lot of stereotypes that . . . men kind of get stuck with.

This special treatment bothered some respondents. Getting assigned all the "discipline problems" can make for difficult working conditions, for example. But many men claimed this differential treatment did not cause distress. In fact, several said they liked being appreciated for the special traits and abilities (such as strength) they could contribute to their professions.

Furthermore, women's special treatment sometimes enhanced—rather than poisoned—the men's work environments. One Texas librarian said he felt "more comfortable working with women than men" because "I think it has something to do with control. Maybe it's that women will let me take control more than men will." Several men reported that their female colleagues often cast them into leadership roles. Although not all savored this distinction, it did enhance their authority and control in the workplace. In subtle (and not-too-subtle) ways, then, differential treatment contributes to the "glass escalator" men experience in nontraditional professions.

Even outside work, most of the men interviewed said they felt fully accepted by their female colleagues. They were usually included in informal socializing occasions with the women—even though this frequently meant attending baby showers or Tupperware parties. Many said that they declined offers to attend these events because they were not interested in "women's things," although several others claimed to attend everything: The minority men I interviewed seemed to feel the least comfortable in these informal contexts. One social worker in Arizona was asked about socializing with his female colleagues:

> I: So in general, for example, if all the employees were going to get together to have a party, or celebrate a bridal shower or whatever, would you be invited along with the rest of the group?
>
> R: They would invite me, I would say, somewhat reluctantly. Being a black male, working with all white females, it did cause some outside problems. So I didn't go to a lot of functions with them . . .
>
> I: You felt that there was some tension there on the level of your acceptance . . . ?
>
> R: Yeah. It was OK working, but on the outside, personally, there was some tension there. It never came out, that they said, "Because of who you are we can't invite you" (laughs), and I wouldn't have done anything anyway. I would have probably respected them more for saying what was on their minds. But I never felt completely in with the group.

Some single men also said they felt uncomfortable socializing with married female colleagues because it gave the "wrong impression." But in general, the men said that they felt very comfortable around their colleagues and described their workplaces as very congenial for men. It appears unlikely, therefore, that men's underrepresentation in these professions is due to hostility towards men on the part of supervisors or women workers.

Discrimination from "Outsiders"

The most compelling evidence of discrimination against men in these professions is related to their dealings with the public. Men often encounter negative stereotypes when they come into contact with clients or "outsiders"—people they meet outside of work. For instance, it is popularly assumed that male nurses are gay. Librarians encounter images of themselves as "wimpy" and asexual. Male social workers describe being type-cast as "feminine" and "passive." Elementary school teachers are often confronted by suspicions that they are pedophiles. One kindergarten teacher described an experience that occurred early in his career which was related to him years afterwards by his principal:

> He indicated to me that parents had come to him and indicated to him that they had a problem with the fact that I was a male. . . . I recall almost exactly what he said. There were three specific concerns that the parents had: One parent said, "How can he love my child; he's a man." The second thing that I recall, he said the parent said, "He has a beard." And the third thing was, "Aren't you concerned about homosexuality?"

Such suspicions often cause men in all four professions to alter their work behavior to guard against sexual abuse charges, particularly in those specialties requiring intimate contact with women and children.

Men are very distressed by these negative stereotypes, which tend to undermine their self-esteem and to cause them to second-guess their motivations for entering these fields. A California teacher said,

> If I tell men that I don't know, that I'm meeting for the first time, that that's what I do, . . . sometimes there's a look on their faces that, you know, "Oh, couldn't get a real job?"

When asked if his wife, who is also an elementary school teacher, encounters the same kind of prejudice, he said,

> No, it's accepted because she's a woman. . . . I think people would see that as a . . . step up, you know. "Oh, you're not a housewife, you've got a career. That's great . . . that you're out there working. And you have a daughter, but

you're still out there working. You decided not to stay home, and you went out there and got a job." Whereas for me, it's more like I'm supposed to be out working anyway, even though I'd rather be home with [my daughter].

Unlike women who enter traditionally male professions, men's movement into these jobs is perceived by the "outside world" as a step down in status. This particular form of discrimination may be most significant in explaining why men are underrepresented in these professions. Men who otherwise might show interest in and aptitudes for such careers are probably discouraged from pursuing them because of the negative popular stereotypes associated with the men who work in them. This is a crucial difference from the experience of women in nontraditional professions: "My daughter, the physician," resonates far more favorably in most people's ears than "My son, the nurse."

Many of the men in my sample identified the stigma of working in a female-identified occupation as the major barrier to more men entering their professions. However, for the most part, they claimed that these negative stereotypes were not a factor in their own decisions to join these occupations. Most respondents didn't consider entering these fields until well into adulthood, after working in some related occupation. Several social workers and librarians even claimed they were not aware that men were a minority in their chosen professions. Either they had no well-defined image or stereotype, or their contacts and mentors were predominantly men. For example, prior to entering library school, many librarians held part-time jobs in university libraries, where there are proportionally more men than in the profession generally. Nurses and elementary school teachers were more aware that mostly women worked in these jobs, and this was often a matter of some concern to them. However, their choices were ultimately legitimized by mentors, or by encouraging friends or family members who implicitly reassured them that entering these occupations would not typecast them as feminine. In some cases, men were told by recruiters there were special advancement opportunities for men in these fields, and they entered them expecting rapid promotion to administrative positions.

I: Did it ever concern you when you were making the decision to enter nursing school, the fact that it is a female-dominated profession?

R: Not really. I never saw myself working on the floor. I saw myself pretty much going into administration, just getting the background and then getting a job someplace as a supervisor and then working, getting up into administration.

Because of the unique circumstances of their recruitment, many of the respondents did not view their occupational choices as inconsistent with a male gender role, and they generally avoided the negative stereotypes directed against men in these fields.

Indeed, many of the men I interviewed claimed that they did not encounter negative professional stereotypes until they had worked in these fields for several years. Popular prejudices can be damaging to self-esteem and probably push some men out of these professions altogether. Yet, ironically, they sometimes contribute to the "glass escalator" effect I have been describing. Men seem to encounter the most vituperative criticism from the public when they are in the most female-identified specialties. Public concerns sometimes result in their being shunted into more "legitimate" positions for men. A librarian formerly in charge of a branch library's children's collection, who now works in the reference department of the city's main library, describes his experience:

R: Some of the people [who frequented the branch library] complained that they didn't want to have a man doing the storytelling scenario. And I got transferred here to the central library in an equivalent job . . . I thought that I did a good job. And I had been told by my supervisor that I was doing a good job.

I: Have you ever considered filing some sort of lawsuit to get that other job back?

R: Well, actually, the job I've gotten now ... well, it's a reference librarian; it's what I wanted in the first place. I've got a whole lot more authority here. I'm also in charge of the circulation desk. And I've recently been promoted because of my new stature, so ... no, I'm not considering trying to get that other job back.

The negative stereotypes about men who do "women's work" can push men out of specific jobs. However, to the extent that they channel men into more "legitimate" practice areas, their effects can actually be positive. Instead of being a source of discrimination, these prejudices can add to the "glass escalator effect" by pressuring men to move *out* of the most female-identified areas, and *up* to those regarded as more legitimate and prestigious for men.

Conclusion: Discrimination Against Men

Both men and women who work in nontraditional occupations encounter discrimination, but the forms and consequences of this discrimination are very different. The interviews suggest that unlike "nontraditional" women workers, most of the discrimination and prejudice facing men in the "female professions" emanates from outside those professions. The men and women interviewed for the most part believed that men are given fair—if not preferential—treatment in hiring and promotion decisions, are accepted by supervisors and colleagues, and are well-integrated into the workplace subculture. Indeed, subtle mechanisms seem to enhance men's position in these professions—a phenomenon I refer to as the "glass escalator effect."

The data lend strong support for Zimmer's (1988) critique of "gender neutral theory" (such as Kanter's [1977] theory of tokenism) in the study of occupational segregation. Zimmer argues that women's occupational inequality is more a consequence of sexist beliefs and practices embedded in the labor force than the effect of numerical underrepresentation per se. This study suggests that token status itself does not diminish men's occupational success. Men take their gender privilege with them when they enter predominantly female occupations: this translates into an advantage in spite of their numerical rarity.

This study indicates that the experience of tokenism is very different for men and women. Future research should examine how the experience of tokenism varies for members of different races and classes as well. For example, it is likely that informal workplace mechanisms similar to the ones identified here promote the careers of token whites in predominantly black occupations. The crucial factor is the social status of the token's group—not their numerical rarity—that determines whether the token encounters a "glass ceiling" or a "glass escalator."

However, this study also found that many men encounter negative stereotypes from persons not directly involved in their professions. Men who enter these professions are often considered "failures" or sexual deviants. These stereotypes may be a major impediment to men who otherwise might consider careers in these occupations. Indeed, they are likely to be important factors whenever a member of a relatively high status group crosses over into a lower status occupation. However, to the extent that these stereotypes contribute to the "glass escalator effect" by channeling men into more "legitimate" (and higher paying) occupations, they are not discriminatory.

Women entering traditionally "male" professions also face negative stereotypes suggesting they are not "real women" (Epstein 1981; Lorber 1984; Spencer and Podmore 1987). However, these stereotypes do not seem to deter women to the same degree that they deter men from pursuing nontraditional professions. There is ample historical evidence that women flock to male-identified occupations once opportunities are available (Cohn 1985; Epstein 1988). Not so with men. Examples of occupations changing from predominantly female to predominantly male are very rare in our history. The few existing cases—such as medicine—suggest that redefinition of the occupations as appropriately "masculine" is necessary before men will consider joining them (Ehrenreich and English 1978).

Because different mechanisms maintain segregation in male- and female-dominated occupations, different approaches are needed to promote their integration. Policies intended to alter the sex composition of male-dominated occupations—such as affirmative action—make little sense when applied to the "female professions." For men, the major barriers to integration have little to do with their treatment once they decide to enter these fields. Rather, we need to address the social and cultural sanctions applied to men who do "women's work" which keep men from even considering these occupations.

One area where these cultural barriers are clearly evident is in the media's representation of men's occupations. Women working in traditionally male professions have achieved an unprecedented acceptance on popular television shows. Women are portrayed as doctors ("St. Elsewhere"), lawyers ("The Cosby Show," "L.A. Law"), architects ("Family Ties"), and police officers ("Cagney and Lacey"). But where are the male nurses, teachers, and secretaries? Television rarely portrays men in nontraditional work roles, and when it does, that anomaly is made the central focus—and joke—of the program. A comedy series (1991–1992) about a male elementary school teacher ("Drexell's Class") stars a lead character who *hates children!* Yet even this negative portrayal is exceptional. When a prime time hospital drama series ("St. Elsewhere") depicted a male orderly striving for upward mobility, the show's writers made him a "physician's assistant," not a nurse or nurse practitioner—the much more likely "real life" possibilities.

Presenting positive images of men in nontraditional careers can produce limited effects. A few social workers, for example, were first inspired to pursue their careers by George C. Scott, who played a social worker in the television drama series, "Eastside/Westside." But as a policy strategy to break down occupational segregation, changing media images of men is no panacea. The stereotypes that differentiate masculinity and femininity, and degrade that which is defined as feminine, are deeply entrenched in culture, social structure, and personality (Williams 1989). Nothing short of a revolution in cultural definitions of masculinity will effect the broad scale social transformation needed to achieve the complete occupational integration of men and women.

Of course, there are additional factors besides societal prejudice contributing to men's underrepresentation in female-dominated professions. Most notably, those men I interviewed mentioned as a deterrent the fact that these professions are all underpaid relative to comparable "male" occupations, and several suggested that instituting a "comparable worth" policy might attract more men. However, I am not convinced that improved salaries will substantially alter the sex composition of these professions unless the cultural stigma faced by men in these occupations diminishes. Occupational sex segregation is remarkably resilient, even in the face of devastating economic hardship. During the Great Depression of the 1930s, for example, "women's jobs" failed to attract sizable numbers of men (Blum 1991:154). In her study of American Telephone and Telegraph (AT&T) workers, Epstein (1989) found that some men would rather suffer unemployment than accept relatively high paying "women's jobs" because of the damage to their identities this would cause. She quotes one unemployed man who refused to apply for a female-identified telephone operator job:

> I think if they offered me $1000 a week tax free, I wouldn't take that job. When I . . . see those guys sitting in there [in the telephone operating room], I wonder what's wrong with them. Are they pansies or what? (Epstein 1989: 577)

This is not to say that raising salaries would not affect the sex composition of these jobs. Rather, I am suggesting that wages are not the only—or perhaps even the major—impediment to men's entry into these jobs. Further research is needed to explore the ideological significance of the "woman's wage" for maintaining occupational stratification.[3]

At any rate, integrating men and women in the labor force requires more than dismantling barriers to women in male-dominated fields. Sex segregation is a two-way street. We must also confront and dismantle the barriers men face in predominantly female occupations. Men's experiences in these nontraditional occupations reveal just how culturally embedded the barriers are, and how far we have to travel before men and women attain true occupational and economic equality.

Notes

1. According to the U.S. Census, black men and women comprise 7 percent of all nurses and librarians, 11 percent of all elementary school teachers, and 19 percent of all social workers (calculated from U.S. Census 1980: Table 278, 1–197). The proportion of blacks in social work may be exaggerated by these statistics. The occupational definition of "social worker" used by the Census Bureau includes welfare workers and pardon and parole officers, who are not considered "professional" social workers by the National Association of Social Workers. A study of degreed professionals found that 89 percent of practitioners were white (Hardcastle 1987).

2. In April 1991, the Labor Department created a "Glass Ceiling Commission" to "conduct a thorough study of the underrepresentation of women and minorities in executive, management, and senior decision-making positions in business" (U.S. House of Representatives 1991:20).

3. Alice Kessler-Harris argues that the lower pay of traditionally female occupations is symbolic of a patriarchal order that assumes female dependence on a male breadwinner. She writes that pay equity is fundamentally threatening to the "male worker's sense of self, pride, and masculinity" because it upsets his individual standing in the hierarchical ordering of the sexes (1990:125). Thus, men's reluctance to enter these occupations may have less to do with the actual dollar amount recorded in their paychecks, and more to do with the damage that earning "a woman's wage" would wreak on their self-esteem in a society that privileges men. This conclusion is supported by the interview data.

References

Bielby, William T., and James N. Baron
1984 "A woman's place is with other women: Sex segregation within organizations." In *Sex Segregation in the Workplace: Trends, Explanations, Remedies*, ed. Barbara Reskin, 27–55. Washington, D.C.: National Academy Press.

Blum, Linda M.
1991 *Between Feminism and Labor: The Significance of the Comparable Worth Movement*. Berkeley and Los Angeles: University of California Press.

Carothers, Suzanne C., and Peggy Crull
1984 "Contrasting sexual harassment in female-dominated and male-dominated occupations." In *My Troubles Are Going to Have Trouble with Me: Everyday Trials and Triumphs of Women Workers*, ed. Karen B. Sacks and Dorothy Remy, 220–227. New Brunswick, N.J.: Rutgers University Press.

Cohn, Samuel
1985 *The Process of Occupational Sex-Typing*. Philadelphia: Temple University Press.

Ehrenreich, Barbara, and Deirdre English
1978 *For Her Own Good: 100 Years of Expert Advice to Women*. Garden City, N.Y.: Anchor Press.

Epstein, Cynthia Fuchs
1981 *Women in Law*. New York: Basic Books.
1988 *Deceptive Distinctions: Sex, Gender and the Social Order*. New Haven: Yale University Press.
1989 "Workplace boundaries: Conceptions and creations." *Social Research* 56: 571–590.

Freeman, Sue J. M.
1990 *Managing Lives: Corporate Women and Social Change*. Amherst, Mass.: University of Massachusetts Press.

Grimm, James W., and Robert N. Stern
1974 "Sex roles and internal labor market structures: The female semi-professions." *Social Problems* 21: 690–705.

Hardcastle, D. A.
1987 "The social work labor force." Austin, Tex.: School of Social Work, University of Texas.

Hodson, Randy, and Teresa Sullivan
1990 *The Social Organization of Work*. Belmont, Calif.: Wadsworth Publishing Co.

Jacobs, Jerry
1989 *Revolving Doors: Sex Segregation and Women's Careers*. Stanford, Calif.: Stanford University Press.

Kanter, Rosabeth Moss
1977 *Men and Women of the Corporation*. New York: Basic Books.

Kessler-Harris, Alice
1990 *A Woman's Wage: Historical Meanings and Social Consequences*. Lexington, Ky.: Kentucky University Press.

Lorber, Judith
1984 *Women Physicians: Careers, Status, and Power*. New York: Tavistock.

Martin, Susan E.
1980 *Breaking and Entering: Police Women on Patrol*. Berkeley, Calif.: University of California Press.
1988 "Think like a man, work like a dog, and act like a lady: Occupational dilemmas of policewomen." In *The Worth of Women's Work: A Qualitative Synthesis*, ed. Anne Statham, Eleanor M. Miller, and Hans O. Mauksch, 205–223. Albany, N.Y.: State University of New York Press.

Phenix, Katharine
1987 "The status of women librarians." *Frontiers* 9: 36–40.

Reskin, Barbara
1988 "Bringing the men back in: Sex differentiation and the devaluation of women's work." *Gender & Society* 2: 58–81.

Reskin, Barbara, and Heidi Hartmann
1986 *Women's Work, Men's Work: Sex Segregation on the Job*. Washington, D.C.: National Academy Press.

Reskin, Barbara, and Patricia Roos
1990 *Job Queues, Gender Queues: Explaining Women's Inroads into Male Occupations*. Philadelphia: Temple University Press.

Schmuck, Patricia A.
1987 "Women school employees in the United States." In *Women Educators: Employees of Schools in Western Countries*, ed. Patricia A. Schmuck, 75–97. Albany, N.Y.: State University of New York Press.

Schreiber, Carol
1979 *Men and Women in Transitional Occupations*. Cambridge, Mass.: MIT Press.

Spencer, Anne, and David Podmore
1987 *In a Man's World: Essays on Women in Male-Dominated Professions*. London: Tavistock.

Strauss, Anselm L.
1987 *Qualitative Analysis for Social Scientists*. Cambridge, England: Cambridge University Press.

U.S. Bureau of the Census
1980 *Detailed Population Characteristics*, Vol. 1, Ch. D. Washington, D.C.: Government Printing Office.

U.S. Congress. House
1991 *Civil Rights and Women's Equity in Employment Act of 1991*. Report. (Report 102-40, Part I.) Washington, D.C.: Government Printing Office.

U.S. Department of Labor. Bureau of Labor Statistics
1991 *Employment and Earnings*. January. Washington, D.C.: Government Printing Office.

Williams, Christine L.
1989 *Gender Differences at Work: Women and Men in Nontraditional Occupations*. Berkeley, Calif.: University of California Press.

Yoder, Janice D.
1989 "Women at West Point: Lessons for token women in male-dominated occupations." In *Women: A Feminist Perspective*, ed. Jo Freeman, 523–537. Mountain View, Calif.: Mayfield Publishing Company.

York, Reginald O., H. Carl Henley, and Dorothy N. Gamble
1987 "Sexual discrimination in social work: Is it salary or advancement?" *Social Work* 32: 336–340.

Zimmer, Lynn
1988 "Tokenism and women in the workplace." *Social Problems* 35: 64–77.

ARTICLE 20

Jennifer Pierce

Rambo Litigators: Emotional Labor in a Male-Dominated Occupation

> *Litigation is war. The lawyer is a gladiator and the object is to wipe out the other side.*
> —Cleveland lawyer quoted in *The New York Times*

A recent spate of articles in *The New York Times* and a number of legal dailies characterized some of America's more flamboyant and aggressive trial lawyers as "Rambo litigators."[1] This hypermasculine, aggressive image is certainly not a new one. In popular culture and everyday life, jokes and stories abound that characterize lawyers as overly aggressive, manipulative, unreliable, and unethical individuals.[2] What jokes, as well as the popular press, fail to consider is that such behavior is not simply the result of individual failings but is actually required and reinforced by the legal profession itself.

Legal scholar Carrie Menkel-Meadow (1985) suggests that the adversarial model with its emphasis on "zealous advocacy" and "winning" encourages a "macho ethic" in the courtroom (pp. 51–54). Lawyers and teachers of trial lawyers argue that the success of litigators depends on their ability to manipulate people's emotions (Brazil 1978; Turow 1987). Trial lawyers must persuade judges and juries, as well as intimidate witnesses and opposing counsel in the courtroom, in deposition, and in negotiations. The National Institute of Trial Advocacy, for example, devotes a three-week training seminar to teaching lawyers to hone such emotional skills, thereby improving their success in the courtroom (Rice 1989). This chapter makes this aspect of lawyering explicit by examining the emotional dimension of legal work in a particular specialty of law—litigation. Sociological studies of the legal profession have yet to seriously examine the emotional dimension of lawyering.[3] Although a few studies make reference to the emotional dimension of work, it is not the central focus of their research.[4] For example, Nelson (1988) reduces lawyering to three roles—"finders, minders and grinders," meaning "lawyers who seem to bring in substantial clients . . . lawyers who take care of the clients who are already here and there are the grinders who do the work" (senior partner quoted in Nelson 1988, p. 69). Nelson's reduction of these roles to their instrumental and intellectual dimensions neglects the extent to which instrumental tasks may also contain emotional elements.

The sparse attention other sociological studies have given to this dimension of lawyering is contradicted by my 15 months of field research (from 1988 to 1989) at two large law firms in San Francisco—six months at a private firm (Lyman, Lyman, and Portia) and nine months in the legal department of a large corporation (Bonhomie Corporation).[5] Litigators make use of their emotions to persuade juries, judges, and witnesses in the courtroom and in depositions, in communications

From *Masculinities in Organizations,* Cheng (ed.), pp. 1–27. Sage Publications, 1993. © Sage Publications. Reprinted by permission.

with opposing counsel, and with clients. However, in contrast to the popular image, intimidation and aggression constitute only one component of the emotional labor required by this profession. Lawyers also make use of strategic friendliness, that is, the use of charm or flattery to manipulate others. Despite the apparent differences in these two types of emotional labor, both use the manipulation of others for a specific end—winning a case. Although other jobs require the use of manipulation to achieve specific ends, such labor may serve different purposes and be embedded in a different set of relationships. Flight attendants, for example, are friendly and reassuring to passengers so as to alleviate their anxiety about flying (Hochschild 1983). However, flight attendants' friendliness takes the form of deference: Their relationship to passengers is supportive and subordinate. By contrast, in litigation, the goal of strategic friendliness is to *win over* or dominate another. As professionals who have a monopoly over specialized knowledge, attorneys hold a superordinate position with respect to clients, witnesses, and jurors and a competitive one with other lawyers. If trial lawyers want to win their cases, they must be able to successfully manipulate and ultimately dominate others for their professional ends.

By doing whatever it takes within the letter of the law to win a case, lawyers effectively fulfill the goal of zealous advocacy: persuading a third party that the client's interests should prevail. In this way, intimidation and strategic friendliness serve to reproduce and maintain the adversarial model. At the same time, by exercising dominance and control over others, trial lawyers also reproduce gender relations. The majority of litigators who *do dominance* are men (88 percent of litigators are male) and those who defer are either female secretaries and paralegals,[6] other women, or men who become feminized in the process of losing. In addition to creating and maintaining a gendered hierarchy, the form such emotional labor takes is gendered. It is a masculinized form of emotional labor, not only because men do it but because dominance is associated with masculinity in our culture. West and Zimmerman (1987) argue, for example, that displays of dominance are ways for men to "do gender."[7] Similarly, psychoanalytic feminists equate masculinity with men's need to dominate women (Chodorow 1978; Benjamin 1988). In the case of trial lawyers, the requirements of the profession deem it appropriate to dominate women as well as other men. Such *conquests* or achievements at once serve the goals of effective advocacy and become the means for the trial lawyer to demonstrate a class-specific form of masculinity.

Gamesmanship and the Adversarial Model

Popular wisdom and lawyer folklore portray lawyering as a game, and the ability to play as gamesmanship (Spence 1988). As one of the trial attorneys I interviewed said,

> The logic of gamesmanship is very interesting to me. I like how you make someone appear to be a liar. You know, you take them down the merry path and before they know it, they've said something pretty stupid. The challenge is getting them to say it without violating the letter of the law.

Lawyering is based on gamesmanship—legal strategy, skill, and expertise. But trial lawyers are much more than chess players. Their strategies are not simply cerebral, rational, and calculating moves but highly emotional, dramatic, flamboyant, and shocking presentations that invoke sympathy, distrust, or outrage. In my redefinition of the term, *gamesmanship* involves the utilization of legal strategy through a presentation of an emotional self designed specifically to influence the feelings and judgment of a particular legal audience—the judge, the jury, the witness, or opposing counsel. Furthermore, in my definition, the choices litigators make about selecting a particular strategy are not simply individual, they are institutionally constrained by the structure of the legal profession, formal and informal professional norms such as the American Bar Association's

(1982) *Model Code of Professional Responsibility* and training in trial advocacy through programs sponsored by the National Institute of Trial Advocacy.

The rules governing gamesmanship derive from the adversarial model that underlies the basic structure of our legal system. This model is a method of adjudication that involves two advocates (e.g., the attorneys) presenting their case to an impartial third party (i.e., the judge and the jury) who listens to evidence and argument and declares one party the winner (Menkel-Meadow 1985; Luban 1988). As Menkel-Meadow (1985) observes, the basic assumptions that underlie this set of arrangements are "advocacy, persuasion, hierarchy, competition and binary results (win or lose)." She writes, "The conduct of litigation is relatively similar . . . to a sporting event—there are rules, a referee, an object to the game, and a winner is declared after play is over" (p. 51).

Within this system, the attorney's main objective is to persuade the impartial third party that his client's interests should prevail (American Bar Association 1982, p. 34). However, clients do not always have airtight, defensible cases. How, then, does the *zealous advocate* protect his clients interests and achieve the desired result? When persuasion by appeal to reason breaks down, an appeal to emotions becomes tantamount (Cheatham 1955, pp. 282–283). As legal scholar John Buchan (1939) writes, "The root of the talent is simply the *power to persuade*" [italics added] (pp. 211–213). By appealing to emotions, the lawyer becomes a "con man."[8] He acts "as if" he has a defensible case, he puffs himself up, he bolsters his case. Thus, the successful advocate must not only be smart, but as famous turn-of-the-century trial lawyer Francis Wellman (1903/1986, p. 13) observes, he must also be a "good actor." In his book, *The Art of Cross-Examination*, first published in 1903 and reprinted to the present, Wellman describes how carefully the litigator must present himself to the judge and jury:

> The most cautious cross-examiner will often elicit a damaging answer. Now is the time for the greatest self-control. If you show by your face how the answer hurt, you may lose by that one point alone. How often one sees a cross-examiner fairly staggered by such an answer. He pauses, blushes . . . [but seldom regains] control of the witness. With the really experienced trial lawyer, such answers, instead of appearing to surprise or disconcert him, will seem to come as a matter of course, and will fall perfectly flat. He will proceed with the next question as if nothing happened, or else perhaps give the witness an incredulous smile, as if to say, "Who do you suppose would believe that for a minute?" (pp. 13–14).

More recently, teacher and lawyer David Berg (1987) advises lawyers to think of themselves as actors, and the jury, an audience. He writes,

> Decorum can make a difference, too. . . . *Stride* to the podium and *exude confidence*, even if there is a chance that the high school dropout on the stand is going to make you look like an idiot. *Take command* of the courtroom. Once you begin, do not grope for questions, shuffle through papers, or take breaks to confer with co-counsel. Let the jury know that you are prepared, that you do not need anyone's advice, and that *you care* about the case . . . because if *you don't care, the jurors won't care*. (1987, p. 28, italics added)

Wellman (1903/1986) and Berg (1987) make a similar point: Trials are the enactment of a drama in the courtroom, and attorneys are the leading actors. Appearance and demeanor are of utmost importance. The lawyer's manner, his tone of voice, his facial expressions are all means to persuade the jury that his client is right. Outrageous behavior is acceptable, as long as it remains within the letter of the law. Not only are trial lawyers expected to act but with a specific purpose in mind: to favorably influence feelings of the jurors. As Berg points out, "if you don't show you care, the jurors won't care."

This emphasis on acting is also evident in the courses taught by the National Institute for Trial Advocacy (NITA) where neophyte litigators learn the basics in presenting a case for trial. NITA's emphasis is on "learning by doing" (Kilpatrick, quoted in Rice 1989). Attorneys do not simply read about cases but practice presenting them in a simulated courtroom with a judge, a jury, and witnesses. In this case, doing means acting. As one of the teacher–lawyers said on the first day of class, "Being a good trial lawyer means being a good actor.... Trial attorneys love to perform." Acting, in sociological terms, translates into emotional labor, that is, inducing or suppressing feelings in order to produce an outward countenance that influences the emotions of others. Teacher–lawyers discuss style, delivery, presentation of self, attitude, and professionalism. Participants, in turn, compare notes about the best way to "handle" judges, jurors, witnesses, clients, and opposing counsel. The efforts of these two groups constitute the teaching and observance of "feeling rules" or professional norms that govern appropriate lawyerlike conduct in the courtroom.

The three-week course I attended[9] took students through various phases of a hypothetical trial—jury selection, opening and closing statements, and direct and cross-examination. Each stage of the trial has a slightly different purpose. For example, the objective of jury selection is to uncover the biases and prejudices of the jurors and to develop rapport with them. On the other hand, an opening statement sets the theme for the case, whereas a direct examination lays the foundation of evidence for the case. Cross-examination is intended to undermine the credibility of the witness, whereas closing represents the final argument. Despite the differing goals that each of these phases has, the means to achieve them is similar in each case, that is, the attempt to persuade a legal audience favorably to one's client through a particular emotional presentation of self.

In their sessions on direct and cross-examination, students were given primarily stylistic, as opposed to substantive, responses on their presentations. They were given finer legal points on the technicalities of their objections—the strength or weakness of their arguments. But in the content analysis of my field notes, I found that 50 percent to 80 percent of comments were directed toward the attorney's particular style. These comments fell into five categories: (a) personal appearance, (b) presentation of self (nice, aggressive, or sincere manner), (c) tone and level of voice, (d) eye contact, and (e) rapport with others in the courtroom.

For example, in one of the sessions, Tom, a young student–lawyer in the class, did a direct examination of a witness to a liquor store robbery. He solemnly questioned the witness about his work, his special training in enforcing liquor laws, and how he determined whether someone was intoxicated. At one point when the witness provided a detail that Tom had not expected, rather than expressing surprise, Tom appeared nonchalant and continued with his line of questions. At the end of his direct, the teacher–lawyer provided the following feedback:

> Good background development of a witness. Your voice level was appropriate but try modulating it a bit more for emphasis. You also use too many thank you's to the judge. You should ingratiate yourself with the judge but not overly so. You also made a good recovery when the witness said something unexpected.

When Patricia, a young woman attorney, proceeded nervously through the same direct examination, opposing counsel objected repeatedly to some of her questions, which flustered her. The teacher–lawyer told her,

> You talk too fast. And you didn't make enough eye contact with the judge. Plus, you got bogged down in the objections and harassment from opposing counsel. You're recovery was too slow. You've got to be more forceful.

In both these examples, as in most of the sessions that I observed, the focus of the comments was not on the questions asked but on *how* the questions were asked. Tom was told to modulate his voice; Patricia was told not to talk so fast. In addition, the teacher–lawyer directed their attention to rapport with others in the courtroom. Tom was encouraged not to be overly ingratiating with the judge, whereas Patricia was told to pay more attention to the judge. Moreover, the teacher commended Tom for his "recovery," that is, regaining self-composure and control of the witness. He criticized Patricia, on the other hand, for not recovering well from an aggressive objection made by opposing counsel.[10]

In my fieldwork at NITA and in the two law offices, I found two main types of emotional labor: intimidation and strategic friendliness. Intimidation entails the use of anger and aggression, whereas strategic friendliness uses politeness, friendliness, or playing dumb. Both forms are related to gamesmanship. Each involves an emotional presentation of self that is intended to favorably influence the feelings of a particular legal audience toward one's client. Many jobs appear to require strategic friendliness and intimidation. Domestic workers, for example, sometimes "play dumb" so as not to alienate their white female employers (Rollins 1985). For domestic workers, however, this strategy is a means for someone in a subordinate position to survive a degrading job. By contrast, for litigators, strategic friendliness, like intimidation, is a means for an individual with professional status to control and dominate others in an effort to win one's case. Although both the litigator and the domestic worker may play dumb, in each job, the behavior serves different goals that are indicative of their divergent positions in relationship to others.

Intimidation and strategic friendliness not only serve the goals of the adversarial model, but they exemplify a masculine style of emotional labor. They become construed as masculine for several reasons. First, emotional labor in the male-dominated professional strata of the gendered law firm is interpreted as masculine, simply because men do it. Ruth Milkman (1987), for example, suggests that "idioms of sex-typing can be applied to whatever women and men happen to be doing" (p. 50). Male trial attorneys participate in shaping this idiom by describing their battles in the courtroom and with opposing counsel as "macho," "something men get into," and "a male thing." In addition, by treating women lawyers as outsiders and excluding them from professional networks, they further define their job as exclusively male.

In addition, the underlying purpose of gamesmanship itself, that is, the control and domination of others through manipulation, reflects a particular cultural conception of masculinity. Connell (1987), for example, describes a hegemonic form of masculinity that emphasizes the domination of a certain class of men—middle- to upper-middle class—over other men and over women. Connell's cultural conception of masculinity dovetails neatly with feminist psychoanalytic accounts that interpret domination as a means of asserting one's masculinity (Chodorow 1978; Benjamin 1988). The lawyers I studied also employed a ritual of degradation and humiliation against other men and women who were witnesses or opposing counsel. The remainder of this chapter describes the two main components of emotional labor—intimidation and strategic friendliness—the purpose of each, and shows how these forms become construed as masculine. These forms of emotional labor are explored in practices, such as cross-examination, depositions, jury selection, and in opening and closing statements.

Intimidation

The first and most common form of emotional labor associated with lawyers is intimidation. In popular culture, the tough, hard-hitting, and aggressive trial lawyer is portrayed in television shows, such as *L.A. Law* and *Perry Mason* and in movies, such as *The Firm*, *A Few Good Men*, and *Presumed Innocent*. The news media's focus on famous trial attorneys such as Arthur Liman, the prosecutor of Oliver North in the Iran-Contra trial, also reinforces this image. Law professor Wayne Brazil (1978) refers to this style of lawyering as the *professional combatant*. Others have used terms such as *Rambo litigator, legal terrorists*, and *barbarians of the bar* (Margolick 1988; Miner 1988; Sayler 1988). Trial attorneys themselves call litigators from large law firms "hired guns" (Spangler 1986). The central figure that appears again and again in these images is not only intimidating but strongly masculine. In the old West, hired guns were sharpshooters, men who were hired to kill other men. The strong, silent movie character Rambo is emblematic of a highly stylized, super masculinity. Finally, most of the actors who play tough, hard-hitting lawyers in the television shows and movies mentioned above are men. Thus, intimidation is not simply a form of emotional labor associated with trial lawyers, it is a masculinized form of labor.

Intimidation is tied to cultural conceptions of masculinity in yet another way. In a review of the literature on occupations, Connell (1987) observes that the cult of masculinity in working-class jobs centers on physical prowess and sexual contempt for men in managerial or office positions (p. 180). Like the men on the shop floor in Michael Burawoy's (1979) study who brag about how much they can lift or produce, lawyers in this study boast about "destroying witnesses," "playing hardball," "taking no prisoners," and about the size and amount of their "win." In a middle-class job such as the legal profession, however, intimidation depends not on physical ability but on mental quickness and a highly developed set of social skills. Thus, masculinizing practices, such as aggression and humiliation, take on an emotional and intellectual tone specific to middle-class occupations and professions.

This stance is tied to the adversarial model's conception of the "zealous advocate" (American Bar Association 1982). The underlying purpose of this strategy is to intimidate, scare, or emotionally bully the witness of opposing counsel into submission. A destructive cross-examination is the best example.[11] Trial attorneys are taught to intimidate the witness in cross-examination, "to control the witness by never asking a question to which he does not already know the answer and to regard the impeachment of the witness as a highly confrontational act" (Menkel-Meadow 1985, p. 54). Wellman (1903/1986) describes cross-examination in this way:

It requires the greatest ingenuity; a habit of logical thought; clearness of perception; infinite patience and self-control; the power to read men's minds intuitively, to judge of their characters by their faces, to appreciate their motives; ability to act with force and precision; a masterful knowledge of the subject matter itself; an extreme caution; and, above all *the instinct to discover the weak point in the witness under examination* . . . It is a *mental duel* between counsel and witness. (p. 8, italics added)

Berg (1987) echoes Wellman's words when he begins his lecture on cross-examination by saying, "The common denominator for effective cross-examination is not genius, however. It's a combination of preparation and an instinct for the jugular" (p. 27). Again, cross-examination involves not only acting mean but creating a specific impression on the witness.

In the sections on cross-examination at NITA, teachers trained lawyers how to *act mean*. The demonstration by the teachers on cross-examination best exemplified this point. Two male instructors reenacted an aggressive cross-examination in a burglary case. The prosecutor relentlessly hammered away, until the witness couldn't remember any specific details about what the burglar looked like. At its conclusion, the audience clapped vigorously. Three male students who had been asked to comment on the section responded unanimously and enthusiastically that the prosecutor's approach has been excellent. One student commentator said, "He kept complete control of the witness." Another remarked, "He blasted the witness's testimony." And the third added, "He destroyed the witness's credibility." The fact that a destructive cross-examination served as the demonstration for the entire class underlines the desirability of aggressive behavior as a model for appropriate lawyerlike conduct in this situation. Furthermore, the students' praise for the attorney's tactics collectively reinforce the norm for such behavior.

Teachers emphasized the importance of using aggression on an individual level as well. Before a presentation on cross-examination, Tom, one of the students, stood in the hallway with one of the instructors trying to "psyche himself up to get mad." He repeated over and over to himself, "I hate it when witnesses lie to me, it makes me so mad!" The teacher coached him to concentrate on that thought, until Tom could actually evoke the feeling of anger. He said to me later in an interview, "I really felt mad at the witness when I walked into the courtroom." In the actual cross-examination, each time the witness made an inconsistent statement, Tom became more and more angry: "First, you told us you could see the burglar, now you say your vision was obstructed! So, which is it, Mr. Jones?" The more irate he became, the more intimidated and confused the witness became, until he completely backed down and said, "I don't know," in response to every question. The teacher characterized Tom's performance as "the best in the class," because it was the "the most forceful" and "the most intimidating." Students remarked that he deserved to "win the case."

NITA's teachers also used mistakes to train students in the rigors of cross-examination. For example, when Laura cross-examined the same witness in the liquor store case, a teacher commented on her performance:

> Too many words. You're asking the witness for information. Don't do that in cross-examination. You tell them what the information is. You want to be destructive in cross-examination. When the other side objects to an answer, *you were too nice. Don't be so nice!* [italics added]. Next time, ask to talk to the judge, tell him, "This is crucial to my case." You also asked for information when you didn't know the answer. Bad news. You lost control of the witness.

By being nice and losing control of the witness, Laura violated two norms underlying the classic confrontational cross-examination. A destructive cross-examination is meant to impeach the witness's credibility, thereby demonstrating to the jury the weakness in opposing counsel's case. In situations that call for such an aggressive cross-examination, being nice implies that the lawyer likes the witness and agrees with his or her testimony. By not being aggressive, Laura created the wrong impression for the jury. Second, Laura lost control of the witness. Rather than guiding the witness through the cross with leading questions[12] that were damaging to opposing counsel's case, she allowed the witness to make his own points. As we will see in the next section of the chapter, being nice can also be used as a strategy for controlling a witness; however, such a strategy is not effective in a destructive cross-examination.

Laura's violation of these norms also serves to highlight the implicitly masculine practices used in cross-examination. The repeated phrase, "keeping complete control of the witness," clearly signals the importance of dominating other women and men. Furthermore, the language used to describe obtaining submission—"blasting the witness," "destroying his credibility," or pushing him to "back down"—is quite violent. In addition, the successful control of the witness often takes on the character of a sexual conquest. One brutal phrase used repeatedly in this way is "raping the witness." Within this discursive field, men who "control," "destroy," or "rape" the witness are seen as "manly," whereas those who lose control are feminized as "sissies" and "wimps" or, in Laura's case, as "too nice."

The combative aspect of emotional labor carries over from the courtroom to other lawyering tasks, such as depositions. Attorneys not only "shred" witnesses in the courtroom but in depositions as well. When I worked at this private firm, Daniel, one of the partners, employed what he called his "cat and mouse game" with one of the key witnesses, Jim, in a deposition that I attended. During the deposition, Daniel aggressively cross-examined Jim. "When did you do this?" "You were lying, weren't you?" Jim lost his temper in response to Daniel's hostile form of interrogation—"You hassle me, man! You make me mad!" Daniel smiled and said, "I'm only trying to get to the truth of the situation." Then, he became aggressive again and said, "You lied to the IRS about how much profit you made, didn't you, Jim!" Jim lost his temper again and started calling Daniel a liar. A heated interchange between Daniel and opposing counsel followed, in which opposing counsel objected to Daniel's "badgering the witness." The attorneys decided to take a brief recess.

When the deposition resumed, Daniel began by accusing John, the other attorney, of withholding crucial documents to the case, while pointing his index finger at him. Opposing counsel stood up and started yelling in a high-pitched voice, "Don't you ever point your finger at me! Don't you ever do that to me! This deposition is over . . . I'm leaving." With that he stood up and began to cram papers into his briefcase in preparation to leave. Daniel immediately backed down, apologized, and said, "Sit down, John, I promise I won't point my finger again." He went on to smooth the situation over and proceeded to tell John in a very calm and controlled voice what his objections were. John made some protesting noises, but he didn't leave. The deposition continued.

In this instance, the deposition, rather than the courtroom, became the *stage* and Daniel took the leading role. His cross-examination was confrontational and his behavior with the witness and opposing counsel was meant to intimidate. After the deposition, Daniel boasted to me and several associates about how mad he had made the witness and how he had "destroyed his credibility." He then proceeded to reenact the final confrontation by imitating John standing up and yelling at him in a falsetto voice. In the discussion that followed, Daniel and his associates gave the effects of his behavior on the "audience" utmost consideration. Hadn't Daniel done a good job forcing the witness to lose control? Hadn't he controlled the situation well? Didn't he make opposing counsel look like a "simpering fool"?

The reenactment and ensuing discussion reveal several underlying purposes of the deposition. First, it suggests that the deposition was not only a fact-finding mission for the attorney but a show designed to influence a particular audience—the witness. Daniel effectively flustered and intimidated the witness. Second, Daniel's imitation of John with a falsetto voice, "as if" he were a woman, serves as a sort of "degradation ceremony" (Garfinkel 1956). By reenacting the drama, he ridicules the man on the other side before an audience of peers, further denigrating him by inviting collective criticism and laughter from colleagues. Third, the discussion of the strategy builds up and elevates Daniel's status as an attorney for his aggressive, yet rational control of the witness and the situation. Thus, the discussion creates a space for collectively reinforcing Daniel's intimidation strategy.

In addition to highlighting the use of intimidation in depositions, this example also illustrates the way aggression as legal strategy or rule-governed aggression (Lyman 1987; Benjamin 1988) and masculinity become conflated, whereas aggression, which is not rule governed, is ridiculed as feminine. John shows his anger, but it is deemed inappropriate, because he loses control of the situation. Such a display of hostility does not serve the interests of the legal profession, because it does not achieve the desired result—a win for the case. As a result, Daniel and his associate regard John's behavior—his lack of control, his seeming hysteria and high voice, with contempt. This contempt takes on a specific sexual character. Just as the working class "lads" in Paul Willis's (1977) book, *Learning to Labor*, denigrate the "earholes" or sissies for their feminine attributes, Daniel and his colleagues ridicule John for his femalelike behavior. Aggression as legal strategy or maleness is celebrated; contempt is reserved for aggression (or behavior) that is not rule governed and behavior that is also associated with the opposite sex.

Attorneys also used the confrontational approach in depositions at Bonhomie Corporation. In a deposition I sat in on, Mack, a litigator, used an aggressive cross-examination of the key witness.

Q: What were the names of the people that have migrated from one of the violators, as you call it, to Bonhomie Corporation?

A: I don't remember as of now.

Q: Do you have their names written down?

A: No.

Q: Well, if you don't remember their names and they're not written down, how can you follow their migration from one company to another?

A: You can consider it in the process of discovery that I will make some inquiring phone calls.

Q: Did you call anyone to follow their migration?

A: Well, I was unsuccessful as of yet to reach other people.

Q: Who have you attempted to call?

A: I can't tell you at this time. I have a list of processes in my mind to follow.

Q: Do you recall who you called and were not able to reach?

A: No.

Q: What's the list of processes in your mind to follow?

A: It's hard to describe.

Q: In other words, you don't have a list?

A: [quietly] Not really.

Q: Mr. Jensen, instead of wasting everyone's time and money, answer the question yes or no!

Opposing Counsel: Don't badger the witness.

Q: Answer the question, Mr. Jensen, yes or no!

Opposing Counsel: I said, don't badger the witness.

Q: Mr. Jensen, you are still required to answer the question!

A: [quietly] No.

In this case, Mack persisted in badgering the witness, who provided incoherent and vague answers. In response to the question, "Well, if you don't remember their names and they're not written down, how can you follow their migration from one company to another?" the witness gave the vague reply: "You can consider it in the process of discovery that I will make some inquiring phone calls." As the witness became more evasive, the attorney became more confrontational, "Answer the question, Mr. Jensen, yes or no!" By using this approach, the lawyer succeeded in making the witness appear even more uncooperative than he actually was and eventually pushed him to admit that he didn't have a list.

Later, in the same deposition, the attorney's confrontational tactics extended to opposing counsel.

Q: Let's change the subject. Mr. Jensen, can you tell me what representations were made to you about the reliability of the Bonhomie Corporation's spider system?

A: Nancy, the saleslady, said they use it widely in the United States, and could not be but very reliable. And, as we allege, fraudulent, and as somebody referred to it, was the, they wanted to give us the embrace of death to provide us more dependency, and then to go on and control our operation totally [sic].

Q: Who said that?

A: My attorney.

Q: When was that?

Opposing Counsel: Well, I . . .

Mack: I think he's already waived it. All I want to know is when it was supposedly said.

A: Well . . .

Opposing Counsel: I do use some great metaphors.

Mack: Yes, I know, I have read your complaint.

Opposing Counsel: Sorry?

Mack: I have read your complaint. That will be all for today, Mr. Jensen.

Here, the attorney did not stop with badgering the witness. When the witness made the statement about the "embrace of death," Mack was quick to find out who said it. And when opposing counsel bragged about his "great metaphors," Mack parried back with a sarcastic retort, "Yes, I know, I have read your complaint." Having had the final word, he abruptly ended the deposition. Like the other deposition, this one was not only an arena for intimidating the witness but for ridiculing the attorney on the other side. In this way, intimidation was used to control the witness and sarcasm to dominate opposing counsel. In doing so, Mack had achieved the desired result—the witness's submission to his line of questioning and a victory over the other side. Furthermore, in his replay of the deposition to his colleagues, he characterized his victory as a "macho blast against the other side," thereby underscoring the masculine character of his intimidation tactics.

Strategic Friendliness

> Mr. Choate's appeal to the jury began long before final argument.... His manner to the jury was that of a *friend* [italics added], a friend solicitous to help them through their tedious investigation; never an expert combatant, intent on victory, and looking upon them as only instruments for its attainment. (Wellman 1903/1986, pp. 16–17)

The lesson implicit in Wellman's anecdote about famous 19th-century lawyer Rufus Choate's trial tactics is that friendliness is another important strategy the litigator must learn and use to be successful in the courtroom. Like the use of aggression, the strategic use of friendliness is another feature of gamesmanship and, hence, another component of emotional labor. As Richard, one of the attorney–teachers at NITA stated, "Lawyers have to be able to vary their styles, they have to be able to have multiple speeds, personalities and style." In his view, intimidation did not always work and he proposed an alternative strategy, what he called "the toe-in-the-sand, aw shucks routine." Rather than adopting an intimidating stance vis-à-vis the witness, he advocated "playing dumb and innocent." "Say to the witness, 'Gee, I don't know what you mean. Can you explain it again?' until you catch the witness in a mistake or an inconsistent statement." Other litigators, such as Leonard Ring (1987), call this the "low-key approach." As an illustration of this style, Ring describes how opposing counsel delicately handled the cross-examination of a child witness:

> The lawyer for the defendant ... stood to cross-examine. Did he attack the details of her story to show inconsistencies? Did he set her up for impeachment by attempting to reveal mistakes, uncertainties and confusion? I sat there praying that he would. But no, he did none of the things a competent defense lawyer is supposed to do. He was old enough to be the girl's grandfather ... the image came through. He asked her very softly and politely: "Honey, could you tell us again what you saw?" She told it exactly as she had on my direct. I felt relieved. He still wasn't satisfied. "Honey, would you mind telling us again what you saw?" She did again exactly as she had before. He still wasn't satisfied. "Would you do it once more?" She did. She repeated, again, the same story—the same way, in the same words. By that time I got the message. The child had been rehearsed by her mother the same way she had been taught "Mary Had a Little Lamb." I won the case, but it was a very small verdict. (pp. 35–36)

Ring concludes that a low-key approach is necessary in some situations and advises against adhering rigidly to the prototypical combative style.

Similarly, Scott Turow (1987), lawyer and novelist, advises trying a variety of approaches when cross-examining the star witness. He cautions against adopting a "guerrilla warfare mentality" in cross-examination and suggests that the attorney may want to create another impression with the jury:

> Behaving courteously can keep you from getting hurt and, in the process, smooth the path for a win. [In one case I worked on] the cross examination was conducted with a politesse appropriate to a drawing room. I smiled to show

that I was not mean-spirited. The chief executive officer smiled to show that he was not beaten. The commissioners smiled to show their gratitude that everybody was being so nice. And my client won big. (pp. 40–42)

Being nice, polite, welcoming, playing dumb, or behaving courteously are all ways that a trial lawyer can manipulate the witness to create a particular impression for the jury. I term this form of gamesmanship *strategic friendliness*. Rather than bully or scare the witness into submission, this tactic employs the opposite—friendliness, politeness, and tact. Despite this seeming difference, it shares with the former an emphasis on the emotional manipulation of another person for a strategic end—winning one's case. For instance, the attorney in Ring's account is gentle and considerate of the child witness for two strategic reasons. First, by making the child feel comfortable, he brings to light the fact that her testimony has been rehearsed. Second, by playing the polite, gentle grandfatherly role, he has created a favorable impression of himself with the jury. Thus, he simultaneously demonstrates to the jury that the witness has been rehearsed and that he, as opposing counsel, is a nice guy. In this way, he improves his chances for winning. And, in fact, he did. Although he didn't win the case, the verdict for the other side was "small."

Although strategic friendliness may appear to be a softer approach than intimidation, it carries with it a strongly instrumental element. Consider the reasoning behind this particular approach. Ring's attorney is nice to the child witness not because he's altruistically concerned for her welfare. He utilizes gentility as a strategy to achieve the desired result—a big win in the courtroom. It is simply a means to an end. Although this approach may be less aggressive than intimidation, it is no less manipulative. Like the goal of intimidation, the central goal of this component of gamesmanship is to dominate and control others for a specific end. This end is best summed up by litigator Mark Dombroff (1989) who writes, "So long as you don't violate the law, including the rules of procedure and evidence or do violence to the canons of ethics, winning is the only thing that matters" (p. 13).

This emphasis on winning is tied to hegemonic conceptions of masculinity and competition. Sociologist Mike Messner (1989) argues that achievement in sporting competitions, such as football, baseball, and basketball, serve as a measure of men's self-worth and their masculinity. This can also be carried over into the workplace. For example, in her research on men in sales, Leidner (1993) finds that defining the jobs as competition becomes a means for construing the work as masculine.

For litigators, comparing the number of wins in the courtroom and the dollar amount of damages or settlement awards allows them to interpret their work as manly. At Bonhomie Corporation and at Lyman, Lyman, and Portia, the first question lawyers often asked others after a trial or settlement conference was "Who won the case?" or "How big were the damages?" Note that both Ring and Turow also conclude their pieces with descriptions of their win—"I won the case, but the verdict was small" and "I won big." Trial attorneys who did not "win big" were described as "having no balls," "geeks," or "wimps." The fact that losing is associated with being less than a man suggests that the constant focus on competition and winning is an arena for proving one's masculinity.

One important area that calls for strategic friendliness and focuses on winning is jury selection or *voir dire*. The main purpose of *voir dire* is to obtain personal information about prospective jurors to determine whether they will be fair, "favorably disposed to you, your client, and your case, and will ultimately return a favorable verdict" (Mauet 1980, p. 31). Once an attorney has made that assessment, biased jurors can be eliminated through challenges for cause and peremptory challenges. In an article on jury selection, attorney Peter Perlman (1988) maintains that the best way to uncover the prejudices of the jury "is to conduct *voir dire* in an atmosphere that makes prospective jurors comfortable about disclosing their true feelings" (p. 5). He provides a checklist of strategies for lawyers to use that enable jurors to feel more comfortable. Some of these include the following:

- Given the initial intimidation that jurors feel, try to make them feel as comfortable as possible; approach them in a *natural, unpretentious, and clear manner*.
- Because jurors don't relate to "litigants" or "litigation," humanize the client and the dispute.
- *Demonstrate the sincere* desire to learn of the jurors's feelings. (pp. 5–9, italics added)

Perlman's account reveals that the underlying goal of jury selection is to encourage the jury to open up so that the lawyer can eliminate the jurors he doesn't want and develop a positive rapport with the ones who appear favorable to his case. This goal is supported not only by other writings on jury selection (Cartwright 1977; Blinder 1978; Mauet 1980; Ring 1983) but also through the training offered by NITA. As a teacher–judge said after the class demonstration on jury selection, "Sell your personality to the jury. Try to get liked by the jury. You're not working for a fair jury but one favorable to your side."

At NITA, teachers emphasized this point on the individual level. In their sessions on *voir dire*, students had to select a jury for a case that involved an employee who fell down the steps at work and severely injured herself. (Jurors in the class were other students, in addition to myself.) Mike, one of the students, proceeded with his presentation. He explained that he was representing the wife's employer. He then went on to tell the jury a little bit about himself. "I grew up in a small town in Indiana." Then, he began to ask each of the jurors where they were from, whether they knew the witness or the experts, whether they played sports, had back problems, suffered any physical injuries, and ever had physical therapy. The instructor gave him the following comments:

The personal comments about yourself seem forced. Good folksy approach, but you went overboard with it. You threw stuff out and let the jury nibble and you got a lot of information. But the main problem is that you didn't find out how people *feel* about the case or about their relatives and friends.

Another set of comments:

Nice folksy approach but a bit overdone. Listen to what jurors say, don't draw conclusions. Don't get so close to them, it makes them feel uncomfortable. Use body language to give people a good feeling about you. Good personality, but don't cross certain lines. Never ask someone about their ancestry. It's too loaded a question to ask. Good sense of humor, but don't call one of your prospective jurors a "money man." And don't tell the jury jokes! You don't *win them over* [italics added] that way.

The sporting element to *voir dire* becomes "winning over the jury." This theme also became evident in discussions student lawyers had before and after jury selection. They discussed at length how best "to handle the jurors," "how to get personal information out of them," "how to please them," "how to make them like you," and "how to seduce them to your side." The element of sexual seduction is no more apparent than in the often used phrase, "getting in bed with the jury." The direct reference to sexual seduction and conquest suggests, as it did with the intimidation strategy used in cross-examination, that "winning over the jury" is also a way to prove one's masculinity. Moreover, the desired result in both strategic friendliness and intimidation is similar: obtaining the juror's submission and winning.

Strategic friendliness is used not only in jury selection but in the cross-examination of sympathetic witnesses. In one of NITA's hypothetical cases, a husband's spouse dies of an illness related to her employment. He sues his deceased wife's former employer for her medical bills, her lost wages, and "lost companionship." One of the damaging facts in the case that could hurt his claim for lost companionship was the fact that he had a girlfriend long before his wife died. In typical combative adversarial style, some of the student lawyers tried to bring this fact out in cross-examination to discredit his relationship with his wife. The teacher–judge told one lawyer who presented such an aggressive cross-examination,

> It's too risky to go after him. Don't be so confrontational. And don't ask the judge to reprimand him for not answering the question. This witness is too sensitive. Go easy on him.

The same teacher gave the following comment to another student who had "come on too strong":

> Too stern. Hasn't this guy been through enough already! Handle him with kid gloves. And don't cut him off. It generates sympathy for him from the jury when you do that. It's difficult to control a sympathetic witness. It's best to use another witness's testimony to impeach him.

And to yet another student:

> Slow down! This is a dramatic witness. Don't lead so much. He's a sympathetic witness—the widower—let him do the talking. Otherwise you look like an insensitive jerk to the jury.

In the cross-examination of a sympathetic witness, teachers advised students not to be aggressive but to adopt a gentler approach. Their concern, however, is not for the witness's feelings but how their treatment of the witness appears to the jury. The jury already thinks the witness is sympathetic, because he is a widower. As a result, the lawyers were advised not to do anything that would make the witness appear more sympathetic and them less so. The one student who did well on this presentation demonstrated great concern for the witness. She gently asked him about his job, his marriage, his wife's job, and her illness. Continuing with this gentle approach, she softly asked him whether anyone had been able to provide him comfort during this difficult time. By doing so, she was able to elicit the testimony about the girlfriend in a sensitive manner. By extracting the testimony about the girlfriend, she decreased the jury's level of sympathy for the bereaved widower. How much companionship did he lose, if he was having an affair? At the same time, because she did so in a gentle manner, she increased the jury's regard for her. She presented herself as a nice person. Her approach is similar to Laura's in using "niceness" as a strategy. However, in Laura's case, being nice was not appropriate to a destructive cross-examination. In the case of cross-examining a sympathetic witness, such an approach is necessary.

Opening statements also provide an opportunity for using the nonconfrontational approach. NITA provided a hypothetical case called *BMI v. Minicom*, involving a large corporation that sues a small business for its failure to pay a contract. Minicom signed a contract for a $20,000 order of computer parts from BMI. BMI shipped the computer parts through UPS to Minicom, but they never arrived. According to the law in the case, the buyer bears the loss, typically through insurance, when the equipment is lost in mail. Mark gave an opening statement that portrayed Minicom as a small business started by ambitious, hard-working college friends "on their way to the big league in business." He played up the difficulties that small businesses face in trying to compete with giant corporations. And at a dramatic moment in the opening, he asked the jury to "imagine a world where cruel giants didn't squeeze out small companies like Minicom." The teacher provided the following comments:

> Good use of evocative imagery. BMI as cruel giant. Minicom squeezing in between the cracks. Great highlighting of the injustice of the situation.

The lawyer for Minicom attempted to gain sympathy from the jury by playing up the underdog role of his client—the small company that gets squeezed between the cracks of the cruel, dominating giant.

In his attempt to counter this image, Robert, the lawyer for BMI, used a courteous opening statement. He attempted to present himself as a nice guy. He took off his jacket, loosened his tie, smiled at the jury, and said, in a friendly conversational tone, "This case is about a broken contract. BMI fulfilled their side of the contract. Mr. Blakey, my client, worked round the clock to get the shipment ready for Minicom. He made phone call after phone call to inventory to make sure the parts got out on time. He checked and rechecked the package before he sent it to Minicom." He paused for dramatic emphasis and, looking sincere and concerned, said, "It's too bad UPS lost the shipment, but that's not BMI's fault. And now, BMI is out $20,000." He received the following comments from the teacher:

> Great use of gestures and eye contact. Good use of voice. You made the case sound simple but important. You humanized yourself and the people at BMI. Good building of sequence.

Here, the attorney for BMI tried to play down his client's impersonal, corporate image by presenting himself as a nice guy. Before he began his opening statement, he took off his jacket and loosened his tie to suggest a more casual and ostensibly less corporate image. He smiled at the jury to let them know that he was friendly—not the cruel giant depicted by opposing counsel. He used a friendly conversational tone to begin his opening statement. And he even admitted that it was not fair that the other side didn't get their computer parts. As the teacher's comments suggest, this strategy was most effective for this particular kind of case.

This approach can also be used in closing statements. In a hypothetical case, during which an insurance company alleged that the claimant set fire to his own business, the lawyer for the store owner tried to defuse the insurance company's strategy with a highly dramatic closing statement:

> Visualize Elmwood Street in 1952. The day Tony Rubino came home from the Navy. His father took him outside to show him a new sign he had made for the family business. It read "Rubino & Son." Standing under the sign "Rubino & Son" with his father was the happiest day of his life. [Pause] The insurance company wants you to believe, ladies and gentlemen of the jury, that Tony set fire to this family jewel. "I'll carry on," he told his father, and he did. . . . [With tears in her eyes, the lawyer concludes] You don't set fire to your father's dream.

The teacher's comments for Janine's closing statement were effusive:

> Great! Well thought out, sounded natural. Good use of details and organization. I especially liked "I don't know what it's like to have a son, but I know what it's like to have a father." And you had tears in your eyes! Gave me the closing-argument goose bumps. Pitched emotion felt real, not phony.

Janine's use of sentimental and nostalgic imagery, the son returning home from the Navy, the beginning of a father and son business, the business as the "family jewel" is reminiscent of a Norman Rockwell painting. It also serves to counter the insurance company's allegation that Tony Rubino set fire to his own store. With the portrait the lawyer paints and the concluding line, "You don't set fire to your father's dream," she rallies the jury's sympathy for Tony Rubino and their antipathy for the insurance company's malicious claim against them. Moreover, her emotional presentation of the story is so effective that the instructor thought it "sounded natural" and "felt real, not phony." The great irony here is that this is not a real case—it is a hypothetical case with hypothetical characters. There is no Tony Rubino, no family store, and no fire. Yet Janine's "deep acting" was so convincing that the teacher believed it was true—it gave him "the closing-argument goose bumps."

Strategic friendliness carries over from the courtroom to depositions. Before deposing a particularly sensitive or sympathetic witness, Joe, one of the attorneys in the private firm, asked me whether "there is anything personal to start the interview with—a sort of warm up question to start things off on a personal note?" I had previously interviewed the woman over the phone, so I knew something about her background. I told him that she was a young mother who had recently had a very difficult delivery of her first child. I added that she was worried about the baby's health, because he had been born prematurely. At the beginning of the deposition later that afternoon, Joe said in a concerned voice that he understood the witness had recently had a baby and was concerned about its health. She appeared slightly embarrassed by the question, but with a slow smile and lots of encouragement from him, she began to tell him all about the baby and its health problems. By the time Joe began the formal part of the deposition, the witness had warmed up and gave her complete cooperation. Later, the attorney bragged to me and one of the associates that he had the witness "eating out of his hand."

After recording these events in my field notes, I wrote the following impressions:

> On the surface, it looks like social etiquette to ask the witness these questions, because it puts her at ease. It lets her know he takes her seriously. But the "personal touch" is completely artificial. He doesn't give a shit about the witness as a person. Or, I should say, only insofar as she's *useful* to him.

Thus, something as innocuous as a personal remark becomes another way to create the desired impression with a witness and thereby manipulate him or her. Perhaps what is most ironic about strategic friendliness is that it requires a peculiar combination of sensitivity to other people and, at the same time, ruthlessness. The lawyer wants to appear kind and understanding, but that is merely a cover for the ulterior motive—winning. Although the outward presentation of self for this form of emotional labor differs from intimidation, the underlying goal is the same: the emotional manipulation of the witness for a favorable result.

Conclusion

In this chapter, I have redefined gamesmanship as the utilization of legal strategy through a presentation of emotional self designed specifically to influence the feelings and judgments of a particular legal audience, such as the judge, the jury, opposing counsel, or the witness. Gamesmanship as emotional labor constitutes two main components—intimidation and strategic friendliness. Despite their apparent differences, both share an emphasis on the manipulation of others toward a strategic end, that is, winning a case. Whereas, the object of intimidation is to "wipe out the other side," playing dumb and being polite represent strategically friendly methods for controlling legal audiences and bringing about the desired "win." Furthermore, I have shown that the attempt to dominate and control judges, juries, and opposing counsel not only serves the goals of the adversarial model but also becomes a means for trial lawyers to assert a hegemonic form of masculinity. Lawyers who gain the other side's submission characterize their efforts as a "macho blast," "a male thing," or "something men get into," whereas those who do not are regarded as "sissies" and "wimps." Thus, it is through their very efforts to be successful litigators that emotional labor in this male-dominated profession is masculinized.

This chapter also suggests many questions for future research on the role of masculinity and emotions in organizations. Masculinity is often a taken-for-granted feature of organizational life. Yet the masculinization of occupations and professions has profound consequences for workers located within them. Not only do male litigators find themselves compelled to act in ways they may find morally reprehensible, but women working in these jobs[13] are increasingly marginalized—facing sex discrimination and sexual harassment (Rhode 1988; Rosenberg, Perlstadt, & Phillips 1993). At the same time, because of its informal and seemingly invisible nature, emotional labor too is often unexamined and unquestioned (Fineman 1993). Given that organizations often intrude on emotional life means that the line between the individual and the job becomes a murky one. The litigator who refuses to play Rambo may not only be unsuccessful, he may find himself without a job. Thus, many questions still require our attention. Is emotional labor gendered in other jobs? Under what conditions? When does emotional labor take on racialized or classed dimensions? When is it exploitative and when is it not? And finally, what role, if any, should emotions play in the workplace?

Notes

1. For examples, see Goldberg (1987), Margolick (1988), Miner (1988), and Sayler (1988).

2. For example, see the *National Law Journal*'s (1986) article, "What America Really Thinks About Lawyers."

3. Classic studies on the legal profession have typically focused on the tension between professionalism and bureaucracy. For examples, see Carlin (1962), Smigel (1969), Spangler (1986), and Nelson (1988).

4. For example, in their classic book, *Lawyers and Their Work*, Johnstone and Hopson (1967) describe 19 tasks associated with the lawyering role. In only two of these 19 tasks do Johnstone and Hopson allude to the emotional dimension of lawyering—"emotional support to client" and "acting as a scapegoat" (pp. 119–120).

5. In addition to my field research, I also conducted 60 interviews with lawyers, paralegals, and secretaries, as well as eight interviews with personnel directors from some of San Francisco's largest law firms. Field work and interviews were also conducted at the National Institute of Trial Advocacy where I spent three weeks with litigators during a special training course on trial preparation. These methodological decisions are fully discussed in the introductory chapter to my book, *Gender Trials* (Pierce 1995). Please note, names of organizations and individuals have been changed throughout to protect confidentiality.

6. See Chapter 4, "Mothering Paralegals: Emotional Labor in a Feminized Occupation," in *Gender Trials* (Pierce 1995).

7. West and Zimmerman (1987) conceptualize gender as "a routine accomplishment embedded in everyday interaction" (p. 1).

8. Blumberg (1967) describes lawyers as practicing a "confidence game." In his account, it is the client who is the "mark" and the attorney and other people in the court who collude in "taking him out." In my usage, litigators "con" not only their clients but juries, judges, and opposing counsel as well.

9. Special thanks to Laurence Rose, Lou Natali, and the National Institute of Trial Advocacy for allowing me to attend and observe NITA's special three-week training seminar on trial advocacy. All interpretations of NITA and its practices are my own and are *not* intended to reflect the goals or objectives of that organization.

10. Women were much more likely to be criticized for being "too nice." The significance of women being singled out for these kinds of "mistakes" is examined in Chapter 5, "Women and Men as Litigators," in *Gender Trials* (Pierce 1995).

11. Mauet describes two approaches to cross-examination. In the first, the purpose is to elicit favorable testimony by getting the witness to agree with the facts that support one's case. On the other hand, a destructive cross-examination "involves asking questions which will discredit the witness or his testimony" (1980, p. 240).

12. The proper form of leading questions is allowed in cross-examination but *not* in direct examination. Mauet (1980) defines a leading question as "one which suggests the answer" and provides examples, such as "Mr. Doe, on December 13, 1977, you owned a car, didn't you?" (p. 247). In his view, control comes by asking "precisely phrased leading questions that never give the witness an opening to hurt you" (p. 243).

13. Women trial lawyers negotiate the masculinized norms of the legal profession in a variety of ways. See Chapter 5, "Women and Men as Litigators," in *Gender Trials* (Pierce 1995).

References

American Bar Association (1982). *Model code of professional responsibility and code of judicial conduct*. Chicago: National Center for Professional Responsibility and ABA.

Benjamin, J. (1988). *The bonds of love: Psychoanalysis, feminism and the problem of domination*. New York: Pantheon.

Berg, D. (1987). Cross-examination. *Litigation: Journal of the Section of Litigation, American Bar Association, 14*(1), 25–30.

Blinder, M. (1978). Picking juries. *Trial Diplomacy, 1*(1), 8–13.

Blumberg, A. (1967). The practice of law as confidence game: Organizational co-optation of a profession. *Law and Society Review, 1*(2), 15–39.

Brazil, W. (1978). The attorney as victim: Toward more candor about the psychological price tag of litigation practice. *Journal of the Legal Profession, 3*, 107–117.

Buchan, J. (1939). The judicial temperament. In J. Buchan, *Homilies and recreations* (3rd ed.). London: Hodder & Stoughton.

Burawoy, M. (1979). *Manufacturing consent*. Chicago: University of Chicago Press.

Carlin, J. (1962). *Lawyers on their own*. New Brunswick, NJ: Rutgers University Press.

Cartwright, R. (1977, June). Jury selection. *Trial, 28*, 13.

Cheatham, E. (1955). *Cases and materials on the legal profession* (2nd ed.). Brooklyn, NY: Foundation.

Chodorow, N. (1978). *The reproduction of mothering: Psychoanalysis and the sociology of gender*. Berkeley & Los Angeles: University of California Press.

Connell, R. W. (1987). *Gender and power: Society, the person and sexual politics*. Palo Alto, CA: Stanford University Press.

Dombroff, M. (1989, September 25). Winning is everything! *National Law Journal*, p. 13, col. 1.

Fineman, S. (Ed.). (1993). *Emotions in organizations*. Newbury Park, CA: Sage.

Garfinkel, H. (1956). Conditions of successful degradation ceremonies. *American Journal of Sociology, 61*(11), 420–424.

Goldberg, D. (1987, July 1). Playing hardball. *American Bar Association Journal*, p. 48.

Hochschild, A. (1983). *The managed heart: Commercialization of human feeling*. Berkeley & Los Angeles: University of California Press.

Johnstone, Q., & Hopson, D., Jr. (1967). *Lawyers and their work*. Indianapolis, IN: Bobbs-Merrill.

Leidner, R. (1993). *Fast food, fast talk: Service work and the routinization of everyday life*. Berkeley: University of California Press.

Luban, D. (1988). *Lawyers and justice: An ethical study*. Princeton, NJ: Princeton University Press.

Lyman, P. (1987). The fraternal bond as a joking relationship: A case study of sexist jokes in male group bonding. In M. Kimmel (Ed.), *Changing men: New directions in research on men and masculinity* (pp. 148–163). Newbury Park, CA: Sage.

Margolick, D. (1988, August 5). At the bar: Rambos invade the courtroom. *New York Times*, p. B5.

Mauet, T. (1980). *Fundamentals of trial techniques*. Boston: Little, Brown.

Menkel-Meadow, C. (1985, Fall). Portia in a different voice: Speculations on a women's lawyering process. *Berkeley Women's Law Review*, pp. 39–63.

Messner, M. (1989). Masculinities and athletic careers. *Gender & Society, 3*(1), 71–88.

Milkman, R. (1987). *Gender at work*. Bloomington: University of Indiana Press.

Miner, R. (1988, December 19). Lawyers owe one another. *National Law Journal*, pp. 13–14.

Nelson, R. (1988). *Partners with power*. Berkeley & Los Angeles: University of California Press.

Perlman, P. (1988). Jury selection. *The Docket: Newsletter of the National Institute for Trial Advocacy, 12*(2), 1.

Pierce, J. L. (1995). *Gender trials: Emotional lives in contemporary law firms*. Berkeley & Los Angeles: University of California Press.

Rhode, D. (1988). Perspectives on professional women. *Stanford Law Review, 40*, 1163–1207.

Rice, S. (1989, May 24). Two organizations provide training, in-house or out. *San Francisco Banner*, p. 6.

Ring, L. (1983, July). Voir dire: Some thoughtful notes on the selection process. *Trial, 19*, 72–75.

Ring, L. (1987). Cross-examining the sympathetic witness. *Litigation: Journal of the Section of Litigation, American Bar Association, 14*(1), 35–39.

Rollins, J. (1985). *Between women: Domestics and their employers*. Philadelphia: Temple University Press.

Rosenberg, J., Perlstadt, H., & Phillips, W. (1993). Now that we are here: Discrimination, disparagement and harassment at work and the experience of women lawyers. *Gender & Society, 7*(3), 415–433.

Sayler, R. (1988, March 1). Rambo litigation: Why hardball tactics don't work. *American Bar Association Journal*, p. 79.

Smigel, E. (1969). *The Wall Street lawyer: Professional or organizational man?* (2nd ed.). New York: Free Press.

Spangler, E. (1986). *Lawyers for hire: Salaried professionals at work*. New Haven: Yale University Press.

Spence, G. (1988). *With justice for none*. New York: Times Books.

Turow, S. (1987). Crossing the star. *Litigation: Journal of the Section of Litigation, American Bar Association, 14*(1), 40–42.

Wellman, F. (1986). *The art of cross-examination: With the cross-examinations of important witnesses in some celebrated cases* (4th ed.). New York: Collier. (Original work published 1903).

West, C., & Zimmerman, D. (1987). Doing gender. *Gender & Society, 1*(2), 125–151.

What America really thinks about lawyers. (1986, October). *National Law Journal*, p. 1.

Willis, P. (1977). *Learning to labor*. Farnborough, UK: Saxon House.

ARTICLE 21

Timothy Nonn

Hitting Bottom: Homelessness, Poverty, and Masculinity

In the dangerous and impoverished Tenderloin district of San Francisco live the men we consider failures. Urban deterioration and public neglect has created a "dumping-ground for unwanted individuals" (North of Market Planning Coalition 1992: 4). Low rents attract immigrants, welfare recipients, and low-income workers. The population is about 40 percent white, one-third Asian American, and one-tenth black and Latino, respectively. There are severe problems with homelessness, AIDS, violence, substance abuse, and unemployment.

In studies of men, poor men are rarely the object of research.[1] This article examines the coping mechanisms poor men develop to resolve their status as "failed men": First, to overcome stigmatization and regain self-worth, Tenderloin men develop "counter-masculinities" within distinct groups; second, some men develop new values in response to a multiplicity of masculinities that allow them to transcend separate groups and identify with the Tenderloin community.

Using a snowball sample, twenty men were interviewed during a six-month period, including twelve whites, six blacks, and two Latinos; twelve were heterosexual, and eight were homosexual. Their ages ranged from twenty-nine to fifty-four; the majority had a high-school education. Many had been homeless, but most were now living in single-room occupancy hotels. Twelve were single, seven were divorced or separated, and one was married. Several have left children behind. Their interactions with women at the time of the interview were very limited. Few had contact with families or had long-term relationships with women.

Each interview lasted about two hours and included a questionnaire that examined attitudes about gender, race, and sexuality. In the study, I examined how Tenderloin men, as groups, interacted with other men.

Failed Men

A discussion of failure among men must begin with hegemonic masculinity. R. W. Connell writes:

> Hegemonic masculinity is constructed in relation to women and to subordinated masculinities. These other masculinities need not be as clearly defined—indeed, achieving hegemony may consist precisely in preventing alternatives gaining cultural definition and recognition as alternatives, confining them to ghettos, to privacy, to unconsciousness. (Connell 1987: 186)

Connell defines hegemonic masculinity as men's dominance over women. While individuals may change, men's collective power remains embedded in social and cultural institutions. Michael Messner interprets change among white, middle-class men as a matter of personal life-style rather than a restructuring of power and politics (Messner 1993).

Hegemonic masculinity is the standard by which Tenderloin men are judged. The media refers to them as "thugs and bums."[2] Forced to live amidst poverty, drugs, and violence, they are stripped of or denied access to a masculine identity constructed around the role of "the good

Reprinted with permission of the author.

provider" (see Bernard 1995). As white heterosexuals, they are stripped of an identity associated with privilege and power. As gays or men of color, they are denied access to a masculine ideal associated with heterosexual whites. George, a divorced black Vietnam veteran, says:

> Now, we're talking about that segment of the male population that have been taught some of the same things that all men are taught. So they were straight-up abject failures.[3]

Tenderloin men sometimes refer to each other as "invisible." George describes a homeless man's life:

> I call it the "invisible-man syndrome." That's what you become. Most homeless, but not all, self-medicate. It's that thing that you can turn to when you're suffering. You feel disenfranchised from society. You feel less than human. It tells him—in between those periods where he has some lucidity, in between drug or alcohol bouts—that he is a total failure.

Allan, a forty-six-year-old heterosexual white man, recounts the experience of trying to cash a small check:

> [I went] into the bank to cash a two-dollar check and had to deal with people's feedback. I just want to be invisible. I'm real embarrassed about that. About my economic status. . . . When I was stripped of all those material things that I was taught were the measure of success, and everybody rejected me—even though as a person I hadn't changed—I saw the sort of shallowness. It was very painful and very hard.[4]

Tenderloin men face a lonely end. Before death—having been stripped of everything that qualifies a man for full participation in society—there is the shame of surviving as less than a man. Tenderloin men belong to a "shamed group" (Goffman 1963: 23). David, a heterosexual black homeless man, describes their daily struggle:

> The thing that really hurts and holds people down is when they give completely up. When you give completely up that means you take your energy and give it to drugs or alcohol. . . .
> Some homeless men have lost their self-esteem. They have been down for so long. And the system has played this game of chess with them for so long. They've just said, "Oh, forget it." They say, "We'll sell drugs. So if I go to jail, I still have a home." So it don't make any difference. They feel rejected.[5]

Tenderloin men feel trapped in the role of failure.[6] Many hang out day and night on streets "drinking and drugging," talking and begging. The ubiquitous drug trade, routine violence, and crushing poverty combine to form an atmosphere of continual dread and hopelessness within the neighborhood. The men wait in line for hours at churches to receive food, clothing, and lodging. Because it is equally painful to be seen as to be invisible, they are silent and avoid eye contact. They spend a lot of time waiting. The wait transforms them. They dress in a similar ragged way. They walk and talk in a dispirited way. Their faces have the same blank stare or menacing hardness. Some turn into predators in search of victims.[7] Others turn into victims in search of sympathy. George says:

> Your antenna is up for people feeling sorry for you. Part of you becomes a predator. The predator part wants to take advantage. So you can get resources to continue your downward spiral to total destruction. The other part of you feels ashamed because you have violated every man-code that you were ever taught. So you're stuck on stupid. You get to a point where you don't know what to do. You don't give a shit no more about how you're perceived. You can walk down the street smelling like a billy goat. Stuff hanging all over you. You haven't had access to basic hygiene in days and sometimes weeks. You don't care. And the looks don't bother you anymore because you ain't nobody. The productive citizens have that way of not looking at you anyway because you're the invisible man.

The invisibility of Tenderloin men is part of "a pervasive two-role social process" in which failure and success are interrelated (Goffman 1963: 138). They are stigmatized merely by living in an area decimated by poverty, sex and drug markets, and high levels of crime and violence. William Julius Wilson calls them "the permanent underclass" (Wilson 1987: 7). Samuel, a forty-year-old homosexual black man, describes their plight more poignantly: "You're always going to need a place where the lonely souls can go."[8]

Trapped at the bottom of society and stigmatized as failures, Tenderloin men have limited opportunities to claim an identity that fosters self-worth. Charles, a fifty-year-old white gay man, says: "Once you go in there, it's like being an untouchable. You're stigmatized as being this type of sleazy person that does dope and needles, and the whole thing."[9] After a man is stripped of or denied access to symbols of masculinity that confer power and privilege—job, car, home, and family—life becomes a series of challenges to his existence. Some escape the Tenderloin by getting clean, finding work, and moving out. Others descend further into self-destructive behavior and die. Those who remain must adapt to the Tenderloin.

Counter-Masculinities

Counter-masculinities—developed in response to hegemonic masculinity—are coping mechanisms that provide Tenderloin men with a sense of self-worth.[10] A typology of counter-masculinities was found among three groups of Tenderloin men: heterosexual whites, heterosexual blacks and Latinos, and homosexual blacks and whites.

Heterosexual White Men: Urban Hermits

Heterosexual whites are the only men that do not identify with their own group. In the introduction to this book, Michael Kimmel writes that white men see themselves as "the generic person" because "the mechanisms that afford us privilege are very often invisible to us." To escape from the stigma of failure, the "urban hermit" structures identify around the value of self-sufficiency. Power is interpreted as individual achievement. Oscar, a fifty-year-old divorced heterosexual white man, describes a sense of failure:

> It's a difficult struggle. But you can't blame anybody but yourself. Because it is you yourself. Like with me. It's me myself that has the illness. Not the people of the government. Not the people of the different businesses. And things like that. It's me.[11]

Although receiving disability benefits, Oscar views himself as self-sufficient and criticizes blacks on welfare for lacking motivation. Men of color similarly criticize whites. Ned, a forty-year-old single heterosexual black man, says:

> I feel that most of them have given up. They don't really care or try. I try to respect all men. But it's difficult to understand why a white man would give up on himself given a society that is made for them.[12]

Virtually all heterosexual white men interpret their present hardship as the result of personal failure. Richard Sennett and Jonathan Cobb argue that the "code of respect" in American society demands that "a man should feel responsibility for his own social position—even if, in a class society, he believes men in general are deprived of the freedom to control their lives." Failure is defined according to cultural values in which a man is expected to have the desire and opportunity to work (Sennett and Cobb 1972: 36).

Urban hermits spend most of their time alone in hotel rooms. Many frequent bars and restaurants where they complain that criminals have "taken over" the area and demand that police "clean up the streets."[13] Unable to reconcile belief in white male superiority and life among the disenfranchised, most believe society is falling apart. Frank, a single heterosexual white man, describes whites:

> Their spirits are broken. They're outcasts of their families from all over the country. They're in disarray. They're drifting. Some of them never came back from Vietnam. Some of them are screwed up on drugs. It seems to me that America isn't like it used to be. When I grew up it was changing . . . it was breaking apart. My family broke apart, anyway. It was hard on me. They're outcasts from all over the country, and they gravitate here.[14]

Heterosexual white men experience a high level of cultural shock in moving to the Tenderloin.[15] A walk to the store is a challenge to their self-esteem. They confront black and Latino men who threaten their sense of racial superiority and gays who threaten their sexual identity. Oscar believes gays challenge divine law. He says:

> God decided he wanted a man to look like a man and a woman to look like a woman. It's not his fault if some men act like women and women act like men. It's the fault of the people themselves. The people can go without acting that way if they don't want to and they can act that way if they want to. It's up to them.[16]

Heterosexual whites are confused and angry because others appear to violate social norms. Most retreat into isolation. A few imitate other men's behavior. Brad, a twenty-nine-year-old single, heterosexual white man, admires the "sense of family" among Latinos.[17] Many appreciate the nurturing qualities of gays. But other men criticize whites for not knowing themselves. Miguel, a divorced fifty-year-old heterosexual Latino man, says:

> The white man tries too hard to make friends. ... If you're going to come in here and start trying to be black, they see that already. You're not! But here's a guy and he's trying to talk like us and be cool. It's a front. We know that. Hey, come on. I mean I've studied white folks before, and I know that's not the way white people are supposed to be.[18]

Wanting to belong, and forced to confront their prejudices, heterosexual whites discover that genuineness is vital. But it is difficult for them to adapt. Quinn, a fifty-four-year-old gay white man, says whites are aloof because: "White is right. White isn't going to be criticized. White isn't going to be stopped by police."[19]

The counter-masculinity of the urban hermit discloses an inability to cope with diversity of race, culture, and sexual orientation. As a coping mechanism, it resists the stigma of failure but undermines identity by organizing social relations around poles of independence and dependence. In the Tenderloin, interdependence is both a reality and a necessity. What heterosexual whites view as self-sufficiency, others view as arrogance. Because the urban hermit is seen as an outcast among outcasts, failure and alienation are not overcome through self-sufficiency.

Heterosexual Black and Latino Men: Cool Pose

Heterosexual blacks and Latinos dominate street life and display what Majors and Billson (1992) call "cool pose." Cool pose is a counter-masculinity that structures identity around the value of respect. Power is interpreted as group solidarity in a racist society. Blacks and Latinos establish social position by displaying aggressiveness or showing deference (Almaguer 1991: 80). Miguel claims the system of respect maintains harmony: "You don't have to trust someone. You just respect them." George uses a hypermasculine facade to obtain respect and to fend off predators. He says:

> One of the techniques you use—and this is a prison technique—is getting big. You work out hard. You carry yourself in an intimidating manner. Your body language says, "I'll kill you if you even think about approaching my space."

The mask of hypermasculinity establishes a man's position in his group.[20] Miguel describes putting on his mask:

> Whenever I walk, I look mean. I make my face look like I got an attitude. Like I just got ripped off. I don't look at the person. I look through them. I'm cutting him. And this guy's thinking, "Hmmm. Let me move out of the way." You could get busted. "Oh, you ain't that tough." But out there you gotta act that way.

"Getting busted" means that someone is able to see through a man's mask. Whites have difficulty distinguishing between actual threats and posturing by blacks and Latinos, and often feel threatened. But Jack, a heterosexual black man, explains that cool pose conceals a sense of failure among men of color living in a white-dominated society:

The one thing I hear from white guys is, "You guys act like you're so proud." They don't realize why we're doing it. It's to survive amongst our own peers. We feel just as bad as he does. The white guy resents that; "How in the hell can he act like that and I'm white? I come from the superior race and I can't act like that. I feel dead." They come from two different worlds.[21]

Ned interprets cool pose in relation to a definition of masculinity that excludes black men in American society:

A black man has to be tough out there on the street. The reason they have to be that way is that they don't have any other outlet for their manhood. They can't show their manhood by being a success economically because society simply will not give them a chance. I mean a black man is even lucky to have a full-time—or even a part-time—job. So he has to show his manhood by acting physically tough. Because mentally tough won't get him anywhere. But there has been no reason that white men have had to be physically tough because they've been able to show their manhood through their nine-to-five. Going to work every day. And making a living.

Cool pose is depicted as "a creative strategy devised by African-American males to counter the negative forces in their lives" (Majors and Billson 1992: 105). Yet, the counter-masculinity of cool pose does not allow heterosexual black and Latino men to escape from failure by structuring identity around the value of respect. While the coping mechanism of cool pose weakens the stigma of failure, it undermines identity by organizing social relations around poles of dominance and submission. What heterosexual men of color view as respect, others view as hostility. By adopting an identity based upon fear and violence, men of color in the Tenderloin in part contribute to their own alienation from other groups and society at large. They are further marginalized in an environment where different social groups demand to live in equality with one another.

Homosexual Black and White Men: Perfect Copy

Gays in the Tenderloin blur gender and sexual boundaries by constructing identity around performance of a series of roles. "Perfect copy" of hypermasculinity redefines and subverts masculinity (Butler 1990: 31). Klaus, a thirty-four-year-old gay white man, interprets his experience with heterosexual men in the Tenderloin:

They feel like their manhood or sexuality has been threatened because I'm more butch than they are. I am more of a man than a straight man can be around here. They're threatened. Not only to me but to themselves.[22]

Gays structure identity around the value of acceptance. Power is interpreted as inclusion of persons who challenge gender and sexual categories. Because identity is in flux, and gender and sexual identity are rendered uncertain, "homosexuality undermines masculinity" (Edwards 1990: 114). Larry, a thirty-three-year-old gay white man, says heterosexuals are simultaneously confused and intrigued by gays:

I think [they] are very jealous of gay men because we're so open and free with our feelings. We speak what we have to say. We don't hide our feelings. We cry at sad movies. Heterosexual men think that men don't cry. But if you go drinking with them, get them drunk or high, they're the first ones that throw their legs in the air or whip out their cocks in front of you and say, "Here. Suck this."[23]

Another gay man believes single heterosexuals are in a predicament because they normally rely on women to provide them with gender identity. Charles says:

Most men depend on women to define that role for them. So a man is what a woman defines him to be. So if you don't have a woman in your life to define you as a man, then you have to depend on all these macho apparatuses. Then you have to prove to other men that you are a man.

Transgenders pose a new challenge by further blurring gender and sexual boundaries. Thomas, a twenty-nine-year-old gay black man, says some men respond favorably:

> It seems to be a turn-on. Especially if everything is in order—the appearance is almost perfect. Woman have a lot to do just getting dressed in the morning. Hair, makeup, clothing, shoes. Everything has to be just right. It's not like men. We can just put on a pair of jeans and a T-shirt. And out the door. I've noticed this especially with straight men. They seem to be really impressed.[24]

Identity is a series of roles that gays perfect in daily encounters. Transgenders further complicate identity when "some transgendered persons consider themselves heterosexual, while others consider themselves homosexual" (Koenig 1993: 10). The counter-masculinity of perfect copy challenges hegemonic masculinity through a multitude of replicated masculinities that blur sexual and gender boundaries. Performance of a series of roles creates security in a homophobic society by destabilizing and redefining social relations. But perfect copy of hypermasculine (or hyperfeminine) roles implies a reliance upon hegemonic masculine ideals. While the coping mechanism of perfect copy resists the stigma of failure, it undermines identity by organizing social relations around poles of performance and observation. Perfect copy contributes to further alienation of gays, because what they view as acceptance, others view as licentiousness.

Counter-masculinities are coping mechanisms that aid Tenderloin men in regaining a sense of self-worth while preventing them from overcoming alienation from other groups of men. For Tenderloin men, masculine identity develops around specific value systems in response to the social system of hegemonic masculinity and an immediately hostile environment (Tong 1971: 8). Paradoxically, counter-masculinities offer resistance to hegemonic masculinity while deepening social divisions. Since the contradictions of counter-masculinities stem from inequitable relations of power, what unites men as a group separates them as a community. The urban hermit devalues interdependence in favor of self-sufficiency; cool pose devalues equality in favor of dominance; and perfect copy devalues mutuality in favor of performance. A new value system constructed around shared power is required to unite Tenderloin men into a community.

Versatile Masculinity

Versatile masculinity is a unique masculine identity that emerges from everyday encounters of Tenderloin men as they collectively resolve the contradictions of counter-masculinities. Versatile masculinity allows men to identify with a transcendent set of values without destroying their group identity or value systems. This new set of values—while not distinctively masculine—is the basis of a masculine identity that binds Tenderloin men together in genuine community.

Versatile masculinity is not a fixed identity but a growing capacity for relating to difference.[25] As a fluid construction that sorts and combines practices, values, and attitudes in a strategic movement, it enables men to flourish in a diverse and dynamic environment. Most important, it is not a way of being but a way of becoming in relationships. David calls it being "flexible":

> So many people [were] raised a certain way, and it stays with them. That's the only way they know. Instead of looking over the whole situation and see this and that. That's the way you have to live. Especially if you're living homeless on the streets. You have to be able to be flexible. Maybe this guy does things a different way. Maybe I can help him do this and he can help me do that. That's where you have to come in and learn it. That's what certain people call "streetwise." Streetwise people are just movable. They're just flexible.

Versatile masculinity does not undermine the different values of Tenderloin men but relates them to a transcendent set of values: honesty, caring, interdependence, and respect. H. Richard

Niebuhr writes that ultimate value is not identifiable with a particular mode of being but "is present whenever being confronts being, wherever there is becoming in the midst of plural, interdependent, and interacting existences. It is not a function of being as such but of being in relation to being" (Niebuhr 1970: 106–107).

Similarly, versatile masculinity creates unity from diversity. Jack believes that acceptance of difference is essential to survival:

> All people are equal. All things are relative. If you exterminate Jews, you exterminate me and you. . . . They're all of our cultures, are relative to keep us together. If I'm not afraid to learn about your culture then I got something to learn. Something that is relative. If everybody was alike, we'd be in trouble. We'd be in real trouble.

As marginalized persons, Tenderloin men are innovative survivors who manifest "creative strategies for survival that then open up new possibilities for everyone" (Duberman 1993: 24). But their experience reveals that only after a man has reached bottom—after he is stripped of or denied access to a masculine identity that provides him with a sense of innate superiority—will he change. Quinn says:

> You bottom out. And you go through the bottom of the barrel and you come up again. You learn a different type of survival skills. . . . But going from the bottom and coming through you run into criminals, junkies, crazies, and everything else. . . . It doesn't make you less of a person. Actually, it can make you a stronger person. And more sensitive.

Versatile masculinity includes three conditions: (1) A man must be stripped of or denied access to a hegemonic masculine identity; (2) a man must adopt a counter-masculinity to reconstruct his identity and resist hegemonic masculine values that stigmatize him as a failure; and (3) a man must experience a multiplicity of masculinities that compel him to develop an identity based on acceptance of difference. When these conditions exist, versatile masculinity drives men to overcome their differences and create a community based on the following values.

Honesty

For Tenderloin men, honesty means genuineness. It is a process of "coming to critical consciousness" (hooks 1990: 191). Tenderloin men sometimes discard illusions that contribute to lack of self-esteem. Hank, a thirty-six-year-old divorced, heterosexual white man, says:

> I realized that the only way I was going to get clean and sober, and really become a disciple of Christ, was to clean up my act. To become truly honest. Beginning with admitting to myself that I was full of shit. That I was living a lie. Just a lie.[26]

Brad says:

> I feel like if you're genuine with people there's some recognition within them. Or they see something. I know it's happened to me when I just met somebody who is for real and I've been acting like a fool or not being true to myself. It kind of makes me go, "Oh!" and "Yeah!"

In the Tenderloin, because men use every imaginable act to hide from themselves and society, they can easily recognize genuineness. Quinn says: "An honest person is going to recognize another honest person and see a phony."

Caring

Many Tenderloin men have HIV/AIDS. Samuel, who is beginning to display symptoms, has given himself a final task before he dies. He says:

> I'm having a big struggle with a transvestite named Carol who rips me off every second she has a chance to. I keep going back to her. And I tell her, "You got me, girl. But you didn't really have to do that. If you wanted it, just ask me for it. I'll give it to you. And if not, then you can rip me off." She's turned out to be one of my best friends. It's all she's ever known in her life. She's always lived in the ghetto. This is my personal struggle. My personal fight is to just take that one person and make her realize that she doesn't have to keep two steps ahead of me

in order to get what's mine. Because it's all materialistic. If what I have you need, you can have it. All you have to do is just ask for it.

Poverty, ostracism, and illness have brought men together to provide and receive care from one another. Allan describes his life at one of the worst slum hotels in the Tenderloin:

> At the Victoria, people will come in who are very different from one another, and sit down and talk and joke with one another. I don't think you could say that those interactions are insincere, or [occur] simply because they're close together. They like each other. They've discovered that we're all human beings with the same needs and very interesting differences. It's an acknowledgment that they're worthwhile. The kinds of sharing of people who don't have a lot to give is striking.

The work of caring is rare among men in our society, because compassion is a value identified with women. For Tenderloin men, caring for one another is tremendously empowering.

Interdependence

Men forced to live at the bottom of society feel insignificant and powerless. A common phrase heard on the streets is "the small people." Masculinity is redefined as an identity based on interdependence. Thomas says:

> Here you kind of like take care of your own. You kind of have to take care of each other here just so everybody survives. If one person doesn't survive, there's a big effect on everybody.

Respect

The most important lesson that Tenderloin men learn is respect for the intrinsic worth of each person. Masculinity includes an identification with humanity rather than only with one's group. This process (especially for heterosexual whites) begins with a period of cultural shock. Eduardo, a thirty-three-year-old single, heterosexual Latino man, says new residents overcome fear when they "start standing in the soup lines and staying in hotels. You realize that the homeless are not unlike you or I. They're human. You become part of the community."[27] Larry—who once worked as a male prostitute in the Tenderloin—believes faith overcomes barriers between people. He says:

> Mary Magdalene was a prostitute. There are many women and men in this city that are prostitutes. There's nothing wrong with that. They're human beings first. Their titles come afterward. We weren't born what we are today. We were born human beings first. Then we were educated and trained to become who we are. But before we are what we are, we're humans first. A lot of people have lost that track. Lost that faith. To see what the hell we were or where we came from.

George says we all are faced with a choice:

> Basically, they are human beings. The one thing that we have been given is the ability to make choices. That's what separates us from other animals. Outside forces may have an effect, and usually do have an effect, on the choices we have to make. But the fact is, we get to make those choices. So make those choices as a winner—not so much as a winner—but as a human being.

Summary

Tenderloin men construct new masculine identities to resist a sense of failure and to create a sense of belonging. Versatile masculinity develops from their need to safely coexist in a hostile environment, but it also provides a basis for shared power and love in relationships. The Tenderloin men who transform themselves from "failed men" into human beings display a capacity not merely to survive, but also to flourish in a context of adversity and diversity. This is aptly demonstrated by the tenants of a Tenderloin residential hotel—many of whom were once homeless and substance abusers—who have built a beautiful rooftop garden. A resident says it's "a little bit of magic in the Tenderloin." Another is happy to see "a new spirit in this neighborhood" (Maitland 1993). In the Tenderloin, a small space has gradually emerged where men are free to change.

Notes

1. There are several noteworthy works that examine the lives of poor and working-class men. See Eugene V. Debs, *Walls and Bars* (Chicago: Charles H. Kerr and Company, 1973); George Orwell, *Down and Out in Paris and London* (New York: Berkeley Medallion, 1959); James Agee and Walker Evans, *Let Us Now Praise Famous Men* (Boston: Houghton Mifflin Company, 1939); Studs Terkel, *Hard Times: An Oral History of the Great Depression* (New York: Washington Square Press, 1970); Elliot Liebow, *Tally's Corner* (Boston: Little, Brown and Company, 1967); William Julius Wilson, *The Truly Disadvantaged: The Inner City, the Underclass, and Public Policy* (Chicago: University of Chicago Press, 1987); Lillian Rubin, *Worlds of Pain: Life in the Working-Class Family* (New York: Basic Books, 1976); Richard Sennet and Jonathan Cobb, *The Hidden Injuries of Class* (New York: Vintage Books, 1972).

2. Local newspapers regularly describe Tenderloin residents in derogatory terms. See "Cheap wine ban sought in Tenderloin," *San Francisco Chronicle*, 5 April 1989; "Group wants Tenderloin as family neighborhood," *San Francisco Chronicle*, 21 July 1992; "Community policing," *San Francisco Chronicle*, 20 November 1992.

3. Interview with George on 30 April 1993. All names are fictitious.

4. Interview with Allan on 22 June 1993.

5. Interview with David on 1 May 1993.

6. Interview with Peter, a recently married, forty-eight-year-old heterosexual white man, on 27 July 1993.

7. The term "predator" is commonly used to refer to persons (often drug users) who prey on the more vulnerable sectors of the Tenderloin neighborhood, such as the elderly, children, and tourists.

8. Interview with Samuel on 26 August 1993.

9. Interview with Charles on 28 July 1993.

10. Thomas J. Gershick and Adam S. Miller (1994: 5) similarly interpret masculinities of disabled men as coping mechanisms that rely upon, reformulate, or reject the standard of hegemonic masculinity.

11. Interview with Oscar on 19 June 1993.

12. Interview with Ned on 26 July 1993.

13. Interviews with Oscar on 24 April and 19 June 1993.

14. Interview with Frank on 13 August 1993.

15. Bruno Bettelheim (1960: 120) reports that of Jews sent to Nazi concentration camps, middle-class German men experienced the greatest level of initial shock and were the least adaptable prisoners.

16. Interview with Oscar on 19 June 1993.

17. Interview with Brad on 28 July 1993.

18. Interview with Miguel on 23 July 1993.

19. Interview with Quinn on 29 July 1993.

20. Pleck (1987: 31) defines "hypermasculinity" as exaggerated, extreme masculine behavior.

21. Interview with Jack on 23 April 1993.

22. Interview with Klaus on 13 March 1993.

23. Interview with Larry on 16 July 1993.

24. Interview with Thomas on 28 August 1993.

25. Versatility is defined as "the faculty or character of turning or being able to turn readily to a new subject or occupation," or "many-sidedness." In *The Compact Edition of the Oxford English Dictionary* 1971, Oxford University Press.

26. Interview with Hank on 31 July 1993.

27. Interview with Eduardo on 14 May 1993.

References

Almaguer, Tomas. 1991. "Chicano Men: A Cartography of Homosexual Identity and Behavior." *Differences* 3(2).

Bernard, Jessie. 1995. "The Good-Provider Role." In Michael S. Kimmel and Michael A. Messner, eds., *Men's Lives*. New York: Macmillan.

Bettelheim, Bruno. 1960. *The Informed Heart: Autonomy in a Mass Age*. New York: The Free Press.

Butler, Judith. 1990. *Gender Trouble: Feminism and the Subversion of Identity*. New York: Routledge & Kegan Paul.

Connell, R. W. 1987. *Gender and Power*. Palo Alto, CA: Stanford University Press.

Duberman, Martin. 1993. "A Matter of Difference." *Nation*, 5 July.

Edwards, Tim. 1990. "Beyond Sex and Gender: Masculinity, Homosexuality and Social Theory." In Jeff Hearn and David Morgan, eds., *Men, Masculinities, and Social Theory*. London: Unwin Hyman.

Gershick, Thomas J., and Adam S. Miller. 1994. "Coming to Terms: Masculinity and Physical Disability." In M. Kimmel and M. Messner, eds., *Men's Lives*, 3rd edition. Boston: Allyn and Bacon.

Goffman, Erving. 1963. *Stigma: Notes on the Management of Spoiled Identity*. New York: Touchstone.

hooks, bell. 1990. "Feminism: A Transformational Politic." In Deborah L. Rhode, ed., *Theoretical Perspectives on Sexual Difference*. New Haven: Yale University Press.

Koenig, Karen. 1993. "Transgenders Unite to Fight for Justice and Recognition." *Tenderloin Times*, August.

Maitland, Zane. 1993. "Tenderloin Hotel Has a Rooftop Garden." *San Francisco Chronicle*, 23 July.

Majors, Richard, and Janet Mancini Billson. 1992. *Cool Pose: The Dilemmas of Black Manhood in America*. New York: Lexington Books.

Messner, Michael A. 1993. " 'Changing Men' and Feminist Politics in the United States." *Theory and Society*, August/September.

Niebuhr, H. Richard. 1970. *Radical Monotheism and Western Culture*. New York: Harper Torchbooks.

North of Market Planning Coalition (NOPC). 1992. *Final Report: Tenderloin 2000 Survey and Plan*. San Francisco: NOPC.

Pleck, Joseph H. 1987. "The Theory of Male Sex-Role Identity: Its Rise and Fall, 1936 to the Present." In Harry Brod, ed., *The Making of Masculinities: The New Men's Studies*. New York: Routledge & Kegan Paul.

Sennett, Richard, and Jonathan Cobb. 1972. *The Hidden Injuries of Class*. New York: Vintage Books.

Tong, Ben. 1971. "The Ghetto of the Mind: Notes on the Historical Psychology of Chinese America." *Amerasia Journal*, 1(3). November.

Wilson, William Julius. 1987. *The Truly Disadvantaged: The Inner City, the Underclass, and Public Policy*. Chicago: University of Chicago Press.

ARTICLE 22

Marianne Cooper

Being the "Go-To Guy": Fatherhood, Masculinity, and the Organization of Work in Silicon Valley

Introduction

Driving down a busy freeway into the heart of Silicon Valley, one sees billboards everywhere heralding the arrival of the new economy. Ads for e-tailing, high-speed Internet connections, and dot.com job openings permeate the skyline. Even a sign for *Forbes* magazine announces "high octane capitalism ahead." While it is undeniable that the new economy is here, it is also undeniable that this is largely a male endeavor. A recent report by the American Association of University Women (2000) found that women make up only about 20 percent of information technology professionals and that they receive less than 28 percent of the computer science bachelor's degrees. In fact, Silicon Valley itself is often referred to as the "Valley of the Boys," an appropriate adage now that San Jose boasts the highest number of available single men in the country, surpassing Alaska (Conlin 2000).

It is within this male-dominated, turbo-capitalism environment that the fathers I interviewed negotiate their work and family lives. The intent of my study was to explore the mostly ignored experiences of working fathers. What I discovered through my examination of these men's work and family lives was the emergence of a newly constituted masculinity that coincides with the new way work is organized in the new economy. Two questions addressing both sides of the work–family equation flowed from this discovery: How does this new masculinity articulate with processes of labor control? And, how does it articulate with processes of family life, particularly fathering? Thus, my findings are twofold. First, they show that as a gendered construct, this new masculinity functions as a key mechanism of control in high-tech workplaces that rely on identity-based forms of control. Second, they show that the successful enactment of this new masculinity shapes how these fathers both think about and manage their work and family lives.

Methods

Many researchers report difficulty in recruiting men to participate in studies of this kind (Daly 1992). However, men eagerly responded to my interview request. I obtained a sample of twenty fathers through various methods. Through friends and acquaintances I sent out an e-mail message requesting one-hour interviews with fathers working in high-tech companies to discuss how they balance work and family life. I also sent the same e-mail message to the parents' list server at one large company and a university. I received over thirty e-mail responses. I ruled out those who were self-employed, since I wanted to get information about workplace culture, interactions with co-workers, etc. I ruled in knowledge workers who seemed to have significant industry experience in a variety of companies as well as those who worked for well-known companies in Silicon Valley. I conducted semi-structured open-ended in-

From *Quantative Sociology* 23(4) 2000, pp. 379–405. Copyright © University of California Press.

terviews with the twenty participants. The interviews took place at cafés, homes, and workplaces and lasted between one and two hours. All interviews were tape-recorded and fully transcribed.

The interviewees work in all different types and sizes of high-tech companies. While some work for large companies that make millions of dollars a year, others work for small start-ups. Thirteen interviewees are software engineers, one is a service engineer, one an engineering project manager, three are in sales/business development/management, and two are computer researchers.

My informants ranged in age from thirty to forty-four; the average age was thirty-seven. Though incomes ranged from $60,000 to $200,000, most were concentrated in the $80,000 to $150,000 range. Except for one informant who was Mexican-American and did not have a bachelor's degree, the rest were white and held college degrees. Three participants had Ph.D.s, two had MBAs, three had master's degrees in computer science, and one had a master's degree in math. All fathers are currently married. Seven of their spouses work full-time, four work part-time, three are students, and six are stay-at-home mothers.

A New Masculinity for the New Economy

In recent years, there has been a growing interest in the definition and practice of masculinity reflected by the emergence of the "New Men's Studies" (Carrigan et al. 1985; Brod and Kaufman 1994; Connell 1995; Mac An Ghaill 1996). Much of this scholarship draws upon R. W. Connell's theory of hegemonic masculinity. For Connell (1995), hegemonic masculinity "is the configuration of gender practices which embodies the currently accepted answer to the problem of legitimacy of patriarchy, which guarantees (or is taken to guarantee) the dominant position of men and the subordination of women" (p. 77). While there is a hegemonic form of masculinity, which in the U.S. could be seen as a rich, good-looking, popular, athletic, white, heterosexual man, masculinity is not unitary or homogeneous. Rather, there are "multiple masculinities," some subordinate and some dominant, which are created by differences in ethnicity, race, class, sexual orientation, age, and occupation (Connell 1987).[1] Even hegemonic forms of masculinity are historically and locally contingent. As Connell (1995) points out, hegemonic masculinity "is not a fixed character type, always and everywhere the same. It is, rather, the masculinity that occupies the hegemonic position in a given pattern of gender relations, a position always contestable" (p. 76).

Given that the form and content of hegemonic masculinity is dependent upon the social and historical context in which it operates, it follows that the Silicon Valley context should shape the particular type of masculinity found in the high tech world of the new economy. Indeed, scholars have already established that technical knowledge and expertise are socially defined as masculine (Turkle 1984, 1988; Cockburn 1988; Hacker 1990) and that within these male domains computing cultures possess a specific masculinity (Wright 1996; Kendall 1999, 2000). For example, Wright (1996) found that the masculinity characteristic of engineering and computer cultures is one "requiring aggressive displays of technical self-confidence and hands-on ability for success, defining professional competence in hegemonically masculine terms and devaluing the gender characteristics of women" (p. 86), and Kendall (2000) found that the masculinity enacted by young male participants in an on-line interactive text-based forum was constructed around a "nerd" identity, characterized by qualities like fascination with technology and real or perceived social ineptitude.

This nerd masculinity, common in the high-tech world, is glorified in depictions of Silicon Valley life. Even the success story of the founders of Silicon Valley is a phenomenon often referred to as "The Revenge of the Nerds." Men who in their youth were marginalized for being geeks and nerds came back as adults to get the last laugh. Using their intellect, they launched a technological revolution and in the process of changing the world became very rich and very powerful.

The consequence of the facts that technology is the foundation of the new economy and that those who participate in it enact a masculinity that diverges from traditional masculinity is the emergence of a newly constituted masculinity in the Valley. Here, technical skill and brilliance are more important than looks and athletic ability. In the Valley, competition isn't waged on the basketball court or by getting girls. Here men compete in cubicles to see who can work more hours, who can cut the best code, and who can be most creative and innovative. As one interviewee put it:

> Guys constantly try to out-macho each other, but in engineering it's really perverted because out-machoing someone means being more of a nerd than the other person. It's really geeky. It's really sad. It's not like being a brave firefighter and going up one more flight than your friend. There's a lot of see how many hours I can work whether or not you have a kid. That's part of the thing, how many hours you work. He's a real man, he works ninety-hour weeks; he's a slacker, he works fifty hours a week. (Scott Webster)

Moreover, high-tech companies are organized in ways that deviate from traditional masculinity. Because it is believed that bureaucratically organized companies stifle creativity and out-of-the-box thinking, typical high-tech companies have a flat hierarchy and a less rigid and austere workplace culture (Kunda 1992; Burris 1998). Furthermore, these companies embrace managerial discourses that champion teamwork, adaptability, open communication, and creativity. These qualities run counter to traditionally masculine practices. Alvesson (1998) makes this point, noting that in knowledge intensive jobs,

> there may be limited space for employment of many of the traditionally used sources of male power and male identity associated with bureaucracy and rationality. New discourses advocated by management theorists as well as by corporate practitioners instead construct work and organizations in terms of creativity, intuition, flexibility, flattened hierarchy, social interaction, and team building, etc. (p. 2).

Thus, the Valley is based upon a masculinity that corresponds with what the technology industry needs to satiate and expand its markets.

Ideological reasons, and in some cases biographical ones as well, also underpin this new masculinity. All of the high-tech workers I spoke with profess an egalitarian gender ideology in regard to women in the work force. They feel it is important for more women to go into the high-tech industry, and many of the fathers I interviewed wished they worked with more women. In fact, in an effort to diversify their teams, several said that they go out of their way to recruit women, extending searches longer than necessary to try to find qualified women candidates.

To be sure, the majority of my sample perceive themselves to be qualitatively different from other men in terms of their more enlightened personal attitudes towards and relationships with women. This self-perception is evident through comparisons the interviewees make between themselves and men who they feel are sexist or stereotypically macho.

> I don't drive a pick-up truck and wear tattoos. I'm very modern. I believe in sharing the household work and believe that my wife's career is important. (Rich Kavelin)

> Communication is something that is important to us. So when something goes wrong, when we have a disagreement or a misunderstanding, my wife feels doubly hurt. Because she thinks, well we put such a value on trying to communicate and it failed. I think it makes it worse than if she were married to Joe Six-Pack. (Jay Masterson)

Many interviewees also separated themselves from frat boys and locker room guys, men who they think are sexist and hostile towards women; that's not what kind of men they are. Unlike stereotypical working-class men who openly degrade women and put them down, these men actually feel virtuous for not being sexist like them or completely ignorant about emotions and relationships like most men. These interviewees think of themselves as "modern," not frat boys; progressive, not stupid jocks.

Biography may also underpin this new masculinity. Though not a focal point of my study, my perception is that as nerds, approximately two-thirds of my sample were victims of traditional hegemonic masculinity in their earlier lives. Accordingly, they may also have personal as well as ideological reasons to oppose a traditionally macho masculinity.

Taken together, type of work, ideology, and, in some cases, biography, work against the form of masculinity that remains dominant in much of society. Nonetheless, there is still a hegemonic masculinity in the new economy, but one that takes on somewhat different characteristics. Though the essence of this masculinity is rooted in technical expertise, its other characteristics involve working a lot of hours and working with a small team of *great* people to get things done. James McNichol and Scott Webster, both software engineers, describe the team dynamic:

> James: It's like a sports team. Not in the sense of locker room, but in the sense that there is just a natural order, and everybody gets their place and you work together. There are lots of models that boys grow up with for how that kind of team works and what you do and don't do. Like not questioning the coach and there's a lot of doing and thinking about it afterwards instead of considering the options beforehand. It's not an articulate culture.
>
> Scott: The key element of this whole environment is the team mentality. It's an idea derived from male tradition probably. Even as a contractor you have to live with it too. You have to be part of the team, you can't fall out. If you get injured, you come back as fast as you can or you play with your injury whether it's emotional or physical.

The successful enactment of this masculinity involves displaying one's exhaustion, physically and verbally, in order to convey the depth of one's commitment, stamina, and virility.

> Engineers have this idea that you are out there and you are building something and these small companies are going to do huge things and lots of people are going to get rich and it's gonna happen because we are great. Even under normal circumstances when there are no extraordinary demands you see people working thirty-six hours straight just because they are going to meet the deadline. They are going to get it done and everybody walks around proud of how exhausted they were last week and conspicuously putting in wild hours. It's a status thing to have pizza delivered to the office. So I don't know why it happens, but I really feel like it is kind of a machismo thing, I'm tough, I can do this thing. Yeah I'm tired but I'm on top of it, you guys don't worry about me, I can get my thing done . . . The people who conspicuously overwork are guys and I think it's usually for the benefit of other guys. (Kirk Sinclair)

Theoretically, the knowledge work these men do is gender-neutral. As opposed to manual work that requires physical strength, knowledge work requires only mental ability. Therefore, either men or women can perform knowledge work. Yet, as Leidner (1993) found and the above quotations illustrate, most jobs can be constructed as either masculine or feminine by emphasizing certain aspects of the job and de-emphasizing and reinterpreting other dimensions. The gendering of jobs that are potentially gender-neutral illustrates how gender is constructed through work, how gendered subjectivities are formed. In this case, masculinity is constructed by imbuing knowledge work with a masculine sensibility that isn't intrinsic to the work. Willis (1977) found a similar trend among working class men.

> Manual labor is suffused with masculine qualities . . . The toughness and awkwardness of physical work and effort—for itself and in the division of labour and for its strictly capitalist logic quite without intrinsic heroism and grandeur—takes on masculine heights and depths and assumes a significance beyond itself. Whatever the specific problems, so to speak, of the difficult task they are always essentially masculine problems. It takes masculine capacities to deal with them . . . The brutality of the working situation is partially re-interpreted into a heroic exercise of manly confrontation with *the task*. Difficult, uncomfortable or dangerous

conditions are seen, not for themselves, but for their appropriateness to a masculine readiness and hardiness (p. 150).

The same male "readiness and hardiness" is both needed and glorified in high-tech knowledge work as well.

> There's a certain glamour to heroic efforts. If you look at a well-managed company that delivers a reliable product on time with no fuss, there's no talk of it. But the release of an important product becomes lore when the engineering team worked for a week solid to get it done. Those kind of amazing efforts are talked about. (Kirk Sinclair)

Remarkably, poor planning is reinterpreted as a test of will, a test of manhood for a team of engineers (men). Sheer determination and strength of character achieve the task, releasing a product on time. Presented with an overwhelming challenge, it takes masculine capabilities to complete the mission, to overcome the odds.

A "masculine mystique" permeates descriptions of what the interviewees do at work (Collinson and Hearn 1996a). It's as if these men are digital warriors, out conquering enemies, surmounting insurmountable odds in their quest to win. The interpretation of this work in such masculine terms points to the "doing of gender" in everyday social interactions. Here, masculinity is performed and achieved by infusing the work with masculine meanings that convey to others one's internal strength, competitive spirit, and ability to get the job done.

Gender and the Labor Process

Not surprisingly, the new masculinity and the workplace practices associated with the achievement of this gendered subjectivity benefit the technology industry. Technical brilliance, innovation, creativity, independent work ethics, long hours, and complete dedication to projects are the main requirements for companies trying to position themselves on the cutting edge. This link between gendered subjectivity and labor process conditions suggests that masculinity may then be a way to control worker's participation in the labor process. Despite the likely link between gender and strategies of control, scholars have noted the absence of research about gender in organizations and about how gender works in the dynamic processes of consent and control (Kanter 1977; Acker 1990; Collinson 1992; Collinson and Hearn 1996b; Mac An Ghaill 1996; Pierce 1996; Alvesson and Billing 1997; Lee 1998).

Ignoring gender, most labor process theorists have instead focused on class-based forms of worker control (Braverman 1974; Edwards 1979; Burawoy 1979, 1985). Lee (1998) addresses this lack of gender analysis and develops a feminist theory of production politics which takes account of the role gender plays in the development of control strategies. Lee's theory argues that "factory regimes are gendered institutions in which gender is a central and primary organizing principle of production politics" (p. 165).[2] Lee draws upon Acker's (1992) definition which states that a gendered institution is one in which "gender is present in the processes, practices, images and ideologies, and distributions of power in the various sectors of social life" (p. 567). In applying feminist theory to the shop floor Lee argues that "production relations rely on gender ideology, organization, and identity, factors that also shape the terms and forms of production politics" (p. 165). Lee's addition of a gendered analysis to a literature focused on class challenges the primacy given to class in labor process accounts. In doing so she refutes Burawoy's claim that labor process activities are "independent of the particular people who come to work, of the particular agents of production" (1979, p. 202).[3]

With labor process scholars looking at how gender works on the shop floor (Collinson 1992; Lee 1998), it would make sense for scholars concerned with identity-based forms of control to also pay attention to gender, a key aspect of an individual's identity. Identity-based forms of control, or what Etzioni (1961) termed normative control, is control which works by laying claim to the worker's sense of self, engendering in them a deep personal commitment to the goals and values of the company. As stated by Kunda (1992):

> ... under normative control, membership is founded not only on the behavioral or economic transaction traditionally associated with work organizations, but, more crucially, on an experiential transaction, one in which symbolic rewards are exchanged for a moral orientation to the organization. In this transaction a member role is fashioned and imposed that includes not only behavioral rules but articulated guidelines for experience. In short, under normative control it is the employee's self—that ineffable source of subjective experience—that is claimed in the name of the corporate interest (p. 11).

Thus, this type of control is a self-surveilling one which monitors work behavior by eliciting thoughts, feelings, and emotions that correspond with the interests of the company. However, research on normative control has not looked through a gendered lens (Edwards 1979; Kunda 1992). Instead, it has focused on mechanisms through which organizations attain identity-based consent, like strong workplace cultures, and on the characteristics of the organizational identity without discussing what the gender, racial, or class dimensions of this identity might be.

Kunda (1992) is particularly guilty of this omission in his ethnography of normative control in the engineering division of a high-tech company. Though Kunda convincingly illustrates how the company engineered its culture so as to create a member role that was internalized by employees, his analysis omits the way in which gender intersects with corporate culture, giving rise to a particular type of normative control operating in this firm. In fact, there is no mention that men overwhelmingly dominate engineering divisions. Therefore, Kunda makes the same mistake many other labor theorists do: His argument rests on the assumption that a workplace comprised mostly of men is actually gender-neutral.

Even though Kunda's ethnography is ostensibly not about gender in organizations, it could be read as such. Mumbly (1998) provides this alternative reading, arguing that Kunda unwittingly offers an analysis of the social construction of white-collar masculinity. Through a comparison with Collinson's (1992) ethnography of working-class masculinity, Mumbly highlights the gendered dynamics that Kunda disregards. Mumbly notes that the self-identity of these engineers is so embedded in their work that there is almost no distinction between their private and public selves. Indeed, he illustrates how the acceptance and enactment of organizational membership can lead to a devaluation of family life and can, in its extreme, cause burnout. The type of masculinity constructed among these engineers is rooted in technical expertise, mental ability, and mental, emotional, and physical endurance, not physical prowess. Ultimately, Mumbly illuminates what Kunda doesn't see—that masculine subjectivities are created and constructed through participation in the labor process itself, that normative control is gendered.

Both Mumbly and Lee offer correctives to the literature on the labor process by asserting that gendered discourses, practices, and ideologies are of primary importance in the organization of work. Moreover, they point out that conceptions of masculinity and femininity are reflected in the way work is organized. As workers enter "gendered institutions," they come into contact with specific understandings of femininity and masculinity. They must then negotiate their own gendered subjectivity within the context of an institutional setting.

Masculinity—The Invisible Control Strategy

High-tech companies rely on normative control to manage the white-collar, or knowledge, workers they employ for three reasons. First, with such a tight labor market, workers are not dependent on any one company for the reproduction of their labor power. Consequently, more coercive tactics, already thought to be incompatible with managing educated and highly skilled workers, are untenable because employees would just leave oppressive work environments. Second, normative control is seen to be well-suited to companies that want to encourage creativity and innovation, characteristics which aren't associated with coercive, technical, or bureaucratic styles of control (Kunda and Van Maanen 1999). Third, at this point in the technological revolution, the member role and work behaviors that high-tech companies seek are so pervasive and diffuse throughout Silicon Valley itself that little articulation of these practices is needed in order to guide workers' thoughts and actions. Dylan Fitzgerald describes this collective consciousness:

> My sense is that being in Silicon Valley that [the culture] is already so much around that [description of it] isn't needed. I mean you almost just have to refer to it and everyone goes yeah. They know what you are talking about. And everyone here knew that. They knew they were signing up for a start-up company in Silicon Valley and that was part of the expectation. It was going to involve a commitment to a small group of people whom [sic] are all counting on each other to make the thing work and there was a potentially big financial pay-off if the whole thing worked out.

These workplace practices are so entrenched that interviewees often used the term Silicon Valley as shorthand for what is to them a clearly defined way of being and of doing. Companies can then rely on the internalization of these shared understandings to regulate workers. This is particularly beneficial for smaller companies with limited resources because they don't have to invest a lot of time or money into codifying and perpetuating the culture.

The culture of Silicon Valley is dominated by the logic of the market. A "masculine ethic" (Kanter 1977, p. 22), or the assumption that a worker doesn't have any outside obligations that conflict with their ability to put work first, makes ten-hour days the norm. Yet, this market logic is made palatable because it is cloaked in a youthful playfulness that pervades the Valley. Indeed, young people (mostly men) with technical skills flock here in search of stimulating work and opportunities to strike it rich. But behind the flex-time and casual dress is a culture in which the viewpoint of the shareholder reigns supreme. Beneath the playfulness a serious adult game is being played, a game in which large amounts of money can be won or lost. In order to win in this world, you have to be inventive and brilliant, you have to squash your competitors by cornering the market, and you have to do it all quickly. The pace is intense; if you stop to take a breath you might miss out.

The fast pace, frenzied lifestyle, and devotion to work are norms clearly internalized by my interviewees. This internalization process is evident when my interviewees report feeling pressure to work, but view the pressure as emanating from an internal rather than an external source. Accordingly, the interviewees more often attribute intense work ethics to individual personality traits than to management and co-worker expectations.

For example, Dylan Fitzgerald's daughter had health problems when she was born. As a principal founder of the start-up in which he currently works, he feels he was given a lot of flexibility to take care of family matters. He said that he took five months off for paternity leave and felt no pressure from his co-workers to return. Yet, as we continued the interview it became clear that he in fact had worked during this time and that he was under pressure, but in his view it was his own.

> [After my daughter was born] I didn't come back to work at all for about two months and was part-time for about six months and I was just extremely fortunate to have the flexibility. I'm sure my co-workers would rather have had me back but I didn't get any pressure.
>
> I tried to keep up with e-mail. I tried to keep up with what was going on. I probably came in once or twice a week for particular meetings. But it wasn't that people were pressuring me but my own sense of things that needed to happen, that I knew people were counting on getting done. So there was kind of a self-generating pressure.
>
> I think what really happened was that I worked a couple hours a day, maybe even half-time towards the end. But because I was not actually

meeting any of the deadlines that I had planned for myself, I kept feeling like I wasn't doing what I was supposed to be doing.

In reality, Dylan did not take time off from work. Instead, he worked less than the amount he expected of himself as a member of a start-up. This pattern of actually working when an interviewee stated that he had taken time off for paternity leave occurred several times.

> When I was on paternity leave with my first child, I actually did a fair amount of work. At the time I was writing programs that really ran on a standard PC, so while Brad was sleeping I wrote. Basically I built an entire product so I had no compunction about work because I was actually working. (Alan Payne)

The desire to work all the time is seen by James McNichol as arising out of an addiction to work as well as workplace expectations:

> So I think there are a couple things going on. First, if you are talking about software guys, most of these guys are just addicts. It's one of the most addictive professions that I know. And it attracts addicts so they are just strung out. They just can't withdraw from working. They can't withdraw from programming especially. Second, the level of management in high-tech companies is just for shit. I mean you've got these nerd addict engineers managing other nerd addict engineers. The managers are giving the engineers the message all the time that you've got to work and most of them don't know how to delegate, it's just pitiful, it's just awful. My god, I mean talk about sweatshops, I mean they are oblivious. The managers have no idea what an altered state they are in all the time while they are managing these guys. So I think engineers are getting constant messages that if they are not working all the time then they will be replaced. I mean their entire self-esteem is based on the code they are cutting, it's really sad. But give an addict any free time at all and they will work.

Interestingly, though James thinks that managers pressure people to work, he believes that he works so much because of his own individual desire to work, his own addiction.

> I work way more than anyone gives me the message to work. I give myself the message that I have to work all the time. I struggle with that all the time. I'm just as much an addict as the rest of these guys, but it's just intrinsic to personality types . . . I'm getting better though. It used to be just because I was an addict. I was just anxious as hell unless I was working. This sense of mastery that you have over this piece of computer software is just astounding, it's just unrivalable in the real world. The real world looks like a series of terrible mishaps that you have very little control over. So you know, the lure of spending your time in front of a machine where you just have complete control over is pretty extraordinary.

> I think lately I've gotten much better. I'm working a lot right now because we are very close to bringing out a new product, but I've gotten much better. Hey, when you got here I was fixing my bike, I mean I'm not working right now. It took me a long time to realize that just because I wasn't working 9 to 5 doesn't mean I have to work all the time. I just learned that I had to take time for myself, take time away from work when things weren't busy. And I think that's taken just years and twelve-step programs literally just to learn not to fall into those traps.

Despite James's belief that he works a lot because of his own individual desire to work, it is clear that internal and external pressures go hand in hand. Internal pressure is generated through an implicit comparison to some external Silicon Valley standard of the amount of work that is necessary or required. It seems that the interviewees compare themselves to some real or mythic person (male) who works when they are asleep, who cuts code that doesn't have bugs, who scores the deal that they just lost, who takes his company public while they struggle to get theirs off the ground. The pressure they experience is internal, but it is created through a comparison to an external standard to which they feel they don't quite measure up. Thus, the force causing them to work both surrounds them and is internalized by them, creating normative patterns, understandings, and definitions about work. These normative beliefs are so shared and internalized that the control strategy has no obvious or definite point of origin. Eerily, it is coming from everywhere and nowhere at the same time. This is precisely the self-enforcing type of discipline characteristic of normative control. As Kunda points out, under normative control "discipline is not based on explicit supervision and reward, but rather on peer pressure and more crucially, internalized standards of performance" (p. 90).

High-tech companies rely on normative control, control that depends on the knowledge worker's identity. However, these identities, rooted in work and internalized by the interviewees, are not gender-neutral; rather they are suffused with masculine qualities. Therefore, behaving in accordance with them achieves a specific gendered subjectivity. In other words, the interviewees work in order to become "real men" and become "real men" by working. The masculinity created and constructed by the labor process borrows from, but is not identical to, traditional masculinity. It does not emphasize physical strength, but mental toughness. It does not require hazing women but does require a willingness to be absorbed in one's work that, by effect if not design, excludes both women and family responsibilities. Kunda (1992) misses this step in his examination of high-tech engineers. His analysis of the member role created by the culture of the company overlooks the gendered aspects of this identity. Hence, he misses the point that enactment of this membership role is equivalent to enactment of a particular kind of masculinity, that being a member is tantamount to being a man.

So where do these identifications with work come from? How are they created? Do organizations produce them and/or are there wider structural causes? Though my data cannot offer definitive answers since I did not study any one organization in depth, I can posit some preliminary explanations that future research should more thoroughly examine. As discussed earlier, the culture of Silicon Valley is diffuse, not organizationally bound. Consequently, organizations may not have to actively or consciously engender identities in employees by manufacturing their culture. This culture may already exist a priori, so to speak. In addition, the focus on casual and flexible workplaces eliminates bureaucratic elements. Although this can't, on its own, produce identifications with work, it does get rid of the formal apparatuses, which could otherwise cause the organizational identity to appear external and therefore distinct from one's own identity. Finally, in the new economy, lifetime, even long-term, employment is a thing of the past. For most workers, and particularly for high-tech workers, short-term employment and job-hopping among firms is common practice. In this new type of career structure, one's career is one's own possession, independent of any particular firm. Thus, concern over employability may serve as a powerful tool for creating identities rooted in work.

Fatherhood in the New Economy

This new masculinity is primarily constructed in the public sphere, for it is only by living up to expectations at work that these men can become *genius warriors, tough guys* who get the job done no matter what. It is only in the public arena that they become *heroes* and *go-to guys* by delivering on the projects they *sign up for*. However, as fathers, these men have private lives and personal responsibilities which conflict with these public requirements. Moreover, as "progressive" men, most interviewees are ideologically, if not always practically, committed to fatherhood and a fairer domestic division of labor between themselves and their wives. Though most of my interviewees did less around the house and less with their children than did their wives, the majority of them expressed a sincere interest in being active fathers. Most displayed negative feelings towards the lack of care they received from their own fathers and were consciously trying not to reproduce these distant relationships with their own children.

Thus, the new masculinity contains an internal contradiction: How can anyone simultaneously be the go-to guy at work and at home?

Superdads

Three ways of resolving this contradiction emerged among my interviewees. Seven of them attempt to meet all work and family obligations without sacrificing anything in either sphere. The result is that these Superdads sacrifice themselves. Superdads invest heavily in both career and family. These fathers tend to have a more egalitarian gender ideology, regardless of whether or not their wives stay home. They also possess a care orientation which engenders a strong emotional connection between them and their families.

This care orientation has two components. First, these fathers talk about being attentive to the emotional, physical, and spiritual needs of those around them. Second, this attentiveness coincides with a broader definition of care which includes emotion work and care work, as well as paid work. Superdads seem to notice when caring work like laundry or shopping needs to be done and don't appear to resent doing it. This attentiveness and broader definition of care enables them to anticipate the needs of their family and, most importantly, it enables them to empathize with their wives. Rich Kavelin, a Superdad who works in business development, illustrates this caring orientation when he describes a typical evening at home with his three-month-old son and his wife Joan, a social worker on an eight-month maternity leave:

> When I get home at 6:30 p.m. the baby is essentially my child for the rest of the evening. My wife very often goes out and just hands me the baby and says here he is, he loves you, here's your daddy. She grabs the car keys and splits because she's with the child non-stop for 10 to 12 hours during the day and she needs a little personal time. So she will go out and generally she's out for about an hour or so and I'll hang out with the baby. I'll feed him, play with him, talk to him. When she gets home, it alternates. About half the time I'll make dinner, and half the time she makes dinner. If there are chores to be done like dishes or laundry, I'll pitch in and help with that. So I don't expect her to do everything.

Rich's acknowledgement that his wife both needs and is entitled to "personal time" reflects his ability to empathize with her and to recognize the actual work involved in taking care of a child. In addition, his more egalitarian philosophy is made clear through his desire to share in the caretaking of their son and through his desire to share in the domestic division of labor. The possession of such a care orientation is stressful and overwhelming for Superdads because, in addition to demands at work, these fathers feel responsible for demands at home as well.

Traditionals

Three[4] participants resolved the new masculinity contradiction by approaching work and family through a traditional male model. Despite these interviewees' ideological belief in egalitarianism, especially in the workplace, they didn't seem to practice what they preached at home. In contrast to Superdads, Traditionals divide the domestic division of labor along traditionally gendered lines. They speak about their families in emotionally disconnected ways and talk about caring for their family in a limited fashion, placing more emphasis on work and the income it provides. This curtailed definition of care coincides with an inattention to the needs of those around them. They either don't notice or overlook the work required for family life, leaving it instead for their wives. Unlike Superdads, these fathers appear to lack the ability to sympathize with their wives. They also appear to be less stressed than Superdads because their energy and emotions are less divided between work and home. Interestingly, Traditionals took the least amount of time off for paternity leave.

Unlike Superdad Rich, Edward Vicker, a traditionalist, does relinquish all the caring work to his wife. Edward, an engineering project manager, is married to Jessica, a full-time homemaker who cares for their two young sons. Edward describes their domestic division of labor:

> My wife does most of the home care. Occasionally I'll do some vacuuming and I gotta make sure I pick up my own clothes and keep the closet clean or else she gets on me about that a little bit. She does the general cleaning and I do all the outside stuff, cutting the lawn and maintenance or repairs. I do usually end up loading the dishwasher after dinner cause I normally get done first. See, my wife has it timed perfectly. I go over and I load my dishes in the dishwasher. And by that time the kids are starting to finish a little bit so she starts handing stuff over to the counter to me. So by the time I get out of there, everybody is done and I've got all the dishes to do so that's really the only inside task that I do on a regular basis.

In contrast to Rich, who doesn't expect his wife to do everything around the house and wants to do his part, Edward not only expects his wife to do everything but feels manipulated by her when he does a single domestic task.

Fathers who relinquish their part of the caring work and expect their wives to be responsible for all domestic chores sometimes encounter resistance. In Edward's case, he and his wife have fights about who does more work for the family:

> We fight occasionally. She feels like she's doing more and I feel like I'm doing more. Like in the fall when football season starts, I'll sit down and watch two football games in a row, six hours worth. She isn't very happy about that. She's running around chasing the kids all day and feeding them and then she's like "You don't do anything around here." And I'll say, "I go to work for forty, fifty hours a week." And then she's like "Don't you think I'm working around here?" So it goes back and forth like that.

Ironically, Edward recognizes the work his wife does while he is relaxing on the couch. Yet he detaches himself from any obligation to share in this type of family work because he feels he has already done his part by working at the office.

Transitionals

Between the Superdads and the Traditionals sits the largest group, the Transitionals. Similar to the Traditionals, the Transitionals partially resolve the new masculinity contradiction by reneging on their egalitarian ideology somewhat and instead leaving a lot of the family work to their wives. Yet, like Superdads, the Transitionals want to be involved fathers and are responsible for at least some of the family work. Consequently, Transitionals have a harder time balancing work and family than the Traditionals. However, they are not as conflicted as the Superdads because they hold onto the care orientation more loosely, frequently handing off duties, obligations, and emotion work to their wives. While some Transitionals lean towards being a Superdad, others lean towards being a Traditional.

Like Edward Vicker, Chris Baxter, a Transitional father in business development, also has clashes with his wife when he "backslides into assuming that because she's home full-time she has all this extra time to clean the bathrooms and cook dinner." Chris and his wife Emma have two children, a girl who is seven and a boy who is four. It seems that ideally Chris would like Emma to be a traditional stay-at-home mom. Yet Emma sees motherhood in more professional terms. She is at home to raise the children, not to be a homemaker or a maid. A recent clash over decorating illustrates this tension:

> I think in terms of motherhood, one of the things that I see her having a greater responsibility for than I is home decorating, and sometimes she accepts it and other times she really pushes back. A part of it is that we are both terrible at it. But I think she's better than I am so I kind of push that on her. So I'll say, "You're staying here at home and part of staying at home is making it a wonderful home, right?" And she's like, "I'll sign up for leading the brainstorming on that but I'm not signing up for doing that as well as deciding what to put here and there and finding the contractor, while you just sign up for writing the check be-

cause you are the one working." So although at times it would be nice if she did that, in the end I think it's better if we do it together because then we are both doing it.

Chris is caught between his wish for his wife to be traditional and his knowledge that a more egalitarian partnership is fairer and more rewarding in the long run.

Comparing Superdad Rich, Traditional Edward, and Transitional Chris, it is easy to see the degree to which each possesses a caring orientation. At one end of the spectrum we have Rich. He embraces a caring logic. He sympathizes with his wife, he wants her to have personal time off, and he wants to do a part of the caring work by cooking dinner and helping out with domestic chores. At the other end of the spectrum we have Edward. Edward is unsympathetic towards his wife's feelings. He feels no responsibility or obligation to help with the housework. Instead, he feels that he is entitled to leisure. Chris stands in the middle. He holds on to the care logic loosely, willing to take part in the caring work only after his wife commands him to. At her prompting, he is reminded of how busy she is at home and is then willing to help.

Being the Go-to Guy

Scholars have found that a father's masculinity is called into question when his family obligations encroach upon his work obligations (Pleck 1993; Hochschild 1997; Levine and Pittinsky 1997). These findings suggest that ideas, norms, and expectations about what is and is not masculine have a regulating effect on the thoughts, choices, and actions of fathers. Indeed, an examination of the work–family practices my interviewees engage in shows that the strategies they employ to manage their work and family lives reflect a desire to personify and embody the public aspects of the new masculinity. To maintain the image and the reality that they are go-to guys, these fathers rely on a combination of the following practices: self-sacrifice, silencing work–family conflict, disguising the care they do perform, and turning to women, both at work and at home, to help them mediate between their public and private responsibilities. Moreover, even the way these fathers think about and conceptualize care reflects a desire to make family fit within the demands of the high-tech world, to make family fit within the narrow boundaries of this gendered subjectivity. Thus, the internalization of the Silicon Valley member role not only impacts how these fathers work, but also spills over into how they think about and participate in family life.

Self-Sacrifice

To reconcile their desire to be involved in family life with their desire to be a serious player at work, Superdads, and some Transitionals, pay a tremendous personal cost. By trying to live up to expectations both in the workplace and at home, these fathers sacrifice all personal time. Rich Kavelin articulates the stress this causes in his life:

> The most difficult thing about having a kid has been letting go of personal time. I don't mind the work, it doesn't bother me . . . But now and then I'd like to be able to go play golf with my friends. My wife still has some personal life because we make an extra effort. She goes to girls' night, to ladies' night, she has a mothers' group and support groups. It's actually more important to me that she has a social life because if you think about it I'm here all day. I have people that I interact with at work, adult conversation, and I'm using my mind. Whereas she's at home with somebody who is drooling and spitting up and going "ahhh" so her need for human contact is much higher and I'm okay with that. But every now and then I get a bit grumpy and think, "Why the hell can't I just go get a beer with Neil tonight, I miss my friend Neil."

Like Rich, Dylan Fitzgerald, also a Superdad, is overwhelmed with work and being there for his two-year-old daughter Anna. Dylan feels torn every day between the demands of his job and his desire to be at home with his child. This tension leaves him feeling as if he's underperforming in both realms.

I'm continually feeling like I'm not quite doing what I want to be doing in either place and I'm doing absolutely nothing else that isn't one of those two things. I mean the concept of free time or hobbies, well it seems kind of laughable at this point.

Not only do the Superdads sacrifice personal time, they also survive on minimal amounts of sleep in order to meet conflicting obligations. Often they work during the day, come home to help with dinner and put the kids to bed, then work more after their kids and their spouses fall asleep. Alan Payne, a software engineer, conceptualizes his workday in two shifts.

> In engineering there just isn't a sharp divide between work and family. I've finally been able to turn that to my advantage but it has cost me a lot of sleep because what I do is I work two shifts. I work a shift in the day at the company starting at around 10 a.m. and ending at 6 p.m. Then I come home and spend time with my family. When the kids go to bed, I log on and work another shift from about 10 p.m. to 2 a.m.

By forfeiting sleep and personal time, Superdads constantly scramble to meet competing commitments, which leaves them feeling exhausted and overwhelmed. Rich Kavelin expresses this fatigue:

> I signed up for this life, right . . . and you pay a price if you have a high-paying job or a career that you are really fulfilled by. So my price is that I'm exhausted. I hardly get any sleep.

Superdads attribute their exhaustion to career demands. Yet, what really seems to be causing their fatigue is that they possess a caring orientation within a social world so dominated by the market that there is little space, time, or energy left for care. So within this context, their attentiveness to the emotional and care needs of their families makes their work load triple that of other fathers who aren't as attentive to the needs of those around them. The Superdads' unwillingness to cut back either at work or at home, and their willingness to live a completely insane lifestyle, signify how central both home and work are to their identities. Not wanting to give up either part of their identity, Superdads completely embrace both the public and private requirements of the new masculinity. Accordingly, Superdads lead lives much bigger than a typical Silicon Valley day can hold.

Silencing Conflict and Care

A prerequisite to being a committed team player is a devotion to work that borders on addiction. Therefore, the intrusion of private sphere issues into the public sphere shatters the image that one is an addict, that one is always ready, willing, and able to work. Addiction means you bring work home—you don't bring home to work. This devaluing of private needs and overvaluing of public needs is quite evident in the hesitancy many fathers feel about bringing up work–family conflicts at the workplace. Instead of openly discussing conflicts, most fathers I interviewed keep problems to themselves, thereby conveying the impression that work comes first.

Rich Kavelin managed a recent work–family conflict with silence. His boss wanted him to leave on a business trip the same day that he and his wife needed to meet with their priest to discuss their son's christening. It was the only available day the priest had in months. Here is Rich's description of the incident:

> So here I am talking to the VP on the phone and he's like "We need to do this now, we need to hook up with these guys from X, we need to set this up, here are my contacts, we are going on the 29th," and I looked at my calendar and literally I started to sweat. I'm going "Umm that day is difficult for me, is there any other day we can go?" and he's like "I don't think so Rich, my calendar is pretty full but check with my secretary tomorrow." So I called up the secretary the next day and I was sweating like a horse. I said, "Hey, you gotta get me out of this because my baby is getting christened and if I don't meet with the priest it's not going to happen and my family is going to kill me and my wife will divorce me and I won't have any kids, and life will be terrible." So she looked, and the only day I could replace that with was four

weeks away so I said, "What is he doing in between?" She said, "He's going to Germany for a week, then Mexico, then to England, then to Boston, then California and then he can meet with you in New York." And the guy lives in Pennsylvania and he has two kids and a wife, and I'm going he doesn't have two kids and a wife, he has people that live in his house, that's basically what he has.

Though Rich is willing to express that the day is difficult, he's not willing to explain the real reason he cannot leave, that he has a family conflict. He told me that he didn't want to tell his boss about the christening because right now he's the VP's "go-to guy." The VP depends on him, gives him interesting assignments, and is clearly impressed with Rich's work. Despite Rich's disdain for the way his boss puts work before family, he does not want to jeopardize his position by identifying himself as someone who prioritizes both work and family. It's as if any connection with the private sphere will be a mark against him. Thus, Rich consents to the logic of the market, to the requirements of the new masculinity. He does whatever it takes to convey that he does not have other needs, that he is autonomous and independent and always ready to go when the boss calls.

Like Rich, other fathers dealt with work–family conflict with silence.

I can remember various times when I had to leave in the middle of the day to drop my son off at baseball practice. I might not have been real forthcoming about that because that may seem a little less important to somebody, particularly if they are not a parent. It would be a lot easier for them to understand if I said my son is at his school and the school is going to close in half an hour and I've got to pick him up before it closes. That's like an emergency. But when it sounds like something that is more optional, I might not be so quick to volunteer it. (Stan Espe)

The hesitancy and silence about work–family conflict maintains the idea that these fathers do not have any obligations outside of work. The above quotation also points out that the most legitimate way in which the family can come into the workplace is through an emergency: In emergency situations it is clear that family comes before work. But when things are functioning smoothly in normal, everyday life, family is less of a priority than work.

When personal things come up in people's lives, like losing a parent or something like that, there is absolutely no question that people would get time to go take care of that. Of course there is also the expectation that when just day-to-day stuff comes up, you will be willing to rearrange your family life to put in extra hours that week or spend a Saturday doing work so we get things done on time. So in real crisis situations there would be no question that family life would get taken care of but there might be week-to-week conflict that's just kind of unavoidable given the way the company has set its goals. (Dylan Fitzgerald)

But how often do real crises come up in family life as opposed to the fairly constant crises of the high-tech industry? Though presented as such, this is not an even and fair trade. Instead, workplace demands are met at the expense of care.

In addition to the silence surrounding work–family conflict, there is also silence about paternity leave. A curious discovery is that ten fathers in my sample were given paid time off, ranging from two to three weeks. This paid leave was not an explicit policy or benefit. Rather, these leaves were secretly arranged through managers who granted the leave but didn't inform the human resources department. The other ten took vacation time and unpaid leave. The desire by some managers to give their employees paternity leave could, if discussed openly, be mobilized to institutionalize men's parenting. Regrettably, however, this countervailing force remains shrouded and untouched, a sign of just how inhospitable the high-tech world is to matters of the heart. To be sure, the silence about work–family conflict and about paid paternity leave disguises the care performed by fathers. The secrecy also devalues care by making it a taboo issue, marking it as something that is not worthy of discussion. Taken together, the silencing and disguising of care is a strategy that allows fathers to parent while preserving the idea that their parental duties do not come before their workplace obligations.

Turning to Women in Order to Care

Through Rich's incident with the VP about his son's christening, we can see the way in which women help men mediate between home and work without being detected. Rich feels comfortable telling the secretary the real reason he cannot leave on that date because he has no fear that she will think he is less committed to work or less of a player. He assumes that as a woman, she will understand his predicament. The secretary solves Rich's problem by finding an alternative date which enables him to keep his commitments to his job and to his family. Not only do most fathers rely on the women in their lives, namely their wives, to do much of the actual work involved in family life, but they also rely on their wives for help in negotiating the details of work and family life. A common theme that emerged was that wives often set times at which their husbands had to be home. The wives enforce these times by telling their husbands the time they need to leave work in order to get home on schedule and by calling or paging to remind them. These reminders can also serve as "excuses" for fathers to go home, since it conveys to others that it is the wife, not the husband, who is responsible for the father leaving work. Thus, women become symbols, interpreters, and mediators of care in a world where "real" men are not allowed, or at least are not supposed, to care.

Market Language

The degree to which the new masculinity is internalized and embodied by my interviewees can be seen in the way some fathers draw upon market language and market concepts to make sense of their intimate relationships and personal lives. In describing his relationship with his wife, Chris Baxter said:

> Our pediatrician tells us that we are supposed to go out on a date once a month but we get busy so we go out about once a quarter. We know mentally what we are supposed to do, but whether we execute on that, well it depends.

This statement "once a quarter" reveals a temporal order dominated by the fiscal year. It also reduces an intimate aspect of personal life to a task that if "executed" can be scratched off the "to do" list, analogous to something being moved from the in box to the out box. Sadly, one gets the sense that this task is a low priority, like a non-urgent memo that becomes covered with more important papers on a desk.

Several fathers portrayed their personal lives in contractual terms. In the same way they "sign up" for projects at work, they "signed up" for a particular family life too. Dylan Fitzgerald used this contractual talk:

> I'm very conscious of the fact that if I had an extra two to three hours a day to do work I could be getting more done here, improving the company's odds of succeeding. I'm also very conscious that I'm not spending as much time around the house with my daughter as I committed to when we planned the whole thing out.

It appears that Dylan and his wife carefully planned out caring for their child, in the same way that projects are planned out at work. Like transactions in the market, the care for their child too is arranged on the basis of a contract, with each party agreeing to perform different parts. Now Dylan is caught in the "time bind" (Hochschild 1997), unable to "deliver" in the way he would like in either part of his life.

In a recent article about Silicon Valley life entitled "Running on Valley Time" (Plotnikoff 1999), Scott Epstein, a high-tech marketing executive, uses market language to explain the impact his absence has had on his two young sons. Though he is uncertain about whether or not his long working hours have hurt his children, he is certain that his absence means he has less of an influence over how they are raised.

I think if you asked my kids, "Do you see your daddy very much?" they would say no and that they want to see him more. Because I'm home less, I have less of a say on how my kids are raised. It's harder to push through my thoughts and see them put into action.

His response indicates that he views his influence upon his children in the same way that he views his influence on marketing campaigns. One imagines him sitting down with his wife and presenting her with a meeting agenda which outlines his ideas in bulleted format. He then "pushes through [his] thoughts," and sways her to his viewpoint. The end result of this meeting is that a parenting "strategy," informed by his know-how, is "put into action." Yet Scott is keenly aware from his own work experience that the only way this family project will be kept on track is through persistent monitoring and reinforcement. Such supervision is very time-consuming, so he concedes the project to his wife and instead focuses his influence on pushing through his ideas at work.

The embodiment of the new masculinity can also be seen in the way some fathers shape and curtail their beliefs about care in order that family life does not interfere with the demands of the market. By reshaping and redefining care, family life is made compatible with the bottom line. Eric Salazar expressed this sentiment when he discussed his paternity leave. His supervisor gave him a paid two-week leave when his daughter was born:

On the one hand I was very grateful that I was being paid for the leave and that I wasn't taking it out of vacation or sick time. But at the same time I honestly felt that it was something I deserved. So I was thankful, but I wasn't overwhelmed by the gift from my boss. I think that it's something that really should be the norm. It's never enough, but realistically I think two weeks would be capitalistically fair for the company to offer that.

Eric assesses the needs for his family within the constraints of capitalism. In doing so, we can see how the market creates the terms within which family policies are negotiated. Ultimately, what is fair for capitalism is by default both fair for the family and a suitable practice for a man who is both a father and a serious high-tech worker.

Chris Baxter also reveals the priority given to market needs, at the expense of familial needs, when he discussed which employees are entitled to flexibility in their job:

As a manager I have a much easier time giving extra flexibility to folks I know will get the job done and come in on the weekend because Thursday afternoon they took off to go to their child's check-up or whatever. Somebody missing deadlines, who is always over their budget, they are not going to get that flexibility. I hate to sound like a capitalist but at the end of the day, the company shareholders aren't holding shares so that we have flexible lives. They are holding the shares because they are expecting a return on them. So if you can generate some return and balance your life then it's great. But job one is the return.

For Chris, not only do market demands come before family concerns, but a worker must also earn the privilege to meet family demands by first meeting all market requirements. Interestingly, though he is obviously a free market supporter, Chris tries to distance himself from sounding like a capitalist. Sensing the coldness of his outlook he points to real-world constraints, not his own belief system, to justify his opinion about flexibility. However, it's very clear that his belief system does not stand outside of the market. His thoughts, feelings, and emotions are overlaid with a market sensibility that shapes his understanding of care and its importance relative to the market. By characterizing care needs in a way that is congruent and acceptable to capitalism, these fathers construct family life in a way that is compatible with the workplace expectations of the new masculinity. In this way, care never infringes on the market, but the market continually intrudes upon care.

Given that these fathers work in a "high octane capitalism" environment, it isn't surprising that they try to shape and curtail care practices so they fit within the capitalist paradigm. Yet, what is somewhat astonishing is how deeply the ideology and practices associated with the new masculinity infiltrate the interviewees' lives. Indeed, the use of market language and market concepts to explain one's personal life makes clear the depth to which the new masculinity penetrates. For not only does it influence work and family practice, it also acts upon the interviewees' hearts, minds, psyches, and souls. Thus, the new masculinity is an all-encompassing gendered subjectivity that impacts every part of the interviewees' existence, from work to family to everything in between.

Resistance

The extent to which individual fathers will go to achieve and enact this gendered subjectivity varies. There do seem to be limits to how far some men will go for their job. Several fathers told cautionary tales about absentee fathers whom they refused to be like. Rich Kavelin will not be like his boss, the senior VP who travels all the time. He also will not be like his former boss at a start-up he used to work for:

> The CEO of this start-up company had three kids, 4, 7, 10, nice kids but he never ever ever sees them because he's at work seven days a week. He does triple sevens. He works from 7 in the morning until 7 in the evening 7 days a week. He thought he was a good father because once a year he'd go camping for a week with his kids or one day on a weekend he would take them out to ice cream for two hours and he'd say it's not the quantity of time it's the quality of time. And I'm just thinking, his kids aren't going to have any idea who he is, he doesn't think these little moments matter but they do. I mean the guy was a real shit when it came to his kids, I'm sorry. He's forty and he's bound and determined that he's going to make his multimillions and he thinks he is doing the right thing for his kids, because he thinks he's doing all this for them since one day they will be rich. They will be rich with money but poor as people.

Rich recognizes that his former boss led an "emotionally downsized" life and refuses to buy into "a reduction of needs" ideology (Hochschild 1997). Yet, it remains unclear how Rich will maintain his line in the sand when he wouldn't even tell his current boss about his son's christening.

Not only are there variations among fathers, but individual fathers themselves embrace and resist this gendered subjectivity at different stages in their life course. For example, Kirk Sinclair is a defector from the triple seven world. He works from home and is in charge of sales for a small software company, but formerly he worked as an engineer who wanted to be known in his field. After spending a year as a vice president of engineering in a struggling firm, working so much that he never saw his children, he decided to change his quality of life. Kirk has changed his priorities.

> I still want to be successful financially. I still want to be respected in my field. But I'm not out for fame and glory any longer. And I think I've got a much more reasonable balance of life.

An in-depth look at the process Kirk went through in order to change his life highlights the contours of the new masculinity and its relationship to work and family life. Kirk's reputation was made through his involvement in a start-up called Innovate that was very successful. At that point in his life he personified the Silicon Valley warrior:

> I worked hard at my start-up because I was Ali, that was my log-in name. I was famous at the company and I was infamous. Salespeople and marketing people would come and talk to me, they wanted me to meet with customers and really decisions didn't get made unless I got to play and I just liked it. I liked being in charge, I never had that in my life, and it was just a lot of fun. I got to make decisions that were worth huge amounts of money and I had never done that before.

When his second child Andi was born, he took only a couple of days off from work. This was and continues to be a "sore point" with his wife, who wanted him to take more time off. Kirk's quick return to work stemmed from his desire to get back to the office, not from management expectations.

I had a very supportive management structure above me. The woman who I reported to was a strong family supporter. And it would have been absolutely okay for me not to be there, which is to say, clock out . . . So I can't say that I was under any pressure from the office. I was under a fair bit of pressure from myself. Then I was mostly doing engineering work. There's this kind of machismo culture among young male engineers that you just don't sleep. So Andi was born and I went back to the office and I didn't have a lot of people saying to me "Jesus, what are you doing here?" My boss was saying "Hey, what are you doing here?" but none of my colleagues were surprised that I was there.

Even though Kirk wasn't pressured by his boss to return to work, it seems he was pressured by the cultural expectations of his peer group about the importance of work and its priority over other parts of one's life. Kirk so identified with the cultural expectations about work that he experienced the pressure to return to work as emanating from inside him, not from the environment that surrounded him. For Kirk to be Ali he had to work all the time; he had to be around so that he could participate in all aspects of the company. In his mind, the company could not succeed without him.

When his start-up went public, it was bought by a larger competitor. Unhappy with the management changes that resulted, Kirk left and went to work as the vice president of engineering at a small biotech start-up.

The company was far away and for family reasons we were not going to move. So the commute was 90 minutes each way every day. It was stupid to think that I could pull it off.

If the job had been absolutely great I would have probably toughed it out. But the job just wasn't that great. It was a little company, we weren't doing very well. It was called GS, it was a small biotech company, a very interesting market, exciting field, but we were not set up to succeed.

So the job sucked and the commute was driving me nuts. I would get up at 4 a.m. and be at the office by 6 so that I could beat the commute rush down. I didn't see the kids in the morning and then there would be a board meeting or something so I would stay until 9 or 10 at night, get in the car and drive home and I wouldn't see them when I got home. So really I went for a year seeing them almost not at all and it was a very, very tough year for my wife. I mean every time the phone rang it was me on my cell phone saying I wouldn't be home. She was supportive of me taking the job, it was clear she hated me having that job and I just was not having any fun. It took me a long time to give myself permission to quit that job, to admit that I had made a mistake. So I resigned in October of last year, nine months after I took the job, and was talked into a fairly extended transition that saw me there basically until the end of May. And at that point I was exhausted, emotionally and intellectually, I didn't have anything left so I took all of the next summer off and we traveled a bunch and I just hung out with the kids.

I started looking around for other jobs, there is a lot of hiring going on. I have a good track record and know a lot of people. So lots of other vice president jobs were available at companies that was [sic] venture-backed and you know it was a chance to get on the Innovate rocketship again and make a lot of money. But the problem is that with those jobs you need to be at the office early, they need you to stay late. They need the job to come first and I had spent a year letting a real crappy job come first. The family really suffered. The kids didn't see me. And frankly I didn't want to do that again.

The reason it was so difficult for Kirk to walk away from his job was because he had "signed up" to do the job and in doing so his name and his capabilities became responsible for making it work. Thus, he committed himself mentally and emotionally to getting the job done.

We all knew walking into it that this was something that needed to be turned around, it was broken. I don't know if it's machismo or not, I mean I was committed to make this thing work. And it was very, very hard to quit 'cause I had convinced myself that I would do that job and so I had to convince myself that it was okay to fail.

In order for Kirk to allow himself to quit, he had to renegotiate aspects of his identity. He had to come to terms with the fact that he was not the person (man) to accomplish "the task." The price of success was too high, too costly. Poignantly, he derides himself for even thinking that he could rise to this insane challenge and feels that he set himself up for failure. It is interesting that Kirk's desire to quit is seen and experienced by him as acceptance of failure. In Kirk's mind, then, you either win or lose, you deliver or you don't. What has changed for him now is that his identity is no longer solely based on the paid work he performs, what his colleagues think of him, and whether or not he's the go-to guy.

> Until not too long ago, a huge part of my identity was wrapped up in what I did for a living and was I famous in my field. Did people call me to solicit my opinion on developments in the industry, and now I don't care about that so much, I don't need to see my name in print, I don't need to see my papers cited in other people's papers.

Now, his identity is built more around his family and less around his work.

> With the job I have now, I'm working with people who I intellectually respect, the product is outstanding, it's very easy to sell. I'm getting to do some stuff that is professionally very important and I get to see my kids every morning and be here in the afternoon when they get home. I chose this job not because it's the one that is going to make us rich. It probably won't. On the other hand, it's a good living. I'm having a fun time and I get to be around the kids all the time.

In order for Kirk to resist the organization of work in the Valley he had to reconstruct his identity, particularly his gendered subjectivity. He had to let go of the desire to outperform others, win battles, and be the best. In essence, Kirk had to let go of the public requirements of the new masculinity in order to embrace its private dimensions. He had to let go of being the go-to guy at work in order to be the go-to guy at home. In reordering his life, he revalued care and recognized that he and his family had needs.

Conclusion

The examination of the work–family phenomenon requires a bridging and reworking of different domains of theorizing so that instead of sitting in either the public or the private, analysis can move back and forth between the public and the private, the market and the home. Approached from this viewpoint, my study of fathers employed as knowledge workers in Silicon Valley sought to draw connections among gender, work, and family. Thus, my discovery of a new masculinity led me to question how it articulates with processes of labor control and with processes of family life.

What I found is that fathers internalize the characteristics of the new masculinity, which shapes both how they work and how they parent. To achieve this gendered subjectivity, men must be technically brilliant and devoted to work. They must be tough guys who get the job done no matter what. Fathers so identify with these qualities that their desire to work all the time is experienced by them as emanating from their own personality traits rather than from co-worker or management expectations. Consequently, the type of control these fathers experience is an identity-based one. However, this identity is not gender-neutral. Rather, because workplace practices are suffused with masculine qualities, performance of them achieves a masculinized subjectivity. To maintain this masculine subjectivity, fathers employ work–family practices, such as remaining silent in the face of work and family conflict, which serve to give the impression, if not the reality, that work comes first. Moreover, the embodiment of the go-to guy image impacts how these fathers conceptualize and experience their private lives as evidenced by their use of market language to make sense of their personal relationships as well as their desire to fit family needs within a capitalist paradigm.

These findings have important implications for labor process and work–family scholars. For labor process scholars, my findings highlight the centrality of gender in the organization of work. Therefore, research about processes of control, particularly research on identity-based forms of control, must analyze the gendered dimensions of the phenomenon they describe in order to gain an accurate and complete understanding. For work–family scholars, my findings highlight the need to think about the ways in which gendered subjectivities explain work and family practices. For example, when taken into consideration, gendered subjectivities may account for the failure of people to make use of family-friendly policies even in ostensibly open organizations. In sum, my study illustrates the importance of studying work and family issues in a holistic manner that more accurately reflects the holistic nature of peoples' everyday lives.

Notes

1. Though some scholars take a more essentialized view of masculinity (and femininity), believing that certain practices indicate that a person is a man or woman (Collinson and Hearn 1994), I take a less embodied viewpoint. I agree with Alvesson and Billing (1997), who see masculinity and femininity as "traits or forms of subjectivities (orientations in thinking, feeling, and valuing) that are present in all persons, men as well as women" (p. 85).

2. Lee is working from Burawoy's (1985) theory of factory regimes which entails two components: the labor process, meaning the technical and social organization of production, and the production apparatuses, meaning the institutions that regulate and shape the workplace politics (p. 19).

3. Other scholars have critiqued Burawoy's disregard of the gendered dynamics on the shop floor. See Davies (1990) and Knights (1990).

4. I am invoking the typology Hochschild (1989) used as it conveys and describes the three distinct positions held by the interviewees. The terms Traditional and Transitional come directly from Hochschild (p. 16).

References

Acker, J. (1990). "Hierarchies, Jobs, Bodies: A Theory of Gendered Organizations." *Gender & Society* 4:2 139–158.

Acker, J. (1992). "Gendered institutions: From Sex Roles to Gendered Institutions." *Contemporary Sociology* 21: 139–158.

Alvesson, M. and Billing, Y. D. (1997). *Understanding Gender and Organizations*. London: Sage Publications.

Alvesson, M. (1998). "Gender Relations and Identity at Work: A Case Study of Masculinities and Femininities in an Advertising Agency." *Human Relations* 51:8 969–1006.

American Association of University Women. (2000). "Tech-Savvy: Educating Girls in the New Computer Age." Washington, DC: American Association of University Women. Retrieved May 28, 2000 (http://www.aauw.org/2000/techsavvybd.html).

Braverman, H. (1974). *Labor and Monopoly Capital*. New York: Monthly Review Press.

Brod, H. and Kaufman, M. (1994). *Theorizing Masculinities*. Thousand Oaks: Sage Publications.

Burawoy, M. (1979). *Manufacturing Consent*. Chicago: University of Chicago Press.

Burawoy, M. (1985). *The Politics of Production*. London: Verso.

Burris, B. (1998) "Computerization of the Workplace." *Annual Review of Sociology* 24: 141–157.

Carrigan, T, Connell, R. W. and Lee, J. (1985). "Towards a New Sociology of Masculinity." *Theory and Society* 14: 551–604.

Chatman, J. and O'Reilly, C. (1986). "Organizational Commitment and Psychological Attachment: The Effects of Compliance, Identification, and Internalization on Prosocial Behavior." *Journal of Applied Psychology* 71:3 492–500.

Cockburn, C. (1988). *Machinery of Dominance: Women, Men and Technical Know-how*. Boston: Northeastern University Press.

Collinson, D. L. (1992). *Managing the Shopfloor*. New York: Walter de Gruyter.

Collinson, D. L. and Hearn, J. (1994). "Naming Men as Men: Implications for Work, Organization and Management." *Gender, Work and Organization* 1:1 2–22.

Collinson, D. L. and Hearn, J. (Eds.) (1996a). *Men as Managers, Managers as Men*. London: Sage Publications.

Collinson, D. L. and Hearn, J. (1996b). Breaking the Silence On: On Men, Masculinities and Managements. In D. L. Collinson & J. Hearn (Eds.), *Men as Managers, Managers as Men (pp. 1–24). London: Sage Publications.

Conlin, M. (2000). "Valley of No Dolls." Business Week, March 6.

Connell, R. W. (1987). Gender and Power. Cambridge: Polity Press.

Connell, R. W. (1995). Masculinities. Berkeley: University of California Press.

Daly, K. J. (1998). "Reshaping Fatherhood." In Shifting the Center, edited by S. Ferguson (pp. 384–399). Mountain View, CA: Mayfield Publishing Company.

Daly, K. J. (1992). "The Fit Between Qualitative Research and the Characteristics of Families." Qualitative Methods in Family Research, edited by J. Gilgun, K. Daly, and G. Handel. Newbury Park, CA: Sage.

Davies, S. (1990). "Inserting Gender into Burawoy's Theory of the Labour Process." Work, Employment and Society 4: 391–406.

Edwards, R. (1979). Contested Terrain. USA: Basic Books.

Faludi, S. (1999). Stiffed. New York: William Morrow and Company, Inc.

Hacker, S. (1990). "Doing it the Hard Way": Investigations of Gender and Technology. Boston: Unwin Hyman.

Hochschild, A. (1989). The Second Shift. New York: Avon Books.

Hochschild, A. (1997). The Time Bind. New York: Metropolitan Books.

Kanter, R. M. (1977). Men and Women of the Corporation. New York: Basic Books.

Kendall, L. (2000). "'Oh no! I'm a Nerd!' Hegemonic Masculinity on an Online Forum." Gender & Society 14:2 256–275.

Kendall, L. (1999). "'The Nerd Within': Mass Media and the Negotiation of Identity Among Computer-Using Men." Journal of Men's Studies 7:3 353.

Knights, D. (1990). "Subjectivity, Power and the Labour Process." In D. Knights & W. Willmott, Labour Process Theory (pp. 297–335). London: Macmillan.

Kunda, G. (1992). Engineering Culture. Philadelphia: Temple University Press.

Kunda, G. and Van Maanen, J. (1999). "Changing Scripts at Work: Managers and Professionals." Annals of the American Academy of Political and Social Science 561: 64–80.

Lee, C. K. (1998). Gender and the South China Miracle. Berkeley: University of California Press.

Leidner, R. (1993). Fast Food, Fast Talk. Berkeley: University of California Press.

Mac An Ghaill, M. E. (1996). Understanding Masculinities. Philadelphia: Open University Press.

Mumbly, D. K. (1998). "Organizing Men: Power, Discourse, and the Social Construction of Masculinity(s) in the Workplace." Communication Theory. 8:2 164–179.

Perlow, L. (1995). "Putting the Work Back Into Work/Family." Group and Organization Management 20:2 227–239.

Pierce, J. L. (1996). "Reproducing Gender Relations in Large Law Firms: The Role of Emotional Labor in Paralegal Work." Working in the Service Society, edited by C. Macdonald and C. Sirianni. Philadelphia: Temple University Press.

Pleck, J. (1993). "Are 'Family-Supportive' Employer Policies Relevant to Men?" Men, Work, and Family, edited by J. C. Hood. Newbury Park: Sage Publications.

Plotnikoff, D. (1999). "Running on Valley Time." SV Magazine, October 31, p. 6.

Turkle, S. (1984). The Second Self: Computers and the Human Spirit. New York: Simon and Schuster.

Turkle, S. (1988). "Computational Reticence: Why Women Fear the Intimate Machine." In Technology and Women's Voices: Keeping in Touch, edited by C. Kramarae (pp. 41–61). New York: Routledge Kegan Paul.

Willis, P. (1977). Learning to Labour: How Working Class Kids Get Working Class Jobs. New York: Columbia University Press.

Wright, R. (1996). "The Occupational Masculinity of Computing." In Masculinities in Organizations, edited by C. Cheng (pp. 77–96). Thousand Oaks: Sage Publications.

ARTICLE 23

Kevin D. Henson
Jackie Krasas Rogers

"Why Marcia You've Changed!"
Male Clerical Temporary Workers Doing Masculinity in a Feminized Occupation

To say that organizations are gendered has many meanings, from gender segregation at work to the part organizations play in the cultural reproduction of gender inequality (Acker 1990; Britton 2000). We know that "advantage and disadvantage, exploitation and control, action and emotion, meaning and identity are patterned through and in terms of a distinction between male and female, masculine and feminine" (Acker 1990, 146). Interaction and identity are but two means through which gender is constituted and reproduced in the workplace. Men and women "do gender" (West and Fenstermaker 1995; West and Zimmerman 1987) at work in organizations that are themselves gendered, and organizational imperatives shape interaction that "naturalizes" and essentializes cultural constructions of masculinity and femininity for men and women. This study provides a look at men doing gender in the highly feminized context of temporary clerical employment.

Doing gender "appropriately" in the workplace has consequences, including material ones,

for both women and men. A significant portion of the existing sociological literature explores how women are required to do gender at work, including emotional labor, which often reinforces vulnerability and inequality (Hochschild 1983; Leidner 1993; Pierce 1995; Williams 1989, 1995; Rogers and Henson 1997). Yet, men are also required to do gender on the job, and although less well documented, men do perform emotional labor, albeit subject to a different set of constraints, expectations, and outcomes than women's emotional labor (Pierce 1995; Cheng 1996). Indeed, emotional work is implicated in the microprocesses of doing gender that reinforce, uphold, and even naturalize male dominance and hegemonic masculinity (Collinson and Hearn 1996).[1]

In contrast with Kanter's (1977) position that any token, male or female, is subject to a distinct set of negative experiences, a recent avenue of inquiry has demonstrated how some men "benefit" from their token status in "women's work"— riding the "glass escalator" to more prestigious, better-paid positions within women's professions (Pierce 1995; Williams 1995; Maume 1999). Although men who cross over into women's work are often seen as less manly, this disadvantage has paled in comparison to the material benefits available to (white) male tokens, who self-segregate (or are pushed) into higher pay and higher status specialties or administrative positions in female-dominated professions (see Williams 1989, 1995).

What happens, however, when men find themselves in a female-dominated occupation

Author's Note: An earlier version of this article was presented at the 1999 meeting of the American Sociological Association in Chicago, Illinois. We would like to thank Marjorie L. DeVault, Ronnie J. Steinberg, Judith Wittner, Anne Figert, Christine Bose, and the reviewers of *Gender & Society* for their comments on earlier drafts of this article.

From *Gender & Society* 15(2): 218–238. Copyright © 2001 Sociologists for Women in Society.

289

with limited opportunities to ride the glass escalator? Temporary clerical work is such an occupation. As externalized employment that institutionalizes limited access to internal labor markets, there is no glass escalator to ride in temporary clerical work. Temporary clerical work does not provide the opportunities for men (or women) to elevate their status through additional credentialing, specialization, or promotions. Indeed, upward mobility into permanent employment—hailed as a major benefit by the temporary industry—is extremely elusive (Smith 1998; Rogers 2000).[2] Therefore, male tokens in female-dominated temporary clerical work present an interesting case concerning the gendered nature of work. How does men's gender privilege operate in the absence of opportunities for upward mobility? Does men's presence in a dead-end, female-dominated occupation disrupt the gender order and challenge hegemonic masculinity?

In this article, we argue that although men's presence in temporary clerical work has the potential to challenge the "naturalness" of the gendered organization of work, in everyday practice it is assumed to say more about the essential nature of the individual men. Male clerical temporaries, as with other men who cross over into women's work, fall increasingly short of the ideals of hegemonic masculinity on at least two fronts. First, they face gender assessment through their lack of a "real" job (i.e., a full-time career in "men's work"). Second, their location in a feminized occupation that requires the performance of emphasized femininity, including deference and caretaking behaviors, calls into question their presumed heterosexuality. The resulting gender strategies (Hochschild 1989) these men adopt reveal how male clerical temporary workers "do masculinity" to reassert the feminine identification of the job while rejecting its application to them. In particular, we argue that men in clerical temporary work do masculinity through renaming and reframing the work, distancing themselves from the work with a cover story, and resisting the demands to perform deference. Paradoxically, rather than disrupting the gender order, the gender strategies adopted help reproduce and naturalize the gendered organization of work and reinvigorate hegemonic masculinity and its domination over women and subaltern men.

The Gendered Character of Temporary Clerical Employment

While temporary employment has increased dramatically in the past 15 years in response to employers' demands (Golden and Appelbaum 1992), researchers have only recently begun to systematically document the effects of this trend for workers and workplace relations. The rapid expansion of temporary employment is profoundly changing the experience, meaning, and conditions of work for temporaries who, like other contingent workers, fall through the cracks of existing workplace protections and provision of benefits (Parker 1994; Henson 1996; Rogers and Henson 1997; Rogers 2000).

The clerical sector of temporary employment, like the permanent clerical sector, is predominantly composed of women (Bureau of Labor Statistics 1995). Historically, this association of temporary work with women's work was reflected in the common inclusion of the infantilizing term *girl* in the names of the earliest temporary agencies (e.g., Kelly Girl). While temporary agencies have formally modernized their names (i.e., Kelly Girl became Kelly Services), the continued popular usage of the outdated names accurately reflects the gendered composition of the temporary clerical workforce. Indeed, a survey by the National Association of Temporary Services (1992) estimated that 80 percent of member agency temporaries were women. A recent government survey concluded that "workers employed by temporary help agencies in February 1997 were more likely than other workers to be young, female, Black or Hispanic" (Cohany 1998, 13).

Contemporary clerical temporary employment, like permanent clerical work, is so completely identified as women's work that until recently, it was considered inappropriate employment for a man, even by the temporary industry.

Until the 1960s, in fact, it was common policy within the industry not to accept male applicants for clerical temporary work (Moore 1963, 35). Men, it was asserted, should be seeking a permanent, full-time career-type job—a "real job"—that would allow them to work hard, be financially successful, and take on the idealized (male) breadwinner role (Connell 1987, 1995; Cheng 1996).

Recently, however, men have come to constitute a greater proportion of temporary agency workers, although they are still more likely to be working as industrial than clerical temporaries (see Parker 1994). In fact, the continued numerical predominance of women in both the permanent and temporary clerical workforce often leads to the assumption that clerical temporary workers are women. Indeed, the job of clerical temporary worker is gendered—more specifically feminized—as women's work. Consequently, temporary work, clerical work, and especially temporary clerical work are perceived as women's work.

Given temporaries' low status and vulnerability to work deprivation, the expectations of temporary agencies and clients become de facto job requirements that shape temporary workers' interactions in such a way that one's gender and sexuality are prominently featured as aspects of the work (see Rogers and Henson 1997). For example, the demands of temporary agencies and client companies for particular (gendered or sexy) physical presentations, and the embedded expectations for deference and caretaking behaviors, highlight the gendered (feminized) and sexualized nature of temporary clerical work (Henson 1996; Rogers and Henson 1997). Indeed, the common association of temporary work with promiscuity, or "occupational sleeping around," highlights the ways in which clerical work and temporary work intersect to create a highly feminized job (see Rogers 2000 for a discussion of the gendering of temporary versus clerical work). In other words, temporary clerical work is a gendered (as well as raced, classed, aged, and heterosexualized) occupation that requires workers to do gender (and race, class, and so forth) in certain forms, recreating them and making them appear natural (see West and Zimmerman 1987; Acker 1990, West and Fenstermaker 1995). The type of gender one must "do" in clerical temporary work is primarily white, middle-class, heterosexual femininity. Consequently, while certain exceptions are made, it is nearly impossible to do this brand of femininity appropriately if you are a man or a woman of color. After describing our research methodology, we examine the gendered (feminized) context of clerical temporary employment, the institutionalized challenges to masculinity such employment poses for token men, and the gender strategies token men adopt to buttress their sense of masculinity. Finally, we discuss how these gender strategies reproduce rather than challenge the gender order.

Method

This research is based on in-depth interviews and extensive participant observation from two broader studies on temporary clerical work we conducted in Chicago in 1990–1991 (Henson 1996) and Los Angeles in 1993–1994 (Rogers 2000). During the participant observation component of our studies, each of us worked as a clerical temporary worker for more than one year on a variety of assignments in many different types of organizations. We entered our temporary employment with many common characteristics such as relatively high educational attainment, whiteness, and youthfulness (Kevin was 26; Jackie was 28), yet our different respective genders affected our temporary work experiences in many dissimilar and revealing ways.

In addition to our participant–observation work, each of us conducted open-ended, semi-structured interviews with temporaries and agency personnel, yielding 68 interviews in all (35 in Chicago and 33 in Los Angeles). Our interview participants included 10 temporary agency personnel and one client company representative, but the majority (57) were temporary clerical workers. We located participants of this highly fluid and difficult-to-access workforce through a variety of methods—personal contacts made on assignment, responses to fliers placed at temporary agency offices, and personal referrals. We pursued a grounded theory approach in our research, including an emphasis on theoretical sampling (Glaser and Strauss 1965, 1967). Consequently, we sought out participants who maximized the range of temporary work experiences we studied rather than pursuing a strictly representative sample of the temporary workforce. In the end, our sample of temporary clerical workers included a relatively diverse group of participants, including 20 men and 37 women ranging in age from 20 to 60 (see Table 23.1).[3] Indeed, our sample approximates the age and race distribution of the general temporary workforce. However, our sample differs in at least one important way from the general clerical temporary workforce. We deliberately oversampled for men in this female-dominated occupation. Collectively, our interview participants had worked through more than 40 temporary agencies with individual tenure in temporary employment ranging from a few months to more than 10 years.

We followed flexible open-ended interview schedules, addressing themes that we had identified as salient during our participant–observation work and pursued new themes as they emerged. We both interviewed women and men in our respective locales, and although evidence of participants' negotiation of the "gendered context of the [interview] interaction" emerged (e.g., men talked directly about feeling "less manly" to Jackie but talked more abstractly about feeling like "failures" to Kevin), there was a remarkable overlap and consistency in the substance of participants' responses (see Williams and Heikes 1993). We tape-recorded, transcribed, and analyzed all of the interviews. Although at first we pursued an open coding process focusing on general concepts such as stigmatization and coping strategies, eventually our analysis revealed consistent gendered patterns in our data. All names indicated in the body of the article are pseudonyms.

What's He Doing Here?

Male temporary clerical workers initially disrupt the gendered landscape of an organization since both the permanent and temporary clerical workforces are female dominated. This is reflected in the consistency with which token male clerical temporaries were met with surprise on the job. Indeed, the reaction to token men highlights the almost complete feminization of the work and the associated expectation that temporary workers will be women. The male temporaries we interviewed, for example, universally commented on their experiences as token men in women's work:

> There are areas where I felt that I did not fit in properly because I was a man on a temp assignment. (Michael Glenn, 26-year-old Asian American man)
>
> People are looking at me like, "What are you doing here?" Like they're thinking, "Gee, what's the deal? Shouldn't you be, I don't know, doing something else?" I mean it's like it's sort of fine if you're just out of school. They kind of expect well, you're doing this until you get a regular job. (Harold Koenig, 29-year-old white man)

Similarly, Henson was conscious on more than one of his assignments of steady streams of chuckling female workers conspicuously moving past his workstation, (apparently) to see the male receptionist. While there might be socially acceptable reasons for a young man's location in

■ **TABLE 23.1**
Race/Ethnicity and Gender of Temporary Clerical Workers

Race/Ethnicity	Men	Women
White	13	28
African American	3	7
Asian	1	2
Latino/Latina	1	0
Other	2	0
Total	20	37

temporary work (e.g., "just out of school" or "until you get a regular job"), for men, it is generally employment requiring an explanation.[4]

In fact, the disruption of the taken-for-granted naturalness of workplace gender segregation by the presence of male temporaries was often a source of humor for permanent workers. For example, Henson repeatedly encountered variants of a joke that played on themes of gender and mistaken identity. Permanent workers, especially men, upon seeing him for the first time at a (female) permanent worker's desk, would declare with mock seriousness, "Why (Marcia, Faye, Lucy) you've changed!" The humor of this joke, apparently, derived from the mismatch between the expected gender of the worker and Henson's gender. Another widespread joke, playing on similar themes, was to knowingly misattribute ownership of a permanent female employee's personal (and feminine) belongings to a male temporary through a mock compliment such as, "Nice pumps." Jackie, however, experienced neither the need to explain her employment nor the jokes.

The feminized nature of the work was further highlighted when others failed to recognize a male temporary as the secretary, mistaking him for someone with higher organizational status. Jon Carter, for example, described the confusion callers experienced when they heard his masculine voice at the receptionist's desk: "I get a lot of people, you know, that are confused as to who I am because it's a male voice" (23-year-old gay white man). Henson also experienced being mistaken for a permanent (higher status) new hire. One coworker, realizing his error after warmly welcoming Kevin and introducing himself, quickly pulled back his extended hand and retreated in embarrassment.

Finally, the feminized nature of temporary work was revealed by the extent to which "male" continues to be the verbally marked category. Note, for example, Linda Schmidt's verbal marking of both "male secretaries" and "male temps":

> Roger Piderat. He was a male secretary. He was very good. And then we had a male temp come in. And he was English. He was a nice guy. And he did reception for a while. And he worked at Anne's desk for a while. But he was a very pleasant person too. So we've had male secretaries before. (Linda Schmidt, 38-year-old white woman)

As with women in nontraditional occupations (e.g., female doctors or female lawyers), men in nontraditional (secretarial and clerical) work are the marked category.

The expectation, indeed assumption, that (requested) temporary workers will be women sometimes is expressed as an overt preference for women—or aversion to men—in these positions. Although temporary agencies are legally required to operate under equal opportunity employer legislation (i.e., to hire workers without regard to race, sex, or age), temporaries are nevertheless often placed for non-skill-specific characteristics including their race, gender, age, and physical attractiveness (Henson 1996; Rogers and Henson 1997; Rogers 2000). Cindy Beitz, a temporary counselor, described how client companies sometimes explicitly, and quite illegally, requested female temporaries:

> You can call them and say, "We have a young gentleman who will be coming in there tomorrow for you." And sometimes they will say . . . they'll come out and say, "Well, I don't want him. I told you I wanted a woman." (Cindy Beitz, 33-year-old white woman)

Without prompting, approximately half of the agency representatives mentioned similar illegal requests. Similarly, temporary workers like Irene Pedersen, who were privy to client company–agency interactions, reported overhearing illegal requests:

> I worked on a temp assignment somewhere in the Personnel Department at this company, and the client wanted a temp receptionist. And he would come in and beat on the personnel manager, he didn't want a man. He didn't want anybody who was Black, he didn't want anybody who was this. (Irene Pedersen, 25-year-old white woman)

Temporary workers were often aware, or at least suspected, that personal characteristics such as gender determined their access to jobs. Arnold Finch, for example, hypothesized that he had lost a job because of his gender:

> I was working a temp job and I left there. I did really good work. They wouldn't call me back. The only reason why, I was a male. They only wanted females to work that job. . . . It's just that I guess companies that . . . when somebody comes in the door, they want a pretty, happy, smiling female face behind the counter. (Arnold Finch, 23-year-old white man)

In addition, Henson lost at least one clerical assignment admittedly on the basis of his gender: "The client isn't sure if they want a male temporary or not. Whoever placed the order is going to check and see if it's okay" (Henson's field notes, 1990). Although Kevin had cross-trained in preparation at the agency's office on a specific word processing program (without pay), the assignment was withdrawn. Neither Rogers nor any of the women we interviewed experienced a negative gender screening similar to Henson's—they were the right gender.[5]

Not only is clerical temporary work feminized, it is also heterosexualized, especially for women. Clients, for example, often included demands for particular feminized (even sexy) physical presentations when placing an order for temporary help:

> When we get a position like that in where they say, "She should wear this outfit" or "She should look like this." Whatever. We'll still recommend . . . we can still call men in too, but . . . (Cindy Beitz, 33-year-old white woman)

> They'll ask for blond and blue eyes and stuff like that. Always for the front office. We tell them that we'll send the best qualified. If we send a qualified person and they send 'em back because they're not blond, we obviously wouldn't be able to fill that order. They'll go to another agency that will. (Regina Mason, 44-year-old Latina agency manager)

Indeed, female temporary secretaries, like women serving higher status men in other traditional women's work (MacKinnon 1979; Hall 1993), were often expected to make an offering of their gender, including their sexual attractiveness, as part of the job. Since the agencies' interests are in pleasing clients, even some of the more egregious requests for female temporary workers as sex objects (e.g., for a young, blond woman with great legs) are often honored (Henson 1996; Rogers and Henson 1997; Rogers 2000). Because temporary agencies depend on client companies for revenue, they are under considerable pressure to comply with these client requests. Agencies that assiduously follow the law risk losing their clients.

However, it would be inaccurate to describe the preference for women in temporary secretarial work as simply the desire to employ women as sexual objects. The employers' preference for women is partially explained by employers' essentialized understandings of gender as it relates to workers' capabilities. In other words, client companies and agencies often use a "gender logic" when matching workers with assignments (Hossfeld 1990). Women, in this logic, are often assumed to be innately superior at work calling for certain emotional and relational skills (Hochschild 1983; Leidner 1993; Pierce 1995). In fact, temporary secretaries, as part of the job, are expected to perform emotional labor—to be deferential and nurturing toward managers, coworkers, clients, and agency personnel (Henson 1996; Rogers and Henson 1997). As Pierce (1995, 89) has argued about another feminized occupation (paralegals), "The feminization of this occupation . . . is created not only by employer preference for women, but by the fact that the occupation itself—formally or not—calls for women to cater to men's emotional needs."

Challenges to Masculinity

Men who cross over to work in highly feminized occupations face institutionalized challenges to their sense of masculinity, that is, the extent to which they measure up to the dictates of hegemonic masculinity (Pringle 1993; Pierce 1995; Williams 1989, 1995). Male clerical temporary workers, for example, face gender assessment—highlighting their failure to live up to the ideals of hegemonic masculinity—on at least two fronts. First, they are working temporary rather than permanent, higher paying, full-time jobs ("He should have a real job"), which limits their ability to assume the male breadwinner role. Second, they are doing clerical work (i.e., women's work), including demands for deference and caretaking, which challenges their presumed heterosexuality ("He could be gay"). Yet, unlike the situation of male nurses or elementary schoolteachers (Williams 1989, 1995), clerical temporary work is not a semiprofession with institutionalized room for upward mobility via the glass escalator.

He Should Have a Real Job

Male temporary clerical workers' individual failings, when faced with gender assessment, included questions about their drive, motivation, and competence for male career success (i.e., "Why doesn't he have a real job?"). Indeed, permanent work providing a sufficient financial base to assume the male breadwinner role is a core component of hegemonic masculine identity (Connell 1987, 1995; Kimmel 1994; Cheng 1996). Consequently, men who have jobs that do not allow them to assume the breadwinner role—such as those in part-time or temporary work—are perceived as "less manly" (Epstein et al. 1999; Rogers 2000).

Indeed, the assumption that men, but not women, should hold or desire permanent employment was widely shared by temporary workers, temporary agency staff, and client company supervisors. For example, Dorothy Brooke, a temporary worker, expressed the idea that temporary work was acceptable for women but that men should be striving to get real jobs. In other words, temporary jobs are unsatisfactory jobs that no real man (i.e., white, heterosexual, and middle-class) would or should accept:

> I was surprised by how many older men were working as temporaries. I guess I expected to just see women. But I asked one of these guys if he was looking for full-time work. And he said he was just hoping that one of his temp jobs was going to turn into a full-time job. I thought you've got to have more spunk than that to get a job. (Henson's field notes, 1991)

Likewise, Regina Mason, a temporary agency manager, struggling to explain the anomalous presence of men in temporary work, tapped into gendered industry rhetoric portraying the work as good for women—a "flexible, secondary wage earning job"—but inadequate for men, except on a truly temporary basis (Henson 1996):

> I think that's the trend that men have never thought of working temporary. I mean that's a new thing to men to go work temp. It's the old attitude that men are breadwinners you know so they gotta have stability, permanency, a real job. But we still have a few men working. I think a lot of housewives don't want anything permanent. So they prefer to come in and just do temping so that they can take off when they want to. (Regina Mason, 44-year-old Latina agency manager)

Ironically, while men in temporary employment are curiosities to be pitied, the low-pay, impermanence, and dead-end nature of these jobs is seen as natural or unproblematic for women. Consequently, an agency manager can bemoan the difficulties she has telling men, but not women, "they'd only be getting maybe $8 an hour and not necessarily steady work" (Rogers's field notes, 1994).

The irregularity, uncertainty, and poor remuneration of clerical temporary work challenged male temporaries' abilities to live up to the breadwinner, and self-sufficiency, ideals contained in hegemonic masculinity. Without prompting, most men in the study detailed the challenges temping presented to their sense of masculinity. Kirk Stevens, for example, felt guilty and ashamed about his inability to take on the idealized (male) breadwinner role. An inadequate supply of assignments left Kirk financially dependent on his girlfriend:

> So far, this summer, Natalie, my girlfriend, has been supporting us both. I really can't stand it. She leaves at eight thirty and gets home at five thirty or six and she's totally exhausted. She

can't stay up past eleven at night. And I feel really guilty 'cause she wouldn't have to be working quite so crazy if I were getting any money in at all. But it's difficult for both of us. (Kirk Stevens, 27-year-old white man)

While financial dependence is seen as an unproblematic aspect of low-wage temporary employment for women (i.e., the income is assumed to be secondary), this same dependence among men often challenges male temporary workers' sense of masculinity. In other words, not only is the male temporary worker unable to provide for others but he also finds himself in the painful position of dependence.

The lack of respect accorded to men who fail to live up to the career orientation ideals embodied in hegemonic masculinity was not lost on male temporary workers. Albert Baxter, for example, described his belief that male temporary workers received less respect than female temporaries:

I think men get a little less respect if they're temping. There's that expectation that they should be like career oriented and like moving up in the world and being a businessman and moving himself forward in business. Where women can do that but it's not an expectation. And so I think that, I think that's where that Kelly Girl image, that temporaries are women is. I have noticed that there is a certain amount, looking down upon. I think that's true of temps in general. They're somewhat looked down upon. I think the men maybe more. (Albert Baxter, 31-year-old white man)

Accordingly, male temporary workers sometimes experienced feelings of inferiority and inadequacy when recognized (and judged) as temporary secretaries by others. Denny Lincoln, for example, articulated feelings of inferiority when others assessed him on the basis of his low-wage, low-status temporary employment:

Why are all these people taking $6.50 and $7.00 an hour jobs? Why? Why can't they go out and get a real job? And I think that's what goes through people's minds. Like you have a college degree! What the hell's going on here? There must be something wrong with this guy.

He can't hold a job, he's working for 7 bucks an hour stuffing envelopes. (Denny Lincoln, 39-year-old white man)

Similarly, Bob Johnson described the embarrassment he felt when recognized on a temporary assignment by old college classmates:

Where I work there's a lot of people who I graduated [from college] with on staff. And when they see me, you know, they go, "What are you doing? Why are you working as a secretary?" And you have to explain yourself. Well, I'm trying to find the ideal job. Maybe it's all in my mind because I feel sort of inferior to that because they're kind of established. I feel really inadequate. (Bob Johnson, 23-year-old gay white man)

Bob's reaction reveals his embarrassment about both the impermanence of his employment ("they're kind of established") and its feminization ("Why are you working as a secretary?").

He Could Be Gay

Male temporary workers' failing, when faced with gender assessment, does not stop with questioning their drive, motivation, and competence for male career success. Their location in a female-dominated occupation that requires and produces emphasized femininity, including deferential and nurturing behaviors, also calls into question their presumed heterosexuality, a core component of hegemonic masculinity. When men do deference and caretaking, they are popularly defined as feminine—like women—and therefore gay. As Donaldson (1993, 648) has noted, any type of powerlessness quickly becomes conflated with the popular stereotype of homosexuality. Male clerical temporaries, as with male secretaries (Pringle 1993), nurses (Williams 1989), elementary schoolteachers (Williams 1995), and paralegals (Pierce 1995), are regularly stereotyped as gay. Patsy Goodrich, for example, accepted the construction of male temporary clerical workers, but not male temporary industrial workers, as gay:

But, yeah, I think most of the people [in temporary work] that I know have either been gay men or women. Or lesbian women. I don't really know. I can't think of a straight man that I know that's done it. Except for my brother. But he did the kind where it's like the industrial side. (Patsy Goodrich, 27-year-old white lesbian woman)

Similarly, in searching for an explanation for the presence of some men in temporary clerical work, Connie Young described the male temporary workers in her office as unmasculine or effeminate in appearance:

We've had male temporaries come in to answer the phones and do whatever typing jobs. And, for some reason, all the male temps we've gotten didn't have any masculine features. They're very longhaired, ponytailed, very artsy look. And the men in business suits would look at them and kind of not take them seriously actually. You know like, "Oh, he has an earring." (Connie Young, 25-year-old Asian American woman)

In addition, male temporary workers are feminized as they enter and interact in an organizational environment that requires the performance of emphasized femininity, including deference. Male temporaries' discomfort with the demands for deference, although more limited than the deferential demands made of female temporaries, revealed both the gendered nature of the work and its implicit threat to their sense of masculinity:

It's a manly thing to be in charge. And men should want to be, supposedly in charge and delegating things. If you're a man and you're being delegated to, it somehow makes you less manly. You know what I'm saying? Whereas it seems to be okay for the person delegating to women. And the women, maybe they're just projecting that to get by. It seems that they're more okay with that than men are. I guess I'm saying that it makes me feel less of the manly kind of qualities, like I'm in charge, you know. And men should be like takin' meetings and barking orders instead of just being subservient. (Harold Koenig, 29-year-old heterosexual white man)

Several male temporary workers remarked that they were surprised by the deferential demands of temporary work—as men with male privilege, they had rarely experienced the requirement to enact deference.

Similarly, Kirk Stevens was outraged when he was asked to perform the subservient work of cleaning bathrooms:

I got a phone call saying there was this company that needed me to go out and change the light bulbs And I met the guy and he gives me, you know, the obligatory tour.... And then he gives me a bucket and a mop, some rubber gloves, and he says, "Now what I'd really like you to do, just to start off, is clean, if you could, the bathrooms need cleaning. Could you clean this bathroom?" And it didn't even ... I just ... I just can't believe that I didn't just say. "Go to hell. I'm not going to clean your goddamn bathrooms." (Kirk Stevens, 27-year-old heterosexual white man)

While someone has to clean bathrooms (often work relegated to poor women of color), Kirk Stevens believed he was not the type of person (e.g., white, educated, and male) who should be asked to do so. The negative reactions to deferential demands were strongest (but not exclusive) among white, heterosexual, college-educated men who would fall closest to the cultural ideal of hegemonic masculinity (see Connell 1987, 1995).

Male temporary workers, heterosexual and gay, were aware of the construction of the male temporary as gay. A noted exception, Michael Glenn, positively rather than negatively framed and accepted an essentialized construction of temporary workers as gay:

But temps usually are women or homosexual men. Um, it's not to say that some heterosexual men don't make good temps, but I think it's harder to find. And then you get into the whole psychology of heterosexual men I suppose. *Men are from Mars* and all of that. But heterosexual men are not as great at being people-people.... you have to be flexible. And there's more of a rigidity to a heterosexual male. And then again in the gradations, I would say there's more rigidity for a homosexual male than for a woman. And I'm not even gonna try to place homosexual women. (Michael Glenn, 26-year-old Asian American gay man)

Note how Michael's assertion that gay men excel over heterosexual men at the emotional and relational demands of the job (being flexible and being "people-people") leads him to the conclusion that gay men are more suited to temporary clerical work. Ironically, while gay men come closer than straight men to naturally making good temps in his account, they still do not measure up to (real, i.e., heterosexual) women, leaving the natural gender order intact.

Gender Strategies/ Hegemonic Bargains

The male temporaries we interviewed, faced with gender assessment, adopted three primary gender strategies—renaming and reframing the work, distancing themselves from the work with a cover story, as well as the more risky strategy of resisting demands for deference—to do masculinity in a feminized occupation. Ironically, rather than disrupting the gender order, each of these strategies "enables men to maintain a sense of themselves as different from and better than women—thus contributing to the gender system that divides men from women in a way that privileges men" (Williams 1995, 123). Indeed, each of these gender strategies represents what Chen (1999, 600), modifying Kandiyoti's (1988) "patriarchal bargain" concept, has described as a "hegemonic bargain"—a situation in which a man's "gender strategy involves trading on (or benefiting from) the advantages conferred by his race, gender, sexuality, class, accent, and/or generational status to achieve "unblushing" manhood."

Doing Masculinity—Renaming and Reframing

One of the primary gender strategies male temporaries use to maintain their sense of masculinity is to distance themselves from the feminized aspects of the occupation by renaming or reframing the work. Male temporary secretaries, similar to men in other feminized occupations (Pierce 1995; Pringle 1993; Williams 1989, 1995), described their work in terms perceived to be more masculine, or at the very least, gender-neutral (e.g., word processor, administrative assistant, proofreader, bookkeeper). Steve Woodhead, a 35-year-old white gay man, for example, characterized his temporary work assignment as *bookkeeping*. Steven did not mention the temporary nature of his job, framing it more as an independent contracting arrangement. Indeed, male temporaries displayed an almost pathological avoidance of the term *secretarial*. In contrast, most of the female temporaries we interviewed described their work without hesitation as secretarial.

Occasionally, agency personnel and clients also participated in this project of renaming the work in more masculine terms. For example, on one of Henson's temporary assignments, the supervisor wondered aloud how to refer to the position in a more masculine or gender-neutral way: "Word processor? What should we call you? We're not going to call you secretary" (Henson's field notes, 1990). Whether this renaming was simply a courtesy to individual male temporary workers or a way of reconciling clients' discomfort in seeing men crossing over into women's work is unclear.[6]

In addition, some male temporary workers attempted to reframe the work as masculine by focusing on the technical competencies required on their temporary assignments. Indeed, to be technically competent is to be masculine (Cockburn 1985; Messerschmidt 1996; Wright 1996). Bob Johnson, for example, described his work in terms of the computer environment of software he was required to use on his (secretarial) work assignments:

> That was mostly work with IBM. You know, cause IBM is incredibly popular. So I used my WordPerfect a lot. And then when they didn't have any WordPerfect, they sent me out on proofreading assignments. To proofread these books that no one would ever, ever read. Basi-

cally, it's been a lot of word processing. (Bob Johnson, 23-year-old gay white man)

This focus on the technological aspects (computer) of the work, however, is not just a refusal to name the work. As Cynthia Cockburn (1985, 12) has noted, "Femininity is incompatible with technological competence; to feel technically competent is to feel manly." Therefore, focusing on the technological aspects of the work is part of a gender strategy that bolsters one's sense of power at the same time it reinforces segregation between men's and women's work.

Another reframing technique male temporaries use to maintain their masculinitiy is to borrow the prestige of the employing organization (Pierce 1995; Williams 1995) when describing their work to outsiders, especially other men. A male paralegal in Pierce's (1995) study of gender in law firms described how he used the name of the law firm rather than his job title to impress outsiders. Similarly, Bob Johnson described the unit he was assigned to at a consulting firm in elaborate detail rather than his specific work tasks when asked about his temporary job:

> I work for six managers ... in the change management services division. Companies hire them to do consulting work and they sort of do a lot of work with organizations that are going through organizational change. Implementing new systems. Both in the workforce and in terms of like information technology. Sort of reeducating them and reorganizing them around different responsibilities and different organizational hierarchies. And the other division I work for is integration services. And they're really technical experts. In terms of different [computer] hardware and software configuration systems. (Bob Johnson, 23-year-old gay white man)

Only in follow-up questions did he detail his more mundane day-to-day secretarial tasks: "I do support work. It's a lot of typing up correspondence between clients and interoffice correspondence. A lot of filing. A lot of typing. Answering phones a lot. Most of the time."

Doing Masculinity—Telling the Cover Story

Male temporaries, almost universally, invoked the "cover story" as a gender strategy to buttress their challenged sense of masculinity. The cover story, told to both self and others, invokes an alternative identity and defines one as truly temporary or occupationally transient (Henson 1996). Male clerical temporaries, through telling the cover story both on and off the job, provide an explanation for their apparent lack of drive or competence in obtaining a real (male) job. Steve Woodhead, for example, described how he strategically used his cover story on new assignments: "Oh, I always told them I was an actor. Immediately. Immediately. And they were, like, 'Great! This is wonderful.' So maybe that's what cut the ice, you know. They knew I wasn't just waiting to get a *real job*. 'Why doesn't this guy have a *real job* yet?'" (35-year-old gay white man). Likewise, Harold Koenig said, "I always wanna tell people that I'm just doing this because I'm a writer and I'm really here because of that. But they really don't want to know that. It's like to save your ego" (29-year-old white man). The cover story, then, explains why a man in clerical temporary employment does not have a real job and asserts a more valuable (masculine) social identity.

While permanent workers might also define themselves as occupationally transient (Williams 1989; Garson 1994; Pierce 1995), the organization of temporary work provided workers with the ready-made temporary label. For example, Pierce (1995, 170) noted that male paralegals frequently asserted their occupational transience despite their permanent, full-time status ("I'm planning to go to law school after working as a legal assistant for a few years"). The organization of their work as permanent, however, required that these workers simultaneously demonstrate commitment and noncommitment to their work.

The organization of temporary work, however, presupposes that male temporary workers are uncommitted and facilitates the assumption that there is an underlying reason to be revealed. Note, for example, Henson's failed use of his cover story, in response to direct questioning, in this field note excerpt:

> Someone asked me if I just temped all the time or what I did. And I said, "Well no. I'm a graduate student in Sociology at Northwestern." She asked what I was studying and I said, "Clerical temporary work." Which she thought was really funny. I saw her in the elevator today and she asked, "How's your little study going?" Like, "Sure. That's just your little story." And it is. Because I'm [also] doing it for money. So it is just my little story. But I felt really belittled because she just wasn't taking me seriously. (Henson's field notes, 1991)

Coworkers commonly elicited cover stories from men, but seldom from women. While some women did offer cover stories, their use appeared to be motivated by class rather than gender anxieties (i.e., "What am I doing here with a college degree?").[7] In fact, since women's presence in clerical temporary employment is naturalized, coworkers rarely pressed them for explanations of any sort. On the few occasions when this happened, the question was precipitated by the temporary worker's efforts or exceptional work performance. During her fieldwork, for example, Rogers's presence in temporary clerical work was questioned only once when she was found to possess unusually detailed knowledge about insurance benefits.

Doing Masculinity—Refusing to Do Deference

Finally, men in clerical temporary work often adopted the risky gender strategy of resisting demands for deference in an effort to do masculinity. Deference, however, is part of being a "good" temporary worker for both male and female temporaries (Rogers 1995; Henson 1996; Rogers and Henson 1997). Temporaries must enact subservience and deference, for example, to continue getting assignments. While other researchers (Hochschild 1983; Pierce 1995; Williams 1995) have argued that men in women's work are not required to do deference (or at least in the same way), we believe that there are occupations in which men are required to do deference, including clerical temporary work. While the demands for deference may be different for women and men (and different within genders along dimensions of race, age, and sexual orientation), men were still expected to provide deferential services as clerical temporary workers.

While none of the men reported ever being asked to get coffee, a request many women reported with great irritation, they were still expected to provide deferential services—smiling, waiting, taking orders, and tolerating the bad moods of their supervisors. In other words, women were asked to provide more of the nurturing and caretaking components of deference than men, especially when working for older and more established men. Helen, for example, reported receiving (and resisting) a particularly egregious request for caretaking behavior on one of her assignments:

> They had this glass candy jar this big. And like, "You're supposed to keep that filled with chocolate." Like, "Where do I get the chocolate from?" "Well, you know, just pick something up. Something cheap." Yeah. Like I'm supposed to go and buy a bag of Hershey's Kisses so that the executives can add to their waistlines. I'm like no. And it's been empty ever since I've been there. [Laughs]. (Helen Weinberg, 24-year-old white woman)

Helen, unlike many of the women we interviewed, resisted the most demeaning caretaking requests through a passive "forgetfulness" strategy. Although both female and male temporaries are generally passive in their resistance (Rogers 2000), the significance of deference in temporary employment for masculinity is heightened when we realize that most opportunities for resistance are passive ones.

The refusal to do deference, as doing masculinity, may be so important that male temporary workers risk losing the job rather than feel demeaned. Contrast Helen's forgetfulness strategy above with Bob's overt refusal to do deferential tasks, notably for a female superior:

> At my long-term assignment, this one permanent secretary was out sick. I had my own desk and I had things that had to be done. And this woman comes up to me and she hands me a stack of photocopying to do. And I said, "Excuse me." And she said, "Well this is for you to do." And I said, "Well, thank you, but I have my own work to do. This work has to be done by 5." And she goes, "Well, you are just a temp and blah, blah, blah, blah, blah." I said, "Wait a minute. I am a temporary worker, but I do have a desk and assigned work that has to be done." And she threw this little fit. And throughout the day she was really terse and really just a real bitch to me.... She was just awful. You know that whole mentality of "just a temp, just a temp." (Bob Johnson, 23-year-old gay white man)

Similarly, Pierce (1995, 92) reports a story of a male paralegal who did not successfully do deference and appropriately "manage his own anger" with an ill-behaved male attorney. He confronted the attorney on his abusive behavior, was removed from the case, and eventually pushed to a peripheral position within the firm.

Similarly, Henson discovered the risks in resisting demands for deference when he failed to adopt a submissive demeanor and was removed from an assignment. Near the end of his first week on a (scheduled) long-term assignment at a small medical college, Henson arrived to find a typed message from Shirley, his work-site supervisor, on his chair. The note clearly asserted the hierarchy of power and demanded deference and submission—especially since Shirley worked only a few feet from Henson's desk and could have easily communicated her request verbally:

> "Kevin. RE: Lunch today (12/5). My plans are to be out of the office from about 11:45 AM to 1:00 PM. (If you get hungry early, I suggest you have a snack before I leave at 11:45 AM). Thanks. Shirl."

This annoys me: patronizing and hostile—at least that's the way I take it. So, I very casually and fully aware of the politics, walk to Shirley's door with the note in hand and say, "Oh, about lunch.... That's great! That works out fine with my plans too. No problem." I'm upbeat and polite, but I'm framing it as giving permission or at least as an interaction between equals. (Henson's field notes, 1990)

At the end of the day, Henson said good night to Shirley and left with every intention of returning in the morning. That evening, however, he received a call from his agency counselor: "Hi Kevin. This is Wendy. I don't know how to tell you this, but the college called us today and they said they just didn't think things were working out. They don't want you to come back tomorrow." While Henson had completed the formal work adequately, he had consciously resisted adopting the appropriate submissive demeanor. By refusing to perform deference and doing masculinity instead, he had lost the assignment.

Demands for deference seemed to be the breaking point for the male temporaries in this study. They were no longer able to reframe their way out of their feminized position. Male privilege no longer protected these men from the requirements of the job, including the performance of feminine styles of emotional labor and deference. While men do perform emotional labor and even deference on the job (Hochschild 1983; Pierce 1995), they typically do so in ways that are compatible with hegemonic notions of masculinity. In contrast, male temporaries were required to enact feminine modes of deference. Thus, men's refusals to do deference in temporary clerical work come to serve as proof that men are not suited for temporary clerical work.

Conclusion

Male clerical temporaries, as with other men who cross over into women's work, fail to conform to the dictates of hegemonic masculinity on at least two fronts. First, they are working temporary rather than permanent, higher paying, full-time jobs (i.e., a real job), which limits their ability to assume the male breadwinner role. Second, they are doing clerical work (i.e., women's work), including demands for deference and caretaking, which challenges their presumed heterosexuality.

At first glance, men's presence in a female-dominated job such as temporary clerical work might appear to disrupt the gendered landscape of the workplace. Unlike men in women's semi-professions, however, these men cannot exercise their male privilege by riding the glass escalator to higher paying, more prestigious work. Work that is female dominated and very low status does not provide the credential system and internal labor market necessary for the operation of the glass escalator. Here, occupational specificity makes all the difference in understanding men's interactions in female-dominated work. The experience of male temporary clerical workers neither conforms wholly to Kanter's (1977) theory of tokenism nor to Williams's (1992) glass escalator theory. Rather, these men experience a gendered set of token-related problems that center on maintaining the ideals of hegemonic masculinity.

With little organizational opportunity for upward mobility, men do gender in such a way that they reassert the feminine identification of the job while rejecting its application to them. Through renaming and reframing their individual duties, men distance themselves from the most feminized aspects of the job. Through telling their cover story, men construct their presence in temporary work as truly transient while naturalizing women's numerical dominance in the job. While men's refusal to do female-typed deference places them at risk of job loss individually, the meanings attributed to those actions once again reproduce the gender order as men are confirmed as unsuited for temporary clerical work. Through their gender strategies, male temporary clerical workers strike a hegemonic bargain, retracing the lines of occupational segregation and reinvigorating hegemonic masculinity and its domination over women and subaltern men.

Notes

1. Connell (1987, 1995) argues that hegemonic masculinity is not a static and homogeneous trait or role but is the ascendant (dominant) definition of masculinity at any one time to which other men are measured and, almost invariably, found wanting. Although the specific dictates of hegemonic masculinity vary over time, it is "chiefly, though not exclusively, associated with men located in the uppermost reaches of a society's ascriptive hierarchies" (Chen 1999, 587). The power of hegemonic masculinity lies not so much in the extent to which men actually conform to its (impossible) expectations but rather in the practice of masculinity and the patriarchal dividend they collect (Connell 1987, 1995).

2. Nevertheless, men may have different rates of exit from temporary work into permanent employment gained from sources other than temporary agencies.

3. Although we did not systematically collect data on the sexual orientation of respondents, two women and 10 men in our sample self-identified as lesbian and gay. While we make no claims regarding generalizability on this front, we have marked sexual orientation of the interviewee where it is directly relevant as indicated by the respondents.

4. We would specify white men here, if our sample permitted, since race is theoretically an important part of the construction of the socially acceptable male temporary clerical worker.

5. Women did report negative screenings on the basis of race, age, and perceived attractiveness.

6. We documented no systematic pay differences for jobs that were renamed in more masculine terms. In fact, pay increases were seldom reported and difficult to negotiate (Rogers 2000).

7. Class anxiety is apparent in the men's comments as well. While class is an important component of hegemonic masculinity, it is difficult to unravel gender and class at this intersection.

References

Acker, Joan. 1990. Hierarchies, jobs, bodies: A theory of gendered organizations. *Gender & Society* 4:139–158.

Britton, Dana M. 2000. The epistemology of the gendered organization. *Gender & Society* 14:418–434.

Bureau of Labor Statistics. 1995. *Handbook of labor statistics*. Washington, DC: Government Printing Office.

Chen, Anthony S. 1999. Lives at the center of the periphery, lives at the periphery of the center: Chinese American masculinities and bargaining with hegemony. *Gender & Society* 13:584–607.

Cheng, Cliff. 1996. *Masculinities in organizations*. Thousand Oaks, CA: Sage.

Cockburn, Cynthia. 1985. *Machinery of dominance: Women, men, and technical know-how*. Boston: Northeastern University Press.

Cohany, Sharon R. 1998. Workers in alternative employment arrangements: A second look. *Monthly Labor Review* 121:3–21.

Collinson, David L., and Jeff Hearn. 1996. *Men as managers, managers as men: Critical perspectives on men, masculinities and managements*. Thousand Oaks, CA: Sage.

Connell, R. W. 1987. *Gender and power*. Palo Alto, CA: Stanford University Press.

———. 1995. *Masculinities*. Berkeley: University of California Press.

Donaldson, Mike. 1993. What is hegemonic masculinity? *Theory and Society* 22:643–657.

Epstein, C. F., C. Seron, B. Oglensky, and R. Saute. 1999. *The part-time paradox: Time norms, professional life, family and gender*. New York: Routledge.

Garson, Barbara. 1994. *All the livelong day: The meaning and demeaning of routine work*. Rev. 2d ed. New York: Penguin.

Glaser, Barney G., and Anselm L. Strauss. 1965. *Awareness of dying*. Chicago: Aldine.

———. 1967. *The discovery of grounded theory: Strategies for qualitative research*. Chicago: Aldine.

Golden, Lonnie, and Eileen Appelbaum. 1992. What was driving the 1982–88 boom in temporary employment: Preferences of workers or decisions and power of employers? *Journal of Economics and Society* 51:473–494.

Hall, Elaine, J. 1993. Smiling, deferring, and flirting: Doing gender by giving "good service." *Work & Occupations* 20:452–471.

Henson, Kevin, D. 1996. *Just a temp*. Philadelphia: Temple University Press.

Hochschild, Arlie R. 1983. *The managed heart: Commercialization of human feeling*. Berkeley: University of California Press.

———. 1989. *The second shift*. New York: Avon.

Hossfeld, Karen. 1990. Their logic against them: Contradictions in sex, race, and class in Silicon Valley. In *Women workers and global restructuring*, edited by K. Ward, Ithaca, NY: ILR Press.

Kandiyoti, Deniz. 1988. Bargaining with patriarchy. *Gender & Society* 2:274–290.

Kanter, Rosabeth M. 1977. *Men and women of the corporation*. New York: Basic Books.

Kimmel, Michael S. 1994. Masculinity as homophobia: Fear, shame, and silence in the construction of gender identity. In *Theorizing masculinities*, edited by Harry Brod and Michael Kaufman. Thousand Oaks, CA: Sage.

Leidner, Robin. 1993. *Fast food, fast talk: Service work and the routinization of everyday life*. Berkeley: University of California Press.

MacKinnon, Catharine A. 1979. *Sexual harassment of working women: A case of sex discrimination*. New Haven and London: Yale University Press.

Maume, David J. Jr. 1999. Glass ceilings and glass escalators: Occupational segregation and race and sex differences in managerial promotions. *Work & Occupations* 26:483–509.

Messerschmidt, James W. 1996. Managing to kill: Masculinities and the space shuttle Challenger explosion. In *Masculinities in organizations*, edited by C. Cheng. Thousand Oaks, CA: Sage.

Moore, Mack. A. 1963. The role of temporary help services in the clerical labor market. Ph.D. diss., University of Wisconsin–Madison.

National Association of Temporary Services. 1992. *Report on the temporary help services industry*. Alexandria, VA: DRI/McGraw-Hill.

Parker, Robert E. 1994. *Flesh peddlers and warm bodies: The temporary help industry and its workers*. New Brunswick, NJ: Rutgers University Press.

Pierce, Jennifer. 1995. *Gender trials: Emotional lives in contemporary law firms*. Berkeley: University of California Press.

Pringle, Rosemary. 1993. Male secretaries. In *Doing "women's work": Men in nontraditional occupations*, edited by C. L. Williams. Newbury Park, CA: Sage.

Rogers, Jackie K. 1995. Just a temp: Experience and structure of alienation in temporary clerical employment. *Work and Occupations* 22:137–166.

———. 2000. *Temps: The many faces of the changing workplace*. Ithaca, NY: Cornell University Press.

Rogers, Jackie K., and Kevin D. Henson. 1997. "Hey, why don't you wear a shorter skirt?" Structural vulnerability and the organization of sexual harassment in temporary clerical employment. *Gender & Society* 11:215–237.

Smith, Vicki. 1998. The fractured world of the temporary worker: Power, participation, and fragmentation in the contemporary workplace. *Social Problems* 45:411–430.

West, Candace, and Sarah Fenstermaker. 1995. Doing difference. *Gender & Society* 1:8–37.

West, Candace, and Don H. Zimmerman. 1987. Doing gender. *Gender & Society* 1:125–151.

Williams, Christine L. 1989. *Gender differences at work: Women and men in nontraditional occupations.* Berkeley: University of California Press.

———. 1992. The glass escalator: Hidden advantages for men in the "female" professions. *Social Problems* 39:253–267.

———. 1995. *Still a man's world: Men who do women's work.* Berkeley: University of California Press.

Williams, Christine L., and Joel E. Heikes, 1993. The importance of researcher's gender in the in-depth interview: Evidence from two case studies of male nurses. *Gender & Society* 7:280–291.

Wright, Rosemary. 1996. The occupational masculinity of computing. In *Masculinities in organizations,* edited by C. Cheng. Thousand Oaks, CA: Sage.

ARTICLE 24

Beth A. Quinn

Sexual Harassment and Masculinity: The Power and Meaning of "Girl Watching"

Confronted with complaints about sexual harassment or accounts in the media, some men claim that women are too sensitive or that they too often misinterpret men's intentions (Buckwald 1993; Bernstein 1994). In contrast, some women note with frustration that men just "don't get it" and lament the seeming inadequacy of sexual harassment policies (Conley 1991; Guccione 1992). Indeed, this ambiguity in defining acts of sexual harassment might be, as Cleveland and Kerst (1993) suggested, the most robust finding in sexual harassment research.

Using in-depth interviews with 43 employed men and women, this article examines a particular social practice—"girl watching"—as a means to understanding one way that these gender differences are produced. This analysis does not address the size or prevalence of these differences, nor does it present a direct comparison of men and women; this information is essential but well covered in the literature.[1] Instead, I follow Cleveland and Kerst's (1993) and Wood's (1998) suggestion that the question may best be unraveled by exploring how the "subject(ivities) of perpetrators, victims, and resistors of sexual harassment" are "discursively produced, reproduced, and altered" (Wood 1998, 28).

This article focuses on the subjectivities of the perpetrators of a disputable form of sexual harassment, "girl watching." The term refers to the act of men's sexually evaluating women, often in the company of other men. It may take the form of a verbal or gestural message of "check it out," boasts of sexual prowess, or explicit comments about a woman's body or imagined sexual acts. The target may be an individual woman or group of women or simply a photograph or other representation. The woman may be a stranger, coworker, supervisor, employee, or client. For the present analysis, girl watching within the workplace is [the focus].

The analysis is grounded in the work of masculinity scholars such as Connell (1987, 1995) in that it attempts to explain the subject positions of the interviewed men—not the abstract and genderless subjects of patriarchy but the gendered and privileged subjects embedded in this system. Since I am attempting to delineate the gendered worldviews of the interviewed men, I employ the term "girl watching," a phrase that reflects their language ("they watch girls").

I have chosen to center the analysis on girl watching within the workplace for two reasons. First, it appears to be fairly prevalent. For example, a survey of federal civil employees (U.S. Merit Systems Protection Board 1988) found that in the previous 24 months, 28 percent of the women surveyed had experienced "unwanted sexual looks or gestures," and 35 percent had experienced

---

Author's Note: I would like to thank the members of my faculty writing group—Lisa Aldred, Susan Kollin, and Colleen Mack-Canty—who prove again and again that cross-disciplinary feminist dialogue is not only possible but a powerful reality, even in the wilds of Montana. In addition, thanks to Lisa Jones for her thoughtful reading at a crucial time and to the anonymous reviewers who offered both productive critiques and encouragement.

From *Gender & Society* 16(3): 386–402. Copyright © 2002 Sociologists for Women in Society.

"unwanted sexual teasing, jokes, remarks, or questions." Second, girl watching is still often normalized and trivialized as only play, or "boys will be boys." A man watching girls—even in his workplace—is frequently accepted as a natural and commonplace activity, especially if he is in the presence of other men.[2] Indeed, it may be required (Hearn 1985). Thus, girl watching sits on the blurry edge between fun and harm, joking and harassment. An understanding of the process of identifying behavior as sexual harassment, or of rejecting this label, may be built on this ambiguity.

Girl watching has various forms and functions, depending on the context and the men involved. For example, it may be used by men as a directed act of power against a particular woman or women. In this, girl watching—at least in the workplace—is most clearly identified as harassing by both men and women. I am most interested, however, in the form where it is characterized as only play. This type is more obliquely motivated and, as I will argue, functions as a game men play to build shared masculine identities and social relations.

Multiple and contradictory subject positions are also evidenced in girl watching, most notably that between the gazing man and the woman he watches. Drawing on Michael Schwalbe's (1992) analysis of empathy and the formation of masculine identities, I argue that girl watching is premised on the obfuscation of this multiplicity through the objectification of the woman watched and a suppression of empathy for her. In conclusion, the ways these elements operate to produce gender differences in interpreting sexual harassment and the implications for developing effective policies are discussed.

Previous Research

The question of how behavior is or is not labeled as sexual harassment has been studied primarily through experimental vignettes and surveys.[3] In both methods, participants evaluate either hypothetical scenarios or lists of behaviors, considering whether, for example, the behavior constitutes sexual harassment, which party is most at fault, and what consequences the act might engender. Researchers manipulate factors such as the level of "welcomeness" the target exhibits, and the relationship of the actors (supervisor–employee, coworker–coworker).

Both methods consistently show that women are willing to define more acts as sexual harassment (Gutek, Morasch, and Cohen 1983; Padgitt and Padgitt 1986; Powell 1986; York 1989; but see Stockdale and Vaux 1993) and are more likely to see situations as coercive (Garcia, Milano, and Quijano 1989). When asked who is more to blame in a particular scenario, men are more likely to blame, and less likely to empathize with, the victim (Jensen and Gutek 1982; Kenig and Ryan 1986). In terms of actual behaviors like girl watching, the U.S. Merit Systems Protection Board (1988) survey found that 81 percent of the women surveyed considered "uninvited sexually suggestive looks or gestures" from a supervisor to be sexual harassment. While the majority of men (68 percent) also defined it as such, significantly more men were willing to dismiss such behavior. Similarly, while 40 percent of the men would not consider the same behavior from a coworker to be harassing, more than three-quarters of the women would.

The most common explanation offered for these differences is gender role socialization. This conclusion is supported by the consistent finding that the more men and women adhere to traditional gender roles, the more likely they are to deny the harm in sexual harassment and to consider the behavior acceptable or at least normal (Pryor 1987; Malovich and Stake 1990; Popovich et al. 1992; Gutek and Koss 1993; Murrell and Dietz-Uhler 1993; Tagri and Hayes 1997). Men who hold predatory ideas about sexuality, who are more likely to believe rape myths, and who are more likely to self-report that they would rape under certain circumstances are less likely to see behaviors as harassing (Pryor 1987; Reilly et al. 1992; Murrell and Dietz-Uhler 1993).

These findings do not, however, adequately address the between-group differences. The more one is socialized into traditional notions of sex roles, the more likely it is for both men and women to view the behaviors as acceptable or at least unchangeable. The processes by which gender roles operate to produce these differences remain underexamined.

Some theorists argue that men are more likely to discount the harassing aspects of their behavior because of a culturally conditional tendency to misperceive women's intentions. For example, Stockdale (1993, 96) argued that "patriarchal norms create a sexually aggressive belief system in some people more than others, and this belief system can lead to the propensity to misperceive." Gender differences in interpreting sexual harassment, then, may be the outcome of the acceptance of normative ideas about women's inscrutability and indirectness and men's role as sexual aggressors. Men see harmless flirtation or sexual interest rather than harassment because they misperceive women's intent and responses.

Stockdale's (1993) theory is promising but limited. First, while it may apply to actions such as repeatedly asking for dates and quid pro quo harassment,[4] it does not effectively explain motivations for more indirect actions, such as displaying pornography and girl watching. Second, it does not explain why some men are more likely to operate from these discourses of sexual aggression contributing to a propensity to misperceive.

Theoretical explanations that take into account the complexity and diversity of sexual harassing behaviors and their potentially multifaceted social etiologies are needed. An account of the processes by which these behaviors are produced and the active construction of their social meanings is necessary to unravel both between- and within-gender variations in behavior and interpretation. A fruitful framework from which to begin is an examination of masculine identities and the role of sexually harassing behaviors as a means to their production.

Method

I conducted 43 semistructured interviews with currently employed men and women between June 1994 and March 1995. Demographic characteristics of the participants are reported in Table 24.1. The interviews ranged in length from one to three hours. With one exception, interviews were audiotaped and transcribed in full.

Participants were contacted in two primary ways. Twenty-five participants were recruited from "Acme Electronics," a Southern California electronic design and manufacturing company. An additional 18 individuals were recruited from an evening class at a community college and a university summer school class, both in Southern California. These participants referred three more individuals. In addition to the interviews, I conducted participant observation for approximately one month while on site at Acme. This involved observations of the public and common spaces of the company.

At Acme, a human resources administrator drew four independent samples (salaried and hourly women and men) from the company's approximately 300 employees. Letters of invitation were sent to 40 individuals, and from this group, 13 women and 12 men agreed to be interviewed.[5]

The strength of organizationally grounded sampling is that it allows us to provide context for individual accounts. However, in smaller organizations and where participants occupy unique positions, this method can compromise participant anonymity when published versions of the research are accessed by participants. Since this is the case with Acme, and since organizational context is not particularly salient for this analysis, the identity of the participant's organization is sometimes intentionally obscured.

The strength of the second method of recruitment is that it provides access to individuals employed in diverse organizations (from self-employment to multinational corporations) and in a range of occupations (e.g., nanny, house painter, accounting manager). Not surprisingly,

TABLE 24.1
Participant Demographic Measures

Variable	Men n	Men %	Women n	Women %	Total n	Total %
Student participants and referrals	6	33	12	67	18	42
Racial/ethnic minority	2	33	2	17	4	22
Mean age		27.2		35		32.5
Married	3	50	3	25	6	33
Nontraditional job	1	17	4	33	5	28
Supervisor	0	0	6	50	6	33
Some college	6	100	12	100	18	100
Acme participants	12	48	13	52	25	58
Racial/ethnic minority	2	17	3	23	5	20
Mean age		42.3		34.6		38.6
Married	9	75	7	54	16	64
Nontraditional job	0	0	4	31	4	16
Supervisor	3	25	2	15	5	20
Some college	9	75	9	69	18	72
All participants	18	42	25	58	43	100
Racial/ethnic minority	4	22	5	20	9	21
Mean age		37.8		34.9		36.2
Married	12	67	10	40	22	51
Nontraditional job	1	6	8	32	9	21
Supervisor	3	17	8	32	11	26
Some college	15	82	21	84	36	84

drawing from college courses resulted in a group with similar educational backgrounds; all participants from this sample had some college, with 22 percent holding college degrees. Student samples and snowball sampling are not particularly robust in terms of generalizability. They are, nonetheless, regularly employed in qualitative studies (Connell 1995; Chen 1999) when the goal is theory development—as is the case here—rather than theory testing.

The interviews began with general questions about friendships and work relationships and progressed to specific questions about gender relations, sexual harassment, and the policies that seek to address it.[6] Since the main aim of the project was to explore how workplace events are framed as sexual harassment (and as legally bounded or not), the term "sexual harassment" was not introduced by the interviewer until late in the interview.

While the question of the relationship between masculinity and sexual harassment was central, I did not come to the research looking expressly for girl watching. Rather, it surfaced as a theme across several men's interviews in the context of a gender reversal question:

> It's the end of an average day. You get ready for bed and fall to sleep. In what seems only a moment, the alarm goes off. As you awake, you find your body to be oddly out of sorts.... To your surprise, you find that you have been transformed into the "opposite sex." Even

stranger, no one in your life seems to remember that you were ever any different.

Participants were asked to consider what it would be like to conduct their everyday work life in this transformed state. I was particularly interested in their estimation of the impact it would have on their interactions with coworkers and supervisors. Imagining themselves as the opposite sex, participants were forced to make explicit the operation of gender in their workplace, something they did not do in their initial discussions of a typical workday.

Interestingly, no man discussed girl watching in initial accounts of his workplace. I suspect that they did not consider it to be relevant to a discussion of their average *work* day, even though it became apparent that it was an integral daily activity for some groups of men. It emerged only when men were forced to consider themselves as explicitly gendered workers through the hypothetical question, something they were able initially to elide.[7]

Taking guidance from Glaser and Strauss's (1967) grounded theory and the methodological insights of Dorothy Smith (1990), transcripts were analyzed iteratively and inductively, with the goal of identifying the ideological tropes the speaker used to understand his or her identities, behaviors, and relationships. Theoretical concepts drawn from previous work on the etiology of sexual harassment (Bowman 1993; Cleveland and Kerst 1993), the construction of masculine identities (Connell 1995, 1987), and sociolegal theories of disputing and legal consciousness (Bumiller 1988; Conley and O'Barr 1998) guided the analysis.

Several related themes emerged and are discussed in the subsequent analysis. First, girl watching appears to function as a form of gendered play among men. This play is productive of masculine identities and premised on a studied lack of empathy with the feminine other. Second, men understand the targeted woman to be an object rather than a player in the game, and she is most often not the intended audience. This obfuscation of a woman's subjectivity, and men's refusal to consider the effects of their behavior, means men are likely to be confused when a woman complains. Thus, the production of masculinity though girl watching, and its compulsory disempathy, may be one factor in gender differences in the labeling of harassment.

Findings: Girl Watching as "Hommo-Sexuality"

[They] had a button on the computer that you pushed if there was a girl who came to the front counter.... It was a code and it said "BAFC"— Babe at Front Counter.... If the guy in the back looked up and saw a cute girl come in the station, he would hit this button for the other dispatcher to [come] see the cute girl.

—Paula, police officer

In its most serious form, girl watching operates as a targeted tactic of power. The men seem to want everyone—the targeted woman as well as coworkers, clients, and superiors—to know they are looking. The gaze demonstrates their right, as men, to sexually evaluate women. Through the gaze, the targeted woman is reduced to a sexual object, contradicting her other identities, such as that of competent worker or leader. This employment of the discourse of asymmetrical heterosexuality (i.e., the double standard) may trump a woman's formal organizational power, claims to professionalism, and organizational discourses of rationality (Collinson and Collinson 1989; Yount 1991; Gardner 1995).[8] As research on rape has demonstrated (Estrich 1987), calling attention to a woman's gendered sexuality can function to exclude recognition of her competence, rationality, trustworthiness, and even humanity. In contrast, the overt recognition of a man's (hetero)sexuality is normally compatible with other aspects of his identity; indeed, it is often required (Hearn 1985; Connell 1995). Thus, the power of sexuality is asymmetrical, in part, because being seen as sexual has different consequences for women and men.

But when they ogle, gawk, whistle and point, are men always so directly motivated to disempower their women colleagues? Is the target of the gaze also the intended audience? Consider, for example, this account told by Ed, a white, 29-year-old instrument technician.

> When a group of guys goes to a bar or a nightclub and they try to be manly. . . . A few of us always found [it] funny [when] a woman would walk by and a guy would be like, "I can have her." [pause] "Yeah, OK, we want to see it!" [laugh]

In his account—a fairly common one in men's discussions—the passing woman is simply a visual cue for their play. It seems clear that it is a game played by men for men; the woman's participation and awareness of her role seem fairly unimportant.

As Thorne (1993) reminded us, we should not be too quick to dismiss games as "only play." In her study of gender relations in elementary schools, Thorne found play to be a powerful form of gendered social action. One of its "clusters of meaning" most relevant here is that of "dramatic performance." In this, play functions as both a source of fun and a mechanism by which gendered identities, group boundaries, and power relations are (re)produced.

The metaphor of play was strong in Karl's comments. Karl, a white man in his early thirties who worked in a technical support role in the Acme engineering department, hoped to earn a degree in engineering. His frustration with his slow progress—which he attributed to the burdens of marriage and fatherhood—was evident throughout the interview. Karl saw himself as an undeserved outsider in his department and he seemed to delight in telling on the engineers.

Girl watching came up as Karl considered the gender reversal question. Like many of the men I interviewed, his first reaction was to muse about premenstrual syndrome and clothes. When I inquired about the potential social effects of the transformation (by asking him, Would it "be easier dealing with the engineers or would it be harder?") he haltingly introduced the engineers' "game."

Karl: Some of the engineers here are very [pause] they're not very, how shall we say? [pause] What's the way I want to put this? They're not very, uh [pause] what's the word? Um. It escapes me.

Researcher: Give me a hint?

Karl: They watch women but they're not very careful about getting caught.

Researcher: Oh! Like they ogle?

Karl: Ogle or gaze or [pause] stare even, or [pause] generate a commotion of an unusual nature.

His initial discomfort in discussing the issue (with me, I presume) is evident in his excruciatingly formal and hesitant language. The aspect of play, however, came through clearly when I pushed him to describe what generating a commotion looked like: " 'Oh! There goes so-and-so. Come and take a look! She's wearing this great outfit today!' Just like a schoolboy. They'll rush out of their offices and [cranes his neck] and check things out." That this is as a form of play was evident in Karl's boisterous tone and in his reference to schoolboys. This is not a case of an aggressive sexual appraising of a woman coworker but a commotion created for the benefit of other men.

At Acme, several spatial factors facilitated this form of girl watching. First, the engineering department is designed as an open-plan office with partitions at shoulder height, offering a maze-like geography that encourages group play. As Karl explained, the partitions offer both the opportunity for sight and cover from being seen. Although its significance escaped me at the time, I was directly introduced to the spatial aspects of the engineers' game of girl watching during my first day on site at Acme. That day, John, the current human resources director, gave me a tour of the facilities, walking me through the departments and offering informal introductions. As we entered the design engineering section, a rhythm of heads emerged from its landscape of partitions, and movement started in our direction. I was definitely aware of being on display as several men gave me obvious once-overs.

Second, Acme's building features a grand stairway that connects the second floor—where the engineering department is located—with the lobby. The stairway is enclosed by glass walls, offering a bird's eye view to the main lobby and the movements of visitors and the receptionists (all women). Robert, a senior design engineer, specifically noted the importance of the glass walls in his discussion of the engineers' girl watching.

> There's glass walls around the upstairs right here by the lobby. So when there's an attractive young female... someone will see the girl in the area and they will go back and inform all the men in the area. "Go check it out." [laugh] So we'll walk over to the glass window, you know, and we'll see who's down there.

One day near the end of my stay at Acme, I was reminded of his story as I ventured into the first-floor reception area. Looking up, I saw Robert and another man standing at the top of the stairs watching and commenting on the women gathered around the receptionist's desk. When he saw me, Robert gave me a sheepish grin and disappeared from sight.

Producing Masculinity

I suggest that girl watching in this form functions simultaneously as a form of play and as a potentially powerful site of gendered social action. Its social significance lies in its power to form identities and relationships based on these common practices for, as Cockburn (1983, 123) has noted, "patriarchy is as much about relations between man and man as it is about relations between men and women." Girl watching works similarly to the sexual joking that Johnson (1988) suggested is a common way for heterosexual men to establish intimacy among themselves.

In particular, girl watching works as a dramatic performance played to other men, a means by which a certain type of masculinity is produced and heterosexual desire displayed. It is a means by which men assert a masculine identity to other men, in an ironic "hommo-sexual" practice of heterosexuality (Butler 1990).[9] As Connell (1995) and others (West and Zimmerman 1987; Butler 1990) have aptly noted, masculinity is not a static identity but rather one that must constantly be reclaimed. The content of any performance—and there are multiple forms—is influenced by a hegemonic notion of masculinity. When asked what "being a man" entailed, many of the men and women I interviewed triangulated toward notions of strength (if not in muscle, then in character and job performance), dominance, and a marked sexuality, overflowing and uncontrollable to some degree and natural to the male "species." Heterosexuality is required, for just as the label "girl" questions a man's claim to masculine power, so does the label "fag" (Hopkins 1992; Pronger 1992). I asked Karl, for example, if he would consider his sons "good men" if they were gay. His response was laced with ambivalence; he noted only that the question was "a tough one."

The practice of girl watching is just that—a practice—one rehearsed and performed in everyday settings. This aspect of rehearsal was evident in my interview with Mike, a self-employed house painter who used to work construction. In locating himself as a born-again Christian, Mike recounted the girl watching of his fellow construction workers with contempt. Mike was particularly disturbed by a man who brought his young son to the job site one day. The boy was explicitly taught to catcall, a practice that included identifying the proper targets: women and effeminate men.

Girl watching, however, can be somewhat tenuous as a masculine practice. In their acknowledgment (to other men) of their supposed desire lies the possibility that in being too interested in women the players will be seen as mere schoolboys giggling in the playground. Taken too far, the practice undermines rather than supports a masculine performance. In Karl's discussion of girl watching, for example, he continually came back to the problem of men not being careful about getting caught. He referred to a particular group of men who, though "their wives are [pause] very attractive—very much so," still "gawk like schoolboys." Likewise, Stephan explained that men who are obvious, who "undress [women] with their eyes" probably do so "because they don't get enough women in their lives. Supposedly." A man must be interested in women, but not too interested; they must show their (hetero) sexual interest, but not overly so, for this would be to admit that women have power over them.

The Role of Objectification and (Dis)Empathy

As a performance of heterosexuality among men, the targeted woman is primarily an object onto which men's homosocial sexuality is projected. The presence of a woman in any form—embodied, pictorial, or as an image conjured from words—is required, but her subjectivity and active participation is not. To be sure, given the ways the discourse of asymmetrical sexuality works, men's actions may result in similarly negative effects on the targeted woman as that of a more direct form of sexualization. The crucial difference is that the men's understanding of their actions differs. This difference is one key to understanding the ambiguity around interpreting harassing behavior.

When asked about the engineers' practice of neck craning, Robert grinned, saying nothing at first. After some initial discussion, I started to ask him if he thought women were aware of their game ("Do you think that the women who are walking by . . . ?"). He interrupted, misreading my question. What resulted was a telling description of the core of the game:

> It depends. No. I don't know if they enjoy it. When I do it, if I do it, I'm not saying that I do. [big laugh] . . . If they do enjoy it, they don't say it. If they don't enjoy it—wait a minute, that didn't come out right. I don't know if they enjoy it or not [pause]; that's not the purpose of us popping our heads out.

Robert did not want to admit that women might not enjoy it ("that didn't come out right") but acknowledged that their feelings were irrelevant. Only subjects, not objects, take pleasure or are annoyed. If a women did complain, Robert thought "the guys wouldn't know what to say." In her analysis of street harassment, Gardner (1995, 187) found a similar absence, in that "men's interpretations seldom mentioned a woman's reaction, either guessed at or observed."

The centrality of objectification was also apparent in comments made by José, a Hispanic man in his late 40s who worked in manufacturing. For José, the issue came up when he considered the topic of compliments. He initially claimed that women enjoy compliments more than men do. In reconsidering, he remembered girl watching and the importance of intent.

> There is [pause] a point where [pause] a woman can be admired by [pause] a pair of eyes, but we're talking about "that look." Where, you know, you're admiring her because she's dressed nice, she's got a nice figure, she's got nice legs. But then you also have the other side. You have an animal who just seems to undress you with his eyes and he's just [pause], there's those kind of people out there too.

What is most interesting about this statement is that in making the distinction between merely admiring and an animal look that ravages, José switched subject position. He spoke in the second person when describing both form of looking, but his consistency in grammar belies a switch in subjectivity: you (as a man) admire, and you (as a woman) are undressed with his eyes. When considering an appropriate, complimentary gaze, José described it from a man's point of view; the subject who experiences the inappropriate, violating look, however, is a woman. Thus, as in Robert's account, José acknowledged that there are potentially different meanings in the act for men and women. In particular, to be admired in a certain way is potentially demeaning for a woman through its objectification.

The switch in subject position was also evident in Karl's remarks. Karl mentioned girl watching while imagining himself as a woman in the gender reversal question. As he took the subject position of the woman watched rather than the man watching, his understanding of the act as a harmless game was destabilized. Rather than taking pleasure in being the object of such attention, Karl would take pains to avoid it.

> So with these guys [if I were a woman], I would probably have to be very concerned about my attire in the lab. Because in a lot of cases, I'm working at a bench and I'm hunched over, in which case your shirt, for example, would open at the neckline, and I would just have to be concerned about that.

Thus, because the engineers girl watch, Karl feels that he would have to regulate his appearance if he were a woman, keeping the men from using him in their game of girl watching. When he considered the act from the point of view of a man, girl watching was simply a harmless antic and an act of appreciation. When he was forced to consider the subject position of a woman, however, girl watching was something to be avoided or at least carefully managed.

When asked to envision himself as a woman in his workplace, like many of the individuals I interviewed, Karl believed that he did not "know how to be a woman." Nonetheless, he produced an account that mirrored the stories of some of the women I interviewed. He knew the experience of girl watching could be quite different—in fact, threatening and potentially disempowering—for the woman who is its object. As such, the game was something to be avoided. In imagining themselves as women, the men remembered the practice of girl watching. None, however, were able to comfortably describe the game of girl watching from the perspective of a woman and maintain its (masculine) meaning as play.

In attempting to take up the subject position of a woman, these men are necessarily drawing on knowledge they already hold. If men simply "don't get it"—truly failing to see the harm in girl watching or other more serious acts of sexual harassment—then they should not be able to see this harm when envisioning themselves as women. What the interviews reveal is that many men—most of whom failed to see the harm of many acts that would constitute the hostile work environment form of sexual harassment—did in fact understand the harm of these acts when forced to consider the position of the targeted woman.

I suggest that the gender reversal scenario produced, in some men at least, a moment of empathy. Empathy, Schwalbe (1992) argued, requires two things. First, one must have some knowledge of the other's situation and feelings. Second, one must be motivated to take the position of the other. What the present research suggests is that gender differences in interpreting sexual harassment stem not so much from men's not getting it (a failure of the first element) but from a studied, often compulsory, lack of motivation to identify with women's experiences.

In his analysis of masculinity and empathy, Schwalbe (1992) argued that the requirements of masculinity necessitate a "narrowing of the moral self." Men learn that to effectively perform masculinity and to protect a masculine identity, they must, in many instances, ignore a woman's pain and obscure her viewpoint. Men fail to exhibit empathy with women because masculinity precludes them from taking the position of the feminine other, and men's moral stance vis-à-vis women is attenuated by this lack of empathy.

As a case study, Schwalbe (1992) considered the Thomas–Hill hearings, concluding that the examining senators maintained a masculinist stance that precluded them from giving serious consideration to Professor Hill's claims. A consequence of this masculine moral narrowing is that "charges of sexual harassment . . . are often seen as exaggerated or as fabricated out of misunderstanding or spite" (Schwalbe 1992, 46). Thus, gender differences in interpreting sexually harassing behaviors may stem more from acts of ignoring than states of ignorance.

The Problem with Getting Caught

But are women really the untroubled objects that girl watching—viewed through the eyes of men—suggests? Obviously not; the game may be premised on a denial of a woman's subjectivity, but an actual erasure is beyond men's power! It is in this multiplicity of subjectivities, as Butler (1990, ix) noted, where "trouble" lurks, provoked by "the unanticipated agency of a female 'object' who inexplicably returns the glance, reverses the gaze, and contests the place and authority of the masculine position." To face a returned gaze is to get caught, an act that has the power to undermine the logic of girl watching as simply a game among men. Karl, for example, noted that when caught, men are often flustered, a reaction suggesting that the boundaries of usual play have been disturbed.[10]

When a woman looks back, when she asks, "What are you looking at?" she speaks as a subject, and her status as mere object is disturbed. When the game is played as a form of hommosexuality, the confronted man may be baffled by her response. When she catches them looking, when she complains, the targeted woman speaks as a subject. The men, however, understand her primarily as an object, and objects do not object.

The radical potential of sexual harassment law is that it centers women's subjectivity, an aspect prompting Catharine MacKinnon's (1979) unusual hope for the law's potential as a remedy. For men engaged in girl watching, however, this subjectivity may be inconceivable. From their viewpoint, acts such as girl watching are simply games played with objects: women's bodies. Similar to Schwalbe's (1992) insight into the senators' reaction to Professor Hill, the harm of sexual harassment may seem more the result of a woman's complaint (and law's "illegitimate" encroachment into the everyday work world) than men's acts of objectification. For example, in reflecting on the impact of sexual harassment policies in the workplace, José lamented that "back in the '70s, [it was] all peace and love then. Now as things turn around, men can't get away with as much as what they used to." Just whose peace and love are we talking about?

Reactions to Anti–Sexual Harassment Training Programs

The role that objectification and disempathy play in men's girl watching has important implications for sexual harassment training. Consider the following account of a sexual harassment training session given in Cindy's workplace. Cindy, an Italian American woman in her early 20s, worked as a recruiter for a small telemarketing company in Southern California.

> [The trainer] just really laid down the ground rules, um, she had some scenarios. Saying, "OK, would you consider this sexual harassment?" "Would you . . ." this, this, this? "What level?" Da-da-da. So, um, they just gave us some real numbers as to lawsuits and cases. Just that "you guys better be careful" type of a thing.

From Cindy's description, this training is fairly typical in that it focuses on teaching participants definitions of sexual harassment and the legal ramifications of accusations. The trainer used the common strategy of presenting videos of potentially harassing situations and asking the participants how they would judge them. Cindy's description of the men's responses to these videos reveals the limitation of this approach.

> We were watching [the TV] and it was [like] a studio audience. And [men] were getting up in the studio audience making comments like "Oh well, look at her! I wouldn't want to do that to her either!" "Well, you're darn straight, look at her!"

Interestingly, the men successfully used the training session videos as an opportunity for girl watching through their public sexual evaluations of the women depicted. In this, the intent of the training session was doubly subverted. The men interpreted scenarios that Cindy found plainly harassing into mere instances of girl watching and sexual (dis)interest. The antiharassment video was ironically transformed into a forum for girl watching, effecting male bonding and the assertion of masculine identities to the exclusion of women coworkers. Also, by judging the complaining women to be inferior as women, the men sent the message that women who complain are those who fail at femininity.

Cindy conceded that relations between men and women in her workplace were considerably strained after the training ("That day, you definitely saw the men bond, you definitely saw the women bond, and there was a definite separation"). The effect of the training session, rather than curtailing the rampant sexual harassment in Cindy's workplace, operated as a site of masculine performance, evoking manly camaraderie and reestablishing gender boundaries.

To be effective, sexual harassment training programs must be grounded in a complex understanding of the ways acts such as girl watching operate in the workplace and the seeming necessity of a culled empathy to some forms of masculinity. Sexually harassing behaviors are produced from more than a lack of knowledge, simple sexist attitudes, or misplaced sexual desire. Some forms of sexually harassing behaviors—such as girl watching—are mechanisms through which gendered boundaries are patrolled and evoked and by which deeply held identities are established. This complexity requires complex interventions and leads to difficult questions about the possible efficacy of any workplace training program mandated in part by legal requirements.

Conclusions

In this analysis, I have sought to unravel the social logic of girl watching and its relationship to the question of gender differences in the interpretation of sexual harassment. In the form analyzed here, girl watching functions simultaneously as only play and as a potent site where power is played. Through the objectification on which it is premised and in the nonempathetic masculinity it supports, this form of girl watching simultaneously produces both the harassment and the barriers to men's acknowledgment of its potential harm.

The implications these findings have for anti-sexual harassment training are profound. If we understand harassment to be the result of a simple lack of knowledge (of ignorance), then straightforward informational sexual harassment training may be effective. The present analysis suggests, however, that the etiology of some harassment lies elsewhere. While they might have quarreled with it, most of the men I interviewed had fairly good abstract understandings of the behaviors their companies' sexual harassment policies prohibited. At the same time, in relating stories of social relations in their workplaces, most failed to identify specific behaviors as sexual harassment when they matched the abstract definition. As I have argued, the source of this contradiction lies not so much in ignorance but in acts of ignoring. Traditional sexual harassment training programs address the former rather than the latter. As such, their effectiveness against sexually harassing behaviors born out of social practices of masculinity like girl watching is questionable.

Ultimately, the project of challenging sexual harassment will be frustrated and our understanding distorted unless we interrogate hegemonic, patriarchal forms of masculinity and the practices by which they are (re)produced. We must continue to research the processes by which sexual harassment is produced and the gendered identities and subjectivities on which it poaches (Wood 1998). My study provides a first step toward a more process-oriented understanding of sexual harassment, the ways the social meanings of harassment are constructed, and ultimately, the potential success of antiharassment training programs.

Notes

1. See Welsh (1999) for a review of this literature.

2. For example, Maria, an administrative assistant I interviewed, simultaneously echoed and critiqued this understanding when she complained about her boss's girl watching in her presence: "If he wants to do that in front of other men . . . you know, that's what men do."

3. Recently, more researchers have turned to qualitative studies as a means to understand the process of labeling behavior as harassment. Of note are Collinson and Collinson (1996), Giuffre and Williams (1994), Quinn (2000), and Rogers and Henson (1997).

4. Quid pro quo ("this for that") sexual harassment occurs when a person with organizational power attempts to coerce an individual into sexual behavior by threatening adverse job actions.

5. This sample was not fully representative of the company's employees; male managers (mostly white) and minority manufacturing employees were underrepresented. Thus, the data presented here best represent the attitudes and workplace tactics of white men working in white-collar, technical positions and white and minority men in blue-collar jobs.

6. Acme employees were interviewed at work in an office off the main lobby. Students and referred participants were interviewed at sites convenient to them (e.g., an office, the library).

7. Not all the interviewed men discussed girl watching. When asked directly, they tended to grin knowingly, refusing to elaborate. This silence in the face of direct questioning—by a female researcher—is also perhaps an instance of getting caught.

8. I prefer the term "asymmetrical heterosexuality" over "double standard" because it directly references the dominance of heterosexuality and more accurately reflects the interconnected but different forms of acceptable sexuality for men and women. As Estrich (1987) argued, it is not simply that we hold men and women to different standards of sexuality but that these standards are (re)productive of women's disempowerment.

9. "Hommo" is a play on the French word for man, *homme*.

10. Men are not always concerned with getting caught, as the behavior of catcalling construction workers amply illustrates; that a woman hears is part of the thrill (Gardner 1995). The difference between the workplace and the street is the level of anonymity the men have vis-à-vis the woman and the complexity of social rules and the diversity of power sources an individual has at his or her disposal.

References

Bernstein, R. 1994. Guilty if charged. *New York Review of Books*, 13 January.

Bowman, C. G. 1993. Street harassment and the informal ghettoization of women. *Harvard Law Review* 106:517–580.

Buckwald, A. 1993. Compliment a woman, go to court. *Los Angeles Times*, 28 October.

Bumiller, K. 1988. *The civil rights society: The social construction of victims*. Baltimore: Johns Hopkins University Press.

Butler, J. 1990. *Gender trouble: Feminism and the subversion of identity*. New York: Routledge.

Chen, A. S. 1999. Lives at the center of the periphery, lives at the periphery of the center: Chinese American masculinities and bargaining with hegemony. *Gender & Society* 13:584–607.

Cleveland, J. N., and M. E. Kerst. 1993. Sexual harassment and perceptions of power: An underarticulated relationship. *Journal of Vocational Behavior* 42 (1): 49–67.

Cockburn, C. 1983. *Brothers: Male dominance and technological change*. London: Pluto Press.

Collinson, D. L., and M. Collinson. 1989. Sexuality in the workplace: The domination of men's sexuality. In *The sexuality of organizations*, edited by J. Hearn and D. L. Sheppard. Newbury Park, CA: Sage.

———. 1996. "It's only Dick": The sexual harassment of women managers in insurance sales. *Work, Employment & Society* 10 (1): 29–56.

Conley, F. K. 1991. Why I'm leaving Stanford: I wanted my dignity back. *Los Angeles Times*, 9 June.

Conley, J., and W. O'Barr. 1998. *Just words*. Chicago: University of Chicago Press.

Connell, R. W. 1987. *Gender and power*. Palo Alto, CA: Stanford University Press.

———. 1995. *Masculinities*. Berkeley: University of California Press.

Estrich, S. 1987. *Real rape*. Cambridge, MA: Harvard University Press.

Garcia, L., L. Milano, and A. Quijano. 1989. Perceptions of coercive sexual behavior by males and females. *Sex Roles* 21 (9/10): 569–577.

Gardner, C. B. 1995. *Passing by: Gender and public harassment*. Berkeley: University of California Press.

Giuffre, P., and C. Williams. 1994. Boundary lines: Labeling sexual harassment in restaurants. *Gender & Society* 8:378–401.

Glaser, B., and A. L. Strauss. 1967. *The discovery of grounded theory: Strategies for qualitative research*. Chicago: Aldine.

Guccione, J. 1992. Women judges still fighting harassment. *Daily Journal*, 13 October, 1.

Gutek, B. A., and M. P. Koss. 1993. Changed women and changed organizations: Consequences of and coping with sexual harassment. *Journal of Vocational Behavior* 42 (1): 28–48.

Gutek, B. A., B. Morasch, and A. G. Cohen. 1983. Interpreting social–sexual behavior in a work setting. *Journal of Vocational Behavior* 22 (1): 30–48.

Hearn, J. 1985. Men's sexuality at work. In *The sexuality of men,* edited by A. Metcalf and M. Humphries. London: Pluto Press.

Hopkins, P. 1992. Gender treachery: Homophobia, masculinity, and threatened identities. In *Rethinking masculinity: Philosophical explorations in light of feminism,* edited by L. May and R. Strikwerda. Lanham, MD: Littlefield, Adams.

Jensen, I. W., and B. A. Gutek. 1982. Attributions and assignment of responsibility in sexual harassment. *Journal of Social Issues* 38 (4): 121–136.

Johnson, M. 1988. *Strong mothers, weak wives.* Berkeley: University of California Press.

Kenig, S., and J. Ryan. 1986. Sex differences in levels of tolerance and attribution of blame for sexual harassment on a university campus. *Sex Roles* 15 (9/10): 535–549.

MacKinnon, C. A. 1979. *The sexual harassment of working women.* New Haven: Yale University Press.

Malovich, N. J., and J. E. Stake. 1990. Sexual harassment on campus: Individual differences in attitudes and beliefs. *Psychology of Women Quarterly* 14 (1): 63–81.

Murrell, A. J., and B. L. Dietz-Uhler. 1993. Gender identity and adversarial sexual beliefs as predictors of attitudes toward sexual harassment. *Psychology of Women Quarterly* 17 (2): 169–175.

Padgitt, S. C., and J. S. Padgitt. 1986. Cognitive structure of sexual harassment: Implications for university policy. *Journal of College Students Personnel* 27:34–39.

Popovich, P. M., D. N. Gehlauf, J. A. Jolton, J. M. Somers, and R. M. Godinho. 1992. Perceptions of sexual harassment as a function of sex of rater and incident form and consequent. *Sex Roles* 27 (11/12): 609–625.

Powell, G. N. 1986. Effects of sex-role identity and sex on definitions of sexual harassment. *Sex Roles* 14:9–19.

Pronger, B. 1992. Gay jocks: A phenomenology of gay men in athletics. In *Rethinking masculinity: Philosophical explorations in light of feminism,* edited by L. May and R. Strikwerda. Lanham, MD: Littlefield Adams.

Pryor, J. B. 1987. Sexual harassment proclivities in men. *Sex Roles* 17 (5/6): 269–290.

Quinn, B. A. 2000. The paradox of complaining: Law, humor, and harassment in the everyday work world. *Law and Social Inquiry* 25 (4): 1151–1183.

Reilly, M. E., B. Lott, D. Caldwell, and L. DeLuca. 1992. Tolerance for sexual harassment related to self-reported sexual victimization. *Gender & Society* 6:122–138.

Rogers, J. K., and K. D. Henson, 1997. "Hey, why don't you wear a shorter skirt?" Structural vulnerability and the organization of sexual harassment in temporary clerical employment. *Gender & Society* 11:215–238.

Schwalbe, M. 1992. Male supremacy and the narrowing of the moral self. *Berkeley Journal of Sociology* 37:29–54.

Smith, D. 1990. *The conceptual practices of power: A feminist sociology of knowledge.* Boston: Northeastern University Press.

Stockdale, M. S. 1993. The role of sexual misperceptions of women's friendliness in an emerging theory of sexual harassment. *Journal of Vocational Behavior* 42 (1): 84–101.

Stockdale, M. S., and A. Vaux. 1993. What sexual harassment experiences lead respondents to acknowledge being sexually harassed? A secondary analysis of a university survey. *Journal of Vocational Behavior* 43 (2): 221–234.

Tagri, S., and S. M. Hayes. 1997. Theories of sexual harassment. In *Sexual harassment: Theory, research and treatment,* edited by W. O'Donohue. New York: Allyn and Bacon.

Thorne, B. 1993. *Gender play: Girls and boys in school.* Buckingham, UK: Open University Press.

U.S. Merit Systems Protection Board, 1988. *Sexual harassment in the federal government: An update.* Washington, DC: Government Printing Office.

Welsh, S. 1999. Gender and sexual harassment. *Annual Review of Sociology* 1999:169–190.

West, C., and D. H. Zimmerman, 1987. Doing gender. *Gender & Society* 1:125–151.

Wood, J. T. 1998. Saying makes it so: The discursive construction of sexual harassment. In *Conceptualizing sexual harassment as discursive practice,* edited by S. G. Bingham. Westport, CT: Praeger.

York, K. M. 1989. Defining sexual harassment in workplaces: A policy-capturing approach. *Academy of Management Journal* 32:830–850.

Yount, K. R. 1991. Ladies, flirts, tomboys: Strategies for managing sexual harassment in an underground coal mine. *Journal of Contemporary Ethnography* 19:396–422.

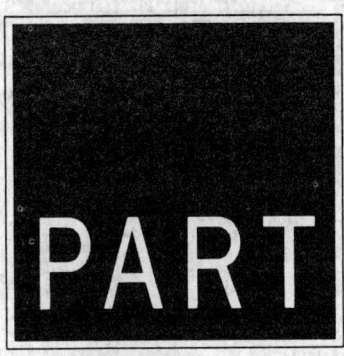

PART FIVE

Men and Health: Body and Mind

Why did the gap between male and female life expectancy increase from two years in 1900 to nearly eight years today? Why do men suffer heart attacks and ulcers at such a consistently higher rate than women do? Why are auto insurance rates so much higher for young males than for females of the same age? Are mentally and emotionally "healthy" males those who conform more closely to the dominant cultural prescriptions for masculinity, or is it the other way around?

The articles in this section examine the "embodiment" of masculinity, the ways in which men's mental and physical health express and reproduce the definitions of masculinity we have ingested in our society. Don Sabo offers a compassionate account of how men will invariably confront traditional stereotypes as they look for more nurturing roles. Ann Fausto-Sterling and Gloria Steinem poke holes in the traditional definitions of masculinity, and especially the putative biological basis for gender expression.

Alongside these dominant cultural conceptions of masculinity, there have always been masculinities that have been marginalized and subordinated. These can often provide models for resistance to the dominant model, as the articles by Robin Kelley, Rafael Diaz, and Thomas Gerschick and Adam Miller suggest.

Image courtesy of www.adbusters.org.

ARTICLE 25

Don Sabo

Masculinities and Men's Health: Moving Toward Post-Superman Era Prevention

My grandfather used to smile and say, "Find out where you're going to die and stay the hell away from there." Grandpa had never studied epidemiology (the study of variations in health and illness in society), but he understood that certain behaviors, attitudes, and cultural practices can put individuals at risk for accidents, illness, or death. This chapter presents an overview of men's health that proceeds from the basic assumption that aspects of traditional masculinity can be dangerous to men's health (Harrison, Chin, & Ficarrotto 1992; Sabo & Gordon 1995). First, I identify some gender differences in relation to morbidity (sickness) and mortality (death). Next, I examine how the risk for illness varies from one male group to another. I then discuss an array of men's health issues and a preventive strategy for enhancing men's health.

Gender Differences in Health and Illness

When British sociologist Ashley Montagu put forth the thesis in 1953 that women were biologically superior to men, he shook up the prevailing chauvinistic beliefs that men were stronger, smarter, and better than women. His argument was partly based on epidemiological data that show males are more vulnerable to mortality than females from before birth and throughout the life span.

From *Nursing Care in the Community*, 2e, J. Cookfair (ed.), St. Louis: Mosby-Year Book. Copyright © 1998, Mosby Year Book, reprinted with permission.

Mortality

From the time of conception, men are more likely to succumb to prenatal and neonatal death than females. Men's chances of dying during the prenatal stage of development are about 12% greater than those of females and, during the neonatal (newborn) stage, 130% greater than those of females. A number of neonatal disorders are common to males but not females, such as bacterial infections, respiratory illness, digestive diseases, and some circulatory disorders of the aorta and pulmonary artery. Table 25.1 compares male and female infant mortality rates across historical time. Though the infant mortality rate decreases over time, the persistence of the higher rates for males than females suggests that biological factors may be operating. Data also show that males have higher mortality rates than females in every age category, from "under one year" through "over 85" (National Center for Health Statistics 1992). In fact, men are more likely to die in 9 out of the 10 leading causes of death in the United States. (See Table 25.2.)

Females have greater life expectancy than males in the United States, Canada, and postindustrial societies (Waldron 1986; Verbrugge and Wingard 1987). This fact suggests a female biological advantage, but a closer analysis of changing trends in the gap between women's and men's life expectancy indicates that social and cultural factors related to lifestyle, gender identity, and behavior are operating as well. Life expectancy among American females is about 78.3 years but 71.3 years for males (National Center for Health

TABLE 25.1
Infant Mortality Rate

Year	Both Sexes	Males	Females
1940	47.0	52.5	41.3
1950	29.2	32.8	25.5
1960	26.0	29.3	22.6
1970	20.0	22.4	17.5
1980	12.6	13.9	11.2
1989	9.8	10.8	8.8

Note: Rates are for infant (under 1 year) deaths per 1,000 live births for all races.

Source: Adapted from *Monthly Vital Statistics Report*, Vol. 40, No. 8, Supplement 2, January 7, 1992, p. 41.

Statistics 1990). As Waldron's (1995) analysis of shifting mortality patterns between the sexes during the 20th century shows, however, women's relative advantage in life expectancy over men was rather small at the beginning of the 20th century. During the mid-20th century, female mortality declined more rapidly than male mortality, thereby increasing the gender gap in life expectancy. Whereas women benefited from decreased maternal mortality, the midcentury trend toward a lowering of men's life expectancy was slowed by increasing mortality from coronary heart disease and lung cancer that were, in turn, mainly due to higher rates of cigarette smoking among males.

The most recent trends show that differences between women's and men's mortality decreased during the 1980s; that is, female life expectancy was 7.9 years greater than that of males in 1979 and 6.9 years in 1989 (National Center for Health Statistics 1992). Waldron explains that some changes in behavioral patterns between the sexes, such as increased smoking among women, have narrowed the gap between men's formerly higher mortality rates from lung cancer, chronic obstructive pulmonary disease, and ischemic heart disease. In summary, it appears that both biological and sociocultural factors are involved with shaping patterns of men's and women's mortality. In fact, Waldron (1976) suggests that gender-related behaviors rather than strictly biogenic factors account for about three-quarters of the variation in men's early mortality.

Morbidity

Whereas females generally outlive males, females report higher morbidity rates, even after controlling for maternity. National health surveys show

TABLE 25.2
Death Rates by Sex and 10 Leading Causes: 1989

	Age-Adjusted Death Rate per 100,000 Population			
Cause of Death	Total	Male	Female	Sex Differential
Diseases of the heart	155.9	210.2	112.3	1.87
Malignant neoplasms	133.0	163.4	111.7	1.45
Accidents and adverse effects	33.8	49.5	18.9	2.62
Cerebrovascular disease	28.0	30.4	26.2	1.16
Chronic liver disease, cirrhosis	8.9	12.8	5.5	2.33
Diabetes	11.5	2.0	11.0	1.09
Suicide	11.3	18.6	4.5	4.13
Homicide and legal intervention	9.4	14.7	4.1	3.59

Source: Adapted from the *U.S. Bureau of the Census: Statistical Abstracts of the United States:* 1992 (112th ed., p. 84), Washington, DC.

that females experience acute illnesses such as respiratory conditions, infective and parasitic conditions, and digestive system disorders at higher rates than males do; however, males sustain more injuries (Givens 1979; Cypress 1981; Dawson & Adams 1987). Men's higher injury rates are partly owed to gender differences in socialization and lifestyle, such as learning to prove manhood through recklessness, involvement in contact sports, and working in risky blue-collar occupations.

Females are generally more likely than males to experience chronic conditions such as anemia, chronic enteritis and colitis, migraine headaches, arthritis, diabetes, and thyroid disease. However, males are more prone to develop chronic illnesses such as coronary heart disease, emphysema, and gout. Although chronic conditions do not ordinarily cause death, they often limit activity or cause disability.

After noting gender differences in morbidity, Cockerham (1995) asks whether women really do experience more illness than men—or could it be that women are more sensitive to bodily sensations than men, or that men are not as prone as women to report symptoms and seek medical care? He concludes, "The best evidence indicates that the overall differences in morbidity are real" and, further, that they are due to a mixture of biological, psychological, and social influences (p. 42).

Masculinities and Men's Health

There is no such thing as masculinity; there are only masculinities (Sabo & Gordon 1995). A limitation of early gender theory was its treatment of "all men" as a single, large category in relation to "all women" (Connell 1987). The fact is, however, that all men are not alike, nor do all male groups share the same stakes in the gender order. At any given historical moment, there are competing masculinities—some dominant, some marginalized, and some stigmatized—each with its respective structural, psychosocial, and cultural moorings. There are substantial differences between the health options of homeless men, working-class men, lower-class men, gay men, men with AIDS, prison inmates, men of color, and their comparatively advantaged middle- and upper-class, white, professional male counterparts. Similarly, a wide range of individual differences exists between the ways that men and women act out "femininity" and "masculinity" in their everyday lives. A health profile of several male groups is discussed below.

Adolescent Males

Pleck, Sonenstein, and Ku (1992) applied critical feminist perspectives to their research on problem behaviors and health among adolescent males. A national sampling of adolescent, never-married males aged 15–19 were interviewed in 1980 and 1988. Hypothesis tests were geared to assessing whether "masculine ideology" (which measured the presence of traditional male role attitudes) put boys at risk for an array of problem behaviors. The researchers found a significant, independent association with seven of ten problem behaviors. Specifically, traditionally masculine attitudes were associated with being suspended from school, drinking and use of street drugs, frequency of being picked up by the police, being sexually active, the number of heterosexual partners in the last year, and tricking or forcing someone to have sex. These kinds of behaviors, which are in part expressions of the pursuit of traditional masculinity, elevate boys' risk for sexually transmitted diseases, HIV transmission, and early death by accident or homicide. At the same time, however, these same behaviors can also encourage victimization of women through men's violence, sexual assault, unwanted teenage pregnancy, and sexually transmitted diseases.

Adolescence is a phase of accelerated physiological development, and good nutrition during this period is important to future health. Obesity puts adults at risk for a variety of diseases such as coronary heart disease, diabetes mellitus, joint disease, and certain cancers. Obese adolescents are also apt to become obese adults, thus elevating long-term risk for illness. National Health and

Nutrition Examination Surveys show that obesity among adolescents increased by 6 percent during 1976–1980 and 1988–1991. During 1988–1991, 22 percent of females of 12–18 years were overweight, and 20 percent of males in this age group were as well (*Morbidity and Mortality Weekly Report* 1994a).

Males form a majority of the estimated 1.3 million teenagers who run away from home each year in the United States. For both boys and girls, living on the streets raises the risk of poor nutrition, homicide, alcoholism, drug abuse, and AIDS. Young adults in their 20s comprise about 20 percent of new AIDS cases and, when you calculate the lengthy latency period, it is evident that they are being infected in their teenage years. Runaways are also more likely to be victims of crime and sexual exploitation (Hull 1994).

Clearly, adolescent males face a spectrum of potential health problems—some that threaten their present well-being, and others that could take their toll in the future.

Men of Color

Patterns of health and illness among men of color can be partly understood against the historical and social context of economic inequality. Generally, because African Americans, Hispanics, and Native Americans are disproportionately poor, they are more apt to work in low-paying and dangerous occupations, reside in polluted environments, be exposed to toxic substances, experience the threat and reality of crime, and worry about meeting basic needs. Cultural barriers can also complicate their access to available health care. Poverty is correlated with lower educational attainment, which, in turn, mitigates against adoption of preventive health behaviors.

The neglect of public health in the United States is particularly pronounced in relation to African Americans (Polych & Sabo 1996). For example, in Harlem, where 96 percent of the inhabitants are African American and 41 percent live below the poverty line, the survival curve beyond the age of 40 for men is lower than that of men living in Bangladesh (McCord & Freeman 1990). Even though African American men have higher rates of alcoholism, infectious diseases, and drug-related conditions, for example, they are less apt to receive health care, and when they do, they are more apt to receive inferior care (Bullard 1992; Staples 1995). Statistics like the following led Gibbs (1988) to describe young African American males as an "endangered species":

- The number of young African American male homicide victims in 1977 (5,734) was higher than the number killed in the Vietnam War during 1963–1972 (5,640) (Gibbs 1988:258).
- Homicide is the leading cause of death among young African American males. The probability of a black male dying from homicide is about the same as that of a white male dying from an accident (Reed 1991).
- More than 36% of urban African American males are drug and alcohol abusers (Staples 1995).
- In 1993 the rate of contracting AIDS for African American males aged 13 and older was almost 5 times higher than the rate for white males (*Morbidity and Mortality Weekly Report* 1994b).

The health profile of Native Americans and Native Canadians is also poor. For example, alcohol is the number-one killer of Native Americans between the ages of 14 and 44 (May 1986), and 42 percent of Native American male adolescents are problem drinkers, compared to 34 percent of same-age white males (Lamarine 1988). Native Americans (10–18 years of age) comprise 34 percent of in-patient admissions to adolescent detoxification programs (Moore 1988). Compared to the "all race" population, Native American youth exhibit more serious problems in the areas of depression, suicide, anxiety, substance use, and general health status (Blum et al. 1992). The rates of morbidity, mortality from injury, and contracting AIDS are also higher (Metler, Conway, & Stehr-Green 1991; Sugarman et al. 1993).

Like those of many other racial and ethnic groups, the health problems facing American and Canadian natives correlate with the effects of poverty and social marginalization, such as dropping out of school, a sense of hopelessness, the experience of prejudice, poor nutrition, and lack of regular health care. Those who care about men's health, therefore, need to be attuned to the potential interplay between gender, race/ethnicity, cultural differences, and economic conditions when working with racial and ethnic minorities.

Gay and Bisexual Men

Gay and bisexual men are estimated to constitute 5 percent to 10 percent of the male population. In the past, gay men have been viewed as evil, sinful, sick, emotionally immature, and socially undesirable. Many health professionals and the wider public have harbored mixed feelings and homophobic attitudes toward gay and bisexual men. Gay men's identity, their lifestyles, and the social responses to homosexuality can impact the health of gay and bisexual men. Stigmatization and marginalization, for example, may lead to emotional confusion and suicide among gay male adolescents. For gay and bisexual men who are "in the closet," anxiety and stress can tax emotional and physical health. When seeking medical services, gay and bisexual men must often cope with the homophobia of health care workers or deal with the threat of losing health care insurance if their sexual orientation is made known.

Whether they are straight or gay, men tend to have more sexual contacts than women do, which heightens men's risk for contracting sexually transmitted diseases (STDs). Men's sexual attitudes and behaviors are closely tied to the way masculinity has been socially constructed. For example, real men are taught to suppress their emotions, which can lead to a separation of sex from feeling. Traditionally, men are also encouraged to be daring, which can lead to risky sexual decisions. In addition, contrary to common myths about gay male effeminacy, masculinity also plays a powerful role in shaping gay and bisexual men's identity and behavior. To the extent that traditional masculinity informs sexual activity of men, masculinity can be a barrier to safer sexual behavior among men. This insight leads Kimmel and Levine (1989) to assert that "to educate men about safe sex, then, means to confront the issues of masculinity" (p. 352). In addition to practicing abstinence and safer sex as preventive strategies, therefore, they argue that traditional beliefs about masculinity be challenged as a form of risk reduction.

Men who have sex with men remain the largest risk group for HIV transmission. For gay and bisexual men who are infected by the HIV virus, the personal burden of living with an AIDS diagnosis is made heavier by the stigma associated with homosexuality. The cultural meanings associated with AIDS can also filter into gender and sexual identities. Tewksbury's (1995) interviews with 45 HIV positive gay men showed how masculinity, sexuality, stigmatization, and interpersonal commitment mesh in decision making related to risky sexual behavior. Most of the men practiced celibacy in order to prevent others from contracting the disease; others practiced safe sex, and a few went on having unprotected sex.

Prison Inmates

There are 1.3 million men imprisoned in American jails and prisons (Nadelmann & Wenner 1994). The United States has the highest rate of incarceration of any nation in the world, 426 prisoners for every 100,000 people (American College of Physicians 1992), followed by South Africa and the former Soviet Union (Mauer 1992). Racial and ethnic minorities are overrepresented among those behind bars. Black and Hispanic males, for example, comprise 85 percent of prisoners in the New York State prison system (Green 1991).

The prison system acts as a pocket of risk, within which men already at high risk of having a preexisting AIDS infection are exposed to conditions that further heighten the risk of contracting HIV (Toepell 1992) or other infections such as tuberculosis (Bellin, Fletcher, & Safyer 1993) or hepatitis. The corrections system is part of an institutional chain that facilitates transmission of HIV and other infections in certain North American populations, particularly among poor, inner-city, minority males. Prisoners are burdened not only by social disadvantage but also by high rates of physical illness, mental disorder, and substance abuse that jeopardize their health (Editor, Lancet 1991).

AIDS prevalence is markedly higher among state and federal inmates than in the general U.S. population, with a known aggregate rate in 1992 of 202 per 100,000 population (Brewer & Derrickson 1992) compared to a total population prevalence of 14.65 in 100,000 (American College of Physicians 1992). The cumulative total of American prisoners with AIDS in 1989 was estimated to be 5,411, a 72 percent increase over the previous year (Belbot & del Carmen 1991). The total number of AIDS cases reported in U.S. corrections as of 1993 was 11,565 (a minimum estimate of the true cumulative incidence among U.S. inmates) (Hammett; cited in Expert Committee on AIDS and Prisons 1994). In New York State, at least 10,000 of the state's 55,000 prisoners are believed to be infected (Prisoners with AIDS/HIV Support Action Network 1992). In Canadian federal penitentiaries, it is believed that 1 in 20 inmates is HIV infected (Hankins; cited in Expert Committee on AIDS and Prison 1994).

The HIV virus is primarily transmitted between adults by unprotected penetrative sex or by needle sharing, without bleaching, with an infected partner. Sexual contacts between prisoners occur mainly through consensual unions and secondarily through sexual assault and rape (Vaid; cited in Expert Committee on AIDS and Prisons 1994). The amount of IV drug use behind prison walls is unknown, although it is known to be prevalent and the scarcity of needles often leads to sharing of needles and sharps (Prisoners with AIDS/HIV Support Action Network 1992).

The failure to provide comprehensive health education and treatment interventions in prisons not only puts more inmates at risk for HIV infection, but also threatens the public at large. Prisons are not hermetically sealed enclaves set apart from the community, but an integral part of society (Editor, Lancet 1991). Prisoners regularly move in and out of the prison system. In 1989, prisons in the United States admitted 467,227 persons and discharged 386,228 (American College of Physicians 1992). The average age of inmates admitted to prison in 1989 was 29.6, with 75 percent between 18 and 34 years; 94.3 percent were male. These former inmates return to their communities after having served an average of 18 months inside (Dubler & Sidel 1989). Within three years, 62.5 percent will be rearrested and jailed. Recidivism is highest among poor black and Hispanic men. The extent to which the drug-related social practices and sexual activities of released or paroled inmates who are HIV positive are putting others at risk upon return to their communities is unresearched and unknown.

Male Athletes

Injury is everywhere in sport. It is evident in the lives and bodies of athletes who regularly experience bruises, torn ligaments, broken bones, aches, lacerations, muscle tears, and so forth. For example, about 300,000 football-related injuries per year require treatment in hospital emergency rooms (Miedzian 1991). Critics of violent contact sports claim that athletes are paying too high a physical price for their participation. George D. Lundberg (1994), editor of the *Journal of the American Medical Association,* has called for a ban on boxing in the Olympics and in the U.S. military. His editorial entreaty, though based on clinical evidence for neurological harm from boxing, is also couched in a wider critique of the exploitative economics of the sport.

Injuries are basically unavoidable in sports, but, in traditional men's sports, there has been a tendency to glorify pain and injury, to inflict injury on others, and to sacrifice one's body in order to "win at all costs." The "no pain, no gain" philosophy, which is rooted in traditional cultural equations between masculinity and sports, can jeopardize the health of athletes who conform to its ethos (Sabo 1994).

The connections between sport, masculinity, and health are evidence in Klein's (1993) study of how bodybuilders use anabolic steroids, overtrain, and engage in extreme dietary practices. He spent years as an ethnographic researcher in the muscled world of the bodybuilding subculture, where masculinity is equated to maximum muscularity and men's striving for bigness and physical strength hides emotional insecurity and low self-esteem.

A nationwide survey of American male high school seniors found that 6.6 percent used or had used anabolic steroids. About two-thirds of this group were athletes (Buckley et al. 1988). Anabolic steroid use has been linked to health risks such as liver disease, kidney problems, atrophy of the testicles, elevated risk of injury, and premature skeletal maturation.

Klein lays bare a tragic irony in American culture—the powerful male athlete, a symbol of strength and health, has often sacrificed his health in pursuit of ideal masculinity (Messner & Sabo 1994).

Men's Health Issues

Advocates of men's health have identified a variety of issues that impact directly on men's lives. Some of these issues may concern you or men you care about.

Testicular Cancer

The epidemiological data on testicular cancer are sobering. Though relatively rare in the general population, it is the fourth most common cause of death among males of 15–35 years accounting for 14 percent of all cancer deaths for this age group. It is the most common form of cancer affecting males of 20–34 years. The incidence of testicular cancer is increasing, and about 6,100 new U.S. cases were diagnosed in 1991 (American Cancer Society 1991). If detected early, the cure rate is high, whereas delayed diagnosis is life threatening. Regular testicular self-examination (TSE), therefore, is a potentially effective means for ensuring early detection and successful treatment. Regrettably, however, most physicians do not teach TSE techniques (Rudolf & Quinn 1988).

Denial may influence men's perceptions of testicular cancer and TSE (Blesch 1986). Studies show that most males are not aware of testicular cancer, and even among those who are aware, many are reluctant to examine their testicles as a preventive measure. Even when symptoms are recognized, men sometimes postpone seeking treatment. Moreover, men who are taught TSE are often initially receptive, but their practice of TSE decreases over time. Men's resistance to TSE has been linked to awkwardness about touching themselves, associating touching genitals with homosexuality or masturbation, or the idea that TSE is not a manly behavior. And finally, men's individual reluctance to discuss testicular cancer partly derives from the widespread cultural silence that envelops it. The penis is a cultural symbol of male power, authority, and sexual domination. Its symbolic efficacy in traditional, male-dominated gender relations, therefore, would be eroded or neutralized by the realities of testicular cancer.

Diseases of the Prostate

Middle-aged and elderly men are likely to develop medical problems with the prostate gland. Some men may experience benign prostatic hyperplasia, an enlargement of the prostate gland that is associated with symptoms such as dribbling after urination, frequent urination, or incontinence. Others may develop infections (prostatitis) or malignant prostatic hyperplasia (prostate cancer). Prostate cancer is the third leading cause of death from cancer in men, accounting for 15.7 deaths per 100,000 population in 1989. Prostate cancer is now more common than lung cancer (Martin 1990). One in 10 men will develop this cancer by age 85, with African American males showing a higher prevalence rate than whites (Greco & Blank 1993).

Treatments for prostate problems depend on the specific diagnosis and may range from medication to radiation and surgery. As is the case with testicular cancer, survival from prostate cancer is enhanced by early detection. Raising men's awareness about the health risks associated with the prostate gland, therefore, may prevent unnecessary morbidity and mortality. Unfortunately, the more invasive surgical treatments for prostate cancer can produce incontinence and impotence, and there has been no systematic research on men's psychosocial reactions and adjustment to sexual dysfunction associated with treatments for prostate cancer.

Alcohol Abuse

Although social and medical problems stemming from alcohol abuse involve both sexes, males comprise the largest segment of alcohol abusers. Some researchers have begun exploring the connections between the influence of the traditional male role on alcohol abuse. Isenhart and Silversmith (1994) show how, in a variety of occupational contexts, expectations surrounding masculinity encourage heavy drinking while working or socializing during after-work or off-duty hours. Some predominantly male occupational groups, such as longshoremen (Hitz 1973), salesmen (Cosper 1979), and members of the military (Pursch 1976), are known to engage in high rates of alcohol consumption. Mass media play a role in sensationalizing links between booze and male bravado. Postman, Nystrom, Strate, and Weingartner (1987) studied the thematic content of 40 beer commercials and identified a variety of stereotypical portrayals of the male role that were used to promote beer drinking: reward for a job well done; manly activities that feature strength, risk, and daring; male friendship and esprit de corps; romantic success with women. The researchers estimate that, between the ages of 2 and 18, children view about 100,000 beer commercials.

Findings from a Harvard School of Public Health (1994) survey of 17,600 students at 140 colleges found that 44 percent engaged in "binge drinking," defined as drinking five drinks in rapid succession for males and four drinks for females. Males were more apt to report binge drinking during the past two weeks than females; 50 percent and 39 percent respectively. Sixty percent of the males who binge three or more times in the past two weeks reported driving after drinking, compared to 49 percent of their female counterparts, thus increasing the risk for accident, injury, and death. Compared to non–binge drinkers, binge drinkers were seven times more likely to engage in unprotected sex, thus elevating the risk for unwanted pregnancy and sexually transmitted disease. Alcohol-related automobile accidents are the top cause of death among 16- to 24-year-olds, especially among males (Henderson & Anderson 1989). For all males, the age-adjusted death rate from automobile accidents in 1991 was 26.2 per 100,000 for African American males and 24.2 per 100,000 for white males, 2.5 and 3.0 times higher than for white and African American females respectively (*Morbidity and Mortality Weekly Report* 1994d). The number of automobile fatalities among male adolescents that results from a mixture of alcohol abuse and masculine daring is unknown.

Men and AIDS

Human immunodeficiency virus (HIV) infection became a leading cause of death among males in the 1980s. Among men aged 25–44 in 1990, HIV infection was the second leading cause of death, compared to the sixth leading cause of death among same-age women (*Morbidity and Mortality Weekly Report* 1993a). Among reported cases of acquired immunodeficiency syndrome (AIDS) for adolescent and adult men in 1992, 60 percent were men who had sex with other men, 21 percent were intravenous drug users, 4 percent were exposed through heterosexual sexual contact, 6 percent were men who had sex with men and injected drugs, and 1 percent were transfusion recipients. Among the cases of AIDS among adolescent and adult women in 1992, 45 percent were intravenous drug users, 39 percent were infected through heterosexual sexual contact, and 4 percent were transfusion recipients (*Morbidity and Mortality Weekly Report* 1993a).

Because most AIDS cases have been among men who have sex with other men, perceptions of the epidemic and its victims have been tinctured by sexual attitudes. In North American cultures, the stigma associated with AIDS is fused with the stigma linked to homosexuality. Feelings about men with AIDS can be mixed and complicated by homophobia.

Thoughts and feelings about men with AIDS are also influenced by attitudes toward race, ethnicity, drug abuse, and social marginality. Centers for Disease Control data show, for example, that men of color aged 13 and older constituted 51 percent (45,039) of the 89,165 AIDS cases reported in 1993. Women of color made up 71 percent of the cases reported among females aged 13 and older (*Morbidity and Mortality Weekly Report* 1994b). The high rate of AIDS among racial and ethnic minorities has kindled racial prejudices in some minds, and AIDS is sometimes seen as a "minority disease." Although African American or Hispanic males may be at greater risk of contracting HIV/AIDS, just as yellow fingers do not cause lung disease, it is not race or ethnicity that confers risk, but the behaviors they engage in and the social circumstances of their lives.

Perceptions of HIV/AIDS can also be influenced by attitudes toward poverty and poor people. HIV infection is linked to economic problems that include community disintegration, unemployment, homelessness, eroding urban tax bases, mental illness, substance abuse, and criminalization (Wallace 1991). For example, males comprise the majority of homeless persons. Poverty and homelessness overlap with drug addiction, which, in turn, is linked to HIV infection. Of persons hospitalized with HIV in New York City, 9–18 percent have been found to be homeless (Torres et al. 1990). Of homeless men tested for HIV at a New York City shelter, 62 percent of those who took the test were seropositive (Ron & Rogers 1989). Among runaway or homeless youth in New York City, 7 percent tested positive, and this rate rose to 15 percent among the 19- and 20-year-olds. Of homeless men in Baltimore, 85 percent admitted to substance use problems (Weinreb & Bassuk 1990).

Suicide

The suicide rates for both African American and white males increased between 1970 and 1989, whereas female rates decreased. Indeed, males are more likely than females to commit suicide from middle childhood until old age (Stillion 1985, 1995). Compared to females, males typically deploy more violent means of attempting suicide (e.g., guns or hanging rather than pills) and are more likely to complete the act. Men's selection of more violent methods to kill themselves is consistent with traditionally masculine behavior (Stillion et al.).

Canetto (1995) interviewed male survivors of suicide attempts in order to better understand sex differences in suicidal behavior. Although she recognizes that men's psychosocial reactions and adjustments to nonfatal suicide vary by race/ethnicity, socioeconomic status, and age, she also finds that gender identity is an important factor in men's experiences. Suicide data show that men attempt suicide less often than women but are more likely to die than women. Canetto indicates that men's comparative "success" rate points toward a tragic irony in that, consistent with gender stereotypes, men's failure even at suicide undercuts the cultural mandate that men are supposed to succeed at everything. A lack of embroilment in traditionally masculine expectations, she suggests, may actually increase the likelihood of surviving a suicide attempt for some men.

Elderly males in North America commit suicide significantly more often than elderly females. Whereas white women's lethal suicide rate peaks at age 50, white men age 60 and older have the highest rate of lethal suicide, even surpassing the rate for young males (Manton, Blazer, & Woodbury 1987). Canetto (1992) argues that elderly men's higher suicide mortality is chiefly owed to gender differences in coping. She writes:

> older women may have more flexible and diverse ways of coping than older men. Compared to older men, older women may be more willing and capable of adopting different coping

strategies—"passive" or "active," "connected" or "independent"—depending on the situation (p. 92).

She attributes men's limited coping abilities to gender socialization and development.

Erectile Disorders

Men often joke about their penises or tease one another about penis size and erectile potency ("not getting it up"). In contrast, they rarely discuss their concerns about impotence in a serious way. Men's silences in this regard are regrettable in that many men, both young and old, experience recurrent or periodic difficulties getting or maintaining an erection. Estimates of the number of American men with erectile disorders range from 10 million to 30 million (Krane, Goldstein, & Saenz de Tejada 1989; National Institutes of Health 1993). The Massachusetts Male Aging Study of the general population of noninstitutionalized, healthy American men between ages 40 and 70 years found that 52 percent reported minimal, moderate, or complete impotence (Feldman et al. 1994). The prevalence of erectile disorders increased with age, and 9.6 percent of the men were afflicted by complete impotence.

During the 1960s and 1970s, erectile disorders were largely thought to stem from psychological problems such as depression, financial worries, or work-related stress. Masculine stereotypes about male sexual prowess, phallic power, or being in charge of lovemaking were also said to put too much pressure to perform on some males (Zilbergeld 1993). In contrast, physiological explanations of erectile disorders and medical treatments have been increasingly emphasized since the 1980s. Today diagnosis and treatment of erectile disorders should combine psychological and medical assessment (Ackerman & Carey 1995).

Men's Violence

Men's violence is a major public health problem. The traditional masculine stereotype calls on males to be aggressive and tough. Anger is a by-product of aggression and toughness and, ultimately, part of the inner terrain of traditional masculinity (Sabo 1993). Images of angry young men are compelling vehicles used by some males to separate themselves from women and to measure their status in respect to other males. Men's anger and violence derive, in part, from sex inequality. Men use the threat or application of violence to maintain their political and economic advantage over women and lower-status men. Male socialization reflects and reinforces these larger patterns of domination.

Homicide is the second leading cause of death among 15- to 19-year-old males. Males aged 15–34 years made up almost half (49 percent, or 13,122) of homicide victims in the United States in 1991. The homicide rate for this age group increased by 50 percent from 1985 to 1991 (*Morbidity and Morality Weekly Report* 1994c).

Women are especially victimized by men's anger and violence in the form of rape, date rape, wife beating, assault, sexual harassment on the job, and verbal harassment (Thorne-Finch 1992). That the reality and potential of men's violence impact women's mental and physical health can be surely assumed. However, men's violence also exacts a toll on men themselves in the forms of fighting, gang clashes, hazing, gay-bashing, intentional infliction of injury, homicide, suicide, and organized warfare.

Summary

It is ironic that two of the best-known actors who portrayed Superman have met with disaster. George Reeves, who starred in the original black-and-white television show, committed suicide, and Christopher Reeve, who portrayed the "man of steel" in recent film versions, was paralyzed by an accident during a high-risk equestrian event. Perhaps one lesson to be learned here is that, behind the cultural facade of mythic masculinity, men are vulnerable. Indeed, as we have seen in this chapter, some of the cultural messages sewn into the cloak of masculinity can put men at risk for illness and early death. A sensible preventive health strategy for the 1990s calls upon men to critically evaluate the Superman legacy, that is, to challenge the negative aspects of traditional masculinity that endanger their health, while hanging on to the positive aspects of masculinity and men's lifestyles that heighten men's physical vitality.

The promotion of men's health also requires a sharper recognition that the sources of men's risks for many diseases do not strictly reside in men's psyches, gender identities, or the roles that they enact in daily life. Men's roles, routines, and relations with others are fixed in the historical and structural relations that constitute the larger gender order. As we have seen, not all men or male groups share the same access to social resources, educational attainment, and opportunity that, in turn, can influence their health options. Yes, men need to pursue personal change in order to enhance their health, but without changing the political, economic, and ideological structures of the gender order, the subjective gains and insights forged within individuals can easily erode and fade away. If men are going to pursue self-healing, therefore, they need to create an overall preventive strategy that at once seeks to change potentially harmful aspects of traditional masculinity and meets the health needs of lower-status men.

References

Ackerman, M. D., & Carey, P. C. (1995). "Psychology's Role in Assessment of Erectile Dysfunction: Historical Procedure, Current Knowledge, and Methods." *Journal of Counseling & Clinical Psychology, 63*(6), 862–876.

American Cancer Society (1991). Cancer facts and figures—1991. Atlanta, GA: American Cancer Society.

American College of Physicians. (1992). The crisis in correctional health care: The impact of the national drug control strategy on correctional health services. *Annals of Internal Medicine, 117*(1), 71–77.

Belbot, B. A., & del Carmen, R. B. (1991). AIDS in prison: Legal issues. *Crime and Delinquency, 31*(1), 135–153.

Bellin, E. Y., Fletcher, D. D., & Safyer, S. M. (1993). Association of tuberculosis infection with increased time in or admission to the New York City jail system. *Journal of the American Medical Association, 269*(17), 2228–2231.

Blesch, K. (1986). Health beliefs about testicular cancer and self-examination among professional men. *Oncology Nursing Forum, 13*(1), 29–33.

Blum, R., Harman, B., Harris, L., Bergeissen, L., & Restrick, M. (1992). American Indian–Alaska native youth health. *Journal of American Medical Association, 267*(12), 1637–1644.

Brewer, T. F., & Derrickson, J. (1992). AIDS in prison: A review of epidemiology and preventive policy. *AIDS, 6*(7), 623–628.

Buckley, W. E., Yesalis, C. E., Friedl, K. E., Anderson, W. A., Streit, A. L., & Wright, J. E. (1988). Estimated prevalence of anabolic steroid use among male high school seniors. *Journal of the American Medical Association, 260*(23), 3441–3446.

Bullard, R. D. (1992). Urban infrastructure: Social, environmental, and health risks to African-Americans. In B. J. Tidwell (Ed.), *The State of Black America* (pp. 183–196). New York: National Urban League.

Canetto, S. S. (1995). Men who survive a suicidal act: Successful coping or failed masculinity? In D. Sabo & D. Gordon (Eds.), *Men's health and illness* (pp. 292–304). Newbury Park, CA: Sage.

Canetto, S. S. (1992). Gender and suicide in the elderly. *Suicide and Life-Threatening Behavior, 22*(1), 80–97.

Cockerham, W. C. (1995). *Medical sociology*. Englewood Cliffs, NJ: Prentice-Hall.

Connell, R. W. (1987). *Gender and power*. Stanford: Stanford University Press.

Cosper, R. (1979). Drinking as conformity: A critique of sociological literature on occupational differences in drinking. *Journal of Studies on Alcoholism, 40*, 868–891.

Cypress, B. (1981). Patients' reasons for visiting physicians: National ambulatory medical care survey, U.S. 1977–78. DHHS Publication No. (PHS) 82-1717, Series 13, No. 56. Hyattsville, MD: National Center for Health Statistics, December, 1981a.

Dawson, D. A., & Adams, P. F. (1987). Current estimates from the national health interview survey: U.S. 1986. Vital Health Statistics Series, Series

10, No. 164. DHHS Publication No. (PHS) 87-1592, Public Health Service. Washington, D.C: U.S. Government Printing Office.

Dubler, N. N., & Sidel, V. W. (1989). On research on HIV infection and AIDS in correctional institutions. *The Milbank Quarterly, 67*(1–2), 81–94.

Editor, (1991, March 16). Health care for prisoners: Implications of "Kalk's refusal." *Lancet, 337,* 647–648.

Expert Committee on AIDS and Prison. (1994). *HIV/AIDS in prisons: Summary report and recommendations to the Expert Committee on AIDS and Prisons* (Ministry of Supply and Services Canada Catalogue No. JS82-68/2-1994). Ottawa, Ontario, Canada: Correctional Service of Canada.

Feldman, H. A., Goldstein, I., Hatzichristou, D. G., Krane, R. J., & McKinlay, J. B. (1994). Impotence and its medical and psychosocial correlates: Results of the Massachusetts Male Aging Study. *Journal of Urology, 151,* 54–61.

Gibbs, J. T. (Ed.) (1988). *Young, black, and male in America: An endangered species.* Dover, MA: Auburn House.

Givens, J. (1979). Current estimates from the health interview survey: U.S. 1978. DHHS Publication No. (PHS) 80-1551, Series 10, No. 130. Hyattsville, MD: Office of Health Research Statistics, November 1979.

Greco, K. E. & Blank, B. (1993). Prostate-specific antigen: The new early detection test for prostate cancer. *Nurse Practitioner, 18*(5), 30–38.

Green, A. P. (1991). Blacks unheard. *Update* (Winter), New York State Coalition for Criminal Justice, 6–7.

Harrison, J., Chin, J., & Ficarrotto, T. (1992). Warning: Masculinity may be dangerous to your health. In M. S. Kimmel & M. A. Messner (Eds.), *Men's lives* (pp. 271–285). New York: Macmillan.

Harvard School of Public Health. Study reported by Wechler, H., Davenport, A., Dowdall, G., Moeykens, B., & Castillo, S. (1994). Health and behavioral consequences of binge drinking in college: A national survey of students at 140 campuses. *Journal of the American Medical Association, 272*(21), 1672–1677.

Henderson, D. C., & Anderson, S. C. (1989). Adolescents and chemical dependency. *Social Work in Health Care, 14*(1), 87–105.

Hitz, D. (1973). Drunken sailors and others: Drinking problems in specific occupations. *Quarterly Journal of Studies on Alcohol, 34,* 496–505.

Hull, J. D. (1994, November 21). Running scared. *Time, 144*(2), 93–99.

Isenhart, C. E., & Silversmith, D. J. (1994). The influence of the traditional male role on alcohol abuse and the therapeutic process. *Journal of Men's Studies, 3*(2), 127–135.

Kimmel, M. S., and Levine, M. P. (1989). Men and AIDS. In M. S. Kimmel & M. A. Messner (Eds.), *Men's lives* (pp. 344–354) New York: Macmillan.

Klein, A. (1993). *Little big men: Bodybuilding subculture and gender construction.* Albany, NY: SUNY Press.

Krane, R. J., Goldstein, I., & Saentz de Tejjada, I. (1989). Impotence. *New England Journal of Medicine, 321,* 1648–1659.

Lamarine, R. (1988). Alcohol abuse among Native Americans. *Journal of Community Health, 13*(3), 143–153.

Lundberg, G. D. (1994, June 8). Let's stop boxing in the Olympics and the United States military. *Journal of the American Medical Association, 271*(22), 1990.

Manton, K. G., Blazer, D. G., & Woodbury, M. A. (1987). Suicide in middle age and later life: Sex and race specific life table and cohort analyses. *Journal of Gerontology, 42,* 219–227.

Martin, J. (1990). Male cancer awareness: Impact of an employee education program. *Oncology Nursing Forum, 17*(1), 59–64.

Mauer, M. (1992). Men in American prisons: Trends, causes, and issues. *Men's Studies Review, 9*(1), 10–12. A special issue on men in prison, edited by Don Sabo and Willie London.

May, P. (1986). Alcohol and drug misuse prevention programs for American Indians: Needs and opportunities. *Journal of Studies of Alcohol, 47*(3), 187–195.

McCord, C., & Freeman, H. P. (1990). Excess mortality in Harlem. *New England Journal of Medicine, 322*(22), 1606–1607.

Messner, M. A., and Sabo, D. (1994). *Sex, violence, and power in sports: Rethinking masculinity.* Freedom, CA: Crossing Press.

Metler, R., Conway, G., & Stehr-Green, J. (1991). AIDS surveillance among American Indians and Alaskan natives. *American Journal of Public Health, 81*(11), 1469–1471.

Miedzian, M. (1991). *Boys will be boys: Breaking the link between masculinity and violence.* New York: Doubleday.

Montagu, A. (1953). *The natural superiority of women.* New York: Macmillan.

Moore, D. (1988). Reducing alcohol and other drug use among Native American youth. *Alcohol Drug Abuse and Mental Health, 15*(6), 2–3.

Morbidity and Mortality Weekly Report. (1993a). Update: Mortality attributable to HIV infection/AIDS among persons aged 25–44 years—United States, 1990–91. *42*(25), 481–486.

Morbidity and Mortality Weekly Report. (1993b). Summary of notifiable diseases United States, 1992. *41*(55).

Morbidity and Mortality Weekly Report. (1994a). Prevalence of overweight among adolescents—United States, 1988–91. *43*(44), 818–819.

Morbidity and Mortality Weekly Report. (1994b). AIDS among racial/ethnic minorities—United States, 1993. *43*(35), 644–651.

Morbidity and Mortality Weekly Report. (1994c). Homicides among 15–19-year-old males—United States. *43*(40), 725–728.

Morbidity and Mortality Weekly Report. (1994d). Deaths resulting from firearm- and motor-vehicle-related injuries—United States, 1968–1991. *43*(3), 37–42.

Nadelmann, P., & Wenner, L. (1994, May 5). Toward a sane national drug policy [Editorial]. *Rolling Stone,* 24–26.

National Center for Health Statistics. (1990). *Health, United States, 1989.* Hyattsville, MD: Public Health Service.

National Center for Health Statistics. (1992). Advance report of final mortality statistics, 1989. *Monthly Vital Statistics Report, 40* (Suppl. 2) (DHHS Publication No. [PHS] 92-1120).

National Institutes of Health. (1993). Consensus development panel on impotence. *Journal of the American Medical Association, 270,* 83–90.

Pleck, J., Sonenstein, F. L., & Ku, L. C. (1992). In R. Ketterlinus, & M. E. Lamb (Eds.), *Adolescent problem behaviors.* Hillsdale, NJ: Lawrence Erlbaum Associates.

Polych, C., & Sabo, D. (1996). Gender politics, pain, and illness: The AIDS epidemic in North American prisons. In D. Sabo & D. Gordon (Eds.), *Men's health and illness.* Newbury Park, CA: Sage, pp. 139–157.

Postman, N., Nystrom, C., Strate, L., & Weingartner, C. (1987). *Myths, men and beer: An analysis of beer commercials on broadcast television, 1987.* Falls Church, VA: Foundation for Traffic Safety.

Prisoners with AIDS/HIV Support Action Network. (1992). *HIV/AIDS in prison systems: A comprehensive strategy* (Brief to the Minister of Correctional Services and the Minister of Health). Toronto: Prisoners with AIDS/HIV Support Action Network.

Pursch, J. A. (1976). From quonset hut to naval hospital: The story of an alcoholism rehabilitation service. *Journal of Studies on Alcohol, 37,* 1655–1666.

Reed, W. L. (1991). Trends in homicide among African Americans. *Trotter Institute Review, 5,* 11–16.

Ron, A., & Rogers, D. E. (1989). AIDS in New York City: The role of intravenous drug users. *Bulletin of the New York Academy of Medicine, 65*(7), 787–800.

Rudolf, V., & Quinn, K. (1988). The practice of TSE among college men: Effectiveness of an educational program. *Oncology Nursing Forum, 15*(1), 45–48.

Sabo, D., & Gordon, D. (1995). *Men's health and illness: Gender, power, and the body.* Newbury Park, CA: Sage.

Sabo, D. (1994). The body politics of sports injury: Culture, power, and the pain principle. A paper presented at the annual meeting of the National Athletic Trainers Association, Dallas, TX, June 6, 1994.

Sabo, D. (1993). Understanding men. In Kimball, G. (Ed.) *Everything You Need to Know to Succeed after College.* Chico, CA: Equality Press, pp. 71–93.

Staples, R. (1995). Health and illness among African-American Males. In D. Sabo and D. Gordon (Eds.), *Men's health and illness.* Newbury Park, CA: Sage, pp. 121–138.

Stillion, J. (1985). *Death and the sexes: An examination of differential longevity, attitudes, behaviors, and coping skills.* New York: Hemisphere.

———. (1995). Premature death among males: Rethinking links between masculinity and health. In D. Sabo & D. Gordon (Eds.), *Men's health and illness.* Newbury Park, CA: Sage, pp. 46–67.

Stillion, J., White, H., McDowell, E. E., & Edwards, P. (1989). Ageism and sexism in suicide attitudes. *Death Studies, 13,* 247–261.

Sugarman, J., Soderberg, R., Gordon, J., & Rivera, F. (1993). Racial misclassification of American

Indians: Its effects on injury rates in Oregon, 1989–1990. *American Journal of Public Health, 83*(5), 681–684.

Tewksbury, (1995). Sexual adaptation among gay men with HIV. In D. Sabo & D. Gordon (Eds.), *Men's Health and Illness* (pp. 222–245). Newbury Park, CA: Sage.

Thorne-Finch, R. (1992). *Ending the silence: The origins and treatment of male violence against women.* Toronto: University of Toronto Press.

Toepell, A. R. (1992). *Prisoners and AIDS: AIDS education needs assessment.* Toronto: John Howard Society of Metropolitan Toronto.

Torres, R. A., Mani, S., Altholz, J., & Brickner, P. W. (1990). HIV infection among homeless men in a New York City shelter. *Archives of Internal Medicine, 150,* 2030–2036.

Verbrugge, L. M., & Wingard, D. L. (1987). Sex differentials in health and mortality. *Women's Health, 12,* 103–145.

Waldron, I. (1995). Contributions of changing gender differences in behavior and social roles to changing gender differences in mortality. In D. Sabo & D. Gordon (Eds.), *Men's health and illness,* Newbury Park, CA: Sage, pp. 22–45.

———. (1986). What do we know about sex differences in mortality? *Population Bulletin of the U.N., No. 18-1985,* 59–76.

———. (1976). Why do women live longer than men? *Journal of Human Stress, 2,* 1–13.

Wallace, R. (1991). Traveling waves of HIV infection on a low dimensional "sociogeographic" network. *Social Science Medicine, 32*(7), 847–852.

Weinreb, L. F., & Bassuk, E. L. (1990). Substance abuse: A growing problem among homeless families. *Family and Community Health, 13*(1), 55–64.

Zilbergeld, B. (1993). *The new male sexuality.* New York: Bantam.

ARTICLE 26

Robin D. G. Kelley

Confessions of a Nice Negro, or Why I Shaved My Head

It happened just the other day—two days into the new year, to be exact. I had dashed into the deserted lobby of an Ann Arbor movie theater, pulling the door behind me to escape the freezing winter winds Michigan residents have come to know so well. Behind the counter knelt a young white teenager filling the popcorn bin with bags of that awful pre-popped stuff. Hardly the enthusiastic employee; from a distance it looked like she was lost in deep thought. The generous display of body piercing suggested an X-generation flower-child—perhaps an anthropology major into acid jazz and environmentalism, I thought. Sporting a black New York Yankees baseball cap and a black-and-beige scarf over my nose and mouth, I must have looked like I had stepped out of a John Singleton film. And because I was already late, I rushed madly toward the ticket counter.

The flower child was startled: "I don't have anything in the cash register," she blurted as she pulled the bag of popcorn in front of her for protection.

"Huh? I just want one ticket for *Little Women*, please—the two-fifteen show. My wife and daughter should already be in there." I slowly gestured to the theater door and gave her one of those innocent childlike glances I used to give my mom when I wanted to sit on her lap.

"Oh god . . . I'm so sorry. A reflex. Just one ticket? You only missed the first twenty minutes. Enjoy the show."

From *Speak My Name: Black Men on Masculinity and the American Dream*, Don Belton (ed.), pp. 12–22, Boston: Beacon. Copyright © 1995. Reprinted by permission of the author.

Enjoy the show? Barely 1995 and here we go again. Another bout with racism in a so-called liberal college town; another racial drama in which I play the prime suspect. And yet I have to confess the situation was pretty funny. Just two hours earlier I couldn't persuade Elleza, my four-year-old daughter, to put her toys away; time-out did nothing, yelling had no effect, and the evil stare made no impact whatsoever. Thoroughly frustrated, I had only one option left: "Okay, I'm gonna tell Mommy!" Of course it worked.

So those five seconds as a media-made black man felt kind of good. I know it's a product of racism. I know that the myth of black male violence has resulted in the deaths of many innocent boys and men of darker hue. I know that the power to scare is not real power. I know all that—after all, I study this stuff for a living! For the moment, though, it felt good. (Besides, the ability to scare with your body can come in handy, especially when you're trying to get a good seat in a theater or avoid long lines.)

I shouldn't admit this, but I take particular pleasure in putting fear into people on the lookout for black male criminality mainly because those moments are so rare for me. Indeed, my *inability* to employ black-maleness as a weapon is the story of my life. Why I don't possess it, or rather possess so little of it, escapes me. I grew up poor in Harlem and Afrodena (the Negro West Side of Pasadena/Altadena, California). My mom was single during my formative preadolescent years, and for a brief moment she even received a welfare check. A hard life makes a hard nigga, so I've been told.

Never an egghead or a dork, as a teenager I was pretty cool. I did the house-party circuit on Friday and Saturday nights and used to stroll down the block toting the serious Radio Raheem boombox. Why, I even invaded movie theaters in the company of ten or fifteen hooded and high-topped black bodies, colonizing the balconies and occupying two seats per person. Armed with popcorn and Raisinettes as our missiles of choice, we dared any usher to ask us to leave. Those of us who had cars (we called them hoopties or rides back in that day) spent our lunch hours and precious class time hanging out in the school parking lot, running down our Die Hards to pump up Cameo, Funkadelic, Grandmaster Flash from our car stereos. I sported dickies and Levis, picked up that gangsta stroll, and when the shag came in style I was with it—always armed with a silk scarf to ensure that my hair was laid. Granted, I vomited after drinking malt liquor for the first time and my only hit of a joint ended abruptly in an asthma attack. But I was cool.

Sure, I was cool, but nobody feared me. That I'm relatively short with dimples and curly hair, speak softly in a rather medium to high-pitched voice, and having a "girl's name" doesn't help matters. And everyone knows that light skin is less threatening to white people than blue-black or midnight brown. Besides, growing up with a soft-spoken, uncharacteristically passive West Indian mother deep into East Indian religions, a mother who sometimes walked barefoot in the streets of Harlem, a mother who insisted on proper diction and never, ever, ever used a swear word, screwed me up royally. I could never curse right. My mouth had trouble forming the words—"fuck" always came out as "fock" and "goddamn" always sounded like it's spelled, not "gotdayum," the way my Pasadena homies pronounced it in their Calabama twang. I don't ever recall saying the word "bitch" unless I was quoting somebody or some authorless vernacular rhyme. For some unknown reason, that word scared me.

Mom dressed me up in the coolest mod outfits—short pants with matching hats, Nehru jackets, those sixties British-looking turtlenecks. Sure, she got some of that stuff from John's Bargain Store or Goodwill, but I always looked "cute." More stylish than roguish. Kinda like W. E. B. Du Bois as a toddler, or those turn-of-the century photos of middle-class West Indian boys who grow up to become prime ministers or poets. Ghetto ethnographers back in the late sixties and early seventies would not have found me or my family very "authentic," especially if they had discovered that one of my middle names is Gibran, after the Lebanese poet Kahlil Gibran.

Everybody seemed to like me. Teachers liked me, kids liked me; I even fell in with some notorious teenage criminals at Pasadena High School because *they* liked me. I remember one memorable night in the ninth grade when I went down to the Pasadena Boys' Club to take photos of some of my partners on the basketball team. On my way home some big kids, eleventh-graders to be exact, tried to take my camera. The ringleader pulled out a knife and gently poked it against my chest. I told them it was my stepfather's camera and if I came home without it he'd kick my ass for a week. Miraculously, this launched a whole conversation about stepfathers and how messed up they are, which must have made them feel sorry for me. Within minutes we were cool; they let me go unmolested and I had made another friend.

In affairs of the heart, however, "being liked" had the opposite effect. I can only recall having had four fights in my entire life, all of which were with girls who supposedly liked me but thoroughly beat my behind. Sadly, my record in the boxing ring of puppy love is still 0–4. By the time I graduated to serious dating, being a nice guy seemed like the root of all my romantic problems. I resisted jealousy, tried to be understanding, brought flowers and balloons, opened doors, wrote poems and songs, and seemed to always be on my knees for one reason or another. If you've ever watched "Love Connection" or read *Cosmopolitan,* you know the rest of the story: I practically never had sex and most of the women I dated left me in the cold for roughnecks. My last girlfriend in high school, the woman I took to my prom, the woman I once thought I'd die for, tried to show me the light: "Why do you always ask me what I want? Why don't you just *tell* me what you want me to do? Why don't you take charge and *be a man?* If you want to be a real man you can't be nice all the time!"

I always thought she was wrong; being nice has nothing to do with being a man. While I still think she's wrong, it's an established fact that our culture links manhood to terror and power, and that black men are frequently imaged as the ultimate in hypermasculinity. But the black man as the prototype of violent hypermasculinity is as much a fiction as the happy Sambo. No matter what critics and stand-up comics might say, I know from experience that not all black men—and here I'm only speaking of well-lighted or daytime situations—generate fear. Who scares and who doesn't has a lot to do with the body in question; it is dependent on factors such as age, skin color, size, clothes, hairstyle, and even the sound of one's voice. The cops who beat Rodney King and the jury who acquitted King's assailants openly admitted that the size, shape, and color of his body automatically made him a threat to the officers' safety.

On the other hand, the threatening black male body can take the most incongruous forms. Some of the hardest brothas on my block in West Pasadena kept their perms in pink rollers and hairnets. It was not unusual to see young black men in public with curlers, tank-top undershirts, sweatpants, black mid-calf dress socks, and Stacey Adams shoes, hanging out on the corner or on the basketball court. And we all knew that these brothas were not to be messed with. (The rest of the world probably knows it by now, too, since black males in curlers are occasionally featured on "Cops" and "America's Most Wanted" as notorious drug dealers or heartless pimps.)

Whatever the source of this ineffable terror, my body simply lacked it. Indeed, the older I got, the more ensconced I became in the world of academia, the less threatening I seemed. Marrying and having a child also reduced the threat factor. By the time I hit my late twenties, my wife, Diedra, and I found ourselves in the awkward position of being everyone's favorite Negroes. I don't know how many times we've attended dinner parties where we were the only African Americans in the room. Occasionally there were others, but we seemed to have a monopoly on the dinner party invitations. This not only happened in Ann Arbor, where there is a small but substantial black population to choose from, but in the Negro mecca of Atlanta, Georgia. Our hosts always felt comfortable asking us "sensitive" questions about race that they would not dare ask other black colleagues and friends: What do African Americans think about Farrakhan? Ben Chavis? Nelson Mandela? Most of my black students are very conservative and career-oriented—why is that? How can we mend the relations between blacks and Jews? Do you celebrate Kwanzaa? Do you put anything in your hair to make it that way? What are the starting salaries for young black faculty nowadays?

Of course, these sorts of exchanges appear regularly in most black autobiographies. As soon as they're comfortable, it is not uncommon for white people to take the opportunity to find out everything they've always wanted to know about "us" (which also applies to other people of color, I'm sure) but were afraid to ask. That they feel perfectly at ease asking dumb or unanswerable questions is not simply a case of (mis)perceived racelessness. Being a "nice Negro" has a lot to do with gender, and my peculiar form of "left–feminist–funny-guy" masculinity—a little Kevin Hooks, some Bobby McFerrin, a dash of Woody Allen—is regarded as less threatening than that of most other black men.

Not that I mind the soft-sensitive masculine persona—after all, it is the genuine me, a product of my mother's heroic and revolutionary child-rearing style. But there are moments when I wish I could invoke the intimidation factor of black-maleness on demand. If I only had that look—that Malcolm X/Mike Tyson/Ice Cube/Larry Fishburne/Bigger Thomas/Fruit of Islam look—I could keep the stupid questions at bay, make college administrators tremble, and scare editors into submission. Subconsciously, I decided that I had to do something about my image. Then, as if by magic, my wish was fulfilled.

Actually, it began as an accident involving a pair of electric clippers and sleep deprivation—a bad auto-cut gone awry. With my lowtop fade on the verge of a Sly Stone afro, I was in desperate need of a trim. Diedra didn't have the time to do it, and as it was February (Black History Month), I was on the chitlin' lecture circuit and couldn't spare forty-five minutes at a barber shop, so I elected to do it myself. Standing in a well-lighted bathroom, armed with two mirrors, I started trimming. Despite a steady hand and what I've always believed was a good eye, my hair turned out lopsided. I kept trimming and trimming to correct my error, but as my flattop sank lower, a yellow patch of scalp began to rise above the surrounding hair, like one of those big granite mounds dotting the grassy knolls of Central Park. A nice yarmulke could have covered it, but that would have been more difficult to explain than a bald spot. So, bearing in mind role models like Michael Jordan, Charles Barkley, Stanley Crouch, and Onyx (then the hip-hop group of the hour), I decided to take it all off.

I didn't think much of it at first, but the new style accomplished what years of evil stares and carefully crafted sartorial statements could not: I began to scare people. The effect was immediate and dramatic. Passing strangers avoided me and smiled less frequently. Those who did smile or make eye contact seemed to be deliberately trying to disarm me—a common strategy taught in campus rape-prevention centers. Scaring people was fun for a while, but I especially enjoyed standing in line at the supermarket with my bald head, baggy pants, high-top Reeboks, and long black hooded down coat, humming old standards like "Darn That Dream," "A Foggy Day," and "I Could Write a Book." Now *that* brought some stares. I must have been convincing, since I adore those songs and have been humming them ever since I can remember. No simple case of cultural hybridity here, just your average menace to society with a deep appreciation for Gershwin, Rodgers and Hart, Van Heusen, Cole Porter, and Jerome Kern.

Among my colleagues, my bald head became the lead subject of every conversation. "You look older, more mature." "With that new cut you come across as much more serious than usual." "You really look quite rugged and masculine with a bald head." My close friends dispensed with the euphemisms and went straight to the point: "Damn. You look scary!" The most painful comment was that I looked like a "B-Boy wannabe" and was "too old for that shit." I had to remind my friend that I'm an OBB (Original B-Boy), that I was in the eleventh grade in 1979 when the Sugar Hill Gang dropped "Rapper's Delight," and that *his* tired behind was in graduate school at the time. Besides, B-Boy was not the intent.

In the end, however, I got more questions than comments. Was I in crisis? Did I want to talk? What was I trying to say by shaving my head? What was the political point of my actions? Once the novelty passed, I began getting those "speak for the race" questions that irritated the hell out of me when I had hair. Why have *black men* begun to shave their heads in greater numbers? Why have so many black athletes decided to shave their heads? Does this new trend have some kind of phallic meaning? Against my better judgment, I found myself coming up with answers to these questions—call it an academician's reflex. I don't remember exactly what I said, but it usually began with black prizefighter Jack Johnson, America's real life "baaad nigger" of the early twentieth century, whose head was always shaved and greased, and ended with the hip-hop community's embrace of an outlaw status. Whatever it was, it made sense at the time.

The publicity photo for my recent book, *Race Rebels,* clearly generated the most controversy among my colleagues. It diverged dramatically from the photo on my first book, where I look particularly innocent, almost angelic. In that first photo I smiled just enough to make my dimples visible; my eyes gazed away from the camera in sort of a dreamy, contemplative pose; my haircut was nondescript and the natural sunlight had a kind of halo effect. The Izod shirt was the icing on the cake. By contrast, the photograph for *Race Rebels* (which Diedra set up and shot, by the way) has me looking directly into the camera, arms folded, bald head glistening from baby oil and rear window light, with a grimace that could give Snoop Doggy Dogg a run for his money. The lens made my arms appear much larger than they really are, creating a kind of Popeye effect. Soon after the book came out, I received several e-mail messages about the photo. A particularly memorable one came from a friend and fellow historian in Australia. In the course of explaining to me how he had corrected one of his students who had read an essay of mine and presumed I was a woman, he wrote: "Mind you, the photo in your book should make things clear—the angle and foreshortening of the arms, and the hairstyle make it one of the more masculine author photos I've seen recently????!!!!!!"

My publisher really milked this photo, which actually fit well with the book's title. For the American Studies Association meeting in Nashville, Tennessee, which took place the week the book came out, my publisher bought a full-page ad on the back cover of an ASA handout, with my mug staring dead at you. Everywhere I turned—in hotel elevators, hallways, lobbies, meeting rooms—I saw myself, and it was not exactly a pretty sight. The quality of the reproduction (essentially a high-contrast xerox) made me appear harder, meaner, and crazier than the original photograph.

The situation became even stranger since I had decided to abandon the skinhead look and grow my hair back. In fact, by the time of the ASA meeting I was on the road (since abandoned) toward a big Black Power Afro—a retro style that at the time seemed to be making a comeback. Worse still, I had come to participate in a roundtable discussion on black hair! My paper, titled "Nap Time: Historicizing the Afro," explored the political implications of competing narratives of the Afro's origins and meaning. Overall, it was a terrific session; the room was packed and the discussion was stimulating. But inevitably the question came up: "Although this isn't directly related to his paper, I'd like to find out from Professor Kelley why he shaved his head. Professor Kelley, given the panel's topic and in light of the current ads floating about with your picture on them, can you shed some light on what is attractive to black men about baldness?" The question was posed by a very distinguished and widely read African-American literary scholar. Hardly the naif, he knew the answers as well as I did, but wanted to generate a public discussion. And he succeeded. For ten minutes the audience ran the gamut of issues revolving around race, gender, sexuality, and the politics of style. Even the issue of bald heads as phallic symbols came up. "It's probably true," I said, "but when I was cutting my hair at three o'clock in the morning I wasn't thinking 'penis.'" Eventually the discussion drifted from black masculinity to the tremendous workloads of minority scholars, which, in all honesty, was the source of my baldness in the first place. Unlike the golden old days, when doing hair was highly ritualized and completely integrated into daily life, we're so busy mentoring and publishing and speaking and fighting that we have very little time to attend to our heads.

Beyond the session itself, that ad continued to haunt me during the entire conference. Every ten minutes, or so it seemed, someone came up to me and offered unsolicited commentary on the photo. One person slyly suggested that in order to make the picture complete I should have posed with an Uzi. When I approached a very good friend of mine, a historian who is partly my Jewish mother and partly my confidante and *always* looking out for my best interests, the first words out of her mouth were, "Robin, I hate that picture! It's the worst picture of you I've ever seen. It doesn't do you justice. Why did you let them use it?"

"It's not that bad," I replied. "Diedra likes it—she took the picture. You just don't like my bald head."

"No, that's not it. I like the bald look on some men, and you have a very nice head. The problem is the photo and the fact that I know what kind of person you are. None of your gentleness and lovability comes out in that picture. Now, don't get a swelled head when I say this, but you have a delightful face and expression that makes people feel good, even when you're talking about serious stuff. The way you smile, there's something unbelievably safe about you."

It was a painful compliment. And yet I knew deep down that she was telling the truth. I've always been unbelievably safe, not just because of my look but because of my actions. Not that I consciously try to put people at ease, to erase conflict and difference, to remain silent on sensitive issues. I can't quite put my finger on it. Perhaps it's my mother's politeness drills? Perhaps it's a manifestation of my continuing bout with shyness? Maybe it has something to do with the sense of joy I get from stimulating conversations? Or maybe it's linked to the fact that my mom refused to raise me in a manner boys are accustomed to? Most likely it is a product of cultural capital—the fact that I *can* speak the language, (re)cite the texts, exhibit the manners and mannerisms that are inherent to bourgeois academic culture. My colleagues identify with me because I can talk intelligently about their scholarship on their terms, which invariably has the effect of creating an illusion of brilliance. As Frantz Fanon said in *Black Skin, White Masks,* the mere fact that he was an articulate *black* man who read a lot rendered him a stunning specimen of erudition in the eyes of his fellow intellectuals in Paris.

Whatever the source of my ineffable lovability, I've learned that it's not entirely a bad thing. In fact, if the rest of the world could look a little deeper, beyond the hardcore exterior—the wide bodies, the carefully constructed grimaces, the performance of terror—they would find many, many brothas much nicer and smarter than myself. The problem lies in a racist culture, a highly gendered racist culture, that is so deeply enmeshed in the fabric of daily life that it's practically invisible. The very existence of the "nice Negro," like the model-minority myth pinned on Asian Americans, renders the war on those "other," hardcore niggas justifiable and even palatable. In a little-known essay on the public image of world champion boxer Joe Louis, the radical Trinidadian writer C. L. R. James put it best: "This attempt to hold up Louis as a model Negro has strong overtones of condescension and race prejudice. It implies: 'See! When a Negro knows how to conduct himself, he gets on very well and we all love him.' From there the next step is: 'If only all Negroes behaved like Joe, the race problem would be solved.'"[1]

Of course we all know this is a bunch of fiction. Behaving "like Joe" was merely a code for deference and patience, which is all the more remarkable given his vocation. Unlike his predecessor Jack Johnson—the bald-headed prize fighter who transgressed racial boundaries by sleeping with and even marrying white women, who refused to apologize for his "outrageous" behavior, who boasted of his prowess in every facet of life (he even wrapped gauze around his penis to make it appear bigger under his boxing shorts)—Joe Louis was America's hero. As James put it, he was a credit to his race, "I mean the human race."[2] (Re)presented as a humble Alabama boy, God-fearing and devoid of hatred, Louis was constructed in the press as a raceless man whose masculinity was put to good, patriotic use. To many of his white fans, he was a man in the ring and a boy—a good boy—outside of it. To many black folks, he was a hero because he had the license to kick white men's butts and yet maintain the admiration and respect of a nation. Thus, despite similarities in race, class, and vocation, and their common iconization, Louis and Johnson exhibited public behavior that reflected radically different masculinities.

Here, then, is a lesson we cannot ignore. There is some truth in the implication that race (or gender) conflict is partly linked to behavior and how certain behavior is perceived. If our society, for example, could dispense with rigid, archaic notions of appropriate masculine and feminine behavior, perhaps we might create a world that nurtures, encourages, and even rewards nice guys. If violence were not so central to American culture—to the way manhood is defined, to the way in which the state keeps African-American men in check, to the way men interact with women, to the way oppressed peoples interact with one another—perhaps we might see the withering away of white fears of black men. Perhaps young black men wouldn't feel the need to adopt hardened, threatening postures merely to survive in a Doggy-Dogg world. Not that black men ought to become colored equivalents of Alan Alda. Rather, black men ought to be whomever or whatever they want to be, without unwarranted criticism or societal pressures to conform to a particular definition of manhood. They could finally dress down without suspicion, talk loudly without surveillance, and love each other without sanction. Fortunately, such a transformation would also mean the long-awaited death of the "nice Negro."

Not in my lifetime. Any fool can look around and see that the situation for race and gender relations in general, and for black males in particular, has taken a turn for the worse—and relief is nowhere in sight. In the meantime, I will make the most of my "nice Negro" status. When it's all said and done, there is nothing romantic or interesting about playing Bigger Thomas. Maybe I can't persuade a well-dressed white couple to give up their box seats, but at least they'll listen to me. For now. . . .

Notes

1. C. L. R. James, "Joe Louis and Jack Johnson," *Labor Action*, 1 July 1946.
2. Ibid.

ARTICLE 27

Anne Fausto-Sterling

How to Build a Man

How does one become a man? Although poets, novelists, and playwrights long past answered with discussions of morality and honor, these days scholars deliberate the same question using a metaphor—that of social construction. In the current intellectual fashion, men are made, not born. We construct masculinity through social discourse, that array of happenings that covers everything from music videos, poetry, and rap lyrics to sports, beer commercials, and psychotherapy. But underlying all of this clever carpentry is the sneaking suspicion that one must start with a blueprint—or, to stretch the metaphor yet a bit more, that buildings must have foundations. Within the soul of even the most die-hard constructionist lurks a doubt. It is called the body.

In contrast, biological and medical scientists feel quite certain about their world. For them, the body tells the truth. (Never mind that postmodern scholarship has questioned the very meaning of the word "truth.") My task in this essay is to consider the truths that biologists extract from bodies, human and otherwise, to examine scientific accounts—some might even say constructions—of masculinity. To do this, I will treat the scientific/medical literature as yet another set of texts open to scholarly analysis and interpretation.

What are little boys made of? While the nursery rhyme suggests "snips and snails, and puppy-dogs tails," during the past seventy years, medical scientists have built a rather more concrete and certainly less fanciful account. Perhaps the single most influential voice during this period has been that of psychologist John Money. Since at least the 1920s, embryologists have understood that during fetal development a single embryonic primordium—the indifferent fetal gonad—can give rise to either an ovary or a testis. In a similar fashion, both male and female external genitalia arise from a single set of structures. Only the internal sex organs—uteri, fallopian tubes, prostates, sperm transport ducts—arise during embryonic development from separate sets of structures. In the 1950s, Money extended these embryological understandings into the realm of psychological development. As he saw it, all humans start on the same road, but the path rapidly begins to fork. Potential males take a series of turns in one direction, potential females in another. In real time, the road begins at fertilization and ends during late adolescence. If all goes as it should, then there are two, and only two, possible destinations—male and female.

But, of course, all does not always go as it should. Money identified the various forks in the road by studying individuals who took one or more wrong turns. From them, he derived a map of the normal. This is, in fact, one of the very interesting things about biological investigators. They use the infrequent to illuminate the common. The former they call abnormal, the latter normal. Often, as is the case for Money and others in the medical world, the abnormal requires management. In the examples I will discuss, management means conversion to the normal. Thus, we have a profound irony. Biologists and physicians use natural biological variation to define normality. Armed with this description, they set out to eliminate the natural variation that gave them their definitions in the first place.

From *Constructing Masculinity*, Maurice Berger, Brian Wallis, and Simon Watson (eds.). Copyright © 1995.

How does all this apply to the construction of masculinity? Money lists ten road signs directing a person along the path to male or female. In most cases these indicators are clear, but, as in any large city these days, sometimes graffiti makes them hard to read and the traveler ends up taking a wrong turn. The first sign is *chromosomal sex*, the presence of an X or a Y chromosome. The second is *gonadal sex*: when there is no graffiti, the Y or the X instructs the fetal gonad to develop into a testis or an ovary. *Fetal hormonal sex* marks the third fork: the embryonic testis must make hormones which influence events to come—particularly the fourth (*internal morphologic sex*), fifth (*external morphologic sex*), and sixth (*brain sex*) branches in the road. All of these, but especially the external morphologic sex at birth, illuminate the road sign for step number seven, *sex of assignment and rearing*. Finally, to become either a true male or a true female in John Money's world, one must produce the right hormones at puberty (*pubertal hormonal sex*), acquire and express a consistent *gender identity and role*, and, to complete the picture, be able to reproduce in the appropriate fashion (*procreative sex*).[1]

Many medical texts reproduce this neat little scheme, and suggest that it is a literal account of the scientific truth, but they neglect to point out how, at each step, scientists have woven into the fabric their own deeply social understandings of what it means to be male or female. Let me illustrate this for several of the branches in the road. Why is it that usually XX babies grow up to be female while XYs become male? Geneticists say that it is because of a specific Y chromosome gene, often abbreviated SDY (for "Sex-Determining Gene" on the Y). Biologists also refer to the SDY as the Master Sex-Determining Gene and say that in its *presence* a male is formed. Females, on the other hand, are said to be the default sex. In the *absence* of the master gene, they just naturally happen. The story of the SDY begins an account of maleness that continues throughout development. A male embryo must activate its master gene and seize its developmental pathway from the underlying female ground plan.

When the SDY gene starts working, it turns the indifferent gonad into a functional testis. One of the first things the testis does is to induce hormone synthesis. It is these molecules that take control of subsequent developmental steps. The first hormone to hit the decks (MIS, or Mullerian Inhibiting Substance) suppresses the development of the internal female organs, which lie in wait ready to unveil their feminine presence. The next, fetal testosterone, manfully pushes over embryonic primordia to develop both the internal and external trappings of physical masculinity. Again, medical texts offer the presence/absence hypothesis. Maleness requires the presence of special hormones; in their absence, femaleness just happens.[2]

Up to this point, two themes emerge. First, masculinity is an active presence which forces itself onto a feminine foundation. Money sometimes calls this "The Adam Principle—adding something to make a male." Second, the male is in constant danger. At any point male development can be derailed: a failure to activate SDY, and the gonad becomes an ovary; a failure to make MIS, and the fetus can end up with fallopian tubes and a uterus superimposed on an otherwise male body; a failure to make fetal testosterone, and, despite the presence of a testis, the embryo develops the external trappings of a baby girl. One fascinating contradiction in the scientific literature illustrates my point. Most texts write that femaleness results from the absence of male hormones, yet at the same time scientists worry about how male fetuses protect themselves from being feminized by the sea of maternal (female) hormones in which they grow.[3] This fear suggests, of course, that female hormones play an active role, after all; but most scientists do not pick up on that bit of logic. Instead, they hunt for special proteins the male embryo makes in order to protect itself from maternally induced feminization. (It seems that mother is to blame even before birth.)

Consider now the birth of a boy-child. He is perfect: Y chromosomes, testes descended into their sweet little scrotal sacs, a beautifully formed penis. He is perfect—except that the penis is very tiny. What happens next? Some medical texts refer to a situation such as this as a social emergency, others see it as a surgical one. The parents want to tell everyone about the birth of their baby boy; the physicians fear he cannot continue developing along the road to masculinity. They decide that creating a female is best. Females are imperfect by nature, and if this child cannot be a perfect or near-perfect male, then being an imperfect female is the best choice. What do the criteria physicians use to make such choices tell us about the construction of masculinity?

Medical managers use the following rule of thumb:

> Genetic females should always be raised as females, preserving reproductive potential, regardless of how severely the patients are virilized. In the genetic male, however, the gender of assignment is based on the infant's anatomy, predominantly the size of the phallus.[4]

Only a few reports on penile size at birth exist in the scientific literature, and it seems that birth size in and of itself is not a particularly good indicator of size and function at puberty. The average phallus at birth measures 3.5 cm (1 to 1.5 inches) long. A baby boy born with a penis measuring only 0.9 inches raises some eyebrows, but medical practitioners do not permit one born with a penis less than 0.6 inches long to remain as a male.[5] Despite the fact that the intact organ promises to provide orgasmic pleasure to the future adult, it is surgically removed (along with the testes) and replaced by a much smaller clitoris which may or may not retain orgasmic function. When surgeons turn "Sammy" into "Samantha," they also build her a vagina. Her primary sexual activity is to be the recipient of a penis during heterosexual intercourse. As one surgeon recently commented, "It's easier to poke a hole than build a pole."

All this surgical activity goes on to ensure a congruous and certain sex of assignment and sex of rearing. During childhood, the medical literature insists, boys must have a phallus large enough to permit them to pee standing up, thus allowing them to "feel normal" when they play in little boys' peeing contests. In adulthood, the penis must become large enough for vaginal penetration during sexual intercourse. By and large, physicians use the standard of reproductive potential for making females and phallus size for making males, although Suzanne J. Kessler reports one case of a physician choosing to reassign as male a potentially reproductive genetic female infant rather than remove a well-formed penis.[6]

At birth, then, masculinity becomes a social phenomenon. For proper masculine socialization to occur, the little boy must have a sufficiently large penis. There must be no doubt in the boy's mind, in the minds of his parents and other adult relatives, or in the minds of his male peers about the legitimacy of his male identification. In childhood, all that is required is that he be able to pee in a standing position. In adulthood, he must engage in vaginal heterosexual intercourse. The discourse of sexual pleasure, even for males, is totally absent from this medical literature. In fact, male infants who receive extensive penile surgery often end up with badly scarred and thus physically insensitive members. While no surgeon finds this outcome desirable, in assigning sex to an intersexual infant, sexual pleasure clearly takes a backseat to ensuring heterosexual conventions. Penetration in the absence of pleasure takes precedence over pleasure in the absence of penetration.

In the world of John Money and other managers of intersexuality, men are made not born. Proper socialization becomes more important than genetics. Hence, Money and his followers have a simple solution to accidents as terrible as penile amputation following infant circumcision: raise the boy as a girl. If both the parents and the child remain confident of his newfound female identity, all will be well. But what counts as good mental health for boys and girls? Here, Money and his coworkers focus primarily on female development, which becomes the mirror from which we can reflect the truth about males. Money has published extensively on XX infants born with masculinized genitalia. Usually such children are raised as girls, receiving surgery and hormonal treatments to feminize their genitalia and to ensure a feminine puberty. He notes that frequently such children have a harder time than usual achieving clarity about their femininity. Some signs of trouble are these: in the toddler years, engaging in rough-and-tumble play, and hitting more than other little girls do; in the adolescent years, thinking more about having a career and fantasizing less about marriage than other little girls do; and, as an adolescent and young adult, having lesbian relationships.

The homologue to these developmental variations can be found in Richard Green's description of the "Sissy Boy Syndrome." Green studied little boys who develop "feminine" interests—playing with dolls, wanting to dress in girls' clothing, not engaging in enough rough-and-tumble play. These boys, he argued, are at high risk for becoming homosexuals. Money's and Green's ideas work together to present a picture of normality. And, surprise, surprise, there is no room in the scheme for a normal homosexual. Money makes a remarkable claim. Genetics and even hormones count less in making a man or a woman than does socialization. In sustaining that claim, his strongest evidence, his trump card, is that the child born a male but raised a female becomes a heterosexual female. In their accounts of the power of socialization, Money and his coworkers define heterosexual in terms of the sex of rearing. Thus, a child raised as a female (even if biologically male) who prefers male lovers is psychologically heterosexual, although genetically she is not.

Again, we can parse out the construction of masculinity. To begin with, normally developing little boys must be active and willing to push one another around; maleness and aggression go together. Eventually, little boys become socialized into appropriate adult behavior, which includes heterosexual fantasy and activity. Adolescent boys do not dream of marriage, but of careers and a professional future. A healthy adolescent girl, in contrast, must fantasize about falling in love, marrying, and raising children. Only a masculinized girl dreams of a professional future. Of course, we know already that for men the true mark of heterosexuality involves vaginal penetration with the penis. Other activities, even if they are with a woman, do not really count.

This might be the end of the story, except for one thing. Accounts of normal development drawn from the study of intersexuals contain internal inconsistencies. How *does* Money explain the higher percentage than normal of lesbianism, or the more frequent aggressive behavior among masculinized children raised as girls? One could imagine elaborating on the socialization theme: parents aware of the uncertain sex of their children subconsciously socialize them in some intermediary fashion. Shockingly for a psychologist, however, Money denies the possibility of subconsciously driven behavior. Instead, he and the many others who interpret the development of intersexual children resort to hormonal explanations. If an XX girl, born with a penis, surgically "corrected" shortly after birth, and raised as a girl, subsequently becomes a lesbian, Money and others do not look to faulty socialization. Instead, they explain this failure to become heterosexual by appealing to hormones present in the fetal environment. Excess fetal testosterone caused the masculinization of the genitalia; similarly, fetal testosterone must have altered the developing brain, readying it to view females as appropriate sexual objects. Here, then, we have the last bit of the picture painted by biologists. By implication, normal males become sexually attracted to females because testosterone affects their brain during embryonic development. Socialization reinforces this inclination.

Biologists, then, write texts about human development. These documents, which take the form of research papers, textbooks, review articles, and popular books, grow from interpretations of scientific data. Often written in neutral, abstract language, the texts have the ring of authority. Because they represent scientific findings, one might imagine that they contain no preconceptions, no culturally instigated belief systems. But this turns out not to be the case. Although based in evidence, scientific writing can be seen as a particular kind of cultural interpretation—the enculturated scientist interprets nature. In the process, he or she also uses that interpretation to reinforce old or build new sets of social beliefs. Thus, scientific work contributes to the construction of masculinity, and masculine constructs are among the building blocks for particular kinds of scientific knowledge. One of the jobs of the science critic is to illuminate this interaction. Once this is done, it becomes possible to discuss change.

Notes

1. For a popular account of this picture, see John Money and Patricia Tucker, *Sexual Signatures: On Being a Man or a Woman* (Boston: Little, Brown and Co., 1975).

2. The data do not actually match the presence/absence model, but this does not seem to bother most people. For a discussion of this point, see Anne Fausto-Sterling, "Life in the XY Corral," *Women's Studies International Forum* 12 (1989): 319–331; Anne Fausto-Sterling, "Society Writes Biology/Biology Constructs Gender," *Daedalus* 116 (1987): 61–76; and Anne Fausto-Sterling, *Myths of Gender: Biological Theories about Women and Men* (New York: Basic Books, 1992).

3. I use the phrase "male hormone" and "female hormone" as shorthand. There are, in fact, no such categories. Males and females have the same hormones, albeit in different quantities and sometimes with different tissue distributions.

4. Patricia Donahue, David M. Powell, and Mary M. Lee, "Clinical Management of Intersex Abnormalities," *Current Problems in Surgery* 8 (1991): 527.

5. Robert H. Danish, Peter A. Lee, Thomas Mazur, James A. Amrhein, and Claude J. Migeon, "Micropenis II: Hypogonadotropic Hypogonadism," *Johns Hopkins Medical Journal* 146 (1980): 177–184.

6. Suzanne J. Kessler, "The Medical Construction of Gender: Case Management of Intersexed Infants," *Signs* 16 (1990).

ARTICLE 28

Gloria Steinem

If Men Could Menstruate

A white minority of the world has spent centuries conning us into thinking that a white skin makes people superior—even though the only thing it really does is make them more subject to ultraviolet rays and to wrinkles. Male human beings have built whole cultures around the idea that penis-envy is "natural" to women—though having such an unprotected organ might be said to make men vulnerable, and the power to give birth makes womb-envy at least as logical.

In short, the characteristics of the powerful, whatever they may be, are thought to be better than the characteristics of the powerless—and logic has nothing to do with it.

What would happen, for instance, if suddenly, magically, men could menstruate and women could not?

The answer is clear—menstruation would become an enviable, boastworthy, masculine event:

Men would brag about how long and how much.

Boys would mark the onset of menses, that longed-for proof of manhood, with religious rituals and stag parties.

Congress would fund a National Institute of Dysmenorrhea to help stamp out monthly discomforts.

Sanitary supplies would be federally funded and free. (Of course, some men would still pay for the prestige of commercial brands such as John Wayne Tampons, Muhammad Ali's Rope-a-dope Pads, Joe Namath Jock Shields—"For Those Light Bachelor Days," and Robert "Baretta" Blake Maxi-Pads.)

From *Outrageous Acts and Everyday Rebellions* by Gloria Steinem, Holt, Rinehart and Winston. Copyright © 1983 by Gloria Steinem.

Military men, right-wing politicians, and religious fundamentalists would cite menstruation ("*men*-struation") as proof that only men could serve in the Army ("you have to give blood to take blood"), occupy political office ("can women be aggressive without that steadfast cycle governed by the planet Mars?"), be priests and ministers ("how could a woman give her blood for our sins?"), or rabbis ("without the monthly loss of impurities, women remain unclean").

Male radicals, left-wing politicians, and mystics, however, would insist that women are equal, just different; and that any woman could enter their ranks if only she were willing to self-inflict a major wound every month ("you *must* give blood for the revolution"), recognize the preeminence of menstrual issues, or subordinate her selfness to all men in their Cycle of Enlightenment.

Street guys would brag ("I'm a three-pad man") or answer praise from a buddy ("Man, you lookin' *good!*") by giving fives and saying, "Yeah, man, I'm on the rag!"

TV shows would treat the subject at length. ("Happy Days": Richie and Potsie try to convince Fonzie that he is still "The Fonz," though he has missed two periods in a row.) So would newspapers. (SHARK SCARE THREATENS MENSTRUATING MEN. JUDGE CITES MONTHLY STRESS IN PARDONING RAPIST.) And movies. (Newman and Redford in "Blood Brothers"!)

Men would convince women that intercourse was *more* pleasurable at "that time of the month." Lesbians would be said to fear blood and therefore life itself—though probably only because they needed a good menstruating man.

Of course, male intellectuals would offer the most moral and logical arguments. How could a woman master any discipline that demanded a sense of time, space, mathematics, or measurement, for instance, without that in-built gift for measuring the cycles of the moon and planets—and thus for measuring anything at all? In the rarefied fields of philosophy and religion, could women compensate for missing the rhythm of the universe? Or for their lack of symbolic death-and-resurrection every month?

Liberal males in every field would try to be kind: the fact that "these people" have no gift for measuring life or connecting to the universe, the liberals would explain, should be punishment enough.

And how would women be trained to react? One can imagine traditional women agreeing to all these arguments with a staunch and smiling masochism. ("The ERA would force housewives to wound themselves every month": Phyllis Schlafly. "Your husband's blood is as sacred as that of Jesus—and so sexy, too!": Marabel Morgan.) Reformers and Queen Bees would try to imitate men, and *pretend* to have a monthly cycle. All feminists would explain endlessly that men, too, needed to be liberated from the false idea of Martian aggressiveness, just as women needed to escape the bonds of menses-envy. Radical feminists would add that the oppression of the nonmenstrual was the pattern for all other oppressions. ("Vampires were our first freedom fighters!") Cultural feminists would develop a bloodless imagery in art and literature. Socialist feminists would insist that only under capitalism would men be able to monopolize menstrual blood. . . .

In fact, if men could menstruate, the power justifications could probably go on forever.

If we let them.

ARTICLE 29

Thomas J. Gerschick
Adam Stephen Miller

Coming to Terms: Masculinity and Physical Disability

Men with physical disabilities are marginalized and stigmatized in American society. The image and reality of men with disabilities undermine cultural beliefs about men's bodies and physicality. The body is a central foundation of how men define themselves and how they are defined by others. Bodies are vehicles for determining value, which in turn translates into status and prestige. Men's bodies allow them to demonstrate the socially valuable characteristics of toughness, competitiveness, and ability (Messner 1992). Thus, one's body and relationship to it provide a way to apprehend the world and one's place in it. The bodies of men with disabilities serve as a continual reminder that they are at odds with the expectations of the dominant culture. As anthropologist Robert Murphy (1990: 94) writes of his own experiences with disability:

> Paralytic disability constitutes emasculation of a more direct and total nature. For the male, the weakening and atrophy of the body threaten all the cultural values of masculinity: strength, activeness, speed, virility, stamina, and fortitude.

This article seeks to sharpen our understanding of the creation, maintenance, and recreation of gender identities by men who, by birth, accident, or illness, find themselves dealing with a physical disability. We examine two sets of social dynamics that converge and clash in the lives of men with physical disabilities. On the one side, these men must deal with the presence and pressures of hegemonic masculinity, which demands strength. On the other side, societal members perceive people with disabilities to be weak.

For the present study, we conducted in-depth interviews with ten men with physical disabilities in order to gain insights into the psychosocial aspects of men's ability to come to terms with their physical and social condition. We wanted to know how men with physical disabilities respond to the demands of hegemonic masculinity and their marginalization. For instance, if men with disabilities need others to legitimize their gender identity during encounters, what happens when others deny them the opportunity? How do they reconcile the conflicting expectations associated with masculinity and disability? How do they define masculinity for themselves, and what are the sources of these definitions? To what degree do their responses contest and/or perpetuate the current gender order? That is, what are the political implications of different gender identities and practices? In addressing these questions, we contribute to the growing body of literature on marginalized and alternative gender identities.

Author's Note: We would like to thank our informants for sharing their time, experiences, and insights. Additionally, we would like to thank the following people for their comments on earlier drafts of this work: Sandra Cole, Harlan Hahn, Michael Kimmel, Michael Messner, Don Sabo, and Margaret Weigers. We, of course, remain responsible for its content. Finally, we are indebted to Kimberly Browne and Erika Gottfried for background research and interview transcriptions. This research was supported by a grant from the Undergraduate Research Opportunity Program at the University of Michigan.

From *Masculinities* 2(1): [pp–pp?]. Copyright © 1994. Reprinted by permission by *Masculinities*.

We will first discuss the general relationship between physical disability and hegemonic masculinity. Second, we will summarize the methods used in this study. Next, we will present and discuss our central findings. Finally, we discuss how the gender identities and life practices of men with disabilities contribute to the politics of the gender order.

Hegemonic Masculinity and Physical Disability

Recently, the literature has shifted toward understanding gender as an interactive process. Thus, it is presumed to be not only an aspect of what one *is*, but more fundamentally it is something that one *does* in interaction with others (West and Zimmerman 1987). Whereas previously, gender was thought to be strictly an individual phenomenon, this new understanding directs our attention to the interpersonal and institutional levels as well. The lives of men with disabilities provide an instructive arena in which to study the interactional nature of gender and its effect on individual gender identities.

In *The Body Silent*, Murphy (1990) observes that men with physical disabilities experience "embattled identities" because of the conflicting expectations placed on them as men and as people with disabilities. On the one side, contemporary masculinity privileges men who are strong, courageous, aggressive, independent, and self-reliant (Connell 1987). On the other side, people with disabilities are perceived to be, and treated as, weak, pitiful, passive, and dependent (Murphy 1990). Thus, for men with physical disabilities, masculine gender identity and practice are created and maintained at the crossroads of the demands of contemporary masculinity and the stigmatization associated with disability. As such, for men with physical disabilities, being recognized as masculine by others is especially difficult, if not impossible, to accomplish. Yet not being recognized as masculine is untenable because, in our culture, everyone is expected to display an appropriate gender identity (West and Zimmerman 1987).

Methods

This research was based on in-depth interviews with ten men. Despite the acknowledged problem of identity management in interviews, we used this method because we were most interested in the subjective perceptions and experiences of our informants. To mitigate this dynamic, we relied on probing questions and reinterviews. Informants were located through a snowball sample, utilizing friends and connections within the community of people with disabilities. All of our informants were given pseudonyms, and we further protected their identity by deleting nonessential personal details. The age range of respondents varied from sixteen to seventy-two. Eight of our respondents were white, and two were African American. Geographically, they came from both coasts and the Midwest. All were "mobility impaired," and most were para- or quadriplegics. Given the small sample size and the modicum of diversity within it, this work must necessarily be understood as exploratory.

We interviewed men with physical disabilities for three primary reasons. First, given the diversity of disabilities and our modest resources, we had to bind the sample. Second, mobility impairments tend to be more apparent than other disabilities, such as blindness or hearing loss, and people respond to these men using visual clues. Third, although the literature in this area is scant, much of it focuses on men with physical disabilities.

Due to issues of shared identities, Adam did all the interviews. Interviews were semi-structured and tape-recorded. Initial interviews averaged approximately an hour in length. Additionally, we contacted all of our informants at least once with clarifying questions and, in some cases, to test ideas that we had. These follow-ups lasted approximately thirty minutes. Each informant received a copy of his interview transcript to ensure that we had captured his perspective accurately. We also shared draft copies of this chapter with them and incorporated their insights into the current version.

There were two primary reasons for the thorough follow-up. First, from a methodological standpoint, it was important for us to capture the experience of our informants as fully as possible. Second, we felt that we had an obligation to allow them to control, to a large extent, the representation of their experience.

Interviews were analyzed using an analytic induction approach (Emerson 1988; Katz 1988; Denzin 1989). In determining major and minor patterns of masculine practice, we used the responses to a series of questions including, What is the most important aspect of masculinity to you? What would you say makes you feel most manly or masculine? Do you think your conception of masculinity is different from that of able-bodied men as a result of your disability? If so, how and why? If not, why not? Additionally, we presented our informants with a list of characteristics associated with prevailing masculinity based on the work of R. W. Connell (1987, 1990a, 1990b, 1991) and asked them to rate their importance to their conception of self. Both positive and negative responses to this portion of our questionnaire guided our insight into how each man viewed his masculinity. To further support our discussion, we turned to the limited academic literature in this area. Much more helpful were the wide range of biographical and autobiographical accounts of men who have physical disabilities (see, for instance, Zola 1982; Callahan 1989; Hahn 1989; Murphy 1990; and Kriegel 1991).

Finally, in analyzing the data we were sensitive to making judgments about our informants when grouping them into categories. People with disabilities are shoehorned into categories too much as it is. We sought to discover what was common among their responses and to highlight what we perceived to be the essence of their views. In doing so, we endeavored to provide a conceptual framework for understanding the responses of men with physical disabilities while trying to be sensitive to their personal struggles.

Disability, Masculinity, and Coming to Terms

While no two men constructed their sense of masculinity in exactly the same way, there appeared to be three dominant frameworks our informants used to cope with their situations. These patterns can be conceived of in relation to the standards inherent in dominant masculinity. We call them the three Rs: *reformulation*, which entailed men's redefinition of hegemonic characteristics on their own terms; *reliance*, reflected by sensitive or hypersensitive adoptions of particular predominant attributes; and *rejection*, characterized by the renunciation of these standards and either the creation of one's own principles and practices or the denial of masculinity's importance in one's life. However, one should note that none of our interviewees *entirely* followed any one of these frameworks in defining his sense of self. Rather, for heuristic reasons, it is best to speak of the major and minor ways each man used these three patterns. For example, some of our informants relied on dominant standards in their view of sexuality and occupation but also reformulated the prevailing ideal of independence.

Therefore, we discuss the *primary* way in which these men with disabilities related to hegemonic masculinity's standards, while recognizing that their coping mechanisms reflected a more complex combination of strategies. In doing so, we avoid "labeling" men and assigning them to arbitrary categories.

Reformulation

Some of our informants responded to idealized masculinity by reformulating it, shaping it along the lines of their own abilities, perceptions, and strengths, and defining their manhood along these new lines. These men tended not to contest these standards overtly, but—either consciously or unconsciously—they recognized in their own condition an inability to meet these ideals as they were culturally conceived.

An example of this came from Damon, a seventy-two-year-old quadriplegic who survived a spinal-cord injury in an automobile accident ten years ago. Damon said he always desired, and had, control of his life. While Damon required round-the-clock personal care assistants (PCAs), he asserted that he was still a very independent person:

> I direct all of my activities around my home where people have to help me to maintain my apartment, my transportation, which I own, and direction in where I go. I direct people how to get there, and I tell them what my needs will be when I am going and coming, and when to get where I am going.

Damon said that his sense of control was more than mere illusion; it was a reality others knew of as well. This reputation seemed important to him:

> People know from Jump Street that I have my own thing, and I direct my own thing. And if they can't comply with my desire, they won't be around. . . . I don't see any reason why people with me can't take instructions and get my life on just as I was having it before, only thing I'm not doing it myself. I direct somebody else to do it. So, therefore, I don't miss out on very much.

Hegemonic masculinity's definition of independence privileges self-reliance and autonomy. Damon required substantial assistance: indeed, some might term him "dependent." However, Damon's reformulation of the independence ideal, accomplished in part through a cognitive shift, allowed him to think otherwise.

Harold, a forty-six-year-old polio survivor, described a belief and practice akin to Damon's. Also a quadriplegic, Harold similarly required PCAs to help him handle daily necessities: Harold termed his reliance on and control of PCAs "acting through others":

> When I say independence can be achieved by acting through other people, I actually mean getting through life, liberty, and the pursuit of happiness while utilizing high-quality and dependable attendant-care services.

As with Damon, Harold achieved his perceived sense of independence by controlling others. Harold stressed that he did not count on family or friends to do favors for him, but *employed* his PCAs in a "business relationship" he controlled. Alternatives to family and friends are used whenever possible because most people with disabilities do not want to burden or be dependent on their families any more than necessary (Murphy 1990).

Social class plays an important role here. Damon and Harold had the economic means to afford round-the-clock assistance. While none of our informants experienced economic hardship, many people with disabilities depend on the welfare system for their care, and the amount and quality of assistance they receive make it much more difficult to conceive of themselves as independent.

A third man who reformulated predominant demands was Brent, a forty-five-year-old administrator. He told us that his paraplegic status, one that he had lived with since he was five years old, had often cast him as an "outsider" to society. This status was particularly painful in his late adolescence, a time when the "sexual revolution" was sweeping America's youth:

> A very important measure of somebody's personhood—manhood—was their sexual ability. . . . What bothers me more than anything else is the stereotypes, and even more so, in terms of sexual desirability. Because I had a disability, I was less desirable than able-bodied people. And that I found very frustrating.

His experiences led him to recast the hegemonic notion that man's relations with a partner should be predominantly physical. As a result, he stressed the importance of emotional relations and trust. This appeared to be key to Brent's definition of his manhood:

> For me, that is my measure of who I am as an individual and who I am as a man—my ability

to be able to be honest with my wife. Be able to be close with her, to be able to ask for help, provide help. To have a commitment, to follow through, and to do all those things that I think are important.

As Connell (1990a) notes, this requires a capacity to not only be expressive, but also to have feelings worth expressing. This clearly demonstrates a different form of masculine practice.

The final case of reformulation came from Robert, a thirty-year-old survivor of a motorcycle accident. Able-bodied for much of his life, Robert's accident occurred when he was twenty-four, leaving him paraplegic. Through five years of intensive physical therapy, he regained 95 percent of his original function, though certain effects linger to this day.

Before his accident, Robert had internalized many of the standards of dominant masculinity exemplified by frequenting bars, leading an active sex life, and riding a motorcycle. But, if our research and the body of autobiographical works from men with physical disabilities has shown anything, it is that coming to terms with a disability eventually changes a man. It appeared to have transformed Robert. He remarked that, despite being generally "recovered," he had maintained his disability-influenced value system:

> I judge people on more of a personal and character level than I do on any physical, or I guess I did; but, you know, important things are guys that have integrity, guys that are honest about what they are doing, that have some direction in their life and know . . . peace of mind and what they stand for.

One of the areas that Robert said took the longest to recover was his sexuality—specifically, his confidence in his sexual ability. While Robert said sexual relations were still important to him, like Brent he reformulated his previous, largely hegemonic notion of male sexuality into a more emotionally and physically egalitarian model:

> I've found a whole different side to having sex with a partner and looking at satisfying the partner rather than satisfying myself; and that has taken the focus off of satisfying myself, being the big manly stud, and concentrating more on my partner. And that has become just as satisfying.

However, reformulation did not yield complete severance from prevailing masculinity's standards as they were culturally conceived. For instance, despite his reformulative inclinations, Robert's self-described "macho" attitude continued in some realms during his recovery. He, and all others we interviewed, represented the complexity of gender identities and practices; no man's masculinity fell neatly into any one of the three patterns.

For instance, although told by most doctors that his physical condition was probably permanent, Robert's resolve was unyielding. "I put my blinders on to all negative insight into it and just totally focused on getting better," he said. "And I think that was, you know, a major factor on why I'm where I'm at today." This typified the second pattern we identified—reliance on hegemonic masculinity's standards. It was ironic, then, that Robert's tenacity, his never-ending work ethic, and his focused drive to succeed were largely responsible for his almost-complete recovery. While Robert reformulated much of his earlier sense of masculinity, he still relied on this drive.

Perhaps the area in which men who reformulate most closely paralleled dominant masculinity was the emphasis they placed on their occupation. Our sample was atypical in that most of our informants were professionally employed on a full-time basis and could, therefore, draw on class-based resources, whereas unemployment among people with disabilities is very high. Just as societal members privilege men who are accomplished in their occupation, Harold said he finds both "purpose," and success, in his career:

> No one is going to go through life without some kind of purpose. Everyone decides. I wanted to be a writer. So I became a writer and an observer, a trained observer.

Brent said that he drew much of his sense of self, his sense of self-esteem, and his sense of manhood from his occupational accomplishments. Initially, Brent denied the importance of the prevailing ideal that a man's occupational worth was derived from his breadwinner status:

> It is not so important to be the breadwinner as it is to be competent in the world. You know, to have a career, to have my name on the door. That is what is most important. It is that recognition that is very important to me.

However, he later admitted that being the breadwinner still was important to him, although he denied a link between his desires and the "stereotypical" conception of breadwinner status. He maintained that "it's still important to me, because I've always been able to make money." Independence, both economic and physical, were important to all of our informants.

Rejection of hegemonic ideals also occurred among men who primarily depended on a reformulative framework. Harold's view of relationships with a partner dismissed the sexually powerful ideal: "The fact of the matter is that I'm not all that upset by the fact that I'm disabled and I'm a male. I mean, I know what I can do." We will have more to say about the rejection of dominant conceptions of sexuality later.

In brief summary, the subset of our informants whose primary coping pattern involved reformulation of dominant standards recognized their inability to meet these ideals as they are culturally conceived. Confident in their own abilities and values, and drawing from previous experience, they confronted standards of masculinity on their own terms. In doing so, they distanced themselves from masculine ideals.

Reliance

However, not all of the men with physical disabilities we interviewed depended on a reformulative approach. We found that many of our informants *were* concerned with others' views of their masculinity and with meeting the demands of hegemonic masculinity. They primarily used the second pattern, reliance, which involves the internalization of many more of the ideals of predominant masculinity, including physical strength, athleticism, independence, and sexual prowess. Just as some men depended on reformulation for much of their masculine definition, others, despite their inability to meet many of these ideals, relied on them heavily. As such, these men did not seem to be as comfortable with their sense of manhood; indeed, their inability to meet society's standards bothered them very much.

This subset of our informants found themselves in a double bind that left them conflicted. They embraced dominant conceptions of masculinity as a way to gain acceptance from themselves and from others. Yet, they were continuously reminded in their interactions with others that they were "incomplete." As a result, the identity behind the facade suffered; there were, then, major costs associated with this strategy.

The tension between societal expectations and the reality of men with physical disabilities was most clearly demonstrated by Jerry, a sixteen-year-old who had juvenile rheumatoid arthritis. While Jerry was physically able to walk for limited distances, this required great effort on his part; consequently, he usually used a wheelchair. He was concerned with the appearance of his awkward walking. "I feel like I look a little, I don't know, more strange when I walk," he said.

The significance of appearance and external perception of manliness is symptomatic of the difficulty men with physical disabilities have in developing an identity and masculinity free of others' perceptions and expectations. Jerry said:

> I think [others' conception of what defines a man] is very important, because if they don't think of you as one, it is hard to think of yourself as one; or, it doesn't really matter if you think of yourself as one if no one else does.

Jerry said that, particularly among his peers, he was not perceived as attractive as the able-bodied teenagers; thus, he had difficulty in male–female relations beyond landing an occasional date. "[The girls believe] I might be a 'really nice person,' but not like a guy per se," he said. "I think to some extent that you're sort of genderless to them." This clearly represents the emasculation and depersonalization inherent in social definitions of disability.

However, Jerry said that he faced a more persistent threat to his autonomy—his independence and his sense of control—from others being "uncomfortable" around him and persisting in offering him assistance he often did not need. This made him "angry," though he usually did not refuse the help out of politeness. Thus, with members of his social group, he participated in a "bargain": they would socialize with him as long as he remained in a dependent position where they could "help" him.

This forced, situational passivity led Jerry to emphasize his autonomy in other areas. For instance, Jerry avoided asking for help in nearly all situations. This was directly tied to reinforcing his embattled manhood by displaying outward strength and independence:

> If I ever have to ask someone for help, it really makes me like feel like less of a man. I don't like asking for help at all. You know, like even if I could use some, I'll usually not ask just because I can't, I just hate asking.... [A man is] fairly self-sufficient in that you can sort of handle just about any situation, in that you can help other people, and that you don't need a lot of help.

Jerry internalized the prevailing masculine ideal that a man should be independent; he relied on that ideal for his definition of manhood. His inability to meet this ideal—partly through his physical condition, and partly from how others treated him—threatened his identity and his sense of manhood, which had to be reinforced even at the expense of self-alienation.

One should not label Jerry a "relier" simply because of these struggles. Being only sixteen years of age—and the youngest participant in our study—Jerry was still developing his sense of masculinity; and, as with many teenagers both able-bodied and disabled, he was trying to fit into his peer group. Furthermore, Jerry will continue to mature and develop his self-image and sense of masculinity. A follow-up interview in five years might show a degree of resolution to his struggles.

Such a resolution could be seen in Michael, a thirty-three-year-old manager we interviewed, who also internalized many of the standards of hegemonic masculinity. A paraplegic from an auto accident in 1977, Michael struggled for many years after his accident to come to terms with his condition.

His struggles had several sources, all tied into his view of masculinity's importance. The first was that, before his accident, he accepted much of the dominant conception of masculinity. A high-school student, farm hand, and football and track star at the time, Michael said that independence, relations with the women he dated, and physical strength were central to his conception of self.

After his accident, Michael's doctors told him there was a 50–50 chance that he would regain the ability to walk, and he clung to the hope. "I guess I didn't understand it, and had hope that I would walk again," he said. However, he was "depressed" about his situation, "but not so much about my disability, I guess. Because that wasn't real yet."

But coming home three months after his accident didn't alleviate the depression. Instead, it heightened his anxiety and added a new component—vulnerability. In a span of three months, Michael had, in essence, his sense of masculinity and his security in himself completely stripped away. He was in an unfamiliar situation; and far from feeling strong, independent, and powerful, he felt vulnerable and afraid: "No one," he remarked, "can be prepared for a permanent disability."

His reliance on dominant masculinity, then, started with his predisability past and continued during his recovery as a coping mechanism to deal with his fears. The hegemonic standard Michael strove most to achieve was that of independence. It was central to his sense of masculinity before and at the time of our interview. Indeed, it was so important that it frustrated him greatly when he needed assistance. Much like Jerry, he refused to ask for it:

> I feel that I should be able to do everything for myself and I don't like it.... I don't mind asking for things that I absolutely can't do, like hanging pictures, or moving furniture, or having my oil changed in my car; but there are things that I'm capable of doing in my chair, like jumping up one step. That I feel like I should be able to do, and I find it frustrating when I can't do that sometimes.... I don't like asking for [help I don't think I need]. It kind of makes me mad.

When asked if needing assistance was "unmanly," Michael replied, "There's probably some of that in there." For both Michael and Jerry, the independence ideal often led to risk-taking behavior in order to prove to themselves that they were more than their social definition.

Yet, much like Robert, Michael had reformulated his view of sexuality. He said that his physical sexuality made him "feel the most masculine"—apparently another reliant response with a stereotypical emphasis on sexual performance. However, it was more complicated. Michael said that he no longer concentrated on pleasing himself, as he did when able-bodied, but that he now had a more partner-oriented view of sexuality. "I think that my compensation for my feeling of vulnerability is I've overcompensated by trying to please my partner and leave little room to allow my partner to please me.... Some of my greatest pleasure is exhausting my partner while having sex." Ironically, while he focused more on his partner's pleasure than ever before, he did so at his own expense; a sense of balancing the needs of both partners was missing.

Thus, sex served multiple purposes for Michael—it gave him and his partner pleasure; it reassured him in his fears and his feelings of vulnerability; and it reconfirmed his masculinity. His sexuality, then, reflected both reliance and reformulation.

While independence and sexuality were both extremely important to Scott, a thirty-four-year-old rehabilitation engineer, he emphasized a third area for his sense of manhood—athletics. Scott served in the Peace Corps during his twenties, working in Central America. He described his life-style as "rigorous" and "into the whole sports thing," and used a mountain bike as his primary means of transportation and recreation. He was also an avid hockey player in his youth and spent his summers in softball leagues.

Scott acquired a polio-like virus when he was twenty-five years old that left him permanently paraplegic, a situation that he did not initially accept. In an aggressive attempt to regain his physical ability, and similar to Robert, Scott obsessively attacked his rehabilitation

> ... thinking, that's always what I've done with all the sports. If I wasn't good enough, I worked a little harder and I got better. So, I kept thinking my walking isn't very good now. If I push it, it will get better.

But Scott's athletic drive led not to miraculous recovery, but overexertion. When ordered by his doctors to scale back his efforts, he realized he could not recover strictly through tenacity. At the time of our interview, he was ambivalent about his limitations. He clearly did not feel like a failure: "I think that if I wouldn't have made the effort, I always would have wondered, could I have made a difference?" Following the athlete's code of conduct, "always give 110 percent," Scott attacked his recovery. But when his efforts were not enough—when he did not "emerge victorious"—he accepted it as an athlete would. Yet, his limitations also frustrated him at times, and in different areas.

For example, though his physical capacity was not what it was, Scott maintained a need for athletic competition. He played wheelchair basketball and was the only wheelchair-participant in a city softball league. However, he did not return to hockey, the sport he loved as a youngster; in fact, he refused to even try the sled-based equivalent.

Here was Scott's frustration. His spirit of athleticism was still alive, but he lamented the fact that he could not compete exactly as before:

[I miss] the things that I had. I played hockey; that was my primary sport for so many years. Pretty much, I did all the sports. But, like, I never played basketball; never liked basketball before. Which is why I think I can play now. See, it would be like the equivalent to wheelchair hockey. Some friends of mine have talked to me about it, [but] I'm not really interested in that. Because it wouldn't be real hockey. And it would make me feel worse, rather than better.

In this respect, Scott had not completely come to terms with his limitations. He still wanted to be a "real" athlete, competing in the same sports, in the same ways, with the same rules, with others who shared his desire for competition. Wheelchair hockey, which he derogatorily referred to as "gimp hockey," represented the antithesis of this for him.

Scott's other responses added to this emphasis. What he most disliked about having a disability was "that I can't do the things that I want to be able to do," meaning he could not ride his bike or motorcycle, he could not play "real" hockey, and he was unable to live a freewheeling, spontaneous life-style. Rather, he had to plan ahead of time where he went and how he got there. The frustration caused by having to plan nearly every move was apparent in almost all of our interviews.

However, on the subject of independence, Scott said "I think I'm mostly independent," but complained that there were some situations where he could not meet his expectations and had to depend on his wife. Usually this was not a "major issue," but "there's still times when, yeah, I feel bad about it; or, you know it's the days where she doesn't feel like it, but she kind of has to. That's what bothers me the most, I guess." Thus, he reflected the general desire among men with disabilities not to be a burden of any kind on family members.

Much of the time, Scott accepted being "mostly independent." His reliance on the ideals of athleticism and independence played a significant part in his conception of masculinity and self. However, Scott learned, though to a limited degree, to let go of some of his previous ideals and to accept a different, reformulated notion of independence and competition. Yet, he could not entirely do so. His emphasis on athletics and independence was still strong, and there were many times when athletics and acceptance conflicted.

However, one should stop short of a blanket assessment of men with disabilities who rely on hegemonic masculinity standards. "Always" is a dangerous word, and stating that "men who rely on hegemonic standards are *always* troubled" is a dangerous assumption. An apparent exceptional case among men who follow a reliant pattern came from Aaron, a forty-one-year-old paraplegic. Rather than experiencing inner turmoil and conflict, Aaron was one of the most upbeat individuals we interviewed. Aaron said that, before his 1976 accident, he was "on top of the world," with a successful business, a commitment to athletics that included basketball shoot-arounds with NBA prospects, and a wedding engagement. Indeed, from the time of his youth, Aaron relied on such hegemonic standards as sexuality, independence, athleticism, and occupational accomplishment.

For example, when asked what masculinity meant to him before his accident, Aaron said that it originally meant sexual conquest. As a teen, he viewed frequent sexual activity as a "rite of passage" into manhood.

Aaron said he had also enjoyed occupational success, and that this success was central to his definition of self, including being masculine. Working a variety of jobs ranging from assembly-line worker to white-collar professional, Aaron said, "I had been very fortunate to have good jobs, which were an important part of who I was and how I defined myself."

According to Aaron, much of his independence ideal came from his father. When his parents divorced, Aaron's father explained to him that, though he was only five, he would have to be "the man of the house." Aaron took this lesson to heart, and strived to fulfill this role both in terms of independence and providing for the family. "My image of manhood was that of a provider," he said, "one who was able to make a contribution to the financial stability of the family in addition to dealing with the problems and concerns that would come up."

His accident, a gunshot wound injuring his spinal cord, left him completely dependent. Predictably, Aaron could not immediately cope with this. "My whole self-image itself was real integrally tied up with the things I used to do," he said. "I found my desire for simple pleasures to be the greatest part of the pain I had to bear."

His pain increased when he left the hospital. His fiancee had left him, and within two years he lost "everything that was important to me"—his house, his business, his savings, most of his friends, and even, for a while, his hope.

However, much as with Robert, Aaron's resiliency eventually turned his life around. Just as he hit bottom, he began telling himself that "if you hold on long enough, if you don't quit, you'll get through it." Additionally, he attacked his therapy with the vengeance he had always devoted to athletics. "I'd never been confronted with a situation in my entire life before that I was not able to overcome by the efforts of my own merit," he said. "I took the same attitude toward this."

Further, he reasserted his sexuality. Though he then wore a colostomy bag, he resumed frequent sexual intercourse, taking the attitude that "this is who I was, and a woman was either going to have to accept me as I was, or she's got to leave me f——— alone."

However, he realized after those five years that his hard work would not be rewarded nor would he be miraculously healed. Figuring that "there's a whole lot of life that I need to live, and this wasn't the most efficient way to live it," he bought a new sport wheelchair, found a job, and became involved in wheelchair athletics. In this sense, a complex combination of all three patterns emerged in Aaron as reliance was mixed with reformulation and rejection.

Furthermore, his soul-searching led him to develop a sense of purpose in his life, and a reason for going on:

[During my recovery] I felt that I was left here to enrich the lives of as many people as I could before I left this earth, and it gave me a new purpose, a new vision, a new mission, new dreams.

Tenacity, the quest for independence, athletics, and sexual activity carried Aaron through his recovery. Many of these ideals, which had their source in his father's teachings, remained with him as he continued to be active in athletics (everything from basketball to softball to scuba diving), to assert his sexuality, and to aim for complete autonomy. To Aaron, independence, both physical and financial, was more than just a personal ideal; it was one that should be shared by all people with disabilities. As such, he aspired to be a role model for others:

The work that I am involved in is to help people gain control over their lives, and I think it's vitally important that I walk my talk. If . . . we hold ourselves out to be an organization that helps people gain control over their lives, I think it's vitally important for me as the CEO of that organization to live my life in a way that embodies everything that we say we're about.

Clearly, Aaron was not the same man he was before his disability. He said that his maturity and his experience with disability "made me stronger," and that manhood no longer simply meant independence and sexual conquest. Manhood also meant

. . . being responsible for one's actions; being considerate of another's feelings; being sensitive to individuals who are more vulnerable than yourself, to what their needs would be; standing up on behalf and fighting for those who cannot speak out for themselves, fight for themselves. It means being willing to take a position and be committed to a position, even when it's inconvenient or costly to take that point of view, and you do it only because of the principle involved.

This dovetailed significantly with his occupation, which was of great importance to him. But as alluded to above, Aaron's emphasis on occupation cannot be seen as mere reliance on the hegemonic conception of occupational achievement. It was more a reformulation of that ideal from self-achievement to facilitating the empowerment of others.

Nevertheless, Aaron's struggle to gain his current status, like the struggle of others who rely on hegemonic masculinity's standards, was immense. Constructing hegemonic masculinity from a subordinated position is almost always a Sisyphean task. One's ability to do so is undermined continuously by physical, social, and cultural weakness. "Understandably, in an effort to cope with this stress (balancing the demands for strength and the societal perception of weakness)," writes political scientist Harlan Hahn, "many disabled men have tended to identify personally and politically with the supposed strength of prevalent concepts of masculinity rather than with their disability" (1989: 3). To relinquish masculinity under these circumstances is to court gender annihilation, which is untenable to some men. Consequently, relying on hegemonic masculinity becomes more understandable (Connell 1990a: 471).

Rejection

Despite the difficulties it presents, hegemony, including that related to gender, is never complete (Janeway 1980, Scott 1985). For some of our informants, resistance took the form of creating alternative masculine identities and subcultures that provided them with a supportive environment. These men were reflected in the final pattern: rejection. Informants who followed this pattern did not so much share a common ideology or set of practices; rather, they believed that the dominant conception of masculinity was wrong, either in its individual emphases or as a practice. One of these men developed new standards of masculinity in place of the ones he had rejected. Another seemingly chose to deny masculinity's importance, although he was neither effeminate nor androgynous. Instead, they both emphasized their status as "persons," under the motto of "people first." This philosophy reflected a key tenet of the Disability Rights Movement.

Alex, a twenty-three-year-old, first-year law student, survived an accident that left him an incomplete quadriplegic when he was fourteen. Before that time, he felt he was an outsider at his private school because he eschewed the superficial, athletically oriented, and materialistic atmosphere. Further, he said the timing of the accident, when many of his peers were defining their social roles, added to this outsider perspective, in that it made him unable to participate in the highly social, role-forming process. "I didn't learn about the traditional roles of sexuality, and whatever the rules are for such behavior in our society, until later," he said. "Because of my physical characteristics, I had to learn a different set of rules."

Alex described himself as a "nonconformist." This simple moniker seemed central to his conception of selfhood and masculinity. Alex, unlike men who primarily reformulate these tenets, rejected the attitudinal and behavioral prescriptions of hegemonic masculinity. He maintained that his standards were his own—not society's—and he scoffed at commonly held views of masculinity.

For example, Alex blamed the media for the idea that men must be strong and attractive, stating "The traditional conception is that everyone has to be Arnold Schwartzenegger... [which] probably lead[s] to some violence, unhappiness, and things like that if they [men] don't meet the standards."

As for the importance of virility and sexual prowess, Alex said, "There is a part of me that, you know, has been conditioned and acculturated and knows those [dominant] values"; but he sarcastically laughed at the notion of a man's sexual prowess being reflected in "making her pass out," and summed up his feelings on the subject by adding, "You have to be willing to do things in a nontraditional way."

Alex's most profound rejection of a dominant ideal involved the importance of fathering, in its strictest sense of the man as impregnator:

> There's no reason why we (his fiancee and himself) couldn't use artificial insemination or adoption. Parenting doesn't necessarily involve being the male sire. It involves being a good parent.... Parenting doesn't mean that it's your physical child. It involves responsibility and an emotional role as well. I don't think the link between parenthood is the primary link with sexuality. Maybe in terms of evolutionary purposes, but not in terms of a relationship.

Thus, Alex rejected the procreation imperative encouraged in hegemonic masculinity. However, while Alex took pride at overtly rejecting prevailing masculinity as superficial and silly, even he relied on it at times. Alex said he needed to support himself financially and would not ever want to be an emotional or economic "burden" in a relationship. On one level, this is a common concern for most people, disabled or not. But on another level, Alex admitted that it tied in to his sense of masculinity:

> If I was in a relationship and I wasn't working, and my spouse was, what could be the possible reasons for my not working? I could have just been fired. I could be laid off. Who knows what happened? I guess . . . that's definitely an element of masculinity, and I guess I am just as influenced by that as, oh, as I guess as other people, or as within my definition of masculinity. What do you know? I have been caught.

A different form of rejection was reflected in Leo, a fifty-eight-year-old polio survivor. Leo, who had striven for occupational achievement since his youth, seemed to value many hegemonic traits: independence, money-making ability, and recognition by peers. But he steadfastly denied masculinity's role in shaping his outlook.

Leo said the most important trait to him was his mental capacity and intelligence, since that allowed him to achieve his occupational goals. Yet he claimed this was not related to the prevailing standard. Rather, it tied into his ambitions from before his disability and his willingness to do most anything to achieve his goals.

Before we label him "a rejector," however, note that Leo was a believer in adaptive technology and personal assistance, and he did not see a contradiction between using personal-care assistants and being independent. This seemed to be a reformulation, just as with Damon and Harold, but when we asked Leo about this relation to masculinity, he flatly denied any connection.

Leo explained his renunciation of masculinity by saying "It doesn't mean a great deal . . . it's not how I think [of things]." He said that many of the qualities on our list of hegemonic characteristics were important to him on an individual level but did not matter to his sense of manhood. Leo maintained that there were "external" and "internal" reasons for this.

The external factors Leo identified were the Women's and Disability Rights Movements. Both provided support and alternatives that allow a person with a disability the freedom to be a person, and not (to use Leo's words) a "strange bird." Indeed, Leo echoed the call of the Disability Rights Movement when he described himself as a "person first." In this way, his humanity took precedence and his gender and his disability became less significant.

Also, Leo identified his background as a contributing factor to his outlook. Since childhood, he held a group of friends that valued intellectual achievement over physical performance. In his youth, Leo said he was a member of a group "on the college route." He remained in academia.

Internally, his view of masculinity came from maturity. He had dealt with masculinity and related issues for almost sixty years and reached a point at which he was comfortable with his gender. According to him, his gender conceptions ranged across all three patterns. This was particularly evident in his sexuality. When younger, he relied on a culturally valued, genital sexuality and was concerned with his potency. He wanted to "be on top," despite the physical difficulties this presented him. At the time of our interview, he had a reformulated sexuality. The Women's Movement allowed him to remain sexually active without worrying about "being on top." He even rejected the idea (but not necessarily the physical condition) of potency, noting that it was "even a funny word—potent—that's power."

Further, his age allowed Leo to let go of many of the expectations he had for himself when younger. For instance, he used to overcompensate with great physical activity to prove his manhood and to be "a good daddy." But, he said, he gradually learned that such overcompensation was not necessary.

The practice of "letting go," as Leo and many of our other informants had done, was much like that described by essayist Leonard Kriegel (1991) who, in a series of autobiographical essays, discussed the metaphor of "falling into life" as a way of coping with a disability and masculinity. Kriegel described a common reaction to coping with disability; that is, attempting to "overcome" the results of polio, in his case, by building his upper-body strength through endless hours of exercise. In the end, he experienced premature arthritis in his shoulders and arms. The metaphor of giving up or letting go of behavioral expectations and gender practices as a way to gain greater strength and control over one's life was prevalent among the men who primarily rejected dominant masculinity. As Hahn notes, this requires a cognitive shift and a change in reference group as well as a source of social support:

> I think, ironically, that men with disabilities can acquire strength by acknowledging weakness. Instead of attempting to construct a fragile and ultimately phony identity only as males, they might have more to gain, and little to lose, both individually and collectively, by forging a self-concept about the concept of disability. Certainly this approach requires the exposure of a vulnerability that has been a primary reason for the elaborate defense mechanisms that disabled men have commonly employed to protect themselves (1989:3).

Thus, men with disabilities who rejected or renounced masculinity did so as a process of deviance disavowal. They realized that it was societal conceptions of masculinity, rather than themselves, that were problematic. In doing so, they were able to create alternative gender practices.

Summary and Conclusion

The experiences of men with physical disabilities are important, because they illuminate both the insidious power and limitations of contemporary masculinity. These men have insider knowledge of what the subordinated know about both the gender and social order (Janeway 1980). Additionally, the gender practices of some of these men exemplify alternative visions of masculinity that are obscured but available to men in our culture. Finally, they allow us to elucidate a process of paramount importance: How men with physical disabilities find happiness, fulfillment, and a sense of self-worth in a culture that has, in essence, denied them the right to their own identity, including their own masculinity.

Based on our interviews, then, we believe that men with physical disabilities depend on at least three patterns in their adjustment to the double bind associated with the demands of hegemonic masculinity and the stigmatization of being disabled. While each of our informants used one pattern more than the others, none of them depended entirely on any one of the three.

To judge the patterns and practices associated with any form of masculinity, it is necessary to explore the implications for both the personal life of the individual and the effect on the reproduction of the societal gender order (Connell 1990a). Different patterns will challenge, comply, or actively support gendered arrangements.

The reliance pattern is reflected by an emphasis on control, independence, strength, and concern for appearances. Men who rely on dominant conceptions of masculinity are much more likely to internalize their feelings of inadequacy and seek to compensate or overcompensate for them. Because the problem is perceived to be located within oneself rather than within the social structure, this model does not challenge, but rather perpetuates, the current gender order.

A certain distancing from dominant ideals occurs in the reformulation pattern. But reformulation tends to be an independent project, and class-based resources play an important role. As such, it doesn't present a formidable challenge to the gender order. Connell (1990a: 474) argues that this response may even modernize patriarchy.

The rejection model, the least well represented in this article, offers the most hope for change. Linked closely to a sociopolitical approach that defines disability as a product of interactions between individuals and their environment, disability (and masculinity) is understood as socially constructed.

Members of the Disability Rights Movement, as a result, seek to reconstruct masculinity through a three-prong strategy. First, they focus on changing the frame of reference regarding who defines disability and masculinity, thereby changing the social-construction dynamics of both. Second, they endeavor to help people with disabilities be more self-referent when defining their identities. To do that, a third component must be implemented: support structures, such as alternative subcultures, must exist. If the Disability Rights Movement is successful in elevating this struggle to the level of collective practice, it will challenge the legitimacy of the institutional arrangements of the current gender order.

In closing, there is much fruitful work to be done in the area of masculinity and disability. For instance, we should expect men with disabilities to respond differently to the demands associated with disability and masculinity due to sexual orientation, social class, age of onset of one's disability, race, and ethnicity. However, *how* and *why* gender identity varies for men with disabilities merits further study. We hope that this work serves as an impetus for others to take up these issues.

References

Callahan, John. 1989. *Don't Worry, He Won't Get Far on Foot*. New York: Vintage Books.

Connell, R. W. 1991. "Live Fast and Die Young: The Construction of Masculinity among Young Working-Class Men on the Margin of the Labor Market." *The Australian and New Zealand Journal of Sociology*, Volume 27, Number 2, August, pp. 141–171.

———. 1990a. "A Whole New World: Remaking Masculinity in the Context of the Environmental Movement." *Gender & Society*, Volume 4, Number 4, December, pp. 452–478.

———. 1990b. "An Iron Man: The Body and Some Contradictions of Hegemonic Masculinity," In *Sport, Men, and the Gender Order*, Michael Messner and Donald Sabo, eds. Champaign, IL: Human Kinetics Publishers, Inc., pp. 83–96.

———. 1987. *Gender and Power: Society, the Person, and Sexual Politics*. Palo Alto, CA: Stanford University Press.

Denzin, Norman. 1989. *The Research Act: A Theoretical Introduction to Sociological Methods*. Englewood Cliffs, NJ: Prentice-Hall.

Emerson, Robert. 1988. "Introduction." In *Contemporary Field Research: A Collection of Readings*, Robert Emerson, ed. Prospect Heights, IL: Waveland Press, pp. 93–107.

Hahn, Harlan. 1989. "Masculinity and Disability." *Disability Studies Quarterly*, Volume 9, Number 3, pp. 1–3.

Janeway, Elizabeth. 1980. *Powers of the Weak*. New York: Alfred A. Knopf.

Katz, Jack. 1988. "A Theory of Qualitative Methodology: The Social System of Analytic Fieldwork." In *Contemporary Field Research: A Collection of Readings*, Robert Emerson, ed. Prospect Heights, IL: Waveland Press, pp. 127–148.

Kriegel, Leonard. 1991. *Falling into Life*. San Francisco: North Point Press.

Messner, Michael A. 1992. *Power at Play: Sports and the Problem of Masculinity*. Boston: Beacon Press.

Murphy, Robert F. 1990. *The Body Silent*. New York: W. W. Norton.

Scott, James C. 1985. *Weapons of the Weak: Everyday Forms of Peasant Resistance*. New Haven: Yale University Press.

West, Candace, and Don H. Zimmerman. 1987. "Doing Gender." *Gender & Society*, Volume 1, Number 2, June, pp. 125–151.

Zola, Irving Kenneth. 1982. *Missing Pieces: A Chronicle of Living with a Disability*. Philadelphia: Temple University Press.

ARTICLE 30

Rafael M. Díaz

Trips to Fantasy Island: Contexts of Risky Sex for San Francisco Gay Men

Promiscuity is famously defined as any amount of sex greater than what you are having. Admittedly, it's an unhelpful word. And yet, "promiscuous" is how many gay men describe at least a part of their life. Some of them mean a kind of innocent, adolescent freedom, but what others really mean is compulsive sex—sex that cannot be credibly taken as political liberation or personal ecstasy because it does not bring joy, cannot be controlled, and is used, exactly like alcohol or drugs, to assuage a non-sexual need. (Jesse Green, "Flirting with Suicide," The New York Times Magazine, 15 September 1996).

In the presence of substantial knowledge about how HIV can be transmitted and prevented—and quite often with strong personal intentions to practice safer sex—a substantial number of gay men in San Francisco engage in unprotected anal intercourse in situations that could potentially result in HIV transmission. As a consequence, the number of new HIV infections in the city, particularly among young gay men and gay men of ethnic minority groups, remains unacceptably high (Lemp et al. 1994; Osmond et al. 1994). Even with promising therapeutic regimens in sight, every new infection represents a costly tragedy—personal, interpersonal, societal, and financial. Understanding the nature and context of unprotected sexual practices in situations where HIV could be transmitted (labeled "risky sex"), especially those that occur in the presence of knowledge and skills to avert further infection, is of utmost importance to the work of HIV prevention (Kelly et al. 1991).

From *Sexualities* 2(1): 89–112. Copyright © 1999 Sage Publications. Reprinted by permission of Sage Publications Ltd.

Based on psychosocial models of behavior change, behavioral scientists have uncovered important correlates and predictors of risky sex, such as perceived self-efficacy and peer norms for safer sex (Coates et al. 1988). Consequently, prevention programs aimed at promoting self-efficacy and reinforcing social norms for safer sex have been effective in promoting condom use, at least modestly, among vulnerable populations (Bandura 1994). Research on predictors of sexual risk behavior to date, however, has been limited by two serious shortcomings. First, models of behavior change have typically focused on personal (mostly cognitive) variables that predict intentions to practice safer sex, rather than contextual variables that compete against the enactment of safer sex intentions (see critique of behavior change models in Díaz 1998: Chapter 3). By focusing on cognitive predictors of personally formulated intentions, research has missed the situational factors that weaken or break down personal intentionality in sexual practices.

Second, research findings on correlates and predictors of sexual risk have been based mostly on comparisons between men who remain consistently safe (typically labeled the "low-risk" group) and men who, within a given period of time, report at least one instance of unprotected intercourse (typically labeled the "high-risk" group). Such between-group analyses, though useful and somewhat valid, ignore the intra-individual circumstances that might explain episodes of unprotected sex in risky situations for men who otherwise possess all the necessary knowledge, motivation, and skills to practice safer sex. New research is needed on the contexts, situations, and circumstances that undermine men's actual attempts, motivation, and ability to protect themselves against HIV infection.

Overview

We report the results of a qualitative analysis of intra-individual variability in the practice of safer sex. The analysis is based not on comparisons between individuals or groups, but rather on comparisons between sexual episodes—risky and safe, protected and unprotected—within individuals' sexual lives. Thirty interviews, conducted in the context of the San Francisco AIDS Foundation Qualitative Interview Study (QIS; described in the following Methodology section), were included in the analysis. Ten individual interviews were selected from each of the three ethnic groups sampled in QIS: 10 African-American, 10 Latino, and 10 non-Latino White/Caucasian men. All 30 men had reported at least one instance of unprotected anal sex in the last 12 months prior to the study screening interview; the majority of them reported episodes of both protected and unprotected anal intercourse.

Analyses of individual interviews yielded a number of reasons why many gay men in San Francisco engage from time to time in the practice of unprotected anal intercourse, quite often with full awareness of the risks involved. Explicit reasons ranged from an "I just didn't care anymore" attitude stemming from exhaustion about the epidemic, to well-reasoned assessment of acceptable risks (e.g., "He told me he was negative, I'm also negative, and I was the top"). Implicit reasons ranged from misguided assumptions of partners' HIV serostatus, to blatant distortions of biomedical fact ("my HIV doesn't infect others").

Rather than a "grocery list" of stated and/or implied reasons for risky sex, however, I want to propose a more integrated conceptual framework for understanding unprotected sexual behavior in this vulnerable group of men. Specifically, and based on systematic comparisons of individuals' narratives for their protected and unprotected sexual episodes reported in QIS, I would like to propose, and document with data from interview transcripts, that risky sexual behavior is likely to occur and re-occur in person–situation contexts that have the following six person–situation characteristics:

1. A painful and powerful emotional need-state prior to the sexual encounter, such as extreme feelings of restlessness, loneliness, or despair.
2. The objectification and even "de-humanization" of a sexual partner in fantasy-like fashion, where the partner is seen mostly in terms of satisfying sexual and/or non-sexual personal needs.
3. Sexual activity that seems disconnected or split from the rest of the personal self, that is, sexual behavior that is not well integrated to the cognitive and affective domains of the individual. The sexual split can be extreme, as in the case where the individual's sexual behavior is observed as occurring independently, "on its own," or occurring to someone who the self is detachedly observing.
4. The use and abuse of drugs and/or alcohol to facilitate, maintain, and justify sexual activity that is ultimately experienced as frightening, undesirable, and/or dissonant with personal values and beliefs. In these situations, and mostly through the attributions regarding their effects on the particular individual, the use of substances facilitates the split of sexual behavior.
5. Perceptions of low sexual control or low sense of responsibility throughout the sexual

episode. Control and responsibility for events in the sexual encounter are attributed to substances, circumstances, or the other partner.
6. Negative emotional states—such as guilt and regret—after the sexual encounter, especially those self-deprecatory ruminations that stem from pathologizing world views that prevent individuals from instructive self-observation.

My major claim is that this conceptual framework—labeled Trips to Fantasy Island—is useful to understand the intra-individual variability in safer sex behavior for the majority of the interviews in the study. My major cautionary note is that this framework should *not* be used to further pathologize individuals who engage in unprotected intercourse, whether risky or not. More often than not, reasons for unprotected intercourse are embedded within an ecology of personal, interpersonal, and social circumstances that create contexts or situations that increase the probability of HIV transmission (Rotello 1997). It follows that "risky" behavior cannot be understood as a property of individuals or as a product of individual deviance and/or pathology, but it is rather the outcome of structural, cultural, personal, and situational factors that meaningfully (and at times oppressively) interact and shape sexual encounters between men. Moreover, when these contextual factors or ecology are taken into account, what appears to an outsider as "risky" sexual behavior appears to the individual as a subjectively powerful and meaningful experience. As evident in the remainder of the article and explicitly discussed in the conclusion, the powerful emotions that initiate the "trips" are closely connected to elements of the culture that shape perceptions of self and give meaning to sexual encounters. Also, it must be kept in mind that the narratives gathered for this analysis were provided by individuals who in other contexts and situations were perfectly capable of practicing safer sex.

The label "Trips to Fantasy Island" underscores the fact that, for many of the risky episodes I studied, men were engaging in sexual activity in an attempt to fulfill or solve, in fantasy-like fashion, what is basically a non-sexual perceived need, whether it is intimacy, masculinity, or self-worth. Thus, at a very basic level, the Fantasy Island framework formalizes a familiar observation, namely that many individuals come to sexual encounters in search of experiences other than simply sex, such as interpersonal connectedness, social acceptance, or personal affirmation. In fact, sexuality can be said to be socially and culturally constructed, to the extent that for a given group or society sex becomes a place, for example, to restore feelings of masculinity–femininity, or assert power, or feel attractive, or experience social connectedness. Psychologically, in those cases where the need for connectedness, affirmation, or self-worth is so great and deeply felt, such needs seem to overpower the concern for safety or health. By the same token, it is not surprising that such needs are really pressing in cultures that worship physical attractiveness, or that demand that masculinity be proven, or where rampant prejudice and discrimination promote social alienation and isolation.

Even though the framework is indeed psychological and developed by someone trained in psychology, I think of it as "contextualized," because it refers to person–situation contexts rather than to cognitive or behavioral constructs that are independent of actual situations. In the Fantasy Island framework, all psychological constructs—emotions, perceptions, and behaviors—become meaningful and integrated only when considered in their whole person–situation context; otherwise, with what we all know about HIV, the sexual episodes would seem totally absurd and crazy.

Not all instances of unprotected intercourse can be explained or understood within this conceptual framework. The framework is offered as only one—yet, in my view, useful—window or perspective to understand the re-occurrence of unprotected risky sexual behavior in the presence of substantial knowledge, motivation, and skills to practice safer sex.

Methodology

Eliciting Sexual Narratives

Men in the study were recruited to participate in an in-depth interview study (QIS) sponsored by the San Francisco AIDS Foundation (SFAF), a well-known non-profit private organization that provides a wide range of HIV/AIDS-related services in the city. Interviews were conducted at the Center for AIDS Prevention Studies (CAPS), a research group affiliated with the University of California San Francisco. Trained interviewers asked men about a diverse set of topics such as family history, participation in gay community, social support networks, and patterns of sexual activity, among others. Somewhere around the second third of the in-depth interview, individual participants were asked to report the frequency of anal intercourse in the past 12 months, and the number of those episodes that were unprotected, with no use of condoms. Study participants were also asked about the number of incidents where condoms might have failed or broken. Questions about the frequency of anal intercourse, though at times shifting abruptly the content of the interviews, served as a good introduction to elicit participants' narratives of selected sexual episodes.

Participants were asked first to describe a sexual episode that involved the use of condoms (i.e. protected sex) and, immediately after, they were asked to describe a sexual episode that involved no condoms at all (i.e. unprotected sex). Narratives about the sexual episodes—including details about setting, location, partners, substance use, emotions, and actual behaviors—were elicited in the following fashion, as in these two examples, taken from two different interviews:

> I would like for you to describe the most recent sexual encounter with another man when you engaged in anal intercourse with a condom that did not break. Try to remember as much about what happened before, during, and after the event. Keeping in mind that I'm interested in your thoughts and feelings. Just tell me about that day, what you were doing and feeling before you had sex, who it was with, what you talked about, things like that. (Case 13)

> If you would could you talk about the last time that you had anal sex with a condom. The last time you fucked with a condom, what was that like? With whom? Where were you? How'd you feel? What was the day like? How did you lead up to having sex with this person? Where'd you meet up? Things like that. (Case 05)

Similar questions were then asked for the unprotected-sex episodes and, in a few cases, about the episode that involved condom break.

Coding the Interview Transcripts

The narratives of sexual episodes were transcribed (varying in length from one to about fifteen single-spaced pages) and coded under the following categories:

1. Setting/situation
2. Partner characteristics
3. Stated emotions prior, during, and after the episode
4. Actual sexual behavior
5. Associated cognitions
6. Substance use: type and amount, reported effects, and attributions of influence
7. Perceptions and assessments of HIV risk
8. Communication: verbal and non-verbal
9. Disclosure of HIV status
10. Gender attributions
11. Decision-making/intentionality
12. Strategies to reduce risk
13. Attitudes towards condoms
14. Perceptions of responsibility/control

For each of the 30 selected interviews, text from both protected and unprotected episodes was categorized under the same categories. Our goal—one that we easily achieved—was to categorize exhaustively the majority of text given for the sexual episodes.

The Contexts of Risky Sex

In the following sections, and based on the voices and subjective experiences of study participants,

I offer some empirical support for the six hypothesized dimensions, factors, or characteristics of unprotected sexual encounters. Most of these factors are present, in different degrees and combinations, in the narratives of many of the unprotected sexual episodes examined. These six factors constitute the major areas of difference between protected and unprotected events within individuals' sexual lives. I propose that, taken together, the six factors create a particular context of sexual risk, labeled Trips to Fantasy Island, which can explain or give meaning to a large proportion of risky sex reported in the study. All names given to the respondents are fictitious, and are used only for the purpose of ease of presentation; Appendix 1 contains a list of cases cited, listed with their respective fictitious names and information regarding age, ethnicity, and HIV serostatus.

(1) *Negative emotions prior to the sexual encounter*
One of the most striking differences between the protected and unprotected sexual episodes was the emotional state of participants immediately prior to the risky sexual encounter. In contrast to the protected episodes, risky episodes contained a certain emotional heaviness or "thickness" that was not present in the descriptions of protected encounters. The emotional heaviness typically referred to a need-state, a sense of personal isolation, or insecurity that somehow would be relieved by the sexual encounter. Even though at times men expressed this emotional state as "I was very horny" or "I had to have it [sex] that night," further inquiry revealed a set of negative emotions connected to non-sexual needs prior to the sexual encounter.

In the context of the unprotected episodes, men talked about feeling lonely, frustrated, anxious, unattractive, disappointed, drained by multiple losses and, some of them, even highly ambivalent about having sex at all or about entering situations they perceived as potentially dangerous and emotionally unsafe. Consider, for example, the contrasting descriptions of Larry, a 40-year-old Caucasian, HIV-positive gay man.

For the protected episode:

Larry: Things at the time were really good. I was feeling really upbeat.

Int.: How had you been feeling during the day while you were getting ready?

Larry: Excited.

Int.: And your mood was . . .

Larry: Real upbeat, real, a bit anxious, you know.

Int.: Did you have anything particularly stressful at that time in your life?

Larry: No, thankfully I had just gotten rid of that stressful, yucky roommate, so no.

For the unprotected episode, Larry reported the following emotions:

Int.: What had your mood been like during the day as you were getting ready for this date?

Larry: Actually to be real honest with you, I was very anxious about it in a bad way because I always feel terribly afraid to take my clothes off the better looking a man is. And I almost, I really had been thinking of ways to lie out of it. So I wouldn't have to go. 'Cause he was so terribly attractive to me, I didn't want him to see me naked. So I had been feeling real anxious.

While Larry confessed being a bit anxious prior to his protected encounter, his "real anxious" and "terribly afraid" state accompanied his unprotected event. The fear, anxiety, and ultimate ambivalence about meeting his sexual partner manifested both his desire and fear of having sex with someone he considered extremely attractive. Sex with this partner, described by Larry as "tragically handsome" (see next section), involved a test of his personal attractiveness. In the context of a very poor body self-image, Larry ventured to have sex with this handsome "looker," as if sex with this man would validate his own sense of personal attractiveness. In fact, later on in the interview, Larry confessed that he fantasized about this partner telling other people how good and exciting he had been in bed.

Quite often, negative emotional states prior to the unprotected events were connected to feelings of social isolation, loneliness, disappointed love, and accompanying feelings of longing and craving for flesh-to-flesh contact. Michael, a 30-year-old HIV-negative Latino gay man who was pretty upset about the general disconnection between sex and intimacy in his life, and his inability to find a romantic partner, described it in the following way:

Michael: It was during a period when there was this guy who I really had grown to like a lot and I told him that I wanted to be in a relationship with him and he didn't feel the same way, and I was very disappointed. That was on a Saturday. And on Sunday night—Sundays tend to be like, I don't know why, but Sunday afternoon and evening feel depressing to me, and lonely. And so that evening I went out to the bar to see a show and have a couple of drinks . . . I went there for a couple hours and didn't run into any of my friends, didn't get any attention from anyone, and left after a couple of hours feeling pretty low, I think. I was down about 'J' and I was feeling lonely. And from there I decided to go home but instead I ended up going out cruising out to a park.

Int.: What would you say were the things that led you to not use a condom that night?

Michael: Um, more than anything else was that sense that I get when I'm in the midst of being sexually predatory of like just being very single-minded and wanting to find that person and to seduce them and to have sex with them. Um, and I think it's sort of a single-minded strange thing I feel that was happening in the left part of the brain, somehow it's not accessible to use it at that point. That was part of it. I don't know how much my down mental state had to do with it but I do know my mental state has a lot do with when I pursue sex because pursuing sex is often what I do to fill up loneliness and I know in general pursuing sex like that is about loneliness. I don't know how much not using a condom was about that . . .

With a decreased sense of personal control, and driven by his longing for social connection, Michael found himself in the cruising park having unprotected sex with someone he didn't feel attracted to. In a state he described as "trance-like," and somewhat desperately, Michael attempted to assuage his feelings of loneliness and isolation in the context of an anonymous and unsafe sexual encounter. While quite connected with and articulate about his own emotional states in retrospect, at the time of the encounter Michael felt outside himself: "I just felt like I was just being kind of swept along on the events and that I was not in control of myself."

In what is perhaps an extreme illustration of the point under discussion, Rick, a 38-year-old HIV-positive Caucasian gay man, spoke of his need to find in sex the physical pain that would match his emotional pain. Rick was able to find this physical pain in an anonymous encounter, being penetrated (without condoms) by a man with a larger than normal penis ("donkey-like," "biggest cock I've ever seen") in a cruising park setting. In his own words:

Int.: How had you been feeling that day? What had that day been like for you, beforehand?

Rick: Well, it really, it was a messed up day. I had my house burglarized, my brand new stereo system taken, my TV taken, my VCR taken, my books taken, my rifles taken, kept my clothes and all my paperwork. But all my material stuff was taken, my telephone taken . . . I was wanting something that size [referring to his partner's penis], maybe smaller, I needed somebody to inflict pain on me. That's going back to my adolescence, at least half my life, whenever, whenever, whenever I hurt on the inside, I want to hurt on the outside, too. So that's when I basically, I go out for anal sex. Because it doesn't really hurt, it feels good. It's twisted, but it's a fact.

(2) *Fantasy partner* More often than not, and in sharp contrast to partners for protected sexual events, partners of risky sexual encounters were described in fantasy-like fashion. Fantasies ranged from Hollywood star-like handsome men, to butcher-type, straight-looking men. Interestingly, and in most cases, fantasies were meaningfully connected to the emotional need-state described as preceding the sexual event. For example, a Latino man who is usually on top in anal intercourse, under the influence of drugs becomes an "eager bottom," and thus longs to be penetrated by a "straight-looking" man. In another example, terribly down on account of his varicose veins and plain physical looks, a gay man searches for an encounter with a "tragically handsome man," an exotic-looking "Harry Belafonte with a beard." Another man goes to the Castro (gentrified gay neighborhood) "to get away from it all" and sees his potential sexual partner as a prince-like charmer who helps him forget the ghetto-like horrors of the Tenderloin (poor section of town) and who, in his view, "probably doesn't have HIV" because he looks so clean, decent, smart, and well-educated. In all cases, the partner is unrealistically polarized, in fantasy-like fashion, to exaggerate the quality most needed to satisfy the individual's unmet need—be it physical attractiveness, masculinity, or escaping the devastating consequences of poverty. Let us consider in more detail the nature of fantasy-like sexual partners, by contrasting Larry's sexual partners for both the protected and unprotected sexual episodes he reported in the interview.

For the protected episode, Larry described his partner as follows:

Larry: . . . I really liked him. I liked being with him and so I was pretty excited and he was enough of what I liked, like sensitive and passionate and erotic and kissing and touching . . . we met at the Aliveness project which was an HIV/AIDS/Wellness community dining resource center in Minneapolis. . . . He looked older than me, but he was like 34. . . . White guy.

Int.: Is that a typical type for you?

Larry: Yeah, white, dark hair, bearded, yeah.

On the other hand, for the unprotected event, Larry describes his sexual partner, not at all according to his "type" described above, but rather according to a fantasy that involves god-like physical beauty in a man of color. Not unlike many other examples in the study, Larry has mixed feelings about his fantasy partner and acknowledges feeling used and abused. However, he is powerfully drawn to this exotic, dark, mysterious, and good-looking partner to whom he totally surrenders control:

I do, like, one black guy every five years, is my average. This guy was so tragically handsome, black guy, bearded black guy. Right, but he's just a macho pig. I'm sure "here's a little honky-boy hole to poke," you know. That's the way I felt. I had a picture of him in my brain because, I mean he's a looker . . . he looks like somebody really famous he looks like. I can't think. Kind of on the order of Harry Belafonte with a beard, yeah. He's not a love-maker, he's just a "sexer." . . . I really, I really have to say that a lot of it is, maybe it's even kind of like, you know, um, worshipping him because he's so hot, you know, so gorgeous, I have to please him, you know, I have to do what he wants me to do. I have to make him say, you know, when he gossips about me to other people about what he did with me, well he was good in bed. You know there's a lot of that stuff going on in my head at that time. Make him wanna see me again, you know.

Eduardo, a 31-year-old, HIV-positive Latino gay man, gave the following account of his unprotected sexual partner:

He was an Italian guy in North Beach, you know he's very "macho" and straight and, you know, has a girlfriend, and no one would ever know that he was doing something like this but he felt like doing it tonight. Because he had been partying too. He had been doing coke the night before with his friends. . . . He was very attractive, very, I would never thought if I saw him on the street, you know, that he would do something like this . . . having sex with a guy. He looked like very, like he coulda been a butcher or a cook in like an Italian restaurant. Sort of burly, hairy, short, stocky, muscular, I could see him with like a wife and kids.

Paradoxically, early in the interview, Eduardo had complained about all those "Latino macho men" who pretend they are straight and say, "Oh, you're just sucking my dick or I'm gonna fuck you and I have a wife and kid so it doesn't mean that I'm gay." . . . Eduardo had also confessed his attraction to Latino straight men who, however, could be dangerous ("beat you up or they pull a knife, a gun") if approached for sex. Like many other Latino gay men, Eduardo struggles with the masculine "macho" ideal, the pressures of needing to prove masculinity especially in sexual intercourse, and the imposition of a cultural gender-definition of homosexuality where homosexuals are seen as less than or "failed" men (Díaz 1998). His fantasy partner thus involved a type of man to whom he felt very attracted but who also represented many of the "macho" qualities he so indignantly scorned about his Latino upbringing. The butcher-looking guy, coupled with the ingestion of multiple drugs, allowed Eduardo to lower his anxiety and act out the straight man fantasy in a physically safer context, though definitely unsafe with respect to HIV transmission. Not surprisingly, the power of the masculinity fantasy overpowered the health concern, much to his dismay after the whole thing was over.

For some men in the Tenderloin, struggling with the multiple and devastating effects of poverty, racism, and HIV, the fantasy partner became a travel companion to a cleaner, safer, healthier space, an oasis away from a troubled urban desert. In the fantasy, of course, HIV could not be part of that oasis which the men so badly needed for rejuvenation and rest. Therefore, in those fantasy-like situations, the partner was assumed HIV-negative or there was simply no talk of HIV, or of condoms, which have come to represent HIV.

Vincent, a 29-year-old, HIV-negative, African-American man from the Tenderloin, told us about going to the Castro "just to get away" and hang out at "The Pendulum," a gay bar where guys "are trying to have something better." The fantasy partner involved in his unprotected episode was described, as Vincent sorted out his reasons for not using condoms:

Vincent: Yeah. And the other person too, I think, at least somebody that, you know, they look pretty clean and decent. You know what I mean it's kinda easy to like not use a condom too.

Int.: What can you, what's that mean? Because I probably have a different idea, you know, what . . . ?

Vincent: Well, when you meet a handsome guy and then they don't show any signs of sickness. I mean, you know. More or less that.

Int.: And that's sort of a way of keeping a little note in your mind that, so, being handsome is one of those things that makes a person seem more likely as not being someone at risk.

Vincent: [?] Smarter,

Int.: So what about things like, you were talking about earlier, people have certain kind of values that you really appreciate to bettering yourself and things like that. Does that also figure into what you think about a person's HIV status and whether you're more likely to . . . ?

Vincent: Yeah.

Int.: So what kind of person is that? Because it comes out in conversation, right?

Vincent: Yeah, it comes out.

Int.: Can you tell from other things like the way they carry themselves, wear their hair?

Vincent: Their hygiene is a lot.

Int.: So if you get near them and they don't smell so great.

Vincent: No way.

Int.: So how 'bout things like if people are professionals.

Vincent: Yeah, man. That would play a good part.

(3) *Non-integrated sex* When study participants described their sexual behavior in protected and unprotected episodes, important differences emerged other than condom use. During the unprotected sex episodes, for lack of better words, sex seemed more disconnected and less integrated to the cognitive and affective domains of the person. In the context of risky episodes, sex was often described as purely physical, just sex, isolated from caresses, kisses, or other signs of interpersonal intimacy—in the words of one participant, "wham-bam, thank you, Sir." In contrast to more playful and affectionate adventures—many of them casual or anonymous—encountered in safer sex episodes, for the unprotected sex encounters, men described feeling like "hunks of meat" or "a robot" or a "sex machine."

Larry's encounter with his bearded Harry Belafonte lookalike did not sound like fun at all:

> He didn't really want to kiss me much or suck my cock, you know, and then I didn't like it because when I'd suck his, he'd shove it at me and I'm like, "Let go of my ears, I know what I'm doing," you know. And, um, and then I just let him throw my legs up like I was some hunk of meat and fuck me violently. And I hated it. I could hardly wait to go after it was over.

In the context of his risky episode, and in more extreme form, Michael spoke about his sexuality as split-off from the rest of his self—he felt as if his sexuality was coming from a very different and isolated part of his brain. In contrast to his playful and affectionate safe encounter at a public cruising beach, Michael described himself as a sexual predator who dehumanized his partner in the risky episode:

Int.: Was there anything about him or the specific circumstances, that setting?

Michael: He was very dehumanized to me. I was definitely only seeing him as someone who might be able to get me off and he was not a full human being to me. That was different from the earlier incident [the protected sexual encounter] that I was telling you about. Part of it has to do with it being nighttime and not being able to see their face but also part of it is I think that it's easier to dehumanize someone for me when I don't feel like I'm really attracted to them. When I feel like I could walk away from that encounter and it wouldn't be a big loss for me, or it wouldn't be difficult, I think it was a lot easier for me to dehumanize someone. When someone is attractive in whatever way you have curiosity about them, you kind of wonder with them but if you knew that you're just with them to have sex and you're not even attracted to them I think they become less than human.

Int.: Like there won't be a romantic fantasy or desire?

Michael: Yeah. There won't be a romantic fantasy or desire and I don't feel obliged to take them in any way around being safe, I feel a lot less obliged to be wanting to take care of them like when I do when I'm with someone I know or like or am attracted to.

It is very important to note that, in the context of this paper, "integrated" sex does not mean sex within boyfriend relationships and, conversely, "non-integrated sex" does not automatically refer to casual or anonymous encounters. That would be a misunderstanding of the point I am trying to convey. In fact, I witnessed descriptions of non-integrated sex in the context of lover relationships and, conversely, a lot of integrated sex in the context of anonymous casual encounters. The central point I am trying to make is that, more often than not, in the context of risky episodes—which happened either with boyfriends or with casual partners—sexuality was described in terms that stressed its "physicality" in a somewhat isolated fashion from other aspects or possible characteristics of a sexual encounter. Also, non-integrated sex in risky situations, while often occurring in contexts that were emotionally charged, could not be described as playful and/or affectionate, involving the whole person.

To stress my point, here is the description of a sexual encounter within a complex lover relationship that, in my view, typifies what I mean by non-integrated sex. Joseph, a 31-year-old HIV-negative Latino gay man, originally from Los Angeles, recounted the following episode that happened prior to a break-up with his troubled lover. His description emerged as he attempted to compare both his protected and unprotected episodes, at the interviewer's request. The sexual split that characterizes this risky episode, in Joseph's point of view, was prompted by the use of speed; other parts of the narrative, however, suggest that relationship issues, other than heavy substance use, might also have played a part in promoting the sexual split. And so the interview goes:

Int.: In the two sorts of sexual events that you've described [protected and unprotected], what's a—how are they alike? Could you compare them and how were they different for you?

Joseph: Well, whereas the experiences with speed [the risky encounter], you know, there was that sexual feeling of—that overwhelming sexual feeling. You know, it's a very kind of, you know, tactile, very sensory feeling. And although I loved him, you know, although when I was on speed, you know, that really kind of didn't mean a lot. You know, at the time it was not something that I thought about. And now, it's more like a, more spiritual, more bonding, more—you know, kind of back and forth and more of an emotional as well as sensory experience now, where there it was just kind of like this sexual frenzy, where it might have—could not have even been him, it could have been just anyone.

Similar feelings of being overpowered by split-off physical sensations were reported by David, a 29-year-old, HIV-negative Latino gay man, when explaining the context and circumstances that led to his risky episode. His encounter, while not involving the use of drugs, includes many of the hypothesized elements of a risk, such as experiences of loneliness and longing prior to the encounter and an overwhelming set of physical sensations that clouded his judgment and undermined his perceptions of sexual control:

David: That particular day I can't remember exactly, but I know when I go up there [a cruising park], you know, I'm really longing for, you know, contact and really longing to have a connection . . . I mean I'll go over there and substitute, you know, sex, for, you know, being touched or something that's non-sexual just because sex is easier to find than intimacy . . . I said okay, just for a moment. You know, just for, you know, a few minutes because it felt pretty intense. And still sort of that intensity of the connection, no barrier. Not a lot of lubrication. I mean he was—you know, it was just mainly spit, and, you know, so there was a bit more friction and so it was just like sort of overcome with those sensations . . . I was like, Shit! this guy wants to get fucked and you don't have a condom . . . I mean at the time I was overcome with the feelings and the intensity of it . . . Just the intensity of the sensation, it being different than with a condom and a lot of lube. You know, just spit.

This closer look at the voices and subjective experiences of study participants begins to clarify some defining characteristics of what I have called "non-integrated sex":

1. An extreme or exclusive focus on the physicality or physical sensations of a sexual encounter.

2. The relative absence of interpersonal expressions of nurturance, warmth, and other manifestations of intimacy and, at times, sex that can be characterized as forceful or coercive.
3. An objectification of the partner as a purely physical object of pleasure, to the point that men might feel like "hunks of meat" or ignore important aspects of the individual partner, that is, "it could have been just anyone."
4. Reduced levels of verbal communication during the sexual encounter, especially about HIV, in favor of keeping the given fantasy alive and unchallenged.

(4) *Substance use* A detailed examination of QIS transcripts reveals that more often than not, unprotected sex was accompanied by the use or abuse of substances, mostly drugs, and more specifically, potent stimulants of the central nervous system, such as cocaine or crystal meth (speed). It is important, however, to realize that there is not a direct relationship between substance use and risky sex. In fact, the interview transcripts do contain plenty of evidence regarding unprotected sex without substance use, as well as safer sex in the presence of heavy use of substances.

The task ahead of us is to understand those specific contexts, situations, and circumstances where drugs become important predictors of unprotected sex. My working hypothesis is that drugs will facilitate risky behavior in the context of trips to Fantasy Island, especially when men attribute to the drug powerful effects that are congruent with the purpose of such trips. I propose that drugs become predictors of risky sex, for example, when men believe that drugs make them more courageous to meet partners they ambivalently both want and fear, or when drugs are believed to alleviate anxiety or numb judgment in emotionally loaded situations, allowing them to do what they would not do otherwise for reasons of principle, personal commitment, or safety. In other words, I believe that the use of drugs predicts risky behavior when attributions of drug effects on the particular individuals are consonant with Fantasy Island goals, such as "it makes me an eager bottom," "it makes me have compulsive sex—I was like a robot," "it just breaks this thing about anal sex," or "I was just too stoned to care."

Let us examine with more detail the use of alcohol and drugs in the context of specific unprotected sexual episodes. Consider, for example, John's attributions of the effects of speed on his personality and sexual activity. John, a 35-year-old, HIV-positive Caucasian gay man, confesses that he goes on five-day-long speed runs that end up in risky sexual encounters.

John: When I'm on crystal I'm up for five days at a time. It's usually the last two days that I'm on crystal, like let's say I was up, you know, first day I'm like coming up, the next day I usually go dancing, you know, and then like the third, fourth, or fifth day would be when I'd have sex . . .

. . [I] go out, get high, go dancing, come home, get on the sex line, that would be a typical night for me.

Sex for John, however, means multiple anonymous encounters with "two to fifteen people in twenty-four hours . . . with people I've never met before, with people I'll never see again." While he talks openly and frankly about his sex life, John is also very harsh and judgmental about his sexual behavior, reporting that he is disgusted by it all:

John: . . . I feel pretty disgusting when I come down completely from it.

Int.: And disgusting about what?

John: Just what I've done and myself. And I mean it's pretty harsh to have sex with, you know, two to fifteen people in twenty-four hours.

Int.: Um hm. Harsh on the physical self?

John: Mentally. That's just disgusting. You know, I, people I've never met before, people I'll never see again. Whatever.

Int.: So when you're coming down that's when you get that sort of sense of the feeling of disgusting, so to speak.

John: When I've completely come down. Yes.

Setting aside the specific reasons that lead John to pursue what he considers unsatisfying and compulsive sexual encounters, it is important to examine how drug use—and specifically crystal use—facilitates and allows him to do it. How does the drug allow John to do what he considers harsh and disgusting when he is sober? John's attributions of crystal's effects on him contain some important clues to answer this question. First of all, John believes that, under the influence of crystal, he becomes "a different person than what I am right now." As such, the drug facilitates a split between sexual behavior and his affect and cognitions; a split from the more reflective self—cognitively and affectively—that he presents in the interview. If nothing else, the drug may in fact facilitate a silencing of his harsh self-judgments. Second, in John's attribution, crystal has the special ability to make "ugly" things look glamorous, as if possessing an alchemic power of transformation very conducive to the production of Fantasy Island contexts:

John: The way I feel makes me, on crystal, makes me a totally different person than what I am right now. I mean like I'm, I usually hang around with my, some girlfriends of mine that were on crystal and I haven't done it for a long, long time. And I could just see the way I used to be in them just how your whole thinking process changes and . . .

Int.: How did they look to you?

John: Well, they look glamorous but they're just, just, what they're talking about and how "spacey" they were and it's just kind of ugly to me, really an ugly thing.

Drugs, and in particular speed, facilitate many of the hypothesized elements involved in the construct trips to Fantasy Island. In John's case, speed facilitated the split of sexual behavior and moral reasoning—under the influence of speed he could do what he labels "ugly" and "disgusting" things. As a matter of fact, with speed, John goes on the ultimate cognitive–sexual split, on "auto-pilot":

John: Having sex when I'm on crystal is like masturbating, I can do it again, and again, and again and it doesn't give me any great satisfaction it's just like, you know, I get the eternal hard-on and, you know? So, anyways.

Int.: So is that—?

John: It's auto-pilot-sex type thing.

For others, speed facilitates the numbing of the emotional pain that brought about in the first place the whole fantasy encounter; speed may also facilitate the focus on physicality, isolating sexual sensations away from other interpersonal, affective concerns. By promoting the intensification of physical sensations during a sexual encounter, speed helps men shift and refocus their attention away from emotion or health concerns to the point of "I just don't care anymore."

I want to illustrate further and provide empirical support for these claims through the words of Harvey, a 34-year-old, HIV-positive African-American bisexual man, as he speaks of the circumstances leading to his unprotected sexual episode. Like many other men on trips to Fantasy Island, Harvey started his own trip with feelings of emotional pain, hurt, and loneliness brought about by the cruel sexual manipulations of one of his African-American friends:

Int.: How had you been feeling? What was your mood like during the day?

Harvey: Uh, stress. I needed to get out. At least do something. I just needed to get out and do something, I was stressed out.

Int.: You said you were feeling horny?

Harvey: Yeah. Stressed out, horny.

Int.: And you're feeling anxious?

Harvey: Yeah.

Int.: Did you have anything particularly stressful happen yesterday that caused this feeling?

Harvey: Um, one of my friends still calls me. He was talking dirty with me and then said, "Oh, I was just playin' wit ya," and hung the phone up! Uh, we sittin' there talkin' dirty for like about forty-five minutes on the phone, I'm going like, "OK." He said, "Are you ready? I'm comin' over there." "OK." Then he say, "Oh, I'm just joking with you." I said, "You're joking!" I said, "OK. I'll talk to you later." "The jokes I was playin' wit you." I had to go find somebody, I was already aroused, ready to go. I just wanted to go do something.

When Harvey goes out on his expedition, he finds a willing fantasy partner, a "White leather-stud" that offers him an oasis of relief from the interpersonal hurt he had just experienced with his African-American buddy. The partner, in Harvey's words: "He's a stud. He's into leather, he's a stud here. Anything but Black, I think I can't deal with." The "stud" partner, purposefully chosen as White, already stoned with 90cc of injected speed, gives Harvey the drugs—both speed and cocaine—to facilitate the split, the numbing of pain, the focus on physicality needed for his Fantasy Island adventure:

Harvey: That speed helped me to [laughs]. It helped me have my face sorta pale, I mean sorta hot. My cheeks was hot and I had to like run to the bathroom like three times. I never done speed. I went to the bathroom three times and I got an erection! I went to the bathroom and I got erection! I'm going like, I ain't gonna haggle with this. I say, "It's on!" It was on!

Int.: Did you feel you needed the drugs to have sex last night?

Harvey: Yeah. To take away the pain. Yes. But I was just horny I just didn't know what I really wanted; man or woman I's gonna get it good as I can get. Gonna go out there and get it. And I was out on Folsom, just "on."

Int.: Were you comfortable with how you handled that and how he did?

Harvey: Actually at the time I was so high I didn't care. I'm just being honest with you.

Int.: So you'd say you were higher than you were the other time [the protected event] we talked?

Harvey: Yeah.

Int.: Did being higher make a difference for you in not bothering to talk about condoms or to use one?

Harvey: Yeah. It did cuz I was in the heat of passion of both drugs mixing and so you don't really think, the only thing you thinkin' about is just doin' it. Gettin' off! . . . I was too stoned in my mind, I didn't give a care. I mean I didn't care.

This split of sexuality and self, as a result of drug use, even though subjectively experienced in many different ways, was quite prevalent in the risky episodes of QIS. For some men, like Larry and Eduardo, drugs are seen as the only way to break down their psychological barriers and fears about anal sex. For others, drugs allow them to focus narrowly on the sexual satisfaction, isolating or even protecting their sexual desire from other intrusive, potentially disturbing, thoughts or feelings. "When I smoke, nothing else is on my mind but what I want [meaning sex]"—said Mike, a 28-year-old, African-American HIV-negative gay man.

The split can be quite dramatic for some men, like in the case of Bob, a 35-year-old, Caucasian HIV-positive bisexual man, who describes himself as a robot when high on cocaine:

Cocaine is the kind of drug that makes me compulsive to have sex. I really can't have sex unless I got a buzz on. I mean if I'm still thinking kind of clearly, you know what I mean? If I know what I'm doing it's, like, it doesn't feel right. I was, like, I was a robot.

Finally, for some men, encountering and facing their demons (such as issues of physical attractiveness) in the sexual context of Fantasy Island means a feat of courage. As an Iron John, on his way to fight the proverbial dragon, Larry finds a little help in alcohol:

> I was at home alone and I started drinking that beer so I would finally get on that bus to go over there. You know, it seemed better to bolster my confidence with a little alcohol than to bail out and lie.

(5) *Perceptions of low sexual control* A common denominator for many of the unprotected sexual episodes I studied—whether attributed to substances, difficult circumstances, or coercive partners—was a decreased sense of personal control over the whole situation, including one's own sexual behavior. Some men felt that they could not think clearly, or that they were not totally there, or that events seemed to just happen on their own.

I want to let the QIS men speak for themselves:

Larry

Int.: Did you feel like you even had a choice?

Larry: Um, not really, I felt that I had to give him that because that was what he was expecting and that's what he wanted, you know and that it would be awkward if I refused.

Int.: Did, uh, you feel that he made the decision about not using the condom?

Larry: Oh, definitely, one hundred percent, could care less.

Eduardo

I'm very in control, but I don't think I am when I've been doing crystal. Had I been a little more clearer thinking, I think I probably wouldn't have gone over there.

Joe

But in that kind of sexual frenzy where everything's moving really fast, it didn't happen. I mean we hadn't planned it . . . I was kind of angry, you know, that, you know, where it was uncomfortable and then he was not listening to me, he was not—we were not communicating well. I was telling him to stop and he wouldn't . . . It just happened, you know.

Michael

It [sex] was very strange, I felt like kind of almost disembodied and again it was kind of the sexual trance that I will sometimes go into. Uh, I just felt like I was just kind of being swept along on the events and that I was not in control of myself.

Mike

I was so high I didn't care. I was in the heat of passion of both drugs mixing and so you don't really think, the only thing you thinking about it's just doin' it. Getting off!

David

Just, like, the body takes over. The mind and reason just goes out the window and it's just like oh my God this feels good. I can't stop, it's just at least for me it's been that way. You know.

(6) *Negative emotions following the sexual encounter* Lastly, I found a substantial amount of unprotected sex to be followed by feelings of depression, guilt, self-hatred, and disgust. With a few notable exceptions, where the unprotected episodes were seen as turning points in their lives, I found many men engaged in painful, self-deprecatory, and regretful rumination about their risky encounters rather than a critical self-reflection about the situations and circumstances that put them at risk or as lessons to be learned for future encounters.

Jesse Greene's comments about "sex that doesn't bring joy," quoted at the beginning of this article, became poignantly clear when listening to men's feelings about "the morning after." Some of the painful feelings were associated with fears about HIV infection following a risky encounter, as evidenced by Michael's interview transcript:

Int.: Um, tell me more about not using the condom?

Michael: I was uh, very shocked immediately afterwards. And I was particularly like frightened that he had, after I had been fucking him, turned around and gone down on me again. I kept thinking about that and I was obsessing about him being HIV-positive and like almost as if he wanted to turn around and clean me up of that somehow, that he felt a sudden remorse or something, so I started obsessing about that.

Int.: And you said that you had some anxiety about his HIV status, afterward?

Michael: Oh! Yeah! A lot!

Int.: How did you feel afterward?

Michael: I felt horrible. It was really horrible. I would say that it was like a big turning point for me around a lot of stuff about my sex and what kind of sex I have and what kind of sex I need. I felt really guilty that after like eight years of taking care of myself around condoms during fucking that I'd slipped that way so I was definitely beating myself up for a while afterwards . . . the effect of not using a condom was a tremendous one, I think for months I was a wreck around that incident.

Painful after-feelings, however, were typically associated with men's puzzlement about doing something they would not do if they had been in their "right mind." In some cases, men felt used, dirty and/or cheap, and had to go home to wash up or literally flush their fantasy partners out of their bodies. In Eduardo's words:

just thought, "Wow! I should not have done that [unsafe sex], but I did." So I pretty much felt hideous . . . I felt gross. I thought people must be looking at me thinking, Oh, my God, look at this guy, he's been up for two days and he looks like, used, or something.

. . . I just felt really gross.

. . . I mean inside too, I felt like, "What are you doing? Why are you doing this? Why are you continuing to do this?"

In contrast to a description of his protected event as "afterglow city," this is how Larry felt after his troubling risky episode:

Thank god it didn't hurt. He wasn't too big and I don't know, it was just the right time for me. It didn't hurt physically, but I felt real disgusted as I was walking to the bus, you know. It was a very empty act for me, you know and I felt real, I felt dirty and cheap [. . .] Yeah, yeah, I felt like, why the fuck did I do that? You know, and I couldn't wait to get to the bathroom, you know and just get him out of me.

In John's case, as he comes down from his crystal runs, the feelings of disgust—about his out-of-control sex with so many strangers in one night—are so intense that he must alleviate his anxiety with additional drugs:

Int.: So when you're coming down that's when you get that sort of sense of the feeling of disgusting, so to speak.

John: When I've completely come down. Yes.

Int.: Um hm. And then was the feeling afterwards of, you called it disgusting?

John: See that comes down after I've had a nap or something like, you know, when I first sleep. So, and usually I'd take some painkillers or, like valiums and alcohol on the way down, you know.

In Conclusion: Individual Pathology or Oppressive Culture?

The risk of sexual transmission of HIV is not randomly distributed in the population; rather, the epidemic is increasingly shaped by the boundaries of poverty, racism, and homophobia. In the perspective of the larger social context, the virus spreads not at random, but within pockets of powerlessness and alienation created by social injustice, inequality, and oppression. Similarly, the risk for HIV is not randomly distributed within individual lives. There are times when, for reasons discussed here, individuals are more vulnerable to act in ways that overpower principles and personal standards of safer sex behavior. There are indeed pockets of powerlessness within individual lives, created by powerful emotional states, different types of partners, and volatile interpersonal situations. More often than not, these are congruent with the social forces that shape, regulate, and give meaning to gay men's sexuality.

It would be very simplistic to attribute the sexual contexts and events described as "Trips to Fantasy Island" to individual pathology or psychological dysfunction. In fact, I want to argue that the non-sexual needs experienced so deeply by the men interviewed, are social and cultural in origin. The non-sexual needs described in connection to the sexual episodes clustered around four specific themes: (1) the need to validate one's sense of physical attractiveness; (2) the need to restore a wounded sense of masculinity; (3) the need to alleviate painful experiences of loneliness and social isolation; and (4) the need to get away, find relief or escape, at least temporarily, from difficult situations brought about by poverty, racism, interpersonal rejection, and AIDS. These "needs" can be traced to sociocultural factors, such as a certain obsession with masculinity and physical beauty found in gay culture, or the perceived lack of models and support to integrate love and sex, intimacy and sexual passion, in long-term gay relationships. The split of sexuality from the cognitive and social domains is perhaps one of the most devastating sequelae of societal homophobia, where closeted sexual lives had to be constructed as the domain of the secret, shameful, and forbidden—what you do with strangers in strange places at strange hours (Díaz 1998). Such negative construction of sexuality in the face of pervasive homophobia does not simply disappear after coming out or moving into the gay neighborhood.

The Fantasy Island analysis leads to the conclusion that the origins of (so-called) risky sexual behavior can be found in elements of our culture, rather than in individuals' pathological impulsiveness or defiant risk-taking. The cultural elements that provide and promote the described contexts of risk, even though experienced subjectively as psychological states, motivations, and feelings, are more truly a reflection of oppressors in our lives such as homophobia, machismo, sexual silence, poverty, and racism. Those forces converge in a deeply felt sense that something is terribly wrong with us, and many of us go to sexual encounters to find a sense of relief.

Acknowledgements

The research for this article was commissioned and financed by the San Francisco AIDS Foundation, based on data collected in the Qualitative Interview Study (QIS), between January and June 1996. I thank members of the QIS team, in particular, René Durazzo, Ron Stall, Andy Williams, Michael Crosby, and George Ayala for their insightful comments and suggestions, as well as for their collegial support in the writing of this manuscript. I also thank Miguel Casuso for coding all the interview transcripts included in this analysis.

References

Bandura, Albert (1994). "Social Cognitive Theory and Exercise of Control over HIV Infection," in R. DiClemente and J. Peterson (eds) *Preventing AIDS: Theories and Methods of Behavioral Interventions*, pp. 25–59. New York: Plenum Press.

Coates, Tom; Stall, Ron; Catania, Joseph; and Kegeles, Susan (1988). "Behavioral Factors in HIV Infection," *AIDS* 2 (Suppl. 1): S239–246.

Díaz, Rafael (1998). *Latino Gay Men and HIV: Culture, Sexuality & Risk Behavior*. New York: Routledge.

Kelly, Jeffrey; Kalichman, Seth; Kauth, Michael; Kilgore, Hilda; Hood, Harold; Campos, Peter; Rao, Stephin; Brasfield, Ted; and St Lawrence, Janet (1991). "Situational Factors Associated with AIDS Risk Behavior, Lapses and Coping Strategies Used by Gay Men Who Successfully Avoid Lapses," *American Journal of Public Health* 81(10): 1335–1338.

Lemp, George; Hirozawa, Ane; Givertz, Daniel; Nicri, Giuliano; Anderson, Laura; Lindergren, Mary Lou; Janssen, Robert; and Katz, Mitchell (1994). "Seroprevalence of HIV and Risk Behaviors among Young Homosexual and Bisexual

Men: The San Francisco/Berkeley Young Men's Survey," *Journal of the American Medical Association* 272: 449–454.

Osmond, Dennis; Page, Kimberly; Wiley, James; Garrett, Karen; Sheppard, Haynes; Moss, Andrew; Schrager, Lewis and; Winkelstein, Warren (1994). "HIV Infection in Homosexual and Bisexual Men 18–29 Years of Age: The San Francisco Young Men's Health Study," *American Journal of Public Health* 84: 1933–1937.

Rotello, Gabriel (1997). *Sexual Ecology: AIDS and the Destiny of Gay Men.* New York: Dutton.

Bob: 35-year-old, Caucasian, HIV positive.
David: 29-year-old, Latino, HIV positive.
Eduardo: 31-year-old, Latino, HIV positive.
Harvey: 34-year-old, African American, HIV positive.
Joseph: 31-year-old, Latino, HIV negative.
John: 35-year-old, Caucasian, HIV positive.
Larry: 40-year-old, Caucasian, HIV positive.
Michael: 30-year-old, Latino, HIV negative.
Mike: 28-year-old, African American, HIV negative.
Rick: 38-year-old, Caucasian, HIV positive.
Vincent: 29-year-old, African American, HIV negative.

Appendix 1

Study Participants Quoted in the Text
(All names, arranged in alphabetical order, are fictitious)

PART SIX

Men in Relationships

Why do many men have problems establishing and maintaining intimate relationships with women? What different forms do male–female relational problems take within different socioeconomic groups? How do men's problems with intimacy and emotional expressivity relate to power inequities between the sexes? Are rape and domestic violence best conceptualized as isolated deviant acts by "sick" individuals, or are they the illogical consequences of male socialization? This complex web of male–female relationships, intimacy, and power is the topic of this section.

And what is the nature of men's relationships with other men? Do men have close friendships with men, or do they simply "bond" around shared activities and interests? How do competition, homophobia, and violence enter into men's relationships with each other? For example, a student recently commented that when he goes to the movies with another male friend, they always leave a seat between them, where they put their coats, because they don't want anyone to think they are there "together."

But what are the costs of this emotional and physical distance? And what are the costs of maintaining emotionally impoverished relationships with other men? How is this emotional distance connected to men's intimate relationships with women? Is it related to Billy Crystal's line in *When Harry Met Sally* that women and men can never be friends because "the sex thing always gets in the way"?

Lillian Rubin begins this section with a psychoanalytic interpretation of male–female relational problems. Early development differences, rooted in the social organization of the nuclear family (especially the fact that it is women who care for infants) have set up the fundamental emotional and sexual differences between women and men that create problems for heterosexual couples. Articles by Karen Walker and Peter Nardi suggest the different ways men—both straight and gay—develop and sustain their friendships with each other.

The problems in male–female relationships—that such relationships can be distorted by insecurity, anger, the need for control, the need to assert and demonstrate manliness—can take an ugly turn, as described by Tim Beneke and Terry Kupers in their powerful essays, which invite men to think about rape. Jason Schultz's essay, however, gives us room for hope that the next generation of men, now in their 20s, may struggle with these issues in new and different ways, and develop very different ideas about male–female relationships.

381

"We've been wandering in the desert for forty years. But he's a man—would he ever ask directions?"

Copyright © 1999. Peter Steiner, The New Yorker Collection. All Rights Reserved.

ARTICLE 31

Lillian B. Rubin

The Approach–Avoidance Dance: Men, Women, and Intimacy

For one human being to love another, that is perhaps the most difficult of all our tasks, the ultimate, the last test and proof, the work for which all other work is but preparation.

—Rainer Maria Rilke

Intimacy. We hunger for it, but we also fear it. We come close to a loved one, then we back off. A teacher I had once described this as the "go away a little closer" message. I call it the approach–avoidance dance.

The conventional wisdom says that women want intimacy, men resist it. And I have plenty of material that would *seem* to support that view. Whether in my research interviews, in my clinical hours, or in the ordinary course of my life, I hear the same story told repeatedly. "He doesn't talk to me," says a woman. "I don't know what she wants me to talk about," says a man. "I want to know what he's feeling," she tells me. "I'm not feeling anything," he insists. "Who can feel nothing?" she cries. "I can," he shouts. As the heat rises, so does the wall between them. Defensive and angry, they retreat—stalemated by their inability to understand each other.

Women complain to each other all the time about not being able to talk to their men about the things that matter most to them—about what they themselves are thinking and feeling, about what goes on in the hearts and minds of the men they're relating to. And men, less able to expose themselves and their conflicts—those within themselves or those with the women in their lives—either turn silent or take cover by holding women up to derision. It's one of the norms of male camaraderie to poke fun at women, to complain laughingly about the mystery of their minds, wonderingly about their ways. Even Freud did it when, in exasperation, he asked mockingly, "What do women want? Dear God, what do they want?"

But it's not a joke—not for the women, not for the men who like to pretend it is.

> The whole goddamn business of what you're calling intimacy bugs the hell out of me. I never know what you women mean when you talk about it. Karen complains that I don't talk to her, but it's not talk she wants, it's some other damn thing, only I don't know what the hell it is. Feelings, she keeps asking for. So what am I supposed to do if I don't have any to give her or to talk about just because she decides it's time to talk about feelings? Tell me, will you: maybe we can get some peace around here.

The expression of such conflicts would seem to validate the common understandings that suggest that women want and need intimacy more than men do—that the issue belongs to women alone; that, if left to themselves, men would not suffer it. But things are not always what they seem.

From *Intimate Strangers* by Lillian B. Rubin, New York: HarperCollins. Copyright © 1983. Reprinted with permission of the Rhoda Weyr Agency.

And I wonder: "If men would renounce intimacy, what is their stake in relationships with women?"

Some would say that men need women to tend to their daily needs—to prepare their meals, clean their houses, wash their clothes, rear their children—so that they can be free to attend to life's larger problems. And, given the traditional structure of roles in the family, it has certainly worked that way most of the time. But, if that were all men seek, why is it that, even when they're not relating to women, so much of their lives is spent in search of a relationship with another, so much agony experienced when it's not available?

These are difficult issues to talk about—even to think about—because the subject of intimacy isn't just complicated, it's slippery as well. Ask yourself: What is intimacy? What words come to mind, what thoughts?

It's an idea that excites our imagination, a word that seems larger than life to most of us. It lures us, beckoning us with a power we're unable to resist. And, just because it's so seductive, it frightens us as well—seeming sometimes to be some mysterious force from outside ourselves that, if we let it, could sweep us away.

But what is it we fear?

Asked what intimacy is, most of us—men and women—struggle to say something sensible, something that we can connect with the real experience of our lives. "Intimacy is knowing there's someone who cares about the children as much as you do." "Intimacy is a history of shared experience. It's sitting there having a cup of coffee together and watching the eleven o'clock news." "It's knowing you care about the same things." "It's knowing she'll always understand." "It's him sitting in the hospital for hours at a time when I was sick." "It's knowing he cares when I'm hurting." "It's standing by me when I was out of work." "It's seeing each other at our worst." "It's sitting across the breakfast table." "It's talking when you're in the bathroom." "It's knowing we'll begin and end each day together."

These seem the obvious things—the things we expect when we commit our lives to one another in a marriage, when we decide to have children together. And they're not to be dismissed as inconsequential. They make up the daily experience of our lives together, setting the tone for a relationship in important and powerful ways. It's sharing such commonplace, everyday events that determines the temper and the texture of life, that keeps us living together even when other aspects of the relationship seem less than perfect. Knowing someone is there, is constant, and can be counted on in just the ways these thoughts express provides the background of emotional security and stability we look for when we enter a marriage. Certainly a marriage and the people in it will be tested and judged quite differently in an unusual situation or in a crisis. But how often does life present us with circumstances and events that are so out of the range of ordinary experience?

These ways in which a relationship feels intimate on a daily basis are only one part of what we mean by intimacy, however—the part that's most obvious, the part that doesn't awaken our fears. At a lecture where I spoke of these issues recently, one man commented also, "Intimacy is putting aside the masks we wear in the rest of our lives." A murmur of assent ran through the audience of a hundred or so. Intuitively we say, "yes." Yet this is the very issue that also complicates our intimate relationships.

On the one hand, it's reassuring to be able to put away the public persona—to believe we can be loved for who we *really* are, that we can show our shadow side without fear, that our vulnerabilities will not be counted against us. "The most important thing is to feel I'm accepted just the way I am," people will say.

But there's another side. For, when we show ourselves thus without the masks, we also become anxious and fearful. "Is it possible that someone could love the *real* me?" we're likely to ask. Not the most promising question for the further development of intimacy, since it suggests that, whatever else another might do or feel, it's we who have trouble loving ourselves. Unfortunately, such misgivings are not usually experienced consciously. We're aware only that our discomfort has risen, that we feel a need to get away. For the person who has seen the "real me" is also the one who reflects back to us an image that's usually not wholly to our liking. We get angry at that, first at ourselves for not living up to our own expectations, then at the other, who becomes for us the mirror of our self-doubts—a displacement of hostility that serves intimacy poorly.

There's yet another level—one that's further below the surface of consciousness, therefore, one that's much more difficult for us to grasp, let alone to talk about. I'm referring to the differences in the ways in which women and men deal with their inner emotional lives—differences that create barriers between us that can be high indeed. It's here that we see how those early childhood experiences of separation and individuation—the psychological tasks that were required of us in order to separate from mother, to distinguish ourselves as autonomous persons, to internalize a firm sense of gender identity—take their toll on our intimate relationships.

Stop a woman in mid-sentence with the question, "What are you feeling right now?" and you might have to wait a bit while she reruns the mental tape to capture the moment just passed. But, more than likely, she'll be able to do it successfully. More than likely, she'll think for a while and come up with an answer.

The same is not true of a man. For him, a similar question usually will bring a sense of wonderment that one would even ask it, followed quickly by an uncomprehending and puzzled response. "What do you mean?" he'll ask. "I was just talking," he'll say.

I've seen it most clearly in the clinical setting where the task is to get to the feeling level—or, as one of my male patients said when he came into therapy, to "hook up the head and the gut." Repeatedly when therapy begins, I find myself having to teach a man how to monitor his internal states—how to attend to his thoughts and feelings, how to bring them into consciousness. In the early stages of our work, it's a common experience to say to a man, "How does that feel?" and to see a blank look come over his face. Over and over, I find myself listening as a man speaks with calm reason about a situation which I know must be fraught with pain. "How do you feel about that?" I'll ask. "I've just been telling you," he's likely to reply. "No," I'll say, "you've told me what happened, not how you *feel* about it." Frustrated, he might well respond, "You sound just like my wife."

It would be easy to write off such dialogues as the problems of men in therapy, of those who happen to be having some particular emotional difficulties. But it's not so, as any woman who has lived with a man will attest. Time and again women complain: "I can't get him to verbalize his feelings." "He talks, but it's always intellectualizing." "He's so closed off from what he's feeling, I don't know how he lives that way." "If there's one thing that will eventually ruin this marriage, it's the fact that he can't talk about what's going on inside him." "I have to work like hell to get anything out of him that resembles a feeling that's something besides anger. That I get plenty of—me and the kids, we all get his anger. Anything else is damn hard to come by with him." One woman talked eloquently about her husband's anguish over his inability to get problems in his work life resolved. When I asked how she knew about his pain, she answered:

I pull for it, I pull hard, and sometimes I can get something from him. But it'll be late at night in the dark—you know, when we're in bed and I can't look at him while he's talking and he doesn't have to look at me. Otherwise, he's just defensive and puts on what I call his bear act, where he makes his warning, go-away faces, and he can't be reached or penetrated at all.

To a woman, the world men live in seems a lonely one—a world in which their fears of exposing their sadness and pain, their anxiety about allowing their vulnerability to show, even to a woman they love, is so deeply rooted inside them that, most often, they can only allow it to happen "late at night in the dark."

Yet, if we listen to what men say, we will hear their insistence that they *do* speak of what's inside them, *do* share their thoughts and feelings with the women they love. "I tell her, but she's never satisfied," they complain. "No matter how much I say, it's never enough," they grumble.

From both sides, the complaints have merit. The problem lies not in what men don't say, however, but in what's not there—in what, quite simply, happens so far out of consciousness that it's not within their reach. For men have integrated all too well the lessons of their childhood—the experiences that taught them to repress and deny their inner thoughts, wishes, needs, and fears; indeed, not even to notice them. It's real, therefore, that the kind of inner thoughts and feelings that are readily accessible to a woman generally are unavailable to a man. When he says, "I don't know what I'm feeling," he isn't necessarily being intransigent and withholding. More than likely, he speaks the truth.

Partly that's a result of the ways in which boys are trained to camouflage their feelings under cover of an exterior of calm, strength, and rationality. Fears are not manly. Fantasies are not rational. Emotions, above all, are not for the strong, the sane, the adult. Women suffer them, not men—women, who are more like children with what seems like their never-ending preoccupation with their emotional life. But the training takes so well because of their early childhood experience when, as very young boys, they had to shift their identification from mother to father and sever themselves from their earliest emotional connection. Put the two together and it does seem like suffering to men to have to experience that emotional side of themselves, to have to give it voice.

This is the single most dispiriting dilemma of relations between women and men. He complains, "She's so emotional, there's no point in talking to her." She protests, "It's him you can't talk to, he's always so darned rational." He says, "Even when I tell her nothing's the matter, she won't quit." She says, "How can I believe him when I can see with my own eyes that something's wrong?" He says, "Okay, so something's wrong! What good will it do to tell her?" She cries, "What are we married for? What do you need me for, just to wash your socks?"

These differences in the psychology of women and men are born of a complex interaction between society and the individual. At the broadest social level is the rending of thought and feeling that is such a fundamental part of Western thought. Thought, defined as the ultimate good, has been assigned to men; feeling, considered at best a problem, has fallen to women.

So firmly fixed have these ideas been that, until recently, few thought to question them. For they were built into the structure of psychological thought as if they spoke to an eternal, natural, and scientific truth. Thus, even such a great and innovative thinker as Carl Jung wrote, "The woman is increasingly aware that love alone can give her her full stature, just as the man begins to discern that spirit alone can endow his life with its highest meaning. Fundamentally, therefore, both seek a psychic relation one to the other, because love needs the spirit, and the spirit love, for their fulfillment."[1]

For a woman, "love"; for a man, "spirit"—each expected to complete the other by bringing to the relationship the missing half. In German, the word that is translated here as spirit is *Geist*. But *The New Cassell's German Dictionary* shows that another primary meaning of *Geist* is "mind, intellect, intelligence, wit, imagination, sense of reason." And, given the context of these words, it seems reasonable that *Geist* for Jung referred to a man's highest essence—his mind. There's no ambiguity about a woman's calling, however. It's love.

Intuitively, women try to heal the split that these definitions of male and female have foisted upon us.

> I can't stand that he's so damned unemotional and expects me to be the same. He lives in his head all the time, and he acts like anything that's emotional isn't worth dealing with.

Cognitively, even women often share the belief that the rational side, which seems to come so naturally to men, is the more mature, the more desirable.

> I know I'm too emotional, and it causes problems between us. He can't stand it when I get emotional like that. It turns him right off.

Her husband agrees that she's "too emotional" and complains:

> Sometimes she's like a child who's out to test her parents. I have to be careful when she's like that not to let her rile me up because otherwise all hell would break loose. You just can't reason with her when she gets like that.

It's the rational-man–hysterical-woman script, played out again and again by two people whose emotional repertoire is so limited that they have few real options. As the interaction between them continues, she reaches for the strongest tools she has, the mode she's most comfortable and familiar with: She becomes progressively more emotional and expressive. He falls back on his best weapons: He becomes more rational, more determinedly reasonable. She cries for him to attend to her feelings, whatever they may be. He tells her coolly, with a kind of clenched-teeth reasonableness, that it's silly for her to feel that way, that she's just being emotional. And of course she is. But that dismissive word "just" is the last straw. She gets so upset that she does, in fact, seem hysterical. He gets so bewildered by the whole interaction that his only recourse is to build the wall of reason even higher. All of which makes things measurably worse for both of them.

> The more I try to be cool and calm her the worse it gets. I swear, I can't figure her out. I'll keep trying to tell her not to get so excited, but there's nothing I can do. Anything I say just makes it worse. So then I try to keep quiet, but ... wow, the explosion is like crazy, just nuts.

And by then it *is* a wild exchange that any outsider would agree was "just nuts." But it's not just her response that's off, it's his as well—their conflict resting in the fact that we equate the emotional with the nonrational.

This notion, shared by both women and men, is a product of the fact that they were born and reared in this culture. But there's also a difference between them in their capacity to apprehend the *logic* of emotions—a difference born in their early childhood experiences in the family, when boys had to repress so much of their emotional side and girls could permit theirs to flower.... It should be understood: Commitment itself is not a problem for a man; he's good at that. He can spend a lifetime living in the same family, working at the same job—even one he hates. And he's not without an inner emotional life. But when a relationship requires the sustained verbal expression of that inner life and the full range of feelings that accompany it, then it becomes burdensome for him. He can act out anger and frustration inside the family, it's true. But ask him to express his sadness, his fear, his dependency—all those feelings that would expose his vulnerability to himself or to another—and he's likely to close down as if under some compulsion to protect himself.

All requests for such intimacy are difficult for a man, but they become especially complex and troublesome in relations with women. It's another of those paradoxes. For, to the degree that it's possible for him to be emotionally open with anyone, it is with a woman—a tribute to the power of the childhood experience with mother. Yet it's that same early experience and his need to repress it that raises his ambivalence and generates his resistance.

He moves close, wanting to share some part of himself with her, trying to do so, perhaps even yearning to experience again the bliss of the infant's connection with a woman. She responds, woman style—wanting to touch him just a little more deeply, to know what he's thinking, feeling, fearing, wanting. And the fear closes in—the fear of finding himself again in the grip of a powerful woman, of allowing her admittance only to be betrayed and abandoned once again, of being overwhelmed by denied desires.

So he withdraws.

It's not in consciousness that all this goes on. He knows, of course, that he's distinctly uncomfortable when pressed by a woman for more intimacy in the relationship, but he doesn't know why. And, very often, his behavior doesn't please him any more than it pleases her. But he can't seem to help it.

Notes

1. Carl Gustav Jung, *Contributions to Analytical Psychology* (New York: Harcourt, Brace & Co., 1928), p. 185.

"I'm Not Friends the Way She's Friends": Ideological and Behavioral Constructions of Masculinity in Men's Friendships

Karen Walker

Contemporary ideologies about men's friendships suggest that men's capacity for intimacy is sharply restricted. In this view, men have trouble expressing their feelings with friends. Whether due to the development of the masculine psyche or cultural prescriptions, men are viewed as highly competitive with friends. Because of their competition, they are unlikely to talk about intimate matters such as feelings and relationships. The literature on gender differences in friendship suggests that the ideologies reflect actual behavior. Researchers have found that men limit verbal self-disclosure with friends, especially when compared to women (Caldwell & Peplau 1982; Rubin 1985; Sherrod 1987; Aukett, Ritchie, & Mill 1988; Swain 1989; Reid & Fine 1992). Men share activities with friends (Rubin 1985; Swain 1987). On the other hand, there are also suggestions that the degree of self-disclosure among men may be underestimated (Hacker 1981; Wright 1982; Rawlins 1992), particularly among men from particular groups (Franklin 1992). My research on friendship shows that men and women share the stereotypes about gender differences in friendship, but in specific friendships, men discuss their relationships and report relying on men friends for emotional support and intimacy (Walker 1994). In addition, many activities of friendship—seeing friends for dinner, sharing ritual events, and visiting—are things both men and women do. Barry Wellman (1992) argues that there has been a widespread "domestication" of male friendship, with men seeing friends in their home in much the same way women do.

In much of the literature on gender differences in friendship, ideology has been mistaken for behavior. In part, researchers seem to have made this mistake because they have asked general, instead of specific, questions about friendship.[1] As a result, they have elicited good representations of what respondents *believe* their behavior is—beliefs that are shaped by the respondents' own ideologies. What they have sometimes failed to elicit is information about specific friendships in which variations from the ideologies may be substantial. Because researchers report what respondents tell them, it is easy to understand why researchers make this mistake. What becomes more difficult to understand is how the confusion between the ideology of friendship and friendship behavior comes to be constructed in everyday life. Why do men maintain their belief that men are less open than women in the face of considerable evidence that they do discuss their feelings with their friends? This is even more crucial because the stereotype of intimate friendship that men believe characterizes women's friendship is currently highly valued. Feminist scholars and writers have successfully revalued women's intimate relationships to the detriment of earlier ideals that privileged male bonding. While not all respondents in this study positively evaluated the stereotype of women's openness

From *Masculinities* 2(2): 38–55. Copyright © 1994 by Men's Studies Association. Reprinted with permission.

with friends, many did, as evidenced by one professional man who said:

> I mean, we [men] talk about sports and politics sometimes, any kind of safe [topic], if you will. Not that any [every] kind of interaction needs to be intimate or this and that, but it's much different when you talk to women. Women catch on. I remember once seeing Robert Bly, and he said something that is really so in my experience, that women get to the heart of things and that they get there so quickly that it makes you, uh, it can put men into a rage because women are able to articulate these kinds of things that men can't.

Given the belief that being intimate and "getting to the heart of things" is good, and given the evidence that men are more intimate in practice than the ideology suggests, *why don't men challenge the ideology?*

There seem to be several answers to this question. First, when men do not conform to the masculine ideals about how they should act with their friends, they are occasionally censured. In the practice of masculine friendship, the positive evaluation of feminine intimacy disappears. Because of their friends' reactions, men come to see their behavior as anomalous and bad, and they do not reevaluate the extent to which the ideology of masculine friendship accurately reflects behavior.

Second, social class influences men's capacities for conforming to gender ideologies. Professional men are somewhat more likely than working-class men to conform to gendered norms with respect to intimate behavior (Franklin 1992; Walker 1994). Also, professional men's social class makes them—with other middle-class men—the primary groups on which cultural stereotypes are based. Literature written specifically about men's friendships often relies on research of middle-class men, particularly college-aged men (Caldwell and Peplau 1982; Rubin 1985; Swain 1989; Rawlins 1992; Reid and Fine 1992). Very recently, some researchers have noted that men who are other than middle-class or white may have different types of friendships from the ideology (Franklin, 1992; Hansen, 1992), but the knowledge of the existence of other forms of masculine friendship among working-class African American and white men has not influenced the ideology of friendship.

Third, there *are* gender differences in behavior, and these differences reinforce stereotypes about gendered forms of friendship, even if the differences differ substantively from the substance of the ideology. For instance, male respondents in this study used the telephone somewhat differently from the ways women used it. Through their use of the telephone men constructed their masculinity, and in so doing they reinforced their notions that men are not open. As I will show, men claimed they called their friends for explicitly instrumental reasons—to make plans, get specific information, and so on—but not to find out how friends were, which they connected to women's telephone use. These practices generally supported the idea that women were better at maintaining friendships and talking to friends about feelings even though men's telephone conversations often included talk about personal matters. But a desire to talk to friends about personal matters was rarely the motive for phone calls.

In this article I examine the ways gender ideology about friendships is maintained through four behaviors and men's interpretations of those behaviors: telephone use, jokes, the use of public space, and how men talk about women. It is only when we understand how men behaviorally construct gender within friendship that we can begin to understand how men use these behavioral constructions to support ideological constructions of masculine friendship practices.

Method of Study

This paper relies on research from a study of men's and women's same-gender and cross-gender friendships. I interviewed 9 working-class and 10 professional men (as well 18 working-class and 15 middle-class women). Within each class I individually interviewed some men who were friends with other respondents in the study. Interviewing friends allowed me to gather information on group interaction that would have been unavailable had I interviewed isolated individuals. In addition, I was able to explore issues that were most salient to groups of friends. Finally, by interviewing friends I could examine the extent to which friends agree on what their interactions were like. This was particularly important when there was a discrepancy between behavior and ideology: Some men did not report on behavior that contradicted the masculine ideology of friendship either because they were unwilling to disclose that their behavior did not match the cultural ideal or because such behavior was somewhat meaningless to them, and they forgot it.

Respondents ranged in age from 27 to 48. Class location was determined by both life style and individuals' work. Thus, working-class respondents tended to have high school educations or less, although one self-employed carpenter had a four-year degree in accounting. Working-class men were in construction and some service occupations. Most working-class men lived in densely populated urban neighborhoods in row houses or twins in Philadelphia. Professional respondents had graduate degrees, and they worked as academics, administrators, lawyers, and therapists. Professionals lived in the suburbs of Philadelphia or in urban apartments.

Interviews were semistructured, and respondents answered both global questions about their friendship patterns as well as questions about activities and topics of conversations in which they engaged with each friend they named. The use of in-depth interviews that included both global and specific questions allowed me to gather data indicating the frequent discrepancies between cultural ideologies of masculine friendships and actual behaviors. In addition, in-depth interviews allowed me to compare working-class and professional respondents' experiences.

Recently, Christine Williams and Joel Heikes (1993) have observed that male nurses shaped responses to interview questions in ways that took into account the gender of the interviewer. In this study, my status as a woman interviewer appeared to have both positive and negative implications for data collection. On the one hand, being a woman made it more likely that men admitted behavior that contradicted gender ideology. Sociologists studying gender and friendship have consistently argued that men do not engage in self-disclosure with other men (Caldwell & Peplau 1982; Reid & Fine 1992). Other research shows that men are likely to be more self-disclosing with women than with men (Rubin 1985; O'Meara 1989). While my research shows that men engaged in self-disclosure more frequently with friends than the literature suggests, they did so with men they considered close friends. Frequently close friends were people they knew for a long time or people with whom they spent much time. Wright (1982) notes that long-time men friends engage in self-disclosure. I suspected that certain kinds of disclosures that men made during the interviews might have been more difficult to make to an unknown man instead of to me, an unknown woman.

On the other hand, respondents suggested that they more heavily edited their responses to questions about how they discussed women with their men friends than they did other questions. They frequently sprinkled their responses with comments recognizing my gender, "You don't have a gun in there, do you? (laugh)" or "I don't mean to be sexist here." I suspected that responses were much more benign than they would have been if I were a man. Thus, when I discuss men's talk about women below I believe that my data underestimate the extent to which men's talk about women constructs gender tensions.

Behavioral Construction of Masculinity

In recent years sociologists of gender have come to emphasize the active construction of gender. Gender is seen as an ongoing activity fundamental to all aspects of social life rather than a static category in which we place men or women (Connell 1987; West & Zimmerman 1987; Leidner 1991). One advantage of a social constructionist perspective is that it allows researchers to explore both the ideological as well as the behavioral construction of gender. Gender is constructed *ideologically* when men and women believe that certain qualities, such as intimacy, characterize one gender rather than another. The way men and women interpret life and its meaning for them is deeply influenced by their ideological beliefs. Gender is constructed *behaviorally* in the activities men and women do and the way they do them.

Sometimes ideology and behavior match—such as when men talk about gender differences in telephone use and report behavior that differs from women's behavior. Sometimes ideology and behavior do not match. When there is a mismatch, the interesting problem of how ideology is sustained when behavior contradicts it emerges. I argue that, in the specific case of friendship, specific behaviors supported men's gendered ideologies. Men discounted or ignored altogether evidence that discredited a distinctly masculine model of friendship. This occurred because gender is a category culturally defined by multiple qualities. When men included themselves in the masculine gender category based on some behavior, they tended unreflectively to accept as given the cultural boundaries of the entire category *even if other of their behaviors contradicted those boundaries.*

Among respondents there were several ways masculinity was constructed in the activities of friendship. First, where men met, particularly working-class men, became a mark of masculinity. Second, the way men used the telephone distinguished masculine from feminine behavior. Third, men used jokes in particular ways to establish masculinity and also to manage tensions between actual behavior and gender ideologies. Finally, men friends talked about women in ways that emphasized the differences and tensions between men and women.

There are class differences in the behaviors that form particular patterns of masculinity. Differential financial constraints, the social expectations of particular kinds of work, and lifestyle differences played roles in shaping particular forms of masculinity. The use of jokes was somewhat more elaborated among working-class men than among professional men, but reports of jokes and joking behavior emerged in both groups. Professional men talked about wives and the strains of work and family differently from working-class men; as I will discuss, this resulted from different work experiences.

Besides class differences, which I will address throughout the article, there were individual differences. All men did not engage in all the behaviors that I argue contribute to the construction of masculinity. One professional man said that while he talked "about what specific women are like," he did not talk about women in general and men who talked about what women are generally like "would not be my friends." Other men did not report the use of jokes and joking behavior in their friendships. Sociology frequently avoids discussion about individuals who do not participate in the behaviors that the sociologist argues shows the existence of meaningful social patterns. Unfortunately, doing so often reifies behavioral differences. This is a particular problem in the discussion of gender because there is currently (and happily for the existence of a lively, informed debate) a very close link between the results of social research on gender and broad social and political debates about men's and women's differences.

I wish, therefore, to give the reader a general indication of the individual variability in the gendered behaviors in which men engaged. In all the behaviors discussed below at least half, and frequently more, of the men participated in the behaviors whereas few women did. There were, however, individual exceptions to these behaviors, and those exceptions point to a flexibility in gendered behavior that, while not as expansive as many would wish, is broader than we frequently recognize. Current social theory about gender emphasizes the agentic nature of the construction of gender. It is a practice in which men and women have a considerable range of actions from which to choose. At given historical points, certain actions may be dictated more than others, and therefore individual men and women may frequently act in ways that conform to current ideology. But even when cultural ideology demands close adherence to particular practices, the practical nature of gender means that some individuals will not conform. Further, the multiplicity of practices that create gender enables individuals to maintain their positions within gender categories without much difficulty.

Men's Use of Public Space

The use of public space for informal and apparently unplanned socializing is much more common among men than among women, and it marks the gender boundaries between men and women. The frequent use of public space by working-class men for informal socializing emerges in ethnographies of men's groups (Liebow 1967; Kornblum 1974; Anderson 1976; Whyte 1981). Working-class men in this study met in public spaces such as local bars and playgrounds. There they talked about work and family, and they made informal connections with other men. Sometimes they picked up side work, sometimes they hung out. At the time of our interview, one working-class man said that he spent some of his time at a local bar selling advertisements in a book to raise money for a large retirement dinner for a long-time coach of a community football team. He also spent time there drinking and talking to friends.

Working-class men also met in semipublic spaces such as gyms or clubs. While membership in these spaces was frequently restricted, the spaces themselves functioned in similar ways to public spaces. Men met regularly and informally in public and semipublic spaces one or more times a week. Unlike women who made definite plans to meet friends occasionally in bars, the men assumed because of past practice that on particular nights of the week they would meet friends.

Wellman (1992) suggests that the use of public space for male socializing is diminishing, and men's friendships are becoming domesticated as their friendships move into the home and hence more like women's. This phenomenon of domestication was evident among professional respondents, most of whom reported socializing infrequently in public spaces. But it was not evident among the working-class respondents in this study. All but one of the working-class respondents had been brought up in the same communities in which they lived when I interviewed them. Among these men there were long-time, continuous patterns of public socializing. While Wellman's point is important, the domestication of male friendship seems to be influenced by circumstances in men's lives and is probably occurring unevenly. Further, barring significant structural changes in working-class men's formal and informal work lives, the domestication of male friendships is unlikely to be complete.

Men's Telephone Use

Discussions of men's telephone use as a construction of gender make the most sense when contrasted with women's telephone use. Many men noted that their wives used the telephone very differently from them. A few, primarily working-class men, stated that they disliked talking on the telephone, and they used it only for instrumental reasons (e.g., to make appointments or get specific information). Other men, both professional and working class, said their wives called friends just to see how they were doing and then talked for a long time, whereas men did not do so. Thus men ideologically constructed gender through their understandings of telephone practices. In addition, both men and women constructed gender behaviorally through using the telephone in different ways.

Telephone use differed slightly by class and work experiences, but even accounting for the effects of class and work, there were substantial gender differences. Men frequently reported that the purpose of their most recent telephone calls with friends was instrumental: lawyers discussed cases, men discussed upcoming social plans, and some working-class men made plans to do side work together. Because of this instrumental motive for telephone calls to friends, many professional men reported that their frequent telephone contact was from their offices during working hours. Men rarely reported that they called friends just to say "hi" and find out how they were. One professional man, Mike,[2] reported differences between his wife and himself in being friends:

> I'm not friends the way she's friends. *How are you friends differently?* I don't work on them. I don't pick the phone up and call people and say, "How are you?"

While Mike reported that, in fact, he did call one friend to find out how he was doing at least once a year, most telephone contact was initiated when friends made plans to visit from out of town or he had business matters to discuss with friends. One result of this behavior was tremendous attrition in his friendship network over time. Mike was a gregarious man who reported many past and current friends, but he tended to lose touch with past friends once business reasons for keeping in touch with them diminished, even those who continued to live in Philadelphia. He only reported talking to two friends six or more times a year on the telephone. One of those friends was a man with whom he had professional ties, and they called one another when they did business. The other friend, Gene, was one of the few men who called friends for social conversations. The fairly frequent calls between Gene and Mike may have been initiated by Gene.

Gil, a working-class man, usually spoke to friends on the phone to arrange meetings. Although he kept in touch with two friends largely through telephone use (he worked two jobs during the week and one of his friends worked on weekends—theirs was a telephone friendship), he said:

> I don't talk to them a long time because I'm not a phone person. I'd rather see them in person because I don't like holding the phone and talking because you really can't think of things to say too often on the phone, but when you're in person you can think of more things, cause I like prefer sitting and talking to a person face-to-face . . . I'll talk to people 10, 15 minutes sometimes, but I prefer not to if I can. But some you just can't get off the phone, no matter what you do. And you're like, "Uh, great, well, I'll talk to you a little bit later." And they go into another story. You know [my friend] Cindy will do that, Cindy is great for that. Now Joanne [my wife] can talk on the phone for two to three hours . . . And then the person she's with is not too far away so she could just walk over and talk, you know.

Peter, a young working-class man, reported that he "avoided the phone as much as possible." He did not call friends to chat, and he only used the telephone for social chats with one friend, a woman:

> I'm not a phone person, but yeah, I do [talk to a specific friend] because she talks on the phone, she likes the phone so . . . She'll talk and I'll yes and no (laughs).

Peter did not do side jobs with other men, thus his reasons for using the telephone were sharply limited. Peter and Gil both reported that their telephone preferences were different from those of women they knew. Their general comment "I'm not a phone person" was a representation of their identity, and it was substantiated by their behavior that differs from women's behavior. Typically, working-class men spoke on the telephone once or twice a week to those with whom they did side jobs. One man who ran a bookmaking business with a friend reported that they spoke several times a day about business. Men spoke much less frequently than that to friends for other reasons.

Although most men reported calling friends for instrumental reasons, many men reported that their telephone conversations were not limited to the reason for the call. During telephone calls men discussed their families or their work after they finished with their business. During telephone calls made to discuss social plans several men discussed infertility problems with their wives. Another complained to a friend about his marital problems during a phone call initiated to plan side work. One man called a friend to make plans for a birthday dinner for the caller's wife. During the conversation he told his friend how many feelings the interview I had with him had stirred up (the friend had referred me to him). These conversations, then, had several functions for men's friendships. The telephone was primarily considered a tool for business or to make social plans, but it was also used as means of communicating important personal information. Most men, however, deemphasized the telephone's function in the communication of personal information.

About one fourth of the men reported that they did call friends simply to find out how they were. Most of the time these men reported calling out-of-town friends with whom they lacked other regular means of contact, and most of the time their calls were infrequent—one to three times a year. In one exception, a professional man regularly called friends to see how they were (and sometimes became irritated and upset when the friends did not reciprocate by initiating some percentage of the telephone calls). He talked with one local friend once a week for no other reason than to keep in touch, but this pattern was unique. The friend he called had limited mobility, and the men rarely saw one another. The telephone was a primary vehicle for their friendship. In this instance, the two men's calls differed little from some women's calls.

There was tremendous variation in telephone use among men, but the variation does not erase the differences across genders. While only one quarter of the men in this study reported that they ever called friends to visit over the telephone and three quarters called for instrumental reasons, over four-fifths of the women reported that they called friends to visit. Also, men's reported frequency of telephoning friends was consistently lower than women's. Whereas two-thirds of all women reported that they spoke with at least one friend three or more times a week, less than one quarter of the men did so.

The finding that men use the telephone less than women and that women use it for social visiting has been noted by others (Rakow 1991; Fischer 1992). Fischer (1992) argues:

research shows that, discounting their fewer opportunities for social contact, women are more socially adept and intimate than men, for whatever reasons—psychological constitution, social structure, childhood experiences or cultural norms. The telephone therefore fits the typical female style of personal interaction more closely than it does the typical male style (p. 235).

Fischer's comments may hold a clue about how ideologies of gender are maintained despite the evidence of intimate behaviors among men. Men and women both see the telephone as something women use more than men, and they see it as a way women are intimate. Men's telephone practices provided evidence to respondents that men are incapable of intimacy whereas women are very intimate with friends. Although women used the telephone more often for intimate conversation than men, men used opportunities at work and in public hangouts to talk intimately (one respondent reported that when they got together in the bar "we're worse than a bunch of girls when it comes to that [talking about their spouses]!"). Although telephone patterns are a poor measure of intimacy in friendship, men used them as such. Several men commented on hearing their wives call friends and talk about personal information. Doing so substantiated their impressions of women's friendships. Also, because the men focused on the reasons for their calls rather than on the contents of telephone calls, telephone use acted to provide confirmation that stereotypes about friendship are true.

Men's Jokes

Men's use of jokes is another way in which men construct their masculinity. In his ethnography, *America's Working Man*, David Halle (1984) points to several functions jokes serve among men: they reaffirm values of friendship and generosity, they ritually affirm heterosexuality among men whose social circumstances create a level of physical and emotional intimacy culturally regarded as unmasculine, and they mediate disputes. These functions were evident in the way working-class men talked about jokes and humor in their friendships. They were less evident among the professional men, for reasons suggested by Halle.

Men friends, particularly working-class men, used harsh teasing as a form of social control to reinforce certain behaviors. One working-class man said that he and his friends were the worst "ball breakers" in the world. If a man did not show up at the bar or at some social event then my respondent said they heard about it from all their friends. Among these men the friendship group was highly valued, but also, like many contemporary friendships, somewhat fragile. Work and family responsibilities that kept men away from the friendship group might put a friend at risk of being teased.

Other men said that the failure to reciprocate favors, such as help with household projects, might be a basis for teasing friends. This was a particularly important way of defusing tension as well as reaffirming values of friendship for working-class men. They frequently depended on friends to help them attain higher standards of living: friends provided craft services whose prices are high in the formal market and thus many working-class people's material lives were somewhat improved through the help of friends. Failure to reciprocate had implications not only for friendship but also for family income. Jokes about a friend's failure to reciprocate became a public statement about his failure to conform to recognized norms, and they were a way for someone to handle his anger at his friend.

Another way jokes constructed masculinity was to highlight an activity that was outside the purview of men's activities that they nonetheless did. For instance, Greg and Chris were friends from law school who saw each other seven or eight times a year. One of those times was a yearly shopping trip to buy Christmas presents. Men generally claimed they did not shop—those who did usually said they went to hardware stores when they were doing a project with a friend. The shopping trip Greg and Chris went on was a traditional joke between them both. It began in law school when Greg asked Chris to go with him to buy a negligee for Greg's girlfriend. When they got to the store Chris ran away and Greg was left feeling terribly embarrassed. Ever since, they went shopping once a year, but both men downplayed the shopping aspect of the trips and highlighted the socializing. They said they did not accomplish very much on their trips. They also said they used the time to buy gag gifts for people instead of serious gifts. Turning the shopping spree into a joke subverted the meaning of shopping as something women do, and the trip became a ritual reaffirmation of masculinity.

Jokes were sometimes used as pseudoinstrumental reasons to call friends on the phone when men lacked instrumental reasons; they thus maintained the masculinity of men's telephone practices. Men called each other and told one another jokes and then moved into more personal topics. Gene, for instance, befriended Al's lover, Ken, before Al died of AIDS. During Al's illness Gene was an important source of support for both men, and he continued to keep in touch with Ken after Al's death. They talked regularly on the telephone, but most of the conversations initiated by Ken began with jokes. After Ken and Gene had exchanged jokes the two men moved on to other topics, including their feelings for Al.

Finally, men used jokes to exaggerate gender differences and denigrate women. Gene considered himself sympathetic to women's issues. He said that he and his friends

> will tell in a joking way, tell jokes that are hostile towards feminism or hostile towards women. It's like there's two levels of it. One is, we think the joke is funny in and of itself or we think the joke is funny because it's so outrageously different from what's politically correct. You know, so we kind of laugh about it, and then we'll laugh that we even had the gall to tell it.

Not all men mentioned the importance of humor to friendship, the existence of jokes among friends, or the tendency to tease friends, but about half the respondents indicated that jokes and teasing were part of their friendship. Also, jokes and joking behavior were not limited solely to men. A few women also told jokes and engaged in joking behavior with their friends, but men emphasized the behavior as part of their friendships, whereas women did not. Also, women reported using jokes in a much more restricted way than men. For men, jokes are an elaborated code with multiple meanings and functions.

Men Talk About Women

Finally, men constructed masculinity through their behavior with men friends through their talk about what women are like. While not every man reported that he engaged in discussions about women with his friends, most men did. Comments about women emphasized men's and women's differences. Men, for instance, discussed how their wives had higher housekeeping standards than they, their wives' greater control over child rearing, and their greater propensity to spend money impulsively; they also discussed women's needs for relationships. These comments helped men interpret their relationships with their wives and served to reassure men that their experiences were not unusual.

> We would talk about like how long it would take them to get dressed . . . my wife took exceptionally long to get dressed, four or five hours in the bathroom. Um, but I mean, I don't think I talk a whole lot about women, when I did I guess I generalized and that kind of stuff, like how a wife expects a husband to kind of do everything for her. (Working-class man)

> What we talked about was the differences, differences we have with our wives in terms of raising kids. . . . And how sometimes we feel, rightly or wrongly, we both agreed that we didn't have quite as much control over the situation or say in the situation as we might have liked . . . That's something that a lot of my friends who have younger kids, I've had that discussion with. I've talked to them about it in terms of something that I think mothers, in particular, have a different input into their child's lives than do fathers. (Professional man)

Through these sorts of discussions with men friends—some brief and jocular, some more sustained and serious—men defined who women are, and who they were, in contrast, as men. These discussions with friends frequently reinforced stereotypes about women and men.

Women were spendthrifts:

> One individual may call me up and say, "Geez, my wife just went out and bought these rugs. I need that like a hole in the head. You know, this is great, I have these oriental rugs now, you know, I'm only going to spill coffee on it." (Professional man)

Women attempted to control men's free time:

> [We might talk about] how much we're getting yelled at or in trouble or whatever, you know what I mean, for not doin' stuff around the house, or workin' over somebody else's house too much or staying out at the bars too late. (Working-class man)

Women were manipulative:

> Sometimes they seem, they don't know what they want, or what they want is something different than what they tell you they want. You know, tough to figure out, [we say] that they can be manipulative . . . Conniving. (Professional man)

Men evaluated women's behaviors and desires through such talk. They reported that such talk was a way of getting feedback on their marital experiences. Talking with friends frequently relieved the tensions men felt in their cross-gender relationships, and it did so without requiring men to change their behaviors vis-à-vis women. Men rarely reported that they accommodated themselves to their wives because their friends suggested that they should: in an unusual case, one working-class man said his friend told him that women needed to be told, "I love you," all the time, and he thought his friend had been helpful in mitigating some strains in his marriage through their talk.

More frequently, men's jokes and comments about women—about their demands for more housekeeping help, their ways with money, and their desires to have men home more often—

served to delegitimize women's demands. Men talked about women as unreasonable; as one man above said, "everybody needs time away." This tendency to delegitimize wives' demands was more apparent among working-class men than among the professional men. Professionals reported that their jobs, not unreasonable wives, prevented them from greater involvement in child care, and they sometimes talked with friends about this as an inevitable part of professional life. The effect, however, was similar because talk among both professional and working-class men friends supported the status quo. Instead of becoming a problem to be solved, professional men and their friends determined that professional life unfortunately, but inevitably, caused men to limit their family involvement. (One man who consistently seemed to play with the boundaries of masculinity had tried to solve the problem through scheduling his work flexibly along the lines that a friend had suggested. He reported that he still did not have enough time for his family.)

These four behaviors: using public spaces for friendship socializing, men's telephone practices, joking, and talking about women in particular ways are some ways that men construct masculinity in their friendships. There are many others. Discussions of sports, for instance, are one obvious other way men construct their masculinity, and such discussions were common among respondents. Like women's telephone use and ease with intimacy, men's talk about sports has become part of our cultural ideology about gendered friendships. Not all respondents, however, participated in such talk, and of those who did, some did not enjoy such talk but engaged in it because it was expected.

Cultural Ideology of Men and Friendship

When I began this article I asked not only how men construct masculinity through their behaviors but also why there was a discrepancy between the cultural ideology of men's friendship's, which maintains that men do not share intimate thoughts and feelings with one another, and reports of specific behaviors that show that they do. It is in part by recognizing that the construction of gender is an ongoing activity that incorporates many disparate behaviors that this question becomes answerable. While one behavior in an interaction may violate the norms of gender ideology, other behaviors are simultaneously conforming to other ideologies of masculinity. When men reflect back on their behavior they emphasize those aspects of their behavior that give truth to their self-images as men. The other behavior may be reported, but, in this study, it did not discredit men's gender ideologies.

Second, as I noted earlier, masculinity is frequently reified, and behavior that does not conform does not affect the overall picture of masculinity. Men belong in the gender category to which they were assigned at birth, and their past in that category reassures them that they belong there. Occasionally respondents recognized that men do things that contradict gender ideology. One man told me about a friend of his who "does thoughtful things for other men." When I asked what he did, and he said:

> Uh, remembers their birthdays. Will buy them gifts. Uh, and does it in a way that's real, I think, really, uh, I don't know, it's not uh, it's not uh, feminine in the sense of, feminine, maybe in the perjorative sense . . . I mean, I remember that John, uh, John's nurturing I saw, not that I was a recipient of it so much although I was in his company a lot and got to see him. Uh, I thought, boy, this guy's a, this guy's a real man, this guy. This guy's all right, you know.

Though my respondent identified his friend's behavior as different, almost feminine, he made sure to tell me that the man is a "real man." This seemed problematic for him, his language became particularly awkward, full of partial sentences. But in the end, the fact that his friend was a man and that my respondent liked and respected him enabled him to conclude, "this guy's a real man."

At other times, recognition that behavior contradicts gender ideology elicits censure instead of acceptance. When men censure one another for such behavior, they reinforce the idea that such behavior is anomalous and should not be expressed. For instance, Gene, who consciously worked at intimacy with his friends, told me about sitting and drinking with a friend of his one night when Gene was depressed. His friend asked him how things were going and Gene told him he was depressed because he was feeling financial pressures. Gene felt "house poor" and upset with himself for buying a house that would cause him to feel such pressures when he had determined that he would not do such a thing. His friend's response was, "Oh, that's the last time I ask you how you're feeling." On an earlier occasion Gene called his gay friend in California on the telephone crying because he had just broken off with a woman he had been dating. His friend comforted him at the time, but later he said, "I didn't know you had it in you [to express yourself like that]." Gene believed that men had greater difficulties with self-disclosure than women, and these events acted as support for his beliefs instead of counterexamples. In both cases friends had let him know his self-disclosing behavior was either intolerable or unusual. His gay friend seemed to admire Gene's ability to call him up in tears by giving him a back-handed compliment, but this was a man who had rejected many norms of heterosexuality, and who saw Gene as participating in hegemonic masculinity (Connell 1987) and teased him for it. Gene's interpretation of these events coincided with his friends: he was behaving in ways men normally did not.

In another case, Anna, a woman respondent, told me about her husband Tom's experience with his best friend. Anna had been diagnosed with a serious chronic illness that had profound consequences for her lifestyle, and Tom was depressed about it. One night he went out with two friends, Jim, Tom's best friend, and another man who was unhappy about his recent divorce. According to Anna, Jim commented that he wished he did not know either Tom or the other man at the time because they were both so depressed. From this, Anna said she and Tom concluded that men did not express their feelings and were not as intimate with one another as women were.

These sorts of events reinforce men's notions that men are emotionally distant. Self-disclosure and attempts to express one's feelings are seen as anomalous, even if desirable—desirable because the contemporary evaluation on friendship as defined primarily by feminists is that women have better friendships than men. Women, by the way, also reported occasions when their friends were unsympathetic to their expressions of distress. The conclusions women and men drew about their unsympathetic friendship differed, however. Women concluded that particular friends lacked sympathy. Unlike men, they did not think their expressive behavior was inappropriate or unusual.

Conclusion

I have conceptualized gender as an ongoing social creation rather than a role individuals learn or a personality type they develop that causes differences in behavior. Individuals construct gender on an ideological and a behavioral level. On a behavioral level, many social acts contribute to the overall construction of masculinity. Men do not talk on the phone unless they have something specific they wish to find out or arrange. Men friends joke around together. Men hang out in bars. Men also talk about women and their wives in ways that distinguish women from men and define gender tensions and men's solutions to them. Some of these behaviors have become part of the cultural ideology of men's friendships. Respondents, for instance, talked generally about differences between men's and women's telephone use. Some also said that women stayed home with their friends whereas men went out. But the relationship between behavior and ideology is not so direct and simple that behaviors in which most men participate become part of the cultural ideology. To the extent that talking about women, for instance, is perceived as sharing personal information, then talking about women is something men do not recognize as characteristic of their friendships.

Because so many actions construct masculinity and gender is a practice over which individuals have some control, the failure to conform to the cultural ideology of masculine friendship does not necessarily threaten either the cultural ideology or the individual's position in the masculine gender category. This becomes particularly important in understanding why the many men who share personal information with friends continue to believe that men are inexpressive and find intimacy difficult. I have found that the exchange of intimate information is something most respondents, men and women, engaged in, but most people also did it with selected friends. Furthermore, talking about personal matters or sharing feelings frequently constituted a small portion of all friendship interactions. Thus, for men whose identities included a notion that they, as men, were not open with friends, the times when they were open were insignificant. There were many other activities of friendship that men preferred to emphasize.

It is useful to expand the debate over gender differences in friendship to include behaviors other than intimacy that has dominated the recent literature on gender and friendship (Miller 1983; Rubin 1985; Sherrod 1987; Swain 1987; Allan 1989; Rawlins 1992). The narrowness of the debate has limited our understandings of why men's friendships have been meaningful and important to them. Working-class men's reliance on friends for services and material support becomes invisible. The importance of joking behavior as a communicative style and its functions in maintaining stable relationships for both working-class and professional men disappear. Finally, the narrow debate over intimacy obscures some implications of how men talk to one another about women for gender relations and inequality.

A version of this article was presented at the 1993 annual meetings of the American Sociological Association in Miami. The author gratefully acknowledges the comments of Robin Leidner and Vicki Smith.

Notes

1. Some researchers have made this mistake as part of a more general positive evaluation of women. Some of this literature is explicitly feminist and draws on literature which emphasizes and dichotomizes gender differences.

2. All names of the respondents have been changed.

References

Allan, G. (1989). *Friendship: Developing a sociological perspective*. Boulder, CO: Westview.

Anderson, E. (1976). *A place on the corner*. Chicago: University of Chicago Press.

Aukett, R., Ritchie, J., & Mill, K. (1988). Gender differences in friendship patterns. *Sex Roles, 19*, 57–66.

Caldwell, M. A., & Peplau, L. A. (1982). Sex differences in same-sex friendships. *Sex Roles, 8*, 721–732.

Connell, R. W. (1987). *Gender and power*. Palo Alto, CA: Stanford University Press.

Fischer, C. (1992). *America calling: A social history of the telephone to 1940*. Berkeley: University of California Press.

Franklin, C. W. II (1992). Friendship among Black men. In P. Nardi (Ed.), *Men's friendships* (pp. 201–214). Newbury Park, CA: Sage.

Hacker, H. M. (1981). Blabbermouths and clams: Sex differences in self-disclosure in same-sex and cross-sex friendship dyads. *Psychology of Women Quarterly, 5*, 385–401.

Halle, D. (1984). *America's working man: Work, home, and politics among blue-collar property owners*. Chicago: University of Chicago Press.

Hansen, K. V. (1992). Our eyes behold each other: masculinity and intimate friendship in antebellum New England. In P. Nardi (Ed.), *Men's friendships* (pp. 35–58). Newbury Park, CA: Sage.

Kornblum, W. (1974). *Blue collar community*. Chicago: University of Chicago Press.

Leidner, R. (1991). Serving hamburgers and selling insurance: Gender, work, and identity in interactive service jobs. *Gender & Society, 5*, 154–177.

Liebow, E. (1967). *Tally's corner: A study of Negro streetcorner men*. Boston: Little, Brown.

Miller, M. (1983). *Men and friendship*. Boston: Houghton Mifflin.

O'Meara, J. D. (1989). Cross-sex friendship: Four basic challenges of an ignored relationship. *Sex Roles, 21,* 525–543.

Rakow, L. F. (1991). *Gender on the line: Women, the telephone, and community life.* Urbana, IL: University of Illinois Press.

Rawlins, W. (1992). *Friendship matters: Communication, dialectics, and the life course.* New York: Aldine de Gruyter.

Reid, H. M., & Fine, G. A. (1992). Self-disclosure in men's friendships. In P. Nardi (Ed.), *Men's friendships* (pp. 132–152). Newbury Park, CA: Sage.

Rubin, L. (1985). *Just friends: The role of friendship in our lives.* New York: Harper & Row.

Sherrod, D. (1987). The bonds of men: Problems and possibilities in close male relationships. In H. Brod (Ed.), *The making of masculinities* (pp. 213–239). Boston: Allen and Unwin.

Swain, S. (1989). Covert intimacy: Closeness in men's friendships. In B. Risman & P. Schwartz (Eds.), *Gender and intimate relationships,* (pp. 71–86). Belmont, CA: Wadsworth.

Walker, K. (1994). Men, women and friendship: what they say; what they do. *Gender & Society, 8,* 246–265.

Wellman, B. (1992). Men in networks: Private communities, domestic friendships. In P. Nardi (Ed.), *Men's friendships* (pp. 74–114). Newbury Park, CA: Sage.

West, C., & Zimmerman, D. (1987). Doing gender. *Gender & Society, 1,* 125–151.

Whyte, W. F. (1981). *Street corner society: The social structure of an Italian slum* (3rd ed.). Chicago: The University of Chicago Press.

Williams, C. L., & Heikes, E. J. (1993). The importance of researcher's gender in the in-depth interview: Evidence from two case studies of male nurses. *Gender & Society, 7,* 280–291.

Wright, P. (1982). Men's friendships, women's friendships and the alleged inferiority of the latter. *Sex Roles, 8,* 1–20.

The Politics of Gay Men's Friendships

Peter M. Nardi

Towards the end of Wendy Wasserstein's Pulitzer Prize–winning play, *The Heidi Chronicles*, a gay character, Peter Patrone, explains to Heidi why he has been so upset over all the funerals he has attended recently: "A person has so many close friends. And in our lives, our friends are our families" (Wasserstein 1990: 238). In his collection of stories, *Buddies*, Ethan Mordden (1986: 175) observes: "What unites us, all of us, surely, is brotherhood, a sense that our friendships are historic, designed to hold Stonewall together.... It is friendship that sustained us, supported our survival." These statements succinctly summarize an important dimension about gay men's friendships: Not only are friends a form of family for gay men and lesbians, but gay friendships are also a powerful political force.

Mordden's notion of "friends is survival" has a political dimension that becomes all the more salient in contemporary society where the political, legal, religious, economic, and health concerns of gay people are routinely threatened by the social order. In part, gay friendship can be seen as a political statement, since at the core of the concept of friendship is the idea of "being oneself" in a cultural context that may not approve of that self. For many people, the need to belong with others in dissent and out of the mainstream is central to the maintenance of self and identity (Rubin 1985). The friendships formed by a shared marginal identity, thus, take on powerful political dimensions as they organize around a stigmatized status to confront the dominant culture in solidarity. Jerome (1984: 698) believes that friendships have such economic and political implications,

Reprinted by permission of the author.

since friendship is best defined as "the cement which binds together people with interests to conserve."

Suttles (1970: 116) argues that:

> The very basic assumption friends must make about one another is that each is going beyond a mere presentation of self in compliance with "social dictates." Inevitably, this makes friendship a somewhat deviant relationship because the surest test of personal disclosure is a violation of the rules of public propriety.

Friendship, according to Suttles (1970), has its own internal order, albeit maintained by the cultural images and situational elements that structure the definitions of friendship. In friendship, people can depart from the routine and display a portion of the self not affected by social control. That is, friendships allow people to go beyond the basic structures of their cultural institutions into an involuntary and uncontrollable exposure of self—to deviate from public propriety (Suttles 1970).

Little (1989) similarly argues that friendship is an escape from the rules and pieties of social life. It's about identity: who one is rather than one's roles and statuses. And the idealism of friendship "lies in its detachment from these [roles and statuses], its creative and spiritual transcendence, its fundamental skepticism as a platform from which to survey the givens of society and culture" (Little 1989: 145). For gay men, these descriptions illustrate the political meaning friendship can have in their lives and their society.

The political dimension of friendship is summed up best by Little (1989: 154–155):

[T]he larger formations of social life—kinship, the law, the economy—must be different where there is, in addition to solidarity and dutiful role-performance, a willingness and capacity for friendship's surprising one-to-one relations, and this difference may be enough to transform social and political life.... Perhaps, finally, it is true that progress in democracy depends on a new generation that will increasingly locate itself in identity-shaping, social, yet personally liberating, friendships.

The traditional, nuclear family has been the dominant model for political relations and has structured much of the legal and social norms of our culture. People have often been judged by their family ties and history. But as the family becomes transformed into other arrangements, so do the political and social institutions of society. For example, the emerging concept of "domestic partnerships" has affected a variety of organizations, including insurance companies, city governments, private industry, and religious institutions (Task Force on Family Diversity final report 1988).

For many gay people, the "friends as family" model is a political statement, going beyond the practicality of developing a surrogate family in times of needed social support. It is also a way of refocusing the economic and political agenda to include nontraditional family structures composed of both romantic and nonromantic nonkin relationships.

In part, this has happened by framing the discussions in terms of gender roles. The women's movement and the emerging men's movement have highlighted the negative political implications of defining gender roles according to traditional cultural norms or limiting them to biological realities. The gay movement, in turn, has often been one source for redefining traditional gender roles and sexuality. So, for example, when gay men exhibit more disclosing and emotional interactions with other men, it demonstrates the limitations of male gender roles typically enacted among many heterosexual male friends. By calling attention to the impact of homophobia on heterosexual men's lives, gay men's friendships illustrate the potentiality for expressive intimacy among all men.

Thus, the assumptions that biology and/or socialization have inevitably constrained men from having the kinds of relationships and intimacies women often typically have can be called into question. This questioning of the dominant construction of gender roles is in itself a sociopolitical act with major implications on the legal, religious, and economic order.

White (1983:16) also sees how gay people's lives can lead to new modes of behavior in the society at large:

> In the case of gays, our childlessness, our minimal responsibilities, the fact that our unions are not consecrated, even our very retreat into gay ghettos for protection and freedom: all of these objective conditions have fostered a style in which we may be exploring, even in spite of our conscious intentions, things as they will someday be for the heterosexual majority. In that world (as in the gay world already), love will be built on esteem rather than passion or convention, sex will be more playful or fantastic or artistic than marital—and friendship will be elevated into the supreme consolation for this continuing tragedy, human existence.

If, as White and others have argued, gay culture in the post-Stonewall, sexual liberation years of the 1970s was characterized by a continuous fluidity between what constituted a friend, a sexual partner, and a lover, then we need to acknowledge the AIDS decade of the 1980s as a source for restructuring of gay culture and the reorganization of sexuality and friendship. If indeed gay people (and men in particular) have focused attention on developing monogamous sexual partnerships, what then becomes the role of sexuality in the initiation and development of casual or close friendships? Clearly, gay culture is not a static phenomenon, unaffected by the larger social order. Certainly, as the moral order in the AIDS years encourages the re-establishment of more traditional relationships, the implications for the ways sexuality and friendships are organized similarly change.

Friends become more important as primary sources of social and emotional support when illness strikes; friendship becomes institutionally organized as "brunch buddies" dating services or "AIDS buddies" assistance groups; and self-help groups emerge centering on how to make and keep new friends without having "compulsive sex." While AIDS may have transformed some of the meanings and role of friendships in gay men's lives from the politicalization of sexuality and friendship during the post-Stonewall 1970s, the newer meanings of gay friendships, in turn, may be having some effect on the culture's definitions of friendships.

Interestingly, the mythical images of friendships were historically more male-dominated: bravery, loyalty, duty, and heroism (see Sapadin 1988). This explained why women were typically assumed incapable of having true friendships. But today, the images of true friendship are often expressed in terms of women's traits: intimacy, trust, caring, and nurturing, thereby excluding the more traditional men from true friendship. However, gay men appear to be at the forefront of establishing the possibility of men overcoming their male socialization stereotypes and restructuring their friendships in terms of the more contemporary (i.e., "female") attributes of emotional intimacy.

To do this at a wider cultural level involves major sociopolitical shifts in how men's roles are structured and organized. Friendships between men in terms of intimacy and emotional support inevitably introduce questions about homosexuality. As Rubin (1985: 103) found in her interviews with men: "The association of friendship with homosexuality is so common among men." For women, there is a much longer history of close connections with other women, so that the separation of the emotional from the erotic is more easily made.

Lehne (1989) has argued that homophobia has limited the discussion of loving male relationships and has led to the denial by men of the real importance of their friendships with other men. In addition, "the open expression of emotion and affection by men is limited by homophobia.... The expression of more tender emotions among men is thought to be characteristic only of homosexuals" (Lehne 1989: 426). So men are raised in a culture with a mixed message: strive for healthy, emotionally intimate friendships, but if you appear too intimate with another man you might be negatively labelled homosexual.

This certainly wasn't always the case. As a good illustration of the social construction of masculinity, friendship, and sexuality, one need only look to the changing definitions and concepts surrounding same-sex friendship during the nineteenth century (see Smith-Rosenberg 1975; Rotundo 1989). Romantic friendships could be erotic but not sexual, since sex was linked to reproduction. Because reproduction was not possible between two women or two men, the close relationship was not interpreted as being a sexual one:

> Until the 1880s, most romantic friendships were thought to be devoid of sexual content. Thus a woman or man could write of affectionate desire for a loved one of the same gender without causing an eyebrow to be raised (D'Emilio and Freedman 1988: 121).

However, as same-sex relationships became medicalized and stigmatized in the late nineteenth century, "the labels 'congenital inversion' and 'perversion' were applied not only to male sexual acts, but to sexual or romantic unions between women, as well as those between men" (D'Emilio and Freedman, 1988: 122). Thus, the twentieth century is an anomaly in its promotion of female equality, the encouragement of male–female friendships, and its suspicion of intense emotional friendships between men (Richards 1987). Yet, in ancient Greece and the medieval days of chivalry, comradeship, virtue, patriotism, and heroism were all associated with close male friendship. Manly love, as it was often called, was a central part of the definition of manliness (Richards 1987).

It is through the contemporary gay, women's, and men's movements that these twentieth century constructions of gender are being questioned. And at the core is the association of close male friendships with negative images of homosexuality. Thus, how gay men structure their emotional lives and friendships can affect the social and emotional lives of all men and women. This is the political power and potential of gay friendships.

References

D'Emilio, John, and Freedman, Estelle. (1988). *Intimate Matters: A History of Sexuality in America*. New York: Harper & Row.

Jerome, Dorothy. (1984). Good company: The sociological implications of friendship. *Sociological Review*, 32(4), 696–718.

Lehne, Gregory K. (1989 [1980]). Homophobia among men: Supporting and defining the male role. In M. Kimmel and M. Messner (Eds.), *Men's Lives* (pp. 416–429). New York: Macmillan.

Little, Graham. (1989). Freud, friendship, and politics. In R. Porter and S. Tomaselli (Eds.), *The Dialectics of Friendship* (pp. 143–158). London: Routledge.

Mordden, Ethan. (1986). *Buddies*. New York: St. Martin's Press.

Richards, Jeffrey. (1987). "Passing the love of women": Manly love and Victorian society. In J. A. Mangan and J. Walvin (Eds.), *Manliness and Morality: Middle-Class Masculinity in Britain and America (1800–1940)* (pp. 92–122). Manchester, England: Manchester University Press.

Rotundo, Anthony. (1989). Romantic friendships: Male intimacy and middle-class youth in the northern United States, 1800–1900. *Journal of Social History*, 23(1), 1–25.

Rubin, Lillian. (1985). *Just Friends: The Role of Friendship in Our Lives*. New York: Harper & Row.

Sapadin, Linda. (1988). Friendship and gender: Perspectives of professional men and women. *Journal of Social and Personal Relationships*, 5(4), 387–403.

Smith-Rosenberg, Carroll. (1975). The female world of love and ritual: Relations between women in nineteenth-century America. *Signs*, 1(1): 1–29.

Suttles, Gerald. (1970). Friendship as a social institution. In G. McCall, M. McCall, N. Denzin, G. Suttles, and S. Kurth, *Social Relationships* (pp. 95–135). Chicago: Aldine.

Task Force on Family Diversity. (1988). *Strengthening Families: A Model for Community Action*. City of Los Angeles.

Wasserstein, Wendy. (1990). *The Heidi Chronicles*. San Diego: Harcourt, Brace, Jovanovich.

White, Edmund. (1983). Paradise found: Gay men have discovered that there is friendship after sex. *Mother Jones*, June, 10–16.

Men on Rape

Tim Beneke

Rape may be America's fastest growing violent crime; no one can be certain because it is not clear whether more rapes are being committed or reported. It *is* clear that violence against women is widespread and fundamentally alters the meaning of life for women; that sexual violence is encouraged in a variety of ways in American culture; and that women are often blamed for rape.

Consider some statistics:

- In a random sample of 930 women, sociologist Diana Russell found that 44 percent had survived either rape or attempted rape. Rape was defined as sexual intercourse physically forced upon the woman, or coerced by threat of bodily harm, or forced upon the woman when she was helpless (asleep, for example). The survey included rape and attempted rape in marriage in its calculations. (Personal communication)
- In a September 1980 survey conducted by *Cosmopolitan* magazine to which over 106,000 women anonymously responded, 24 percent had been raped at least once. Of these, 51 percent had been raped by friends, 37 percent by strangers, 18 percent by relatives, and 3 percent by husbands. 10 percent of the women in the survey had been victims of incest. 75 percent of the women had been "bullied into making love." Writer Linda Wolfe, who reported on the survey, wrote in reference to such bullying: "Though such harassment stops short of rape, readers reported that it was nearly as distressing."

From *Men on Rape* by Timothy Beneke. Copyright © 1982 by Timothy Beneke. Reprinted by permission of St. Martin's Press, LLC.

- An estimated 2–3 percent of all men who rape outside of marriage go to prison for their crimes.[1]
- The F.B.I. estimates that if current trends continue, one woman in four will be sexually assaulted in her lifetime.[2]
- An estimated 1.8 million women are battered by their spouses each year.[3] In extensive interviews with 430 battered women, clinical psychologist Lenore Walker, author of *The Battered Woman*, found that 59.9 percent had also been raped (defined as above) by their spouses. Given the difficulties many women had in admitting they had been raped, Walker estimates the figure may well be as high as 80 or 85 percent (personal communication). If 59.9 percent of the 1.8 million women battered each year are also raped, then a million women may be raped in marriage each year. And a significant number are raped in marriage without being battered.
- Between one in two and one in ten of all rapes are reported to the police.[4]
- Between 300,000 and 500,000 women are raped each year outside of marriage.[5]

What is often missed when people contemplate statistics on rape is the effect of the *threat* of sexual violence on women. I have asked women repeatedly, "How would your life be different if rape were suddenly to end?" (Men may learn a lot by asking this question of women to whom they are close.) The threat of rape is an assault upon the meaning of the world; it alters the feel of the human condition. Surely any attempt to comprehend the lives of women that fails to take issues of violence against women into account is misguided.

Through talking to women, I learned: *The threat of rape alters the meaning and feel of the night.* Observe how your body feels, how the night feels, when you're in fear. The constriction in your chest, the vigilance in your eyes, the rubber in your legs. What do the stars look like? How does the moon present itself? What is the difference between walking late at night in the dangerous part of a city and walking late at night in the country, or safe suburbs? When I try to imagine what the threat of rape must do to the night, I think of the stalked, adrenalated feeling I get walking late at night in parts of certain American cities. Only, I remind myself, it is a fear different from any I have known, a fear of being raped.

It is night half the time. If the threat of rape alters the meaning of the night, it must alter the meaning and pace of the day, one's relation to the passing and organization of time itself. For some women, the threat of rape at night turns their cars into armored tanks, their solitude into isolation. And what must the space inside a car or an apartment feel like if the space outside is menacing?

I was running late one night with a close woman friend through a path in the woods on the outskirts of a small university town. We had run several miles and were feeling a warm, energized serenity.

"How would you feel if you were alone?" I asked.

"Terrified!" she said instantly.

"Terrified that there might be a man out there?" I asked, pointing to the surrounding moonlit forest, which had suddenly been transformed into a source of terror.

"Yes."

Another woman said, "I know what I can't do and I've completely internalized what I can't do. I've built a viable life that basically involves never leaving my apartment at night unless I'm directly going some place to meet somebody. It's unconsciously built into what it occurs to women to do." When one is raised without freedom, one may not recognize its absence.

The threat of rape alters the meaning and feel of nature. Everyone has felt the psychic nurturance of nature. Many women are being deprived of that nurturance, especially in wooded areas near cities. They are deprived either because they cannot experience nature in solitude because of threat, or because, when they do choose solitude in nature, they must cope with a certain subtle but nettlesome fear.

Women need more money because of rape and the threat of rape makes it harder for women to earn money. It's simple: if you don't feel safe walking at night, or riding public transportation, you need a car. And it is less practicable to live in cheaper, less secure, and thus more dangerous neighborhoods if the ordinary threat of violence that men experience, being mugged, say, is compounded by the threat of rape. By limiting mobility at night, the threat of rape limits where and when one is able to work, thus making it more difficult to earn money. An obvious bind: women need more money because of rape, and have fewer job opportunities because of it.

The threat of rape makes women more dependent on men (or other women). One woman said: "If there were no rape I wouldn't have to play games with men for their protection." The threat of rape falsifies, mystifies, and confuses relations between men and women. If there were no rape, women would simply not need men as much, wouldn't need them to go places with at night, to feel safe in their homes, for protection in nature.

The threat of rape makes solitude less possible for women. Solitude, drawing strength from being alone, is difficult if being alone means being afraid. To be afraid is to be in need, to experience a lack; the threat of rape creates a lack. Solitude requires relaxation; if you're afraid, you can't relax.

The threat of rape inhibits a woman's expressiveness. "If there were no rape," said one woman, "I could dress the way I wanted and walk the way I wanted and not feel self-conscious about the responses of men. I could be friendly to people. I wouldn't have to wish I was ugly. I wouldn't have to make myself small when I got on the bus. I wouldn't have to respond to verbal abuse from men by remaining silent. I could respond in kind."

If a woman's basic expressiveness is inhibited, her sexuality, creativity, and delight in life must surely be diminished.

The threat of rape inhibits the freedom of the eye. I know a married couple who live in Manhattan. They are both artists, both acutely sensitive and responsive to the visual world. When they walk separately in the city, he has more freedom to look than she does. She must control her eye movements lest they inadvertently meet the glare of some importunate man. What, who, and how she sees are restricted by the threat of rape.

The following exercise is recommended for men.

> Walk down a city street. Pay a lot of attention to your clothing; make sure your pants are zipped, shirt tucked in, buttons done. Look straight ahead. Every time a man walks past you, avert your eyes and make your face expressionless. Most women learn to go through this act each time we leave our houses. It's a way to avoid at least some of the encounters we've all had with strange men who decided we looked available.[6]

To relate aesthetically to the visual world involves a certain playfulness, spirit of spontaneous exploration. The tense vigilance that accompanies fear inhibits that spontaneity. The world is no longer yours to look at when you're afraid.

I am aware that all culture is, in part, restriction, that there are places in America where hardly anyone is safe (though men are safer than women virtually everywhere), that there are many ways to enjoy life, that some women may not be so restricted, that there exist havens, whether psychic, geographical, economic, or class. But they are *havens*, and as such, defined by threat.

Above all, I trust my experience: no woman could have lived the life I've lived the last few years. If suddenly I were restricted by the threat of rape, I would feel a deep, inexorable depression. And it's not just rape; it's harassment, battery, Peeping Toms, anonymous phone calls, exhibitionism, intrusive stares, fondlings—all contributing to an atmosphere of intimidation in women's lives. And I have only scratched the surface; it would take many carefully crafted short stories to begin to express what I have only hinted at in the last few pages. I have not even touched upon what it might mean for a woman to be sexually assaulted. Only women can speak to that. Nor have I suggested how the threat of rape affects marriage.

Rape and the threat of rape pervade the lives of women, as reflected in some popular images of our culture.

"She Asked for It"—Blaming the Victim[7]

Many things may be happening when a man blames a woman for rape.

First, in all cases where a woman is said to have asked for it, her appearance and behavior are taken as a form of speech. "Actions speak louder than words" is a widely held belief; the woman's actions—her appearance may be taken as action—are given greater emphasis than her words; an interpretation alien to the woman's intentions is given to her actions. A logical extension of "she asked for it" is the idea that she wanted what happened to happen; if she wanted it to happen, she *deserved* for it to happen. Therefore, the man is not to be blamed. "She asked for it" can mean either that she was consenting to have sex and was not really raped, or that she was in fact raped but somehow she really deserved it. "If you ask for it, you deserve it," is a widely held notion. If I ask you to beat me up and you beat me up, I still don't deserve to be beaten up. So even if the notion that women asked to be raped had some basis in reality, which it doesn't, on its own terms it makes no sense.

Second, a mentality exists that says: a woman who assumes freedoms normally restricted to a man (like going out alone at night) and is raped is doing the same thing as a woman who goes out in the rain without an umbrella and catches a cold. Both are considered responsible for what happens to them. That men will rape is taken to be a legitimized given, part of nature, like rain or snow. The view reflects a massive abdication of responsibility for rape on the part of men. It is so much easier to think of rape as natural than to acknowledge one's part in it. So long as rape is regarded as natural, women will be blamed for rape.

A third point. The view that it is natural for men to rape is closely connected to the view of women as commodities. If a woman's body is regarded as a valued commodity by men, then of course, if you leave a valued commodity where it can be taken, it's just human nature for men to take it. If you left your stereo out on the sidewalk, you'd be asking for it to get stolen. Someone will just take it. (And how often men speak of rape as "going out and *taking* it.") If a woman walks the streets at night, she's leaving a valued commodity, her body, where it can be taken. So long as women are regarded as commodities, they will be blamed for rape.

Which brings us to a fourth point. "She asked for it" is inseparable from a more general "psychology of the dupe." If I use bad judgment and fail to read the small print in a contract and later get taken advantage of, "screwed" (or "fucked over"), then I deserve what I get; bad judgment makes me liable. Analogously, if a woman trusts a man and goes to his apartment, or accepts a ride hitchhiking, or goes out on a date and is raped, she's a dupe and deserves what she gets. "He didn't *really* rape her" goes the mentality—"he merely took advantage of her." And in America it's okay for people to take advantage of each other, even expected and praised. In fact, you're considered dumb and foolish if you don't take advantage of other people's bad judgment. And so, again, by treating them as dupes, rape will be blamed on women.

Fifth, if a woman who is raped is judged attractive by men, and particularly if she dresses to look attractive, then the mentality exists that she attacked him with her weapon so, of course, he counter-attacked with his. The preview to a popular movies states: "She was the victim of her own *provocative beauty*." Provocation: "There is a line which, if crossed, will *set me off* and I will lose control and no longer be responsible for my behavior. If you punch me in the nose then, of course, I will not be responsible for what happens: you will have provoked a fight. If you dress, talk, move, or act a certain way, you will have provoked me to rape. If your appearance *stuns* me, *strikes* me, *ravishes* me, *knocks me out*, etc., then I will not be held responsible for what happens; you will have asked for it." The notion that sexual feeling makes one helpless is part of a cultural abdication of responsibility for sexuality. So long as a woman's appearance is viewed as a weapon and sexual feeling is believed to make one helpless, women will be blamed for rape.

Sixth, I have suggested that men sometimes become obsessed with images of women, that images become a substitute for sexual feeling, that sexual feeling becomes externalized and out of control and is given an undifferentiated identity in the appearance of women's bodies. It is a process of projection in which one blurs one's own desire with her imagined, projected desire. If a woman's attractiveness is taken to signify one's own lust and a woman's lust, then when an "attractive" woman is raped, some men may think she wanted sex. Since they perceive their own lust in part projected onto the woman, they disbelieve women who've been raped. So long as men project their own sexual desires onto women, they will blame women for rape.

And seventh, what are we to make of the contention that women in dating situations say "no" initially to sexual overtures from men as a kind of pose, only to give in later, thus revealing their true intentions? And that men are thus confused and incredulous when women are raped because in their sexual experience women can't be believed? I doubt that this has much to do with men's perceptions of rape. I don't know to what extent women actually "say no and mean yes"; certainly it is a common theme in male folklore. I have spoken to a couple of women who went through periods when they wanted to be sexual but were afraid to be, and often rebuffed initial sexual advances only to give in later. One point is clear: the ambivalence women may feel about having sex is closely tied to the inability of men to fully accept them as sexual beings. Women have been traditionally punished for being openly and freely sexual; men are praised for it. And if many men think of sex as achievement of possession of a valued commodity, or aggressive degradation, then women have every reason to feel and act ambivalent.

These themes are illustrated in an interview I conducted with a 23-year-old man who grew up in Pittsburgh and works as a file clerk in the financial district of San Francisco. Here's what he said:

"Where I work it's probably no different from any other major city in the U.S. The women dress up in high heels, and they wear a lot of makeup, and they just look really *hot* and really sexy, and how can somebody who has a healthy sex drive not feel lust for them when you see them? I feel lust for them, but I don't think I could find it in me to overpower someone and rape them. But I definitely get the feeling that I'd like to rape a girl. I don't know if the actual act of rape would be satisfying, but the *feeling* is satisfying.

"These women look so good, and they kiss ass of the men in the three-piece suits who are *big* in the corporation, and most of them relate to me like 'Who are *you*? Who are *you* to even *look* at?' They're snobby and they condescend to me, and I resent it. It would take me a lot longer to get to first base than it would somebody with a three-piece suit who had money. And to me a lot of the men they go out with are superficial assholes who have no real feelings or substance, and are just trying to get ahead and make a lot of money. Another thing that makes me resent these women is thinking, 'How could she want to hang out with somebody like that? What does that make her?'

"I'm a file clerk, which makes me feel like a nebbish, a nerd, like I'm not making it, I'm a failure. But I don't really believe I'm a failure because I know it's just a phase, and I'm just doing it for the money, just to make it through this phase. I catch myself feeling like a failure, but I realize that's ridiculous."

What Exactly Do You Go Through When You See These Sexy, Unavailable Women?

"Let's say I see a woman and she looks really pretty and really clean and sexy, and she's giving off very feminine, sexy vibes. I think, 'Wow, I would love to make love to her,' but I know she's not really interested. It's a tease. A lot of times a woman knows that she's looking really good and she'll use that and flaunt it, and it makes me feel like she's laughing at me and I feel *degraded*.

"I also feel dehumanized, because when I'm being teased I just turn off, I cease to be human. Because if I go with my human emotions I'm going to want to put my arms around her and kiss her, and to do that would be unacceptable. I don't like the feeling that I'm supposed to stand there and take it, and not be able to hug her or kiss her; so I just turn off my emotions. It's a feeling of humiliation, because the woman has forced me to turn off my feelings and react in a way that I really don't want to.

"If I were actually desperate enough to rape somebody, it would be from wanting the person, but it would be a very spiteful thing, just being able to say, 'I have power over you and I can do anything I want with you,' because really I feel that *they* have power over *me* just by their presence. Just the fact that they can come up to me and just melt me and make me feel like a dummy makes me want revenge. They have power over me so I want power over them. . . .

"Society says that you have to have a lot of sex with a lot of different women to be a real man. Well, what happens if you don't? Then what are you? Are you half a man? Are you still a boy? It's ridiculous. You see a whiskey ad with a guy and two women on his arm. The implication is that real men don't have any trouble getting women."

How Does It Make You Feel Toward Women to See All These Sexy Women in Media and Advertising Using Their Looks to Try to Get You to Buy Something?

"It makes me hate them. As a man you're taught that men are more powerful than women, and that men always have the upper hand, and that it's a man's society; but then you see all these women and it makes you think, 'Jesus Christ, if we have all the power how come all the beautiful women are telling us what to buy?' And to be honest, it just makes me hate beautiful women because they're using their power over me. I realize they're being used themselves, and they're doing it for money. In *Playboy* you see all these beautiful women who look so sexy and they'll be giving you all these looks like they want to have sex so bad; but then in reality you know that except for a few nymphomaniacs, they're doing it for the money; so I hate them for being used and for using their bodies in that way.

"In this society, if you ever sit down and realize how manipulated you really are it makes you pissed off—it makes you want to take control. And you've been manipulated by women, and they're a very easy target because they're out walking along the streets, so you can just grab one and say, 'Listen, you're going to do what I want you to do,' and it's an act of revenge against the way you've been manipulated.

"I know a girl who was walking down the street by her house, when this guy jumped her and beat her up and raped her, and she was black and blue and had to go to the hospital. That's beyond me. I can't understand how somebody could do that. If I were going to rape a girl, I wouldn't hurt her. I might *restrain* her, but I wouldn't *hurt* her. . . .

"The whole dating game between men and women also makes me feel degraded. I hate being put in the position of having to initiate a relationship. I've been taught that if you're not aggressive with a woman, then you've blown it. She's not going to jump on *you*, so *you've* got to jump on *her*. I've heard all kinds of stories where the woman says, 'No! No! No!' and they end up making great love. I get confused as hell if a woman pushes me away. Does it mean she's trying to be a nice girl and wants to put up a good appearance, or does it mean she doesn't want anything to do with you? You don't know. Probably a lot of men think that women don't feel like real women unless a man tries to force himself on her, unless she brings out the 'real man,' so to speak, and probably too much of it goes on. It goes on in my head that you're complimenting a woman by actually staring at her or by trying to get into her pants. Lately, I'm realizing that when I stare at women lustfully, they often feel more threatened than flattered."

Notes

1. Such estimates recur in the rape literature. See *Sexual Assault* by Nancy Gager and Cathleen Schurr, Grosset & Dunlap, 1976, or *The Price of Coercive Sexuality* by Clark and Lewis, The Women's Press, 1977.

2. *Uniform Crime Reports*, 1980.

3. See *Behind Closed Doors* by Murray J. Strauss and Richard Gelles, Doubleday, 1979.

4. See Gager and Schurr (above) or virtually any book on the subject.

5. Again, see Gager and Schurr, or Carol V. Horos, *Rape*, Banbury Books, 1981.

6. From "Willamette Bridge" in *Body Politics* by Nancy Henley, Prentice-Hall, 1977, p. 144.

7. I would like to thank George Lakoff for this insight.

Rape and the Prison Code

Terry A. Kupers

The prisoner is in "the hole" of a high-security unit in a state prison. He is a slight, gay man in his early twenties who does not display any of the posturing and bravado that is characteristic of so many prisoners. Convicted of drug dealing, he was consigned to a high-security prison because he carried a gun. But in prison, without a gun, his physical size and inexperience in hand-to-hand combat make him an easy mark. He explains to me that, since the time he arrived at the prison, he has been brutalized and raped repeatedly. His overt homosexuality seems to pose a threat to tough prisoners, and they regularly single him out for abuse. And he was told that, if he snitched to a guard, he would be killed. He tried talking to a seemingly friendly correctional officer about his plight, but the officer only insisted that he reveal the name of the prisoner who had raped him. He seemed more interested in busting a guilty tough than in helping his man figure out a way to be safe "inside."

This prison does not have a protective custody unit, a "safer" cell block where potential victims might be placed for their own protection—a place for child molesters, policemen who are serving time, snitches, and others who would not survive on the main line. After suffering rape after rape and multiple injuries from beatings, this man determined that the best way to stay alive while serving his time was to be locked up in the hole. So he hit a guard and, as predicted, he was placed in solitary confinement. He cries as he tells me in private how lonely he feels and how seriously he is contemplating suicide.

The rate of occurrence of rape behind bars is unknown, because many cases go unreported. The Federal Bureau of Prisons estimates that between 9 and 20 percent of prisoners become victims of sexual assault (Polych, 1992), and Daniel Lockwood (1980) reports that 28 percent of prisoners in two New York prisons report that, while in custody they have been the victims of sexual assault. But these figures do not include the huge number of men who "consent" to having sex with a tougher con or consent to having sex with many other prisoners only because they are very afraid that, if they do not they will be repeatedly beaten or perhaps even killed. In my view, this kind of coerced sex also constitutes rape.

The prevalence of AIDS in prison is also very high, and it is rising (Polych, 1992). Considering how much crime is drug related, this is not surprising. But this problem greatly magnifies the damage done by rape and multiplies the terror connected with sexual assault.

The New Prisoner's Dread

Hans Toch interviewed prisoners who had suffered emotional crises as they entered the prison world and discovered that, in many cases, concerns about the violence of prison initiation rites was a major precipitant of their psychological stress. According to one man, "When you're a new fish you're nothing. So you've got pressure coming from all sides. When you first come in, anyway, their first intention when they look at you is that they're going to make this man my pussy, my girl and shit.... They aggravate you. They

From "Rape and the Prison Code" as it appears in *Prison Masculinities*, edited by Dan Sabo et al. Reprinted by permission of Temple University Press. Copyright © 2001 by Temple University. All rights reserved.

say, 'We're going to test this motherfucker.'" This prisoner assumes, with good reason, that the prisoners aggravate him specifically to lure him to the back of the cell block where they can beat him and sodomize him. "So you come along back from the cell and shit, and you lock in [each prisoner is permitted to remain in his cell and lock the door during certain periods when prisoners are being let out to the day room or the yard] and see these guys, big guys, running down" (1992:82–83).

The Problem with Snitching

For the victim of rape, reporting the assault to security staff is not a simple matter. Even if the victim asks to lock up—to be transferred to a protective custody unit—the perpetrator may retaliate by killing, or by arranging for another prisoner to kill, the snitch. In addition, Toch (1992) describes prisoners' need to appear as "manly men." They must not display any sign of weakness lest other prisoners attack them. According to the code, snitching is the worst offense, but being a punk (the victim of rape or the voluntary passive partner of "butt fucking") or displaying weakness of any kind is not much better—and all are punishable by repeated beatings, rapes, or even death. Moreover, it is not at all clear to the violated male prisoner that the staff will maintain confidentiality, much less protect him if he snitches.

I have spoken to many prisoners who report that, when they have told correctional officers that they were raped, the officers have insisted that they reveal the name of the assailant. The situation is even sadder for the victim who suffers from a serious mental illness and does not really understand the code or the possible ramifications of snitching. These prisoners are especially vulnerable to victimization and rape. And when an officer demands that they give the name of the rapist, they are very likely to comply without realizing that they are violating the code and putting themselves in grave danger. I have talked to several mentally disturbed prisoners who were raped, went to a guard to ask what they should do, and ended up answering the guard's questions about who committed the rape. Once the word gets out that they have snitched, there is no way for the authorities to protect them.

Systemic Factors

Conditions of confinement are very important factors. A recent lawsuit illustrates how overcrowding and relative understaffing can lead to rape. I was asked to give an opinion about a young man who was raped by two gang members in a protective custody unit of a county jail. He was suing the county for not providing adequate protection. I examined the man and reviewed his file, including school reports and past psychiatric records. There seemed to be a pattern of vulnerability. For example, he had on occasion been the victim of mean pranks by classmates who first "suckered" him into engaging in behaviors at school that would lead to punishment and then laughed at him for being stupid enough to give in to their goading only to get caught. This hapless young man was clearly a potential victim. And after examining him, I concluded that he was suffering from severe post-traumatic stress disorder secondary to rape while he was in jail.

How was it possible, in a protective custody unit, for two gang members who had spent many years in prison to rape a vulnerable man who had never been to prison and never committed a violent crime? The victim, who had given the police the names of his accomplices at the time of his arrest, had asked to be placed in the unit because he feared he would be killed if other prisoners found out he had snitched. The two men who raped him, who were bigger and stronger than he was, had been returned from state prison to this jail only because they had to go to court to stand trial for gang-related violence inside prison. But they had been "outed" by their gangs (perhaps they were perceived as snitches). In other words, because they were in trouble with their gangs and therefore in grave danger anywhere in the correctional system, they had been placed in the protective custody unit.

At the time of the rape, a single officer was responsible for observing a day room, a dining area, and two floors of cells with open doors. It was not possible, at any given time, for that officer to observe the entire unit. In fact, the victim told me that the rape took place over a forty-five-minute time span, in a second floor cell, while the officer was in the day room, where she was unable to see inside the cells on the second floor.

The victim should not have been housed with the men who raped him. But in an overcrowded system, it is unlikely that prisoners of different security levels who are identified as being in need of protective custody will be further segregated—staff members are so far behind classifying the new prisoners that the assignment to protective custody is considered classification enough. And this is just one of the many ways that overcrowding can lead to heightened violence and mental decompensation in correctional settings.

The Code

Rape is not an isolated event in prison. It is part of a larger phenomenon: the hierarchical ranking of prisoners by their fighting ability and manliness. Jack Henry Abbott, who has spent most of his teen years and adult life behind bars, describes the process: "This is the way it is done. If you are a man, you must either kill or turn the tables on anyone who propositions you with threats of force. It is the custom among young prisoners. In so doing, it becomes known to all that you are a man, regardless of your youth. I had been trained from a youth spent in gladiator school (juvenile detention hall) for this. It was inevitable then that a youth in an adult penitentiary at some point will have to attack and kill, or else he most certainly will become a punk—even though it may not be well known he is a punk. If he cannot protect himself, someone else will" (1982:94).

The code, with some changes over time, permeates prison culture. Thus, Irwin and Austin point out that, in the first half of the twentieth century, the prisoners essentially operated prisons in the United States. They cooked, served meals, landscaped, performed building maintenance, and worked in prison industries. "Collectively, prisoners developed their own self-contained society, with a pronounced stratification system, a strong convict value system, unique patterns of speech and bodily gestures, and an array of social roles. . . . Importantly, their participation in this world with its own powerful value system, the convict code, gave them a sense of pride and dignity. It was them against what they perceived as a cruel prison system and corrupt society. . . . However, society was more accepting of the ex-convict than it is now and apparently most did not return to prison" (1994:66).

The situation is very different today. The "war on drugs" that rages in the inner cities: society's "law and order" sensibility; harsher sentences, including state and federal "three strikes legislation"; huge racial disparities in arrests and sentencing; the waning of prison rehabilitation programs; massive overcrowding of jails and prisons; racial and gang tensions in prison; and high recidivism rates have combined to change the code significantly. For instance, the prisoners no longer operate the prison, and there is less solidarity among prisoners of different races and ages. Still, some parts of the prison code remain the same.

One commandment continues to stand out: "Thou shalt not snitch!" Snitching can be a capital offense in prison. "And you had better not show any signs of weakness, or else others will pounce on you and rape or kill you!" The rules go on and on. For example, if a weapon is found in a double cell, each of the cellies is interrogated separately and encouraged—better, coerced—to snitch on the other in order to receive a pardon for having the weapon in the cell. In other words, the security officers manipulate the code to put teeth in their interrogations. They know that a prisoner who snitches and beats the rap will be attacked by other prisoners. Staff members use the code to maintain order in the prison.

Prison is an extreme environment. The men have to act tough, lift weights, and be willing to fight to settle grudges. Any sign of weakness leads to being labeled a victim, and weaklings are subject to beatings and sodomy. Of course, in this milieu, prisoners do not talk to each other about their pains, their vulnerabilities, or their neediness—to do so with the wrong man could lead to betrayal and death. Consequently, a lot of men choose to spend their time in their cells. Touring a high-security prison in the middle of the day, one is struck by the large number of prisoners lying in their bunks with the lights out—just trying to "do the time and stay alive."

This aspect of the code is not ironclad. I cite here some of the worst-case scenarios. In fact, in my tours through prisons and my interviews with prisoners, I have been impressed by a certain warmth and friendship in spite of the danger. For example, it is not rare for a prisoner to report that he was only able to survive in prison because another prisoner offered him the support and help he needed.

Politically conscious prisoners and activists in the growing prison movement on the outside are trying to build on the camaraderie and feelings of solidarity among prisoners. The goal is to help all prisoners understand that animosity toward other prisoners is misguided and that they must stand together against their real oppressors. The male dominance hierarchy, interracial animosities, and intergang battles are the obstacles that must be overcome in this organizing and consciousness-raising project.

There is even consensual sex in prison. Many men find partners, have sex as a sexual outlet in an all-male world, and do not consider themselves gay before or after release. Sex between mutually consenting prisoners can be quiet and unproblematic. There is even affection—sometimes great affection—but this kind of innovation in male intimacy does not attract the kind of media attention that rape receives. In contrast, prison rape is not about affection at all. It is about domination. A prisoner is either a "real man" who subdues and rapes an adversary, or he is a "punk."

There are four obvious structural elements of the prison code:

1. There is a hierarchy of domination wherein the toughest and the most dominant men rule those who are less dominant. Of course, the hierarchy does not begin or end with the prisoners. The security officers wield power over the prisoners; the warden dominates the security officers; and at the other end of the hierarchy, more than a few prisoners have been known to rape women or beat them and their children. Every prisoner knows his place in the hierarchy and maintains his place by proving himself when challenged.

2. There is a sharp line between those at the top of the hierarchy, the dominants, and those at the bottom of the heap, the weaklings and punks. The rape victims I have described are at the bottom.

3. The bottom is defined in terms of the feminine. Whether a man is known as a loser, a weakling, a snitch, a faggot, or a punk, he is accused of being less than a man—in other words, a woman. Jean Genet describes a man he knew at Mettray reform school: "Bulkaen, on the other hand, was a little man whom Mettray had turned into a girl for the use of the big shots, and all his gestures were the sign of nostalgia for his plundered, destroyed virility" (1966:144). When one man beats up another and sodomizes him, the message is clear: "I, the dominant man, have the right and the power to use you, the loser, sexually, as if you were a woman and my slave."

4. There is a narrowing of personal possibilities, as if the only way to survive is to conform to the rigid hypermasculine posturings of the prison culture. Sanyika Shakur, also known as Monster Kody Scott, a leader of the Crips of South Central Los Angeles, tells the story of a vicious fight between cell mates that occurred at the beginning of his first prison term. Fat Rat began punching B.T. B.T. tried pleading with Fat Rat to stop; after all, they were both Crips from South Central. Fat Rat would not listen, and the more B.T. pleaded, the more Fat Rat gloried in his dominance—calling B.T. "bitch"

and "pussy" and proceeding to humiliate him. According to Shakur, "Fat Rat, like me, was uncut street, straight out of the bush. The only language Fat Rat knew or respected or could be persuaded by was violence. Everything else was for the weak. Action and more action—anything else paled in comparison" (1993:295).

Notice that, in these four elements, the structure of masculine domination in prison mirrors the outside world. This is why films such as *An Innocent Man* and *The Shawshank Redemption* strike such resonant chords in many free men's minds. In both films a successful, middle-class man is framed for a crime he did not commit, sent to prison, and forced to fight in order to avoid rape. In *An Innocent Man,* Tom Selleck avoids rape by killing another prisoner. Middle-class male viewers shudder as Tim Robbins is repeatedly raped in *The Shawshank Redemption*. Of course, on the outside, especially among middle- and upper-class men, dominance is not based solely on physical prowess or gang affiliation. It depends more on one's level of affluence or status in the corporate world, in academia, or in the professions. And the literal threat of "butt fucking" is not as omnipresent as it is in prison; rape is more of a symbol. (Of course, for women the threat is literal.) Thus, men on the outside keep their cards close to their chests in order to avoid "being shafted" and try to avoid giving other men the impression that they might be womanly or gay. A man needs a friend who will "watch his back." And on the outside, there are women to play the role of underdog, so men can rape and oppress women instead of raping each other. But there is also, just as in prison, the ever-present hierarchy, the sharp line between winners and losers, the perpetual fear of being betrayed or defeated and falling to the bottom of the heap (this is one reason that so many men become workaholics), the castigation of those at the bottom as womanly or queer, and the narrowing and constricting of men's possibilities in the interest of maintaining the image of a "real man."

In prison, the penalty for falling to the bottom of the heap is literal. The trick for someone who is not a tough guy is to find a "third alternative," neither "pitcher" nor "catcher," neither king of the mountain nor bottom of the heap. For example, some frail intellectuals make themselves invaluable to other prisoners by becoming knowledgeable about law and learning their way around the law library. They become immune to gladiatorial battles because they have a commodity to sell—law is an invaluable resource in a correctional setting, where many prisoners are very involved in attempts to win habeas corpus motions and appeals of their convictions—so the prison toughs leave them alone.

There are other ways to create a third alternative. I met a slim, blond, effeminate man in a maximum-security prison in the Midwest. He was wearing a flowing red gown that reached to the floor, and he had a shawl draped across his chest in a way that did not allow assessment of the size of his breasts. He wore makeup and sported a very seductive female pose. He explained that, because he had been beaten and raped several times upon arrival at the prison, he decided to become the "woman" of one prison tough. He performed sexual favors for this one man, so that all other prisoners would leave him alone for fear of retaliation by his "sugar daddy." There was coercion involved, so his sex acts were not exactly performed by mutual consent. But at least there were no more beatings and rapes. Still, the exceptions to the "top dog"/"punk" dichotomy merely serve to prove the general rule of domination.

Isolation

Shakur writes, "Fat Rat had a reputation for being a 'booty bandit,' and thrived on weak men with tight asses" (1993:293). The booty bandit, the rapist on the prowl for potential victims, preys on isolated prisoners. This is one reason that prisoners are so intent on joining a gang or a group that eats together and lifts weights together. The loner is a potential victim, especially if he cannot defend himself. Men who lack social skills, for instance mentally disordered and timid prisoners, are easily victimized. And after they are raped, they keep it secret. The tendency on the part of these prisoners to isolate themselves thus works against their recovery from the violation and the resulting post-traumatic stress disorder.

Shame plays a big part not only in victims' refusal to report rapes but also in maintaining their isolation. When a boy is shamed, for instance by an alcoholic father or critical mother, he goes to his room. He does not seek the support of other members of the family. In the school yard, the boy who loses a fight or "chickens out" does not seek the support of his friends to heal his wounds; he keeps to himself, and the wounds fester. Shame leads to isolation, and in isolation there is little hope of transcending shame. In prison, it can be dangerous to speak frankly to others about one's pains—again, the code. After being defeated in a fight, especially if a man is raped, he keeps to himself; perhaps he remains in his cell all day in the dark. But this is precisely the kind of response that deepens depression or leads to chronic post-traumatic stress disorder (Pelka, 1993).

It is not only the individual's shame that makes life in prison unbearable. There is also the prisoners' contempt for a weakling. If a man tries to take his own life and fails, and there are visible scars on his wrist or neck, he is labeled a weakling and is likely to be victimized and possibly raped. Many prisoners suffering from mental disorders are raped.

The code in prison is based on intimidation. Positive outlets for the need to feel powerful are scarce. The demeaned of the land are willing to demean those who are even lower in the hierarchy than they are. And even some of the most demeaned of the prisoners, when eventually they leave prison, find themselves acting abusively toward others.

References

Abbott, Jack Henry. 1982. *In the Belly of the Beast: Letters from Prison.* New York: Vintage.

Genet, Jean. 1966. *Miracle of the Rose.* New York: Grove Press.

Irwin, John, and James Austin. 1994. *It's about Time: America's Imprisonment Binge.* Belmont, Calif.: Wadsworth.

Lockwood, Daniel. 1980. *Prison Sexual Violence.* New York: Elsevier Horth Holland.

Pelka, Fred. 1993. "Raped: A Male Survivor Breaks His Silence." *Changing Men* 25 (Winter/Spring): 41–44.

Polych, C. 1992. "Punishment within Punishment: The AIDS Epidemic in North American Prisons." *Men's Studies Review* 9 (1): 13–17. Quoting T. Hammet, *Update: AIDS in Correctional Facilities* (Washington, D.C.: National Institute of Justice, 1989).

Shakur, Sanyika. 1993. *Monster: The Autobiography of an L.A. Gang Member.* New York: Atlantic Monthly Press.

Toch, Hans. 1992. *Mosaic of Despair: Human Breakdowns in Prison.* Washington, D.C.: American Psychological Association.

PART SEVEN

Male Sexualities

How do many men learn to desire women? What are men thinking about when they are sexual with women? Are gay men more sexually promiscuous than straight men? Are gay men more obsessed with demonstrating their masculinity than straight men, or are they likely to be more "effeminate"? Recent research indicates that there are no simple answers to these questions. It is increasingly clear, however, that men's sexuality, whether homosexual, bisexual, or heterosexual, is perceived as an experience of their gender.

Since there is no anticipatory socialization for homosexuality and bisexuality, future straight and gay men receive the same socialization as boys. As a result, sexuality as a gender enactment is often a similar internal experience for all men. Early socialization teaches us—through masturbation, locker-room conversations, sex-ed classes and conversations with parents, and the tidbits that boys will pick up from various media—that sex is private, pleasurable, guilt provoking, exciting, and phallocentric, and that orgasm is the goal toward which sexual experience is oriented.

The articles in this section explore how male sexualities express the issues of masculinity. Michael Messner describes how he "became" 100 percent straight, and M. Rochlin's questionnaire humorously challenges us to question the normative elements of heterosexuality. Robert Staples, Tomas Almaguer, and Susan Cochran and Vickie Mays examine elements of black male and gay male sexuality, exploring the intersection among sexuality, race and ethnicity, and gender. Julia O'Connell Davidson and Jacqueline Sanchez Taylor examine the recent phenomenon of sex tourism, and raise important questions about masculinity on the one hand and global sex trafficking, globalization, and consumer culture on the other.

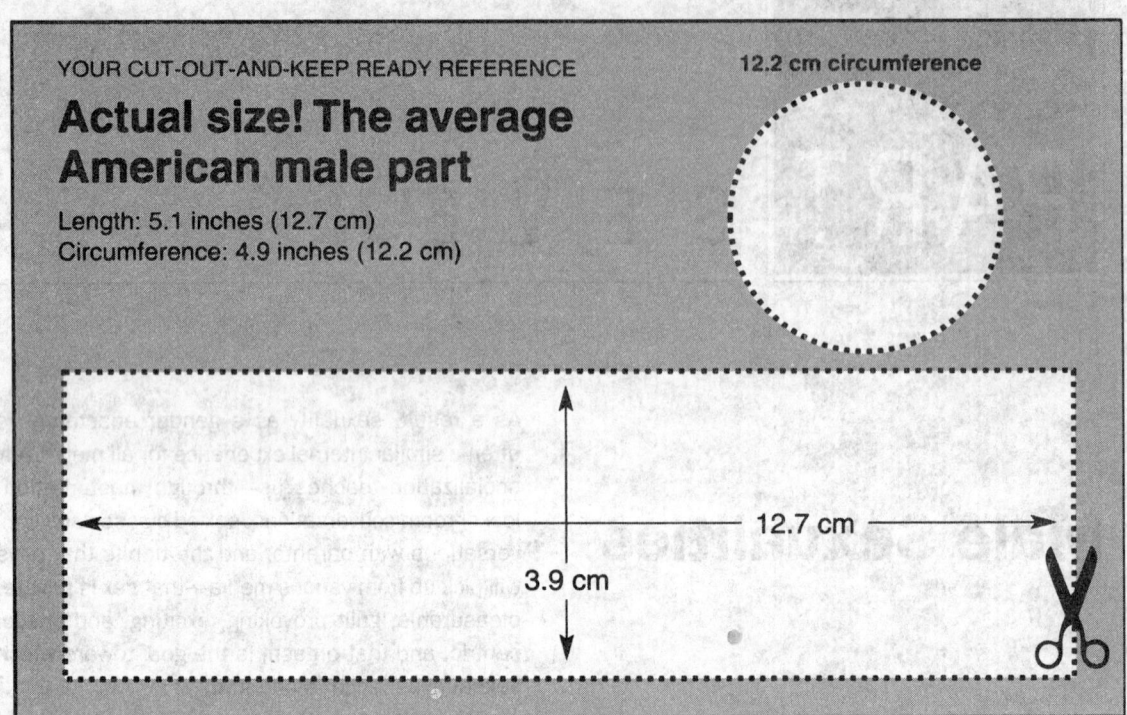

ARTICLE 36

Michael A. Messner

Becoming 100 Percent Straight

In 1995, as part of my job as the President of the North American Society for the Sociology of Sport, I needed to prepare an hour-long presidential address for the annual meeting of some 200 people. This presented a challenge to me: how might I say something to my colleagues that was interesting, at least somewhat original, and above all, not boring. Students may think that their professors are especially dull in the classroom but, believe me, we are usually much worse at professional meetings. For some reason, many of us who are able to speak to our classroom students in a relaxed manner, using relatively jargon-free language, seem to become robots, dryly reading our papers—packed with impressively unclear jargon—to our yawning colleagues.

Since I desperately wanted to avoid putting 200 sport studies scholars to sleep, I decided to deliver a talk which I entitled "Studying up on sex." The title, which certainly did get my colleagues' attention, was intended as a play on words, a double entendre. "Studying up" has one generally recognizable colloquial meaning, but in sociology it has another. It refers to studying "up" in the power structure. Sociologists have perhaps most often studied "down"—studying the poor, the blue- or pink-collar workers, the "nuts, sluts and perverts," the incarcerated. The idea of "studying up" rarely occurs to sociologists unless and until we live in a time when those who are "down" have organized movements that challenge the institutional privileges of elites. For example, in the wake of labor movements, some sociologists like C. Wright Mills studied up on corporate elites. Recently, in the wake of racial and ethnic civil rights movements, some scholars like Ruth Frankenberg have begun to study the social meanings of "whiteness." Much of my research, inspired by feminism, has involved a studying up on the social construction of masculinity in sport. Studying up, in these cases, has raised some fascinating new and important questions about the workings of power in society.

However, I realized that when it comes to understanding the social and interpersonal dynamics of sexual orientation in sport we have barely begun to scratch the surface of a very complex issue. Although sport studies have benefited from the work of scholars such as Helen Lenskyj (1986, 1997), Brian Pronger (1990), and others who have delineated the experiences of lesbians and gay men in sports, there has been very little extension of their insights into a consideration of the social construction of heterosexuality in sport. In sport, just as in the larger society, we seem obsessed with asking "how do people become gay?" Imbedded in this question is the assumption that people who identify as heterosexual, or "straight," require no explanation, since they are simply acting out the "natural" or "normal" sexual orientation. We seem to be saying that the "sexual deviants" require explanation, while the experience of heterosexuals, because we are considered normal, seems to require no critical examination or discussion. But I knew that a closer look at the development of sexual orientation or sexual identity reveals an extremely complex process. I decided to challenge myself and my colleagues by arguing that although we have begun to "study up" on corporate elites in sport, on whiteness, on

From *Inside Sports*, Jay Coakley and Peter Donnelly (eds.), pp. 104–110, Routledge Copyright © 1999. Reprinted by permission.

masculinity, it is now time to extend that by studying up on heterosexuality.

But in the absence of systematic research on this topic, where could I start? How could I explore, raise questions about, and begin to illuminate the social construction of heterosexuality for my colleagues? Fortunately, for the previous two years I had been working with a group of five men (three of whom identified as heterosexual, two as gay) mutually to explore our own biographies in terms of the earlier bodily experiences that helped to shape our gender and sexual identities. We modeled our project after that of a German group of feminist women, led by Frigga Haug, who created a research method which they call "memory work." In short, the women would mutually choose a body part, such as "hair," and each would then write a short story based on a particularly salient childhood memory that related to their hair (for example, being forced by parents to cut one's hair, deciding to straighten one's curly hair in order to look more like other girls, etc.). Then the group would read all of the stories and discuss them one by one in the hope of gaining a more general understanding of, and raising new questions about, the social construction of "femininity." What resulted from this project was a fascinating book called *Female Sexualization* (Haug 1987), which my men's group used as the inspiration for our project.

As a research method, memory work is anything but conventional. Many sociologists would argue that this is not really a "research method" at all. The information that emerges from the project cannot be used very confidently as a generalizable "truth," and in this sort of project the researcher is simultaneously part of what is being studied. How, my more scientifically oriented colleagues might ask, is the researcher to maintain his or her objectivity? My answer is that in this kind of project objectivity is not the point. In fact, the strength of this sort of research is the depth of understanding that might be gained through a systematic group analysis of one's experience, one's subjective orientation to social processes. A clear understanding of the subjective aspect of social life—one's bodily feelings, emotions, and reactions to others—is an invaluable window that allows us to see and ask new sociological questions about group interaction and social structure. In short, group memory work can provide an important, productive, and fascinating insight on social reality, though not a complete (or completely reliable) picture.

As I pondered the lack of existing research on the social construction of heterosexuality in sport, I decided to draw on one of my own stories from my memory work in the men's group. Some of my most salient memories of embodiment are sports memories. I grew up as the son of a high school coach, and I eventually played point guard on my dad's team. In what follows, I juxtapose my story with that of a gay former Olympic athlete, Tom Waddell, whom I had interviewed several years earlier for a book on the lives of male athletes (Messner and Sabo 1994).

Many years ago I read some psychological studies that argued that even for self-identified heterosexuals it is a natural part of their development to have gone through "bisexual" or even "homosexual" stages of life. When I read this, it seemed theoretically reasonable, but did not ring true in my experience. I have always been, I told myself, 100 percent heterosexual! The group process of analyzing my own autobiographical stories challenged the concept I had developed of myself, and also shed light on the way in which the institutional context of sport provided a context for the development of my definition of myself as "100 percent straight." Here is one of the stories:

> When I was in the 9th grade, I played on a "D" basketball team, set up especially for the smallest of high school boys. Indeed, though I was pudgy with baby fat, I was a short 5'2", still prepubescent with no facial hair and a high voice that I artificially tried to lower. The first day of practice, I was immediately attracted to a boy I'll call Timmy, because he looked like the boy who played in the *Lassie* TV show. Timmy was short, with a high voice, like me. And like me, he had no facial hair yet. Unlike me, he was very skinny. I liked Timmy right away, and soon we

were together a lot. I noticed things about him that I didn't notice about other boys: he said some words a certain way, and it gave me pleasure to try to talk like him. I remember liking the way the light hit his boyish, nearly hairless body. I thought about him when we weren't together. He was in the school band, and at the football games, I'd squint to see where he was in the mass of uniforms. In short, though I wasn't conscious of it at the time, I was infatuated with Timmy—I had a crush on him. Later that basketball season, I decided—for no reason that I could really articulate then—that I hated Timmy. I aggressively rejected him, began to make fun of him around other boys. He was, we all agreed, a geek. He was a faggot.

Three years later, Timmy and I were both on the varsity basketball team, but had hardly spoken a word to each other since we were freshman. Both of us now had lower voices, had grown to around six feet tall, and we both shaved, at least a bit. But Timmy was a skinny, somewhat stigmatized reserve on the team, while I was the team captain and starting point guard. But I wasn't so happy or secure about this. I'd always dreamed of dominating games, of being the hero. Halfway through my senior season, however, it became clear that I was not a star, and I figured I knew why. I was not aggressive enough.

I had always liked the beauty of the fast break, the perfectly executed pick and roll play between two players, and especially the long twenty-foot shot that touched nothing but the bottom of the net. But I hated and feared the sometimes brutal contact under the basket. In fact, I stayed away from the rough fights for rebounds and was mostly a perimeter player, relying on my long shots or my passes to more aggressive teammates under the basket. But now it became apparent to me that time was running out in my quest for greatness: I needed to change my game, and fast. I decided one day before practice that I was gonna get aggressive. While practicing one of our standard plays, I passed the ball to a teammate, and then ran to the spot at which I was to set a pick on a defender. I knew that one could sometimes get away with setting a face-up screen on a player, and then as he makes contact with you, roll your back to him and plant your elbow hard in his stomach. The beauty of this move is that your own body "roll" makes the elbow look like an accident. So I decided to try this move. I approached the defensive player, Timmy, rolled, and planted my elbow deeply into his solar plexus. Air exploded audibly from Timmy's mouth, and he crumbled to the floor momentarily.

Play went on as though nothing has happened, but I felt bad about it. Rather than making me feel better, it made me feel guilty and weak. I had to admit to myself why I'd chosen Timmy as the target against whom to test out my new aggression. He was the skinniest and weakest player on the team.

At the time, I hardly thought about these incidents, other than to try to brush them off as incidents that made me feel extremely uncomfortable. Years later, I can now interrogate this as a sexual story, and as a gender story unfolding within the context of the heterosexualized and masculinized institution of sport. Examining my story in light of research conducted by Alfred Kinsey a half-century ago, I can recognize in myself what Kinsey saw as a very common fluidity and changeability of sexual desire over the life course. Put simply, Kinsey found that large numbers of adult, "heterosexual" men had previously, as adolescents and young adults, experienced sexual desire for males. A surprisingly large number of these men had experienced sexual contact to the point of orgasm with other males during adolescence or early adulthood. Similarly, my story invited me to consider what is commonly called the "Freudian theory of bisexuality." Sigmund Freud shocked the post-Victorian world by suggesting that all people go through a stage, early in life, when they are attracted to people of the same sex.[1] Adult experiences, Freud argued, eventually led most people to shift their sexual desire to what he called an appropriate "love object"—a person of the opposite sex. I also considered my experience in light of what lesbian feminist author Adrienne Rich called the institution of compulsory heterosexuality. Perhaps the extremely high levels of homophobia that are often endemic in boys' and men's organized sports led me to deny and repress my own homoerotic desire through a direct and overt rejection of Timmy, through homophobic banter with male peers, and the resultant stigmatization of the feminized Timmy. Eventually I considered my experience in the light of what radical theorist Herbert Marcuse called the sublimation of homoerotic desire into an aggressive, violent act as serving to construct a clear line of demarcation between self and other. Sublimation, according to Marcuse, involved the driving underground, into the unconscious, of sexual desires that might appear dangerous due to their socially stigmatized status. But sublimation involves more than simple repression into the unconscious. It involves a transformation of sexual desire into something else—often into aggressive and violent acting out toward others. These acts clarify the boundaries between oneself and others and therefore lessen any anxieties that might be attached to the repressed homoerotic desire.

Importantly, in our analysis of my story, the memory group went beyond simply discussing the events in psychological terms. The story did perhaps suggest some deep psychological processes at work, but it also revealed the importance of social context—in this case, the context of the athletic team. In short, my rejection of Timmy and the joining with teammates to stigmatize him in ninth grade stands as an example of what sociologist R. W. Connell calls a moment of engagement with hegemonic masculinity, where I actively took up the male group's task of constructing heterosexual/masculine identities in the context of sport. The elbow in Timmy's gut three years later can be seen as a punctuation mark that occurred precisely because of my fears that I might be failing in this goal.

It is helpful, I think, to compare my story with gay and lesbian "coming out" stories in sport. Though we have a few lesbian and bisexual coming out stories among women athletes, there are very few from gay males. Tom Waddell, who as a closeted gay man finished sixth in the decathlon in the 1968 Olympics, later came out and started the Gay Games, an athletic and cultural festival that draws tens of thousands of people every four years. When I interviewed Tom Waddell over a decade ago about his sexual identity and athletic career, he made it quite clear that for many years sports was his closet:

> When I was a kid, I was tall for my age, and was very thin and very strong. And I was usually faster than most other people. But I discovered rather early that I liked gymnastics and I liked dance. I was very interested in being a ballet dancer . . . [but] something became obvious to me right away—that male ballet dancers were effeminate, that they were what most people would call faggots. And I thought I just couldn't handle that . . . I was totally closeted and very concerned about being male. This was the fifties, a terrible time to live, and everything was stacked against me. Anyway, I realized that I had to do something to protect my image of myself as a male—because at that time homosexuals were thought of primarily as men who wanted to be women. And so I threw myself into athletics—I played football, gymnastics, track and field . . . I was a jock—that's how I was viewed, and I was comfortable with that.

Tom Waddell was fully conscious of entering sports and constructing a masculine/heterosexual athletic identity precisely because he feared being revealed as gay. It was clear to him, in the context of the 1950s, that being known as gay would undercut his claims to the status of manhood. Thus, though he described the athletic closet as "hot and stifling," he remained there until several years after his athletic retirement. He even knowingly played along with locker room discussions about sex and women as part of his "cover."

> I wanted to be viewed as male, otherwise I would be a dancer today. I wanted the male, macho image of an athlete. So I was protected by a very hard shell. I was clearly aware of what I was doing . . . I often felt compelled to go along with a lot of locker room garbage because I wanted that image—and I know a lot of others who did too.

Like my story, Waddell's points to the importance of the athletic institution as a context in which peers mutually construct and reconstruct narrow definitions of masculinity. Heterosexuality is considered to be a rock-solid foundation of this concept of masculinity. But unlike my story, Waddell's may invoke a dramaturgical analysis.[2] He seemed to be consciously "acting" to control and regulate others' perceptions of him by constructing a public "front stage" persona that differed radically from what he believed to be his "true" inner self. My story, in contrast, suggests a deeper, less consciously strategic repression of my homoerotic attraction. Most likely, I was aware on some level of the dangers of such feelings, and was escaping the risks, disgrace, and rejection that would likely result from being different. For Waddell, the decision to construct his identity largely within sport was to step into a fiercely heterosexual/masculine closet that would hide what he saw as his "true" identity. In contrast, I was not so much stepping into a "closet" that would hide my identity; rather, I was stepping out into an entire world of heterosexual privilege. My story also suggests how a threat to the promised privileges of hegemonic masculinity—my failure as an athlete—might trigger a momentary sexual panic that can lay bare the constructedness, indeed, the instability of the heterosexual/masculine identity.

In either case, Waddell's or mine, we can see how, as young male athletes, heterosexual masculinity was not something we "were," but something we were doing. It is significant, I think, that although each of us was "doing heterosexuality," neither of us was actually "having sex" with women (though one of us desperately wanted to). This underscores a point made by some recent theorists that heterosexuality should not be thought of simply as sexual acts between women and men. Rather, heterosexuality is a constructed identity, a performance, and an institution that is not necessarily linked to sexual acts. Though for one of us it was more conscious than for the other, we were both "doing heterosexuality" as an ongoing practice through which we sought to do two things:

- avoid stigma, embarrassment, ostracism, or perhaps worse if we were even suspected of being gay;
- link ourselves into systems of power, status, and privilege that appear to be the birthright of "real men" (i.e., males who are able to compete successfully with other males in sport, work, and sexual relations with women).

In other words, each of us actively scripted our own sexual and gender performances, but these scripts were constructed within the constraints of a socially organized (institutionalized) system of power and pleasure.

Questions for Future Research

As I prepared to tell this sexual story publicly to my colleagues at the sport studies conference, I felt extremely nervous. Part of the nervousness was due to the fact that I knew some of them would object to my claim that telling personal stories can be a source of sociological insights. But a larger part of the reason for my nervousness was due to the fact that I was revealing something very personal about my sexuality in such a public way. Most of us are not accustomed to doing this, especially in the context of a professional conference. But I had learned long ago, especially from feminist women scholars, and from gay and lesbian scholars, that biography is linked to history. Part of "normal" academic discourse has been to hide "the personal" (including the fact that the researchers are themselves people with values, feelings, and yes, biases) behind a carefully constructed facade of "objectivity." Rather than trying to hide or be ashamed of one's subjective experience of the world, I was challenging myself to draw on my experience of the world as a resource. Not that I should trust my experience as the final word on "reality." White, heterosexual males like me have made the mistake for centuries of calling their own experience "objectivity," and then punishing anyone who does not share their worldview by casting them as "deviant." Instead, I hope to use my experience as an example of how those of us who are in dominant sexual/racial/gender/class categories can get a new perspective on the "constructedness" of our identities by juxtaposing our subjective experiences against the recently emerging worldviews of gay men and lesbians, women, and people of color.

Finally, I want to stress that in juxtaposition neither my own nor Tom Waddell's story sheds much light on the question of why some individuals "become gay" while others "become" heterosexual or bisexual. Instead, I should like to suggest that this is a dead-end question, and that there are far more important and interesting questions to be asked:

- How has heterosexuality, as an institution and as an enforced group practice, constrained and limited all of us—gay, straight, and bi?
- How has the institution of sport been an especially salient institution for the social construction of heterosexual masculinity?
- Why is it that when men play sports they are almost always automatically granted masculine status, and thus assumed to be heterosexual, while when women play sports, questions are raised about their "femininity" and sexual orientation?

These kinds of questions aim us toward an analysis of the working of power within institutions—including the ways that these workings of power shape and constrain our identities and relationships—and point us toward imagining alternative social arrangements that are less constraining for everyone.

Notes

1. The fluidity and changeability of sexual desire over the life course is now more obvious in evidence from prison and military populations, and single-sex boarding schools. The theory of bisexuality is evident, for example, in childhood crushes on same-sex primary schoolteachers.

2. Dramaturgical analysis, associated with Erving Goffman, uses the theater and performance to develop an analogy with everyday life.

References

Haug, Frigga (1987) *Female Sexualization: A Collective Work of Memory*, London: Verso.

Lenskyj, Helen (1986) *Out of Bounds: Women, Sport and Sexuality*, Toronto: Women's Press.

——— (1997) "No fear? Lesbians in sport and physical education," *Women in Sport and Physical Activity Journal* 6(2): 7–22.

Messner, Michael A. (1992) *Power at Play: Sports and the Problem of Masculinity*, Boston: Beacon Press.

——— (1994) "Gay athletes and the Gay Games: An interview with Tom Waddell," in M. A. Messner and D. F. Sabo (eds), *Sex, Violence and Power in Sports: Rethinking Masculinity*, Freedom, CA: The Crossing Press, pp. 113–119.

Pronger, Brian (1990) *The Arena of Masculinity: Sports, Homosexuality, and the Meaning of Sex*, New York: St. Martin's Press.

ARTICLE 37

M. Rochlin

The Heterosexual Questionnaire

1. What do you think caused your heterosexuality?
2. When and how did you decide you were a heterosexual?
3. Is it possible that your heterosexuality is just a phase you may grow out of?
4. Is it possible that your heterosexuality stems from a neurotic fear of others of the same sex?
5. If you have never slept with a person of the same sex, is it possible that all you need is a good Gay lover?
6. Do your parents know that you are straight? Do your friends and/or roommate(s) know? How did they react?
7. Why do you insist on flaunting your heterosexuality? Can't you just be who you are and keep it quiet?
8. Why do heterosexuals place so much emphasis on sex?
9. Why do heterosexuals feel compelled to seduce others into their lifestyle?
10. A disproportionate majority of child molesters are heterosexual. Do you consider it safe to expose children to heterosexual teachers?
11. Just what do men and women *do* in bed together? How can they truly know how to please each other, being so anatomically different?
12. With all the societal support marriage receives, the divorce rate is spiraling. Why are there so few stable relationships among heterosexuals?
13. Statistics show that lesbians have the lowest incidence of sexually transmitted diseases. Is it really safe for a woman to maintain a heterosexual lifestyle and run the risk of disease and pregnancy?
14. How can you become a whole person if you limit yourself to compulsive, exclusive heterosexuality?
15. Considering the menace of overpopulation, how could the human race survive if everyone were heterosexual?
16. Could you trust a heterosexual therapist to be objective? Don't you feel s/he might be inclined to influence you in the direction of her/his own leanings?
17. There seem to be very few happy heterosexuals. Techniques have been developed that might enable you to change if you really want to. Have you considered trying aversion therapy?
18. Would you want your child to be heterosexual, knowing the problems that s/he would face?

Copyright © 1984, *Changing Men*. Used by permission.

ARTICLE 38

Robert Staples

Stereotypes of Black Male Sexuality: The Facts Behind the Myths

It is difficult to think of a more controversial role in American society than that of the black male. He is a visible figure on the American scene, yet the least understood and studied of all sex–race groups in the United States. His cultural image is typically one of several types: the sexual superstud, the athlete, and the rapacious criminal. That is how he is perceived in the public consciousness, interpreted in the media, and ultimately how he comes to see and internalize his own role. Rarely are we exposed to his more prosaic role as worker, husband, father, and American citizen.

The following essay focuses on the stereotypical roles of black male heterosexuality, not to reinforce them, but to penetrate the superficial images of black men as macho, hypersexual, violent, and exploitative. Obviously, there must be some explanation for the dominance of black men in the nations' negative statistics on rape, out-of-wedlock births, and premarital sexual activity. This is an effort to explore the reality behind the image.

Black Manhood

As a starting point, I see the black male as being in conflict with the normative definition of masculinity. This is a status which few, if any, black males have been able to achieve. Masculinity, as defined in this culture, has always implied a certain autonomy and mastery of one's environment. It can be said that not many white American males have attained this ideal either. Yet, white males did achieve a dominance in the nuclear family. Even that semblance of control was largely to be denied black men. During slavery he could receive the respect and esteem of his wife, children, and kinsmen, but he had no formal legal authority over his wife or filial rights from his children. There are numerous and documented instances of the slave-owning class's attempts to undermine his respect and esteem in the eyes of his family.[1]

Beginning with the fact that slave men and women were equally subjugated to the capricious authority of the slaveholder, the African male saw his masculinity challenged by the rape of his woman, sale of his children, the rations issued in the name of the woman and children bearing her name. While those practices may have presaged the beginning of a healthier sexual egalitarianism than was possible for whites, they also provoked contradictions and dilemmas for black men in American society. It led to the black male's self-devaluation as a man and set the stage for internecine conflict within the black community.

A person's sex-role identity is crucial to their values, life style, and personality. The black man has always had to confront the contradiction between the normative expectations attached to being male in this society and the proscriptions on his behavior and achievement of goals. He is subjected to societal opprobrium for failing to live up to the standards of manhood on the one hand and for being super macho on the other. It is a classical case of "damned if you do and damned if you don't." In the past there was the assertion that black men were effeminate because they were

Reprinted from *Changing Men*, Winter 1986. Copyright © 1986.

raised in households with only a female parent or one with a weak father figure. Presently, they are being attacked in literature, in plays, and at conferences as having succumbed to the male chauvinist ideal.

Although the sexual stereotypes apply equally to black men and women, it is the black male who has suffered the worst because of white notions of his hypersexuality. Between 1884 and 1900 more than 2,500 black men were lynched, the majority of whom were accused of sexual interest in white women. Black men, it was said, had a larger penis, a greater sexual capacity, and an insatiable sexual appetite. These stereotypes depicted black men as primitive sexual beasts, without the white male's love for home and family.[2] These stereotypes persist in the American consciousness.

It is in the area of black sexual behavior, and black male sexuality in particular, that folk beliefs are abundant but empirical facts few. Yet public policy, sex education, and therapeutic programs to deal with the sex-related problems of black people cannot be developed to fit their peculiar needs until we know the nature and dynamics of black sexual behavior. Thus, it is incumbent upon researchers to throw some light on an area enmeshed in undocumented myths and stereotypes.

Sexuality of the Male Adolescent

The Kinsey data, cited by Bell,[3] reveal that black males acquire their knowledge about condoms at a later age than white males. The white male learns about sexual intercourse at a later age than black males. Because of poorer nutrition, the black male reaches puberty at a later age than his white male counterpart. A critical distinction between black and white males was the tendency of the more sexually repressed white male to substitute masturbation, fellatio, and fantasy for direct sexual intercourse. Masturbation, for instance, was more likely to be the occasion of the first ejaculation for the white male while intercourse was for the black male. A larger percentage of white males reported being sexually aroused by being bitten during sexual activity, seeing a member of the opposite sex in a social situation, seeing themselves nude in the mirror or looking at another man's erect penis, hearing dirty jokes, reading sadomasochistic literature, and viewing sexy pictures. Conversely, black males tended to engage in premarital intercourse at earlier ages, to have intercourse, and to reach orgasm more frequently. As Bell notes in his analysis of these data, the black male's overabundance of sexuality is a myth. The sexuality of black and white men just tends to take different forms and neither group has any more self-control or moral heroism than the other.

Among young black American males, sexual activity begins at an earlier age, is more frequent, and involves more partners. Apparently white males are more likely to confine their associations in the adolescent years with other men. Larson and his associates found that black male adolescents were twice as likely to be romantically involved with women as white males.[4] The kind of rigid gender segregation found in white culture is largely absent from black society. For example, blacks are less likely to be associated with all male clubs, organizations, or colleges.

The sexual code of young black males is a permissive one. They do not, for example, divide black women into "good" (suitable for marriage) and "bad" (ineligible for marriage) categories. In the lower income groups, sexual activity is often a measure of masculinity. Thus, there is a greater orientation toward premarital sexual experimentation. In a study of premarital sexual standards among blacks and whites in the 1960s, Ira Reiss found that the sexual permissiveness of white males could be affected by a number of social forces (e.g., religion), but the black male was influenced by none of them.[5] Leanor Johnson and this author found that few black male adolescents were aware of the increased risk of teenage pregnancy, but there was an almost unanimous wish not to impregnate their sexual partner. Another survey of black male high school students reported their group believed that a male respects his partner when he uses a condom.[6]

Poverty and the Black Father

The period of adolescence, with its social, psychological and physical changes (particularly sex-role identity and sexuality), is the most problematic of the life cycle stages. The prolongation of adolescence in complex technological society and the earlier onset of puberty have served to compound the problem. While adolescents receive various messages to abandon childlike behavior, they are systematically excluded from adult activity such as family planning. This exclusion is justified not only by their incomplete social and emotional maturity, but by their lack of marketable skills which are necessary to command meaningful status-granting jobs. Unskilled adolescents are further disadvantaged if they are members of a minority racial group in a racially stratified society.

Parenthood at this stage of the life cycle is most undesirable. Yet, recent upsurges in teenage pregnancy and parenthood have occurred, specifically among females younger than 14. Approximately 52 percent of all children born to black women in 1982 were conceived out of wedlock. Among black women under age 20, about 75 percent of all births were out of wedlock compared with only 25 percent of births to young white women.[7] Although the rate of white out-of-wedlock pregnancy is increasing and that of non-whites decreasing, black unwed parenthood remains higher than that of whites.

Because life and family support systems of black males are severely handicapped by the effects of poverty and discrimination, the consequences of becoming a father in adolescence are more serious for the minority parent. Many family planning agencies offer counseling to the unwed mother, while the father is usually involved only superficially or punitively—as when efforts are made to establish legal paternity as a means for assessing financial responsibility. This omission, however, is not unique to black males. It is, perhaps, the single fact of inadequate economic provision which has resulted in the social agencies' premature conclusion that unwed fathers are unwilling to contribute to the future of their child and the support of the mother. Furthermore, sociological theory purports that slavery broke the black man's sense of family responsibility. Thus, it is assumed that black women do not expect or demand that black men support them in raising their children.

Family Planning

Recent evidence, however, suggests that the matrifocality of present theory and social services is myopic. Studies have demonstrated that most unwed fathers are willing to face their feelings and responsibilities.[8] The findings suggest that unmarried black males do not consider family planning a domain of the female, but rather a joint responsibility to be shared by both parents.[9]

Throughout the world one of the most important variables affecting birth rates is the male attitude toward family planning and the genesis of this attitude. Too often we are accustomed to thinking of reproduction as primarily a female responsibility. Since women are the main bearers and main rearers of children in our society, we tend to believe that they should be primarily concerned with planning the size of a family and developing those techniques of contraception consistent with the family's earning power, their own health and happiness, and the psychological well-being of their children.

However, in a male-dominated world it is women who are given the burden of having and raising children, while it is often men who determine what the magnitude of that burden should be. Unfortunately, the male's wishes in regard to the size of his family are not contingent on the effect of childbearing on the female partner, but are often shaped by his own psychological and status concerns.

Within many societies there is an inseparable link between men's self-image and their ability to have sexual relations with women and the subsequent birth of children from those sexual acts. For example, in Spanish-speaking cultures this masculine norm is embedded in the concept of "machismo." "Machismo," derived from the

Latin word "masculus," literally means the ability to produce sperm and thus sire—abilities which define the status of a man in society. In male-dominated society other issues involved in reproduction are subordinated to the male's desire to affirm his virility, which in turn confirms his fulfillment of the masculine role. The research literature tells us that the male virility cult is strongest in countries and among groups where the need for family planning is greatest.

Thus, we find that in underdeveloped countries—and among low-income ethnic groups in industrialized societies, including much of the black population in the U.S.—men are resistant to anything but natural controls on the number of children they have. Studies show that males who strongly believe that their masculine status is associated with their virility do not communicate very well with their wives on the subject of family planning. As a result the wives are less effective in limiting their families to the number of children they desire.

Sexual Aggression

Sexual attacks against women are pervasive and sharply increasing in this country. The typical rapist is a black male and his victim is most often a black female. However, the most severe penalties for rape are reserved for black males accused of raping white women. Although 50 percent of those convicted for rape in the South were white males, over 90 percent of those executed for this crime in that region were black. Most of their alleged victims were white. No white male has ever been executed for raping a black woman.[10]

As is probably true of white females, the incidence of rape of black women is underreported. Lander reported that an eight-year-old girl has a good chance of being exposed to rape and violence if she is a member of the black underclass.[11] While widespread incidents of this kind are rooted in the sexist socialization of all men in society, it is pronounced among black men who have other symbols of traditional masculinity blocked to them. Various explanations have been put forth to explain why black men seem to adopt the attitudes of the majority group toward black women. Poussaint believes that because white men have historically raped black women with impunity, many black males believe they can do the same.[12]

Sexual violence is also rooted in the dynamics of the black dating game. The majority of black rape victims know their attacker—a friend, relative, or neighbor. Many of the rapes occur after a date and are what Amir describes as misfired attempts at seduction.[13] A typical pattern is for the black male to seek sexual compliance from his date, encounter resistance which he thinks is feigned, and proceed to forcibly obtain his sexual gratification from her. Large numbers of black men believe sexual relations to be their "right" after a certain amount of dating.

Rape, however, is not regarded as the act of a sexually starved male but rather as an aggressive act toward females. Students of the subject suggest that it is a long-delayed reaction against authority and powerlessness. In the case of black men, it is asserted that they grow up feeling emasculated and powerless before reaching manhood. They often encounter women as authority figures and teachers or as the head of their household. These men consequently act out their feelings of powerlessness against black women in the form of sexual aggression. Hence, rape by black men should be viewed as both an aggressive and political act because it occurs in the context of racial discrimination which denies most black men a satisfying manhood.

Manhood in American society is closely tied to the acquisition of wealth. Men of wealth are rarely required to rape women because they can gain sexual access through other means. A female employee who submits to the sexual demands of a male employer in order to advance in her job is as much an unwilling partner in this situation as is the rape victim. The rewards for her sexual compliance are normatively sanctioned, whereas the rapist does not often have the resources to induce such sexual compliance. Moreover, the concept of women as sexual property is at the root of rape. This concept is peculiar to capitalistic, western societies rather than African nations (where the incidence of rape is much lower). For black men, rape is often an act of aggression against women because the kinds of status men can acquire through success in a job is not available to them.

Recommendations

To address the salient issues in black male sexuality, I offer the following recommendations:

1. An educational program for black men must be designed to sensitize them to the need for their responsibility for, and participation in, family planning. This program will best be conducted by other men who can convey the fact that virility is not in and of itself the measure of masculinity. Also, it should be emphasized that the use of contraception—or obtaining a vasectomy—does not diminish a male's virility.
2. An overall sex education program for both sexes should begin as early as kindergarten, before the male peer group can begin to reinforce attitudes of male dominance. Sex education courses should stress more than the physiological aspects in its course content. Males should be taught about the responsibility of men in sex relations and procreation. Forms of male contraception should be taught along with female measures of birth control.
3. The lack of alternative forms of role fulfillment available to many men, especially in industrialized societies, must be addressed. In cases of unemployment and underemployment, the male often resorts to the virility cult because it is the only outlet he has for a positive self-image and prestige within his peer group. Thus, we must provide those conditions whereby men can find meaningful employment.
4. Lines of communication must be opened between men and women. A supplement to the educational program for men should be seminars and workshops involving both men and women. Hopefully, this will lead to the kind of dialogue between men and women that will sensitize each of them to the feelings of the other.

Notes

1. Robert Staples, *The Black Family: Essays and Studies*. (Belmont, CA: Wadsworth, 1978.)

2. Robert Staples, *Black Masculinity*. (San Francisco: The Black Scholar Press, 1982.)

3. Alan P. Bell, "Black Sexuality: Fact and Fancy" in R. Staples, ed., *The Black Family: Essays and Studies*, pp. 77–80.

4. David Larson, et al., "Social Factors in the Frequency of Romantic Involvement Among Adolescents." *Adolescence* 11: 7–12, 1976.

5. Ira Reiss, *The Social Context of Premarital Sexual Permissiveness*. (New York: Holt, Rinehart and Winston, 1968.)

6. Leanor Johnson and Robert Staples, "Minority Youth and Family Planning: A Pilot Project." *The Family Coordinator* 28: 534–543, 1978.

7. U.S. Bureau of the Census, *Fertility of American Women*. (Washington, D.C.: U.S. Government Printing Office, 1984.)

8. Lisa Connolly, "Boy Fathers." *Human Behavior* 45: 40–43, 1978.

9. B. D. Misra, "Correlates of Males' Attitudes Toward Family Planning" in D. Bogue, ed., *Sociological Contributions to Family Planning Research*, pp. 161–167. (Chicago: Univ. of Chicago Press, 1967).

10. William J. Bowers, *Executions in America*. (Lexington Books, 1974.)

11. Joyce Lander, *Tomorrow's Tomorrow: The Black Woman*. (Garden City, New York: Doubleday, 1971.)

12. Alvin Poussaint, *Why Blacks Kill Blacks*. (New York: Emerson-Hall, 1972.)

13. Menachim Amir, "Sociocultural Factors in Forcible Rape" in L. Gross, ed., *Sexual Behavior*, pp. 1–12. (New York: Spectrum Publications, 1974).

ARTICLE 39

Tomás Almaguer

Chicano Men: A Cartography of Homosexual Identity and Behavior

The sexual behavior and sexual identity of Chicano male homosexuals is principally shaped by two distinct sexual systems, each of which attaches different significance and meaning to homosexuality. Both the European-American and Mexican/Latin-American systems have their own unique ensemble of sexual meanings, categories for sexual actors, and scripts that circumscribe sexual behavior. Each system also maps the human body in different ways by placing different values on homosexual erotic zones. The primary socialization of Chicanos into Mexican/Latin-American cultural norms, combined with their simultaneous socialization into the dominant European-American culture, largely structures how they negotiate sexual identity questions and confer meaning to homosexual behavior during adolescence and adulthood. Chicano men who embrace a "gay" identity (based on the European-American sexual system) must reconcile this sexual identity with their primary socialization into a Latino culture that does not recognize such a construction: there is no cultural equivalent to the modern "gay man" in the Mexican/Latin-American sexual system.

How does socialization into these different sexual systems shape the crystallization of their sexual identities and the meaning they give to their homosexuality? Why does only a segment of homosexually active Chicano men identify as "gay"? Do these men primarily consider themselves *Chicano* gay men (who retain primary emphasis on their ethnicity) or *gay* Chicanos (who place primary emphasis on their sexual preference)? How do Chicano homosexuals structure their sexual conduct, especially the sexual roles and relationships into which they enter? Are they structured along lines of power/dominance firmly rooted in a patriarchal Mexican culture that privileges men over women and the masculine over the feminine? Or do they reflect the ostensibly more egalitarian sexual norms and practices of the European-American sexual system? These are among the numerous questions that this paper problematizes and explores.

We know little about how Chicano men negotiate and contest a modern gay identity with aspects of Chicano culture drawing upon more Mexican/Latin-American configurations of sexual meaning. Unlike the rich literature on the Chicana/Latina lesbian experience, there is a paucity of writings on Chicano gay men.[1] There does not exist any scholarly literature on this topic other than one unpublished study addressing this issue as a secondary concern (Carrillo and Maiorana). The extant literature consists primarily of semi-autobiographical, literary texts by authors such as John Rechy, Arturo Islas, and Richard Rodriguez.[2] Unlike the writings on Chicana lesbianism, however, these works fail to discuss directly the cultural dissonance that Chicano homosexual men confront in reconciling their primary socialization into Chicano family life with the sexual norms of the dominant culture. They

---

An edited version of the original article appeared in *Differences: A Journal of Feminist Cultural Studies* 3:2(1991), pp. 75–100. Reprinted with permission. I gratefully acknowledge the valuable comments on an earlier version of this article by Jackie Goldsby, David Halperin, Teresa de Lauretis, Bob Blauner, Carla Trujillo, Patricia Zavella, Velia Garcia, and Ramón Gutiérrez.

offer little to our understanding of how these men negotiate the different ways these cultural systems stigmatize homosexuality and how they incorporate these messages into their adult sexual practices.

In the absence of such discussion or more direct ethnographic research to draw upon, we must turn elsewhere for insights into the lives of Chicano male homosexuals. One source of such knowledge is the perceptive anthropological research on homosexuality in Mexico and Latin America, which has direct relevance for our understanding of how Chicano men structure and culturally interpret their homosexual experiences. The other, ironically, is the writings of Chicana lesbians who have openly discussed intimate aspects of their sexual behavior and reflected upon sexual identity issues. How they have framed these complex sexual issues has major import for our understanding of Chicano male homosexuality. Thus, the first section of this paper examines certain features of the Mexican/Latin-American sexual system which offer clues to the ensemble of cultural meanings that Chicano homosexuals give to their sexual practices. The second section examines the autobiographical writings of Chicana lesbian writer Cherríe Moraga. I rely upon her candid discussion of her sexual development as ethnographic evidence for further problematizing the Chicano homosexual experience in the United States.

The Cartography of Desire in the Mexican/Latin-American Sexual System

American anthropologists have recently turned their attention to the complex meaning of homosexuality in Mexico and elsewhere in Latin America. Ethnographic research by Joseph M. Carrier, Roger N. Lancaster, Richard Parker, Barry D. Adam, and Clark L. Taylor has documented the inapplicability of Western European and North American categories of sexual meaning in the Latin-American context. Since the Mexican/Chicano population in the U.S. shares basic features of these Latin cultural patterns, it is instructive to examine this sexual system closely and to explore its impact on the sexuality of homosexual Chicano men and women.

The rules that define and stigmatize homosexuality in Mexican culture operate under a logic and a discursive practice different from those of the bourgeois sexual system that shaped the emergence of contemporary gay/lesbian identity in the U.S. Each sexual system confers meaning to homosexuality by giving different weight to the two fundamental features of human sexuality that Freud delineated in the *Three Essays on the Theory of Sexuality*: sexual object choice and sexual aim. The structured meaning of homosexuality in the European-American context rests on the sexual object-choice one makes—i.e., the biological sex of the person toward whom sexual activity is directed. The Mexican/Latin-American sexual system, on the other hand, confers meaning to homosexual practices according to sexual aim—i.e., the act one wants to perform with another person (of either biological sex).

The contemporary bourgeois sexual system in the U.S. divides the sexual landscape according to discrete sexual categories and personages defined in terms of sexual preference or object choice: same sex (homosexual), opposite sex (heterosexual), or both (bisexual). Historically, this formulation has carried with it a blanket condemnation of all same-sex behavior. Because it is non-procreative and at odds with a rigid, compulsory heterosexual norm, homosexuality traditionally has been seen as either 1) a sinful transgression against the word of God, 2) a congenital disorder wracking the body, or 3) a psychological pathology gripping the mind. In underscoring object choice as the crucial factor in defining sexuality in the U.S., anthropologist Roger Lancaster argues that "homosexual desire itself, without any qualifications, stigmatizes one as a homosexual" (116). This stigmatization places the modern gay man at the bottom of the homosexual sexual hierarchy. According to Lancaster, "the object-choice of the homosexual emarginates him from male power, except insofar as he can serve as a negative example and . . . is positioned outside the operational rules of normative (hetero)sexuality" (123–124).

Unlike the European-American system, the Mexican/Latin-American sexual system is based on a configuration of gender/sex/power that is articulated along the active/passive axis and organized through the scripted sexual role one plays.[3] It highlights sexual aim—the act one wants to perform with the person toward whom sexual activity is directed—and gives only secondary importance to the person's gender or biological sex. According to Lancaster, "it renders certain organs and roles 'active,' other body passages and roles 'passive,' and assigns honor/shame and status/stigma accordingly" (123). It is the mapping of the body into differentiated erotic zones and the unequal, gender-coded statuses accorded sexual actors that structure homosexual meaning in Latin culture. In the Mexican/Latin-American context there is no cultural equivalent to the modern gay man. Instead of discrete sexual personages differentiated according to sexual preference, we have categories of people defined in terms of the role they play in the homosexual act. The Latin homosexual world is divided into *activos* and *pasivos* (as in Mexico and Brazil) and *machistas* and *cochóns* (in Nicaragua).

Although stigma accompanies homosexual practices in Latin culture, it does not equally adhere to both partners. It is primarily the anal–passive individual (the *cochón* or *pasivo*) who is stigmatized for playing the subservient, feminine role. His partner (the *activo* or *machista*) typically "is not stigmatized at all and, moreover, no clear category exists in the popular language to classify him. For all intents and purposes, he is just a normal . . . male" (Lancaster 113). In fact, Lancaster argues that the active party in a homosexual drama often gains status among his peers in precisely the same way that one derives status from seducing many women (113). This cultural construction confers an inordinate amount of meaning to the anal orifice and to anal penetration. This is in sharp contrast to the way homosexuality is viewed in the U.S., where the oral orifice structures the meaning of homosexuality in the popular imagination. In this regard, Lancaster suggests the lexicon of male insult in each context clearly reflects this basic difference in cultural meaning associated with oral/anal sites (111). The most common derisive term used to refer to homosexuals in the U.S. is "cocksucker." Conversely, most Latin American epithets for homosexuals convey the stigma associated with their being anally penetrated.

Consider for a moment the meaning associated with the passive homosexual in Nicaragua, the *cochón*. The term is derived from the word *colchón* or mattress, implying that one gets on top of another as one would a mattress, and thereby symbolically affirms the former's superior masculine power and male status over the other, who is feminized and indeed objectified (Lancaster 112). *Cochón* carries with it a distinct configuration of power, delineated along gender lines that are symbolically affirmed through the sexual role one plays in the homosexual act. Consequently, the meaning of homosexuality in Latin culture is fraught with elements of power/dominance that are not intrinsically accorded homosexual practices in the U.S. It is anal passivity alone that is stigmatized and that defines the subordinate status of homosexuals in Latin culture. The stigma conferred to the passive role is fundamentally inscribed in gender-coded terms.

> "To give" (*dar*) is to be masculine, "to receive" (*recibir, aceptar, tomar*) is to be feminine. This holds as the ideal in all spheres of transactions between and within genders. It is symbolized by the popular interpretation of the male sexual organ as active in intercourse and the female sexual organ (or male anus) as passive. (Lancaster 114)

This equation makes homosexuals such as the *pasivo* and *cochón* into feminized men; biological males, but not truly men. In Nicaragua, for example, homosexual behavior renders "one man a machista and the other a cochón. The machista's honor and the cochón's shame are opposite sides of the same coin" (Lancaster 114).

Male Homosexual Identity and Behavior in Mexico

Some of the most insightful ethnographic research on homosexuality in Mexico has been conducted by anthropologist J. M. Carrier. Like other Latin American specialists exploring this issue, Carrier argues that homosexuality is construed very differently in the U.S. and in Mexico. In the U.S., even one adult homosexual act or acknowledgment of homosexual desire may threaten a man's gender identity and throw open to question his sexual identity as well. In sharp contrast, a Mexican man's masculine gender and heterosexual identity are not threatened by a homosexual act as long as he plays the inserter's role. Only the male who plays the passive sexual role and exhibits feminine gender characteristics is considered to be truly homosexual and is, therefore, stigmatized. This "bisexual" option, an exemption from stigma for the "masculine" homosexual, can be seen as part of the ensemble of gender privileges and sexual prerogatives accorded Mexican men. Thus it is primarily the passive, effeminate homosexual man who becomes the object of derision and societal contempt in Mexico.

The terms used to refer to homosexual Mexican men are generally coded with gendered meaning drawn from the inferior position of women in patriarchal Mexican society. The most benign of these contemptuous terms is *maricón*, a label that highlights the non-conforming gender attributes of the (feminine) homosexual man. Its semantic equivalent in the U.S. is "sissy" or "fairy" (Carrier, "Cultural Factors" 123–124). Terms such as *joto* or *puto*, on the other hand, speak to the passive sexual role taken by these men rather than merely their gender attributes. They are infinitely more derogatory and vulgar in that they underscore the sexually non-conforming nature of their passive/receptive position in the homosexual act. The invective associated with all these appellations speaks to the way effeminate homosexual men are viewed as having betrayed the Mexican man's prescribed gender and sexual role. Moreover, it may be noted that the Spanish feminine word *puta* refers to a female prostitute while its male form *puto* refers to a passive homosexual, not a male prostitute. It is significant that the cultural equation made between the feminine, anal-receptive homosexual man and the most culturally-stigmatized female in Mexican society (the whore) share a common semantic base.[4]

Carrier's research suggests that homosexuality in Mexico is rigidly circumscribed by the prominent role the family plays in structuring homosexual activity. Whereas in the U.S., at least among most European-Americans, the role of the family as a regulator of the lives of gay men and lesbians has progressively declined, in Mexico the family remains a crucial institution that defines both gender and sexual relations between men and women. The Mexican family remains a bastion of patriarchal privilege for men and a major impediment to women's autonomy outside the private world of the home.

The constraints of family life often prevent homosexual Mexican men from securing unrestricted freedom to stay out late at night, to move out of their family's home before marriage, or to take an apartment with a male lover. Thus their opportunities to make homosexual contacts in other than anonymous locations, such as the balconies of movie theaters or certain parks, are severely constrained (Carrier, "Family Attitudes" 368). This situation creates an atmosphere of social interdiction which may explain why homosexuality in Mexico is typically shrouded in silence. The concealment, suppression, or prevention of any open acknowledgment of homosexual activity underscores the stringency of cultural dictates surrounding gender and sexual norms within Mexican family life. Unlike the generally more egalitarian, permissive family life of white middle-class gay men and lesbians in the U.S., the Mexican family appears to play a far more important and restrictive role in structuring homosexual behavior among Mexican men ("Family Attitudes" 373).

Given these constraints and the particular meanings attached to homosexuality in Mexican culture, same-sex behavior in Mexico typically unfolds in the context of an age-stratified hierarchy that grants privileges to older, more masculine men. It is very significant that in instances where two masculine, active men enter into a homosexual encounter, the rules that structure gender-coded homosexual relations continue to operate with full force. In these exchanges one of the men—typically he who is defined as being more masculine or powerful—assumes the active, inserter role while the other man is pressed into the passive, anal-receptive role. Moreover, men who may eventually adopt both active and passive features of homosexual behavior typically do not engage in such reciprocal relations with the same person. Instead, they generally only play the active role with one person (who is always viewed as being the more feminine) and are sexually passive with those they deem more masculine than themselves ("Cultural Factors" 120–121).

In sum, it appears that the major difference between bisexually active men in Mexico and bisexual males in the U.S. is that the former are not stigmatized because they exclusively play the active, masculine, inserter role. Unlike in the North American context, "one drop of homosexuality" does not, ipso facto, make a Mexican male a *joto* or a *maricón*. As Carrier's research clearly documents, none of the active inserter participants in homosexual encounters ever considers himself a "homosexual" or to be "gay" ("Mexican Male" 83). What may be called the "bisexual escape hatch" functions to insure that the tenuous masculinity of Mexican men is not compromised through the homosexual act; they remain men, *hombres*, even though they participate in this sexual behavior. Moreover, the Mexican sexual system actually militates against the construction of discernable, discrete "bisexual" or "gay" sexual identities because these identities are shaped by and draw upon a different sexual system and foreign discursive practices. One does not, in other words, become "gay" or "lesbian" identified in Mexico because its sexual system precludes such an identity formation in the first place. These "bourgeois" sexual categories are simply not relevant or germane to the way gender and sexual meanings are conferred in Mexican society.

Implications for Chicano Gay Men in the U.S.

The emergence of the modern gay identity in the U.S. and its recent appearance in Mexico have implications for Chicano men that have not been fully explored. What is apparent, however, is that Chicanos, as well as other racial minorities, do not negotiate the acceptance of a gay identity in exactly the same way white American men do. The ambivalence of Chicanos vis-à-vis a gay sexual identity and their attendant uneasiness with white gay/lesbian culture do not necessarily reflect a denial of homosexuality. Rather, I would argue, the slow pace at which this identity formation has taken root among Chicanos is attributable to cultural and structural factors which differentiate the experiences of the white and non-white populations in the U.S.

Aside from the crucial differences discussed above in the way homosexuality is culturally constructed in the Mexican/Latin-American and European- or Anglo-American sexual systems, a number of other structural factors also militate against the emergence of a modern gay identity among Chicano men. In this regard, the progressive loosening of familial constraints among white, middle-class homosexual men and women at the end of the nineteenth century, and its acceleration in the post–World War II period, structurally positioned the white gay and lesbian population to redefine their primary self-identity in terms of their homosexuality. The shift from a family-based economy to a fully developed wage labor system at the end of the nineteenth century dramatically freed European-American men and women from the previously confining social and economic world of the family. It allowed both white men and the white "new woman" of the period to transgress the stifling gender roles that previously bound them to a compulsory heterosexual norm.[5] Extricating the nuclear family from its traditional role as a primary unit of production enabled homosexually inclined individuals to forge a new sexual identity and to develop a culture and community that were not previously possible. Moreover, the tremendous urban migration ignited (or precipitated) by World War II accelerated this process by drawing thousands of homosexuals into urban settings where the possibilities for same-sex intimacy were greater.

It is very apparent, however, that the gay identity and communities that emerged were overwhelmingly white, middle class, and male-centered. Leading figures of the first homophile organizations in the U.S., such as the Mattachine Society, and key individuals shaping the newly emergent gay culture were primarily drawn from this segment of the homosexual population. Moreover, the new communities founded in the postwar period were largely populated by white men who had the resources and talents needed to create "gilded" gay ghettos. This fact has given the contemporary gay community—despite its undeniable diversity—a largely white, middle class, and male form. In other words, the unique class and racial advantages of white gay men provided the foundation upon which they could boldly carve out the new gay identity. Their collective position in the social structure empowered them with the skills and talents needed to create new gay institutions, communities, and a unique sexual subculture.

Despite the intense hostility that, as gay men, they faced during that period, nevertheless, as white gay men, they were in the best position to risk the social ostracism that this process engendered. They were *relatively* better situated than other homosexuals to endure the hazards unleashed by their transgression of gender conventions and traditional heterosexual norms. The diminished importance of ethnic identity among these individuals, due principally to the homogenizing and integrating impact of the dominant racial categories which defined them foremost as white, undoubtedly also facilitated the emergence of gay identity among them. As members of the privileged racial group—and thus no longer viewing themselves primarily as Irish, Italian, Jewish, Catholic, etc.—these middle-class men and women arguably no longer depended solely on their respective cultural groups and families as a line of defense against the dominant group. Although they may have continued to experience intense cultural dissonance leaving behind their ethnicity and their traditional family-based roles, they were now in a position to dare to make such a move.

Chicanos, on the other hand, have never occupied the social space where a gay or lesbian identity can readily become a primary basis of self-identity. This is due, in part, to their structural position at the subordinate ends of both the class and racial hierarchies, and in a context where ethnicity remains a primary basis of group identity and survival. Moreover, Chicano family life requires allegiance to patriarchal gender relations and to a system of sexual meanings that directly militate against the emergence of this alternative basis of self-identity. Furthermore, factors such as gender, geographical settlement, age, nativity, language usage, and degree of cultural assimilation further prevent, or at least complicate, the acceptance of a gay or lesbian identity by Chicanos or Chicanas respectively. They are not as free as individuals situated elsewhere in the social structure to redefine their sexual identity in ways that contravene the imperatives of minority family life and its traditional gender expectations. How they come to define their sexual identities as gay, straight, bisexual or, in Mexican/Latin-American terms, as an *activo*, *pasivo*, or *macho marica*, therefore, is not a straightforward or unmediated process. Unfortunately, there are no published studies to date exploring this identity formation process.

However, one unpublished study on homosexual Latino/Chicano men was conducted by Hector Carrillo and Horacio Maiorana in the spring of 1989. As part of their ongoing work on AIDS within the San Francisco Bay Area Latino community, these researchers developed a typology capturing the different points in a continuum differentiating the sexual identity of these men. Their preliminary typology is useful in that it delineates the way homosexual Chicanos/Latinos integrate elements of both the North American and Mexican sexual systems into their sexual behavior.

The first two categories of individuals, according to Carrillo and Maiorana, are: 1) Working-class Latino men who have adopted an effeminate gender persona and usually play the passive role in homosexual encounters (many of them are drag queens who frequent the Latino gay bars in the Mission District of San Francisco); and 2) Latino men who consider themselves heterosexual or bisexual, but who furtively have sex with other men. They are also primarily working class and often frequent Latino gay bars in search of discrete sexual encounters. They tend to retain a strong Latino or Chicano ethnic identity and structure their sexuality according to the Mexican sexual system. Although Carrillo and Maiorana do not discuss the issue, it seems likely that these men would primarily seek out other Latino men, rather than European-Americans, as potential partners in their culturally circumscribed homosexual behavior.

I would also suggest from personal observation that these two categories of individuals occasionally enter into sexual relationships with middle-class Latinos and European-American men. In so doing, these working-class Latino men often become the object of the middle-class Latino's or the white man's colonial desires. In one expression of this class-coded lust, the effeminate *pasivo* becomes the boyish, feminized object of the middle-class man's colonial desire. In another, the masculine Mexican/Chicano *activo* becomes the embodiment of a potent ethnic masculinity that titillates the middle-class man who thus enters into a passive sexual role.

Unlike the first two categories of homosexually active Latino men, the other three have integrated several features of the North American sexual system into their sexual behavior. They are more likely to be assimilated into the dominant European-American culture of the U.S. and to come from middle-class backgrounds. They include 3) Latino men who openly consider themselves gay and participate in the emergent gay Latino subculture in the Mission district; 4) Latino men who consider themselves gay but do not participate in the Latino gay subculture, preferring to maintain a primary identity as Latino and only secondarily a gay one; and, finally, 5) Latino men who are fully assimilated into the white San Francisco gay male community in the Castro District and retain only a marginal Latino identity.

In contrast to the former two categories, Latino men in the latter three categories are more likely to seek European-American sexual partners and exhibit greater difficulty in reconciling their Latino cultural backgrounds with their gay lifestyle. In my impressionistic observations, these men do not exclusively engage in homosexual behavior that is hierarchically differentiated along the gender-coded lines of the Mexican sexual system. They are more likely to integrate both active and passive sexual roles into their sexuality and to enter into relationships in which the more egalitarian norms of the North American sexual system prevail. We know very little, however, about the actual sexual conduct of these individuals. Research has not yet been conducted on how these men express their sexual desires, how they negotiate their masculinity in light of their homosexuality, and, more generally, how they integrate aspects of the two sexual systems into their everyday sexual conduct.

In the absence of such knowledge, we may seek clues about the social world of Chicano gay men in the perceptive writings of Chicana lesbians. Being the first to shatter the silence on the homosexual experience of the Chicano population, they have candidly documented the perplexing issues Chicanos confront in negotiating the conflicting gender and sexual messages imparted by the coexisting Chicano and European-American cultures. The way in which Chicana lesbians have framed these problems, I believe, is bound to have major significance for the way Chicano men reconcile their homosexual behavior and gay sexual identity within a Chicano cultural context. More than any other lesbian writer's, the extraordinary work of Cherríe Moraga articulates a lucid and complex analysis of the predicament that the middle-class Chicana lesbian and Chicano gay man face in this society. A brief examination of her autobiographical writings offers important insights into the complexities and contradictions that may characterize the experience of homosexuality for all Chicanos and Chicanas in the U.S.

Cherríe Moraga and Chicana Lesbianism

An essential point of departure in assessing Cherríe Moraga's work is an appreciation of the way Chicano family life severely constrains the Chicana's ability to define her life outside of its stifling gender and sexual prescriptions. As a number of Chicana feminist scholars have clearly documented, Chicano family life remains rigidly structured along patriarchal lines that privilege men over women and children.[6] Any violation of these norms is undertaken at great personal risk because Chicanos draw upon the family to resist racism and the ravages of class inequality. Chicano men and women are drawn together in the face of these onslaughts and are closely bound into a family structure that exaggerates unequal gender roles and suppresses sexual non-conformity.[7] Therefore, any deviation from the sacred link binding husband, wife, and child not only threatens the very existence of *la familia* but also potentially undermines the mainstay of resistance to Anglo racism and class exploitation. "The family, then, becomes all the more ardently protected by oppressed people and the sanctity of this institution is infused like blood into the veins of the Chicano. At all costs, la familia must be preserved," writes Moraga. Thus, "we fight back . . . with our families—with our women pregnant, and our men as indispensable heads. We believe the more severely we protect the sex roles within the family, the stronger we will be as a unit in opposition to the anglo threat" (*Loving* 110).

These cultural prescriptions do not, however, curb the sexually non-conforming behavior of certain Chicanos. As in the case of Mexican homosexual men in Mexico, there exists a modicum of freedom for the Chicano homosexual who retains a masculine gender identity while secretly engaging in the active homosexual role. Moraga has perceptively noted that the Latin cultural norm inflects the sexual behavior of homosexual Chicanos: "Male homosexuality has always been a 'tolerated' aspect of Mexican/Chicano society, as long as it remains 'fringe' . . . But lesbianism, in any form, and male homosexuality which openly avows both the sexual and the emotional elements of the bond, challenge the very foundation of la familia" (111). The openly effeminate Chicano gay man's rejection of heterosexuality is typically seen as a fundamental betrayal of Chicano patriarchal cultural norms. He is viewed as having turned his back on the male role that privileges Chicano men and entitles them to sexual access to women, minors, and even other men. Those who reject these male prerogatives are viewed as non-men, as the cultural equivalents of women. Moraga astutely assesses the situation as one in which "the 'faggot' is the object of Chicano/Mexicano's contempt because he is consciously choosing a role his culture tells him to despise. That of a woman" (111).

The constraints that Chicano family life imposed on Moraga herself are candidly discussed in her provocative autobiographical essays "La Guera" and "A Long Line of Vendidas" in *Loving in the War Years*. In recounting her childhood in Southern California, Moraga describes how she was routinely required to make her brother's bed, iron his shirts, lend him money, and even serve him cold drinks when his friends came to visit their home. The privileged position of men in the Chicano family places women in a secondary, subordinate status. She resentfully acknowledges that "to this day in my mother's home, my brother and father are waited on, including by me" (90). Chicano men have always thought of themselves as superior to Chicanas, she asserts in unambiguous terms: "I have never met any kind of Latino who . . . did not subscribe to the basic belief that men are better" (101). The insidiousness of the patriarchal ideology permeating Chicano family life even shapes the way a mother defines her relationships with her children: "The daughter must constantly earn the mother's love, prove her fidelity to her. The son—he gets her love for free" (102).

Moraga realized early in life that she would find it virtually impossible to attain any meaningful autonomy in that cultural context. It was only in the Anglo world that freedom from oppressive gender and sexual strictures was remotely possible. In order to secure this latitude, she made a necessary choice: to embrace the white world and reject crucial aspects of her Chicana upbringing. In painfully honest terms, she states:

> I gradually became anglocized because I thought it was the only option available to me toward gaining autonomy as a person without being sexually stigmatized. . . . I instinctively made choices which I thought would allow me greater freedom of movement in the future. This meant resisting sex roles as much as I could safely manage and that was far easier in an anglo context than in a Chicano one. (99)

Born to a Chicana mother and an Anglo father, Moraga discovered that being fair-complexioned facilitated her integration into the Anglo social world and contributed immensely to her academic achievement. "My mother's desire to protect her children from poverty and illiteracy" led to their being "anglocized," she writes; "the more effectively we could pass in the white world, the better guaranteed our future" (51). Consequently her life in Southern California during the 1950s and 1960s is described as one in which she "identified with and aspired toward white values" (58). In the process, she "rode the wave of that Southern California privilege as far as conscience would let me" (58).

The price initially exacted by anglicization was estrangement from family and a partial loss of the nurturing and love she found therein. In reflecting on this experience, Moraga acknowledges that "I have had to confront that much of what I value about being Chicana, about my family, has been subverted by anglo culture and my cooperation with it. . . . I realized the major reason for my total alienation from and fear of my classmates was rooted in class and culture" (54). She poignantly concedes that, in the process, "I had disavowed the language I knew best—ignored the words and rhythms that were closest to me. The sounds of my mother and aunts gossiping—half in English, half in Spanish—while drinking cerveza in the kitchen" (55). What she gained, on the other hand, was the greater autonomy that her middle-class white classmates had in defining their emergent sexuality and in circumventing burdensome gender prescriptions. Her movement into the white world, however, was viewed by Chicanos as a great betrayal. By gaining control of her life, Moraga became one of a "long line of vendidas," traitors or "sell-outs," as self-determined women are seen in the sexist cultural fantasy of patriarchal Chicano society. This is the accusation that "hangs above the heads and beats in the hearts of most Chicanas, seeking to develop our own autonomous sense of ourselves, particularly our sexuality" (103).

Patriarchal Chicano culture, with its deep roots in "the institution of heterosexuality," requires Chicanas to commit themselves to Chicano men and subordinate to them their own sexual desires. "[The Chicano] too, like any other man," Moraga writes, "wants to be able to determine how, when, and with whom his women—mother, wife, and daughter—are sexual" (110–111). But "the Chicana's sexual commitment to the Chicano male [is taken as] proof of her fidelity to her people" (105). "It is no wonder," she adds, that most "Chicanas often divorce ourselves from conscious recognition of our own sexuality" (119). In order to claim the identity of a Chicana lesbian, Moraga had to take "a radical stand in direct contradiction to, and in violation of, the women [sic] I was raised to be" (117); and yet she also drew upon themes and images of her Mexican Catholic background. Of its impact on her sexuality Moraga writes:

> I always knew that I felt the greatest emotional ties with women, but suddenly I was beginning to consciously identify those feelings as sexual. The more potent my dreams and fantasies

became and the more I sensed my own exploding sexual power, the more I *retreated* from my body's messages and into the region of religion. By giving definition and meaning to my desires, religion became the discipline to control my sexuality. Sexual fantasy and rebellion became "impure thoughts" and "sinful acts." (119)

These "contrary feelings," which initially surfaced around the age of twelve, unleashed feelings of guilt and moral transgression. She found it impossible to leave behind the Catholic Church's prohibitions regarding homosexuality, and religious themes found their way into how she initially came to define herself as a sexual subject—in a devil-like form. "I wrote poems describing myself as a centaur: half-animal/half-human, hairy-rumped and cloven-hoofed, como el diablo. The images emerged from a deeply Mexican and Catholic place" (124).

As her earliest sexual feelings were laden with religious images, so too were they shaped by images of herself in a male-like form. This is understandable in light of the fact that only men in Chicano culture are granted sexual subjectivity. Consequently, Moraga instinctively gravitated toward a butch persona and assumed a male-like stance toward other women.

> In the effort to avoid embodying la chingada, I became the chingón. In the effort not to feel fucked, I became the fucker, even with women. ... The fact of the matter was that all those power struggles of "having" and "being had" were played out in my own bedroom. And in my psyche, they held a particular Mexican twist. (126)

In a candid and courageously outspoken conversation with lesbian activist Amber Hollibaugh, Moraga recounts that:

> ... what turned me on sexually, at a very early age, had to do with the fantasy of capture, taking a woman, and my identification was with the man. ... The truth is, I do have some real gut-level misgivings about my sexual connection with capture. It might feel very sexy to imagine "taking" a woman, but it has sometimes occurred at the expense of my feeling, sexually, like I can surrender myself to a woman; that is, always needing to be the one in control, calling the shots. It's a very butch trip and I feel like this can keep me private and protected and can prevent me from fully being able to express myself. (Moraga and Hollibaugh 396)

Moraga's adult lesbian sexuality defined itself along the traditional butch/femme lines characteristic of lesbian relationships in the post-war period.[8] It is likely that such an identity formation was also largely an expression of the highly gender-coded sexuality imparted through Chicano family life. In order to define herself as an autonomous sexual subject, she embraced a butch, or more masculine, gender persona, and crystallized a sexual desire for feminine, or femme, lovers.

The Final Frontier: Unmasking the Chicano Gay Man

Moraga's experience is certainly only one expression of the diverse ways in which Chicana lesbians come to define their sense of gender and experience their homosexuality. But her odyssey reflects and articulates the tortuous and painful path traveled by working-class Chicanas (and Chicanos) who embrace the middle-class Anglo world and its sexual system in order to secure, ironically, the "right to passion expressed in our own cultural tongue and movements" (136). It is apparent from her powerful autobiographical writings, however, how much her adult sexuality was also inevitably shaped by the gender and sexual messages imparted through the Chicano family.

How this complex process of integrating, reconciling, and contesting various features of both Anglo and Chicano cultural life is experienced by Chicano gay men has yet to be fully explored. Moraga's incisive and extraordinarily frank autobiographical account raises numerous questions about the parallels in the homosexual development of Chicana lesbians and Chicano gay men. How, for example, do Chicano male homosexuals internalize and reconcile the gender-specific prescriptions of Chicano culture? How does this primary socialization impact on the way they define their gender personas and sexual identities? How does socialization into a patriarchal gender system that privileges men over women and the masculine over the feminine structure intimate aspects of their sexual behavior? Do most Chicano gay men invariably organize aspects of their sexuality along the hierarchical lines of dominance/subordination that circumscribe gender roles and relationships in Chicano culture? My impression is that many Chicano gay men share the Chicano heterosexual man's underlying disdain for women and all that is feminine. Although it has not been documented empirically, it is likely that Chicano gay men incorporate and contest crucial features of the Mexican/Latin-American sexual system into their intimate sexual behavior. Despite having accepted a "modern" sexual identity, they are not immune to the hierarchical, gender-coded system of sexual meanings that is part and parcel of this discursive practice.

Until we can answer these questions through ethnographic research on the lives of Chicano gay men, we must continue to develop the type of feminist critique of Chicano male culture that is so powerfully articulated in the work of lesbian authors such as Cherríe Moraga. We are fortunate that courageous voices such as hers have irretrievably shattered the silence on the homosexual experience within the Mexican American community. Her work, and that of other Chicana lesbians, has laid a challenge before Chicano gay men to lift the lid on their homosexual experiences and to leave the closeted space they have been relegated to in Chicano culture. The task confronting us, therefore, is to begin interpreting and redefining what it means to be both Chicano and gay in a cultural setting that has traditionally viewed these categories as a contradiction in terms. This is an area of scholarly research that can no longer be left outside the purview of Chicano Studies, Gay and Lesbian Studies, or even more traditional lines of sociological inquiry.

Notes

1. See, for example, the writings by Chicana and Latina lesbians in Ramos; Alarcón, Castillo, and Moraga; Moraga and Anzaldúa; and Anzaldúa. See also the following studies on Latinas: Arguelles and Rich; Espin; and Hidalgo and Hidalgo-Christensen.

2. See Bruce-Novoa's interesting discussion of homosexuality as a theme in the Chicano novel.

3. There is a rich literature documenting the ways in which our sexuality is largely structured through sexual scripts that are culturally defined and individually internalized. See, for example, Gagnon and Simon; Simon and Gagnon; and Plummer. What is being referred to here as the Mexican/Latin-American sexual system is part of the circum-Mediterranean construction of gender and sexual meaning. In this regard, see the introduction and essays in Gilmore. For further discussion of this theme in the Mexican context, see Alonso and Koreck. Their essay, which uses many of the same sources as the present essay, explores male homosexual practices in Mexico in relation to AIDS.

4. In "Birth of the Queen," Trumbach has perceptively documented that many of the contemporary terms used to refer to homosexual men in Western Europe and the United States (such as queen, punk, gay, faggot, and fairy) also were at one time the slang term for prostitutes (137). See also Alonso and Koreck, 111–113.

5. For a broad overview of the development of a gay and lesbian identity and community in the United States, see D'Emilio; D'Emilio and Freedman; and Katz. A number of articles in the important anthology edited by Duberman, Vicinus, and Chauncey document the white middle class–centered nature of gay/lesbian identity construction and community formation.

6. Some of the very best research in Chicano studies has been conducted by Chicana feminists who have explored the intersection of class, race, and gender in Chicanas' lives. Some recent examples of this impressive scholarship include Zavella; Segura; Pesquera; and Baca-Zinn.

7. This solidarity is captured in the early Chicano movement poster fittingly entitled "La Familia." It consists of three figures in a symbolic pose: a Mexican woman, with a child in her arms, is embraced by a Mexican man, who is centrally positioned in the portrait and a head taller. This poster symbolized the

patriarchal, male-centered privileging of the heterosexual, nuclear family in Chicano resistance against white racism. For a provocative discussion of these themes in the Chicano movement, see Gutiérrez.

8. For an interesting discussion of the butch/femme formulation among working-class white women at the time, see Davis and Kennedy; and Nestle.

References

Adam, Barry D. "Homosexuality without a Gay World: Pasivos y Activos en Nicaragua." *Out/Look* 1.4 (1989): 74–82.

Alarcón, Norma. "Chicana's Feminist Literature: A Re-vision Through Malintzin/or Malintzin: Putting Flesh Back on the Object." Moraga and Anzaldúa 182–190.

Alarcón, Norma, Ana Castillo, and Cherríe Moraga, eds. *Third Woman: The Sexuality of Latinas*. Berkeley: Third Woman, 1989.

Alonso, Ana Maria, and Maria Theresa Koreck. "Silences: 'Hispanics,' AIDS, and Sexual Practices." *differences: A Journal of Feminist Cultural Studies* 1.1 (1989): 101–124.

Anzaldúa, Gloria. *Borderlands/La Frontera: The New Mestiza*. San Francisco: Spinsters, 1987.

Arguelles, Lourdes, and B. Ruby Rich. "Homosexuality, Homophobia, and Revolution: Notes Toward an Understanding of the Cuban Lesbian and Gay Male Experience, Part 1." *Signs: Journal of Woman in Culture and Society* 9 (1984): 683–699.

———. "Homosexuality, Homophobia, and Revolution: Notes Toward an Understanding of the Cuban Lesbian and Gay Male Experience, Part 2." *Signs: Journal of Women in Culture and Society* 11 (1985): 120–136.

Baca-Zinn, Maxine. "Chicano Men and Masculinity." *The Journal of Ethnic Studies* 10.2 (1982): 29–44.

———. "Familism Among Chicanos: A Theoretical Review." *Humboldt Journal of Social Relations* 10.1 (1982–83): 224–238.

Blackwood, Evelyn, ed. *The Many Faces of Homosexuality: Anthropological Approaches to Homosexual Behavior*. New York: Harrington Park, 1989.

Bruce-Novoa, Juan. "Homosexuality and the Chicano Novel." *Confluencia: Revista Hispanica de Cultura y Literatura* 2.1 (1986): 69–77.

Carrier, Joseph M. "Cultural Factors Affecting Urban Mexican Male Homosexual Behavior." *The Archives of Sexual Behavior: An Interdisciplinary Research Journal* 5.2 (1976): 103–124.

———. "Family Attitudes and Mexican Male Homosexuality." *Urban Life: A Journal of Ethnographic Research* 5.3 (1976): 359–376.

———. "Gay Liberation and Coming Out in Mexico." Herdt 225–253.

———. "Mexican Male Bisexuality." *Bisexualities: Theory and Research*. Ed. F. Klein and T. Wolf. New York: Haworth, 1985. 75–85.

Carrillo, Hector, and Horacio Maiorana. "AIDS Prevention Among Gay Latinos in San Francisco: From Behavior Change to Social Change." Unpublished ms., 1989.

Davis, Madeline, and Elizabeth Lapovsky Kennedy. "Oral History and the Study of Sexuality in the Lesbian Community: Buffalo, New York, 1940–1960." Duberman 426–440.

D'Emilio, John. "Capitalism and Gay Identity." Snitow, Stansell, and Thompson 100–113.

———. *Sexual Politics, Sexual Communities: The Making of a Homosexual Minority in the United States, 1940–1970*. Chicago: U of Chicago P, 1983.

D'Emilio, John, and Estelle B. Freedman. *Intimate Matters: A History of Sexuality in America*. New York: Harper, 1988.

Duberman, Martin Bauml, Martha Vicinus, and George Chauncey Jr., eds. *Hidden from History: Reclaiming the Gay and Lesbian Past*. New York: NAL, 1989.

Espin, Oliva M. "Cultural and Historical Influences on Sexuality in Hispanic/Latin Women: Implications for Psychotherapy." *Pleasure and Danger: Exploring Female Sexuality*. Ed. Carol Vance. London: Routledge, 1984, 149–163.

———. "Issues of Identity in the Psychology of Latina Lesbians." *Lesbian Psychologies*. Ed. Boston Lesbian Psychologies Collective. Urbana: U of Illinois P, 1987. 35–55.

Freud, Sigmund. *Three Essays on the Theory of Sexuality*. 1905. *The Standard Edition of the Complete Psychological Works of Sigmund Freud*. Trans. and ed. James Strachey. Vol. 7. London: Hogarth, 1953. 123–243.

Gagnon, John H., and William Simon. *Sexual Conduct: The Social Sources of Human Sexuality*. Chicago: Aldine, 1973.

Gilmore, David D., ed. *Honor and Shame and the Unity of the Mediterranean*. No. 22, Washington: American Anthropological Association, 1987.

Goldwert, Marvin. "Mexican Machismo: The Flight from Femininity." *Psychoanalytic Review* 72.1 (1985): 161–169.

Gutiérrez, Ramón. "Community, Patriarchy, and Individualism: The Politics of Chicano History and the Dream of Equality." Forthcoming in *American Quarterly*.

Herdt, Gilbert, ed. *Gay and Lesbian Youth*. New York: Haworth, 1989.

Hidalgo, Hilda, and Elia Hidalgo-Christensen. "The Puerto Rican Lesbian and the Puerto Rican Community." *Journal of Homosexuality* 2 (1976–77): 109–121.

———. "The Puerto Rican Cultural Response to Female Homosexuality." *The Puerto Rican Woman*. Ed. Edna Acosta-Belen. New York: Praeger, 1979. 110–123.

Islas, Arturo. *Immigrant Souls*. New York: Morrow, 1990.

———. *The Rain God: A Desert Tale*. Palo Alto, CA: Alexandrian, 1984.

Katz, Jonathan Ned. *Gay/Lesbian Almanac: A New Documentary*. New York: Harper, 1983.

Lancaster, Roger N. "Subject Honor and Object Shame: The Construction of Male Homosexuality and Stigma in Nicaragua." *Ethnology* 27.2 (1987): 111–125.

Martin, Robert K. "Knights-Errant and Gothic Seducers: The Representation of Male Friendship in Mid-Nineteenth Century America." Duberman 169–182.

Moraga, Cherríe. *Loving in the War Years: Lo que nunca pasó por sus labios*. Boston: South End, 1983.

Moraga, Cherríe, and Gloria Anzaldúa, eds. *This Bridge Called My Back: Writings by Radical Women of Color*. Watertown, MA: Persephone, 1981.

Moraga, Cherríe, and Amber Hollibaugh. "What We're Rollin Around in Bed With: Sexual Silences in Feminism." Snitow, Stansell, and Thompson 394–405.

Nestle, Joan. "Butch–Fem Relationships: Sexual Courage in the 1950s." *Heresies* 12 (1981): 21–24.

Newton, Esther. "The Mythic Mannish Lesbian: Radcliffe Hall and the New Woman." Duberman 281–293.

Parker, Richard. "Youth Identity, and Homosexuality: The Changing Shape of Sexual Life in Contemporary Brazil." Herdt 269–289.

———. "Masculinity, Femininity, and Homosexuality: On the Anthropological Interpretation of Sexual Meanings in Brazil." Blackwood 155–164.

Paz, Octavio. *Labyrinth of Solitude: Life and Thought in Mexico*. New York: Grove, 1961.

Pesquera, Beatriz M. "Work and Family: A Comparative Analysis of Professional, Clerical and Blue-Collar Chicana Workers." PhD diss. U of California, Berkeley, 1985.

Plummer, Kenneth. "Symbolic Interaction and Sexual Conduct: An Emergent Perspective." *Human Sexual Relations*. Ed. Mike Brake. New York: Pantheon, 1982. 223–244.

Ramos, Juanita, ed. *Compañeras: Latina Lesbians*. New York: Latina Lesbian History Project, 1987.

Rechy, John. *City of Night*. New York: Grove, 1963.

———. *Numbers*. New York: Grove, 1967.

———. *Rushes*. New York: Grove, 1979.

———. *The Sexual Outlaw*. New York: Grove, 1977.

Rodriguez, Richard. *Hunger of Memory: The Education of Richard Rodriguez, An Autobiography*. Boston: Godine, 1982.

———. "Late Victorians: San Francisco, AIDS, and the Homosexual Stereotype." *Harper's Magazine* Oct. 1990: 57–66.

Rupp, Leila J. "Imagine My Surprise: Woman's Relationships in Mid-Twentieth Century America." Duberman 395–410.

Segura, Denise. "Chicana and Mexican Immigrant Women in the Labor Market: A Study of Occupational Mobility and Stratification." PhD diss. U of California, Berkeley, 1986.

———. "Chicana and Mexican Immigrant Women at Work: The Impact of Class, Race, and Gender on Occupational Mobility." *Gender and Society* 3.1 (1989): 37–52.

———. "The Interplay of Familism and Patriarchy on Employment Among Chicana and Mexican Women." *Renato Rosaldo Lecture Series* 5 (1989): 35–53.

Simon, William, and John H. Gagnon. "Sexual Scripts: Permanence and Change." *Archives of Sexual Behavior* 15.2 (1986): 97–120.

Smith-Rosenberg, Carroll. "Discourses of Sexuality and Subjectivity: The New Woman, 1870–1936." Duberman 264–280.

Snitow, Ann, Christine Stansell, and Sharon Thompson, eds. *Powers of Desire: The Politics of Sexuality*. New York: Monthly Review, 1983.

Taylor, Clark L. "Mexican Male Homosexual Interaction in Public Contexts." Blackwood 117–136.

Trumbach, Randolph. "The Birth of the Queen: Sodomy and the Emergence of Gender Equality in Modern Culture, 1660–1750." Duberman 129–140.

Zavella, Patricia. *Women's Work and Chicano Families: Cannery Workers of the Santa Clara Valley*. Ithaca: Cornell University Press, 1987.

ARTICLE 40

Susan D. Cochran
Vickie M. Mays

Sociocultural Facets of the Black Gay Male Experience

Prior to the appearance of AIDS in this country, studies on the sexual preferences and behaviors of gay men generally ignored the specific experiences of Black men (Bell, Weinberg, and Hammersmith 1981). With the press of the AIDS epidemic to develop baseline information on men's intimate behaviors, this tendency rarely to study Black gay men, or to do so in the same manner as White gay men, persists. While many researchers may recognize the importance of possible cultural differences, their approach has been to assume that Black gay men would be more like White gay men than Black heterosexuals. Questionnaires, sampling procedures, and topics of focus have been more consistent with White gay men's experiences (see Becker and Joseph 1988, for a comprehensive review of behavior change studies). This proclivity has resulted in an emergence of comparisons between Black and White men using White gay standards of behavior that may be obscuring our understanding of important psychosocial determinants of sexual behaviors in Black gay men. Given the differences that have been observed in family structure and sexual patterns between Black and White heterosexuals, there is no empirical basis upon which to assume that Black gay men's experience of homosexuality would perfectly mimic that of Whites (Bell, Weinberg, and Hammersmith 1981). Indeed, very little is known empirically about the lives of Black gay men (Mays and Cochran 1987), though there are some indications, discussed below, that they are more likely to engage in activities that place them at greater risk for HIV infection.

In the absence of any data we need to proceed cautiously with assumptions that imply anything other than [that] same-sex *activities* of Black gay men resemble those of White gay men. This caution is particularly true for AIDS studies that purport to study psychosocial behavior. Studies of this type report not only on behavior but also attempt to describe motivations and circumstances that lead to the behavior. In the absence of a set of questions or framework incorporating important cultural, ethnic, and economic realities of Black gay men, interpretations emanating from a White gay male standard may be misleading.

Development of a Black Gay Identity

In recent years, researchers (Spanier and Glick 1980; Staples 1981; Guttentag and Secord 1983) have noted differences between Whites and Blacks in their intimate heterosexual relationships. Differential sociocultural factors presumably influence the development and specific structure of sexual behavior within Black heterosexual relationships. These factors include the unavailability of partners of the same ethnic group, fewer social and financial resources, residential immobility,

An abridged version of the article "Epidemiologic and Sociocultural Factors in the Transmission of HIV Infection in Black Gay and Bisexual Men" printed in *A Sourcebook of Gay/Lesbian Health Care,* M. Shernoff and W. A. Scott (eds.), Washington, D.C.: National Gay and Lesbian Health Foundation, 2nd ed. Copyright © 1988 by the National Gay and Lesbian Health Foundation. Reprinted by permission.

and lack of employment opportunities. Many of these same conditions may surround the formation, maintenance, and functioning of Black gay male relationships.

Popular writings in past years by Black gay men describe the difficulty in finding other Black gay men for potential partners, the lack of a visible Black gay community, an absence of role models, and the dearth of Black gay male social or professional organizations (Soares 1979; Beame 1983). While gay bars, gay baths, and public places existed where White gay men gathered, some of these were off limits to Black gay men either due to actual or perceived racism within the White gay community or the danger of passing through White neighborhoods in order to participate in gay community activities. Thus, expectations that the experiences of Black gay men are identical to those of White gay men seem unwarranted.

In examining differences between Blacks and Whites in the emergence of a homosexual orientation, Bell, Weinberg, and Hammersmith (1981) found that, for the White males, pre-adult sexual feelings appeared to be very important. In contrast, among Black males, childhood and adolescent sexual activities, rather than feelings, were stronger predictors of the development of adult homosexual sexual orientation. Thus, Blacks started to act at an earlier age on their sexual inclinations than Whites did (Bell, Weinberg, and Hammersmith 1981). This would be consistent with Black–White differences in the onset of heterosexual sexual activity if socioeconomic status is not statistically controlled for (Wyatt, personal communication).

The typical conceptualization of sexual orientation is that individuals are located in terms of their sexual feelings and behaviors on a bipolar dimension where one extreme is heterosexuality, the other is homosexuality, and lying somewhere in between is bisexuality (Bell and Weinberg 1978). This definition does not include ethnicity or culture as an interactive factor influencing the expression of sexual behavior or sexual orientation. For example, Smith (1986) makes a distinction between Black gays and gay Blacks complicating the demarcation between homosexuality and bisexuality:

> Gay Blacks are people who identify first as being gay and who usually live outside the closet in predominantly white gay communities. I would estimate that they amount to roughly ten percent of all Black homosexuals. Black gays, on the other hand, view our racial heritage as primary and frequently live "bisexual front lives" within Black neighborhoods. (p. 226)

These two groups are probably quite different in both social activities and sexual behaviors. The Black gay man, strongly identified with Afro-American culture, will often look and behave much like the Black heterosexual man except in his sexual behavior. The extent to which his same-sex partners are integrated into his family and social environment may be a function of his class status (Soares 1979). It has long been noted by Blacks that there are differences, both in values and behaviors, between middle-class and working-class Blacks. There is no reason to assume that within the Black gay community such diversity would not persist. While Smith (1986) has described the Black gay community in only two dimensions we would be remiss if we stopped here. There is a growing population of Black gays who have forged an identity acknowledging both statuses:

> At times I cried just remembering how it is to be both Black and gay during these truly difficult times. But here we are, still proud and living, with a culture all our own. (Sylvester, p. 11, 1986)

We know less about the behavior of Black men who identify as bisexual and least about those Black men who engage in same-sex sexual behavior but identify as exclusively heterosexual. When the factor of social class is added the distinction between homosexuality and heterosexuality may become even more blurred. Among lower socioeconomic Black men, those engaged in same-sex sexual activities, regardless of their sexual object choices, may appear on the surface no different from Black heterosexuals. If the support systems of Black gay men are like those of Black lesbians (Cochran and Mays 1986), fewer economic resources result in a greater reliance on a Black social network (both gay and heterosexual) for tangible and emotional support, a strong tendency to live in predominantly ethnic neighborhoods, and the maintenance of emotionally and economically close family ties.

This extensive integration into the Black heterosexual world may not only be a function of fewer economic resources, but also of ethnic identification. The culture of gay life, generally perceived to be White, may not be synonymous with the norms of Black culture. Choices of how to dress, what language to use, where to live, and whom to have as friends are all affected by culture. The White gay community, while diverse, has developed norms concerning language, social behavior, and other demarcations (Warren 1974) that may not mesh well with certain subgroups of Black gays. For example, in the past there has been a heavy emphasis in the gay White community (except among the middle-aged, middle-class closeted gay men) on socializing in public places—bars, beaches, and resorts (Warren, 1974). In contrast, the Black gay community places greater emphasis on home entertainment that is private and not public, perhaps as a holdover from the days when discrimination in many public places was common. This pattern of socializing would facilitate the development of a distinct Black gay culture (Soares 1979).

It is perhaps this difference in socializing that has frustrated health educators attempting to do AIDS education through the social network in gay bars. Generally, they have found that they do not reach a significant number of Black men using this technique. An understanding of the Black gay community makes salient that risk reduction strategies should focus on "risk behaviors" and *not* "risk groups." Emphasizing risk reduction strategies that rely on group membership requires a social and personal identification by Black men that for many may not be relevant.

Sexual Behavior

Bell and Weinberg, in a 1978 study comparing sexual activities of White and Black gay men, found that Blacks were more likely to report having engaged in anal sex, both passively and actively, than White gay men. In terms of our current knowledge of AIDS, this appears to be one of the highest risk factors for contracting the HIV virus (Friedland and Klein 1987).

A second aspect of Black gay men's sexuality is that they may be more bisexual in their behaviors than White gay men. Evidence for this comes again from Bell and Weinberg (1978) who reported that Black gay men were significantly more likely to have engaged in heterosexual coitus (22 percent) in the previous twelve months than White gay men (14 percent). This seems to be borne out nationally by the AIDS statistics. Among male homosexual/bisexual AIDS patients, Black men are more likely than White men to be classified as bisexual (30 percent versus 13 percent) rather than homosexual (70 percent versus 87 percent). Due to the intense homophobia in the Black community and the factors we discussed above, men may be more likely to remain secretive regarding their homosexual activities (Mays and Cochran 1987). This may provide a mode of transmission of the AIDS virus outside of an already identified high-risk group.

There are several other differences between Black and White gay men noted in the Kinsey Institute data that have implications for contracting the HIV virus. Looking at sexual behavior both pre- and post-Stonewall, Black gay men, in comparison to White gay men, were more likely to be sexually active across ethnic boundaries and less likely to report that their sexual partners were strangers (Bell and Weinberg 1978; Gebhard and Johnson 1979). Sexual practices post-Stonewall underwent profound change in the gay community. Black gay men were a part of that change

(Bell and Weinberg 1978; Gebhard and Johnson 1979). However, these differences in meeting partners or choice of partners remain. They are apparently less malleable to change than specific risk-related sexual behaviors.

While the 1978 Bell and Weinberg study was conducted on a small sample in the San Francisco area, it is suggestive of the need for further research to assess the prevalence of risk behaviors and strategies most effective for decreasing risk. Indeed, a recent report of ethnically based differences in syphilis incidence rates (Landrum, Beck-Sague, and Kraus 1988) suggests Black gay men are less likely than White gay men to be practicing "safer sex." Sexual behavior has multiple determinants and it is important that variables such as culture, ethnic identification, and class be incorporated into health education programs designed to promote sexual behavior change by Black men.

Intravenous Drug Use

IV drug use is more common in the Black community (Gary and Berry 1985), which may explain the higher than expected prevalence of Blacks in the co-categories of IV drug user and homosexual/bisexual male. HIV infection is endemic among IV drug users in the urbanized Northeast who themselves are most likely to be Black (Ginzburg, MacDonald, and Glass 1987). Ethnic differences exist between the percentage of homosexual/bisexual men with AIDS who are also IV drug users; for White gay and bisexual men with AIDS, 9 percent have histories of IV drug use, while for Blacks the figure is 16 percent. Black gays and bisexual men who do not use IV drugs may also be at increased risk because they are more likely than Whites to be sexual partners of Black men who are IV drugs users. In the Bell and Weinberg study (1978), 22 percent of White men had never had sex with a Black man, whereas for Black respondents, only 2 percent had never had sex with a White man.

Alcohol as a Cofactor

Recently, alcohol use has been implicated as a cofactor facilitating the occurrence of high risk sexual behavior among gay men (Stall et al. 1986). In predicting alcohol use among Black gay and bisexual men, one might expect that normative use patterns will be influenced by what is common behavior in both the Black community and gay community.

Norms for alcohol use in the Black community reflect a polarization of attitudes, shaped on the one hand by traditional religious fundamentalism and rural southern heritage and on the other by a focus on socializing in environments where drinking is common, such as bars, nightclubs, and home parties (Herd 1986). This latter norm is more prevalent in urban Black communities. Blacks and Whites vary in small ways in their drinking patterns, although Blacks are more likely to suffer negative consequences, including alcohol-related mortality and morbidity, from their drinking than are Whites. Current rates of mortality due to liver cirrhosis indicate that rates are 10 times higher in Black men aged 25–34 as compared to White males. While drinking is found across all socioeconomic groups of Blacks, health and social problems associated with drinking have been found more often in low income urban Blacks (Lex 1987). Similarly, for this group it was found that Black males 30–59 were most likely to use alcohol to face the stress of everyday life situations. This is the group most affected by HIV infection.

Within the gay male community, alcohol abuse is a serious problem (Icard and Traunstein 1987). This may result from both the sociocultural stress of discrimination and the tendency for gay-oriented establishments to be drinking establishments as well. Thus, gay men frequently socialize in environments where alcohol consumption is normative.

Black gay and bisexual men, depending upon their relative identification with the Black or gay community, would be expected to demonstrate behavior consistent with these norms. For some, this might mean a high level of abstinence apart from social drinking consistent with other Black Americans; for others, alcohol consumption might more closely resemble that of White gay men with concomitantly higher rates of alcohol dependency.

Crossing Traditional Risk Groups' Boundaries

Early AIDS epidemiologic tracking programs conceptualize the disease as a result of the gay lifestyle (Mays 1988). Indeed, now discarded names for different manifestations of the illness included Gay-related Immunodeficiency Disease and Gay Cancer. This focus on discrete risk factors continues to the present, although the additional populations of IV drug abusers, hemophiliacs, persons born in Haiti and Central Africa, and recipients of blood transfusions after 1978 have been added to the list. For Whites, this approach is highly successful, describing the presumed HIV transmission vector in 94 percent of cases; for native-born Blacks, the percentage of cases accurately labeled by a single risk factor (including the combination of IV drug use and male homosexual sexual contact) drops to 88 percent (Cochran 1987). This underscores the reality that sociocultural factors varying across ethnic groups strongly influence individuals' behavior, and by this their risk of contracting HIV.

For Black gay and bisexual men, the reliance on highly specified risk groups (or factors) ignores the fundamental nature of their behavioral location in society. The multiplicity of their identities may indirectly increase their risk for HIV infection by exposing them to more diverse populations (Grob 1983).

First, as Blacks, they are behaviorally closer to two epicenters of the AIDS epidemic: IV drug users and foreign-born Blacks (primarily those from Haiti and Central Africa where HIV infection is more common). Social and behavioral segregation by ethnic status is still a reality of the American experience and Black gay and bisexual men suffer, like other Blacks, from pervasive racism. As we noted above, if their social support systems are similar to what we know of Black lesbians (Cochran and Mays 1986), extensive integration into the Black heterosexual community is common. Behaviorally, this may include both IV drug use and heterosexual activity with HIV infected individuals. Thus Black gay and bisexual men are at increased risk for HIV infection simply by virtue of being Black.

Second, as men who have sex with other men, Black gay and bisexual men are often members of the broader gay community in which ethnicity probably reflects the general U.S. population (84 percent White). Black gay and bisexual men may have relatively open sexual access to White men, although racism in the community may preclude other forms of socializing (Icard 1985). Data from the Bell and Weinberg study (1978) suggest several interesting differences, as well as similarities, between White and Black gay men. Blacks reported equivalent numbers of sexual partners, both lifetime (median = 100–249 partners) and in the previous 12 months (median = 20–50), as Whites. Although they were significantly less likely than White gay men to engage in anonymous sexual contacts (51 percent versus 79 percent of partners), more than two-thirds reported that more than half their sexual partners were White men. In contrast, none of the White respondents reported that more than half their partners were Black. It should be kept in mind, however, that a greater percentage of the White sample (14 percent) was recruited at bath houses than the Black sample (2 percent). Nevertheless, at least sexually, Black gay men appear to be well integrated into the gay community. Therefore, Black gay and bisexual men are also at higher risk for HIV infection because they are behaviorally close to another epicenter of the AIDS epidemic: the gay male community.

Third, as a social grouping unto itself, the Black gay and bisexual male community may be more diverse than the White gay community (Icard 1985). Some men identify more closely with the Black community than the gay community (Black gay men); others find their primary emotional affinity with the gay community and not the Black community (gay Black men). To the extent that this diversity of identity is reflected in behavioral diversity as well, HIV transmission may be greatly facilitated (Denning 1987).

Thus Black gay and bisexual men are individuals often located behaviorally at the crossroads of HIV transmission. Their multiple social identities make it more likely that the practicing of high-risk behavior, whether sexual or needle-sharing, will occur in the presence of HIV.

Perceptions of Risk

There may be a reluctance among Black gay and bisexual men to engage in risk reduction behaviors because of the perception by some members of the Black community that AIDS is a "gay White disease," or a disease of intravenous drug users (Mays and Cochran 1987). In addition, many risk reduction programs are located within outreach programs of primarily White gay organizations. These organizations often fail to attract extensive participation by Black gay men.

Research findings suggest that the personal perception of being at risk is most often influenced by accurate knowledge of one's actual risk and personal experiences with the AIDS epidemic (McKusick, Horstman, and Coates 1985). There may be a variety of reasons why Black gay and bisexual men do not see themselves as at risk. These include the notion of relative risk and a lack of ethnically credible sources for encouraging risk perceptions (Mays and Cochran 1988). Relative risk refers to the importance of AIDS in context with other social realities. For example, poverty, with its own attendant survival risks, may outweigh the fear of AIDS in a teenager's decision to engage in male prostitution. Economic privilege, more common in the White gay community, assists in permitting White gay men to focus their energies and concerns on the AIDS epidemic. For Black gay men of lesser economic privilege other pressing realities of life may, to some extent, diffuse such concerns. Credible sources relate to the issues that we have presented here of ethnic identification. Black gay men who are emotionally and behaviorally distant from the White community may tend to discount media messages from White sources.

References

Bakeman, R., J. Lumb, R. E. Jackson, and P. N. Whitley. 1987. "The Incidence of AIDS among Blacks and Hispanics." *Journal of the National Medical Association* 79: 921–928.

Beame, T. 1983. "Racism from a Black Perspective." In *Black Men/White Men: A Gay Anthology*, M. J. Smith ed. San Francisco: Gay Sunshine Press.

Becker, M. H. and J. G. Joseph. 1988. "AIDS and Behavioral Change to Reduce Risk: A Review." *American Journal of Public Health* 78: 394–410.

Bell, A. P. and M. S. Weinberg. 1978. *Homosexualities: A Study of Diversity among Men and Women*. New York: Simon & Schuster.

Bell, A. P., M. S. Weinberg, and S. K. Hammersmith. 1981. *Sexual Preference: Its Development in Men and Women*. Bloomington: Indiana University Press.

Bureau of the Census. 1983. "General Population Characteristics, 1980." U.S. Department of Commerce: U.S. Government Printing Office.

Centers for Disease Control, Acquired Immunodeficiency Syndrome (AIDS) Weekly Surveillance Report, United States AIDS Activity, Center for Infectious Diseases, April 4, 1988.

Centers for Disease Control. 1987. "Human Immunodeficiency Virus Infection in the United States: A Review of Current Knowledge." *Morbidity and Mortality Weekly* 36 (Suppl. no. S-6): 1–48.

Cochran, S. D. 1987. "Numbers That Obscure the Truth: Bias in Data Presentation." Paper presented at the meetings of the American Psychological Association, New York, August.

Cochran, S. D. and V. M. Mays. 1986. "Sources of Support among Black Lesbians." Paper presented at the meetings of the American Psychological Association, Washington, D.C., August.

Cochran, S. D., V. M. Mays, and V. Roberts. 1988. "Ethnic Minorities and AIDS." In *Nursing Care of Patients with AIDS/ARC*, A. Lewis ed., pp. 17–24. Maryland: Aspen Publishers.

Denning, P. J. 1987. "Computer Models of AIDS Epidemiology." *American Scientist* 75: 347–351.

Friedland, G. H. and R. S. Klein. 1987. "Transmission of the Human Immunodeficiency Virus." *New England Journal of Medicine* 317: 1125–1135.

Friedman, S. R., J. L. Sotheran, A. Abdul-Quader, B. J. Primm, D. C. Des Jarlais, P. Kleinman, C. Mauge, D. S. Goldsmith, W. El-Sadr, and R. Maslansky. 1987. "The AIDS Epidemic among Blacks and Hispanics." *The Milbank Quarterly* 65, Suppl. 2.

Gary, L. E. and G. L. Berry. 1985. "Predicting Attitudes toward Substance Use in a Black Community: Implications for Prevention." *Community Mental Health Journal* 21: 112–118.

Gebhard, P. H. and A. B. Johnson. 1979. *The Kinsey Data: Marginal Tabulations of the 1938–1963 Interviews Conducted by the Institute for Sex Research*. Philadelphia: W. B. Saunders Co.

Ginzburg, H. M., M. G. MacDonald, and J. W. Glass. 1987. "AIDS, HTLV-III Diseases, Minorities and Intravenous Drug Abuse." *Advances in Alcohol and Substance Abuse* 6: 7–21.

Gottlieb, M. S., H. M. Schanker, P. Fan, A. Saxon, J. D. Weisman, and I. Posalki. 1981. "Pneumocystic Pneumonia—Los Angeles." *Morbidity and Mortality Weekly Report* 30: 250–252.

Grob, G. N. 1983. "Diseases and Environment in American History." In *Handbook of Health, Health Care, and the Health Professions*, D. Mechanic, ed., pp. 3–23. New York: Free Press.

Guttentag, M. and P. F. Secord. 1983. *Too Many Women: The Sex Ratio Question*. Beverly Hills, Calif.: Sage Publications.

Herd, D. 1986. "A Review of Drinking Patterns and Alcohol Problems among U.S. Blacks." In *Report of the Secretary's Task Force on Black and Minority Health*: Volume 7, M. Heckler ed. USDHHS.

Icard, L. 1985. "Black Gay Men and Conflicting Social Identities: Sexual Orientation versus Racial Identity." *Journal of Social Work and Human Sexuality* 4: 83–93.

Icard, L., and D. M. Traunstein. 1987. "Black, Gay, Alcoholic Men: Their Character and Treatment." *Social Casework* 68: 267–272.

Landrum, S., C. Beck-Sague, and S. Kraus. 1988. "Racial Trends in Syphilis among Men with Same-Sex Partners in Atlanta, Georgia." *American Journal of Public Health* 78: 66–67.

Lex, B. W. 1987. "Review of Alcohol Problems in Ethnic Minority Groups." *Journal of Consulting and Clinical Psychology* 55 (3): 293–300.

Macdonald, D. I. 1986. "Coolfont Report: A PHS Plan for the Prevention and Control of AIDS and the AIDS Virus." *Public Health Reports* 101: 341–348.

Mays, V. M. 1988. "The Epidemiology of AIDS in U.S. Blacks: Some Problems and Projections." Unpublished manuscript.

Mays, V. M. and S. D. Cochran. 1987. "Acquired Immunodeficiency Syndrome and Black Americans: Special Psychosocial Issues." *Public Health Reports* 102: 224–231.

———. "Issues in the Perception of AIDS Risk and Risk Reduction Activities by Black and Hispanic Women." *American Psychologist* 1988; 43: 11.

McKusick, L., W. Horstman, and T. J. Coates. 1985. "AIDS and Sexual Behavior Reported by Gay Men in San Francisco." *American Journal of Public Health* 75: 493–496.

Morgan, W. M. and J. W. Curran. 1986. "Acquired Immunodeficiency Syndrome: Current and Future Trends." *Public Health Reports* 101: 459–465.

Samuel, M. and W. Winkelstein. 1987. "Prevalence of Human Immunodeficiency Virus in Ethnic Minority Homosexual/Bisexual Men." *Journal of the American Medical Association* 257: 1901 (letter).

Smith, M. C. 1986. "By the Year 2000." *In the Life: A Black Gay Anthology*, J. Beam ed. Boston: Alyson Publications.

Soares, J. V. 1979. "Black and Gay." In *Gay Men: The Sociology of Male Homosexuality*, M. P. Levine, ed. New York: Harper & Row Publishers.

Spanier, G. B. and P. C. Glick. 1980. "Mate Selection Differentials between Whites and Blacks in the United States." *Social Forces* 58: 707–725.

Stall, R. S., L. McKusick, J. Wiley, T. J. Coates, and D. G. Ostrow. 1986. "Alcohol and Drug Use during Sexual Activity and Compliance with Safe Sex Guidelines for AIDS: The AIDS Behavioral Research Project." *Health Education Quarterly* 13: 359–371.

Staples, R. 1981. *The Changing World of Black Singles*. Connecticut: Greenwood Press.

Sylvester. 1986. Foreword. In *In the Life: A Black Gay Anthology*, J. Beam, ed. Boston: Alyson Publications.

Warren, C. A. B. 1974. *Identity and Community Formation in the Gay World*. New York: John Wiley & Sons.

ARTICLE 41

Julia O'Connell Davidson
Jacqueline Sanchez Taylor

Fantasy Islands:
Exploring the Demand for Sex Tourism

In a useful review of prostitution cross-culturally and historically, Laurie Shrage observes that "one thing that stands out but stands unexplained is that a large percentage of sex customers seek (or sought) sex workers whose racial, national, or class identities are (or were) different from their own" (Shrage 1994: 142). She goes on to suggest that the demand for African, Asian, and Latin American prostitutes by white Western men may "be explained in part by culturally produced racial fantasies regarding the sexuality of these women" and that these fantasies may be related to "socially formed perceptions regarding the sexual and moral purity of white women" (ibid: 48–50). Kempadoo also draws attention to the "over-representation of women of different nationalities and ethnicities, and the hierarchies of race and color within the [international sex] trade" and observes, "That sex industries today depend upon the eroticization of the ethnic and cultural Others suggest we are witnessing a contemporary form of exoticism which sustains postcolonial and post-cold war relations of power and dominance" (Kempadoo 1995: 75–76).

This chapter represents an attempt to build on such insights. Drawing on our research with both male and female Western heterosexual sex tourists in the Caribbean,[1] it argues that their sexual taste for "Others" reflects not so much a wish to engage in any specific sexual practice as a desire for an extraordinarily high degree of control over the management of self and others as sexual, racialized, and engendered beings. This desire, and the Western sex tourist's power to satiate it, can only be explained through reference to power relations and popular discourses that are simultaneously gendered, racialized, and economic.

White Western Men's Sex Tourism

Empirical research on sex tourism to Southeast Asia has fairly consistently produced a portrait of Western male heterosexual sex tourists as men whose desire for the Other is the flip side of dissatisfaction with white Western women, including white Western prostitute women. Lee, for example, explores the demand for sex tourism as a quest for racially fantasized male power, arguing that this is at least in part a backlash against the women's movement in the West: "With an increasingly active global feminist movement, male-controlled sexuality (or female passivity) appears to be an increasingly scarce resource. The travel advertisements are quite explicit about what is for sale: docility and submission" (Lee 1991: 90; see also Jeffreys 1997). Western sex tourists' fantasies of "docile" and "willing" Asian women are accompanied, as Kruhse-Mount Burton (1995: 196) notes, by "a desexualization of white women . . . who are deemed to be spoiled, grasping and, above all, unwilling or inferior sexual partners." These characteristics are also attributed to white prostitute women. The sex tourists interviewed

From *Sun, Sex and Gold: Tourism and Sex Work in the Caribbean* K. Kempadoo, ed. Lanham, MD: Rowan and Littlefield, 1999. © Rowan & Littlefield, reprinted by permission.

by Seabrook (1997: 3) compared Thai prostitutes "very favorably with the more mechanistic and functional behavior of most Western sex workers." Kruhse-Mount Burton states that where many impose their own boundaries on the degree of physical intimacy implied by the prostitution contract (for example refusing to kiss clients on the mouth or to engage in unprotected penetrative and/or oral sex) and are also in a position to turn down clients' requests to spend the night or a few days with them is likewise experienced as a threat to, or denial of, traditional male identity.

Though we recognize that sex tourism provides Western men with opportunities "to reaffirm, if only temporarily, the idealized version of masculine identity and mode of being," and that in this sense sex tourism provides men with opportunities to manage and control both themselves and others as engendered beings, we want to argue that there is more to the demand for sex tourism than this (ibid: 202). In the remainder of this chapter we therefore interrogate sex tourists' attitudes toward prostitute use, sexuality, gender, and "race" more closely, and further complicate matters by considering white Western women's and black Western men and women's sex tourism to the Caribbean.

Western Sexuality and Prostitute Use

Hartsock observes that there is "a surprising degree of consensus that hostility and domination, as opposed to intimacy and physical pleasure" are central to the social and historical construction of sexuality in the West (Hartsock 1985: 157). Writers in the psychoanalytic tradition suggest that the kind of hostility that is threaded through Western sexual expression reflects an infantile rage and wish for revenge against the separateness of those upon whom we depend. It is, as Stoller puts it, "a state in which one wishes to harm an object," and the harm wished upon objects of sexual desire expresses a craving to strip them of their autonomy, control, and separateness—that is, to dehumanize them, since a dehumanized sexual object does not have the power to reject, humiliate, or control (Stoller 1986: 4).

The "love object" can be divested of autonomy and objectified in any number of ways, but clearly the prostitute woman, who is in most cultures imagined and socially constructed as an "unnatural" sexual and social Other (a status which is often enshrined in law), provides a conveniently ready dehumanized sexual object for the client. The commercial nature of the prostitute–client exchange further promises to strip all mutuality and dependency from sexual relations. Because all obligations are discharged through the simple act of payment, there can be no real intimacy and so no terrifying specter of rejection or engulfment by another human being. In theory, then, prostitute use offers a very neat vehicle for the expression of sexual hostility and the attainment of control over self and others as sexual beings. Yet for many prostitute users, there is a fly in the ointment:

> Prostitute women may be socially constructed as Others and *fantasized* as nothing more than objectified sexuality, but in reality, of course, they are human beings. It is only if the prostitute is imagined as stripped of everything bar her sexuality that she can be *completely* controlled by the client's money/powers. But if she were dehumanized to this extent, she would cease to exist as a person. . . . Most clients appear to pursue a contradiction, namely to control as an object that which cannot be objectified. (O'Connell Davidson 1998: 161)

This contradiction is at the root of the complaints clients sometimes voice about Western prostitutes (Graaf et al. 1992: Plumridge and Chetwynd 1997). It is not always enough to buy access to touch and sexually use objectified body parts. Many clients want the prostitute to be a "lover" who makes no claims, a "whore" who has sex for pleasure not money, in short, a person (subject) who can be treated as an object. This reflects, perhaps, deeper inconsistencies in the discourses which surround prostitution and sexuality. The prostitute woman is viewed as acting in a way wholly inconsistent with her gender identity. Her perceived sexual agency degenders her (a woman who takes an impersonal, active, and instrumental approach to sex is not a "real" woman) and dishonors her (she trades in something which is constitutive of her personhood and cannot honorably be sold). The prostitute-using man, by contrast, behaves "in a fashion consistent with the attributes associated with his gender (he is active and sexually predatory, impersonal, and instrumental), and his sexual transgression is thus a minor infraction, since it does not compromise his gender identity" (O'Connell Davidson 1998: 127). A paradox thus emerges:

> The more that men's prostitute use is justified and socially sanctioned through reference to the fiction of biologically determined gender roles and sexuality, the greater the contradiction implicit in prostitution. In order to satisfy their "natural" urges, men must make use of "unnatural" women. (ibid: 128)

All of this helps to explain the fact that, even though their sexual interests may be powerfully shaped by a cultural emphasis on hostility and domination, prostitute use holds absolutely no appeal for many Western men.[2] Fantasies of unbridled sexual access to willingly objectified women are not necessarily fantasies of access to prostitute women. Meanwhile, those who do use prostitutes in the West imagine and manage their own prostitute use in a variety of different ways (see O'Connell Davidson 1998). At one extreme are men who are actually quite satisfied with brief and anonymous sexual use of women and teenagers who they imagine as utterly debased and objectified "dirty whores." (For them, the idea of using a prostitute is erotic in and of itself.) At the other extreme are those who regularly visit the same prostitute woman and construct a fiction of romance or friendship around their use of her, a fiction which helps them to imagine themselves as seen, chosen, and desired, even as they pay for sex as a commodity. Between these two poles are men who indulge in a range of (often very inventive) practices and fantasies designed to create the illusion of balance between sexual hostility and sexual mutuality that they personally find sexually exciting. How does this relate to the demand for sex tourism?

Let us begin by noting that not all Western male sex tourists subjectively perceive their own sexual practices abroad as a form of prostitute use. This reflects the fact that even within any one country affected by sex tourism, prostitution is not a homogeneous phenomenon in terms of its social organization. In some countries sex tourism has involved the maintenance and development of existing large-scale, highly commoditized sex industries serving foreign military personnel (Truong 1990; Sturdevant and Stoltzfus 1992; Hall 1994). But it has also emerged in locations where no such sex industry existed, for instance, in Gambia, Cuba, and Brazil (Morris-Jarra 1996; Perio and Thierry 1996; Sanchez Taylor 1997). Moreover, even in countries like Thailand and the Philippines, where tourist-related prostitution has been grafted onto an existing, formally organized brothel sector serving military demand, tourist development has *also* been associated with the emergence of an informal prostitution sector (in which prostitutes solicit in hotels, discos, bars, beaches, parks, or streets, often entering into fairly protracted and diffuse transactions with clients).

This in itself gives prostitution in sex tourist resorts a rather different character to that of prostitution in red-light districts in affluent, Western countries. The sense of difference is enhanced by the fact that, in many places, informally arranged prostitution spills over into apparently noncommercial encounters within which tourists who do not self-identify as prostitute users can draw local/migrant persons who do not self-identify as prostitutes into profoundly unequal and exploitative sexual relationships. It also means that sex tourism presents a diverse array of opportunities for sexual gratification, not all of which involve straightforward cash for sex exchanges in brothels or go-go clubs or on the streets, and so provides the sex tourist with a veritable "pic 'n' mix" of ways in which to manage himself as a sexual and engendered being. He can indulge in overt forms of sexual hostility (such as selecting a numbered brothel prostitute from those on display in a bar or brothel for "short time" or buying a cheap, speedy sexual service from one of many street prostitutes), or he can indulge in fantasies of mutuality, picking up a woman/teenager in an ordinary tourist disco, wining and dining and generally simulating romance with her for a day or two and completely denying the commercial basis of the sexual interaction. Or, and many sex tourists do exactly this, he can combine both approaches.

Now it could be argued that, given the fact that Western men are socialized into a view of male sexuality as a powerful, biologically based need for sexual "outlets," the existence of multiple, cheap, and varied sexual opportunities is, in itself, enough to attract large numbers of men to a given holiday resort. However, it is important to recognize the numerous other forms of highly sexualized tourism that could satisfy a wish to indulge in various sexual fantasies and also a desire for control over the self as a sexual and engendered being. Sex tourists could, for example, choose to take part in organized holidays designed to facilitate sexual and romantic encounters between tourists (such as Club 18–30 and other singles holidays), or they could choose to take all-inclusive holidays to resorts such as Hedonism or destinations renowned for promiscuous tourist–tourist sex, such as Ibiza or Cap d'Azur. These latter offer just as many opportunities for anonymous and impersonal sex in a party atmosphere as well as for intense but ultimately brief and noncommitted sexual romances. What they do not offer is the control that comes from paying for sex or the opportunity to indulge in racialized sexual fantasies, which helps to explain why sex tourists reject them in favor of sexual experience in what they term "Third World" countries. This brings us to questions about the relationship between the construction of "Otherness" and sex tourism.

"Otherness" and Western Men's Sex Tourism

For obvious reasons, sex tourists spend their time in resorts and *barrios* where tourist-related prostitution is widespread. Thus they constantly encounter what appear to them as hedonistic scenes—local "girls" and young men dancing "sensuously," draping themselves over and being fondled by Western tourists, drinking and joking with each other, and so on. Instead of seeing the relationship between these scenes and their own presence in the resort, sex tourists tend to interpret all this as empirical vindication of Western assumptions of "non-Western peoples living in idyllic pleasure, splendid innocence or Paradise-like conditions—as purely sensual, natural, simple and uncorrupted beings" (Kempadoo 1995: 76). Western sex tourists (and this is true of black as well as white informants) say that sex is more "natural" in Third World countries, that prostitution is not really prostitution but a "way of life," that "They" are "at it" all of the time.

This explains how men who are not and would not dream of becoming prostitute users back home can happily practice sex tourism (the "girls" are not really like prostitutes and so they themselves are not really like clients, the prostitution contract is not like the Western prostitution contract and so does not really count as prostitution). It also explains the paranoid obsession with being cheated exhibited by some sex tourists, who comment on their belief that women in certain sex tourist resorts or particular brothels or bars are "getting too commercial" and advise each other how to avoid being "duped" and "exploited" by a "real professional," where to find "brand new girls," and so on (see O'Connell Davidson 1995; Bishop and Robinson 1998).

It also points to the complex interrelations between discourses of gender, "race," and sexuality. To begin with, the supposed naturalness of prostitution in the Third World actually reassures the Western male sex tourist of his racial or cultural superiority. Thus we find that sex tourists continue a traditional Western discourse of travel which rests on the imagined opposition between the "civilized" West and the "barbarous" Other (Grewal 1996: 136; Kempadoo 1996: 76; see also Brace and O'Connell Davidson 1996). In "civilized" countries only "bad" women become prostitutes (they refuse the constraints civilization places upon "good" women in favor of earning "easy money"), but in the Third World (a corrupt and lawless place where people exist in a state of nature), "nice girls" may be driven to prostitution in order to survive ("they have to do it because they've all got kids" or "they're doing it for their families"). In the West, "nice girls" are protected and supported by their menfolk, but in the Third World, "uncivilized" Other men allow (or even demand that) their womenfolk enter prostitution. In interviews, Western male sex tourists contrast their own generosity, humanity, and chivalry against the "failings" of local men, who are imagined as feckless, faithless, wife-beaters, and pimps. Even as prostitute users, Other men are fantasized as inferior moral beings who cheat and mistreat the "girls."

In this we see that sex tourism is not only about sustaining a male identity. For white men it is also about sustaining a *white* identity. Thus, sex tourism can also be understood as a collective behavior oriented toward the restoration of a generalized belief about what it is to be white: to be truly white is to be served, revered, and envied by Others. For the black American male sex tourists we have interviewed, sex tourism appears to affirm a sense of Western-ness and so of inclusion in a privileged world. Take, for example, the following three statements from a 45-year-old black American sex tourist. He is a New York bus driver and ex-vice cop, a paid-up member of an American-owned sex tourist club, Travel & the Single Male, and he has used prostitutes in Thailand, Brazil, Costa Rica, and the Dominican Republic:

> There's two sides to the countries that I go to. There's the tourist side and then there's the real people, and I make a habit of going to the real people, I see how the real people live, and when I see something like that . . . I tend to look at the little bit I've got at home and I appreciate it. . . .
>
> I've always been proud to be an American. . . . I always tip in US dollars when I arrive. I always keep dollars and pesos, because people tend to think differently about pesos and dollars. . . .

> They always say at hotels they don't want you to bring the girls in; believe me, that's crap, because you know what I do? Reach in my pocket and I go anywhere I want.

Meanwhile, sexualized racisms help the sex tourist to attain a sense of control over himself and Others as engendered and racialized sexual beings. Here it is important to recognize the subtle (or not so subtle) variations of racism employed by white Western men. The sex tourists we have interviewed in the Caribbean are not a homogeneous group in terms of their "race" politics, and this reflects differences of national identity, age, socioeconomic background, and racialized identity. One clearly identifiable subgroup is comprised of white North American men aged forty and above, who, though perhaps not actually affiliated with the Klan, espouse a white supremacist worldview and consider black people their biological, social, and cultural inferiors. They use the word "nigger" and consider any challenge to their "right" to use this term as "political correctness." As one sex tourist complained, in the States. "You can't use the N word, nigger. Always when I was raised up, the only thing was the F word, you can't use the F word. Now you can't say cunt, you can't say nigger."

For men like this, black women are imagined as the embodiment of all that is low and debased, they are "inherently degraded, and thus the appropriate partners for degrading sex" (Shrage 1994: 158). As unambiguous whores by virtue of their racialized identity, they may be briefly and anonymously used, but they are not sought out for longer term or quasi-romantic commercial sexual relationships. Thus, the sex tourist quoted above told us that when he and his cronies (all regular sex tourists to the Dominican Republic) see another American sex tourist "hanging round" with a local girl or woman who has the phenotypical characteristics they associate with African-ness, they call out to him, "How many bananas did it take to get her down out of the tree?" and generally deride him for transgressing a racialized sexual boundary which should not, in their view, by openly crossed.

The Dominican females that men like this want sexual access to are light skinned and straight haired (this is also true in Cuba and in the Latin American countries where we have undertaken fieldwork). They are not classified as "niggers" by these white racists, but instead as "LBFMs" or "Little Brown Fucking Machines," a catch-all category encompassing any female Other not deemed to be either white or "African." The militaristic and imperialist associations of this term (coined by American GIs stationed in Southeast Asia) simultaneously make it all the more offensive and hostile and all the more appealing to this type of sex tourist, many of whom have served in the armed forces (a disturbing number of whom have also been or currently are police officers in the United States) and the rest of whom are "wanna-be vets"—men who never made it to Vietnam to live out their racialized–sexualized fantasies of masculine glory.

Shrage and Kruhse-Mount Burton's comments on the relationship between fantasies of hypersexual Others and myths about white women's sexual purity are also relevant to understanding this kind of sex tourist's worldview. An extract from an article posted on an Internet site written by and for sex tourists entitled "Why No White Women?" is revealing:

Q: Is it because white women demand more (in terms of performance) from their men during Sex? and white men cannot deliver?

A: In my case, it's just that my dick is not long enough to reach up on the pedestal they like to stand on.

If whiteness is imagined as dominance, and woman is imagined as subordination, then "white woman" becomes something of a contradiction. As Young notes, "For white men, white women are both self and other: they have a floating status. They can reinforce a sense of self through common racial identity or threaten and disturb that sense through their sexual Otherness" (Young 1996: 52). White supremacists have to place white women on a pedestal (iconize them as racially, morally, and sexually pure), since whiteness and civilization are synonymous and "civilization" is constructed as the rejection of base animalism. But keeping them on their pedestal requires men to constantly deny what they imagine to be their own needs and nature and thus white women become the object of profound resentment.

Not all Western male sex tourists to the Caribbean buy into this kind of overt, denigrating racism. In fact, many of them are far more strongly influenced by what might be termed "exoticizing" racisms. Younger white Europeans and North Americans, for example, have been exposed to such racisms through the Western film, music, and fashion industries, which retain the old-school racist emphasis on blackness as physicality but repackage and commoditize this "animalism" so that black men and women become the ultimate icons of sporting prowess, "untamed" rebelliousness, "raw" musical talent, sexual power and so on (see hooks 1992, 1994; Young 1996). As a consequence, many young (and some not so young) white Westerners view blackness as a marker of something both "cool" and "hot."

In their own countries, however, their encounters with real live black people are not only few and far between, but also generally something of a disappointment to them. As one British sex tourist to Cuba told us, black people in Britain are "very standoffish. . . . They stick to their own, and it's a shame, because it makes divisions." What a delight it is for men like this to holiday in the Caribbean, then, where poverty combined with the exigencies of tourist development ensure that they are constantly faced by smiling, welcoming black folk. The small black boy who wants to shine their shoes; the old black woman who cleans their hotel room; the cool, young, dreadlocked black man on the beach who is working as a promoter for some restaurant or bar; the fit, young black woman soliciting in the tourist disco—all want to "befriend" the white tourist. Finally, interviews with black American male sex tourists suggest that they too sexualize and exoticize the women they sexually exploit in the Third World ("Latin women are hot," "Latin girls love sex").

Both the sexualized racism that underpins the category LBFM and the exoticizing sexualized racism espoused by other sex tourists help to construct the Other prostitute as the embodiment of a contradiction, that is, as a "whore" who does it for pleasure as much as for money, an object with a subjectivity completely attuned to their own, in short, the embodiment of a masturbatory fantasy. Time and again Western sex tourists have assured us that the local girls really are "hot for it," that Third World prostitutes enjoy their work and that their highest ambition is to be the object of a Western man's desire. Their belief that Third World prostitutes are genuinely economically desperate rather than making a free choice to prostitute for "easy money" is clearly inconsistent with their belief that Third World prostitutes are actually acting on the basis of mutual sexual desire, but it is a contradiction that appears to resolve (at least temporarily) an anxiety they have about the relationship between sex, gender, sexuality, and "race."

The vast majority of the sex tourists we have interviewed believe that gender attributes, including sexual behavior, are determined by biological sex. They say that it is natural for women to be passive and sexually receptive as well as to be homemakers, child rearers, dependent upon and subservient toward men, which is why white Western women (prostitute and nonprostitute alike) often appear to them as unsexed. Thus the sex tourist quoted at the beginning of this chapter could only explain women's presence on traditional male terrain by imagining them as sexually "unnatural" ("Most of these girls are dykes anyways"). White women's relative economic, social, and political power as well as their very whiteness makes it hard for Western male sex tourists to eroticize them as nothing more than sexual beings. Racism/ethnocentrism can collapse such tensions. If black or Latin women are naturally physical, wild, hot, and sexually powerful, there need be no anxiety about enjoying them as pure sex. Equally, racism settles the anxieties some men have about the almost "manly" sexual power and agency attributed to white prostitutes. A Little Brown Fucking Machine is not unsexed by prostituting, she is "just doing what comes naturally." Since the Other woman is a "natural" prostitute, her prostitution does not make her any the less a "natural woman." All these points are also relevant to understanding the phenomenon of female sex tourism.

"Otherness" and Female Sex Tourism

Western women's sexual behavior abroad (both historically and contemporaneously) is often viewed in a rather different light compared to that of their male counterparts, and it is without doubt true that Western women who travel to Third World destinations in search of sex differ from many of the Western male sex tourists discussed above in terms of their attitudes toward prostitution and sexuality. Few of them are prostitute users back home, and few of them would choose to visit brothels while abroad or to pay street prostitutes for a quick "hand job" or any other sexual service (although it should be noted that some women do behave in these ways). But one of the authors' (Sanchez Taylor) ongoing interview and survey research with female sex tourists in Jamaica and the Dominican Republic suggests that there are also similarities between the sexual behavior of Western women and men in sex tourist resorts.

The Caribbean has long been a destination that offers tourist women opportunities for sexual experience, and large numbers of women from the United States, Canada, Britain, and Germany as well as smaller numbers of women from other European countries and from Japan (i.e., the same countries that send male sex tourists) engage in sexual relationships with local men while on holiday there (Karch and Dann 1981; Chevannes 1993; Pruitt and LaFont 1995). Preliminary analysis of data from Sanchez Taylor's survey of a sample of 104 single Western female tourists in Negril, Sosúa, and Boca Chica shows that almost 40 percent had entered into some form of sexual relationship with a local man.³ The survey data further suggest that these were not chance encounters but rather that the sexually active female tourists visit the islands in order to pursue one or more sexual relationships. Only 9 percent of sexually active women were on their first trip; the rest had made numerous trips to the islands, and over 20 percent of female sex tourists reported having had two or more different local sexual partners in the course of a two- to three-week stay. Furthermore female sex tourists, as much as male sex tourists, view their sexual experiences as integral to their holiday—"When in Jamaica you have to experience everything that's on offer," one black American woman explained, while a white woman working as a tour representative for a U.S. package operator said: "I tell my single women: come down here to love them, fuck them, and leave them, and you'll have a great time here. Don't look to get married. Don't call them."

Like male sex tourists, these women differ in terms of their age, nationality, social class, and racialized identity, including among their ranks young "spice girl" teenagers and students as well as grandmothers in their sixties, working-class as well as middle-class professionals, or self-employed women. They also differ in terms of the type of sexual encounters they pursue and the way in which they interpret these encounters. Some are eager to find a man as soon as they get off the plane and enter into multiple, brief, and instrumental relationships; others want to be romanced and sweet-talked by one or perhaps two men during their holiday. Around 40 percent described their relationships with local men as "purely physical" and 40 percent described them as "holiday romances." Twenty percent said that they had found "true love." Almost all the sexually active women surveyed stated that they had "helped their partner(s) out financially" by buying them meals, drinks, gifts, or by giving cash, and yet none of them perceived these relationships as commercial sexual transactions. Asked whether they had ever been approached by a gigolo/prostitute during their stay in Jamaica, 90 percent of them replied in the negative. The data collected in the Dominican Republic revealed similar patterns of denial.

The informal nature of the sexual transactions in these resorts blurs the boundaries of what constitutes prostitution for Western women just as it does for Western men, allowing them to believe that the meals, cash, and gifts they provide for their sexual partners do not represent a form of payment for services rendered but rather an expression of their own munificence. It is only when women repeatedly enter into a series of extremely brief sexual encounters that they begin to acknowledge that, as one put it, "It's all about money." Even this does not lead them to view themselves as prostitute users, however, and again it is notions of difference and Otherness that play a key role in protecting the sex tourist from the knowledge that they are paying for the sexual attentions they receive. As Others, local men are viewed as beings possessed of a powerful and indiscriminate sexuality that they cannot control, and this explains their eagerness for sex with tourist women, regardless of their age, size, or physical appearance. Again, the Other is not *selling* sex, just "doing what comes naturally."

As yet, the number of black female sex tourists in Sanchez Taylor's survey and interview sample is too small to base any generalizations upon,⁴ but so far their attitudes are remarkably consistent with those voiced by the central character in Terry Macmillan's 1996 novel *How Stella Got Her Groove Back,* in which a black American woman finds "love and romance" with a Jamaican boy almost half her age and with certainly less than half her economic means.⁵ Stella views her own behavior in a quite different light from that of white male sex tourists—she disparages an older white male tourist as "a dirty old man who probably has to pay for all the pussy he gets" (Macmillan 1996: 83). It is also interesting to note the ways in which Macmillan "Otherizes" local men: the Jamaican boy smells "primitive"; he is "exotic and goes with the island"; he is "Mr. Expresso in shorts" (ibid: 142, 154). Like white female sex tourists interviewed in the course of research, Macmillan further explains the young Jamaican man's disinterest in Jamaican women and so his sexual interest in an older American woman by Otherizing local women through the use of derogatory stereotypes. Thus, Jamaican women are assumed to be rapacious, materialistic, and sexually instrumental—they only want a man who owns a big car and house and money—and so Jamaican men long for women who do not demand these things (i.e., American women who already possess them).

Like their male counterparts, Western female sex tourists employ fantasies of Otherness not just to legitimate obtaining sexual access to the kind of young, fit, handsome bodies that would otherwise be denied to them and to obtain affirmation of their own sexual desirability (because the fact is that some female sex tourists are themselves young and fit looking and would be easily able to secure sexual access to equally appealing male bodies at home), but also to obtain a sense of power and control over themselves and others as engendered, sexual beings and to affirm their own privilege as Westerners. Thus they continually stress their belief that people in the Caribbean "are different from Westerners." Sexual life is one of the primary arenas in which this supposed difference is manifest. More than half of the female sex tourists surveyed in Jamaica stated that Jamaicans are more relaxed about teenage sex, casual sex, and prostitution than Westerners. In response to open-ended questions, they observed that "Jamaican men are more up front about sex," that "Jamaicans are uninhibited about sex," that "Jamaicans are naturally promiscuous," and that "sex is more natural to Jamaicans." In interviews, female sex tourists also reproduced the notion of an opposition between the "civilized" West and the "primitive" Third World. One Scots grandmother in her early forties described the Dominican Republic as follows: "It's just like Britain before its industrial phase, it's just behind Britain, just exactly the same. Kids used to get beat up to go up chimneys, here they get beaten up to go polish shoes. There's no difference."

Western female sex tourists' racisms, like those of male sex tourists, are also many-layered and nuanced by differences in terms of nationality, age, and racialized identity. There are older white American female sex tourists whose beliefs about "race" and attitudes toward interracial sex are based upon an ideology that is overtly white supremacist. The black male represents for them the essence of an animalistic sexuality that both fascinates and repels. While in their own country they would not want to openly enter a sexual relationship with a black man, in a holiday resort like Negril they can transgress the racialized and gendered codes that normally govern their sexual behavior, while maintaining their honor and reputation back home. As one Jamaican gigolo commented:

> While they are here they feel free. Free to do what they never do at home. No one looking at them. Get a Black guy who are unavailable at home. No one judge them. Get the man to make they feel good then they go home clean and pure.

This observation, and all the sexual hostility it implies, is born out by the following extract from an interview with a 45-year-old white American woman from Chicago, a regular sex tourist to Negril:

> [Jamaican men] are all liars and cheats.... [American women come up Negril because] they get what they don't get back home. A girl who no one looks twice at back home, she gets hit on all the time here, all these guys are paying her attention, telling her she's beautiful, and they really want her.... They're obsessed with their dicks. That's all they think of, just pussy and money and nothing else.... In Chicago, this could never happen. It's like a secret, like a fantasy and then you go home.

When asked whether she would ever take a black boyfriend home and introduce him to her friends and family, she was emphatic that she would not—"No, no, never. It's not like that. This is something else, you know, it's time out. Like a fantasy." This is more than simply a fantasy about having multiple anonymous sexual encounters without getting caught and disgraced. It is also a highly racialized fantasy about power and vengeance. Women like the sex tourist quoted above are looking for black men with good bodies, firm and muscle-clad sex machines that they can control, and this element of control should not be overlooked. It is also important to female sex tourists who reject white supremacist ideologies, and there are many of these, including white liberals and young white women who value Blackness as a "cool" commodity in the same way that many young white men do, and black American and black British female sex tourists.

These latter groups do not wish to indulge in the overtly hostile racialized sexual fantasy described by the woman quoted above, but they do want to live out other fantasies, whether they be "educating and helping the noble savage," or being the focus of "cool" black men's adoring gaze, or being the central character of a Terry Macmillan novel.[6] No matter what specific fantasy they pursue, female sex tourists use their economic power to initiate and terminate sexual relations with local men at whim, and within those relationships, they use their economic and racialized power to control these men in ways in which they could never command a Western man. These are unaccustomed powers, and even the female sex tourists who buy into exoticizing rather than hostile and denigrating racisms appear to enjoy them as such.

For white women, these powers are very clearly linked to their own whiteness as well as to their status and economic power as tourist women. Thus they contrast their own experience against that of local women (remarking on the fact that they are respected and protected and not treated like local women) *and* against their experience back home (commenting on how safe they feel in the Caribbean walking alone at night and entering bars and discos by themselves, observing that local men are far more attentive and chivalrous than Western men). Take, for example, the comments of "Judy," a white American expatriate in the Dominican Republic, a woman in her late fifties and rather overweight:

> When you go to a disco, [white] men eye up a woman for her body, whatever. Dominicans don't care because they love women, they love women. It's not that they're indifferent or anything. They are very romantic, they will never be rude with you, while a white man will say something rude to you, while Dominican men are not like that at all. A white man will say to me, like, "slut" to me and I have been with a lot of Dominican men and they would never say anything like that to you. They are more respectful. Light cigarettes, open doors, they are more gentlemen. Where white men don't do that. So if you have been a neglected woman in civilization, when you come down here, of course, when you come down here they are going to wipe you off your feet.

The Dominican Republic presents women like Judy with a stage upon which to simultaneously affirm their femininity through their ability to command men and exact revenge on white men by engaging sexually with the competition, i.e., the black male. For the first time she is in a position to call the shots. Where back home white female sex tourists' racialized privilege is often obscured by their lack of gender power and economic disadvantage in relation to white men, in sex tourist resorts it is recognized as a source of personal power and power over others. Meanwhile, their beliefs about gender and sexuality prevent them from seeing themselves as sexually exploitative. Popular discourses about gender present women as naturally sexually passive and receptive, and men as naturally indiscriminate and sexually voracious. According to this essentialist model of gender and sexuality, women can never sexually exploit men in the same way that men exploit women because penetrative heterosexual intercourse requires the woman to submit to the male—she is "used" by him. No matter how great the asymmetry between female tourist and local male in terms of their age or economic, social, and racialized power, it is still assumed that the male derives benefits from sex above and beyond the purely pecuniary and so is not being exploited in the same way that a prostitute woman is exploited by a male client. This is especially the case when the man so used is socially constructed as a racialized, ethnic, or cultural Other and assumed to have an uncontrollable desire to have sex with as many women as he possibly can.

Conclusion

The demand for sex tourism is inextricably linked to discourses that naturalize and celebrate inequalities structured along lines of class, gender, and race/Otherness; in other words, discourses that reflect and help to reproduce a profoundly hierarchical model of human sociality. Although sex tourists are a heterogeneous group in terms of their background characteristics and specific sexual interests, they share a common willingness to embrace this hierarchical model and a common pleasure in the fact that their Third World tourism allows them either to affirm their dominant position within a hierarchy of gendered, racialized, and economic power or to adjust their own position upward in that hierarchy. In the Third World, neocolonial relations of power equip Western sex tourists with an extremely high level of control over themselves and others as sexual beings and, as a result, with the power to realize the fantasy of their choosing. They can experience sexual intimacy without risking rejection; they can evade the social meanings that attach to their own age and body type; they can transgress social rules governing sexual life without consequence for their own social standing; they can reduce other human beings to nothing more than the living embodiments of masturbatory fantasies.

In short, sex tourists can experience in real life a world very similar to that offered in fantasy to pornography users: "Sexuality and sexual activity are portrayed in pornography as profoundly distanced from the activities of daily life. The action in pornography takes place in what Griffin has termed 'pornotopia,' a world outside real time and space" (Harstock 1985: 175). To sex tourists, the resorts they visit are fantasy islands, variously peopled by Little Brown Fucking Machines, "cool" black women who love to party, "primitive smelling" black studs who only think of "pussy and money," respectful Latin gentlemen who love women. All the sex tourist has to do to attain access to this fantasy world is to reach into his or her pocket, for it is there that the sex tourist, like other individuals in capitalist societies, carries "his social power as also his connection with society" (Marx 1973: 94). That the Western sex tourist's pocket can contain sufficient power to transform others into Others, mere players on a pornographic stage, is a testament to the enormity of the imbalance of economic, social, and political power between rich and poor nations. That so many Westerners *wish* to use their power in this way is a measure of the bleakness of the prevailing model of human nature and the human sociality that their societies offer them.

Notes

1. In 1995 we were commissioned by ECPAT (End Child Prostitution in Asian Tourism) to undertake research on the identity, attitudes, and motivations of clients of child prostitutes. This involved ethnographic fieldwork in tourist areas in South Africa, India, Costa Rica, Venezuela, Cuba, and the Dominican Republic. We are currently working on an Economic and Social Research Council-funded project (Award no. R 000 23 7625) which builds on this research through a focus on prostitution and the informal tourist economy in Jamaica and the Dominican Republic. Taking these projects together, we have interviewed some 250 sex tourists and sexpatriates and over 150 people involved in tourist-related prostitution (women, children, and men working as prostitutes, pimps, procurers, brothel keepers, etc.)

2. The fact that not all men are prostitute users is something that is often forgotten in radical feminist analyses of prostitution which, as Hart has noted, encourage us to view "either all men as prostitutes' clients or prostitutes' clients as somehow standing for/being symbolic of men in general" (Hart 1994: 53).

3. Because the survey aims to support exploration and theory development in a previously underre-

searched field, purposive (nonprobability) sampling methods were employed (Arber 1993: 72). Sanchez Taylor obtained a sample by approaching all single female tourists in selected locations (a particular stretch of beach, or a given bar or restaurant) and asking them to complete questionnaires.

4. Four out of eighteen single black British and American female tourists surveyed had entered into sexual relationships with local men. Sanchez Taylor also interviewed four more black female sex tourists.

5. In Negril, gigolos often refer to black American female sex tourists as "Stellas," after this fictional character.

6. Macmillan hints at the transgressive elements of a black Western female sex tourist's excitement—Stella's desire for the "primitive"-smelling younger man makes her feel "kind of slutty," but she likes the feeling.

References

Arber, Sarah. "Designing Samples." *Researching Social Life*, ed. Nigel Gilbert, 68–92. London: Sage, 1993.

Bishop, Ryan and Lillian S. Robinson. *Night Market: Sexual Cultures and the Thai Economic Miracle.* New York: Routledge, 1998.

Brace, Laura and Julia O'Connell Davidson. "Desperate Debtors and Counterfeit Love: The Hobbesian World of the Sex Tourist." *Contemporary Politics* 2.3 (1996): 55–78.

Chevannes, Barry. "Sexual Behaviour of Jamaicans: A Literature Review." *Social and Economic Studies* 42.1 (1993).

Graaf, Ron de, Ine Vanwesenbeck, Gertjan van Zessen, Straver Visser, and Jan Visser. "Prostitution and the Spread of HIV." *Safe Sex in Prostitution in The Netherlands*, 2-24, Amsterdam: Mr A. de Graaf Institute, 1992.

Grewal, Inderpal. *Home and Harem: Nation, Gender, Empire and the Cultures of Travel*. London, Leicester University Press 1996.

Hall, C. Michael. "Gender and Economic Interests in Tourism Prostitution: The Nature, Development and Implications of Sex Tourism in South-East Asia." *Tourism: A Gender Perspective*, ed. Vivien Kinnaird and D. Hall. London: Routledge, 1994.

Hart, Angie, "Missing Masculinity? Prostitutes' Clients in Alicante, Spain." *Dislocating Masculinity: Comparative Ethnographics*, ed. Andrea Cornwall and Nancy Lindisfarne, 48–65. London: Routledge, 1994.

Harstock, Nancy. *Money, Sex, and Power.* Boston: Northeastern University Press, 1985.

hooks, bell. *Black Looks: Race and Representation*. London: Turnaround; Boston: South End Press, 1992.

——*Outlaw Culture: Resisting Representations*. London; Routledge, 1994.

Jeffreys, Sheila. *The Idea of Prostitution*. Melbourne: Spinifex, 1997.

Karch, Cecilia A. and G. H. S. Dann, "Close Encounters of the Third Kind." *Human Relations* 34 (1981): 249–68.

Kempadoo, Kamala. "Prostitution, Marginality, and Empowerment: Caribbean Women in the Sex Trade." *Beyond Law* 5.14 (1994): 69–84.

——"Regulating Prostitution in the Dutch Caribbean." Paper presented at the 20th annual conference of the Caribbean Studies Association, Caraçao, Netherlands Antrilles, May 1995.

——"Dominicanas en Curaçao: Miros y Realidades." *Genero y Sociedad* 4.1 (May–August 1996): 102–30.

Kruhse-Mount Burton, Suzy. "Sex Tourism and Traditional Australian Male Identity." *International Tourism: Identity and Change*, ed. marie-Françoise Lanfant, John Allcock, and Edward Bruner, 192–204. London: Sage, 1995.

Lee, Wendy. "Prostitution and Tourism in South-East Asia." *Working Women: International Perspectives on Labour and Gender Ideology*, ed. N. Redclift and M. Thea Sinclair, 79–103. London: Routledge, 1991.

Macmillan, Terry. *How Stella Got Here Groove Back*. New York: Penguin, 1996.

Marx, Karl. *Grundisse*. Harmondsworth, England: Penguin, 1973.

Morris-Jarra, Monica. "No Such Thing as a Cheap Holiday." *Tourism in Focus 26* (autumn 1996): 6–7.

O'Connell Davidson, Julia. *Prostitution, Power and Freedom*. Cambridge: Polity Press, 1998.

Perio, Gaelle and Dominique Thierry. *Tourisme Sexuel au Bresil et en Colombie*. Rapport D'Enquete, TOURGOING, 1996.

Plumridge, Elizabeth and Jane Chetwynd. "Discourses of Emotionality in Commercial Sex." *Feminism & Psychology* 7.2 (1997): 165–81.

Pruitt, Deborah and Suzanne LaFont. "For Love and Money: Romance Tourism in Jamaica." *Annals of Tourism Research* 22.2 (1995): 422–40.

Sanchez Taylor, Jacqueline. "Marking the Margins: Research in the Informal Economy in Cuba and the Dominican Republic." Discussion Paper No. 597/1, Department of Sociology, University of Leicester, 1997.

Seabrook, Jeremy. *Travels in the Skin Trade: Tourism and the Sex Industry*. London: Pluto Press, 1997.

Shrage, Laurie, *Moral Dilemmas of Feminism*. London: Routledge, 1994.

Steller, Robert, *Perversion: The Erotic Form of Hatred*, London: Karnac, 1986.

Sturdevant, Saundra and Brenda Stolzfus. *Let the Good Times Roll: Prostitution and the U.S. Military in Asia*. New York: The New Press, 1992.

Truong, Than Dam. *Sex, Money and Morality: The Political Economy of Prostitution and Tourism in South East Asia*. London: Zed Books, 1990.

Young, Lola. *Fear of the Dark: "Race," Gender and Sexuality in the Cinema*. London: Routledge, 1996.

PART EIGHT

Men in Families

Are men still taking seriously their responsibilities as family breadwinners? Are today's men sharing more of the family housework and childcare than those in previous generations? The answers to these questions are complex, and often depend on which men we are talking about and what we mean when we say "family."

Many male workers long ago won a "family wage," and with it made an unwritten pact to share that wage with a wife and children. But today, as Barbara Ehrenreich argues in her influential book *The Hearts of Men*, increasing numbers of men are revolting against this traditional responsibility to share their wages, thus contributing to the rapidly growing impoverishment of women and children. Ehrenreich may be correct, at least with respect to the specific category of men who were labeled "yuppies" in the 1980s. But if we are looking at the growing impoverishment of women and children among poor, working-class, and minority families, the causes have more to do with dramatic shifts in the structure of the economy—including skyrocketing unemployment among young black males—than they do with male irresponsibility. Increasing numbers of men have no wage to share with a family.

But how about the new dual-career family? Is this a model of egalitarianism, or do women still do what sociologist Arlie Hochschild calls "the second shift"—the housework and childcare that comes after they get home from work. In this section, Francine Deutch examines dual-career families and observes how men get out of sharing housework and childcare. Deutch makes clear that equality will come only when we have dual career and dual-carer families.

Also in flux are notions of fatherhood, and how this role may be changing. Are men becoming more nurturing and caring fathers, developing skills, like the men in Hollywood films such as *Three Men and a Baby*, or simply loving their children more than life itself, as in *Ransom, Jingle All the Way*, and so many others? The articles in this section cause us to expand the debate about fatherhood, recognizing the variety of fatherhoods that are evidenced by different groups of men, such as gay fathers (Brian Miller) and black fathers (Michael Hanchard). Lionel Cantú describes the family experiences of gay Mexican men, and thereby deepens our understanding of the meaning of "family."

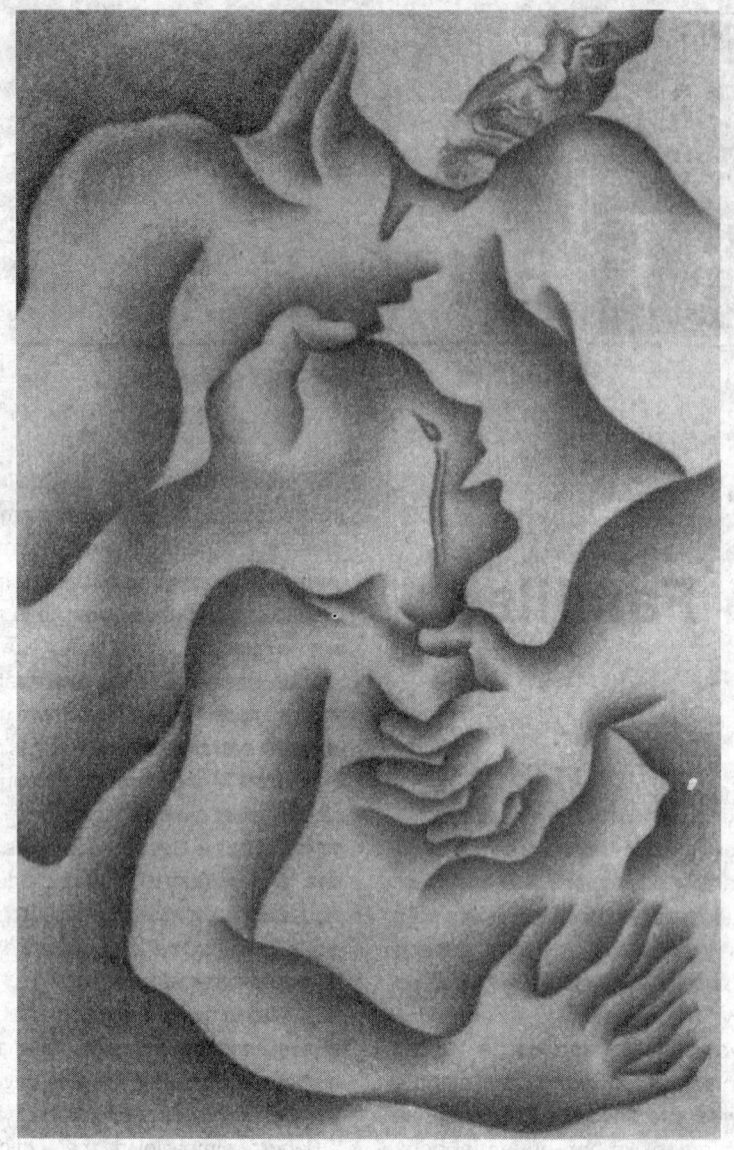

Trying to Kill the Womanly Feelings in his Heart, study from *Powerplay,* Copyright Judy Chicago 1986, prismacolor on hand-made paper, 15" × 10". Collection of Jeffrey Bergen, ACA Galleries, New York, NY. Photo: © Donald Woodman.

ARTICLE 42

Francine M. Deutsch

Strategies Men Use to Resist

Women's ambivalence alone certainly doesn't account for the unequal division of labor at home. The unequal men are hardly fighting to do an equal share of the work. In part, they feel entitled to their wives' domestic services, entitled to pursue unfettered careers, and entitled to relax after their day at the job. Yet they don't feel as entitled as their fathers did. They recognize that their wives are out doing paid labor as well. The men in my study virtually never justified their lack of involvement in household work by invoking some inherent right or privilege they held as men. Although even recent statistics show that women do much more of the household labor, the raw spoken claim of male privilege seems to have become taboo.[1] Men do resist, but their strategies are largely indirect. They include: passive resistance, strategic incompetence, strategic use of praise, the adherence of inferior standards, and denial.[2]

Passive Resistance

"Just say nothing!" seems to be the motto of some men who resist their wives' efforts to involve them in household work. The most obvious form of passive resistance is simply to ignore the request. When I asked one father how he responded to his wife's entreaties, he answered, "In one ear, and out the other."

Obliviousness can be another form of passive resistance. Ethan sits with his coffee oblivious to his children's requests for juice. Another mother reports a similar scene at her house:

From *Halving it All* by Francine Deutsch, Cambridge, MA: Harvard University Press, 1999.

He plants himself on the couch. As soon as he's home from work sometimes . . . If there's something going on with kids, the kids could be screaming and yelling. He's totally oblivious to it. I'm listening to it (while preparing dinner) and I have to come out here and say something to them.

Sometimes men give in and perform a particular household duty, but their grouchiness while doing so becomes another form of passive resistance:

He'll help do dishes once in a while . . . He might put up a stink, but he'll end up doing it. I think I . . . try to sleaze out of it (responsibility when at home) as much as I can . . . I try to dicker or make an excuse or something as my first response, but I usually end up, perhaps somewhat nastily, taking care of them (household chores).

Passive resistance is effective because it requires so much energy to overcome. Women, already tired from their double day, may give up the struggle if the cost of getting help looks higher than the benefits of that help. Having to ask a husband to pour the juice when a child asks may feel like more effort than it's worth. As one mother put it: "I have to direct him and it's easier for me to just do it." The sulking, unpleasant compliance of a husband who clearly resents doing a chore will probably cloud whatever satisfaction his wife feels in getting help. Small wonder that the next time she may very well shrink from trying to obtain his help.

Incompetence

Ruining the laundry, leaving grease on the dishes, ignoring children when one is supposed to be watching them, and forgetting to pick them up from activities are all examples of the strategy of incompetence. Incompetence has its rewards. It allows men to justify the gender-based distribution of domestic labor.

> Getting the kids dressed—these buttons are so tiny I can't do these tiny buttons . . . Poor kids, they're always getting dressed backwards.
> Dinnertime. Mom is the cook. When the kids hear that Daddy's going to be making dinner, they'd rather eat out. I'm not talented. I'm just not very good in the kitchen.
> I just don't possess the tools to deal with girls' clothing, whereas she can.

Women may think twice about trying to get their husbands to take more responsibility at home when the way they carry out those responsibilities creates more problems than it solves: "From time to time he's taken on laundry, but that always ends up really a disaster, something being stained or shrunk, so I don't want him to do laundry."

Ruined laundry or mismatched children's outfits may be annoying, but incompetent care for children can be downright frightening. One mother recounted an incident in which her husband forgot her specific instructions to pick up his eight-year-old son before the older one so that the younger child wouldn't be waiting alone. The eight-year-old did end up waiting on a corner for his father, not alone only because another mother discovered his predicament and waited with him. Not surprisingly, she concludes, "Sometimes I don't trust (my husband) . . . He just doesn't pay attention."

Likewise, another mother explained why she worries when her husband watches their two-year-old:

> The other day he was outside with her and he was sitting there reading the newspaper. I never do that, never sit there and read a newspaper, not because I have to see everything that she does. It was more of a safety thing . . . I would like to feel more confident that when he's alone with her he is watching out for her safety-wise. I sometimes think he's not as conscious of safety.

One might argue that men's "incompetence" in household chores is not a strategy, but simply reflects their lack of skill because of the way they were raised. Boys aren't taught how to take care of children and how to do laundry. According to this argument, even if their incompetence functions to relieve them of domestic responsibility, it doesn't mean that the incompetence is by design. There are two flaws in this argument.

First, although women may be socialized to feel the responsibility for childcare, many have not learned any of the necessary skills before they actually become parents. The difference between them and their husbands is that they know they have no choice. They have to learn how to button those tiny buttons, how to feed solid food, and how to soothe a crying infant. Although these women may have begun parenthood as incompetently as their husbands, the expectations that they and others hold for them as mothers mean that they simply learn what is necessary to learn.

Second, the skills in question can readily be learned. If one took the descriptions of men's incompetence at face value, one would wonder how these men held down jobs. Can it really be the case that a machinist or a man who holds a Ph.D. is incapable of running a washing machine? Women and men often say that women are the managers at home because the women are more organized, but how then do these "disorganized" men manage at work? If a man "forgot" important responsibilities at work the way the father just described "forgot" to pick up his eight-year-old son, he might soon be out of a job.

At heart the issue is not competence, but motivation. If someone wants to learn how to cook, do laundry, take care of children, and manage the household chores she or he can certainly do so. The equally sharing (and alternating-shift) fathers make eminently clear that competence in household skills is not the exclusive domain of women. Some women are not fooled by their husband's cries of incompetence. Listen to this mother's take on what happens when she asks for some help:

> He plays, you know, "How do you do this kind of thing?" and asks me fifteen questions so it would almost be easier for me to do it myself than to sit there and answer all his questions. That makes me angry because I feel like he's just playing stupid because he doesn't want to do it.

The strategy of incompetence often works. Like passive resistance, it is a way of making the cost of the struggle over the work at home too high. This mother sums it up succinctly: "If they act incompetent, then we have to act competent . . . I have this fear that if I didn't do it, then it wouldn't get done or it would be done incompetently." It is a fear that has basis in fact.

Praise

The flip side of men's self-portrayals of incompetence is their praise of their wives' skill in domestic labor. Although praise may be a sincere expression of appreciation, a benefit to its recipient, praise at home may also have the insidious effect of keeping the work within women's domain. The underlying message from men to their wives may sometimes be: "You're so good at it, you should do it." Sometimes the message is hardly subtle: "It would be a struggle for me to do the laundry. I don't think I do it as well as Roz. I think she is better with sort of the *peasant* stuff of life." And the father who said the kids wanted to eat out when they heard Dad was the cook told me: "I only eat to survive, but Dale is just wonderful. She makes these fabulous dinners." In a few couples men used the praise they heaped on their wives to justify why childcare was divided traditionally in their households:

> I definitely wasn't as good as Roz. Roz's just good. She's good if they get a splinter. She's just good at all that stuff.
>
> She's wonderful (as a mother) . . . Some women, like I say, are geared to be business-women; Florence is geared to be a mother. She loves it. She's good at it. I feel real lucky to have her as a partner because it takes a lot of the burden off me.

Praise can be insidious precisely because women do derive satisfaction from a job well done at home and from receiving recognition for it. Ironically, praise may undermine women's struggle for more help because they don't want to lose the self-esteem they derive from husbands' admiring accolades.

Different Standards

Another strategy men use to resist work at home is to maintain different and lower standards. Their spoken or unspoken claim is that they don't care as much as their wives if the house is clean, if a nutritious dinner is served, or if children have after-school activities.

There are three ways that couples might respond to this difference. First, men could raise their standards to meet their wives'. This rarely happens among the unequal couples. Second, women could lower their standards, which occasionally does occur among this group. Most commonly, however, the difference in standards becomes a driving force behind an unequal division. The person who cares more takes the responsibility and does the work.[3]

Women usually care more about keeping the house neat and clean because they, and not their husbands, are judged to be lacking if the house is a mess: "He wouldn't care if it wasn't dusted once every six months. I care because it's a reflection on me. Now that's another problem. Why should it be a reflection on me? He lives here too. But if anybody comes in here and the house is dirty, they're going to think that I'm a slob." Nonetheless, women are lowering their standards for household care, as sales of paper plates have increased and sales of floor wax have declined.[4]

The problem of what children need is a more troubling one. When the welfare of children is involved, women often feel they can't compromise their standards. Denise gave up a camping trip because she thought one parent should be home with her kids. Other mothers changed their jobs so they could meet the school bus when their husbands wouldn't do it or take their children to the after-school activities that they cared about more than their husbands did.

Denial

Just as a magician tricks us by directing our gaze elsewhere while he makes his move, some fathers deny there is a problem by focusing attention elsewhere while their wives do the work at home. Denial takes a variety of forms. Men exaggerate their own contributions by comparing themselves to previous generations, attribute greater contributions of their wives to their wives' personalities or preferences, and obscure who's doing what by invoking rules and patterns that sound fair and equal.

Men often recall their own fathers' roles at home in order to understand their superior contributions. Ironically, some men who do far less than their wives even see themselves as progressive role models. One father in a dual-earner family said he did 35 percent of the childcare; his wife said 25 percent. Nevertheless, he sees himself as a model of equality. His exaggerated view of his contributions seems to stem from his implicit comparison to himself and his father. When I asked why mothers usually did more at home, he said, "Because of the roles of our parents." (His analysis, of course, ignores that his wife leads a very different life from that of his mother, who was never employed outside the home.) He went on to describe his own contributions in glowing terms:

> We've joked and talked about many of the things that I try and do as far as helping and participating . . . I'm hoping that as our girls are selecting mates later in life, they remember how much I helped out and how caring and listening I was . . . One of the advantages for kids that I'm involved with parenting (is) that they will expect their spouses will be involved. I'm a strong advocate of equal rights of women.

No doubt he is a loving and caring father, but he is far from contributing an equal share at home. He does help out, but his enthusiasm for the benefits of their modern division of labor must be considered in light of the inequality between him and his wife and her response to their division: "Sometimes I get overwhelmed and tired, real tired." By focusing on what he is doing that his father didn't, this man seems to miss what his wife is doing that he is not.

Men sometimes obscure an unequal division of labor by talking about and perhaps thinking about themselves and their wives as interchangeable. When I asked men to describe a typical day, indicating who did what, they sometimes used the word "we." "We get the kids ready for school." "We unloaded the dishwasher." Invariably, on further investigation, "we" meant that their wives were doing it.

Men also suggested by a false interchangeability between themselves and their wives by invoking a rule for dividing household labor that ostensibly applied equally to each, but actually worked in their favor. For example, parents commonly reported that whoever was available did the task at hand. Although that might sound like an equitable procedure, it is not if the father arranges to be unavailable. Consider this family. The father describes the division of responsibility at night: "As far as helping with the homework it's fairly equal . . . We both tend to try to help out—whoever's free that night . . . It's not you're going to do the help in math or I'm going to help in math. It's who's free." That sounds equitable, but listen to his wife's description of what happens in the evening:

> That's been a bone of contention lately. Sawyer goes out a lot . . . He still runs a lot at night so that leaves me to deal with the homework . . . She (one of their children) needs a lot of help with math, so that any homework issues I've been dealing with, and getting the youngest ready for bed.

He goes out, so guess who is available?

Finally, fathers sometimes engage in denial when they acknowledge an inequity in the distribution of labor but attribute it to personality characteristics or personal preferences of their wives. Men exaggerated their wives' enjoyment of the family work. For example, this 75–25 father told me: "Cooking relaxes her. She likes to do it and she likes to keep busy for the most part." But when I talked to his wife, she *complained* that he didn't make dinner when he got home from work early.

By imagining their wives' desire and need to do the domestic labor, these men avoid acknowledging the inequity within the couple. This denial allows them to resist not only the work, but also the guilt they might feel if they viewed the situation accurately.

Clearly, men in the unequal families resist the work at home. But the unequal men are not villains. In fact, most are helpers, not slackers. They do relinquish some male privileges, even while they resist giving up others.[5] However, they also ignore the need for their help, feign incompetence, manipulate their wives with praise, discourage them with very low household and parental standards, and avoid work by denying that there is any conflict at all. All of these strategies work to relieve men of household work without their having to admit directly that they simply don't feel responsible for it. Despite the time their wives spend earning a paycheck, the unequal men often feel entitled to avoid picking up the slack at home. The myth implicitly promulgated by these men is that their wives do the work at home not simply because they are women, but because they notice it, they're better at it, and they enjoy it more.

Although these work-resisting strategies are used mostly by the unequal husbands, the equally sharing husbands are not perfect either. Some resist giving up at least a few traditional male privileges. Housework, in particular, seemed an area of contention. For example, in one of the most explicitly feminist equally sharing couples I interviewed, the father's "incompetence" in doing laundry sounded remarkably familiar. Even in the most equal of households, there may be vestiges of the old ways. Still, even if there are some pockets of resistance, for the most part the equally sharing fathers honor their wives' claims to equality.

Strong Women and Reasonable Men

Strong women and reasonable men resolve the conflict over domestic work by inventing equality. Equally sharing mothers are an assertive crew. They communicate in a clear and direct manner, and use whatever clout they have to elicit their husbands' cooperation. Their husbands acknowledge the strength of these women in establishing equality at home:

> Sally is very strong. There's no question about that. I think it's partly that Sally... makes it that we both share. She feels very strongly about that.

> I think the most important reason is that Bernice absolutely, completely insists on it.

However, part of the reason these women appear strong is their success, and although women's strength may be necessary in the fight for equality, it is not sufficient. The strength and assertiveness of the equally sharing mothers is matched by the sense of fairness evident in the behavior of the equally sharing fathers. Equally sharing men have relinquished male privileges to which at least some had initially felt entitled.

In fact, the equally sharing women may argue for principles of equality because they sense they have a shot at success with their husbands. The unequally sharing mothers, realizing the futility of trying for equality in their families, settle for trying to get their husbands to do a bit more. The equally sharing mothers may not have to resort to meltdowns because their husbands have already responded. The rage of the unequal women may express more than the frustration of trying to do the impossible. It may be the rage of impotence at their failure to get more help.[6]

Compare the experience of the equally sharing mothers who won the battles for equality to that of Madeline, a legal services attorney with two children, who began parenthood with strong views about equal sharing. She and her husband agreed that when their first child was born each of them would take parental leave, and subsequently each of them would cut back on paid work to care for their new baby to avoid using too much daycare. Her husband, Aaron, was thrilled with his equally sharing role in the early years of parenting: "I was very excited about it. I had a paternity leave and . . . did sole care . . . and then worked a three- or four-day week for another year . . . There was a lot of time when I was just with my son and I considered that a privilege." Equal sharing was initially achieved in this family with little conflict. But perhaps signs of the dénouement were evident in the meaning Aaron ascribed to his sharing. The language he uses as he enthusiastically describes his role as a new parent is telling. It is the language of personal choice: "It was just great. It completely felt like my own choice and not something that I should do or that I had to do."

It is difficult to imagine a mother speaking these words. No matter how thrilled she is at spending time with a new infant, there is no denying that caring for a new baby is something she "should do." Aaron expresses the thrill of parenting at the same time that he asserts his entitlement not to do it. He immerses himself in parenthood the first time around because he wants to, not because he feels ultimately that it is his responsibility to do so. Thus, after their second child was born, when his career was getting off the ground and he had less passion and energy for parenting, he felt entitled to refuse to do it. He refused to take parental leave or cut back to part-time work. His wife told me:

> If you had come a year after William was born, then you would have found us struggling more about whose responsibility was what. I was feeling very much like Aaron was reneging on the commitment that we made about being with William . . . I had made my commitment and he wasn't keeping his part of the bargain.

Madeline was every bit as assertive as the equally sharing mothers. Yet, although she fought for her belief in equal responsibility for childcare clearly and directly, today she compromises her career while her husband takes a helper role at home. Aaron's analysis of what happens in "society" aptly describes what happened in his own family:

"I think probably men feel they have the option to invest or not invest, whereas I think women feel they're the bottom line and they can't count on anyone else to do that."

Madeline may not appear as strong as other equally sharing mothers simply because she failed. Her husband did not honor her claims of equality. Aaron differed from the equally sharing men because those men accepted the justice of their wives' claims, even if they hadn't internalized as strong a feeling of responsibility for family life as their wives had. One extraordinarily honest equally sharing father acknowledged that although he "irrationally" wished his wife would create a more traditional family life, "rationally" he recognized that it wouldn't be fair: "I'm hardly a raging feminist, but I do have enough sense to see that that's a completely unfair distribution of labor."

Thus a sense of fairness motivates some of the equally sharing men to accept their wives' well-argued claims. Moreover, that sense of fairness drives some of the men to share even without a struggle. Let's not forget Paul, the father of five, who jumped in to help without prompting from his wife. His sense of fairness and love for his wife dictated that it wouldn't be right to shirk while she worked.

The sense of entitlement that men and women bring to marriage affects the content and conduct of their conflicts, but it also changes and develops over time. Feelings of entitlement lead women to fight for principles, make clear and rational demands, and back them up with power-assertive strategies. But the feelings of entitlement expressed by the equally sharing mothers can also be a product, rather than a precursor, of their success. When their husbands accept principles of equality, respond to their demands, or indicate that their relationships are more important than male privilege, they promote a feeling of entitlement in their wives.

For example, consider Paul's wife, Mary, the equally sharing mother of five who didn't demand equality or even fight for it. When I asked her whether she or Paul had more leisure time, she reflected for a few seconds (indicating there wasn't much difference between them) and then replied, "I don't know, maybe he has a little bit more," adding in a light-hearted tone, "I'll have to do something about that." Once achieved, equality feels like a right.

Conversely, when the unequal husbands resist, they undermine their wives' sense of entitlement to their help. Listen to this mother's story:

> There's some things that aren't worth fighting over. I always know when (my husband) has been babysitting for a couple of hours because the living room looks like a demolition derby has come through. And the bathroom looks the same way . . . the dirty diapers are in there and all the dirty clothes are all over the bathroom floor . . . So I just have learned that it's not worth wasting all kinds of extra energy. I just kind of do it, not necessarily that I like it. *He helps much more than a lot of fathers help.*

The futility of some struggles leads women to give up and to read just their expectations. Instead of comparing their husbands' contributions to their own, they shift to comparing their husbands' contributions to those of other men. It is precisely that focus on within-gender comparison that maintains different senses of entitlement between men and women.[7] If a husband does more than his peers, his wife may then conclude she is getting a good deal. But although she may be getting a good deal relative to other women, it's not so good when you compare it to what her husband is getting. The shift in comparisons, however, allows women to live with resistant husbands and not feel exploited.[8]

Men's senses of entitlement are also, in part, products of the struggle with their wives. When you look at the equally sharing men now, they all seem eminently reasonable. For some, the reasonable stance was born out of serious strife with their wives. Interestingly, sometimes these men don't mention the conflicts that led up to their equally sharing role. For example, the husband who had expected his wife to "cook, clean, . . . and box his collars" made no mention of the strikes his wife used to get him to change. His transformation occurred so thoroughly that now his explanation for equal sharing refers only to his own sense of responsibility to do right by his children.

Discovering themselves acting like egalitarians, equally sharing fathers often pat themselves on the back for their enlightened stance. Meanwhile, their wives tout their own assertiveness and strength. Although they look like they have always been strong women and reasonable men, it is important not to forget that female strength and male reason are qualities that are sustained, lost, or developed in the creation of family life.

Life-Styles of Gay Husbands and Fathers

Brian Miller

The words "gay husband" and "gay father" are often regarded as contradictions in terms. This notion is hinted at in Anita Bryant's widely quoted non sequitur, "Homosexuals recruit because they cannot reproduce." Researchers estimate, however, that in America there are six million gay husbands and fathers (Schulenberg 1985; Bozett 1987). Why do these men marry and have children? How do they organize their lives? What are their difficulties and joys as a consequence of their behavior?

To address these questions, 50 gay husbands and fathers were contacted in 1976 by means of multiple-source chain-referral samples. At first interview, 24 of the men were living with their wives; three years later at the second interview, only three had intact marriages. Approximately two-thirds of the respondents have been followed and all of them are now separated (Humphreys and Miller 1980a). To show the modal developments in gay husbands' and fathers' life-styles, the data are organized along a four-point continuum: Covert Behavior, Marginal Involvement, Transformed Participation, and Open Endorsement.

Covert Behavior

Early in adult life, gay husbands and fathers tend to regard their homosexual feelings as nothing more than genital urges. They are reluctant to refer to either themselves or their behavior as gay: "I hate labels" is a common response to questions about sexual orientation. These men have unstable self-concepts—one day thinking they are homosexual and another day thinking they are not. Their reluctance to label their same-sex activity as homosexual is not because they hate labels per se; indeed they strive to present themselves to others under a heterosexual label. Rather, they dislike a label that calls attention to behaviors they would prefer to forget.

Premarital homosexual experiences are often explained away with "It's only a phase" or "God, was I drunk last night!" These men report such activities prior to marriage as arranging heterosexual double-date situations in which they would perform coitus in the back seat of the car, for example, while fantasizing about the male in the front seat. Others report collaborating with a buddy to share a female prostitute. These ostensibly heterosexual acts allowed the men to buttress their sense of heterosexuality while gratifying homosexual urges. During the premarital period, respondents discounted gay life-styles and romanticized heterosexual family living as the only way to achieve the stable home life, loyal companionship, and fatherhood they desired.

These men married in good faith, thinking they could overcome their gay desires; they did not believe they were deceiving their spouses. In fact, most men broached the issue of their homosexual feelings to their wives before marriage, but the information was usually conveyed in an oblique manner and downplayed as inconsequential. This kept their future wives from thinking that they might be marrying homosexuals. Wives' denials of their husbands' homosexuality were further facilitated by the fact that half the women, at their nuptials, were pregnant by the men they were marrying.

Revised and updated from an article in *Gay Men: The Sociology of Male Homosexuality* by Martin P. Levine. New York: Harper & Row, 1979.

In the early years of marriage, high libido provided husbands with easy erections for coitus. Respondents report, however, that this situation tended to deteriorate shortly after the birth of the first child. Increasingly, they found themselves fantasizing about gay erotica during coitus.

Marriage engulfs the men in a heterosexual role, making them marginal to the gay world. Their social isolation from others who share their sexual interests burdens them with "I'm-the-only-one-in-the-world" feelings. These men, realizing their behavior is inconsistent with their heterosexual reputation, try to reduce their anxiety and guilt by compartmentalizing gay and nongay worlds. One respondent said: "I never walk in the door without an airtight excuse of where I've been." Some men avoid the strain of remembering stories by intimidating the wife into silence: "She knows better than to question my whereabouts. I tell her, 'I get home when I get home; no questions asked.'" In these respects, respondents have parallels to their adulterous heterosexual counterparts (Libby and Whitehurst 1977).

Extramarital sex for respondents usually consists of clandestine, impersonal encounters in parks, tearooms, or highway rest stops, with hitchhikers or male hustlers. (Regarding this, single gays sometimes comment, "Married gays give the rest of us a bad name.") Occasionally, furtiveness itself becomes eroticized, making the men sexually dysfunctional in calmer contexts. Recreational, gay scenes such as dances, parties, and gay organizations are not used by respondents, primarily because they dread discovery and subsequent marital dissolution. Many are further limited by fears that their jobs would be threatened, by lack of geographical access to gay institutions, or by religious scruples. In fact, these men are largely unaware of gay social events in their communities and have little idea of how to participate in them. They tend to be ideologically ambivalent about the gay world, sometimes thinking of it as exotic, and other times condemning it as "superficial, unstable, full of blackmail and violence." Given their exposure to only the impersonal homosexual underground, and not to loving gay relationships, their negative perception is somewhat justified. As long as they remain marginal to the gay world, the likelihood of their participation in safe, fulfilling gay relationships remains minimal (Miller and Humphreys 1980).

Some men regard their homosexual desires not as an orientation, but as a compulsion: "I don't want to do these things, but I'm driven to do them." Other accounts that explain away their homosexual behavior, emphasize its nonseriousness, and minimize its consequences include the following. (1) "I might be okay if my wife learned to give good blow jobs." (2) "I only go out for it when I'm drunk or depressed." (3) "I go to the truck-stop and meet someone. We're just a couple of horny married guys relieving ourselves. That's not sex. [It] doesn't threaten my marriage like adultery would." (4) "Sex with men is a minor aspect of my life that I refuse to let outweigh more important things."

The respondent who gave this last account also presented conflicting evidence. He spent time, effort, and anxiety in rearranging his schedule to accommodate sex, spending money on his car and fuel to search for willing men, constructing intricate stories to fool work associates and family, and buying his wife penance gifts. He also experienced near misses with police and gay bashers. Still, he viewed all this as only a "minor aspect" of his life.

Another rationalization is "I'm not really homosexual since I don't care if it's a man, woman or dog that's licking my cock. All I want is a hole." Further questioning, however, made clear that this respondent was not looking for just any available orifice. He stated that it was equally important that he persuade the most attractive man available to fellate him.

Another account is the "Eichmann dodge." Men may claim, like Eichmann, that they are the victims of other men's desire, inadvertently caught up and swept along by the events, thereby absolving themselves of responsibility. Men stating this rationalization, however, are often skilled at seducing others into making the first move. Some gay husbands and fathers claim that they limit themselves to one special "friendship" and that no one else of their sex could excite them. If they think of homosexuality at all, they conceive it as promiscuous behavior done by degenerates, not by people like themselves who are loyal and who look conventional.

These accounts help respondents deny homosexuality while practicing it. They find it difficult to simultaneously see themselves as worthwhile persons and as homosexuals, and to reconcile their masculine self-image with the popular image of gays as effeminate. The most they can acknowledge is that they get together with other men to ejaculate and that they fantasize about men during sex with their wives. In spite of their rationalizations, however, these men report considerable anxiety and guilt about maintaining their compartmentalized double lives.

Respondents are reluctant to rate their marriages as "happy," typically referring to them as "duties." The ambivalence is expressed by one who said: "My wife is a good person, but it's funny, I can't live with this marriage and I can't live without it." Respondents report conflict with wives who object to the disproportionate time these men spend away from home, neglecting parental responsibilities. The men view alternatives to marriage as limited, not seeing life in the gay world as a viable option. They find it difficult to talk about their children and express guilt that their work and sex schedules do not allow them to spend as much time with their children as they would like. Nevertheless, most of the men report that their children are the main reason for remaining married: "In this horrible marriage, [the children] are the consolation prize."

Marginal Involvement

Respondents at this point on the continuum engage in homosexual behavior and have a gay self-identity. However, these men are marginal to the gay community since they have heterosexual public identities, and are often living with their wives. Still, they are much more comfortable with their homoerotic desires than are those in the Covert Behavior group and are more disclosing about their sexual orientation to other gays.

Compared with men in the previous group, Marginally Involved respondents have an expanded repertoire of sexual outlets. They sometimes compile telephone-number lists of sex partners and have limited involvement with small networks of gay friends. The men maintain secrecy by using post office boxes or separate office phones for gay-related business. Fake identities and names may be constructed to prevent identification by sexual partners. Employing male "masseurs" or maintaining a separate apartment for gay sex provide other relatively safe outlets. Consequently, these men are less likely to encounter police entrapment or gay bashers. Gay bars are somewhat inaccessible since they often start too late, and the men cannot regularly find excuses for extended absences from home. Some men resort to lunch-hour or presupper "quickies" at the baths.

In spite of these measures, respondents report many facade-shattering incidents with heterosexuals. Such difficulties include being caught on the street with a gay friend whose presence cannot be explained, blurting out praise about an event, then remembering it was attended with a gay friend, not one's wife, and transferring body lice or a venereal disease from a hustler to the wife, an especially dangerous occurrence in this time of AIDS (Pearson 1986). Many respondents, however, continue to deny wives' knowledge about their homosexuality: "I don't think my wife really knows. She's only mentioned it a couple of times, and only when she was too drunk to know what she was saying."

Men who travel as part of their business or who have loosely structured working hours enjoy relative freedom. For them, absences and sexual incidents may be more easily covered. A minority of men, specifically those in artistic and academic fields, are able to mix their heterosexual and homosexual worlds. Their circle is that of the relatively wealthy and tolerant in which the epithet "perversion" is replaced by the more neutral "eccentricity," and variant behavior is accepted as long as the man is discreet and does not "rub the wife's nose in it." Several respondents socialize openly with similarly situated men or with gay sex partners whom wives and others ostensibly know as merely work assistants or friends of the family.

Because Marginally Involved respondents are "out" to some audiences and not to others, they sometimes resemble, as one man said, "a crazy quilt of contradictions." This is emphasized by playing word games with questioners or with those who try to penetrate their defenses. Playing the role of the eccentric and giving mixed messages provide a smokescreen for their emotional whereabouts from both gays and nongays.

This adjustment, however, is tenuous and respondents are often ambivalent about maintaining their marriages. They fantasize about life as a gay single, and entertain ideas of divorce. The guilt these respondents experience is sometimes reflected in what might be called Santa Claus behavior. They shower their children—and sometimes their wives—with expensive gifts to counteract feelings that they have done a terrible thing to their family by being homosexual: "It's the least I can do for having ruined their chance to grow up in a normal home." Using credit cards to manage guilt has many of these men in serious debt and laboring as workaholics.

Like men in the first category, these men regret that performing their breadwinner, husband, and homosexual roles leaves little time for the father role. Nevertheless, they are reluctant to leave their marriages, fearing permanent separation from their children. They also fear community stigma, ambivalently regard the gay world, and are unwilling to endure the decreased standard of living necessitated by divorce.

Over time, it becomes increasingly difficult for these men to reconcile their discordant identities as husband and as homosexual. Although some are able to routinize compartmentalization, others find sustaining the necessary maneuvers for secrecy to be not worth it. Conspiracies of silence and denial within the families become strained, if not transparent. Respondents tend to seek closure by communicating, directly and indirectly, their orientational needs to wives and by becoming more explicit in their methods of making gay contacts. Others are exposed by vice arrests or by being victimized by men they solicit. Most wives are surprised by the direct confrontation. Respondents are surprised that their wives are surprised since respondents may have thought their wives already knew, and tacitly accepted it. Initially wives often react with disbelief, revulsion, and anger: "I feel betrayed." This frequently gives way to a feeling of couple solidarity, that "we can conquer the problem together." When this is the adaptation, respondents do not come out of the closet so much as take their wives into the closet with them.

Couples try a variety of techniques to shore up the marriages. Respondents may seek therapy to "cure" their homosexuality. Some men generously offer wives the freedom to experience extramarital affairs, too, although it appears this is done mostly to relieve respondents' guilt since they know that wives are unlikely to take them up on the offer. When wives do not put the offer to the test, respondents further console their guilt by interpreting this as evidence that the wives are "frigid" or low in "sex drive," although data from the wives dispute this characterization (Hays and Samuels 1988).

Some couples try instituting new sexual arrangements: a *ménage à trois,* or the husband is allowed out one night a week with gay friends. In the former interaction, wives tend to report feeling "used" and, in the latter, men tend to report feeling they are on a "leash."

Sexual conflicts spill into other domestic areas. Tardiness or missed appointments lead to wives' suspicions and accusations and general marital discord. One man calls this compromise period "white-knuckle heterosexuality." By negotiating ground rules that reinstate partial denial and by intellectualizing the situation, some couples maintain for years the compromise period. This uneasy truce ends if ground rules are repeatedly violated and when the wife realizes (1) that her husband finds men sexier than herself, (2) that he is unalterably gay, (3) that her primary place as object of permanent affection is challenged, and (4) that she has alternatives and can cope without the marriage. Wives gradually come to resent romanceless marriages with men who would rather make love to another man, and the homosexual husbands come to resent, as one man said, being "stifled in a nuptial closet."

Couples who remain married after disclosure tend not to have rejected divorce, but rather to have an indefinite postponement of it: "After the children leave home." "After the finances are in order." Other considerations that keep the couples together include religious beliefs, family pressure, wives' dependence, and the perceived nonviability of the gay world.

In most cases, the immediate impetus for ending the marriage is the husband's establishment of a love relationship with another man. As such relationships intensify, men begin to reconstruct the gay world as favorable for effecting companionship and social stability. It is usually wives, however, who take action to terminate the marriages. Painful as this experience is, it somewhat eases the men's guilt for causing marital dissolution.

Transformed Participation

Respondents who reach this point on the continuum engage in homosexual behavior and have self-identities—and to a limited extent, public identities—that reflect acceptance of their behavior. These men generally have come out as gay and left their wives.

Acculturation into the gay world involves three areas of concern for respondents: (1) disadvantage of advanced age and late arrival on the scene, (2) the necessity of learning new gay social definitions and skills, and (3) the need to reconcile prior fantasies to the realities of the gay world. Once respondents no longer live with wives and children, they begin to increase their contacts with the gay world and their marginality to it decreases. They may now subscribe to gay publications, join gay religious congregations, and go to gay social and political clubs and private gay parties. They experience a rapid expansion of gay consciousness and skills and take steps to form close friendships with others of their sexual orientation.

Moving out of the closet, these men report a stabilization of self-concept and a greater sense of psychological well-being. Their attitudes toward homoerotic behavior become more relaxed and better integrated into their everyday lives. Most experience a change in body image, exemplified by improved physical fitness and increased care with their appearance. Many report the elimination of nervous and psychosomatic disorders such as ulcers, excessive fatigue, and back aches, as well as substance abuse.

These respondents' sexual orientation tends to be known by significant others with two exceptions: their employers and children. Secrecy sometimes exists with employers since respondents believe the legal system does not protect their interests should they be dismissed for being gay (Levine 1981).

Relatively little openness about homosexuality also exists with these respondents' children. Typically, only older children (if any) are told, and it is not considered a topic for general discussion. There is fear that, if the man's gayness becomes known in the community, his employer might find out or his ex-wife might become irked and deny him child visits. Successful legal appeal for gay people in such matters is difficult, a situation these men perceive as legally sanctioned blackmail.

In line with this, most respondents, rather than living with their children, have visiting schedules with them. They do not have the financial resources either to persuade their ex-wives to relinquish the children or to hire care for them while devoting time to their own careers.

Men who are able to terminate marriages without their spouse's discovering their homosexuality avoid this problem. However, fear of subsequent exposure and loss of children through a new court order remains and prompts some men to stay partially closeted even after marital dissolution. In spite of these fears, the degree of passing and compartmentalization of gay and nongay worlds is much less for men at this point on the continuum than for those who are Covert and Marginal.

Open Endorsement

Respondents who reach this point on the continuum not only engage in homosexual behavior and have a self-identity reflective of the behavior but also openly champion the gay community. Although they come from the full range of economic backgrounds, they tend to have high social and occupational resources. Some have tolerant employers; some are full-time gay activists; others are self-employed, often in businesses with largely gay clienteles.

Proud of their newfound identity, these men organize their world, to a great extent, around gay cultures. Much of their leisure, if not occupation, is spent in gay-related pursuits. They have experienced unhappy marriages and divorce, the struggle of achieving a gay identity, and now feel they have arrived at a satisfactory adjustment. These men, consequently, distinguish themselves in ideology from respondents in other categories. For example, what the others refer to as "discretion," men in this category call "duplicity" and "sneaking around." Moreover, what closeted men see as "flaunting," openly gay respondents call "being forthright" and "upfront."

Respondents' efforts in constructing this new life are helped not only by having a gay love relationship, but by the Gay Liberation Movement (Humphreys and Miller 1980b). Parallel processes are at work whereby the building of a personal gay identity is facilitated by the larger cultural context of increasing gay pride and diversification of gay institutions and heritage (Harry and DeVall 1978; and Murray 1979; Adam 1987). Still, coming out is not easy or automatic. This is partly due to the fact that there is no necessary conjunction among sexual behavior fantasy, self-identity, and object of affectional attachment. Although there is a strain toward consistency for most people among these components of sexuality, this is not invariably so. The ways these components change over time and the combinations in which they link with each other are multiple (Simon and Gagnon 1969; Miller 1983).

Men who reach the Open Endorsement point often have fears that their father and ex-husband statuses could distance them from single gays. Sometimes respondents fear that single gays, similar to nongays, regard them with confusion, curiosity, or pity. Integrating gay and father roles requires patience, since it is often difficult for respondents to find a lover who accepts him and his children as a "package deal," and the gay father may feel he has not enough time and energy to attend to both children and a lover. Selecting a lover who is also a gay father is a common solution to this situation.

Most respondents who have custody of their children did not experience court custody battles but gained custody because the mother did not want the children or because the children, being allowed to choose, chose to live with their fathers. Respondents who live with their children are more likely to have a close circle of gay friends as their main social outlet, rather than participating primarily in gay commercial establishments (McWhirter and Mattison 1984).

Men at this point on the continuum have told their children about their homosexuality. They report children's reaction to be more positive than expected and, when there is a negative reaction, it generally dissipates over time (Miller 1979). Children's negative reactions centered more on the parent's divorce and subsequent household changes than on the father's homosexuality per se. Daughters tend to be more accepting of their father's homosexuality than sons, although most children feel their father's honesty brings them closer together. Children report few instances of neighborhood homophobia directed against them, possibly because the children try to disclose only to people they know will react favorably. There is no indication that the children of gay fathers are disproportionately homosexual themselves although, of the children who turned out to be gay, there were more lesbian daughters than gay sons.

Wives and relatives sometimes worry that gay men's children will be molested by him or his gay friends. Evidence from this study supports earlier research findings that indicate such fears are unwarranted (Bozett 1987).

Discussion

The general tendency is for the Covert Behavior respondents to move toward Open Endorsement. There are several caveats, however, about this movement. For example, the continuum should not be construed as reifying transient states into types. Additionally, movement out of marriage into an openly gay identity is not unilateral. There are many negotiations back and forth, in and out of the closet. There is not a finite number of stages; not everyone becomes publicly gay and not everyone passes through every step. Few respondents move easily or accidentally through the process. Rather, each level is achieved by a painful search, negotiating with both oneself and the larger world.

The event most responsible for initiating movement along the continuum and reconstructing gay fathers' perceptions of the gay community is the experience of falling in love with another man. By contrast, factors hindering movement along the continuum include inability to perceive the gay world as a viable alternative as well as perceived lack of support from other gays, economic difficulty, family pressure, poor health, wives' dependence, homophobia in respondents or community, and moral/religious scruples.

This study has several findings. Gayness and traditional marital relationships are perceived by the respondents as discordant compared to relationships established when they move into the gay world. Although respondents perceive gayness as incompatible with traditional marriage, they perceive gayness as compatible with fathering. Highly compartmentalized life-styles and deceit sometimes repress open marital conflict, but unresolved tension characterizes respondents' marriages. In contrast, men who leave their spouses and enter the gay world report gay relationships to be more harmonious than marital relationships. They also report fathering to be more salient once having left their marriages. Men who come out perceive less discrimination from family, friends, and co-workers than those who are closeted anticipate. Wives tend to be upset by their husbands' revelations, but respondents are typically surprised by the positive reactions of their children and their parents.

Future prospects for gay fathers hinge largely on the success of the gay liberation movement. If these men can politicize their status, if they can see their difficulties stemming from social injustice and society's homophobic conditioning rather than personal inadequacy, and if they can redefine themselves, not as deviants, but as an oppressed minority, self-acceptance is improved. This helps lift their depression and externalize anger—anger about prejudice and about wasting their precious early years in the closet. Further, it minimizes their guilt and eases adjustment into the gay community (Miller 1987).

As the gay liberation movement makes alternatives for fathering available within the gay community, fewer gays are likely to become involved in heterosexual marriages and divorce. Adoption, surrogate parenting, and alternative fertilization are some of the new ways single gays can now experience fatherhood (Miller 1988). If current trends continue, there will be a proliferation of family life-styles so that parenthood becomes available to all regardless of sexual orientation.

References

Adam, B. (1987). *The rise of a gay and lesbian movement.* Boston: Hall.

Bozett, F. W. (1987). *Gay and lesbian parents.* New York: Praeger.

Harry, J. & DeVall, W. (1978). *The social organization of gay males.* New York: Praeger.

Hays, D. & Samuels, A. (1988). Heterosexual women's perceptions of their marriages to bisexual or homosexual men. In F. W. Bozett (Ed.), *Homosexuality in the family.* New York: Haworth.

Humphreys, L. & Miller, B. (1980a). Keeping in touch: Maintaining contact with stigmatized respondents. In W. Shaffir, R. Stebbins, & A. Turowetz (Eds.), *Field work experience: Qualitative approaches in social research.* New York: St. Martin's.

Humphreys, L. & Miller, B. (1980b). Identities in the emerging gay culture. In J. Marmor (Ed.), *Homosexual behavior: A modern reappraisal.* New York: Basic.

Levine, M. (1981). Employment discrimination against gay men. In P. Stein (Ed.), *Single life.* New York: St. Martin's.

Libby, R. & Whitehurst, R. (1977). *Marriage and alternatives.* Glenview, IL: Scott, Foresman.

McWhirter, D. & Mattison, A. (1984). *The male couple.* Englewood Cliffs, NJ: Prentice-Hall.

Miller, B. (1979). Gay fathers and their children. *Family Coordinator* 28: 544–552.

Miller, B. (1983). Foreword. In M. W. Ross (Ed.), *The married homosexual man.* London: Routledge & Kegan Paul.

Miller, B. (1987). Counseling gay husbands and fathers. In F. W. Bozett (Ed.), *Gay and lesbian parents.* New York: Praeger.

Miller, B. (1988). Preface. In F. W. Bozett (Ed.), *Homosexuality in the family.* New York: Haworth.

Miller, B. & Humphreys, L. (1980). Lifestyles and violence: Homosexual victims of assault and murder. *Qualitative Sociology* 3: 169–185.

Murray, S. (1979). The institutional elaboration of a quasi-ethnic community. *International Review of Modern Sociology* 9: 165–177.

Pearson, C. (1986). *Good-by, I love you.* New York: Random House.

Schulenberg, J. (1985). *Gay parenting.* New York: Doubleday.

Simon, W. & Gagnon, J. (1969). On psychosexual development. In D. Goslin (Ed.), *Handbook of socialization theory and research.* New York: Rand McNally.

ARTICLE 44

Lionel Cantú

A Place Called Home: A Queer Political Economy: Mexican Immigrant Men's Family Experiences

Introduction

Driving the Interstate 5 Freeway near San Diego and the San Onofre border checkpoint there are large yellow signs graphically depicting a fleeing family (father leading, mother, and child—legs flailing behind). The almost surreal signs are meant to warn motorists of the danger of "illegal" immigrant families trying to cross the busy lanes. This image reveals not only the extreme risks that many immigrants are willing to take to get to the United States but also the way in which we imagine these immigrants. While most motorists probably do not think of a sexual message when they see the warning sign, it's there for us to see; if we only really look. The sign is symbolic at multiple levels: a nuclear family unit, heteronormative in definition, a threat to the racial social order by virtue of its reproductive potential. The sign is also symbolic of the current state of international migration studies: sexuality is an implicit part of migration that has been overlooked—ignored.

In this chapter I examine some of the ways in which sexuality, understood as a dimension of power, has shaped the lives, intimate relationships, and migratory processes of Mexican men who immigrate to the U.S. More specifically, I utilize ethnographic data to examine how traditional family relations and alternative support systems such as "chosen families" (Weston 1991) influence migration among Mexican immigrant men who have sex with men (MSMs). The men whom I interviewed and introduce in this essay had a variety of sexual identities both prior to and after migration. An important part of my research, therefore, is to examine from a queer materialist perspective dimensions which shape the social relations of families of origin and families of choice, and thus the intimate context by which identity itself is shaped. I argue for a theoretical move towards a *queer political economy* in order to understand the dynamics which shape "the sexuality of migration" and the fluidity of identities in a global context.

Border Crossers: Family, Migration, Identity

The immigrant men who I interviewed for my research ranged in age from their early twenties to early forties and lived in the greater Los Angeles area. I met these men during my dissertation research fieldwork from 1997 through December of 1999 by making initial contacts through organizations, fliers, and friends and then using a snowball sampling technique to meet others. While each of these men's stories were in their own way unique, there were also similarities that became more evident as my research progressed.

From *Queer Families, Queer Politics: Challenging Culture and the State*, ed. M. Bernstein and R. Reimann. Copyright © 2001 Columbia University Press. Reprinted by permission of the publisher.

Most of the men came from the Pacific states of Mexico and approximately two-thirds came from the state of Jalisco. About half described their communities of origin as small cities or towns, with only a couple describing their origins as rural; but migration to larger cities (such as Guadalajara or border cities like Tijuana) prior to migrating to the United States was also a common experience. All the men included here were 16 years old or older when they immigrated. Most came from lower-middle-class Mexican backgrounds and had at least a high school education. Like many of their straight counterparts, many were undocumented. Only two of the men who I met were not working at the time of their interview; one man was unable to work due to health reasons related to AIDS/HIV, the other was looking for work. Several of the men were actually holding down more than one job; one full-time and one part-time. The average income of the men was $20,000–25,000. English fluency ranged among the men relative to their time in the United States, but none was completely fluent in English. Due in part to this, the men interviewed reported daily lives that were for the most part Spanish speaking. In addition, nearly all estimated that more than 75 percent of their social circles were Latino.

In the following pages I will introduce six of the twenty men whom I formally interviewed. I selected these particular interviews as representative of the range of experiences related to me. However, the interview excerpts included below should not be considered representative of all Mexican immigrant men who have sex with men (MSMs) to the United States—the diversity of experiences is far greater than can be captured here. The men I have included identified as either bisexual or homosexual (gay) at the time of the interviews. In addition, I do not include the voice of transgendered Mexican immigrants, although some of the men do have experience with cross-dressing. Yet the voices represented here do reveal the complexity of the sexuality of migration and the importance of including sexuality in our analysis. I will first provide a general description of these men and then discuss their experiences as they relate to family, migration, and sexual identity.

- *Lalo* is a 33-year-old immigrant from Guadalajara, Jalisco. The fifth of nine children, Lalo comes from what he describes as a "very poor" class background. He migrated to the United States in 1983 and is a legal resident who currently lives in Fountain Valley.
- *Armando* is a 32-year-old Mexican national born in the state of Jalisco where he spent eight years in a seminary studying to be a priest. He is the oldest of eight children (four boys and four girls). He moved to the United States in 1995 and is an undocumented immigrant. He currently lives in Santa Ana but lived in Los Angeles with his brother when we met.
- *Gabriel* is a 23-year-old undocumented immigrant who has lived in the Orange County area for the past five years where he works as a Medical Assistant. The fourth of six children, Gabriel moved to the U.S. from Nayarit, Mexico in 1993 when he was 18. Gabriel lives in Fullerton.
- *Paco*, a native of La Piedad, Michoacan, is 30 years old and now lives in Tustin. He is the youngest of six children (four sisters and a brother). Paco's father died three months after he was born. Paco is a legal resident of the United States, although he immigrated illegally in 1990.
- *Roberto* is in his early forties and has lived in the U.S. since migrating from Mexico in 1994. The fourth of five children, he comes from a prestigious and well-to-do family in Nayarit, Mexico. Although never married, Roberto has a teenaged son who lives in Mexico with his mother. Roberto now lives in the San Fernando Valley and works as an AIDS educator for a Latino community organization.
- *Manuel* is 30 years old, identifies as bisexual, and is currently unemployed, although he worked as a registered nurse in Guadalajara,

Mexico. He is the third of eight children (seven boys and one girl) and grew up in Tlaquepaque, a town famous for its artisans and now considered part of the Guadalajara metro area. A Jehovah's Witness, he considers himself to be very religious. Due to his HIV status he moved to the U.S. in 1996 to be with his family and is an undocumented immigrant. He lives with his family in Santa Ana, who know of his condition but are not aware of his sexual identity.

- *Carlos* migrated from Guadalajara in 1990 and is currently seeking political asylum in the U.S. based on his sexual orientation. Because Carlos was an active member of the Democratic Revolutionary Party (PRD), an opposition party to Mexico's ruling Institutional Revolutionary Party (PRI), he fears that he may be imprisoned or murdered if he returns to Mexico. He now lives in Los Angeles.

Family Life in Mexico

Social scientists have historically given great focus to the role of *la familia* in Latino culture. Scholarship often points to Latino "familism," defined as the value and preservation of the family over individual concerns (Moore and Pachon 1985; Williams 1990), as the contentious source of both material and emotional support and patriarchal oppression. The stereotype is problematic for a number of reasons, not the least of which is the fact that the same argument could be made of most families regardless of their cultural context. Thus, in this section, while I discuss how the early family lives of Mexican immigrant MSMs influenced migratory processes, my aim is not to reproduce a cultural pathology of *la familia* but, rather, to examine the family as a site where normative constructions of gender and sexuality are reproduced and in which the dynamics of migration are materially embedded.

During my interviews most of the men remembered their lives as children in Mexico fondly. Yet, even when memories of early family life were positive, the daily lessons of normative masculinity which these men learned often resulted in emotional conflicts. I asked them to share with me their memories of family life and educational experiences in order to better understand the processes by which normative gender roles and sexuality are learned. Most early childhood memories were shared with smiles and consisted of generally carefree days; playing typical games and going to school. Most also reported that they were good students who received awards for their scholarship and genuinely seemed to have enjoyed school. However, even men like Paco, who reported that his childhood was "a great time . . . a very beautiful stage of my life," expressed a sense of inner conflict rooted in normative definitions of masculinity.

These conflicts were even more pronounced for men like Lalo whose memories of early life in Mexico were not good ones. Recounting his childhood Lalo told me:

> As I child I was very mischievous. I was sexually abused when I was seven by the neighbor, a man of forty. It was a childhood experience that affected me greatly. This person continued to abuse me, he would give me money, later I would go looking for him myself and I was like his "boyfriend" until I was nine. I knew what he was doing was wrong so I never told anyone.

Paternostro (1998) reports that child sexual abuse by a family member is a common phenomenon in Latin America (whether it is more prevalent there than in other countries is debatable). In fact Lalo was not the only man I interviewed who was sexually abused as a child, but he was the most forthcoming about the experience. Later in the interview he explained that he was also abused by two older male cousins and when he told his father about the abuse his father's response was to rape him for being a *maricón*.

None of the sexually abused men, including Lalo, remember connecting these experiences to homosexuality at the time of their occurrence; in part because they didn't really know what homosexuality was. Lalo explained that although he had never heard the word "homosexual," words like *maricón* and *joto* were commonly heard in his home. However, Lalo related these terms to effeminate men or *vestidas* like the man in his neighborhood who dressed like a woman. Many informants related similar experiences. As Carlos explained: "Across from us lived the town *maricón*. In every town there is a drunk and the *maricón*, and the *maricón* lived across the street." As children the question of what a *maricón* was remained somewhat of a mystery; although they knew it wasn't anything "good." For instance, it wasn't until later that Lalo started to understand what "homosexual" meant. He explained:

> After about the age of twelve or thirteen there was a lot of sexual play among the boys of the *colonia*. We would masturbate one another. There were about twelve of us in the group and we would form a circle and masturbate one another. Later, couples would form and we would penetrate one another. Now they are all grown up and married but there was a lot of sexual play when we were kids.... There were some boys who would refuse to join us, saying, "that's for *marciones*" or "you're going to be a *joto* or a woman." It was then that I started to understand but I never thought that I was going to be like a woman.

Masculine discourse that devalues the feminine and equates homosexuality to the feminine is, of course, not particular to Mexican culture (cf. Fellows 1996; Murray and Roscoe 1998). However, as Lalo explained, homosexuality and femininity are not popularly understood as synonymous. "Being a *joto* is to not be man. Neither a man nor a woman, it is to be an abomination, a curse." Prieur's (1998) recent work on male-to-female transgendered residents of Mexico City supports Lalo's analysis and suggests that class perspectives are an important dimension of its construction. Thus, the relationship of homosexuality to the feminine is more complex than a synonymous equation implies. Homosexuality is not only the opposite of masculinity, it is a corruption of it, an unnatural form which by virtue of its transgression of the binary male/female order poses a threat that must be contained or controlled.

The liminal/marginal location of homosexuality, perhaps best understood as shaped by what Almaguer (1993) refers to as a sex/gender/power axis, is reproduced through messages in everyday life. Discussing his daily chores at home, Paco said:

> My duties at home in particular, well, they were almost never designated to us. I liked very much to sweep, mop, wash the dishes, and when [my mother and sisters] would make cake I always liked to be there when they were preparing it. But only when my mom and my sisters were there, because my brother would often be in the United States. I always liked to help my mom and my sisters, but when my brother would get there, I always had to hide or not do it because he would tell me "You are not a woman to be doing that, that's for the *maricones*." Then, since I was scared of him, I wouldn't do it anymore. But it was what I liked to do, up till now; I like cleaning very much and chores like that. I like to cook very much, I like to have everything clean—I've always liked that.

When I asked Paco to discuss the issue of "women's work" in more detail, he explained:

> In Mexico they say "Oh, a homosexual person or a *maricón* or a *joto* are those persons that are dressed like women." They always have a little of that mentality. For example, there were times that a guy named Luis would pass by and he always left his nails long and his hair long like a woman. He had a bag, and he would put on women's pants or a woman's blouse, and he might have put on makeup but not a lot, but obviously he would go around like a woman. Then all the people, well, they said things, but in my family one time I heard my mother call him, she would call them *frescos* [fresh], there goes that *fresco*, I would hear my mom say that. Then I would get angry when I would hear that, because I would say "Well, I am not like that, but I am attracted to young men."

Armando expressed learning the same type of sex/gender message through child's play. Armando explained that he liked to play with paper dolls and more than anything liked to cut out the clothes, yet he hid when he did so. When I asked him why, Armando replied:

> It's the only game I remember playing secretly. I knew my parents wouldn't like it. I thought it was perfectly normal, it was only bad because it was something that little girls do.

The struggle which Paco and Armando relate in attempting to negotiate the perceived contradictions of sex, gender, and sexual identities was a common theme of many of my interviews. Participants expressed a certain sense of isolation or "not belonging" and not wanting to disappoint their families. Even learning to emulate normative gender and sexual performances was not, in itself, sufficient to resolve these conflicts. For some men, these tensions were a catalyst for migration itself.

Leaving Home

One of the questions that I asked immigrant interviewees was what their top three reasons for immigrating were. After analyzing the answers given, it became clear that sexuality was indeed influencing reasons for migration and that "family" dynamics were often linked to these reasons. However, understanding how sexuality actually influenced these decisions was not always as clear cut as having people respond, "it was my sexuality"—although that sometimes happened. For example, Lalo told me, "Ninety percent of the reason I migrated was because of my sexuality." Such reasons obviously resonate with D'Emilio (1993) and Rubin's (1992) model of rural to urban migration by "gay" men and women seeking greater anonymity and "gay life" in the cities. Yet, in order to understand how sexuality is linked to other socioeconomic dimensions more fully, one must attempt to connect the micro with the meta and macro dimensions of life. That is to say, one cannot separate individual reasons for migration from the larger processes that shape people's everyday lives and perceived "choices." Several themes did arise from the interviews, sometimes from the same source, and are implicated in a queer political economy in different ways.

For example, all of the men I interviewed, in one form or another, gave financial reasons for migrating to the United States. And indeed, immigration scholars have traditionally placed a great deal of emphasis on economic reasons for migration, yet to a great degree their vision of the economic realm is extremely limited. The social inequalities of sexuality, like race and gender, are integrally linked to the economic structures of society. Groups that are marginalized as sexual minorities are constrained by the limits of discrimination and prejudice which may limit their socioeconomic opportunities. Thus, when an immigrant who is part of a sexual minority says that they immigrated for financial reasons, sexuality must be part of the analysis. For instance, even one of the people I interviewed in Mexico who owned his own pesticide and fertilizer business felt the constraints of heterosexism. Business networks, he explained, depend upon having the right image, which means a wife, children, and social events tied to church and school. Clearly as a gay man he was outside this world. His class privilege and the fact that he is his own "boss," however, permit him to remain in Mexico relatively free from some of the pressures that drive others to migrate.

Thus, while men like Lalo clearly migrate to escape a sense of sexual oppression, for others the decision to migrate to the United States is influenced by a combination of sexual liberation and economic opportunities. For example, Gabriel moved to the U.S. from Nayarit, Mexico when he was 18 but explained that he had begun to prepare himself for immigrating at 16. When I asked him why, he explained that he had two major reasons for coming to the U.S.:

> First, I wanted a better level of education. And the second reason was sexuality. I wanted to be able to define myself and have more freedom with respect to that. I wanted to come here to live, not to distance myself from my family but to hide what I already knew I had. I knew I was gay but I thought I might be able to change it.

I needed to come here and speak to people, to learn more about it, because in Mexico it's still very taboo. There isn't so much liberation.

Gabriel's experience reveals how the tension of sexual desire versus "not wanting to distance" oneself from family may serve as a migratory "push." Yet while he clearly moved to the United States seeking a more liberal sexual environment it was not just a "personal" matter, it was also because he felt he had limited economic opportunities as a "gay" man in Mexico. Staying in Mexico might very well have meant either attempting to create a heteronormative family or dealing with social and economic discrimination as a gay man.

Sometimes homosexual relationships might have subtle influences such as serving to establish or expand social networks, or they might have a more direct influence driving migration itself. For instance, Roberto explained to me that he was quite happy with his life in Mexico as a civil servant but that people had begun to gossip about his sexual orientation and he feared for his job security, especially since he had recently learned that he was HIV positive. Roberto had met a man from the United States who was vacationing in Mexico and had maintained a friendly relationship with him. When the American suggested to Roberto that he move to the U.S. to live with him, Roberto took advantage of the opportunity and moved to Los Angeles. Although he is no longer in a relationship with the American, they continue to be friends. In this case, new (transnational) social bonds are created similar to the kinship networks that migration scholars argue facilitate migration, yet these are not "blood-based" but rather based on affiliation—transnational gay networks.

Finding Their Way Home

Adapting to life in the United States is difficult for any migrant, but for immigrants who migrate to the United States expecting a gay utopia like Lalo, the reality of life in the United States can be quite a blow. Indeed Lalo had returned to Mexico for two years after first migrating to the United States because of his disillusionment, but returned when he realized that his prospects as a gay man were limited in Mexico. Thus, for Lalo, "home" was no longer Jalisco. While there are a number of important aspects of an immigrant's experiences adapting to their new "home," in this section I focus on how sexuality might be related to a migrant's adaptation and incorporation. Specifically, I am concerned here with kin networks and the home as mechanisms for adaptation.

In her research on gay and lesbian kin relations, Weston (1991) demonstrates how gays and lesbians construct "chosen" families based on shared affinities and relationships of both material and emotional support. Kinship (biological) plays a central role in migration as a means by which immigrants receive support and acquire important knowledge for survival and adaptation (cf. Chavez 1992). While the Mexican men I interviewed often utilized kinship networks to these ends they also depended upon networks which were similar to those described by Weston. About half of the immigrants I spoke with utilized pre-existing gay networks to migrate to the United States. They were people like Lalo who migrated with the help of a gay compatriot already living in Los Angeles, and like Roberto who came with the help of a gay American. But even some of those who utilized kin networks for initial migration also used gay networks for meeting other gay Latino men, finding gay roommates, job contacts, and other types of information. The existence and use of these alternative networks depended to a large extent on how the men identified sexually, to what extent they were "out of the closet," and to some extent on their ability to speak English (and thus expand their networks into the mainstream gay world).

For instance, although Paco migrated and found his first job using kinship networks, he was soon able to develop a gay network as well.

> My second job was in a company where they made pools. I obtained that job through a [gay] friend, an American, who is the person, the third person that I have to thank about my legal

status here in this country. He helped me get the job because it was the company of a friend of his. In the morning I would clean the offices and then I would go to the warehouse and take inventory or I would clean the warehouse or cut fiberglass, or things like that. And they paid me well at that time but I worked only a few hours. So after that, since they said "Oh, you clean so well," and they had some very beautiful houses, over in Laguna Beach. Sometimes I would stay over because I could not finish in the weekend. The owners of the company were gay. They would go to San Francisco, or wherever they were going, they always traveled on the weekend, they left me the key. "Here is the stereo and here is the television," and everything like that because I had to sleep over. Then I would go home when they returned on Sundays.

Ironically, Paco is one of the people who assured me that sexuality had not influenced his migratory experiences in the least. This excerpt, however, reveals that gay social networks were an aid for finding work. In addition, Paco shares a home with a lesbian niece and has allowed other gay immigrants to stay with him temporarily until they are able to move on.

Carlos also made use of gay networks in a similar manner. When he migrated to the United States he first lived for two months in Watsonville, California, with a brother and then went to live with his two sisters—who are lesbians—in Milwaukee for two years. He then moved to Los Angeles after meeting and starting a relationship with a gay man. Like Paco, Carlos revealed that his gay friends had helped him find work and even helped him out financially. "Because of my gay friends, I have never gone without," he said.

Both Paco's and Carlos's experiences also point to the fact that sexuality is an important dimension of immigrant household arrangements. While recent immigration literature has discussed the importance of household arrangements as "landing pads" for migrant adaptation (cf. Chavez 1992, 1994), the sexual dimensions of these arrangements are missing from the analyses. For an individual who has migrated to the United States seeking a more liberal sexual environment, it makes little sense to live in a home constrained by heteronormative relations. While about half of the Mexican men I interviewed originally lived with family members when they migrated, most had formed alternative living arrangements as soon as they were able to. Lalo's home exemplifies this alternative type of arrangement.

When I first met Lalo he was living in Santa Ana in an apartment which he shared with three other immigrant men, all gay. Since our first meeting, Lalo has moved twice and has had a number of different roommates, always gay Latino immigrant men. Sometimes the men, especially if they were recent immigrants, would stay only a short time until they found another place to live. It was clear that Lalo's home was a "landing pad," but it was one where Latino men could be openly gay, support one another, and share information which was essential for adaptation. Although the men did not explicitly define these relations as "family," they did sometimes refer to each other affectionately as siblings (sometimes as "sisters" and sometimes as "brothers"). Regardless of how these relationships were labeled it was clear that an alternative support system had been created. It is precisely in this type of living arrangement that many men discover the space which transforms the way they think about themselves and their sexual identities.

Migrating Identities

One of the contributions of postmodern and postcolonial literature (including Queer Theory) is that identity is no longer understood as something inherently fixed and stable. Rather, identity is understood as mutable and plural; that is, the subject is the intersection of multiple identities (race/ethnicity, gender, sexuality, etc.) that change and have salience at different moments in time and place. Given the dramatic sociospatial changes which immigrants experience, their sexual identities therefore cannot be assumed to be stable. As Iain Chambers (1994: 25) puts it, "Identity is formed on the move." The effects of migration upon the sexual identities of Mexican immigrant

MSMs are ultimately linked to their emotional and material relationships to their biological families and the degree to which they have been able to resolve the normative sexuality and gender conflicts that fed their desire to migrate.

I asked the men I interviewed if they felt that they had changed at all since migrating to the United States. Nearly all of the men responded with a resounding yes. The changes they described generally centered around racial, gender, sexual, and class identities. Most of the men inevitably referred to a more liberal sexual environment as a reason for their transformations. Migrating to the United States was for many men one step in a series towards what might be called a "journey to the self." For Gabriel, the desire to live in a place where he could develop his human potential as a "gay man" was a driving force in his decision to immigrate. He adds:

> I have two names, Gabriel Luis, and my family calls me Luis. I've always said that Luis is the person who stayed in Mexico. Once I came here, Gabriel was born. Because, like I've told you, once I was here I defined myself sexually and I've changed a lot emotionally, more than anything emotionally, because I found myself.

This journey of "self-discovery" is intimately linked to resistance to the normative gender and sex regimes described earlier. While earlier scholarship asserted that Mexican male sexual identities were based on the active or passive (*activo/pasivo*) role of the participant (where only the passive was deemed homosexual), more recent research, including my own, finds that Mexican sexual identities are more complex.

Most informants remembered first being aware of their attraction to boys or men in early childhood. Some remembered being attracted to the same sex as young as age four, but the majority of recollections were a bit later. Carlos remembered, "I was around eight years old. I could recognize the beauty of men. But from then on it was an issue of denial." The pressure to conform, or as Lalo described, "la lucha de no querer ser gay" (the struggle of not wanting to be gay) took a toll on most of the men who I interviewed, perhaps most eloquently described by Armando.

Armando explained that he had been tormented by schoolmates after around the fourth grade. They would call him *joto* and *maricón*. He explains:

> But I learned how to hide it better, so it wasn't noticeable. I no longer isolated myself, instead I would mix with the troublemakers at school so that their reputation would rub off on me and so no one would tell me anything anymore. A new student arrived who was even more obvious than me and to a certain extent he was my salvation. Everyone focused their attention on him and it was a load off of me. It gave me the opportunity to get closer to the other students and do everything that they did, to act like them, have girlfriends and not be the "good boy" anymore—to take on the heterosexual role.

Armando would later join a seminary in an attempt to escape his sexual feelings and began to lift weights so that his appearance was more masculine. Eventually, however, he realized he needed to face who he "really" was.

> I feel that I lost a lot of my essence as a homosexual during that time. I see it like that now. At that time I only wanted to be part of a group, to be accepted. It's horrible to feel marginalized, in a corner, abnormal. In my attempts to be like everyone else wanted me to be I lost much of my self.

Two months after migrating to the United States seeking the freedom to be a gay man he confessed to a cousin who he was staying with that he was gay. She told him that she accepted and loved him as he was but that he needed to talk to his brothers. Armando told his brothers one by one and they all accepted his homosexuality (although it was by no means easy). He then decided to tell his widowed mother. At the time of our interview it had been five months since he had written his mother a five-page letter explaining his struggle to accept himself. A month later Armando's mother wrote him back asking forgiveness and assuring him that he would have her support and unconditional love. Armando has been able to successfully integrate his calling to service with his desire to be true to himself. He now works as an AIDS educator and program coordinator for an organization that serves gay Latino men.

Like Armando, other men who migrated to the United States also came out to their families and some found acceptance as well. In some of these men's cases it seems that the acceptance is in part tied to a reversal in family roles. Where once they were dependent upon their families for support, now their families are dependent upon them. Thus, while Almaguer (1993) has argued that economic interdependence stifles a gay identity from forming among Latino MSMs, my research reveals that it may actually facilitate familial acceptance. For instance, since migrating to the United States Lalo has also gained acceptance from the family who threw him out of the house. He explained to me that he has sent money to Mexico to have his mother's house repaired and to pay for his brother's tuition and that his family now respects him. Lalo related:

> I'm much more secure now. I'm not afraid to say I'm a homosexual. I'm content being gay and I can help others. I'm stronger and have achieved a lot of things.

Thus the transformation in economic roles and physical separation has allowed Lalo the opportunity to be both gay and "accepted" by his family.

There were, however, a couple of men who I interviewed who were openly gay prior to migrating to the United States. In both cases these men had upper-class backgrounds. The difference which class makes in mitigating the effects of homophobia is significant and needs to be studied more closely. For example, when I asked Roberto about his son he laughed out loud and said:

> Oh my son! My son was the product of an agreement. His mother knew that I was gay. My partner of ten years and I lived together [in Tepic, Nayarit] and she lived in front of us. She knew of my relationship with Alejo and the three of us would go out to dance. In a small town, well, it was known that she was the friend of "the boys."
> We would go out to dance, she would come to our home to watch television, listen to music, or have a drink. Then one day she told me flat-out that she wanted to have my baby. Then between the jokes I began to understand and between the jokes we ended up in bed. We had sex for two or three months and one day she called me and told me she was pregnant. I was 23 or 24 and was completely out of the closet with my family and I didn't care about anything.

Without a doubt, Roberto's class privilege allowed him to not "care about anything" as an openly gay man. In all probability it also shaped his gay social networks, which allowed him to migrate to the United States as well.

To be clear, for those men who do not have such privileges in Mexico, migrating to the United States does not necessarily afford them these privileges either. While there may be more space to be "gay" in the United States, migrating has its costs. Carlos lamented:

> Being away from Mexico creates a strong nationalistic feeling with a lot of nostalgia. You begin to notice how different the system is here than in Mexico. An economic system that changes your life completely. A system where one forgets about other things that in Mexico were a priority. Here one lives life from the perspective of money. Working and making enough money to pay your bills is more important than having friends and doing what you like. In Mexico it's very different. It's more important to have friends, one lives less a slave to the clock. One forgets these things and becoming aware of that has made me very sad.

Discovering the virulence of racism in the United States seems to counterbalance any feelings of sexual liberation. I asked the men, in an open-ended manner, if they had ever experienced discrimination (without defining the type). Nearly all of the men responded in ways similar to Carlos: "For being Latino, for not speaking English perfectly, for the color of my skin." The irony, of course, is that in their attempts to escape one form of bigotry, most of the Mexican men I interviewed discovered that not only had they not entirely escaped it but they now faced another. As Lalo said, "It wasn't true that homosexuals are free, that they can hold hands, or that Americans like Mexicans." Under these circumstances the role of a support system becomes all the more important and for queer Latino immigrant men this often means that new "families" must be created.

Building Family

I was naively surprised by the responses I got when asked immigrant men about their future plans. I suppose that I had allowed myself to become so immersed in the migration literature that I was expecting to hear something more along the lines of "return to Mexico and start my own business." More common, however, were responses like Paco's:

> I want to be anywhere close to the person I love, to support me. If it's in Mexico, a lot better because I would have my family and that person near me. But, more than anything, right now I worry a lot for my own person and for the partner who I think will be what I wait for in my life. And I see myself in a relationship with a lot of affection, and maybe by then, living with that person, together. And maybe even to get married.
>
> *Q: So your plans for the future are to have a partner?*
>
> A stable partner, be happy, and give them all my support, and I would little help that person shine, succeed in anything I could help. I will try to do it all the time. If he accomplishes more than I have it will make me very happy because in that aspect I am not egotistical. And still more things that are positive; get more involved in helping people that need me, in every aspect. Be happy, make my partner happy, above all make myself happy, and my family, my friends, all the people that like me, and I like.

This type of response does not exclude dreams of material wealth and entrepreneurship, but it centers and gives priority to affective dimensions—to building new families. The desire for stable relationships reflects not only the difficulty of maintaining such relationships in Mexico, but also the isolation that these men feel in the United States. This isolation which gay Mexican immigrant men feel is due in some measure to language difficulties, but racial and class issues also play into it. For instance, Carlos explained to me that although he was in a relationship at the time of our interview he didn't see much of a future in it.

> I don't have many expectations for my relationship because my partner is not Latino. I think that, ideally, for a stable relationship I need to be with a Latino ... someone who identifies as Latino. Someone intelligent and a little more cultured. Someone who has the capacity to go to an art or photography exhibit and enjoy it. Someone open-minded, open to learning from other cultures and who is financially independent.

The problem, of course, is that the social location of Mexican immigrant MSMs in the United States is a marginal one. "Stability" is not easily established and "financial independence" may take years to accomplish, if at all. The problem is exacerbated by the fact that there are few public spaces where Latino gay men can openly meet one another. Thus, creating family or even a sense of community depends in no small part upon the ability of queer Latinos to build a new "home" with limited resources and little external support.

Conclusion

"Who do you turn to for support?" I asked the men I interviewed. The standard response was "family and friends." Yet it is clear from my discussions with these men, and the data presented here, that these relationships (whether biological or chosen) were sometimes strained, always evolving, and ultimately negotiated. A queer materialist analysis of the experiences of Mexican immigrant men who have sex with men reveals the ways in which dimensions of family, migration, and sexual identity intersect and are embedded within a political economy. Many of the men interviewed felt marginalized by heteronormative definitions of masculinity reproduced through and embodied in the traditional family. These norms, reproduced in daily activities since childhood, marginalize not only men with "feminine" characteristics but also those able to "pass" who were instilled with a fear of "discovery." Associations of femininity to homosexuality created a sense of confusion in some men who, although they were attracted to men, did not identify as feminine. The economic liability that derived from not creating a heteronormative family unit as an adult also influenced the immigration process. These strict gender/sex regimes were powerful enough to drive many men to migrate to the United States in search of a more liberal environment.

A queer political economy perspective of migration also aids in unveiling how sexuality has shaped processes and strategies for adaptation such as social networks and household arrangements. Alternative relations to biological families are created based on sexual orientation, which serve as systems of support. The members of these "chosen families" assist one another through the trials and tribulations of being a queer Mexican immigrant man. Such assistance takes a variety of forms, including helping with migration itself, sharing knowledge and resources such as job information, and even sharing households.

New economic arrangements mean that some men find that they are empowered to "come out" to their biological families as gay men and maintain a level of acceptance and respect from their loved ones. Shared space is also an important dimension linked to the futures of these gay men. Faced with a sense of isolation and a deep desire to form the stable relationships which they were prevented from having in Mexico, space becomes the base for adaptation, community, and shared futures. Thus, for many men who have come to identify as "gay," new family structures become a means by which dreams may be realized.

Although my focus has been on Mexican immigrant men, there are larger implications that need to be explored. When we understand sexuality as a dimension of power (that intersects with other dimensions such as race, gender, and class) in which certain groups are privileged over others, then these implications become more visible. For instance, Argüelles and Rivero (1993) argue that some immigrant women have migrated in order to flee violent and/or oppressive sexual relationships or marriage arrangements which they contest. Little research has been conducted of Latinas in general, far less exists on the intersections of migration and sexuality (regardless of sexual orientation). While it is clear that biological families reproduce normative constructions of gender and sexuality, the ways in which these norms and power relations influence different groups of people in terms of migration and identity are not understood. The research presented here is, hopefully, a step towards the development of a queer materialist paradigm by which the sexual dimensions of migration can be understood and by which further research may be conducted.

Note

This chapter represents part of a larger dissertation research project entitled "Border Crossings: Mexican Men and the Sexuality of Migration. The author gratefully acknowledges the comments and suggestions of the editors and Nancy Naples, as well as the funding support of the Social Science Research Council's Sexuality Fellowship Program and the Ford Foundation which made this research possible. In addition, the author wishes to express his gratitude to the men who participated in this project.

References

Almaguer, Tomás. 1993. "Chicano Men: A Cartography of Homosexual Identity and Behavior" in *The Lesbian and Gay Studies Reader,* edited by Abelove, Barale, and Halperin. New York: Routledge.

Anzaldúa, Gloria. 1987. *Borderlands/La Frontera: The New Mestiza.* San Francisco: Aunt Lute.

Argüelles, Lourdes and Anne M. Rivero. 1993. "Gender/Sexual Orientation Violence and Transnational Migration: Conversations with Some Latinas We Think We Know." *Urban Anthropology,* 22 (3–4): 259–276.

Bennett, James R. 1996. Introduction to "Materialist Queer Theory: A Working Bibliography" in *The Material Queer,* edited by Donald Morton. Boulder, CO: Westview Press.

Cantú, Lionel (Forthcoming) "Entre Hombres/Between Men: Latino Masculinities and Homosexualities" in *Gay Masculinities,* edited by Peter Nardi. Newbury Park, CA: Sage.

Cantú, Lionel. 1999. "Border Crossings: Mexican Men and the Sexuality of Migration." Dissertation manuscript. University of California, Irvine.

Carrier, Joseph. 1995. *De Los Otros: Intimacy and Homosexuality Among Mexican Men.* New York: Columbia University Press.

Chambers, Iain. 1994. *Migratory, Culture, Identity.* New York: Routledge.

Chavez, Leo. 1992. *Shadowed Lives: Undocumented Immigrants in American Society.* San Diego, CA: Harcourt Brace Jovanovich College Publishers.

Chavez, Leo. 1994. "The Power of the Imagined Community: The Settlement of Undocumented Mexicans and Central Americans in the United States." *American Anthropologist,* 96 (1): 52–73.

Cousins, Mark and Athar Hussain. 1984. *Michel Foucault.* New York: Macmillan.

D'Emilio, John. 1993 [1983]. "Capitalism and Gay Identity" in *Lesbians, Gay Men, and the Law,* edited by W. B. Rubenstein. New York: New Press.

Donovan, Josephine. 1992. *Feminist Theory.* New York: Continuum.

Engels, Frederick. 1993. *The Origin of the Family, Private Property and the State.* New York: International Publishers.

Fellows, Will (ed.). 1996. *Farm Boys: Lives of Gay Men from the Rural Midwest.* Madison: University of Wisconsin Press.

Foucault, Michel. 1978. *The History of Sexuality: An Introduction,* trans. Robert Hurley. New York: Pantheon.

Gluckman, Amy and Betsy Reed (eds.). 1997. *HomoEconomics: Capitalism, Community, and Lesbian and Gay Life.* New York: Routledge.

Gutmann, Matthew C. 1996. *The Meanings of Macho: Being a Man in Mexico City.* Berkeley: University of California Press.

Hennessy, Rosemary and Chrys Ingraham (eds.). 1997. *Materialist Feminism: A Reader in Class, Difference, and Women's Lives.* New York: Routledge.

Herdt, Gilbert H. 1994. [1981]. *Guardians of the Flutes: Idioms of Masculinity.* New York: McGraw-Hill.

Hondagneu-Sotelo, Pierrette. 1994. *Gendered Transitions: Mexican Experiences of Immigration.* Los Angeles: University of California Press.

Hondagneu-Sotelo, Pierrette and Michael Messner. 1994. "Gender Displays and Men's Power: 'The New Man' and the Mexican Immigrant Man" in *Theorizing Masculinities,* edited by Harry Brod and Michael Kaufman. Thousand Oaks, CA: Sage Publications.

Ingram, Gordon Brent, Anne-Marie Bouthillette, and Yolanda Retter. 1997. *Queers In Space: Communities, Public Places, Sites of Resistance.* Seattle, WA: Bay Press.

Jagose, Annamarie. 1996. *Queer Theory: An Introduction.* New York: New York University Press.

McIntosh, Mary. 1968. "The Homosexual Role." *Social Problems,* 16 (69): 182–192.

Martin, Biddy. 1988. "Feminism, Criticism, and Foucault" in *Feminism and Foucault: Reflections on Resistance,* edited by Irene Diamond and Lee Quinby. Boston: Northeastern University Press.

Massey, Douglas S. and Kristin Espinosa. 1995. "What's Driving Mexico–US Migration? A Theoretical, Empirical, and Policy Analysis." Unpublished paper.

Massey, Douglas S., Jaoquin Arango, Graeme Hugo, Ali Kouaouci, Adela Pellegrino, and J. Edward Taylor. 1993. "Theories of International Migration: Review and Appraisal." *Population and Development Review,* 19 (3): 431–467.

Moore, Joan and Harry Pachon. 1985. *Hispanics in the United States.* Englewood Cliffs, NJ: Prentice-Hall.

Morton, Donald (ed.). 1996. *The Material Queer.* Boulder, CO: Westview Press.

Murray, Stephen O. 1995. *Latin American Male Homosexualities.* Albuquerque: University of New Mexico Press.

Murray, Stephen O. and Will Roscoe (eds.). 1998. *Boy-Wives and Female Husbands: Studies in African Homosexualities.* New York: St. Martin's Press.

Paternostro, Silvana. 1998. *In the Land of God and Man: Confronting Our Sexual Culture.* New York: Dutton.

Pedraza, Silvia. 1991. "Women and Migration: The Social Consequences of Gender." *Annual Review of Sociology,* 17: 303–325.

Prieur, Annick. 1998. *Mema's House, Mexico City: On Transvestites, Queens, and Machos.* Chicago, IL: University of Chicago Press.

Rubin, Gayle. 1992 [1984]. "Thinking Sex: Notes for a Radical Theory of the Politics of Sexuality" in *The Lesbian and Gay Studies Reader*, edited by Abelove, Barale, and Halperin. New York: Routledge.

Seidman, Steven (ed.). 1996. *Queer Theory/Sociology*. Cambridge, MA: Blackwell Publishers.

Weeks, Jeffrey. 1977. *Coming Out: Homosexual Politics in Britain from the Nineteenth Century to the Present*. London: Quartet.

Weston, Kath. 1991. *Families We Choose: Lesbians, Gays, Kinship*. New York: Columbia University Press.

Williams, Norma. 1990. *The Mexican American Family: Tradition and Change*. Dix Hills, NY: General Hall Publishers.

Wood, Charles, H. 1982. "Equilibrium and Historical Structural Perspectives on Migration." *International Migration Review*, 16 (2): 298–319.

ARTICLE 45

Michael C. Hanchard

On "Good" Black Fathers

After observing my then two-year-old daughter and I playing with each other at a summer event during graduate school, a black woman graduate student I knew walked up to us with a big smile and said, "It's so nice to see a black man who spends so much time with his child," adding a serious tone that reduced her voice to a conspiratorial whisper: "There's not too many black men who spend time with their children these days, you know," before she walked away. My daughter, oblivious to the exchange, continued with her demand that I flip her one more time (for the third time!). I was stunned.

How could this woman make such a statement, I thought to myself, when she herself was a product of a household with a responsible father (of whom she often spoke)? Had the dynamics of black communities—middle- and working-class—changed that much over the course of one generation to make the term *black father* an oxymoron, and cavorting with my daughter an exception? Like many other people in the United States, black or otherwise, I had heard and read the statistics and data on the number of black men who helped produce children but who were not "heading households," which has come to be understood as not living with the mother of his child. This has also come to be equated with, I believe, being an absent, irresponsible or non-parent.

These two assumptions are not, however, only part of the rhetoric about the crisis of black fatherhood. They are inextricably related to more general assumptions about fatherhood, domesticity, and masculinity in these United States. Rarely, though, are discussions about black fatherhood linked to a broader conjuncture of societal forces that have shaped the present moment. Consequently, relations between black women, black men, and their children are rarely considered against the backdrop of rising divorce rates, family dysfunction, and cultural conservatism in the nation as a whole.

Embedded in my fellow graduate student's comments to me during that afternoon barbecue were parts of this discussion, the presumptions about the culpability of black men in impeding our ability to reproduce and nurture ourselves. That moment in which I was identified as a presence in my daughter's life became a barometer and lightning rod for black male parenting. In contrast to most mothers I know, who are automatically considered parents, young fathers like myself who are also parents are often treated like some sort of novelty. The fact of my blackness made my public act of parenting seem like an even greater novelty. While the widely voiced concern can be attributed to the circumstances under which black men, as fathers and individuals, find themselves at the present time, it is also a variation on a recurrent theme over the course of U.S. history, politics, and public policy about the very ability of African-Americans to care for themselves as a people, from slave quarters in Mississippi to the south side of Chicago, from Strivers Row in Harlem to Shaker Heights in Cleveland and points elsewhere. Whereas once African-Americans, like other people of African descent, were considered intellectually incapable of attending to their own self-governance, they are now interpreted by many who hold conservative as well as liberal

From *Faith of Our Fathers: African-American Men Reflect on Fatherhood*, Andre C. Willis (ed.), pp. 74–89, New York: Penguin. Copyright © 1997. Reprinted by permission.

positions as being culturally incapable—that is, without the moral and ethical imperatives—to raise and take care of families. The so-called "crisis of the black male," a topic of debate among members of black communities and their attendant institutions, policy makers, the religious right, rap musicians, and others, is often segregated from society at large by a language that assumes that black men and the communities that spawned them can be interpreted only through the lens of slavery and discrimination, as if these two features of U.S. society and culture affected only black people.

As those of any color who are involved in the lives of children know, parenting involves much more than an afternoon barbecue or any other public event in which people who supposedly love one another perform the usual niceties of hugging, kissing, and embracing in ways that suggest to the world outside that all is well within. Biographies of celebrities both living and dead, talk shows, television documentaries, and published research by specialists on families have provided ample grounds for suggesting that while the image of a loving, mutually supportive family with two ever-present parents is not an absolute myth, there are few actual families that resemble the conventional, "traditional" model of the nuclear family. At the same time, those individuals and families whose lives do not resemble the mythic family are not, by definition, either bad people or bad parents.

Most people fall somewhere in between the models for families that more closely resemble a facade on a Hollywood movie lot than an actual case of domesticity or the entirely dysfunctional ensembles of disfigured humanity that family arrangements sometimes turn out to be. Most parents struggle with issues of divorce, fidelity, time and budgetary constraints, ornery relatives, and other thorny subjects within the context of their families and individual identities. Black people are no different.

What does distinguish black fathers, mothers, and their children from the present "crisis of the family" is that black people have struggled through various crisis and moments—as families and individuals—ever since their arrival into the New World as slaves four centuries ago. The very condition of slavery presupposed the absence or negation of family, since slavery operated on the premise that slaves belonged to no one other than slave owners themselves. From the dawn of slavery, people of African descent in the United States resisted their comprehensive but incomplete domination at the hands of slave masters by maintaining whatever possible links with family members on other plantations, or by forging familial ties where these were none, such as those between shipmates and their offspring.

I briefly recall this history simply to suggest that the present "crisis" of the black family in general and black males in particular has a prior history, and it is but a variation on a theme. With this in mind, I would like to make a basic point about the need to recognize the creative responses African-American communities have had to the responsibilities of fatherhood that have not fit within the parameters of the mythic constructions of fatherhood, the family, masculinity, and domesticity. Discussions of black fatherhood that attempt to force black males into a model of parenting that few people—male or female—white, black, or otherwise, adhere to in the contemporary United States should be viewed with suspicion against this historical and contemporary backdrop. Unfortunately, as my own personal example suggests, members of the African-American community, often in an effort to portray a sense of the cohesiveness and respectability so often denied by broader society, reproduce the same myths about parenting and family responsibility that imprison them within the very stereotypes they have been struggling for so long to break free of.

While I do not want to suggest that we ignore or dismiss nasty legacies of domestic and other forms of violence within black communities, teenage pregnancies, and a litany of other maladies that have been perpetrated and perpetuated by black men, I do want to suggest that we view discussions about the "crisis of the black male" with skepticism as long as the more general crises weighing over black people are ignored. Ultimately, the debates about the black male are less about black maleness and responsibility than about the variety of racially and economically discriminatory circumstances, both inside and outside black communities, that black males often find themselves in and react to, regardless of their parenting status.

An example of the ways in which the stereotypes of black dysfunction plague even the most successful black families regardless of their specific circumstances again comes from a personal experience, involving a girlfriend of my daughter. This child, whom I will call Rachel, was my daughter's best friend in the first grade. Donna (for the purposes of this essay), Rachel's mother, was a hard-working woman. She not only raised Rachel but worked at a demanding managerial job, held leadership positions in church and community organizations, and raised her stepson's infant daughter in her home. Neither Donna nor her husband was wealthy by any means, but they were able to provide not only for themselves but for their extended family as well, in both material and spiritual terms. They lived in a modest one-family home in the black section of a very segregated city. Donna would sometimes allow several days to pass before reading through the material in the school folder that Rachel brought home every day, which included past homework and exercises as well as information about upcoming school events. Like most working parents I know, regardless of socioeconomic status, it was a constant struggle to juggle domestic and professional responsibilities. With perhaps the exception of male single parents, I believe it is safe to say that women parents have greater home responsibilities than their male counterparts, and Donna was no exception.

Ms. Mason, her daughter's teacher, reprimanded Rachel one day for not having her folder materials checked by a parent, one of the rules of her classroom. After receiving a note from Rachel's teacher on the matter, Donna immediately called my wife and told her something like the following: "The next time I brought Rachel to school, I had a talk with the teacher, to let her know that just because I hadn't looked at her folder did not mean I didn't check her homework," adding "because I'm a good black parent."

A good black parent. What does that mean? There are several conditions that these four words could imply. A black person cannot simply be a parent; they are a black parent. But to be a black parent is simply not enough; one must be a good black parent. How does being a good black parent differ from being a good white parent, or simply a white or any other hued parent? What links Donna and me in this example is the manner in which both of us lurk between the categories already created for us and acted upon in a racist society. The identities of our lives are multiple: parent, spouse, counsel, friend, son and daughter, and so on. The stereotypes that we supposedly inhabit are singular: suspect parent. We are suspect parents because we are suspect human beings, suspected by the ideologies of racial discrimination to be something less than the norm, less than ideal.

Donna is a prime example of how black people both in and out of conventional families respond to these stereotypes of negativity. There is little doubt, I think, in her statement about her ability to be a good parent or the ability of others in her position to do the same. There is doubt, though, about the capability of certain members of white society to see her that way. This, unfortunately, is part of the legacy of black performance in public life in the United States. One of the cultural responses of blacks in virtually every profession since emancipation has been that black people must be nearly perfect in their undertakings, lest a little slip-up here or there (unchecked class assignments, for example) be taken as not only individual incompetence but a collective shortcoming. This is echoed in the personal narratives, biographies of people like Benjamin O. Davis of the U.S. Army, sports legends Jackie Robinson and Joe Louis, performers like Wilma

Rudolph and Lena Horne. It is also echoed in everyday people's daily lives, as Donna's example illustrates.

The example of her life is instructive because of the way in which it combines the activities of both conventional nuclear and extended families (community, in a word) that extends beyond narrower definitions of family. First, given the realities of teenage pregnancy, the ravages of crack, undereducation, unemployment, and other plagues of working-class black communities, black mothers and fathers cannot afford—I repeat, cannot afford—to operate exclusively under the nuclear family rubric. In no way am I declaring myself "anti-family" in the way that political and cultural conservatives claim that leftists advocate. I realize that families of all colors have had to adjust and adapt to the changing realities of the 1990s in the United States, where even middle- and upper-middle-class parents no longer operate with the assurance that their children will be able to fare as well as or better than they have. Black communities must not allow the focus on "the crisis of the black family" to obscure the larger problems of this precarious time. Simply put, if the majority of U.S. communities, which includes African-Americans, are neither products of nor participants in a two-parent family, then why should African-Americans be expected to adhere to a more restrictive notion of family that serves as an ideal more than a reality and, ultimately, was designed with another group of people in mind?

All this relates to the politics of black fatherhood since, invariably, black men who sire and/or nurture children can be fathers only in relation to their children, husbands and/or lovers in relation to their wives and/or companions, sons in relation to their parents. When viewed in isolation, black fatherhood becomes a fetish of machismo and conventional masculinity rather than a practical component of family life within immediate and extended families and communities. When viewed in isolation, the black family becomes but another receptacle for dominant values and ideals that do not work for the dominant social group in the first place but are utilized to tell African-Americans, once again, that they don't measure up.

A recent example of the effects of distorted images upon African-American males comes from the state of New Jersey, where then Republican governor Christine Whitman started a controversy in March 1995 during an interview when she stated that young black ghetto men in Newark proudly considered siring children out of wedlock a matter of adding "jewels to the crown." Ms. Whitman, who is certainly no ghetto dweller, obtained this information from a black mother in Newark who informed her that this was the reality of black male parental responsibility in that city.

The governor has had to respond to the outcry over this statement from a variety of sources in black communities in New Jersey, including young black fathers who have children out of wedlock and are responsible parents. Participants in the Young Fathers' Program in Newark,[1] a program that had been in existence eight years prior to Ms. Whitman's statement, as well as other collectives of young fathers, have informed the governor of the seriousness of their programs and their good-parenting practices regardless of their marital status. In a meeting with the governor in June of the same year, several members of the Young Fathers' Program and lifelong Newark residents told Ms. Whitman that they had never heard of the "jewels in the crown" phrase uttered by the young black mother.

At various times in the ensuing months, the governor reiterated that she had been merely repeating something said to her. It was a statement she neither confirmed nor endorsed. During her June meeting with Young Fathers' Program participants, she stated, "I didn't stigmatize anybody."

While she may have made what one would call an "honest mistake" (certainly impolitic), she still misses the point, but she does so in a way that is useful for this article. Those young men were already stigmatized by the fact that they did not operate within the conventional two-family model. Her statement, to my mind, can be viewed only as naive or disingenuous when seen in the context of two arenas of public debate that relate to this controversy, family values and the disintegration of the black family.

More subtle indignations, however, emerge when we consider the fact that a white, female governor who preside[d] over some of the most blighted and underfunded cities in the entire country would accept the comments of one person of any race to characterize the behavior of an entire class of individuals. Would she have relayed these comments in such an offhand, unmediated manner if the individuals in question were young white men from Princeton or Upper Montclair, New Jersey, two of the state's most affluent neighborhoods? Would she have even believed the comments of a single person from the neighborhood? We may never know the answer to these two questions, but it is significant that in most cases involving white parenting such questions are rarely posed. My guess is that part of the reason she relied so easily upon one black mother's depiction of unwed fathers is because it corresponded so easily with common assumptions about young black men.

Tellingly, in her June 1995 meeting with the program participants she explained that her statement was a rendering of "a comment that someone said to me, by someone who said this was what happened, whether it was on her block or what, I don't know." Ironically, her explanation reveals the pressures of what I shall call "racial translation," which are often imposed upon blacks in their interaction with whites in the United States. Before making such a statement, wouldn't it have made sense for Ms. Whitman to determine whether her informant was talking about young black men in general or a few on the woman's block? This is a depressingly familiar scenario in which the comments of one black individual as "racial translator" become the opinion of depiction of black people as a whole, much in the same way that the negative actions of one or several black individuals are often perceived as being symptomatic of black communities or the entire black race.

The similarities between the responses of these young black fathers and Donna are striking. Both felt the need to respond to others' characterizations that did not correspond with the realities of their daily lives. Like my own identity as a father, their identities as parents reside somewhere in between stereotypes and the starkest cases of parental neglect and abuse. What distinguishes these young men from Donna and myself is that poverty, undereducation, and unemployment render them socially naked. They do not have the trappings of middle-class respectability that would shield them from the accusations and characterizations of irresponsibility in the way that middle-class whites or minorities do. One only has to think of the surprise and shock echoed in voices and journalistic reports when a case of middle-class abuse is uncovered (parents who lock their infant children in the house to go on a vacation, for example) to obtain a sense of what notions of middle-class respectability can obscure. This is not restricted to young black men, either; the poor in general are symbolically victimized by these characterizations, as they are deemed to be the underside of what good parenting is all about.

In an age where both parents work and only 3 percent of families in the United States rely solely on a male breadwinner, parents who live with their children don't always have ample time to spend with them. In many middle- and upper-middle-class households (black and white) it is not uncommon to find nannies performing the functions of parents, who spend less and less time at home. Years of neglect and inattention have taken their toll on many prep school-educated Ivy League-bound adolescents, just as it has upon the "latchkey" children in working-class homes who are alone, locked inside their homes while their parents are at work. I mention these things to suggest what should be an obvious point; *no class or race has a monopoly on good or bad parenting*. Seemingly "external" societal factors have as much impact upon family dynamics as internal ones.

When one adds relational discord, physical and psychoemotional violence, incest, alcoholism, poverty, depression, and a range of other personal travails that have domestic repercussions, some children are better off without their biological or adoptive parents. This further erodes the all-or-nothing distinctions made between parents who live with their children and those who do not. The behavioral imprint left upon children in dysfunctional households can affect not only immediate family members but successive generations as well. With males of any color, children who witnessed or experienced physical and non-physical violence are likely to reproduce such violence in their own families.

At a conference in Fort Lauderdale, Florida, in October 1994, six present and former professional football players—all black—participated in a forum on domestic violence against women. Having witnessed their fathers break the arms and blacken eyes of their mothers and traumatize everyone in their presence at the same time, several of these men in turn heaped similar forms of violence upon their girlfriends and spouses. This cycle, as these men came to recognize, has to be broken before there are any realistic prospects for improved family dynamics among people of African descent. The reason I mention these particular men is to suggest that such labels, for example, "wife beater," could apply to a broad array of males, from the aforementioned men to O. J. Simpson. Eradicating domestic and other forms of intracommunity violence often means coming to terms with memories of violence inflicted upon them by a previous generation—by mothers, fathers, relatives, or family friends.

To discuss "the black family" without consideration of the myriad forms of violence and its consequences for black men as well as black women is to engage in the sort of blissful denial of negative, abusive "family values" that have existed as long as families have. Such violence has often operated as a primary cause of drug abuse, predation by young males, teenage runaways, suicide, depression, among other phenomena that characterize what family specialists refer to as "at-risk youth." If we are concerned with the preservation of family values—"African," "Afro-centric," or otherwise—let us make sure about just what it is we are preserving.

Here is where more complex understandings of the relationship between family and community become crucial for deeper probings of the politics of black fatherhood. In much of black conservative discussions about responsibility for teenage pregnancy (public statements and writings by Stanley Crouch and Glenn Loury provide two examples), there is often a nostalgic evocation of a bygone era when young women were sanctioned within black communities for having children out of wedlock. Suspending for the moment whether this was actually true even in some (certainly not all) black communities, or whether this was or is viable coping strategy for young teenage mothers, there is virtually no mention in this rhetoric of popular community sanctions against woman beaters or men who too readily and too violently spank their children. Should this nostalgic rhetoric be preserved? Should the silence about these issues be preserved? As usual, women political and cultural activists remain at the forefront of this discussion within the black community. Billye Avery, founder of the National Black Women's Health Project, is one example of a black woman political activist who has worked on these issues, often to the deaf ears of her male counterparts in the struggle for racial equality. Queen Latifah and Karyn White, two popular contemporary artists, have both produced effective music and videos on the theme of domestic violence within black families.[2] Certainly there are others, created largely by black women, that address domestic-violence issues, but there needs to be an ongoing dialogue about these issues in black communities and institutions. Family coherence should not be confused with individual abuse, intimidation, and oppression. Nor should discussion of the failings of particular black men in this regard be automatically considered a threat to the black male.

All of these concerns, from notions of community and extended families to domestic violence, impact upon black fathers and the politics of their being. An example of this occurred while riding a bus one day with two young black men from a summer program, which I was mentoring. I became the mediator in an argument about "proper" parenting philosophies for black men, a discussion that was prompted, I believe, by the presence of my daughter Jenna.

One young man from Kentucky stated that if he were a parent, he would raise his boy and girl children differently since boys, men in the making, had to be taught not to cry, not wear their emotions on their sleeves and commit other acts that would make them be perceived as weak. In contrast, the other young man, who hailed from Boston, said that he would not raise his girl child any differently from his son, since men too need to cry and express their emotions. "Plus," he added with emphasis, "it's rough out here on the sisters these days. They've got to be tough, too. They need all the help they can get."

And so they do. The task for progressive black males, as fathers, lovers, friends, and "brothers" in both senses of the term, is to understand black masculinity as merely one facet of their humanity. Like me, these two young men exist somewhere in between negative stereotypes and ideal types. Together, in dialogue, they were not only coming to terms with what it meant to be responsible black men in the contemporary United States, but with what it meant to be fuller human beings.

Notes

1. The Young Fathers' Program was founded in 1987 after a successful pilot program initiated in 1986. The program, which is housed in the New Jersey Medical School in Newark, is designed to assist young black and latino men between fifteen and twenty-three in meeting the emotional, financial, and social demands of fatherhood. Its services include educational and employment training for young men and their families, family support and counseling to reduce the risk of neglect and abuse within these families. As of June 1995, approximately one thousand young fathers have utilized the program's services. For more information contact (201) 982-5277.

2. See Queen Latifah's 1993 hit "U.N.I.T.Y." and Karyn White's incisive 1995 production, aptly entitled "I'd Rather Be Alone." Both ably capture the problems inherent in static categorizations of the nuclear family which do not address the reasons why, in some instances, it is healthier for people not to be in their nuclear family relationships, ones that cause unnecessary emotional and physical disfigurement.

PART NINE

Masculinities in the Media

Men are daily bombarded with images of masculinity—in magazines, television, movies, music, even the Internet. We see what men are supposed to look like, act like, be like. And social scientists are only now beginning to understand the enormous influence that the media have in shaping our ideas about what it means to be a man.

For one thing, it's clear that the media can create artificial standards against which boys as well as girls measure themselves. Just as idealized human female models can only approximate the exaggeratedly large breasts and exaggeratedly small waistline of Barbie, virtually no men can approach the physiques of the cartoon version of Tarzan or even G.I. Joe. The original G.I. Joe had the equivalent of 12.2-inch biceps when he was introduced in 1964. Ten years later, his biceps measured 15.2 inches. By 1994, he had 16.4-inch biceps, and today his biceps measure 26.8 inches—nearly 7 inches larger than Mark McGwire's 20-inch muscles. "Many modern figures display the physiques of advanced bodybuilders and some display levels of muscularity far exceeding the outer limits of actual human attainment," notes Dr. Harrison Pope, a Harvard psychiatrist.

Media masculinities create standards against which men measure themselves. No wonder we often feel like we fail the test of physical manhood. At the same time, the media encourage us to evaluate and judge the manhood of others by those same standards. As the articles in this section suggest, we are constantly "seeing" masculinity, in the movies (Peter Lehman), in commercials (Lance Strate), in pornography (Richard Fung), and especially in sports (Shari Lee Dworkin and Faye Linda Wachs). Any effort to understand—let alone transform—masculinity must take account of the ways in which we see ourselves reflected through the lenses that record our fantasy lives.

ARTICLE 46

Shari Lee Dworkin
Faye Linda Wachs

The Morality/Manhood Paradox: Masculinity, Sport, and the Media

In a world where women do not say no, the man is never forced to settle down and make serious choices. His sex drive—the most powerful compulsion in his life is never used to make him part of civilization as the supporter of a family. If a woman does not force him to make a long-term commitment—to marry—in general, he doesn't. It is maternity that requires commitment. His sex drive only demands conquest, driving him from body to body in an unsettling hunt for variety and excitement in which much of the thrill is in the chase itself. (Gilder, 1986, p. 47)

Journalists articulated the "body panic" surrounding HIV/AIDS and sport in ways that framed heterosexual women as the virulent agents and heterosexual men as the "innocent" victims. These accounts are readily acceptable because they simultaneously produce and reproduce a gender regime that privileges heterosexual male "promiscuity" and devalues, pathologizes, or criminalizes other forms of sexuality. (McKay, 1993, p. 77)

On November 7, 1991, Earvin "Magic" Johnson announced that he had tested positive for the HIV virus. The public registered immediate shock and dismay that arguably one of the greatest and most beloved players in NBA history contracted the highly stigmatized virus. After Johnson, a self-identified heterosexual, made his announcement, once-quiet HIV/AIDS information hot lines were suddenly jam-packed with millions of concerned inquiries as to who gets HIV and how. Johnson became a national spokesman for safe sex and began to urge abstinence, citing his unsafe "accommodation" of thousands of women. More than four years later, on February 22, 1996, professional diver Greg Louganis announced that he had AIDS and that he had been HIV-positive during the 1988 Seoul Olympics. Mainstream news coverage focused on the now infamous "blood in the pool" incident after Louganis struck his head on a springboard and still went on to win an Olympic gold. Although no shock or dismay was expressed vis-à-vis Louganis, concern was expressed that Louganis, who identifies as gay, had not informed others of his HIV status—and what effect his virus may have had on the doctors who stitched his bleeding head and on others in the pool. During the same month, on February 11, 1996, white working-class professional boxer Tommy Morrison let the public hear his own HIV story. Morrison expressed shock, regretfully blamed his "fast lane lifestyle," and is described by friends as the "world's biggest bimbo magnet." This chapter examines paradoxes that juxtapose

From *Masculinities, Gender Relations, and Sport*, Jim McKay, Michael A. Messner, and Don Sabo, eds. Sage Publication, 2000. © 2000 by Sage Publications, Inc. Reprinted by permission.

the public perception of athletes as role models against media accounts rife with "moral" turpitude. These paradoxes are particularly timely in the wake of recent attention paid to AIDS in sport. Our exploration of the widespread print media coverage of these prominent sports figures reveals cultural and historical assumptions about masculinity, sexuality, and HIV/AIDS.

In U.S. mainstream culture, athletes and sports have specific cultural meanings. Athletes in mediated sports are role models, heroes, and are often featured as successful individuals. Our analysis of dominant print media coverage of these athletes' HIV announcements highlights two important and interrelated issues surrounding bodies, morality, sexuality, and masculinity (the Appendix contains citations to all articles examined in this study). First, a contradiction between dominant norms of morality and masculinity becomes apparent. Second, the complexity of current and historical dynamics of race/class/gender/sexuality are explicated.

Hegemonic Masculinity, Sport, and Bodies

Hegemonic masculinity provides cultural icons or mythic images of masculinity that privilege the most powerful half of multiple dichotomous social locations. Hegemonic masculinity, the most dominant form of masculinity (white, middle-class, heterosexual) in a given historical period, is defined in relation to femininity and subordinated masculinities (Connell, 1987). As Foucault (1979) demonstrated, individuals live at the intersection of multiple hierarchicalized dualities, some of which are privileged, others of which are stigmatized. An individual's social location is determined by his or her positioning within multiple and fragmented hierarchies and dualities. For example, African Americans historically have been framed by the media as being "closer to nature" (Collins, 1990). Within sport, African American male athletes are assumed to be "natural" athletes, whereas white men are praised for their intelligence and hard work (Edwards, 1973). Although at times both privileged and subordinated male bodies may be said to enjoy male privilege and are seen as physically superior to female athletes, marginalized masculinities are indubitably stigmatized through comparisons with white middle-class norms (Majors, 1990). The body, then, and its discursive interpretations, are sites at which the material effects of power can be explored (Foucault, 1979). It is a tangible enactment and representation of these intersections.

In Western thought, the athletic male body has been a mark of power and moral superiority for those who bear it (Synnott, 1993; Dutton, 1995). Those who have these characteristics, along with other such as the "correct" race and class status, are assumed to be inherently "morally" superior. Which bodies are marked as superior is not static, but is contested. At the turn of the 20th century, the definition of morality was being debated within and between many social institutions, especially religious, medical, legislative, psychiatric, and social welfare agencies. The definition of morality was influenced by religious norms of good versus evil, prohibitions on non-procreative sex (Katz, 1995b), and the Protestant work ethic that stressed hard work, individualism, and self-abnegation (Turner, 1984). This definition privileged the white, heterosexual middle class as "moral" against assumptions made about subordinated "others."

When urbanization and industrialization created changes in economic opportunities at the turn of the 20th century, many of these changes presented challenges to ideologies of gender and the position defined as hegemonic masculinity. The creation of white-collar occupations, an expanding middle class, and greater acceptance of women in the workforce facilitated a crisis in the definition of masculinity. Women's increasing presence in the public sphere, coupled with changes in men's work, fed fears of social feminization. The rise of competitive team sports in the United States is said to be a backlash, a means for white middle-class men to reaffirm symbolically their physical and moral superiority over women and socially subordinated men (Messner, 1988; Crosset, 1990; Kimmel, 1990). The sports that were popularized in the United States did not promote any type of masculinity and femininity but rather reflected specifically middle-class ideals of masculinity and femininity (Gorn & Goldstein, 1993). Individuals who participated in hegemonic sports were deemed heroes by virtue of their participation. Their bodies became signifiers of power and masculinity. With this power came the assumption of not only physical but also moral superiority.

In recent decades, most of the American public have increasingly experienced sport through the mass media (Wenner, 1989; Sage, 1990). This is not surprising, as sport and the mass media have enjoyed a mutually beneficial or "symbiotic" relationship over the last century (Jhally, 1989; McChesney, 1989). Mediated sports function largely to naturalize values and points of view that are generally consistent with cultural hegemony and come to appear as "common sense" (Jhally, 1989). Ideologies about gender, race, class, and sexuality are reproduced explicitly in media texts, in the assumptions that underlie the text, and in which sports and athletes are valued as culturally significant (Duncan & Hasbrook, 1988; Duncan, Messner, & Jensen, 1994; Kane, 1988, 1996; Messner, Duncan, & Wachs, 1996). For example, numerous works demonstrate how women and femininity are constructed as inferior through mediated sports and how men and masculinity are implicitly defined and constructed as superior (Theberge, 1987; Duncan & Hasbrook, 1988; Kane & Snyder, 1989; Whitson, 1990; Nelson, 1994; Kane, 1995; Messner et al., 1996). Furthermore, other works demonstrate how mediated sports reinforce stigmatizations of marginalized masculinities (Pronger, 1990; Messner & Solomon, 1993; Cole & Denny, 1994; Lule, 1995; Cole & Andrews, 1996; Wachs & Dworkin, 1997; Dworkin & Wachs, 1998). Although some works have examined HIV in sport (King, 1993; McKay, 1993; Cole & Denny, 1994), the cultural paradox that simultaneously represents male athletes as "moral" leaders and protects male privileges that are inconsistent with dominant norms of morality has not yet been problematized.

Given that sport is one of the most powerful socializing institutions for masculinity (Messner, 1992b) that privileges male heterosexual bodies, it provides an interesting forum for exploring norms of sexual behavior. Some scholars have argued that hegemonic male sexuality contributes to sexually aggressive locker room talk (Curry, 1991; Kane & Disch, 1993), violence against women (Kane & Disch, 1993; Messner & Sabo, 1994; Nelson, 1994; Crosset, Benedict, & McDonald, 1995), violence against other men (Messner, 1988; Young, 1993), and [. . .] difficulty in having lasting intimate relationships with women (Connell, 1990; Messner, 1992b; Klein, 1993). To be a man in our culture (and in sport in particular) is to have an assumed naturally aggressive sexual virility that brings with it access to multiple women's bodies. The case of athletes with HIV/AIDS presents a compelling arena in which to explore the discourse on masculinity and sexuality, and specifically "promiscuity" or "virility." Without the stigma that comes with HIV/AIDS, sexually active (heterosexual) men, by definition, are adhering to masculinity successfully. Given that HIV/AIDS is associated with the gay community (Weeks, 1985; Connell, 1987; Sontag, 1989; Watney, 1989; Patton, 1990) and carries a heavy "moral" stigma, we ask: How does the dominant print media frame male athletes and their concomitant normative sexual privilege when they acquire the highly socially stigmatized virus HIV? How will the public discourse—in our example, print media coverage—frame these announcements in the mass cultural discourse given its dual tendency to support hegemonic masculinity and stigmatize and blame infected (and often othered) bodies as immoral? How does mainstream media coverage reconcile hero status, dominant norms of masculinity, and morality in the body of the HIV-positive athlete? For which men?

Methodology

We used textual analysis to explore how cultural discourses that define gendered norms of sexuality shape and constrain men's and women's behaviors. Foucault (1979) observed that power operates both constitutively and repressively. Power operates to constitute dominant discourses, whereby some assumptions shape the acceptable public discourse and appear as common sense; this leaves many potentialities outside the realm of the fathomable. This constitution of power then creates a basis for power to operate repressively, whereby it seems "natural" to accept certain behaviors as "normal" and "moral" while policing "deviant" and "immoral" behaviors (Foucault, 1979). We explored dominant print media framings as one of power's material effects. Our interest was to deconstruct dominant assumptions about male and female sexual agency that survey and police "public" bodies and acts. We also explore the tensions and contradictions within these assumptions.

To explore these assumptions, we performed a textual analysis on all available articles from the *Los Angeles Times, The New York Times,* and *The Washington Post* that followed the HIV-positive announcements of professional basketball player Earvin "Magic" Johnson, Olympic diver Greg Louganis, and professional boxer Tommy Morrison. Articles were coded for content, tone, and implications and were cross-coded for validity. Out of the initial read of the articles emerged two areas for analysis. First, articles were analyzed as to how the status of the HIV-positive athlete was framed: Was he framed as a hero or as a "carrier"? The selective usage of the word hero in titles and/or bodies of articles demonstrates the morality/manhood paradox and reveals how the social location of individuals predetermines their access to hero status. Second, articles were coded for how men's and women's sexual agency is framed. This theme demonstrates how mainstream media coverage maintains this paradox by reinforcing cultural discourses that protect norms of hegemonic masculinity and male (hetero) sexual privilege while blaming and stigmatizing women and subordinated men.

Due to the enormous number of articles on Magic Johnson, many of which focused exclusively on his career, we limited our collection to all articles for three months following his announcement and 10% of the articles that appeared thereafter. Three mainstream newspapers were chosen from three major cities in the United States to represent the dominant or mainstream print media's treatment of gender norms, sexuality, and HIV/AIDS. Indeed, other newspapers, such as *USA Today,* may have large circulations, and the gay and alternative press might offer different framings of these events. However, the selected newspapers garner prestige and respect as mainstream media sources and, as such, are valuable sites in which to analyze dominant discourses on these subjects.

One striking feature of the HIV-positive announcements of Johnson, Louganis, and Morrison is the vast difference in the number of articles written. There are more than 100 articles about Magic Johnson, 12 articles about Greg Louganis, and 8 articles about Tommy Morrison. Perhaps the difference in sheer number of articles highlights not only Magic Johnson's celebrity status within the basketball community but also the fact that basketball is part of the triad of sports that reinforces hegemonic masculinity and is one of the most watched sports in our culture. By contrast, the fewer number of articles about Louganis and Morrison may reflect their lesser popularity as individuals or the status of the sports in which they participate. Furthermore, one cannot ignore the effect of the symbiotic relation between sports and the mass media (Jhally, 1989; Sage, 1990). Sport is promoted by the mass media as a means for targeting the hard-to-reach male middle-class market aged 18 to 45 years. Hence, sports that are considered middle-class and "masculine appropriate" (Kane, 1988) garner the bulk of media coverage (Messner, 1988; Jhally, 1989).

Boxing is a blood sport that has been widely contested as violent and immoral. Participation in such a sport has been largely linked to working-class men, who have been disproportionately represented in the sport since its inception (Gorn & Goldstein, 1993). Although boxing is widely accepted, popularized, and aired in mainstream sports media, it still retains stigma through its historical association with the working class. Thus, although Morrison participates in a sport with heavy doses of physical contact that aids the status of boxing in terms of hegemonic masculinity, its popularity suffers because it is not a team sport with signifiers linked to the dominant class. Although it is true that Morrison is hardly the equivalent of Johnson in terms of the success of his career, it is interesting to note that he received almost as much coverage as did Louganis despite his being a mediocre professional compared to Louganis, who dominated his sport for most of his career.

The relative lack of coverage of Louganis likely reflects that diving, which involves no direct physical confrontation, is not linked to the construction of hegemonic masculinity. In general, team sports are considered male-appropriate, whereas sports that emphasize grace are associated with femininity (Kane, 1988). Male team sports often involve overcoming opponents' defenses and asserting mastery and control of the field of play. The "female-appropriate" sports, like gymnastics and figure skating, involve one receiving an individual score that (in theory) is in no way dependent on the other participants' actions. Men who participate in sports that are not "masculine-appropriate" do not acquire the status of hegemonic masculinity; indeed, their participation may even mark them as less than masculine. Greg Louganis participates in an individual, graceful sport. His athletic body does not have the same status as an exemplar of hegemonic masculinity. Furthermore, as a gay man, he is linked to a number of negative body stigmatizations, especially the (assumed to be) diseased body. Thus, all of these factors contributed to keeping the mainstream media from more in-depth coverage of his announcement.

The "Hero" and the "Whore": Privileging and Protecting Hegemonic Masculinity

In mainstream Western culture, AIDS is associated with the gay community (Weeks, 1985; Connell, 1987; Sontag, 1989; Watney, 1989; Eisenstein, 1994) and other marginalized subpopulations and is therefore highly stigmatized. Despite the widespread invisibility and marginalization of gay men with AIDS, Magic Johnson, a self-identified heterosexual man, was not stigmatized when he publicly announced he had contracted the HIV virus. He was framed by the mainstream American print media unequivocally as a hero and was lauded for courageously battling a socially stigmatized illness (Wachs & Dworkin, 1997). Although coverage of Johnson's announcement may destabilize popular assumptions around AIDS and sexual identity through its statements that "straights can get it too," racist ideologies of black male sexuality most likely linger in the public imagination. As is demonstrated by the print media coverage, ideologies reveal a way in which power relations operate to reproduce the stigmatization of subordinated men and women while protecting the privileges of dominant social categories.

More than 100 articles covered Magic Johnson's announcement. Although the primary framing and content of 27 was that Magic Johnson is a hero, numerous other articles also framed him as a hero through reference to his exemplary career and described his profound influence in professional basketball. Articles titled "Magic Johnson's Legacy" (Berkow, *The New York Times*, 11/8/91) and "A Career of Impact, a Player of Heart" (Brown, *The New York Times*, 11/8/91) ran the day after his announcement. Off the court, Johnson was framed as a hero to at-risk subpopulations, sports fans, activists, the medical community, and the public at large. One article featured Los Angeles Mayor Bradley's comparison of this news to the assassination of former President Kennedy (Thomas, *The New York Times*, 11/9/91). Other articles stated that Magic Johnson "became a hero to a new set of fans—the community of activists and medical professionals" (Harris, *Los Angeles Times*, 11/8/91) and "I think he's obviously a hero to many Americans . . . so I think he would have a tremendous impact" (Cimons, *Los Angeles Times*, 11/11/91).

Johnson's hero status was even openly conferred by President George Bush: "President Bush on Friday described Los Angeles Lakers basketball star Earvin (Magic) Johnson as 'a hero to me' and 'to everyone (who) loves sports'" (Gerstenzang & Cimons, *The Los Angeles Times,* 11/9/91). This status conferral was also reflected in the titles of several articles in which the words hero and icon became synonymous with Johnson: "Los Angeles Stunned as Hero Begins Future With HIV" (Mathews, *The Washington Post,* 11/9/91), "An Icon Falls and His Public Suffers the Pain" (Murphy & Griego, *Los Angeles Times,* 11/8/91). Furthermore, Johnson was framed as a hero for gracefully and honestly dealing with a socially stigmatized illness. For example, he was described as handling his announcement as a "gentleman" (Gerstenzang & Cimons, *Los Angeles Times,* 11/9/91) "with grace and candor," and as a "challenge to fans to put aside shock and dismay" (Kindred, *Los Angeles Times,* 11/8/91). Despite the long negative history of HIV/AIDS, when Magic was found to have contracted the disease, the press reported, "You don't have to avoid Magic Johnson. He is not contaminated. He is not a leper. He is still Magic Johnson" (Downey, *Los Angeles Times,* 11/8/91). These articles demonstrate the media's willingness to remove the stigma of HIV/AIDS when it was contracted by a self-identified heterosexual sports star.

Other articles framed Johnson as a hero for his role as an educator about HIV/AIDS to the heterosexual community and the role he would play as a national spokesman for AIDS. For example, the *Los Angeles Times* and *The Washington Post* published articles titled "Announcement Hailed as a Way to Teach Public" (Harris, *Los Angeles Times,* 11/8/91) and "Hero's Shocker Leaves Teens Grasping for Answers" (Shen, *The Washington Post,* 11/9/91). Johnson was credited with bringing AIDS to the general public's attention and for putting AIDS on the national agenda, for example, "An Epidemic the Public Might Finally Confront: Johnson Could Help End Stigma of AIDS" (Gladwell, *The Washington Post,* 11/10/91), "Legend's Latest Challenge: Sports Hero's Message May Resonate" (Gladwell & Muscatine, *The Washington Post,* 11/8/91), and "They say he can help shatter myths about HIV, AIDS" (Harris, *Los Angeles Times,* 11/8/91).

However, given the fact that the social discourse that has surrounded AIDS has been one of individual blame, it is interesting to note that Magic Johnson was not vilified for the risk at which he put himself, nor the risk at which he put the numerous people with whom he was physically intimate. The way in which the blame for AIDS transmission was framed shows how the discourse on sexuality serves to exonerate heterosexual men, blame women, and marginalize gay men. Magic Johnson's "promiscuity" was not problematized as his responsibility or his "risk" but rather was blamed on aggressive female groupies. As McKay (1993) argued, the media coverage of Johnson privileged and protected virile male heterosexuality in sport, while making consistent references to "wanton" women who wait for the athletes. What is implied is that any "normal man" would have done the same thing (e.g., "boys will be boys"). Magic Johnson's "promiscuity" is not only blamed on women, but he is painted as a kind man who is quoted as "accommodating" as many women as possible. In one article, Magic Johnson was quoted as saying, "There were just some bachelors that almost every woman in Los Angeles wanted to be with: Eddie Murphy, Arsenio Hall and Magic Johnson. I confess that after I arrived in L.A. in 1979 I did my best to accommodate as many women as I could" (Editor, "Sorry but Magic Isn't a Hero," *New York Times,* 11/14/91). A second article agreed: "The groupies, the 'Annies.' They are the ancient entitlements of the locker room, the customary fringe benefits of muscles" (Callahan, *The Washington Post,* 11/10/91). It is assumed that sports stars, as icons of masculinity, have a right to abundant sexual access to women's bodies.

Four years later, when white, working-class, heterosexual, professional boxer Tommy Morrison announced his HIV-positive status, he was not similarly valorized. Rather than elevating Morrison to hero status for overcoming the stigma of the illness, mainstream print media coverage treated him as a tragic figure, who, through his own "ignorance" about HIV transmission, destroyed a promising career. However, heterosexual masculine privilege was protected, through a reassignment of blame to women's sexual aggressiveness. As in the coverage of Johnson, women were framed as pursuers in the Morrison coverage, and Morrison is framed as a man who is unable to resist temptation. For example, one article pointed to the women who "wait outside the door fighting over who was going to get Tommy that night" (Romano, *The Washington Post*, 2/16/96) as the problem, not Morrison's pursuit of these women or his failure to practice safe sex. Although Morrison was blamed on an individual level for making "irrational, immature decisions," in his fast-lane lifestyle, he clearly was not framed as the pursuer, threat, or sexual agent, but rather as the "world's biggest bimbo magnet." Although the articles held Morrison accountable for his ignorance of HIV/AIDS, he was not held responsible for the risk at which he may have put others. One article highlighted how Morrison's inner circle summed up the situation: "It wasn't uncommon for me to go to his hotel room and find three or four women outside the door fighting over who was going to get Tommy that night. We had groupies all the way up to career women" (Romano, *The Washington Post*, 2/16/96). As in their treatment of Johnson, the media confirmed Morrison's heterosexuality and affirmed his sexual desirability to women through his acquiescence to temptation—what any "normal" man also would have done.

"Normal" under Western ideals of masculinity can include sexual conquest with multiple desirable women. Because sports define and reproduce ideologies of masculinity, it is hardly surprising that athletes are expected to demonstrate their masculinity off as well as on the field. Even when media framings call men into question for their actions, agency and responsibility are displaced onto the bodies of women, while masculine privilege is protected. As noted, women are framed as aggressive groupies who are responsible for tempting men, whereas men are framed as doing what "any normal" man would have done. Reminiscent of 19th century ideologies of gender and sexuality, these ideologies featured cultural narratives that claimed that men's sexual appetites were naturally more powerful and aggressive than women's. Given this claim, it is women who were (and are still) held responsible for controlling men's sexuality (Gilder, 1973). Repopularized during the Reagan and Bush era by leading conservative thinkers such as George Gilder (1986), these ideologies are maintained, reinforced, and celebrated under the rubric of "family values." This conceptual framework refers to women as the "moral guardians of civilization" through the expectation that they will not elicit, provoke, or satisfy male desire outside of heterosexual monogamous marriage. Hence, when mainstream media coverage presents Magic Johnson and other athletes as having "accommodated" as many "bimbos" as they could, the implication is that these men were merely yielding to aggressive females who are depicted as "out of control." Thus, through the framing of female groupies as responsible for tempting male sports stars into "promiscuity," the norm of aggressive male (hetero)sexual conquest common under masculinity remains unproblematized. Furthermore, the idea that women are responsible for control of men's morality means that male athletes are still presumed to be inherently moral. As we show, when individual athletes' morality is called into question, media frames do not link the "moral" transgressions to the norms of hegemonic masculinity but to each man's subordinate status.

Blaming Marginalized Masculinities

The mainstream print media coverage of Greg Louganis reveals a compelling contrast to the coverage of Johnson and Morrison. Although "shock" and "surprise" were abundantly referenced with regard to Johnson's and Morrison's announcements, there were no references to shock or surprise in the print media when Greg

Louganis made his HIV-positive announcement. Unlike the articles on Morrison and Johnson, which featured phrases like "he got it from heterosexual sex," there were no inquiries as to how Louganis could have contracted the virus. The assumed linkage between homosexuality and AIDS was so profound that none of the 11 articles on Louganis even posed the question as to how he contracted HIV/AIDS. We argue that the profound questioning as to how self-identified heterosexual men contracted the virus, coupled with the lack of inquiry into how Louganis could have contracted the disease, works to reinforce the idea that HIV/AIDS is a "natural" and expected part of the gay life course (Weeks, 1985; Watney, 1989; Wachs & Dworkin, 1997; Dworkin & Wachs, 1998). This works to perpetuate the historic assumption that gay bodies are inherently diseased and immoral.

The athletes also were framed differently vis-à-vis the risk of transmission they present to others. Although the "blame" or responsibility for the pollution of the bodies of Magic Johnson and Tommy Morrison was placed on the aggressive women who pursued successful male sports stars, there is no corollary absolution of blame or fault for Greg Louganis. There was no discussion surrounding male groupies who may have pursued Louganis. Furthermore, Magic Johnson and Tommy Morrison's threat to women was nearly always discussed in relation to their wife and fiancée, respectively; they generally were not presented as a threat to their numerous other sex partners. In contrast, the print media did not even begin to ponder the men Greg Louganis may have infected in sex, nor did they ever mention his long-term partner. Several stories, however, expressed concern for the presumably heterosexual divers and doctor who came into contact with Louganis and his blood during the 1988 Olympics. All articles that covered Louganis's announcement discussed this incident and the potential risk of transmission. In this way, gay men and "promiscuous" women are viewed as the virulent agents or problematic vehicle for transmission (Treichler, 1988) while hegemonic masculinity, and the norm of virile male (hetero)sexuality is protected and reaffirmed.

Although data show how heterosexual masculinity is protected at the expense of women and gay men, print media coverage simultaneously subtly reinvigorates the link between blame and working-class and minority status. Johnson was presented as being an African American man with "special" importance as an educator and role model for minority communities. Although he was lauded more generally for raising public awareness on heterosexual AIDS and its prevention, numerous articles focused specifically on this special importance. For example, one article highlighted that the National Minority AIDS Council wanted Johnson to lobby for much-needed increases in financing for health care and prevention (Gross, *The New York Times*, 11/13/91), whereas Johnson himself "has indicated that his personal efforts will focus on AIDS education in the black community" (Harris, *Los Angeles Times*, 11/13/91). Articles claimed, "He speaks best for African Americans" (Gross, *The New York Times*, 11/13/91) and focused explicitly on how "the message" would be loudest for those "who need to hear it most," as quoted in an article titled "Magic's Loud Message for Young Black Men" (Specter, *The New York Times*, 11/8/91, p. B12). Although funding and education are of paramount importance in often-overlooked minority communities whose AIDS rates are disproportionately high, the suggestion that African Americans "need to hear it most" can all too easily become a historical "reminder" that links minorities to stereotypes of excess and a lack of control (Adam, 1978; Collins, 1990). Similarly, articles cited Morrison's poor rural upbringing and broken home and concurrently noted his "irresponsible, irrational, immature decisions," how he "lacked the discipline to say no" (Romano, *The Washington Post*, 2/16/96), and his "ignorance" (Vecsey, *The New York Times*, 2/16/96).

We find it ironic that in the furor over cases involving sexual assaults and athletes, particularly athletes in hegemonic sports, the norm of male sexual conquest in sport goes largely unquestioned (Curry, 1991; Nelson, 1994; Crossett et al., 1995). However, when an athlete acquires a highly stigmatized, potentially deadly virus such as HIV/ AIDS, which historically is associated with the gay community, "mistakes" and "ignorance" regarding male (hetero)sexuality are abundantly recognized by the media. Print media coverage of both Morrison and Johnson simultaneously displaced blame onto the bodies of women and framed the two men as having made bad "choices" or "mistakes." For instance, articles on Morrison noted his "ignorance" around proper HIV and AIDS transmission information, quoted him as saying that he thought he had a "better chance of winning the lottery than contracting this disease," and featured how he "lacked the discipline to say no" (Romano, *The Washington Post*, 2/16/96). An article on Johnson featured a young man who was cited in a *Los Angeles Times* article as saying, "It is good [Magic Johnson] is not ashamed he made a mistake" (Almond & Ford, 11/18/91, *Los Angeles Times*). What, however, is the mistake, precisely—is it "promiscuity"? Or is it "getting caught" conforming to the norm of male sexual conquest only when men have acquired HIV? Instead of highlighting how hegemonic masculinity in sport fuels the discourse on male sexual conquest as part of its cultural norm, popular discourse embraces the idea that it is the individual athlete's bad decision making or ignorance that is to blame.

We also argue that the transgression does not just stand on its own as a bad "individual" decision, but becomes available as a negative signifier of subordinate social categories, that is, in the same way that male privilege is protected while women are blamed, we argue that white middle-class heterosexuality is protected, whereas working-class, black, and gay male sexualities are blamed. The social location of white middle-class heterosexuals is left out of the picture, and working-class, black, and gay male sporting bodies are featured in the spotlight as "guilty."

Because the dominant position remains unscrutinized by the mainstream media press, it becomes the "normal" or moral category against which the "other" categories are negatively compared. Indeed, this is the case because working-class and minority men are the ones held up in the sports limelight due to a limited structure of opportunity that disproportionately funnels subordinated men into a sports career (Edwards, 1973; Messner, 1992b). By featuring Morrison's working-class background and "ignorance," along with Johnson's "mistakes" and his role in speaking to African Americans who "need to hear it most," the print media reinforces "others'" bad individual decision making. Those in the dominant race, class, and sexuality position remain the invisible good against which the "bad" sexually excessive and/or out of control "other" is juxtaposed.

Myths in Sport: Productive Bodies, Moral Men?

We have noted the historical significance of how the muscled male body has been associated with moral superiority (Dutton, 1995). Male athletes who display this body and are successful at culturally valued sports receive widespread public attention and are elevated to the status of hero. As "heroes" with cultural fame and popularity, these athletes enjoy numerous social and economic privileges, one of which is the assumption of morality. Yet, simultaneously, one of the social privileges that (heterosexual) men in hegemonic sports are said to enjoy is access to the bodies of numerous women. We are left with a paradox between "moral" standards of heterosexual monogamy and how to attain high status under dominant norms of masculinity. For "fallen heroes" in sport, print media coverage rarely if ever acknowledges norms in sport or in U.S. culture at large that equate masculinity with sexual prowess. Sexual access to women is a cultural privilege associated with being a man, yet, in turn, the powerful then use this privilege to stigmatize subordinated masculinities and women while dominant men remain invisible to the watchful media eye.

Our analysis of print media coverage of the HIV announcements of Magic Johnson, Tommy Morrison, and Greg Louganis is consistent with those who argue that our culture gradually will add to the list of "others" who have been tagged as "deserving AIDS," to distinguish them from "innocent" victims (Eisenstein, 1994). The lack of inquiry into how Louganis acquired HIV, coupled with concern for the threat of transmission only to the heterosexual public, reinforces a tendency to blame gay sexuality for HIV transmission. It is also notable that lesbians are often left out of the discourse on HIV/AIDS, and sexuality in general, because popular culture tends to render lesbians and the kinds of sex they have invisible (Butler, 1993; Kane & Lenskyj, 1998). For Morrison and Johnson, media frames that emphasize "better decision making" for individual "promiscuous" black and working-class bodies reinvigorate negative stigmatizations as to which bodies are inherently "bad" or immoral. Heterosexual male privilege is protected, and "immorality" is linked to "other" categories. Johnson and Morrison are simultaneously featured for behaving "as any normal" man would, while also highlighting their "ignorant" individual decisions and "mistakes" amid discussions of their class and race, respectively. Thus, it is masculinity that is privileged as "normal," whereas it is the social categories of otherness upon which the responsibility for "deviance" is subtly foisted. Thus, dominant coverage works to displace blame onto the bodies of gay, working-class, and black male, and what becomes implied is that through the proper education and assimilation (to heterosexual middle-class values), "the problem" will be solved. This is consistent with Cole and Denny's (1994) argument that such rhetoric "obscures the responsibility of multinational capitalism and the Reagan–Bush administration for the erosion of social welfare programs and the neglect of AIDS" (p. 123). Furthermore, we argue that the articles reinvigorate a white, heterosexual, middle-class moral gaze on gay, black, and working-class manhood.

Afterward: "God Saved Me": Family Values, Masculinity, and Sexual Conquest

Rather than revealing the paradox between the dominant norms of morality and masculinity, the position of sports stars with AIDS demonstrates how the social location of individuals defines their moral status, not their behavior. Although gay male bodies with HIV are featured often in the media as decaying, diseased, and unproductive (Crimp, 1990), recently, Magic Johnson's body was featured as healing, healthy, and productive. Johnson even announced that the virus in his blood has dropped to "undetectable levels," proof that "God" has "saved him" (Editor, *The New York Times*, 4/5/97). Whereas earlier articles featured Johnson as a spokesman for safe sex, later articles featured his pro-God, promonogamy, profamily rhetoric. Whereas gay men are not framed as having the option of "being saved" from HIV, Johnson, a self-identified newly monogamous heterosexual, is lauded for battling the virus to a level at which it is undetectable. Instead of seeing Johnson as having access to the finest medical care in the world due to his class status, his body is held up as morally deserving of beating the stigmatized illness. Once Johnson renounces his "fast-lane lifestyle" in favor of marriage, family, and monogamy, he is saved. The power of this rhetoric also underlies the critiques of Morrison as irresponsible and assumes that a fast-lane lifestyle is the culprit. The discourse on risk assumes that particular lifestyles and family statuses are safe, and others are dangerous. By conflating lifestyle with risk, erroneous information about HIV transmission is perpetuated (Dworkin & Wachs, 1998). Furthermore, these assumptions reproduce ideologies that privilege particular family forms and relationships and stigmatize others. By contrast, Louganis and other gay men, even if monogamous or family-oriented, are rarely if ever featured for courageously battling HIV or for educating the public; rather, media accounts seem to imply that they "deserve" their fate (Wachs & Dworkin, 1997). For instance, whereas Johnson has become an acclaimed national spokesman and educator for people with HIV/AIDS, a U.S. senator attempted to ban Greg Louganis from speaking on a college campus, citing his talk as "immoral" (Associated Press, *Los Angeles Times*, 1/26/97). Because mainstream print media have identified (assumed to be) immoral acts that require blame, and they have reassigned this blame to "others," coverage of HIV/AIDS announcements reveals the paradox between manhood in hegemonic sports and dominant notions of morality. This is accomplished without ever problematizing hegemonic masculinity in sport or long-held mythic ideals associated with gender, family, and sexuality.

Appendix
Print Media Coverage of HIV Announcements by Prominent Athletes
Magic Johnson

11/8/91 Aldridge, David. Lakers Star Put Imprint on Finals, Records, Money. *The Washington Post*, p. C1.

11/8/91 Araton, Harvey. Riley Leads the Prayers. *The New York Times*, p. B11.

11/8/91 Berkow, Ira. Magic Johnson's Legacy. *The New York Times*, p. B11.

11/8/91 Bonk, Thomas. Even Hearing News Was Not Believing It. The *Los Angeles Times*, p. C1.

11/8/91 Brown, Clifton. A Career of Impact, A Player With Heart. *The New York Times*, p. B11.

11/8/91 Cannon, Lou. Basketball Star Magic Johnson Retires With AIDS Virus. *The Washington Post*, p. A1.

11/8/91 Castaneda, Ruben, & Rene Sanchez. Johnson's AIDS Virus Revelation Moves Teenagers, Fans. *The Washington Post*, p. D1.

11/8/91 Downey, Mike. Earvin Leaves NBA, But His Smile Remains. The *Los Angeles Times*, p. C1.

11/8/91 Gladwell, Malcolm, & Alison Muscatine. Legend's Latest Challenge. *The Washington Post*, p. A1.

11/8/91 Harris, Scott. Announcement Hailed as a Way to Teach Public. The *Los Angeles Times*, p. A32.

11/8/91 Heisler, Mark. Magic Johnson's Career Ended by HIV-Positive Test. The *Los Angeles Times*, p. A1.

11/8/91 Kindred, Dave. Magic's Gift for Inspiring Us Tests Reality. The *Los Angeles Times*, p. B7.

11/8/91 Murphy, Dean E., & Tina Griego. An Icon Falls and His Public Suffers the Pain. The *Los Angeles Times*, p. A1.

11/8/91 Specter, Michael. Magic's Loud Message for Young Black Men. *The New York Times*, p. B12.

11/8/91 Springer, Steve. Through the Years, He Stayed the Same. The *Los Angeles Times*, p. C1.

11/8/91 Stevenson, Richard W. Basketball Star Retires on Advice of His Doctors. *The New York Times*, p. A1.

11/8/91 Thomas, Robert McG., Jr. News Reverberates Through Basketball and Well Beyond It. *The New York Times*, p. B13.

11/9/91 Bonk, Thomas, & Janny Scott. "Don't Feel Sorry for Me," Magic Says. The *Los Angeles Times*, p. A1.

11/9/91 Cannon, Lou, & Anthony Cotton. Johnson's HIV Caused by Sex: "Heterosexual Transmission" Cited; Wife Is Pregnant. *The Washington Post*, p. A1.

11/9/91 Editor. A Magical Cure for Lethargy. The *Los Angeles Times*, p. B5.

11/9/91 Lacey, Marc, & Hugo Martin. Student's Cry a Bit, Learn Life Lessons. The *Los Angeles Times*, p. A26.

11/9/91 Gerstenzang, James, & Marlene Cimons. Bush Calls Johnson a Hero, Defends Administration's Policy on AIDS. The *Los Angeles Times*, p. A26.

11/9/91 Horovitz, Bruce. Sponsors May Use Magic in Ads to Encourage Safe Sex. The *Los Angeles Times*, p. D1.

11/9/91 Mathews, Jay. Los Angeles Stunned As Hero Begins Future With HIV. *The Washington Post*, p. A12.

11/9/91 McMillen, Tom. Magic, Now and Forever. *The New York Times*, p. 23

11/9/91 Shen, Fern. Hero's Shocker Leaves Teens Grasping for Answers. *The Washington Post*, p. A1.

11/9/91 Specter, Michael. When AIDS Taps Hero, His "Children" Feel Pain. *The New York Times*, p. A1.

11/9/91 Stevenson, Richard W. Johnson's Frankness Continues. *The New York Times*, p. 33.

11/9/91 Thomas, Robert McG., Jr. A Day Later, It Remains a Shock Felt Around the World. *The New York Times*, p. A33.

11/10/91 Aldridge, David. For Moments Like These. *The Washington Post*, p. D4.

11/10/91 Callahan, Tom. What It Boils Down to Is Playing With Fire. *The Washington Post*, p. D2.

11/10/91 Gladwell, Malcolm. An Epidemic the Public Might Finally Confront. *The Washington Post*, p. A1.

11/10/91 Jones, Robert A. A Shock That Shifted the World. The *Los Angeles Times*, p. A3.

11/10/91 Lipsyte, Robert. A Jarring Reveille for Sports. *The New York Times*, p. S1.

11/10/91 McNeil, Donald. On the Court or Off, Still Magic. *The New York Times*, p. E9.

11/10/91 Muscatine, Alison. Magic's Revelations Transcends Sports. *The Washington Post*, p. D1.

11/11/91 Chase, Marilyn. Johnson Disclosure Underscores Facts of AIDS in Heterosexual Population. *The Wall Street Journal*, p. B1.

11/11/91 Cimons, Marlene. White House May Name Johnson to AIDS Panel. The *Los Angeles Times*, p. A1.

11/11/91 Horovitz, Bruce. Advertisers Try to Handle This Magic Moment Carefully. The *Los Angeles Times*, p. D1.

11/13/91 Gross, Jane. For Anyone but Johnson, a Daunting Pile of Requests for Help. *The New York Times*, p. A14.

11/13/91 Harris, Scott. Johnson Brings New Stature to AIDS Funding. The *Los Angeles Times*, p. A1.

11/14/91 Editor. Converse's AIDS Efforts Features Magic Johnson. *The New York Times*, p. D10.

11/14/91 Editor. Sorry but Magic Isn't a Hero. *The New York Times*, p. B19.

11/18/91 Almond, Elliot, & Andrea Ford. Wild Ovation Greets Magic at Lakers Game. The *Los Angeles Times*, p. A1.

11/31/91 Editor. Keep Magic in the Mainstream. *The New York Times*, p. B7.

1/1/92 Araton, Harvey. Advertisers Shying From Magic's Touch. *The New York Times*, p. 44.

1/14/92 French, Mary Ann. Magic, Rewriting the Rules of Romance. *The Washington Post*, p. B1.

4/5/97 Editor. Johnson's HIV Level Drops (AIDS Virus in Earvin "Magic" Johnson Is Significantly Reduced). *The New York Times*, p. 36.

Greg Louganis

2/23/95 Longman, Jere. Doctor at Games Supports Louganis. *The New York Times*, p. B15.

2/23/95 Sandomir, Richard. Louganis, Olympic Champion, Says He Has AIDS. *The New York Times*, p. B11.

2/23/95 Weyler, John. Olympic Diver Louganis Reveals That He Has AIDS. The *Los Angeles Times*, p. A1.

2/24/95 Boxall, Bettina, & Frank Williams. Louganis Disclosure Greeted With Sadness. The *Los Angeles Times*, p. B1.

2/24/95 Editor. Louganis: Breaks His Silence, Another World-Famous Athlete Disclosed He Has AIDS. The *Los Angeles Times*, p. B6.

2/24/95 Longman, Jere. Olympians Won't Have to Take H.I.V. Test. *The New York Times*, p. B7.

2/24/95 Vecsey, George. Tolerance, Not Blame, For Louganis. *The New York Times*, p. B7.

2/26/95 Longman, Jere. Olympian Blood: Debate About HIV Tests Sparked by Diver With AIDS. *The New York Times*, p. 2.

2/28/95 Quintanilla, Michael. The Truth Shall Set You Free. The *Los Angeles Times*, p. E11.

3/5/95 Alfano, Peter. The Louganis Disclosure: AIDS in the Age of Hype. *The New York Times Magazine*, p. E1.

5/5/95 Ammon, Richard. Gay Athletes. The *Los Angeles Times*, p. M5.

1/26/97 Associated Press. Senator Seeks to Ban Louganis. The *Los Angeles Times*.

Tommy Morrison

2/12/96 Eskenazi, Gerald. Morrison Suspension: An HIV Concern. *The New York Times*, p. B6.

2/13/96 Eskenazi, Gerald. Morrison Confirms Positive HIV Test. *The New York Times*, p. B13.

2/13/96 Springer, Steve. Magic Johnson Plans to Call Boxer. The *Los Angeles Times*, p. A9.

2/13/96 Springer, Steve, & Earl Gustkey. Boxer's HIV Test Heats Up Debate Over Risk to Others. The *Los Angeles Times*, p. A1.

2/14/96 HIV Test for Morrison Ref. *The New York Times*, p. B11.

2/16/96 Eskenazi, Gerald. Remorseful Morrison Has Words of Caution. *The New York Times*, p. B7.

2/16/96 Romano, Lois. Heavyweight Deals With Serious Blow. *The Washington Post*, p. A1.

2/16/96 Vecsey, George. Morrison Didn't Pay Enough Attention. *The New York Times*, p. B20.

9/20/96 Kawakami, Tim. HIV-Positive Morrison Says He'll Fight Again. The *Los Angeles Times*, p. C9.

References

Adam, B. (1978). *The survival of domination: Inferiorization and everyday life*. New York: Elsevier North-Holland.

Butler, J. (1993). *Bodies that matter: On the discursive limits of "sex."* Boston: Routledge & Kegan Paul.

Cole, C. L., & Andrews, D. L. (1996). Look, it's NBA Showtime! A Research Annual. *Cultural Studies*, (1), 141–181.

Cole, C. L., & Denny, H., III. (1994). Visualizing deviance in post-Reagan America: Magic Johnson, AIDS and the promiscuous world of professional sport. *Critical Sociology*, 20(3), 123–147.

Collins, P. H. (1990). *Black feminist thought: Knowledge, consciousness, and the politics of empowerment*. New York: HarperCollins.

Connell, R. W. (1987). *Gender and power: Society, the person, and sexual politics*. Stanford, CA: Stanford University Press.

Connell, R. W. (1990). An iron man: The body and some contradictions of hegemonic masculinity. In M. Messner & D. Sabo (Eds.), *Sport, men, and the gender order: Critical feminist perspectives* (pp. 83–96). Champaign, IL: Human Kinetics.

Crimp, D. (1990). *AIDS demographics*. Seattle, WA: Bay.

Crosset, T. (1990). Masculinity, sexuality, and the development of early modern sport. In M. Messner & D. Sabo (Eds.), *Sport, men and the gender order: Critical feminist perspectives* (pp. 45–54). Champaign, IL: Human Kinetics.

Crosset, T., Benedict, J., & McDonald, M. A. (1995). Male student athletes reported for sexual assault: Survey of campus police departments and judicial affairs offices. *Journal of Sport and Social Issues*, 19, 126–140.

Curry, T. J. (1991). Fraternal bonding in the locker room: A profeminist analysis of talk about competition and women. *Sociology of Sport Journal*, 8, 119–135.

Duncan, M. C., & Hasbrook, C. A. (1988). Denial of power in televised women's sports. *Sociology of Sport Journal*, 5, 1–21.

Duncan, M. C., Messner, M. A., & Jensen, K. (1994). *Gender stereotyping in televised sports: A follow-up to the 1989 study*. Los Angeles: Amateur Athletic Foundation.

Dutton, K. (1995). *The perfectible body: The Western ideal of male physical development*. New York: Continuum.

Dworkin, S. L., & Wachs, F. L. (1998). "Disciplining the body": HIV positive male athletes, media surveillance, and the policing of sexuality. *Sociology of Sport Journal*, 15, 1–20.

Edwards, H. (1983). *Sociology of sport*. Belmont, CA: Dorsey.

Eisenstein, Z. (1994). *The color of gender: Reimaging democracy*. Berkeley: University of California Press.

Foucault, M. (1979). *Discipline and punish: The birth of the prison.* New York: Vintage.

Gilder, G. (1973). *Sexual suicide.* New York: Quadrangle.

Gilder, G. (1986). *Men and marriage.* Gretna: Pelican.

Gorn, E. J., & Goldstein, W. (1993). *A brief history of American sports.* New York: Hill & Wang.

Jhally, S. (1989). Cultural studies and the sports/media complex. In L. A. Wenner (Ed.), *Media, sports, and society* (pp. 41–57). Newbury Park, CA: Sage.

Kane, M. J. (1988). Media coverage of the female athlete before, during, and after Title IX: *Sports Illustrated* revisited. *Journal of Sport Management, 2,* 87–99.

Kane, M. J. (1995). Resistance/transformation of the oppositional binary: Exposing sport as a continuum. *Journal of Sport and Social Issues, 19,* 191–218.

Kane, M. J. (1996). Media coverage of the post Title IX athlete: A feminist analysis of sport, gender, and power. *Duke Journal of Gender Law and Policy, 3,* 95–127.

Kane, M. J., & Disch, L. J. (1993). Sexual violence and the reproduction of male power in the locker room: The "Lisa Olsen incident." *Sociology of Sport Journal, 10,* 331–352.

Kane, M. J., & Lenskyj, H. (1998). Media treatment of female athletes: Issues of gender and sexualities. In L. Wenner (Ed.), *MediaSport: Cultural sensibilities and sport in the media age* (pp. 186–201). Boston: Routledge & Kegan Paul.

Kane, M. J., & Snyder, E. (1989). Sport typing: The social "containment" of women in sport. *Arena Review, 13,* 77–96.

Katz, J. (1995b). *The invention of heterosexuality.* New York: Penguin.

Kimmel, M. (1990). Baseball and the reconstitution of American masculinity, 1880–1920. In M. Messner & D. Sabo (Eds.), *Sport, men and the gender order: Critical feminist perspectives* (pp. 55–66). Champaign, IL: Human Kinetics.

King, S. (1993). The politics of the body and the body politic: Magic Johnson and the ideology of AIDS. *Sociology of Sport Journal, 10,* 270–285.

Klein, A. (1993). *Little big men: Bodybuilding subculture and gender construction.* Albany: State University of New York Press.

Lule, J. (1995). The rape of Mike Tyson: Race, the press and symbolic stereotypes. *Critical Studies in Mass Communication, 12,* 176–195.

Majors, R. (1990). Cool pose: Black masculinity in sports. In M. Messner & D. Sabo (Eds.), *Sport, men and the gender order: Critical feminist perspectives* (pp. 109–114). Champaign, IL: Human Kinetics.

McChesney, R. W. (1989). Media made sport: A history of sports coverage in the United States. In L. A. Wenner (Ed.), *Media, sports, and society* (pp. 49–69). Newbury Park, CA: Sage.

McKay, J. (1993). "Marked men" and "wanton women": The politics of naming sexual "deviance" in sport. *Journal of Men's Studies, 2*(1), 69–87.

Messner, M. A. (1988). Sport and male domination: The female athlete as contested ideological terrain. *Sociology of Sport Journal, 5,* 197–211.

Messner, M. 91992a). Like family: Power, intimacy, and sexuality in male athletes' friendships. In P. Nardi (Ed.), *Men's friendships.* Newbury Park, CA: Sage.

Messner, M. A. (1992b). *Power at play: Sports and the problem of masculinity.* Boston: Beacon.

Messner, M. A., Duncan, M. C., & Wachs, F. L. (1996). The gender of audience-building: Televised coverage of women's and men's NCAA basketball. *Sociological Inquiry, 66,* 422–439.

Messner, M. A., & Sabo, D. (Eds.). (1994). *Sex, violence and power in sports: Rethinking masculinity.* Freedom, CA: Crossing.

Messner, M. A., & Solomon, W. S. (1993). Outside the frame: Newspaper coverage of the Sugar Ray Leonard wife abuse story. *Sociology of Sport Journal, 10,* 119–134.

Nelson, M. B. (1994). *The stronger women get, the more men love football: Sexism and the American culture of sports.* Orlando, FL: Harcourt Brace.

Patton, C. (1990). *Inventing AIDS.* Boston: Routledge & Kegan Paul.

Pronger, B. (1990). *The arena of masculinity: Sport, homosexuality, and the meaning of sex.* New York: St. Martin's Press.

Sage, G. (1990). *Power and ideology in American sport: A critical perspective.* Champaign, IL: Human Kinetics.

Sontag, S. (1989). *AIDS and its metaphors.* New York: Farrar, Straus & Giroux.

Synnott, A. (1993). *The body social: Symbolism, self and society.* Boston: Routledge & Kegan Paul.

Theberge, N. (1987). Sport and women's empowerment. *Women's Studies International Forum, 10,* 387–393.

Treichler, P. (1988). AIDS, gender and biomedical discourse: Current contests for meaning. IN E. Fee & D. Fox (Eds.), *AIDS: the burden of history* (pp. 190–266). Berkeley: University of California Press.

Turner, B. (1984). *The body and society: Explorations in social theory.* Oxford, UK: Basil Blackwell.

Wachs, F. L., & Dworkin, S. L. (1997). There's no such thing as a gay hero: Magic = hero, Louganis = carrier: Sexual identity and media framing of HIV positive athletes. *Journal of Sport and Social Issues, 21,* 335–355.

Watney, S. (1989). *Policing desire: Pornography, AIDS, and the media.* Minneapolis: University of Minnesota Press.

Weeks, J. (1985). *Sexuality and its discontents: Meanings, myths, and modern sexualities.* Boston: Routledge & Kegan Paul.

Wenner, L. A. (1989). Media, sports, and society: The research agenda. In L. A. Wenner (Ed.), *Media, sports, and society* (pp. 13–48). Newbury Park, CA: Sage.

Whitson, D. (1990). Sport in the social construction of masculinity. In M. Messner & D. Sabo (Eds.), *Sport, men and the gender order: Critical feminist perspectives* (pp. 19–29). Champaign, IL: Human Kinetics.

Young, K. (1993). Violence, risk, and liability in male sports culture. *Sociology of Sport Journal, 10,* 373–396.

ARTICLE 47

Peter Lehman

In an Imperfect World, Men with Small Penises Are Unforgiven
The Presentation of the Penis/Phallus in American Films of the 1990s

Reservoir Dogs (1992) begins with a dark screen as we hear a man saying, "Let me tell you what 'Like a Virgin's all about. It's all about a girl who digs a guy with a big dick. It's her song. It's a metaphor for big dicks." After he finishes, the blank screen yields to the image of a group of men sitting in a restaurant talking. One of them (played by Quentin Tarantino, the film's writer and director) has spoken the lines we just heard. Moments later, amid the wandering conversation, he says, "You guys are like making me lose my train of thought. I was saying something. What was it? . . . What the fuck was I talking about?" After one of his companions puts him back on track, he continues, "Let me tell you what 'Like a Virgin's about. It's all about this . . . regular fuck machine. I'm talking morning, day, night—dick, dick, dick, dick, dick, dick." "How many dicks is that?" someone asks. "A lot," another answers.

Both the question and the answer are oddly appropriate for the talk about penises that characterizes several recent American films as well as the news media in the 1990s. In *Running Scared: Masculinity and the Representation of the Male Body* (Lehman 1993), I argued that work on the representation of the penis is important since, until very recently, nearly all critical attention has been focused on the phallus. This nearly exclusive attention to the symbolic realm has had the unfortunate effect, among others, of perpetuating the very phallic mystique that such work seeks to deconstruct. The penis in our culture either is hidden from sight, or its representation is carefully regulated for specific ideological purposes. Centering the penis may seem the ultimate patriarchal tyranny, but it is no coincidence that the most traditional men have been comfortable with the silence surrounding the penis and its absence or careful regulation within representation. Silence about and invisibility of the penis contribute to a phallic mystique. The penis is and will remain centered until such time as we turn the critical spotlight on it; paradoxically, we have to center the penis so that eventually it may be decentered. Richard Dyer's 1982 article, "Don't Look Now: The Male Pin-Up," began important work on the penis/phallus relationship and the manner in which it structures certain notions of masculinity and representations of the male body. As Barbara de Genevieve (1991) puts it, "To unveil the penis is to unveil the phallus is to unveil the social construction of masculinity" (p. 4). It is within this perspective that it is important that we understand the chatter and joking about penises in films of the 1990s.

When the penis is shown in our culture, such representations are carefully regulated, as in the pornographic discourse that attempts to make an impressive spectacle of the penis or in contempo-

Author's Note: I would like to thank Chris Holmlund, Robert Eberwein, Melanie Magisos, Russell Merritt, and William Luhr for their comments and revision suggestions. I am particularly indebted to an anonymous reviewer for *Men and Masculinities*.

From *Men and Masculinities* 1(2): 123–137. Copyright © 1998 Sage Publications, Inc. Reprinted by permission of Sage Publications, Inc.

rary medical discourse that attempts to represent the "normal" or statistically average penis. What these and other discourses do is suppress anything resembling the variety and range of actual penises, which thus remain mysterious and become the subject of curiosity, the object of scorn and humor, or the unseen object of phallic worship. It is precisely within this context that we can understand the seemingly unlimited public appetite for gossip and information surrounding the Bobbitt case and other news stories that center discussion of penises. Predictably, some people felt that Howard Stern reached an all-time television low during his 1993 New Year's eve show when he waved $15,000 in front of John Bobbitt as enticement to drop his pants and let the nation see what a reattached penis looked like (Ring out the old 1994, 33). Yet, such antics seem to me not far removed from recent newspaper articles in Oakland, Tucson, San Antonio, and Phoenix about new surgical techniques for penis enlargement (Hosteteler 1994; Kanigel 1995; Schmidt 1995) or a recent *Arizona Daily Star* story with a large headline, "Urologist Debunks Myths Surrounding the Area below Men's Belts" (Cobb 1994, C6). One of the myths is, predictably, "Myth 7: Penis size matters."

We have created an environment in which inquiring minds want to know, laugh, snicker, speculate, and worship the hidden penis. Lisa Kemler, one of Lorena Bobbitt's lawyers, remarked after the case, "This case was not about a penis. . . . Everyone was so consumed with that. But that's not what this case is really about. It was really about a life" (Bobbitt cleared 1994, 1A). She is, of course, correct on both counts. The reason, however, that everyone was too "consumed" with the penis is that the one real taboo that remains in our culture is that disallowing of anything resembling a mature and explicit representation of the actual organ that is the subject of all this media attention, be it in the news or the movies—for such representation would destroy the cherished patriarchal myth that the penis can sustain such never-ending fascination and be worthy of setting entire narratives in motion or dominating a trial involving life-and-death issues and matters of the most profound social and cultural importance.

I have elsewhere documented in detail how American films of the 1970s and 1980s have been laced with chatter about the penis (Lehman 1990), frequently taking the form of fleeting penis-size jokes, and while the 1990s promises to continue this pattern (there are, for example, two such jokes in 1994's *Mrs. Doubtfire*), there exists a significant variation of which *Reservoir Dogs* is a prime example. Talk about the penis has been occurring nearer the beginning of some films and, in several extreme instances, even sets the narrative events in motion. This development is not entirely without precedent. *The Witches of Eastwick* (1987) begins with three women talking about their penis-size preferences, and, in a variation that involves no language, the plot of *Robocop* (1987) is set in motion when a female police officer is distracted by looking at a man's penis as he finishes urinating. Similarly, the entire narrative momentum in *Hard to Kill* (1990) begins when Steven Seagal awakens from a coma of many years immediately after a nurse lifts the sheets and sighs about the waste of his impressive sexual endowment. Clint Eastwood's *Unforgiven* (1992) and *A Perfect World* (1993) are currently the most significant films to conform to this pattern, but before turning attention to them, I want to return to *Reservoir Dogs*.

The gangster in *Reservoir Dogs* completes his interpretation (which, despite his occupation, is something of a scholarly analysis) of "Like a Virgin" as follows:

> Then one day she meets this John Holmes motherfucker and it's like "Whoa baby." I mean this cat is like Charles Bronson in *The Great Escape*—he's big in tunnels . . . pain, pain . . . it hurts. It shouldn't hurt . . . but when this cat fucks her it hurts—it hurts just like it did the first time. See, the pain is reminding the fuck machine what it was like to be a virgin—hence, "Like a Virgin."

Viewers of the film, like the Harvey Keitel character, may complain that they've "got Madonna's big dick coming out of [their] left ear" since this constant chatter about big dicks seems distracting in relation to the gangster story that is "coming out of [their] right" ear.

Although in many films this chatter about penises occurs only once, such is not the case in *Reservoir Dogs*. Once the gangster story proper begins, we are treated to another dick-talking session, this time as a group of the gangsters drive to a big meeting where they will be briefed by their leader. The driver announces his desire to tell a story. When the others continue talking, he yells, "Shut up! I'm trying to tell a story here." The story is about a woman who seeks vengeance on her lover.

> So anyway, one night she plays it real cool. She waits for this bag of shit to get real drunk. He falls asleep on the fucking couch. She sneaks up on him and she puts whacko glue on his dick and glues his dick to his belly.

"Jesus Christ!" the Keitel character exclaims amid general groans of disgust. "They had to call the paramedics to cut the prick loose," the driver concludes, and they all share a good laugh. The film cuts to the leader addressing the men, "You guys like to tell jokes and giggle and kid around, huh? Giggling like a bunch of young broads in a school yard."

Once again, the film viewer is likely to feel like there is someone's dick coming out of one ear while the gangster story is coming out of the other. What do these dicks have to do with the gangster story? *Reservoir Dogs* is a remarkable and coherent film and one that has been read by Robert Hilferty (1992) as possessing a homosexual subtext. In any case, whether homosexual or not, the film deals centrally with the intimacies of male bonding, and talk about the penis relates to that context. The dick talk in this film is linked to both age and generation; the young men feel a need to talk about penises, which relates to the notions of masculinity they struggle with. The older man either ignores them or scolds them for this type of behavior. For the younger man seated on Keitel's left, big dicks are an important part of masculinity, while for the older man seated on his right, they seem to hold no interest; he leafs through his address book during the conversation, muttering to himself. This seating arrangement suggests that the masculine obsession with penility is replaced by senility with advancing age. When the penis is no longer central to masculinity, only its decline and ruin are left.

Despite this rich context for the dick talking in *Reservoir Dogs*, I would caution against an overly thematic reading, especially of the metaphoric kind the character played by the film's director offers of "Like a Virgin." Like many recent films, *Reservoir Dogs* seems to sense some connection between penises and its subject matter, but it does not know precisely what that connection is. What makes *Reservoir Dogs* unique in this regard is that it gives formal expression to this somewhat bizarre state of affairs. Indeed, in both cases the characters doing the dick talking voice their frustration with the manner in which they are interrupted ("What the fuck was I saying?" and "I'm trying to tell a story here."), and their stories themselves appear like digressions and interruptions in the film. And other characters make this clear in both cases. Keitel's character is literally distracted from his conversation with the boss in the restaurant, and the boss scolds the men for acting like giggling schoolgirls immediately following the second dick discussion. Indeed, Keitel's left and right ear dilemma neatly summarizes the cacophonic disruption that such digressive talk creates in most of these films. The filmmakers need to talk about penises (which they never show) for reasons that are not fully clear even to them, although such talk interrupts their films and the stories they are trying to tell. While such talk in *Reservoir Dogs* is far from being totally digressive, it interrupts the film's narration in a manner mirroring that in which the narrators of the penis stories are themselves interrupted.

In *True Lies* (1994), by contrast, the filmmakers seem to know exactly why they talk about penis size. In that film, a pathetic used-car salesman masquerades as a glamorous spy who is like the one played by Arnold Schwarzenegger. When caught and asked why he engaged in such behavior, he blurts out, "I'm not a spy. I'm nothing. ... I have to lie to women to get laid and I don't score much. I got a little dick; it's pathetic." He then wets his pants. This "nothing" man, the pretender to the true masculinity that Schwarzenegger represents, is primarily marked by the "little dick" and secondarily by his inability, due to fear, to control his bladder. The character reappears briefly at the end of the film when he once again wets his pants.

In my earlier analysis of the virtual epidemic of penis-size jokes in Hollywood films of the 1970s, 1980s, and early 1990s, I hypothesized that their presence could be accounted for in a number of quite different ways including fear of the collapse of the alleged dramatic visual marker of sexual difference, veiled homoerotic desire given a heterosexual veneer by the women who frequently tell the jokes and make the judgments, and, in relation to the last point, male masochism that revels in being judged against a phallic standard and found lacking (Lehman 1993).

While I still believe that all those dynamics are present, it now seems to me that two additional things have to be considered. First, *True Lies* makes dramatically clear that to maintain our belief in the powerful phallic sexuality of an Arnold Schwarzenegger, we have to believe in the pathetic failed sexuality of men with small penises. How can we worship big penises in a world without small penises? (It might be interesting, incidentally, to consider the comic pairing of Schwarzenegger and Danny DeVito in *Twins*, 1988, and *Junior*, 1994, from this perspective—the presence of the small man even further dramatizes Schwarzenegger's large stature.) Second, my analysis of 1970s and 1980s penis-size jokes and chatter reveals an entrenched binary opposition between big and small penises, with small men being the pathetic objects of the jokes and large men being the, frequently implicit, desirable ideal. Something new, however, is emerging in some 1990s films that unexpectedly breaks this dichotomy and suggests that the ideal of the large penis may not be what it's cracked up to be and may, in fact, even be dangerous.

When the function of the penis is to serve as the privileged sign of visual sexual difference, the logical direction of crisis about penis size is that which emerges in Michel Foucault's (1980) edition of *Herculine Barbin: Being the Recently Discovered Memoirs of a Nineteenth-Century French Hermaphrodite*. Two medical documents referring to Adelaide Herculine Barbin are of particular interest here. Dr. Chesnet examined Barbin when as a teenager "she" was living in a convent. Much attention is given to what he calls a "penial body," which measures four to five centimeters. "This little member, which because of its dimensions is as far removed from the clitoris as it is from the penis in its normal state, can, according to Alexina, swell, harden, and lengthen" (p. 126). Later in the report, he refers to "a sort of imperforate penis, which might be a monstrously developed clitoris" (p. 127). In a published autopsy report in Foucault, E. Goujon makes similar observations. At one point, Barbin's sexual organ is described as a "large clitoris rather than a penis; in fact, among women we sometimes see the clitoris attain the size of the index finger" (p. 131). When the dimensions of the penis are given later, it is again noted that "in size [it] did not exceed the clitoris of some women," and it is finally simply referred to as "the erectile organ (penis or clitoris)" (pp. 131–135). The crisis surrounding the penis in the Barbin case is that the external organ is presumed to be the visual marker of sexual difference, and size is key to distinguishing between it and a clitoris.

Something much different is happening in *True Lies*, in which the small penis serves to set off not the clitoris but the large penis. In effect, these penis-size jokes no longer pretend to be about the collapse of sexual difference or about female pleasure. If in Foucault's analysis, Barbin is sacrificed to the nineteenth-century need to determine an individual's true sex, the pathetic used-car salesman with the "little dick" is sacrificed on the altar of late-twentieth-century worship of true masculinity—such is our need to believe in Schwarzenegger's masculinity. The small penis, in other words, far from being an embarrassment for masculinity, becomes its very ground. By making fun of some characters whose penises do not measure up to the phallic mystique, we ensure that mystique with the implicit assumption that some do measure up. Hence, rather than reveal the gap between the penis and the phallus, such films revel in its denial.

As in *Reservoir Dogs,* however, the penis talk in *True Lies* takes place within a complex context. The scenes of high-tech tracking and interrogation of Schwarzenegger's wife's sexual activities reveal how desperately insecure his masculinity is. He may seem like the phallic ideal in comparison to the used-car salesman, but the ideal is not what it seems to be. The true masculinity that Schwarzenegger embodies is itself a form of true lies. He requires the highest technology the government can offer and is assisted by a SWAT team when he captures his wife, who is about to engage in infidelity. He then breaks her down in an interrogation scene in which he stands behind a two-way mirror. Although critics frequently singled out this scene as particularly misogynistic, it in fact can be read quite the opposite. The extremes to which Schwarzenegger goes to catch his wife and wring a confession from her expose an astonishing level of insecurity. The dynamics of the scene enable the audience to laugh at Schwarzenegger and his male partner rather than simply identify with them and enjoy the powerful manner in which they brutally terrorize the woman. Nevertheless, by the end of the film, when he rises into view at a skyscraper to rescue his daughter who has been kidnapped, he appears to have a powerful jet between his legs. As outrageous as the phallic imagery of the plane is, Schwarzenegger commands it masterfully.

Clint Eastwood's *Unforgiven* and *A Perfect World* are particularly interesting films to analyze within this context of 1990s films that grapple with the penis/phallus conundrum for two reasons. They foreground and integrate these issues narratively and thematically, and since Eastwood himself has been one of the major stars to shape and embody masculinity in cinema since the mid-1960s, these films in part reflect back on his star persona.

Unforgiven begins in midaction with a cowboy slashing the face of a whore. Another prostitute explains, "All she done when she seen he had a teensy little pecker is give a giggle. That's all." This event sets the entire narrative in motion since the prostitutes offer a bounty for the guilty man and his companion. If the cowboy at the beginning of the film is found to be literally lacking in the privileged cultural sign of masculinity, we quickly find that all the men are symbolically plagued by similar problems. William Munny (Clint Eastwood) has trouble mounting his horse due to his age, and the young cowboy who somewhat maniacally assembles the posse and leads them is, for all practical purposes, blind. In another image closely related to the film's opening emphasis on the penis, an Eastern writer becomes so scared during a tense confrontation that he wets his pants. Thus, like *True Lies,* the film contains references to and images of perhaps the two most humiliating possibilities surrounding the dual functions of the penis as a sexual and a urinary organ: sexual smallness and loss of bladder control due to fear. The image of masculinity that permeates *Unforgiven* is one of men with small penises who piss in their pants and have trouble mounting and staying on their horses and even seeing who they are shooting at and pursuing.

This integration of a reference to a small penis into complex and carefully developed imagery about the myth of masculinity within the Western genre recalls Robert Altman's similar integration of a penis-size joke in *McCabe and Mrs. Miller* (1971). Dennis Bingham (1994) notes that the script for *Unforgiven* was written by David Webb Peoples in 1975 and that it was "apparently inspired" by Altman's film (p. 232). Although the consequences in Altman's film are much different, once again a prostitute laughs at a cowboy with a small penis, this time when another whore whispers in her ear and indicates with her fingers the man's sexual smallness. As I have shown in a detailed analysis of that film (Lehman 1990,

119–123), Altman not only weaves this joke into a complex critique of the mystique of the Western hero but also into a comparison with the female body, since the dialogue makes clear that one of the whores is sexually small both in her vagina and her breasts.

Similarly, in *Unforgiven* Eastwood extends his careful development of male body imagery to a comparison with the female body. After Munny is beaten in a fight, he regains consciousness to see the scarred whore from the opening scene nursing him. "I must look kinda like you now, huh?" Munny remarks. "You don't look nothing like me, Mister," she quickly responds. Although Munny later calls himself ugly and tries to reassure her that she is "a beautiful woman," her initial response is unsentimentally accurate. In Hollywood films, when a beautiful woman's face is scarred, it nearly always indicates a loss of power stemming from the cultural assumption that women derive power from the passive possession of beauty. When a man's face is similarly disfigured, it nearly always means that he is a tough, active character, the scars proving that he has been tested and survived. He is, in other words, more powerful as a result of his scarred face. The scarred whore in *Unforgiven* hires others to avenge the irreparable loss she has suffered; the battered Munny does the job just fine himself, emerging as a powerful, demonic figure. The cosmetic damage he has suffered is, to say the least, not just like that of the woman.

But the body imagery in *Unforgiven* is even further complicated not by contrasting the male body with the female body but, rather, by unexpectedly contrasting the film's initial emphasis on the cowboy with the small penis with a gunslinger with a large one. During a jail conversation, the sheriff, Little Bill Daggett (Gene Hackman), whose name is of no small interest here, tells the Eastern writer about a gunfighter who died in a shoot-out with "English Bob," the man whose biography he is writing. The gunfighter was nicknamed "Two-Gun Corky," even though he only carried one gun. "Corky never carried two guns, although he should have," the sheriff observes before explaining how he got the nickname. "He had a dick that was so big, it was longer than the barrel on that Walker colt that he carried." Corky's mistake, we are told, was "to stick that thing of his into this French lady that English Bob here was kinda sweet on." Corky is killed in an ensuing fight when the gun he is using blows up in his hand. The sheriff draws the moral, "You see though, if Corky had had two guns instead of just a big dick; he would have been there right to the end to defend himself." I will return to this image of the large penis as posing a danger to its possessor after considering *A Perfect World*.

Although the comparisons with *Unforgiven* were inevitable, very few critics saw much of a connection between that film and *A Perfect World,* Eastwood's next directorial effort. The former appeared to be a film of epic range that looked back on much of the history of the genre and on Eastwood's persona as it was developed in the films of Sergio Leone and Don Diegel, while the latter appeared to be a minor action film with none of the ambitious sweep of its predecessor. Yet, penis size emerges overtly once again in *A Perfect World,* and it is once again woven into the fabric of the film. The convict who escapes from prison with Butch Haynes (Kevin Costner) is represented from the outset as revolting. This is in keeping with a tradition within the male action film, which I have analyzed elsewhere in relation to *The Man Who Shot Liberty Valance,* in which the hero and the villain are similar to each other (Luhr and Lehman 1977). In this variation, the escapees are the "bad" male system, but there is a dichotomy within that system with a good male (Haynes) and a bad male (his companion). They are further contrasted with a "good" male system, the law, which is also composed of the good lawman, Red Garnett (Clint Eastwood), and a sleazy officer who sexually harasses a young woman assigned to the case.

In a pivotal scene that is once again near the beginning of the film, Haynes leaves the boy they have kidnapped with his partner in the car and goes into a store. At Haynes's instructions, the boy, in the front seat, holds a cocked gun pointed at the head of the man sitting in the back seat. The boy has no pants on since he was kidnapped in his underpants. The man talks to the boy about shooting and surmises that he has never shot a gun before. Leaning forward, he tells the boy that they are going to have a "man-to-man" talk, asks him whether he is a man, and, saying, "Let's see what you got down there," reaches down to his underpants, pulls the hand out, looks down, and observes, "Kinda puny ain't it?" The boy, distracted by looking down, is disarmed. The man then begins to molest him. The boy escapes from the car and runs into a field followed by the man, who now appears absolutely diabolical and degenerate. Moments later Haynes kills him.

A truly remarkable scene, however, occurs later in the film when Haynes is alone with the boy in the car. When the boy is reluctant to undress and put on a pair of new pants in front of him, Haynes asks, "Are you embarrassed because I might see your pecker?" "It's puny," the boy replies. When Haynes guesses who told him that, he says, "Let me see," assuring the boy that he will tell him the truth. In a two-shot through the car door window, we see the profile of the boy's head as he pulls down his underpants and Haynes leans forward, looks directly down at his groin, and reports, "Hell no, Philip. Good size for boy your age." We then see a close-up of the boy beaming with pride. The spectacle of an actor of Costner's importance looking at a penis for the express purpose of determining its size in a scene that not only shows him looking but also announces in a dialogue why he is looking is undoubtedly the most narratively and visually centered example to date within a virtual epidemic of such penis preoccupied scenes within Hollywood films. Why is it there?

At one level, the scene uniquely dramatizes why penis-size anxiety so riddles our culture. It condenses a long, drawn out, psychoanalytic experience for boys into a few brief, dramatic moments. The "bad" convict plants the idea in the little boy's mind that he is sexually inadequate, linking the "puny" penis to symbolic issues of masculinity, including guns and shooting. The "good" convict eliminates that anxiety from the boy's psyche (much like he literally eliminates the bad convict from the narrative), in effect making him feel good about himself. The manner in which the boy smiles indicates just how important this moment is. The scene is intensely emotional since it dramatizes how important it is for the boy's psychic development that he feel good about his penis and also how fundamentally good and humane Haynes is for reversing the damage done by the bad convict. Since the little boy's father has abandoned the family, Haynes becomes a kind of good-father figure here, giving the boy what he needs and what he himself never had when he was growing up. For all the talk and joking about penis size that riddles recent Hollywood films, *A Perfect World* provides a rare, serious, indeed profound context for that preoccupation. It is no exaggeration to say that the scene, in its extremely condensed and dramatic form, may help explain why the subject has been so pervasive, if less integrated, in so many other movies. Male subjectivity is, in this scene, formed around the penis. From this perspective, penis size does matter, and for a boy to feel good about his penis is important. Haynes fulfills both literal and symbolic functions of the absent father in this film and, for the fulfillment of the latter, the penis-size scene is crucial— for if *Unforgiven* unlooses an ugly and "bad" masculinity resulting from the cowboy with a small penis who cuts up a whore, *A Perfect World* suggests that Haynes (the good version of such a bad cowboy) has prevented the formation of precisely such a masculinity within the boy.

But the scene functions in yet another way that shows just how much the good and bad male systems are like each other in the male action film. There are many ways that Haynes could fulfill the function of the good father by relieving the boy's anxiety. Like his evil partner, however (they are two sides of the same coin), Haynes affirms the very importance of penis size in masculine identity. By telling the boy that he will evaluate him and tell him the truth, Haynes implies that the answer could be that he is indeed "puny" and that looking at the flaccid penis is important to determine whether this is the case. He makes the boy feel good, in other words, because his penis is of good size. Yet, he could tell the boy, for example, that penis size does not matter and that growing up to be a man has nothing to do with big or small penises. As Michael Renov (1980) has shown in a different context, when films present two male systems (one good and one bad), the bad within the good system goes unnoticed because we are so glad to see the evil male get his punishment. In *A Perfect World*, we are so likely to be overjoyed with the manner in which Haynes stops the damage to the boy's psyche begun by his partner that we do not notice that, in the process, he emphasizes and affirms the same principle.

Although we may miss the connection between Haynes and his evil partner in that particular scene because it is structured to make us identify with Haynes's good-guy version of the persona, part of what makes *A Perfect World* so complex is the disturbing manner in which other scenes virtually insist on us seeing the connection. This aspect of the film reaches its zenith in the scene with the black family. After seeing the father slap his son, Haynes literally goes into a sadistic, murderous rage that is only contained by Philip when he shoots him. Although reminiscent of, for example, the murderous rage that Ethan Edwards in *The Searchers* bears toward his niece (Lehman 1990), this is one of the most extreme and graphically disturbing instances in all of the action cinema of the normally hidden bad part emerging within a "good" character. This exact same complexity lies at the center of *Unforgiven*, in which Gene Hackman's character is simultaneously highly likable and frighteningly egomaniacal and sadistic. And, of course, William Munny himself swings between poles of kindness and generosity (e.g., his treatment of the scarred whore when she offers him sex) and the most vicious and brutally excessive masculinity when he turns his murderous rage loose at the film's climax.

Before returning to *Unforgiven*, however, I want to detour through *The Last Seduction* (1994), another film in which a major portion of the narrative is set in motion by penis size. A young man in a bar tries to pick up a woman, who turns him down without showing any interest. He leans over and whispers in her ear that he is "hung like a horse." He then turns to walk away and she calls him back, referring to him as "Mr. Ed." Staring at his groin she asks him to show her. She tells him to sit down, unzips his pants, then puts her hand in and feels around. When he asks her what she is doing, she says "looking for a certain horse-like quality." Apparently satisfied that he has it, she invites him to bed. It is all downhill from there for this well-hung, confident stud. By the time the film is over, he is framed by the woman for murders he did not commit and for which capital punishment awaits him. Similarly, after she is taken into custody by a black private detective, she manages to kill him and escape by convincing him to show her whether it is true that all black men are well hung. He takes off his seat belt to unzip his pants and, in an appropriation of phallic machinery worthy of Schwarzenegger in *True Lies*, she crashes the car so hard that his body is thrown through the windshield.

The fate of the central character in *The Last Seduction* and, to a lesser extent, that of the private detective bear comparison with that of the well-hung gunfighter described in *Unforgiven*. Nearly all the penis-size jokes and references I have traced through so many films of the 1970s, 1980s, and early 1990s either make fun of small ones or glorify big ones. *Unforgiven* and *The Last Seduction*, on the other hand, imply that being too small is not the only danger. Indeed, it is literally dangerous to be too big—it can kill a man. It is within this context that the scene in the car between Haynes and the boy in *A Perfect World* can be most fully understood. The film does not glorify the alleged phallic power of the large penis but, rather, implies the importance of the "normal" penis to the psychic development of the boy. As soon as the concept of normality is invoked, however, one can be either above or below the norm, have either too much or too little. Just like one can be too smart for one's own good, apparently in the 1990s one can also be too big for one's own good. Being normal is safest.

The continuing preoccupation with penis size in Hollywood films of the 1990s causes critical bewilderment and misjudgment in those rare instances in which reviewers acknowledge it. In his *New Yorker* review of *Nell*, Terrence Rafferty (1994) accuses the film of being hopelessly muddled and writes,

> In the nuttiest scene, Jerry and Paula try to cure Nell of her fear of men . . . by giving her a glimpse of the good Doctor's penis; he strips in the moonlight, Nell giggles girlishly, and her lifelong phobia vanishes into the night air. (p. 108)

Although countless other scenes could qualify for the dubious distinction of being the "nuttiest" in this film, the scene is indeed ludicrous for all the reasons Rafferty (1994) suggests: Nell is instantly cured and, as he goes on to note, she remains entirely pure and innocent. I, however, would emphasize an aspect of the scene that Rafferty overlooks: it is also shot and edited in a ludicrous manner. We see a frontal view of Jerry as he approaches Nell with a towel wrapped around his waist. We get the predictable penis-size joke when Paula urges Jerry on by telling him that "it's no big deal," and he responds self-deprecatingly by adding, "believe me, it's no big deal." He then takes his towel off for the benefit of Nell, who watches from the lake in which she is swimming. As soon as he takes the towel off, however, he sits down and we only see him in profile. One might very well wonder by what logic a man wishing to display his penis sits down to do so. Although Paula says seeing a penis is "no big deal," Hollywood thinks otherwise. Although it may be no big deal for Paula, it is for the audience of this film, who must be protected from its sight. Needless to say, the same is not true for the sight of Nell's nude body, over which the camera lingers long and lovingly—and, of course, innocently.

What is this "nutty" scene doing in the film? I think it can only be understood within Hollywood's current preoccupation with talking about the penis while keeping it covered up. It is precisely this structure that guarantees that penises are a big deal. *Nell*, along with such films as *True Lies, Unforgiven, A Perfect World,* and *The Last Seduction,* conforms to a deep-seated need in current Hollywood films to narratively center the penis and circle around it in a manner so extreme that audiences may soon begin to wonder just how much longer this can go on without showing penises.

Robert Cauthorn's (1994) positive review of *The Last Seduction* is revealing in this regard. Like Rafferty's (1994) review of *Nell*, Cauthorn's review of *The Last Seduction* is generally very perceptive. He complains, however, of "several glaring flaws."

> Chief among these is a somewhat juvenile take on sex that conflicts with the movie's more sophisticated spirit. Bridget has this thing for asking men to whip out their penises at inappropriate moments, and the men slavishly respond. "The Last Seduction" actually uses one such scene to resolve a critical moment. (p. E14)

He might very well add that if one instance resolves a crucial scene, the other actually sets the narrative in motion. Just like it is not particularly helpful to call the penis scene in *Nell* the "nuttiest" scene in the film, it is not helpful to call the penis scenes in *The Last Seduction* "juvenile." Such critical responses brush over an important cultural preoccupation that must be understood.

If *Reservoir Dogs, Unforgiven,* and *A Perfect World* all indicate that the answer to the question, "How many dicks is that?" in recent Hollywood films is "a lot," they also indicate that the answer to the related question we might pose, "What is the meaning of all these dicks?" may be varied and complicated. In most films, like *Mrs. Doubtfire,* the dick talk merely supplies fleeting and usually forgettable moments that equate masculinity with big penises and small penises with its pitiable and/or comic collapse. Something much more complex is happening in *Reservoir Dogs, The Last Seduction, Unforgiven,* and *A Perfect World.* All of these films explore and question the place of the penis in the formation of male subjectivity or within the construction of mythic, phallic masculinity.

The dangers associated with the large penis in *The Last Seduction* and *Unforgiven* may reveal a growing awareness among filmmakers that we have long confused the penis with the phallus in our culture. Both the sexually predatory young man in *The Last Seduction* and Two-Gun Corky in *Unforgiven* act on an arrogant assumption of, respectively, their sexual and physical prowess based on their large penises. The young man presumes he will be able to conquer the woman he desires, and Corky presumes that he will be able to kill all his opponents with one gun. Both men have confused their literal endowment with symbolic power, and both are sadly mistaken. Indeed, the manner in which Corky's gun backfires in his hand bears comparison with the car crash that kills the private "dick" in *The Last Seduction*. The woman driving the car is keenly aware of this male confusion when she seizes phallic power and crashes the car, forcibly ejecting the man at precisely the moment that he has unbuckled his seat belt to show her his presumably large penis. As this scene shows, even the large penis and the phallus are two separate things, and the woman with no penis can seize the phallus just as well as any man and perhaps better than a man who feels secure in his endowment. Near the end of *The Last Seduction*, we learn that the overly confident, well-hung young man had years earlier fallen in love with and married a woman who he did not know was actually a man—his endowment and his powers are clearly quite separate!

It is, of course, too soon to predict whether the very recent notion that big penises pose a deadly threat to their possessors will become a trend in Hollywood films. Both *Unforgiven* and *A Perfect World*, however, reveal a 1990s continuing preoccupation with the importance of penis size and the undesirability of small ones, as well as a new caution against the usual reification of the "big dick" as the desired alternative. On the contrary, these films seem to desire a concept of normality in which either extreme is dangerous. As such, their insistence on the importance of the "normal" penis is much like their insistence on "normal" forms of masculinity. Coming from Clint Eastwood, who somewhat gloriously personified powerful, phallic masculinity for a quarter century, this desire to abandon the excesses of such a form of masculinity has added significance. Dennis Bingham (1994) notes of stars like Eastwood and Schwarzenegger that "machismo cannot hold for long and eventually must call attention to its own considerable artifice" (p. 245). But Eastwood wants to do more than expose the artifice; he seems to have developed an almost nostalgic desire for a masculine norm that makes machismo appear grotesque. If only Haynes in *A Perfect World* had had a normal family life with a father, if only the little boy he kidnaps had such a normal life with such a father, if only Munny at the beginning of *Unforgiven* was normal and had not grown too soft, if only we lived in a perfect world where both literally and symbolically masculinity and male sexuality were all in the "normal" range, no one would be unforgiven.

References

Bingham, Dennis. 1994. *Acting male: Masculinities in the films of James Stewart, Jack Nicholson, and Clint Eastwood.* New Brunswick, NJ: Rutgers University Press.

Bobbitt cleared as temporarily insane in attack. 1994. *The Arizona Daily Star,* 22 January, 1A–5A.

Cauthorn, Robert. 1994. Review of *The Last Seduction. Arizona Daily Star,* 18 November, E14.

Cobb, Nathan. 1994. Urologist debunks myth surrounding the area below men's belts. *Arizona Daily Star,* 19 January, 6C.

Dyer, Richard. 1982. Don't look now: The male pin-up. *Screen* 23 (34): 61–73.

Foucault, Michel. 1980. *Herculine Barbin: Being the recently discovered memoirs of a nineteenth-century French hermaphrodite,* translated by Richard McDougall. New York: Pantheon.

Genevieve, Barbara de. 1991. Masculinity and its discontents. *Camerawork* 18 (3/4): 3–5.

Hilferty, Robert. 1992. Review of *Reservoir Dogs. Cineaste* 19 (4): 79–81.

Hosteteler, Darrin. 1994. A groin concern. *New Times,* 5–11 January, 5.

Kanigel, Rachele. 1995. Penile surgery risky process, study warns. *Oakland Tribune,* 26 April, A9–A10.

Lehman, Peter. 1990. Texas 1868/America 1956: The searchers. In *Close viewings: An anthology of new film criticism,* edited by Peter Lehman. Tallahassee: Florida State University Press.

———. 1993. *Running scared: Masculinity and the representation of the male body.* Philadelphia: Temple University Press.

Luhr, William, and Peter Lehman. 1977. *Authorship and narrative in the cinema: Issues in contemporary aesthetics and criticism.* New York: G. P. Putnam.

Rafferty, Terrence. 1994. Review of *Nell, The New Yorker,* 19 December, 108.

Renov, Michael. 1980. From identification of ideology: The male system of Hitchcock's *Notorious. Wide Angle* 4 (1): 30–37.

Ring out the old, gross out the new. 1994. *Newsweek,* 17 February, 33.

Schmidt, Becky Whitestone. 1995. Men unzipping wallets to change penis size. *Arizona Daily Star,* 15 May, B8. Originally published in *San Antonio Express-News.*

ARTICLE 48

Lance Strate

Beer Commercials:
A Manual on Masculinity

Jocks, rock stars, and pick-up artists; cowboys, construction workers, and comedians; these are some of the major "social types" found in contemporary American beer commercials. The characters may vary in occupation, race, and age, but they all exemplify traditional conceptions of the masculine role. Clearly, the beer industry relies on stereotypes of the man's man to appeal to a mainstream, predominantly male target audience. That is why alternate social types, such as sensitive men, gay men, and househusbands, scholars, poets, and political activists, are noticeably absent from beer advertising. The manifest function of beer advertising is to promote a particular brand, but collectively the commercials provide a clear and consistent image of the masculine role; in a sense, they constitute a guide for becoming a man, a rulebook for appropriate male behavior, in short, a manual on masculinity. Of course, they are not the only source of knowledge on this subject, but nowhere is so much information presented in so concentrated a form as in television's 30-second spots, and no other industry's commercials focus so exclusively and so exhaustively on images of the man's man. Most analyses of alcohol advertising acknowledge the use of masculine characters and themes, but only focus on their persuasive function (see, for example, Finn & Strickland 1982, 1983; Jacobson, Atkins, & Hacker 1983; Atkin 1987; Hacker, Collins, & Jacobson 1987). In my own research on beer commercials (Postman et al. 1987; Strate 1989, 1990), the ads are analyzed as a form of cultural communication and a carrier of social myths, in particular, the myth of masculinity. A similar approach is taken by Craig (1987) in his analysis of Super Bowl advertising, and by Wenner (1991) in his analysis of beer commercials and television sports. A major concern in my research has been the relationship between alcohol advertising and drinking and driving, a problem especially among young, unmarried men. Drawing on that research, I will discuss here the ways in which the myth of masculinity is expressed in beer commercials.

Myths, according to semioticians such as Roland Barthes (1972), are not falsehoods or fairy tales, but uncontested and generally unconscious assumptions that are so widely shared within a culture that they are considered natural, instead of recognized as products of unique historical circumstances. Biology determines whether we are male or female; culture determines what it *means* to be male or female, and what sorts of behaviors and personality attributes are appropriate for each gender role. In other words, masculinity is a social construction (Kimmel 1987a; Fejes 1989). The foundation may be biological, but the structure is manmade; it is also flexible, subject to change over time and differing significantly from culture to culture. Myth, as a form of cultural communication, is the material out of which such structures are built, and through myth, the role of human beings in inventing and reinventing masculinity is disguised and therefore naturalized (and "biologicized"). The myth of masculinity is manifested in myriad forms of mediated and nonmediated communication; beer commercials are only one such

In *Men, Masculinity, and the Media,* Steve Craig (ed.), pp. 78–92. Copyright © 1992 Sage Publications. Reprinted by permission of Sage Publications, Inc.

form, and to a large extent, the ads merely reflect preexisting cultural conceptions of the man's man. But in reflecting the myth, the commercials also reinforce it. Moreover, since each individual expression of a myth varies, beer ads also reshape the myth of masculinity, and in this sense, take part in its continuing construction.

Myths provide ready-made answers to universal human questions about ourselves, our relationships with others and with our environment. Thus, the myth of masculinity answers the question: What does it mean to be a man? This can be broken down into five separate questions: What kinds of things do men do? What kinds of settings do men prefer? How do boys become men? How do men relate to each other? How do men relate to women? Let us now consider the ways in which beer commercials answer these questions.

What kinds of things do men do? Although advertisers are prevented from actually showing an individual drinking beer in a television commercial, there is no question that drinking is presented as a central masculine activity, and beer as the beverage of choice. Drinking, however, is rarely presented as an isolated activity, but rather is associated with a variety of occupational and leisure pursuits, all of which, in one way or another, involve overcoming challenges. In the world of beer commercials, men work hard and they play hard.

Physical labor is often emphasized in these ads, both on and off the job. Busch beer features cowboys riding horses, driving cattle, and performing in rodeos. Budweiser presents a variety of blue-collar types, including construction workers, lumberjacks, and soldiers (as well as skilled laborers and a few white-collar workers). Miller Genuine Draft shows men working as farm hands and piano movers. But the key to work is the challenge it poses, whether to physical strength and endurance, to skill, patience, and craftsmanship, or to wit and competitive drive in the business world. The ads do associate hard work with the American dream of economic success (this theme is particularly strong in Budweiser's campaign), but it is also presented as its own end, reflecting the Puritan work ethic. Men do not labor primarily out of economic necessity nor for financial gain, but rather for the pride of accomplishment provided by a difficult job well done; for the respect and camaraderie of other men (few women are visible in the beer commercial workplace); for the benefit of family, community, and nation; and for the opportunity to demonstrate masculinity by triumphing over the challenges work provides. In short, work is an integral part of a man's identity.

Beer is integrated with the work world in three ways. *First,* it is represented in some commercials as the product of patient, skillful craftsmanship, thus partaking of the virtues associated with the labor that produced it; this is particularly apparent in the Miller beer commercials in which former football player Ed Marinaro takes us on a tour of the Miller brewery. In effect, an identity relationship between beer and labor is established, although this is overshadowed by the identification between beer and nature discussed below. *Second,* beer serves as a reward for a job well done, and receiving a beer from one's peers acts as a symbol of other men's respect for the worker's accomplishment—"For all you do, this Bud's for you." Beer is seen as an appropriate reward not just because drinking is pleasurable, but because it is identified with labor, and therefore can act as a substitute for labor. Thus, drinking beer at the end of the day is a symbolic reenactment of the successful completion of a day's work. And *third,* beer acts as a marker of the end of the work day, the signal of quitting time ("Miller time"), the means for making the transition from work to leisure ("If you've got the time, we've got the beer"). In the commercials, the celebration of work completed takes on a ritualistic quality, much like saying grace and breaking bread signal the beginning of meal time; opening the can represents the opening of leisure time.

The men of beer commercials fill their leisure time in two ways: in active pursuits usually conducted in outdoor settings (e.g., car and boat racing, fishing, camping, and sports; often symbolized by the presence of sports stars, especially in Miller Lite ads) and in "hanging out," usually in bars. As it is in work, the key to men's active play is the challenge it provides to physical and emotional strength, endurance, and daring. Some element of danger is usually present in the challenge, for danger magnifies the risks of failure and the significance of success. Movement and speed are often a part of the challenge, not only for the increased risk they pose, but also because they require immediate and decisive action and fine control over one's own responses. Thus, Budweiser spots feature automobile racing; Michelob's music video-like ads show cars moving in fast-motion and include lyrics like "I'm overheating, I'm ready to burn, got dirt on my wheels, they're ready to turn"; Old Milwaukee and Budweiser commercials include images of powerboat, sailboat, and canoe racing; Busch beer features cowboys on galloping horses; and Coors uses the slogan, "The Silver Bullet won't slow you down." Activities that include movement and speed, along with displays of coordination, are particularly troubling when associated with beer, in light of social problems such as drinking and driving. Moreover, beer commercials portray men as unmindful of risks, laughing off danger. For example, in two Miller Genuine Draft commercials, a group of young men are drinking and reminiscing; in one they recall the time when they worked as farm hands, loading bales of hay onto a truck, and the large stack fell over. In the other, the memory is of moving a piano, raising it up by rope on the outside of a building to get it into a third-story apartment; the rope breaks and the piano crashes to the ground. The falling bales and falling piano both appear dangerous, but in the ads the men merely joke about the incidents; this attitude is reinforced visually as, in both cases, there is a cut from the past scene to the present one just before the crash actually occurs.

When they are not engaged in physical activity, the men of beer commercials frequently seek out symbolic challenges and dangers by playing games such as poker and pool, and by watching professional sports. The games pose particular challenges to self-control, while spectator sports allow for vicarious participation in the drama of challenge, risk, and triumph. Even when they are merely hanging out together, men engage in verbal jousts that contain a strong element of challenge, either in the form of good-natured arguments (such as Miller Lite's ongoing "tastes great—less filling" conflict) or in ribbing one another, which tests self-control and the ability to "take it." A sense of proportion and humor is required to overcome such challenges, which is why jokers and comedians are a valued social type in the myth of masculinity. Women may also pose a challenge to the man's ability to attract the opposite sex and, more important, to his self-control.

The central theme of masculine leisure activity in beer commercials, then, is challenge, risk, and mastery—mastery over nature, over technology, over others in good-natured "combat," and over oneself. And beer is integrated into this theme in two ways: one obvious, the other far more subtle. At the overt level, beer functions in leisure activities as it does in work: as a reward for challenges successfully overcome (the race completed, the big fish landed, the ribbing returned). But it also serves another function, never explicitly alluded to in commercials. In several ways drinking, in itself, is a test of mastery. Because alcohol affects judgment and slows reaction time, it intensifies the risks inherent in movement and speed, and thereby increases the challenge they represent. And because it threatens self-control, drinking poses heightened opportunities for demonstrating self-mastery. Thus beer is not merely a reward for the successful meeting of a challenge in masculine work and leisure, but is itself an occasion for demonstrating mastery, and thus, masculinity. Beer is an appropriate award for overcoming challenge because it is a challenge itself, and thereby allows a man to symbolically reenact his feat. It would be all but suicidal for advertisers to present drinking as a challenge by which the masculine role can be acted out; instead, they associate beer with other forms of challenge related to the myth of masculinity.

What kinds of settings do men prefer? In beer commercials, the settings most closely associated with masculinity are the outdoors, generally the natural environment, and the self-contained world of the bar. The outdoors is featured prominently as both a workplace and a setting for leisure activity in ads for Busch beer, Old Milwaukee, Miller Genuine Draft, and Budweiser. As a workplace, the natural environment provides suitable challenge and danger for demonstrating masculinity, and the separation from civilization forces men to rely only on themselves. The height of masculinity can be attained when the natural environment and the work environment coincide, that is, when men have to overcome nature in order to survive. That is why the cowboy or frontiersman is the archetypical man's man in our culture. Other work environments, such as the farm, factory, and office, offer their own form of challenge, but physical danger is usually downplayed and the major risk is economic. Challenge and danger are also reduced, but still present, when nature is presented as a leisure environment; male bonding receives greater emphasis, and freedom from civilization becomes freedom for men to behave in a boyish manner.

In the ads, nature is closely associated with both masculinity and beer, as beer is presented as equivalent to nature. Often, beer is shown to be a product that is natural and pure, implying that its consumption is not harmful, and perhaps even healthy. Moreover, a number of beers, including Rolling Rock, Heineken's Old Style, and Molson's Golden, are identified with natural sources of water. This identification is taken even further in one Busch beer commercial: We see a cowboy on horseback, herding cattle across a river. A small calf is overcome by the current, but the cowboy is able to withstand the force of the river and come to the rescue. The voice-over says, "Sometimes a simple river crossing isn't so simple. And when you've got him back, it's your turn. Head for the beer brewed natural as a mountain stream." We then see a six-pack pulled out of clear running water, as if by magic. The raging water represents the power and danger of nature, while the mountain stream stands for nature's gentler aspect. Through the voice-over and the image of the hand pulling the six-pack from the water, beer is presented as identical with the stream, as bottled nature. Drinking beer, then, is a relatively safe way of facing the challenge of raging rivers, of symbolically reenacting the taming of the frontier.

Beer is identified with nature in a more general way in the ads for Old Milwaukee, which are usually set in wilderness environments that feature water, such as the Florida Everglades, and Snake River, Wyoming. In each ad, a group of men is engaged in recreational activities such as high-speed air-boating, flat-bottom boat racing, or fishing. Each commercial begins with a voice-over saying something like, "The Florida Everglades and Old Milwaukee both mean something great to these guys." Each ad includes a jingle, which says, "There's nothing like the flavor of a special place and Old Milwaukee beer." In other words, Old Milwaukee is equivalent to the special place. The place is special because it is untouched by civilization, allowing men to engage in forms of recreation not available elsewhere. It therefore must be fairly inaccessible, but since beer is presented as identical to the place, drinking may act as a substitute for actually going there.

Beer is also identified with nature through animals. For example, the symbol of Busch beer, found on its label and in its commercials, is a horse rearing on its hind legs, a phallic symbol that also evokes the idea of the untamed. And in another Busch ad, a young rodeo rider is quickly thrown from his mount; trying to cheer him up, an older cowboy hands him a beer and says, "Here. This one don't buck so hard." Thus, the identification of beer and nature is made via the horse. Drinking beer is like rodeo-riding, only less strenuous. It is a challenge that the rider can easily overcome, allowing him to save face and reaffirm masculinity. Budweiser beer also uses horses as a symbol: The Budweiser Clydesdales, a breed of "draft" horse. Whereas the Busch Stallion represents the frontier wilderness, the Clydesdales stand for the pastoral. Also, Colt 45 malt liquor, by its very name, invokes images of the Old West, horses, and of course guns, another phallic symbol. Another way in which beer is identified with nature and animals is through Budweiser's "Spuds McKenzie" and Stroh's "Alex," both dogs that behave like humans; both are in turn identified with masculinity as they are male characters, and canines are the animals most closely associated with masculinity.

As a setting for masculine activity, the bar runs a close second to nature, and many commercials seem to advertise bar patronage as much as they do a particular brand of beer. Of course, the drinking hall has a venerable history in Western culture as a center for male socializing and tests of skill, strength, and drinking ability. It is a setting featured prominently in the myths and legends of ancient Greece, and in Norse and Old English sagas. The pub is a popular setting in British literature, as is the saloon in the American Western genre. Like its predecessors, the bar of the beer commercial is presented as a male-dominated environment, although it sometimes serves as a setting for male-female interaction. And it is generally portrayed as a relaxed and comfortable context for male socializing, as well as a place where a man can find entertainment and excitement. The bars are immaculate and smokeless, and the waitresses and bartenders are always friendly; thus, along with nature, bars are the ideal male leisure environment. The only exception is the Bud Light bar, where men who are so uninformed as to ask for "a light" rather than a specific brand are subjected to pranks by the bartenders; still, even in this case the practical jokes are taken in stride, reaffirming the customer's masculinity.

It is worth noting that in the romanticized barroom of beer commercials, no one ever pays for his drinks, either literally or in terms of alcohol's effects. In other words, there are no consequences to the men's actions, which is consistent with the myth of masculinity's tendency to ignore or downplay risk and danger. The bar is shown as a self-contained environment, one that, like the outdoors, frees men from the constraints of civilization, allowing them to behave irresponsibly. Moreover, most settings featured as drinking-places in beer commercials are probably places that people would drive to—and drive home from. Because the action is confined to these settings, however, the question of how people arrived and how they will get home never comes up.

How do boys become men? In the world of beer commercials, boys become men by earning acceptance from those who are already full-fledged members of the community of men. Adult men are identified by their age, their size, their celebrity, and their positions of authority in the work world and/or status in a bar. To earn acceptance, the younger man must demonstrate that he can do the things that men do: take risks, meet challenges, face danger courageously, and dominate his environment. In the workplace, he demonstrates this by seizing opportunities to work, taking pride in his labor, proving his ability, persisting in the face of uncertainty, and learning to accept failure with equanimity. Having proven that he can act out the masculine role, the initiate is rewarded with beer. As a reward, beer symbolizes the overcoming of a challenge, the fulfilling of the requirements for group membership. The gift of beer also allows the adult male to show his acceptance of the initiate without becoming emotional. Beer then functions as a symbol of initiation and group membership.

For example, one of Budweiser's most frequently aired commercials during the 1980s features a young Polish immigrant and an older foreman and dispatcher. In the first scene, the dispatcher is reading names from a clipboard, giving workers their assignments. Arriving late, which earns him a look of displeasure from the foreman, the nervous young man takes a seat in the back. When he is finally called, the dispatcher stumbles over the immigrant's foreign name. The young man walks up to the front of the room, corrects the dispatcher's mispronunciation—a risky move, given his neophyte status, but one that demonstrates his pride and self-confidence. He receives his assignment, and the scene then shifts to a montage of the day's work. At the beginning, he drops a toolbox, spilling its contents, a mishap noted by the foreman; by the end of the day, however, he has demonstrated his ability and has earned the respect of his co-workers. The final scene is in a crowded tavern; the young man walks through the door, making his way to the bar, looking around nervously. He hears his name called, turns around, and the foreman, sitting at the bar, hands him a beer. In both the first and final scene, the immigrant begins at the back of the room, highlighting his outsider status, and moves to the front as he is given a chance to prove himself. The commercial's parallelism is not just an aesthetic device, but a mythic one as well. Having mastered the challenge of work, the neophyte receives the reward of a beer, which is both a symbol of that mastery and an invitation to symbolically reenact his feat. By working hard and well, he gains acceptance in the work world; by drinking the beer, he can also gain acceptance into the social world of the bar. The foreman, by virtue of his age, his position of authority, and his position sitting at the bar in the center of the tavern, holds the power of confirmation in both worlds.

The theme of initiation is also present in a subtle way in the Bud Light ads in which someone orders "a light," is given a substitute such as lamp or torch, and then corrects himself, asking for a "Bud Light." As one of the commercials revealed, the bartenders play these pranks because they are fed up with uninformed customers. The bizarre substitutions are a form of hazing, an initiation into proper barroom etiquette. The mature male is familiar with brands of beer, knows what he wants, and shows decisiveness in ordering it. Clearly, the individuals who ask for "a light" are inexperienced drinkers, and it is important to keep in mind that, to the barroom novice (and especially to the underage drinker), bars and bartenders can seem very threatening. While the substitute "lights" come as a surprise to the patrons, and thus threaten their composure, they are a relatively mild threat. The customers are able to overcome this challenge to their self-control, correct their order, and thereby gain entry into barroom society.

The biological transition from childhood to adulthood is a gradual one, but in traditional cultures, it is symbolized by formal rituals of initiation, rites of passage which mark the boundary between childhood and adulthood, clearly separating these two social positions. In our own culture, there are no initiation rites, and therefore the adolescent's social position is an ambiguous one. A number of events and activities do serve as symbols of adulthood, however. The commercials emphasize entry into the work world as one such step; financial independence brings the freedom of adulthood, while work is an integral part of the adult male's identity. As a symbol of initiation into the work world, beer also functions as a symbol of adulthood. And although this is never dealt with in the commercials, drinking in and of itself is a symbol of adulthood in our culture, as is driving, particularly in the eyes of underage males. Bars are seen as exclusively adult environments, and so acceptance in bars is a further sign of manhood. In the commercials, bars and workplaces complement each other as environments in which initiation into adulthood can be consummated.

How do men relate to each other? In beer commercials, men are rarely found in solitary pursuits (and never drink alone), and only occasionally in one-to-one relationships, usually involving father-son or mentor-protégé transactions. The dominant social context for male interaction is the group, and teamwork and group loyalty rank high in the list of masculine values. Individualism and competition, by contrast, are downplayed, and are acceptable only as long as they foster the cohesiveness of the group as a whole. Although differences in status may exist between members of the group and outsiders, within the group equality is the rule, and elitism and intellectualism are disdained. This reflects the American value of egalitarianism and solidifies the importance of the group over individual members. The concept of group loyalty is extended to community and to country, so that patriotism is also presented as an important value for men.

The emotional tenor of relationships among men in beer commercials is characterized by self-restraint. Generally, strong emotions are eschewed, especially overt displays of affection. In the workplace, mutual respect is exhibited, but respect must be earned through ability and attitude. In leisure situations, humor is a major element in male interactions. Conversations among men emphasize joking, bragging, storytelling, and good-natured insults. The insults are a form of symbolic challenge; taking a ribbing in good spirit is a demonstration of emotional strength and self-mastery. By providing a controlled social context for the exchange of challenges and demonstrations of ego strength and self-control, the group provides continuous reinforcement of the members' masculinity. Moreover, gathering in groups provides men with the freedom to act irresponsibly; that is, it allows men to act like boys. This is particularly the case in the Miller Lite ads that feature retired sports stars, comedians, and other celebrities.

In beer commercials, drinking serves several important functions in promoting group solidarity. Beer is frequently the shared activity that brings the group together, and in the ads for Miller Genuine Draft, sharing beer acts as a reminder of the group's identity and history. Thus, beer becomes a symbol of group membership. It also serves as a means for demonstrating the group's egalitarian values. When one man gives a beer to another, it is a sign of acceptance, friendship, or gratitude. In this role, beer is also a substitute for overt display of affection. Although the commercials never deal with why beer takes on this role, the answer lies in the effects of alcohol. Certainly, its function as mood enhancer can have a positive influence on group interaction. And, as previously discussed, alcohol itself constitutes a challenge, so that drinking allows each member of the group to publicly demonstrate his masculinity. Alcohol also lowers inhibitions, making it easier for men to show their affection for one another. The well-known saying that you cannot trust a man who does not drink reflects the popular conception that under the influence of alcohol, men become more open and honest. Moreover, the effects of drinking on physical coordination make a man less of an immediate threat. All these properties contribute to beer's role as a medium of male bonding and a facilitator of group solidarity.

In general, men are not portrayed as loners in beer commercials, and in this respect the ads differ markedly from other expressions of the myth of masculinity. There are no isolated Marlboro men in the Busch frontier, for example. When he saves the calf from being swept away by the river, the Busch cowboy appears to be on his own, but by the time he is ready for his reward, another cowboy has appeared out of nowhere to share his beer. In another Busch ad, a jingle with the following lyrics is heard: "There's no place on earth that I'd rather be, than out in the open where it's all plain to see, if it's going to get done it's up to you and me." In this way, the ideal of individual self-reliance that is so central to the American myth of the frontier is transformed into group self-reliance. In the world of beer commercials, demonstrating one's masculinity requires an audience to judge one's performance and confirm one's status. Moreover, the emphasis the ads place on beer drinking as a group activity undermines the idea that it is in any way problematic. One of the most widespread stereotypes of problem drinkers is that they are solitary and secretive loners. The emphasis on the group in beer commercials plays on the common misconception that drinking, when it is done socially and publicly, cannot be harmful.

How do men relate to women? Although the world of beer commercials is often monopolized by men, some of the ads do feature male-female interaction in the form of courtship, as well as in more established relationships. When courtship is the focus, the image of the man's man gives way to that of the ladies' man, for whom seduction is the highest form of challenge. And while the obvious risk in courtship is rejection by the opposite sex, the more significant danger in beer ads is loss of emotional self-control. The ladies' man must remain cool, confident, and detached when faced with the object of his desires. This social type is exemplified by Billy Dee Williams, who plays on his romantic image in Colt 45 commercials. Strangely enough, Spuds McKenzie, Budweiser's "party animal," also fits into this category, insofar as he, like Alex, is treated like a human being. In his ads, Spuds is surrounded by the Spudettes, three beautiful young women who dance with him, serve him, even bathe him. The women are attractive enough to make most males salivate like Pavlov's dogs, but Spuds receives their attentions with casual indifference (and never betrays the insecurities that haunt his cousin Snoopy when the *Peanuts* dog assumes his "Joe Cool" persona). While the commercials do not go so far as to suggest bestiality, there is no question that Spuds is a stud.

Emotional control is also demonstrated by the male's ability to divide his attention. For example, in one Michelob commercial, a young woman is shown leaning over a jukebox and selecting a song; her expression is one of pure pleasure, and she seems lost in thought. Other scenes, presumably her memories, show her dancing in the arms of a handsome young man. His arms are around her neck, and he is holding in one hand, behind her back, a bottle of beer. This image emphasizes the difference between the myths of masculinity and femininity; her attention is focused entirely on him, while his interests extend to the beer as well as the woman. According to the myth of masculinity, the man who loses control of his emotions in a relationship is a man who loses his independence, and ultimately, his masculinity; dividing attention is one way to demonstrate self-control. Michelob also presents images of ladies' men in the form of popular musicians, such as the rock group Genesis, rock star Eric Clapton, and popular vocalist Frank Sinatra. Many male pop stars have reputations as sexual athletes surrounded by groupies; in the ads, however, they function as modern troubadours, providing a romantic backdrop for lovers and facilitating social interaction. Acting, like Spuds McKenzie, as mascots for the beer companies, they imply that the beer they are identified with serves the same functions.

By far the most sexist of beer commercials, almost to the point of farce, are the Colt 45 ads featuring Billy Dee Williams. One of these, which is divided into three segments, begins with Williams saying: "There are two rules to remember if you want to have a good time: Rule number one, never run out of Colt 45. Rule number two, never forget rule number one." In the next segment, Williams continues: "You want to know why you should keep plenty of Colt 45 on hand? You never know when friends might show up." As he says this, he opens a can and a woman's hand reaches out and takes it. In the third segment, he concludes, "I don't claim you can have a better time with Colt 45 than without it, but why take chances?" As he says this, the camera pulls back to reveal Williams standing, and an attractive woman sitting next to him. The ad ends with a picture of a Colt 45 can and the slogan, "The power of Colt 45: It works every time." There are a number of ways to interpret this pitch. First, malt liquor has a higher alcohol content than beer or ale, and therefore is a more *powerful* beverage. Second, the ad alludes to alcohol's image as an aphrodisiac, despite the fact that it actually reduces male potency. As noted, the Colt 45 pistol is a phallic symbol, while the slogan can be read as a guarantee against impotency—"it works every time." Third, it can be seen as referring to alcohol's ability to make men feel more confident about themselves and more interested in the opposite sex. And fourth, it plays on the popular notion that getting a woman drunk increases her desire for and willingness to engage in sex. Williams keeps Colt 45 on hand not just for himself, but for "friends," meaning "women." His secret of seduction is getting women to drink. In the ad, the woman is eager to drink Colt 45, implying that she will be just as eager to make love. The idea that a woman who drinks is "looking for it" is even clearer in a second ad.

This commercial begins with the title "Billy Dee Williams on Body Language." Moving through an outdoor party, Williams says, "You know, body language tells you a lot about what a person is thinking. For instance, that means she has an interest in the finer things in life." As he says this, the camera pans to show an attractive woman sitting at a bar alone, holding her necklace. She shifts her position and strokes her hair, and Williams says, "That means she also wants a little fun in her life, but only with the right man." At this point, the woman fills her glass with Colt 45, as Williams says, "And now she's pouring Colt 45 and we all know what that means." He then goes over to her and asks if she would mind if he joined her, and she replies, "You must have read my mind." Williams responds, "Something like that," and the ad ends with the same slogan as the first. What is implied in this commercial is that any woman who would sit by herself and drink must be looking to get picked up; she is sending out signals and preparing herself to be seduced. And although she is making herself approachable, she must wait for Williams to make the first move. At the same time, the woman appears to be vain, fondling her jewelry and hair. And in both ads, the women are seated while Williams stands. This portrayal of the woman's woman, based on the myth of femininity, is the perfect counterpart to Williams' image as a ladies' man.

When the commercials depict more established relationships, the emphasis shifts from romance and seduction to male activities in which women are reduced largely to the role of admiring onlookers. Men appear to value their group of friends over their female partners, and the women accept this. Women tend to be passive, not participating but merely watching as men perform physical tasks. In other words, they become the audience for whom men perform. For the most part, women know their place and do not interfere with male bonding. They may, however, act as emotional catalysts for male interaction, bringing men together. Occasionally, a woman may be found together with a group of men, presumably as the girlfriend or wife of one of the group members. Here, the presence of women, and their noninterference, indicates their approval of masculine activity and male bonding, and their approval of the role of beer in these situations. Even when a group of men acts irresponsibly and/or boyishly, the presence of a woman shows that this behavior is socially sanctioned.

Alternate images of femininity can be found in beer commercials, but they are generally relegated to the background; for the most part, the traditional roles of masculinity and femininity are upheld. One exception is a Michelob Light ad that features Madeline Kahn. Introduced by a male voice-over, "Madeline Kahn on having it all," she is lying on her side on a couch, wearing an expensive-looking gown and necklace, and holding a bottle of beer. Kahn does a short humorous monologue in which she acknowledges her wealth and glamour, and the scene shifts to a shot of the beer, as the male voice-over says, "Michelob Light. You *can* have it all." While this represents something of a concession to changing conceptions of femininity, the advertisers hedge their bets. The male voice-over frames, and in a sense controls, Kahn's monologue, while Kahn's position, lying on her side, is a passive and seductive one. To male viewers, the commercial can easily imply that "having it all" includes having a woman like her.

Conclusion

In the world of beer commercials, masculinity revolves around the theme of challenge, an association that is particularly alarming, given the social problems stemming from alcohol abuse. For the most part beer commercials present traditional, stereotypical images of men, and uphold the myths of masculinity and femininity. Thus, in promoting beer, advertisers also promote and perpetuate these images and myths. Although targeted at an adult audience, beer commercials are highly accessible to children; between the ages of 2 and 18, American children may see as many as 100,000 of these ads. They are also extremely attractive to children: humorous, exciting, and offering answers to questions about gender and adulthood. And they do have an impact, playing a role in social learning and attitude formation (Wallack, Cassady, & Grube 1990). As Postman

(1979) argues, television constitutes a curriculum, one that children spend more time with than in schoolrooms. Beer commercials are a prominent subject in television's curriculum, a subject that is ultimately hazardous to the intellectual as well as the physical health of the young. The myth of masculinity *does* have a number of redeeming features (facing challenges and taking risks are valuable activities in many contexts), but the unrelenting one-dimensionality of masculinity as presented by beer commercials is clearly anachronistic, possibly laughable, but without a doubt sobering.

References

Atkin, C. K. (1987). Alcoholic-beverage advertising: Its content and impact. *Advances in Substances Abuse (Suppl.) 1*, 267–287.

Barthes, R. (1972). *Mythologies* (A. Lavers, Ed. and Trans.). New York: Hill & Wang. (Original work published 1957).

Craig, S. (1987, March). Marketing American masculinity: Mythology and flow in the Super Bowl telecasts. Paper presented at the annual meeting of the Popular Culture Association, Montreal.

Fejes, F. (1989). Images of men in media research. *Critical Studies in Mass Communication, 6*(2), 215–221.

Finn, T. A., & Strickland, D. (1983). The advertising and alcohol abuse issue: A cross media comparison of alcohol beverage advertising content. In M. Burgeon (Ed.), *Communication yearbook* (pp. 850–872). Beverly Hills, CA: Sage.

Hacker, G. A., Collins R., & Jacobson, M. (1987). *Marketing booze to blacks.* Washington, DC: Center for Science in the Public Interest.

Jacobson, M., Atkins, R., & Hacker, G. (1983). *The booze merchants: The inebriating of America.* Washington, DC: Center for Science in the Public Interest.

Kimmel, M. (Ed.). (1987). *Changing men: New directions in research on men and masculinity.* Newbury Park, CA: Sage.

Strate, L. (1989). The mediation of nature and culture in beer commercials. *New Dimensions In Communications, Proceedings of the 47th Annual New York State Speech Communication Association Conference 3*, 92–95.

Strate, L. (1990, October). The cultural meaning of beer commercials. Paper presented at the Advances in Consumer Research Conference, New York.

Wenner, L. (1991). One part alcohol, one part sport, one part dirt, stir gently: Beer commercials and television sports. In L. R. Vande Berg & L. A. Wenner (Eds.), *Television criticism: Approaches and applications.* New York: Longman.

ARTICLE 49

Richard Fung

Looking for My Penis: The Eroticized Asian in Gay Video Porn

Several scientists have begun to examine the relation between personality and human reproductive behavior from a gene-based evolutionary perspective. . . . In this vein we reported a study of racial difference in sexual restraint such that Orientals > whites > blacks. Restraint was indexed in numerous ways, having in common a lowered allocation of bodily energy to sexual functioning. We found the same racial pattern occurred on gamete production (dizygotic birthing frequency per 100: Mongoloids, 4; Caucasoids, 8; Negroids, 16), intercourse frequencies (premarital, marital, extramarital), developmental precocity (age at first intercourse, age at first pregnancy, number of pregnancies), primary sexual characteristics (size of penis, vagina, testis, ovaries), secondary sexual characteristics (salient voice, muscularity, buttocks, breasts), and biologic control of behavior (periodicity of sexual response predictability of life history from onset of puberty), as well as in androgen levels and sexual attitudes.[1]

This passage from the *Journal of Research in Personality* was written by University of Western Ontario psychologist Philippe Rushton, who enjoys considerable controversy in Canadian academic circles and in the popular media. His thesis, articulated throughout his work, appropriates biological studies of the continuum of reproductive strategies of oysters through chimpanzees and posits that degree of "sexuality"—interpreted as penis and vagina size, frequency of intercourse, buttock and lip size—correlates positively with criminality and sociopathic behavior and inversely with intelligence, health, and longevity. Rushton sees race as the determining factor and places East Asians (Rushton uses the word *Orientals*) on one end of the spectrum and blacks on the other. Since whites fall squarely in the middle, the position of perfect balance, there is no need for analysis, and they remain free of scrutiny.

Notwithstanding its profound scientific shortcomings, Rushton's work serves as an excellent articulation of a dominant discourse on race and sexuality in Western society—a system of ideas and reciprocal practices that originated in Europe simultaneously with (some argue as a conscious justification for[2]) colonial expansion and slavery. In the nineteenth century these ideas took on a scientific gloss with social Darwinism and eugenics. Now they reappear, somewhat altered, in psychology journals from the likes of Rushton. It is important to add that these ideas have also permeated the global popular consciousness. Anyone who has been exposed to Western television or advertising images, which is much of the world, will have absorbed this particular constellation of stereotyping and racial hierarchy. In Trinidad in the 1960s, on the outer reaches of the empire, everyone in my schoolyard was thoroughly versed in these "truths" about the races.

From *Asian American Sexualities: Dimensions of the Gay and Lesbian Experience*, Russell Leong (ed.). Copyright © 1995. Reproduced by permission of Taylor & Francis-Routledge, Inc.

Historically, most organizing against racism has concentrated on fighting discrimination that stems from the intelligence–social behavior variable assumed by Rushton's scale. Discrimination based on perceived intellectual ability does, after all, have direct ramifications in terms of education and employment, and therefore for survival. Until recently, issues of gender and sexuality remained a low priority for those who claimed to speak for the communities.[3] But antiracist strategies that fail to subvert the race–gender status quo are of seriously limited value. Racism cannot be narrowly defined in terms of race hatred. Race is a factor in even our most intimate relationships.

The contemporary construction of race and sex as exemplified by Rushton has endowed black people, both men and women, with a threatening hypersexuality. Asians, on the other hand, are collectively seen as undersexed.[4] But here I want to make some crucial distinctions. First, in North America, stereotyping has focused almost exclusively on what recent colonial language designates as "Orientals"—that is East and southeast Asian peoples—as opposed to the "Orientalism" discussed by Edward Said, which concerns the Middle East. This current, popular usage is based more on a perception of similar physical features—black hair, "slanted" eyes, high cheek bones, and so on—than through a reference to common cultural traits. South Asians, people whose backgrounds are in the Indian subcontinent and Sri Lanka, hardly figure at all in North American popular representations, and those few images are ostensibly devoid of sexual connotation.[5]

Second, within the totalizing stereotype of the "Oriental," there are competing and sometimes contradictory sexual associations based on nationality. So, for example, a person could be seen as Japanese and somewhat kinky, or Filipino and "available." The very same person could also be seen as "Oriental" and therefore sexless. In addition, the racial hierarchy revamped by Rushton is itself in tension with an earlier and only partially eclipsed depiction of *all* Asians as having an undisciplined and dangerous libido. I am referring to the writings of the early European explorers and missionaries, but also to antimiscegenation laws and such specific legislation as the 1912 Saskatchewan law that barred white women from employment in Chinese-owned business.

Finally, East Asian women figure differently from men both in reality and in representation. In "Lotus Blossoms Don't Bleed," Renee Tajima points out that in Hollywood films:

> There are two basic types: the Lotus Blossom Baby (a.k.a. China Doll, Geisha Girl, shy Polynesian beauty, et al.) and the Dragon Lady (Fu Manchu's various female relations, prostitutes, devious madames).... Asian women in film are, for the most part, passive figures who exist to serve men—as love interests for white men (re: Lotus Blossoms) or as partners in crime for men of their own kind (re: Dragon Ladies).[6]

Further:

> Dutiful creatures that they are, Asian women are often assigned the task of expendability in a situation of illicit love.... Noticeably lacking is the portrayal of love relationships between Asian women and Asian men, particularly as lead characters.[7]

Because of their supposed passivity and sexual compliance, Asian women have been fetishized in dominant representation, and there is a large and growing body of literature by Asian women in the oppressiveness of these images. Asian men, however—at least since Sessue Hayakawa, who made a Hollywood career in the 1920s of representing the Asian man as sexual threat[8]—have been consigned to one of two categories: the egghead/wimp, or—in what may be analogous to the lotus blossom-dragon lady dichotomy—the kung fu master/ninja/samurai. He is sometimes dangerous, sometimes friendly, but almost always characterized by a desexualized Zen asceticism. So whereas, as Fanon tells us, "the Negro is eclipsed. He is turned into a penis. He *is* a penis,"[9] the Asian man is defined by a striking absence down there. And if Asian men have no sexuality, how can we have homosexuality?

Even as recently as the early 1980s, I remember having to prove my queer credentials before being admitted with other Asian men into a Toronto gay club. I do not believe it was a question of a color barrier. Rather, my friends and I felt that the doorman was genuinely unsure about our sexual orientation. We also felt that had we been white and dressed similarly, our entrance would have been automatic.[10]

Although a motto for the lesbian and gay movements has been "we are everywhere," Asians are largely absent from the images produced by both the political and the commercial sectors of the mainstream gay and lesbian communities. From the earliest articulation of the Asian gay and lesbian movements, a principal concern has therefore been visibility. In political organizing, the demand for a voice, or rather the demand to be heard, has largely been responded to by the problematic practice of "minority" representation on panels and boards.[11] But since racism is a question of power and not of numbers, this strategy has often led to a dead-end tokenistic integration, failing to address the real imbalances.

Creating a space for Asian gay and lesbian representation has meant, among other things, deepening an understanding of what is at stake for Asians in coming out publicly.[12] As is the case for many other people of color and especially immigrants, our families and our ethnic communities are a rare source of affirmation in a racist society. In coming out, we risk (or feel that we risk) losing this support, though the ever-growing organizations of lesbian and gay Asians have worked against this process of cultural exile. In my own experience, the existence of a gay Asian community broke down the cultural schizophrenia in which I related on the one hand to a heterosexual family that affirmed my ethnic culture and, on the other, to a gay community that was predominantly white. Knowing that there was support also helped me come out to my family and further bridge the gap.

If we look at commercial gay sexual representation, it appears that the antiracist movements have had little impact: the images of men and male beauty are still of *white* men and *white* male beauty. These are the standards against which we compare both ourselves and often our brothers—Asian, black, native, and Latino.[13] Although other people's rejection (or fetishization) of us according to the established racial hierarchies may be experienced as oppressive, we are not necessarily moved to scrutinize our own desire and its relationship to the hegemonic image of the white man.[14]

In my lifelong vocation of looking for my penis, trying to fill in the visual void, I have come across only a handful of primary and secondary references to Asian male sexuality in North American representation. Even in my own video work, the stress has been on deconstructing sexual representation and only marginally on creating erotica. So I was very excited at the discovery of a Vietnamese American working in gay porn.

Having acted in six videotapes, Sum Yung Mahn is perhaps the only Asian to qualify as a gay porn "star." Variously known as Brad Troung or Sam or Sum Yung Mahn, he has worked for a number of different production studios. All of the tapes in which he appears are distributed through International Wavelength, a San Francisco–based mail order company whose catalog entries feature Asians in American, Thai, and Japanese productions. According to the owner of International Wavelength, about 90 percent of the Asian tapes are bought by white men, and the remaining 10 percent are purchased by Asians. But the number of Asian buyers is growing.

In examining Sum Yung Mahn's work, it is important to recognize the different strategies used for fitting an Asian actor into the traditionally white world of gay porn and how the terms of entry are determined by the perceived demands of an intended audience. Three tapes, each geared toward a specific erotic interest, illustrate these strategies.

Below the Belt (1985, directed by Philip St. John, California Dream Machine Productions), like most porn tapes, has an episodic structure. All the sequences involve the students and *sense* of an all-male karate *dojo*. The authenticity of the setting is proclaimed with the opening shots of a gym full of *gi*-clad, serious-faced young men going through their weapons exercises. Each of the main actors is introduced in turn; with the exception of the teacher, who has dark hair, all fit into the current porn conventions of Aryan, blond, shaved, good looks.[15] Moreover, since Sum Yung Mahn is not even listed in the opening credits, we can surmise that this tape is not targeted to an audience with any particular erotic interest in Asian men. Most gay video porn exclusively uses white actors; those tapes having the least bit of racial integration are pitched to the specialty market throughout outlets such as International Wavelength.[16] This visual apartheid stems, I assume, from an erroneous perception that the sexual appetites of gay men are exclusive and unchangeable.

A Karate dojo offers a rich opportunity to introduce Asian actors. One might imagine it as the gay Orientalist's dream project. But given the intended audience for this video, the erotic appeal of the dojo, except for the costumes and a few misplaced props (Taiwanese and Korean flags for a Japanese art form?) are completely appropriated into a white world.

The tape's action occurs in a gym, in the students' apartments, and in a garden. The one scene with Sum Yung Mahn is a dream sequence. Two students, Robbie and Stevie, are sitting in a locker room. Robbie confesses that he has been having strange dreams about Greg, their teacher. Cut to the dream sequence, which is coded by clouds of green smoke. Robbie is wearing a red headband with black markings suggesting script (if indeed they belong to an Asian language, they are not the Japanese or Chinese characters that one would expect). He is trapped in an elaborate snare. Enter a character in a black *ninja* mask, wielding a *nanchaku*. Robbie narrates: "I knew this evil samurai would kill me." The masked figure is menacingly running the nanchaku chain under Robbie's genitals when Greg, the teacher, appears and disposes of him. Robbie explains to Stevie in the locker room: "I knew that I owed him my life, and I knew I had to please him [long pause] in any way that he wanted." During that pause we cut back to the dream. Amid more puffs of smoke, Greg, carrying a man in his arms, approaches a low platform. Although Greg's back is toward the camera, we can see that the man is wearing the red headband that identifies him as Robbie. As Greg lays him down, we see that Robbie has "turned Japanese"! It's Sum Yung Mahn.

Greg fucks Sum Yung Mahn, who is always face down. The scene constructs anal intercourse for the Asian Robbie as an act of submission, not of pleasure: unlike other scenes of anal intercourse in the tape, for example, there is no dubbed dialogue on the order of "Oh yeah... fuck me harder!" but merely ambiguous groans. Without coming, Greg leaves. A group of (white) men wearing Japanese outfits encircle the platform, and Asian Robbie, or "the Oriental boy," as he is listed in the final credits, turns to lie on his back. He sucks a cock, licks someone's balls. The other men come all over his body; he comes. The final shot of the sequence zooms in to a close-up of Sum Yung Mahn's headband, which dissolves to a similar close-up of Robbie wearing the same headband, emphasizing that the two actors represent one character.

We now cut back to the locker room. Robbie's story has made Stevie horny. He reaches into Robbie's pants, pulls out his penis, and sex follows. In his Asian manifestation, Robbie is fucked and sucks others off (Greek passive/French active/bottom). His passivity is pronounced, and he is never shown other than prone. As a white man, his role is completely reversed: he is at first sucked off by Stevie, and then he fucks him (Greek active/French passive/top). Neither of Robbie's manifestations veers from his prescribed role.

To a greater extent than most other gay porn tapes, *Below the Belt* is directly about power. The hierarchical dojo setting is mild for its evocation of dominance and submission. With the exception of one very romantic sequence midway through the tape, most of the actors stick to their defined roles of top or bottom. Sex, especially anal sex, as punishment is a recurrent image. In this genre of gay pornography, the role-playing in the dream sequence is perfectly apt. What is significant, however, is how race figures into the equation. In a tape that appropriates emblems of Asian power (karate), the only place for a real Asian actor is as a caricature of passivity. Sum Yung Mahn does not portray an Asian, but rather the liberalization of a metaphor, so that by being passive, Robbie actually becomes "Oriental." At a more practical level, the device of the dream also allows the producers to introduce an element of the mysterious, the exotic, without disrupting the racial status quo of the rest of the tape. Even in the dream sequence, Sum Yung Mahn is at the center of the frame as spectacle, having minimal physical involvement with the men around him. Although the sequence ends with his climax, he exists for the pleasure of others.

Richard Dyer, writing about gay porn, states that:

> although the pleasure of anal sex (that is, of being anally fucked) is represented, the narrative is never organized around the desire to be fucked, but around the desire to ejaculate (whether or not following from anal intercourse). Thus, although a level of public representation of gay men may be thought of as deviant and disruptive of masculine norms because we assert the pleasure of being fucked and the eroticism of the anus, in our pornography this takes a back seat.[17]

Although Tom Waugh's amendment to this argument—that anal pleasure is represented in individual sequences[18]—also holds true for *Below the Belt*, as a whole the power of the penis and the pleasure of ejaculation are clearly the narrative's organizing principles. As with the vast majority of North American tapes featuring Asians, the problem is not the representation of anal pleasure per se, but rather that the narratives privilege the penis while always assigning the Asian the role of bottom; Asian and anus are conflated. In the case of Sum Yung Mahn, being fucked may well be his personal sexual preference. But the fact remains that there are very few occasions in North American video porn in which an Asian fucks a white man, so few, in fact, that International Wavelength promotes the tape *Studio X* (1986) with the blurb "Sum Yung Mahn makes history as the first Asian who fucks a non-Asian."[19]

Although I agree with Waugh that in gay as opposed to straight porn "the spectator's positions in relation to the representations are open and in flux,"[20] this observation applies only when all the participants are white. Race introduces another dimension that may serve to close down some of this mobility. This is not to suggest that the experience of gay men of color with this kind of sexual representation is the same as that of heterosexual women with regard to the gendered gaze of straight porn. For one thing, Asian gay men are men. We can therefore physically experience the pleasures depicted on the screen, since we too have erections and ejaculations and can experience anal penetration. A shifting identification may occur despite the racially defined roles, and most gay Asian men in North America are used to obtaining pleasure from all-white pornography. This, of course, goes hand in hand with many problems of self-image and sexual identity. Still, I have been struck by the unanimity with which gay Asian men I have met, from all over this continent as well as from Asia, immediately identify and resist these representations. Whenever I mention the topic of Asian actors in American porn, the first question I am asked is whether the Asian is simply shown getting fucked.

Asian Knights (1985, directed by Ed Sung, William Richhe Productions), the second tape I want to consider, has an Asian producer–director and a predominantly Asian cast. In its first scenario, two Asian men, Brad and Rick, are seeing a white psychiatrist because they are unable to have sex with each other:

Rick: We never have sex with other Asians. We usually have sex with Caucasian guys.

Counselor: Have you had the opportunity to have sex together?

Rick: Yes, a coupla times, but we never get going.

Homophobia, like other forms of oppression, is seldom dealt with in gay video porn. With the exception of safe sex tapes that attempt a rare blend of the pedagogical with the pornographic, social or political issues are not generally associated with the erotic. It is therefore unusual to see one of the favored discussion topics for gay Asian consciousness-raising groups employed as a sex fantasy in *Asian Knights*. The desexualized image of Asian men that I have described has seriously affected our relationships with one another, and often gay Asian men find it difficult to see each other beyond the terms of platonic friendship or competition, to consider other Asian men as lovers.

True to the conventions of porn, minimal counseling from the psychiatrist convinces Rick and Brad to shed their clothes. Immediately sprouting erections, they proceed to have sex. But what appears to be an assertion of gay Asian desire is quickly derailed. As Brad and Rick make love on the couch, the camera cross-cuts to the psychiatrist looking on from an armchair. The rhetoric of the editing suggests that we are observing the two Asian men from his point of view. Soon the white man takes off his clothes and joins in. He immediately takes up a position at the center of the action—and at the center of the frame. What appeared to be a "conversion fantasy" for gay Asian desire was merely a ruse. Brad and Rick's temporary mutual absorption really occurs to establish the superior sexual draw of the white psychiatrist, a stand-in for the white male viewer, who is the real sexual subject of the tape. And the question of Asian–Asian desire, though presented as the main narrative force of the sequence, is deflected, or rather reframed from a white perspective. Sex between the two Asian men in this sequence can be related somewhat to heterosexual sex in some gay porn films, such as those produced by the Gage brothers. In *Heatstroke* (1982), for example, sex with a woman is used to establish the authenticity of the straight man who is about to be seduced into gay sex. It dramatizes the significance of the conversion from the sanctioned object of desire, underscoring the power of the gay man to incite desire in his socially defined superior. It is also tied up with the fantasies of (female) virginity and conquest in Judeo–Christian and other patriarchal societies. The therapy session sequence of *Asian Knights* also suggests parallels to representations of lesbians in straight porn, representations that are not meant to eroticize women loving women, but rather to titillate and empower the sexual ego of the heterosexual male viewer.

Asian Knights is organized to sell representations of Asians to white men. Unlike Sum Yung Mahn in *Below the Belt*, the actors are therefore more expressive and sexually assertive, as often the seducers as the seduced. But though the roles shift during the predominantly oral sex, the Asians remain passive in anal intercourse, except that they are now shown to want it! How much this assertion of agency represents a step forward remains a question.

Even in the one sequence of *Asian Knights* in which the Asian actor fucks the white man, the scenario privileges the pleasure of the white man over that of the Asian. The sequence begins with the Asian reading a magazine. When the white man (played by porn star Eric Stryker) returns home from a hard day at the office, the waiting Asian asks how his day went, undresses him (even taking off his socks), and proceeds to massage his back.[21] The Asian man acts the role of the mythologized geisha of "the good wife" as fantasized in the mail-order bride business. And, in fact, the "house boy" is one of the most persistent white fantasies about Asian men. The fantasy is also a reality in many Asian countries where economic imperialism gives foreigners, whatever their race, the pick of handsome men in financial need. The accompanying cultural imperialism grants status to those Asians with white lovers. White men who for various reasons, especially age, are deemed unattractive in their own countries, suddenly find themselves elevated and desired.

From the opening shot of painted lotus blossoms on a screen to the shot of a Japanese garden that separates the episodes, from the Chinese pop music to the chinoiserie in the apartment, there is a conscious attempt in *Asian Knights* to evoke a particular atmosphere.[22] Self-conscious "Oriental" signifiers are part and parcel of a colonial fantasy—and reality—that empowers one kind of gay man over another. Though I have known Asian men in dependent relations with older, wealthier white men, as an erotic fantasy the house boy scenario tends to work one way. I know of no scenarios of Asian men and white house boys. It is not the representation of the fantasy that offends, or even the fantasy itself, rather the uniformity with which these narratives reappear and the uncomfortable relationship they have to real social conditions.

International Skin (1985, directed by William Richhe, N'wayvo Richhe Productions), as its name suggests, features a Latino, a black man, Sum Yung Mahn, and a number of white actors. Unlike the other tapes I have discussed, there are no "Oriental" devices. And although Sum Yung Mahn and all the men of color are inevitably fucked (without reciprocating), there is mutual sexual engagement between the white and nonwhite characters.

In this tape Sum Yung Mahn is Brad, a film student making a movie for his class. Brad is the narrator, and the film begins with a self-reflexive "head and shoulders" shot of Sum Yung Mahn explaining the scenario. The film we are watching supposedly represents Brad's point of view. But here again the tape is not targeted to black, Asian, or Latino men; though Brad introduces all of these men as his friends, no two men of color ever meet on screen. Men of color are not invited to participate in the internationalism that is being sold, except through identification with white characters. This tape illustrates how an agenda of integration becomes problematic if it frames the issue solely in terms of black–white, Asian–white mixing; it perpetuates a system of white-centeredness.

The gay Asian viewer is not constructed as a sexual subject in any of this work—not on the screen, not as a viewer. I may find Sum Yung Mahn attractive, I may desire his body, but I am always aware that he is not meant for me. I may lust after Eric Stryker and imagine myself as the Asian who is having sex with him, but the role the Asian plays in the scene with him is demeaning. It is not that there is anything wrong with the image of servitude per se, but rather that it is one of the few fantasy scenarios in which we figure, and we are always in the role of servant.

Are there then no pleasures for an Asian viewer? The answer to this question is extremely complex. There is first of all no essential Asian viewer. The race of the person viewing says nothing about how race figures in his or her own desires. Uniracial white representations in porn may not in themselves present a problem in addressing many gay Asian men's desires. But the issue is not simply that porn may deny pleasures to some gay Asian men. We also need to examine what role the pleasure of porn plays in securing a consensus about race and desirability that ultimately works to our disadvantage.

Though the sequences I have focused on in the preceding examples are those in which the discourses about Asian sexuality are most clearly articulated, they do not define the totality of depiction in these tapes. Much of the time the actors merely reproduce or attempt to reproduce the conventions of pornography. The fact that, with the exception of Sum Yung Mahn, they rarely succeed—because of their body type, because Midwestern-cowboy-porn dialect with Vietnamese intonation is just a bit incongruous, because they groan or gyrate just a bit too much—more than anything brings home the relative rigidity of the genre's codes. There is little seamlessness here. There are times, however, when the actors appear neither as simulated whites nor as symbolic others. There are several moments in *International Skin*, for example, in which the focus shifts from the genitals to hands caressing a body; these moments feel to me more "genuine." I do not mean this in the sense of an essential Asian sexuality, but rather a moment is captured in which the actor stops pretending. He does not stop acting, but he stops pretending to be a white porn star. I find myself focusing on moments like these, in which the racist ideology of the text seems to be temporarily suspended or rather eclipsed by the erotic power of the moment.

In "Pornography and the Doubleness of Sex for Women," Joanna Russ writes:

> Sex is ecstatic, autonomous and lovely for women. Sex is violent, dangerous and unpleasant for women. I don't mean a dichotomy (i.e., two kinds of women or even two kinds of sex) but rather a continuum in which no one's experience is wholly positive or negative.[35]

Gay Asian men are men and therefore not normally victims of the rape, incest, or other sexual harassment to which Russ is referring. However, there is a kind of doubleness, of ambivalence, in the way that Asian men experience contemporary North American gay communities. The "ghetto," the mainstream gay movement, can be a place of freedom and sexual identity. But it is also a site of racial, cultural, *and* sexual alienation sometimes more pronounced than that in straight society. For me sex is a source of pleasure, but also a site of humiliation and pain. Released from the social constraints against expressing overt racism in public, the intimacy of sex can provide my (non-Asian) partner an opening for letting me know my place—sometimes literally, as when after we come, he turns over and asks where I come from.[24] Most gay Asian men I know have similar experiences.

This is just one reality that differentiates the experiences and therefore the political priorities of gay Asians and, I think, other gay men of color from those of white men. For one thing we cannot afford to take a libertarian approach. Porn can be an active agent in representing *and* reproducing a sex–race status quo. We cannot attain a healthy alliance without coming to terms with these differences.

The barriers that impede pornography from providing representations of Asian men that are erotic and politically palatable (as opposed to correct) are similar to those that inhibit the Asian documentary, the Asian feature, the Asian experimental film and videotape. We are seen as too peripheral, not commercially visible—not the general audience. *Looking for Langston* (1988),[25] which is the first film I have seen that affirms rather than appropriates the sexuality of black gay men, was produced under exceptional economic circumstances that freed it from the constraints of the marketplace.[26] Should we call for an independent gay Asian pornography? Perhaps I do, in a utopian sort of way, though I feel that the problems in North America's porn conventions are manifold and go beyond the question of race. There is such a limited vision of what constitutes the erotic.

One major debate about race and representation has shifted from an emphasis on the image to a discussion of appropriation and control of production and distribution—who gets to produce the work. But as we have seen in the case of *Asian Knights*, the race of the producer is no automatic guarantee of "consciousness" about these issues or of a different product. Much depends on who is constructed as the audience for the work. In any case, it is not surprising that under capitalism, finding my penis may ultimately be a matter of dollars and cents.

Notes

I would like to thank Tim McCaskell and Helen Lee for their ongoing criticism and comments, as well as Jeff Nunokawa and Douglas Crimp for their invaluable suggestions in converting the original spoken presentation into a written text. Finally, I would like to extend my gratitude to Bad Object-Choices for inviting me to participate in "How Do I Look?"

1. Phillipe Rushton and Anthony F. Bogaert, University of Western Ontario, "Race versus Social Class Difference in Sexual Behavior: A Follow-up Test of the r/K Dimension," *Journal of Research in Personality* 22 (1988): 259.

2. Feminists of color have long pointed out that racism is phrased differently for men and women. Nevertheless, since it is usually heterosexual (and often middle-class) males whose voices are validated by the power structure, it is their interests that are taken up as "representing" the communities. See Barbara Smith, "Toward a Black Feminist Criticism," in *All the Women Are White, All the Blacks Are Men, But Some of Us Are Brave:*

Black Women's Studies (Old Westbury, N.Y.: The Feminist Press, 1982), 182.

3–4. The mainstream "leadership" within Asian communities often colludes with the myth of the model minority and the reassuring desexualization of Asian people.

5. In Britain, however, more race–sex stereotypes of South Asians exist. Led by artists such as Pratibha Parmar, Sunil Gupta, and Hanif Kureishi, there is also a growing and already significant body of work by South Asians themselves, which takes up questions of sexuality.

6. Renee Tajima, "Lotus Blossoms Don't Bleed: Images of Asian Women," *Anthologies of Asian American Film and Video* (New York: A distribution project of Third World Newsreel, 1984), 28.

7. Ibid, 29.

8. See Stephen Gong, "Zen Warrior of the Celluloid (Silent) Years: The Art of Sessue Hayakawa," *Bridge* 8, no. 2 (Winter 1982–1983): 37–41.

9. Frantz Fanon, *Black Skin, White Masks* (London: Paladin, 1970), 120. For a reconsideration of this statement in the light of contemporary black gay issues, see Kobena Mercer, "Imaging the Black Man's Sex," in *Photography/Politics: Two*, ed. Pat Holland, Jo Spence, and Simon Watney (London: Comedia/Methuen 1987); reprinted in *Male Order: Unwrapping Masculinity*, ed. Rowena Chapman and Jonathan Rutherford (London: Lawrence and Wishart 1988), 141.

10. I do not think that this could happen in today's Toronto, which now has the second largest Chinese community on the continent. Perhaps it would not have happened in San Francisco. But I still believe that there is an onus on gay Asians and other gay people of color to prove our homosexuality.

11. The term *minority* is misleading. Racism is not a matter of numbers but of power. This is especially clear in situations where people of color constitute actual majorities, as in most former European colonies. At the same time, I feel that none of the current terms are really satisfactory and that too much time spent on the politics of "naming" can in the end be diversionary.

12. To organize effectively with lesbian and gay Asians, we must reject self-righteous condemnation of "closetedness" and see coming out more as a process or a goal, rather than as a prerequisite for participation in the movement.

13. Racism is available to be used by anyone. The conclusion that—because racism = power + prejudice—only white people can be racist is Eurocentric and simply wrong. Individuals have varying degrees and different sources of power, depending on the given moment in a shifting context. This does not contradict the fact that, in contemporary North American society, racism is generally organized around white supremacy.

14. From simple observation, I feel safe in saying that most gay Asian men in North America hold white men as their idealized sexual partners. However, I am not trying to construct an argument for determinism, and there are a number of outstanding problems that are not easily answered by current analyses of power. What of the experience of Asians who are attracted to men of color, including other Asians? What about white men who prefer Asians sexually? How and to what extent is desire articulated in terms of race as opposed to body type or other attributes? To what extent is sexual attraction exclusive and/or changeable, and can it be consciously programmed? These questions are all politically loaded, as they parallel and impact the debates between essentialists and social constructionists on the nature of homosexuality itself. They are also emotionally charged, in that sexual choice involving race has been a basis for moral judgment.

15. See Richard Dyer, *Heavenly Bodies: Film Stars and Society* (New York: St. Martin's Press 1986). In his chapter on Marilyn Monroe, Dyer writes extensively on the relationship between blondness, whiteness, and desirability.

16. Print porn is somewhat more racially integrated, as are the new safe sex tapes—by the Gay Men's Health Crisis, for example—produced in a political and pedagogical rather than a commercial context.

17. Richard Dyer, "Coming to Terms," *Jump Cut*, no. 30 (March 1985): 28.

18. Tom Waugh, "Men's Pornography, Gay vs. Straight," *Jump Cut*, no. 30 (March 1985): 31.

19. *International Wavelength News* 2, No. 1 (January 1991).

20. Tom Waugh, "Men's Pornography, Gay vs. Straight," 33.

21. It seems to me that the undressing here is organized around the pleasure of the white man in being

served. This is in contrast to the undressing scenes, in, say, James Bond films, in which the narrative is organized around undressing as an act of revealing the woman's body, an indicator of sexual conquest.

22. Interestingly, the gay video porn from Japan and Thailand that I have seen has none of this Oriental coding. Asianness is not taken up as a sign but is taken for granted as a setting for the narrative.

23. Joanna Russ, "Pornography and the Doubleness of Sex for Women," *Jump Cut*, no. 32 (April 1986): 39.

24. Though this is a common enough question in our postcolonial, urban environments, when asked of Asians it often reveals two agendas: first, the assumption that all Asians are newly arrived immigrants and, second, a fascination with difference and sameness. Although we (Asians) all supposedly look alike, there are specific characteristics and stereotypes associated with each particular ethnic group. The inability to tell us apart underlies the inscrutability attributed to Asians. This "inscrutability" took on sadly ridiculous proportions when during World War II the Chinese were issued badges so that white Canadians could distinguish them from "the enemy."

25. Isaac Julien (director), *Looking for Langston* (United Kingdom: Sankofa Film and Video 1988).

26. For more on the origins of the black film and video workshops in Britain, see Jim Pines, "The Cultural Context of Black British Cinema," in *Blackframes: Critical Perspectives on Black Independent Cinema*, ed. Mybe B. Cham and Clair Andrade-Watkins (Cambridge, Mass.: MIT Press 1988), 26.

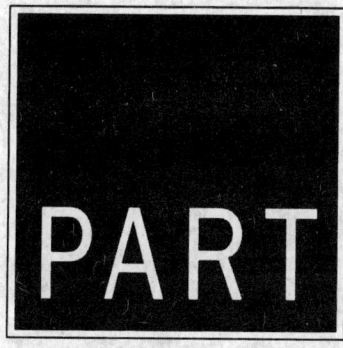

PART TEN

Men, Movements, and the Future

Q: Why did you decide to record again?

A: Because *this* housewife would like to have a career for a bit! On October 9, I'll be 40, and Sean will be 5 and I can afford to say, "Daddy does something else as well." He's not accustomed to it—in five years I hardly picked up a guitar. Last Christmas our neighbors showed him "Yellow Submarine" and he came running in, saying, "Daddy, you were singing . . . Were you a Beatle?" I said, "Well—yes, right."

—John Lennon, interview for *Newsweek*, 1980

Are men changing? If so, in what directions? Can men change even more? In what ways should men be different? We posed many of these questions at the beginning of our exploration of men's lives, and we return to them here, in the book's last section, to examine the directions men have taken to enlarge their roles, to expand the meaning of masculinity, to change the rules.

The articles in this section address the possibility and the direction of change for men: how shall we, as a society, address the questions raised by men's increasing exploration of the meaning of our lives? R. W. Connell situates current discussions of men changing in the larger context of globalization. bell hooks argues that feminists, and especially African American feminists, need to see men as potential allies, while Robert Reid-Farr describes the gender politics of the Million Man March. The "Statement of Principles" of the National Organization for Men Against Sexism (NOMAS) provides an alternative way to frame these issues of gender, sexual, and racial equality. And Michael Kimmel's essay explores a variety of recent events in the continuing redefinition of masculinity and suggests some of the ways we can transform masculinity in the future.

ARTICLE 50

bell hooks

Men: Comrades in Struggle

Feminism defined as a movement to end sexist oppression enables women and men, girls and boys, to participate equally in revolutionary struggle. So far, contemporary feminist movement has been primarily generated by the efforts of women—men have rarely participated. This lack of participation is not solely a consequence of anti-feminism. By making women's liberation synonymous with women gaining social equality with men, liberal feminists effectively created a situation in which they, not men, designated feminist movement "women's work." Even as they were attacking sex role divisions of labor, the institutionalized sexism which assigns unpaid, devalued, "dirty" work to women, they were assigning to women yet another sex role task: making feminist revolution. Women's liberationists called upon all women to join feminist movement but they did not continually stress that men should assume responsibility for actively struggling to end sexist oppression. Men, they argued, were all-powerful, misogynist oppressors—the enemy. Women were the oppressed—the victims. Such rhetoric reinforced sexist ideology by positing in an inverted form the notion of a basic conflict between the sexes, the implication being that the empowerment of women would necessarily be at the expense of men.

As with other issues, the insistence on a "woman only" feminist movement and a virulent anti-male stance reflected the race and class background of participants. Bourgeois white women, especially radical feminists, were envious and angry at privileged white men for denying them an equal share in class privilege. In part, feminism provided them with a public forum for the expression of their anger as well as a political platform they could use to call attention to issues of social equality, demand change, and promote specific reforms. They were not eager to call attention to the fact that men do not share a common social status; that patriarchy does not negate the existence of class and race privilege or exploitation; that all men do not benefit equally from sexism. They did not want to acknowledge that bourgeois white women, though often victimized by sexism, have more power and privilege, are less likely to be exploited or oppressed, than poor, uneducated, nonwhite males. At the time, many white women's liberationists did not care about the fate of oppressed groups of men. In keeping with the exercise of race and/or class privilege, they deemed the life experiences of these men unworthy of their attention, dismissed them, and simultaneously deflected attention away from their support of continued exploitation and oppression. Assertions like "all men are the enemy," "all men hate women" lumped all groups of men in one category, thereby suggesting that they share equally in all forms of male privilege. One of the first written statements which endeavored to make an anti-male stance a central feminist position was the "Redstockings Manifesto." Clause III of the manifesto reads:

> We identify the agents of our oppression as men. Male supremacy is the oldest, most basic form of domination. All other forms of exploitation and oppression (racism, capitalism, imperialism, etc.) are extensions of male

From *Feminist Theory: From Margin to Center,* by bell hooks, Boston: South End Press. Copyright © 1984 South End Press. Reprinted by permission.

supremacy: men dominate women, a few men dominate the rest. All power situations throughout history have been male-dominated and male-oriented. Men have controlled all political, economic, and cultural institutions and backed up this control with physical force. They have used their power to keep women in an inferior position. All men receive economic, sexual, and psychological benefits from male supremacy. All men have oppressed women. (1970, p. 109)

Anti-male sentiments alienated many poor and working class women, particularly non-white women, from feminist movement. Their life experiences had shown them that they have more in common with men of their race and/or class group than bourgeois white women. They know the sufferings and hardships women face in their communities; they also know the sufferings and hardships men face and they have compassion for them. They have had the experience of struggling with them for a better life. This has been especially true for black women. Throughout our history in the United States, black women have shared equal responsibility in all struggles to resist racist oppression. Despite sexism, black women have continually contributed equally to anti-racist struggle, and frequently, before contemporary black liberation effort, black men recognized this contribution. There is a special tie binding people together who struggle collectively for liberation. Black women and men have been united by such ties. They have known the experience of political solidarity. It is the experience of shared resistance struggle that led black women to reject the anti-male stance of some feminist activists. This does not mean that black women were not willing to acknowledge the reality of black male sexism. It does mean that many of us do not believe we will combat sexism or woman-hating by attacking black men or responding to them in kind.

Bourgeois white women cannot conceptualize the bonds that develop between women and men in liberation struggle and have not had as many positive experiences working with men politically. Patriarchal white male rule has usually devalued female political input. Despite the prevalence of sexism in black communities, the role black women play in social institutions, whether primary or secondary, is recognized by everyone as significant and valuable. In an interview with Claudia Tate (1983), black woman writer Maya Angelou explains her sense of the different role black and white women play in their communities:

> Black women and white women are in strange positions in our separate communities. In the social gatherings of black people, black women have always been predominant. That is to say, in the church it's always Sister Hudson, Sister Thomas, and Sister Wetheringay who keep the church alive. In lay gatherings it's always Lottie who cooks, and Mary who's going to Bonita's where there is a good party going on. Also, black women are the nurturers of children in our community. White women are in a different position in their social institutions. White men, who are in effect their fathers, husbands, brothers, their sons, nephews, and uncles say to white women or imply in any case: "I don't really need you to run my institutions. I need you in certain places and in those places you must be kept—in the bedroom, in the kitchen, in the nursery, and on the pedestal." Black women have never been told this. . . .

Without the material input of black women, as participants and leaders, many male-dominated institutions in black communities would cease to exist; this is not the case in all-white communities.

Many black women refused participation in feminist movement because they felt an anti-male stance was not a sound basis for action. They were convinced that virulent expressions of these sentiments intensify sexism by adding to the antagonism which already exists between women and men. For years black women (and some black men) had been struggling to overcome the tensions and antagonisms between black females and males that is generated by internalized racism (i.e., when the white patriarchy suggests one group has caused the oppression of the other). Black women were saying to black men, "we are not one another's enemy," "we must resist the socialization that teaches us to hate ourselves and one another." This affirmation of bonding between black women and men was part of anti-racist struggle. It could have been a part of feminist struggle had white women's liberationists stressed the need for women and men to resist the sexist socialization that teaches us to hate and fear one another. They chose instead to emphasize hate, especially male woman-hating, suggesting that it could not be changed. Therefore no viable political solidarity could exist between women and men. Women of color, from various ethnic backgrounds, as well as women who were active in the gay movement, not only experienced the development of solidarity between women and men in resistance struggle, but recognized its value. They were not willing to devalue this bonding by allying themselves with anti-male bourgeois white women. Encouraging political bonding between women and men to radically resist sexist oppression would have called attention to the transformative potential of feminism. The anti-male stance was a reactionary perspective that made feminism appear to be a movement that would enable white women to usurp white male power, replacing white male supremacist rule with white female supremacist rule.

Within feminist organizations, the issue of female separatism was initially separated from the anti-male stance; it was only as the movement progressed that the two perspectives merged. Many all-female sex-segregated groups were formed because women recognized that separatist organizing could hasten female consciousness-raising, lay the groundwork for the development of solidarity between women, and generally advance the movement. It was believed that mixed groups would get bogged down by male power trips. Separatist groups were seen as a necessary strategy, not as a way to attack men. Ultimately, the purpose of such groups was integration with equality. The positive implications of separatist organizing were diminished when radical feminists, like Ti Grace Atkinson, proposed sexual separatism as an ultimate goal of feminist movement. Reactionary separatism is rooted in the conviction that male supremacy is an absolute aspect of our culture, that women have only two alternatives: accepting it or withdrawing from it to create subcultures. This position eliminates any need for revolutionary struggle and it is in no way a threat to the status quo. In the essay "Separate to Integrate," Barbara Leon (1975) stresses that male supremacists would rather feminist movement remain "separate and unequal." She gives the example of orchestra conductor Antonia Brico's efforts to shift from an all-women orchestra to a mixed orchestra, only to find she could not get support for the latter:

> Antonia Brico's efforts were acceptable as long as she confined herself to proving that women were qualified musicians. She had no trouble finding 100 women who could play in an orchestra or getting financial backing for them to do so. But finding the backing for men and women to play together in a truly integrated orchestra proved to be impossible. Fighting for integration proved to be more a threat to male supremacy and, therefore, harder to achieve.
>
> The women's movement is at the same point now. We can take the easier way of accepting segregation, but that would mean losing the very goals for which the movement was formed. Reactionary separatism has been a way of halting the push of feminism. . . .

During the course of contemporary feminist movement, reactionary separatism has led many women to abandon feminist struggle, yet it remains an accepted pattern for feminist organizing, e.g. autonomous women's groups within the peace movement. As a policy, it has helped to marginalize feminist struggle, to make it seem more a personal solution to individual problems, especially problems with men, than a political movement which aims to transform society as a whole. To return to an emphasis on feminism as revolutionary struggle, women can no longer allow feminism to be another arena for the continued expression of antagonism between the sexes. The time has come for women active in feminist movement to develop new strategies for including men in the struggle against sexism.

All men support and perpetuate sexism and sexist oppression in one form or another. It is crucial that feminist activists not get bogged down in intensifying our awareness of this fact to the extent that we do not stress the more unemphasized point which is that men can lead life affirming, meaningful lives without exploiting and oppressing women. Like women, men have been socialized to passively accept sexist ideology. While they need not blame themselves for accepting sexism, they must assume responsibility for eliminating it. It angers women activists who push separatism as a goal of feminist movement to hear emphasis placed on men being victimized by sexism; they cling to the "all men are the enemy" version of reality. Men are not exploited or oppressed by sexism, but there are ways in which they suffer as a result of it. This suffering should not be ignored. While it in no way diminishes the seriousness of male abuse and oppression of women, or negates male responsibility for exploitative actions, the pain men experience can serve as a catalyst calling attention to the need for change. Recognition of the painful consequences of sexism in their lives led some men to establish consciousness-raising groups to examine this. Paul Hornacek (1977) explains the purpose of these gatherings in his essay "Anti-Sexist Consciousness-Raising Groups for Men":

> Men have reported a variety of different reasons for deciding to seek a C-R group, all of which have an underlying link to the feminist movement. Most are experiencing emotional pain as a result of their male sex role and are dissatisfied with it. Some have had confrontations with radical feminists in public or private encounters and have been repeatedly criticized for being sexist. Some come as a result of their commitment to social change and their recognition that sexism and patriarchy are elements of an intolerable social system that needs to be altered . . .

Men in the consciousness-raising groups Hornacek describes acknowledge that they benefit from patriarchy and yet are also hurt by it. Men's groups, like women's support groups, run the risk of overemphasizing personal change at the expense of political analysis and struggle.

Separatist ideology encourages women to ignore the negative impact of sexism on male personhood. It stresses polarization between the sexes. According to Joy Justice, separatists believe that there are "two basic perspectives" on the issue of naming the victims of sexism: "There is the perspective that men oppress women. And there is the perspective that people are people, and we are all hurt by rigid sex roles." Many separatists feel that the latter perspective is a sign of co-optation, representing women's refusal to confront the fact that men are the enemy—they insist on the primacy of the first perspective. Both perspectives accurately describe our predicament. Men *do* oppress women. People *are* hurt by rigid sex role patterns. These two realities co-exist. Male oppression of women cannot be excused by the recognition that there are ways men are hurt by rigid sex roles. Feminist activists should acknowledge that hurt—it exists. It does not erase or lessen male responsibility for supporting and perpetuating their power under patriarchy to exploit and oppress women in a manner far more grievous than the psychological stress or emotional pain caused by male conformity to rigid sex role patterns.

Women active in feminist movement have not wanted to focus in any way on male pain so as not to deflect attention away from the focus on male privilege. Separatist feminist rhetoric suggested that all men shared equally in male privilege, that all men reap positive benefits from sexism. Yet the poor or working class man has been socialized via sexist ideology to believe that there are privileges and powers he should possess solely because he is male often finds that few if any of these benefits are automatically bestowed him in life. More than any other male group in the United States, he is constantly concerned about the contradiction between the notion of masculinity he was taught and his inability to live up to that notion. He is usually "hurt," emotionally scarred because he does not have the privilege or power society has taught him "real men" should possess. Alienated, frustrated, pissed off, he may attack, abuse, and oppress an individual woman or women, but he is not reaping positive benefits from his support and perpetuation of sexist ideology. When he beats or rapes women, he is not exercising privilege or reaping positive rewards; he may feel satisfied in exercising the only form of domination allowed him. The ruling class male power structure that promotes his sexist abuse of women reaps the real material benefits and privileges from his actions. As long as he is attacking women and not sexism or capitalism, he helps to maintain a system that allows him few, if any, benefits or privileges. He is an oppressor. He is an enemy to women. He is also an enemy to himself. He is also oppressed. His abuse of women is not justifiable. Even though he has been socialized to act as he does, there are existing social movements that would enable him to struggle for self-recovery and liberation. By ignoring these movements, he chooses to remain both oppressor and oppressed. If feminist movement ignores his predicament, dismisses his hurt, or writes him off as just another male enemy, then we are passively condoning his actions.

The process by which men act as oppressors and are oppressed is particularly visible in black communities, where men are working class and poor. In her essay "Notes for Yet Another Paper on Black Feminism, or Will The Real Enemy Please Stand Up?" (1979) black feminist activist Barbara Smith suggests that black women are unwilling to confront the problem of sexist oppression in black communities:

> By naming sexist oppression as a problem it would appear that we would have to identify as threatening a group we have heretofore assumed to be our allies—Black men. This seems to be one of the major stumbling blocks to beginning to analyze the sexual relationships/sexual politics of our lives. The phrase "men are not the enemy" dismisses feminism and the reality of patriarchy in one breath and also overlooks some major realities. If we cannot entertain the idea that some men are the enemy, especially white men and in a different sense Black men, too, then we will never be able to figure out all the reasons why, for example, we are beaten up every day, why we are sterilized against our wills, why we are being raped by our neighbors, why we are pregnant at age twelve, and why we are at home on welfare with more children than we can support or care for. Acknowledging the sexism of Black men does not mean that we become "manhaters" or necessarily eliminate them from our lives. What it does mean is that we must struggle for a different basis of interaction with them.

Women in black communities have been reluctant to publicly discuss sexist oppression, but they have always known it exists. We too have been socialized to accept sexist ideology and many black women feel that black male abuse of women is a reflection of frustrated masculinity—such thoughts lead them to see that abuse is understandable, even justified. The vast majority of black women think that just publicly stating that these men are the enemy or identifying them as oppressors would do little to change the situation; they fear it could simply lead to greater victimization. Naming oppressive realities, in and of itself, has not brought about the kinds of changes for oppressed groups that it can for more privileged groups, who command a different quality of attention. The public naming of sexism has generally not resulted in the institutionalized violence that characterized, for example, the response to black civil rights struggles. (Private naming, however, is often met with violent oppression.) Black women have not joined the feminist movement not because they cannot face the reality of sexist oppression; they face it daily. They do not join feminist movement because they do not see in feminist theory and practice, especially those writings made available to masses of people, potential solutions.

So far, feminist rhetoric identifying men as the enemy has had few positive implications. Had feminist activists called attention to the relationship between ruling class men and the vast majority of men, who are socialized to perpetuate and maintain sexism and sexist oppression even as they reap no life-affirming benefits, these men might have been motivated to examine the impact of sexism in their lives. Often feminist activists talk about male abuse of women as if it is an exercise of privilege rather than an expression of moral bankruptcy, insanity, and dehumanization. For example, in Barbara Smith's essay, she identifies white males as "the primary oppressor group in American society" and discusses the nature of their domination of others. At the end of the passage in which this statement is made she comments: "It is not just rich and powerful capitalists who inhibit and destroy life. Rapists, murderers, lynchers, and ordinary bigots do too and exercise very real and violent power because of this white male privilege." Implicit in this statement is the assumption that the act of committing violent crimes against women is either a gesture or an affirmation of privilege. Sexist ideology brainwashes men to believe that their violent abuse of women is beneficial when it is not. Yet feminist activists affirm this logic when we should be constantly naming these acts as expressions of perverted power relations, general lack of control over one's actions, emotional powerlessness, extreme irrationality, and in many cases, outright insanity. Passive male absorption of sexist ideology enables them to interpret this disturbed behavior positively. As long as men are brainwashed to equate violent abuse of women with privilege, they will have no understanding of the damage done to themselves, or the damage they do to others, and no motivation to change.

Individuals committed to feminist revolution must address ways that men can unlearn sexism. Women were never encouraged in contemporary feminist movement to point out to men their responsibility. Some feminist rhetoric "put down" women who related to men at all. Most women's liberationists were saying "women have nurtured, helped, and supported others for too long—now we must fend for ourselves." Having helped and supported men for centuries by acting in complicity with sexism, women were suddenly encouraged to withdraw their support when it came to the issue of "liberation." The insistence on a concentrated focus on individualism, on the primacy of self, deemed "liberatory" by women's liberationists, was not a visionary, radical concept of freedom. It did provide individual solutions for women, however. It was the same idea of independence perpetuated by the imperial patriarchal state which equates independence with narcissism and lack of concern with triumph over others. In this way, women active in feminist movement were simply inverting the dominant ideology of the culture—they were not attacking it. They were not presenting practical alternatives to the status quo. In fact, even the statement "men are the enemy" was basically an inversion of the male supremacist doctrine that "women are the enemy"— the old Adam and Eve version of reality.

In retrospect, it is evident that the emphasis on "man as enemy" deflected attention away from focus on improving relationships between women and men, ways for men and women to work together to unlearn sexism. Bourgeois women active in feminist movement exploited the notion of a natural polarization between the sexes to draw attention to equal rights effort. They had an enormous investment in depicting the male as enemy and the female as victim. They were the group of women who could dismiss their ties with men once they had an equal share in class privilege. They were ultimately more concerned with obtaining an equal share in class privilege than with the struggle to eliminate sexism and sexist oppression. Their insistence on separating from men heightened the sense that they, as women without men, needed equality of opportunity. Most women do not have the freedom to separate from men because of economic inter-dependence. The separatist notion that women could resist sexism by withdrawing from contact with men reflected a bourgeois class perspective. In Cathy McCandless's essay "Some Thoughts About Racism, Classism, and Separatism," she makes the point that separatism is in many ways a false issue because "in this capitalist economy, none of us are truly separate" (1979). However, she adds:

Socially, it's another matter entirely. The richer you are, the less you generally have to acknowledge those you depend upon. Money can buy you a great deal of distance. Given enough of it, it is even possible never to lay eyes upon a man. It's a wonderful luxury, having control over who you lay eyes on, but let's face it: most women's daily survival still involves face-to-face contact with men whether they like it or not. It seems to me that for this reason alone, criticizing women who associate with men not only tends to be counterproductive, it borders on blaming the victim. Particularly if the women taking it upon themselves to set the standards are white and upper or middle class (as has often been the case in my experience) and those to whom they apply these rules are not.

Devaluing the real necessities of life that compel many women to remain in contact with men, as well as not respecting the desire of women to keep contact with men, created an unnecessary conflict of interest for those women who might have been very interested in feminism but felt they could not live up to the politically correct standards.

Feminist writings did not say enough about ways women could directly engage in feminist struggle in subtle, day-to-day contacts with men, although they have addressed crises. Feminism is politically relevant to the masses of women who daily interact with men both publicly and privately, if it addresses ways that interaction, which usually has negative components because sexism is so all-pervasive, can be changed. Women who have daily contact with men need useful strategies that will enable them to integrate feminist movement into their daily life. By inadequately addressing or failing to address the difficult issues, contemporary feminist movement located itself on the periphery of society rather than at the center. Many women and men think feminism is happening, or happened, "out there." Television tells them the "liberated" woman is an exception, that she is primarily a careerist. Commercials like the one that shows a white career women shifting from work attire to flimsy clothing exposing flesh, singing all the while "I can bring home the bacon, fry it up in the pan, and never let you forget you're a man" reaffirm that her careerism will not prevent her from assuming the stereotyped sex object role assigned women in male supremacist society.

Often men who claim to support women's liberation do so because they believe they will benefit by no longer having to assume specific, rigid sex roles they find negative or restrictive. The role they are most willing and eager to change is that of economic provider. Commercials like the one described above assure men that women can be breadwinners or even "the" breadwinner, but still allow men to dominate them. Carol Hanisch's essay "Men's Liberation" (1975) explores the attempt by these men to exploit women's issues to their own advantage, particularly those issues related to work:

> Another major issue is the attempt by men to drop out of the work force and put their women to work supporting them. Men don't like their jobs, don't like the rat race, and don't like having a boss. That's what all the whining about being a "success symbol" or "success object" is really all about. Well, women don't like those things either, especially since they get paid 40% less than men for working, generally have more boring jobs, and rarely are even allowed to be "successful." But for women working is usually the only way to achieve some equality and power in the family, in their relationship with men, some independence. A man can quit work and pretty much still remain the master of the household, gaining for himself a lot of free time since the work he does doesn't come close to what his wife or lover does. In most cases, she's still doing more than her share of the housework in addition to wife work and her job. Instead of fighting to make his job better, to end the rat race, and to get rid of bosses, he sends his woman to work—not much different from the old practice of buying a substitute for the draft, or even pimping. And all in the name of breaking down "role stereotypes" or some such nonsense.

Such a "men's liberation movement" could only be formed in reaction to women's liberation in an attempt to make feminist movement serve the opportunistic interests of individual men. These men identified themselves as victims of sexism, working to liberate men. They identified rigid sex roles as the primary source of their victimization and though they wanted to change the notion of masculinity, they were not particularly concerned with their sexist exploitation and oppression of women. Narcissism and general self-pity characterized men's liberation groups. Kanisch concludes her essay with the statement:

> Women don't want to pretend to be weak and passive. And we don't want phony, weak, passive acting men any more than we want phony supermen full of bravado and little else. What women want is for men to be honest. Women want men to be bold—boldly honest, aggressive in their human pursuits. Boldly passionate, sexual and sensual. And women want this for themselves. It's time men became boldly radical. Daring to go to the root of their own exploitation and seeing that it is not women or "sex roles" or "society" causing their unhappiness, but capitalists and capitalism. It's time men dare to name and fight these, their real exploiters.

Men who have dared to be honest about sexism and sexist oppression, who have chosen to assume responsibility for opposing and resisting it, often find themselves isolated. Their politics are disdained by antifeminist men and women, and are often ignored by women active in feminist movement. Writing about his efforts to publicly support feminism in a local newspaper in Santa Cruz, Morris Conerly explains:

> Talking with a group of men, the subject of Women's Liberation inevitably comes up. A few laughs, snickers, angry mutterings, and denunciations follow. There is a group consensus that men are in an embattled position and must close ranks against the assaults of misguided females. Without fail, someone will solicit me for my view, which is that I am 100% for Women's Liberation. That throws them for a loop and they start staring at me as if my eyebrows were crawling with lice.

> They're thinking, "What kind of man is he?" I am a black man who understands that women are not my enemy. If I were a white man with a position of power; one could understand the reason for defending the status quo. Even then, the defense of a morally bankrupt doctrine that exploits and oppresses others would be inexcusable.

Conerly stresses that it was not easy for him to publicly support feminist movement, that it took time:

> . . . Why did it take me some time? Because I was scared of the negative reaction I knew would come my way by supporting Women's Liberation. In my mind I could hear it from the brothers and sisters. "What kind of man are you?" "Who's wearing the pants?" "Why are you in that white shit?" And on and on. Sure enough, the attacks came as I had foreseen but by that time my belief was firm enough to withstand public scorn.
>
> With growth there is pain . . . and that truism certainly applied in my case.

Men who actively struggle against sexism have a place in feminist movement. They are our comrades. Feminists have recognized and supported the work of men who take responsibility for sexist oppression—men's work with batterers, for example. Those women's liberationists who see no value in this participation must re-think and re-examine the process by which revolutionary struggle is advanced. Individual men tend to become involved in feminist movement because of the pain generated in relationships with women. Usually a woman friend or companion has called attention to their support of male supremacy. Jon Snodgrass introduces the book he edited, *For Men Against Sexism: A Book of Readings* (1977), by telling readers:

> While there were aspects of women's liberation which appealed to men, on the whole my reaction was typical of men. I was threatened by the movement and responded with anger and ridicule. I believed that men and women were oppressed by capital, but not that women were oppressed by men. I argued that "men are op-

pressed too" and that it's workers who need liberation! I was unable to recognize a hierarchy of inequality between men and women (in the working class) not to attribute it to male domination. My blindness to patriarchy, I now think, was a function of my male privilege. As a member of the male gender case, I either ignored or suppressed women's liberation.

My full introduction to the women's movement came through a personal relationship.... As our relationship developed, I began to receive repeated criticism for being sexist. At first I responded, as part of the male backlash, with anger and denial. In time, however, I began to recognize the validity of the accusation, and eventually even to acknowledge the sexism in my denial of the accusations.

Snodgrass participated in the men's consciousness-raising groups and edited the book of readings in 1977. Towards the end of the 1970s, interest in male anti-sexist groups declined. Even though more men than ever before support the idea of social equality for women, like women they do not see this support as synonymous with efforts to end sexist oppression, with feminist movement that would radically transform society. Men who advocate feminism as a movement to end sexist oppression must become more vocal and public in their opposition to sexism and sexist oppression. Until men share equal responsibility for struggling to end sexism, the feminist movement will reflect the very sexist contradictions we wish to eradicate.

Separatist ideology encourages us to believe that women alone can make feminist revolution—we cannot. Since men are the primary agents maintaining and supporting sexism and sexist oppression, they can only be successfully eradicated if men are compelled to assume responsibility for transforming their consciousness and the consciousness of society as a whole. After hundreds of years of anti-racist struggle, more than ever before non-white people are currently calling attention to the primary role white people must play in anti-racist struggle. The same is true of the struggle to eradicate sexism—men have a primary role to play. This does not mean that they are better equipped to lead feminist movement; it does mean that they should share equally in resistance struggle. In particular, men have a tremendous contribution to make to feminist struggle in the area of exposing, confronting, opposing, and transforming the sexism of their male peers. When men show a willingness to assume equal responsibility in feminist struggle, performing whatever tasks are necessary, women should affirm their revolutionary work by acknowledging them as comrades in struggle.

References

Angelou, Maya. 1983. "Interview." In *Black Women Writers at Work*, edited by Claudia Tate. New York: Continuum Publishing.

Hanisch, Carol. 1975. "Men's Liberation," In *Feminist Revolution* (pp. 60–63). New Paltz, NY: Redstockings.

Hornacek, Paul. 1977. "Anti-Sexist Consciousness-Raising Groups for Men." In *A Book of Readings for Men Against Sexism*, edited by Jon Snodgrass. Albion: Times Change Press.

Leon, Barbara. 1975. "Separate to Integrate." In *Feminist Revolution* (pp. 139–144). New Paltz, NY: Redstockings.

McCandless, Cathy. 1979. "Some Thoughts About Racism, Classism, and Separatism." In *Top Ranking*, edited by Joan Gibbs and Sara Bennett (pp. 105–115). New York: February Third Press.

"Redstockings Manifesto." 1970. In *Voices from Women's Liberation*, edited by Leslie B. Tanner (p. 109). New York: Signet, NAL.

Smith, Barbara. 1979. "Notes for Yet Another Paper on Black Feminism, or Will the Real Enemy Please Stand Up?" *Conditions: Five* 2 (2): 123–127.

Snodgrass, Jon (ed.). 1977. *For Men Against Sexism: A Book of Readings*. Albion, CA: Times Change Press.

ARTICLE 51

The National Organization for Men Against Sexism

Statement of Principles

The National Organization for Men Against Sexism is an activist organization of men and women supporting positive changes for men. NOMAS advocates a perspective that is pro-feminist, gay-affirmative, and committed to justice on a broad range of social issues including race, class, age, religion, and physical abilities. We affirm that working to make this nation's ideals of equality substantive is the finest expression of what it means to be men.

We believe that the new opportunities becoming available to women and men will be beneficial to both. Men can live as happier and more fulfilled human beings by challenging the old-fashioned rules of masculinity that embody the assumption of male superiority.

Traditional masculinity includes many positive characteristics in which we take pride and find strength, but it also contains qualities that have limited and harmed us. We are deeply supportive of men who are struggling with the issues of traditional masculinity. As an organization for changing men, we care about men and are especially concerned with men's problems, as well as the difficult issues in most men's lives.

As an organization for changing men, we strongly support the continuing struggle of women for full equality. We applaud and support the insights and positive social changes that feminism has stimulated for both women and men. We oppose such injustices to women as economic and legal discrimination, rape, domestic violence, sexual harassment, and many others. Women and men can and do work together as allies to change the injustices that have so often made them see one another as enemies.

One of the strongest and deepest anxieties of most American men is their fear of homosexuality. This homophobia contributes directly to the many injustices experienced by gay, lesbian, and bisexual persons, and is a debilitating restriction for heterosexual men. We call for an end to all forms of discrimination based on sexual–affectional orientation, and for the creation of a gay-affirmative society.

We also acknowledge that many people are oppressed today because of their race, class, age, religion, and physical condition. We believe that such injustices are vitally connected to sexism, with its fundamental premise of unequal distribution of power.

Our goal is to change not just ourselves and other men, but also the institutions that create inequality. We welcome any person who agrees in substance with these principles to membership in the National Organization For Men Against Sexism.

Copyright © 1991 *The National Organization For Men Against Sexism.*

ARTICLE 52

Michael S. Kimmel

Clarence, William, Iron Mike, Tailhook, Senator Packwood, Spur Posse, Magic . . . and Us

A Second Look

The title of this essay, published first in 1993, drew its examples from the early 1990s, as Americans launched into a decade that may be best remembered as one in which we took a crash course on male sexuality. From the national teach-in on sexual harassment that emerged from Clarence Thomas's confirmation hearings, to accusations about sexual harassment against Senator Robert Packwood, to the U.S. Navy Tailhook scandal, to Magic Johnson's revelation that he is infected with the HIV virus, to William Kennedy Smith and Mike Tyson's date rape trials—we've had a steady discussion about troubling aspects of male sexuality, a sexuality that seems to be more about predatory conquest than pleasure and connection.

Hopes that the second half of the decade and the first years of the new millennium might be a bit different, however, were misplaced. This essay now really should be titled: "Clarence, William, Iron Mike, Tailhook, Senator Packwood, Spur Posse, Magic, VMI, the Citadel, Woody, Iron Mike (again), Aberdeen, Marv, Latrell, President Clinton, Columbine, Eminem, Gary, The Roman Catholic Church, Hootie, the Air Force Academy . . . and Us."

Not a week seems to go by without another in the seemingly endless parade of "men behaving badly," men who embody the seamier side of male sexuality—entitlement, predation, violence.

When confronted by this parade, many men react defensively. "Men on Trial" has been the common headline linking these disparate cases. "Save the Males!" buttons proliferated at the Citadel. While President Clinton and Monica Lewinsky became standard targets of derision on late-night TV, others in the list were lionized as heroes.

But it's not men on trial here; it's masculinity, or, rather, the traditional definition of masculinity, which leads to certain behaviors that we now see as politically problematic and often physically threatening. Under prevailing definitions, men have and are the politically incorrect sex. Perhaps we should slap a warning label on penises across the land: WARNING: OPERATING THIS INSTRUMENT CAN BE DANGEROUS TO YOUR AND OTHERS' HEALTH.

But why have these issues emerged now? And why are sexual harassment and date rape particularly dominant as matters of concern today? Since it is certain that we will continue to face these issues for the foreseeable future, how can we better understand them? What can we do to address them? How can we change the meanings of masculinity so that sexual harassment and date rape will disappear from our workplaces and our relationships?

Copyright © 2003 by Michael Kimmel. Reprinted by permission.

The Social Construction of Male Sexuality

To speak of transforming masculinity is to begin with an examination of how men are sexual in our culture. As social scientists see it, sexuality is less a product of biological urges and more about the meanings that we attach to those urges, meanings that vary dramatically across cultures, over time, and among a variety of social groups within any particular culture. Sexual beings are made, not born. John Gagnon, a well-known theoretician of this approach, argues that:

> People learn when they are quite young a few of the things that they are expected to be, and continue slowly to accumulate a belief in who they are and ought to be through the rest of childhood, adolescence, and adulthood. Sexual conduct is learned in the same ways and through the same processes; it is acquired and assembled in human interaction, judged and performed in specific cultural and historical worlds.

And the major item in that assemblage, the chief building block in the social construction of sexuality, is gender. We experience our sexual selves through a gendered prism. The meanings of sex to women and men are very, very different. There really are a "his" and "hers" when it comes to sex. To offer one example: think about the difference in the way we view a man or a woman who has a lot of different sexual partners: one is a stud and the other a slut.

The rules of masculinity and femininity are strictly enforced. And difference equals power. The difference between male and female sexuality reproduces men's power over women, and, simultaneously, the power of some men over other men, especially of the dominant, hegemonic form of manhood—white, straight, middle-class—over marginal masculinities. Those who dare to cross over—women who are sexually adventurous and men who are sexually passive—risk being seen as gender, not sexual, non-conformists. And we all know how homophobia links gender non-conformity to homosexuality. The stakes are high if you don't play along.

Sexual behavior confirms manhood. It makes men feel manly. The psychologist Robert Brannon has identified the four traditional rules of American manhood: (1) No Sissy Stuff: men can never do anything that even remotely suggests femininity. Manhood is a relentless repudiation and devaluation of the feminine; (2) Be a Big Wheel: manhood is measured by power, wealth, and success. Whoever has the most toys when he dies, wins; (3) Be a Sturdy Oak: manhood depends on emotional reserve. Dependability in a crisis requires that men not reveal their feelings, and (4) Give 'em Hell: exude an aura of manly daring and aggression. Go for it. Take risks.

These four rules lead to a sexuality built around accumulating partners (scoring), emotional distance, and risk taking. In locker rooms and playgrounds across the country, men are taught that the goal of every encounter with women is to score. Men are supposed to be ever ready for sex, constantly seeking sex, and constantly seeking to escalate every encounter so that intercourse will result, since, as one of my students once noted, "It doesn't count unless you put it in."

The emotional distancing of the sturdy oak is considered necessary for adequate male sexual functioning, but it leads to some strange behaviors. For example, to keep from ejaculating "too soon," men may devise a fascinating array of distractions, such as counting, doing multiplication tables in their heads, or thinking about sports.

Risk-taking is a centerpiece of male sexuality. Sex is about adventure, excitement, danger—taking chances. Responsibility is a word that seldom turns up is male sexual discourse. And this, of course, has serious medical side effects: STDs, possibility of impregnation, and AIDS—currently the most gendered disease in American history.

To reign in this constructed male "appetite," women have been assigned the role of asexual gatekeeper; women decide, metaphorically and literally, who enters the desired garden of earthly delights, and who doesn't. A woman's sexual agency, her sense of entitlement to desire, is drowned out by the incessant humming of the male's desire that propels him ever forward. A man's job is to wear down her resistance. One fraternity at a college I was lecturing at last year offered seminars to pledges on dating etiquette that appropriated the business advice book "Getting to Yes."

Sometimes that hum is so loud it drowns out the actual voice of the real lwoman a man is with. Men suffer from socialized deafness, a hearing impairment that strikes only when women say no. For example, some campus men's groups offer seminars to other men about how to spike women's drinks with "roofies"—basically using the drug Rohiypnol to render women unconscious, and consequently more "compliant." I'm sure I'm not the first person to point out that having sex with someone who is unconscious is actually closer to necrophilia than it is to sex. I certainly wouldn't imagine it counts on the male's scorecard.

Who Are the Real Sexual Revolutionaries

Of course, a lot has changed along the frontiers of the sexual landscape in the past two decades. We've had a sexual revolution, after all. But as the dust is settling from the sexual revolution, what emerges in unmistakably finer detail is that women, not men, are the real sexual pioneers of our era. We men like to think that the sexual revolution, with its promises of more access to more partners with less emotional commitment, was tailor-made for male sexuality's fullest flowering. In fact, women's sexuality, not men's, has changed in the past two decades. Women now feel capable—no, more than that, entitled—to sexual pleasure. They have learned to say yes to their own desires, claiming, in the process, sexual agency.

And men? We're still dancing the same tired dance of the sexual conquistadors. Look, for a minute, at those late-night and cable TV shows, like "The Man Show" or those "new" men's magazines like Maxim or Stuff. Men seem to need to feel reassured that although women are working alongside men in every conceivable field of endeavor they remain, underneath it all, potential sexpots ready to jump on trampolines in bikinis, or fetishized consumer goods, or oversized mammary glands in too-tight tops. Consider also those "reality" shows like The Bachelor, in which women literally and symbolically prostrate themselves on the altar of masculinity to get some media-defined version of "Mr. Right"—handsome, rich and vacuous—to marry them. (Even The Bachelorette, which pretends to reverse roles, makes women into the object of men's attraction, for which men are supposed to compete. This is hardly a role reversal. What it shows is that women are equally capable of objectifying men—not quite the revolution one might have expected.)

Some might argue that this simply confirms that women can have male sex and that male sexuality was victorious because we've convinced women to be more like us. But then why are so many men wilting in the face of desiring women? Why are sex therapists offices crammed with men who complain not of premature ejaculation (the most common sexual problem twenty years ago—a sexual problem that involves being a bit over-eager) but of what therapists euphemistically call "inhibited desire"—that is, men who don't want to have sex now that all these women are able to claim their sexual rights.

And that's not to mention all those legions of men who found themselves literally wilting, clambering now for Viagra, not to help pump their erections, but their libidos. It appears that many men believe that Viagra is a foolproof aphrodisiac, guaranteed to enable them to achieve functioning erections even in the absence of sexual desire. It does no such thing; it enables the erection to be achieved and sustained only in the presence of the experience of desire. It makes desire "actionable," but it does not replace it. Only in the most "hydraulic" model of male sexuality—ten inches, hard as steel, goes all night—could Viagra be seen as priming the pump.

Date Rape and Sexual Predation, Aggression, and Entitlement

As women have claimed the right to say yes, they've also begun to assert their rights to say no. Women are now demanding that men be more sexually responsible and accountable for their sexual behaviors. And, yes, it is women who have changed the rules of sexual conduct. What used to be (and in many places still is) called male sexual etiquette—forcing a woman to have sex when she says no, conniving, coercing, pushing, ignoring her efforts to get you to stop, getting her so drunk that she loses the ability (or consciousness) that one needs to consent—is now defined as date rape.

In one recent study, 45 percent of all college women said that they had had some form of sexual contact against their will. A full 25 percent had been pressed or forced to have sexual intercourse against their will. That many of these women don't call it rape nor see themselves as rape victims has been offered as proof that feminist women inflate the numbers to generate a date-rape hysteria on campus that douses all sexual energy with the cold shower of political correctness. To the contrary, I think that the fact that most women neither see the interaction as rape nor see themselves as rape victims indicates that women, as well as men, essentially subscribe to the notion that men are uncontrolled sexual predators who don't take no for an answer and will take whatever they can get away with. Since the women are experiencing what men call "dating behavior," how can they see it as anything else?

But consider, for a moment, the testimonies of those women who were the victims of such dating etiquette. Patricia Bowman, who went home with William Kennedy Smith from Au Bar in Palm Beach, Florida, testified that when she told Smith that she'd called her friends and was going to call the police, he responded "You shouldn't have done that. Nobody's going to believe you." And, indeed, the jury didn't. I did.

But they weren't allowed to hear the testimony of three other women who claimed Smith sexually assaulted them. Their testimony would have established a pattern not of criminal assault, but of Smith's obvious belief in sexual entitlement, that he was entitled to press his sexual needs on women despite their resistance, because he didn't particularly care what they felt about it.

And Desiree Washington knows all about men who don't listen when a woman says no. Mike Tyson's aggressive masculinity in the boxing ring was sadly translated into a vicious misogyny with his ex-wife Robin Givens and a predatory sexuality, as evidenced by his behavior with Washington. Tyson's "grandiose sense of entitlement, fueled by the insecurities and emotions of adolescence," as writer Joyce Carol Oates put it, led to a behavior with women that was as out of control as his homosocial behavior inside the ring.

Tyson's case underscores our particular fascination with athletes (or, in the case of Marv Albert, of the announcers-turned-celebrities who hang around athletes and who believe that athletic entitlement rubs off on them too). There's an almost expected equation in American life between athletes and sexual aggression. Barely a week goes by in which the sports pages do not tell of yet another athlete like Christian Peters, the former Nebraska lineman, or Randy Moss, the star receiver for the Minnesota Vikings (who was tossed off the Notre Dame team before he even arrived for sexual assaults in high school, and starred at Marshall, where he was also accused of rape.). The Center for the Study of Sport and Society at Northeastern University posts the names of all athletes accused of sexual assault—and they have to update it weekly. And what about Latrell Sprewell, who, when upset by his coach's working the team too hard in practice, decided to try and strangle him? In high schools, colleges, and professional teams, we're getting the message that our young male athletes, trained for fearless aggression on the field, are translating that to a predatory sexual aggression in relationships with women. Columnist Robert Lipsyte calls it the "varsity syndrome"—"winner take all, winning at any cost, violence as a tool, aggression as a mark of masculinity." The very qualities we seek in our athletes are exactly the qualities we do not want in young men today—respect for others, compassion, the ability to listen, attention to process and not the end goal. Our task is to make it clear that what we want from our athletes when they are on the playing field is NOT the same as what we want from them when they are playing the field.

Men in Groups

Athletes only illustrate the problem—the problem of male entitlement that seems to flow unquestioningly to men in groups. Most athletes, after all, play on teams; thus much of their social life and much of a player's public persona is constructed through association with teammates. Another homosocial preserve, fraternities, is the site of most gang rapes that occur on college campuses, according to psychologist Chris O'Sullivan, who has been studying gang rape for several years. At scores of campus and corporate workshops over the past fifteen years, women have shared the complaint that, while individual men may appear sympathetic when they are alone with women, they suddenly turn out to be macho louts capable of the vilest misogynist statements when they are in groups of other men. I'm sure that the members of the U.S. Navy Tailhook Association, or the staff sergeants at the Aberdeen training ground, or the cadets at the U.S. Air Force Academy are decent, law-abiding, and law-upholding family men when they are alone or with their families. They are sworn to uphold honor, integrity, and the American way of life, to put themselves in harm's way, and to sacrifice their lives, if need be, to preserve our freedoms. But put those same guys together at a convention or in their barracks after the lights are out, and they become a marauding gang of masculinist thugs who should be prosecuted for felonious assault, not merely slapped on their collective wrists and met with a resigned "boys will be boys" shrug.

It was true that the members of Spur Posse, a group of relatively affluent Southern California adolescent boys are also "regular guys." This made their sexual predation and homosocial competition as chilling as it was revealing of something sinister at the heart of American masculinity. Before a large group of young women and girls—one as young as ten!—came forward to claim that members of Spur Posse had sexually assaulted and raped them, these guys would have been seen as typical high school fellas. Members of the group competed with one another to have sex with the largest number of girls, and kept elaborately coded scores of their exploits by referring to various athletes' names as a way to signify the number of their conquests. Thus a reference to "Reggie Jackson" would immediately be understood to mean 44, the number of his jersey, or a "David Robinson" would signify 50 conquests. In this way, the boys could publicly compete with each other without the young women understanding that they were simply the currency in this male-male competition.

When some of these young women accused the boys of assault and rape, many residents of their affluent suburb were shocked. The boys' mothers, particularly, winced when they heard that their fifteen year-old sons had had sex with as many as 50 young girls. A few expressed outrage. But the boys' fathers glowed with pride. "That's my boy," they declared in chorus. They accused the girls of being sluts. And sometimes we wonder where the kids get their attitudes.

Spur Posse is only one example of a recent spate of cases in which masculine sexual entitlement is offered to boys as part of their birthright. Transforming a rape culture is going to mean transforming a view of women as the means through which men can compete, trying to better their positions on the homosocial ladder of success and status.

Masculine Fragility

What is it about groups that seem to bring out the worst in men? I think it is because the animating condition for most American men is a deeply rooted fear of other men—a fear that other men will see us as weak, feminine, and not manly. The fear of humiliation, of losing in the competitive ranking among men, of being dominated by other men—these are the fears that keep men in tow and reinforce traditional definitions of masculinity as a false means of safety. Homophobia—which I take to be more than the fear of homosexual men but really the fear of other men—keeps men acting like men. It keeps us exaggerating adherence to traditional norms so that no other men will get the wrong idea that we might really be that most dreaded person of all: the sissy.

But don't take my word for it. Listen to my favorite gender theorist in America today, Eminem. When asked in a recent interview why he uses homophobic epithets in his raps, Eminem poignantly illustrated the role of "gay-baiting" in peer interactions. In his view, calling someone a "faggot" is not a slur on the other man's sexuality but on his gender. "The lowest degrading thing that you can say to a man . . . is to call him a faggot and try to take away his manhood," said America's premier rap artist. "Call him a sissy. Call him a punk. 'Faggot' to me doesn't necessarily mean gay people. 'Faggot' to me just means taking away your manhood." (In his hit movie, 8 Mile, it's the fear of being humiliated by other men in rap competitions that animates Eminem's desire to strive; and when he is victorious, the movie closes with his song about taking your "one shot" despite the obvious restrictive burdens of wives and children.)

That fear of being seen as a sissy, of being gay-baited, taunted, and bullied because one is not a "real man" is certainly what lies behind so much adolescent masculine risk-taking and violence. A recent survey asked high school students what they were most afraid of. The girls answered that they were most afraid of being assaulted, raped, killed. The boys? They said they were most afraid of "being laughed at."

Boys laugh at each other, tease each other, make fun of each other, and bully each other constantly. When we've confronted the myriad school shootings that have occurred since 1992 (there have been 28 cases), several constants stand out. All 28 cases were committed by boys. All but one was committed by a white boy in a suburban or rural school. And yet we speak of "teen violence," "youth violence," "violence in the schools"—but no one manages to call it "boys' violence," although that is what it is.

Try a little thought experiment: Imagine that all the killers in all the school shootings in recent years (Littleton, Colorado; Pearl, Mississippi; Paducah, Kentucky; Springfield, Oregon; and Jonesboro, Arkansas) were all black girls from poor families who lived instead in New Haven, Boston, Chicago, or Newark. I believe we'd now be having a national debate about inner-city poor black girls. The entire focus would be on race, class, and gender. The media would invent a new term for their behavior, as they did with "wilding" a decade ago after the attack on the Central Park jogger. We'd hear about the culture of poverty; about how life in the city breeds crime and violence; about some putative natural tendency among blacks toward violence. Someone would even blame feminism for causing girls to become violent in vain imitation of boys. Yet the obvious fact that all these school killers were all middle-class white boys seems to have escaped everyone's notice.

Even more central is another striking consistency in the stories that have emerged about the boys who did commit the violence: All had stories of being constantly bullied, beaten up, and, most significantly for this analysis, "gay baited." All seem to have stories of being mercilessly and constantly teased, picked on, and threatened. And, most strikingly, it was not because they were gay (none of them was gay as far as the public can tell), but because they were different from the other boys—shy, bookish, an honor student, a "geek" or a "nerd."

For example, young Andy Williams, who shot several classmates in Santee, California, was described as "shy" and was "constantly picked on" by others in school. (They stole his clothes, his money, and his food, beat him up regularly, and locked him in his locker, among other daily taunts and humiliations.) Classmates described Gary Scott Pennington, who killed his teacher and a custodian in Grayson, Kentucky, in 1993, as a "nerd" and a "loner" who was constantly teased for being smart and wearing glasses. Barry Loukaitas, who killed his algebra teacher and two other students in Moses Lake, Washington, in 1996, was an honor student who especially loved math; he was also constantly teased and bullied and described as a "shy nerd." And Evan Ramsay, who killed one student and the high school principal in Bethel, Alaska, in 1997, was also an honor student who was teased for wearing glasses and having acne.

Fourteen year-old Michael Carneal was a shy and frail freshman at Heath High School in Paducah, Kentucky, barely 5 feet tall, weighing 110 pounds. He wore thick glasses and played in the high school band. He felt alienated, pushed around, and picked on. He was said to be very upset when students called him a "faggot" and almost cried when the school gossip sheet labeled him as "gay." On Thanksgiving 1997, he stole two shotguns, two semiautomatic rifles, a pistol, and 700 rounds of ammunition, and after a weekend of showing them off to his classmates, brought them to school hoping that they would bring him some instant recognition. "I just wanted the guys to think I was cool," he said. When the cool guys ignored him, he opened fire on a morning prayer circle, killing three classmates and wounding five others. Now serving a life sentence in prison, Carneal told psychiatrists weighing his sanity that "people respect me now."

And at Columbine High School, the nation's most infamous school shooting, this connection was not lost on Evan Todd, a 255-pound defensive lineman on the Columbine football team, an exemplar of the jock culture that Dylan Klebold and Eric Harris found to be such an interminable torment. "Columbine is a clean, good place, except for those rejects," Todd said. "Sure we teased them. But what do you expect with kids who come to school with weird hairdos and horns on their hats? It's not just jocks; the whole school's disgusted with them. They're a bunch of homos. . . . If you want to get rid of someone, usually you tease 'em. So the whole school would call them homos." In the videotape made the night before the shootings, Harris says, "People constantly make fun of my face, my hair, my shirts." Klebold adds, "I'm going to kill you all. You've been giving us shit for years."

What Klebold said he had been receiving for years apparently included constant gay baiting, being called "queer," "faggot," "homo," being pushed into lockers, grabbed in hallways, and mimicked and ridiculed with homophobic slurs. For some boys, high school is an interminable torment, a constant homophobic gauntlet, and they may respond by becoming withdrawn and sullen, using drugs or alcohol, becoming depressed or suicidal, or acting out in a blaze of over-compensating violent "glory."

The prevalence of this homophobic bullying, teasing, and violence is staggering. Probably the most common putdown in America's high schools and middle schools today is "that's so gay." And as we've seen it has less to do with sexual orientation than it does with gender. We are the gender police, making sure that other boys stay in line.

Men's fears of being judged a failure as a man in the eyes of other men leads often to a certain homosocial element within any heterosexual encounter: men often will use their sexual conquest as a form of currency to gain status among other men. Such homosocial competition contributes to the strange hearing impairment that leads us to hear "no" as "yes," to escalate an encounter, to always go for it, to score. And this is occurring just as women are learning to say "yes" to their own desires, to hear their own voices. Instead of our socialized deafness, we need to become what Langston Hughes called "articulate listeners": we need to trust women to tell us what they want and when they want it, as well as what they don't want. And we need to listen to our own inner voices, our own real desires and needs. We need to ignore the voices telling us to prove something that cannot be proved, and listen to the voices telling us to genuinely connect with another person, and experience the desires and passions that can happen between two equals.

Saving the Males

If men are afraid of what other men will think of them, they're also afraid of what women will do to them—just by their mere presence. Supporters of the male-only admissions policy at the Citadel distributed buttons that said "Save the Males!"—as if the presence of women on campus would dilute the mystical bonding that takes place among the male cadets. At the Citadel and VMI, the nation's last remaining state-supported all-male colleges, women were seen as such a "toxic kind of virus" that, according to Maj. Gen. Josiah Bunting III, the current Commandant of Cadets at VMI, admitting women cadets would make it impossible for men to become men. Not only did school leaders claim that women were physically incapable of withstanding the brutality, violent hazing, and "adversative" educational methodologies employed at these schools (despite the presence of women at West Point and in the actual military for more than 25 years), but they also claimed that the presence of women would so pollute the environment that the men would not be able to experience the bonding necessary to become "citizen soldiers." Imagine a masculinity so fragile, so threatened, so besieged that simply the proximity of a woman would make proving manhood impossible!

That also seems to be the fear William (Hootie) Johnson expresses in his intransigent refusal to allow women to become members of the Augusta National Golf Club. When their male-only policy was exposed by Martha Burk, a Washington D.C.-based feminist activist, Hootie's growling resistance reminded me of those southern military schools: baffled by the desire of women to join and gruffly resistant to allowing them to do so. Here was the head of the nation's premier country club, the site of its most prestigious golf tournament, acting like the Little Rascals defending their all-boy clubhouse with a hand-painted wooden sign that said "No Gurls Allowed."

What could possibly be so scary about women's presence? I'll give you a hint. It's not women's presence that is threatening to men; it's their equality. There are plenty of women at VMI and the Citadel—they cook the food and serve it, they clean the barracks and teach the classes, and they are graduate students and counselors. And there are plenty of women at Augusta National. Just who do you think serves all those cocktails at the 19th hole? Who prepares the food, serves the meals, makes the beds in the guestrooms? Women are all over the place, but are not allowed to wear the fabled cadet uniform or the heralded green blazer. Happily, the Supreme Court saw through this male-bonding pretext and demanded that VMI (and the Citadel) either open their doors to women or cease receiving federal and state funds. (Their vote was 7-1 against VMI, with only Justice Scalia dissenting. Clarence Thomas had to recuse himself since his son attended VMI.) And eventually, there will even be a woman member at Augusta National. Maybe it'll be Carly Fiorina, the CEO of Hewlett-Packard. Or maybe it'll be Shirley Tilghman, President of Princeton University. Obviously the male cadets at VMI and the Citadel and the captains of industry at Augusta National do not need saving from women. They need to be saved from themselves—and from their outmoded ideas about male entitlement and male privilege.

From the Bedroom to the Boardroom

Men's fears and opposition to women's equality is found frequently in the workplace. Male doctors rarely are upset by female nurses or administrators, only by female doctors; male corporate executives don't mind female secretaries, only female colleagues. But they'd better get used to it because women have utterly transformed the public arena, in particular the workplace. As with sexuality, the real revolution in the past thirty years has been women's dramatic entry into the labor force in unprecedented numbers. Women are in the workforce to stay, and men had better adjust to having them around.

That means the cozy boys' club—a.k.a. the workplace—has been penetrated by women, at a time when that arena is more suffused with doubt and anxiety than ever before. In a downwardly spiraling economy, the current generation of college students are, themselves, downwardly mobile. The fastest growing job category in the U.S. economy today is not "doc com millionaire;" in fact, of all jobs created in the decade 2000-2010, over four-fifths will be in entry level service and sales jobs. Most Americans are less successful than their own parents were at the same age—and this will continue for their entire working lives. It literally takes two incomes to earn what one income earned thirty years ago (the actual income of a family of four in the United States in 2003, in constant dollars, is within $10 of what it was in 1973). Most middle-class Americans cannot afford to buy the house in which they grew up.

Since men derive so much of our identity in the public sphere, as workers, breadwinners, and providers, this is important to us. There are fewer and fewer "big wheels" and more and more men who will feel they have to prove themselves, who feel damaged, injured, powerless. And now here come women into that arena, in unprecedented numbers. It is virtually impossible for a man to go through his entire working life without a woman colleague, co-worker, or supervisor. Just when our breadwinner status is most threatened, women appear on the scene as easy targets for men's anger.

This may help explain men's defensiveness and resistance to women's equality in the workplace: it feels like a loss to us. Recently I appeared on a television talk show opposite three "angry white males" who felt they had been the victims of workplace discrimination. The show's title, no doubt to entice a large potential audience, was "A Black Woman Stole My Job." In my comments to these men, I invited them to consider what the word "my" meant in that title. Where did they get the idea that it was their job? Why wasn't the title of the show "A Black Woman Got the Job" or "A Black Woman got a Job"? Because, to these men, that job was rightfully theirs. They were entitled to it, and when some "other" person—black, female—got the job, that person was really taking "their" job. But by what right is a job a male's job? Only by his sense of entitlement, which he now perceives as threatened by the movement toward workplace gender equality.

This potent combination of women's increased entry into the workplace, men's declining fortunes, and men's sense of entitlement is what I often think of as the political economy of sexual harassment. I'm not referring to the generally less common form of quid pro quo harassment, by which sex is exchanged or demanded in return for promotions, hiring, or other job perks. I'm thinking more of the far more pervasive "hostile environment," in which women are reminded that although they may be in the workplace, they still don't belong there because it is still really a man's world. The placing of sexual harassment on the national agenda affords men a rare opportunity to do some serious soul searching. What is sexual harassment about? And why is it in men's interests to help put an end to it?

One thing that sexual harassment is usually not about, although you couldn't convince the U.S. Senate of this, is a matter of one person telling the truth and the other person lying. Sexual harassment cases are difficult and confusing precisely because there are often a multiplicity of truths. "His" truth might be what appears to him to be an innocent indication of sexual interest or harmless joking with the "boys in the office" (even if those "boys" happen to include women workers). "Her" truth is that those seemingly innocent remarks cause stress, anxiety about promotion, potential firing, and sexual pressure.

Clarence Thomas asserted during the course of his testimony that "At no time did I become aware, either directly or indirectly, that she felt I had said or done anything to change the cordial nature of our relationship." And there is no reason to assume that he would have been aware of it. But that doesn't mean his words or actions did not have the effect that Professor Hill states, but only that she was successful in concealing the resulting trauma from him—a concealment that women have carefully developed over the years in the workplace.

Why should this surprise us? Women and men often experience the same event differently. Men experience their behavior from the perspective of those who have power; women from the perspective of those upon whom that power is exercised.

If an employer asks an employee for a date, and she declines, perhaps he has forgotten about it by the time he gets to the parking lot. No big deal, he says to himself. You ask someone out and she says no. You forget about it. In fact, repairing a wounded male ego often requires that you forget about it. But the female employee? She is now frozen, partly with fear, wondering: What if I said yes? Would I have gotten promoted? Would he have expected more than a date? Will I now get fired? Will someone else get promoted over me? What should I do? And so, she will do what millions of women do in that situation: she calls her friends, who counsel her to let the matter rest, and get on with her work. And she remembers, for a long, long time. Who, therefore, is likely to have a better memory: those in power or those against whom that power is deployed?

This is precisely the divergence in experience that characterizes the controversies that led Senator Bob Packwood to resign from the U.S. Senate. Long a public supporter of women's causes, Senator Packwood also apparently chased numerous women around office desks, clumsily trying to have affairs with them. He claims now that alcoholism caused this behavior and that he doesn't remember. You can be sure the women remember.

And what Senator Packwood did so clumsily, it appears former President Clinton did with a sort of effortless ease. Although he was pilloried by a vengeful gaggle of ardent right-wingers, and many Americans were shocked by the allegations of sexual predation that followed him from the Arkansas governor's mansion to the White House, most of the country actually agreed with his claim that he "did not have sexual relations with that woman, Monica Lewinsky." Monica Lewinsky reminded me of those girls in high school who protected their reputations as "good girls" by doing "everything but"—when everything but meant everything but intercourse. Since the only thing that actually "counted" on one's cosmic sexual scorecard was "it," then these girls remained "technical virgins" and their reputations were unsullied. A survey published in the Journal of the American Medical Association backed this up; over two-thirds of Americans surveyed said that "sexual relations" was limited to sexual intercourse and that all other sexual activities did not count. He was telling the truth after all! "Faithful" to his marriage vows in their letter, if not in their spirit, President Clinton also came to represent a certain cavalier predatory male sexuality—delighting in the chase of unavailable women, and using his position as governor and president essentially as a terrific way to meet girls.

Using one's position to hit on women is the kernel of what is objectionable about sexual harassment. It's particularly volatile because it often fuses two levels of power: the power of employers over employees and the power of men over women. Thus what may be said or intended as a man to a woman is also experienced in the context of superior and subordinate, or vice versa. Sexual harassment in the workplace results from men using their public position to demand or extract social relationships. It is the confusion of public and private, bringing together two arenas of men's power over women. Not only are men in positions of power in the workplace, but we are socialized to be the sexual initiators and to see sexual prowess as a confirmation of masculinity.

Sexual harassment is also a way to remind women that they are not yet equals in the workplace, that they really don't belong there. Harassment is most frequent in those occupations and workplaces where women are new and in the minority, such as surgeons, firefighters, and investment bankers. "Men see women as invading a masculine environment," says Louise Fitzgerald, a University of Illinois psychologist. "These are guys whose sexual harassment has nothing whatever to do with sex. They're trying to scare women off a male preserve."

During the Tailhook hearings, Barbara Pope, the only woman on the NIS investigation panel, began to mutter about old-boy networks, foot dragging, and clubbiness, all of which hampered the investigation. "What you don't understand, Barbara," Rear Admiral Mac Williams admonished her, "is that men in the Navy don't want women in the Navy."

"Mac, you don't get it," she replied. "Yes, some men don't want women in the Navy. Things were easier when women weren't there. But if men can't accept women and integrate women into the military, then they shouldn't be there."

When the power of men is augmented by the power of employer over employee, it is easy to understand how humiliating and debilitating sexual harassment can be, and how individual women would be frightened about seeking redress. The workplace is not a level playing field. Subordinates rarely have the resources to complain against managers, whatever the problem.

Some men were confused by Professor Hill's charges, and others have become furious about the issue of sexual harassment because it feels as though women are changing the rules. What used to be routine behavior for men in the workplace is now being defined as sexual harassment. "Clarence Thomas didn't do anything wrong, that any American male hasn't done," commented Dale Whitcomb, a 32-year-old machinist, probably unaware of how right he was. The fact that two-thirds of the men surveyed said they would be complimented if propositioned by a woman at work, gives some idea of the vast gulf between women's and men's perceptions of workplace sexual conduct.

Although men surely do benefit from sexual harassment, I believe that we also have a stake in ending it. First, our ability to form positive and productive relationships with women colleagues in the workplace is undermined. So long as sexual harassment is a daily occurrence and women are afraid of their superiors in the workplace, innocent men's behaviors may be misinterpreted. Second, men's ability to develop social and sexual relationships that are both ethical and exciting is also compromised. If a male boss dates a subordinate, can he really trust that the reason she is with him is because she wants to be? Or will there always be a lingering doubt whether she is there because she is afraid not to be, or because she seeks to please him because of his position?

As men, we should work to end sexual harassment. It is more important than ever to desexualize the workplace, and to begin to listen to women-to listen with a compassion that understands that women's and men's experiences are different, and that men, too, can benefit from the elimination of sexual harassment.

AIDS as a Mens Disease

Surely, men will benefit from the eradication of AIDS. Although we rarely think about HIV in this way, we need to hold this disease up to the gender lens, and to see it through the prism of masculinity. AIDS is one of American men's chief health problems, among the largest causes of death for men aged 35-44 nationwide. AIDS is, perhaps, the most gendered disease in American history. No other disease has ever attacked one gender so disproportionately, except those diseases, like hemophilia, that are sex-linked (to which only males or females are susceptible). AIDS could affect both men and women equally, and throughout the rest of the world (except the United States, Western Europe, and Canada) the rates of infection reach gender parity; that is, in the 80 percent of HIV infections worldwide, half are women and half men. And remember, from unprotected heterosexual intercourse, women are actually more at risk for HIV transmission than men are. But in the United States, over 85 percent of people with AIDS are men.

Let me be clear that I am not saying that one should not be compassionate for women AIDS patients. Of course one must recognize that women are as likely as men to get AIDS from engaging in the same high-risk behaviors. But that's precisely my point: Women don't engage in such behaviors at rates anything like those of men.

One is put at risk for contracting AIDS by engaging in specific high-risk behaviors that ignore potential health risks for more immediate pleasures. For example, sharing needles is both a defiant flaunting of health risks and an expression of community among IV drug users. And the capacity for high-risk behavior—unprotected anal intercourse with large numbers of partners, and the ability to "take it," despite any potential pain—is also a confirmation of masculinity.

And so is accumulation—of money, property, or sexual conquests. It's curious that one of America's most lionized heroes, Magic Johnson, doesn't seem to have been particularly compassionate about the possibility of infecting any of the 2,500 women with whom he reported having sex. Johnson told Sports Illustrated that as a single man, he tried to "accommodate as many women as I could, most of them through unprotected sex." Accommodate? When he protested that his words were misunderstood, he told The New York Times: "I was a bachelor, and I lived a bachelor's life. And I'm paying the price for it. But you know I respect women to the utmost." (I suppose that Wilt Chamberlain, who boasts in his autobiography that he slept with over 20,000 women, respected them almost ten times as much.)

Who Asked For It?

The victims of men's adherence to these norms of masculinity—AIDS patients, rape victims, victims of sexual harassment—did not become victims intentionally. They did not "ask for it." And they certainly do not deserve blame. That some women today are also sexual predators, going to swank bars or waiting outside athletes' locker rooms or trying to score with male subordinates at work, doesn't make William Kennedy Smith, Mike Tyson, Magic Johnson, or Clarence Thomas any less predatory. When predatory animals threaten civil populations, we warn people to stay indoors until the wild animals can be caught. When it's men on the prowl, women engage in a voluntary curfew, unless they want to risk being attacked.

And the men—the date rapists, the sexual harassers, the spreaders of AIDS—are not "perverts" or "deviants" who have strayed from the norms of masculinity. They are, if anything, overconformists to destructive norms of male sexual behavior. Until we change the meaning of manhood, sexual risk-taking and conquest will remain part of the rhetoric of masculinity. And we will scatter the victims, both women and men, along the wayside.

But wait, you might say. The outcomes are pretty varied. On the one hand, VMI and the Citadel lost in court, Clinton was impeached and Packwood resigned, and Iron Mike was convicted in both real court and in the court of public opinion. On the other hand, Magic Johnson remains lionized, Clarence Thomas was confirmed, and William Kennedy Smith was acquitted. Augusta National remains all male, Spur Posse went unpunished, Marv Albert got his job back, and Latrell Sprewell stars for the Knicks whereas his coach got fired. And while a few heads will roll at the Air Force, the structure of male sexual entitlement will remain untouched. Didn't male sexuality actually triumph? I don't think so. Following those proceedings, we've heard a growing critique coming from all sides that has paralleled these formal legal vindications of the men's behaviors. Thomas's confirmation hasn't chilled women's outrage at sexual harassment; in fact, it has fueled it, and currently organizations and corporations are scrambling to put into place procedures to curtail workplace harassment. In an op-ed essay in The New York Times, novelist Mary Lee Settle commented that Anita Hill had, "by her heroic stance, given not only me but thousands of women who have been silenced by shame the courage and the need to speak out about what we have tried for so long to bury and forget." Smith's acquittal may have dampened some victims' impulses to press charges, but date rape is getting the widest hearing it's ever had. And immediately after Magic's revelations of sexual prowess, questions were raised about those faceless 2,500 women and their HIV status.

The Sexual Politics of Safety

The Sexual Bill of Rights and Responsibilities

What links all of these struggles—against sexual harassment, date and acquaintance rape, HIV infection—is that all of them require a sexual politics of safety. The politics of safety may be the missing link in the transformation of men's lives, in their capacity for change. Safety is more than the absence of danger, although that isn't such a bad goal either. Safety is proactive. It is the creation of a space in which all people, women and men, gay and straight, of every color, can experience the fullness of their beings, work to their potential, and express themselves fully.

Think for a moment about how the politics of safety affects the three areas I have discussed in this essay. What is the best way to prevent AIDS? To use sterile needles for intravenous drug injections and to practice "safer sex." Sterile needles and safer sex share one basic characteristic: they both require that men act responsibly. This is not one of the cardinal rules of manhood. Safer sex programs encourage men to have fewer partners, to avoid certain particularly dangerous practices, and to use condoms when having any sex that involves the exchange of bodily fluids. In short, safer sex programs encourage men to stop having sex like men. To men, you see, "safer sex" is an oxymoron, one of those juxtapositions of terms that produce a nonsensical outcome. That which is sexy is not safe, that which is safe is not sexy. Sex is about danger, risk, excitement; safety is about comfort, softness, and security.

Seen this way, it is not surprising to find, as some researchers have found, that one-fourth of urban gay men report that they have not changed their unsafe sexual behaviors. What is, in fact, astonishing is that slightly more than three-fourths *have* changed and are now practicing safer sex.

What heterosexual men could learn from the gay community's response to AIDS is how to eroticize that responsibility—something that women have been trying to teach men for decades. Making safer sex into sexy sex has been one of the great transformations of male sexuality accomplished by the gay community. And straight men could also learn a thing or two about caring for one another through illness, supporting one another in grief, and maintaining a resilience in the face of a devastating disease and the callous indifference of the larger society.

Safety is also the animating condition for women's expression of sexuality. While safety may be a turnoff for men (comfort, softness, and security are the terms of postorgasmic detumescence, not sexual arousal), safety is a precondition for sexual agency for women. Only when women feel safe can they give their sexuality full expression. For men, hot sex leaves a warm afterglow; for women, warmth builds to heat, but warmth is not created by heat.

This perspective helps explain that curious finding in the sex research literature about the divergence of women's and men's sexualities as they age. We believe that men reach their sexual peak at around eighteen, and then go into steady, and later more precipitous, decline for the rest of their lives; while women hit their sexual stride closer to thirty, with the years between twenty-seven and thirty-eight as their peak years. Typically, we understand these changes as having to do with differences in biology—that hormonal changes find men feeling soft and cuddly just as women are getting all steamed up. But aging does not produce such changes in every culture; that is, biology doesn't seem to work the same way everywhere.

What biological explanations leave out is the way that men's and women's sexualities are related to each other, and the way that both are shaped by the institution of marriage. Marriage makes one's sexuality more predictable—the partner, the timing, the experience—and it places sex *always* in the context of the marital relationship. Marriage makes sex safer. No wonder women find their sexuality heightening—they finally feel safe enough to allow their sexual desires to be expressed. And no wonder men's sexuality deflates—there's no danger, risk, or excitement left.

Safety is a precondition for women's sexual expression. Only when a woman is certain, beyond the shadow of a doubt, that her "no" means "no," can she ever say "yes" to her own sexual desires. So if we men are going to have the sexual relationships with exciting, desiring women that we say we want, then we have to make the environment safe enough for women to express their desires. We have to make it absolutely certain to a woman that her "no" means "no"—no matter how urgently we feel the burning of our own desires.

To do this we will need to transform the definition of what it means to be a real man. But we have to work fast. AIDS is spreading rapidly, and date rape and sexual harassment are epidemic in the nation's colleges and workplaces. As AIDS spreads, and as women speak up about these issues, there are more and more people who need our compassion and support. Yet compassion is in relatively short supply among American men, since it involves the capacity of taking the role of the other, of seeing ourselves in someone else's shoes, a quality that contradicts the manly independence we have so carefully cultivated.

Sexual democracy, just like political democracy, relies on a balance between rights and responsibilities, between the claims of the individual and the claims of the community. When one discusses one's sexual rights—that each person, every woman and man, has an equal right to pleasure—men understand immediately what you mean. Women often look delighted and a little bit surprised. Add to the Bill of Sexual Rights a notion of responsibility, in which each of us treats sexual partners as if they had an integrity equal to our own, and it's the men who look puzzled. "Responsibility? What's that got to do with sex? I thought sex was about having fun."

Sure it is, but it's also political in the most intimate sense. Sexual democracy doesn't have to mean no sex. It means treating your partner as someone whose lust is equal to yours and also as someone whose life is equally valuable. It's about enacting in daily life one's principles, claiming our rights to pleasure, and making sure that our partners also feel safe enough to be able to fully claim theirs. This is what we demand for those who have come to America seeking refuge—safety—from political tyranny. Could we ask any less for those who are now asking for protection and refuge from millennia of sexual tyranny?

CODA

It's been ten years since I wrote the first draft of this essay—ten years in which dramatic progress has been matched by equally dramatic setbacks. Despite a noticeable increase in the number of men who have become active in these campaigns—organizing campus groups against sexual assault, rape, and harassment, as well as programming to engage other men in these efforts—the majority continue to believe that transforming a rape culture is "women's work."

And why shouldn't they believe it? After all, most of the programming we do around sexual assault and date rape on campus focuses entirely on the women. To be sure, we tell the men "don't do it, or else." But that's often the end of the conversation with men. The women, however, are given heavy responsibilities. We tell them what to wear and what not to wear, which parties to attend and which to avoid, what to drink and what not to drink, how late to stay out and how to get themselves home. We tell them to always go to parties with a trusted friend, to never lose sight of that friend, even to follow each other into the bathroom, and to make sure to taste each other's drinks.

Now let me be completely clear here: women must do all of these things to reduce their risk of sexual assault. But what such measures imply about men is that unless women compromise their liberties, remain eternally vigilant, and modify their activities, we men will be all over them in an instant. By pitching our safety programs entirely to women, we assume an utterly unsavory—and unfair—image of men as testosterone-crazed sexual predators.

I think we can do better than this. Part of transforming a rape culture means transforming masculinity, encouraging and enabling men to make other choices about what we do with our bodies, and insisting that men utilize their own agency to make different sorts of choices. To ignore men, to believe that women alone will transform a rape culture, freezes men in a posture of defensiveness, defiance, and immobility.

Nowhere is this better expressed than on a "splash guard" that a colleague devised for Rape Awareness Week at his university, which I have been taking to campuses around the country. For those who don't know, a splash guard is the plastic grate that is placed in men's public urinals to prevent splatter. These simple devices are placed in urinals all over campus. And if used as directed, you would see that my colleague's version comes with a helpful little slogan: "You hold the power to stop rape in your hand."

Note

My thinking on these issues has benefitted enormously from collaborative work with Michael Kaufman and the late Martin Levine. The material in the sections on sexual harassment and AIDS draws from that collaborative work, and I am grateful to them for their insights and support.

ARTICLE 53

Robert Reid-Pharr

It's Raining Men

Notes on the Million Man March

Perhaps the most curious feature of the 1995 Million Man March was the way that this massive political demonstration, at least twice the size of the historic 1963 March on Washington, actually worked to reinforce the racial commonsense of the nation. At a moment when the enemies of Black America had consolidated with frightening determination, Minister Louis Farrakhan, his supporters, and even his detractors encouraged the notion that at the root of the difficulties facing Black Americans is a certain male lack—an inability, or unwillingness, to take responsibility as *men* to stand up for community and self.

It was probably an unintended irony that the rhetoric of the march organizers echoed Daniel Patrick Moynihan's infamous 1965 report, "The Negro Family: The Case for National Action," with its diagnosis of pathologies plaguing black families and communities. This resonance, which went largely unremarked, is central to the way the march forced so many of us to rehearse the assorted racial, sexual, and political identities by which we define ourselves and that define us. "Who are you?" the march asked. "Black or not-black? Man or not-man?"

It should be clear to most observers that the way Farrakhan and the other march organizers answered these questions—with appeals to a revitalized patriarchy—worked to reinforce traditional gender norms. What is less obvious is the way that this black spectacle restaged the *racial* commonsense of the nation, the same commonsense that animates much of the conservative rhetoric about issues and policies most directly associated with black communities, especially affirmative action and welfare. In the face of shrinking public resources and an evangelical zeal to "reinvent" (read: dismantle) government, Black Americans were once again advised that self-help is the best medicine. The black man was instructed to return home and start providing for kith and kin, to stop making excuses about the scarcity of legitimate well-paying jobs, and to access his inner manhood, that great and mysterious wellspring of masculinity hidden deep within his psyche, waiting to be harnessed to the project of a beautiful black tomorrow. This all-powerful masculinity was offered as the solution to, and compensation for, the stark curtailments of resources and opportunities that confront Black American men (and everyone else) in this country.

In this light, at a celebration of black masculinity predicated on the absence of black women, it is interesting to consider the question of black gay men's participation in the event. For, if the real message of the march was that it is going to take a heroic black masculinity to restore order to our various communities, especially poor and working-class communities, then it follows that black gay men are irrelevant, or even dangerous, to that project. And, if the march itself was intended to re-create a masculine community of agency and responsibility through the archetypical figures of father and son, then the surreptitious presence of the lover threatened to undo the logic of the event itself.

From Robert Reid-Pharr. *Black Gay Man Essays.* New York: NYU Press, 2001. © 2001 by NYU. Reprinted with permission.

In the weeks prior to the march, the gay press was full of speculation over the proper stance black gay men should take toward Farrakhan, the other march organizers, and the march itself. The National Black Lesbian and Gay Leadership Forum vacillated on the question, finally encouraging gay men to attend and to make their presence known. Activists staged a premarch rally and tried to convince Ben Chavis, the march's executive director, to agree to have an openly gay speaker address the crowd from the podium.

The debate revolved around the question of whether black gay men should support an event so closely identified with Minister Louis Farrakhan, who has made no secret of his homophobia. (In Oakland, California, in 1990 Farrakhan told a crowd, "If God made you for a woman, you can't go with a man . . . you know what the penalty of this is in the Holy Land? Death.") More to the point, black gay men, even if they stayed home, were again confronted with a rather awkward set of questions. Faced with a celebration of a stable—that is, Afrocentric, bourgeois, and heterosexual—black masculinity, gay men who felt compelled by the march had to decide among a number of plausible responses. They could reject the event itself as "not truly black" because of the homophobia and misogyny in which it trafficked. They could think of the march as representative of a flawed blackness that might be repaired by making a significant black gay presence visible at the event (which many did) or by intervening with the march organizers (which a few attempted). And, finally, they could acknowledge the basic logic of Farrakhan's rhetoric. For, if the definition of blackness hinges on heterosexuality, then either blackness and homosexuality are incommensurable (and black gays are not really black) or the notion of blackness is untenable, as witnessed by the undeniable existence of large numbers of black gay men.

This last position, of course, is most difficult to accept. It flies directly in the face of much within contemporary black gay and lesbian thought, which most often represents black gays and lesbians as integral, if beleaguered, members of the black family—witness *Brother to Brother, Home Girls, Sister Outsider,* works shepherded by Essex Hemphill, Barbara Smith, and Audre Lorde, respectively. Indeed, the gay response to the march dramatizes the fact that there are remarkably few spaces—even those inhabited by black gays and lesbians—in which one might contest the most basic assumptions that underlie American race and gender identity. Even in the midst of raucous and intense disagreement, the idea of race emerges unscathed. Indeed, blackness has been bolstered, insofar as we all were forced, at least those of us who are black *and* otherwise, to scurry for cover under the great black mantle, to fly our colors, the good old red, black, and green, even as we attempted to resist the homophobic assumptions that structured the event.

More than a political demonstration with concrete political demands, Farrakhan's march was a sort of race spectacle. Following Guy Debord, we should look to locate its meaning not in the striking images it produced or in our individual responses but in the social relationships constructed by and through these images. Debord doubts that transcendence can be located within the spectacle. For him, spectacles are never progressive events; rather, they represent and reaffirm the larger society. Debord writes, "For what the spectacle expresses is the total practice of one particular economic and social formation's *agenda*. It is also the historical moment by which we happen to be governed."

His point is well taken. Those of us interested in progressive politics desperately need to reconsider the efficacy of the marches, protests, and demonstrations that convulsed the American public sphere in the past century, as well as the ways in which their themes (civil rights, antiwar, gay pride) are constrained by the nature of the event. Mustering enthusiasm for these events requires a fair dose of ignorance about the contentiousness that invariably surrounds them—disagreements that most often turn on the organizers' unwillingness to push the boundaries of their political and social agendas. I am reminded here of the successful struggle initiated by Anna Arnold Hedgeman to have women included among the speakers on the platform at the 1963 march, as well as the significant opposition to Bayard Rustin's leadership in its planning because of his homosexuality and his ties to leftists. That march has become an important part of the American national memory because it so clearly articulated the rather limited language and values of a liberal America. Indeed, King's "I Have a Dream" speech receives much of its force from the evocation of an ethos that is at once Christian and American nationalist, supporting, in the process, a liberal integrationist agenda that insists upon the expansiveness—and expansion—of the nation.

Mass public spectacles have been a regular means by which changing ideas of race have been disseminated to the American populace. As early as 1895, Booker T. Washington called for black reconciliation with the very whites who were the architects of segregation, disfranchisement, and systematic racist terror, thereby rearticulating the emerging racialist—and segregationist—commonsense. Washington's particular genius, evident in his Atlanta Cotton States Exposition speech, was his ability to articulate a conservative racial politics to whites, particularly white southerners, while captivating many blacks with a message that spoke to their basic desire to be admitted as equal participants in American public life. "In all things that are purely social," he argued, "we can be as separate as the fingers, yet one as the hand in all things essential to mutual progress."

It is a compelling irony that the sensibility behind Washington's words should so deeply inform the 1995 rhetoric of Louis Farrakhan. Specifically, both men call for black self-sufficiency, if not self-determination; both swallow, more or less whole, frankly segregationist notions about the proper interaction between the races; and both, oddly enough, subscribe to the myth of America. As Farrakhan proclaimed at the march:

> There's no country like this on Earth. And certainly if I lived in another country, I might never have had the opportunity to speak as I speak today. I probably would have been shot outright, and so would my brother Jesse, and so would Maulana Karenga, and so would Dr. Ben Chavis and Reverend Al Sharpton and all the wonderful people that are here. But because this is America, you allow me to speak even though you don't like what I may say.

Of all the curiosities uttered by minister Farrakhan during the march, including the extended numerological analysis, the excoriation of presidents past and present, the religious rhetoric of atonement, and so forth, I was least prepared for this hackneyed bit of American exceptionalism. It was tempting to read this gesture as mere anomaly, the kind of unnecessary bombast that cushions overly long or ambitious speeches. But I suggest we take this piece of Farrakhan's rhetoric seriously—indeed, that we recognize in it the key to his success that day, as he spoke to the assembled masses on the Mall and to the nation.

Minister Farrakhan's particular talent is his ability to sensitize wildly diverse black audiences to their very real oppression while steering them not simply away from a critique of the political and economic structures of the United States but toward a reinvestment in the very ideological processes that work to create and maintain those structures. It is true that Farrakhan regularly points out the evil of the American enterprise: slavery, segregation, disfranchisement, continued and continual racial degradation. But, instead of leading his followers toward radical critique, Farrakhan chooses instead to return again and again to an essentially therapeutic mode in which he plays the role of the good father come back to set the (national) house in order.

At the Million Man March—"a glimpse of heaven," as the Nation of Islam's newspaper, *The Final Call,* had it—Louis Farrakhan put himself forward as the emblem, the ideal type, if you will, of a newly emergent black masculinity. He appeared as a shining exemplar of a renewed Black Man, striking the posture of the stern, if gentle, father, savior, patriarch, messiah. He scorned our enemies while asking us only to look inward, to find the evil therein and to cast it out. If we did so, he prophesied, if only we could learn to humble ourselves, we would surely see a new dawn of cleanliness and order, the Black Millennium. He stood, then, as a sort of Emersonian representative man, embodying a masculinity so pure that simply by gazing upon it one could extinguish the fires of ambiguity and uncertainty that rage in the hearts of black men across America.

The agreement on the part of the march's organizers to discourage black women's participation implicitly shored up Farrakhan's myth making. I never could quite understand why a demonstration about the plight of Black Americans had to be gendered in the first place. (Wouldn't two Million Black People beat one Million Black Men?) With this strategy—an obvious insult to black women—the march organizers showed themselves to be concerned primarily with lending a certain ontological stability to men whose identities are increasingly complex. The injunction to keep the women at home helped channel public debates about the march into familiar territory, the ongoing "crisis of Black American gender relations." In that sense, the sexist rhetoric and the many responses it provoked simply represented business as usual. It was a forceful restatement à la Moynihan of the terms we have used to discuss (Black) American cultural, political, and economic life since at least the 1960s.

Fundamental changes in American political and economic life are currently being debated in a conversation still largely dominated by the Republican right and their Democratic look-alikes. What is disconcerting about this is the way rhetorics of blackness (such as Ronald Reagan's "welfare queen" and George Bush's "Willie Horton") have been coupled not simply with critiques of black communities but also with even blistering attacks on affirmative action, welfare, education, social service initiatives, and so forth. While the march was still in progress, President Clinton made a speech at the University of Texas in which, after distancing himself from Farrakhan, he praised the black men who attended the event for taking responsibility for themselves and for *their* communities. He then went on to make a rather predictable speech on race relations in which he suggested, among other things, that it is not racism that motivates a mother to pull her child close when she passes a black man in a crime-ridden neighborhood.

What is disturbing about this line of argument is not only the crude manner in which it reaffirms the myth of the Dangerous Black Man, The Black Beast, but the way that it reiterates a racialist logic that stands at the root of this country's many woes. The idea that there are discrete black communities beset by black problems that can and should be solved exclusively by black people is precisely the logic of segregation, no matter how empowered individual black people may feel in the process of its articulation. What connects Clinton and Farrakhan, then, is that neither has yet seen his way clear of the pernicious racialism that increasingly dominates American public life.

Despite my reservations about the ideological underpinnings of the march, it would be untrue to say that I do not understand what drew hundreds of thousands of individuals to Washington on that October day. I went, full of skepticism yes, but also expectant, even hopeful. The first thing that struck me was that it was *not* a march but more of a *happening*. I am accustomed to marches on Washington with thousands of people—singly or in more or less well-organized groups—streaming down Pennsylvania Avenue en route to the Mall. Usually the architects of the mass action try to divvy up the crowd into state-based bodies, collectivities of gender and race, various political and social organizations, groups of students, dignitaries, and so forth. The Million Man March had none of this. The few banners and signs that dotted the crowds were largely homemade, expressing local and specific concerns. Moreover, there were surprisingly few individuals who could be clearly identified as members of the Nation of Islam or even as Muslim. The emphasis was on similarity, the incredible and moving oneness we all shared.

I should acknowledge here how exciting, titillating even, this oneness actually felt. The beauty of the men was startling. It hung in the air like the smoke of incense, intoxicating us all, calling into existence a fantastic vision of community—a glimpse of heaven, indeed. The entire event, not to mention the debates that framed it, was wholly overdetermined by a kind of black-inflected homoeroticism. It seemed that we men could enact millions of tiny instances of love and desire—a touch, a glance, murmurings of "Pardon me brother," "Excuse me sir"—precisely because the women were absent. What remained was a sort of naked masculinity.

A teenaged boy comes up to me. I see his baggy clothes, his corn-rowed hair, the cocky lilt in his walk, before I see him. His face is flushed as if he has just witnessed something beautiful and terrible both, like he has just survived a natural disaster or awakened from some horrible fever. He takes my hand, places his other arm around my shoulder, and says, "All this unity, all this love," presses close to me for an instant, then releases me and keeps moving. I am stunned, caught up in the moment. I imagine that I really have seen this boy, that he has seen me. I am no longer afraid but, on the contrary, rather giddy, glad to be here, to have been part of all this.

At Union Station, I buy a disposable camera and begin taking snapshots of other anomalies in the crowd: women, the elaborately dressed, the not-black. In looking back over these pictures, now as then, I think that there is something incredibly satisfying about seeing reflected, if only for a brief while and through a deeply flawed lens, an image of an equitable, just, and peaceful community. It felt like freedom, a new beginning. Indeed, for a moment, I felt that I had regained that which was lost, had seen beyond the horizon.

Still, as Paul Gilroy has suggested, it is unsettling that the notion of (black) freedom seems so inevitably dependent on polarities of sex and gender and is so often accompanied by a certain desperate insistence on black sexual potency. It seems that the idea of freedom has been so overwritten by fantasies of race and gender that it has become nearly impossible to imagine it without reference to those same fantasies. "The Black Man," as the rhetoric of both the right and the left would have it, is the most *unfree* of American citizens. As huge numbers of black men in this country languish in prisons or under the stewardship of assorted probation and parole boards; as black men continue to be over-represented in the drug trade and among the legions of persons with chronic illnesses—H.I.V., cancer, heart disease, alcoholism, depression—as we give our lives over to violence or to a certain silent despair, we have become the very emblems of the ugliness, the bestiality, the barbarism by which the rest of America, particularly white America, can view itself as liberal and free. The image in my mind now is of Rodney King's beating: the endless blows, the irrationality of the white policemen's rage as they labored to drive this black beast even deeper into their collective unconscious. It is possible to chart the past several decades of American cultural and political life by lining up our black male martyrs, criminals, and infamous celebrities: King, Malcolm, Medgar Evers, Louis Farrakhan, Clarence Thomas, Mike Tyson, Willie Horton, Yusef Hawkins, O. J. Simpson, Abner Louima. The list grows continually.

If freedom were truly the ultimate goal of the march, then it was freedom of a discrete, limited kind: freedom from the crushing burden of images—the criminal, the addict, the vengeful lover, the victim, the invalid. Instead, we were presented with an ocean of men, orderly, directed, clean-cut, and remarkably eloquent. Even in their silences. At the march, in the act of rethinking and reenacting our disparate identities, we felt an intimation of some larger notion.

Here, then, despite the regressive racial and gender politics that framed the Million Man March, there were countless improvisational moments of transcendence. The reality of all public spectacles is that the outcome is never certain; no one can confidently predict what its attendees will take away from it, what meanings its many participants will attribute to it. The sad part is that the march organizers evinced so little respect for this wondrously messy and ambiguous process. Once again we were urged to mount the tired horse of black patriarchy. Ministers Farrakhan and Chavis worked to yoke the energy of the event to a simplistic—and segregationist—racial ideology. I still yearn, then, for a vision of the good, for a public dialogue and a civic life that celebrates multiplicity, that prizes ambiguity, that recognizes the play of identity and difference that makes possible community as well as change.

CONTRIBUTORS

JUDI ADDELSTON, Ph.D., received her doctorate at the City University of New York Graduate School and University Center in 1996. She is currently a professor of psychology at Valencia Community College in Orlando, Florida. In addition, she has a private practice in marriage and family therapy and mental health counseling.

TOMÁS ALMAGUER is Associate Professor of American Studies at the University of California, Santa Cruz, and Associate Professor of Sociology and American Culture at the University of Michigan, Ann Arbor. His book, *Racial Fault Lines: The Historical Origins of White Supremacy*, was published by University of California Press.

TIM BENEKE is a freelance writer and editor living in the San Francisco Bay Area. He is the author of *Men on Rape* and *Proving Manhood*.

A. AYRES BOSWELL is a supervisor at a foster care agency in New York City. She works with abused and neglected children, trying to achieve permanency in the children's lives by reunification with their birth parents or by locating adoptive resources.

LIONEL CANTÚ, Assistant Professor of Sociology at the University of California, Santa Cruz, specialized in sexuality influences on migration. His dissertation, "Border Crossings: Mexican Men and the Sexuality of Migration," analyzed Mexican Men who have sex with men, and how sexual identity changes in different cultural contexts. He died at the age of 36 in 2002.

ROCCO L. (CHIP) CAPRARO, Senior Associate Dean and Assistant Professor of History, is the founding coordinator of the men's studies program and founding director of the rape prevention education program for men at Hobart and William Smith Colleges, Geneva, New York. He received his B.A. from Colgate University and his Ph.D. from Washington University, and is a consultant and public speaker in the areas of gender and diversity, with an emphasis on masculinity, and is currently writing a brief history of rock and roll from a men's studies perspective.

ANTHONY S. CHEN is Assistant Professor of Sociology and Public Policy at the University of Michigan, Ann Arbor. Chen is interested in social inequality, American political development, and public policy, with a special focus on regulation; he is currently completing a book entitled, *From Fair Employment to Affirmative Action: Jobs, Politics, and Civil Rights in the United States, 1941–1972*. He received his B.A. from Rice University and his M.A. and Ph.D. in sociology from the University of California, Berkeley. His article was originally his M.A. thesis, which he wrote under the supervision of Arlie Hochschild.

JUDY CHICAGO is an artist, author, feminist, and educator. One of the pioneers of Feminist Art, her installation, "The Dinner Party" (1974–1979) was a monumental media project, a symbolic history of women in Western Civilization. Subsequent projects have included "The Birth Project," "The Holocaust Project," and "Powerplay". She lives in New Mexico.

SUSAN D. COCHRAN currently teaches at California State University, Northridge.

MARIANNE COOPER is a doctoral student in sociology at the University of California, Berkeley. Her article, *Being the "Go-To-Guy": Fatherhood, Masculinity, and the Organization of Work in Silicon Valley*, grew out of the research she conducted for her master's thesis. Her research was supported by the Cal@Silicon Valley fellowship.

ANGELA COWAN is a postgraduate student in the Department of Sociology at the University of Newcastle. Her thesis topic is an investigation of the discursive world of young children. She is a trained primary school schoolteacher and has worked as an observer on a number of psychiatric research projects.

TIMOTHY JON CURRY is in the Department of Sociology at the Ohio State University.

JULIA O'CONNELL DAVIDSON is Professor of Sociology at the University of Nottingham in the

United Kingdom with a focus on gender, race, class and global inequalities, and contract, employment relations, selfhood, and human rights. She has conducted studies of entrepreneurial prostitution, sex tourism, and children's involvement in the global sex trade.

FRANCINE M. DEUTSCH is Professor of Psychology at Mount Holyoke College, and the author of *Halving It All: How Equality Shared Parenting Works* (1999, Harvard University Press), a study of the division of domestic labor among dual-earner couples. Her articles on gender and the family have been published in *Journal of Personality* and *Social Psychology, Psychology of Women Quarterly, Sex Roles, Journal of Family Issues,* and *Current Directions in Psychology*. Her most recent research examines the gendered life plans of Chinese college seniors in the People's Republic of China, and plans for egalitarian marriage among graduating college seniors in the U.S.A.

RAFAEL M. DIAZ is a social worker and developmental psychologist who is on the faculty of AIDS Prevention Studies at University of California, San Francisco. His current research project is a "sociocultural model of HIV risk in Latino gay men."

SHARI LEE DWORKIN is a Post-Doctoral Research Fellow at the HIV Center for Clinical and Behavioral Studies (New York State Psychiatric Institute and Columbia University, Mailman School of Public Health) where she carries out gender, sexuality, and HIV research. Her journal articles have appeared in *Sociological Perspectives, the Sociology of Sport Journal,* and *The Journal of Sport and Social Issues*. She was guest coeditor (with Michael A. Messner) of a special issue of *Sociological Perspectives* on gender and sport (Winter, 2002) and currently serves on the editorial board of *Gender and Society*. She is coauthor of *Built to Win: The Female Athlete as Cultural Icon* (April, 2003, University of Minnesota Press).

MARTÍN ESPADA is the author of seven books of poetry, including *City of Coughing and Dead Radiators* and *Imagine the Angels of Bread*. A former tenant lawyer, he teaches literature at University of Massachusetts, Amherst.

YEN LE ESPIRITU is Professor of Ethnic Studies at the University of California, San Diego. She is the author of *Asian American Panethnicity: Bridging Institutions and Identities, Filipino American Lives,* and *Asian American Women and Men: Labor, Laws, and Love*. She is also serving as the President of the Association of Asian American Studies.

ANNE FAUSTO-STERLING is Professor of Biology and Women's Studies in the Division of Biology and Medicine at Brown University. She is the author of *Myths of Gender: Biological Theories about Women and Men,* and has also written broadly about the role of race and gender in the construction of scientific theory and the role of such theories.

JULES FEIFFER is a syndicated cartoonist and was a regular contributor to *The Village Voice*.

ANN FERGUSON is Assistant Professor of Women's Studies and African American Studies at Smith College. She received her Ph.D. in Sociology from University of California at Berkeley.

MICHELLE FINE, Distinguished Professor of Social Psychology at the Graduate Center, CUNY, has taught there since 1990. Her work concerns questions of social injustice in schools, prisons, and communities. She draws from feminist psychology, critical race, and Marxist thought. She looks at the spaces of possibility in which youth struggle for what could be and against what is; the relation of scholarship and activism; and questions of theory, ethics, and method in participatory research.

RICHARD FUNG is a writer, independent video artist, and cultural cricic in Toronto, Canada. He has produced tapes including "Fighting Chance: Gay Asian Men and HIV" (1980) and "My Mother's Place" (1990), while contributing articles to *Fuse* magazine and *Moving the Image: Independent Asian Pacific American Media Arts* (1991).

THOMAS J. GERSCHICK is Associate Professor of Sociology at Illinois State University. His research focuses on identity, and marginalized and alternative masculinities.

JULIA MARUSZA HALL received her Ph.D. from the University at Buffalo, State University of New York. Hall is the author of articles that have appeared in *Anthropology, Education Quarterly*, and *The Urban Review*, among others. She currently teaches Social Foundations of Education at D'Youville College in Buffalo, New York.

MICHAEL C. HANCHARD is a Professor of Political Science at Northwestern University. He is the author of *Orpheus and Power: Afro-Brazilian Social Movements in Rio de Janeiro and Sao Paolo, 1945–1988*. He is currently working on a project on race, modernity, and the politics of the African dispora.

KEVIN D. HENSON is Associate Professor of Sociology at Loyola University Chicago. He is the author of *Just a Temp* (1996) and co-editor of *Unusual Occupations* (2000). His research focuses on gender and nonstandard employment. He has written about the role of clerical temporary employment in recreating racial and gender inequalities, and is currently working on a project on traveling nurses.

BELL HOOKS is a writer and lecturer who speaks on issues of race, class, and gender. She teaches at CUNY Graduate Center. Her books include *Ain't I a Woman*, *Feminist Theory*, and *Talking Back*. Her column, "Sisters of the Yam," appears monthly in *Z* magazine.

ELLEN JORDAN is Senior Lecturer in the Department of Sociology at the University of Newcastle. She was for many years a teacher in primary schools. Her major research interests are women's work in nineteenth-century Britain and gender construction in early childhood.

ROBIN D. G. KELLEY is a Professor of History and Africana at New York University and the author of *Hammer and Hoe: Alabama Communists During the Great Depression* (1990) and *Race Rebels* (1994).

MICHAEL S. KIMMEL is Professor of Sociology at SUNY at Stony Brook. His books include *Changing Men* (1987), *Men Confront Pornography* (1990), *Men in the United States* (1992), *Manhood in America* (1996), *The Politics of Manhood* (1996) and *The Gendered Society* (2000). He is the editor of *masculinities*, a scholarly journal, and national spokesperson for the National Organization for Men Against Sexism (NOMAS).

BARBARA KRUGER is an artist in New York City.

TERRY A. KUPERS practices psychiatry in Oakland, California, and is Institute Professor at The Wright Institute in Berkeley. He consults with several public mental health agencies, and has testified in many class action lawsuits about the psychological consequences of harsh prison conditions, the quality of mental health services "Inside," and the issue of prison rape in men's and women's prisons. He is active in the National Organization for Men Against Sexism, California Prison Focus, Critical Resistance and Stop Prisoner Rape (website: www.spr.org). His books include *Revisioning Men's Lives: Gender, Intimacy and Power* (Guilford, 1992) and *Prison Madness: The Mental Health Crisis Behind Bars and What We Must Do About It* (Wiley/Jossey-Bass, 1999). He is also co-editor of *Prison Masculinities* (Temple University Press, 2001).

PETER LEHMAN is a Professor in the Interdisciplinary Humanities Program and the Hispanic Research Center at Arizona State University. He is author of *Running Scared: Masculinity and the Representation of the Male Body* and the editor of *Defining Cinema*.

PETER LYMAN is University Dean of Libraries at the University of California, Berkeley.

PAT MAHONY is Professor of Education at Roehampton Institute, London. She has worked for many years in the areas of equal opportunities and teacher education. Her books include *Schools for the Boys?*, *Promoting Quality and Equality in Schools*, and *Changing Schools*.

MANNING MARABLE is Professor and Director of the Center for African American Studies at Columbia University.

VICKIE M. MAYS currently teaches at University of California, Los Angeles.

JAMES MESSERSCHMIDT is Professor of Sociology in the Criminology Department at the University of Southern Maine. His research interests focus on the interrelation of gender, race, class, and crime. In addition to numerous articles and book chapters, he is the author of *The Trial of Leonard Peltier* (South End Press, 1983), *Capitalism, Patriarchy, and Crime: Toward a Socialist Feminist Criminology* (Rowman & Littlefield, 1986), *Masculinities and Crime: Critique and Reconceptualization of Theory*

(Rowman & Littlefield, 1993), *Crime as Structured Action: Gender, Race, Class, and Crime in the Making* (Sage, 1997), *Criminology* (3rd edition), with Piers Beirne (Westview, 1999), and *Nine Lives: Adolescent Masculinities, the Body, and Violence* (2000, Westview Press).

MICHAEL A. MESSNER is Professor of Sociology and Gender Studies at the University of Southern California. He is co-editor of *Through the Prism of Difference: Readings on Sex and Gender* (1997). His books include *Power at Play: Sports and the Problem of Masculinity* (1992), and *Politics of Masculinities: Men in Movements* (1997).

ADAM STEPHEN MILLER was a master's degree student in journalism at University of Michigan and an organizer of an Internet disability support group. He died in 1997.

BRIAN MILLER is a psychotherapist in West Hollywood, California. He writes a popular advice column for the gay community called "Out for Good." Besides gay husbands and fathers, he has researched victims of anti-gay violence.

ALREDO MIRANDÉ is Professor of Sociology and Ethnic Studies at the University of California, Riverside. He is the author of *The Age of Crisis, La Chicana, The Chicano Experience,* and *Gringo Justice.*

PETER M. NARDI is Professor of Sociology at Pitzer College. He has published articles on AIDS, anti-gay crimes and violence, magic and magicians, and alcoholism and families. His books include *Men's Friendships* (1993) and *Growing Up Before Stonewall* (1994), with David Sanders and Judd Marmor. He has served as co-president of the Los Angeles chapter of the Gay and Lesbian Alliance Against Defamation.

TIMOTHY NONN received his Ph.D. at the Graduate Theological Union in Berkeley and wrote a dissertation on faith and masculinity among poor men. He has a background in community organizing among rural and urban poor and refugees. He has published several articles on religion, gender, and poverty.

JENNIFER PIERCE is Associate Professor of American Studies at the University of Minnesota. She is author of *Gender Trials: Emotional Lives in Contemporary Law Firms* (California 1995).

BETH A. QUINN is an Associate Professor in the Department of Sociology at Montana State University-Bozeman. She received her Ph.D. in Criminology, Law, and Society from the University of California-Irvine. Drawing primarily on feminist and masculinity theories and neo-institutional organizational theory, her research focuses on legal complaint-making and discrimination law. This research has been published in journals such as *Law and Social Inquiry* and *Gender & Society*. She is currently exploring how human resources understand and deal with sexual harassment law.

ROBERT REID-PHARR is Professor of English at the Graduate Center of the City University of New York. He is the author of two books: *Conjugal Union, the Body, the House and the Black American* (Oxford 1999) and *Black Gay Man: Essays* (NYU 2001). He lives in Brooklyn.

M. ROCHLIN is the creator of "The Heterosexual Questionnaire."

JACKIE KRASAS ROGERS'S research interests include gender and racial inequality in work and employment. She explores issues of inequality and employment in her book entitled, *Temps: The Many Faces of the Changing Workplace*. The book documents and analyzes the experiences both of temporary clerical workers and temporary lawyers. Presently, Professor Rogers is working as part of an interdisciplinary research team funded by the National Science Foundation to investigate the underrepresentation of women in the information technology field. Her work has appeared in *Gender & Society* and *Work & Occupations*.

LILLIAN B. RUBIN is a Research Associate at the Institute for the Study of Social Change at University of California, Berkeley, and a psychotherapist in private practice. Her books include *Intimate Strangers, Just Friends, Erotic Wars, Worlds of Pain*, and, most recently, *Families on the Fault Line* and *The Transcendant Child*.

DON SABO is a Professor of Social Sciences at D'Youville College in Buffalo, New York. He has co-authored *Humanism in Sociology, Jock: Sports &*

Male Identity, and *Sport, Men and the Gender Order: Critical Feminist Perspectives*. His most recent books include, *Sex, Violence and Power in Sports: Rethinking Masculinity*, and *Men's Health & Illness: Gender, Power & the Body*. He has conducted many national surveys on gender issues in sport, is a trustee of the Women's Sports Foundation, and co-authored the 1997 Presidents' Council on Physical Fitness and Sports report "Physical Activity & Sport in the Lives of Girls."

RITCH C. SAVIN-WILLIAMS is Professor of Human Development at Cornell University. He is co-editor, with Kenneth M. Cohen, of *The Lives of Lesbians, Gays, and Bisexuals* (Harcourt Brace 1996).

JASON SCHULTZ is a third-year law student at the University of California at Berkeley (Boalt Hall). He graduated from Duke University in 1993 with a degree in public policy studies and honors in women's studies. While at Duke, he volunteered at the Durham County Rape Crisis Center and helped organize Men Acting For Change, a profeminist men's activist group committed to ending violence against women.

JOAN Z. SPADE is Associate Professor of Sociology at Lehigh University. Her previous publications have focused on the interstices of work and family, including the effects of men's and women's parental values. She is currently examining the effects of grouping students in middle schools.

ROBERT STAPLES is in the Department of Sociology at the University of California, San Francisco. He has written widely on black families and gender issues, including his book, *Black Masculinity*.

GLORIA STEINEM is a founding editor of *Ms.*, and the author of *Outrageous Acts and Everyday Rebellions* and *Revolution from Within*.

LANCE STRATE is Assistant Professor of Communications at Fordham University. He is co-author, with Neil Postman, Christine Nystrom, and Charles Weingartner of *Myths, Men and Beer: An Analysis of Beer Commercials on Broadcast Television* and is working on a book on the relationship between media and concepts of the hero.

JACQUELINE SANCHEZ TAYLOR is a researcher on adult sex tourism and child sexual exploitation in Latin America, India, South Africa, and the Caribbean. Her Ph.D. focuses on sexual economic exchanges between female tourists and local men in Jamaica and the Dominican Republic. She is currently a sociology lecturer at the University of Leeds.

FAYE LINDA WACHS is an Assistant Professor of Sociology in the Behavioral Sciences Department at Cal Poly Pomona. Current research projects include a content and textual analysis of men's and women's health and fitness magazines, and interviews with women who participate in sports historically considered "male appropriate." Past projects have examined gender relations in the field of coed softball, and media coverage of HIV+ athletes.

KAREN WALKER has completed her doctorate in the Department of Sociology at the University of Pennsylvania. She is Vice Presidnet of Research at Public/Private Ventures in Philadelphia.

LOIS WEIS is the author or co-author of numerous books and articles pertaining to social class, race, gender and schooling in the United States. Her most recent books include *Silenced Voices and Extraordinary Conversations: Re-Imagining Schools* (Teachers College Press, 2003, with Michelle Fine); *The Unknown City: The Lives of Poor and Working Class Young Adults* (Beacon Press, 1998, with Michelle Fine); *Speed Bumps: A Student Friendly Guide to Qualitative Research* (Teachers College Press, 2000, with Michelle Fine); and *Beyond Black and White: New Faces and Voices in US Schools* (State University of New York Press, 1997, with Maxine Seller). She sits on numerous editorial boards and is the editor of the *Power, Social Identity, and Education* book series with SUNY Press.

CHRISTINE L. WILLIAMS is Professor of Sociology at the University of Texas at Austin. She is author of *Gender Differences at Work* (1989), *Still a Man's World* (1997), and editor of *Doing "Women's Work": Men in Nontraditional Occupations* (1993).

培文书系人文科学英文影印系列 同期推出

文化研究导论
Introducing Cultural Studies
Elainl Baldwin 等 著

■内容简介

这本文化研究导论修订版系统地概述了文化研究的概念、理论和最新的研究。正文从文化理论的讲述开始，然后细述文化的多维性，加强了文化研究跨学科的本性，包括空间、时间、政治、人体和视觉文化等。文化研究导论提供给大学生和研究生多种的训练，包括对于文化研究、英国、地理、社会学、通讯和媒介研究这些领域详细地介绍。

ISBN 7-301-08038-7
定价：45.00 元
（16 开 468 页）
原著书号：0-13-123283-5
（Prentice Hall 2003）
原著定价：£23.99

文化原理与通俗文化导论
Cultural theory and Popular culture: *An Introduction*
John Storey 著

■内容简介

本书是经过作者约翰·斯托里全面广泛修正的第三版，和前两版一样为读者清楚地呈现了关于通俗文化的各种研究理论和研究方法。除这些理论之外，新增加了涉及同性恋理论的部分。对原有的浪漫文学、女性杂志、女权运动、男性研究四部分进行了扩展，增加了新的材料及插图。同时保留前两版的特色，并使用与通俗文化的正文和惯例相关的合适的例子。新版继续保留学生和讲演者最喜欢的内容，适合大学本科生和研究生在文化研究、媒介研究、传播学、文化社会学、通俗文化和其他有关主题方面进行学习。

ISBN 7-301-08050-6
定价：25.00 元
（16 开 240 页）
原著书号：0-582-42363-5
（Prentice Hall 2001）
原著定价：$38.90

女性与学术研究：起源及影响
Women's Studies in the Academy: Origins and Impact
Robyn L. Rosen 著

■内容简介

本书是一部女性研究方面的著作，涉及历史、科学、社会学，经济学等多个重要的学术领域，分析了女性为获得接受高等教育的权利而不断抗争的历史，说明了女权扩张在学术领域里产生的碰撞，以及妇女地位的变化。作者首先从历史视角展开对女性研究发展的考察，指出女性教育要求的根源在于妇女在政治、法律权利上的抗争。历史维度确立后，作者继续探讨了女性研究领域的成就，展示女性研究对学术进步的巨大影响。在方法论上，作者认为在探询和回答相关问题时，学者们的思维方式与态度大多会受其专业学术训练的深刻影响，而本书最有意义的目的则是有助于学生学会批判思考。

ISBN 7-301-07364-X
定价：52.00 元
（16 开 558 页）
原著书号：013092928X
（Prentice Hall 2004）
原著定价：$52.67

北京大学出版社人文社科类图书重点经销商

省份	店名	电话	地址
北京	北大书店	010-62757515 010-62752015	北京大学校内博实商场2楼
	海淀图书城北大读者服务部	010-62534449 010-62523168	北京市海淀图书城5号2层
	三联书店	010-64002710	北京市东城区美术馆东街22号
	涵芬楼书店	010-85117603	北京市东城区王府井大街36号
	风入松书店	010-62625941	北京大学南门外资源东楼地下室
	国林风书店	010-82618384	北京市海淀区西大街36号 昊海楼地下一层
	万圣书店	010-62768750	北京海淀区清华北大教师楼4—5号楼二层
	北京大学新华书店	010-62753275	北京大学三角地
	清华大学新华书店	010-62782410	清华大学校内
	人民大学出版社读者服务部	62510566-230	北京市中关村大街31号
	北京师范大学出版社读者服务部	010-58808104	北京市新街口外大街19号
天津	天津南开大学出版社书店	022-23507092	天津市卫津路94号南开大学校内
	天津南开区书香缘书店	022-23509858	南开大学新图书馆一楼外跨楼梯间书香缘书店
	天津市新华书店高等教育书店	022-23526801	天津大学院内（老图书馆西侧）
河南	郑州二七区新世纪法律书店	0371-6955389	郑州市大学路33号付4号
	三联书店郑州分销店	0371-5367851	郑州市文化路56号（文化路与农业路交汇处金国商厦3楼）
	河南大学出版社书店	0378-2825010	开封市明伦街85号
陕西	西安科技法律书店	029-85218448	西安市长安南路280号
	陕西万邦文化传播有限公司	029-82222531	西安市东大街383号方汇大厦一层万邦书城
广东	汕头三联商务文化中心	0754-8165365	汕头市长平路105号1-2楼
	深圳市新文海图书有限公司	0755-25910358	深圳市八卦三路522栋一楼
	珠海市文华书城有限公司	0756-8881203	珠海市拱北迎宾南路1013号国际大厦负一层国际大厦书城
	广东学而优书店有限公司	020-89027101	广州市海珠区新港西路91-93号
湖南	湖南弘道文化传播有限公司	0731-4431522	长沙市解放中路定王台文化广场15H
浙江	杭州华宝斋古籍书社	0571-88256044	杭州市登云路639号杭州文化商城B区228号
	生活.读书.新知三联书店杭州分销店	0571-88989020	杭州市文三西路沁雅花园康恒大厦
	杭州博大教育图书发行有限公司	0571-86721090	杭州下沙高教园区2号大街18号月雅苑10-1-102号
甘肃	甘肃纸中城邦书业有限公司	0931-8831085	兰州市城关区东岗西路462号
	兰州安宁高教书店	0931-7766637	兰州市安宁东路935号
	兰州学源理工科技图书有限公司	0931-8840555	兰州市七里河区兰工坪路1号
河北	河北大学出版社书店	0312-5033223	河北保定合作路1号
	石家庄学步书店	0311-3800874	石家庄市红旗大街389号

地区	书店	电话	地址
山西	山西尔雅书店有限公司	0351-7231473	山西省太原市双塔西街130号
	太原市文杰大学书店有限公司	0351-4132420	太原市并州路东坡斜巷1号
	山西省外文书店—学府购书中心	0351-7018919	太原市坞城路36号山大旧校门
宁夏	银川市新华书店—宁大店	0951-5018005	银川市解放东街47号
	银川周末文汇书店	0951-5042547	银川市解放西街111号（公安厅对面）
山东	三联书店济南分销店	0531-6096766	济南市院前大街泉城路商业设施F3-8号
江西	南昌市青苑书店	0791-8592290	南昌市洪都北大道图书城1号
福建	厦门华文图书有限公司	0592-2185998	厦门大学图书馆一楼（厦门大学963号信箱）
	福建省厦门市晓风书屋	0592-5816123	厦门市思明南路416-12号
	厦门对外图书交流中心	0592-5054027	厦门市湖滨南路809号
安徽	安徽省导航图书有限公司	0551-5107801	合肥市东至路5号炮院招待所
	合肥考试书店-格致书店	0551-3600141	中国科技大学东区活动中心
	中国科技大学出版社读者服务部	0551-3607380	安徽省合肥市金寨路96号科大东区出版社一楼
四川	西南书局	028-86511882	成都市梨花街2号四川书市2楼7号
	弘文书局	028-86129612	成都市人发西路101号
重庆	重庆大学出版社书店	023-65111509	重庆市沙坪坝正街174号
	重庆精典文化传播有限公司精典书店	023-63734260	重庆市渝中区民权路17号
上海	上海交大昂立图书有限公司	021-32260589	上海市徐汇区广元西路43号惠谷电脑城地下室
	上海季风图书有限公司	021-32260589	上海市陕西南路215号
	上海复旦经世书局	021-65642857	上海杨浦区国权路579号
	上海财大书店	021-65163862	上海中山北路369号
	上海鹿鸣书店	021-65647139	上海国权路334号
广西	广西师范大学出版社大学书店	0773-5806955	桂林市普陀路44号
	广西南国书店	0771-2615485	广西南宁市中山路99号
贵州	贵阳西南风文化发展有限公司	0851-5933050	贵阳市延安东路130号
	贵州西西弗	0851-5811504	贵州市富水南路196号金林广场A栋11楼4号
湖北	湖北政博书刊发行有限公司（图书）	027-87388263	武汉市楚雄大道268-A13号
	湖北三新图书公司	027-87870493	武汉市洪山区楚雄大街龙家湾270号
云南	云南清华实业公司	0871-5314348	昆明12.1大街158号(云南师大)
	昆明新知图书城有限责任公司	0871-4184679	云南省昆明市新闻路348号（云南省图书批发市场四楼）
吉林	长春学人书店	0431-5676686	长春市人民大街4696号
	长春联合图书城	0431-2722234	长春市宽城区芙蓉路1号
	吉林大学出版社书店	0431-5676648	长春市朝阳区永昌路9号
内蒙古	内蒙古大学出版社书店	0471-4990657	呼和浩特市赛罕区昭乌达路凯旋广场88号
辽宁	东北财经大学出版社图书代办站	0411-84712239	大连市黑石礁
江苏	南京大学出版社书店	025-83320583	南京市汉口路22号
	南京先锋书店	025-83325082	南京市广州路12号2楼
黑龙江	哈尔滨工业大学出版社书店	0451-6412461	哈尔滨市南岗区教化街21号

北京大学出版社教材经销商名录

省 份	单 位	联系人	电 话
北京	北京齐贤合力图书有限公司	王凤林	010-63797744
	北京清华文泉图书有限公司	王 岳	010-62783932
	北京泓源昕辰图书经销有限公司	胡文凯	010-82630078
	北京乘云阁图书有限公司	吴文聚	010-63772357
广东	广州理念书业有限公司	胡杨柳	020-83798116
浙江	金华捷达教材调剂站	曾建华	0579-2101028
	宁波天行图书发展公司	黄潮洋	0574-87450681
	杭州高教书店有限公司	郑志伟	0571-87970945
湖南	长沙风景旅游文化公司	李柏伟	0731-4431500
	长沙书局	宋 武	0731-2222629
江苏	江苏唐风图书公司	宋 宁	025-86633629
	徐州科瑞书店	姚 斌	0516-83867109
	江苏畅想源图书公司	高红新	025-83202461
黑龙江	黑龙江财经书店	刘丹君	0451-82732336
吉林	长春学人书店	吴 凤	0431-5676686
辽宁	沈阳理想书店	陈 林	024-8619841
	大连佳诚考试书店	石 杰	0411-4670294
	沈阳现代教育书店	孙德萱	024-88112726
上海	上海经济二店	蒋鉴丽	021-62867889
安徽	合肥市三人行书屋	陈 群	0551-4233589
四川	四川海华科技文化有限责任公司	敖 波	028-85459726
	四川桃李芳华图书发行有限公司	蔡晓春	028-85455171
重庆	重庆财经书店	罗世林	023-63607672
陕西	陕西弘文教科图书有限公司	张治诚	029-85255275
	西安科技法律书店	雷 鸣	029-85218448
河南	洛阳育科图书教材有限公司	李小申	0379-4272783
	河南省黄河教育图书供应社	王亚林	0371-5966764
天津	南开大学出版社高校图书代办站	李金保	022-23507092
山东	山东金融书店	韩 冬	0531-8966754
	山东天平法律书店	郑 卫	0531-8545647
	济南中元图书有限公司	沈正路	0531-2861755
福建	福大高校图书代办站	王愫明	0591-7893417
	三明高等教育书店	马 腾	0598-8398113
江西	江西弘苑书店	戴小华	0791-8593531
	江西高校出版社图书代办站	李建民	0791-8503827
河北	河北润才书店	刘胜利	0317-5062463
	河北省教育图书教材店有限公司	刘国良	0311-7084040
	河北正元书店有限公司	闫殿龙	0316-2951420
山西	太原市文杰大学书店有限公司	李建刚	0351-4132420
	太原华拓图书有限公司	武长虹	0351-7063789
新疆	新疆福路交通图书有限公司	李广禄	0991-5812005
	乌鲁木齐市财经图书有限公司	窦少华	0991-2620533
甘肃	兰州财经书店	徐 山	0931-8508814
湖北	湖北政博图书公司	李方林	027-50248986
	武汉高文图书公司	田金生	027-87197858
贵州	贵州新知专业图书有限责任公司	吴 斌	0851-8128076

市场营销中心联系名录

主任：张涛

副主任：潘建 刘宗彦

地区	联系人	电话
北京	经理：潘建（兼）	62752018
	经理：刘梓盈	62767313
	助理：宋诗安	62752018
	助理：黄英	62767313
陕西、河南、天津	经理：饶勇	62757439
	助理：陈志国	62752935
广东、浙江、湖南	经理：刘宗彦（兼）	62759712
	助理：宗秀菊	62757317
江苏、东三省、内蒙古	经理：王林冲	62767314
	助理：郗雨	62757438
上海 安徽 四川 重庆	经理：谢尚楹	62757299
	助理：李瑞芳	62752954
山东、福建、海南、江西	经理：张志国	62752013
	助理：许秀文	62757295
河北、山西、新疆、甘肃、青海、宁夏	经理：梁滨	62757298
	助理：陈志国	62752935
湖北、云南、贵州、广西	经理：张继承	62757295
	助理：许秀文	62750694

北京大学出版社培文教育文化公司

地址：北京市海淀区中关村北大街118号1号楼1209室

邮编：100871　　　　　　　　　　　联系人：孙明卉

网址：http://cbs.pku.edu.cn　　　　电子信箱：pw@pup.pku.edu.cn

电话：010-58874097　　　　　　　　传真：010-58874098

欲获取相关教学辅导资料的教师烦请填写如下支持表，传真或 E-MAIL 给我们，以确此教辅只被教师获得。

培生教育出版集团北京办事处
Pearson Education Beijing Office
电话：8610–88817788–2301
　　　8610–88817788–2302
　　　8610–88816659
传真：8610–88817499
E–mail：service@pearsoned.com.cn

北京大学出版社培文教育文化公司
地址：北京市海淀区中关村 118 号
　　　1 号楼 1209 室
邮编：100871
电话：010–58874097
传真：010–58874098
E–mail：pw@pup.pku.edu.cn

教辅资料支持表

兹证明＿＿＿＿＿＿＿＿＿＿大学(English Name)＿＿＿＿＿＿＿系/院＿＿＿＿＿学年（学期）开设的＿＿＿＿＿＿＿＿＿＿课程，采用＿＿＿＿＿＿＿＿＿出版社出版的＿＿＿＿＿＿（英文原版/简体中文版）作为主要教材任课教师为＿＿＿＿＿＿，学生＿＿＿个班共＿＿＿人。

任课教师可选择以下所需教辅资料的 2–3 种，并注明所需资料的形式。

教学辅导资料种类
☐ 教师指导手册 (Instructor's Manual)
☐ 习题解答 (Solution Manual)
☐ 题库 (Test Bank)
☐ 幻灯片 (PowerPoint Slides)

教学辅导资料提供形式
☐ E–file (须拷贝)
☐ 印刷手册
☐ 网上注册后下载　(PearsonEd 推荐使用)

英文书名 (Title)：＿＿＿＿＿＿＿＿＿＿＿＿＿＿＿＿＿＿＿＿＿＿＿＿＿＿＿＿＿＿
版次 (Edition)：＿＿＿＿＿＿＿＿＿＿＿　作者 (Author)：＿＿＿＿＿＿＿＿＿＿＿
课程名称 (Course Name)：＿＿＿＿＿＿＿＿＿＿＿＿＿＿＿＿＿＿＿＿＿＿＿＿＿
年级／程度 (Year/Level)：＿＿＿＿＿＿＿　院／系 (School/Fac)：＿＿＿＿＿＿＿＿
必修课 (Required)：　　☐ 是　　　☐ 否

联系地址 (Adress)：＿＿＿＿＿＿＿＿＿＿＿＿＿　邮编 (Zip Code)：＿＿＿＿＿＿＿
电话 (Tel)：＿＿＿＿＿＿＿＿　传真 (Fax)：＿＿＿＿＿＿＿　E–mail：＿＿＿＿＿＿＿

系/院主任：　　　　　（签字）

（系/院办公室章）

年　　月　　日

培文书系·最新书目

←人文科学系列

英文影印版

历史人文系列
- 全球通史:从史前到21世纪(第7版)(上)
- 全球通史:从史前到21世纪(第7版)(下)
- 西方文明遗产(第9版)(上)
- 西方文明遗产(第9版)(下)
- 世界文明的源泉(第3版)(上)
- 世界文明的源泉(第3版)(下)
- 伦理学:理论与实践(第8版)
- 世界宗教(第9版)

艺术人文系列
- 艺术:让人成为人(第7版)
- 西方文化中的音乐简史

中文翻译版

历史人文系列
- 全球通史:从史前到21世纪(第7版)(上)
- 全球通史:从史前到21世纪(第7版)(下)

艺术人文系列
- 艺术:让人成为人(第7版)
- 西方文化中的音乐简史

社会科学系列→

英文影印版

社会学系列
- 审视自我:社会学经典、当代和跨文化阅读(第6版)
- 社会变迁(第5版)
- 社会与政治原理:经典读本
- 社会科学:社会研究导论(第12版)
- 医学社会学(第9版)
- 政治社会学导论(第4版)
- 大众传媒(第7版)

文化研究系列
- 文化研究导论(第1版)
- 文化原理与通俗文化导论(第3版)
- 女性与学术研究
- 男性的世界(第6版)
- 女性的世界

心理学系列
- 心理学:大脑,人,世界(第2版)
- 心理学的历史与体系(第6版)
- 心理学史:观点与背景(第3版)
- 教育心理学:理论与实践(第7版)
- 社会心理学(第11版)
- 语言心理学
- 变态心理学(第12版)
- 心理学与生活(第17版)
- 发展心理学:婴儿、孩童与青春期(第5版)
- 心理测量(第4版)
- 终身发展心理学(第3版)
- 应用心理学与人力资源管理(第6版)

中文翻译版

心理学系列
- 社会心理学(第5版)
- 心理学的邀请(第3版)
- 投资心理学(第2版)